D0960641

DICTIONARY OF THE LITURGY

DICTIONARY OF THE LITURGY

By

REV. JOVIAN P. LANG, OFM

Illustrated

CATHOLIC BOOK PUBLISHING CO.
New York

IMPRIMI POTEST: Robert J. Karris, O.F.M.
Privincial Minister

NIHIL OBSTAT: John J. Quinn, M.A.
Censor Librorum

IMPRIMATUR: Patrick J. Sheridan
Vicar General, Archdiocese of New York

The Nihil Obstat and Imprimatur are official declarations that a book or pamphlet is free of doctrinal or moral error. No implication is contained therein that those who have granted the Nihil Obstat and Imprimatur agree with the contents, opinions or statements expressed.

ACKNOWLEDGMENTS

We wish to thank the copyright holders of the works from which the relatively few quotations in this Dictionary are taken. Those not identified in place are the following:

Scriptural quotations are taken from the *New American Bible with Revised New Testament* © 1986 by the Confraternity of Christian Doctrine, Washington, DC. All rights reserved.

Liturgical quotations are taken from the *Sacramentary* and the *Liturgy of the Hours* © 1973, 1985 and 1970, 1973, 1975 respectively by the International Commission on English in the Liturgy (ICEL), Washington DC. All rights reserved.

DEDICATION

To the Sacred Heart of Jesus

To the Sacred Heart Province of the Order of Friars Minor

Library of Congress Cataloging-in-Publication Data
Lang, Jovian
Dictionary of the Liturgy / by Jovian P. Lang; illustrated.
p. cm.
Includes bibliographical references.
ISBN 0-89942-273-X :
1. Catholic Church—Liturgy—Dictionaries.
2. Liturgics—Dictionaries. I. Title.
BV173.L26 1989
264' .02' 003—dc20 89-17407
CIP

(T-273)

PREFACE

THE liturgical renewal of the Second Vatican Council is almost completed at this time, clearly indicating that there is a pressing need for a dictionary of the Liturgy in English. This Dictionary is written primarily for the average Catholic, although it in no way excludes our Christian friends of other denominations, who are also interested in the Liturgy because it relates to many of their services. Numerous Catholics are on liturgical committees and involved in activities during liturgical services as lectors, chanters, music directors, team-workers with the Rite of Christian Initiation of Adults (RCIA), and so forth. All these people will find in this book valuable explanations and practical initiation into the various matters of liturgical appeal that have developed in the past twenty-five years.

Since the present Dictionary places this material at the fingertips of all Christians, it should be well received also by priests, seminarians, professors of Liturgy and their students, sisters, brothers, and members of secular institutes. It can take persons with comparatively little knowledge of the Liturgy through the initial steps to a richer explanation of some of the more complicated aspects of the present Liturgy. It can also be used effectively by all those who have built up a strong interest in the Liturgy already. We have tried to achieve a balance of words and ideas between the old (pre-Vatican II Liturgy) and the new (post-Vatican II Liturgy). Many new and innovating ideas in printed and audiovisual forms are emerging from various presses and even from the Vatican. An attempt has been made to include the most recent releases (1989).

Among the many features found in the Dictionary, the following may be singled out.

- Clear explanations and accurate interpretations are provided for everything related to the Liturgy—words, rites, gestures, themes, prayers, service books, sacred vessels, vestments, music, art, and much more. The liturgical implications of words that have broader meanings in religion are also explained, e.g., grace, magic, life, mysticism, death. Similarly, the relationship of broad topics to the Liturgy is described in entries such as: Liberation and Liturgy; Culture and Worship; the Domestic Church; and several entries on various Eastern Rites.
- Summaries are provided for the main parts of all liturgical rites of the Church together with an explanation of the meaning of each rite.
- Every part of the Eucharistic Celebration is explained in detail.
- The liturgical renewal is explained from several different aspects, integrating it with the postconcilar documents of the Liturgy.

• Besides a brief history of each feast of our Lord and our Lady, together with its liturgical meaning, a short biography of every Saint in the liturgical calendar is furnished with the date and theme of the celebration.

• The liturgical use for each Book of the Bible is set forth, and the relationship between it and the Liturgy is clearly specified.

• Major liturgical themes, such as joy, penance, peace, thanksgiving, and the various virtues are treated in detail.

• Popular prayer texts not readily accessible in liturgical books, for example, the *Ave Maris Stella* and the *Jesu Dulcis Memoria,* are reproduced for the benefit of the reader.

• Illustrations abound—some are explanatory, others decorative—and there is a full-color section on the Mass.

• Special charts and tables as well as a select chronology of major events in the history of the Liturgy are included and will be found particularly helpful to solve the many reference questions in Liturgy asked of librarians.

• Cross references are inserted when more related material can be found elsewhere in the text. Asterisks are used to denote words that have an entry of their own.

• A select bibliography will be helpful, particularly to those who need extra material for a further explanation of some of the definitions found in this encyclopedic Dictionary.

• In phonetic fashion the correct pronunciation of all defined entries is spelled out.

Since I have been working on this Dictionary for more than a few years, there have been several secretaries entering the information on files. To each of them I owe a great deal of thanks: Julie Wolff; Patricia Wiecezak; Linda Hadjoglou; and Patricia Frame. My deepest appreciation goes to the editor of Catholic Book Publishing Company, Anthony Buono, who has done a yeoman's work in helping with the specialized types of explanations and definitions, Biblical entries, and particularly with material coming from the French and Italian languages, with which the author is unfamiliar. He checked the entries, suggesting others that should be included, and assembled the chronology. It was he who was responsible for all the in-house work that is necessary to make a book of this nature come together in a proper fashion. To Robert Cavalero, the publisher, who was present when this project was first discussed and has offered continuous help in its completion, my fondest regards. Despite the variety of delays, over which we had no control, we hope that this Dictionary will in many ways satisfy an evident need for the public for whom it is intended.

Rev. Jovian Peter Lang, OFM

ALPHABETIZATION AND CROSS-REFERENCE

System of Alphabetization: Entries in the Dictionary are arranged *word by word,* not letter by letter. Therefore, *All Souls* precedes *Alleluia;* nothing comes before something. When several words are in an entry, they file alphabetically together with inverted headings, e.g., *Cross, Adoration of; Cross Bearer; Cross, Pectoral.* However, a subdivision of an entry follows that entry before all other entries, e.g., *Bible; Bible—Canon; Bible and Liturgy.*

Method of Cross-reference: An asterisk (*) after a word indicates that the word is defined under an entry of its own, which is identical or very similar to it. When helpful, *See* and *See also* cross-references are used.

PRONUNCIATION

For purposes of pronunciation, a simple system of phonetic spelling has been devised and included in parentheses for every entry defined. The accented syllable is indicated by capital letters, and the pronunciation for the letters is as follows.

uh = a, e, i, o, u unaccented (the Schwa)
a = hat
ah = father
ai = aisle, ice
aw = awful, for
ay = ape; care
e = get (short)
ee = eve
i = pit (short)
o = odd (short)
oh = no
oi = noise, joy
ow = cow
oo = boot

u = foot, book (accented, long)
uh = culture, cut (accented, short)
yuh = nature (unaccented, short)
yoo = use, unite (accented, long)
uhr = further
ch = church
sh = shame, wish
zh = vision
g = get
j = judge
k = cow; key
kw = quick
w = witch
hw = which

ABBREVIATIONS

A	Year A, of the three-year cycle of Sunday readings
AA	*Apostolicam Actuositatem* (Decree on the Apostolate of the Laity)
AAS	*Acta Apostolicae Sedis*
Acts	Acts of the Apostles
A.D.	*Anno Domini* (In the year of our Lord)
Am	Amos, The Book of
B	Year B, of the three-year cycle of Sunday Readings
Bar	Baruch, The Book of
B.C.	Before Christ
BCL	Bishops' Committee on the Liturgy
bef.	before
C	Year C, of the three-year cycle of Sunday readings
C1	Eucharistic Prayer for Masses with Children I
C2	Eucharistic Prayer for Masses with Children II
C3	Eucharistic Prayer for Masses with Children III
Can.	Canon (of the new *Code of Canon* Law)
CCD	Confraternity of Christian Doctrine
CD	*Christus Dominus* (Decree on the Pastoral Office of Bishops in the Church)
1 Chr	Chronicles, The First Book of
2 Chr	Chronicles, The Second Book of
Col	Colossians, The Epistles to the
1 Cor	Corinthians, First Epistle to the
2 Cor	Corinthians, Second Epistle to the
Dn	Daniel, The Book of
Dt	Deuteronomy, The Book of
DV	*Dei Verbum* (Constitution of Divine Revelation)
EACW	*Environment and Art in Catholic Worship*
Eccl	Ecclesiastes, The Book of
ed(s)	editor(s)
EI	*Enchiridion of Indulgences*
EM	*Eucharisticum Mysterium*
EP I	Eucharistic Prayer I
EP II	Eucharistic Prayer II
EP III	Eucharistic Prayer III
EP IV	Eucharistic Prayer IV
Eph	Ephesians, The Epistle to the
Est	Esther, The Book of
Ex	Exodus, The Book of
Ez	Ezekiel, The Book of
Ezr	Ezra, The Book of
FC	*Familiaris Consortio* (Apostolic Exhortation on the Family)
Gal	Galatians, The Epistle to the
GCD	*General Catechetical Directory*
GILH	General Instruction on the Liturgy of the Hours
GIRM	General Instruction of the Roman Missal
Gn	Genesis, The Book of
Hb	Habakkuk, The Book of
Heb	Hebrews, The Epistle to the
Hg	Haggai. The Book of
Hos	Hosea, The Book of
ICEL	International Commission on English in the Liturgy
IOE	*Inter Oecumenici* (First Instruction on the Proper Implementation of the Constitution on the Sacred Liturgy)
Is	Isaiah, The Book of
Jas	James, The Epistle of
Jb	Job, The Book of
Jdt	Judith, The Book of
Jer	Jeremiah, The Book of
Jgs	Judges, The Book of
Jl	Joel, The Book of
Jn	John, The Gospel According to
1 Jn	John, The First Epistle of
2 Jn	John, The Second Epistle of
3 Jn	John, The Third Epistle of
Jon	Jonah, The Book of
Jos	Joshua, The Book of
Jude	Jude, The Epistle of
1 Kgs	Kings, The First Book of
2 Kgs	Kings, The Second Book of
Lam	Lamentations, The Book of

LFMI	Lectionary for Mass, Introduction
LG	*Lumen Gentium* (Constitution on the Church)
LI	*Liturgicae Instaurationes* (Third Instruction on the Proper Implementation of the Constitution on the Sacred Liturgy)
Lk	Luke, The Gospel According to
Lv	Leviticus, The Book of
Mal	Malachi, The Book of
1 Mc	Maccabees, The First Book of
2 Mc	Maccabees, The Second Book of
MC	*Marialis Cultus* (Apostolic Constitution on Devotion to Mary)
MD	*Mediator Dei* (Encyclical on the Sacred Liturgy)
Mi	Micah, The Book of
Mk	Mark, The Gospel According to
Mt	Matthew, The Gospel According to
Na	Nahum, The Book of
NCCB	National Council of Catholic Bishops
NCD	*National Catechetical Directory: Sharing the Light of Faith*
Neh	Nehemiah, The Book of
Nm	Numbers, The Book of
no(s).	number(s)
Not	*Notitiae*
NT	New Testament
Ob	Obadiah, The Book of
Opt. Mem.	Optional Memorial
OT	Old Testament
p(p).	page(s)
PC	*Perfectae Caritatis* (Decree on the Appropriate Renewal of the Religious Life)
Phil	Philippians, The Epistle to the
Phlm	Philemon, The Epistle to
Prv	Proverbs, The Book of
Ps(s)	Psalms, The Book of
1 Pt	Peter, The First Epistle of
2 Pt	Peter, The Second Epistle of
R 1	Eucharistic Prayer for Masses of Reconciliation I
R 2	Eucharistic Prayer for Masses of Reconciliation II
RM	Roman Missal
Rom	Romans, The Epistle to the
Ru	Ruth, The Book of
Rv	Revelation, The Book of
SC	*Sacrosanctum Concilium* (Constitution on the Sacred Liturgy)
Sir	Sirach, The Book of
1 Sm	Samuel, The First Book of
2 Sm	Samuel, The Second Book of
Song	Song of Songs
St(s).	Saint(s)
Tb	Tobit, The Book of
1 Thes	Thessalonians, First Epistle to the
2 Thes	Thessalonians, Second Epistle to the
Ti	Titus, The Epistle to
1 Tm	Timothy, First Epistle to
2 Tm	Timothy, Second Epistle to
UR	*Unitatis Redintegratio* (Decree on Ecumenism)
USCC	United States Catholic Conference
vol(s).	volume(s)
Wis	Wisdom, The Book of
(Year) I	Year I of the two-year cycle of weekday readings
(Year) II	Year II of the two-year cycle of weekday readings
Zec	Zechariah, The Book of
Zep	Zephaniah, The Book of

— A —

Abacus. *See* CREDENCE TABLE.

Abbess (AB-uhs). The elected superioress of a community of nuns of certain orders, particularly of Benedictine tradition. Her authority varies according to the constitution and rules of her order. A new formula for the blessing of an abbess, to take place during Mass, was promulgated on November 9, 1970 (AAS 63:710).

Abbey (AB-ee). A monastery ruled by an abbot* or an abbess,* usually composed of a number of buildings: church, guesthouse, dormitory, chapter house, workshops, etc. Here the Religious dedicated to God serve Him by a life of work and prayer according to their Rule.

Abbot (AB-uht). Elected by professed members of the community, this superior of a monastery of monks of Orders like the Benedictines, with a fixed location, is in charge of both spiritual and temporal affairs according to the Rule of the Order. His authority is quasi-episcopal. A new formula for the blessing of an abbot, to take place during Mass, was promulgated on November 9, 1970 (AAS 63:710).

Abel (AY-buhl). The religious and just son of Adam and Eve whose sacrifice pleased God yet aroused the murderous envy of his brother Cain. He was a shepherd and offered the firstlings of his flock to the Lord (Gn 4:2-8). In the Liturgy,* Abel is mentioned in the Canon of the Mass (Eucharistic Prayer I*) and serves as a model of those who offer themselves to God with Jesus in the Sacrifice of the Eucharist.*

Abjuration (ab-joo-RAY-shuhn). Official act of renouncing apostasy, heresy, or schism. It is still in force in exceptional cases, but adults who become Catholics are usually not required to make an act of abjuration, since they publicly profess the Catholic Faith. This act implies the renunciation of any error contrary to Catholicism.

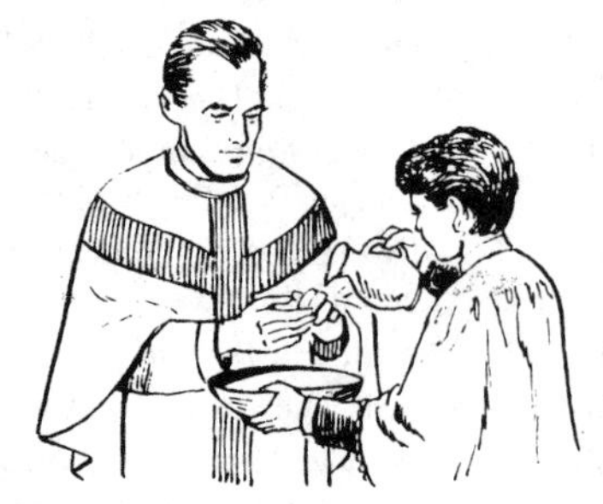

Ablutions (uh-BLOO-shuhnz). Liturgical actions that consist in washing or purifying one's body (or part of it), thus figuratively one's inner self, or some object. They occur at Baptism,* at the rite of Washing the Feet* on Holy Thursday,* and at Mass.* After the preparation of the bread* and wine* to be consecrated, the celebrant washes his fingers to cleanse them. This ritual symbolizes that he must be pure in heart and mind to offer the Sacrifice. He asks God to give him that purity.

After Communion,* if particles adhere to his fingers, he purifies them over the paten.* The vessels are washed by the priest,* deacon,* or acolyte* after Communion or after Mass, usually at the credence table.* The chalice is washed with wine and water, or with water only, which is then drunk by the celebrant or deacon. This liquid mixture is also called the ablution.

Hand-washing as a practical necessity is prescribed outside of Mass after actions that soil the hands, e.g., distributing candles on Candlemas* Day, ashes,* palms,* anointing during Baptism,* Confirmation,* Holy Orders,* Anointing of the Sick,* Dedication of a Church.*

Abraham (AY-bruh-ham). "The Father of believers." At God's command he left his home in Ur of the Chaldees about 2000 B.C. and settled in Palestine. God made a Covenant* with him and promised him a great posterity. In his old age his wife Sarah bore him a son (Isaac) in fulfillment of God's promise (Gn 11–25). In the Liturgy,* Abraham is mentioned in Eucharistic Prayer I* and exemplifies faith in God's goodness, in accord with St. Paul's motto: "My just one shall live by faith" (Heb 10:38).

Absolution (ab-suh-LOO-shuhn). The remission of sin and the punishment due to sin. In the Rite of Penance,* a priest possessing valid orders and jurisdiction* may absolve a penitent who has confessed sin, who is contrite and promises to make satisfaction.

The Penitential Rite* at Mass is not an absolution properly so-called; it is only a petition for pardon. As such, it is a Sacramental*

that takes away venial sin. *See also* GENERAL ABSOLUTION.

Abstinence (AB-sti-nuhn[t]s). Refraining from eating meat or food prepared with meat on certain days as commanded by the Church,* to remind us of Jesus' redeeming Death (on a Friday), to prepare for the celebration of certain feasts, to win heavenly graces, and to practice the virtue of penance (to atone for sin and for help in the firm purpose of amendment). "Days of abstinence" in the United States include Ash Wednesday,* Good Friday* and Fridays of Lent. On other Fridays of the year, all are exhorted to perform acts of devotion, self-denial, and charity in the spirit of piety and penance, and particularly for peace; abstinence from meat is especially recommended but under no obligation by law. Canon Law for the world prescribes abstinence on all Fridays (Canon 1251).

The rule of abstinence allows eggs, dairy products, and condiments (even if they are made from the fat of animals). This rule is not based on scientific data; for instance, fish, shellfish, frog, waterhen, turtle, and beaver may be eaten. Abstinence is compulsory from the age of fourteen. Some faithful,* however, are dispensed from it: the sick, and in some countries, soldiers.

Those in orders or institutes of Christian perfection may observe different abstinence regulations according to their rule of life.

Acclamations (ak-luh-MAY-shuhnz). Brief formulas of greeting, prayer, and faith that constitute the people's response to the greeting or invitation of the celebrant* or his ministers* in any liturgical action. They represent the minimum external requirement for the active participation* of the people. Some of the most common ones are: "Amen,"* "Alleluia,"* "Thanks be to God,"* "Glory to You, Lord,"* "Praise to You, Lord Jesus Christ,"* "Holy, holy, holy,"* and "Hosanna in the highest. . . ."*

The Missal of Paul VI has reintroduced two ancient forms of acclamations. The *Gospel Acclamation,* after the Responsorial Psalm* (or the Second Reading* when there is one), is directed to the Gospel,* honoring Christ Who will "evangelize" the assembly. It enshrines a short Biblical sentence, praising Christ in His function of Teacher and Revealer, or it recalls a Scriptural axiom characteristic of the feast or the day. The people customarily make the acclamation by singing or reciting "Alleluia" before and after the text used. In Lent,* four different acclamations replace the "Alleluia."

The *Memorial Acclamation* is sung or recited by the people immediately after the consecration* of the bread and wine. There are four versions in English—each a paraphrase of the formula of St. Paul: "As often as you eat this bread and drink the cup, you proclaim the death of the Lord until he comes" (1 Cor 11:26). This acclamation is a wonderful manifestation at the very heart of the Eucharistic Prayer* of the active participation of the faithful in the Mass, an expression of their baptismal priesthood.* *See also* RESPONSES.

Accommodation (uh-kom-uh-DAY-shuhn). One of the traditional four senses of Scripture: literal, spiritual, sensus plenior, and the accommodated sense. It is the application to any Scripture passage of a more or less arbitrary meaning, a simple adaptation of the text to another subject, sometimes conserving its first or original meaning and sometimes making allusion to it. In the Liturgy,* the Church makes frequent use of accommodation. If done judiciously, it can aid understanding and impart edification.

Achilleus, St. (ah-ki-LAY-uhs, saynt*). 1st century. Roman soldier who became Christian and quit the service. The bas-relief of his martyrdom is the oldest such representation known. *Liturgical celebration:* May 12 (Opt. Mem.); *theme:* courage in professing the Faith.

* Hereinafter, the word "St." will no longer be phoneticized.

Acolytes (AK-uh-laits). Formerly, this term referred to clerics in Minor Orders, specifically the highest of the four minor orders in the Western Church. Effective 1973, these orders have been abolished and replaced by two *ministries* that are open to lay people: acolyte* and reader.* The acolyte ministry is instituted for service of the altar.* An acolyte prepares the altar and the sacred vessels* at the beginning of the Liturgy of the Eucharist,* assists the celebrant* and deacon* at Mass especially, and at other liturgical functions. After Communion* or Mass he may purify the chalice*

and other vessels. He may also act as extraordinary minister of Communion* and expose the Blessed Sacrament.*

In a broad sense, the altar boy or server is known as an acolyte; he usually carries out the duties once entrusted to the order of acolyte—offering the cruets of water and wine to the celebrant, lighting the candles, carrying lighted candles, and performing other minor duties.

Acta Apostolicae Sedis (AHK-tuh ah-puh-STOH-lee-chay SAY-dis). The official journal of the Holy See* and the ordinary vehicle for promulgating liturgical as well as other laws. The law goes into effect three months after the date of the issue in which the law appears, unless the nature of the law requires an immediate effective date or unless the law itself specifies a date. *See also* LITURGICAL LAW, SOURCES OF.

Action Mass (AK-shuhn mas). That type of Mass full of extensive active participation of the congregation. Stressing spontaneity and improvisation, like (dancing,) dialogue homilies, and nonscriptural readings, such formats may be counter to official liturgical legislation.

Actions and Gestures. *See* ATTITUDES; ORIENTATION; POSTURE IN WORSHIP.

Actions, Liturgical. *See* LITURGICAL ACTIONS

Active Participation of the Faithful. *See* LITURGY—PARTICIPATION.

Acts of the Apostles (AKS uhv thee uh-PAH-suhlz). Fifty-first Book of the Bible* and fifth of the New Testament, written by St. Luke* the Evangelist in the 70's or 80's of the first century. It continues the narrative of the early Church from the Ascension* of Christ to the first imprisonment of St. Paul,* a period of about thirty-three years.

Liturgical use: This Book is read primarily during the Easter Season.* The Church sets before us the history of the primitive community with its accent on the joy and fervor of the Christians stemming from the knowledge of Christ's Resurrection.* We are thus encouraged to live our Faith with the same trust and boldness of our brothers and sisters of apostolic times.

Ad Gentes (ahd JEN-tez). Latin title (from the first two words "To the nations") of the *Decree on the Missionary Acitivity of the Church* issued by the Second Vatican Council* on December 7, 1965. It makes the point that missionary activity and the Liturgy* go together. Missionary activity is nothing more nor less than the appearance—that is, the epiphany—and the fulfillment of God's will in the world and its history; there through missions God is clearly unfolding the History of Salvation.* Missionary activity makes Christ the Author of Salvation* present through preaching the Word and celebrating the Sacraments,* of which the Eucharist* is the center and crowning point. *See also* VATICAN COUNCIL, SECOND.

Ad Libitum (ad LIB-i-tuhm). Latin phrase meaning "at one's choice." It is used whenever there is a choice of text or ritual in the liturgical rites reformed by Vatican II.* *See also* OPTIONS.

Ad Multos Annos (ahd MUHL-tohs AHN-ohs). Latin formula meaning "for many years to come" expressing the greeting and best wishes that the consecrated bishop* addresses three times to the consecrator and the abbot* addresses once to the bishop who blesses him. Now used for other circumstances as well—for example, the ordination of priests.*

Adaptation, Liturgical (ad-uhp-TAY-shuhn, luh-TUHR-ji-kuhl; li-). The principle endorsed by Vatican II* whereby the Roman Liturgy* is to be renewed in a general fashion by addressing a new cultural era in the Universal Church,* or in a particular way made to accord with the culture of every Local Church.* Without sacrificing the essential message of the Liturgy,* the Roman Rite* must give way to new cultural expressions, to reinterpretations, modifications, and variations.

A universal Roman Rite means unity in essentials and diversity in cultural forms. The Council set two conditions for admitting into the Liturgy elements from the people's traditions and culture. One is negative: ". . . anything . . . which is not indissolubly bound up with superstition and error." The other is positive: ". . . so long as they harmonize with its [the Liturgy's] true and authentic spirit" (SC 37).

Liturgical adaptation entails not only Liturgy but also theology, exegesis, sociology, anthropology, psychology, linguistics, and the arts. In addition, interdisciplinary consultation must be carried on to insure proper adaptation. Large-scale adaptation of rites is left to the Episcopal Conferences* to carry out, with the approval of the Holy See,* whether they be in a racial or a national setting.

The new liturgical books* have specified areas wherein priests or those conducting liturgical actions may improvise or adapt the Liturgy to those present—choice of readings and prayers,* changing forms of address, variable admonitions,* etc. These amount to what might be called accommodations.

There is also a more radical type of adaptation called indigenization, which the Council authorized (SC 40). It takes place in three phases: (1) The competent territorial ecclesiastical authority has the task of determining which elements from the tradition and culture of individual peoples might appropriately be admitted into Divine worship and submitting them to the Holy See.* (2) Preliminary experiments are to be conducted over a period of time by limited groups. (3) The genius and talents of the races or nations are to be respected, as all of this is carried out with the technical assistance of experts in the field. Thus in the words of Paul VI, "adaptation of the Christian life in the fields of pastoral, ritual, didactic, and spiritual activities is not only possible; it is even favored by the Church" (Address of 7/31/69).

It must, however, be borne in mind that adaptation must never be seen exclusively in terms of culture; the Biblical foundation essential to any Christian adaptation must always be taken into account.

Adaptation is sometimes understood to be Western ideas and forms adjusted to local customs of that country; indigenization is much stronger. Therefore an attempt should be made to create a native expression of Christianity, incarnating the Gospel* in the particular cultural contexts. True inculturation is of supreme importance if the Church's teachings and rituals are to be meaningful. In some countries serious and satisfactory steps have been taken in this regard, for instance, Africa, India, Latin America, and Southeast Asia. *See also* CULTURE AND WORSHIP; NATIVE CUSTOMS.

Addai and Mari, Anaphora of (AD-dai and MA-ree, uh-NAF-uh-ruh uhv). One of the three anaphoras proper to the East Syrian Church, and the most frequently used. It is known as the "Anaphora of the Apostles," because it is attributed to Sts. Addai and Mari, the evangelizers of Mesopotamia according to tradition. Composed about 200 A.D., it is of the highest importance for the early history of the Liturgy.*

The anaphora includes the Introductory Dialogue* to the Preface,* the Sanctus* (probably a later addition), and the post-Sanctus. It lacks the Institution Narrative* but has the Anamnesis,* the second Epiclesis,* the Intercessions,* and the concluding Doxology.* A notable feature is that it is addressed to Christ* instead of God the Father.*

Addresses (Allocutions), Papal. See LITURGICAL LAW, SOURCES OF.

Admission to Candidacy for the Diaconate and Presbyterate, Rite of (uhd-MISH-uhn too KAN-duh-duh-see fohr thuh dai [dee]-AK-uh-nuht [nayt] and prez-BIT-uh-rayt, rait uhv). Once the Rite of Tonsure* was suppressed, together with its juridical effects of becoming a cleric* and being incardinated in a diocese* or forming a contractual relationship with the Ordinary,* a new rite was instituted whereby the person aspiring to the diaconate publicly declares his intention to enter Holy Orders.* Thus the individual becomes an official candidate for the diaconate* or priesthood.* Although no formal testimonial letters are compulsory, among the requirements would be the lack of mental and physical defects, the presence of good qualities, indications of an authentic vocation, and a desire to dedicate one's life to the service of the Church for God and the good of souls. Seminarians aiming for the transitional diaconate should be twenty years old and already into their theological program of studies.

Spiritually the individual's first public expression of intention for Holy Orders earmarks him as one preparing for a specific ministry in the Church community. Therefore it

presumes a maturity whereby he is capable not only of dedicating himself to the service of God and the faithful but of assuming the responsibilities of the diaconate and/or priesthood. When the candidate's proper Ordinary accepts the declaration on behalf of the Church, a spiritual bond is established between the two by this Admission. Professed Religious of clerical congregations state their intention to their major superior.

During the rite the bishop (or major superior) at a public celebration within the Mass or a suitable Liturgy of the Word* presides over the ceremony. It is never joined to an ordination or the institution of ministries; the choice of a feast day would be more seemly than an ordinary weekday. Alternate Scriptural texts may be chosen in accordance with the occasion. The Homily,* developed from these Scriptural passages, relates to vocation—the call from God and man's response. Standing before the bishop and the community, the candidate answers the questions put to him by the bishop concerning his intention to minister in the Church and to prepare well for it. The celebration concludes with a prayer for the candidates and a brief litany,* which includes the patron saints* of the candidates.

Admonitions (ad-muh-NISH-uhnz). Introduction and invitations addressed to the Eucharistic assembly* by the celebrant* and commentator* for the purpose of accommodating the celebration to the needs of the local community. These admonitions enable the people to be drawn into a fuller understanding of the sacred action, or any of its parts, and lead them into a true spirit of participation.*

The most important of these admonitions are those that the General Instruction on the Roman Missal invites the celebrant to compose and proclaim. He is invited to introduce the faithful* to the day's Mass at the very beginning of the celebration; to the Liturgy of the Word,* before the Readings;* to the Eucharistic Prayer,* before the Preface;* finally he is invited to bring the entire function to a conclusion, in his own words, before the Dismissal.*

Also important are those admonitions set down in the Order of the Mass itself before certain portions of the rite, e.g., before the Penitential Rite* or the Lord's Prayer.* These do not have to be expressed verbatim as given, but may be adapted to the circumstances. Most important of all, the admonitions must not be allowed to develop into sermons or homilies;* brevity must be cultivated and wordiness avoided.

Adoration (ad-uh-RAY-shuhn). Any of several religious acts (reverences, postures, prayers, sacrifices), performed by mind, body, and will, recognizing God alone, the supreme being, worthy of our homage. Adoration is one of the four ends of prayer* and of the Sacrifice of the Mass* (which is the highest form of adoration since it commemorates the greatest act of adoration by which Jesus gave Himself to God the Father). *See also* LATRIA; MASS; PETITION; PRAYER; REPARATION; THANKSGIVING; WORSHIP.

Adoration, Eucharistic (ad-uh-RAY-shuhn, yoo-kuh-RIS-tik). Worship of the Blessed Sacrament,* acknowledging Christ's real presence* there as incarnate God. Reverential practices varied during the centuries. After the 12th century, a strong cult honoring the Eucharistic species developed. With the institution of the feast of Corpus Christi* came processions,* monstrances,* and the Forty Hours' Devotion.*

Nocturnal adoration emerged from the latter and honors the exposed Blessed Sacrament during the night hours. Such devotion is fostered by the Nocturnal Adoration Society.

Perpetual Adoration is practiced by Religious Orders and eucharistic confraternities whose members continually worship the Eucharist exposed or in the tabernacle* in accordance with their Constitutions or the regulations of their Institute. Therefore perpetual adoration in parish churches is not permitted. *See also* FORTY HOURS' DEVOTION.

Adoration of the Cross. *See* CROSS.

Adoro Te Devote (uh-DOH-roh tay day-VOH-tay). The Latin title (meaning "Devoutly I Adore You") of a hymn attributed to St. Thomas Aquinas* (1225-1274). It is one of the five beautiful hymns the Angelic Doctor composed in honor of Jesus in the Blessed Sacrament* at the specific request of Pope Urban IV (1261-1264) for the new Feast of Corpus Christi* in 1264. Some doubt exists about the accuracy of this authorship, but the hymn is attributed to St. Thomas by the *Missal of Pius V** (1570).

The hymn itself is a simple, most personal, and deeply felt prayer to the Sacramental Lord, and it is found in the *Roman Missal** as one of the prayers for thanksgiving after Mass. It is also used for liturgical processions* and Benediction of the Blessed Sacrament.* The following is one of numerous translations that exist.

Hidden God, devoutly I adore You,
Truly present underneath these veils:
All my heart subdues itself before You,
Since it all before You faints and fails.

Not to sight, or taste, or touch be credit,
Hearing only do we trust secure;
I believe, for God the Son has said it—
Word of Truth that ever shall endure.

On the cross was veiled Your Godhead's splendor,
Here Your manhood lies hidden too;
Unto both alike my faith I render,
And, as sued the contrite thief, I sue.

Though I look not on Your wounds with Thomas,
You, my Lord, and You, my God, I call:
Make me more and more believe Your promise,
Hope in You, and love You over all.

O memorial of my Savior dying,
Living Bread, that gives life to man;

Make my soul, its life from You supplying,
Taste Your sweetness, as on earth it can.

Deign, O Jesus, Pelican of heaven,
Me, a sinner, in Your Blood to lave,
To a single drop of which is given
All the world from all its sin to save.

Contemplating, Lord, Your hidden presence,
Grant me what I thirst for and implore,
In the revelation of Your essence
To behold Your glory evermore.

Adult Baptism. *See* BAPTISM.

Adult Catechumenate. *See* CATECHUMENATE; RITE OF CHRISTIAN INITIATION OF ADULTS.

Advent (AD-vent). Signifying coming or arrival, this Season begins the Church Year* on the fourth

Sunday before Christmas* to prepare Christians ascetically and liturgically for the appearance of the Lord. It begins on the Sunday closest to the Feast of St. Andrew* (November 30) and therefore falls from November 27 to December 3. Primarily penitential in spirit, the Season also reflects the joy of anticipation. The expectation not only recalls Christ's first appearance on earth but also reflects His second coming. For the people of God there should be the third coming between these two, namely, His current presence in the hearts of all the faithful* by His grace.*

Since Advent is this time of preparation, it becomes a time of desire, longing, and expectancy. The spiritual hunger that consumes us at this time is to be quelled by the way the Church prepares us for Christ's coming in a threefold manner.

(a) The Old Testament, particularly through the prophet Isaiah* and with many Messianic prophecies, does much to reveal God. As there is a progressive revelation, simultaneously with this develops our longing for the Redeemer.

(b) Then comes John the Baptist,* the herald and forerunner of the Savior's Advent in history. He shows us that Advent is a time of conversion. His words lead us to a genuine reformation.

(c) Since our salvation is built on a human framework, it is not too surprising that God chose to work through a woman—thus the immaculately conceived Mary* becomes the Mother of God. What better model could we have than she who bodily contained and sheltered Him, a most perfect example of God's indwelling!

In Isaiah, John, and Mary we have models of our longing, repentance, and intimacy with God. On the last seven days the O Antiphons* are intoned, with holy desires, in which enters the great anguish that our Lord has planted in our hearts: the anguish for salvation of souls. But the horizon lights up; He, for Whom the "nations cry," is coming.

Advent Wreath (AD-vent reeth). Formed from sprigs of green foliage in a circular shape, which surround four candles, the wreath sits on a table or altar, or hangs from the ceiling. Lighting a distinct candle on each of the four Sundays of Advent* symbolizes the coming of Christ, the Light of the world. Family prayers are recited and hymns sung each day or each week.

Agape (ah-GAH-pay; AH-gah-pay). In the early Church a common evening meal called the "love feast," at first connected to a Eucharistic Liturgy, but soon separated because of scandal. It was a prayerful meal with charitable overtones; the poor were invited gratuitously. Defunct by the 8th century, it has revived after Vatican II,* e.g., in a common breakfast on days of recollection. *See also* EUCHARIST.

Agatha, St. (A-gah-thuh). ? - c.250. Sicilian Virgin* martyred under Decius. Her cult spread quickly and she is named in the Canon of the Mass (EP I*). Patroness of Nurses. *Liturgical celebration:* February 5 (Memorial); *theme:* bearing witness to Christ.

Age, Canonical. *See* CANONICAL AGE.

Aggiornamento (uh-jor-nuh-MEN-toh). An Italian word for "updating" that became the watchword for the Second Vatican Council,* whose task was to bring the Church *up-to-date* in a legitimate fashion. The liturgical aggiornamento or renewal was the very first work completed by the Council and set the tone for the renewal in the other ecclesiastical fields.

Agnes, St. (AG-nes). ?-304. Roman Virgin* martyred at an early age under Diocletian. Her cult spread widely and she is mentioned in the Canon of the Mass (EP I*). She is the Patroness of the Children of Mary Sodality. *Liturgical celebration:* January 21 (Memorial); *theme:* loyalty to the Faith.

Agnus Dei (AHG-noos, or AH-nyoos, DAY-ee). A small piece of wax, the size of a medal, derived from the paschal candle* or candles of the Purification,* stamped with an image of the Lamb of God and blessed by the Pope* in the first year of his pontificate and every seventh year thereafter. This Sacramental* protects against Satan, temptation, sudden death, and various illnesses and helps one through difficulties. *See also* LAMB OF GOD.

Aisle (ail). That architectural division of a church, on either side of the nave,* separated by series of columns or pillars. Inappropriately the passageway between rows of chairs or pews.

Akathist Hymn (AK-uh-thist him). The most celebrated liturgical hymn in honor of the Blessed Virgin used by the Byzantine Church.* It is called "Akathist" (=to be recited "without sitting down") out of reverence for the Incarnation* (announced by the Angel) in the same way that Christians stand when listening to the Gospel.* The content is made up of a brief hymn and 24 long and short strophes, each beginning with a succeeding letter of the Greek alphabet and concluding alternatively with "Rejoice, O Virgin Spouse" and "Alleluia."* The hymn is sung at the Office in part on the first four Sundays of Lent* and in toto on the 5th Saturday of Lent.

Alb (alb). A full-length white linen garment, usually gathered by a cincture,* worn by the principal clergy* over the cassock* or habit at liturgical functions. Based on the Greco-Roman tunic, it symbolizes the purity consonant with the celebration of Mass* and resembles the white robe with which Herod, in derision, ordered Christ to be covered.

Albert, St. (AL-bert). 1206-1280. German Dominican and Bishop of Ratisbon. Called "the Great" and the "Universal Doctor" because of his encyclopedic knowledge of both sacred and secular sciences. Taught St. Thomas Aquinas.* He is a Doctor of the Church* and the Patron of Scientists and Medical Technicians. *Liturgical celebration:* November 15 (Memorial); *theme:* to reach God through the human sciences.

Alcuin (AL-koo-in). c. 735-804. Priest-educator of the Palace School and advisor to Charlemagne on religious and educational matters. He was devoted to the study of the sciences, the Faith, and the Liturgy,* and is known as the author of the Carolingian Liturgical Reform. It was Alcuin who revised the *Roman Lectionary** in Gaul and reconciled the *Gregorian Sacramentary** (sent to Charlemagne by Pope Hadrian I) with the surviving Gallican customs by adding an Appendix to it.

Alexandrian Rite (a-lek-ZAND-ree-uhn rait). One of the Eastern rites known as the Liturgy of St. Mark. It also contains elements of the Byzantine Rite* of St. Basil and the liturgies of Sts. Mark,* Cyril of Alexandria,* and Gregory of Nazianzen.* There are two branches: the Copts, who celebrate it in Coptic and Arabic, and the Ethiopians, who celebrate it in Geez.

Aliturgical Days (ay-luh-TUR-ji-kuhl; -li-; dayz). Days on which the Eucharistic Sacrifice may not be celebrated. In the early Church* weekdays were aliturgical. Many still are in the Eastern Church. Recently in the Roman rite* Good Friday* and Holy Saturday* were, but with the Easter Vigil* reinstated now, only Good Friday is aliturgical.

All Saints (awl saynts). A Holy Day of Obligation* (November 1) to honor all Saints in a common feast, even those unrecorded. In the East such a feast honored the martyrs* as early as the 4th century, and was later enlarged to include nonmartyrs, celebrated either in an Easter* period or on the octave day of Pentecost.* In the West relics of martyrs were moved from some catacombs to the Pantheon,* and Boniface IV consecrated the building on May 13, 610, under the title of All Martyrs and All Saints and of Our Lady. This title was changed to All Saints in 835 by Gregory III when he dedicated a chapel in honor of All Saints in the Vatican Basilica, and at that time the date was changed to November 1.

All Souls (awl sohls). A commemoration of all the faithful departed on November 2. When it falls on

Sunday, the Masses are of the commemoration, and the Office is of the Sunday. Three Masses were formerly allowed to be celebrated by each priest, but one intention was stipulated for all the Poor Souls and another for the Pope's intention. This permission was granted by Benedict XV during the World War of 1914-1918 because of the great slaughter of that war, and because, since the time of the Reformation and the confiscation of church property, obligations for anniversary Masses which had come as gifts and legacies were almost impossible to continue in the intended manner. Some canonists believe Canon 905 of the New Code has abolished this practice. However, the *Sacramentary,** printed prior to the Code, provides three separate Mass texts for this date.

Most Christians felt that besides funeral or anniversary rites there should be an opportunity when the ordinary people, good Christians, but not canonized, could be prayed for in the hope that God would allow them also to share in the victory of the risen Christ. At the funeral service Christian hope* gives a strong testimony in the anticipated blessed resurrection. Therefore, this solemn memorial day, having been celebrated on different dates in various localities, became fixed on November 2, around the start of the 11th century when Odilo of Cluny chose that date for the commemoration in all the Cluniac houses. It spread from there and was eventually adopted in Rome by the 14th century.

Alleluia (ah-luh-LOO-yuh). From the Hebrew *hallelujah* (Praise the Lord). A very ancient liturgical acclamation of jubilation used in the Psalms,* and now at the Mass* and in the Liturgy of the Hours.* It is a joyful response to a chant used on festival occasions. As its use grew, it detached itself from psalmody* and launched out on an independent existence, usually as a joyous, ecstatic cry, sometimes more spontaneous than liturgical. Christians and Jews alike embellished the word musically so that sometimes especially the last syllable became a pure, wordless chant of joy, almost as if the people were "speaking with tongues."

This Alleluia was understood to be a foretaste of the elect's eternal gladness, not only an expression of the Praise of God. The Western Church suppresses the Alleluia during the Lenten Season* and formerly for funerals. Therefore, at Vespers* before Lent the Alleluia is frequently repeated since it will not be used again until Easter.* Then it is joyfully repeated again on the vigil of Easter in what is sometimes termed the great Alleluia. As St. Augustine said, "We are an Easter people and Alleluia is our cry." (*See also* EASTER.)

Historically it has been used not only as an act of worship but sometimes as a war cry, a signal, a magic formula, a joyous exclamation, a song of plowmen and boatmen, and perhaps also in a nursery.

Alleluia Verse (ah-luh-LOO-yuh vuhrs). Formerly the chant sung after the Gradual* between the

Al-le - lu - ia.
Al-le - lu - ia.
Al-le - lu - ia.

Epistle* and the Gospel,* now it introduces the theme of the Gospel, primarily in the content of the verse selected. Musically florid, the Alleluia is sung twice, and a verse from the Psalms* or some Scriptural text is inserted before the Alleluia is repeated a last time. The congregation is to join in this joyful acclamation. And those who sing it should be affected inwardly, causing them to meditate on how they should praise God and rejoice in Him.

The norm in the General Instruction of the Roman Missal (no. 39, 1975) reads: "If not sung, the *Alleluia* or the Verse before the Gospel may be omitted." However, the Introduction to the *Ordo Lectionum Missae* (Order of Readings for Mass) reads: "The *Alleluia* or the Verse before the Gospel must be sung and during it all stand." The Bishops' Committee on the Liturgy* in the United States has interpreted the conflicting norms in this way. According to Canon 20 of the 1983 *Code of Canon Law* the latter law has derogated from the former law. The deduction is: since the acclamation must be sung, it follows that it may not be recited; then it must be omitted if it is impossible to sing it. The Congregation for Divine Worship and the Discipline of the Sacraments promulgated the variations to be introduced in new editions of liturgical books according to the norms of the new *Code of Canon Law* in 1983, and did not make this change in number 39 of the GIRM.

Alma Redemptoris Mater (AHL-mah ray-demp-TOH-rees MAH-ter). Latin title ("Mother Benign of our Redeeming Lord") for one of the Marian Antiphons that conclude the Hour of Night Prayer* in the Divine Office.* The Latin text is attributed to Herman the Cripple (1013-1054), and many English translations exist. The following is one version:

Mother benign of our Redeeming Lord,
Star of the sea and portal of the skies,
Unto your fallen people help afford—
Fallen but striving still anew to rise.

You who did once, while wondering worlds adored,
Bear your Creator, Virgin then as now,
O by your holy joy at Gabriel's word,
Pity the sinners who before you bow.

See also FINAL ANTIPHONS OF OUR LADY

Alms. *See* COLLECTION.

Aloysius Gonzaga, St. (a-loo-WISH-uhs guhn-ZAH-guh). 1568-1591. Italian Jesuit scholastic. Model cleric who died from a plague contracted while caring for the sick. Patron of Catholic Youth. *Liturgical celebration:* June 21 (Memorial); *theme:* purity and penance.

Alpha and Omega (AL-fuh and oh-MEG-uh;-MEE-guh;-MAY-guh). The first and last letters of the Greek alphabet, often in conjunction with the cross in ecclesiastical decoration, denote the Divinity of Christ and symbolize Him as the beginning and end of all things.

Alphabet, Liturgical Use (AL-fuh-bet, luh-TUR-ji-kuhl; li-; yoos). Besides being symbols of Christ, the letters of the Hebrew, Greek, and Latin alphabets are found in calendars, the Psalms,* and the Lamentations* of Jeremiah. The entire Roman and Greek alphabets are traced by the bishop on two outlined beams of a St. Andrew's cross on the floor of a church during its consecration. The choir sings to extol the sanctity of the House of God, which the Alpha and Omega* signify as belonging to the Divine Christ.

Alphonsus Liguori, St. (al-FON-suhs lig-U-ree). 1696-1787. Neapolitan Missionary, Bishop, and Moral Theologian who founded the Order of the Most Holy Redeemer (Redemptorists). He is a Doctor of the Church* and Patron of Confessors and Moralists. *Liturgical celebration:* August 1 (Memorial); *theme:* zeal for souls.

Altar (AWL-tuhr). A table or structure used for offering sacrifice. For

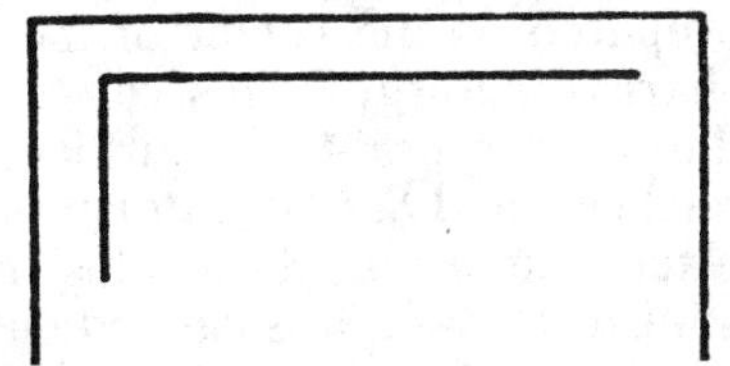

Catholics, the place for the central sacrifice, the Eucharist,* attended by the faithful* as the sacrificial meal consisting of their witness, readings,* a homily,* and prayer.* Since the Christian community is the essential factor in honoring God, the celebration may be held in a variety of places. Nevertheless, the altar is central to the service and should be the cynosure of all eyes. Recent liturgical changes take this into account and stipulate the following.

In churches, consecrated buildings, the altar is either fixed—that is, attached to the floor so as to be immovable—or movable.

Fixed altars should have natural stone for the table. The Bishops' Conference* may authorize other solid material. The rest of the altar must be durable and solid. Such altars should be consecrated and the inclusion of relics* of Saints* in an altar stone* is commended.

Movable altars ought to be of solid material, dignified and suitable for sacrifice, and acceptable in the local culture. They may be consecrated, but it is sufficient to bless them.

When Mass is celebrated outside a church, e.g., in multipurpose halls, homes, etc., a suitable table is utilized, properly covered, with no obligation of an altar stone.*

The main altar, or even the movable altar outside a church, should be freestanding, so that it can be circled and Mass can be celebrated facing the community, all of whom should be able to see the mensa, the top of the altar. On it will be the gifts of bread and wine and the *Sacramentary.**

Altars are to be covered with at least one altar cloth.* Candles* and a cross* are part of the appurtenances for the celebration.

Minor altars, apart from the nave* in the chapels in the aisles,* should be limited.

Altar, Blessing of an. *See* CHURCH DEDICATION.

Altar Boy. *See* ACOLYTE.

Altar Cards (AWL-tuhr kardz). Three convenient memory aids for the celebrant* of Mass that became part of the altar appurtenances in the 16th century. The card at the

Epistle* side contained the prayers for the Washing of the Hands.* The card in the center of the altar contained the parts of the Ordinary* of the Mass recited there. The card at the Gospel* side contained the Prologue of St. John,* which was known as the "Last Gospel" and was recited at the end of the Mass. In the wake of the Liturgical Renewal* of Vatican II, altar cards have been rendered obsolete.

Altar Cloth (AWL-tuhr klawth). Formerly three blessed linen cloths were prescribed; now at least one cloth should cover the altar out of respect for the banquet of the Lord. Its size, shape, and adornment should suit the structure of the altar. With the corporal,* it provides clean absorbent material to be used if consecrated wine is spilled.

Altar, Consecration of (AWL-tuhr, kon-suh-KRAY-shuhn uhv). The now more simple rite of anointing the altar once in five places during song and incensation, with the insertion of relics* as recommended. In the early Church* the custom developed of celebrating Mass* at gravesites of martyrs* and eventually building churches and altars over the tomb of martyrs; thus the use of relics in an altar, especially one consecrated for this purpose of the sacrifice of the Mass, became Church law by the end of the 16th century.

The recent laws found in the General Instruction of the Roman Missal (no. 265) indicate that the altar stone is no longer required on movable altars. This perhaps reflects the realization that the Church, the celebrating community, makes the altars sacred and the church a place of worship, and not the opposite. Consequently, homes and multipurpose halls can be used for Christian Liturgy,* with any appropriate table being used as an altar.

Altar, Decoration of (AWL-tuhr, dek-uh-RAY-shuhn uhv). All requisites for worship ought to be beautiful and worthy, noble and simple, to enhance the dignity of the sacred place. An artistic appearance should be combined with cleanliness, quality, and simplicity. Besides the altar cloth,* cross,* and candles,* flowers are permitted on or near the altar. However, the penitential aspect of Lent* and Advent* is heightened by their absence. Yet the tabernacle, separate from the altar of sacrifice, may be graced with fresh flowers all year (*Notitiae 11* (1975), 196-201).

Altar of Repose. *See* REPOSITORY.

Altar, Preparation of (AWL-tuhr, prep-uh-RAY-shuhn uhv). The General Instruction of the Roman Missal (no. 49) indicates that when the Liturgy of the Eucharist* begins "first the altar, the Lord's table, is prepared as the center of the Eucharistic Liturgy." This consists in the corporal,* purificator,* Chalice,* and *Sacramentary** being placed upon it. Since this is a ministerial task, it is carried out by a person other than the celebrant* —a deacon* or an acolyte.* Such

manner of acting constitutes a return to the original preparing of the altar when a linen cloth was spread upon the table and then the bread and wine brought by ministers and people were placed upon it. During the Middle Ages the preparation became more elaborate.

The *Rite of Dedication of a Church and an Altar* (ch. 4, no. 4) indicates the reason for this preparation: "The Christian altar is by its very nature properly the table of sacrifice and of the Paschal banquet. It is a unique altar on which the Sacrifice of the Cross* is perpetuated in Mystery* throughout the ages until Christ comes; a table at which the Church's children gather to give thanks to God and receive the Body and Blood* of Christ." Hence, its preparation at this part of the Mass indicates that something new is beginning. Just as the lectern was the main focus of the Liturgy of the Word,* so the altar is now the main focus of the Liturgy of the Eucharist. *See also* ALTAR; PREPARATION OF THE GIFTS; LITURGY OF THE EUCHARIST.

Altar Rails (AWL-tuhr raylz). Ornamental railings of various materials that separate the sanctuary* from the nave* of the church. Kneeling communicants use these as Communion* rails. Current legislation leads one to sense a desire to eliminate them. A higher floor level or distinctive structure and decor should mark off the sanctuary from the nave (GIRM, 258).

Altar Societies (AWL-tuhr suh-SAI-uh-teez). Parish organizations that help maintain the altar and liturgical appurtenances by the services and donations of their members.

Altar Stone (AWL-tuhr stohn). (1) The top slap or mensa of a fixed altar. (2) An inch-thick stone big enough to hold the chalice* and paten* and containing relics,* formerly placed on movable altars to fulfill the law that Mass be celebrated over relics.* Now no longer prescribed (GIRM, 265).

Altar, Stripping the (AWL-tuhr, STRIP-ing thee). Performed now without ceremony on Maundy Thursday* and Good Friday.* The cloth and movable objects are removed from the altar. Formerly done reciting Psalm 22. This action recalls Christ being stripped before crucifixion and our mourning for Him till Mass on the Easter Vigil.*

Altar, Veneration of the (AWL-tuhr, ven-uh-RAY-shuhn uhv thee). When the celebrant* and ministers* come to the sanctuary* at Mass,* they greet the altar. As a first sign of veneration, the priest or ordained ministers *kiss* the altar. This is an outgrowth of two practices that prevailed in secular society at the time of the primitive Church.* The pagans used the kiss as a sign of greeting to show their reverence for temples and images of the gods. Another custom existed of kissing the table before the family meal because those who would partake of it were hosts or guests of the household gods.

Thus, the reason behind the veneration is that the altar is a symbol of Christ ("Christ, the Head and Teacher, is the true altar"—*Rite of Dedication of a Church and an Altar,* ch. 2, no. 2). It is also the symbol of the Christian community ("Christians who give themselves to prayer, offer petitions to God, and present sacrifices of supplication, are the living stones from which the Lord Jesus builds the Church's altar"—*ibid.).*

A third influence on the use of the kiss for reverencing the altar was the cult of the Martyrs,* which led to the placing of their relics* beneath the altar. Hence, kissing the altar mean greeting the Saints* whose relics were there and the whole Church Triumphant.* Kissing the altar thus constitutes a greeting that indicates the common table is sacred to the action of the assembly.*

Originally, the altar was kissed only three times at Mass: at the beginning, during the Canon,* and before the Dismissal.* During the 14th century, kissing the altar became far more frequent and remained so up to the reform of Vatican II.* Today, it occurs only at the beginning and at the end of Mass.

A second sign of veneration is also used at times. The priest may *incense* the altar. This is a symbol of honor and deep reverence. The ascending smoke serves as a representation of the prayer* by the congregation* rising to the throne of the Divine Majesty. Furthermore, the grains of sand personify the individual Christians being poured out and consumed as they serve the Lord. *See also* ALTAR; INCENSATION; INCENSE; KISS.

Altarpiece (AWL-tuhr-pees). An ornamental carving or religious painting or fresco hung above, placed upon, or set behind an altar.* The current trend toward noble simplicity may cause such pieces to fall into desuetude.

Amalarius of Metz (ah-muh-LA-ree-uhs uhv mets). c. 775-850. A pupil of Alcuin* who was active in the Carolingian Renewal. His major work on "Ecclesiastical Offices" attempted among other things to foster the fusion of Roman and Gallican ceremonial practices. He is a basic source of the history of the Liturgy* in his time. His explanations of the Liturgy tended to be allegorical and gave rise to the allegorical explanations of the Middle Ages.

Ambo. *See* LECTERN.

Ambrose, St. (AM-brohz). c. 340-397. One of the four great Latin Fathers* and Doctors* of the Western Church. Bishop of Milan from 374 on, he wrote pastoral works on Scripture, the priesthood, the teachings of the Faith, and hymnology. He influenced the Liturgy of Milan that became known as the "Ambrosian Rite."* He is the Patron of Chandlers and Learning. *Liturgi-*

cal celebration: December 7 (Memorial); *theme:* Christian courage and wisdom.

Ambrosian Rite (am-BROH-zhuhn ;-zhee-uhn; rait). Some think St. Ambrose,* Bishop of Milan, shaped the principal characteristics of this rite, perhaps more accurately called Milanese Rite, a non-Roman Rite used in Milan and the surrounding territory. Although it has been exempted from many of the obligations of the *Roman Missal** and *Breviary,** in 1976 the *Missal* was revised according to the Second Vatican Council,* and in 1983-84, the *Divine Office.* These changes incorporate many of the features of the reformed Roman Rite, while reflecting the tradition of the Church in Milan. Some differences are: the procession of gifts in preparation for Mass* occurs before the Creed, the litany is chanted by the deacon,* a different order is followed for some of the ceremonies, Baptism is given by immersion, and some variations are introduced in the *Liturgy of the Hours.**

Ambry (AM-bree). Also aumbry. Today a niche in the sanctuary wall where the holy oils* are stored.

Amen (AY-men; AH-men). OT: acceptance of or assent to another's statement. NT: reinforces significance of an assertion. Liturgy: a Hebrew acclamation of agreement, now proclaimed by the congregation, at the end of the priest's prayers, at the end of the various parts of the Mass stressing the people's assent to what has just been said. It is especially obvious at the end of the Eucharistic Prayer*—the great Amen.* Also, since it is the response at the time of the administration of the Eucharist* to the people, it is the means by which communicants make a public affirmation of their faith in the presence of the Lord.

Amendment, Purpose of. *See* CONTRITION; PENANCE, RITE OF.

Amice (AM-uhs). An oblong white linen vestment worn by a minister over the neck and shoulders and secured by two tapes. When the habit has a capuche, the amice is worn over the head and dropped down with the hood upon arrival at the altar. Optional today only if the collar of the alb* or the chasuble* is so made as to take the place of the amice, covering the minister's secular dress—or for Religious, the capuche.

Amidah. *See* EIGHTEEN BLESSINGS, THE

Amos, The Book of (AY-muhs, thuh buk uhv). Thirty-seventh Book of the Old Testament* and third of the Minor Prophets,* the Book of Amos was composed about the 8th century. Amos was a shepherd of Tekoa in Judah. He was sent by God to preach against religious, moral, and social evils that were rampant in the Kingdom of Israel. His Book (9 chapters) concludes with a vision of God's punishment of Israel and the preservation of a remnant that will restore to the House of David its past splendor.

Liturgical use: In the *Roman Missal,** this Book is read on 15th Sun.

(B) and 25th and 26th Sundays (C), and on Weekdays after 13th Sun. (II). In the *Liturgy of the Hours,** it is used on the first three days after the 18th Sunday. *Meaning:* Amos shows that Divine punishment is never completely destructive; it is part of the hidden plan of God to bring salvation to human beings. The perversity of the human will may retard but it cannot totally frustrate this design of a loving God.

Amphora (AM[P]-fuh-ruh). Ancient jar or vase, usually made of clay, with a large oval body, narrow neck, and two handles reaching almost to its mouth. In the early Church,* it was used to hold wine for the Eucharist.* Christian symbols* adorn such vases when they are found in the catacombs.*

Ampule. *See* OIL STOCKS.

Ampullae. *See* CRUETS.

Anamnesis (an-am-NEE-sis). The essential part of the Eucharistic Prayer* after the Consecration* that commemorates the Lord's Passion,* Resurrection,* and Ascension* into heaven. Coming immediately after the Memorial Acclamation* of the people, it continues the notion of memorial by recalling the saving actions of God in Christ. At the same time, it has an obvious connection with the concepts of praise, blessing, and thanksgiving based on the remembered good deeds of God—which have been previously expressed. The Anamnesis also takes for granted the fact that the saving action of Christ works here and now in the hearts of those present at the celebration bringing them close to God and to one another.

Anaphora (uh-NAF-uh-ruh). A Greek word meaning offering; liturgically the term used in the Eastern Rite* for that part of the Mass* in the Western Liturgy,* formerly called the Canon,* now described as the Eucharistic Prayer.* For a full explanation, *see* EUCHARISTIC PRAYER.

Anastasia, St. *See* CHRISTMAS.

Anastasimatarion (an-uh-sta-see-muh-TA-ree-uhn). A liturgical book* of the Greek Church containing the text and music for the Sunday Office.*

And Also with You. *See* GREETING; LORD BE WITH YOU, THE.

André Bessette, Bl. (AHN-dray buh-SET, BLES-uhd). 1845-1937. Born near Quebec, André became a Brother of the Congregation of the Holy Cross and because of poor health was an illiterate, assigned as doorkeeper at the College of Notre Dame, Montreal. His piety and willingness to help others charmed the students and their parents. His great devotion to St. Joseph* brought about the chapel that eventually grew into the great basilica to St. Joseph in Montreal, visited by pilgrims from all over the world. His feast is part of the Proper* for the United States. *Liturgical celebration:* January 6 (Opt. Mem.); *theme:* devotion to St. Joseph and love for the poor.

Andrew, St. (AN-droo). ? - 70. A native of Bethsaida in Galilee and fisherman by trade, Andrew was a disciple of St. John the Baptist.* He

joined Jesus as a member of the Apostolic College and took his brother Peter* with him. With Philip* he presented the Gentiles to Christ and before the miracle of the loaves he pointed out to Christ the boy with the loaves and the fish. After the dispersion of the Apostles he preached in Greece and other countries before being martyred in Patras, Greece, by crucifixion on a cross made in the form of an X. He is the Patron of Fishermen. *Liturgical celebration:* November 30 (Feast); *theme:* sharing Christ's Cross.

Andrew Kim, St. (AN-droo kim) **and Companion Martyrs.** 19th cent. Unusual as it may seem, the evangelization of Korea began during the 17th century through a group of lay persons.* A strong vital Christian community flourished there under lay leadership until missionaries arrived from France in 1836. During the terrible persecutions that occurred in the 19th century, this Christian community had 103 martyrs,* outstanding among them being their first Korean priest and pastor Andrew Kim, and a lay apostle Paul Chong Hasang. The others were a few bishops and priests but mostly laity, married and single, young and old, who suffered torture to consecrate the beginnings of the Church of Korea with their blood. *Liturgical celebration:* September 20 (Memorial); *theme:* valiant struggle during persecution is the seed of Christianity.

Angela Merici, St. (AN-juh-luh muh-REE-chee). 1470-1540. Born in Desenzano in Lombardy, Angela became a Franciscan Tertiary and called together girls whom she instructed in charitable works. In 1535, under the patronage of St. Ursula, she founded a Congregation of women who instructed poor girls in the Christian life. It was the first teaching Order for women approved by the Church. *Liturgical celebration:* January 27 (Opt. Mem.); *theme:* fidelity to Divine teaching.

Angelic Hymn. *See* GLORY TO GOD.

Angelical Salutation. *See* HAIL MARY.

Angels (AYN-juhlz). A word that comes from the Greek for "messengers" and denotes free spirits not dependent on matter, created to honor and serve God. The existence

of angels was defined by the Church* during Lateran Council IV (1215) and Vatican Council I (1870). Since angels are free, they are able to sin. Hence, devils, angels by nature, are called fallen angels.

Angels differ in perfection of nature and grace and normally are considered to be grouped in nine different choirs: archangels, angels, principalities, dominations, powers, virtues, thrones, cherubim, and seraphim.

In the Old Testament* their principal activities were divided between praising God and acting as messengers to human beings. In the New Testament* they are related to Christ's kingship* over creation, and are usually connected with the events in His life, such as adoring Jesus at His Birth,* ministering to Him during His Public Life, and being messengers at the time of His Resurrection.* Paul,* in his Epistles, makes clear that the angels are subordinate to Christ. They pertain to Christ's salvific relation to the world, and their spiritual presence and influence are felt by the world at large.

Formerly each of the three archangels mentioned in the Bible and venerated by the Church had a separate feast day, but the recent liturgical change brought the three together on the 29th of September: Sts. Michael,* Raphael,* and Gabriel.* The idea that guardian angels, from the choir named angels, are appointed by God for each person reached acceptance; their feast is celebrated on October 2. The role of the angels in connection with the end of the world is significantly explained in the Book of Revelation.*

The various sections of the Mass reflect the work of the angels or their activities. They are invoked at the Blessing of the Incense* and in all the Prefaces,* and our voices are joined with theirs during the singing of the Holy, Holy, Holy.*

The Glory to God* is called the Angelic Hymn since it was sung by the angels on the night of Christ's Birth.

At the solemn moment after Consecration in the First Eucharistic Prayer,* the invocation reads: "Almighty God, / we pray that your angel may take this sacrifice / to your altar in heaven." The assumption is that the angels surround the priest and the altar, uniting with him in adoration of the Victim, Who is resting on the altar, Jesus Christ Himself. This holy angel carries and presents the sacred gifts of the earthly altar to God the Father, so that they may be accepted by Him with kindness since they constitute the sacrifice of praise of the Church Triumphant.*

In the *Liturgy of the Hours** for the Feasts of angels, the Psalms* in which the Divine messengers are mentioned have been chosen for recitation. Antiphons,* responses,* and readings* are taken from the various Prophets* and Scriptural sections that touch upon their work.

Angelus (AN-juh-luhs). A devotional practice in honor of the Incarnation,* using the Hail Mary,* commemorating the archangel Gabriel's annunciation to Mary, and recited thrice daily, morning (6:00 A.M.) noon, and evening (6:00 P.M.) while a bell is rung. Consisting of three versicles with their responses,

each followed by the Hail Mary,* it concludes with a brief verse and a prayer. The name derives from the first Latin word of the opening verse, *Angelus Domini,* "The angel of the Lord." The total prayer sums up the history of the Incarnation of the Word. In short, it is a primitive structure of a *Daytime Prayer** without a hymn or a short reading,* and with the Psalms supplanted by the Hail Mary.*

During the Easter Season* the Angelus is replaced by the anthem *Regina Caeli** ("Queen of Heaven") with its verse and prayer.

Originating in the 13th century, this devotion grew into general use by the 17th century. There is a daily ringing of the bell* during its recitation, with three strokes, three times tolled, followed by a long ringing until the final prayer is completed. The Angelus is said kneeling, the *Queen of Heaven* is recited standing.

Pope Callistus III (1455-1458) determined the intention that Christians should have in this devotion, namely, protection of Christendom against the Turks. (We thus see the Christian reply to the appeal of the Muezzin for the Moslem prayer.)

Pope Paul VI (in 1974) indicated the underlying and truly Christian intention for saying this prayer: "Its simple structure, its Biblical character, its historical origin which links it to the prayer for peace and safety, and its quasi-liturgical rhythm which sanctifies different moments during the day, . . . and its reminder of the Paschal Mystery,* in which recalling the Incarnation of the Son of God we pray that we may be led 'through His Passion and Cross to the glory of His Resurrection' " (MC, 41).

The text of the *Angelus* in the *Enchiridion of Indulgences** is as follows:

℣. The Angel of the Lord declared unto Mary,
℟. And she conceived of the Holy Spirit.
Hail Mary . . .

℣. Behold the handmaid of the Lord.
℟. Be it done unto me according to your word.
Hail Mary . . .

℣. And the Word was made flesh,
℟. And dwelt among us.
Hail Mary . . .

℣. Pray for us, O holy Mother of God,
℟. That we may be made worthy of the promises of Christ.

Let us pray: Pour forth, we beg You, O Lord, Your grace into our hearts: that we, to whom the Incarnation of Christ Your Son was made known by the message of an Angel, may by His Passion and Cross be brought to the glory of His Resurrection. Through the same Christ our Lord. Amen.

Anima Christi (AH-nee-mah KRIS-tee). Latin name (meaning "Soul of Christ") of a beautiful and popular Eucharistic prayer that is found in the *Roman Missal** section on "Thanksgiving after Mass." Of unknown authorship, it was popularized by St. Ignatius Loyola* and its recitation carries a partial indulgence* (EI, 10).

Those who pray the *Anima Christi* unite themselves with Christ's sacrifice, which is the supreme act of worship and praise of God. They are led to see the Eucharist* as the source of salvation, redemption, sanctification, and joy.

For them, the Eucharist truly becomes a lasting memorial of Christ's Passion* (and implicit Resurrection*), which brings human beings pardon of sins, protection from evil, and strength for daily life on the way to a blessed eternity.

The translation given in the *Enchiridion of Indulgences** is as follows:

Soul of Christ, sanctify me.
Body of Christ, save me.
Blood of Christ, inebriate me.
Water from the side of Christ, wash me.
Passion of Christ, strengthen me.
O good Jesus, hear me.
Within Your wounds, hide me.
Separated from You let me never be.
From the malignant enemy, defend me.
At the hour of death, call me.
To come to You, bid me,
That I may praise You in the company
Of Your Saints, for all eternity. Amen.

Ann, St. (an). 1st century B.C. Since early Christian times, churches were dedicated in honor of St. Ann, mother of the Blessed Virgin Mary.* The Fathers of the Church frequently extolled her virtues, holiness, and privileges. She is the Patroness of Cabinetmakers, Housewives, and Women in Labor. *Liturgical celebration:* July 26 (Memorial); *theme:* fulfillment of God's promise.

Anniversary (an-uh-VUHR-suh-ree). A liturgical celebration of an annual remembrance of a specific event in the life of the Church,* keeping in mind that grace is liberated at this stage in time, to achieve the continual efficacy intended.

The liturgical cycle creates a rhythm that brings back the same feasts year by year, celebrated as anniversaries of historical or conventional dates.

(1) The Temporal Cycle (Proper of the Season*) commemorates the anniversaries of the more important events of the life of Jesus Christ, His Birth,* the Adoration of the Magi,* the Presentation,* His Death,* Resurrection,* Ascension,* etc.

(2) In the Sanctoral Cycle (Proper of the Saints*), there are anniversaries of various events in the life of Mary* as well as the death of the Saints, that is, the day of their birth in heaven.

(3) On the anniversaries of the election and installation of the reigning Pontiff, specific prayers are offered for the Pope,* either by means of a special Votive* Mass in his honor or with the orations of the Mass of the day selected from that Mass. A remembrance should certainly be added to the invocations for the General Intercessions* or Prayer of the Faithful.

(4) On the anniversary of the election, transfer, episcopal ordination, or installation of the Diocesan Bishop,* a special petition is included in the General Intercessions during Mass. In most cases the oration from the Mass for the Bishop may also be used.

(5) On the anniversary of their sacerdotal ordination, all priests may choose the Votive Mass for this

particular purpose, provided the rank of the day allows it.

(6) Anniversaries for marriages may be celebrated regularly, but in most instances they occur primarily on the 25th or the 50th wedding anniversary. A special Votive Mass may be used, and after the Gospel* an opportunity exists for the married couple to renew their vows.

(7) On the first anniversary of the death or burial of a person, the anniversary Mass for the Dead may be celebrated. Many communities and fraternities have at least one day during the year on which the anniversary of all the deceased members of their group is celebrated.

(8) The dedication* of a church, namely, the day it was consecrated or blessed, is regularly celebrated on its anniversary. This custom has its origin from the Jews who purified the second Temple of Zerubbabel in the year 165 B.C. under Judas Maccabeus. They had a feast of purification that was celebrated each year on the 25th of the month of Kasleu. In like manner the Christians celebrated the anniversary of the dedication of their churches, an obligation for the community of that place itself.

(a) The annual anniversaries of the dedication of four great basilicas of Rome occur in the Universal Church calendar. November 9: the Archbasilica of St. John Lateran*; November 18: the two basilicas of St. Peter* at the Vatican and St. Paul-outside-the-walls; and August 5: the basilica of St. Mary Major.*

(b) All the churches in the diocese celebrate the anniversary of their cathedral.* Normally this occurs on the very anniversary day of the dedication.

(c) Any consecrated church has the obligation of celebrating its anniversary, usually on the date of the consecration. However, the bishop may fix an anniversary date for all the consecrated churches in his diocese. Then all in the diocese celebrate the anniversary of their church on the same day.

Some other aspects of Church life are also commemorated, such as Baptism,* First Holy Communion,* Confirmation,* and Religious Profession,* as well as acknowledgment of the choir, the school, the religious education program, etc. Such celebrations vary from the elaborate recitation of an Hour from the *Liturgy of the Hours** with a concelebrated Mass at the regular parish Mass to other religious activities or devotions, sometimes in conjunction with more secular festivals.

Announcements (uh-NOWN[T]S-muhnts). Announcements at Mass* should be about public worship or possibly some explanation of the parish calendar. Some have become unduly long, incorporating the proclamation of banns,* civil enactments, society meetings, and appeals, and have thus reduced the sacred character they were to have. Today most announcements can be made through the use of posters and bulletin boards, or printed in

parish bulletins or monthly magazines. Thus verbal announcements can be minimal. The proper place for them according to present legislation is following the Prayer after Communion,* prior to the Concluding Rite* (that is, the Greeting* and Final Blessing*) and never before or after the Homily.*

Annunciation of the Lord (uh-nun[t]-see-AY-shun uhv thuh lawrd). Nine months before Jesus' Birth,* the Archangel Gabriel* was sent by God to announce to the Virgin Mary* that she was to be the Mother of the promised Redeemer. On this same day, God the Son, the Second Person of the Blessed Trinity, by the power of the Holy Spirit* assumed a human body and became the Son of Mary.

This is therefore a double feast—the Annunciation of the Maternity of Mary and the Incarnation* of the Son of God. The Liturgy* emphasizes that the Incarnation contained in germ the entire divinization of humankind. It also shows Christ making an act of obedience to the Father on coming into the world and Mary welcoming Christ in faith; it thus urges us to do likewise. *Liturgical celebration:* March 25 (Solemnity); *theme:* conforming oneself to Christ.

Anointing (uh-NOINT-ing). In a religious ceremony the daubing of holy oil upon a person or object for a sacral purpose. The major significance of anointing is to convey the spirit of Christ Who is simultaneously the source of the spirit and the paragon of living as a Christian. In the Old Testament* kings, priests, and prophets were anointed, i.e., made sacred. Such unctions are used in the Sacraments* in a twofold manner: (1) to confer them, as in Confirmation* and Anointing of the Sick*; (2) as part of the ceremony, as in Baptism* and Holy Orders.*

In the case of the sick the oil's medicinal quality acquires a remedial significance in the Sacrament. The baptismal anointing strengthens the candidates for their fight with any evil power they may meet as they are plunged into the waters of life. Through anointing, the priest's hands are made sacred since he will celebrate the Eucharist* and handle the sacred elements. By anointing the bishop* on his head, it is as if his total body is anointed, and thus he becomes sacrosanct. Cult objects like altars* and church walls are also consecrated with oil. Some blessed oils (for instance, those of St. Serapion) are employed as Sacramentals.*

Anointing of the Sick (uh-NOINT-ing uhv thuh sik). The proper current term for the Sacrament* formerly known as Extreme Unction. Since the Sacrament is for the sick and not only for the dying, the former term is a misnomer and tends to alarm the ailing person. The Sacrament's purpose is to strengthen the spiritual health of the sick even to remission of sins, should they be unable to confess.

Occasionally the ill have recovered physical health also.

Serious illness or old age is sufficient reason to receive the Sacrament. It may be repeated after a recovery, or if the danger increases. Anointing before a major operation or of unconscious Christians is allowed. It is administered by anointing the forehead and hands with blessed olive oil* (or another vegetable oil in certain circumstances) while reciting the formula.

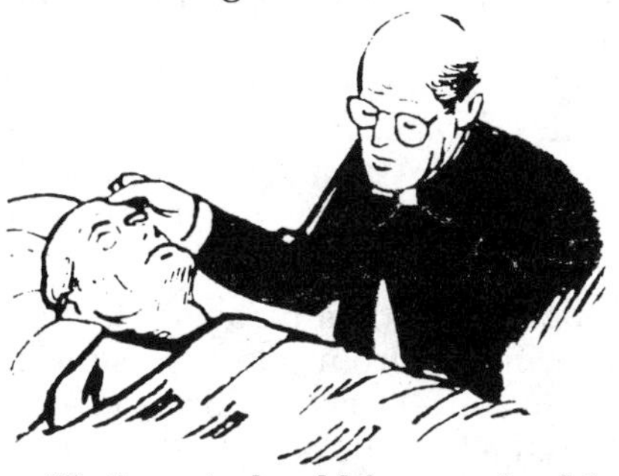

Viaticum* should be received by all in danger of death. The continuous rite is available to permit an ill person to receive the Penance Rite,* Viaticum, and Anointing in one service. *See also* PASTORAL CARE OF THE SICK; VIATICUM.

Anselm, St. (AN-selm). 1033-1109. Born in Piedmont, Italy, Anselm became a Benedictine, Abbot* of a monastery, and Archbishop of Canterbury in 1093. He wrote philosophical and theological works that have earned for him the titles of the Father of Scholastic Theology and a Doctor of the Church.* *Liturgical celebration:* April 21 (Opt. Mem.); *theme:* faith aiding understanding.

Ansgar, St. (ANZ-gahr). 801-865. Born at Corbie, he was first a monk, then a missionary to Denmark and Sweden before becoming Bishop of Hamburg and finally Bremen. He is the Apostle of Scandinavia. *Liturgical celebration:* February 3 (Opt. Mem.); *theme:* walking in the light of God's truth.

Antependium (ant-i-PEN-dee-uhm). A decorative and protective veil or hanging for the front of the altar,* covering its entire length from top to bottom and varying in color according to the ecclesiastical season* or feast.* First used in the 5th century (4th in the East), it has now become obsolete. The term is also used of hangings for the pulpit and lectern.*

Anthem (AN-thum). Sacred vocal, usually choral, music. Liturgically today in Catholic circles it refers only to the rhythmic invocations to the Blessed Virgin Mary at the end of Night Prayer.* *See also* FINAL ANTIPHONS OF OUR LADY.

Anthony the Abbot, St. (AN-thuh-nee thee AB-uht). c. 250-356. Born in Egypt, Anthony sold all he had and retired to the desert at 18. He is called the Patriarch of Monks because he was the first Abbot* to establish a stable rule for his family of monks dedicated to Divine Service. He is the Patron of Basketmakers, Brush Makers, Butchers, and Gravediggers. *Liturgical celebration:* January 17 (Memorial); *theme:* self-denial and love for God.

Anthony Claret, St. (AN-thuh-nee cla-RAY). 1807-1870. Spanish priest and missionary to Catalonia and the Canary Islands. Founded Missionary Sons of the Immaculate Heart of Mary (Claretians). Later as Archbishop of Santiago de Cuba he founded the Teaching Sisters of Mary Immaculate. *Liturgical celebration:* October 24 (Opt. Mem.); *theme:* missionary zeal.

Anthony of Padua, St. (AN-thuh-nee uhv PAD-oo-uh). 1195-1231. A native of Lisbon, he is called "of

Padua" because of his long residence in the latter city. Priest and Doctor,* he is venerated as one of the greatest Franciscan Saints—a profound theologian, brilliant preacher, and formidable foe of

heresy. He is the Patron of Barren Women, the Poor, Searchers for Lost Articles, and Travelers. *Liturgical celebration:* June 13 (Memorial); *theme:* giving good example.

Anthony Zaccaria, St. (AN-thuh-nee za-kuh-RAI-uh). 1502-1539. Born in Cremona, Italy, Anthony gave up his practice of medicine to embrace the Religious Life. Later he founded the Order of Clerks Regular of St. Paul, called Barnabites. *Liturgical celebration:* July 5 (Opt. Mem.); *theme:* grasping the wisdom of Christ.

Anticipated Sunday Mass. *See* SUNDAY MASS OBLIGATION.

Anticipation (an-tis-uh-PAY-shuhn). Technical term referring to the custom of reciting the Office of Readings* for any date on the preceding day, during the night hours after Evening Prayer* has been said (*See* GILH, 59).

Antimension (an-ti-MEN-zhi-uhn). Also Antimensium. Used in Eastern Churches, particularly Byzantine, this square cloth held relics* and was placed on the altar of sacrifice. Formerly, when relics were required for the celebration of Mass on a portable altar, the Ordinary* could permit its use in the Latin Rite.

Antiochene Rite (an-TEE-oh-keen rait). One of the five principal rites used by the Eastern Christian Churches. Its origin goes back to the *Apostolic Constitutions** and the Liturgy of St. James of Jerusalem.* It is celebrated in Syriac and Malayalam by the *Malankarese* in India; in Syriac and Arabic by the *Maronites* in Lebanon, Cyprus, Egypt, Syria as well as in the United States, Brazil, and Australia; and in Syriac and Arabic by the *Syrians* in Asia, Africa, the Americas, and Australia.

Antiphon (AN-tuh-fuhn). A short text, usually from Scripture, sung or recited as a refrain before and after a Psalm,* canticle,* or psalm-verse in the Liturgy.* The antiphon was introduced into the Mass with a primarily ornamental function at particular rites: during the Processional Chants* (Entrance Antiphon,* Offertory Antiphon,* and Communion Antiphon*) and the Intervenient Chants* (Gradual,* Alleluia Verse,* and Tract*).

It was also inserted into the Liturgy of the Hours* with an essentially psalmic function. Antiphons help to bring out the literary form of the Psalm; they transform the Psalm into a personal prayer; they highlight a sentence that might otherwise not attract the attention it deserves; they suggest an individual quality in a Psalm in accord with different contexts; indeed, as long as extravagant accommodated meanings are avoided, they are of great value in helping bring about an understanding of the typological meaning or the meaning appropriate to the feast; and they can also add pleasure and variety to the recitation of the Psalms *(see* GILH, 113ff).

The term antiphon is also used at times as a synonym for anthem.*

Antiphonal Chant (an-TIF-uh-nuhl chant). Alternate choirs chanting verses of the Psalms.* Originally the singing of the refrain by choirs between psalm-verses* sung by soloists.

Antiphonary (an-TIF-uh-ner-ee). The liturgical book* containing the words and music for the choral singing of the Liturgy of the Hours.* *See also* LECTIONARY; LITURGY OF THE HOURS.

Apocrypha (uh-POK-ruh-fuh). Writings, presumably of sacred origin, purporting to be Scriptural and composed around the time of Christ, but not classed as authentic

or canonical. Non-Catholic Christians use the term "Pseudepigrapha" for the apocrypha of the OT. They reserve the term "Apocrypha" for the religious books used by both Jews and Christians that were not originally included in the collection of inspired writings—all of Tobit,* Judith,* 1 and 2 Maccabees,* Wisdom,* Baruch,* and Ecclesiasticus (Sirach*), and parts of Esther* and Daniel.* Catholics call these "Deuterocanonical."

The Liturgy* makes use of parts of the deuterocanonical books. It also includes a few selections from the apocryphal books, for example, 4 Esdras. *See also* BIBLE.—CANON.

Apology. *See* PENITENTIAL RITE.

Apostle (uh-POS-uhl). (1) A Greek word that means an authorized representative of the sender, in this case, men called by Jesus and sent in His name into the world; the Apostles formed a collegial community under Peter* as a nucleus working together to establish His one true Church.* The threefold office conferred on them was to rule, teach, and sanctify, using Sacramental power to "make disciples of all nations" (Mt 28:19).

Attributed to them was their own confirmation in grace, individual infallibility, and universal jurisdiction* under Peter, the first Pope.* Their names were: Peter, Matthew,* James the Greater,* James the Less,* John,* Judas, Andrew,* Philip,* Bartholomew,* Thomas,* Jude,* and Simon.* To succeed Judas, Matthias* was chosen by lot according to the norm: one who traveled with Jesus from His Baptism* to the Ascension* and could testify to the Resurrection* (Acts 1:21-22). Paul* received a special call from Christ (1 Cor 9:1; 15:9-10) and so, though celebrated with Peter on June 29, more properly fits the second definition below.

(2) The broader sense of apostle refers to those who first established the Church in various countries, e.g., Boniface* in Germany. Recent Biblical studies indicate that both men and women were apostles in the Church.

(3) This term also applies to the Epistle* read during the Liturgy of

the Eastern Churches, always chosen from one of the Apostles or Acts,* never the Old Testament.

Apostles. *See* SAINTS, LITURGICAL CATEGORIES OF.

Apostles' Creed. *See* PROFESSION OF FAITH.

Apostleship of Prayer (uh-POS-uhl-ship uhv prayr). A worldwide association to unite its members in prayer for their own intentions and those of the Holy Father, and to foster their devotion to the Sacred Heart* of Jesus, especially in His Sacrament of Love. The essential practice is a Morning Offering*—a prayer and sacrifice to be lived throughout each day. Through the Immaculate Heart of Mary* the members offer our Lord all their prayers, works, joys, and sufferings. They offer them in union with Christ's own offering of Himself in the Holy Sacrifice of the Mass,* being offered at every moment of the day, somewhere in the world. Thus, the Apostleship of Prayer makes the Mass the very center of the members' day, and it is intimately linked with the Liturgical Movement.*

Two other practices are encouraged but not required: (1) Mass and Communion of Reparation at regular times, especially on the First Friday*; and (2) the daily recitation of the Rosary,* or at least one decade of it.

Apostolate (uh-POS-tuh-layt,-luht). The vocation of an apostle to "make disciples of all nations" (Mt 28:19). All Catholics are called to participate in "extending the kingdom of Christ throughout the world for the glory of God the Father . . . and to direct the whole universe to Christ" (AA, 2). The *liturgical apostolate** is an especially effective way in which all members of the Church can fulfill their apostolate. By living the Liturgy* they can bring Christ into their lives and to the world. Thus, it is incumbent upon pastors* to promote an active and complete participation by the laity,* and upon priests to grasp fully the import of their performance of sacred actions, living the liturgical life* in such a manner that the members of the Church entrusted to them may share in it and radiate it to others.

Apostolic Blessing. *See* BLESSING, APOSTOLIC.

Apostolic Constitutions (a-puh-STOL-ik kon-sti-TOO-shuhnz). A collection of Church law (in eight books) supposedly from the early Church, but actually compiled in the 4th century by a Syrian and probably Semi-Arian writer. It is largely based on the *Didascalia Apostolorum,** the *Didache,** the *Apostolic Tradition** of Hippolytus, and the Antiochene Liturgy.* Nonetheless, it offers an interesting description of liturgical practices of the Church of Syria in the 4th century.

Apostolic Constitutions, Papal. *See* LITURGICAL LAW, SOURCES OF.

Apostolic Epistles, Papal. *See* LITURGICAL LAW, SOURCES OF.

Apostolic Exhortations, Papal. *See* LITURGICAL LAW, SOURCES OF.

Apostolic Letters, Papal. *See* LITURGICAL LAW, SOURCES OF.

Apostolic See (a-puh-STOL-ik see). Title of the bishopric of Rome. The Pope,* bishop of Rome, with his offices, enjoys supreme authority over liturgical matters, e.g., confirming adaptations, approving decrees of the National Conferences of Bishops,* granting the faculty to experiment, and reviewing rituals.

Apostolic Tradition (a-puh-STOL-ik truh-DI-shuhn). A treatise on Church order generally regarded as the work of St. Hippolytus* in 215. This invaluable work (1) deals with the consecration of bishops, the Eucharistic Liturgy,* ordination* of priests and deacons, and various blessings*; (2) lists laws for the laity*; and (3) sets down various ecclesiastical practices.

Only extracts of the original work exist, but there are complete translations extant in Coptic, Arabic, Ethiopic, and Latin. It is of great importance for the history of the Liturgy and the history of the Roman community in the 3rd century.

Apostolicam Actuositatem (ah-pohs-TOH-lee-kahm ahk-too-oh-zee-TAH-tem). Latin title (from the first two words "Apostolic Activity") of the *Decree on the Apostolate of the Laity* issued by the Second Vatican Council* on November 18, 1965. It stresses that the laity* are made sharers in the priestly, prophetic, and kingly office of Christ. Thus, in all they do they may offer up spiritual sacrifices and bear witness to Christ in all the earth. The Sacraments,* the Eucharist* above all, bring to them and sustain that charity or love* which is the soul of all apostolic activity. The effectiveness of the apostolate depends on the laity's personal vital union with Christ, which is nurtured in the Church from the spiritual resources that all the faithful share, above all from a devout participation* in the Liturgy.* *See also* VATICAN COUNCIL, SECOND.

Appearances of Bread and Wine (uh-PIR-uhn[t]s-uhz uhv bred and wain). The outward physical characteristics of the Bread* and Wine* that remain after the Consecration* at Mass.* The substance of the consecrated Bread and Wine has become the Body and Blood of Jesus, but the appearances of both are unchanged. The Bread still looks, feels, smells, and tastes like bread, and the Wine looks, feels, smells, and tastes like wine. They are termed the Sacred Species.* *See also* CONSECRATION; EUCHARISTIC ELEMENTS; PRESENCE, REAL; TRANSUBSTANTIATION.

Appropriation (uh-proh-pree-AY-shuhn). A way of speaking (resulting from the limitations of human language and the finite nature of the human mind) that is widely used in the Liturgy* as well as in Catholic teaching. Found in Sacred Scripture* and in ecclesiastical writers and preachers, appropriation attributes certain names, qualities, and operations to one Person of the Blessed Trinity* in preference to but not to the exclusion of the others.

The areas of attribution are usually listed as: (1) names: the Father

as God *(Theos)* and the Son as Lord *(Kyrios);* (2) attributes: the Father as endowed with eternity, power, and unity; the Son, with beauty, equality, and wisdom; and the Holy Spirit, with goodness, happiness, and harmony; (3) operations: the Father as efficient cause, the Son as exemplary cause; and the Holy Spirit as final cause, and (4) worship: the Father as the recipient of adoration and praise, the Son as the mediator, and the Holy Spirit as the Advocate—in accord with the formula: "To the Father through the Son in the unity of the Holy Spirit."

Appropriation is concerned not with the inner life of the Persons of the Trinity but with the outward life. It is based on the resemblance or affinity of the appropriated attribute with the properties of the Persons to Whom it is attributed. As such, it can aid the human mind and heart to understand in some way the Divine Persons and their relations with their creatures. *See also* ACCOMMODATION; GOD.

Apse (aps). Architecturally the extremity of the nave* or choir,* usually constructed in a semicircle and roofed with a half dome, covering the altar* and sanctuary.* In some churches side-apses occur at the ends of the aisles.* Side chapels or chevets sometimes surround the apse. To achieve the effect of bringing the people closer to the altar, modern churches are built without an apse.

Archangels. *See* ANGELS.

Archbishop (ahrch-BISH-uhp). Title for the bishop* who has the highest authority over an ecclesiastical province, usually consisting of several suffragan dioceses. Occasionally termed metropolitan (mother city), he convenes the provincial council, acts as a judge of appeals from the suffragan sees, and guards the doctrine and discipline in the province. It may also refer to the honorary title for a bishop of an important diocese who does not have metropolitan jurisdiction.

Archconfraternities *See* CONFRATERNITIES.

Archdiocese (ahrch-DAI-uh-sis, -ses, -seez). The diocese* over which an archbishop,* who has rank and ceremonial prestige, rules.

Archeologism (ahr-kee-AHL-uh-jiz-uhm). Exaggerated zeal for antiquity in liturgical matters. It is also termed "antiquarianism," and as such has been proscribed by the Church.* Thus Pius XII observed: "The Liturgy* of the early ages is most certainly worthy of all veneration. But ancient usage must not be esteemed more suitable and proper, either in its own right or in its significance for later times and new situations, on the simple ground that it carries the savor and aroma of antiquity. The more recent liturgical rites likewise deserve reverence and respect. . . .

"Assuredly, it is a wise and most laudable thing to return in spirit and affection to the sources of the sacred Liturgy. For research in this field of study, by tracing it back to its origins, contributes valuable assistance toward a more thorough and careful investigation of the significance of feastdays and of the meaning of the texts and sacred ceremonies employed on their occasion. But it is neither wise nor laudable to reduce everything to antiquity by every possible device" (MD, 61-62).

Archeology, Liturgical (ahr-kee-AHL-uh-jee, luh-TUHR-ji-kuhl; li-). The study of Christian monuments to unearth information about the Liturgy* of antiquity (the first six centuries) through the excavation of sites, reconstruction of inscriptions, and study of building methods. Monuments include the catacombs,* cemeteries, church baptisteries and monasteries, sculpture, paintings, mosaics, frescoes, engravings, miniatures, textiles, implements for worship, glass, cups, medals, and rings.

Liturgical archeology has been one of the most important parts of the historical science of Liturgy, which was created in the 17th century and served to open the eyes of both clergy* and laity* to the value and riches of the Liturgy, its importance in the Church's tradition, the precise meaning of rites and prayers, the correct distinction between what is essential and what is nonessential, and the unity and diversity of its euchological patrimony.

Indeed, archeological discoveries have often given rise to renewed interest in the history of the Liturgy, which has been mentioned by Pius XII and the Second Vatican Council* as playing an important role in the liturgical renewal (MD, 4-5; SC, 23. 50. 62).

Architectural Environment (ahr-kuh-TEK-chuh-ruhl en-VAI-ruhn-muhnt). Laws for architecture of

places of worship closely relate to those pertaining to Art and Liturgy.* Whatever revision is necessary in laws that refer to worthy and well planned construction of sacred buildings and altars should take place. The intent is to achieve a setting in keeping with the reformed Liturgy. The result should be able to satisfy those who have rediscovered personal prayer and intense meditation as well as to fulfill the needs of those who celebrate with new and vital forms of worship.*

Archpriest (AHRCH-preest). A term that designates a priest* who holds a preeminent position. Today it is used by custom for the unofficially designated experienced priest who assists at the first Mass* of a newly ordained.

Arcosolium (ahr-ko-SOH-lee-uhm). An arched recess in dirt or rock that formed a place of burial in the catacombs.* Celebrations of the Eucharist* took place on the slab that closed the grave.

Arculae (AHRK-oo-lay). Small containers used by the faithful* to carry the Blessed Sacrament* during the persecutions in the Early Church. Fashioned out of gold or other precious metal, they were early forms of the pyx.*

Armenian Rite (ar-MEE-ni-uhn rait). This is substantially the

Liturgy of St. Basil* translated into classical Armenian, with modifications from the Antiochene Rite* and additions from the Latin Mass.* It is considered an older form of the Byzantine Rite,* and is celebrated in the Near East, Europe, Africa, the Americas, and Australasia.

Art and Liturgy (ahrt and LIT-uhr-jee). The word art comes from the Latin *ars* meaning "ability," "talent," and "know-how." Originally, it referred to a practical know-how possessed by the good worker, who labored with method and precision to produce a perfect work. This good worker was an "artisan," and an "artist" was someone concerned with aesthetic perfection or beauty in the sphere of the Fine Arts.

"Art is the experience of universality. It cannot be only an object or a means. It is a primary word, in the sense that it comes first and is at the basis of every other word. It is a word of the origin, which seeks, beyond the immediacy of experience, for the first and ultimate meaning of life. It is a knowledge expressed in lines, images, and sounds, symbols that the mind knows how to recognize as projections about the mystery of life, beyond the limits that the mind cannot surpass: openness to the depths, to the heights, and to what is inexpressible about existence, paths that lead humans freely toward mystery and impart to them the anxiety that has no other words by which to be expressed.

"Hence art is religious because it leads human beings to have a consciousness of that disquietude that lies at the basis of their being, which neither science with the objective formality of its laws nor technology with the programmatic that saves at the cost of errors will

ever be able to pacify" (John Paul II, address of June 17, 1985).

More formally, art can be defined as "the aptitude for perceiving and experiencing sensibly in things the quality by which they are able to cause aesthetic pleasure" (C. Vaggini). As such art permeates the Liturgy* in all its manifestations: mime, gesture, choreography, speech, song, instrumental music, architecture, painting, plastic art, the goldsmith's craft, and other lesser arts. It is there in its twofold aspect of practical know-how and aesthetic perfection.

"The Church has called the arts into the service of the Liturgy, entrusting to them the task of aiding the dialogue of human beings with God and placing in sacred edifices those artistic forms that, 'by means of adequate language and in conformity with liturgical requirements, raise the spirit to God' (GS, 62) in a worship that disposes persons to mutual love and to the sole service of Almighty God" (John Paul II, discourse of May 2, 1986).

Hence, the elements of the Liturgy should be covered with beauty according to the laws of aesthetics, which is the science of beauty. Ancient and accepted essential conditions of beauty are the unity and integrity of the object, the proportion and order of its parts, and its splendor. The end of Art and

Liturgy is to beautify the cult for the greatest glory of God and the education of the souls that they elevate toward uncreated Beauty. Therefore current liturgical legislation embodies the following principles.

Holy Mother Church, always a patron of fine art, in judging art decides if it is fit for sacred use—not whether or not it is fine art. She admits all styles of art from every race and region, and contemporary art that offers due reverence. Since good taste rather than sumptuous display is the goal, bishops are to consult with the Diocesan Commission for Art* they appointed and other experts. Schools to train artists, who will use their talents to serve God's glory in the Church, should be established. Seminarians are expected to study the history, development, and principles of art.

Ascension (uh-SEN-shuhn). A Holyday of Obligation* commemorating Christ's return to heaven under His own power forty days after His Resurrection.* It marks the close of the visible mission of Jesus on earth, the reappearance in heaven of His total humanity glorified, placed in the position of honor at His Father's side eternally. It is from this seat of glory that He sent the Spirit on Pentecost* and will come to the final general judgment of all people. Formerly the paschal candle* was extinguished at the end of the Gospel* this day to symbolize His ascent. Now it is lighted during Baptisms and funerals to recall Christ's Death, Resurrection, and Ascension.

The theme of the Ascension is that Christ has passed beyond our sight, not to abandon us but to be our hope. He is the beginning, the

Head of the Church; where He has gone we hope to follow. Our hope is strong because Christ, although gone physically, has not left us spiritually. He is present in His Signs—in His ministers,* in His assembly,* in His Word, and especially in His Eucharist* (by His Real Presence). In this way, Christ will be with us until the end of the world. Hence, we must continue to carry out the task given each of us and labor to build His Kingdom until He comes again.

Ash Wednesday. *See* ASHES, BLESSED.

Ashes, Blessed (ASH-uhz, blest). Ashes, as a Jewish sign of penitence, were accepted by Christians and are used now primarily as a Sacramental* on Ash Wednesday, the first day of Lent.* Derived from burning the palms* from the previous year, the ashes are blessed and imposed on the faithful (in America on the forehead) during the ceremony after the Homily* of the Mass.* Outside Mass they are blessed and imposed during a Liturgy of the Word.*

This outward popular symbol of private or public sorrow, sadness, or penance* is a proof of humility, the result of human frailty, a remembrance of our mortality, that we are made of dust and will return to dust. However, a second formula also allows another concept more in keeping with the Lenten period, namely, penance, contrition,* and the striving after perfection.* "Turn away from sin and be faithful to the gospel."

In the early Christian era ashes were imposed on public penitents, sprinkled on their penitential clothes. When this custom was discontinued, the present rite appeared.

On Ash Wednesday, the opening day of Lent, in keeping with its penitential spirit, Catholics observe a day of fasting* and abstinence.*

Ashes are used in two different ways in the consecration of a church.* They are sprinkled on the floor in the form of a cross and mixed with the Gregorian water* sprinkled on the altar and in the church during the ceremony.

Asperges. *See* SPRINKLING.

Aspergill. *See* SPRINKLER.

Aspirations. *See* INVOCATIONS.

Assembly, Liturgical (uh-SEM-blee, luh-TUHR-ji-kuhl; li-). All who come together to celebrate a liturgical function form the liturgical assembly. Although the priest* is the president of the assembly, the faithful* are described as "a holy nation, a chosen race, a royal priesthood." At Mass* they offer the victim not only *through* the hands of the priest but *with* him. Offering themselves, they become one body, listening to the Word of God, praying, singing, offering sacrifice and communicating at the Lord's table as one united body. Evidence of this is their corporate action and posture.

In this connection, the assembly must have a quality that is essential to the Church, a *hierarchical* structure of persons differing in rank and function. The *distribution of roles* is of the highest importance as a sign, clearly manifesting that the assembly is not a haphazard gathering of people, but a manifestation of the Church, the fundamental doer, actor, and minister of the Liturgy.*

The assembly provides the priest who presides, the deacon* who ministers to him, the acolytes* who assist him, the readers* who proclaim God's Word, the extraordinary ministers* who administer Christ's Body and Blood (to those physically present as well as to those who are unable to be there but nonetheless belong to it), the choirs* who create the mood of the celebration,* the ushers* who insure the good physical order of the celebration, and various others. *See also* ATTITUDES; LITURGY—PARTICIPATION; POSTURE IN WORSHIP.

Assist at Mass (uh-SIST at mas). To be present at Mass* with more than *devout attendance*—to be present with *active participation.** To assist at Mass on Sundays and Holy Days of Obligation* is the first of the Commandments (or Precepts) of the Church.* *See also* LITURGY—PARTICIPATION.

Assistant Priest (uh-SIS-tuhnt preest). (1) A priest who helps prelates during solemn liturgical functions. Ordinarily he aids the bishop*; protonotaries* and abbots* may utilize an assistant priest* when they celebrate pontifically. A

blind priest must be so assisted. At a newly ordained priest's first Mass,* such an archpriest* may be employed. (2) A curate who helps the pastor* of a parish. The current more acceptable term is associate pastor.*

Associate Pastor (uh-SOH-shee-ayt, -shuht, PAS-tuhr). One who has the care of souls under the leadership of the pastor*; occasionally still called assistant pastor.

Associations, Pious (uh-soh-shee-AY-shuhnz, PAI-uhs). Organizations of clerics or laity* with certain Christian goals, e.g., corporal or spiritual works of mercy or fostering a devotion. Regulated by Canon law, they would seem to fall under the section *Societies of Apostolic Life* and are popularly known as: secular third orders; confraternities; pious unions. *See also* CONFRATERNITIES.

Assumption of Mary (uh-SUHM[P]-shuhn uhv MAYR-ee). A Holyday of Obligation* (August 15) celebrating the dogma* of Faith that the Mother of God was taken up to heaven, soul and body, after her earthly life. Backed primarily by tradition,* this dogma is based upon her sinlessness, her Motherhood of Christ, her concomitant virginity, and her participation in the redemptive work. Because of the above and even though sinless, she accepted death as her Son did; yet she was spared bodily corruption and has joined her Son in corporal glory.

By the Feast of the Assumption, the Church not only enables us to render due honor to Mary for her part in the Redemption* but also reminds us of a valuable truth. Just as Mary's Motherhood constituted a grace for the whole world, leading to its salvation through her Son, so her personal Assumption into heaven inaugurated the assumption of all humankind in God. Like Mary, we bear within our bodies—which are the temples of the Holy Spirit*—the seeds of eternity. And her Assumption foreshadows our own entry, body and soul, into heaven for all eternity.

Asterisk (AS-tuh-risk). The typographical sign corresponding to a small star with eight points used in liturgical books* to indicate the interval between the two halves of every versicle in the Psalms.* In responsories* it distinguishes the refrain, and in antiphons* it identifies the suitable point for beginning intonation.

Athanasian Creed. *See* PROFESSION OF FAITH.

Athanasius, St. (a-thuh-NAY-shuhs). (295-373). Outstanding exponent and defender of the true Faith. He served as an expert at the Council of Nicaea (325) where he helped preserve the Church's teaching on the Divinity of Christ in opposition to the Arian heresy. He served as Bishop of Alexandria for forty-five years, undergoing exile five times and enduring many other privations. He is one of the great Doctors* of the Eastern Church. *Liturgical celebration:* May 2 (Memorial); *theme:* belief in the Divinity of Christ.

Atrium (AY-tree-uhm). The forecourt or entrance to a Christian basilica.* The center is usually open with the sides roofed to the colonnades.

Attending Non-Catholic Services (uh-TEND-ing non-KATH-[uh-]lik SUHR-vuh-suhz). New norms and principles for Catholics attending other than Catholic services are explained in the 1967 *Directory,* and Vatican II's *Decree on Ecumenism** and *Decree on the Eastern Catholic Churches.** These decrees recognize that activities and spiritual endowments of other churches are also derived from Christ and return to Him. In drawing up these norms, the Church took into account the variety of Anglican, Protestant, Orthodox, and other religious traditions, along with local and cultural diversity, reciprocity, the eventual peril of proselytism or indifferentism, and the tolerance required while growth in ecumenical harmony takes place.

Thus, Catholics may, without fear of compromising their Faith, worship with others in joint prayer services using the church buildings and objects at the same function and may follow the strictly Sacramental and liturgical practices of a given church or worshiping community. The local Ordinary* sets the norms whereby Catholics may participate in the prayers for unity, for common concerns, and in any services of a national or community interest. These are generally encouraged, and as such are considered the sharing of others' *spiritual activities* and resources.

During many ecumenical conferences, the worship of various churches has been studied and presented in order to develop a greater understanding of each group's Liturgy.* Sometimes a hybrid type of worship, including traditions from various representatives, is presented, so that all may be pleased. However, true ecumenical worship will more probably develop as people become creative in sharing unfamiliar ways of prayer, until this converges toward a liturgical worship that is mutually enriching, as it discovers the common origins in Liturgy. Although the Orthodox and Catholics cannot participate in the full Eucharistic communion at an ecumenical worship of the Eucharist,* yet the service symbolizes much and allows all to profess a faith common to all, something perhaps unimaginable fifty years ago.

When sharing in the *liturgical worship* is a question, then the special principles of the *Decree on Ecumenism,* number 8, must be observed. By this we mean that Sacramental actions of an individual church or community are celebrated according to its liturgical books or defined norms. Such services may be attended by Catholics occasionally and, when they find the prayers and hymns agreeing with their Catholic Faith, they may join in these. As yet, reception of Communion* has not been allowed. A Catholic may be a godparent* at a

Christian baptismal service, as long as a representative of that community is also a witness. A Catholic may attend as well as be a witness* at a non-Catholic wedding service. *See also* UNITATIS REDINTEGRATIO.

Attitudes (AT-uh-t[y]oodz). Composed of body and soul, we should render homage to God by both interior and exterior worship.* Therefore, the body also plays an important part, because our devotion to God ought to be expressed externally as well. In various cultures the form of expression will vary. Thus, during a liturgical act expressing love of God, Christians will show it in their community action by a certain bodily ritual.

Bodily posture symbolizes a variety of degrees and types of respect for persons or things, even outside of the Liturgy.* All kinds of actions from a slight bow* to complete prostration have been used and conventions have grown up about the meaning of the individual positions. During the centuries, even in the Christian religion, depending upon a variety of circumstances, some ambivalence has occurred as to which posture signifies the greatest honor. Should one stand before God or kneel since "at the name of Jesus, every knee should bend" (Phil 2:9)?

Accordingly, cultural or temperamental differences have occasioned a great variety of liturgical attitudes during the history of the Church. Formerly since the eastward direction was looked upon as hope, rebirth, and light, and the westward direction as being the opposite, even the churches were built in such a way that the priests would be facing the East. Now with the priest facing the people, a westward position is taken in all churches having been built in the earlier tradition. For a full understanding of the proper postures, *see* POSTURE IN WORSHIP.

Attrition (uh-TRISH-uhn). Sorrow for one's sins, based on faith* but arising from a supernatural motive that is less than perfect love* for God. It is also termed imperfect contrition. Attrition suffices for receiving the remission of sins in the Sacraments of Reconciliation,* adult Baptism,* and the Anointing of the Sick* when one is unable to go to confession. Some of the motives for attrition are: (1) fear of loss of heaven, the pains of hell, God's punishments in this life, or God's judgment at death; (2) sense of having disobeyed and been ungrateful to God; or (3) regret over lost merits or graces. *See also* CONTRITION.

Audiovisuals. *See* MASS MEDIA.

Augustine of Canterbury, St. (uh-GUS-tin uhv KAN-tuhr-ber-ee). ? - 605. Italian missionary, sent by Pope Gregory the Great* in 597 to convert the people of England. He erected a monastery at Canterbury and established his Episcopal See there. Aided by King Ethelbert, Augustine converted many to the Faith and established numerous dioceses. He is known as Apostle of England. *Liturgical celebration:* May 27 (Opt. Mem.); *theme:* spreading the Faith to others.

Augustine of Hippo, St. (uh-GUS-tin uhv HIP-oh). 354-430. Born at Tagaste, present-day Algeria, Augustine searched ceaselessly for the truth until the age of thirty-five. Then, with the help of his mother's prayers, he was converted to the Faith at Milan and baptized by St. Ambrose.* At 41, he became Bishop of Hippo in North Africa and guided his flock for thirty-four years. Augustine left voluminous works that have been the admiration of the ages, and his sublime knowledge has made him one of the four great Fathers and Doctors* of the Latin Church. He is the Patron of Brewers, Printers, and Theologians. *Liturgical celebration:* August 28 (Memorial); *theme:* the search for God through His Church.

Authority (uh-THOR-uh-tee). Society assumes to itself the right to regulate its members toward its aim and goal. In most societies God is considered the source of authority, and it passes from Him to the society.

Since God Himself founded the Catholic Church,* He structured it Himself and passed on the authority to its leaders. The Sacred Liturgy* depends totally on the authority of the Church, in this case, the Apostolic See.* Naturally some delegation of this power is transferred to the bishops or the National Conference of Bishops.*

Ave Maria. *See* HAIL MARY.

Ave Maris Stella (AH-vay MAH-rees STEL-lah). Latin title ("Hail, Star of Ocean") of a popular liturgical hymn of unknown origin dating back to the 9th century and frequently attributed to St. Bernard.* It is found in ancient codices of the Divine Office* for Evening Prayer* on feasts of Mary.* In concise and beautiful fashion, this classic hymn depicts Mary as our guide to Jesus and offers petitions to her under some of her greatest titles.

There are over twenty English translations of *Ave Maris Stella,* of which the following is one:

Hail, thou star of ocean,
God's own Mother blest,
Ever sinless Virgin,
Gate of heavenly rest.

Oh! by Gabriel's Ave,
Uttered long ago,
Eva's name reversing,
'Stablish peace below.

Break the captive's fetters,
Light on blindness pour;
All our ills expelling,
Every bliss implore.

Show thyself a Mother;
May the Word Divine,
Born for us thine Infant,
Hear our prayers through thine.

Virgin all excelling,
Mildest of the mild;
Freed from guilt preserve us
Meek and undefiled.

Keep our lives all spotless,
Make our way secure,
Till we find in Jesus,
Joy for evermore.

Through the highest heaven
To the Almighty Three,
Father, Son, and Spirit,
One same glory be.

Ave Regina Caelorum (AH-vay ray-JEE-nah chay-LOH-room). Latin title ("Hail O Queen of Heaven") of a popular Marian antiphon.* It comprises a series of acclamations honoring the Blessed Virgin formerly assigned to be recited in the Liturgy* from February 2 to Holy Thursday* inclusively. It dates from the 12th century, and its author is unknown. The following is one of the many English translations:

Hail, O Queen of heaven enthroned!
Hail, by angels Mistress owned!
Root of Jesse, Gate of morn,
Whence the world's true Light was born.

Glorious Virgin, joy to you,
Loveliest whom in heaven they view:
Fairest where all are fair,
Plead with Christ our sins to spare.

See also FINAL ANTIPHONS OF OUR LADY.

Ave Verum (AH-vay VE-room). Opening Latin words of the first line of a short Eucharistic hymn *Ave verum corpus natum* ("Hail, true Body truly born") of unknown authorship and dating to the 14th century. It is a splendid expression of deep reverence for the Blessed Sacrament* and strong belief in the Real Presence of Jesus.

During the Middle Ages the *Ave Verum* was sung at the elevation of the Host during the Consecration,* although not prescribed by any liturgical rubric.* In time, it came to be used most often at Benediction of the Blessed Sacrament* and during processions* in honor of the Eucharistic Jesus. It may also be sung as an Offertory Song* or a Communion Song* at Mass. The following is one of several translations:

Hail, true Body, truly born
Of the Virgin Mary mild,
Truly offered, wracked and torn,
On the Cross for all defiled,
From Whose love-pierced, sacred side
Flowed Your true Blood's saving tide:
Be a foretaste sweet to me
In my death's great agony,
O my loving, gentle One,
Sweetest Jesus, Mary's Son.

Azyme. *See* UNLEAVENED BREAD.

— B —

Baldachin (BOL-duh-kuhn, BAL-). (1) Properly applied it should refer to the dome-shaped canopy woven from the rich fabrics of the East (the name is derived from the Italian *baldacco,* which means Bagdad), carried by means of movable poles, and held over the Blessed Sacrament,* relics,* or eminent persons during a procession* to protect from the sun or rain. Also called an umbella, which serves as an umbrella-like covering during processions. (2) It also improperly describes any type of canopy over a main altar,* commonly made of stone, metal, or wood. Such a canopy may be suspended from the ceiling or supported by columns. When used to cover a throne, it may even be projected from a wall. The term ciborium* is more correctly used in this case.

Current legislation states that there is to be no baldachin over a bishop's chair, unless it is a valuable work of art from the past that is being preserved.

Balsam; balm (BOL-suhm; bahm). A viscous aromatic resinous fluid acquired by cutting certain trees or plants. Together with olive oil it comprises one of the ingredients of the chrism,* which is blessed on Holy Thursday* and used for administration of Confirmation* and Baptism,* and during other blessings* of the Church. Since it is a curative agent for muscles and healing wounds, symbolically it indicates the grace* received that preserves Christians from the evils of the world and allows them to lead virtuous and devout lives.

Banner (BAN-uhr). Liturgically, a ceremonial standard, made of cloth, rectangular in shape and

adorned with pictures, religious emblems, or some symbol, usually attached to a crossbar at the top of a rod that is capped with a cross or statue. Its primary purpose usually is to be carried in a procession,* particularly to identify persons or groups, in honor of Saints*; and even in processions of the Blessed Sacrament,* one banner for the Confraternity of the Blessed Sacrament is carried in front of the procession before the cross.

Recently, there has been an upsurge in the popularity of banners to be used in church activities other than processions. They are used in many public religious functions to single out a specific group of people, to demonstrate certain ideas from Scripture, to highlight the liturgical theme of the Season* or the Feast, to identify the motto of some special religious group, to aid the students of a religious education class to understand the presentation, etc.

Primarily, banners are not intended to be cloth coverings for the walls or used to obscure the fine architectural lines of a church. All of the rules and regulations that have been sent out by Vatican II* concerning art* and its use in churches must be applied to banners also. Currently banners seem to be acceptable in churches, as long as they meet the requirements of fine art. Decorative art, as it pertains to Liturgy,* cannot be considered of small importance. Ruskin claims that no art is of higher order than decorative art. Such art is used on banners.

Certain originality, fine contours, careful relationship of subjects to the details, appreciation of proper color combinations—all are part of a proper realization of the purpose behind liturgical art and result in well-defined, beautiful banners that can be of help in the performance of any liturgical action. It is to be hoped that Catholic art will have the grace and ability that Greek art had at its zenith. Such art can be produced only as a result of meditative, tasteful, and artistic ability. *See also* ART AND LITURGY.

Banns (banz). Official public announcements of those planning to marry, with the intent to assure that they are free to marry, that no impediments exist for a valid and lawful marriage. Historically they began about the 8th century, and in the 13th century the law was extended to the entire Church,* indicating that a threefold publication was required, on three consecutive Sundays or holydays. Today such announcements may be posted on church doors or published in parish bulletins. Those aware of an impediment are obliged in conscience to inform the clergy.* Banns are continued by custom in the United States and need not be dispensed by the Ordinary,* especially if for good reasons the freedom to marry cannot be known in another manner.

Such public banns may also be announced for persons intending to receive Holy Orders (Canon 1051).

Banquet (BAN-kwuht). In the Bible,* the Messianic Banquet is a figure of the joys of the Messianic Kingdom. Isaiah* (25:6) states that Yahweh* is preparing a banquet for those who are redeemed. Jesus describes the joys of heaven in the figure of a banquet: "Many will come from the east and the west, and will recline . . . at the banquet in the kingdom of heaven" (Mt 8:11). He implies the same thing in the Parable of the Banquet (Lk 14:15-24) and portrays the Last Supper* as an anticipated Messianic Banquet, which He will share with His disciples in the Kingdom of His Father (Mt 26:29; Lk 22:16-18).

This theme is one of the basic characteristics of the Mass.* The Eucharist* is at the same time: (1) a sacrifice in which the Sacrifice of the Cross is perpetuated; (2) a Memorial of the Death and Resurrection* of the Lord, Who said: "Do this in memory of me" (Lk 22:19); and (3) a Sacred Banquet in which, through the Communion* of the Body and Blood of Christ, the People of God share the benefits of the Paschal Sacrifice, renew the New Covenant that God has made with human beings once and for all through Christ's Blood, and in faith and hope foreshadow and anticipate the Eschatological Banquet in the Kingdom of the Father, proclaiming the Lord's Death until He comes. In the Eucharistic Meal, Christ nourishes Christians, not only with His Word but especially with His Body and Blood, effecting a transformation that impels them toward greater love of God and neighbor.

Baptism (BAP-tiz-uhm). In the Christian initiation rites* this is the first Sacrament* a person may receive, which opens the door to all the other Sacraments. Baptism is the cleansing by water of all sins, bringing about a rebirth and sanctification in Christ, which incorporates the person into the Church.* By means of it the person passes from the death of sin into life, and its celebration should reflect the joy of the resurrection.

Validity of the Sacrament demands (1) the use of water that moves in a cleansing action during the ceremony, (2) the Trinitarian invocation: "I baptize you in the name of the Father, and of the Son, and of the Holy Spirit," and (3) the intention of the officiant that the person through this action should be baptized in the Church.

Effects of Baptism

The benefits or effects of Baptism include the remission of original and personal sin, together with all punishment due to sin, and the infusion of Divine grace,* including the virtues of faith,* hope,* and love.* Becoming a Christian or being incorporated into Christ, the person enters the Catholic Church and is given a share in Christ's priesthood,* which brings with it the power to co-offer the Eucharist with the celebrant.* The baptized is marked with a baptismal character that never disappears even though one may fall from faith. Most fundamental of all the Sacraments, Baptism allows the reception of the others, which continue to enrich the person spiritually, increasing the grace already received.

Bishops,* priests,* and deacons* are the ordinary ministers of the Sacrament. In danger of death, when no deacon or priest is available, any Christian, indeed anyone with the right intention, may administer Baptism. Proper catechesis* should prepare adults for entry into the Church. Parents, godparents,* relatives, friends, and neighbors should take an active part in the celebration and should be instructed about their role.

True or natural water should be used, clean, warmed if necessary, and blessed for this specific rite. Both the rite of immersion, more suitable to symbolize the person's participation in the Death and Resurrection of Christ, and the rite of infusion (pouring the water) are allowed by the Catholic Church.

In the baptistry* where the baptismal font* has been placed, sufficient room should exist to accommodate a reasonable number of people. Certain rites to be performed outside the baptistry are normally celebrated in various areas of the church convenient to the attending congregation.

The National Conference of Catholic Bishops* may make adaptations. During the ceremony itself, the minister, in accordance with the circumstances he faces, can freely make a variety of choices allowed in the rite.

Owing to their natural relationship, parents have an important ministry in Baptism, more so than the godparents.* Instructions are to be given to the parents prior to the celebration, which they are expected to attend. Besides joining in prayer with the congregation, the parents explicitly ask that the child be baptized, sign the child with the Sign of the Cross, renounce Satan and profess their Faith, carry the child to the font, hold the lighted candle, and are recipients of the special blessing for mothers and fathers. Therefore, they are to accept their responsibilities of educating the child and preparing it properly for the reception of the other Sacraments of initiation: Confirmation* and Holy Eucharist.*

Concerning the time and place of the Baptism of children, the child in danger of death is baptized without delay. Otherwise, Baptism occurs within the first weeks after birth at a time when the parents may be present and properly prepared. Normally it takes place on a Sunday, which commemorates the Lord's Resurrection,* and during a Mass,* so that a larger community may be present.

Structure of the Rite

The rite begins with the reception of the children, which allows the parents and godparents to express their desire that the child be baptized, especially by tracing the Sign of the Cross on the foreheads of the children. The Liturgy of the Word* follows, which includes reading of one or more selections from the Scriptures and a brief Homily* followed by General Intercessions* (Prayer of the Faithful). Then the prayer of exorcism precedes the anointing for Baptism, followed by the laying on of hands.

Moving to the font, the celebrant blesses the water of Baptism, receives the renunciation of sin and the profession of faith from the parents and godparents, and follows with a final interrogation of the parents and godparents. The actual Baptism may occur by immersion or infusion while he recites the invocation of the Blessed Trinity.

This is followed by the anointing with the chrism,* the clothing with a white garment and the holding of the lighted candle; then the prayer over the ears and mouth may be performed. The last mentioned, the ephphetha,* is optional in the United States. The ceremony concludes with the celebrant referring to the continuation of the Christian initiation, with the recitation of the Lord's Prayer,* and with the final blessings over the mother, father, and congregation.

If a child has already been baptized in a hospital or at home because of danger of death, and has returned to health, such a child is brought to the church for a special rite. The ceremonies normally used during the Baptism are adapted, leaving out solely the act of Baptism.

Adult Baptism

Adult Baptism is only one small portion of the total initiation rites* found in the *Rite of Christian Initiation.* If the initiation takes place at

the customary time, this Sacrament is received after the blessing of the water on the Easter Vigil.* If it does not occur then, the celebration should reflect the Easter spirit, employing the ritual Mass from the *Sacramentary.**

The rite of the Baptism itself proceeds in this manner. The candidates and their godparents assemble around the font or approach it while the Litany* is being sung. Thereupon the water is blessed in the font. A choice of three formulas exists to ask the elect to renounce Satan. Following the anointing with the oil of catechumens* on the breast, each candidate is asked to profess the Faith. Immediately thereafter the candidate is baptized. This may take place either by total or partial immersion or by infusion or pouring.

Confirmation* follows; if, for some serious reason, it is not conferred, the candidates are anointed on the crown of the head with sacred chrism at this point. The rite continues with the clothing of each neophyte in a white garment (this action is sometimes omitted). The final part of the Baptism is the action of the godparents approaching the Easter candle to light a candle to be given to the neophyte.* *See also* RITE OF CHRISTIAN INITIATION OF ADULTS.

Baptism of Blood

If a nonbaptized person is martyred for the Faith, it is commonly presupposed that the heroism obtains the grace of justification, thereby completely remitting all sin and entitling the person to immediate entrance to heaven. Implicitly there is an act of perfect love for God through suffering this martyrdom.

Baptism of Desire

In the case of Baptism by desire a nonbaptized person's desire, whether expressed or not, to be baptized (that is, to want to do what God expects of human beings even though the person is unaware of what God's normal requirement is) constitutes the reception of the Sacrament.

Vatican Council II,* in the *Constitution on the Church** (16), states it simply thus: "Those who through no fault of their own do not know the Gospel of Christ or of His Church, but who nevertheless seek God with a sincere heart, and, moved by grace, try in their actions to do His will as they know it through the dictates of their conscience—those too may achieve eternal salvation." *See also* BORN AGAIN.

Baptism, Conditional (BAP-tiz-uhm, kuhn-DISH-uhn-uhl). Since Baptism* can be received only once, when there is doubt about a person's ability to receive a valid Baptism, the minister precedes the Baptism with a conditional sentence, for instance, "If you are alive," since a person may be dead or unconscious; or "If you are not baptized" when a person has been baptized in another Christian religion but there is serious doubt whether or not the Sacrament* had been properly administered.

Baptism of the Lord (BAP-tiz-uhm uhv thuh lawrd). In celebrating the Baptism* of Jesus by John in the river Jordan, we advert to the fact that God is inaugurating a new age of salvation (the sky opened); Jesus, through the symbol of the dove,* is to be the representative of God's new people according to the Spirit; and the voice authenticates the fact that Jesus is that Servant of the Lord* foretold by the Prophets.* Our tradition recognizes the institution of Sacramental Baptism at this instance insofar as water through contact with the humanity of Christ is given sanctifying power. His baptism then becomes an archetype of Christian Baptism, so that through the Sacrament each Christian becomes a Child of God by receiving the Spirit and therefore is pleasing to the Father. This feast marks the end of the Christmas Season.*

Liturgical celebration: on the Sunday after the Epiphany,* unless the week of the Epiphany is omitted that year; if so, it is celebrated on the Monday after Epiphany (Feast); *theme:* Jesus, the Man for Others, asks us to accept our own calling in life.

Baptismal Font (Bap-TIZ-muhl fahnt). A water basin placed on a pedestal containing baptismal water for the administration of Baptism.* Modern fonts are generally made of stone or marble, divided into two parts. One part holds

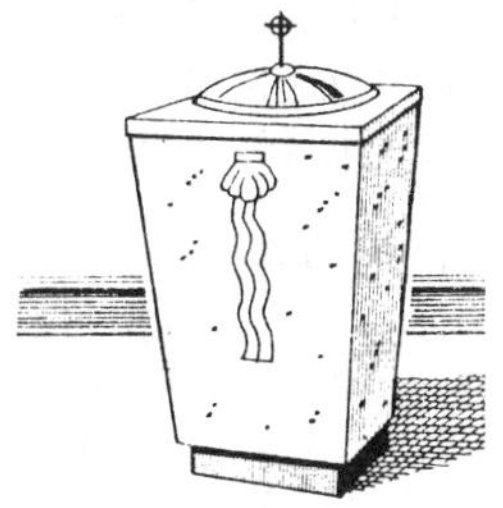

the baptismal water and the other part is used as a receptacle to receive the baptismal water that drips from the head of the person baptized and is drained into a piscina* dug into the ground. Should there not be two compartments, the water is gathered in a basin and emptied into another piscina.

Current legislation opts for something of a small pool in which a person may descend and be totally immersed. By law each parish church should have at least a baptismal font.

Baptismal Name (bap-TIZ-muhl naym). The Christian name given to each person at the time of Baptism.* Traditionally this name is chosen from among the Saints* so that this canonized person can serve as a patron and model for the child. By imitating the virtues and holiness of the Saint, the newly baptized expect the Saints to be their advocates to watch over their souls and bodies until they too join their Patron Saint* in heaven. *See also* PATRON SAINTS.

Baptismal Promises (Vows) (bap-TIZ-muhl PROM-uhs-uhz, vahooz). Prior to the actual Baptism,* the adult (or parents and sponsors in the name of the child to be baptized) expresses a profession of Christian Faith. To deepen the appreciation or the significance of this rite of Baptism, since 1951 a renewal of such promises is made during the Easter Vigil* Liturgy. Frequently, a solemn renewal of these promises occurs at the end of a mission or a retreat,* and when receiving First Communion* or the Sacrament of Confirmation.* Basically it expresses a detachment from Satan and all his enticements and a turning toward the Lord.

Baptismal Water (bap-TIZ-muhl WAWT-uhr, WOT-uhr). Blessed water used in the rite of Baptism.* Water blessed on the Easter Vigil* before the Baptisms that are to take place that night. The oil of catechumens* and the chrism* are added to it. Since Vatican Council II,* except during Easter Time,* water may be blessed during each baptismal liturgy. Only in case of an emergency will unblessed water suffice for the valid reception of the Sacrament.*

Baptistery (Baptistry) (BAP-tuh-stree). That part of the church or separate building reserved for the administration of Baptism.* At one time, particularly when adult Baptism flourished, baptisteries were quite ornate. Eventually, as Baptism by infusion developed, the area became smaller and the use of the font was sufficient. Today the regulations call for the baptistery to be in the front part of the church toward the left, somewhat lower than the altar.*

This allows for ease of incorporating Baptism into the Liturgy of the Mass as is the current practice. So that the living waters of Baptism may be symbolized better, running water is preferred and currently there is a move toward a type of baptistery that existed before—a pool with steps that would allow the person to be immersed.

Barnabas, St. (BAHR-nuh-buhs). ?-61. Born at Cyprus, Barnabas was among the first of the faithful at Jerusalem. He preached the Faith at Antioch and then was the companion of St. Paul* on the First Missionary Journey. After attending the Council of Jerusalem (49/50), Barnabas returned to Cyprus and made many converts. He died a martyr in 61 with the Gospel of Matthew,* written by his own hand, on his chest. *Liturgical celebration:* June 11 (Memorial); *theme:* proclaiming the Gospel* by word and deed.

Bartholomew, St. (bahr-THAHL-uh-myoo). Born in Cana, Bartholomew (called Nathanael in John's* Gospel) was brought to Jesus by the Apostle Philip.* He was selected by Jesus to be an Apostle* and after the Ascension he preached the Gospel* in India and was martyred there. A tradition says that he was flayed

alive in Armenia. He is the Patron of Plasterers. *Liturgical celebration:* August 24 (Feast); *theme:* loyal faith.

Baruch, The Book of (buh-ROOK, BA-ruhk, thuh buk uhv). Thirty-second Book of the Old Testament* and fourth of the Prophetic Books. It is ascribed to the secretary of Jeremiah,* but it is more probably the pious reflection of a later Jewish writer upon the circumstances of the exiles in Babylon as he knew them from the Book of Jeremiah. His purpose was to portray for his own and later generations the spirit of repentance that prompted God to bring the Exile to an end. It is thought that the five compositions it comprises were used in the Jewish liturgy during the 2nd century B.C. by communities dispersed in the pagan world.

Liturgical use: In the *Roman Missal,** this Book is read on the 2nd Sunday of Advent* (C), on the Easter Vigil,* on Friday and Saturday of the 26th Week in Ordinary Time* (I), and in the Rite of Penance.* In the *Liturgy of the Hours,** it is read on Friday and Saturday of the 29th Week in Ordinary Time. *Meaning:* Baruch shows that aversion from God brings Divine punishment but repentance and conversion to God leads to Divine mercy and restoration.

Basil, St. (BAY-zuhl, BA-zuhl). 330-379. One of the four great Fathers and Doctors* of the East, Basil was born at Cappadocia in Asia Minor. He became a monk and combated the Arian heresy with great zeal. He wrote the famous Basilian Rule of Monasticism and framed the Basilian Liturgy. He is the Patron of Hospital Administrators. *Liturgical celebration:* January 2 (Memorial); *theme:* honor for and love of the Trinity.

Basilica (buh-SIL-i-kuh, -ZIL). Historically this was a public building intended for use as a forum, where justice was meted out, commercial affairs were transacted, and one could idle away time. In the 4th century this term was applied to churches, and many Roman churches took the classic basilic form, that is, adapting a large ancient hall to the necessity of the Christian community and liturgical life.

One entered through the atrium,* and passed through the narthex* or large vestibule immediately before the entrance of the church proper. The wide central nave* usually had clerestories with some aisles along the sides. Columns supported the roof and helped to focus the atten-

tion upon the altar* that was placed in front of the apse,* which was a polygonal recess placed in the back, taking the form of a semicircular niche vaulted in demi-cupola, sheltering the area.

The bishop* occupied the apse surrounded by his clergy,* and this area was called the presbytery.* Usually each side of the apse had a small room containing furniture and shelter for the clergy before and after services, comparable to our modern sacristies.* Some of the larger basilicas had beautifully adorned transepts.* The rare beauty of such a specialized architectural form can still be appreciated in some of the older churches. Throughout the centuries some churches emulated this architectural type in their construction.

Major Basilicas

In Rome four basilicas are called patriarchal in memory of the four principal patriarchal cathedrals. Each is called an archbasilica.* For the patriarch of the West (the Pope), Saint John Lateran is designated—the mother and the first among all the churches of the cities and the world. For the patriarch of Constantinople, it is the largest church in Christendom, St. Peter in the Vatican, which is designated. Besides housing the sepulcher of St. Peter, it is that place where great papal solemnities are celebrated: crowning of the supreme Pontiffs, beatifications* and canonizations* of the Saints.* St. Paul Outside-the-Walls is the basilica for the patriarch of Alexandria, now administered by the Benedictines. The largest edifice consecrated to the Mother of God is St. Mary Major, the basilica for the patriarch of Antioch.

Special privileges are accorded these four basilicas: (a) a papal altar, used only by the Pope or, with his permission, by a cardinal*; (b) a papal throne, used only by the Pope; (c) a holy door, significant during the jubilee* years; (d) a red velvet flag, worked with gold wire, and a silver hand bell; (e) the chapter,* clergy serving the basilica, has the privilege of wearing the cappa.*

Outside of Rome, the St. Francis of Assisi church in Assisi is also a major basilica with a papal altar and throne.

Minor Basilicas

When the patriarch of Jerusalem was recognized, the basilica of St. Lawrence Outside-the-Walls was assigned to him. When the indulgenced pilgrimage to the Roman basilicas was instituted it was necessary to add two more basilicas since a visit to seven churches was required. Therefore, the basilica of the Holy Cross and that of St. Sebastian (the Basilica of the Apostles) were added to their number.

Many other churches throughout the world have been given the title of minor basilica by the Pope, which confers on them some of the privileges of the major basilicas. *See also* CHURCHES.

Beatification (bee-at-uh-fuh-KAY-shuhn). A declaration by the Sovereign Pontiff proclaiming that a deceased person is Blessed* (in heaven) and authorizing a public cult, inferior to that of sainthood, for such a person. It signifies the attainment of heaven because of a holy life of martyrdom. Before this can happen, a long process of examining the reputation for holiness—through the life, virtues, and writings—of the Blessed must occur with arduous scrutiny.

Reforms in 1969 allow greater responsibility to the local Ordinary,* who, sometimes with the National Conference of Catholic Bishops,* gathers evidence of the sanctity of the person involved in order to submit it to the Sacred Congregation for Sainthood Causes. Thereupon, either the local bishop or the Congregation will do the follow-up work. Sufficient evidence should exist of the heroic sanctity of the person and scientific and medical evidence of authentic miracles is required.

Once the decree* of beatification is signed by the Pope, the person may be called Blessed and a solemn pronouncement occurs in St. Peter's Basilica where an image of the Blessed is uncovered and a song of thanksgiving performed. A solemn Mass* is celebrated. The Pope enters the basilica later in the day to venerate the relics* and usually assists at the Benediction* of the Blessed Sacrament. Since the cult* of this Blessed is authorized only for certain places and certain groups,

the decree indicates which regions or Religious Institutes are affected. *See also* CANONIZATION.

Beatitudes (bee-at-uh-T[Y]OODZ). Eight blessings pronounced by Jesus at the beginning of the Sermon on the Mount* (Mt 5:3-12). In the first three Beatitudes are listed the faults that must be corrected if human beings are to be perfect—the love of riches, pride, and desire for pleasure. In the next three Beatitudes are found the virtues that must regulate our relations with God, our neighbor, and ourselves—justice, mercy, and purity. In the last two Beatitudes, Christ urges His followers to be zealous in spreading the Gospel* and peace,

and He promises that they will be rewarded with honor and power in the Kingdom of God for all that they have had to suffer for Him.

Liturgical use: In the *Roman Missal,** the Gospel of the Beatitudes is used on the Feast of All Saints,* 4th Ordinary Sunday (A), Monday of 10th Ordinary Week, Common of Holy Men and Women, Mass for Peace and Justice, Mass for Persecuted Christians, and in the Rites of Confirmation,* Penance,* Marriage,* Anointing of the Sick,* and Funerals.* *Meaning:* The Beatitudes have rightly been termed the *Magna Charta* of Christianity, for they set forth the Christian Rule of Life. As such, they have also been characterized with good reason as "Eight Words for Eternity."

Bede the Venerable, St. (beed thuh VEN-uhr-uh-buhl). 673-735. Born in Jastrow, England, Bede joined the Benedictines and was ordained in 702. Because of the enormous amount of his writings, full of sacred doctrine, he was called "Venerable"* while still living. He is rightly known as the Father of English History and is a Doctor of the Church.* *Liturgical celebration:* May 25 (Opt. Mem.); *theme:* love for Church teaching.

Beheading of John the Baptist. *See* JOHN THE BAPTIST, ST.

Bells (belz). The use of bells for religious purposes predates the 6th century when they became quite common. At their signal the Religious were wakened or called to liturgical services. At first they were small, but later they became quite huge, so that belfries and campaniles* frequently marked churches. Casting these metal cups that were either struck or rung became a fine technique, in which their shape and the amount of various metals determined the tone.

The ringing of bells has primarily the practical purpose of signaling an event. Before the invention of watches and small clocks, it was used to invite people to services, or to indicate when a particular action at the services—such as the Consecration*—was taking place. It was only in the 13th century that small bells were used to make the people aware of Consecration and Communion* within the church, usually because they may have been in a location where they could not see the liturgical action readily.

Bell-ringing would also remind people of devotional practices, such as the Angelus* and Evening Prayer.* Furthermore, it could be a call to prayer for the departed, as when a bell would be rung to announce the death of a person or during a person's burial, or the bringing of viaticum* to a sick person. The ringing was also used to indicate festive occasions, such as an important feast for the area, some solemn occasion, or the presence of a high dignitary.

Invented in Flanders in the 15th century, chimes consist of a group of bells of different sizes, tuned with precision, on which various musical airs may be played. They may range as much as five or six octaves.

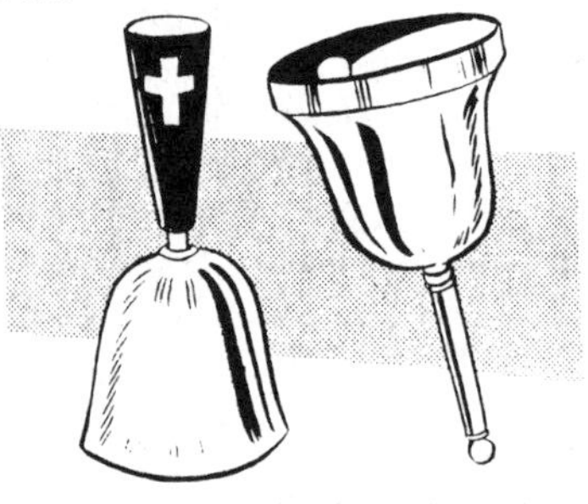

Ordinarily church-bells are limited to ecclesiastical use, except in a time of emergency when their secular use is of benefit to all in the area. Church laws deem it fitting that each church make use of bells that are blessed or consecrated according to the approved liturgical rite. Thus, the ringing of bells also becomes a Sacramental* by which the faithful seek Divine protection from evil spirits, from violent storms, or from other catastrophes.

The *Sacramentary* indicates that a small hand bell may be rung on three occasions during Mass: a little before the Consecration* as a signal to the people, and at each elevation (GIRM, 109). However, in a proper architectural setting and a well-ordered service, there would be little need for a bell to announce the Consecration and approaching Communion.* To commemorate the sorrow of the Church at the Passion and Death of Christ, bells are not rung from the *Glory to God** on Holy Thursday* until the same prayer is sung on the Easter Vigil.*

Benedicamus Domino. *See* LET US PRAISE THE LORD.

Benedicite Dominum. *See* CANTICLE OF THE THREE YOUNG MEN.

Benedict, St. (BEN-uh-dikt). 480-547. Born in Nursia, Umbria (Italy), and educated at Rome, Benedict retired to Subiaco where he lived as a hermit. When disciples gathered around him, he established a community of monks at Monte Cassino and composed the Benedictine Rule, which was eventually adopted throughout Europe. He is the Father of Western Monasticism. He is the Patron of Poison Sufferers and Speleologists. *Liturgical celebration:* July 11 (Memorial); *theme:* serving the Lord in work and prayer.

Benediction (ben-uh-DIK-shuhn). This liturgical action is a Eucharistic devotion in which the Blessed Sacrament* is exposed, raised aloft, and the minister, tracing the Sign of the Cross* with it, blesses the adorers.

The rite proceeds in this manner. With the people present, a Eucharistic hymn is sung as the minister comes to the altar, where he places the ciborium* or monstrance* on the altar table. Sometimes, especially if the exposition is lengthy, the monstrance would be placed on a throne. In particular

circumstances, for the purpose of exposition and reposition only, that is, without Benediction,* an acolyte,* or one of the extraordinary ministers* of Holy Communion, or someone deputed by the Ordinary* may act as minister.

The Eucharist* is incensed, and a period of adoration follows, in which prayers, songs, and readings, freqently from the Scriptures—as well as a Homily* or exhortations—endeavor to develop for the faithful a more clear understanding of the Eucharistic Mystery. Some periods of silence are also apropos.

After this period of adoration, the minister (a priest* or deacon*) kneels at the altar while another Eucharistic hymn is sung. This is usually the *Tantum Ergo,* the last two stanzas of the hymn *Pange Lingua** from Evening Prayer of the Feast of Corpus Christi.* The versicle and response formerly said between the hymn and the prayer are now omitted.

After a prayer is chanted by the minister, he puts on the humeral veil.* With this veil covering his hands he grasps the ciborium* or monstrance making the Sign of the Cross over the people, during which a small bell is usually rung. Custom in the United States has this action followed by the singing or recitation of the Divine Praises.* Thereupon the Blessed Sacrament is reposed in the tabernacle while the people sing another appropriate hymn or acclamation.

The devotion developed from the desire to look upon the Sacred Host and grew rapidly as a custom from the 15th century. Truly the veneration of the Blessed Sacrament as an object of adoration is laudable, yet such worship should not denigrate the fact that we go to God through Jesus Christ in the Sacrifice of the Mass and Communion. Worship of the Blessed Sacrament, reserved after Mass, does extend the grace of this sacrifice.

In recent years, the regulations were relaxed with regard to the Eucharistic fast* and the hour at which Mass may be celebrated. Thus afternoon and evening devotions sprang up around the celebration of the Mass instead of continuing the practice of Benediction.

Benedictus. *See* CANTICLE OF ZECHARIAH.

Benedixit Deus in Saecula. *See* BLESSED BE GOD FOR EVER.

Berakah (be-RAH-kah; be-rah-KAH). Transliteration of the Hebrew word for a blessing or benediction, it designates any prayer that begins and/or ends with the euchological formula "Blessed are You, O Lord, our God, King of the universe." It can also refer to a formula of a general blessing. In Hebrew it indicated to bless God by rendering thanks to Him for a particular act. Hence, in the New Testament this word is translated interchangeably by *eucharistein* (to give thanks) and *eulogein* (to bless).

Some liturgists such as J. P. Audet maintain that *berakah* was at the basis of the Eucharist, which consisted of: (1) a blessing *(berakah);* (2) the anamnesis* or memorial of the wonders of God;

and (3) a final blessing in the form of a doxology.*

Others such as Ligier and Rouwhorst have recourse to Hebrew formulas of table prayers that were probably in use at the time of Christ. They give this outline: (1) initial blessing with the breaking and distribution of bread; (2) dining of those at table; and (3) a final formula called *Birkat-ha-Mazon* that may be at the basis of our Eucharistic Prayer* and was itself divided into (a) a short blessing ("Blessed are You, O Lord, our God Who nourish the whole world"); (b) a solemn rendering of thanks (for the gift of the Promised Land,* the Covenant,* the Law,* life,* and salvation*); and (c) a prayer of supplication in the form of a blessing that expresses trust in the great and beneficent God Who today, tomorrow, and forever will heap His blessings on Israel.

Bernard, St. (BUR-nuhrd; buhr-NAHRD). 1090-1153. Confessor,* Abbot,* and Doctor of the Church,* Bernard was the guiding light of the Church in the 12th century. Born at Dijon in France, he became a Cis-

tercian Monk at the age of twenty-two. Appointed Abbot of the Monastery of Clairvaux, he was the arbiter of his century. Preacher of the Second Crusade, he wrote many pages on the Blessed Virgin and on Jesus Christ. He is the Patron of Chandlers and Skiers. *Liturgical celebration:* August 20 (Memorial); *theme:* zeal for the Church.

Bernardine, St. (BUR-nuhr-duhn; bur-nuhr-DEEN). 1380-1444. Born in Tuscany of noble parentage, Bernardine joined the Franciscan Order and became one of its chief glories. He preached everywhere devotion to the Name of Jesus and fostered learning and discipline in his Order. He is the Patron of Advertisers, Communications Personnel, and Public Relations. *Liturgical celebration:* May 20 (Opt. Mem.); *theme:* devotion to the Holy Name of Jesus.

Betrothal (bi-TROH-thuhl, bi-TRO-thuhl). A solemn promise by a mutual agreement between man and woman to marry. More than becoming engaged, the couple makes an agreement in writing, signed by each party, the pastor, and two witnesses. Although uncommon in the United States, a simple ceremonial rite may be used.

The existence of such an agreement imposes by natural law the obligation to keep the engagement in conscience and in justice but does not give either party the right to demand the celebration of the marriage. It only permits one to institute action in reparation for any injury or harm effectively caused. Therefore, it would also not be an impediment to either person marrying another party. *See also* ENGAGEMENT.

Bible (BAI-buhl). A collection of sacred books, which were composed under the positive influence of the Holy Spirit by men chosen by God, and which have been accepted by the Church as inspired. It is the most authorized, most admirable, and most important book in the world because it is the only "Divine book," the word of God in human language.

The Bible is composed of many books (it is really a "library" of books), some by unknown authors, written over the course of more than a thousand years—from about 950 B.C. to 100 A.D.

The Bible is incomparable as far as all other "sacred" literature is concerned because (1) it is the unique revelation of God; (2) it is inspired by God in a unique way (2 Tm 3:16); (3) it discloses God's saving plan for time and eternity; and (4) it centers on God incarnate in Jesus Christ, Savior of the world (Heb 1:1-2).

Other names for the Bible are: Holy or Sacred Scripture(s), Holy Writ, the Sacred Writings, the Good Book, and the Word of God.

The word Bible comes from the Greek term *biblia,* which means "books." The Book of Daniel* (9:2) refers to the writings of the Prophets as *ta biblia* in Greek, translated as "Scriptures." The sacred writer of the First Book of Maccabees* (12:9) calls them the "sacred books." This usage was accepted by the Christians and by the 5th century A.D. came to be applied to all the sacred writings. St. Jerome* (d. 400) called the Bible "the Divine Library." By the 13th century *the books* became *the book*—stressing the unity of all the books contained therein.

The two main parts of the Bible are the Old Testament* and the New Testament.* The word "testament" is used here in the sense of "agreement" or "covenant." The Old Testament is a record of the *old*

agreement between God (Yahweh*) and His chosen people, the Hebrews. It describes the remote preparation for the coming of the Messiah.* The New Testament is a record of the *new agreement* made by God with the whole human race through the Life, Death, and Resurrection* of Jesus Christ, the Son of God made Man.

In the Bible as we know it, there are seventy-three books: forty-six in the Old Testament and twenty-seven in the New.

BOOKS OF THE OLD TESTAMENT

First Eight Books

Pentateuch	**Remaining Books**
Genesis	Joshua
Exodus	Judges
Leviticus	Ruth
Numbers	
Deuteronomy	

Historical Books

1 Samuel	Nehemiah
2 Samuel	Tobit
1 Kings	Judith
2 Kings	Esther
1 Chronicles	1 Maccabees
2 Chronicles	2 Maccabees
Ezra	

Sapiential (or Didactic) Books

Job	Song of Songs
Psalms	Wisdom
Proverbs	Sirach
Ecclesiastes	

Prophetic Books

Major Prophets	Amos
Isaiah	Obadiah
Jeremiah	Jonah
Lamentations	Micah
Baruch	Nahum
Ezekiel	Habakkuk
Daniel	Zephaniah
Minor Prophets	Haggai
Hosea	Zechariah
Joel	Malachi

BOOKS OF THE NEW TESTAMENT

Historical Books

Gospel of Matthew
Gospel of Mark
Gospel of Luke
Gospel of John
Acts of the Apostles

Didactic Books

Epistles of Paul

Major Epistles
Romans
1 Corinthians
2 Corinthians
Galatians

Captivity Epistles
Ephesians
Philippians
Colossians

First Epistles
1 Thessalonians
2 Thessalonians

Pastoral Epistles
1 Timothy
2 Timothy
Titus
Philemon

Non-Pauline Epistle

Hebrews

Catholic Epistles

James
1 Peter
2 Peter
1 John
2 John
3 John
Jude

Prophetic Book

Book of Revelation

The Catholic Church is the official interpreter of the Bible. As the people of God—both of the Old Covenant *in figure* and of the New Covenant *in reality*—she wrote the Sacred Scriptures. As the Church of Christ, she has interpreted them. And as the Church of Christians, she has always treasured them.

She encourages her members to study the Scriptures for she knows that they can discover nothing but what will make the Bible a greater force in her life and that of her members. And she knows that "ignorance of the Scriptures is ignorance of Christ." *See also* DEI VERBUM; TESTAMENT, NEW; TESTAMENT, OLD.

Bible—Canon (BAI-buhl—KAN-uhn). The word canon stems from a reed that in olden times was used for measuring, so it came to mean a rule of faith, and eventually something immutable. By the 4th century the term signified the official list of inspired writings, those with Divine authorship. In 1546 the Council of Trent defined the Biblical canon, actually listing each book, forty-six in the Old Testament, twenty-seven in the New Testament, with a total of seventy-three. At the same time, it declared the Vulgate* to be the sole authentic translation for use in public readings, disputations, sermons, and expositions—hence, for use in the Liturgy.* In 1963, the Second Vatican Council* approved the use of the vernacular* in liturgical celebrations (SC, 36), paving the way for the National Conferences of Bishops* to approve vernacular texts for use in the Liturgy. *See also* BIBLE AND LITURGY; BIBLE, VERSIONS OF.

Bible and Liturgy (BAI-buhl and LIT-uhr-jee). The Liturgy* has fittingly been called "the Bible in action." For the Bible pervades every part of the liturgical rites of the Church. We find in this public worship Biblical passages (Readings*), Biblical chants (Antiphons*), Biblical formulas (Greetings,* Acclamations,* and Institution Narrative), Biblical allusions (Prayers*), and Biblical instruction (Homily*).

This is not very strange when we consider that the Bible is God's Word to us and that it was first written with worship* in mind. Indeed, it was the Word of God that formed God's people and that continues to do so today.

By the same token, it is the Liturgy that provides the perfect forum for God's Word to be proclaimed, understood, and loved. The Liturgy presents the true background for the interpretation and appreciation of God's Word.

In the new Liturgy of the Mass, the Church has brought the Liturgy of the Word* into closer relationship with the Liturgy of the Eucharist* and has increased the number of Scripture readings contained therein. The Liturgy of the Word consists of the readings from the Bible and the songs occurring between them. The Homily, the Profession of Faith* (Creed), and the Prayer of the Faithful* develop and conclude it.

In the readings God speaks to His people, reveals to them the Mysteries of redemption* and salvation,* and provides them with spiritual nourishment; and Christ Himself, in the form of His Word, is present in the midst of His faithful. The people appropriate this Divine Word to themselves by their singing, and testify to their fidelity to God's Word by their profession of faith. Strengthened by the Word of God, they intercede, in the Prayer of the Faithful, for the needs of the entire Church and for the salvation of the whole world.

The liturgical use of Scripture should be important to Christians since it is read publicly in both the celebration of the Eucharist and the Liturgy of the Hours.* Between the Mass and the Liturgy of the Hours, within a two-year period, almost all of the Books of Scripture can be found, each not in its totality. Naturally there is some interrelationship of the readings at Mass and in the Divine Office, each complementing the other. The Psalms* from the Old Testament form an integral part of the Liturgy of the Hours. The Gospels* for the most part are reserved for the Mass. For a complete description of the use of the Bible in these liturgical services consult chapter six of the *General Instruction of the Liturgy of the Hours.* (See individual books of the Bible for their liturgical use and meaning.)

In liturgical functions, the *Lectionary,** containing Biblical readings for worship, may be carried in procession, be incensed, and be given a prominent place in the sanctuary during the service or even outside of it. As such, it, the Word of God, can be properly venerated by the faithful. *See also* EPISTLE; GOSPEL; LECTIONARY; PSALTER; READINGS.

Bible Service (BAI-buhl SUHR-vuhs). Planned according to traditional principles of worship* and incorporating the reading of the Bible as the Word of God, this prayer service received official recognition in the *Constitution on the Sacred Liturgy** (35,4) of Vatican Council II.* Although the format is rather free, ordinarily it follows the pattern of the Liturgy of the Word* with an entrance rite, the readings, usually followed by a homily, some prayers, song, silence, and normally some general intercessions. Theologically and historically it is similar to a synagogue service, or the assembly prayers that eventually grew into the Divine Office, the term for the present Liturgy of the Hours.*

An advantage to this type of service is that an ordained minister is not necessarily required, since lay people can perform the various actions and preach without giving a

homily. When interest in the Bible grew after the Second World War, many of these Bible services were organized, especially around the liturgical Seasons,* such as Advent* and Lent,* and the vigils in preparation for the greater feasts. At one time the term Bible Vigil was also used for these services. Furthermore, at that time, prior to the relaxation of the laws in relation to Communion* and the time for the celebration of the Mass, it became a satisfactory substitute for evening devotions.

Bible, Versions of (BAI-buhl, VUHR-zhuhnz uhv). Translations into the vernacular of the Bible or any part thereof. Originally the Old Testament* was written in Hebrew, with some books in Greek and parts of some in Aramaic. Early Christians used the Septuagint,* the Greek version of the Old Testament. Then for liturgical services, when a Latin version became necessary, St. Jerome* translated the Old and New Testament into what was called a common tongue in those days, and hence his work was entitled the *Vulgate.**

In the United States, the following Biblical translations are approved for liturgical use: *The New American Bible; Revised Standard Version, Catholic Edition;* and *Jerusalem Bible.* The Grail translation for the psalmody* is also approved. The American Bishops are presently seeking a new translation of the Bible that would be pastorally suitable for children.

Bible Vigil. *See* BIBLE SERVICE.

Biblical Inspiration. *See* INSPIRATION.

Bidding Prayer. *See* GENERAL INTERCESSIONS.

Bination (bai-NAY-shuhn). The same priest* celebrating the Holy Sacrifice of the Mass* twice on the same day. The ordinary rule is one Mass per day. For pastoral reasons, the bishops grant permission to offer more than one Mass a day, particularly in the case of Sundays* and Holy Days of Obligation,* if several people might otherwise not fulfill their obligation. *See also* TRINATION.

Biretta (buh-RET-uh). A square stiff brimless headgear with three or four ridges on the top surface,

formerly worn at ceremonial occasions by secular and some religious clergy.* The color denotes the cleric's rank. No longer obligatory in Mass,* its use in the United States has virtually disappeared.

Birth of John the Baptist. *See* JOHN THE BAPTIST, ST.

Birth of Mary. *See* MARY, BLESSED VIRGIN—FEASTS.

Birthday (BUHRTH-day). For secular concerns, this means the day of one's birth into the world. For the Liturgy,* it refers to the day of birth into heaven—hence the day of death in this world and passage to new life. Accordingly, the celebration of the feast of Saints* is usually assigned to the date on which they died.

If the day of a Saint's birth into heaven is impeded by the existence of a Solemnity,* Feast,* or Obligatory Memorial,* the feast is assigned to the closest free day, either before or after the birthday; or it may be assigned to the anniversary of the transfer of the Saint's body; or in the case of several Eastern Saints (St. Ignatius of Antioch,* for example), the day on which they are venerated in their own region is used.

Bishop (BISH-uhp). In the Sacrament of Holy Orders,* this is the highest rank or the fulfillment of the priesthood, consisting primarily of the power of ordaining others to the same priesthood and episcopacy. In the Apostolic Era the bishop was the liturgical minister performing practically all liturgical services. As converts increased it became necessary for him to have help from priests* and deacons.* Bishops are successors of the Apostles,* in charge of local churches throughout the world; their responsibility embraces the mission of the Church to bring salvation to all. They have a threefold function: teaching; sanctifying (by means of the Sacraments* and the Sacrifice); and being leaders of the people, that is, pastors.*

A residential bishop is in charge of the local Church or diocese* and is called the *Ordinary of the place.*

A coadjutor or an auxiliary bishop will help the Ordinary of the diocese. At times the coadjutor may have the right of succession. Retired bishops give up their administrative powers but may help in a diocese if they so desire. Bishops who do not actually rule a certain section of the Church receive a title from a former diocese and hence are called titular bishops.

Bishop, Episcopal Ordination of (BISH-uhp, i-PIS-kuh-puhl ohr-duh-NAY-shuhn uhv). Through episcopal ordination a priest* enters the college of bishops, receiving his power by the laying on of hands from the bishops who have received their Order in an unbroken succession from the Apostles.* The new rite occurs in the revised ceremonies after the Gospel* in the Liturgy,* and includes an exhortation, certain ritual questions, prayers, a brief Litany of the Saints,* and the imposition of hands.* Following the ordination prayer of Hippolytus* recited by the ordaining bishops, the anointing of the new bishop occurs, and he is enthroned (if he is a local Ordinary) in his own cathedral.*

Bishops' Committee on the Liturgy (BISH-uhps kuh-MIT-ee on thuh LIT-uhr-jee). In the United States that special group of experts appointed by the National Conference of Catholic Bishops* to aid them in attaining the liturgical dimensions in relation to the liturgical apostolate called for in the *Constitution on the Liturgy** as it deals with liturgical science, sacred music,* art,* pastoral practice, the restoration, experimentation, adaptation,* and development of the Liturgy,* the revision of liturgical books,* and any other aspect of the regulation of sacred Liturgy in the country. *See also* LITURGICAL COMMISSIONS.

Bishops' Conferences. *See* NATIONAL CONFERENCE OF CATHOLIC BISHOPS.

Black Mass. *See* SATANISM.

Blase, Blessing of St. (blayz, BLES-ing uhv). On the feast of St. Blase of Sebaste, the day after Candlemas,* the rite of blessing throats occurs, with the priest* holding two crossed candles under the person's chin while saying: "Through the intercession of Saint Blase, bishop and martyr, may God deliver you from every disease of the throat and from every other illness. In the name of the Father, and of the Son, ✠ and of the Holy Spirit." Each person responds: "Amen." Legend has it that St. Blase cured a child who had choked on a fishbone.

Blase, St. (blayz). ?-317. Blase devoted his early years to the study of philosophy and went on to practice medicine before becoming Bishop of Sebaste in Armenia (Turkey). He was beheaded after terrible tortures under Licinius in 317. In the Middle Ages his cult* spread widely and he is invoked against diseases of the throat. *Liturgical celebration:* February 3 (Opt. Mem.); *theme:* peace in this life and happiness in eternity.

Blessed. *See* BEATIFICATION; CANONIZATION.

Blessed Ashes. *See* ASHES, BLESSED.

Blessed Be God for Ever (BLES-uhd bee god fawr EV-uhr). An acclamation* recited by the people* during the Preparation of the Gifts* at Mass* in response to the prayers of praise *(berakah*)* at the preparation of the bread and wine when there is no singing. The Latin is: *Benedixit Deus in saecula. See also* PREPARATION OF THE GIFTS.

Blessed Bread (blest bred). Ordinary bread that in some areas is customarily brought up at the Preparation of the Gifts* to be blessed at

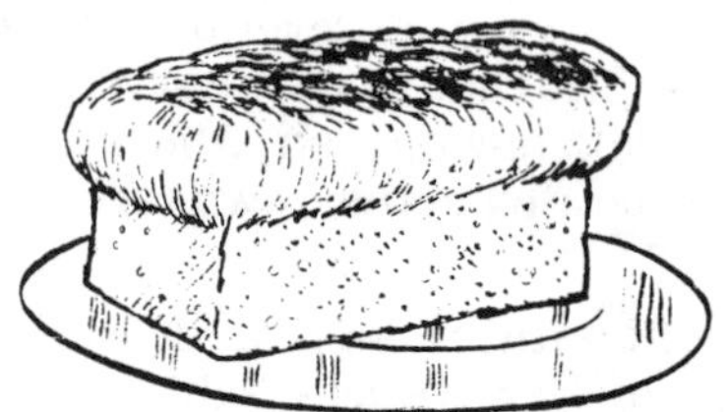

the end of the Eucharistic Prayer* and distributed later. Not a consecrated host, it represents primarily the unity and love that should exist among Christians and on occasion is given to the catechumens,* who are not allowed to receive the Eucharist.* Blessing of bread occurs on Easter,* and also on feasts of certain Saints.* Bread was always highly esteemed since it is the matter of the Eucharist, and many customs arise, such as signing bread with a cross before cutting it, hot-cross buns on Good Friday,* and so forth.

Blessed Sacrament. *See* EUCHARIST.

Blessed Virgin Mary on Saturday. *See* MARY, BLESSED VIRGIN—MEMORIAL ON SATURDAY.

Blessing. (BLES-ing). A word with a variety of meanings, yet only God blesses, for, strictly speaking, a blessing means that God looks favorably upon persons or things.

(A) The action of God who blesses, expressing His kindness toward human beings, the favor He grants to them, and the gifts that come from it. Examples are the Divine blessings from the time of the Creation, then through the Patriarchs, Noah, Abraham,* Isaac, and in the New Testament,* where we find Christ blessing children, bread and fish, bread and wine at the Last Supper,* until His final blessing of the Apostles on His Ascension* day.

(B) Not in the strict sense, one can consider it an act of blessing God, singing His praises, saying something good, thereby expressing admiration, adoration,* and thanksgiving. Psalms* and canticles* invite all creatures to bless the Lord. Catholic Liturgy* invokes such blessings, as in the Preface acclamation,* "Blessed is he who comes in the name of the Lord"; and "Let us praise [bless] the Lord" at certain times in the Liturgy of the Hours.*

(C) Jesus granted the power to bless to His disciples, especially to give peace, and usually it was given with an invocation and the imposition of hands.*

A blessing then is a sacred rite by which the Church draws Divine favors down upon persons and objects of worship or things of nature, and sanctifies their use. It always includes a formula and the Sign of the Cross,* which materialize the thought and the will of the one authorized to bless. Such a liturgical blessing brings down God's favor upon humankind, as in the Blessing* at the end of Mass. It may also be a formula worded, with a sign, that indicates the sanctification of an object, such as the blessing of a book or a Christmas tree.

Currently the law of the Church specifies two types of liturgical blessings: (1) *constitutive,* which permanently bring about the dedication of a person or an object in the service of the Church, for example, the bishop* or an altar*; and (2) *invocative,* which ask God to help those who are in need or who use blessed objects, for instance, the blessing for the sick or the blessing of a ship.

In conclusion one might say that a liturgical blessing is usually composed of words and actions, and ordinarily the Sign of the Cross, which are expected to sanctify or consecrate a person, thing, or activity.

In 1987 an interim translation of that part of the *Roman Ritual** pertaining to blessings* was completed. Besides a foreword explaining the theological and liturgical bases for blessings, the majority of the volume consists of formularies of blessings divided into five sections: (a) for persons; (b) for buildings and different activities of Christians; (c) for elements and objects that have direct relationship to liturgical life and celebrations; (d) for objects meant to foster devotion; (e) for blessings for various needs and occasions. Each rite comprises two essential parts: a short reading from Scripture and the praise of God's goodness along with a petition for Divine help. When a more solemn blessing might be in order, a second formulary is given. The appendix contains petitions that, owing to their nature, cannot be inserted into the group of blessings above.

Two Books of Blessings are planned for publication in the United States. One is a regular edition as used by bishops,* priests,* and deacons.* The other is a home/family edition, entitled *Catholic Household Blessings and Prayers.* The latter contains extracts from the official *Book of Blessings* plus other prayers that can be used in the home or in other places outside the church by clergy* or lay ministers.

(D) Formerly, only ministers of God could perform blessings as an action of the Church; the laity* could perform them as private actions. A typical example would be parents blessing their children. However, the Second Vatican Council* decreed: "Let provision be made that some Sacramentals,* at least in special circumstances and at the discretion of the Ordinary,* be administered by qualified lay persons" (SC, 79). Accordingly, the Sacred Congregation for Divine Worship* has been examining this aspect, and in 1972 stated that it is good for lay people to make use of blessings, especially those which refer to their daily lives and activities *(Notitiae,* April 1972).

In other words, the laity, by virtue of their universal priesthood* received through Baptism* and Confirmation,* may celebrate blessings, which are indicated in their respective orders of blessing, as long as they use the Rite and Formularies provided for lay persons. They exercise this ministry by virtue of their office, e.g., parents on behalf of their children, or because they exercise special liturgical ministries or fulfill a particular charge in the Church.* Some Religious* or catechists* with proper pastoral formation frequently give these blessings at the discretion of the local Ordinary. Thus, the consecration* (blessing) of a chapel* is performed by the bishop* of the place; blessings that affect the life of the community are carried out by the pastor, his assistant, deacon, acolyte,* or reader*; and blessings in the life of the family are performed by the parents.

(E) Besides the Easter* proclamation on the Solemnity of the Epiphany* and the Christmas* Proclamation *(Roman Martyrology*),* the following are some blessings included in the American edition of the *Book of Blessings:* Of parents before childbirth; of mothers on Mother's Day; of fathers on Father's Day; of foster parents and adopted children; on the occasion of a birthday; of parents after a miscarriage; of a person suffering from substance abuse; of a victim of crime or oppression; of teachers; of students; of a meeting; of an ecumenical gathering; of an interreligious (interfaith) gathering; at the inauguration of a public official; of fishing boats and gear; of seeds at the time of planting; of food on Holy Saturday*; of food on Thanksgiving Day*; of throats; upon visiting a cemetery on All Souls* Day; of an Advent* wreath; of a Christmas* crèche or manger scene; of a Christmas tree; of a home on the Solemnity of the Epiphany; of a home in the Easter Season*; of foods and other elements related to religious devotion (e.g., bread,* wine,* flowers,* candles,* oil*).

Blessing, Apostolic (BLES-ing, a-puh-STOL-ik). A papal blessing, usually bestowed during Mass* on special occasions, such as the Feast

of Sts. Peter and Paul,* Easter,* or the Pope's election. Twice a year bishops* may give it. Priests* may impart it at the end of a mission, a retreat, or a series of Lenten sermons, as well as when someone is dying. When the necessary conditions are fulfilled, even those who hear it on the radio or television may gain a plenary indulgence.*

Blessing, Final. *See* FINAL BLESSING.

Blessing, Nuptial. *See* NUPTIAL BLESSING.

Blessing of a Church. *See* CHURCH DEDICATION.

Blessing of an Altar. *See* CHURCH DEDICATION.

Blessing of Houses. *See* HOUSES, BLESSING OF.

Blessing of St. Blase. *See* BLASE, BLESSING OF ST.

Blood, Baptism of. *See* BAPTISM.

Boat, Incense (boht, IN-sens). A small oblong receptacle, usually in the shape of a little vessel, which holds the incense* that is transferred to the thurible* with a spoon.*

Body and Blood of Christ (BOD-ee and bluhd uhv kraist). This feast is also known by its Latin name: Corpus Christi. To recall the institution of the Eucharist on Holy Thursday,* when sorrow over the Passion,* the prime thought during Holy Week,* hinders a proper celebration, this feast was established and is celebrated on the Thursday (or Sunday) after Trinity Sunday.* It owes its origin to the progressive development of worship and devotion to the Blessed Eucharist during the Middle Ages and to a revelation to St. Juliana of Liège where it was

first celebrated as a local feast; in 1264 it was extended to the Universal Church.*

A prominent aspect of this feast is the procession,* which is to follow the Mass. A Host consecrated during the Mass is placed in the monstrance* and carried with lights,* incense, and under a canopy* to several stations where the Eucharistic blessing may be given.

The procession is not to take place within the body of the church. If an outdoor procession cannot be held on Corpus Christi, then in the cathedral church or some other appropriate places, some kind of public celebration—for instance, celebration of the Mass or Adoration of the Blessed Sacrament with Scripture readings, songs, homily, and meditation—should take place.

On this feast, we give special thanks and praise to God for this sublime gift of His Body and Blood that Christ left to us at the Last Supper: (1) The living *Memorial* of His Passion, Death, and Resurrection,* which brings us its sacrificial and saving power until the end of time. (2) The great *Sacrament* by which we encounter the living risen Christ and receive strength in holiness so that all peoples may come to walk in the light of one faith, in one communion of love. (3) The sacred *Banquet* in which all are fed at God's table and grow into the holiness of the risen Christ. *See also* EUCHARIST.

Body of Christ or **Body of the Church.** *See* MYSTICAL BODY OF CHRIST.

Bonaventure, St. (BON-uh-ven-chuhr). 1218-1274. Born in Tuscany, Bonaventure entered the Franciscan Order and lectured at the University of Paris, where he became the close friend of St. Thomas Aquinas.* Known as the Seraphic Doctor, he was named General of the Franciscan Order and Cardinal of Albano. He is regarded as the greatest exponent of Mystical Theology in the Middle Ages. *Liturgical celebration:* July 15 (Memorial); *theme:* the virtue of love.

Boniface, St. (BON-uh-fuhs). 673-754. Born in England, Boniface became a Benedictine monk. He preached in Germany and later was consecrated first Bishop of Germany by Pope Gregory II. He continued to travel and established monasteries in Bavaria, Thuringia, and Franconia. While preaching the Gospel to the Frisians (Holland), he was killed by pagans. He is known as the Apostle of Germany. *Liturgical celebration:* June 5 (Memorial); *theme:* courage to profess the Faith.

Book of Hours (buk uhv owrz). (1) A liturgical book with only the daytime Hours,* exclusive of the Office of Readings.* The most comparable thing we have today of this nature is *Christian Prayer.** (2) More usually, a devotional prayer book of medieval times that held some offices, Psalms,* and prayers, which were supplemental to the then *Divine Office,* and most commonly used by worshipful laity.* *See also* CHRISTIAN PRAYER.

Book of (the) Gospels. *See* LECTIONARY.

Books, Liturgical. *See* LITURGICAL BOOKS.

Bookstand. *See* CUSHION.

Born Again (bawrn uh-GEN). The term that describes how a person conceived in sin is regenerated by Baptism* as a child of God and thus may inherit heaven (Jn 3:5). Catholics consider it supernatural regeneration; to Protestants, it usually signifies a new experiential feeling about Christ, brought about through Baptism or some instant but permanent conversion from sin to dedicated service of God. *See also* BAPTISM.

Bow Your Heads . . . (bow yawr hedz). The full text is "Bow your heads and pray for God's blessing," which is a free translation of the Latin words *"Humiliate capita vestra Deo"* (literally, "Bow your heads before God"). It is the invitation the deacon* addresses to the assembly* at the end of the Mass* so that its members may receive the Blessing* in its more solemn forms (Solemn Blessing* and Prayer over the People*).

Bowing (BOW-ing). An inclination of the head, or the head with the body, which entered into liturgical use as a mark of supplication and adoration toward God, denoting respect or reverence toward human beings and things, or as a simple expression of greeting. Reverencing the name of Jesus has Scriptural foundation (Phil 2:10). Through the years the use of bows was much augmented, until recent legislation. The former three bows, with the body inclining more or less deeply, have been changed to only two, the bow of the head and the bow of the body. The former is made when the three Divine Persons are mentioned together, and at the names of Jesus,* Mary,* and the Saint* honored at Mass* that day; also at the Consecration.* The bow of the body is made before an altar when the Blessed Sacrament is not present, and at specified words during the Mass. *See also* POSTURE IN WORSHIP.

Bread (bred). (1) As one of the elements of the Eucharist,* this bread is baked from pure wheatmeal. Although Christ most probably used the unleavened bread that was customary at the Paschal meal, leavened bread was used in the celebration thereafter for many centuries. By the 11th century, unleavened bread was in general use in the Western Church, leavened in the East. Valid matter for Catholics is bread from wheat flour, whether leavened or unleavened. Church law, however, forbids as illicit the use of leavened bread in the Latin rites of the Church. Once the bread is consecrated, it is frequently called the Host, from the Latin word *hostia* meaning "victim," namely, Christ as our sacrificial offering. (*See also* UNLEAVENED BREAD.)

(2) Bread becomes a symbol of union when loaves are presented as an offering of a newly consecrated bishop* or at a canonization Mass, or when the bread blessed at the Preparation of the Gifts* is later distributed to the people for consumption at home. (*See also* BLESSED BREAD.)

(3) Bread becomes the symbol of sacrifice when the faithful bring bread to be blessed at the Sunday parish Mass. The *Roman Ritual** contains blessings for bread, even those in honor of certain Saints* for protection against hazards to health.

Breaking of (the) Bread (BRAYK-ing uhv (thuh) bred). (1) *Biblical:* This practice has its roots in the Old Testament* practice whereby the head of the family presiding at a meal recited an opening blessing and then broke and distributed the bread first, before other food. Jesus did this at the multiplication of loaves and at the Last Supper.* Its purpose was to express fellowship or fraternity. Since the Eucharist* was initially merged with such meals, the expression "breaking of (the) bread" was applied to the Eucharist, but each time the phrase occurs in the New Testament,* it does not necessarily mean the Eucharistic or Sacramental rite.

(2) *Liturgical:* Another term, fraction, refers to breaking the Hosts during the Mass after the Our Father,* when the Sign of Peace* is completely finished, during the singing of the Lamb of God.* The purpose is to obtain small pieces for Communion of the community from the fairly large Hosts. Even if small Hosts are used for the congregation, the large Host is broken in two, and in the Roman Rite* a small particle is broken off one of the halves and placed in the chalice.* Whenever large Hosts are used, the Breaking of the Bread is necessarily prolonged and thus shows clearly that the Eucharist is a sign of unity

and charity, because one bread is being distributed among the members of one family.

Variations of the Breaking of the Bread occur in other rites; in the Eastern Rite* it is broken into four parts, one of which is placed in the chalice. The Host is divided into nine portions in the Mozarabic Rite,* and two particles are put into the chalice. The action signifies the distribution of one Lord to many, and, for some, it took on the meaning of the violent breaking of the Lord's body upon the Cross.

There are four fundamental actions to the Eucharistic Liturgy: (1) *Taking:* In the Preparation of the Gifts,* the priest takes the bread,* wine,* and water,* as "Jesus took bread" and "took the cup." (2) *Blessing:* The great prayer of praise and thanksgiving by the Church, from the Preface* to the Great Amen,* corresponds to the second action of Christ: a blessing, when He gave thanks and praise over the bread and the cup. (3) *Breaking:* This third action, breaking the bread, signifies the unity among Christians. (4) *Giving:* This fourth action of Christ, giving Himself to His Apostles,* is replicated by the priest giving the Body and Blood of Christ to the faithful, which thus actually produces the unity signified by the Breaking of the Bread. Thus the latter two actions are celebrated together in the Communion Rite.* Since the words of the institution are not the actions of Christ, but His authority to us to perform the act in His memory, to break the Host at the words of the institution would distort seriously the Church's long tradition in celebrating the four fundamental acts of the Eucharist. *See also* EUCHARIST.

Breviary (BREE-v[y]uh-ree, BREEV-ee-uhr-ee). Official book of the Divine Office, which contains the prayers by which the Church gives praise to God every day of the year and every hour of the day. Before the 11th century, all the elements that make up a *Breviary* were in distinct volumes, e.g., Psalter,* Lectionary* (collection of readings), Martyrology,* Homiliary (collection of patristic expositions), Antiphonary,* and Hymnary (metrical hymns sung in the Divine Office). The *Breviary,* i.e., compendium, brought all these into one volume, so that the Office could be said readily outside of choir. Sick persons, travelers, and clerics constantly moving needed an abbreviated and portable book to satisfy their obligation of daily prayers. Eventually an abbreviated Breviary of the Friars Minor, similar to that of the Roman Curia, became the version approved by the Council of Trent and was published in 1568. In 1911, Pius X ordered a redistribution of the Psalms and a combination of the Sanctoral and Temporal Cycles.* After Vatican II,* the *Breviary* was changed to the four-volume *Liturgy of the Hours.** Many still tend to call it the *Breviary. See also* LITURGY OF THE HOURS.

Bridget, St. (BRI-jit). 1303-1373. Born into the royal house of Sweden, Bridget married Prince Ulfo and gave birth to eight children, one of whom was St. Catherine of Sweden. After her husband's death in 1344, Bridget joined the Third Order of St. Francis, and ultimately founded the Order of the Most Holy Savior. She wrote many works in which she related her mystical experiences. *Liturgical celebration:* July 23 (Opt. Mem.); *theme:* love for Christ's Passion.

Brief, Apostolic (BREEF, ap-uh-STOL-ik). A term in use from the 15th century that refers to a papal letter written in relatively simple style concerning a matter of lesser importance. Briefs have been used in the past to legislate on matters that affect the Liturgy,* for example, applying indulgences to actions or prayers that have a bearing on the Liturgy.* *See also* BULL, PAPAL; LITURGICAL LAW, SOURCES OF.

Bruno, St. (BROO-noh). 1035-1101. Born in Cologne, Germany, and educated at Paris, Bruno became a priest and taught theology. Seeking to lead a solitary life, he retired to the desert hills of Dauphany with six of his followers and formed the nucleus of the Order of the Carthusians. At the urgent request of Pope Urban II, he assisted him in meeting the needs of the Church and died in Squillace, Calabria. *Liturgical celebration:* October 6 (Opt. Mem.); *theme:* remaining faithful to God amid the changes of this world.

Bugia (BOO-jee-uh). A low candlestick consisting of a small plate and a metal or porcelain socket in which the candle is placed. Equipped with a kind of handle so that it could be carried without the wax falling, it provided additional light for reading the *Missal** at the Mass of a bishop* or other church dignitary. Its use was abolished in 1968. The name bugia stemmed from Bougie, Algeria, one of the sources of wax. *See also* CANDLESTICK.

Bull, Papal (BUL, PAY-puhl). Name popularly given to a large number of Pontifical documents, which usually are the most solemn and deal with matters of most importance. The name is derived from the Latin *bulla,* which refers to the leaden seal affixed to the parchment on which the document is written, rather than the document itself. On one side of the seal is the image of the reigning Pope and on the other that of Sts. Peter* and Paul.*

Papal bulls concern doctrinal decisions, canonizations,* disciplinary questions, jubilees,* and the like—some of which have to do with the Liturgy.* *See also* LITURGICAL LAW, SOURCES OF.

Burial. *See* FUNERAL RITES AND CEREMONIES; MASS OF CHRISTIAN BURIAL.

Burse (buhrs). (1) A case to hold the folded corporal* used at Mass.* Two pasteboards about eight to ten

inches square are covered with cloth and held together on three sides. The upper cloth matches the color* of the vestment for Mass; apart from Mass it is the color of the stole* the priest is wearing. Today its use is optional. (2) A smaller leather case for holding the pyx* that is used to carry Communion* to the sick.

Byzantine Rite (BIZ-uhn-teen, bi-ZAN-tain, rait). Syrian in origin, this rite was brought from Caesarea and Antioch to Constantinople. At first in the Greek tongue, later it employed national languages, both ancient and modern. It embodies the most important and lasting of the liturgical work done in Palestinian monasteries. After the Roman, it is the most widely used rite, having three forms: (1) the liturgy of St. James,* modified by St. Basil*; (2) St. John Chrysostom's* later modification, the common Eucharistic service of Constantinople; (3) the Liturgy of the Presanctified, during which the distribution of the Blessed Sacrament* consecrated on the preceding Sunday occurs.

— C —

Cajetan, St. (KAJ-uh-tuhn). 1480-1547. Born at Vicenza, Cajetan studied law at Padua and became a priest. He founded the Congregation of Clerks Regular (Theatines) to help the work of the apostolate by spreading a fresh spirit of devotion among the clergy.

He contributed greatly to the reform of morals in the 16th century. *Liturgical celebration:* August 7 (Opt. Mem.); *theme:* fidelity in seeking the Kingdom of God.

Calamus. *See* TUBE.

Calendar (KAL-uhn-duhr). A method of dividing the lunar or solar year, or both, into a table of the months, weeks, and days of the year, in which the names of the feasts* to be celebrated and of the Saints* to be honored are inscribed. The civil calendar of the Romans, namely the Julian Calendar, was established by Julius Caesar in 45 B.C. and remained in vogue until replaced by the Gregorian Calendar in 1582.

The Julian Calendar was the basis of the Christian calendar, but because the Julian year was 365 days and six hours, adjustment was required eventually since the six hours added too much year after year. By the Middle Ages the calendar was not synchronous with the seasonal dates, particularly Easter* (scheduled for the Sunday following the first full moon after the vernal equinox). Thus in 1582, Pope Gregory XIII reformed the calendar, canceling ten days from that year (October 5 became October 15) to counteract the extra days that had accumulated. He also instituted the present system of a leap year each fourth year, except in the century year unless it is divisible by four hundred, which has brought about a year that fits quite well in the tropical year.

In addition, the Gregorian Calendar restored New Year's Day to January 1. In the 6th century, Dionysius Exiguus had set the beginning of the Christian Era at March 25 of the year 1 (which he erroneously miscalculated as the 753rd year from the founding of Rome instead of the 758th).

Almost all Catholic countries quickly accepted the Gregorian Calendar, but some few were sluggish, not adopting it until the 20th century. Recent discussions concerning the possibility of a perpetual calendar, one that would stipulate a specific Sunday for Easter and bring greater regularity to the Gregorian Calendar, have taken place. Vatican Council II* has not opposed this "World Calendar," provided it maintains a seven-day week with Sunday (and no days outside the week) and provided that the other Christian Churches agree.

The celebrations in the calendar developed by giving new meaning to pre-Christian feasts or these were totally supplanted by Christian feasts. The feast can be movable, calculated by the date of Easter, which affects the beginning of Lent,* Ascension,* Pentecost,* etc.

Immovable feasts are the anniversaries of the burial of Martyrs* and Saints. Thus the Christian Calendar, will list the feasts of our Lord, Mysteries of the Faith, and names of Saints. Besides the Roman Calendar, which is obligatory for the whole Church, each diocese,* Religious Order, and Particular Church* may have celebrations in its own particular calendar, with the approbation of the Congregation for Divine Worship.* A directory or ordo* is published each year for the country, the diocese, or a group of dioceses, giving the instructions for public worship. *See also* CHURCH YEAR; ORDO.

Callistus I, St. (kuh-LIS-tuhs). ?-222. Callistus is reputed to have been a slave who was ordained a deacon by Pope Zephyrinus after obtaining his freedom. In 217 he succeeded Zephyrinus in the Chair of St. Peter and fought against the Adoptionist and Modalist heresies. He also provided for the burial of the Martyrs* in the catacombs and instituted the Ember Day* fasts. Callistus suffered martyrdom under the reign of Alexander Severus and was buried on the Aurelian Way. *Liturgical celebration:* October 14 (Opt. Mem.); *theme:* serving others in accord with God's will.

Camillus de Lellis, St. (kuh-MIL-uhs duh LEL-is). 1550-1614. Born in the Kingdom of Naples, Camillus was a professional soldier before being ordained and dedicating himself to the care of the sick. He founded the *Order of Hospitallers,* which established hospitals and cared for the sick. He died a victim of his charity and is the Patron of Hospitals, Nurses, and the Sick. *Liturgical celebration:* July 18 (Opt. Mem.); *theme:* serving Christ in others, especially the sick.

Campanile (cam-puh-NEE-lee; -NEE[UH]L). Any bell-tower or bell-steeple, the detached bell-tower that originated in Italy. The Leaning Tower of Pisa is a campanile.

Candelabrum (kan-duh-LAH-bruhm; -LA-bruhm; -LAY-bruhm). Although it may refer to the hanging chandelier for lamps used in early churches, today it is a candlestick

with many branches, not suspended but standing before or on the altar.* It referred to the seven-branched candlesticks during the Middle Ages, but today it describes any multiple candleholder. In medieval times candelabra were of huge dimensions, in silver, bronze, wrought iron, and sculptured wood. Today most are in gilded bronze and are used primarily during Benediction* and Tenebrae.*

Candidacy to Diaconate and Presbyterate. *See* ADMISSION TO CANDIDACY FOR THE DIACONATE AND PRESBYTERATE, RITE OF.

Candle Bearers (KAN-duhl BAYR-uhrz). Acolytes,* usually positioned on both sides of the processional cross, who hold the candles during processions.*

Candle, Paschal. *See* PASCHAL CANDLE.

Candlemas. *See* PRESENTATION OF THE LORD.

Candles and Lights (KAN-duhlz and laits). Because of pagan customs of using lights to restrain demons, the use of candles or lights in Christian worship* in the early centuries was solely for practical reasons. However, by the 4th century popular customs arose to use candles for honorary reasons, such as carrying them ahead of the celebrant* as a sign of respect, and eventually for religious purposes, giving symbolic emphasis to the candle, as a symbol of Christ. Today artificial lighting has taken over the utilitarian need of lights in worship.

Throughout the centuries, there were occasions when many candles were merely of ornamental value, used largely for decoration, as were the candelabra.* Among the religious or ceremonial uses of lamps or candles were: (a) placing them before the shrines of Martyrs,* before relics* and sacred images,* (b) carrying them during processions* particularly of the Eucharist,* and (c) lighting them for the celebration of liturgical functions, e.g., during the celebration of the Sacraments,* the Liturgy of the Hours,* and certain blessings.*

Candles as ornaments next to the crucifix on altars are a continuation of the honorary function of lighting. At first the candles carried in procession prior to the celebration of a liturgical function were placed on the ground surrounding the altar rather than upon it. Candles at Mass* became obligatory only in the 17th century. In an ordinary Mass two lighted candles are required. In a more festive Mass, six are allowed and a seventh is added at a pontifical Mass celebrated by the Ordinary.* These candles, as well as the Paschal Candle,* should be at least 65 percent beeswax unless the Episcopal Conference* determines otherwise.

Symbolically, the candle represents Christ as the light of the world (Easter Vigil*). Illumination by candlelight is usually a sign of joy.

Candles for liturgical use are to be made of material that can provide a living flame without being noxious or smoky and that does not stain altarcloths and coverings. To safeguard authenticity and the full symbolism of light, electrical bulbs are banned. It is also most unfitting that electric vigil lights be used for devotional purposes. In the United States, oil lamps may be used only in the case of the sanctuary light.*

The blessing of the Paschal Candle occurs during the vigil of Easter*; candles used during liturgical services otherwise are blessed on Candlemas.* On the feast of St. Blase* the candles blessed the previous day are used for the blessing of throats.

A candle can be considered a Sacramental,* and it is burned by the faithful before relics, shrines,* and images of Christ or the Saints.* As such it is a show of honor by the person who lights it, believing it is the proper way of offering thanksgiving or obtaining aid in seeking the fulfillment of a petition.

Blessed candles are lit during storms; they burn during a person's final hours, or are placed beside the corpse. The blessing of St. Blase occurs with two crossed candles. For the use of the lamp or candle at the tabernacle, *see* SANCTUARY LIGHT.

Candlestick (KAN-duhl-stik). A prop or support on which is placed a wax candle, and thus a very practical, useful article. Candlesticks used during processions* are smaller, less ornate and lightweight, made from various metals or wood. Some candlesticks, particularly those that hold the Paschal Candle* during the Easter Season,* are large and ornate as is also the candelabrum.* When it became proper to place candles on the altar,* for Mass,* Benediction,* and the Liturgy of the Hours,* a more ornate and heavy candlestick was provided. Not only does it serve as a proper holder of the candle, but it will catch wax drippings if necessary.

Formerly, a small hand candlestick (bugia*) was used in certain liturgical functions for the reading of certain rituals by bishops,* abbots,* and other superiors. For the most part it was a sign of honor, much as the candles that are carried before the celebrant, or beside the Book of Gospels.*

Canon (KAN-uhn). A cleric who belongs to a cathedral chapter or staff appointed by a bishop and has a place in the sanctuary* for the performance of the more solemn liturgical functions in the cathedral in common with the other canons. Collegiate canons are members of a collegiate chapter who fulfill the duties committed to them by the law or the diocesan bishop. Canons exist primarily in Europe and are not found in the United States.

Canon — Bible. *See* BIBLE — CANON.

Canon Law. *See* LITURGICAL BOOKS; LITURGICAL LAW.

Canon of the Mass. *See* EUCHARISTIC PRAYER.

Canon of the Mass, Saints of. *See* SAINTS IN EUCHARISTIC PRAYER I.

Canonical Age (kuh-NON-i-kuhl ayj). For the licit or valid reception of the Sacraments,* the acceptance of the ecclesiastical offices, and the imposition of certain duties upon their subjects, ecclesiastical law may require a specific age. Thus Marriage* cannot be contracted until adulthood, a priest* cannot be ordained until twenty-five (a bishop* until thirty), or a novice master appointed until thirty-five. Abstinence* begins at fourteen; fasting* commences at eighteen and ceases at sixty.

Canonical Hours (kuh-NON-i-kuhl owrz). The Church* sets times for the proper recitation of liturgical prayer, the Liturgy of the Hours,* formerly the Divine Office. Ascribing prayer to specified times was inherited from Judaism, and monastic tradition soon gave the hours the form that they maintained until Vatican Council II.* These were seven, based on Psalm 118:164: "Seven times a day, I praise you": Matins with Lauds, Prime, Terce, Sext, None, Vespers,

Compline. In monasteries, Matins could be separated from Lauds, and recited early, about 2:00 A.M., Lauds at 6:00 A.M., and Prime and Terce before the community Mass*; at midday, Sext and None were recited; in the evening, Vespers, and for night prayer, Compline. Lauds with Matins and Vespers were called major hours; the others, minor hours.

Since Vatican Council II a new terminology occurs and a different approach is taken. The intention was to allow at least some of the canonical hours to be prayed with a congregation in church, therefore not reserved to priests* and Religious.* The new structure then maintains the two major hours, Morning Prayer* (Lauds) and Evening Prayer* (Vespers) as the hinges upon which the daily Office turns. The Office of Readings,* comparable to the former Matins, may be said at any suitable time of the day, even anticipated.* The Daytime Prayer* takes the place of the former minor hours. In private recitation there is usually only one such hour, termed Daytime Prayer; for monastic settings, there are three sections to it, similar to the former Terce, Sext, and None. Night Prayer* is similar to the former Compline. *See also* LITURGY OF THE HOURS.

Canonization (kan-uhn-i-ZAY-shuhn). Etymologically, the inscribing of a name in the Canon or Catalog of Saints.* This declaration by the Pope* raises a deceased person to complete honors of the altar, sainthood, since the person has gone through the process of beatification* previously. Whereas beatification allows public commemoration, canonization requires it throughout the Universal Church.*

Over the centuries, the rules varied much with regard to canonization. By the 10th century it was regulated by Rome,* and the formal process was instituted. Besides proof of the extraordinary life and/or martyrdom for the Faith, scientifically proved miracles are demanded to ascertain that the person is truly in heaven.

Formerly the local bishops gathered information and sent the evidence to the Congregation of Rites,* which then conducted its own investigation; thereafter the cause was introduced. Several discussions followed and eventually the decree* of beatification occurred. Later proof of new miracles was required, confirming the sanctity of the person before canonization took place. Since 1969 the local Ordinary* or the territorial Conference of Bishops* gathers most of the information and works together with the Congregation for the Causes of Saints in a concerted effort to simplify the process. Further clarifications may be done either by the Congregation or by the local bishop.

Along the path to canonization, three titles are conferred on the candidates: (1) "Servant of God": given when a person is adjudged worthy to have life and virtues examined for canonization. (2) "Blessed": given to a Servant of God who has had at least two miracles substantiated, that is, performed at the invocation of the Blessed's name. (It was customary to use "Venerable" for non-Martyrs.)* (3) "Saint": given to a "Blessed" who has completed the process.

Canonization confers a sevenfold honor: (1) inscription of name in the Catalogue of Saints and reception of public veneration; (2) invocation in the public prayers of the Church; (3) dedication of churches in the Saint's honor; (4) celebration of Mass* and Divine Office*; (5) assignment of feastday; (6) pictorial representation with heavenly light of glory; and (7) public veneration of relics.* *See also* BEATIFICATION.

Canopy (KAN-uh-pee). This is the more familiar English word for the baldachin,* the umbrella-like covering of precious cloth attached to four or six staffs and carried over persons or objects of special honor. Basically it is a portable baldachin. *See also* BALDACHIN.

Canticle (KAN-ti-kuhl). A lyric or song of thanksgiving not from the Psalms* and composed by a famous person of the OT or NT. The *Liturgy of the Hours** includes both *minor* and *major* canticles. The 35 *minor canticles* occur between the two Psalms in Morning Prayer* and after the two Psalms in Evening Prayer.* At Morning Prayer, in addition to the series of OT canticles introduced into the Breviary by Pius V* a number of other canticles have been added. At Evening Prayer, something entirely new has been introduced—a series of canticles from the NT Epistles and the Book of Revelation.* Thus, each weekday of the four-week Psalter* has its own proper canticle and each Sunday one of two sections of the canticle of the Three Young Men.*

The *minor canticles of the OT* include the well-known Canticle of Hannah* (1 Sm 2:1-10), Canticle of Miriam* (Ex 15:1-4a, 8-13, 17-18), and Canticle of the Three Young Men* (Dn 3:57-88, 56) as well as the canticles of Moses (Dt 32:1-12), David (1 Chr 29:10-13), Tobit (13:1-8 and 13:8-15), Judith (Jdt 16:2-3a, 13-15), Solomon (Wis 9:1-6, 9-11), Sirach (Sir 36:1-5, 10-13), Isaiah (Is 2:2-5; 12:1-6; 26:1-4, 7-9, 12; 33:13-16; 38:10-14, 17-20; 40:10-17; 42:10-16; 45:15-25; 61:10—62:5; 66:10-14a), Jeremiah (Jer 14:17-21; 31:10-14), Ezekiel (Ez 36:24-28), Azariah (Dn 3:26, 27, 29, 34-41 and 8:52-57), and Habakkuk (Hb 3:2-4, 13a, 15-19). (Twelve of these canticles recur in Appendix I: Canticles and Gospels for Vigils together with 21 additional ones.)

The *minor canticles of the NT* include the well-known Alleluia Canticle* (Rv 19:1-7), the Canticle of the Lamb* (Rv 4:11; 5:9, 10, 12), and the Canticle of Christ's Self-Emptying* (Phil 2:6-11) as well as the canticles of the Body of Christ (Col 1:12-20), the Divine Plan (Eph 1:3-10), the Mystery of Christ (1 Tm 3:16), the Passion of Christ (1 Pt 2:21-24), God's Judgment (Rv 11:17-18; 12:10b-12a), and God's Glory (Rv 15:3-4).

The *major canticles* are the Gospel canticles of the NT: the Canticle of Our Lady* (Lk 1:46-55), the Canticle of Zechariah* (Lk 1:67-79), and the Canticle of Simeon* (Lk 2:29-32). They form as it were the climax of Morning Prayer, Evening Prayer, and Night Prayer* respectively. When they are sung the choir stands; each verse is intoned, and at solemn functions the incensing of the altar occurs during the singing of the Canticle of Our Lady or the Canticle of Zechariah.

Canticle of Canticles. *See* SONG OF SONGS.

Canticle of Hannah (KAN-ti-kuhl uhv HAN-nuh). Song of the mother of the OT Prophet Samuel in gratitude for God's gift of a son. It praises God's transcendence and power, which are visible in His works. He brings strength out of weakness, fecundity out of sterility, and life out of death. This hymn had great influence on the *Magnificat** and is used in the *Liturgy of the Hours* at Morning Prayer* of Wednesday of Week II.

Canticle of Miriam (KAN-ti-kuhl uhv MIR-ee-uhm). Also known as the Canticle of the Exodus and the ancient Canticle of Moses (Ex 15:1-4a, 8-13, 17-18). Some Scripture scholars regard only verses 19-21 as the Canticle of Miriam and 1-18 as the Canticle of Moses. It celebrates God's saving power miraculously delivering His people from their sins and leading them to the victorious conquest of the Promised Land. It is used in the *Liturgy of the Hours* at Morning Prayer* of Saturday of Week I.

Canticle of Our Lady (KAN-ti-kuhl uhv owr LAY-dee). Ascribed by most scholars to Mary* and by some to Elizabeth,* this song from Luke (1:46-55), sung or recited during Evening Prayer* each day, is still popularly known as the *Magnificat,* its first word in Latin. It leans heavily on the Canticle of Hannah* (1 Sm 2:1-10) and the major themes of OT piety, expressing praise of God's power and holiness, gratefulness for His magnificence, for His loving kindness toward the poor, and for Mary's humility while passing judgment upon the rich; it concludes with the acknowledgment of God's largesse in rescuing Israel, His servant.

Thus, the *Magnificat,* totally imbued with the faith and hope of Israel, has become the Church's song of predilection for praising the ineffable gratuitousness of the Lord's salvific intervention toward the poor and the lowly. In Evening Prayer* it is preceded and followed by its own proper antiphon.* When sung, it has a special form of intonation, and on solemn occasions the altar and choir are incensed.

The text is as follows:

My soul proclaims the greatness of the Lord,
my spirit rejoices in God my Savior
for He has looked with favor on His lowly servant.

From this day all generations will call me blessed:
the Almighty has done great things for me,
and holy is His Name.

He has mercy on those who fear Him
in every generation.

He has shown the strength of His arm,
He has scattered the proud in their conceit.

He has cast down the mighty from their thrones,
and has lifted up the lowly.

He has filled the hungry with good things,
and the rich He has sent away empty.

He has come to the help of His servant Israel
for He has remembered His promise of mercy,
the promise He made to our fathers,
to Abraham and His children for ever.

Canticle of Simeon (KAN-ti-kuhl uhv SIM-ee-uhn). This lyrical statement was made by Simeon at the Presentation of the Lord* in the Temple, Lk 2:29-31. It could be an Early Church liturgical hymn that Luke placed on his lips. Also known for its opening words in Latin, *Nunc dimittis ("Now, you let go"),* it has been used daily since the 4th century in Christian worship by Roman Catholics at Night Prayer,* and by others at Evening Prayer.*

The text is as follows:

Lord, now you let Your servant go in peace;
Your word has been fulfilled:

my own eye have seen the salvation
which You have prepared in the sight of every people:

a light to reveal You to the nations
and the glory of Your people Israel.

Canticle of the Three Young Men (KAN-ti-kuhl uhv thuh three yuhng men). Song of Shadrach, Meshach, and Abednego in the fiery furnace (Dn 3:57-88, 56). Part of a passage not accepted by some Christians as canonical but found in the Septuagint* and Vulgate* (Dn 3:24-90), which also includes the Prayer of Azariah (Abednego) (Dn 3:26, 27, 29, 34-41, 52-57). It calls on all creatures to praise God for His unflagging goodness and mighty works. Also known as the *Benedicite Dominum* from its opening words in Latin ("Bless the Lord"), it is used in the *Liturgy of the Hours* at Morning Prayer* for Sunday of Week I and II and Tuesday of Week IV.

Canticle of Zechariah (KAN-ti-kuhl uhv zek-uh-RAI-uh). Accredited to Zechariah, this lyric passage was said at the birth of his son, John the Baptist,* and is frequently referred to as the *Benedictus,* its opening word in Latin ("Blessed"). Having been unable to speak after the angel's announcement of the conception of John, at this moment Zechariah breaks forth in this acknowledgment of the Incarnation* and the Redemption,* thanks God for accomplishing the promises He has made, and prophesies the mission of this child who is called the Prophet of the Most High.

Each day at Morning Prayer,* this canticle is recited or sung, and it has the same privileges as the Canticle of Our Lady.* Zechariah's canticle is incorporated in many other church liturgies.

The text is as follows:

Blessed be the Lord, the God of Israel;
He has come to His people and set them free.

He has raised up for us a mighty savior,
born of the house of His servant David.

Through His holy Prophets He promised of old
that He would save us from our enemies,
from the hands of all who hate us.

He promised to show mercy to our fathers
and to remember His holy Covenant.

This was the oath He swore to our father Abraham:
to set us free from the hands of our enemies,
free to worship Him without fear,
holy and righteous in His sight
all the days of our life.

You, my child, shall be called the prophet of the Most High;
for you will go before the Lord to prepare His way,
to give His people knowledge of salvation
by the forgiveness of their sins.

In the tender compassion of our God
the dawn from on high shall break upon us,
to shine on those who dwell in darkness and the shadow of death,
and to guide our feet into the way of peace.

Cantillation (kan-tuh-LAY-shuhn). Recitative-melodic chanting of liturgical texts indicating the musical pointing of the text by the simple inflection of the voice. *See also* CHANT.

Cantor. *See* CHANTER.

Capitulary (kuh-PICH-oo-ler-ee). A book containing special lists of Biblical pericopes chosen for liturgical use, indicated by the first and last word. It preceded the use of the LECTIONARY.*

Capitulum (kuh-PICH-oo-luhm). Latin word for "chapter," which originally referred to a "little chapter," a short reading from Scripture recited in the Liturgy* (in the *Liturgy of the Hours** after the Psalms*). The new Office calls it "[Short] Reading."

The word chapter then went on to be used for an official assembly of religious or canons, since an assembly opened its meeting with the reading of a little chapter. It was then extended to a congregational group or college of canons entrusted with elective, liturgical, and administrative tasks in a cathedral* or collegiate church.

Cappa (KAHP-puh). A large choir mantle, similar to the cope* worn by cardinals,* bishops,* and clergy serving basilicas* and by canons* in some cathedrals.* This choir dress is made of violet wool for bishops, red for cardinals, with a large hood and now a shortened train. It is a sign of jurisdiction and is used whenever the prelate celebrates or presides from the throne.*

Capsula (KAP-suh-luh). Round metal receptacle in which is reserved the large Host* for Benediction* or Exposition* of the Blessed Sacrament.* The capsula is kept in the tabernacle.* *See also* LUNULA.

Cardinal (KAHRD-uhn-uhl; KAHRD-nuhl). As a prince of the Church,* the cardinal, a member of the Sacred College of Cardinals, belongs to the senate of the Roman Pontiff and assists him as a counselor and aids in the government of the Church. Appointed by the Pope,* he receives his red hat at a Consistory.*

There are three orders in the Sacred College: (a) *Cardinal Bishop.* The office of this highest rank is held by the cardinals who are the titular bishops of the neighboring dioceses of Rome. (b) *Cardinal Priest.* The second rank today consists of the largest number of cardinals who also are residential bish-

ops in most of the dioceses in the world. They are provided with a title that places them at the head of a church in Rome, which enjoys their patronage. (c) *Cardinal Deacon.* The lowest rank was the office originally held by the seven deacons of the Roman church, who took care of the poor. Today, the Cardinal Deacons are those who perform their duties at the various administrative offices within the Vatican.*

Carols (KAR-uhlz). Traditional rhythmic simple songs, not hymns, usually unpolished for informal singing. Although such carols exist for many Seasons of the Church Year,* usually the term is confined to such songs used at Christmas.* In medieval times, the carol introduced a more jovial element into acts of worship* in contrast to Gregorian Chant.* The miracle and mystery plays of the 13th century and the popularization of the Christmas crib* by St. Francis of Assisi* provided some of the early occasions for the singing of carols.

Casimir, St. (KAS-uh-meer). 1458-1484. Son of King Casimir IV of Poland and Elizabeth of Austria, Casimir was a prince of Lithuania. Amid the moral dangers of the court, he was a shining example of genuine piety with particular regard to chastity, kindness to the poor, and zeal for the Faith. He had special devotion to the Blessed Sacrament* and to the Blessed Virgin Mary.* The young prince died of consumption while on a journey to Lithuania. He is a Patron of Poland. *Liturgical celebration:* March 4 (Opt. Mem.); *theme:* serving God in holiness and justice.

Cassock (KAS-uhk). With long narrow sleeves, this close-fitting

ankle length garment fastens in front from neck to foot and is worn as an undergarment during liturgical functions. However, it is also the overgarment for both indoors and outdoors for clerics in Catholic countries. Others such as acolytes,* chanters,* choir members, and certain other ecclesiastical persons also wear the cassock. Diocesan priests* wear black (white in tropical countries); bishops,* purple; cardinals,* red; the Pope,* white.

Catacombs (KAT-uh-kohmz). Underground cemeteries in which the Christians of Rome buried their dead during the first three centuries. These were regarded as sacrosanct by the Romans (as was every burial place). Hence, Christians were safe here during persecutions, and they began to celebrate the Eucharist* atop the tombs of Martyrs.*

After the invasion of the barbarians, Christians buried their dead in city churches and no longer needed the catacombs, which became places of pilgrimage because of the presence of Martyrs and early Popes* there. However, by the 9th century, knowledge of the catacombs disappeared. A chance discovery of a catacomb in 1578 renewed interest in the catacombs, and the work of G. B. de Rossi in the

19th century brought them back into the public consciousness.

There were something like forty catacombs and twenty-five have been discovered – along the Appian Way, the Nomentine, and the Ardeatine. They are still being explored by scholars and providing much information about primitive Christian life,* art,* and worship* through their carvings, artifacts, and inscriptions.

Catafalque (KAT-uh-falk). This term has two meanings: (1) An ornamental and temporary structure sometimes used in funerals to hold the coffin of the deceased. (2) A pall-covered coffin-shaped structure used at Masses for the Dead* celebrated after burial to simulate the presence of the deceased. Contemporary liturgists consider the second use of the catafalque to be inappropriate, and it is now obsolescent.

Catechesi Tradendae (kah-te-KAY-zee trah-DEN-day). Latin title (from the first two words "Handing on Catechesis") of the *Apostolic Exhortation on Catechesis in Our Time* issued by Pope John Paul II on October 16, 1979. The document points out that catechesis is intrinsically linked with the whole of liturgical and Sacramental life, for it is in the Sacraments,* especially in the Eucharist,* that Jesus works in fullness for the transformation of human beings. Indeed, Sacramental life is impoverished and very soon turns into hollow ritualism if it is not based on serious knowledge of the meaning of the Sacraments, and catechesis becomes intellectualized if it fails to come alive in Sacramental practice.

Catechesis and Liturgy (kat-uh-KEE-suhs and LIT-uhr-jee). Catechesis is one of the four forms of the Ministry of the Word that devolves on the Church* and every Christian: (1) Evangelization,* (2) Catechesis, (3) Liturgy,* and (4) Theology (GCD, 17ff)—all of which are totally connected with one another in the concrete reality of pastoral ministry. Catechesis is a procedure of teaching and achieving the spiritual formation of those who have already been evangelized and accepted the Faith with the purpose of making each person's "faith become living,

conscious, and active through the light of instruction" (CD, 14).

Catechetical activity must meet the variety of circumstances and diverse audiences that exist. Catechesis occurs at various age levels, for baptized children, preadolescents, and adolescents as well as young adults and adults. It may also serve different groups, with varied cultural, racial, and ethnic backgrounds, and with many lingual, vocational, and geographical variations in their backgrounds.

The concern for catechesis, under proper ecclesiastical authority, pertains to all the members of the Church in proportion to the role of each. Parents above others are obliged to form their children in the faith and practice of the Christian life by word and example; godparents and those who take the place of parents have a similar obligation (Canon 774).

To attain the proper catechetical formation for everyone under his jurisdiction, the pastor* may employ the services not only of the clerics who belong to the parish but also of the members of Institutes of Consecrated Life and Societies of Apostolic Life, the laity,* and properly educated catechists, without detriment to the role that parents should play in family catechesis. Any communication media, teaching aids, and helps that will enable the faithful to learn the Catholic Faith more completely, and thus practice it more suitably, should be used in accord with the talents, age, characteristics, and condition of life of the persons being catechized.

Mutual Assistance

From the earliest times, "the Church has recognized that Liturgy and catechesis support one another. Prayer and the Sacraments* call for informed participants; fruitful participation in catechesis calls for the spiritual enrichment that comes from liturgical participation" (NCD, 36).

Liturgical celebrations have informative and educative values. At the same time, " 'every liturgical celebration, because it is an action of Christ the priest and of His Body the Church, is a sacred action surpassing all others. No other action of the Church can match its claim to efficacy, nor equal the degree of it' (SC, 7). And the more mature a Christian community becomes in faith, the more it lives its worship in spirit and in truth in its liturgical celebrations, especially at the Eucharist.*

"Therefore, catechesis must promote an active, conscious, genuine participation* in the Liturgy of the Church, not merely by explaining the meaning of the ceremonies but also by forming the minds of the faithful for prayer, for thanksgiving, for repentance, for praying with confidence, for a community spirit, and for understanding correctly the meaning of Creeds—all of which are necessary for a true liturgical life" (GCD, 25).

Liturgy as Catechesis in Action

As the culminating expression of tradition and life, Liturgy is an inexhaustible source of catechesis. It enables us to gather into one all the aspects of the Mystery of Christ, by speaking in concrete terms to the mind as well as the senses.

The Liturgy is *catechesis in action.* It celebrates and expresses the Mystery of Christ as a mystery of salvation that is realized today in the Church, in a Sacramental, significative, and efficacious action. Those who participate in it are enabled to penetrate more deeply into the Mystery of Christ and comprehend its extension and its wondrous unity.

Indeed, the whole past and future of the History of Salvation* are concentrated in the *present* of the liturgical celebrations. At the same time, the worshiping community and the individual members gather the fruits of the Redemption* and commit themselves to insure that it is extended ever more to humankind for eternal life. This attitude is expressed in a universal form especially in the Eucharistic Prayer.* In the Prayer of the Faithful* it is set forth in a more local form, in accord with the needs of the moment and those of the concrete praying community.

In this way, the Liturgy is rendered actual and made a vital part of the lives of all who participate in it. When properly understood, this aspect constitutes the greatest catechesis of all.

Accordingly, Pope Pius XI called the Liturgy the forum where "the ordinary and privileged teaching of the Church is given": "People are instructed in the truths of the Faith and brought to appreciate the inner joys of religion far more effectually by the annual celebration of our sacred Mysteries than by any pronouncement, however weighty, of the teaching Church. . . . People are composed of body and soul. Thus, they need the external festivities [of the Liturgy] so that the sacred rites—in all their beauty and variety—may stimulate them to drink more deeply of the fountain of God's teaching, that they may make it a part of themselves and use it with profit for their spiritual lives" *(Encyclical on the Kingship of Christ).*

Liturgical Catechesis

The Liturgy is a *dialogue in action*—God is intervening through it in our lives today. We, too, then are part of the History of Salvation. Liturgical celebrations constitute a profession of faith in action. The liturgical texts are themselves richly interwoven with Biblical expressions and become precious formulas for faith and prayer.

The liturgical prayers and chants inculcate spiritual attitudes of filial piety, adoration,* thanksgiving, offering, and contrition.* They express in praise and prayer the most vivid sentiments of faith,* hope,* and love* of believers.

The Congregation for Divine Worship and the Discipline of the Sacraments* has counseled all to be mindful that the liturgical renewal should be the concern of the whole Church. It requires "a study of its meaning and practice for the Christian education of the people to the end that the Liturgy may become vital, touch the soul, and meet its needs" (LI, 13).

Celebrants have a golden opportunity for liturgical catechesis *within the Liturgy itself.* They can make use of *admonitions** at important parts of the liturgical action. They can give a brief introduction to the celebration, inserting it into the Liturgical Year of the Church—indicating what attitude the particular service is trying to inculcate in the people.

They can also situate the *readings** for the people. A judicious word will provide a minimum Biblical knowledge that enables the listeners to respond more deeply and positively to God's Word (and His presence among them in that Word) on the day in question.

The Homily* provides a special time for instruction and enlightenment. The homilist can clarify liturgical signs* and actions, inculcating in the people liturgical attitudes and enabling them to apply the Liturgy to their lives.

Before the *Eucharistic Prayer,** celebrants can bring the people into the action by pointing out the particular reason for offering thanks and praise to God through Christ on that day—for celebrating the living Memorial of Christ's Death and Resurrection.*

Apart from the celebration, the greatest way to impart liturgical catechesis is by insuring that the liturgies are well prepared. This

means getting together a Liturgy Committee* that is a true cross-section of the community and working with its members to devise celebrations that will be particularly geared for the parish.* This entails, among other things, choosing the appropriate options, selecting the right hymns, and composing truly relevant petitions for the Prayer of the Faithful—petitions that will be appreciated by the community in question for they affect that community.

Other ways of communicating liturgical catechesis are through the parish school and CCD programs, through arranging little "Liturgy Meetings" for the parishioners from time to time, and through running articles on Liturgy in the Parish Bulletin or Monthly Newsletter.

Every catechesis should lead the people to greater participation in the Liturgy. In turn, every Liturgy should enable them to bring their Christian witness to the world. This "living the Liturgy" will then reach full cycle with their more active participation in the next Liturgy. *See also* GRAVISSIMUM EDUCATIONIS.

Catechumen (kat-uh-KYOO-muhn). A learner, accepted into the catechumenate,* being taught the principles of Christianity to qualify for formal entry into the Church.*

Catechumenate (kat-uh-KYOO-muhn-uht). That process of the initiation rites,* undergone for a period of time determined by the Ordinary,* in which pastoral formation by the Church* aids unbaptized adults to prepare for the Sacraments of Christian Initiation. A fourfold plan is involved in achieving this purpose:

(a) A complete instruction, usually accommodated to the Liturgical Year* and enhanced by Scriptural celebrations, brings these adults to an understanding of the beliefs and obligations they will accept, together with the Mystery* of salvation they want to share.

(b) The faithful,* primarily through sponsors and godparents, give example and support in teaching them how to live the Christian way of life. Through the practice of virtue,* a progressive change in morals and outlook develops, so that, though experiencing human division, the catechumen savors the joy that the Lord gives without measure.

(c) Through fitting liturgical rites, the Church cleanses the catechumens a bit at a time and strengthens them, particularly while they attend the celebrations of the Word. Technically they should be present only during the Liturgy of the Word* with the faithful and be dismissed after the Mass of the Catechumens,* before the Eucharistic celebration starts.

(d) During this period they learn how to become involved actively with others in spreading the Gospel,* building up the Church through the testimony of their lives in their profession of faith, thus partaking in an apostolic role from the beginning. *See* RITE OF CHRISTIAN INITIATION OF ADULTS.

Cathedra. *See* CHAIR (CATHEDRA).

Cathedral (kuh-THEE-druhl). In a diocese,* the principal church* in which the bishop usually officiates. In this church the Ordinary* has his fixed chair* (from the Latin and Greek *cathedra)* permanently erected in the cathedral church as a sign of authority. Thus the cathedral is the parish* seat of the entire diocese,* or the mother church of all the other churches.

The bishop at his episcopal throne is aided by the canonically appointed clerics who service the cathedral in celebrating the liturgical functions there.

The anniversary of the cathedral's dedication and the feast of the Mystery* or the Saint,* in whose honor the cathedral has been consecrated, are celebrated by all the clergy of the diocese. Ordinarily, all solemnities of a diocesan character are presided over by the bishop in the cathedral, such as the blessing of holy oils* on Holy Thursday* and ordinations.*

Cathedral Office (kuh-THEE-druhl OF-uhs, AWF-). This term describes regular public services of a church, apart from the Eucharist.* Originally, this consisted only of two regular gatherings, one in the evening and one in the morning for prayer; however, on the evenings of Sundays and great feasts, a vigil or night office also occurred.

With the growth of monasticism, these two or three daily prayer times gave way to the seven or eight canonical hours, structured on the continuous reading of the Scriptures in the Psalter,* thus eliminating most elements of public prayer.

There is presently much interest in the cathedral office, particularly since it might be a vital method to develop public devotion.* A creative application of the principles of the cathedral office might produce a form of the Liturgy of the Hours* that could be integrated properly with the Eucharist,* the Church Year,* and the design of everyday life.

Catherine of Siena, St. (KATH-uh-rin uhv see-EN-uh). 1347-1380. A Dominican tertiary from Siena, Italy, Catherine pacified the civil discords of her country, vigorously fought for the rights and freedom of the Roman Pontiff, and promoted the renewal of religious life. She was imprinted with the sacred Stigmata (the marks of Christ's wounds on the body) and composed works of doctrine and spiritual inspiration, making her a Doctor* of the Church. She is the Patroness of Nurses. *Liturgical celebration:* April 29 (Memorial); *theme:* sharing the Mystery* of Christ's Death.

Catholicity (kath-uh-LIS-uh-tee). A distinctive mark of the Church* indicating universality, instituted for and accommodated to all people, places, and times; physically universal by existing in the whole world with no difference of doctrine and under one obedience. Liturgically the multiple and varied ritual forms adapt to the character and

culture of all people, yet there is one Faith, one Sacrifice in the same Sacraments.*

Cecilia, St. (suh-SEEL-yuh). ?-230. A Roman by birth, Cecilia was forced to marry Valerian, a pagan. She converted him and his brother Tiburtius to the Faith. Although married, she preserved her virginity by the consent of her husband and died a Martyr* for love of Christ. She is the Patroness of Musicians, Organ Builders, Poets, and Singers. *Liturgical celebration:* November 22 (Memorial); *theme:* witnessing to Christ by one's life.

Celebrant (SEL-uh-bruhnt). The clergyman, deacon,* priest,* or bishop,* who officiates at a liturgical function. In the chapters of a cathedral* or a collegiate church, as well as in choirs of monasteries and Religious houses the officiating priest is called the hebdomadary,* since he fulfills the office for one week, celebrating the various parts of the Liturgy of the Hours* and the Eucharist.* Each member of the community takes a turn at this function. The hebdomadary's prerogative is to convey the prayers of all to God, like the great priests of the New Law, who assume the responsibility of collective prayer and of the sacrifice of our Mediator. Such a one is the ambassador for the community.

The recent understanding of the corporate nature of the Church and of worship* makes everyone an active participant in the celebration of the Eucharist and other liturgical services. Such a communal character of celebrating leads to the choice of the term President, since the function of the minister seems not to celebrate on behalf of or apart from the congregation, but to preside over it. *See also* CONCELEBRATION.

Celebrant, Private Prayers of (SEL-uh-bruhnt, PRAI-vuht prayrz uhv). Prayers of confession and imploration recited inaudibly by the celebrant* during the Eucharist.* Also known as liturgical "apologies," they were once quite numerous in the Order of Mass but have been greatly reduced in the *Roman Missal** of Paul VI. They occur at the Preparation of the Gifts*: "Lord God, we ask you to receive us . . ."; during the Communion Rite*: at the commingling: "May this mingling . . ."; before Communion: "Lord Jesus Christ, Son . . ."; or "Lord Jesus Christ, with faith in your love and mercy . . ."; and at the cleansing of the sacred vessels: "Lord, may I receive these gifts in purity of heart. . . ."

Celebration (sel-uh-BRAY-shuhn). Observance of some religious, patriotic, or social occasion, especially by ceremonies or festivities. When people celebrate a ceremony, a feast, or an anniversary, they live an event fully, they give it its full dimension, they perform it solemnly. Celebration entails a public, festive, visible, and ritual aspect.

The word *celeber* in Latin means "numerous," "in great number." A celebrated place is one that is much frequented. A celebrated feast is one that crowds flock to. Persons or feasts can be called "celebrated" because they are known to a large number. Therefore celebration signifies affluence, reunion of many, gathering, assembly, and thereby solemnity or feast.

Celebration in the liturgical sense entails coming together to commemorate the announcement and actuation of the Mystery of Christ in the *today* of the Church.* It recalls the basic Biblical reality of the People of God,* brought together by God to carry out the life of the Covenant.* A celebration is an action that unites the People of the Covenant with their God and enables them to share His life. It does so with the aid of the Word of God and the Sacrifice/Sacrament of Christ.

These culminate in a *presence* of God among His people, whose supreme realization is the presence of Christ among His people.

A liturgical celebration is never the private function of a few people; it is always the celebration of the whole Church, "the many brothers and sisters" (Rom 8:29) for whom Christ shed His Blood (Mt 26:28) and whom He leads to the unity of the Trinity. All that the Liturgy* announces in its celebration it also effects: every announcement is a realization. Only in the celebration and through the celebration that constitutes the fullness of time of the Church does Christ continue to remain in the midst of His people and does the Father in Christ continue to pitch His tent among us in the Holy Spirit.

As a celebration, the Liturgy is also *prayer* in action.* It is the prayer of the entire social body that constitutes the Church, the prayer of a people united around its priest in the unity of the Father, the Son, and the Holy Spirit. As such it is the manifestation of the Church.

At the same time, this act of celebration also brings into play the bodies of all present. Standing,* bowing,* kneeling,* with hands extended or joined,* Christians at liturgical celebrations pray in a rare human fullness. Through the bodily manifestation of their inner feelings they communicate with each other in their adherence to the Lord.

Finally, the body expresses itself in song, through which joy and suffering, humility and tenderness, thanksgiving and supplication achieve their highest expression: joy becomes the jubilation of a community, and the suffering of one is assumed by all.

Whenever a liturgical celebration takes place, the celebrant* always exercises a function of bringing people together like Christ and in Him in the unity of the Holy Spirit. At the same time, the assembly* becomes ever more what it is: the People of God,* the Body of Christ,* and the Temple of the Holy Spirit.

A liturgical celebration has various degrees in accord with its importance: Solemnity, Feast, or Memorial. *See* FEASTS; MEMORIALS; SOLEMNITIES.

Celebration of the Word. *See* LECTIONARY.

Celebret (SEL-uh-bret). A credential from a bishop* or religious superior declaring that the bearer is a priest* in good standing, so that he may obtain permission to celebrate Mass* in another diocese.*

Cemetery (SEM-uh-ter-ee). A burial place of Christians, considered a sacred place where they await the resurrection. A cemetery that is primarily Catholic is usually consecrated by the bishop.* Where the Church does not own the cemetery, each grave must receive a blessing at the moment of burial by the priest* who recites the assigned prayer, while he sprinkles and incenses it, as well as the coffin. Usually Catholics are buried in the ground; however, they may be buried in mausoleums, and recently permission has been granted for cremation.*

Censer. *See* THURIBLE.

Censor (SEN-suhr). The bishop* appoints a cleric to study written material and other communication media that deal with spiritual topics. If the material passes muster, "nihil obstat," which means "nothing impedes (publication)," is printed on the verso of the title page with the name of the censor. All liturgical books* by virtue of their content must be perused by a censor. *See also* IMPRIMATUR.

Cerecloth (SI[UH]R-klawth). A linen cloth, waxed on the bottom side, that is placed atop the altar* before the altar cloth* is spread over it. The cerecloth is kept there until all traces of holy oils* used in consecration of the altar are gone. Formerly, it was an altar covering placed beneath three altar cloths, and the wax prevented any drops of the Precious Blood* from seeping into the altar stone. It is also called a chrismale.

Ceremonial (ser-uh-MOH-nee-uhl). The set of rules that govern religious ceremonies and worship*; usually it refers to the book that contains the succession of acts that constitute a ceremony or group of ceremonies.

The *Roman Ceremonial* treats of Papal ceremonies, such as the election of the Pope,* canonization* of Saints,* creation of cardinals,* celebration of Mass* and Divine Office* by the Pope, and any general rules governing pontifical ceremonies.

The *Ceremonial of Bishops* deals with the ceremonies celebrated or presided over by the bishop* of the diocese.* Besides the general principles that govern the action of the bishop and his ministers* at such functions, it treats specifically of the offices and duties of the Ordinary* and each of his ministers in some detail. Sections describe the rules for Mass and Divine Office, anniversaries of the bishop's election and episcopal ordination, and also liturgical honors due to bishops and even civil authorities.

Were we to try to distinguish between ceremonial and ritual,* we would say the ceremonial accentuates the external acts, whereas the ritual details more specifically the formula of prayer to be used. Naturally there is much overlapping, since both liturgical books* must involve the specialty of each other. *See also* RITUAL.

Ceremonies. *See* RITES AND CEREMONIES.

Ceremonies, Master of. *See* MASTER OF CEREMONIES.

Chair (Cathedra) (chayr; kuh-THEE-druh). The seat or throne occupied by the local bishop* in his church; hence the name cathedra. At first it was placed in the vertex of the apse,* where he presided at celebrations and preached. As altars began to have retables, the framework on the wall-side of the altar table for a picture, the positioning of the chair at that spot was impossible, so it was moved to the Gospel side. Today it will still be there, if the present architectural features of the building do not allow it in its original and proper place at the head of the apse.* Should the bishop sit during a liturgical function, such as ordination,* a faldstool* is used in front of the altar.

As the word Seat or See (Holy See) is a word in the current language of the Church, the word Chair is also found in the Roman Liturgy* and signifies not only the material piece of furniture but also episcopal authority. For instance, when the Pope speaks *ex cathedra*, his formal pronouncement on doctrine carries infallibility. To use a throne to symbolize authority predates Christian times. The feast of the Chair of Saint Peter,* our first Pope* and bishop, is celebrated each year on February 22.

With the growth of the Church, a chair for the celebrant* to use when he presides over the assembly became a necessity. If possible it is to be placed behind the altar in the middle, but not on a throne. He remains at the chair from the beginning of the Eucharistic celebration through the Liturgy of the Word*; he may even preach the Homily* there. He returns to the chair after Communion,* and remains there until the end. Chair for Preaching: *see* LECTERN.

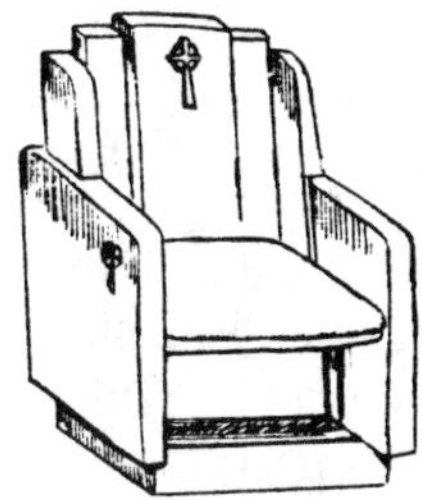

Chair of St. Peter (chayr uhv saynt PEE-tuhr). This feast originally celebrated on February 22 commemorates St. Peter's pontifical authority in Rome, where he arrived to teach and rule as bishop* of that city. It is believed that he held this position for about 25 years. Pope Paul IV instituted a feast of Peter's Chair at Rome to be observed on January 18; so February 22 marked the founding of the Church at Antioch where Peter had been bishop before coming to Rome. In 1961 the duplicate feast was eliminated, and the original date is retained to honor Peter as the Bishop of the Church of Rome, differing from the celebration of June 29 when we honor him as the first Vicar of Christ, the ruler of the Universal Church.* *Liturgical celebration:* February 22 (Feast); *theme:* love for the Liturgy means love for its original home, Rome. *See also* PETER, APOSTLE, ST.

Chair of Unity Octave. *See* WEEK OF PRAYER FOR CHRISTIAN UNITY.

Chaldean Rite (kal-DEE-uhn rait). This rite is listed as a separate and distinct one by the Sacred Congregation for the Oriental Rites. It was derived from the Antiochene Rite.* Its members are descendants of the Nestorians who returned to Christian unity in 1692. They are found in the Middle East as well as in Europe, Africa, and the Americas. The liturgical languages are Syriac and Arabic. Some are also Syro-Malabarese descendants of the St. Thomas Christians of Malabar, India. These use a westernized form of the Chaldean Rite. *See also* EASTERN RITE.

Chalice (CHAL-is). A sacred vessel in which the Eucharistic wine is consecrated at Mass.* Cup shaped, it consists of three parts: the cup, the base, and a nob or node separating the two.

At first chalices were made of glass, but by the 9th century practically all of them were of precious metals. Until recent Vatican II* legislation, at least the inner part of the cup was gold-plated. Now chalices may be made of nonabsorbent material, solid and worthy, in the judgment of the Conference of Bishops* in the region. Before it is used, a chalice is to be consecrated. Formerly this was done by a bishop,* but now it may be consecrated by a priest.*

Eventually, there may be a return to the ministerial chalice that has two handles, so that it may be more easily distributed to the faithful* when Communion* is given under both species. *See also* PATEN; SACRED VESSELS.

Chalice Veil (CHAL-is vayl). A square cloth of silk large enough to cover the chalice* and paten* when they are on the credence table* and it is draped naturally over them. Usually it matches the color* of the vestment of the day, but it may always be white. Decorative symbols may be used in a modest manner.

Chancel (CHAN-suhl). That area of the church assigned to officiating clergy.* The term was derived from the Latin, meaning crossbar, lattice, or screen. In the early centuries such a balustrade or railing was used; it was also common at the beginning of the 20th century. In fact, it substituted for altar rails.* During the Middle Ages a taller choir screen was used. At first it comprised only the area around the altar, the space known as the sanctuary*; it was expanded to include the choir as that became a popular feature. *See also* SANCTUARY.

Chant (chant). Liturgical music* sung during a religious service. It can vary from a recitative to an extremely florid piece, which could be handled only by a trained choir or a soloist. The chants are formulas that can be used with any text, unless they are quite florid. With the advent of vernacular* worship,* particularly since Vatican II,* liturgical chant is employed less and less, with more care taken in a meaningful expression of a text being read.

Chant can have a threefold purpose: (a) To invite the participation of the people during acclamations* and litanies.* (b) To interpret more fully the sometimes long ceremony, such as the distribution of Communion.* (c) To create a restful moment between readings, such as the Responsorial Psalm.* It enhances the solemnity and beauty of the liturgical text, which it sometimes also clarifies. *See also* GREGORIAN CHANT.

Chanter (CHANT-uhr). A singer, lay or cleric, who sets the pitch, intones and leads the singing, formerly particularly the unaccompanied singing during the Divine Office* or the Sacrifice of the Mass.* This leader of the choir intones hymns,* psalms,* antiphons,* and any singing at liturgical functions. His job is essential for the proper performance of the Office and the Liturgy.* Today, commonly called a leader of song, such a person would stand at a lectern* other than the pulpit, and direct the congregation in its singing while also intoning certain parts of the Responsorial Psalms,* etc. In this latter position the chanter may be called a psalmist.*

Chants of the Ordinary (chants uhv thee OR-duhn-er-ee). This term refers to the unvarying parts of the Mass* that are rendered chorally: the Kyrie (Lord, Have Mercy*), Gloria (Glory to God*), Creed* (We Believe), Sanctus and Benedictus (Holy, Holy, Holy* and Blessed), and Agnus Dei (Lamb of God*). These pieces comprise the Mass as a musical work.

Chants of the Proper (chants uhv thuh PROP-uhr). This term refers to the variable Mass* texts that are set to music: Entrance Antiphon,* Communion Antiphon,* Responsorial Psalm,* Alleluia Verse,* and Sequence.* In the pre-Vatican II Mass there was also an Offertory Antiphon* and a Gradual* in place of the Responsorial Psalm (which used to give way to a Tract* from Septuagesima* to Easter*).

These antiphons were also longer and were combined with a psalm-verse (and other verses from the same Psalm could be added). *See also* SIMPLE GRADUAL.

Chapel (CHAP-uhl). So called because of the cloak or cape of St. Martin of Tours in a shrine that took its name from the diminutive of cappa (cappella). Eventually the name also designated the little apses provided with an altar that were built at the ends of the side aisles of churches or around the aisles themselves. These side chapels may have special purposes, the reservation of the Blessed Sacrament,* a shrine, or a treasury for relics.* The term also describes a small place for liturgical service, and hence could include oratories in institutions, private residences, or cemeteries. *See also* CATHEDRAL; CHURCHES; ORATORY.

Chaplain (CHAP-luhn). A priest* especially appointed by ecclesiastical authority to minister to the spiritual needs of a particular group by conducting religious services for them. Such may be Religious communities, associations, confraternities,* institutions, soldiers, collegians, prisoners, sick persons in hospitals or homes, orphans, etc. The pastoral care chaplains offer their subjects varies with the jurisdiction given them from the Ordinary.*

Chaplet. *See* ROSARY.

Character (Sacraments) (KAR-ik-tuhr). Usually defined as the indelible seal impressed on the soul through the Sacraments of Baptism,* Confirmation,* and Holy Orders.* This sign, which most likely lasts even into eternity, signifies that the recipient relates in a special and unique way to Christ. More specifically, one might say that it is a spiritual power to receive or generate something sacred.

This configuration to Christ brings with it the ability to participate in the Priesthood* of Christ, thus deputing to the recipient the privilege of participating in the public worship* of the Church. Initially, the Priesthood* begins when the character is imprinted by the Sacraments of Baptism and Confirmation. Thus the faithful* too offer to God together with the priest the Eucharistic Sacrifice.

Charismatic Movement. *See* NEO-PENTECOSTALISM; PENTECOSTAL MOVEMENT.

Charles Borromeo, St. (chahrlz bor-roh-MAY-oh). 1538-1584. Born in Lombardy, Charles became proficient in both civil and canon law. At twenty-two years of age, he was made Cardinal-Archbishop of Milan by his uncle Pope Pius IV and went on to become one of the great reformers of the Church in the 16th century, according to the norms instituted by the Council of Trent. He

erected many monasteries, founded a host of charitable institutions, and was a model bishop.* He is the Patron of Seminarians and Catechists. *Liturgical celebration;* November 4 (Memorial); *theme:* renewal of the Church through individual renewal.

Charles Lwanga, St. (chahrlz luh-WAHN-guh). ?-1886. Between 1885 and 1887 many Christians were martyred in Uganda by King Mwanga. Among them were Charles Lwanga, the chief of the royal pages, and twenty-one of his companions. As their leader, Charles exhorted them by his words and left them an example by his death—since he was the first to be buried alive. Twelve others followed him on that same day, June 3, 1886; the rest were killed between May 26, 1886, and June 27, 1887. *Liturgical celebration:* June 3 (Memorial); *theme:* living the Christian Faith.

Chasuble (CHAZ-uh-buhl; CHAS-). The sleeveless liturgical outer garment used primarily for the celebration of Mass.* Worn over all the other vestments, this tent-like garment covers the entire body with only an opening for the wearer's head. Throughout the centuries, it took on a variety of shapes and sizes with the current interest reverting to the Gothic. At first without decoration, the chasuble, ample and supple by nature, fell lightly around the body. Eventually, especially as it grew less ample, symbolic ornamentation occurred in a number of ways.

This garment is the distinctive sign of the priestly office, symbolizing Christ's yoke. Although it should be made of silk and the color* of the liturgical day, the latest regulations permit the Episcopal Conference* to regulate the material and design according to the culture of the regions, as long as liturgical dignity reigns. Currently a combined chasuble-alb design is in vogue.

In the United States the chasuble-alb may be used in concelebrations,* Masses for special groups, celebrations outside a sacred place, and in similar cases when, by reason of the place or persons, it seems advisable. In this case the stole worn on top of the chasuble-alb should be of the color of the Mass. In other Masses the regular norms are to be followed. *See also* VESTMENTS.

Chasuble-Alb. *See* CHASUBLE.

Children, Communion of. *See* COMMUNION.

Children, Mass for. *See* MASS FOR CHILDREN AND SPECIAL GROUPS.

Chimes. *See* BELLS.

Chinese Rites. (chai-NEEZ raits). Controversy that arose among missionaries and theologians in the 18th century regarding the legitimacy of the toleration or adaptation of traditional customs by Jesuit missionaries in China and in the Coast of Malabar, India. This tolerant attitude was first adopted by Father Matteo Ricci (1552-1610). Arriving in China in 1582, he largely Christianized certain expressions and customs of Confucianism, particularly those pertaining to the veneration of Confucius and ancestors. Roberto de Nobili (1577-1656) did the same thing in India for various Brahmin customs.

Advocates of these rites contended that they were civil ceremonies that did not express superstitious beliefs, especially in the upper classes, and that evangelization* would be severely handicapped if converts could not retain customs so central to their national life. However, opponents of these rites argued that the Church cannot compromise and that the rites were inextricably bound up with superstitious beliefs.

Accordingly, the practices were denounced to the Holy See* and first regulated for the Malabarese Rites with much understanding (1623) and then for China in a more reserved fashion and with manifold distinctions (decrees of 1645 and 1656). When the controversy flared up anew at the turn of the century, the Chinese Rites were condemned by the Holy Office (1704). This condemnation was confirmed by the Apostolic Constitution of Clement XI in 1715 and later by Benedict XIV in 1762, bringing to a virtual halt the evangelization of the upper classes in the Far East.

The question was taken up anew in a more relaxed atmosphere and in changed circumstances in the 20th century and the purely civil character of the customs was recognized both for China (1939) and for India (1940). Vatican II* affirmed the need to evangelize in a way that avoids syncretism but is suited to the sociocultural pattern of each nation. *See also* ADAPTATION, LITURGICAL; CULTURE AND WORSHIP.

Chi-Rho (kai-roh; kee). Monogram formed by the first and second letters of the Greek spelling for Christ. They resemble the English letters X and P and signify Christ—especially in His victory over sin and death.

Choirs (Architecture) (kwairz [ahr-kuh-TEK-chuhr]). Originally the choir was that part of the church that was reserved for the clergy,* in which the faithful* did not enter, i.e., the chancel* or the sanctuary,* usually at the east end of the building. Later on this area was subdivided so that the choir was the enclosure reserved for the clergy who assisted at liturgical ceremonies without taking a direct part in carrying out the rites. The other section, the sanctuary, contained the altar* and consisted of the place occupied by the clergy appointed to perform the sacred functions.

The choir then became the place where choir monks and choir nuns, members of Religious Institutes or Orders of men or women obliged to recite the *Liturgy of the Hours** daily in common, perform this duty.

Most choirs are comprised of stalls, rows of seats facing each other from the two sides of the choir, with a bookrest in front of each row and the individual seats divided by arm rests.

In the last two centuries, the singers who formed a musical choir, frequently in robes and surplice,* made use of this area, but it separated the congregation* from the altar.

Since the 13th century, some churches made use of a choir loft, either above the sanctuary or at the entrance of the church (the west end), in which both the organ and the musical choir performed. Modern church architecture will endeavor to place the choir in view of the congregation, but not obstructing its vision of the sanctuary. *See also* CHANCEL; SANCTUARY.

Choirs (Music) (kwairz [MYOO-zik]). At first this word was used to designate the monastic men or women who sang the Divine Office* in Gregorian Chant.* Eventually the monastic choirs grew in size with additional singers, for example, boy sopranos from the monastic schools. Later, professional singers without clerical status formed the great cathedral choirs. After the Reformation and Counter-Reformation, the liturgical character of

Catholic choirs diminished, until they became almost secular. Women were employed to sing the soprano and alto parts; the choir chose florid musical numbers rather than liturgical ones.

Liturgical changes occurring after Vatican Council II* insisted that choirs add beauty and solemnity to the Liturgy* and should assist and encourage singing by the congregation.* Sometimes the choir is to lead the people in sung prayer, either alternating or reinforcing the sacred song of the congregation, or enhancing it by an elaborate musical piece. Delay in attaining this goal occurred until some capable and competent musicians wrote a satisfactory repertory for the new rites in the vernacular.* In some areas guitar music became popular in certain groups; many congregations found it easier to join in with the singing. In certain geographical districts, the congregations opted for some of the great Church music of the Protestant tradition.

Post-Vatican II choirs may be made up of men, boys, or women—alone or in combination with one another. The choristers exercise a true liturgical ministry and should not only be trained in music but also be given an adequate liturgical and spiritual formation. In this way, their ministry will not only add beauty to the sacred action and edify the faithful* but also obtain a genuine spiritual benefit for the choir members themselves.

Choirs of Angels (kwairz uhv AYN-juhlz). A term often used in the Preface* at Mass,* it refers to the whole company of angels* arranged in hierarchic order (traditionally spoken of as nine choirs), in union with whom we sing God's praises. *See also* ANGELS.

Chrism (KRIZ-uhm). A blend of olive oil* and balsam,* blessed during the morning Mass of the Chrism on Holy Thursday* by a bishop in a Cathedral Church, and used at liturgical anointings of persons (Baptism,* Confirmation,* Holy Orders*) and of things (altars,* bells,* churches, sacred vessels,* and baptismal water*). The oil stock is marked SC. Anointing with chrism implies abundance of grace* and dedicated service to God. *See also* HOLY OILS.

Chrism Mass. *See* HOLY THURSDAY.

Chrismale. *See* CERECLOTH.

Christ (kraist). This term, derived from the Greek, signifies "anointed" and translates the Hebrew word for *Messiah.** The Hebrew king was anointed with holy oil*; so was the high priest (2 Sm 12:7; Ex 29:21). In

the Bible, it is the title given to the one who, in the future, will come to restore Israel (Dn 9:25-26). Although Jesus hardly ever used the title Himself, He presented Himself as the expected Messiah (Mk 14:62).

As King, Priest, and Prophet par excellence, Jesus the God-Man is the Messiah. By reason of the Incarnation,* He has received in His humanity the fullness of power, sweetness, and joy that was symbolized by the oil of consecration in the ancient rites. The Psalmist, for example, said of the Messiah-King: "You love justice and hate wickedness;

therefore God, your God, has anointed you with the oil of gladness above your fellow kings" (Ps 45:8). Jesus clearly explained the symbolism when He applied the text of Isaiah to Himself: "The Spirit of the Lord is upon me; therefore he has anointed me" (Lk 4:18; Is 61:1). The Spirit* with His seven gifts (cf. Is 11:2) is at the origin of the conception of Jesus in the womb of Mary* (Lk 1:35).

The primitive Church proclaimed Jesus as the Messiah (Christ) (Acts 2:36; 3:20; 4:26). In time, however, the title lost its Messianic force and became a *personal* name: Jesus Christ, Christ Jesus, or simply Christ (1 Cor 1:13, 17; Rom 1:1, 6, 8). This title then went on to become a *cultic* name for Jesus by its use in worship* (2 Tm 1:10; Ti 1:4).

The Liturgy* transmits this anointing of Jesus to all the faithful.* It progressively carries out the interpenetration of the Spirit of God on all humankind. In this way, Christians achieve what their name signifies: they become other "Christs," other "anointed ones," of the Divine Spirit. *See also* JESUS CHRIST.

Christ the King (kraist thuh king). Instituted by Pius XI, this feast was celebrated on the last Sunday of October to foster the awareness of Christ's dominion over all people and to establish peace among nations. After Vatican Council II* the feast was transferred to the last Sunday of the Liturgical Year,* the Sunday before Advent,* on which day the human race is consecrated to the Sacred Heart* through the Litany of the Sacred Heart* and a prayer recited before the Blessed Sacrament.*

This feast celebrates Christ's Kingship in an altogether non-

worldly way. Jesus was anointed by the Father with the oil of gladness as the Eternal Priest and Universal King. As Priest He offered His life on the altar of the Cross and redeemed the human race by this one perfect sacrifice of peace. As King He claims dominion over all creation, that He may present to the almighty Father a Kingdom of truth* and life,* a Kingdom of holiness* and grace,* a Kingdom of justice,* love,* and peace.* *See also* QUAS PRIMAS.

Christening (KRIS-uhn-ing). Another term for the ceremony of Baptism and naming of the child. *See also* BAPTISM.

Christian Burial, Mass of. *See* MASS OF CHRISTIAN BURIAL.

Christian Name. *See* BAPTISMAL NAME.

Christian Prayer (KRIS-chuhn prayr). An abbreviated version of the *Liturgy of the Hours,** available in one volume, patterned after the presently approved Divine Office. By virtue of the constitution of their institute, Religious* may use this Breviary; also the diocesan clergy* if the bishop* has duly approved its use. Thus it is recognized as the public prayer of the Church.

Formerly, prior to Vatican Council II,* such vernacular versions were called the *Short Breviary, Short Office,* or the *Little Office of the Blessed Virgin Mary,* especially for Religious women. The temporal cycle of the Liturgical Year* was emphasized in such Breviaries, which included a few of the major feasts and usually allowed fewer Psalms* throughout the week. *Christian Prayer,* however, has the same structure as far as the psalmody is concerned as the *Liturgy of the Hours,* but one edition eliminates the Office of Readings. The readings that are available in the other edition are selective. *See also* BOOK OF HOURS; LITTLE OFFICE OF THE BLESSED VIRGIN MARY.

Christian Unity, Week of Prayer for. *See* WEEK OF PRAYER FOR CHRISTIAN UNITY.

Christian Year. *See* CHURCH YEAR.

Christifideles Laici (kris-tee-fee-DAY-lez LAI-ee-chee). Latin title (from the first two words "Lay followers of Christ") of the Apostolic *Constitution on the Vocation and Mission of the Lay Faithful in the Church* issued by Pope John Paul II on December 30, 1988. Among other things, it stresses the clear distinction that exists between the liturgical ministries exercised by the ordained and those exercised by lay persons. *See also* LAITY; UNIVERSAL PRIESTHOOD.

Christmas (KRIS-muhs). The feast of the Nativity of the Lord on December 25 commemorates the redemptive Mystery of the entrance of Christ into this world. This feast is characterized by the celebration of three Masses, one at midnight, one at dawn, and another during the day. The oldest one is the Mass of the day, the third one, which was celebrated in the Basilica of St. Peter already in the 4th century.

The second Mass, which used to have a commemoration of St. Anastasia, was said by the Popes for many years at the Basilica of St. Anastasia, a church used by the Greeks who lived in Rome. Although that Mass was in honor of St. Anastasia, today the second Mass on Christmas at dawn is truly of an incarnational nature, probably built upon the practice of having a Mass at Jerusalem for those who were returning from Bethlehem from the midnight Mass.

The midnight Mass is the most recent and proclaims the dogma of the Maternity of Mary.* It was sung in the Basilica of St. Mary Major, which had been rebuilt with a crypt containing a replica of the crib* built in imitation of the grotto of the Nativity in Bethlehem. The Mass of Christmas Eve, when there is an evening Mass the day before Christmas, is of an anticipatory nature to the Feast of the Incarnation of Christ, a typical vigil.* All priests are allowed to celebrate the three Masses on Christmas and take stipends* for them.

The most common spiritual sense attributed to this feast is related to the three births: the eternal birth of the Word in the bosom of the splendor of the paternal glory*; the temporal birth in the humility of the flesh; the final return on the day of judgment. Some devotional books substitute the spiritual birth of Christ in our souls for the last of these, which might be proper to encourage devotion, but is foreign to the sense of the triple Liturgy.

Christmas Crib. *See* CRIB.

Christmas Season (KRIS-muhs SEE-zuhn). Many consider that the cycle* of Christmas begins with the first Sunday of Advent* and lasts through the Advent Season* to Christmas Eve also. Surely it starts with Christmas Eve and takes in the Octave of Christmas and concludes with Feast of the Baptism of the

Lord,* usually on the Sunday after the Epiphany.* Celebrated as the vigil, Christmas Eve, the day before Christmas, was a day of fast* and abstinence* until 1966.

Many customs in various countries occur, especially in the evening hours, for instance, the appearance of St. Nicholas* (Santa Claus). The decoration of the Christmas tree with lights and ornaments reminds Christians of Christ, the Light of the World and the Tree of Life. Devotion around the crib,* popularized by St. Francis of Assisi,* includes the reading of the Christmas Gospel,* singing of hymns,* a prayer, and the singing of carols.* These traditional songs in the vernacular are frequently sung by carolers on the streets and in the neighborhoods. The climax of the evening is the midnight Mass.

After the celebration of the Masses on Christmas, the feast is extended by an octave, which still includes the Feasts of St. Stephen,* St. John the Evangelist,* and the Holy Innocents.* Undoubtedly, one of the reasons for their inclusion is that these Saints have a direct link with the Nativity of Christ being celebrated.

On December 26, the Church puts before us St. Stephen,* the first adult to bear witness with his life to the Incarnate Christ. On December 27, she remembers St. John the Evangelist, the unparalleled herald of the Incarnation ("The Word was made flesh and dwelt among us"). Then on December 28, we celebrate the Holy Innocents, the infants who unknowingly gave their lives for the Incarnate Word (thus showing that martyrdom is always a gift of God).

The next three days celebrate the Mass of the Christmas Season (with a commemoration of St. Thomas of Canterbury* on December 29 and St. Sylvester* on December 31).

The Octave includes the Feast of the Holy Family* celebrated on the occurring Sunday (or on December 30 when there is none) and concludes with the Solemnity of the Mother of God* on the Octave Day, January 1. This used to be (from the 15th century until 1961) the Feast of the Circumcision, but its Marian character has now been restored.

The season includes Epiphany, formerly always celebrated on January 6 with its octave. Now the octave has been suppressed, and an option allows the celebration of Epiphany on the Sunday after the Octave Day of Christmas. Should that occur on January 7 or 8, the Feast of the Baptism of the Lord* is celebrated the following Monday, and Epiphany week is omitted that year.

The feasts of the Liturgical Year* place before our minds the sign of some hidden sacred reality that must be applied to all of us. During the Christmas Season this hidden sacred reality is the light, the life, and the joy beaming from Christ, the "Sun of Justice," upon humankind in the darkness of ignorance and sin (Mal 4:2).

This Mystery of our salvation is to be honored not as something that happened 2,000 years ago, but as something present, for while the act itself (Christ's birth and manifestation) is past, its effects are very present. The hidden reality in this Mystery is ultimately Christ and His saving action. He is present in the Mystery of Christmas-Epiphany, constantly interceding for us and communicating Himself in holy symbols.

We meditate on and celebrate the Christmas Mystery as happening now to us and embrace its mystical effects with an open heart. After the time of waiting (Advent), we enjoy a fuller realization of Christ's presence in us. In the Word made flesh, we see that God is no stranger to the human condition; in the Infant born in a stable to simple working people, we come to understand that God Who is infinitely great is also one of us.

The readings* of this season provide the salient features of this Infant. He is the Servant of Yahweh and the Prince of Peace, whom Isaiah* foretold. He is the Light and the Logos which is greater than human reason and perfects it (John). In Him we encounter the Ultimate Transcendent Reality: He reveals the Father (Heb 1) Who is gracious to human beings (Titus). This Father comforts and consoles us (Is 52) and promises to unite us His adopted children in Jerusalem, symbols of the Church and brotherly love (Gal 4; Is 68).

Christmas celebrates the Father's gift to us: the revelation of His loving presence. This knowledge has been given to us through Israel and the Prophets* and supremely through Christ His Son. It must continue to be made manifest through Christ-in-us; "from his fullness we have all received" (Jn 1:16).

Christus Dominus (KREES-toos DOH-mee-noos). Latin title (from the first two words "Christ the Lord") of the *Decree on the Pastoral Office of Bishops in the Church* issued by the Second Vatican Council* on October 28, 1965. It stipulates that bishops* are to work constantly toward the faithful's* deeper knowledge and living of the Paschal Mystery* through the Eucharist* in order to fashion the one Body, closely bound together in the unity of Christ's charity.

Since all priests share with the bishop the one priesthood* of Christ, in their work of sanctifying they celebrate the Eucharistic Sacrifice* as the center and high point of the whole life of the Christian community. They also strive to strengthen the faithful* by advocating the devout and frequent reception of the Sacraments* and an intelligent and intense participation in the Liturgy.* *See also* VATICAN COUNCIL, SECOND.

Chronicles, First and Second (KRON-i-kuhlz, fuhrst and SEK-uhnd). Thirteenth and Fourteenth Books of the Old Testament* and Fifth and Sixth Historical Books. The two books of Chronicles were written in the 5th century B.C. by the "Chronicler" (probably Ezra the Scribe). He recounts events already recorded in the Books of Samuel* and Kings*—but from a completely different point of view. He stresses that despite the calamities that have befallen the chosen people God is faithful to His promises and will fulfill them through the people of Judah. And he bases his assurance of this fact on the great achievements of David and Solomon, the reforms of Jehoshaphat, Hezekiah, and Josiah, and the deeds of those who remained faithful to the Lord.

In this connection, the Chronicler presents David as the real founder of the Temple and its ritual, describes the beginning of the Temple and its worship and attributes both to David as the central figure of Jewish history, portrays Jerusalem as the holy city, inculcates the sacralization of history, and stresses the unbending law of retribution.

Liturgical use: The Books of Chronicles are used sparingly in the *Roman Missal**: on the Assumption,* Vigil Mass and Common of the Blessed Virgin* (transferal of the ark to the city of David), the Dedication of a Church* (transferral of the ark to the Temple of Solomon), Saturday of the 11th Week in Ordinary Time* (II) and the Common of Martyrs (no sin without punishment and no punishment without sin), and the 4th Sunday of Lent* (B) (destruction of Jerusalem and ultimate deliverance). In the *Liturgy of the Hours,** it is used only four times: Thursday of the 14th Week (preparations for building the Temple), Friday of the 15th Week (Josaphat obtains God's help), the Annunciation* and the Common of the Blessed Virgin (Messianic prophecy about the Son of David). It also gives rise to a minor canticle.*

Meaning: Infidelity to God brings disastrous consequences. Yet God is faithful to His promises (He will send the Messiah*) and rewards fidelity to Himself. He dwells in His Temple and accepts the sacrifices of His people.

Chronista. *See* PASSION.

Church and Liturgy (chuhrch and LIT-uhr-jee). The Greek word *ekklesia* originally denoted the assembly of free citizens called together by convocation *(ek-kaleo).* In this sense, the Church is the assembly* of the People of God* convoked by God and for God in view of a celebration* of the Covenant.*

In the OT Israel was born as the People of God on the "Day of the Assembly" (Dt 9:10; 10:14; 18:16) when it consented to the Covenant with Yahweh* (Ex 24). The (Hebrew word) *qahal** of Yahweh was translated by the (Greek) *ekklesia* of the Lord in the Septuagint.* Thus, the People of God became a people in a *liturgical covenant;* it has a liturgical identity.

The Church of the NT is the assembly of the dispersed children of God (Jn 11:52), brought together into the unity of the Trinity (Jn 17:11, 21, 22) by the Blood of Christ (Acts 20:28). The Church was rendered fruitful at the Cross* by the Spirit, the water, and the Blood (Jn 19:30, 34; 1 Jn 5:6-8)—at the heart of the unique sacrifice of the New Covenant. The Church was born at Pentecost* in the effusion of the Holy Spirit, as an assembly celebrating the wondrous deeds of God (Acts 2:11).

St. Peter* sets forth the liturgical titles of the assembly at Sinai when he tells the faithful: "You are 'a chosen race, a royal priesthood, a holy nation, a people of his own, so that you may announce the praises' of him who called you out of darkness into his wonderful light. Once you were 'no people' but now you are God's people" (1 Pt 2:9-10).

Hence, the very nature of the Church is liturgical, and it is in the celebration of the Liturgy* that the Church most completely expresses what she is and what she is becoming: the People-Bride united with the Bridegroom and made fruitful by the Spirit and initiated into the Trinitarian exchange, the ultimate reality of the Liturgy.

In its rites and in its words as well as in the unity and multiplicity of its forms, the Liturgy is a special manifestation of the Church: the expression and realization of her mystery of communion and salvation. It is above all in her liturgical celebrations that the Church appears more clearly and efficaciously as "a kind of Sacrament* or sign and instrument of intimate union with God and of the unity of humankind" (LG, 1), "simultaneously manifesting and exercising the mystery of God's love for human beings" (GS, 45).

The Liturgy "daily builds up those who are within into a holy temple in the Lord, into a dwelling place for God in the Spirit, to the mature measure of the fullness of Christ. At the same time, it marvelously strengthens their power to preach Christ and thus shows forth the Church to those who are outside as a sign lifted up among the nations under which the scattered children of God may be gathered together, until there is one sheepfold and one shepherd" (SC, 2).

Within the sphere of the History of Salvation,* the Paschal Mystery* of Christ gives forth "the wondrous Sacrament of the whole Church" (SC, 5). To accomplish the work of our redemption "Christ is always present in His Church. . . . Christ always associates the Church with Himself in His great work. . . . In the Liturgy the whole public worship is performed by the Mystical Body* of Jesus Christ, that is, by the Head and His members" (SC, 7).

"Liturgical actions are not private functions but are celebrations of the Church, which is the 'Sacrament of unity,' namely the holy people united and ordered under their bishops. . . . They pertain to the whole body of the Church; they manifest it and have effects upon it" (SC, 26). Indeed, "the preeminent manifestation of the Church consists in the full, active participation* of all God's holy people in these liturgical celebrations, especially the Eucharist,* in a single prayer, at one altar,* at which there presides the bishop* surrounded by his college of priests* and by his ministers" (SC, 41).

The Church is most manifested when she acts as the Sacrament of Christ in the world, through the seven modalities of grace* by which people come in contact with the Paschal Mystery of the Lord in space and time—the Sacraments.* But all the Sacraments are oriented toward the Eucharist as to their completion and their end: "The celebration of Mass, the action of Christ and the People of God arrayed hierarchically, is for the Universal and the Local Church* as well as for each person the center of the whole Christian life" (RM, 1). Every Sacrament introduces them into an essential aspect of the

Church, as the earthly presence of salvation.*

At the same time, "the Church is also manifested when the Liturgy of the Hours* is celebrated. As a community, the Church must express its nature as a community by its prayer as well as in other ways" (GILH, 9). "Public and private prayer by the People of God is rightly considered to be among the principal duties of the Church" (GILH, 1).

The Liturgy of the Hours celebrated in the local community is the type and realization of Christian prayer,* understood as a response to the Word of God,* as the exercise of the priesthood of Christ, and as the actuation and manifestation of the Church.

The Liturgy "does not exhaust the entire activity of the Church." Evangelization,* conversion,* and commitment to all the works of charity, piety, and the apostolate* are also needed (SC, 9). "Nevertheless, the Liturgy is the summit toward which the activity of the Church is directed; at the same time, it is the fount from which all her power flows" (SC, 10).

The Church centers her life around the Liturgy and by means of the Liturgy. The work of salvation is realized in the Liturgy. The Church is built up and constructed through the full, active, and conscious participation of her members in the Liturgy, especially the Eucharist.

Church, Catholic (chuhrch, KATH-uh-lik). Generally, the society of true Christians, those who believe in Jesus Christ, profess His doctrine, participate in His Sacraments,* and are under the direction of lawful pastors,* particularly the Bishop of Rome. Thus is the Catholic Church defined by the Council of Trent.

Gleaned from the Scriptures, there may be various senses to a broad definition:

(a) *The community of believers,* that is, the Church of the Gospel,* which exists everywhere the true Gospel is preached.

(b) *The Kingdom of God,* since it fulfills the ancient prophecies concerning the reign of the Messiah.*

(c) *The Mystical Body of Christ,** insofar as it unites all who are sanctified by the grace of Christ. He, their invisible head, recognizes them as His visible members. Therefore it includes the faithful* on earth, the souls in purgatory, and the Saints* in paradise.

Vatican Council II* acknowledged the Council of Trent's definition as the objective statement identifying the Roman Catholic Church. Yet its own subjective qualification would include everyone who is baptized and professes faith in Jesus Christ. By His providence, He confers special blessings on these His chosen People of God.

Liturgically speaking, the Church is referred to as the assembly* of believers congregating for instruction and worship.* Thus the twofold mission of the Church is accomplished, the sanctification of human beings and the glory of God. *See also* CHURCH AND LITURGY.

For the church as an edifice, *see* CHURCHES.

Church, Consecration of. *See* CHURCH DEDICATION.

Church Dedication (chuhrch ded-uh-KAY-shuhn). Current terminology favors a "Dedication" of a Church and an Altar over the "Consecration" of a Church or Altar. Formerly the solemn blessing was termed the consecration; the simple blessing, a dedication.

The church building is an image of the Church,* built from living stones; it is the place where the Eucharist* is kept, the place where Christians assemble to hear the Word of God,* to pray and praise the Lord, and to celebrate the holy Mysteries. The altar,* at which the people of God partake in the Lord's Sacrifice to be refreshed by a holy Sacrament, stands as a sign of Christ Himself, the priest, victim, and altar of His own sacrifice. Consequently, the rite of the Dedication of a Church and an Altar is a most solemn liturgical service. Although it was revised and simplified in 1961, further revisions for adaptation to contemporary conditions were deemed advisable and took effect in 1977.

Laying of the Cornerstone

As the construction of a new church starts, the celebration of a rite—to seek God's blessing on the work and thus remind people that the physical structure is a visible sign of the living Church—is desirable. The blessing and laying of the cornerstone or foundation stone occurs, unless the style of the building disallows a cornerstone. In that case at least the blessing of the site should be celebrated.

Usually the bishop* of the diocese performs the rite, approaching the construction site together with the people in procession* if that is possible. Otherwise the people assemble with the bishop at the site of the new church. After readings from the *Lectionary** and a Homily,* the bishop sprinkles the site of the new church, sprinkles the cornerstone and incenses it. Then a stonemason fixes the stone with mortar. Throughout appropriate hymns may be sung. General Intercessions* and a prayer by the bishop conclude the ceremony.

Dedication of a Church

Any building destined permanently as a church for the community of faithful* and for performing sacred functions should be dedicated to God in a solemn rite, since it is a sign of the pilgrim Church on earth reflecting the Church in heaven. To be dedicated the church must have a titular: the Trinity,* Christ under some Mystery* or Title, the Holy Spirit,* the Blessed Virgin Mary,* an angel,* or a Saint* in the *Roman Martyrology.** It is appropriate that authentic relics* of Martyrs* or other Saints be placed beneath the altar.

In preparation for the celebration, ordinarily performed by the bishop, a day should be chosen when many people can participate. The Divine Office* for that day is from the Dedication of a Church at the rank of a Solemnity,* and the Mass* with its various prayers and anointings is proper, except for the

readings from the *Lectionary,* which are from the Common of the Dedication of a Church.

Parts of the Rite

(a) *Entrance into the Church.* Comparable to Palm Sunday,* the entrance may be by procession, solemn entrance, or a simple entrance. There is a formal handing over of the building to the bishop, e.g., with legal documents, the keys, the plan of the building. That is followed by the blessing of water, which is used to sprinkle the people (the spiritual temple), the walls of the church, and the altar.

(b) *Liturgy of the Word.* After the appropriate readings,* the bishop gives a Homily,* and the Profession of Faith* occurs, followed by the Litany of the Saints.*

(c) *Prayer of Dedication and the Anointings.* Following the Litany, the relics of the Saints are deposited under the altar by the bishop who then recites the prayer of dedication.

Standing before the altar, the bishop then pours chrism* on it and anoints the middle of the altar and

each of its four corners. Then he moves to the walls of the church signing with chrism the twelve (or four) crosses there. He may allow a priest* to anoint the walls instead. The bishop incenses the altar, then sits while the ministers incense the people and the walls. The deacon* receives from the bishop a lighted candle, with which he lights the candles on the altar for the celebration of the Eucharist.* Meanwhile festive lighting occurs throughout the church as a symbol of rejoicing.

(d) *Liturgy of the Eucharist.* This part continues as usual, except that there may be an inauguration of the Blessed Sacrament* chapel, should there be such an area in the church.

Certain rites in the dedication express visibly the invisible work of the Lord as accomplished through the Church. Anointing the altar with chrism symbolizes Christ, the anointed one, the high priest Who sacrificed His life for all. Anointing the church denotes that it is dedicated entirely and perpetually to Christian worship.* Incense* burned on the altar connotes that the sacrifice of Christ, as an odor of sweetness, ascends to God; similarly the prayers of the people waft upward, pleasing and acceptable at the throne of God.

Incensing the church indicates that it is a house of prayer, second only to the People of God* who were incensed first. Covering and decorating the altar signifies that it is a table of sacrificial banquet, the Lord's table from which the community is refreshed with the Body and Blood* of Christ. Lights* on the altar and in the church represent Christ as the Light of Nations, shining in the Church and thus to the entire human family.

The anniversary of any church's dedication is celebrated as a Solemnity; however, the dedication of a cathedral church* is celebrated by the other churches in the diocese as a Feast.*

Dedication of a Church Already in General Use

This special rite exists for churches in which the sacred Mysteries have been celebrated, but the churches were not dedicated. The chief differences that occur are: the rite of opening the doors to the church is omitted; handing the church over to the bishop is omitted, observed, or adapted depending upon the circumstances; sprinkling the walls of the church, purificatory by nature, is omitted; instead of the proper First Reading from the *Lectionary,* another suitable reading is chosen from the Common.*

Should it be necessary to have a consecration of an altar alone, the rite is comparable to that of a Dedication of a Church and an Altar with appropriate changes made throughout.

Blessing of a Church

Private oratories,* chapels,* or sacred buildings may be chosen for Divine worship only for a time. In that case rather than being dedicated, they are blessed in a much simpler ceremony. After the usual entrance into the church, the bishop blesses water and then sprinkles the people with it and purifies the walls of the new church or oratory. Returning to the sanctuary, he sprinkles the altar, unless it has already been blessed or dedicated.

The proper Mass continues as usual with the readings taken from the Common of a Dedication of a Church or the Mass of the day. After the General Intercessions,* the altar is blessed in a very simple and short prayer, followed by an incensation. Then the altar is covered and decorated for the Liturgy of the Eucharist, which is interrupted only if the chapel of the Blessed Sacrament is to be inaugurated as mentioned above.

Blessing of an Altar

Should it be necessary to bless a movable altar alone, the Mass of the day is said. Everything proceeds as usual until after the General Intercessions, when according to the rite the bishop blesses the altar, which was entirely uncovered from the beginning of the ceremony. The antiphon* or an appropriate song is sung; the bishop addresses the people and blesses the altar with a short prayer. After the bishop sprinkles the altar with holy water and incenses it, the ministers cover the altar with a cloth and decorate it for the celebration of Mass, which proceeds as usual from this point.

Church Furnishings (chuhrch FUHR-nish-ingz). For proper liturgical celebrations, the Church insists on proper furnishings and objects of varying importance, all of which reveal the character of their sacred use and are quite distinguishable from profane appurtenances. Some examples, described elsewhere in this book, are the credence table,* benches, pulpits,* bookstands, and confessionals.*

Recent legislation admits all styles and types of materials and ornamentation as time and the advance of technical arts allow. Adaptations, particularly with regard to the material and form, are under the supervision of the territorial bishops.*

Church Militant (chuhrch MIL-uh-tuhnt). The faithful* on earth who have been incorporated into the

Mystical Body of Christ* by Baptism* and who are united with Christ's visible successor, the Sovereign Pontiff. They are still struggling to win their eternal reward, and so they conduct the Liturgy* on earth for the glory of God and the redemption of His people. *See also* COMMUNION OF SAINTS, THE.

Church Suffering (chuhrch SUF-[uh-]ring). The faithful* who are saved but are now undergoing purification before entering heaven. They can no longer gain merits for themselves but can be aided by the prayers and sacrifices of the Church Militant,* especially liturgical celebrations, such as the Eucharist,* and prayers based on the Liturgy.* *See also* COMMUNION OF SAINTS, THE.

Church Triumphant (chuhrch trai-UM-fuhnt). The faithful* who have attained heavenly glory* and now take part in the "heavenly Liturgy,* which is celebrated in the heavenly city of Jerusalem* toward which we journey as pilgrims, where Christ is seated at the right hand of God, a minister of the holies and of the true tabernacle" (SC, 8). *See also* COMMUNION OF SAINTS, THE.

Church Unity Octave. *See* WEEK OF PRAYER FOR CHRISTIAN UNITY.

Church Year (chuhrch yeer). The span of time, one solar year long, comprising fifty-two weeks beginning with the First Sunday of Advent* and ending with the Saturday of the 34th week in Ordinary Time.* It memorializes the redemptive Mysteries* of Christ and their efficacy in sanctifying the Saints,* thus inviting all the faithful* to honor them and live in a similar spirit. The year is composed of two cycles,* running simultaneously: (1) the temporal commemorates the Mysteries of Christ; (2) the sanctoral, remembering the Blessed Virgin Mary* and the Saints, developed from annual celebrations of the martyrdom of the local heroes of the Faith. It soon expanded to include Saints other than Martyrs.

The temporal cycle consists of several seasons, Advent,* Christmas Season,* Lent,* Easter Season,* and Ordinary Time.* The last one begins after the Feast of the Baptism of the Lord* and extends until Ash Wednesday*; it picks up again the Monday after Pentecost* and concludes with the Saturday before Advent. Early in Christianity Sunday* brought the assembly* together for the Eucharistic celebration of the Paschal Mystery.* As Sunday dominated the week, so Easter was preeminent to the year as a whole.

The sanctoral cycle is ordinarily arranged by the date of the death of the Saint, celebrated annually, together with several feasts of our Lady, all of which are differentiated by various ranks.

In this fashion the Church Year consecrates time in two ways, honoring Christ and those who followed

Him closely. The calendar year and the months have practically no significance to the Church Year. *See also* CYCLES.

Churches (CHUHRCH-uhz). Sacred buildings, dedicated to liturgical worship,* decreed by law to welcome the total Christian community for their social rite of honoring God. Since churches are meant for all, they are to be distinguished from an oratory,* which is for a particular community, usually Religious, and from a chapel,* which is primarily for private use.

Historically, rooms and private houses were used by the early Christians, especially during the persecutions. The first Christian churches followed the plans of a basilica.* The bishop's throne was situated in the circular end of the basilica; around him were the benches for the clergy.* The entrance faced the apse,* directing the attention of all to the altar,* situated between the clergy and the people. Thus the church was divided into three successive enclosures: the sanctuary,* the choir,* and the nave.* The term church basically refers to a parish church, the focal point of all pastoral ministry. It would include the cathedral,* the seat of the bishop*, and in other cities the collegiate church, serviced by canons,* secular priests.

Recent legislation insists that in renovating or reconstructing churches, and in building new churches, care be taken that they be suitable for the active participation* of the faithful* and the proper performance of the Liturgy.* Besides the freestanding altar,* an ambo* and a presidential chair* should be provided. *See also* BASILICA; CHAPEL; CONVENTUAL CHURCH; ORATORY.

Churching of Women (CHUHRCH-ing uhv WIM-uhn). The blessing* of a woman after childbirth—the liturgical opportunity for her to thank God for motherhood and to seek the blessing of the priest.* Such a thanksgiving service should put to rest any idea that defilement might be incurred in childbirth. Holding on to the end of the priest's stole,* the mother is actually brought back into the church* or symbolically introduced into the church, where she gives praise and thanksgiving. The priest intercedes for her offspring, so that they may attain everlasting happiness. This liturgical rite is infrequently performed in the United States.

Ciborium (suh-BOHR-ee-uhm). (1) This sacred vessel is a covered container in which are reserved the small hosts* used for distribution of Communion.* In the early centuries it had various forms, made of box-

wood, copper, ivory, and other metals. Today it may be made from any noble and solid metal or durable material that the local bishops consider suited to sacred use. Eventually, a base was added for easy handling and for exposition.

At first a ciborium was small, used primarily for holding the hosts for the sick. Frequent Communion, subsequent to the Council of Trent, demanded larger ciboria, usually looking much like a chalice with a lid. Today, with Eucharistic ministers* aiding in the distribution of Communion, several smaller, more flat, cuplike vessels, some shaped like deep dishes, which fit one on top of another, are more popular and useful. (*See also* PYX.)

(2) A structure of stone, marble, or metal surmounting an altar,* domeshaped, or like a canopy* supported by pillars, designed to accent the altar. *See also* BALDACHIN.

Cincture (SINK-chuhr). A lengthy cord, usually of linen or hemp, tied at the waist to gather and confine the full, long flowing alb.* Also called a girdle, it symbolizes chastity and is usually white, but it may be also of the liturgical color* of the day. With modern form-fitting albs, the cincture is currently used primarily by Religious who need a fuller alb to cover their habit. The term also refers to the sash or belt of certain religious habits.

Circular Letters. *See* LITURGICAL LAW, SOURCES OF.

Circumcision of the Lord, Feast of (suhr-kuhm-SIZH-uhn uhv thuh Lawrd, feest uhv). A feast* that commemorates the day on which Jesus received His Name when He was circumcised eight days after His birth. It was kept on the Octave Day of Christmas,* January 1. It is now supplanted by the Solemnity of Mary, Mother of God, although the Gospel about the circumcision of Jesus has been retained. *See also* MARY, BLESSED VIRGIN—FEASTS.

Clapper (KLAP-uhr). An instrument constructed with an attachment so as to bring two surfaces of wood together, thus making a knocking sound. It may be used to supplant the ringing of bells* in church after the Gloria* on Holy Thursday* until the Gloria of the Easter Vigil.*

Clare, St. (klayr). 1193-1253. Born in Assisi, Clare followed her fellow-citizen St. Francis* in a life of poverty for God. She founded the Second Franciscan Order (known as the "Poor Clares") and led a life of austerity filled with charity and piety. She is the Patroness of Television. *Liturgical Celebration:* August 11 (Memorial); *theme:* love of the spirit of poverty.

Clement, St. (KLEM-uhnt). ?-100. Clement was a Roman Jew converted by Sts. Peter* and Paul.* He accompanied Paul to Rome and according to Tertullian was ordained Bishop by St. Peter. In the year 91, he became the third successor of St. Peter in the See of Rome. He wrote a famous Epistle to the Corinthians that was placed in rank next to the canonical books of the Bible.* He died a Martyr during the reign of Trajan. He is the Patron of Marble Workers and Stonecutters. *Liturgical celebration:* November 23 (Opt. Mem.); *theme:* praise of God's glory and power in His servants.

Clementine Instruction (KLEM-uhn-tain in-STRUHK-shuhn). Instruction of Pope Clement XII in

1731 that regulated the Forty Hours' Devotion* until the appearance of the revised rite for Benediction* and Exposition of the Blessed Sacrament in 1973.

Clementine Liturgy (KLEM-uhn-tain LIT-uhr-jee). The manner of celebrating the Eucharist* according to Book Eight of the apocryphal *Apostolic Constitutions** purported to be the work of Pope Clement* of Rome. Actually Book Eight derives from the *Apostolic Tradition** of Hippolytus* and was written about 380. Although never used as a rite by any congregation, this liturgy greatly influenced many of the later Eastern Rites.

Clergy (KLUR-jee). The collective name for the clerics in Holy Orders,* namely, deacons,* priests,* and bishops* who are set apart from the laity* by ordination, so as to become leaders in the Church.* They enjoy a hierarchic or ministerial portion of the one priesthood* of Christ, different from the universal priesthood of the laity.*

The cleric, a member of the clergy, is a man whose duty is to serve God principally and exclusively as opposed to lay persons, for whom Divine service, while remaining the final object of their earthly activity, still occupies only a temporal and transitory place in their daily life. Entrance into the ranks of the clergy presupposes a renunciation of worldly affairs. In return the Church insures the material support of her clerics by giving them a share in the offerings received from the faithful in the celebration of Divine worship.*

Those in the clerical state share in the ministries of sanctifying, teaching, and governing the Church. Their obligations include holiness of life, acquiring and developing the necessary knowledge and culture, perpetual celibacy (in the west), performance of Divine service conformable to the Order received, and the wearing of ecclesiastical dress.

Accordingly, life in seminaries should be thoroughly influenced by the spirit of the Liturgy,* and sufficient liturgical training should exist that the seminarians may be able to understand the sacred rites and take part in them wholeheartedly.

After Vatican Council II,* besides transitional deacons (those intending to become priests) permanent deacons may be ordained from the laity, even among married men, should the Episcopal Conference* so decide. *See also* BISHOPS; DEACONS; PRIESTS.

Closed Times (klohzd taimz). Certain periods of the Church Year* have restrictions concerning the celebration of Marriage.* Should Marriage take place during Advent* or Lent,* the distinctive nature of these liturgical seasons should be taken into account by less solemnity in the Marriage.

Cloth, Communion. *See* COMMUNION CLOTH.

Clothing of Monastics. *See* INVESTITURE.

Clown Ministry (klown MIN-uh-stree). The word ministry includes

nonliturgical functions. Clowns may definitely perform in the religious education of children, when visiting the sick or those confined to nursing homes, and homes for the elderly; and even in certain celebrations for small children, pastoral reasons could readily suggest clowns or mimes. Ordinarily it would be inappropriate for clowns to function at Mass* or other liturgical rites. Approaches that might derogate from the nature of the Liturgy* are to be avoided, such as those mentioned by John Paul II to the Congregation for Divine Worship*: "rites invented outside the established norms, and attitudes unfavorable to a sense of the sacred, of beauty, and of recollection."

As *Environment and Art in Catholic Worship* indicates, ritual movement and gestures can "subtly, yet really, contribute to an environment which can foster prayer or which can detract from prayer." Clown ministry during the Liturgy may personalize the Liturgy too much and detract from the prayerful atmosphere necessary for the community in worship. As also stated in EACW, a work of art is to be appropriate by "bearing the weight of mystery, awe, reverence and wonder which the liturgical action expresses; it must clearly serve ritual action, which has its own structure, rhythm and movement."

Coadjutor Bishop. *See* BISHOP.

Collect. *See* OPENING PRAYER.

Collection (kuh-LEK-shuhn). Gift offerings, usually contributions of money gathered during Mass* after the Profession of Faith* and before the Prayer over the Gifts.* In the early Church, the bread,* wine,* and water* were actually brought to the altar* at this time, and eventually other gifts were included, such as gold, oil, fruits, candles, and other useful items for the support of the church and its charitable activities. Such a procession of gifts was discontinued in the 10th century, when it was readily replaced by donations of money.

Recently, it has become customary for the faithful to bring up the bread, wine, and water, and in some instances other symbols that befit the particular Liturgy. Ordinarily the money collected is placed near the altar, thus showing the penitential nature of the alms received, which are used to procure the requisites for public worship,* to maintain the upkeep of the church and school, to supply sufficient pastoral care, and to aid the poor, whom we always have with us.

The people's offering of monetary gifts is a symbol of their inner readiness to give God all of themselves with their hopes and disappointments, their work and leisure and their whole everyday lives.

Colors (KUHL-uhrz). Colors have a symbolic meaning in Liturgy.* They suggest the Mystery* or the feast* or signify the sentiment of the special occasion for which the Mass* is celebrated. Since the linens are always white, the colors refer only to the vestments and altar ornaments. At first, the only liturgical color was white, but by the 9th century, other colors were established. In the new Liturgy these traditional colors are retained.

(a) *White.* In the Offices and Masses of the Christmas* and Easter* seasons, feasts of the Lord, except His Passion,* celebrations of Mary,* the angels,* the Saints* who were not Martyrs,* All Saints,* John the Baptist,* John the Evangelist,* Chair of Peter,* and Conversion of Paul.* In the United States white may be used in Masses for the dead.

(b) *Red.* For Palm Sunday,* Good Friday,* Pentecost,* celebrations of the Passion,* feasts of the Apostles and Evangelists* except John, and feasts of Martyrs.*

(c) *Green.* For Ordinary Time.*

(d) *Violet.* During Advent* and Lent*; it may be used also during Offices and Masses for the dead.

(e) *Black.* May be used in Masses for the dead.

(f) *Pink.* On the 3rd Sunday of Advent and the 4th Sunday of Lent.

(g) *Gold* or a more precious vestment may be used on special occasions, even if it does not conform to the proper color.

The color for Votive Masses* may be that most fitting to the Mass itself or it may conform to the color of the day or season. Masses for Various Occasions* are in the color of the day or season.

The traditional meaning assigned to each color is as follows: white—purity and integrity of life; red—offering of one's life for God; green—hope and the vitality of the life of faith; violet—penance; black—mourning; pink—anticipatory joy in a time of penance; gold—highest celebration or great solemnity.

Blue is not approved for the Season of Advent or for feasts of Mary (BCL Newsletter, 12/87).

Colossians, Epistle to the (kuh-LOSH-uhnz; -LOS[H]-ee-uhnz; i-PIS-uhl too thuh). Fifty-eighth Book of the Bible* and twelfth of the New Testament.* Written by St. Paul* during his first Roman captivity (61-63) to the Christians at Colossae, a town in Asia Minor east of Ephesus, this Epistle has as its theme the preeminence of Christ. To counter errors that have been spread about, Paul sets forth in clear terms the true doctrine concerning Christ, our Redeemer, head of the Mystical Body,* the Church, and draws up rules for an ideal Christian life. Between these two positive sections he inserts a condemnation of the false teachings.

Liturgical use: This book is read mainly during the Christmas Season* and in Ordinary Time.* In the *Roman Missal** it occurs principally on the 15th, 16th, 17th, and 18th Ordinary Sundays (Year C) and during the 22nd and 23rd Ordinary Weeks (I). It is also read on Easter Sunday,* Christ the King* (C), and Masses for Various Needs and Occasions* as well as in the Rite of Penance.* In the *Liturgy of the Hours,** it is read during the Christmas Season and gives rise to a minor canticle.* *Meaning:* Through Christ, God created the world and through Him He is bringing it back to Himself. Only in union with Christ is there hope of salvation for the world.

Columban, St. (kuh-LUHM-buhn). 525-615. Born in Ireland, Columban was well trained in the

classics and theology. Becoming a monk, he went to France and founded many monasteries of strict discipline there as well as in Switzerland and Italy. He is also known by his list of penances and his Rule. Many of his companions went on to become great founders also and helped to create a bulwark of faith against the onrush of the pagans in the Dark Ages. *Liturgical celebration:* November 23 (Opt. Mem.); *theme:* seeking God above all things.

Coming, Second. *See* PAROUSIA.

Commandments (kuh-MAN[D]-muhnts). Liturgy* requires a conversion* on the part of those who take part in it. This conversion entails a serious examination of conscience* in the light of the Word of God,* which among other things sets before us the Commandments of God on which to judge ourselves.

The Greatest Commandment

The Greatest Commandment is:

"You shall love the Lord, your God, with all your heart, with all your soul, and with all your mind. This is the greatest and the first commandment. The second is like it: You shall love your neighbor as yourself. There is no other commandment greater than these" (Mt 22:37-39; Mk 12:30-31).

Already in the Old Testament* God enjoined the commandment of love (Dt 6:4-5). Vatican II* says: "The greatest commandment in the Law is to love God with one's whole heart and one's neighbor as oneself. Christ made this commandment of love of neighbor His own and enriched it with a new meaning. For He wanted to equate Himself with His brothers and sisters as the object of this love when He said: 'As long as you did it for one of My least brothers or sisters, you did it for Me' (Mt 25:40). Assuming human nature, He bound the whole human race to Himself as a family through a certain supernatural solidarity and established charity as the mark of His disciples, saying, 'This is how all will know that you are My disciples, if you have love for one another (Jn 13:35)' " (AA, 8). *(See also* LOVE.)

The Ten Commandments

The Ten Commandments make more specific the Greatest Commandment. Three of the Commandments spell out the relation of human beings to God (the love and worship they owe to Him), while the last seven make more precise the relation of human beings to each other (the love and justice due to others).

The Ten Commandments were given by God to Moses on Mount Sinai and were revered by the Israelites. Christ said He came not to abolish the Law—especially the Commandments—but to perfect it. For the Commandments simply transcribe the basic moral precepts that God has written on the human heart (as St. Paul notes in Romans 2:14-16).

The usual Catholic rendering of the Commandments is:

1. I, the Lord, am your God. You shall not have other gods besides Me.

2. You shall not take the name of the Lord, your God, in vain.
3. Remember to keep holy the Sabbath day.
4. Honor your father and your mother.
5. You shall not kill.
6. You shall not commit adultery.
7. You shall not steal.
8. You shall not bear false witness against your neighbor.
9. You shall not covet your neighbor's wife.
10. You shall not covet your neighbor's goods.

Precepts (or Commandments) of the Church

Christ entrusted the Church* with the right to make laws: "Whatever you bind on earth shall be bound in heaven" (Mt 18:18). Included in this right of the Church is the authority to demand observance of her laws and to impose sanctions upon transgressors.

The phrase Precepts of the Church refers primarily to laws that enable Catholics to carry out the Ten Commandments and are used in catechetical instruction and examination of conscience. Their purpose is to assure at least the minimum of conformity among all the faithful* of the community.

Originally, in the 15th century, there were ten such laws in imitation of the Ten Commandments. In the 16th century, St. Peter Canisius* listed five Precepts in his Catechism while St. Robert Bellarmine* enumerated six. This variation still holds from country to country.

In the United States, catechisms followed the directive of the Third Council of Baltimore (1886) and listed six Precepts. In 1975, the American Bishops published the *Basic Teachings for Catholic Religious Education,* which gave the Precepts in an updated and fuller form and listed seven.

From time to time the Church has listed certain specific duties of Catholics. Among those expected of Catholic Christians today are the following. (Those traditionally mentioned as Precepts of the Church are marked with an asterisk.)

1. To keep holy the day of the Lord's Resurrection: to worship God by participating in Mass every Sunday and Holy Day of Obligation;* to avoid those activities that would hinder renewal of soul and body on the Sabbath (e.g., needless work and business activities, unnecessary shopping, etc.). [See Can. 1246-1248.]

2. To lead a Sacramental life: to receive Holy Communion frequently and the Sacrament of Reconciliation regularly —minimally, to receive the Sacrament of Reconciliation at least once a year (annual confession is obligatory only if serious sin is involved);* —minimally also, to receive Holy Communion at least once a year, between the First Sunday of Lent and Trinity Sunday.* [See Can. 989 and 920.]

3. To study Catholic teaching in preparation for the Sacrament of Confirmation, to be confirmed, and then to continue to study and advance the cause of Christ. [See Can. 890 and 229.]

4. To observe the marriage laws of the Church;* to give religious training, by example and word, to one's children: to use parish schools

and catechetical programs. [See Can. 1063-1072 and 796.]

5. To strengthen and support the Church*—one's own parish community and parish priests, the worldwide Church and the Pope. [See Can. 222.]

6. To do penance, including abstaining from meat and fasting from food on the appointed days.* [See Can. 1249-1251.]

7. To join in the missionary spirit and apostolate of the Church. [See Can. 781.]

Commemoration. *See* SAINTS, COMMEMORATION OF.

Commemoration of the Living and the Dead. *See* EUCHARISTIC PRAYER; INTERCESSIONS.

Commemoration of the Saints. *See* SAINTS, COMMEMORATION OF.

Commendation of the Dying (kom-uhn-DAY-shuhn uhv thuh DAI-ing). In the *Roman Ritual** under this title, prayers,* litanies,* aspirations,* psalms,* and readings* from Scripture are provided, so that Christians may express fellowship with a dying brother or sister and assist the sick person to imitate Christ and accept suffering and death in the hope of resurrection and eternal life in heaven. The ceremony should be adapted to the spiritual and physical condition of the sick person, the others who may be present, and in consideration of any other circumstances.

Unless the situation was sudden and unexpected, it is presumed that the sick person has already received the pastoral care of the sick and the Rite of Anointing.* If not, the continuous rite* of Penance, Anointing, and Viaticum should be employed. The reception of these Sacraments* should occur while the individual is capable of participating. Thus the person may enter into the Paschal Mystery* of Christ by celebrating his or her personal Pasch, a passage from life to death, and then from death to eternal life. *See also* PASTORAL CARE OF THE SICK.

Commentaries. *See* ADMONITIONS.

Commentator (KOM-uhn-tayt-uhr). A cleric* or lay person* in this role exercises a genuine liturgical function and should be properly trained to perform the duty correctly, orderly, and in the true spirit of the Liturgy.* Standing in a suitable place before the people, not at the pulpit or lectern,* the Commentator with remarks carefully prepared, in a clear and succinct manner, delivers explanations and directives to the people, thus introducing the celebration and helping the people to understand it better. As the congregation becomes more familiar with the Liturgy, the explanations, whose purpose is a more active and intelligent participation* by the assembly,* may be less necessary; yet the Commentator's responsibility in leading and directing the response of the faithful* continues to be significant.

Most important of all, the Commentator coordinates the active roles of all present and molds the people into a real assembly*—a community of persons united in heart and mind for the purpose of performing the sacred Liturgy. The Commentator is a person who is skilled at directing others and has a talent for communication of any kind, one who has a good idea of the Liturgy and an ability to remain in the background while "stage managing."

Commingling (kuh-MIN-gling). (1) The ritual act at Mass* that consists of dropping into the chalice of Precious Blood a particle of the Eucharistic Bread after the Breaking of the Bread.* In the 8th century a Syrian Pope introduced this rite. Since the double consecration* of the bread and wine represented the Death of Christ, it was considered necessary to symbolize the Resurrection* with the bread of immortality in Communion.* This concept was accomplished by reuniting the Body and Blood before Communion, in a kind of symbolic reenactment of the Lord's Resurrection.

Centuries before this, any priest at Rome, unable to celebrate with the Pope, would receive a small piece of bread called Fermentum* consecrated at the Papal Liturgy and would drop it in his chalice* as a sign of unity. At a later period in history the priest would place bread consecrated at a previous celebration into the chalice to symbolize the continuity of the Eucharistic sacrifice.

The Church* has given no explanation of this action. One noted liturgist (A-M. Roguet) believes that it symbolizes the fact that "in reality, if we receive in Communion *either* the Consecrated Bread alone *or* the Bread and the Chalice, we receive in either case the whole Christ, Who is living and glorious."

(2) The word may refer to the mixture of water and wine at the time of the Preparation of the Gifts.* *See also* FERMENTUM.

Commissions, Liturgical. *See* LITURGICAL COMMISSIONS.

Common of the Mass (KOM-uhn uhv thuh mas). The parts of Mass* that remain the same in every celebration—also known as the Ordinary.* *See also* MASS, ORDINARY OF THE.

Common of the Saints (KOM-uhn uhv thuh saynts). That group of texts placed in the *Liturgy of the Hours** and *Roman Missal** for those Saints* or feasts* that do not have an assigned text completely of their own. They are divided into various categories: Dedication of a Church*; the Blessed Virgin Mary*; Apostles*; Martyrs*; Pastors*; Doctors*; Virgins*; Holy Men*; Holy Women*; Religious*; Teachers*; Those who Worked for the Underprivileged.* *See also* SAINTS, LITURGICAL CATEGORIES OF.

Common Prayer. *See* PARALITURGY.

Common Priesthood. *See* PRIESTHOOD.

Communicant (kuh-MYOO-ni-kuhnt). In the exact sense, one who partakes of the Eucharist.* Usually it may also apply to the active members of the Church; those meeting minimal standards, such as receiving annual Communion.* In a very broad sense, it is synonymous for Church member.

Communicantes (kuh-moo-ni-KAHN-tez). In Eucharistic Prayer I* this is the first Latin word and identifying name of a paragraph that the celebrant* says right after the commemoration of the living and asserts the union with the Saints* in offering the Eucharistic Sacrifice.

Besides Mary* and Joseph,* twelve apostles and twelve Martyrs venerated in Rome in the early Church are listed. In the new form the recitation of all the Saints is optional. Special variable forms occur for certain major feasts, e.g., Christmas,* Epiphany,* and Easter.* *See also* EUCHARISTIC PRAYER; SAINTS IN EUCHARISTIC PRAYER I.

Communicatio in Sacris. *See* ATTENDING NON-CATHOLIC SERVICES.

Communio et Progressio (kuh-MOO-nee-oh et proh-GRES-ee-oh). Latin title (from the first three words "Communion and Progress") of the *Pastoral Instruction on the Media of Social Communication* issued by the Pontifical Commission on the Media of Social Communication on January 29, 1971, at the direction of the Second Vatican Council.* It sets forth basic doctrinal principles and general pastoral guidelines concerning the media and the Church, including the Liturgy.*

In this connection, the document states that the most desirable and fitting broadcasts are those of the celebration of Mass* and other sacred rites. Everything about the Liturgy itself and the technical details must be prepared with absolute care. The diversity of the audience must be taken into consideration as also, in the case of international broadcasts, regional religious opinions and customs.

Communion (kuh-MYOO-nyuhn). That part of the Eucharistic Sacrifice during which individual Christians really unite themselves with Jesus Christ by receiving His risen and glorified Body and Blood* under Sacramental signs. Holy Communion* is an act by which the Victim offered to God, and accepted by Him, is consumed by the priest* and the faithful,* that they may unite themselves to God and receive His graces.

All the faithful, after the age of reason, are obliged to receive Communion once a year during Paschal Time,* or in the United States sometime between the First Sunday of Lent* and Trinity Sunday.*

The reception of Communion is expected to bring about a similarity to Christ in the communicant. This special union of the soul with Christ entices a person to perform acts of love for God and neighbor. Another purpose is to curb disorderly passions, particularly those against chastity. One further effect is to take away the personal guilt of lesser sins and the temporal punishment due to sins already forgiven. Finally, a pledge of future resurrection and blessedness is given.

Worthy and fruitful reception of Communion, however, entails diligent preparation on the part of the

receivers. (1) They should be free from all mortal sins. (2) They should be sorry for all venial sins and strive to overcome them. (3) They should be fasting from foods and liquids (except water) for one hour before receiving. (4) They should participate fully, consciously, and actively in the Eucharist* at which they receive.

Communion may be received by the faithful at altar rails,* at a Communion station,* or at a Communion table.*

Communion under Both Species

Instead of distributing only the Sacred Host to the laity,* Communion administered under both species allows them to receive the consecrated wine also. Such was the normal practice from the beginning until about the 12th century.

In recent years the Church has restored Communion under both species in many situations, particularly since the laity have a renewed understanding of the Eucharist and recognize the importance of full participation in the liturgical action of the Mass.

Besides the 14 situations listed in number 242 of GIRM, the bishops in the United States have extended this privilege to all members of the faithful present on those occasions, at funeral Masses, and Masses for special family observances, on days of special religious or civil significance, on Holy Thursday* and the Easter Vigil,* and at weekday Masses.

Although Communion under both kinds is permissible by intinction,* that is, the host being dipped into the Precious Blood and then received, or from a tube, or from a spoon, in the United States much pressure has been placed upon the communities to receive from the chalice, since the words of the Scripture read, "Take and drink."

We can enumerate the benefits of receiving Communion under both kinds—that is, under the Sacred Species of Bread and Wine—in part as follows: (1) It stresses the *meal aspect* of the Eucharist and makes it more understandable. (2) It makes the connection between the Eucharistic Meal and the Heavenly Banquet in the Father's Kingdom easier to grasp (see Mt 26:27-29). (3) It shows more clearly how the New and Eternal Covenant is ratified in the Blood of the Lord and strongly reminds us of both Old and New Testament images that speak of *an agreement sealed in blood* between God and human beings. (4) It recalls the *roots* of the Mass *in the Jewish Passover Meal,* a ritual ceremony in which the drinking of wine took place at designated intervals and was accompanied by brief prayers or explanations (see 1 Cor 10:16). (5) It brings out the special, festive, joyful *banquet notion* of the Mass. We celebrate in the context of a sacred meal our Lord's Resurrection* from sin and death as well as our own. Bread is a staple food, and wine adds a sign of specialness and festivity.

Communion in the Hand

The optional practice of Communion in the hand was voted on favorably by the Bishops in the United

States and approved by the Congregation for Divine Worship* in 1977. A thorough catechesis at the parochial level was planned and proper materials were prepared by the Bishops' Committee on the Liturgy* for all to use in the explanation.

Presuming the proper catechesis, the decision to implement the optional practice and the time of so doing was in the hands of the local Ordinary.* No limitations on account of age were established. In all cases the practice is an option, the communicant's personal choice. Should Communion be distributed by intinction, it may not be given in the hand, nor may the communicant dip the Host into the chalice.

We can enumerate the benefits of receiving Communion in the hand in part as follows: (1) It teaches that *our entire body,* including hand as well as tongue, *shares equally in* the *goodness of God's creation* and in the holiness achieved through Christ's entrance into the world as the Word made flesh (see Gn 2:31; Jn 1:14-16). (2) It reminds us that through the Sacraments of Christian Initiation (Baptism,* Confirmation,* and Eucharist*) we have become temples of the living God (see 2 Cor 6:16), a chosen race, a royal priesthood, a holy nation (see 1 Pt 2:9). We are cleansed and consecrated, rendered sharers in Christ's priesthood, and made a new creation. (3) It forms a positive, human, understandable response to Jesus' invitation to "take and eat." We actually reach out, receive the Lord's Body into our hands, and then communicate ourselves. (4) It appears to be a *more mature* and *adult gesture.* In our culture, normally only infants and the infirm receive food into their mouths from another's hand. (5) It is a more relaxed and hygienic method of distributing Communion. (6) It links together the *presentation of the gifts* and the *reception of the Lord.* The same hands that brought forward and offered the bread and wine earlier in the Mass now receive back these transformed gifts.

First Communion

The occasion when a child (usually) receives Holy Communion for the first time is termed First Communion. Pope St. Pius X* set the age for this reception at about the seventh year.

In conjunction with the First Communion is the involvement of the parents during the preparatory period for the child. The parents are central to the proper religious formation of the child, and therefore much religious education programming is spent to influence the parental function in this regard.

Frequent Communion

After the turn of the century Pope St. Pius X tried to develop the practice of frequent and even daily Communion. Although this practice was very common in the early Church, it fell into disuse—mostly because of heresies. As of today it has been gradually restored, based on our need to support ourselves with Eucharistic Bread as our daily food. A person may receive the Eucharist again the same day only during the celebration of the Mass in which the person participates (Canon 917).

Spiritual Communion

Spiritual Communion is a private devotion that purports to receive Christ spiritually, that is, by desire, when to receive Him Sacramentally is impossible. Emphatic in the reform of the Liturgy is the reception of Communion as integral to the liturgical celebration, thus expressing the active presence of Christ and the union of His members with Him and one another. Hence the Eucharist continues in its long-lasting effect as a source of continuous presence in the life of the faithful. Therefore, the older understanding of a need for spiritual Communion seems more or less superfluous and a distraction from the proper understanding of the Eucharist. *See also* EUCHARIST; MASS.

Communion Antiphon (kuh-MYOO-nyuhn AN-tuh-fuhn). A verse from the Bible* that was the refrain for a Psalm that the choir sang at Mass* during the distribution of Communion* to the faithful,* which ordinarily lasted quite some time. When daily Communion diminished with the passage of time, the Psalm disappeared and only the Antiphon* was retained, recognized as a "people's part" of the Proper.* Now the practice of singing the Antiphon or another appropriate song during the distribution of Communion is reestablished by the liturgical reform. If no singing occurs, the Antiphon is recited by the congregation, by a reader, or by the celebrant* after his Communion, before the Communion of the congregation.

Communion Cloth (kuh-MYOO-nyuhn klawth). Replaced now by the Communion Plate,* this long linen cloth was attached to the altar rail in such a way that it could catch particles from the Eucharistic Bread that could fall during its distribution to the faithful.*

Communion in the Hand. *See* COMMUNION.

Communion Fast. *See* FAST, EUCHARISTIC.

Communion of Saints, The (kuh-MYOO-nyuhn uhv saynts, thuh). The communion of faith and love that unites all the baptized in the unity of the Father, the Son, and the Holy Spirit—this is the union of the faithful* on earth (the Church Militant*), the Blessed* in heaven (the Church Triumphant*), and the souls in purgatory (the Church Suffering*) with Christ their Head. It is an active union—a sharing of spiritual goods among the members of the Mystical Body.*

All its true members are called "saints" because they are so in reality or are called to be so by their regeneration in Baptism.* They are also united by the promise of the same good—which some already possess, some are secure of possessing, and the rest, in a state of uncertainty, are laboring to possess. Secondly, they are united by partaking in the prayers* and good works* of each other. For prayers, good works, Sacraments,* and sacrifice* are common goods of the Church.

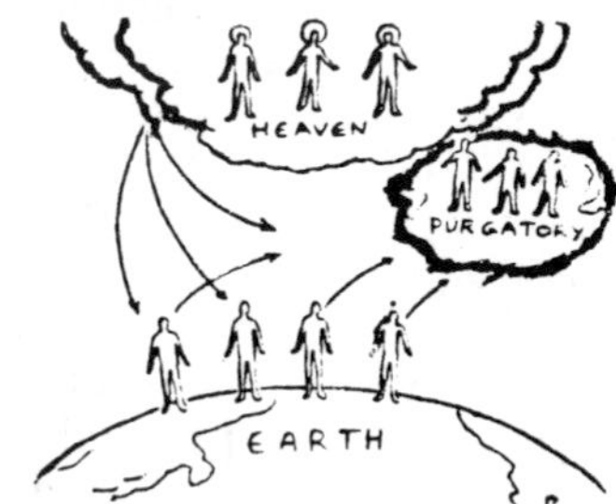

This union is concretized in the communion of the members of the assembly* gathered around the altar* to participate in "holy things"—the Body and Blood* of Christ. By means of the Sacrament, this union is extended to all believers throughout the world. It is expressed by the interchange of spiritual goods and mutual aid. It is also expressed by the union with the diocesan bishop,* with the whole body of bishops, and with the Pope.*

Thus, the Liturgy* provides the best means by which we can maintain our spiritual unity with the Blessed in heaven, the Poor Souls in purgatory, and other Christians on earth and receive the benefits of that communion. The Eucharistic Prayers* bear witness to this communion in their own way: EP I by two series of prayers before and after the Consecration* and EP II, III, and IV by a single prayer text.

We communicate with the Saints in heaven by honoring their memory, by joining with them in blessing and praising God, and by asking them to obtain blessings for us and intercede in our favor. We communicate with the souls in purgatory by praying for them, offering up the Holy Sacrifice for them, and performing good works on their behalf.

Communion of the Sick (kuh-MYOO-nyuhn uhv thuh sik). Even apart from the imminent danger of death, when it is obligatory for Catholics to receive Communion,* sick persons, prisoners, and others who find it difficult to get to church are encouraged to request Communion at least now and then. There is a long history in the Church of deacons* and laity* being entrusted with this duty. If pastoral care prompts it, Confession* and the Anointing of the Sick* may precede Communion.

Communion may be brought to the sick at any hour of any day ex-

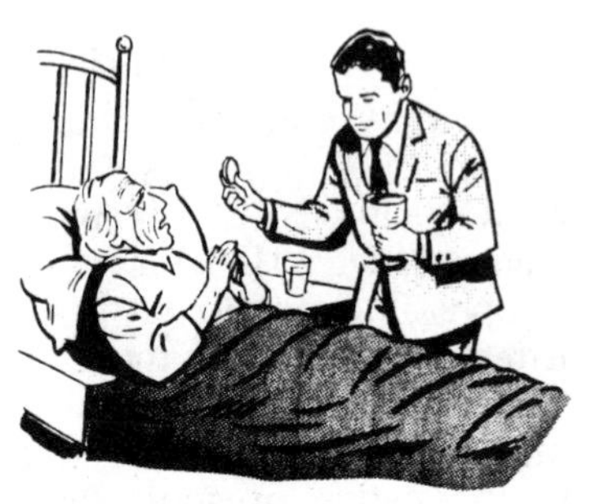

cept Holy Saturday* (when only Viaticum* may be brought) by the priest or deacon whose office this is. However should they be impeded, Eucharistic Ministers* may distribute Communion to the sick according to the special rite they should follow. If the sick cannot receive in the form of bread, they may receive in the form of wine. The length of the Eucharistic fast, ordinarily one hour from solid food and beverages (except water), does not obligate the sick, the aged, sick or elderly priests and those persons who care for them, and the family, if they cannot conveniently observe the full one hour fast.

Communion Outside of Mass (kuh-MYOO-nyuhn OWT-said; owt-SAID; uhv mas). Since Communion* received during Mass is a more perfect participation in the Eucharistic Sacrifice, the People of God* should be encouraged to receive Communion during the Eucharistic Celebration itself; yet priests may not refuse Communion to those who ask for it outside of Mass. Those who cannot attend the community's celebration ought to have this privilege, even though they are not sick or prisoners. Ordinarily the proper place for Communion outside of Mass is the church* or oratory* where the Eucharist is celebrated or reserved. Other places, even private homes, are suitable when the persons cannot leave the place.

The rite begins with the Greeting,* then the Penitential Rite* comparable to that used in the Mass, the Liturgy of the Word,* the Lord's Prayer,* and the Lamb of God* follow. After the distribution of Communion a Prayer after Communion* and the Final Blessing* occur. In many areas where there is a scarcity of priests, public worship* is given in this fashion by a deacon* or an authorized lay minister.*

Communion Plate (kuh-MYOO-nyuhn playt). A projecting handle on this saucer-like metal gilded plate makes it easy to hold it under the chin of the communicant to catch any fragment that might fall from the Sacred Host.* Since the optional practice of Communion* in the hand began in the United States, the Communion plate is hardly ever used. Individual miniature bronze patens on sale for use in the reception of Holy Communion are not authorized or approved.

Communion Procession (kuh-MYOO-nyuhn pruh-SESH-uhn). One of the five processions* that take place at Mass.* At least from the time of St. Augustine* it has been customary to sing a psalm during the procession of communicants, culminating in the choice of songs permitted today, as indicated under Communion Song.* The Communion Procession is the one procession at Mass in which the whole assembly* can take part physically as well as spiritually.

We go to acclaim Jesus in the Eucharist,* the Jesus Who comes to us in a special presence. We receive Him from His minister thus sharing in this sacred Meal that brings us all together and concluding the sacrificial part of the rite. That is why the Church wants us to sing as we go.

Communion Rails. *See* ALTAR RAILS.

Communion Rite. *See* MASS—COMMUNION RITE.

Communion Silence (kuh-MOO-nyuhn SAI-luhntz). The silence after the distribution of Communion* called for by the new Order of Mass.* At this point, the people may spend some time in silent prayer (GIRM, 23, 56j, 121), each one praising God in his or her heart and praying. This is a "silent prayer but in community" (A.M. Roguet, *The New Mass).* Then the Prayer after Communion* serves to sum up the unspoken sentiments of all.

As an alternative to silent prayer, a psalm or hymn of praise may also be sung. *See also* MASS—COMMUNION RITE; SILENCE.

Communion Song (kuh-MYOO-nyuhn song). A song during the Communion* of the priest* and people,* which expresses the spiritual union of the communicants who join their voices in a single song, shows the joy of all, and makes the Communion Procession* an act of solidarity. The song begins when the priest receives Communion and continues as long as convenient.

The choice of texts for the Communion Song is governed by the same rules as the Entrance Song.* This song should foster a sense of unity. It should be simple and not demand great effort. It gives expression to the joy of unity in the Body of Christ* and the fulfillment of the Mystery* being celebrated. During the seasons of Advent,* Christmas,* Lent,* and Easter,* it is preferable that most songs used at Communion be seasonal in nature. During Ordinary Time,* however, topical songs may be used, provided they do not conflict with the Paschal character of every Sunday.*

Communion Station (kuh-MYOO-nyuhn STAY-shuhn). An area designated for the reception of Communion* by the faithful.* In modern church architecture altar rails* no longer exist; in reconstruction they are abandoned. Therefore, certain places within the church are designated for the distribution of Communion, arranged in such a fashion that the congregation may approach the ministers readily and then return to the pews. Should the communicants be many, Eucharistic Ministers* are employed and several such spots are indicated. *See also* ALTAR RAILS.

Communion Table (kuh-MYOO-nyuhn TAY-buhl). In early centuries Communion* was received at the altar,* which was truly a Communion table; however, when the sanctuary* developed and the laity* were forbidden in that area, Communion rails* were prescribed and were used to symbolize the Communion table. They are now falling into desuetude. *See also* ALTAR RAILS.

Communion under Both Kinds. *See* COMMUNION.

Communion with the Catholic Church. *See* RECEPTION OF BAPTIZED CHRISTIANS.

Community (kuh-MYOO-nuht-ee). (a) Generally speaking it is a

group of people united by certain characteristics, such as proximity, goals and values, interdependence, authority, and permanence.

(b) Christian theology extends human life communally to the Divine community of the Father and the Son and the Holy Spirit; the love of charity given by the Spirit animates the Mystical Body of Christ.*

(c) Religious have this idea also for they share mutual interests and needs, dwelling together, sharing a common table, and unite with each other in liturgical worship.*

(d) Such a sense of community is to be encouraged within the parish,* particularly in the common celebration of the Sunday Eucharist.*

Community Mass (kuh-MYOO-nuht-ee mas). Celebrated for a Religious community not obligated to the Divine Office* in choir. However, even some Religious communities who are obliged to choir will have a community Mass rather than a conventual Mass.* It should be celebrated with full participation by all the members of the community, with the priests* concelebrating, but not being obliged to do so.

Competentes. *See* ELECT.

Compline. *See* NIGHT PRAYER.

Concelebration (kuhn-sel-uh-BRAY-shuhn). Celebration of Mass* by many bishops* and/or many priests* who associate themselves with the one and same liturgical Sacrifice* of the principal celebrant, consecrating the same bread and wine.

Vatican Council II* revived the traditional concelebration, which truly shows the unity of the Sacrifice, the hierarchical nature of the Church, the collegiate character of the priesthood,* and the unity of the People of God.* Thus a concelebrated Liturgy* signifies unity to the faithful* and keeps them aware that they are the One Body of Christ.*

In the early Church concelebration was somewhat common, but it had a different history at various places. In effect, it avoided the duplication of liturgical roles and followed the principle of distribution of such roles. In this form all participated and each priest did not confect the Sacrament by himself alone.

Besides the times that the rite is prescribed, it is also allowed at both Masses on Holy Thursday,* at the blessing of an Abbot,* during councils and synods; furthermore, the Ordinary* may decide whether concelebration is suitable in other situations, namely conventual Masses,* principal Masses in churches, meetings of priests and Religious, etc.

Because the dignity of the rite may demand it, a bishop may regulate the number of concelebrants, especially at regional or national meetings or conventions. In such cases it is more appropriate to designate a specific number of concelebrants, who would be truly representative of the entire group. In this way a pastoral consideration is given to the ritual problems that could occur. In such cases the non-concelebrating priests should be offered the opportunity to celebrate at another time each day.

Although priests are not obliged to concelebrate, most will prefer to concelebrate at a scheduled Mass rather than to celebrate a Mass without a congregation.

The rubrics for concelebration are contained in GIRM, numbers 153-208. Briefly, the concelebrants, clad in liturgical vestments* as indicated in number 161, or the chasuble-alb,* which has been approved, with the stole* worn over it, reverence the altar* and kiss it. Then they move to their chairs near the altar or, only if no other suitable place is available, in the first pews of the church, where they follow the actions of the celebrant during the Liturgy of the Word.* Remaining in their places until the Preparation of the Gifts,* some of the concelebrants, when the altar is not large enough to hold all the Hosts necessary, may hold ciboria in their hands during the Eucharistic Prayer.* When it begins, the concelebrants come to the altar and stand in a location that does not obstruct the people's view, unless the number of concelebrants is too large. In that case, only those who will proclaim an individual part of the Eucharistic Prayer will be with the principal celebrant at the altar.

The concelebrants are to hold their hands, or at least their right

hand, outstretched toward the offerings during the Epiclesis.* During the Institution Narrative,* each of them *may* extend his right hand, with the palm facing to the side, toward the Host and the Chalice. The concelebrants bow profoundly during the genuflection of the celebrant after both consecrations. Certain parts of the Eucharistic Prayer are recited together, but the concelebrants do so softly or inaudibly so that the voice of the celebrant dominates. Only the main celebrant raises the Bread at the Doxology,* while the deacon* (or, if no deacon, a concelebrant) elevates the Chalice. Other ciboria and chalices are not to be elevated by anyone.

At the *This is the Lamb of God,** only the principal celebrant shows the Host to the assembly. Following the reception of Communion* under both species, the concelebrants may help in the distribution of Communion to the faithful. If the number of concelebrants is large, they may receive while others are distributing to the faithful. Concelebrants not helping to distribute Communion return to their seats immediately. The Mass is concluded as usual; the concelebrants reverence the altar as they leave, but do not kiss it.

Concerts in Church, Musical. *See* MUSICAL CONCERTS IN CHURCH.

Conciliar Documents. *See* LITURGICAL LAW, SOURCES OF.

Concluding Rite. *See* MASS—CONCLUDING RITE.

Concordat cum Originali. *See* LITURGICAL BOOKS; NIHIL OBSTAT.

Concurrence (kuhn-KUHR-uhn[t]s). When two Offices—the one of the day and the one of the morrow—meet at Evening Prayer,* concurrence takes place. If a Solemnity* and a Feast* of the Lord concur in this manner, the Evening Prayer of the day holding the higher rank in the table of liturgical days takes precedence. Should both days have the same rank, Evening Prayer is of the current day. *See also* ORDER OF PRECEDENCE.

Conditional Baptism. *See* BAPTISM, CONDITIONAL.

Conference of Bishops. *See* NATIONAL CONFERENCE OF CATHOLIC BISHOPS.

Confession. *See* PENANCE, RITE OF.

Confession at Mass. *See* PENITENTIAL RITE.

Confession, Public. *See* PENANCE, RITE OF.

Confession, Seal of. *See* SEAL OF CONFESSION.

Confessional (kuhn-FESH-uhn-uhl). The place or the furniture used in administering the Rite of Penance.* Until the Middle Ages the confessor sat on a chair or a bench between the altar* and the Communion rail,* with the penitent next to him. The rite also took place in the priest's residence.

In the 16th century the confessional became a separate compartment, a highly decorated piece of furniture, a box-like structure, with a roof, ordinarily having three compartments, the middle one for the priest and the two on the sides for the kneeling penitents. Because of the importance of secrecy, a grille separates the penitent from the priest. Current legislation grants the penitent the option of receiving the Sacrament traditionally in such a confessional or in a more casual and familiar setting. *See also* RECONCILIATION ROOM.

Confessor (kuhn-FES-uhr; KON-fes-uhr). (1) The priest* who hears confessions of the faithful and has jurisdiction to absolve them, that is, he is qualified to perform the Rite of Penance.* He may absolve from censures and grant dispensations. More properly, this name should rather belong to the penitent who confesses or acknowledges his or her sins.

Many Catholics, at the encouragement of masters of the spiritual life, may choose a regular confessor, one to whom they open their consciences and confess with regularity. Such a situation allows the regular confessor to direct the spiritual effort along the needs of the penitent, whose state of soul, difficulties, problems, and graces he understands. He may console, advise, encourage, and set up objectives that the penitent can achieve. Thus the confessor frequently fulfills the role of spiritual director also. (*See also* PENANCE, RITE OF.)

(2) (KON-fes-uhr). A title formerly given to a male saint who had not suffered martyrdom for the Faith but attested to the Faith by his way of life, in some cases having suffered persecution, but not death. Eventually this name applied to all Christian males who had rendered witness to our Lord by the sanctity of their lives. Currently the term is not used and the Saints are referred to by some other apt title, such as: Pope,* Bishop,* Deacon,* Priest,* Doctor,* Abbot,* Religious,* Holy Man.* *See also* SAINTS, LITURGICAL CATEGORIES OF.

Confirmation (kon-fuhr-MAY-shuhn). One of the Sacraments of Christian Initiation*; those baptized receive this Sacrament ordinarily from a bishop,* by the laying on of hands and anointing with chrism* with a specific formula: *N., be sealed with the Gift of the Holy Spirit.*

Baptism* incorporates people into Christ, to the dignity of adopted children of God. Strengthened by the Holy Spirit in Confirmation, they become a more perfect image of the Lord, profess the Faith perseveringly, and bear witness to the Lord in the world, while working for growth of the Body of Christ.* Eventually they receive the Eucharist,* whereby they may attain eternal life and aver unity in God's people. Coming to the full stature of Christ through these Sacraments of Christian Initiation, they carry out the mission of the People of God* in the Church.*

Distinct ritually from Baptism, Confirmation is the complement to Baptism that perfects it and orientates the confirmed toward the Eucharist.* This anointing consecrates the person in a twofold manner: (a) *priestly,* allowing the person to be brought more deeply into the Eucharistic worship to take part more intensely in the Paschal Mystery*; (b) *prophetic,* fortifying the Christian to bear witness before the world to Christ, his or her Savior and the Founder of the Church.

Thus one encounters Christ in a mature manner to adhere to Christian commitment and community.

This Sacrament is still under study, so as to bring it into closer union with Christian Initiation. Intimately connected with this study is the problem of the desirable age for reception, *later* to stress it as a Sacrament of maturity or *earlier* to reinstitute the proper order of Christian Initiation.

Celebration of the Sacrament

To stress the fundamental connection of the Sacrament with Christian Initiation, it normally takes place within Mass.* Thus baptized persons after Confirmation may complete their initiation through participation in the Eucharist. The proper Mass allows appropriate texts from the *Lectionary** during the Liturgy of the Word.* After the Gospel* the candidates are presented to the bishop, who then gives a brief Homily* on the readings.*

The Baptismal promises* are renewed, and the imposition of hands by the bishop and the priests who assist follows. Then each candidate is anointed with chrism* during the recitation of the formula, and the Sign of Peace* is given to each individual. Where there is a necessity, extraordinary ministers* may be designated to assist the bishop, who then perform this same anointing in like manner. After the General Intercessions,* the Liturgy of the Eucharist* proceeds, with the Profession of Faith* omitted, since the baptismal promises were renewed.

Should those to be confirmed not have made their First Communion,* or under other special circumstances, Confirmation may be celebrated outside Mass. In that

case the rite is very similar to the above, with the exclusion of the Liturgy of the Eucharist.*

Adult converts being initiated into the Church* ordinarily receive the three Sacraments of Christian Initiation at the same service. If the bishop is not present, the priest who conferred Baptism administers Confirmation to the individual. By force of Canon Law or a particular concession, priests may also validly confirm (Canons 882-888).

Since all baptized persons should complete their Christian Initiation before death, any person in danger of death, having reached the age of reason, ought to be strengthened by Confirmation prior to receiving Viaticum,* if possible after the requisite catechesis. Shortened formulas exist for cases of necessity.

Confirmation Name (kon-fuhr-MAY-shuhn naym). A name that may be taken by a person upon receiving the Sacrament of Confirmation.* It may be the first name of the sponsor or any other name. This optional custom serves as a sign that the person confirmed is entering upon a new way of life and is ready to bear closer witness to Christ, aided by the Sacramental character* and the power of the Holy Spirit.*

Confiteor. *See* PENITENTIAL RITE.

Confraternities (kon-fruh-TUHR-nuht-eez). Associations of the faithful,* constituting moral persons, whose special object is the promotion of public worship,* usually in a specific form. They are distinct from third orders, which are attached to a Religious Order, and from pious unions that have a charitable or pious object, but without any relation to public worship. A group of officers lead and guide the corporate structure in its common activities.

Each parish is expected to have a Confraternity of Christian Doctrine and a Confraternity of the Blessed Sacrament. Archconfraternities have received the right from the Holy See to affiliate confraternities of the same kind. *See also* ASSOCIATIONS, PIOUS.

Congregation for (the Sacraments and) Divine Worship. *See* CONGREGATION FOR DIVINE WORSHIP AND THE DISCIPLINE OF THE SACRAMENTS.

Congregation for Divine Worship and the Discipline of the Sacraments (kon-gruh-GAY-shuhn fawr di-VAIN WUR-ship and thuh DIS-uh-plin uhv thuh SAK-ruh-muhnts). This is one of the nine (previously, twelve) Roman congregations that help the Pope* in governing the Church. Known as the Congregation of Rites in the 19th century, it retained this name when changes were made by Pope Paul VI in the organization of the Curia in 1967. In 1969 its title was changed to Congregation for Divine Worship. Later in 1975 it received the title: Congregation for the Sacraments and Divine Worship. On April 5, 1984, Pope John Paul II for pastoral reasons divided the Congregation into two distinct Dicasteries: the Congregation for the Sacraments and the Congregation for Divine Worship with one Pro-Prefect for both.

One Dicastery dealt with the Sacraments,* the other with Divine Worship,* having authority over liturgical and extraliturgical questions. Besides approving calendars and interpreting liturgical norms, it handles doctrinal, ritual, and pastoral aspects of the Liturgy.* Local Episcopal Conferences* communicate with it on all liturgical adaptations. Furthermore under its purview fall also sacred music* and art,* the development of the liturgical apostolate,* and contact with the pastoral and liturgical institutes.

Pope John Paul II reunited these two congregations under the title of Congregation for Divine Worship and the Discipline of the Sacraments in 1988.

Congregation of Rites. *See* CONGREGATION FOR DIVINE WORSHIP AND THE DISCIPLINE OF THE SACRAMENTS.

Congregational Singing (kon-gruh-GAY-shuhn-uhl SING-ing). Hymns sung by a worshiping assembly* is the hallmark of Christianity, which followed the Jewish tradition. Despite a framework in the Church for congregational singing, much of it had been left to talented choirs.* Preservation of the Latin language with the focus on Gregorian Chant* hindered congregational participation. *The Constitution on the Liturgy** called for such singing to be skillfully fostered in liturgical functions so that the assembly could participate as it should. With the adoption of the vernacular, many were encouraged but met further obstacles: the reluctance of Catholics to sing in public, the poor translations and lack of suitable hymns and music; and little time for agreements to be met with regard to taste and standards. Progress has been slow, but the efforts continue. Remember that earlier fine church music was the result of centuries of development. *See also* CAROLS; CHOIRS (MUSIC); MUSIC.

Conopaeum (kon-uh-PAY-uhm). A veil that adorns the tabernacle* where the Blessed Sacrament* is reserved. An opening in the front of the veil, which may be of the color* of the day as well as white or gold, allows access to the tabernacle.

Consecration (kon-suh-KRAY-shuhn). That formalized action with Jesus' words of institution of the Eucharist,* repeated by the priest as the culminating moment of the Mass during which the substance of the bread and wine is changed into the Body and Blood of Christ,* yet with the appearance of bread and wine persisting. This action is called the Transubstantiation,* which confects the same sacrifice Christ instituted at the Last Supper. As St. Ambrose* said, it is Christ Himself who consecrates in the priest. (*See also* EPICLESIS.)

The Eucharistic Prayer* is the heart of the Mass, and the Consecration or Institution Narrative* is the heart of the Eucharistic Prayer—it is essential for the celebration of the Eucharist. However, we cannot divorce these words of consecration from the rest of the text without narrowing our understanding of the celebration and even fostering false notions about the Mass.

The entire Eucharistic Prayer is a consecratory, thanksgiving prayer of praise. At the Last Supper, Jesus remembered God's wondrous works in the past and realized that these wonders were to culminate in Him. What He was about to do that night at table, the next day on the Cross, and the third day from the empty tomb were the greatest interventions of God in human history. Hence, He praised the Father for them, gave thanks, and offered Himself to His followers under the form of Bread and Wine. Then He told them to do the same—as a living Memorial of Him.

At the Consecration specifically, and throughout the whole Eucharistic Prayer, all that God has accomplished in creation and Salvation History is fulfilled, signified, and made present in the person of the crucified and risen Christ. Christ's words constitute a sacred promise and through the power of the Holy Spirit* they accomplish what they signify: His Eucharistic Body and Blood, His Real Presence* with all the riches of the Kingdom.

The words used in the Institution Narrative are reflected in the Biblical accounts of the Last Supper,* which, scholars assert, borrowed the phrasing of these words from Eucharistic Celebrations of the Apostolic Church. However, even the Institution Narratives (some eighty in all among the Eucharistic Prayers of the various Rites of the Church) exhibit differences among them. All show a concern for Biblical tradition but they do not strive for literal exactitude.

The elevation of the consecrated Host dates from the 13th century when the faithful rarely received Communion* and replaced it by wanting to "see" the Host.* The elevation of the chalice with the consecrated Wine and the genuflections after the consecration of the Host and the Wine appeared in the late 14th century and were prescribed universally by the Missal of Paul V in 1570.

All present Eucharistic Prayers in the Roman Rite have the same words of institution. The phrase "Mystery of Faith"* has been removed from the words over the chalice, and the sacrificial phrase "which will be given for you" (Lk 22:19 and 1 Cor 11:24) has been added to the words over the host.

Consecration, Act of (kon-suh-KRAY-shuhn, akt uhv). An act by which something is separated from common and profane usage and converted to sacred usage. Also an act by which someone or something is dedicated to the service and worship* of God by prayers,* rites,* and ceremonies.* *See also* CONSECRATION.

Consecration of a Church. *See* CHURCH DEDICATION.

Consecration of Altars. *See* ALTAR, CONSECRATION OF.

Consecration of Bishops. *See* BISHOP, EPISCOPAL ORDINATION OF.

Consecration of Churches. *See* CHURCH DEDICATION.

Consecration of Virgins (kon-suh-KRAY-shuhn uhv VUHR-jinz). An old Latin rite whereby in a solemn ceremony women who take a public vow of perpetual virginity are consecrated to Christ and His Church. The English version of the new rite was approved in 1975. Pertaining to either the active or the contemplative life, one form of the rite is for Religious, the other for lay women. The bishop* admits the latter when he has sufficient evidence of a dedicated life of a suitable candidate.

In order that the sign value be achieved, the ceremony is to take place after the Liturgy of the Word* during a Ritual Mass in a cathedral* with faithful attending. An insignia, such as a ring or veil, may be conferred. In the case of Religious, this ceremony is combined with the final perpetual Religious profession, taking place during a Ritual Mass, after the proclamation of their vows. Americans make little use of this consecration.

Consecration to the Sacred Heart. *See* SACRED HEART, CULT OF.

Consent (kuhn-SENT). That free act of the will by which a person does, accepts, or refuses something. Each Sacrament* administered to adults must have their consent. Lack of consent would render the administration illicit. In Matrimony,* however, the consent of both parties is required even for the validity; it must be expressed and thus constitutes the sacred sign.

Consistory (kuhn-SIS-t[uh-]ree). A gathering of cardinals* with the Pope* (secret) or with others present (public) to promulgate papal decisions, e.g., the naming of cardinals or the canonization* of Saints.

Constitution on Divine Revelation. *See* DEI VERBUM.

Constitution on the Church. *See* LUMEN GENTIUM.

Constitution on the Church in the Modern World. *See* GAUDIUM ET SPES.

Constitution on the Sacred Liturgy (con-stuh-TOO-shuhn; TYOO-shuhn; on thuh SAY-kruhd LIT-uhr-jee). Since the intent of the Second Vatican Council* was to be a renewal in the life of the Church, of extreme importance was the task of Paul VI to look at the celebration of the Liturgy.* His predecessor, Pius XII, with some encyclicals, particularly *Mediator Dei,** gave a strong boost to all liturgical progress. Paul VI then took up the work outlined by the Council and began with the Liturgy because of its central position and the spiritual and pastoral potential it had for the entire Church. In promulgating this Constitution (entitled *Sacrosanctum Concilium),* he described it as "the first subject to be examined and also the first, in a certain sense, because of its intrinsic value in the life of the Church."

Primarily a pastoral document, the Constitution presents broad principles to govern the adaptation of the Liturgy, so that it can become a form of worship* and sanctification genuinely corresponding to the needs of Christians. The commission appointed by Paul VI to completely overhaul the Liturgy, aware of the liturgical apostolate that existed already in many countries, realized that four points repeatedly accentuated themselves as truly important: the pastoral* character of Liturgy; the Liturgy's importance for the missions*; the need to incorporate the vernacular* into the

Liturgy; and a strong desire to return to concelebration.*

Although *Mediator Dei* will remain a basic authoritative analysis of the Liturgy, the Constitution is a more dramatic form of teaching. Guided by a vision of the essentials in the liturgical Mystery,* Vatican II, a pastoral Council, formulated the essentials in a striking and forceful manner, thus producing an enlightened revision of legislation unparalleled in Church history.

In the introduction, the Council indicates that its several aims are actually cogent reasons for undertaking the reform and promotion of the Liturgy. The following is an outline of the Constitution:

I. General Principles for the Restoration and Promotion of the Sacred Liturgy
   1. The nature of the Sacred Liturgy and its importance in the Church's life
   2. The promotion of liturgical instruction and active participation
   3. The reform of the Sacred Liturgy
      a) General principles
      b) Principles drawn from the hierarchic and communal nature of the Liturgy
      c) Principles for adapting the Liturgy to the culture and traditions of nations
   4. Promotion of liturgical life in dioceses and parish
   5. Promotion of pastoral-liturgical action

II. The Mystery of the Holy Eucharist
III. The Other Sacraments and the Sacramentals
IV. The Divine Office
V. The Liturgical Year (Appendix on the revision of the Calendar [Fixed Easter])
VI. Sacred Music
VII. Sacred Arts and Furnishings

Chapter 1 deals with the nature of the Liturgy and its importance in the life of the Church. It is from this section that the majority of quotations come concerning the place of Liturgy in our lives. Perhaps the most important change that resulted from the Second Vatican Council was the promotion of the faithful's participation* in Church life. To bring about such a change, this first document of the Council stresses the faithful's participation in the Liturgy, with the resultant liturgical significance of the parish* and the diocese.* Pastoral life in liturgical action is promoted, and therefore special instructions for clerics in formation and priests already working in the Lord's vineyard are included. Regulations concerning the adaptation of the text and ritual are also set forth where necessary, and it has taken decades for these principles to be fulfilled in accord with the basic principle that Liturgy is an action of the whole Church, involving not only ordained ministers but also the body of the faithful.

Chapter 2 deals with the place of the Holy Eucharist* in Liturgy, emphasizing again how important it is that the community of believers should not be silent spectators but should fully collaborate with the priest in the celebration of the Mass.* The rites are to be simplified by discarding certain elements and restoring others. A more rich fare from the Bible* is called for, resulting in the several cycles that we now use, and thus the Liturgy of the Word* is amplified, together with the Homily* to explain it; the intimate link between the Liturgy of the Word and the Liturgy of the Eucharist* is clarified, thus making these the two important parts of the Mass. To allow for even more thoughtful participation, the vernacular* is allowed and concelebration* approved.

After insuring that the Mass is the center of the Sacramental system, chapter 3 takes up the other Sacraments,* indicating first of all their purpose, the fact that they are signs that instruct us, their relationship

to the Sacramentals,* and how the Sacraments and Sacramentals are to be revised, allowing also the vernacular in their celebration. Then each of the other Sacraments is taken up one by one, with a description of the type of revision required. Regulations concerning the Sacramentals, Religious Profession,* and burial* rites conclude the chapter.

Reaffirming the Divine Office* as *the* liturgical prayer of the entire Church, chapter 4 insists on its importance to the pastoral life with an invitation to the faithful to celebrate the Hours also. The revised Breviary contains similar material, but rearranged in such a way as to simplify regulations. Great importance is attached to the choral celebration by those obliged to it, and an invitation is extended to the laity to join them. The adoption of the vernacular should be a great aid toward the conscious participation in the Liturgy by clerics and nonclerics alike.

Key concepts in the Constitution are the terms *Mystery of Christ** and *Paschal Mystery,** which offer a more unified and Christocentric approach to the Liturgical Year,* the topic of chapter 5. The Liturgical Year unfolds the whole Mystery of Christ, from Incarnation* to Ascension,* including the hope of the coming of the Lord. Through the Paschal Mystery, the fulfillment of God's plan for reconciliation of humankind takes place. The Temporal Cycle* centers on the saving Mysteries of Christ. Since the Pasch is the culmination of Christ's efforts, preparation for it is of utmost necessity. Each Sunday is also described as a little Easter, or a weekly Easter. Although the Sanctoral Cycle* is assigned a subordinate place in the Liturgical Year, it in no way derogates the cult of the Saints. There is to be no opposition between the Temporal and the Sanctoral cycles. In the Saints, Christ relives His Paschal Mystery. The Church contemplates Christ in His Saints. The variety of their sanctity reflects the infinite riches of Christ.

The strong musical tradition of the Church is treated in chapter 6, facing up to the problems that will result from allowing the vernacular. The teaching and practice of music* in seminaries is accentuated, with the understanding that Gregorian Chant* may still be used in conjunction with the Latin language, but probably performed more by special choirs. The singing by the faithful is to be fostered in every way possible, so that the use of sacred music, which makes any liturgical action more holy, can be continually developed. Composers are to cultivate sacred music and increase the repertoire.

The last chapter treats of the sacred arts* and furnishings. As patron of Fine Arts throughout the centuries, the Church has constantly made use of the work of artists, as long as they are in accordance with the Faith and piety. Her treasury of art does in no way indicate that she has adopted any particular style of art as her own; rather she has admitted styles from every period, relating to the natural dispositions of her peoples and the needs that various rites might call for. The bishops, together with their trained artists and craftsmen on commissions, are to strive after noble beauty rather than sumptuous display in all art works, including the architecture, the pictures and statues, and the articles and vestments used in the celebration of liturgical actions. *See also* MEDIATOR DEI.

Constitutions, Apostolic. *See* APOSTOLIC CONSTITUTIONS.

Constitutions, Conciliar. *See* LITURGICAL LAW, SOURCES OF.

Consultation on Common Texts. *See* LECTIONARY.

Contemplation (kon-tuhm-PLAY-shuhn). Concentration on spiritual things as a form of private devotion, a state of mystical awareness of God's being. In itself, contemplation is a liturgical act—it comes from the Latin *cum templo,* meaning to be with (or live in) the temple. And in the heavenly Jerusalem where God Himself will be the temple (Rv 21:22), contemplation and vision will be perfect.

However, on earth contemplation and Liturgy* must of necessity be set apart. The community celebration of the Covenant*—despite the presence in it of moments of silence—cannot be the place or the moment for a "contemplative" encounter with God, as will be the case in the heavenly Liturgy. Hence, our celebrations must be prepared for and followed by times of personal prayer wherein the riches of expression and content can be assimilated according to the rhythm and needs of each person. The Liturgy contains all that is needed for the spiritual life, but we are able to obtain it only by making use of contemplation apart from liturgical celebrations. *See also* LIFE; LITURGY AND CONTEMPLATIVE LIFE; PRAYER.

Continuous Reading. *See* LECTIO CONTINUA; READINGS.

Continuous Rite. *See* PASTORAL CARE OF THE SICK.

Contrition (kon-TRISH-uhn). Heartfelt sorrow and aversion for sin committed along with the intention of sinning no more. Contrition is the first of the four parts of the Sacrament of Penance* and is followed by confession,* an act of penance (satisfaction), and absolution.*

To be sorry for sins for human reasons, such as shame or loss of job, is *natural* contrition, which does not suffice for forgiveness from God. *Supernatural* contrition must be based on motives of faith: the goodness of God that was offended and the justice of God to which we are liable for our sins.

Supernatural contrition is "perfect" if the motive of sorrow is true love of God as the highest Good and our greatest Benefactor, Whom we have offended by our sins and to Whom we have shown ourselves ungrateful. It is called perfect because love of God is the highest and most perfect motive of repentance. As the traditional Act of Contrition states: " . . . because they [my sins] offend You, my God, Who are all-good and deserving of all my love."

Supernatural contrition is "imperfect" when it is based on motives still of faith but not love of God for His own sake. (This also is contained in the traditional Act of Contrition: ". . . because I dread the loss of heaven and the pains of hell.") Such motives are acknowledgment of God's justice and fear of His just punishment (here or hereafter) if we do not turn from our sins and strive to serve Him. Imperfect contrition (also called "attrition") with

Sacramental Confession* suffices for forgiveness of sin.

In practice, our contrition often is mixed. We love God but our love leaves something to be desired. And we fear God but not without trust in His mercy and love. As love grows, it drives out fear. *See also* PENANCE, RITE OF.

Contrition, Act of (kon-TRISH-uhn, akt uhv). A formula that expresses sorrow* for sin and a firm resolution to sin no more. When celebrating the Sacrament of Reconciliation,* the penitent says an act of contrition before receiving absolution.* The new rite gives ten acts of contrition and notes that any other one may also be used. The traditional Act of Contrition is as follows:

> O my God, I am heartily sorry for having offended You, and I detest all my sins, because of Your just punishments, but most of all because they offend You, my God, Who are all good and deserving of all my love. I firmly resolve, with the help of Your grace, to sin no more and to avoid the near occasions of sin.

Those who say any act of contrition can gain a partial indulgence.*

Conventual Church (kuhn-VEN-choo-uhl chuhrch). A church connected to a clerical Religious house, though not a typical parish church, may be granted the status of a church, for the pastoral care of the faithful. *See also* CHURCHES; ORATORY.

Conventual Mass (kuhn-VEN-choo-uhl mas). As part of the Office,* this Mass is to be celebrated daily in those communities obliged to the recitation of the Divine Office. Although conventual Masses do not have their own form of celebration, it is most fitting that they be sung, with the full participation* of all the members of the community. All the priests who are not bound to celebrate individually for the pastoral care of the faithful* ought to concelebrate* at this Mass, if possible. All members of the community, even those priests who celebrate individually for others, may communicate under both species. *See also* COMMUNITY MASS.

Conversion (kuhn-VUHR-zhuhn; -shuhn). Conversion is a change of heart, and in the context of religion it is a "turning to God" or a "returning to Him." It is also a gift of God, the result of His intervention in revealing the distance of human beings from Him—a distance called sin.

Jesus came to call people to repent and believe—that is, to be converted: "Reform your lives and believe in the Good News" (Mk 1:15).

While He was on earth, He was the means through Whom grace for conversion was dispensed and conversion was achieved. Now the Liturgy* is the major means through which the grace is dispensed and conversion is achieved, especially in the Sacrament of Penance.*

The Liturgy provides a means for conversion (Penitential Rite* at Mass), calls us to repentance (Ash

Wednesday, Reading I*; 3rd Ordinary Sunday, B, Reading I; 1st Sunday of Lent, B, Gospel*). It prays for conversion as a gift of God (Prayer over the People,* no. 6) and instructs us about the qualities of conversion.

Conversion must be sincere and durable (Saturday of 3rd Week of Lent, I, Reading I), and it is connected with faith (1st Sunday of Lent, B, Gospel; 15th Ordinary Sunday, B, Gospel). Finally, conversion is an element of eschatological joy,* originating in God's mercy (24th Ordinary Sunday, C, Gospel). *See also* PENANCE, RITE OF.

Conversion of St. Paul (kuhn-VUHR-zhuhn; shuhn; uhv saynt pawl). With this liturgical feast we commemorate Saul's conversion while journeying to Damascus, about five years after the Resurrection.* It constituted a great miracle because this soul-shaking experience was not sought by him but was the result of Divine intervention. This event was of supreme importance to Christianity, because through his uncompromising spirit, the new Church of Christ shook off the Judaic bonds allowing the development of God's Kingdom to spread to the Gentiles. Saul, whose name was changed to Paul on his first missionary journey, spread the Faith of Christ to Europe, and even to Rome. Through his efforts the Church became what we all know it is by nature—catholic, universal. Furthermore, the feast stresses the doctrine of the Mystical Body* as we listen to Christ's words to him; "Saul, Saul, why do you persecute Me?" *Liturgical celebration:* January 25 (Feast); *theme:* the act of conversion is not enough; it must be lasting. *See also* PAUL, APOSTLE, ST.

Cope (kohp). A long semicircular cloak, open in the front and reaching down to the heels, fastened at the breast with a clasp, with a hood or a nonfunctional one, taking the form of a shield. Originally, it was used as a protection from the cold and rain, hence the attached hood.

Never used by the celebrant at Mass,* it is the usual garment for processions,* benediction,* the archpriest,* the solemn singing of Liturgy of the Hours,* and during other services as each rite indicates.

Corinthians, First Epistle to the (kuh-RIN-thee-uhnz, fuhrst i-PIS-uhl too thuh). Fifty-third Book of the bible* and seventh of the New Testament.* This first Epistle was written by St. Paul* from Ephesus about the year 56 to put an end to disorders in the Corinthian Church (where Paul had spent 18 months) and to answer questions put to him in a letter from that community. It deals with dissensions, moral irregularities, marriage and celibacy, conduct at religious gatherings, the Eucharist,* spiritual gifts (charisms) and their function in the Church, Christian love, and the resurrection of the body.

Liturgical Use: This Epistle is used extensively throughout the *Roman Missal,** for example, on the early Sundays of Ordinary Time,* Easter,* Pentecost,* Christ the King,* and from Thursday of the

21st Week in Ordinary Time to Saturday of the 24th Week (Year II). In the *Liturgy of the Hours** it is used in the Commons and on the Feast of the Holy Trinity.* *Meaning:* This magnificent Epistle affirms the new spirit of the Gospel* in all its originality and freedom and places it against the practices of Judaism and the errors of the paganism of Paul's time. In the hymn in honor of Christian love (ch. 13), the religious thought reaches the height attained by Jesus Himself in His exaltation and praise of love.

Corinthians, Second Epistle to the (kuh-RIN-thee-uhnz, SEK-uhnd i-PIS-uhl too thuh). Fifty-fourth Book of the Bible* and eighth of the New Testament.* St. Paul* wrote this Epistle from Macedonia toward the close of his third missionary journey, about 57 A.D. In it he defends his life and ministry, urges that the collection—already requested and begun—be made for the poor Christians in Jerusalem, and replies to his bitter opponents. This Epistle is intensely personal and hotly polemical. Paul stresses that he is a true apostle of Jesus, and that his sincerity and authority have been amply attested by extraordinary visitations from heaven and unparalleled labors and sufferings in behalf of the Gospel.*

Litugical Use: This Epistle is used frequently in the *Roman Missal,** for example, from the 7th through the 14th Sunday in Ordinary Time (B), on Trinity Sunday* (A), and during the 10th and 11th Weeks (Year I); in the *Liturgy of the Hours,** it is read on the 16th and 17th Sundays in Ordinary Time, August 6, and the Commons. *Meaning:* This Epistle deals in passing with the most sublime truths: the Trinity,* the role of the Holy Spirit,* the opposition of the two Covenants,* etc. Above all, it provides the experience, the mystique, the spirituality, and the theology of the apostolate, accentuates the power of the Word of God,* and pinpoints the active solidarity that should characterize all Christians.

Cornelius, St. (kawr-NEEL-yuhs). ?-253. Cornelius became Pope in 251 and fought against the Novatian schismatics. With the help of St. Cyprian* of Carthage, he was

able to uphold his papal authority and maintain unity in the Church. Exiled by the Emperor Gallus, Cornelius died at Civitavecchia in Italy. *Liturgical celebration:* September 16 (Memorial); *theme:* zeal for Church unity.

Cornerstone (KAWR-nuhr-stohn). One of the first stones placed in the foundation of a church during its construction, usually in a corner of the building. Engraved with the name and date, the stone may contain in its cavity souvenirs of the time and circumstances, e.g., coins or medals of the year, the account of the ceremony with signatures, including the date, the reigning Pope,* the President, the pastor* of the parish,* the mayor of the city, the bishop* who blessed the site, the architect, and perhaps important lay people of the church council. Having been blessed, the cornerstone, symbolizing Christ as the Foundation of the Church, is set in place according to the ritual for the Dedication of a Church and an Altar, in the *Roman Pontifical.** *See also* CHURCH DEDICATION.

Coronation of a Pope (kor-uh-NAY-shun [kawr-] uhv uh pohp). A liturgical ceremony whereby the newly elected Pope* had the papal tiara* placed on his head to symbolize his jurisdiction, his powers to teach, to sanctify, and to rule. After Pope Paul VI gave away his tiara to the poor and thus freed the ecclesiastical ceremonies from elaborate observances, subsequent Popes were not crowned, but were installed instead by the formal investiture with the pallium* during the Mass concelebrated with the college of cardinals.

Coronation of the Blessed Virgin (kor-uh-NAY-shuhn [kawr-] uhv thuh BLES-uhd VUHR-juhn). A rite consisting of the solemn placing of a crown of wrought metal on the head of a statue of the Blessed Virgin. Once placed there the crown remains permanently on the statue. Crowning statues of Madonnas is very old, but this ceremony originated in the 18th century. In 1981, the Church issued a new rite replacing the one found in the *Roman Pontifical.** *See also* MARY, BLESSED VIRGIN—ORDER OF CROWNING AN IMAGE OF.

Corporal (KAWR-puhr-uhl). A sacred cloth of white linen around twenty inches square upon which the chalice,* paten,* and ciboria* are placed during Mass.* When not in use, it is folded three times each way so as to form nine equal squares and placed in the burse.* All vessels that actually contain the Blessed Sacrament*—chalice, paten, ciborium, and monstrance*—must be placed on a corporal.

The Byzantine Rite* makes use of a different and larger corporal called the *eileton* or the Greek corporal. This is a square, two-piece linen cloth that takes the place of an altar cloth; it contains relics* and is beautifully adorned. Priests of the Roman Rite* had obtained permission to use this corporal when celebrating Mass away from the church.

Corpus Christi. *See* BODY AND BLOOD OF CHRIST.

Cosmas and Damian, Sts. (KOZ-muhs and DAY-mee-uhn). ?-283. Cosmas and Damian were brother physicians probably born in Arabia. They cured many of the faithful at Aegea in Cilicia more by faith in Jesus Christ than by their own natural abilities. They suffered martyrdom during the reign of Diocletian and gained a widespread cult among the early Christians. They are Patrons of Barbers, Pharmacists, Physicians, and Surgeons. *Liturgical celebration:* September 26 (Opt. Mem.); *theme:* Christ's sacrifice gives meaning to all martyrdom.

Council, Second Vatican. *See* VATICAN COUNCIL, SECOND.

Covenant (KUHV-[uh]-nuhnt). The Covenant (a formal, solemn, and binding agreement) is at the heart of God's loving design from all eternity: although He has no need of human beings, He freely desires to bind Himself to a people with the very intimacy of a marriage bond. The Liturgy,* Work of God* and Work of His People, is the integral or complete action in which is sealed the Covenant that God never ceases proposing to human beings. We can thus define Liturgy as the encounter of God and His People for the celebration of their Covenant.

In the History of Salvation,* the liturgies are distinguished by the covenant that they celebrate. "Again and again You offered a Covenant to [human beings]," says Eucharistic Prayer IV. The liturgies of the so-called pagan religions can be referred in all their positive aspects to the Covenant sealed with Noah (Gn 9:8-17). The Covenant concluded with Abraham* (Gn 15 and 17) and consummated in the sacrifice of Isaac (Gn 22) was destined to disappear for the benefit of a single people.

Israel was born as the People of Yahweh at the solemn liturgy of the Covenant at Sinai. This was the day of the Assembly* (Dt 9:10; 10:4; 18:16) when Moses, taking the blood of the sacrifice, poured half on the altar* that represented God and the other half on the people, saying: "This is the blood of the Covenant which the Lord has made with you in accordance with these words of his" (Ex 24:8).

The notorious infidelity of the People who became the ally of Yahweh—one thinks of the golden calf incident (Ex 32)—did not prevent the Sinaitic Covenant, renewed (Ex 34), from being actualized in the daily, weekly, and annual celebrations of Israel. But even more, the liturgical renewal of the Covenant was directed toward the future, in the expectation of the new Covenant promised by the Prophets (Jer 31:31-34), and of that "Angel of the Covenant" who was to come into His Temple, to be the initiator of a pure offering that could be presented to God from the rising of the sun to its setting (Mal 3:1,3,4; see 1:11).

Jesus, God and Man, *is* the Covenant. He came to inaugurate "by one offering" the Liturgy of the new People of God, which is the Church.* At the Last Supper,* this true Servant of Yahweh* (see Is 52:13—53:12), this Lamb of God who mounted Calvary* to take away the sins of the world (see Jn 1:29), left His Apostles the Sacrament of His sacrifice, the Memorial of the New Covenant. Manifestly, the words that consecrated the wine into His Blood refer to the Sinaitic Covenant: "This is my blood of the Covenant which will be shed on behalf of many for the forgiveness of sins" (Mt 26:28; see Ex 24:8).

After Calvary, the Liturgy—centered on the Eucharist*—enables members of the Church to enter into the new and eternal Covenant, until it is consummated in the heavenly Jerusalem. Then, "the formula of the Covenant" will be perfectly applied: "They will be his people and God himself will always be with them as their God" (Rv 21:3;

see Ex 6:7; Lv 26:12; Dt 26:17f; Jer 7:23; 11:4; 30:22; 31:1-33; 32:38; Ez 11:20; 14:11; 37:27; 2 Cor 6:16).

Cowl (KOWL). A hood worn over the head by monks and Religious to protect the head and shoulders against the rigors of cold weather. It is also and more correctly the flowing garment, having ample sleeves and a hood, presented to a monk upon making his solemn vows.

Creativity in Liturgy (kree-uh-TIV-uh-tee in LIT-uhr-jee). Although this explanation refers primarily to the Eucharistic Liturgy,* comparable situations may well occur in other liturgical actions, where it is expected that the celebrant will act accordingly.

(1) *Presidential Introductions.* In his role as president of the assembly,* the priest should use personal creativity in (a) introducing the Liturgy of the day before the celebration begins; (b) the Penitential Rite*; (c) the Liturgy of the Word* before the readings; (d) the Eucharistic Prayer*; (e) the Lord's Prayer*; (f) the Sign of Peace*; (g) Holy Communion*; (h) the final announcement before the Dismissal.*

Normally done by the president of the congregation, they may also be performed by the deacon* or the commentator.* Although they are not obligatory, most of them aid the assembly in joining in the Mystery* of the celebration.* Each admonition* has a purpose, and the literary genre should be succinct and pointed.

(2) *The Homily.* This is a privileged area for creativity and presents the challenge and demand of much study of the *Lectionary,** inquiry into contemporary exegesis, study groups, etc. *See also* HOMILY.

(3) *General Intercessions.* All throughout the introduction, petitions, responses, and conclusion, creative initiative should be used, so that timeliness and spontaneity fulfill the needs of the present assembly. (*See also* GENERAL INTERCESSIONS.)

(4) *The Diaconal Announcements.* Only if a deacon or another designated minister is absent would the president make these. They pertain to the reminders given to the assembly with regard to the position of prayer,* the meaning of the music* as it relates to the celebration, etc.

(5) *Music.* Talented creativity should be used not only in composing new music but also in selecting the proper music most suited to the particular function and community. In selecting and arranging music in any liturgical celebration, the meaning and purpose of each of the songs is important in making the choice so that it is appropriate to the tenor of the liturgical action. *See also* MUSIC.

Credence Table (KREED-uhn[t]s TAY-buhl). A movable table to the side of the altar* upon which are placed the things needed for sacred functions, particularly the Mass,* such as the chalice,* cruets,* basin, and finger cloth* or towel.

Credo. *See* PROFESSION OF FAITH.

Creed. *See* PROFESSION OF FAITH.

Cremation (kri-MAY-shuhn). The destruction of the human corpse by fire. Both the new *Order of Christian Funerals* (no. 15) and the new *Code of Canon Law* (1176) state that funeral rites are to be granted to those who have chosen cremation, unless there is evidence that their choice was dictated by anti-Christian motives, such as a sectarian spirit, hatred of the Catholic religion or the Church, or a denial of Christian doctrine. Furthermore, every precaution is to be taken against the danger of scandal or religious indifferentism.

Crib (krib). A manger, which represents the feeding box that held the Christ Child at His birth. Popularized by St. Francis of Assisi,* it is erected in churches at Christmas time in memory of the birth of Christ at the stable in Bethlehem. Many Christians also have such representations in their homes.

Crosier. *See* CROZIER.

Cross (kraws, kros). As a symbol of the Passion of Christ, the Cross is the most honored of all Christian images. Since it signifies the saving act of Christ and all its power, it stands not only for the redemptive act of Jesus but for the strength to bear the trials of life by following Christ.

The crucifix, a Cross with an image of Christ on it, was not used in the early centuries while crucifixion was still customary. After that, triumphal crosses became popular, showing the glory* won by Christ on the Cross, depicting Him in robes, without nails, with a royal crown, etc. Recent liturgical revival somewhat favors this so-called cameo-cross, depicting Christ glorified and ruling from the Cross. After the Reformation, crucifixes of the suffering or dead Christ appeared. Honor and reverence are paid to the Cross with incense, bowing,* and on Good Friday* by genuflection.*

A blessed Cross is a Sacramental* and used in many ways. Placed on mountaintops, in fields, and similar localities, it becomes a sign of Christ's sovereignty. Many men and women Religious wear it as part of their habit. It is attached to Rosary* beads, placed in the hands of a dying person, and used for many liturgical blessings.* During the Eucharistic sacrifice, the crucifix is either on the altar or nearby. At present a custom is developing of carrying a Cross during the entrance procession* for Mass, which is placed on or near the altar, if another Cross is not already there.

Finding of the True Cross

Several legends exist on the finding of the Cross, but they have little historical accuracy. Yet there is evidence, especially from St. Cyril of Jerusalem,* that the Cross had been found; others indicate that veneration of the Cross occurred by the last half of the 4th century. Most legends indicate that it was found in the early part of the 4th century. Regardless of the authenticity of the legends, the Church has accepted the identity of the true Cross from the 4th century.

Relics of the True Cross

According to St. Cyril of Jerusalem, by the middle of the 4th century pilgrims had taken relics* of the Cross to various parts of the world. Later on several documents indicate that fragments of the true Cross were given to various people throughout the world. The catalog of known relics of the Cross estimates that they would comprise only about one-third of the Cross that would have been used in the crucifixion.

Cross, Adoration of the. *See* VENERATION OF THE CROSS.

Cross Bearer (kraws, kros, BAYR-uhr). At ceremonial or liturgical occasions the person, usually an acolyte,* who carries the processional Cross.*

Cross, Pectoral (kraws, kros, PEK-t[uh-]ruhl). Worn on the breast and hanging from the neck by means of a string or chain, this cross became part of the costume of all bishops around the 12th century. Of gold or of gilded silver, it contains some relics of martyrs* or other Saints,* and often a particle of the true Cross.* Precious stones frequently decorate it. Popes, bishops, and certain other prelates may wear it everywhere, during liturgical functions or over street clothes. *See also* INSIGNIA, PONTIFICAL.

Cross, Processional (kraws, kros, pruh-SESH-uhn-uhl). A portable crucifix, mounted on a staff, which is used in liturgical processions at the head of the vested members of the clergy.

Cross, Sign of the. *See* SIGN OF THE CROSS.

Cross, Stations of the. *See* STATIONS OF THE CROSS.

Cross, Triumph of the. *See* TRIUMPH OF THE CROSS.

Cross, Veneration of the. *See* VENERATION OF THE CROSS.

Crown (krown). (1) A circular ornament used as a headdress or as a sign of distinction or victory. On Christ the King* it illustrates His majestic power and, on Mary* it proclaims she is Queen, above all angels and Saints.* In ecclesiastical symbols, it signifies the glory* that the Saints have won as they now reign triumphant with Christ.

(2) The crown of thorns was a wreath of torture mockingly put on the head of Christ by the soldiers. In the 13th century, St. Louis IX* constructed a shrine for it in Paris, Sainte-Chapelle. The crown's authenticity is uncertain, but its veneration arouses ardent devotion to the Passion of Christ.

(3) Besides the fifteen-decade Rosary* of the Blessed Virgin Mary, other similar devotions are termed crowns. There are nine such similar forms of prayer, in which the same formulas are repeated a certain number of times, determined by enchained or threaded beads. The series and number of prayers vary, depending on the intent of each devotion. For instance, in the Angelic Crown, nine groups of three beads for Hail Mary's* and one for the Our Father* are recited in honor of St. Michael* and the nine choirs of angels. *See also* ROSARY.

Crozier (KROH-zhuhr). A pastoral staff used by bishops* as the insignia of their dignity and jurisdiction. With a history of many forms, this ornamental staff today is shaped like a shepherd's crook, of gilded or silver plated metal about a man's height, near six feet. Bishops carry it at solemn pontifical rites. Certain abbots* and other privileged prelates may also be entitled to the crozier.

Crucifix. *See* CROSS.

Cruets (KROO-uhts). Vessels or bottles, usually in the form of jugs, having a handle and a beak, made of glass or metal, intended to contain the wine and water for Mass.*

The acolyte* carries them on a tray from the credence table* to the altar* for the Preparation of the Gifts* and ablution of the chalice* after Communion.* The tray serves as a basin while the priest washes his hands after the Preparation of the Gifts. Cruets usually have a metal cover or a glass stopper to protect the contents from insects.

The term sometimes refers to the containers for the holy oils. *See also* OIL STOCK.

Crypt (kript). An underground vault or room, usually excavated under the choir,* used as a burial place. It may have an altar or two and be used for religious services.

Cult (kuhlt). (1). That group of actions by which human beings worship God, or which, through the ministry of the Church,* sanctifies souls. Usually this worship refers to a Eucharistic cult, the participation of all in Mass* and Holy Communion,* in which the real presence* of Christ is adored as true God in the Sacrament.* When it pertains to veneration of the Saints,* it is usually spelled cultus.

(2) An exclusive religious group, of uncommon belief, playing up some peculiar ritual or practice. *See also* WORSHIP.

Culture and Worship (KUHL-chuhr and WUHR-shuhp). Among other things, culture consists of behavior patterns in various aspects of human work and thought. In worship* there is a formation element, which involves cultural patterns, whereby people respond to God and a transformation occurs between them. A structural pattern of worship is related to cultural patterns, and it is incumbent on society to recognize a common culture that can provide satisfactory patterns for understanding, responding, and communicating during worship.

The God-human relationship must be taken into account in all liturgical revision. Never should the Church be so cut off from the concerns of the world* and life that worship would become static, become unable to move with the times. On the other hand, she may not allow herself to be so accommodated to life and molded by cultural patterns that she might forget the extent of the Divine she should advocate. Worship must both affirm and resist certain aspects of culture to achieve the necessary balance.

Today, traditional patterns are disparaged and new possibilities explored; this action uncovers many other culture traditions which should be respected. Furthermore, there is strong concern for genuine and honest personal relationship in our technological society, which might tend to keep people apart even though communication is much improved. Hence the Church, starting from her Christian belief in practice today, should explore the current climate and seek for discernment, not according to some final set pattern of her own but constantly being open to new possibilities. Thus without jeopardizing her own Divine dimension, she can maintain a balance that is vital to Christian worship. *See also* ADAPTATION, LITURGICAL; NATIVE CUSTOMS; WORSHIP.

Cup. See CHALICE.

Curate. *See* ASSOCIATE PASTOR.

Curé of Ars. *See* JOHN VIANNEY, ST.

Curial Documents. *See* LITURGICAL LAW, SOURCES OF.

Cushion (KUSH-uhn). A pillow upon which the *Sacramentary** rests when placed on the altar. In many areas it is replaced by a bookstand.

Customs (KUHS-tuhmz). (1) For customs to have juridical value, they must last for at least forty years, be reasonable, be accepted by the legislator, and be introduced by a community having legal capacity. Since the Holy See* has reserved exclusively to itself all rights in liturgical matters, it is difficult—indeed, practically impossible—to introduce a legitimate custom in Liturgy.*

(2) Conventional mode or form of action of peoples is to be taken into consideration in various liturgical activities, primarily the initiation rites* and the music in mission lands, the rite of burial, Lenten practices, and sacred furnishings. The Church allows variations and adaptations in liturgical books* to suit different groups in regions and permits revisions in the Liturgical Year* to preserve traditional customs or disciplines in certain areas, all of which are submitted to the Apostolic See by the competent territorial ecclesiastical authority for approval. *See also* ADAPTATION, LITURGICAL.

Cycle, Alternate Two-Year. *See* TWO-YEAR CYCLE OF READINGS, ALTERNATE.

Cycles (SAI-kuhlz). (1) Those periods of the Church Year* that prepare for and develop the great Mysteries* of Christ. The Christmas* cycle begins with Advent* and continues to the Feast of the Baptism of the Lord.* The Easter* cycle used to start with Ash Wednesday* and conclude with Pentecost*; now it begins with the Easter Vigil.* Outside these major cycles is the period of Ordinary Time,* which extends from the Christmas cycle to Ash Wednesday and then picks up after Pentecost until Advent begins again. The term Proper of the Season* is more popular today for this type of cycle. (*See also* ADVENT; CHRISTMAS SEASON; EASTER SEASON; LENT; ORDINARY TIME; PROPER OF THE SEASON.)

(2) The *Lectionary** has cycles, three for Sundays, with various

readings* for each Sunday in three consecutive years, after which the three cycles are then repeated. The first three letters of the alphabet designate the cycles; the number of the C Year is always equally divisible by three. The different seasons and the theme of each liturgical season determine which principle, semicontinuous or thematic, applies. Harmony between the Old* and New* Testament readings led to certain choices. Common themes, best illustrated during Advent, Lent, and Easter Season, allow another kind of harmonization. Sundays in Ordinary Time have no particular theme, so the New Testament readings are arranged semicontinuously, while the Old Testament readings relate to the Gospel.*

For weekdays outside of Advent, Lent, and Easter Season, there is a two-year cycle of the First Readings,* but the Gospels remain the same each year. The first series is for the odd-numbered years, the second series for the even years. Thematic choices depend on a theme for the particular season, e.g., Baptism* and Penance* in Lent; otherwise the semicontinuous principle prevails.

(3) The *Liturgy of the Hours** also has cycles of Readings (both Biblical and non-Biblical). A One-Year Cycle of Readings is incorporated into the four-volume work with a First Reading from the Fathers* and Doctors* of the Church as well as ecclesiastical writers. There is also an Alternate Two-Year Cycle of Readings* that has not yet been published in full. A listing of the Biblical Readings appears in *Christian Prayer** and the full text is given in *Christian Readings* an unofficial but approved six-volume edition. The non-Biblical Readings have not been listed, but *Christian Readings* offers a representative series.

(4) There is a four-week cycle of Psalms* said in the *Liturgy of the Hours** or *Christian Prayer**; thus, except for the few Psalms omitted in the cycle, the Book of Psalms is recited in a period of four weeks. The first week of the cycle starts on the first Sunday in Advent, Lent, Easter, and Ordinary Time. Psalms for Morning Prayer,* Evening Prayer,* and Night Prayer* express the theme of the hour. Sundays have Psalms associated with the Paschal Mystery*; Fridays have penitential Psalms. Psalms concerned with the History of Salvation* are used in Advent, Christmas, Lent, and Easter seasons.

See also FIRST READING; LECTIONARY; PSALTER; READINGS; SECOND READING; TWO YEAR-CYCLE OF READINGS, ALTERNATE.

Cyprian, St. (SIP-ree-uhn). 210-258. Born in Carthage of wealthy pagan parents, Cyprian was converted, ordained, and subsequently made bishop of that city in 249. In a short ten-year span, he led his flock through a two-year persecution under Decius, defended the unity of the Church against two schismatical sects, was the soul of the city's morale during a devastating plague, and experienced exile during which he kept up the spirits of his people by constant correspondence. Cyprian was martyred under Emperor Valerian in 258 and is one of the Fathers of the Church. *Liturgical celebration:* September 16 (Opt. Mem.); *theme:* zeal for Church unity.

Cyril and Methodius, Sts. (SIR-uhl and me-THOH-dee-uhs). 826-

869; 827-883. Cyril and Methodius, Apostles to the Slavs, were born in Thessalonica and educated in Constantinople. They evangelized Moravia, Bohemia, and Bulgaria and prepared liturgical texts in what would subsequently be known as the Cyrillic alphabet. They were summoned to Rome and consecrated bishops by Pope Hadrian II. Cyril died there in 869.

Methodius went to Pannonia where he continued to preach the Gospel* and also formulated the Slav alphabet. He also preached in Moravia and Poland and died in Velehrad, Czechoslovakia. Cyril and Methodius are Patrons of the Unity of the Eastern and Western Churches. *Liturgical celebration:* February 14 (Memorial); *theme:* unity of faith and worship. *See also* SLAVORUM APOSTOLORUM.

Cyril of Alexandria, St. (SIR-uhl uhv al-ig-ZAN-dree-uh). 370-444. Born in Alexandria, Cyril lived the monastic life, was ordained a priest, and succeeded his uncle as bishop of that city in 412. He became the glory of the Church in Egypt and is principally renowned for his strenuous defense of the Divine Maternity of the Blessed Virgin Mary* against the Nestorians. Cyril wrote many works explaining and defending the Catholic Faith and is a Doctor* of the Church. *Liturgical celebration:* June 27 (Opt. Mem.); *theme:* devotion to Mary Mother of God.

Cyril of Jerusalem, St. (SIR-uhl uhv juh-ROOZ-uh-lem). 315-386. Born near Jerusalem, Cyril succeeded Maximus as bishop of that city in 348. He was a staunch foe of Arianism and vigorously defended Christ's Divinity, leading to his incurring repeated exiles. In his famous *Catecheses* he explained to his people the true teaching of the Faith and of Scripture, and of the traditions of the Church. He is a Doctor* of the Church. *Liturgical celebration:* March 18 (Opt. Mem.); *theme:* true knowledge of Christ and His Mysteries.

— D —

Daily Communion (DAY-lee kuh-MYOO-nyuhn). The practice whereby the faithful* receive Communion* every day. This practice flourished in the early Church and for centuries thereafter. However, with the passage of time it fell into disuse owing to a decline in piety and the spread of heresies. St. Pius X* restored the practice in 1905, and the Second Vatican Council* warmly recommended that everyone who participates at Mass* should receive Communion (provided, of course, the conditions for reception are met) (SC, 55). *See also* COMMUNION.

Dalmatic (dal-MAT-ik). The outer vestment worn by the deacon,* and sometimes by a bishop* under the chasuble* if he pontificates. Although it was originally something like an alb,* now with wide short sleeves and open at the side it reaches below the knees. In color and material, it corresponds with the chasuble.

Damasus I, St. (DAM-uh-suhs). 305-384. Born in Rome of Spanish ancestry, St. Damasus governed the Church from 366 to 384. He commissioned St. Jerome* to translate the Bible* into Latin, combated the Apollinarist and Macedonian heresies, and confirmed the Council of Constantinople, which had condemned Arianism. He also promoted the cult of martyrs* whose burial places he adorned with sacred verse. *Liturgical celebration:* December 11 (Opt. Mem.); *theme:* love for and imitation of martyrs.

Damian, St. *See* COSMAS AND DAMIAN, STS.

Dancing, Liturgical (DAN[T]S-ing; DAHN[T]S-ing; luh-TUHR-ji-kuhl; li-). Rhythmic movement to music during a religious ceremony. Historically sacred dancers have long been featured in liturgical worship.* Throughout the years dance in many places was closely combined with formal worship.

In the Old Testament,* dancing was part of worship: "All the women went after her [Miriam] with timbrel and dances" (Ex 15:20-21). David "danced with all his might before the Lord" (2 Kgs 6:14). The Psalms* show dancing in the Temple (Ps 149:9; 150:4; Jer 20:4; Song 7:1). During early Christian times, vigils* of martyrs* were celebrated with dance. In the Middle Ages, dance and formal worship were combined during the chief liturgical seasons. Today dance still occurs before the Seville cathedral high altar on the feasts of the Immaculate Conception* and the Body and Blood of Christ* and in Shrovetide.

Dance as an art* expresses human feelings and is especially adapted to signify joy.* Dance becomes prayer* by disclosing itself in a movement that engages the whole being, soul and body. Thus we speak of a prayer of the body, which asserts praise and indicates petition* by movement.

After Vatican Council II,* renewed interest arose in liturgical dance, using gesture,* music,* and rhythmic movement in relation to the Scriptural theme. Because the body reflects the soul, dancing should express the faith* and adoration* in such a way that it becomes prayer. As in other matters, it too comes under the competent Church authority.

In some cultures dancing is more acceptable and truly reflects religious values. Except as described above, dance has rarely been an integral part of the official worship. Those who condemn religious dance believe it conduces little to worship and might degenerate into disorders. Where cultures have dancing reflective of religious values, ritual dance would be permitted, because the *Constitution on the Sacred Liturgy** respects and fosters the talents and genius of various peoples, even admitting it into the Liturgy,* as long as it brings a genuine and authentic spirit. Such an act well received in one culture cannot be accepted by another. Many think that the traditional reserve of Latin worship would bar dance from religious worship, though it may take place outside of the Liturgy.

To introduce artistic ballet into the Liturgy is contrary to the norm that in all Liturgy there should be participation,* rather than a performance one might attend. Amorous dancing should never be introduced into liturgical celebrations. Priests are to be excluded from the dance. Religious dancing outside the Liturgy is permissible as long as it occurs in areas that are not strictly liturgical *(see Not* 11, pp. 202-5).

Daniel, The Book of (DAN-yuhl, thuh buk uhv). Thirty-fourth Book of the Old Testament* and fourth of the Major Prophets.* It takes its name, not from the author, who is actually unknown, but from its hero, a young Jew taken early to Babylon, where he lived at least until 538 B.C. Strictly speaking, the Book does not belong to the prophetic writings but rather to a distinctive type of literature known as "apocalyptic," of which it is an early specimen. Apocalyptic writing enjoyed its greatest popularity from 200 B.C. to 100 A.D., a time of distress and persecution for Jews, and later for Christians. Although it was subsequent in time to the prophetic, apocalyptic literature had its roots in the teaching of the Prophets, who often pointed ahead to the Day of the Lord, the consummation of history. For both prophet and apocalyptist, Yahweh* was the Lord of history, and He would ultimately vindicate His people.

This work was composed during the bitter persecution carried out by Antiochus IV Epiphanes (167-164) and was written to strengthen and comfort the Jewish people in their ordeal. It contains stories originating in and transmitted by popular traditions, which tell of the trials and triumphs of the wise Daniel and his three companions.

Liturgical Use: In the *Roman Missal** this book is read in Ordinary Time* on the 33rd Sunday (B), Christ the King* (B), and the whole 34th Week (I) as well as in Lent,* on the Monday of the 2nd Week, Tuesday of the 3rd Week, and Monday and Wednesday of the 5th Week, plus August 6 and September 29, Masses for Persecuted Christians and For Any Need. In the *Liturgy of the Hours,** it is read on the entire 32nd Week in Ordinary Time* and gives rise to three minor canticles.* *Meaning:* Daniel stresses that God controls events on behalf of the righteous in such a way that the Kingdom of God will ultimately triumph. Hence, the people of faith can resist temptation and conquer adversity of every kind.

Days of Abstinence. *See* ABSTINENCE.

Days of Prayer (dayz uhv prayr). This more general term is used today for the Rogation and Ember Days, on which the Church gives thanks in a public manner to the Lord and prays for the needs of people, for productive land, and for the labor of humankind. The time and manner of observing these days are adapted to the various regions and needs of people by the competent authority, the Episcopal Conference.* It sets the norm for the celebration, as to time and frequency.

The National Conference of Catholic Bishops in the United States has specified Thanksgiving Day* and

Labor Day,* and then asked the local Ordinaries to designate the times when days of prayer are to be observed at least for the following: (a) the general needs of humankind; (b) the fruits of the earth; (c) world justice and peace; (d) human rights and equality. The existing Masses for Various Needs and Occasions* together with the readings* and chants* from the *Lectionary** offer ample choices to fit the purpose of the various observances. *See also* INDEPENDENCE DAY MASS; ROGATION DAYS.

Daytime Prayer (DAY-taim prayr). The third of the Canonical Hours of the Divine Office* has been changed by Vatican Council II.* One Little Hour, Prime, was abrogated. The three other Little Hours, Terce, Sext, and None, are classified as Daytime Prayer. The obligation indicates that only one of these need be said; everyone is encouraged to say all three parts of this Daytime Prayer. The three parts are preserved in choir. Certain variations occur depending upon whether it is Midmorning, Midday, or Midafternoon. *See also* LITURGY OF THE HOURS.

De Profundis (day proh-FOON-dees). First words in Latin of Psalm 130: "Out of the depths," used to indicate this well-known hymn, which has been used from antiquity as a penitential Psalm and for the commemoration of the dead. It is recited in the Office for the Dead,* in Evening Prayer I of Sunday of the Fourth Week in the Psalter,* Evening Prayer II for Christmas,* Evening Prayer I for the Feast of the Sacred Heart,* and Night Prayer* for Wednesday. *See also* PENITENTIAL PSALMS.

De Sacramentis (day sahk-rah-MEN-tees). Latin title ("Concerning the Sacraments") of a famous 4th-century work on the Sacraments* attributed to St. Ambrose.* It deals with Baptism,* Confirmation,* and the Eucharist.* Its liturgical importance is gauged by the fact that it constitutes the earliest witness to the text of Eucharistic Prayer I* (the Roman Canon*).

Deacon (DEE-kuhn). A man, who serves the community, ordained in the first of the three orders of Holy Orders*; the others are the priesthood and the episcopacy. His ministry is one of liturgical and pastoral service to the Church and charitable works of mercy.

There are two types of deacons: transitional and permanent. (a) *Transitional.* One who plans to be a deacon temporarily, since his intent is to become a priest.* Historically, the deacon served as an administrative assistant to the bishop* and also enjoyed a prominent liturgical role. By the Middle Ages, the diaconate declined considerably in importance, becoming rather a final stage in preparation for priesthood. With the restoration of the diaconate after Vatican Council II,* the transitional deacon fulfills the same ministry as permanent deacons.

(b) *Permanent.* A person who makes a lifelong commitment to serve as deacon, either as a celibate or in the married diaconate.

Obligations

Those aspiring to this order seek admission freely through a written petition, followed by acceptance of the competent ecclesiastical superior. They are to receive the ministries of lector* and acolyte.* The Ordinary* performs the rite of admission and confers the ministries, with the proper intervals as established by law. Before ordination to the diaconate, a public commitment to celibacy is celebrated in a special rite; this action makes entering marriage invalid. A married deacon who loses his wife may not enter a new marriage.

Transitional deacons must complete the course of study prescribed by the norms prior to ordination. For permanent deacons the theological study that must precede ordination is decided by the Episcopal Conference* and approved by the Sacred Congregation for Catholic Education. Transitional deacons are bound to celebrate the Liturgy of the Hours*; permanent deacons should recite at least that part of the Liturgy of the Hours determined by the Episcopal Conference.

Ministry

The deacon's liturgical ministry varies in style and mode as follows: "(1) assisting the President of the Eucharistic Assembly; (2) making intercessions and offering petitions for the people; (3) inviting and exhorting the people to pray and make ritual gestures; (4) presiding at celebrations, especially in those situations in which there is neither priest nor bishop; (5) ministering certain Sacraments*; (6) blessing* objects and persons within certain liturgical celebrations; (7) proclaiming and preaching the Word of God*; (8) assisting the bishop in episcopal and cathedral liturgies" *(The Deacon [Study Text VI],* USCC, p. 42).

A. *Christian Initiation.* During evangelization* the deacon may conduct inquiry classes and discussion groups and help in teaching the manner of prayer. During the catechumenate* he works closely with the priests, enriching the celebrations of the Word, leading sessions in catechesis, and exercising the liturgical functions during the catechumenal rites. During the enlightenment* he shares in judging the readiness of the catechumens, presents the catechumens to the community, and leads the intercessions. The deacon assists in the rite of initiation during the Paschal Vigil.* During the Mystagogia* he continues a catechesis of enlightenment.

Prior to the solemn Baptism of infants that he may perform, the deacon should prepare families to help them in the Christian formation of their children.

B. *The Ministry of the Word.* Although reading the Gospel and

preaching at the Liturgy is his most solemn ministry, he can extend that in many ways at informal meetings, adult education, and religious education.

Preaching depends on faculties and diocesan norms. When he presides, the deacon may preach at Baptism,* Matrimony,* Benediction of the Blessed Sacrament,* wake service or other Christian burial service apart from Mass, visitation of the sick and when giving Viaticum,* and during the celebration of the Liturgy of the Hours.

Again depending upon faculties and norms, the deacon may preach at any celebration of the Eucharist,* when he is not the presiding minister at a celebration of a Sacrament,* at retreats, days of recollection, missions, etc., and when homilies take place at an ecumenical service.

C. *In the celebration of the Eucharist.* After preparing the altar* for the necessary liturgical items, the deacon, vested in alb* and stole* (over his left shoulder) and a dalmatic,* if desired, walks before the priest in the procession* carrying the Book of Gospels.* During the Introductory Rite,* the deacon may assist the priest in the Incensation,* the Rite of Sprinkling,* and the Introduction. During the Liturgy of the Word,* he proclaims the Gospel, may preach unless the presiding minister does, and leads the General Intercessions.*

During the Liturgy of the Eucharist,* besides preparing the altar, he assists with the gifts and helps the priest with the chalice* and *Sacramentary** during the Eucharistic Prayer.* He invites the people to exchange a Sign of Peace.* At the Doxology* he elevates the chalice* and during the Lamb of God* assists in breaking the bread* and readying the chalices for Communion* under both kinds. After Communion he takes care of the vessels.

In the Concluding Rite,* after he has made the announcements,* and the priest has given the Blessing,* he may dismiss the people. If a Solemn Blessing or Prayer over the People* is said, the deacon directs the people to bow their heads. During concelebrated Masses the deacon should perform all these functions in the usual way, his duties not being preempted by a concelebrating priest.

D. *Other Liturgical Celebrations.* (1) The deacon is a minister during the Rite of Benediction. (2) Following the Rite of Marriage* in the *Roman Ritual,* a deacon, in the absence of a priest, may accept the vows of a properly prepared couple, as long as he has the proper delegation. (3) In the communal forms of reconciliation he may exhort the people to Penance,* leading them in the Intercessions* and by proclaiming the Gospel. In penitential celebrations of a non-Sacramental nature, he may be the leader. (4) During the Liturgy of the Hours,* especially when Morning and Evening Prayer are part of the parish community life, the deacon may preside. (5) Pastoral care of the aged, sick, and dying is a prominent activity of deacons in many places. Although he may not administer the Sacrament of Anointing,* the deacon is minister in the Communion of the Sick and of Viaticum. (6) Except for the Eucharist itself, all the other rites of Christian burial may be celebrated by a deacon.

Deaconess (DEE-kuh-nis). A woman officially chosen for certain functions in the early Church.* Elderly women, usually widows, aided the Church in service to Christian women, particularly in caring for the sick and the poor, instructing women catechumens,* and maintaining order in the women's part of the Church. More importantly they helped during Baptism* by immersion for women during the unclothing and anointing, but as adult baptisms declined, the office of deaconess soon died out.

It would seem that the order or office of deaconess existed in the East, but the ministry of deaconesses was quite restricted in function. In the West we have no proof that such an order or office existed. Its possible revival is intimately connected with the ordination of women.

Dead, Mass for the. *See* MASS OF CHRISTIAN BURIAL.

Dead, Office for the. *See* OFFICE FOR THE DEAD.

Dead, Rite for Burial of. *See* MASS OF CHRISTIAN BURIAL.

Death (deth). Human death has found meaning in the Paschal Mystery* worked by Christ. Through Baptism,* Christians share in the redemptive Death and Resurrection* of the Lord Jesus. Each participation in the Eucharist* prepares, in the celebration of the new Passover, for one's own "passage" (passover) to life eternal.

The Sacrament of the Anointing of the Sick,* in comforting those who suffer, also orients them to death. A final celebration of the Sacrament of Reconciliation* and Communion* received as Viaticum* constitutes the ultimate preparation for the "passage." Thus, four Sacraments* give its true meaning to the death of a Christian (Baptism, Eucharist, Penance, and Anointing of the Sick): the crucial moment opening out to true life,* just as the Death of Christ on the Cross* terminated in the Resurrection.

After the death of the faithful, the Church* celebrates the Liturgy of the Dead* to accompany them on the "passage" by recommending them to God. (*See* FUNERAL RITES AND CEREMONIES; MASS OF CHRISTIAN BURIAL.)

The Liturgy* also speaks of the spiritual death of sin, which is the result of sin that reached "maturity" (Tuesday of 6th Week in Ordinary Time,* II, Reading I*). In His Death, Jesus overcame this death and became the model of the new person. Henceforth those who are in Christ cannot be touched by this spiritual death (Easter Vigil,* Epistle; 5th Sunday of Lent,* A, Reading II; Easter* Sunday, Reading II).

Through the Sacrament of Penance, Christ's merits are applied to Christians dead in sin, and they inspire such Christians to put on new life. The Eucharist, according to the Prayer after Communion,* enables properly disposed Christians to pass "from death to life" (Friday of 4th Week of Lent); it "[frees] us from our sinful ways and [brings] us new life" (Friday of 1st Week of Lent).

Death of Christ. *See* GOOD FRIDAY.

Declaration on Christian Education. *See* GRAVISSIMUM EDUCATIONIS.

Declaration on Religious Freedom. *See* DIGNITATIS HUMANAE.

Declaration on the Relationship of the Church to Non-Christian Religions. *See* NOSTRA AETATE.

Declarations. *See* LITURGICAL LAW, SOURCES OF.

Decoration of an Altar. *See* ALTAR, DECORATION OF.

Decree on Ecumenism. *See* UNITATIS REDINTEGRATIO.

Decree on Priestly Formation. *See* OPTATAM TOTIUS.

Decree on the Apostolate of the Laity. *See* APOSTOLICAM ACTUOSITATEM.

Decree on the Appropriate Renewal of Religious Life. *See* PERFECTAE CARITATIS.

Decree on the Eastern Catholic Churches. *See* ORIENTALIUM ECCLESIARUM.

Decree on the Life and Ministry of Priests. *See* PRESBYTERORUM ORDINIS.

Decree on the Media of Social Communication. *See* INTER MIRIFICA.

Decree on the Missionary Activity of the Church. See AD GENTES.

Decree on the Pastoral Office of Bishops in the Church. *See* CHRISTUS DOMINUS.

Decrees, Concilar and Curial. *See* LITURGICAL LAW, SOURCES OF.

Decretal Letters. *See* LITURGICAL LAW, SOURCES OF.

Dedication of a Church. *See* CHURCH DEDICATION.

Dedication of St. John Lateran (ded-uh-KAY-shuhn uhv saynt jon LAT-uh-ruhn). The Basilica of St. John Lateran is the cathedral* church of the archdiocese of Rome and was the seat of church government until the 13th century, when the Pope* moved to the Vatican.* Within its walls four Ecumenical Councils were held. It was erected by Constantine on land originally belonging to the Laterani family. Its first title was Basilica of the Holy Savior. Because of its large baptistry,* the catheral became the baptismal church of ancient Rome and the baptistry was dedicated to St. John the Baptist.* Consequently the current name evolved: the Basilica of St. John Lateran.

Church buildings are special, not because of their size or artistic decoration, but because people gather there to celebrate the Life, Death, and Resurrection* of Christ; the place is made holy by the presence of the Lord among His people. *Liturgical celebration:* November 9 (Feast); *theme:* church buildings are symbols of something greater, namely, the people who give them life.

Dedication of St. Mary Major. *See* MARY, BLESSED VIRGIN—FEASTS.

Dedication of the Churches of Sts. Peter and Paul (ded-uh-KAY-shuhn uhv thuh CHUHRCH-uhz uhv saynts PEE-tuhr and pawl). This is an anniversary celebration of the consecration of the two basilicas* in Rome, identifying the spot of each Apostle's martyrdom and tomb, that of St. Peter* in the Basilica of St. Peter and that of St. Paul* in the Basilica of St. Paul Outside the Walls. In Rome there are two principal churches: St. John Lateran, the mother of all the churches on earth, the church proper to the Bishop of Rome as head of the local community; on the other hand, the Basilica of St. Peter is the church of non-Romans, those pilgrims who journey to the eternal city, and where celebrations that express the universal character of the Roman Church are celebrated.

Although these anniversaries were celebrated as early as the 12th century, the present St. Peter's was consecrated on November 18, 1626, and after St. Paul's Basilica was destroyed in 1823, the present church was consecrated on December 10, 1854. *Liturgical celebration:* November 18 (Opt. Mem.); *theme:* Peter and Paul, offspring of the Divine seed, lead us to the heavenly Jerusalem.

Dei Verbum (DAY-ee VER-boom). Latin title (from the first two words "The Word of God") of the *(Dogmatic) Constitution on Divine Revelation* issued by the Second Vatican Council* on November 18, 1965. It declares that Sacred Tradition* and Sacred Scripture* make up the one deposit of the Word of God* entrusted to the Church.* Holding fast to this, the entire holy people, united to their bishops* in doctrine and communion, persevere together in the Breaking of the Bread* and in prayer.* The Constitution notes that the Church has always revered Sacred Scripture even as she has revered the Body* of the Lord, because, above all in the Liturgy,* she never ceases to receive the Bread of Life* from the table both of God's Word and of Christ's Body and to offer it to the faithful.* Therefore, all preaching must have the Scriptures as its source and norm. *See also* VATICAN COUNCIL, SECOND.

Demonic Possession. *See* EXORCISM.

Denis and His Companions, Sts. (DEN-is and his cum-PAN-yuhns). ? - 250/258. Denis was sent by Pope St. Fabian* to preach the Faith in Gaul along with six other bishops. He organized a church at what is now Paris and was aided by a priest called Rusticus and a deacon named Eleutherius. So effective were they in converting the people to Christ that the pagan priests had them arrested by the Roman authorities. After a long im-

prisonment the three servants of God suffered martyrdom together during the persecution of Decius (250) or that of Valerian (258). Denis is the Patron of Those Possessed. *Liturgical celebration:* October 9 (Opt. Mem.); *theme:* rejection of the power and wealth of the world.

Deo Gratias. *See* THANKS BE TO GOD.

Deosculatorium (day-oh-skoo-lah-TAW-ree-uhm). Alternate name (from the Latin word for "kiss") for the Pax, an object sometimes used at Mass to convey the kiss of peace. *See also* INSTRUMENTUM PACIS.

Deprecatio Gelasii (day-pray-KAH-tsee-oh jay-LAH-see-ee). The Latin name (meaning "intercession of Gelasius") for the earliest extant Latin litany.* It is thought to have been composed during the pontificate of Pope Gelasius (492-96) and it was inserted into the Offices for feasts on Friday by Alcuin.*

Der Balyzeh Fragments (duhr bah-LEE-zay FRAG-muhnts). Fragments of Greek papyri discovered at Der Balyzeh, south of Assiout, in Egypt in 1907. Assigned to the 3rd, 4th, or 6th century by various scholars, these parts of liturgical prayers and a Creed* are important for the history of the Liturgy in Egypt and in general.

Desacralization (dee-say-kruh-lai-ZAY-shuhn; -li-). The loss of a quality of sacred. Places become sacred by virtue of receiving the dedication* or blessing* that liturgical books* provide for this purpose (can. 1205). They lose their dedication or blessing if they suffer major destruction or if they are permanently given over to profane uses. Thus, they cannot function in accord with the definition of a sacred place, that is, one suitable for Divine worship* or for the burial of the faithful. In order for the sacred quality to be restored, the place would have to be dedicated or blessed anew. *See also* SACRILEGE.

Desire for Baptism. *See* BAPTISM.

Deus in Adiutorium (DAY-oos in ahd-yoo-TOH-ree-oom). Second verse of Psalm 70 (Latin for "God, come to my assistance") now used at the beginning of every Hour of the Divine Office* as well as in other liturgical celebrations. *See* INTRODUCTORY VERSE.

Deuterocanonical Books. *See* APOCRYPHA.

Deuteronomy, The Book of (d[y]OO-tuh-RON-uh-mee, thuh buk uhv). Fifth and last book of the Pentateuch (first five Books of the Bible). Although attributed en masse to Moses, they are really the result of a progressive fusion of traditions of diverse origins and times. The name Deuteronomy means "second law." In reality, what it contains is not a new law but a partial repetition, completion, and explanation of the law proclaimed on Mount Sinai. The historical portions of the Book are also a resume of what is related elsewhere in the Pentateuch.

The chief characteristic of this Book is its vigorous oratorical style. In a series of eloquent discourses Moses presents the theme of covenant* renewal in a vital religious framework. He exhorts, corrects, and threatens his people, appealing to their past glory, their historic mission, and the promise of future triumph. His aim is to enforce among the Israelites the Lord's claim to their obedience, loyalty, and love.

Liturgical use: In the *Roman Missal,** this Book is used quite often, for example in Lent*: on the 1st Sunday (C), Saturday of the 1st Week, and Wednesday of the 3rd Week; and in Ordinary Time*: 4th Sunday (B), 9th Sunday (A,B), 22nd Sunday (B), and Friday of the 18th Week to Wednesday of the 19th Week (Year I). In the *Liturgy of the Hours,** it is read during the 2nd and 3rd Weeks in Ordinary Time and gives rise to one minor canticle* in the Psalter.* *Meaning:* God has saved and blessed His chosen people, whom He loves dearly. Hence, we His people should remember this and obey Him so that we may have life and continued blessings.

Devil. *See* EXORCISM.

Devotion (di-VOH-shuhn). The disposition to give willingly, promptly, and earnestly to the worship* and service of God. This attitude of the will exhibits itself by the readiness to honor God in worship or to fulfill His will; thus a person's devotion is grounded in a great love for God. It is not to be confused with the sometimes pleasurable sense of a warmth that comes from prayer, the opposite of aridity.

Devotions. *See* PARALITURGY; PRAYER.

Diaconate. *See* DEACON.

Dialogue (DAI-uh-log; -lahg). That interchange between the congregation and the celebrant* especially during the Penitential Rite,* the Introduction to the Preface,*

and the frequent greeting *The Lord be with you.** Much more than praying the Responses,* dialogue pertains also to the Acclamations,* the Profession of Faith,* the General Intercessions.* and the Lord's Prayer.* Furthermore, the singing or recitation of certain proper parts of the Mass, e.g., Entrance Antiphon* and Communion Antiphon,* tends to build an active participation of the people in the Eucharistic Sacrifice, thus stressing its communal nature. Besides the verbal and singing participation, actions, gestures, and bodily attitudes by the congregation are encouraged.

From 1922 to Vatican Council II* the term Dialogue Mass was used to express this method of participation by the faithful. Now each Mass has such a dialogue form, so there is no specific type of Eucharistic Liturgy called a Dialogue Mass.

The Liturgy itself is termed a dialogue between God and human beings. *See also* ACCLAMATIONS; GENERAL INTERCESSIONS; LITURGY; PENITENTIAL RITE; RESPONSES.

Didache, The (DID-uh-kay, thuh). An early Christian manual on morals and Church practice, known by the first word of its Greek title: *The Teaching (Didache) of the Twelve Apostles.* Its author is unknown and it is dated in the last decades of the 1st century.

The *Didache* had a great influence on the early Church and is still highly regarded because of its information concerning the Liturgy* of the early Church. It gives rules for the celebration of the Eucharist* and Baptism,* reproduces two Eucharistic Prayers,* and describes the ecclesiastical organization of the Church.*

Didascalia Apostolorum (di-dah-SKAH-lee-ah ah-pohs-toh-LAW-rum). Latin title ("The Teaching of the Apostles") of an early-3rd-century Church order originally composed in Greek. The Syrian title is: *The Catholic Teaching of the Twelve Apostles and the Holy Disciples of Our Savior.* Apparently written by a converted Jewish physician, it is modeled after the *Didache** and has been incorporated into the *Apostolic Constitutions.** A complete Syrian text and an incomplete Latin text are extant. The work deals with the duties of a bishop,* penance,* and liturgical worship,* among other things.

Dies Irae (DEE-ez EE-ray). Opening Latin words (meaning "Day of Wrath") and title of the Sequence* that was formerly part of the Mass for the Dead.* It was traditionally ascribed to Thomas of Celano (d. 1260) but is now more usually attributed to an unknown Franciscan of that time. This chant was based on Zep 1:14-16 and presented a rather depressing picture of the Last Judgment. It was very popular at one time and its musical setting is one of the most famous melodies of Gregorian Chant.* This Sequence finds no place in the revised *Roman Missal.**

Dignitatis Humanae (di-nyee-TAH-tees hoo-MAH-nay). Latin title (from the first two words "Human dignity") of the *Declaration on Religious Freedom* issued by the Second Vatican Council* on December 7, 1965. The document states the principle that religious freedom is necessary for human beings so that they may worship* God, and it has to do with immunity from coercion in society. This religious freedom is tantamount to a civil right. Thus, Catholics, like persons of all religious persuasions, have a right to participate in the Liturgy* of the Church. *See also* VATICAN COUNCIL, SECOND.

Dignum et Iustum Est. *See* INTRODUCTORY DIALOGUE.

Diocesan Commission of Art (DAI-os-uh-suhn kuh-MISH-uhn uhv ahrt). The *Constitution on the Sacred Liturgy** calls for commissions to be set up for art,* music,* and Liturgy* in each diocese,* to work in close collaboration; hence they might be best fused into one commission. *See also* LITURGICAL COMMISSIONS.

Diocesan Liturgical Commissions, Federation of. *See* FEDERATION OF DIOCESAN LITURGICAL COMMISSIONS.

Diocese (DAI-uh-sis; -sees; -seez). The territorial area governed by a bishop,* who has received the ecclesiastical jurisdiction for it from the Pope.* More accurately it is that group of the People of God entrusted to the bishop who shepherds them together with his pastors. The comprehensive revision of diocesan boundaries and governance called for by Vatican Council II* has not yet been initiated. *See also* ARCHDIOCESE.

Diptychs (DIP-tiks). Two-leveled folders of wood or metal (from the Greek *diptukon:* folder) on which were written the names of living and departed Christians (including Catechumens*) who were to be remembered in the Canon of the Mass.* The names were read aloud by one of the liturgical ministers, but this practice ceased in the West during the 12th century.

Among the living, the minister cited especially the heads of the churches with which the assembly* was in communion. Therefore, to remove a person's name from the diptychs was tantamount to excommunication. Among the dead, the Saints* held a privileged place: originally, "canonization" meant to be named in the "Canon" of the Mass.

In Eucharistic Prayer I* the diptychs subsist under the form of the *Communicantes** and the *Nobis quoque peccatoribus* ("To us sinners also") which give a long list of Saints, and the Intercessions* for the living and the dead.

Direction, Liturgical. *See* ORIENTATION.

Directories. *See* LITURGICAL LAW, SOURCES OF.

Disabled (dis-AY-buhld). The special needs of the blind, the deaf, and the physically disabled are of concern because full participation* of all members of the community is expected in the acts of worship.* Therefore architectural barriers should be removed in existing buildings, making sure of accessibility, particularly for wheelchairs. Whether the physically disabled are aged, with heart conditions, on crutches or braces, or in wheelchairs, provisions should be made that no aisles are blocked and that access doors are large enough to allow wheelchairs to pass through, whether at the entrance, the penitential room,* the sacristry,* etc.

Railings may be necessary. Large-type hymnals may be necessary; Braille materials and sign language* interpreters might be utilized. The disabled should be able to function in liturgical roles, such as reader,* chanter,* etc. To eliminate physical barriers in church buildings, consult *Mainstreaming Handicapped Persons,* from the Diocesan Office of Worship, Buffalo, New York.

For the blind who can read Braille, it is expected that they should be able to have the neces-

sary books that they need in that format. Most of the Bible* has been produced in Braille, so the *Lectionary** readings could be handled by a blind person. Another method might be prerecording the material, so that an individual would be able to hear the liturgical material through an earplug. For the partially sighted, there are more and more books available in large print; religious material is available through the Xavier Society for the Blind, 154 E. 23rd St., New York, NY 10010.

For the profoundly deaf who never learned to speak naturally, since they cannot articulate easily, following the printed word is possible but sometimes not acceptable. For them worship ought to be visible and meaningful through gestures, signs, finger spelling. Those who are severely deaf after learning to speak find reading quite simple in conjunction with a worship program and will follow the order of service readily with printed material. Usually they will also benefit from sign language. In some areas sign language choirs interpret singing. Some of the hard of hearing can use hearing aids, and for them an induction loop system should be installed in part of the church building to enhance clarity of what is sung or said. In certain places a congregation of deaf people will have services specifically prepared for them, usually by priests who have learned sign language and are most understanding of this handicap.

Not only the blind or deaf but those disabled in other ways should be involved in corporate worship insofar as it is physically possible. Movement prayers can be very important for them. They should be esteemed and allowed to perform a variety of liturgical duties, such as leaders of song,* acolytes,* and readers.*

Dismissal (dis-MIS-uhl). During the Concluding Rite,* that formula pronounced by the celebrant* (or deacon*) to dismiss the faithful* at the end of the holy Sacrifice of the Mass. Formerly, it was: *Go, the Mass is ended (Ite, Missa est).* Historically, there was also a dismissal of the catechumens after the Liturgy of the Word.* As the catechumenate* ceased, so did the latter dismissal.

Currently, several variations of the Dismissal are printed in the *Sacramentary,** but adaptations are allowed (see circular Letter of April 27, 1973): "Go in the peace of Christ"; "The Mass is ended, go in peace"; and "Go in peace to love and serve the Lord." The people answer "Thanks be to God" after each one—giving their assent to what has been done and pledging to carry out the Eucharist in their lives.

Christians who have participated in the Sacrifice of their Lord, which was offered for the salvation of all human beings, and offered with the Church which is the Sacrament of salvation for the world, cannot be content with just going back home, satisfied at having accomplished their duty and obeyed the law. Without transforming themselves into professional missionaries or preachers, they must strive to radiate justice and charity around them.

Formerly if the Mass was followed by another liturgical function, the faithful were not dismissed. On such occasions, the priest said simply: "Let us praise the Lord"* (*Benedicamos Domino),* and all answered: "Thanks be to God."* But even this conclusion is omitted if the Mass is celebrated for a funeral and is followed by the "Final Commendation and Farewell," which is a blessing destined for the body of the deceased.

Dispensation (dis-puhn-SAY-shuhn, -pen-). The relaxation of a law in a particular case by the lawgiver or by an authorized person. The Pope* can grant a dispensation from all purely ecclesiastical laws, while bishops,* Religious superiors, and pastors* can dispense only from some purely ecclesiastical laws. Among the latter are disciplinary laws or laws that refer to the good of the faithful* and their pursuit of perfection in their state of life. Thus, bishops can dispense the faithful from attendance at Mass on Holy Days of Obligation,* fulfillment of fast* and abstinence,* reception of the Sacraments,* observance of marriage laws, and accomplishment of work prescribed for gaining indulgences.* No one, however, can dispense from Divine laws.

Distractions (dis-TRAK-shuhnz). The wanderings of the thoughts and imaginations of people at private or public prayer,* leading to inattention. Involuntary distractions, which are practically impossible to avoid completely in our present state, do not invalidate the prayer. Such distractions arise from a variety of sources, and there are many ways in which to remove them.

The Church* has always striven to encourage those who pray the Liturgy of the Hours* or celebrate the Eucharist* or the Sacraments* to do so with full attention, which is worthy of God and benefits the person praying. She urges all to achieve *full, active, and conscious* participation* at liturgical celebrations and to pray the Liturgy of the Hours with hearts cleansed "of any worthless, evil, or distracting thoughts" and "with attention, reverence, and devotion." However, distractions (even voluntary) on the part of those who minister the Sacraments* do not invalidate the Sacraments.

Diurnal (dai-UHRN-uhl). Service book containing all the Hours of the Liturgy of the Hours* except the Office of Readings* (formerly Matins)—hence a "Day Book."

Dives in Misericordia. *See* MERCY OF GOD.

Divine Office. *See* LITURGY OF THE HOURS.

Divine Praises (di-VAIN PRAYZ-uhz). A sequence of acclamations blessing God,* Jesus Christ,* the Holy Spirit,* the Blessed Virgin,* St. Joseph,* and all the Saints.* Most of the acclamations were written by Luigi Felici, S.J., in 1797 to make reparation for profane language and blasphemy. Recent Popes have added acclamations and granted an indulgence* for their recitation. They are usually recited publicly

after Benediction of the Blessed Sacrament.* The acclamations are:

Blessed be God.
Blessed be His holy Name.
Blessed be Jesus Christ, true God and true Man.
Blessed be His most Sacred Heart.
Blessed be His most Precious Blood.
Blessed be Jesus in the most holy Sacrament of the Altar.
Blessed be the Holy Spirit, the Paraclete.
Blessed be the great Mother of God, Mary most holy.
Blessed be her holy and immaculate conception.
Blessed be the name of Mary, Virgin and Mother.
Blessed be St. Joseph, her most chaste spouse.
Blessed be God in His angels and in his Saints.

Divine Worship. *See* WORSHIP.

Divine Worship, Congregation for (and the Discipline of the Sacraments). *See* CONGREGATION FOR DIVINE WORSHIP AND THE DISCIPLINE OF THE SACRAMENTS.

Divino Afflatu (dee-VEE-noh ahf-LAH-too). Latin title ("By Divine wisdom") of Pope St. Pius X's* constitution* of November 1, 1911, which revised the norms for reciting the Divine Office* and celebrating Mass.* It issued new rules for occurrence* and stipulated that more of the Psalter* be used.

Doctor of the Church (DOK-tuhr uhv thuh chuhrch). A title granted by the Church* to an ecclesiastical author or preacher because of outstanding learning, staunch faith, and sanctity of life. There are presently thirty-two Doctors: four great Doctors of the West (Ambrose,* Augustine,* Gregory the Great,* and Jerome*) and four great Doctors of the East (Athanasius,* Basil the Great,* Gregory Nazianzen,* and John Chrysostom*) as well as the

universal Doctor (Thomas Aquinas*).

The other twenty-three are: Albert the Great,* Alphonsus Liguori,* Anselm,* Anthony of Padua,* Bede the Venerable,* Bernard of Clairvaux,* Bonaventure,* Catherine of Siena,* Cyril of Alexandria,* Cyril of Jerusalem,* Ephrem the Syrian,* Francis de Sales,* Hilary of Poitiers,* Isidore of Seville,* John of the Cross,* John Damascene,* Lawrence of Brindisi,* Leo the Great,* Peter Canisius,* Peter Chrysologus,* Peter Damian,* Robert Bellarmine,* and Teresa of Avila.* All have a liturgical celebration assigned them. *(See* individual listings.)

There is a Common of Doctors* both in the *Roman Missal** and in the *Liturgy of the Hours.** The theme of these liturgical formulas is not only the importance of teaching the Faith but also the greater importance of living that Faith.

Dogma (DAWG-muh; DOG-). A truth of Faith,* contained in Revelation* proposed in and by the Church* either by the teaching of the ordinary and universal Magisterium* (Teaching Office) or by the extraordinary Magisterium (definition by the Pope* or a General Council). Each definition of a new dogma is but the formal expression of a teaching already contained in the Faith. Some dogmas like the Assumption* of Mary have been celebrated in the Liturgy* before they were defined by a Pope or a Council, in accord with the liturgical adage *Lex orandi—lex credendi:** the rule of prayer is the rule of Faith.

D.O.M. Abbreviation for the Latin words *Deo Optimo Maximo* (meaning "To God, the best and the greatest"), which indicates the dedication of a church to God.

Domestic Church (duh-MES-tik chuhrch). A title applied to the Christian couple and the Christian family as a result of the universal priesthood* of believers. The family represents and constitutes a miniature Church,* an "element" of the one and universal Church* that is the whole Body of Christ.* It does so (1) by its honest and moral expression, which combines the ineffable and inexhaustible harmonies of two separate beings into one life; (2) by its Sacramental origin, which raises a fragile and violable natural love to the level of an inviolable and ever-new supernatural love; and (3) by its deontology, that is, by the law that governs it and makes the union from which it takes its origin into an exclusive and perennial society reflecting the union of Christ and His Church.

Christ's sacrificial love, which was constitutive of the Church on the Cross, is daily re-presented in the Eucharist* and the Sacraments.* Thus, by participating in the Eucharist and with the grace of the Sacrament of Matrimony* the Christian couple and the Christian family are built up into a "domestic Church," as a manifestation and realization—in their own way—of the great Church of Christ.

The twofold and unitary dynamism that moves the Church, born from the dead and risen Christ, also

inspires the domestic Church: the *liturgical dynamism* that calls the Church to chant the glory* of God and the *apostolic-missionary dynamism* that summons the Church to reveal and communicate the salvation of Christ to all human beings.

The Christian couple and the Christian family—by virtue not only of their Baptism but also of the specification of the Sacrament of Matrimony—have the grace and the responsibility to share with the visible Church their liturgical, cultural, vision. That is, there exists a "domestic priesthood," which empowers and commits the couple and the family to glorify the Lord, to encounter Him in prayer as a couple and family, and in and through the typical realities of conjugal and family existence as a whole.

In this way every home becomes a spiritual temple, and everything that is part of daily life—joys and sorrows, works and hopes, activity and rest, obligations and delusions, births and deaths—is turned into a "spiritual sacrifice" pleasing to God in Jesus through the Holy Spirit (see LG, 11; FC, 49). *See also* FAMILIARIS CONSORTIO.

Domine, Non Sum Dignus. *See* LORD, I AM NOT WORTHY.

Dominic, St. (DOM-i-nik). 1170-1221. A native of Calaruega in Old Castile, Spain, Dominic was a member of the illustrious house of Guzman. He founded the Order of Preachers, propagated devotion to

the Rosary,* and saved the Church from the growing power of the Albigensian heresy. He led an extremely active life, traveling through France, Spain, and Italy, preaching the Gospel,* lecturing on theology, and establishing houses of his Order. He died at Bologna. He is the Patron of Astronomers. *Liturgical celebration:* August 8 (Memorial); *theme:* preaching Christ to others.

Dominica in Albis (doh-MIN-i-kah in AHL-bis). Latin title for the Sunday after Easter* now known as the Second Sunday of Easter. It is short for *"Dominica in albis depositis* or *deponendis"*—"Sunday for laying aside white vestments." This was the last day on which those newly baptized at the Easter Vigil* could wear the white baptismal garment they had worn for the eight days since their Baptism.* This day is also known as Low Sunday in contrast to the "high feast" of Easter Sunday.

Dominicae Cenae (doh-MIN-ee-chay CHAY-nay). Latin title from the first two words ("The Lord's Supper") of the *Letter on the Mystery and Worship of the Eucharist* issued by John Paul II on February 24, 1980, and directed to bishops,* priests,* and deacons.* The document has much to say about the Eucharist* to everyone. Adoration* of Christ in the Sacrament* of Love must find expression not only in the Eucharist but also in various forms of Eucharistic devotion*: personal prayer before the Blessed Sacrament,* hours of adoration, periods of exposition—short, prolonged, and annual (Forty Hours*)—Eucharistic Processions,* and Eucharistic Congresses.*

For the Church "makes the Eucharist," and the "Eucharist builds up" the Church. The authentic sense of the Eucharist becomes of itself the school of active love of neighbor. The Eucharist is the center and goal of the Sacramental style of the Christian life. Indeed, the Church not only acts but also expresses herself in the Liturgy,* lives by the Liturgy, and draws from the Liturgy the strength for her life. This letter led to the Instruction *Inaestimabile Donum.**

Dominical Letter (duh-MIN-i-kuhl LET-uhr). In the General Roman Calendar* used for computing the liturgical seasons,* a letter from *A* to *G* is affixed to the Sundays of a particular year, beginning with *A* assigned to January 1. In this way the calendar reader can know at a glance what will be the day of the week for any date during the year in question. This arrangement was devised to provide a quick listing of Sundays (hence the name dominical) so as to find the date for Easter,* which governs all Sundays that follow.

A leap year has two dominical letters—the change occurring at the end of February (on the 29th in newer liturgical books and on the 25th in others). In 1988, a leap year, the two dominical letters were *C* and *B*. The need for knowing dominical letters is not as acute as it was when people lacked the proliferation of calendars to provide them with the day of the week for any date of the year.

Dominican Rite (duh-MIN-i-kuhn rait). Owing to their scholarly apostolate the Dominicans drew up a special Liturgy in the 13th century. Characterized by simplicity and beauty, it varied somewhat from the other rites used in the Roman Church. The New Order of the Mass abrogated it.

Dominum et Vivificantem (DOM-ee-noom et vee-vee-fee-KAHN-tem). Latin title (from the first two words "Lord and Giver of Life") of the Encyclical *Lord and Giver of Life* issued by Pope John Paul II on May 30, 1986. It points out that in the Liturgy* there is a new coming of Christ by the power of the Holy Spirit* whereby Christ is constantly present and active in the spiritual life. In this Sacramental reality, Christ, Who has gone away in His visible humanity, comes, is present, and acts in the Church* in such an intimate manner as to make the Church His Body.

The most complete Sacramental expression of the "departure" of Christ through the Mystery of the Cross and Resurrection* is the Eucharist.* In every celebration of the Eucharist, His coming, His salvific presence, is Sacramentally realized: in the Sacrifice* and Communion.* Through the Eucharist the Holy Spirit accomplishes that strength of the inner person spoken of in Ephesians (3:16). Through the Eucharist, individuals and communities, by the action of the Paraclete-Counselor, learn to discover the Divine sense of human life as spoken of by the Second Vatican Council*: that sense whereby Jesus fully reveals human beings to themselves.

Dominus Vobiscum. *See* LORD BE WITH YOU, THE.

Doorkeeper (DAWR-kee-puhr). One of the four Minor Orders* that used to be received by candidates for Holy Orders* before 1972 when it was abolished. The doorkeeper's duties consisted in: calling the people to Divine services by ringing the church bells*; opening and closing

the church; admitting the people and excluding the unruly; insuring the maintenance of proper religious behavior; opening the book for the preacher; and maintaining cleanliness. In time these duties became divided among church custodians, sacristans,* and ushers,* and the office became expendable.

Dormition of the Virgin (dor-MISH-uhn uhv thuh VUHR-juhn). A term that comes from the Latin for "sleep" (*dormir)* and refers to Mary's death and Assumption* into heaven. The Liturgy* had a feast of Mary's "rest" on August 15 as early as the 5th century in Jerusalem. In the 6th century the feast of the Dormition of the Virgin was celebrated on August 15 throughout the Eastern Empire. In the 7th century it was adopted by Rome, and its name was changed to the Assumption.*

Double (DUH-buhl). Former liturgical rank of certain feasts. The term may have originated because the anniversary Office* of a Saint* was added as a double to the Office of the day. During the Middle Ages and up to our day, the term was justified by the fact that at the principal Hours* of the Office the antiphons* of the Psalms were doubled, that is, recited in their entirety both before and after the Psalm whereas on semi-double and simple Offices the antiphons were said completely only once—after the Psalm.

The rank of double comprised four degrees: double of the first class, double of the second class, double major, and double minor. All of these disappeared together with the semi-double at the end of the year 1960 when the present scheme of liturgical ranking went into effect: Solemnity,* Feast,* Memorial,* and Optional Memorial.*

Dove (duhv). A symbol of the Holy Spirit* from Apostolic times that is used frequently in the Liturgy.* This symbol arose from the Gospel account of the Baptism of Jesus* wherein the Holy Spirit descended on Him like a dove (Mt 3:16).

The dove is also a symbol of peace.

Doxology (dok-SOL-uh-jee). In general, it is a prayer of praise expressing glory to God, usually honoring the Trinity.* Specifically, it refers to (a) the lesser doxology said at the end of each psalm, *Glory be to the Father* . . .*; (b) the major doxology, *Glory to God,** said before the Opening Prayer* at Mass; (c) the most solemn doxology that concludes the Eucharistic Prayer*; (d) the final stanzas of the hymns* in the Liturgy of the Hours.*

The most important Doxology is, of course, the one that concludes (and summarizes) the Eucharistic Prayer. The Eucharist is a prayer of praise to the Father through Christ. At the Doxology all human beings—the Saints* in heaven, the deceased

in purgatory, and all living persons here and abroad—united by the action of the Holy Spirit* in a special way during this particular Eucharistic Celebration join Jesus in offering glory and honor to God the Father.

One of the Doxologies of the Eastern Rite spells out some of the Divine benefits in some detail: "Give [Your servants] the *power* of the Holy Spirit, the confirmation and increase of *faith,* and the *hope* of eternal life to come, through our Lord. Through Him be glory to You, Father, with the Holy Spirit forever."

At the end, the congregation registers its assent and approval to the whole Eucharistic Prayer with the Great Amen.*

Dry Mass (drai mas). An abbreviated form of Mass,* popular during the Middle Ages, that utilized all the Mass prayers except the Offertory,* Consecration,* and Communion.* It was used when celebration of the Mass was forbidden, for example when a priest who had not broken his fast was unavailable. In pre-Vatican II days the term was appplied to a step-by-step explanation of the Mass with a run-through of all the prayers and actions.

Dulia (doo-LAI-uh). That type of veneration which honors the Saints and angels, because their friend God manifested Himself in them. It is not the same as the worship of adoration given to God alone. *See also* HYPERDULIA; LATRIA.

Duplication d[y]oop-li-KAY-shuhn). The repetition by the celebrant* of Mass texts intended primarily for the whole congregation or the choir.* This duplication was the accidental result of the conversion from sung Mass to recited Mass that began in the 9th century. The Second Vatican Council* decreed that duplications were to be eliminated and that all persons were to perform only those actions that were required of them by the nature of the Liturgy* (see SC, 28). The renewed Liturgy has eliminated all such duplications.

The term can also be used in place of bination.*

Dying, Commendation of the. *See* COMMENDATION OF THE DYING.

— E —

Easter (EES-tuhr). The yearly celebration of the Resurrection* of Christ is the oldest and most solemn Christian feast, considered the center of the Liturgical Year.* It is also called the Pasch* after the Jewish feast commemorating the emancipation of the Jews from their servitude in Egypt. It was in His last celebration of the Passover, on the first Holy Thursday,* that Christ instituted the Eucharist* and the priesthood* of the New Law. The deliverance of the Jews foreshadowed the Christian Pasch, when Christ the Lamb was sacrificed that the human race would be liberated from the bondage of the devil. Thus Easter becomes the Christian Passover.

Other feasts of the Church Year* depend upon the date of Easter, which occurs on the first Sunday following the first full moon after the vernal equinox. Each Sunday in the year is considered a continuation of Easter in the eyes of the Church.* Its name (in Latin: *Dominica)* derives from *Dominus,* which means "Lord," a title that the primitive Church bestowed on Jesus with respect to His Resurrection.

The importance of Easter is emphasized liturgically by the long preparation of Lent,* by the special ceremonies of Holy Week,* and by the Octave that follows, as well as by the whole Easter Season,* which runs until Pentecost Sunday inclusive.

The characteristic of Easter (and the entire season) is the Paschal Candle* and the frequent reiteration of "Alleluia,"* the chant of joy and victory at Christ's redemption. In the words of Augustine, "We are an Easter people and Alleluia is our

song." There is also the Sequence "Victimae Paschali Laudes"* ("To the Paschal Victim"), a short dramatic hymn celebrating Christ's conquest of death composed in the 11th century.

On the Easter Vigil,* we participated in the Paschal Mystery by celebrating the Sacraments of Baptism* and the Eucharist.* In this "second" Mass of Easter we now give thanks to the Father for the new life given us by Christ's Resurrection *on this day.* For "this is the Day the Lord has made; let us rejoice and be glad."

This is the day when Jesus conquered sin and death and manifested Himself to His disciples; when He made Himself known to two disciples on the way to Emmaus in the "breaking of the bread"; when He gave the Holy Spirit* to His Apostles* for the remission of sins and sent them forth to be His witnesses to the world.

Accordingly, in this Easter Liturgy we renew our Baptismal promises. It is through faith* and Baptism* that we now share in His glorious Resurrection till we fully share in it by partaking in His Ascension* into heaven.

Receiving Communion on Easter is required of all, but the obligation is extended from the first Sunday of Lent* to Trinity Sunday in the United States.* *See also* CALENDAR; CHURCH YEAR; CYCLES.

Easter Duty. *See* PASCHAL TIME.

Easter Proclamation. *See* EXSULTET.

Easter Season (EES-tuhr SEE-zuhn). According to the revised liturgical calendar,* the span of time from Easter* to Pentecost.* In addition to the presence of the Paschal Candle, which shines forth until the Ascension* signifying the Risen Christ, the principal characteristic of this Season is the frequent use of "Alleluia,"* the chant of victory. Hence, these fifty days may be seen as an anticipated celebration of the bliss of heaven. We sing Alleluia, but it is only to lighten our burden. We sing but we never stop moving forward on our heavenly journey.

The joy* is also expressed in the Scriptural Readings* and Mass Prayers. The Gospels* are taken from St. John* and focus on the message of Jesus in the light of Easter. The First Readings* are taken from the Acts of the Apostles* and set before us the history of the primitive community with its accent on the joy and fervor of Christians flowing from the knowledge of Christ's Resurrection.*

The Entrance Antiphons* give prominence to a particular aspect of the Paschal Mystery on each day of the week. *Monday:* Christ is risen. *Tuesday:* the triumph of the Risen Lord at the end of times. *Wednesday:* the psalmodic chant of the redeemed. *Thursday:* the new Exodus. *Friday:* salvation in the blood of the Risen Christ. *Saturday:* new life in Jesus.

Before 1969, the Easter Cycle included the preparation time for Easter, from before Lent to Holy Week inclusive. *See also* CALENDAR; CYCLES; LENT.

Easter Time. *See* EASTER SEASON.

Easter Triduum. *See* SACRED TRIDUUM.

Easter Vigil (EES-tuhr VI-juhl). The celebration of the Paschal Mystery* of Christ restored now on the night of Holy Saturday.* The ceremonies relate to the Resurrection* of the Lord and the Sacraments* of Initiation. It is definitely a celebration to be observed at night, not to begin before nightfall and to end before daybreak on Sunday. Even if the Vigil Mass would occur before midnight, the Mass of the Resurrection, part 4, is celebrated.

1. The Service of Light

No lights are on in the church;* a fire is prepared outside the church or, if not possible, inside the vestibule.* After greeting the congregation the priest* blesses the new fire, symbolic of Christ's Resurrection, coming forth from the tomb and giving light to the world. On the Paschal Candle* the priest traces a cross and the numerals of the current year. Finally the priest lights the candle from the new fire and the deacon* or, if there is no deacon, the priest lifts the Paschal Candle and sings *Christ our Light.*

After walking halfway into the church, he sings the same acclamation, after which the people light their candles from the Easter Candle. Upon arriving at the altar, the acclamation is sung for a third time

and the lights in the church are put on. Immediately thereafter follows the *Exsultet,** the Easter Proclamation, sung while all stand and hold lighted candles. It honors the night on which Christ redeemed us.

2. Liturgy of the Word

For this vigil, seven readings* are provided from the Old Testament* and two from the New.* Should pastoral reasons dictate, the number may be limited to three from the Old Testament, and for serious reasons, only two. The reading from Exodus 14 is always used. The readings deal with creation, Abraham's* sacrifice, the passage through the Red Sea, the new Jerusalem,* salvation offered to all, the fountain of wisdom, and a new heart and a new spirit. The people sing the responses and answer *Amen** after each prayer. The celebration continues with the Glory to God,* the Opening Prayer,* the Epistle,* the Alleluia,* the Gospel,* and the Homily.*

3. Liturgy of Baptism

Usually candidates to be baptized are called forward at this time as the ministers go to the baptismal font.* The blessing of the font occurs even if there are no candidates to be baptized. In that case the Litany that would follow is omitted. The Litany may be sung during the procession to the baptistery,* in which the Paschal Candle is carried first, followed by the candidates with their godparents* and the priest with the ministers. At the baptistery, or if the baptistery could not be seen by the congregation, in the sanctuary,* the priest blesses the baptismal water. The candidates then renounce the devil individually and are baptized, the adults usually being confirmed at that time also.

When this rite is completed, or if there were no baptisms, immediately after the blessing of the water, all present stand with lighted candles and renew their baptismal profession of faith. The priest then sprinkles the people with the blessed water, sometimes called Easter Water, which is subsequently placed in the baptismal font. It is highly valued by the faithful as a Sacramental.* The usual Profession of Faith* is omitted and the General Intercessions* follow immediately.

4. Liturgy of the Eucharist

The conclusion of the ceremony is the resumption of the Mass with the Preparation of the Gifts,* which are brought forward by the newly baptized. The rest of the Mass continues as usual, but with the addition of two Alleluias* following the Dismissal.*

Eastern Rite (EES-tuhrn rait). In the early Christian era the political division of the Roman Empire brought about the dissimilarity between Eastern and Western Christianity. The West was centered in Rome and drew up its Liturgy* from the Roman Rite.* In the East Christianity focused on Alexandria in Egypt and on Antioch in Syria. From these sources came the various Eastern liturgical families. The Eastern Rite then refers to liturgical

families of the East who remained Catholic or Uniate, that is, in communion with Rome, unlike the Orthodox Christians.

The Antiochene* type showed heavy Greek influence on Christianity and through the centuries various other rites developed from it. The Alexandrian* type was more conservative and similar to the Roman Rite and adopted a Coptic vernacular. A derivation of this, called the Ethiopian Rite, resembles American Negro Spirituals. *See also* BYZANTINE RITE; ROMAN RITE.

Ecce Lignum Crucis (EK-chay-LEEN-yoom KROO-chees). First three words in Latin (meaning "Behold the wood of the Cross") of the versicle chanted three times during the unveiling of a large crucifix* on Good Friday* for the Veneration of the Cross.* The versicle is now chanted in the vernacular and reads: "This is the wood of the Cross, on which hung the Savior of the world." The people respond: "Come, let us worship." The rite thus renders worship to Christ Crucified on the liturgical anniversary of His Death.

Ecclesiastes, The Book of (ik-lee-zee-AS-teez, e-klee-, thuh buk uhv). Twenty-fifth Book of the Old Testament* and Fourth Sapiential Book whose title is the Greek translation of the Hebrew name *Qoheleth* meaning, perhaps, "one who convokes an assembly" or the "Preacher." Written about the 3rd

century B.C. by an unknown sage, this Book examines a wide range of human experience only to conclude that all things are vanity except the fear of the Lord and observance of His commandments and that God requites human beings in His own good time.

Liturgical use: In the *Roman Missal,** this Book is read on the 18th Sunday in Ordinary Time* (C) and on the Thursday, Friday, and Saturday of the 25th Week in Ordinary Time (Year II). In the *Liturgy of the Hours,** it is read during the Seventh Week in Ordinary Time. *Meaning:* The author's vain search for success and happiness on earth finds its solution in our Lord's assurance of these things to His followers not in this world but in the bliss of heaven. By stressing the fleeting character of purely earthly pleasures, wisdom, and happiness, Ecclesiastes teaches us to find our happiness only in God and to put our whole trust in Him alone.

Ecclesiasticus, The Book of. *See* SIRACH, THE BOOK OF.

Economy, Divine (ee-KON-uh-mee, duh-VAIN). The plan of salvation decreed by God,* accomplished and revealed in the total unfolding of history by Christ, Who is the center and the culmination of the Divine economy (Eph 1:3-14). The Liturgy* participates in this economy by making present for all time the Mysteries of the Redemption* so that the faithful* are enabled to lay hold of the Lord's power and merits and become filled with grace.* *See also* HISTORY OF SALVATION.

Ecumenical Movement. *See* MOVEMENT, ECUMENICAL.

Ecumenical Worship. *See* ATTENDING NON-CATHOLIC SERVICES.

Editio Typica. *See* TYPICAL EDITION.

Education and Liturgy. *See* CATECHESIS AND LITURGY; LITURGICAL FORMATION.

Eighteen Blessings, The (AY[T]-teen BLES-ingz, thee). In Hebrew *Shemoneh cEsreh* (eighteen); also called *Tephillah* ("Prayer") or *Amidah* ("standing"). A Jewish formulary for weekday prayer dating to 200 B.C. It is composed for the most part of Biblical phrases. The first three and the last three are used also on Sabbaths, festivals, and the Day of Atonement whereas the middle twelve are replaced by other prayers. Many regard this prayer as having influenced early Christian communal prayer and the Divine Office.*

Ejaculations. *See* INVOCATIONS.

Elect (i-LEKT). A catechumen* judged by the community or its representatives as worthy to move to the second stage of Christian Initiation, namely, the period of purification,* normally falling during Lent.*

Elect, Book of the (i-LEKT, buk uhv thee). Artistically designed, elegantly bound, and beautifully illustrated book in which the names of the candidates are inscribed during the Enrollment* in the Rite of Christian Initiation of Adults. *See also* RITE OF CHRISTIAN INITIATION OF ADULTS.

Election (i-LEK-shuhn). The beginning of the second stage of initiation, whereby the catechumens* deemed worthy and ready to take part in the next celebration of the Sacraments* of Initiation are chosen. Usually on the first Sunday of Lent* the bishop* or his delegate confirms the process of selection by the parish.* Just as God chose certain people for specific missions, so the Church acting in the name of God elects these persons.

Elevation (el-uh-VAY-shuhn). After the Consecration* during the Eucharistic Sacrifice, the priest* holds up the Host* for the adoration of the faithful.* This practice probably developed through the popular desire to view the consecrated Host as the Real Presence. A couple of centuries later elevating the chalice after Consecration added symmetry. The bell may be rung before Consecration, and at each elevation.

The purpose of the elevation of the Sacred Host and Chalice is both to symbolize their offering to the Father and to exhibit them for adoration. As such, the elevations provide the members of the assembly* with a few precious moments for expressing heartfelt sentiments of love and adoration for the Risen Lord and Savior and for preparing to proclaim the Mystery of Faith* and acclaim the Risen Jesus publicly in unison at the Memorial Acclamation.*

It is customary to say silently the invocation "My Lord and my God" at the elevation of the Host and "My Jesus, mercy" at the elevation of the Chalice.

Elevation, Little (el-uh-VAY-shuhn, LIT-uhl). Immediately before the Lord's Prayer,* both the Bread* and the Wine* are raised slightly by the priest while he sings or says the Doxology.*

Elizabeth Ann Seton, St. (i-LIZ-uh-buhth an SEE-tuhn). 1774-1821. A Protestant mother of five children, Elizabeth learned of Catholicism in Italy after her husband's death. She was received into the Church in 1805 and by 1809 she started a small group of Sisters of St. Joseph for the education of children in Baltimore. By 1812, this group became the first American Foundation of the Daughters of Charity of St. Vincent de Paul.* Mother Seton became the Superior and kept that position until her death. Besides schools, she opened the first Catholic orphanage in the United States in Philadelphia and made arrangements for the first Catholic hospital in Baltimore. Beatified in 1963, she was canonized in 1975, the first American-born saint, and her feast is part of the Proper* for the United States. *Liturgical celebration:* January 4 (Memorial); *theme:* dedicated service to education and the underprivileged.

Elizabeth of Hungary, St. (i-LIZ-uh-buhth uhv HUHN-guh-ree). 1207-1231. Daughter of King Andrew of Hungary, Elizabeth was married to Louis the Landgrave of Thuringia at the age of fourteen and bore him three children. She devoted herself to prayer and meditation. After her husband's untimely death in 1227, she made arrangements for her children and joined the Third Order of St. Francis.* She spent herself in heroic works of charity and died at the young age of twenty-four. She is the Patroness of Bakers, Franciscan Tertiaries, and Nursing and Nursing Services. *Liturgical celebration:* November 17 (Memorial); *theme:* serving Christ in the poor and the sick.

Elizabeth of Portugal, St. (i-LIZ-uh-buhth uhv POR-chi-guhl). 1271-1336. Daughter of King Peter II of Aragon, and grandniece of St. Elizabeth of Hungary,* Elizabeth was given in marriage to Dionysius I of Portugal and bore him two children. She bravely endured trials and afflictions through prayer and works of charity. When her husband died, she took the habit of the Third Order of St. Francis* and retired to a convent of Poor Clares. After ending a serious dispute between her son and son-in-law, she died in peace. *Liturgical celebration:* July 4 (Opt. Mem.); *theme:* working for true peace among peoples.

Ember Days. *See* DAYS OF PRAYER.

Embolism (EM-buh-liz-uhm). The sequel to the Lord's Prayer* inserted before the Breaking of the Bread* in the Canon of the Mass.* Besides continuing the petition to liberate us from evil arising from sin, it makes an appeal for peace.

Enchiridion of Indulgences (en-ki-RID-ee-uhn uhv in-DUHL-juhn(t)s-uhz). A handbook of indulgences,* listing the prayers and other good works to which indulgences are attached and containing the official Church teaching about indulgences. It was published in Latin as *En-*

chiridion Indulgentiarum in 1968, and an authorized English edition appeared in 1969, edited by Rev. William Barry, C.SS.R. *See also* INDULGENCES.

Encyclicals (in-SIK-li-kuhlz; en-). Taken from the Greek word for "circular," encyclicals are documents addressed by the Pope* to the bishops* of the Church or the general faithful* (sometimes even to all persons of goodwill) to set forth his thoughts about current social and religious topics. They are divided into *encyclical letters* (which may be termed pastoral letters written to the Universal Church*) and *encyclical epistles* (which are more solemn in form and written to only part of the Church).

Encyclicals have been used as vehicles for liturgical teaching and legislation, although they are not legislative in the sense that they modify existing liturgical laws. The most famous *encyclical letter* is Pius XII's *Mediator Dei** (1949), a full-scale treatment of the Liturgy.* The most recent is Paul VI's *Mysterium Fidei** (1965), concerning the doctrine and worship of the Holy Eucharist.* An *encyclical epistle* on the Liturgy is Paul VI's *Mense Maio** concerning prayers to be offered in honor of Mary* during the month of May. *See also* LITURGICAL LAW, SOURCES OF.

Ends of the Mass. *See* MASS.

Engagement (in-GAYJ-muhnt). An expression of commitment to each other by a couple who promise to marry. If a formal contract is signed by the couple and the pastor, bishop,* or witnesses, it is considered a solemn engagement, but not binding in conscience. A format for the ceremony has been developed, but no official rite for engagement exists as yet. Premarital chastity must be kept by the engaged couples. *See also* BETROTHAL.

Enlightenment (en-LAIT-n-muhnt; in-). That period when the elect,* in the final stage of preparation for celebrating the Rite of Initiation,* become involved in a concentrated preparation of the mind, more from a spiritual than catechetical point of view since their minds and hearts are purified through repentance and a profound knowledge of their Savior, Jesus Christ. Various rites help in this intense preparation, particularly the Scrutinies* and the Presentation.*

Enrollment (en-ROHL-muhnt). The inscription of their names in the Book of the Elect* by those candidates elected to take part in the next celebration of the Sacraments of Initiation.* This pledge of their fidelity occurs at the stage of Enlightenment.*

Enthronement (in-THROHN-muhnt). (1) A ceremony during the episcopal ordination. (*See also* INSTALLATION.)

(2) A religious ceremony in which a picture or statue of the Sacred Heart* is formally installed in a home or institution through an act of consecration led by a priest.* It is social and official acknowledgment that the Heart of Jesus reigns over the Christian family.

Entrance Antiphon (EN-truhn[t]s AN-tuh-fuhn, -fahn). From the 6th to the 16th century the entrance song or Introit* consisted of a Psalm* that began and concluded with a short antiphon* whose text was taken from the Psalm itself, from the Epistle* of the day, or even from some non-Biblical source. In the *Missal* of Pius V (1570 to Vatican

II*), the Introit was reduced to the antiphon, one psalm-verse, the "Glory Be,"* and the repetition of the antiphon. In the post-Vatican II *Roman Missal** the text has been further reduced to the antiphon alone.

If there is no singing at the entrance, the Antiphon is recited either by the people, by some of them, or by a reader.* Otherwise it is said by the priest* after the Greeting.*

If there is singing, one may use: (1) the Entrance Antiphon and Psalm of the *Roman Gradual**; (2) the Entrance Antiphon and Psalm of the *Simple Gradual**; (3) songs from other approved collections of psalms and antiphons; (4) other sacred songs chosen in accord with the season or feast.*

The purpose of this "people's part" is to open the celebration, deepen the unity of the people, introduce them to the Mystery* of the season or feast, and accompany the procession.*

Entrance Procession (EN-truhn[t]s pruh-SESH-uhn). The first of five processions* that take place at Mass.* Before the celebration* begins the people of the Assembly* stand and process in spirit with those who are the actors in the drama of the Mass—priest-celebrant,* ministers,* lectors,* extraordinary ministers.* At the same time, they acclaim Jesus (in the person of the celebrant) Who comes to

reenact and re-present His saving Sacrifice* and to invite them to partake of His Sacrificial Meal—to become one in Him.

Entrance Rite. *See* INTRODUCTORY RITES.

Entrance Song (EN-truhn[t]s song). To open the celebration of the Mass,* it is fitting that the people assembled sing together as the celebrant* and ministers* walk to the altar.* Besides deepening the unity among the congregation, the song should introduce them to the feast* or the Mystery* of the season. Usually it is sung alternately by the choir* and the people, or by the chanter* and the people, or it is sung entirely by the choir alone or by the people. Since very little music exists so far in the vernacular for the Antiphon and Psalm of the *Roman Gradual,* usually another song that fits the season or the Mass is chosen, as long as it has approval of the Conference of Bishops.* In case there is no singing, the Entrance Antiphon* in the *Sacramentary** is recited either by the people or by a reader* as the priest enters. Otherwise, after the Greeting,* the priest says it.

Environment. *See* ARCHITECTURAL ENVIRONMENT.

Ephemerides Liturgicae (ef-e-MER-ee-dez li-TOOR-jee-chay). A bimonthly liturgical periodical published by Edizioni Liturgiche at Rome. It has appeared since 1887 and is regarded as one of the liturgical organs that can safely be followed on questions of liturgical practice. *See also* LITURGICAL LAW, SOURCES OF.

Ephesians, Epistle to the (i-FEE-shuhnz, i-PIS-uhl too thee). Fifty-sixth Book of the Bible* and tenth of the New Testament.* One of the "Captivity Epistles" probably written during Paul's first Roman imprisonment, 61-63 A.D. Very similar in theme and language to the Epistle to the Colossians,* but much more abstract, profound, and systematic, this Epistle's central thought is the Church regarded as the Mystical Body of Christ.* Through this Body, God pours out the Divine life of grace* in most generous fashion to its members, the Christians, in and through its head, Jesus Christ. The basic principle of the life of this Body is the spiritual, organic unity of its members with Christ and one another.

Liturgical use: In the *Roman Missal,** extensive use is made of this short Epistle—more than 60 readings are used throughout the year, including the 4th Sunday of Lent* (A, B), 15th, 16th, 17th, 18th, 19th, 20th, and 21st Sundays (B), 2nd Sunday after Christmas,* Epiphany,* Ascension,* Sacred Heart* (B), and Immaculate Conception*; it is also read during the 28th, 29th, and 30th Weeks (Year II). In the *Liturgy of the Hours,** it is used only sparingly (seven times) for the Holy Family,* Ascension, Assumption, and a few Saints as well as the Common* of Holy Men and Women. It also gives rise to a minor canticle* in the Psalter.* *Meaning:* Christians are exhorted to lead the new life that befits those incorporated into the sublime unity of the Mystical Body of Christ, consisting of Christ as Head and those who belong to the Church as His members.

Ephphetha Rite (EF-fuh-thah rait). The rite, at the end of the Enlightenment.* In immediate preparation for the Sacraments of Initiation,* it usually takes place on Holy Saturday.* Resembling the cure of the

deaf mute in Mark 7, this action symbolizes the need of grace for all to hear the Word of God and work toward salvation. Touching each of the elect* on the right and left ear and on the closed mouth with his thumb, the celebrant says "Ephphetha: that is, be opened, that you may profess the Faith you hear, to the praise and glory of God." *See also* RITE OF CHRISTIAN INITIATION OF ADULTS.

Ephrem, St. (EE-fruhm). 306-373. Born of a Christian family at Nisibis in Mesopotamia, Ephrem lived as a hermit and was later ordained a deacon* of Edessa. He founded a theological school and wrote many books in defense of the Catholic Church, about the various Mysteries* of our Lord, and in honor of the Blessed Virgin. His skills as an orator, exegete, and poet earned for him the name of the "Lyre of the Holy Spirit" and the title of Doctor of the Church.* *Liturgical celebration:* June 9 (Opt. Mem.); *theme:* singing the praises of God's Mysteries.

Epiclesis (ep-i-KLAY-sis). Generally, calling upon God's name during any blessing* or consecration*; specifically, that invocation during the Eucharistic Prayers* in which the Church begs that the gifts of human beings, which are to be consecrated, may truly become the Body and Blood of Christ, and then when they are received in Communion* that salvation may come to all who share them. This invocation of the power of God usually asks that the Holy Spirit* be sent during the Eucharistic Sacrifice to change the gifts into the Body and Blood of Christ.

The *General Instruction of the Roman Missal* indicates that the epiclesis is part of the consecratory prayers but also includes the section after the Consecration* (Offering*) that implores that those who receive the Eucharist* share in the fruits of salvation. Thus the former argumentation as to whether Consecration consisted of the words of institution exclusively or of the Epiclesis alone is set aside. *See also* CONSECRATION.

Epiphany (i-PIF-uh-nee). A sign of Divine power. The solemnity in the Christmas* cycle, originating in the East, where its dominant theme was the Baptism of Jesus but had subsidiary themes of the Birth of Christ, the Adoration of the Magi (Wise Men or Kings), and the Miracle at Cana. Later, as it was accepted in the West, the manifestation to the Magi became its central theme. At the same time the East began to accept the feast of Christmas.*

Celebrated on January 6, Epiphany might have been modeled after a pagan festival of the New Year and the winter solstice, which fell on that date. In its fullest meaning this solemnity commemorates the

coming of the Word into the world and His revelation to the nations.

In the mid-fifties when the octave* and vigil* of Epiphany were abolished, the former octave day became the feast of the Baptism of the Lord.* However the new calendar in 1969 moved His baptism to the first Sunday after Epiphany. Since the Epiphany is not observed as a Holy Day of Obligation* in some countries, for instance the United States, it is transferred to the Sunday after the Octave Day of Christmas, the Solemnity of Mary, Mother of God.* In that case, the feast of the Baptism falls on the following Sunday. Should the Epiphany occur on the seventh or eighth of January, so that the feast of the Baptism would coincide with it, the latter is transferred to the following Monday.

Episcopacy (i-PIS-kuh-puh-see). The office of the bishops,* whereby they have ordinary power of government over their dioceses.* It may refer to their period of tenure. Also, it designates a group of bishops in a church or a geographical region. By virtue of the Episcopacy, bishops are autonomous pastors of their faithful, not merely representatives of the Pope.* Their power is restricted to a specified segment of the Church. *See also* BISHOP.

Episcopal Conference. *See* NATIONAL CONFERENCE OF CATHOLIC BISHOPS.

Episcopal Ordination. *See* BISHOP, EPISCOPAL ORDINATION OF.

Epistle (i-PIS-uhl). (1) *Scriptural.* The literary form of a New Testament* writing that presents a doctrine, a public declaration. Written or authorized by an Apostle,* it was ordinarily an official communication of an instructive or corrective nature to one of the churches or perhaps a group of them. This term is in contradistinction to a *letter,* which addresses a special situation dealing with it in a concrete and personal fashion.

(2) *Liturgical.* Before the current *Lectionary** the term usually referred to the reading that followed the Opening Prayer.* In most cases this was taken from what was then considered an Epistle of the New Testament. In the current *Lectionary,** the term Reading* is used instead. Ordinarily in the Sunday cycles, Reading II would be from the Epistles. In the weekday cycles, some of the selections for Reading I are from the Old Testament* and some from the New Testament from these same Epistles or letters. The term Epistle is used in the *Lectionary* on the Easter Vigil* for the choice of the Reading after the Seven Readings from the Old Testament. *See also* READINGS.

Epistulary. *See* LECTIONARY.

Eschatology. *See* LITURGY AND ESCHATOLOGY.

Espousal. *See* BETROTHAL.

Espousals of the Blessed Virgin Mary (is-POW-suhlz; -suhls; uhv thuh BLES-uhd VUHR-juhn MAYR-ee). Feast of Mary that seems to have arisen from popular devotion in the 15th century. By the espousals among the Jews a legal marriage is contracted, and Mary and Joseph became true husband and wife. Pope Leo X permitted the celebration of this feast to the Nuns of the Annunciation in 1517, but it has remained a local feast, never becoming part of the Universal Calendar.* *Liturgical celebration:* January 23; *theme:* marriage of Mary and Joseph and sanctity of married love.

Esther, The Book of (ES-tuhr, thuh buk uhv). Nineteenth Book of the Old Testament* and eleventh of the Historical Books. Written between the 4th and the 2nd centuries B.C., this Book tells the story of a Jewish heroine named Esther. By her courage and love for God and her people, she saves them from being exterminated from the Persian Empire. In this way, the unknown sacred author explains the origin, meaning, and date of the Feast of Purim. He also consoles the Israelites by reminding them that God's providence continually watches over them and never abandons them when they serve Him faithfully or turn to Him in time of trial.

Liturgical use: In the *Roman Missal,** this Book is used only on Thursday of the 1st Week of Lent,* the Common* for Holy Men and Women, and the special Masses for Persecuted Christians and for Any Need. In the *Liturgy of the Hours,** much of the Book is read—during the 29th Week in Ordinary Time.* *Meaning:* This Book brings before us the heroic actions of a devout lover of God and His law. It upholds the traditional spiritual practices of prayer,* fasting,* and chastity, and calls for absolute trust in God, in the face of any danger. Fidelity to His commandments* and His teaching combined with this hope will insure our salvation.*

Et Cum Spiritu Tuo. *See* LORD BE WITH YOU, THE.

Eternal Life (i-TUHRN-uhl laif). Life of endless duration in and with God. God is the source of Life—both natural and supernatural (Responsorial Psalm* for Thursday of 16th Ordinary Week, Year II). Creatures have received a participation in this life: "You are the living God; you have called us to share in your life, and to be happy with you for ever" (Eucharistic Prayer for Masses with Children III*).

In a certain sense, eternal life remains in the future for Christians and will be given them after death (Prayer after Communion* for Queenship of Mary*). But in Jesus Christians live even now their eternal life (Epistle* for Easter Vigil*). "By his birth we are reborn. In his suffering we are freed from sin. By his rising from the dead we receive everlasting life. In his return to you in glory we enter into your heavenly kingdom" (Preface of Sundays in Ordinary Time* IV).

The lives of believers are hidden with Christ in God (Reading II for Easter*: Col 3), in the living God whose temples they are (2 Cor 6:16). Thus they participate in the nature of God (Reading I for Monday of 9th Ordinary Week, Year II) and in a life previously foreign to them. Indeed, they possess a "fullness of life": "You never cease to call us to a new and more abundant life" (Eucharistic Prayer for Masses of Reconciliation I*). And this eternal life consists in the knowledge of the Father and the Son Whom He has sent (Gospel of 7th Sunday of Easter, A).

The Liturgy* is one of the most powerful means for Christians to obtain this life of grace.*

Eucharist (YOO-kuh-rist). This Greek word for thanksgiving is a technical term for the Mass,* since during its institution at the Last Supper* Jesus gave thanks and thus He, in sacrificing His life, offered the supreme act of Christian gratitude to God. In perpetuating the Sacrifice of the Cross, He left us a Sacrament of love, a bond of charity, a sign of unity. Hence the Eucharist is both a Sacrament* and a Sacrifice.* We have the symbolic action by which Christ's unique sacrifice on Calvary becomes visibly present and operative together with the abiding Real Presence* of Christ as a result.

Sacrifice

At the Last Supper in a sacrifice of expiation Jesus offered Himself to the Father at a religious meal, before giving Himself as food and drink to the Apostles.* In this way He instituted a rite of sacrifice that would be accomplished once on the altar of the Cross,* yet He continues to communicate the graces merited for us on Calvary. Full participation* in the Eucharist occurs only when the faithful* are refreshed by receiving Communion* as their spiritual food.

Communion

The Eucharistic Liturgy reaches its fulfillment only when the faithful recognize that it is to be considered a community meal, in which they as participants know that the risen

Lord will be in their midst. This gathering of Christian fellowship is for the very specific purpose of uniting with each other in the consecrated Cup and Bread. Hence Christ, with the Spirit, gives life to the recipients uniting them with Him and the other members of His Mystical Body* in a fellowship of love.

Sacrament

Besides the Sacrifice and Communion mentioned above, one result of the immolation of Christ as victim is the teaching that Christ is truly, substantially, really present under the species of Bread and Wine. Therefore, Christ is totally present as long as any Sacramental sign of the transubstantiated Bread and Wine persists.

Outside of the Sacrifice itself, the Eucharist is preserved in order to be available for the administration of Viaticum.* Secondarily then it is available for distribution of Communion outside of Mass, and to allow adoration of the Lord's presence in the Eucharist reserved in the tabernacle,* or as exposed in a monstrance,* for instance, during Benediction* and Forty Hours' Devotion.* *See also* AGAPE; BANQUET; BERAKAH; COMMUNION; CONSECRATION; MASS; MIRAE CARITATIS; TRANSUBSTANTIATION.

Eucharistic Adoration. *See* ADORATION, EUCHARISTIC.

Eucharistic Celebration. *See* CELEBRATION.

Eucharistic Congress (yoo-kuh-RIS-tic KONG-gruhs). A meeting of members of the Church* from every walk of life to profess some aspect of the Eucharistic Mystery and publicly show their devotion to it in unity and charity. The first such local congress occurred in France

in 1874. By 1881 the first international congress was organized, also in France. Such congresses may be local, regional, national, or international. Internationally they have been held in every continent, the recent ones attended by the then reigning Pope.*

These well organized assemblies are prepared for by a thorough catechesis on the Eucharist* suitable for various groups; a full active participation* in the Liturgy* to build brotherhood and community; research and presentations on topics of concern to contemporary society as they work toward the future of God's Kingdom.*

During the celebration, meetings and conferences investigate the theme and propose practical solutions; opportunities for common prayers and adoration of the Blessed Sacrament* occur; in accordance with the social, local, and religious conditions, Eucharistic processions* take place; the true center and acme of the congress will be the celebration of the Eucharist.*

Eucharistic Devotions (yoo-kuh-RIS-tic di-VOH-shuhnz). Private and public devotions* in honor of the Blessed Sacrament* that are approved and encouraged by the Church.* They originated from the practice of Eucharistic Reservation,* which became customary in order to permit the reception of Communion* on the part of the sick and eventually led to the practice of adoring the Blessed Sacrament and offering it the worship* due to God. Some of these devotions are: Visits to the Blessed Sacrament, the Nine First Fridays,* the Holy Hour,* Benediction,* Eucharistic Processions,* and Nocturnal Adoration.*

The Church highly recommends these devotions since the Eucharistic Sacrifice* is the source and summit of the whole Christian life. She stipulates, however, that "when the faithful* adore Christ present in the Sacrament,* they should remember that this presence derives from the Sacrifice and is directed toward both Sacramental Communion and spiritual Communion*" (EM, 50). Eucharistic devotions constitute a subjective prolongation of Mass and a beginning of one's next Communion. *See also* ADORATION, EUCHARISTIC; BENEDICTION; FIRST FRIDAY DEVOTIONS; HOLY HOUR; RESERVATION OF THE EUCHARIST.

Eucharistic Dove. *See* TABERNACLE.

Eucharistic Elements (yoo-kuh-RIS-tic EL-uh-muhnts). The visible matter of the Sacrament,* bread and wine, which by the words of consecration are changed into the Body and Blood of Christ. The fresh bread used is of wheat—in the Roman Rite, unleavened; in the Eastern Rite, leavened. The wine is to be fermented from the juice of grapes with no additives. The external appearances of the elements remain after the Consecration,* yet they are the Sacramental sign of the Body and Blood of Christ replacing the reality of the bread and wine. The whole and entire reality of Christ is present under the appearance of these elements, and so they become spiritual food, not natural food. Should the elements decompose, the Eucharistic Presence of Christ would cease to exist.

Eucharistic Fast. *See* FAST, EUCHARISTIC.

Eucharistic Heart of Jesus (yoo-kuh-RIS-tic hahrt uhv JEE-zuhs). A feast observed in some places on Thursday after Corpus Christi.* It was instituted by Pope Benedict XV and is intended to commemorate Christ's love for humankind as indicated by the Eucharist* and to help those who participate in it to foster within themselves a similar love through frequent reception of Communion.* For the reception of the Eucharist brings Christians into Sacramental*

contact with the Sacred Heart, since that Heart is an integral element of Our Lord's humanity totally present in the Sacrament of the Altar.* *See also* ENTHRONEMENT; SACRED HEART, CULT OF.

Eucharistic Hymns of St. Thomas (yoo-kuh-RIS-tik himz uhv saynt Tom-uhs). Over the centuries many hymns have been composed in honor of the Blessed Sacrament.* The most famous are the five written by St. Thomas Aquinas* at the specific request of Pope Urban IV for the new Feast of Corpus Christi* (1264). They have been set to music and become classics of music as well as poetry: *Adoro Te Devote,* Lauda Sion,* Pange Lingua** (whose last two stanzas are known as the *Tantum Ergo*), Sacris Sollemnis** (whose last two stanzas are known as the *Panis Angelicus*),* and *Verbum Supernum** (whose last two stanzas are known as the *O Salutaris*).*

The contents of these five hymns, which are at once simple and sublime, graphic and sober, have been termed a complete doctrine of the Blessed Sacrament.

Eucharistic Ministers. *See* EXTRAORDINARY MINISTERS OF HOLY COMMUNION.

Eucharistic Prayer (yoo-kuh-RIS-tic prayr). In the Liturgy of the Eucharist,* the Eucharistic Prayer is the section that used to be called the Canon* of the Mass; it corresponds to the Anaphora* of the Eastern rites. It begins with a Preface* and concludes with the Doxology.*

Among the revisions proposed for the Mass during Vatican Council II,* extra Eucharistic Prayers were adopted to supplement the one Canon prayed in the Roman Rite.* At first three such prayers were chosen for pastoral reasons. Even a perfect prayer would fall short of expressing the fullness of the totality of the Mass, which is a sacrifice, a banquet, a song of praise, and basically a prayer of thanksgiving. Furthermore, alternatives circumvent any monotony that may occur from constant repetition, particularly in the vernacular.*

The format of the new prayers allows the faithful* to respond more frequently to the priest* during the celebration of the Mystery* of salvation. The newer Eucharistic Prayers have a more unified presentation

since they were not subject to additions in past centuries as was the Roman Canon, they are more instructive as to salvation history, and they exhibit a more inclusive role for the Holy Spirit* in the act of Transubstantiation* and of bringing together into one body those who will receive Communion.*

Naturally the character and style of each Eucharistic Prayer is distinctive because of its origin; yet throughout, the same structural pattern occurs. After an *Introductory Dialogue** between the people and the priest, the *Preface** occurs. Such a variety of Prefaces exists that the priest may give thanks and praise to the Lord for our salvation according to the spirit of the time or feast. In the *Acclamation** the people and celebrant sing or recite the *Holy, Holy, Holy.** In the *Epiclesis** all pray that the offerings through God's power and the Holy Spirit may be transformed into the Body and Blood of Christ. Then follows the *Consecration** or *Institution Narrative,** using the words of the Last Supper.

Thereafter the people are asked to proclaim the Mystery of Faith* in one of several brief *Memorial Acclamations.** The *Anamnesis** that follows commemorates the Lord's Passion,* Resurrection,* and Ascension.* After this, the *Epiclesis* is a petition that the communicants will be able to join more fully in this Mystery of the Death and Resurrection of Jesus and thus be united more closely to each other. Through the *Intercessions** both living and dead members of the Church are prayed for as the Sacrifice is being offered. The Eucharistic Prayer concludes with the *Doxology,** a prayer of adoration* to the Trinity, responded to by the congregation with a final Amen.*

Deacons* and the laity* should not say the prayers, especially the Eucharistic Prayers,* or perform actions proper to the priest who is presiding at the Eucharist* (Canon 907). They are expected to answer the Introductory Dialogue and join in with the Acclamations, as mentioned above.

The former Roman Canon is called the first Eucharistic Prayer. The second one is derived from Hippolytus.* Simple and brief it is suitable for children, small groups, and ordinary weekdays. The third, somewhat longer and more rich, emphasizes the idea of sacrifice. Appropriate for Sundays, it becomes an alternative for the first Eucharistic Prayer. The fourth Eucharistic Prayer, the longest, is patterned after the Eastern rites, giving an idea of the Divine plan for salvation; for congregations with a good grasp of Scripture.

In 1980, after an interim trial period from 1975, five more Eucharistic Prayers were approved indefinitely: three for Children's Liturgies and two for Masses of Reconciliation. Both categories contain aspects proper to the purpose for which they were composed. Those for children have an entirely new feature—the insertion of Acclamations for the assembly* throughout the whole prayer. This helps keep the children's attention on what is being done and gives the prayer almost a dialogue form.

More Eucharistic Prayers are being composed and presented for adoption to the Holy See.* *See also* EUCHARISTIC PRAYER I; EUCHARISTIC PRAYER II; EUCHARISTIC PRAYER III; EUCHARISTIC PRAYER IV; EUCHARISTIC PRAYERS FOR MASSES OF RECONCILIATION; EUCHARISTIC PRAYERS FOR MASSES WITH CHILDREN.

Eucharistic Prayer I (yoo-kuh-RIS-tik prayr wuhn). Known also as the Roman Canon,* beginning with the Latin words *Te igitur,* this prayer is of ancient origin, going back to the 5th century and even beyond in its primitive form. From the 11th or 12th century on, it was the only Eucharistic Prayer* used in the whole Western Church until the introduction of the three new Eucharistic Prayers in 1969. It was highly regarded for its theological precision, sobriety of expression, Biblical and Christian terminology, repetition of concepts in clusters of two or three, and its brevity.

This First Eucharistic Prayer recalls the First Gospel, that of Matthew,* because it sets forth a strong sense of the Church,* especially the Church of the Messianic fulfillment. In addition, it contains a theology of offering that is well-exposed and easy to grasp. Following Christ's explicit example and command, bread and wine are chosen from among the gifts God has given us

and are offered to Him as a symbol of the offering of ourselves, of what we possess, and of the whole material creation.

In this offering, we ask God to accept them, bless them, and transform them through His Spirit* into the Body and Blood of Christ. We then pray that they will be given back to us transformed in such a way that we may be united in the Spirit to Christ and to one another, sharing in the Divine Nature. *See also* EUCHARISTIC PRAYER.

Eucharistic Prayer II (yoo-kuh-RIS-tik prayr too). Substantially the text of Hippolytus,* a Eucharistic Prayer* that has come down to us from the primitive Church and dates back to 215. There have been several modifications of the original version—the addition of a Sanctus* and Intercessions,* an alteration in the Doxology,* and the clarification of obscure phrases. It is extremely brief, particularly when compared to the customary Roman Canon.*

Simplicity and clarity mark this Eucharistic Prayer. The overall theme is Christ, in a motif that is established as the prayer addresses the Father in praise and thanksgiving for all that Jesus is and all that He has done for us by forming a new people of God through His Death* and Resurrection.* Thus, this Second Eucharistic Prayer is like the Second Gospel, that of Mark,* by its emphasis on the mighty Son of God overcoming the powers of evil.

Because of its brevity, concise language, and clear concepts, this text should be particularly effective for weekday Masses, home Masses, Masses for the young, and Masses for small groups. *See also* EUCHARISTIC PRAYER.

Eucharistic Prayer III (yoo-kuh-RIS-tik prayr three). The key themes in this Eucharistic Prayer* are sacrifice and the Holy Spirit*—with an obvious connection between the two. The opening section mentions the work of the Spirit in forming a worshiping community that will offer a clean sacrifice to God's glory. A familiar ("from east to west . . .") quotation from the Prophet Malachi,* often used by the Fathers* in writing of the Eucharist,* concludes the section.

Just as the Spirit gathers together a people for worship,* so we ask the Father* in the consecratory invocation to make holy by the power of the Spirit the gifts offered so that they may become Christ's Body and Blood.

A theology of sacrifice is developed in the memorial,* offering,* and communion* invocations,* What is being offered in sacrifice to God is the bread and wine—taken from among the gifts He has given us and considered as symbols of ourselves and of all things—but also, and at the same time, Christ in person.

Offering Christ and His sacrifice to God means consciously uniting ourselves in heart and mind to the offering that Christ makes of Himself, of us, and of the whole world to God.

We are one in the Spirit, one with Christ, one with ourselves, and one with our neighbor. But it is "this sacrifice, which has made our peace with you," that brings about the oneness and enables us to be at peace, love, and union with God, ourselves, and the whole world. Quite naturally the prayer flows then into prayer for those others and for the world around us—asking that all God's children be united in mercy and love. This accent on unity and on the People of God ("You gather a people to yourself . . . the entire people your Son has gained for you . . . your pilgrim Church on earth") has led some writers to regard this as the "Eucharistic Prayer of the Second Vatican Council." This same emphasis also likens this third Eucharistic Prayer to the Third Gospel, that of Luke,* equating the pilgrim Church with the Lucan themes of humanity and reconciliation. *See also* EUCHARISTIC PRAYER.

Eucharistic Prayer IV (yoo-kuh-RIS-tik prayr fohr). The Fourth Eucharistic Prayer—longest of the three new permanent ones though still considerably shorter than the Roman Canon*—is perhaps the most beautiful of the post-Vatican II* texts. It contains real possibilities for teaching since its specific characteristic is a synthetic presentation of the total movement of the History of Salvation.*

Every Eucharistic Prayer is essentially Trinitarian in structure. It is addressed to the Father, centers on the Mystery* of the Son, and seeks extension into our lives and into the world around us through the power of the Holy Spirit.* The Fourth Eucharistic Prayer reflects this outline in its text.

Uniquely, however, among the new texts, it gives a complete picture of human history and a view of the Trinity within the prayer itself. Following the Sanctus,* we speak of the Father creating the human race, of Christ saving humankind, and of the Spirit Who will "complete his work on earth."

Then, logically continuing the text and the theme, we ask the Father that "this Holy Spirit sanctify these offerings" so that they may become "the body and blood of Jesus Christ our Lord."

The memorial,* offering,* and communion* invocations are terse and intertwined with the acclamation.* They too form an explicit Trinitarian prayer. Finally, this Fourth Eucharistic Prayer is closely linked with the Fourth Gospel, that of John,* by several themes, especially the commemoration of Jesus loving His "own" until the end when His Hour dawned. *See also* EUCHARISTIC PRAYER.

Eucharistic Prayers for Masses of Reconciliation (yoo-kuh-RIS-tik prayrz fohr MAS-uhz uhv rek-uhn-si-lee-AY-shuhn). Like the three Eucharistic Prayers for Masses with Children,* these two Anaphoras* feature great unity of composition—their various parts are not juxtaposed but orderly arranged in a single movement of thanksgiving. They are also marked by choices of structure and inspiration stemming from the renewal of Vatican II,* in-

cluding allusions to texts of the Bible and the Council. They also reread the salvific value of the Eucharist in terms of "reconciliation." This reveals itself as a central category of Salvation History* and an excellent hermeneutic key to the work and person of Christ.

Eucharistic Prayer 1 (R1). This prayer is imbued with the idea of forgiveness of sins and reconciliation of God's people to Him through Christ. It possesses a remarkable Preface,* which in poetic language akin to that of the Bible stresses the Divine initiative and traces the main lines of the history of the Covenant* (sealed, broken, and then renewed definitively between God and human beings). In the Institution Narrative,* reconciliation is alluded to ("he was to reconcile all things to himself"). Then at the Anamnesis* it specifies that the Eucharist actualizes the reconciling sacrifice of Christ ("we offer you . . . the sacrifice which restores man to your friendship") in the time of the Church between the definitive and unique past (Death and Resurrection) and the future toward which the whole History of Salvation tends ("look for the coming of that day").

Eucharistic Prayer 2 (R2). This prayer is also suffused with the idea of reconciliation and with Scriptural and Concilar allusions. The Preface is both trinitarian and existential in tone. In contemporary language it identifies the tragic situation of humankind, evokes human peace efforts, relates those efforts to God, and thanks Him for them. The Last Supper* is placed in relation with the sacrifice of the Cross* presented as our liberation. The Anamnesis, more strongly than in the Roman Canon,* states that we can offer God only what He gives us ("We . . . bring you the gift you have given us"). Finally, the Eucharist* is presented as the prefiguration and the pledge of bliss to come: gathering, communion, and banquet of the Kingdom.* *See also* EUCHARISTIC PRAYER.

Eucharistic Prayers for Masses with Children (yoo-kuh-RIS-tik prayrz fohr MAS-uhz with CHIL-druhn). Prepared by the Congregation for Divine Worship* upon the request of many episcopates and at the express desire of Paul VI, these prayers were approved by the Pope on October 26, 1974, and published on November 1. They were used experimentally for some years and then gradually allowed to be inserted into the vernacular editions of the *Sacramentary** (they became part of the English Sacramentary in 1985).

These prayers are much concerned with the problem of "celebration" that renders possible a fuller and more active participation* on the part of the assembly.* They also confer importance on the theme of thanksgiving and make frequent concrete references to Christ and to the love that led Him to His Paschal Mystery.*

They seek to speak a language more accessible to the religious experience of children while at the same time preserving the dignity of the prayer. They do so by avoiding

childish language, especially in the case of the part reserved for the celebrant,* by also avoiding too great a difference between the prayers and the Eucharistic Prayers for adults, and finally by fostering an active participation that nevertheless respects the presidential character of the prayer.

Each of them offers the merit of a great unity of composition: the parts are not juxtaposed but founded on an identical movement of thanksgiving. It is interesting to note that only in this case the Latin text is specifically mentioned as not intended for liturgical use. Naturally, these prayers are also strictly limited to Masses celebrated with children.

Eucharistic Prayer 1 (C1) is the simplest of the three. It is especially adapted for children just beginning to participate in the Eucharist.* The emphasis is placed on thanksgiving, starting from sentiments of admiration and gratitude for all that God has done for humankind. The thanksgiving encompasses the works of nature and those of grace,* which culminate in Christ's redemptive work. The prayer is bathed from end to end in a climate of wonder, joy, and gratitude.

Eucharistic Prayer 2 (C2) stresses the mystery of God's love for us: in creation, in the giving of His Son, in the Church, and in the whole work of Christ, which is the basis for the love possessed by humans. The numerous Acclamations* give the prayer the look of a dialogue, even within the Institution Narrative.* In these Acclamations, the essence of the Sanctus* and the traditional chants of Anamnesis* are found.

Eucharistic Prayer 3 (C3) contains three variables for the Easter Season*—at the Preface,* after the Sanctus, and at the communion epiclesis.* They are included to stir up attention and enrich the prayer. Joy, happiness, life, peace, love, and gratitude form the substance of the prayer. The Anamnesis* is more developed and lyrical than in the first two prayers. It expresses the memorial, Christ's offering of sacrifice, and our communion in this offering; then it invokes the Mystery of Jesus in three periods: in the past: His Death* and Resurrection*; in the Present: He lives with God and us; in the future: He will return. Each stage is marked by an identical acclamation so that children can grasp the character of praise and thanksgiving proper to the whole prayer. *See also* EUCHARISTIC PRAYER.

Eucharisticum Mysterium (ay-oo-kah-REES-tee-koom mee-STER-ee-oohm). Latin title (from the first two words "The Eucharistic Mystery") of the *Instruction on the Worship of the Holy Eucharist* issued by the Sacred Congregation of Rites* on May 25, 1967. The purpose of this most important document is to set forth rules concerning Eucharistic worship* "not only to emphasize the general principles of how to instruct the people in the Eucharist* but also to make more readily intelligible the signs by which the

Eucharist is celebrated as the Memorial of the Lord and worshiped as a permanent Sacrament* of the Church.*" It is divided into three chapters: (1) some general principles of particular importance in instructing the people of God* in the Mystery* of the Eucharist; (2) the celebration of the Memorial of the Lord; and (3) the worship of the Eucharist as a permanent Sacrament. *See also* MYSTERY; VATICAN COUNCIL, SECOND.

Euchologion (yoo-kuh-LOH-jee-uhn). The book that contains the prayers for the Eucharistic Celebration.* The most famous is the Euchologion of Serapion* (d. 360). In the Eastern Church, it refers to the service book for the bishop,* priest,* and deacon* that contains the texts and rubrics for the Liturgy of the Hours,* the Ordinary of the Eucharist,* the Sacraments,* the Office for the Dead,* monastic profession,* consecrations, and blessings. It corresponds to the *Sacramentary,* Ritual,* and Pontifical** in the West.

Euchology (yoo-KOL-uh-jee). In the strict sense, it is the science that studies prayers and the norms that regulate their composition. In the broad sense, it refers to the collection of prayers contained in a liturgical book.

Eulogy (YOO-luh-jee). (1) Although this word may describe a type of biography of Saints portraying their virtues or deeds, usually it refers to the panegyric presented at a funeral. Current instructions prohibit such a funeral eulogy, though the Homily* may show gratitude to God for His gifts to the person.

(2) This Greek word, *Eulogia,* means blessing and has meant the Eucharist,* or the gifts consecrated at the Eucharist, but ordinarily it refers to the blessing given to bread at Mass, or the blessed bread itself. *See also* BLESSED BREAD.

Euouae. Memory aid comprising the vowels in the conclusion of the Glory Be* in Latin *(seculorum. Amen),* used in choral liturgical

books to indicate the ending of every verse of the Psalm* that made up the Introit* (at Mass*) and the Responsory* (in the Divine Office*).

Eusebius of Vercelli, St. (yoo-SEE-bee-uhs uhv ver-CHEL-ee; SEL-ee). 300(?)-371. Born in Sardinia, Eusebius became a member of the Roman clergy and was chosen first bishop of Vercelli, Italy, in 345. He zealously proclaimed the Gospel* in his diocese and established the monastic life there, taking part in some aspects of it himself. He fought tirelessly against Arianism, which denied the Divinity of Christ, and was exiled by Emperor Constantius. After suffering torments and privations of every kind, Eusebius was released from exile and returned to Vercelli in 361 where he labored for ten more years before his death. *Liturgical celebration:* August 2 (Opt. Mem.); *theme:* belief in Christ's divinity.

Evangeliary. *See* LECTIONARY.

Evangelical Counsels (ee-van-JEL-i-kuhl; -ev-uhn; KOWN[T]-

suhlz). Directives based on the words and example of Christ that—although not to be considered as binding upon all—aim to rise above the minimum of Christian obligation and reach up for Christian perfection* as far as that can be attained on earth. The Evangelical Counsels especially recommended by Christ are: (1) voluntary poverty (see Mk 10:17ff), (2) perpetual chastity (see Mt 19:11-12), and (3) perfect obedience (see Mk 9:34). Those who embrace the Counsels publicly as part of a way of life are members of Religious Orders (or congregations) or secular institutes. Others of the faithful* may follow them privately.

Participation* in the Liturgy* is one of the best means for keeping the Counsels. At the same time, the Counsels enhance participation in liturgical celebrations and lead to the performance of good works.* Ultimately, the Counsels flow from love* for God.

Those who do not profess the Counsels by vows or sacred bonds can nonetheless observe the spirit of the Counsels. By being willing to give up unneeded luxuries in order to help the poor, they observe the spirit of voluntary poverty. By keeping themselves pure in thought and deed, they observe the spirit of perpetual chastity. By being obedient to their lawful superiors, they observe the spirit of perfect obedience. *See also* COMMANDMENTS; GOOD WORKS.

Evangelii Nuntiandi (ev-ahn-JEL-ee-ee nuhn-tsee-AHN-dee). Latin title (from the first two words "Proclaimers of the Gospel") of the *Apostolic Exhortation on Evangelization in the Modern World* issued by Pope Paul VI on December 8, 1975. The document points out that evangelization* and Liturgy* go hand in hand. Evangelization must touch life*: the natural life, to which it gives a new meaning, and the supernatural life, which is not the negation but the purification and elevation of the natural life. This supernatural life finds its living expression in the Sacraments* and the radiation of grace* and holiness* that they possess. The role of evangelization is to educate people in the Faith in such a way as to lead each individual Christian to live the Sacraments as true Sacraments of Faith.

Evangelists (i-VAN-juh-lists). Generally, those who proclaim the Gospel.* Specifically, those who wrote the four Canonical Gospels. From Ezekiel's* vision, the apocalyptic beasts symbolize the four evangelists: Matthew,* Mark,* Luke,* and John.* The four symbolic beasts convey distinctive meanings: (1) Man for Matthew, who established Christ as Man through His genealogical table. Mark as lion, since he begins the book with the preaching of John the Baptist* in the desert; a lion that sleeps with its eyes open is a symbol of the Divinity in the tomb. Luke as the ox, because of the ox or calf chosen as a sacrifice in the Temple by Zechariah, and Christ as the sac-

rifice in the New Law. John as the eagle that looks toward and flies into the sun, which represents John's gaze on the eternal generation of the Word, proving His Divinity.

(2) Further, these mystic beasts signify the Son of God as Man in His birth; as Ox in His Death,* the supreme sacrifice, as Lion because of His Resurrection*; and as Eagle through His Ascension.*

(3) Symbolism is carried even farther by denoting the virtues required for salvation. Christians, as reasonable animals, are of necessity human beings (man); they sacrifice (ox) materialistic gratification, display fortitude (lion), and contemplate eternity (eagle).

Evangelization (i-van-juh-luh-ZAY-shuhn). Broadly, the procla-

mation of the Good News* intended to bring everyone by missionary activity to Christianity. More specifically, it is the initial period of the first stage for Christian Initiation, in which the prospective candidates learn the basic message of God with His intent to save all people. Thus with their hearts open to the Lord by the Holy Spirit,* they would be expected to adhere to Him, Who is the Way, the Truth, and the Life.

Evening Mass (EEV-ning mas). By the late 1950s permission for evening Mass on all days of the week could be granted by the local Ordinary* provided he believed it would benefit the faithful* spiritually. On January 10, 1970, the Sacred Congregation for the Clergy permitted the Ordinary to give similar permission that would allow the congregation to fulfill their Sunday obligation at a Saturday evening Mass. This dispensation was ordinarily granted where there was a shortage of priests. The Mass* is of the Sunday, and should include a Homily* and General Intercessions.*

On Saturday evening, to fulfill the Sunday obligation on a day when the feast on Saturday liturgically is of a higher grade than the Sunday, the Mass is nevertheless to be of that Sunday since it carries the precept to attend Mass. The same regulation would obtain on a Sunday evening if a greater feast would occur on Monday. As yet the Congregation has not settled the case when a Holy Day of Obligation* and a Sunday occur either on Saturday or on Sunday evening outside of Advent.* In such an instance a former decision made in 1974 might obtain, namely that the Mass should coincide with the Evening Prayer* prescribed, i.e., the one higher in the table of liturgical days.

When one looks at modern schedules for people, especially those who work odd hours, morning Masses are less suitable than evening celebrations in church. Before these permissions existed, certain groups of people would find it quite difficult to attend Mass on Holy Days during the week and sometimes even on Sundays. The new Code extends this privilege to the entire world. *See also* SUNDAY MASS OBLIGATION.

Evening Prayer (or Evensong) (EEV-ning prayr; EE-vuhn-song). Celebrated as the day draws to a close, this portion of the Liturgy of the Hours,* formerly called Vespers, is one of the two hinges on which the day's Divine Office pivots, and it is therefore to be considered one of the chief Hours. Prayed at this time, it suitably gives thanks for the gifts received that day and reflects on that portion of salvation history when the holy Mysteries* of the Church were instituted by Christ; also it relates to the sacrifice that He offered the next day once and for all to His Father.

Since Evening Prayer is of such importance, its public celebration is encouraged particularly by those living in community. However whenever possible, at least Sunday Evening Prayer ought to be celebrated with the people, particularly on the solemn celebration of Easter.* The psalmody for this Hour was chosen to be suitable for celebration with the people.

In accordance with number 61 of the Roman Calendar* when a Solemnity* or Feast of the Lord* would displace the Sunday Evening Prayer, since the Mass would be of the Sunday, the Evening Prayer would also be of the Sunday in that instance.

Structure

After the Introductory Verse,* a Hymn that sets the tone for that Hour or the day's feast is sung. It should lead easily into the Psalmody,* which consists of two Psalms (or sections thereof) followed by a Canticle* from the Epistles.* Short Readings* occur after the Psalter,* related to the day, season, or feast. Longer Scripture Readings may be chosen, particularly during celebra-

tions with the people, either from the Office of Readings* or from the *Lectionary** for Mass. A Homily* may explain the Reading. Some suitable response to God's word follows, usually a Responsorial Hymn. The Antiphons that precede the Canticle of Our Lady* may vary according to the liturgical feastday or season.

The Intercessions* during the Evening Prayer* are in the form of petitions that follow the example of the Lord's Prayer* and include praise of God. Since the Liturgy of the Hours is a prayer by and for the whole Church, the Intercessions should intercede for general needs of the Church, her ministries, civil authorities, the poor, the sick, peace, and world needs. Particular intentions may be added, but the last intention is always for the dead. In community celebrations either variable or uniform responses may be given.

Then the Lord's Prayer precedes the concluding Prayer, which, for weekdays and Ordinary Time,* is in the Psalter,* otherwise in the Proper. Finally, the priest or deacon dismisses the people as at Mass with a greeting, a blessing, and an invitation to go in peace.

Ex Cathedra. *See* CHAIR (CATHEDRA).

Ex Opere Operantis (eks OH-puh-ray oh-puh-RAHN-tis). A Latin theological formula meaning "from the act of the doer" and referring to the dispositions of the doer or recipient of a Sacrament,* Sacramental,* or indulgence.* The dispositions of the doer or the recipient do not affect the efficacy of a Sacrament, but they do determine the amount of grace* received or not received by that person in the case of a Sacramental or an indulgenced prayer or good work. Of course, even in the case of a Sacrament, the dispositions of the recipient or the minister are important subjectively—but not for the validity of the Sacrament.

Ex Opere Operato (eks OH-puh-ray oh-puh-RAH-toh). A Latin theological formula meaning "from the act done" and referring to the objective manner of operation of the Sacraments,* which does not depend on the subjective attitudes of either the minister or the recipient. As long as no obstacle is placed in the way, all properly administered Sacraments confer the particular grace proper to each.

Exequies. *See* FUNERAL RITES AND CEREMONIES.

Exercises, Pious (EK-suhr-saiz-uhz, PAI-uhs). Extraliturgical forms of piety, such as the practices of meditation, examination of conscience, retreats,* the spiritual exercises of St. Ignatius Loyola,* recitation of the Rosary,* the month of the Sacred Heart,* the month of Mary,* triduums, novenas,* and the Stations of the Cross.*

The Second Vatican Council* stated that such devotions, provided they conform to the laws and norms of the Church, are to be recommended, especially when they are ordered by the Holy See* (SC, 13). However, it went on to say that these devotions are to be drawn up in such a way that they harmonize with the liturgical seasons,* accord with the sacred Liturgy,* are in some way derived from it, and lead the people to it—for the Liturgy is by its very nature superior to them.

Paul VI set forth detailed instructions concerning the qualities of such devotions. They must be Trinitarian, Christological, and ecclesial with a Biblical basis, liturgical orientation, ecumenical character, and anthropological awareness (MC, 24-39). *See also* LITURGICAL SPIRITUALITY; PARALITURGY.

Exodus, The Book of (EK-suhd-uhs; -EG-zuhd; thuh buk uhv). The second book of the Pentateuch (*see* DEUTERONOMY) is called Exodus from the Greek word for "departure," because the central event narrated in it is the departure of the Israelites from Egypt. It continues the history of the chosen people from the point where the Book of Genesis* leaves off. It recounts the oppression by the Egyptians of the ever-increasing descendants of Jacob and their miraculous deliverance by God through Moses, who led them across the Red Sea to

Mount Sinai where they entered into a special Covenant* with God.

These events were of prime importance to the chosen people, for they became thereby an independent nation and enjoyed a unique relationship with God. Through Moses, God gave to the Israelites at

Mount Sinai the "law"; the moral, civil, and ritual legislation by which they were to become a holy people, in whom the promise of a Savior for all humankind would be fulfilled.

Liturgical use: In the *Roman Missal,** this Book is used extensively, for example, on the Easter Vigil,* Pentecost,* and Trinity Sunday* (A) as well as on the 3rd Sunday of Lent* (B, C) and the weekdays of the 15th through 17th Weeks (Year I). In the *Liturgy of the Hours,** it is used during the first three Weeks of Lent and in a minor canticle* in the Psalter.* *Meaning:* Exodus is the Paschal Book par excellence. The wonders of the Exodus prepare for and foretell in their way the even more astounding manifestations of Divine love that established the New Covenant. The Christian Passover, effected by the sacrifice of Jesus our Lord Who is the new Paschal Lamb, is fully substituted for the old as the basis for our faith.* It has obtained for the new people of God an even more profound deliverance—from captivity to sin and the tyranny of the devil.

Exomologesis (ek-soh-mol-uh-JEE-sis). A term (from the Greek word for confession) that refers to the whole penitential rite as well as the public or private confession of sins. (*See* 1 Jn 1:9; Jas 5:16.)

Exorcism (EK-sohr-siz-uhm; EK-suhr-). (1) An act of freeing by symbolic action and invocation places, things, and even persons from the vexation, ravages, obsession, or possession of the evil spirit. Today such solemn exorcism may be performed only by a priest* who has express permission from his bishop.*

(2) In the Rite of Christian Initiation* of Adults, as one becomes a catechumen, there is an exorcism that may occur if in the particular geographical area the Episcopal Conference* so decides. It would depend on the false worship that may be there, the worshiping of spiritual powers, the obtaining of benefits from magical arts.

During the time of evangelization, prior to the catechumenate, minor exorcisms may be celebrated by the priest or deacon* and may be used more than once in various circumstances. The intent is to bring spiritual good to the interested inquirers. During the first Scrutiny another exorcism of the elect takes place. Even in the Rite of Initiation for children, the exorcism takes place during the Scrutinies* or Penitential Rites.

(3) Certain other liturgical exorcisms are used, for instance, during the blessing of a church, or for certain objects such as salt,* water,* and sacred vessels.*

Exorcist (EK-sohr-sist; EK-suhr-). The third of the four Minor Orders,* which were suppressed in 1972. Conferred by the handing over of the book of exorcisms (the *Roman Ritual*),* the order was purely a formality, since exorcism could be performed only by a priest* especially delegated by the local Ordinary.* *See also* MINOR ORDERS.

Experimentation, Liturgical (ek-sper-uh-men-TAY-shuhn, luh-TURH-ji-kuhl; li-). To insure a viable

Liturgy,* liturgical experimentation is necessary as human conditions and cultures change. Vatican Council II* therefore allows truly scientific public efforts drawn from the experience of a specific congregation with regard to its modes, styles, and rites in worship,* to achieve a meaningful and congenial attitude toward its culture. Research and measurement tools of our time ought to make possible the more rapid adaptation of liturgical action as affected by cultural change. Such experimentation is authorized only through the National or International Conferences of Bishops,* as long as it is confirmed by the Holy See.*

In the United States a Subcommittee of the Bishops' Committee on the Liturgy* is appointed to organize proposals and requests. Research centers exist, but they are in need of more financial help and coordination with experts in relevant disciplines. Through liturgical experimentation, our current elements of Liturgy may be added to, eliminated, changed, or modified because of specific cultural situations.

In a more broad sense, this term refers also to other types of activities, namely, assessing in certain places the rites restructured by the Holy See. Territorial authorities authorize specific communities to test and report on such religious services. Some use the term to describe those options that are licit under the present laws, such as a priest* choosing Readings* from supplementary Scriptural Readings for Mass,* musical accompaniment by instruments other than the organ, etc. *See also* ADAPTATION, LITURGICAL.

Exposition of the Holy Eucharist (ek-spuh-ZISH-uhn uhv thee HOH-lee YOO-kuh-rist). The ceremony of exhibiting the Sacred Host* for adoration* by the faithful.* It is considered private when the Eucharist* remains in the ciborium,* brought forward to the tabernacle* door; public, when a large host in a lunula* of a monstrance* is positioned for all adorers to see. Exposition should foster the principal intent of Christ when He instituted the Eucharist to be with us as comfort and food—hence the cult of the Blessed Sacrament must relate to the Mass.*

This devotion developed and grew during the Middle Ages, when there was a strong desire by the people to view the consecrated Host. The feast of Corpus Christi* had its influence on this form of Eucharistic piety also. Modern liturgical reform tends to deprecate such static adoration in favor of the more dynamic action of the Mass. Yet the *Instruction on Eucharistic Worship (Eucharisticum Mysterium**) considers it a valuable practice whereby the faithful may be invited to spiritual communion with Christ. Consequently, it is recommended that parish churches should have at least one period of time each year when the Blessed Sacrament is solemnly exposed, for instance, during Forty Hours' Devotion.* If there are not a sufficient number of worshipers, the Blessed Sacrament is reposed at stated intervals.

Should the Exposition last an entire day or several days, it is to be interrupted during the celebration of Mass.

Some Religious communities and certain other groups practice perpetual Eucharistic adoration, or adoration over extended periods of time. At times the whole community adores, making use of readings, songs, and meditation. At other times at least one or two members of the community are present before the Sacrament, spelling each other, as they pray in the name of the whole community and the Church.

Shorter periods of time for Exposition can be arranged so that prior to Benediction* an appropriate period for readings from the Scripture, songs, prayers, and meditation may occur.

The ordinary minister for Exposition, a priest* or deacon,* blesses the faithful with the Sacrament before reposition. When the ordinary minister is unavailable, the following may expose and repose the Eucharist for the faithful: an acolyte* or special minister of Communion*; a member of a religious community or lay association devoted to Eucharistic adoration, if appointed by the local Ordinary.* It is unlawful for the special ministers to bless the people with the Sacrament. *See also* BENEDICTION; BODY AND BLOOD OF CHRIST; FORTY HOURS' DEVOTION.

Exsultet (eks-SUHL-tet). The first word of the Latin version of the Easter Proclamation, the song of praise sung by the deacon* at the Easter Vigil* in conjunction with the blessing of the Paschal Candle.* The hymn praises the many marvels of God, particularly the Resurrection* of Christ that took place on this night. *See also* EASTER VIGIL; LUCERNARIUM.

External Solemnity. *See* SOLEMNITY.

Extraordinary Ministers of Holy Communion (ik-STROHRD-uhn-er-ee; ek-strah-ORD; MIN-uh-stuhrz uhv HOH-lee kuh-MYOO-nyuhn). That the Eucharist* may be more readily received, authorization was given in 1973 for unordained (therefore extraordinary) persons to distribute Communion.* The local Ordinary* or his delegate appoints them, usually for a definite period of time or permanently. The appointment may be granted for a single occasion.

The circumstances warranting such an appointment are the lack of ordained ministers, a large group of communicants that would lengthen the service unduly, or the spiritual demands of the infirm in homes or hospitals. Good Catholics are to be chosen and they may minister the Sacrament* either within Mass* or outside of Mass. In the latter case they are a great help in distributing Communion to the sick and Viaticum* to the dying. A rite of commissioning these ministers exists.

Extreme Unction. *See* ANOINTING OF THE SICK.

Ezekiel, The Book of (e-ZEE-kee-uhl, thuh buk uhv). Thirty-third Book of the Old Testament* and third of the Major Prophets.* Both priest and prophet, Ezekiel ministered to his fellow exiles from 593 to 563 B.C.; he is the prophet of the Temple and the Liturgy* as well as of the absolute majesty of God. Like Jeremiah,* Ezekiel denounces the false illusions of his people, their moral corruption, and especially the idolatry of their worship. He preaches a religion of the heart, announces a new Covenant,* and insists on the personal responsibility of every member of the people. Called the "father of Judaism," Ezekiel announces the restoration of Israel and the coming of God to reign over His people like a shepherd.

Liturgical use: This Book is well read in the *Roman Missal,** for example, on the Easter Vigil,* Pentecost,* Christ the King* (A), 5th Sunday of Lent* (A), 11th and 14th Sundays in Ordinary Time* (B), and the 23rd and 26th Sundays (A) as well as on the Weekdays of the 19th and 20th Weeks in Ordinary Time (II). In the *Liturgy of the Hours,** it is read on the 24th and 25th Weeks in Ordinary Time and gives rise to a minor canticle* in the Psalter.* *Meaning:* Ezekiel imparts a strong sense of sin, seen as an abomination before God. At the same time, he inculcates in all an equally vivid sense of the gratuity of salvation*: human beings cannot merit forgiveness; it is God Who grants it beyond the boundaries of strict justice and thus heaps confusion upon unrepentant sinners.

Ezra, The Book of (EZ-ruh, thuh buk uhv). Fifteenth Book of the Old Testament* and seventh of the Historical Books. This Book continues the narrative of the Chronicler (*see* CHRONICLES) and tells the story of the return from Babylon and the rebuilding of the Temple. It is most likely the work of Ezra the Scribe who is also its protagonist. Ezra joined with Nehemiah* in fashioning the Jewish community after the Exile. He is regarded by the Talmud as a second Moses—for restoring the Law* to the people.

Liturgical use: This Book is used only three times in the *Roman Missal** (Monday, Tuesday, and Wednesday of the 20th Week in Ordinary Time,* I). In the *Liturgy of the Hours,** it is read only in the Alternate Two-Year Cycle* (Monday and Tuesday of the 11th Week and Tuesday, Wednesday, and Thursday of the 12th Week, II). *Meaning:* God fulfilled His promise to restore His people to their own land. He reestablished the old forms of worship and put an end to compromise with heathenism. Just as He gave new life to His people in the past, so will He continue to give His people new life in the present and for all eternity.

— F —

Fabian, St. (FAY-bee-uhn). ?-250. Fabian was Pope from 236 to 250, succeeding St. Anterus. He sent St. Dionysius and other preachers of the Gospel* into Gaul and condemned Privatus, the originator of a new heresy in Africa. St. Cyprian* of Carthage, who relates this fact, calls St. Fabian an incomparable man. Fabian suffered martyrdom under the Emperor Decius. *Liturgical celebration:* January 20 (Opt. Mem.); *theme:* serving God in faith.

Faculties (FAK-uhl-teez). An authorization granted to bishops* by the Holy See* or to priests* by an Ordinary* to allow them to employ their powers in favor of the faithful* they serve.

(1) As a general term it pertains to the Rite of Penance,* indicating those priests who are empowered to absolve from ecclesiastical censures, sins, even reserved. Through ordination* the priest possesses the power, but may exercise it only after receiving permission from the competent authority, namely, the local bishop. Beyond this all the Sacraments* demand faculties for their licit administration.

This term also refers to the privilege of preaching, which is the prime function of the Pope* and the bishops. Preaching, to proclaim and elucidate the Word of God in a formal manner, is a license given to priests and deacons* only.

Similarly, when one is allowed to impart certain blessings* reserved to a major superior or a bishop, he is said to have faculties. In the revision of ritual blessings there are fewer reserved blessings.

(2) The Pope has powers reserved to himself but may grant *apostolic* faculties (to be interpreted strictly as conceded) as a privilege to certain persons. Some faculties to dispense from the universal law of the Church are given every five years to diocesan bishops. After Vatican Council II* stated that bishops may dispense from law for the spiritual welfare of their subjects, the Pope in 1963 listed the faculties that they have by reason of their office. *See also* CONFESSOR.

Faith (fayth). Faith is "the realization of what is hoped for and evidence of things not seen" (Heb 11:1). It is an act of the understanding and a Divinely infused virtue* whereby we accept as true all that God has revealed, because He has revealed it. The matter of faith is what God has revealed and through His Church* teaches us to believe. The motive is the truthfulness of God. Faith is necessary for salvation.*

It is not enough, however, to hold as true the truths of faith. For faith to be complete, its teachings must bring us into a more personal relationship with God. In other words, we must live according to what we believe. Every religious truth should bind us more closely to God. Faith then becomes our response to God's call to follow Him.

In this connection, the Liturgy* is the most complete and most pefect expression of faith, for it is the active adherence of the ecclesial community to the God of the Covenant.*

Thus, Christian faith is faith in the redeeming love of God, in the Divine and eternal life* of human beings, in the Incarnation* and Resurrection* of Jesus Christ the Savior. Faith is the encounter of Jesus in the Church and the Liturgy. Belief in Christ means practicing the Liturgy. Faith has need of the Liturgy because it is in the Liturgy that Christ comes to us.

By the same token, the Liturgy has need of faith; it is for believers. It celebrates faith. "Christian worship . . . is a work which proceeds from faith and is based on it" (Can. 836).

Faith also refers to the set of beliefs, the Divinely revealed truths. As such, the Faith vitalizes and directs the Liturgy, while in return the Liturgy avows and bears witness to the Faith. *See also* CATECHESIS AND LITURGY.

Faith, Act of (fayth, akt uhv). (1) An act of the understanding and a Divinely infused virtue,* whereby we firmly accept as true all that God has revealed, because He has revealed it. (2) A formula that expresses this assent of the understanding. The Liturgy* makes much use of acts or professions of faith—e.g., the Nicene Creed* at Mass* and variations of it in the Sacraments* (the promises at Baptism*). Indeed, conscious, full, and active participation* in the Liturgy is possible only through genuine acts of faith. The traditional Act of Faith is as follows:

> O my God, I firmly believe that You are one God in three Divine Persons, Father, Son, and Holy Spirit. I believe that Your Divine Son became Man and died for our sins and that He will come to judge the living and the dead. I believe these and all the truths that the Holy Catholic Church teaches, because You have revealed them Who can neither deceive nor be deceived.

Those who say an act of faith can gain a partial indulgence.*

Faith, Profession of. *See* PROFESSION OF FAITH.

Faithful (FAYTH-fuhl). Canon 204 defines faithful as those who, inasmuch as they have been incorporated in Christ through Baptism,* have been constituted as the people of God. Since they have become sharers in Christ's priestly, prophetic, and royal office in their own manner, they are called to exercise the mission that God has entrusted to the Church* to fulfill in the world, in accord with the condition proper to each.

Thus, the faithful are those who have the Faith, those who have put their trust in the God of the Covenant.* Adhering to Christ as Bride to the Bridegroom, they are the people of the new Covenant.* Through Baptism they are made capable of celebrating the Liturgy* and expressing and nourishing their faith* by coming together to "announce the praise of him who

called [them] out of darkness into his wonderful light" (1 Pt 2:9).

The word faithful is also used as a synonym for laity.* *See also* LAITY; UNIVERSAL PRIESTHOOD.

Faithful, Active Participation of the. *See* LITURGY—PARTICIPATION.

Faldstool (FAWLD-stool). A backless, movable, folding chair with arms, used by bishops* in liturgical functions when they are not at the throne.* When kneeling, the bishop may also use it as a support.

Familiaris Consortio (fah-mee-lee-AH-rees kuhn-SAWR-tsee-oh). Latin title (from the first two words "Marriage Fellowship") of the *Apostolic Exhortation on the Family* issued by Pope John Paul II on December 15, 1981. Among the many points this document makes about the family and the Liturgy* are the following: (1) The family is a domestic Church,* a Church in miniature, in such a way that it is a living image and historical representation of the Mystery of the Church.* (2) The Sacrament of Marriage* is the specific source and original means of sanctification for Christian married couples and families. (3) The Christian family's sanctifying role is grounded in Baptism* and has its highest expression in the Eucharist,* to which Christian Marriage is intrinsically connected. (4) Repentance and mutual pardon within the bosom of the Christian family, so much a part of daily life, receive their specific Sacramental expression in Christian Penance.* (5) Family members are transformed into spiritual sacrifices acceptable to God through Jesus (1 Pt 2:5) in view of their baptismal priesthood of the faithful* exercised in the celebration of the Eucharist and the other Sacraments* and in the offering of self to the glory* of God but also in a life of prayer* through prayerful dialogue with the Father, through Jesus, in the Holy Spirit.

Family Prayer (FAM-uh-lee; FAM-lee; prayr). Since the family is the fundamental unit of society and all humans are to be images of God, in the family children learn how to become children of God. Christ the High Priest* has given a priestly role to the Christian Family. Because the baptismal priesthood of the faithful* is exercised in the Sacrament of Marriage,* there is a basis of a priestly vocation and mission for the spouses and the family, by which their daily lives become spiritual sacrifices acceptable to God through Christ. This happens not only when they celebrate the Eucharist* and the other Sacraments,* and whenever they offer themselves to the glory of God, but also when they carry out their prayer life, that is, their prayerful dialogue with the Father* through Jesus,* in the Holy Spirit.*

One characteristic of family prayer is that it is offered in common. Such community prayer occurs as a consequence of and a requirement of the Sacraments of Baptism* and Matrimony. Surely the words of Christ apply to the members of the Christian family: "I say to you, if two of you agree on earth about anything for which they are to pray, it shall be granted to them by my heavenly Father" (Mt 18:19).

The object of family prayer is *family life itself.* Mark the many things that denote God's loving intervention in family history: births and birthday celebrations, wedding anniversaries of the parents, departures, separations and homecomings, important and far-reaching decisions, hopes and disappointments, joys and sorrows, the death of those who are dear, etc. All these mark God's loving intervention in the family's history and offer suitable moments for petition, thanksgiving, trust in the Lord, praise, and adoration.

Since the Christian family is considered the domestic church,* the parents have the specific responsibility of educating their children in prayer. The family's inalienable right to educate the children would include developing religious piety and prayer at home, fulfilling Christ's counsel for common prayer. Parents introduce them gradually to the Mystery* of God and to personal dialogue with Him. By praying together with their children, the father and mother can, exercising their royal priesthood,* penetrate the inmost depths of their children's hearts and thus leave an impression that future events in their lives will never be able to efface.

Fathers and mothers pray together with their children, in preparation for the Sacraments, when they are sick, saying the family Rosary, and thus their example of honesty in thought and action becomes a lesson for life, an act of worship of singular value. Drawing attention to the Sacramentals,* such as blessing the house, automobiles, etc., is one of the concerns of the parents.

Family Prayer and the Liturgy

This prayer life of the domestic church forms a natural introduction for the children to the liturgical prayer of the whole Church. In a sense it prepares them for it and extends liturgical prayer into their personal, family, and social life. Christian families strive to celebrate at home, in a way suited to their members, the times and feasts of the Liturgical Year.* They may use some of the more popular devotions for this purpose, but these will be connected with the liturgical celebrations that they observe in the church with their family.

There is the sanctification of the *day* with family prayers in the morning, evening, and at table; of the *week,* by special devotions at home on specific days such as devotion to the Sacred Heart* on Friday, devotion to Mary* on Saturdays, and participation at Sunday Mass with the reception of Communion as a family; or of the *month,* by having celebrations in honor of the persons to whom each month is dedicated, for example, the holy souls in purgatory during November and the Sacred Heart of Jesus during June.

Some churches have family services, where the Eucharist* is celebrated specifically around a family situation, so that the children and adults may join in a family-oriented liturgy. There is a new *Roman Catholic Daily Office,* particularly the single volume of *Christian Prayer** containing Morning Prayer* and Evening Prayer,* which can be recited by the family either in church or at home and is developed from a popular form of the Divine Office,* which priests are bound to say daily.

The Christian year takes on a greater religious significance if the various seasons are entered into with appropriate family activities. For instance, devotion in connection with the Advent wreath,* doing favors for each other during Advent* in preparation for Christmas*; erection of the crib* and Christmas tree for that season; welcoming the singers on Epiphany*; receiving blessed ashes and choosing proper Lenten activities; bringing the palm from the procession on Passion Sunday* to its place of honor behind the home crucifix; having a special Easter* light at that time; and honoring crucifixes, statues, or pictures at various seasons with fresh flowers and specific devotions.

We accept the fact that the family is the fundamental cell of human society. To fulfill its everyday commitments and to accept all its responsibilities, the Christian family finds its strongest incentive in prayer. The actual participation of family members in the Church's life and mission is directly proportionate to their intensity of prayer and their close union with Christ, the Head of the Church. The aim of the Christian family to transform the

world is possible because of its living union with Christ, nourished by the Liturgy, self-oblation, and prayer.

Fanon (FAN-uhn). Collar-shaped vestment or outer-amice worn by the Pope* at pontifical ceremonies over his amice.* One part of it is over the alb* and the other is over the chasuble.* It is made of two pieces of white silk with an opening in the center so that it may slip over the head. In the past, fanon was also used to designate the maniple*; the cloth in which the congregation formerly brought the Eucharistic gifts to the altar*; the strings of the miter*; the humeral veil*; and processional banners.*

Fast, Eucharistic (fast, yoo-kuh-RIS-tic). Refraining from food and drink for a period of time before the reception of Holy Communion* out of reverence for the Eucharist. Formerly abstinence, even from water, was enjoined from midnight. Since 1953 the regulation has been modified several times so that today the fast is for one hour from foods, solid and liquid, including alcoholic drinks. Medicines and water are exceptions. One should calculate the time from the actual reception, not the beginning of Mass.* For the sick, the aged, and those attending them, the fast does not bind. A priest* who binates* or trinates* may eat or drink between celebrations, even if the intervening time is less than an hour. One may always observe a more severe fast than that which is prescribed.

Fasting (FAST-ing). Abstention, whether complete or partial, from food and drink for religious reasons. Fasting as a means of penance was practiced in the Church from early times with a variety of regulations. At first it meant no food or drink until sunset. Strenuous fasting practices are mitigated in modern times, so that the current rule would allow one main meal, with some food being allowed at the other two mealtimes. The law binds those who are eighteen up to the beginning of their sixtieth year on Ash Wednesday* and Good Friday.* Usually the bishop* gives a local mandate to establish norms that would be opportune and efficacious in his diocese.*

The intent of fasting is penitential in nature and with the purpose of intensifying prayer*; hence as a means to an end, it has psychological and religious value. It may apply to refraining from using certain luxuries and pleasures, such as candy, alchohol, tobacco, television, films, or other entertainment. *See also* ABSTINENCE.

Father, God the. *See* GOD.

Fathers of the Church. *See* PATRISTIC READINGS.

Feasts (feests). (1) Days in the Church Year* commemorating certain events in salvation history, sacred Mysteries,* by which special honor accrues to God, our Savior, the angels, the Blessed Mother, and the Saints.* The celebration consists primarily of the Mass* in honor of the Mystery or Saint and the performance of the Liturgy of the Hours.* The regular occurrence of feasts throughout the year reminds

us to grow in holiness and prepares us for the coming of Christ. Sundays also, as little Easters, reflect the Mystery of Christ, particularly during the various seasons of the year. Thus throughout the year we are kept mindful of the principal Mysteries and persons of Christianity.

(a) Some feasts are *fixed,* that is, they occur each year on the same date, e.g., Christmas,* the Assumption,* and most feasts of the Saints.* Some feasts are attached to a fixed Sunday, for instance, Christ the King.*

(b) Other feasts are *movable,* that is, they fall on different dates each year, dependent on the date assigned Easter* that year. Besides Easter, this would affect Ascension,* Pentecost,* Corpus Christi,* the Holy Trinity,* and the Sacred Heart of Jesus.*

(2) In the current terminology of feasts, the Roman Calendar* divides them into Solemnities,* Feasts,* and Memorials* (obligatory or optional). Sundays* and weekdays* are classed separately. Thus the word *Feast* may have this specific meaning of being second in rank among all feasts.

Although there are feasts of very many Saints in existence, not all of them are celebrated by everyone. Many are celebrated locally by a diocese,* or by the Religious community. Comparatively few Saints are honored throughout the Universal Church* each year, for they must have universal significance for the whole Church.

Feasts in the very specific sense are limited in their celebration to a natural day. Only Feasts of the Lord, when they fall on Sundays, enjoy Evening Prayer I,* for they substitute for the Sunday Office. In the *Liturgy of the Hours* Feasts tend to have more proper parts than Memorials. Unlike Memorials, at the daytime hours, the Feast's proper prayer is said, even though the Psalms* and antiphons* are almost always from the weekday. Night Prayer* is also as on ordinary weekdays. However the Office of Readings,* Morning Prayer,* and Evening Prayer* are the same as on a Solemnity.

Certain feasts are termed Holy Days of Obligation,* and are observed as days of rest by Christians. *See also* CALENDAR; HOLY DAYS OF OBLIGATION; *and Names of individual feasts.*

Federation of Diocesan Liturgical Commissions (fed-uh-RAY-shuhn uhv DAI-os-uh-suhn luh-TUHR-ji-kuhl; li-; kuh-MISH-uhnz). In the wake of the appointment of many liturgical commissions throughout the United States, this Federation was formed in 1971 to promote the Liturgy* as the heart of Christian life, particularly in the parish community. Its goals and purposes are:

"As a professional organization, the Federation is committed to assist the total American hierarchy and individual bishops in their responsibility of positive leadership in liturgical education and development. It will be the task of this Federation:

(a) To foster and coordinate the work of liturgical commissions* as they affect the needs and utilize the resources of their people.

(b) To gather, dispense, and commission catechetical materials that will aid individual commissions in carrying out educational programs in their respective dioceses.

(c) To cooperate with the Bishops' Committee on the Liturgy* and its Secretariat in the sponsoring of national meetings of Diocesan Liturgical Commissions.

(d) To serve, in an advisory capacity, the Bishops' Committee on the Liturgy especially on matters to be proposed to the National Conference of Catholic Bishops.*

(e) To bring results of pastoral experience to the Bishops' Committee on the Liturgy.

(f) To encourage and facilitate the legitimate adaptation* of liturgical rites and ceremonies to the American culture as envisioned by the *Constitution on the Sacred Liturgy** (Nos. 39-40).

(g) To be the medium through which Diocesan Committees can contribute responsibly and effectively in forming and in articulating the voice of priests,* Religious,* and laity* in the development of Liturgy.

In order to accomplish its goals of promoting effective pastoral Liturgy the Federation recognizes its need to solicit the help of the academic community engaged in the pursuit of liturgical studies, of allied sciences, and of Churches and communities separated from us; in turn it will make available its pastoral insights" *(Newsletter BCL,* v.7, no. 7, p. 8).

See also LITURGICAL COMMISSIONS.)

Felicity and Perpetua, Sts. *See* PERPETUA AND FELICITY, STS.

Feminist Liturgical Movement. *See* WOMEN AS MINISTERS.

Ferial. *See* WEEKDAY.

Fermentum (Fur-MEN-tuhm). A term of Biblical origin (Mt 13:33) that in the first centuries of Christianity indicated a particle of the Eucharist.* At Rome around the 4th century, the Pope* (and possibly the bishop* elsewhere) was accustomed to send the fermentum from a Host* consecrated at his Mass* to parish priests* who were unable to take part in the Papal Mass because they were celebrating the Eucharist with their people. The fragment was placed in the priest's chalice at the moment when the *Pax Domini** ("Peace of the Lord") was said—as a sign of unity of Pope and faithful* in Christ. *See also* COMMINGLING.

Ferule (Ferula) (FER-uhl; FER-[y]uh-luh). (1) A rod that was formerly used by priests* of the Vatican Sacred Penitentiary to touch penitents lightly. (2) The name also refers to the staff surmounted by a Cross that both clergy and people used for support during lengthy liturgical ceremonies before sitting was allowed. It continues to be used in choir by Maronite monks as well as by dissident Ethiopian and Coptic monks.

Fidelis of Sigmaringen, St. (fi-DAY-luhs uhv sig-muh-RIN-guhn; -juhn). 1578-1622. Born in Sigmaringen, a German town in the principality of the Hohenzollern, Mark Roy was called "the Christian philosopher" during his student years. After serving as a teacher for three princes and practicing law at Colmar, he entered the Capuchin Order at Fribourg and took the

name Fidelis. Practicing an austere life of penance,* vigils,* and prayer,* he also engaged in continuous preaching of God's Word* and labored for the unity of Christians. Commissioned by the Sacred Congregation for the Propagation of the Faith to preach, together with eight Fathers of his Order, in the canton of the Grisons in Switzerland, he was attacked by a band of fanatics and died at Seewis praying for his assassins. *Liturgical celebration;* April 24 (Opt. Mem.); *theme:* growing in the knowledge of the power of Christ's Resurrection.*

Final Antiphons of Our Lady (FAI-nuhl AN-tuh-fuhnz uhv owr LAY-dee). The four great antiphons in honor of Mary are recited or sung at the end of Night Prayer* in the Liturgy of the Hours.* Until the *Liturgy of the Hours* was promulgated, each of the four was specified for a certain liturgical season. Now all those saying the Divine Office may choose any one of them on any day. Originating in the 11th or 12th centuries, they are of extremely uncertain authorship. Frequently these chants are sung on other occasions also. They are: *Alma Redemptoris Mater (Loving Mother of the Redeemer); Regina Caeli Laetare* (Queen of Heaven, Rejoice); Ave,* Regina Caelorum* (Hail, Queen of Heaven); and Salve Regina* (Hail, Holy Queen).* The last is the most popular.

Final Blessing (FAI-nuhl BLES-ing). The blessing* given by the celebrant* at Mass* before the Dismissal.* It asks for the greatest of all blessings to come upon those who have partaken of the Word of God* and the Body and Blood of Christ* in the Eucharist.* It also recalls Christ's action as He was taking leave of the disciples at His Ascension*: "Then he led them out as far as Bethany, raised his hands, and blessed them" (Lk 24:50).

This Final Blessing is the remnant of an early rite at Rome that included an invitation on the part of the deacon* for the people to bow their heads and a Prayer over the People* on the part of the bishop* with the people answering Amen.* From the 7th century on, a more simple form evolved. At the end of Papal Masses, the Pope* began to bless each section of the congregation as he processed from the altar.* Gradually bishops were allowed to do the same, and from the 11th century on priests* also performed this practice. In 1570, it became part of the rite of Mass in the Missal of Pius V,* with an accompanying text—still given after the Dismissal.

In the present *Roman Missal** the Blessing has been placed before the Dismissal and may take any one of three forms. (1) *Simple Form.* After the Greeting* the celebrant gives a simple blessing in the name of the Father,* and of the Son,* and of the Holy Spirit,* to which the people respond Amen. (2) *Solemn Blessing.* The deacon invites the people to bow their heads and pray for God's blessing. The celebrant pronounces three invocations (according to the season or feast*) each concluded by the people's Amen. Then the celebrant gives a simple blessing to which the people add Amen. (3) *Prayer over the People.* The deacon invites the people to bow their heads and pray for God's blessing. The celebrant says a prayer over the congregation to which all respond Amen. The celebrant gives a simple blessing concluded by Amen.

Finding of the True Cross. *See* CROSS.

Finger Cloth. *See* TOWELS.

Fire (FAI-uhr). A combination of flame, light, and heat, fire is closely allied with life. It is the most suitable symbol we have for the soul within that makes us live. Like fire, life is warm and radiant, never still, eager for the unreachable. Fire is also a symbol of God: "The Lord, your God, is a consuming fire" (Dt 4:24). Jesus came to light a fire on earth (Lk 12:49) and He alone could baptize in the Holy Spirit* and in fire (Mt 3:11). Fire is the symbol of the Spirit and of the ardor of Divine love.

The Easter Vigil* begins with the blessing of the new fire, from which the Paschal Candle* will be lighted. This new fire is the symbol of the Risen Christ, light that sprang up in the darkness, of which the Paschal Candle will be a more durable symbol. The candles* that are used at almost all liturgical rites are discreet symbols of the propagation of the fire of Divine Love in the Holy Spirit and of the life of the Risen Christ, light of the world. *See* EASTER VIGIL

First Blessing (fuhrst BLES-ing). One given by a newly ordained priest* with imposition of hands and the ordinary formula used outside of Mass.* This Sacramental* might be very efficacious since those who receive it and the one who blesses on this occasion are particularly well disposed.

First Communion. *See* COMMUNION.

First Confession. *See* PENANCE, RITE OF.

First Friday Devotions (fuhrst FRAI-dee; -day; di-VOH-shuhnz). Because of a promise made to St. Margaret Mary Alacoque,* many observe the First Fridays by receiving Communion* on nine consecutive First Fridays, usually in honor of the Sacred Heart.* The Votive Mass* for First Fridays in honor of the Sacred Heart has special privileges. The faithful* practice this devotion the year round because the Sacred Heart, among other things, has promised death in the state of grace,* the grace of final perseverance,* and the Sacred Heart as a haven at the hour of death.

First Martyrs of the Church of Rome (fuhrst MAHR-tuhrs uhv thuh chuhrch uhv rohm). For varying and valid reasons, the new reformed Calendar* of the Church has suppressed many names of ancient Martyrs.* In exchange this feast has been inserted into the Calendar on the day following that of Sts. Peter and Paul* in honor of the first Martyrs of the Church of Rome who were put to death at the Vatican Circus at the time of the persecution under Nero (in 64).

Whatever was the real cause of the conflagration that erupted within the confines of the Palatine and the Celius and ravaged the city for six days and seven nights, the wicked Emperor elected to hold Christians responsible for it—most of them slaves, enfranchised, and foreign. The cruelty and injustice of the ensuing repression, which led to the martyrdom of Sts. Peter and Paul and had the victims torn to pieces by wild beasts or burned like living torches, eventually evoked the indignation of even pagans, such as Tacitus. *Liturgical celebration:* June 30 (Opt. Mem.); *theme:* joy in the victory of Christ and His Martyrs.

First Reading (fuhrst REED-ing). During the Jewish synagogue service, the books of Moses (the Law*) were read continuously from one session to another, and the Prophets* were also read "at will." The early Church made use of this tradition by inserting at least one Old Testament* reading in the Liturgy of the Word.* At Rome, this was followed by two New Testament* readings, with the Gospel* as the second of the two. In time, the Old Testament reading was dropped from the Sunday Eucharist, and the Old Testament selections occurred only on weekdays. Vatican II* restored the use of the Old Testament on Sundays.

In the revised Liturgy,* there are always three readings on Sundays and major feasts. The first is usually from the Old Testament. Generally the Old Testament readings were chosen to prepare for the Gospel. In line with ancient tradition, the First Reading during the Easter Season* is taken from the Acts of the Apostles,* a Book that shows how the early Christians bore witness to the Paschal Mystery.*

On weekdays, there are only two readings. During Advent* and Lent* the first is always from the Old Testament and is related to the Gospel. During Ordinary Time both the Old Testament and the New are used with no attempt to harmonize the reading with the Gospel.

The Church wants us to recall that the proclamation of God's Word is always centered on Christ, present through His Word. Old Testament writings prepare for Him; New Testament books speak of Him directly. All of Scripture* calls us to believe once more and to follow.

In the *Liturgy of the Hours,** the Reading is not so much a proclamation to move us to worship as it is in the Mass and the Sacraments; it is a *lectio divina,** a reading and meditating of God's Word. It is primarily didactic. It is meant to be listened to in a spirit of openness and to shape our way of thinking as the Spirit wills. (For the contents of the First Reading, *see* READINGS; TWO-YEAR CYCLE OF READINGS, ALTERNATE.) *See also* EPISTLE; LITURGY OF THE WORD; READINGS; SECOND READING; TWO-YEAR CYCLE OF READINGS, ALTERNATE.

First Saturday Devotions (fuhrst SAT-uhr-dee; -day; di-VOH-shuhnz). Devotion rendered the Immaculate Heart of Mary* on the First Saturday for five consecutive months as a result of her revelations at Fatima. Besides receiving Communion,* after confession, those who practice this devotion are to recite five decades of the Rosary* and meditate on these Mysteries* for fifteen minutes. The Votive Mass* in honor of the Immaculate Heart on First Saturdays has special privileges.

First Thursday Devotions (fuhrst THUHRZ-dee; -day; di-VOH-shuhnz). Christians are asked to receive Communion* and pray for increased vocations to the priesthood* and for continuing strength for priests active in the ministry on the First Thursday of each month. To strengthen this practice, the Votive Mass* in honor of Christ the Eternal High Priest, when celebrated on the First Thursday, has special privileges.

Fish (fish). From early centuries this symbol is found in Christian literature and art to represent Christ. *Ichthus*, the Greek word for fish,

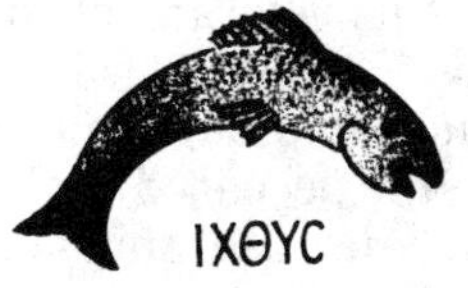

forms an acrostic with the initial letters of: *J*esus *C*hrist, *G*od's *S*on, *S*avior. In the New Testament* fish is connected with Christianity through the multiplication of loaves and fish, Christ feeding His disciples fish after the Resurrection,* and fishermen being called by Jesus to become fishers of humans. By the 4th century the fish was accepted as a Eucharistic symbol.

Fistula. *See* TUBE.

Fixed Feasts. *See* FEASTS.

Flagon (FLAG-uhn). A pitcher of metal or pottery in which is consecrated sufficient wine when many people receive under both species during Mass.*

Flags (flagz). The Catholic assembly for worship* cannot divest itself of its cultural, ethnic, and national identities. Our Liturgy* should always reflect the Church that is truly Catholic. Thus when the national flag of a country appears in church sanctuaries, it is usually accompanied by the papal flag, not as a requirement but as a symbol of loyalty. Although the papal flag is the state flag of Vatican City, it is symbolic of the papacy indicating both sacred and secular power. *Environment and Art in Catholic Worship* (no. 101) seems to indicate that such a decoration is not appropriate as a permanent part of the liturgical environment, but it should be used on particular occasions or holidays.

The national flag is sometimes used as a sign of honor by a nation to one of its veterans at the Rite of Funerals.* Since the white pall* is symbolic of the baptismal garment given to the deceased at the time of Baptism,* its use should be continued during the Mass,* rather than the flag, which would be more appropriately incorporated into graveside rites.

Flectamus Genua (flek-TAH-moos JE-noo-ah). A Latin phrase meaning "Let us kneel," which on certain penitential days was pronounced before the prayer by the celebrant* at Low Mass* and by the deacon* at Solemn High Mass.* The people would kneel together with the celebrant and pray silently for a short time.* When the celebrant or deacon said "Levate" ("Stand"), all would rise and the celebrant would say the prayer.

In the revised Latin *Missal,** the term occurs only on Good Friday* before the General Intercessions.* The rubric states: "The conference of bishops* may provide an acclamation* for the people to sing before the priest's prayer or decree that the deacon's traditional invitation to kneel and pray be continued: Let us kneel—let us stand." The *Sacramentary* adds: "In the United States, if desired, an appropriate acclamation by the people may be introduced before each of the solemn prayers of intercession, or the traditional period of kneeling at each of the prayers (at the invitation of the deacon) may be continued."

Flowers (FLOW-uhrz). A long history of flowers as adornment for altars,* before statues,* at shrines* and other places of pilgrimage exists in the Catholic Church. Thus they were associated with a sense of joy and festivity, and usually excluded on days of penance and during penitential seasons like Advent* and Lent,* even for funerals. But this liturgical custom clashed with the human sense of sorrow at funerals, since flowers express respect and affection.

The new rubrics allow flowers for the decoration of churches. A lack of such decorations during Advent and Lent would heighten the penitential aspect of such seasons. Nevertheless, one would hope that the tabernacle,* apart from the altar of sacrifice, would be graced with fresh flowers all year. Artificial flowers are certainly out of place; cut flowers resemble a form of sacrifice, since they wither and must be replaced.

Floral decorations in Christian art* on buildings, vestments,* vessels,* and ornaments of various kinds appear abundantly and have been symbolically interpreted throughout the centuries. For instance, some of the figurative meanings are: the tulip, prayer; the myrtle, the state of virginity; the hawthorne, hope; the violet, humility; the hyacinth, peace and power.

Font (font). A fixed receptacle, ordinarily of stone, in which baptismal water is stored. When Baptism* occurred more frequently by immersion, the font was quite large, below ground level; the catechumens* would stand in it when water was poured over them. For infants, a font was above ground, enabling the little ones to be immersed easily. However, when Baptism by pouring became more common, the fonts were smaller and raised above ground, so that the child could be held over the font while water was poured; the adult could lean over the basin during the action.

Throughout the ages various shapes have been used for the fonts, all of them in some fashion or other being symbolic of an aspect of Baptism: a tomb from which the sinner rises; the Death and Resurrection* of Jesus through which the sinner is now born again to a new life. In many churches the font may be in a separate section or chapel (baptistery*) or marked off as a sort of closed section of the church.

Small fonts, also called stoups, holding holy water* that the people use in blessing themselves as they enter or leave church, are placed near the doors of the church.

For Ever and Ever (fawr EV-uhr and EV-uhr). Conclusion of the prayers in the Liturgy* as well as many private prayers. It is a translation of the Latin *"Per omnia saeculo saeculorum,"* which literally means "For all the centuries upon centuries" or *"In saecula saeculorum,"* which literally means "For centuries upon centuries." Both Latin phrases may also be translated as "World without end," which has become a hallowed phrase at the end of many traditional prayers.

The conclusion refers to the eternity of God and alludes to the hope of those who say the prayers to which it is appended that the temporal praise they offer now may become eternal praise in heaven. *See also* PRAYER ENDINGS.

For the Kingdom, the Power, and the Glory . . . (fawr thuh KING-duhm, thuh pow-uhr, and thuh GLOH-; GLAW-ree). Doxological acclamation* of the people at the end of the Lord's Prayer* and its embolism* at Mass.* The entire text is: "For the Kingdom, the power, and the glory are yours now and for ever" (in Latin: *Quia tuum est regnum, et potestas, et gloria in saecula).*

This acclamation comes from the Byzantine Rite,* which always appends it to the Our Father, possibly out of a desire not to end the prayer on a negative note: "Deliver us from evil." It is thematically linked to the Lord's Prayer with its request for the full realization of God's Kingdom.*

Forgiveness of Sin. *See* PENANCE, RITE OF.

Formulas, Liturgical (FOHR-myuh-luhz, luh-TUHR-ji-kuhl; li-). The set prayer texts recited or sung during liturgical celebrations, by either the president,* the deacon,* or the congregation.* Their forms vary, some invitational, some responsorial, and others direct prayer, usually addressed to the Father.* Ordinarily their style or pattern is not spontaneous since they are repeated and tend to receive identical responses.

Some examples would be the Acclamations,* the Responsorial Psalms,* the Doxology,* the Presidential Prayers,* Litanies,* Eucharistic Prayers,* and Profession of Faith.* Some are invitational and directive, as frequently happens at Mass,* and usually expect the proper answer. Acclamations of joy occur in the Alleluia.* Liturgical prayer is led by the celebrant,* but active participation* is expected of the deacon and congregation. *See also* LITURGICAL BOOKS.

Fortitude (FAWRT-uh-t[y]ood). One of the four chief moral virtues,* which dispose us to lead moral, or good, lives by aiding us to treat persons and things in the right way—that is, according to the will of God. They are also known as cardinal virtues because they are like hinges on which hang all other moral virtues and our whole moral life.

Fortitude strengthens the will and makes it capable of following what is good, even when it is difficult or arduous. Only those with fortitude, like the Martyrs,* are able to undertake and endure great things. Vices opposed to fortitude are timidity and temerity while virtues allied with it are magnanimity, patience, and perseverance.

Participating in the Liturgy* is an act of the moral virtue of religion that strengthens the other moral virtues including fortitude, as indicated in the article on good works.* *See also* GOOD WORKS; JUSTICE; PRUDENCE; TEMPERANCE; VIRTUES.

Forty Hours Devotion (FAWR-tee owrz di-VOH-shuhn). To honor the forty hours that the body of Christ rested in the tomb, the Blessed Sacrament* is solemnly exposed for this period of time, during which public services, private meditation, and prayer* take place. The devotion developed in the 16th century, and many regulations were made by various Popes.* The devotion was characterized by beginning and ending with a Solemn High Mass,* a procession,* and the Litany of the Saints.*

St. John Neumann,* Bishop of Philadelphia, advocated the devotion in the United States. In the last century because of lack of attendance, frequently the period was interrupted during the night so that it lasted three days. In other situations a shorter period of time was established. Today each parish* is expected to have an extended

period of time for exposition of the Blessed Sacrament whereby due honor and glory is given to the Sacramental Lord. Regulations insist that the devotion is secondary to the Mass, and therefore should be interrupted during the celebration of Mass. *See also* EUCHARIST.

Founders of the Order of Servites, Seven, Sts. (FOWN-duhrs uhv thee AWRD-uhr uhv SER-vaits, SEV-uhn). 13th century. On the feast of the Assumption* in 1233, seven members of a Florentine Confraternity* devoted to the Mother of God were gathered in prayer. The Blessed Virgin* appeared to the young men, exhorting them to devote themselves to her service in retirement from the world. With the approval of their bishop,* these zealous Christians who had once been prominent businessmen of Florence retired to Mount Senario. They founded a new Order which, in recognition of the special manner of venerating the Seven Sorrows of Mary, was called "Servants of Mary," or "Servites."

The group of Seven Brothers was such a unit that only two names are known to us with certainty: St. Bonfiglio Monaldo, who seems to have been the most forceful personality, and St. Alexis Falconieri, who died at the age of more than a hundred in 1310. *Liturgical celebration:* February 17 (Opt. Mem.); *theme:* deep love for Mary, the Mother of God.

Fraction. *See* BREAKING OF (THE) BREAD.

Frances of Rome, St. (FRAN-ses uhv rohm). 1384-1440. Born in Rome of a noble family, Frances was given in marriage at the age of twelve to a nobleman named Lawrence Ponziani and bore him three sons. Although living in calamitous times, she gave her goods to the poor and looked after the sick. Frances was outstanding in her active love for the destitute and in practicing the virtues* of humility and patience. In 1425, she founded the Congregation of the Oblates under the rule of St. Benedict,* and after her husband's death she entered the Congregation in 1437 and went on to become superior. She is the Patroness of Motorists. *Liturgical celebration:* March 9 (Opt. Mem.); *theme:* finding God in all aspects of life.

Frances Xavier Cabrini, St. (FRAN-ses ZAY-vee-uhr, ZAV-yuhr, kuh-BREE-nee). 1850-1917. The Italian-born foundress of the Missionary Sisters of the Sacred Heart had hoped to go to China as a missionary, but through the intervention of her local bishop* and Pope Leo XIII, who approved the rule of the Order she established, she was sent to New York to care for the needs of the Italian immigrants and their children. She, who was considered too sickly to enter the Religious Life, established her own Order and founded sixty-seven convents of her sisterhood in Europe and the Americas by the time she died at sixty-seven years of age. Her Sisters work in orphanages, schools, and hospitals.

Because of the many activities in the United States and the other Americas, Frances made many trips across the ocean. In 1909 she took out enough time from her very busy life to become an American citizen. Her energy, verve, and business sense, together with much trust and faith in the Lord, blessed her many activities, despite her constant illness. She died in Chicago on December 22, 1917, and the lapse of years usually required between death and beatification* and canonization* were dispensed with in her case. Frances was the first American-citizen saint when canonized in 1946. Since Memorials cannot be celebrated fully on December 22, her Memorial* is transferred to November 13 as part of the Proper* for the United States. She is the Patroness of Emigrants and Hospital Administrators. *Liturgical celebration:* November 13 (Memorial); *theme:* sickness is no obstacle to fulfilling the needs of the Church.

Francis de Sales, St. (FRAN-sis duh saylz). 1567-1622. Born in Savoy, Francis became a priest and labored diligently for the restoration of Catholicism in his country. After many victories and conversions, which were the fruits of his apostolic zeal in combating Calvinism, Francis was chosen Bishop* of Geneva. He showed himself to be a true pastor to his clergy* and faithful,* and he strengthened their faith through his writings, deeds, and example. He was the architect of a Christian spirituality that was especially accessible to the laity,* and with St. Frances de Chantal* he founded the Visitation Order. Francis was declared a Doctor* of the Church and the Patron of the Deaf and of Writers. *Liturgical celebration:* February 24 (Memorial); *theme:* the spirit of compassion.

Francis of Assisi, St. (FRAN-sis uhv uh-SEEZ-ee, -SIS-ee). 1182-1226. Born at Assisi in Italy, Francis led a carefree life until the age of twenty-five when he renounced his wealth and committed himself to God. He led a life of evangelical poverty and preached the love of God to all. He founded the Order of Friars Minor, the Second Order of Poor Clares, and the Tertiaries or Third Order of St. Francis (now called the Secular Franciscan Order)—lay people* who practice penance* while living in the world.

Francis was favored by our Lord with the Stigmata and is known as the Seraphic Saint. He has captured the imagination of people of all religious persuasions by his love for God and human beings as well as all His creatures, by his simplicity, directness, and single-mindedness, and by the lyrical aspects of his multifaceted life. Francis was a man possessed of vast spiritual insight and presence, a man whose all-consuming love for Christ and redeemed creation burst forth in all he said and did. He is the Patron of Catholic Action, Ecologists, and Merchants. *Liturgical celebration:* October 4 (Memorial); *theme:* following Christ in poverty and humility.

Francis of Paola (FRAN-sis uhv pay-OH-luh). 1416-1507. Born in Paola, a small city in Calabria,

Francis became a hermit on its outskirts in 1432. In time he founded a Congregation of Hermits, which was later titled the Order of Minims and approved by the Apostolic See* in 1506. After establishing his Congregation also in France, he died at Tours. *Liturgical celebration:* April 2 (Opt. Mem.); *theme:* giving up all worldly possessions out of love for God.

Francis Xavier, St. (FRAN-sis ZAY-vee-uhr; ZAV-yuhr). 1506-1552. Born in Spain, Francis went to study liberal arts in Paris and instead became one of the first Jesuits under St. Ignatius Loyola.* He was ordained at Rome in 1537 and devoted himself to works of charity. In 1541, he traveled to the Orient where for ten years he untiringly proclaimed the Gospel* in India and Japan and converted thousands through his preaching. He died off the coast of China while waiting to gain entry and pursue his ministry there. He is the Patron of the Foreign Missions. *Liturgical celebration:* December 3 (Memorial); *theme:* zeal for the Faith.

Freedom (FREE-duhm). The absence of necessity, coercion, or constraint in one's choice of action. It implies self-mastery and self-determination. The Liturgy* requires a freedom of acting from those who take part in it, for their participation* must be full, active, and "conscious." Without freedom, such outward acts of worship* are valueless for the individual. At the same time, the Liturgy, following the Bible,* says much about freedom.

Christian freedom is that of the children of God (Tuesday after Easter,* Opening Prayer*), for God is the "Father of our freedom" (Friday of 4th Week of Easter, Opening Prayer), and it comes to us from Christ who sets people free (Wednesday of 5th Week of Lent,* Gospel*) and in the Holy Spirit* (January 1, Reading II*).

Christ has obtained for us freedom from sin, from the Jewish Law, and from death (Wednesday of 5th Week of Lent, Gospel). This freedom is not to be regarded so much as "freedom from" as "freedom for"—freedom for implementing Christ's law of love (13th Sunday in Ordinary Time,* C, Reading II), "free to love as Christ teaches" (10th Sunday in Ordinary Time, Alternative Opening Prayer). Hence, the Church prays that God may "free all the world to rejoice in [Christ's] peace" (Christ the King,* Alternative Opening Prayer).

The Church in America also celebrates the day of freedom for the American nation (July 4), indicating that political freedom both derives from and is instituted to insure theological freedom brought by Christ—which is the only real freedom. It insures that we have (1) *freedom of conscience,* the right to direct our destiny in accord with our conscience; (2) *freedom of thought,* the right to seek truth and adhere to it; (3) *freedom of action,* the right to be led by inner conviction rather than subservience; (4) *freedom of speech,* the right to make known and publish our thoughts and artistic creations; and (5) *freedom of the press,* the right to print news and comments on life and to have access to such information.

Hence, Christians strive to use these freedoms in fashioning themselves into the image of Christ, in transforming themselves into Christ's likeness through love* and grace.* *See also* DIGNITATIS HUMANAE.

Frequent Communion. *See* COMMUNION.

Fruits of the Holy Spirit. *See* HOLY SPIRIT.

Fruits of the Mass (froots uhv thuh mas). The Mass* renews the Sacrifice of the Cross, applying the merits from it to souls. Both temporal and spiritual blessings* are derived from the Eucharistic Sacrifice, and the whole Church*—both living and deceased members—benefits from the *general* fruits of the Mass. The *special* fruits are shared first by the priest who celebrates, then by those for whom he offers it in a special way, usually because of receiving a stipend,* and lastly by all those who participate* in the sacrificial Liturgy,* which would include the Universal Church.*

The preceding distinction was developed in the Middle Ages, particularly by Duns Scotus and was accepted by the Church for centuries as the theological principle behind the reception of stipends. A current liturgical theology decries this distinction, and arguments that claim to be derived from the new Code of Canon Law and Paul VI's 1974 apostolic letter *Firma in Traditione* contend that the Church no longer fosters the traditional explanation of the special fruits of the Mass. Paul VI indicates "a more abundant supply of fruits" accrue to the faithful* by virtue of giving a Mass offering but presumably does not say it is a "special fruit of the Mass."

Proponents of this view would claim that the beneficiary of the "supply of fruits" is the donor of the Mass offering, and not the intention for which the priests prays. The new Code and Paul VI do not claim offering a Mass for a certain intention results in any benefit at all for that intention. According to them, the principal beneficiary of Mass offerings is the Church herself, since she gains financially; the secondary beneficiaries are the donors, who profit because of their spiritual disposition, their participation in the Eucharist,* and their sharing of the work and ministry in the Church. Some hesitate to attribute spiritual benefits to the donor's intention because a Mass was applied for it, since God alone answers prayers.

Despite this recent theory, the practice of the Church indicates that the intention of the donor is included in the special benefits or "special fruit" derived from the Mass by the person who offers the stipend. *See also* STIPENDS.

Funeral Rites and Ceremonies (FYOO-nuhr-uhl raits and SER-uh-moh-neez). In accordance with the *Constitution on the Sacred Liturgy** one of the early post-Vatican II* decrees set forth the revised Rites for Burial, that more clearly expressed the Paschal character of Christian death and allowed sufficient variation to fit the traditions and circumstances of various countries. Through Baptism* we became one with the Risen Christ and expect to be welcomed into heaven to join the community of Saints.* At His second coming* we are promised the bodily resurrection.

With the funeral rites, Christians affirm their hope of everlasting happiness without ignoring the feelings of those concerned. Customs and traditions should be allied to the Gospel* in the funeral rites in order to profess this Paschal faith. Through use of the Biblical readings, respect for the dead, hope of reunion with God in heaven, and the witness of Christian living are encouraged.

Prayer in a truly liturgical spirit that expresses faith in eternal happiness for the deceased does not preclude prayer for the relatives who are seeking consolation in their sorrow. Although the Office for the Dead* may not be the custom in many places, the current wake service* is built upon the format of the Office. It is permissible to have Christian funeral rites for those who are cremated.

Catechumens* have the same privileges for Christian burial as Catholics. Children who die before receiving the Baptism* their parents intended to confer on them may be given ecclesiastical rites through permission of the Ordinary.* The Ordinary may allow the funeral rites for baptized members of non-Catholic Churches if their own minister is unavailable, and it would not be contrary to their own will.

In arranging funeral celebrations, every effort should be made to be aware of the circumstances of the deceased's life and death, the sorrow of the relatives and their needs, so that faith in the Paschal Mystery* and the resurrection of the body may be strengthened. Frequently persons attend funerals who rarely or never participate in

the Eucharist,* so it is necessary for the celebrant* to weigh well the choice of Readings* and the presentation during the Homily.* Thus he ministers the Good News of Christ to all. Except for the Mass, deacons* may perform the Funeral Rites, and in some cases a lay person may be deputed to lead the prayers during the Liturgy of the Word* and the Commendation.

In planning the celebration, the priest should consider various circumstances and the wishes of the family, while making generous use of the variety offered in the texts. When the priest celebrates the Funeral Liturgy with meaning and dignity, he shows true concern for the family, supporting them in sorrow, and involving them in the celebration in a loving and thoughtful manner. Relatives or friends may be chosen to be readers* and to bring up the gifts in preparation for the Eucharist.

Although the Rites are usually marked with simplicity, it may be necessary to explain some of the symbolism, which ordinarily reflects the Christian's attitude toward death.* In the United States, vestments* may be black,* violet,* or white*; in most instances white is used to express the gladness that the deceased is on his or her way to heaven. Holy water* relates to the waters of Baptism, and the white covering over the coffin reminds one of the baptismal garment. As the Paschal Candle* was used at Baptism, now it is carried in the funeral procession and placed near the coffin. Although there is hope because of Christ's Resurrection,* all must be sensitive to the grief of the mourners and to the customs they may have.

Since the Rite had to be developed for the entire world, three plans were established. The *first* plan is comparable to the former Roman ritual, in which there were three stations: at the home (or the funeral parlor), at the church, and at the cemetery. This plan is more common in the United States. The *second* plan has only two stations, the cemetery chapel and the grave, more in accord with the German custom, with the Mass being said either before or after the funeral. The *third* plan is celebrated in the home of the deceased conforming to the conditions in Africa. The Conferences of Bishops* may allow for many local variations since the Rite allows great flexibility in any of the plans.

Between the death and the funeral, various opportunities may exist for prayer, primarily at the wake service* or when the body is placed on the bier. These services show vestiges of the Office of the Dead.* (*See* WAKE SERVICE.)

First Plan

The principal parts, or stations, of the first plan are the service in the home, funeral parlor, or wherever else the body may be exhibited before the funeral; Mass celebrated in the Church; the Rite of Final Commendation or the actual burial.

In the home or funeral parlor the priest enters, greets the people present, recites a Psalm,* usually in responsory fashion with them, and adds a prayer.

Since this first station is not the usual custom in the United States, the priest meets the body in the vestibule of the church, greets those present, sprinkles the body with holy water, and recites the prayers that would have been said at the home or funeral parlor. The white pall is placed over the coffin. During a song the body is brought forward in the procession, someone carrying the Paschal Candle,* to the front

of the church where the Opening Prayer* begins the Mass.

After the Liturgy of the Word,* a Homily* tailored to the congregation is given, relating to the Lord's Resurrection and our hope of eternal happiness. A Eulogy* is forbidden. After the General Intercessions* the Liturgy of the Eucharist* begins, and participation by the family or friends at the preparation of the gifts is to be encouraged. Incensation* of the gifts, altar, and body may occur. At Communion* all may receive under both species.

The Final Commendation and Farewell may occur immediately after the Prayer after Communion.* After a brief introduction, there is time for silent prayer, even some words from a relative, and if holy water* and incense* have not been used before, the body is then sprinkled and incensed. As the body is taken away an Antiphon* is sung.

When the Final Commendation is celebrated after the Mass, then at the third station, namely the grave, a prayer is used to bless the grave if necessary. Usually a reading from Scripture with a Responsorial Psalm* follows, and a prayer precedes the Lord's Prayer* said together by all. After another short prayer for the deceased, a prayer may be added for the mourners.

When the priest and congregation come to the cemetery with the body for the Final Commendation and Farewell, rather than having it at the end of Mass, the grave may be blessed, if it has not been blessed before. Then a prayer occurs bidding the deceased farewell, and a relative may speak. A reading from Scripture with a Responsorial Psalm may take place, followed by sprinkling the body with holy water* and incensing it. The final prayer for the deceased is read followed by a prayer for those present.

Second Plan

The second plan excludes the Eucharistic celebration during the Funeral Rites, although Mass might be celebrated at some suitable time without the body being present. The first station in this plan would be at the cemetery chapel where, after the greeting and the song, the Liturgy of the Word* with a Homily* follows. Thereafter the Final Commendation and Farewell follow as described above.

Normally the procession to the grave or tomb takes place immediately and during it Psalms are recited. The second station at the grave or tomb occurs as in the first plan, with the two different possibilities depending upon whether or not the Final Commendation has been said after the Liturgy of the Word.

Third Plan

In the third plan the home of the deceased is used; the Liturgy of the Word occurs comparable to that in a wake service. The local bishop* may grant permission to have the Funeral Mass in the home. Then the Rite of Final Commendation and Farewell is celebrated as in the first plan.

Funeral Rite of Children

There is a rite for baptized children who died before the age of reason, or for a child whom the parents had planned to have baptized,

but death intervened. Festive vestments are used, and Paschal symbolism and the joy of the Christian hope are expressed in this rite. The different plans as for funerals of adults are followed in this situation also, except that the readings and prayers are adapted to the particular situation. A wide range of texts for Funerals of Baptized Children is available. *See also* EULOGY; MASS OF CHRISTIAN BURIAL; OFFICE FOR THE DEAD; WAKE SERVICE.

Revised Edition

The revised *Rite of Funerals,* with its new title *Order of Christian Funerals,* was scheduled to go into effect in the United States as of November 2, 1989. Besides the revised translation of both the text and the rubrics, there is a pastoral rearrangement and contents of the book, plus the addition of supplementary texts to cover pastoral circumstances not in the Latin edition: for example, prayers for a still-born child, for a victim of violent or accidental death, for interment of the ashes after cremation, etc. Morning Prayer* and Evening Prayer* of the *Office for the Dead** are included.

A big advantage for all will be the carefully rearranged presentations of the three plans for greater pastoral effect. It will not be necessary to turn to other sections except to choose a more appropriate presidential prayer.* The general introduction is much improved and includes a section that deals with the ministry of consolation to the deceased and mourners.

— G —

Gabriel the Archangel, St. (GAY-bree-uhl thee AHRK-ayn-juhl). Angels are spirits without bodies, who possess superior intelligence, gigantic strength, and surpassing holiness. They enjoy an intimate relationship to God as His special adopted children, contemplating, loving, and praising Him in heaven. Some of them are frequently sent as messengers to human beings from on high. The Liturgy* celebrates a feast of three Angels who were sent by God to human beings over the course of the ages: Gabriel, Michael,* and Raphael.* They are termed Archangels, the second of nine choirs of Angels, which are in descending order: Seraphim, Cherubim, Thrones, Dominations, Virtues, Powers, Principalities, Archangels, and Angels.

The name Gabriel means "man of God," or "God has shown Himself mighty." It appears first in the prophecies of Daniel* in the Old Testament.* This Angel announced to Daniel the prophecy of the seventy weeks (Dn 9:21-27). His name also occurs in the apocryphal book of Henoch. He was the Angel who appeared to Zechariah to announce the birth of St. John the Baptist* (Lk 1:11). Finally, he announced to

Mary that she would bear a Son who would be conceived of the Holy Spirit,* Son of the Most High, and the Savior of the world (Lk 1:26). He is the Patron of Messengers, Postal Employees, and Radio and Television Workers. *Liturgical celebration:* September 29 (Feast); *theme:* salvation through the protection of the Angels.

Galatians, Epistle to the (guh-LAY-shuhnz, i-PIS-uhl too thuh). Fifty-fifth Book of the Bible* and ninth of the New Testament.* Written about 49 or 50 A.D., this is possibly the most personal and emotional of Paul's Epistles. In it he strongly defends his person and his doctrine. In indignation he asserts the Divine origin of his teaching and of his authority. He shows that justification is not through the Mosaic Law,* but through faith* in Jesus Christ, Who was crucified and Who rose from the dead. He concludes that consequently the Mosaic Law was something transient and not permanent, that it is not an essential part of Christianity. At the same time, he insists on the necessity of the evangelical virtues,* especially love,* the offspring of faith.

Liturgical use: In the *Roman Missal,** this Epistle is read from the 9th through the 14th Sunday in Ordinary Time* (C) and on the days of the 27th and 28th Weeks in Ordinary Time (II) as well as on January 1 and in some feasts of Saints,* the Commons,* and Ritual Masses.* In the *Liturgy of the Hours,** it is used only on the Triumph of the Cross* (September 14) and in the Common of the Blessed Virgin Mary.* *Meaning:* Those who believe in Christ are freed from the prescriptions of the Law, so that we may live in the liberty of love and put ourselves freely at the service of our neighbor. We are transformed by Christ's grace* and become new persons whose dynamism is that of the Holy Spirit.* As it were by instinct, then, we should engage in doing good works* for the benefit of others.

Gallican Rites (GAL-i-kuhn raits). The collective name for the diverse liturgical non-Roman forms of Liturgy* from the 4th to the 8th centuries in Western Europe, primarily in Gaul. The missionaries Christianized Gaul in the early centuries, and many Eastern, Roman, and Celtic influences were felt in the Liturgy. Charlemagne imposed the Roman Rite* to avoid the continuing diversity of liturgical forms.

Subdivisions of these rites include the Ambrosian Rite,* the Celtic Rite for Ireland and Scotland, the Mozarabic Rite* for Spain, and the Gallican Rite in a narrow sense in France. Today remnants remain only of the Ambrosian Rite* in Milan and the Mozarabic in Toledo.

Unlike the concise Roman liturgical forms, the Gallican Rites contain dramatic elements and prolix prayers. Besides variable prayers at the Eucharistic Proclamation and the chanting of the Holy, Holy, Holy,* there was a more intricate ceremonial during the Preparation of the Gifts*; the arrangement for the liturgical year* differed from the Roman Rite. *See also* AMBROSIAN RITE; MOZARABIC RITE.

Garment, White (GAHR-muhnt, hwait). Near the end of the Baptismal Rite, the godparents* clothe the neophytes* with a white garment, while the priest prays that they will bring it unstained to everlasting life, since it symbolizes the fact that the persons were clothed in Christ at Baptism.* *See also* BAPTISM.

Gaudete Sunday (gow-DAY-tay SUN-dee; day). Another name for the Third Sunday of Advent* stemming from the first Latin word of the Entrance Antiphon*: "Gaudete" (Rejoice). This day was very noteworthy in previous times when Advent was much more of a penitential season replete with fasting* and abstinence* and other similar practices. Today the use of the organ,* flowers,* and the rose-colored or silver-colored vestments* are a sign of the joy* that all the Church feels at the nearness of the Redemption.*

Gaudium et Spes (GOW-dee-uhm et spes). Latin title (from the first two words "Joy and Hope") of the (pastoral) *Constitution on the Church in the Modern World* issued by the Second Vatican Council* on December 7, 1965. Among its teachings is the point that the Church by the very fact of carrying out her proper office gives impetus to human and civil culture, contributes to it, and by her activity—the Liturgy*—leads humankind toward freedom of spirit. The document also states that the Church respects new art forms suited to the people of today according to the mentality of the many different nations and regions. These are to be admitted into the sanctuary* wherever, by being expressed in a way adapted and conformed to the demands of the Liturgy, they raise the mind to God.* Moreover, priests* should see to it that the vocation of husbands and wives is encouraged by the preaching of God's Word, worship in Liturgy, and other spiritual helps. *See also* VATICAN COUNCIL, SECOND.

Gelasian Sacramentary (juh-LAY-zee-uhn sak-ruh-MEN-tuh-ree). Name given (since L. Muratori in 1748) to a Vatican manuscript of an early *Sacramentary** originating in the 6th or 7th century. It contains the formulas for the president of the Eucharist* and other celebrations. It was erroneously attributed to Pope Gelasius I (492-496) who is known to have composed Prefaces* and Prayers* for Sacramentaries.

The *Gelasian Sacramentary* is divided into three books: (1) Proper of the Season* (from the Vigil of Christmas* to Pentecost*), including texts for other rites like ordinations,* the catechumenate* and Baptism,* Penance,* Dedication of a Church,* and the Consecration of Virgins*; (2) Proper of the Saints* and the Sundays of Advent*; and (3) Ordinary Sundays, with the Canon* and various celebrations.

A characteristic feature is the presence of two or even three prayers before the Prayer over the Gifts.* It is thought that the *Gelasian Sacramentary* was for use of the parish priests of Rome while the *Gregorian** was for the use of the Pope.* The name *Gelasian of the 8th Century* is given to various copies of a Sacramentary compiled in Gaul around 750, which includes the *Gelasian* contents plus numerous elements taken from Gallican Sacramentaries. The oldest of these is the *Sacramentary of Gellone. See also* GREGORIAN SACRAMENTARY: LEONINE SACRAMENTARY: SACRAMENTARY.

General Absolution (JEN-uhr-uhl ab-suh-LOO-shuhn). In an emergency when private confession* is impossible, the Sacramental absolution of several people at one time. It is used in the third Rite of Reconciliation. *See also* PENANCE, RITE OF.

General Confession (JEN-uhr-uhl kuhn-FESH-uhn). (1) In private confession,* occasionally a penitent may desire to confess all past sins for a certain period, though they may have been previously mentioned and forgiven. Such a general confession is required if a mortal sin had been deliberately concealed in a past confession, or a confession in the past was invalid because of lack of sorrow. A general confession may be spiritually beneficial at the moment of entering a new state of life, such as Marriage,* Holy Orders,* or Religious Life.*

(2) The term also refers to the third Rite of Reconciliation, in which a group of people receive absolution at one time. *See also* GENERAL ABSOLUTION; PENANCE, RITE OF.

General Intercessions (JEN-uhr-uhl in-tuhr-SESH-uhnz). Occurring after the Profession of Faith,* or, if the latter is not prescribed, after the Homily,* these are a series of petitions for all people by which the faithful* exercise their priestly function. Hence, they are also known as the Prayer of the Faithful and should be included in every Mass* with a congregation. The sequence of intentions is usually: the needs of the Church, civil authorities, salvation of the world,* those in need, and the local commu-

nity. On a special occasion, e.g., marriage or funeral, the intentions may relate more closely to the particular celebration.

The priest* invites the people to pray, and the deacon,* chanter,* or reader* sings or proclaims the intentions, to which the people reply by a common response after each or by silent prayer. The celebrant concludes with a prayer, seconded by the faithful's Amen.

Similar intercessions occur during Morning Prayer* and Evening Prayer.*

A more formal expression of the General Intercessions occurs in the Liturgy of Good Friday,* where the celebrant intones solemn intercessory prayers that are followed by silent prayer and concluded with the formal prayer for that intention, assented to by the congregation with their Amen. *See also* INTERCESSIONS.

Genesis (JEN-uh-suhs). The first Book of the Bible* and of the Pentateuch (see Deuteronomy*), the book of beginnings, the beginnings of the people of God and those of the world. The first eleven chapters paint in broad strokes the history of the world, from its beginnings to Abraham,* and form the setting for the History of Salvation.* They delineate the creation of the world and human sinfulness as well as God's promise of restoration. The remaining chapters deal with the pre-history of the chosen people through the great patriarchs Abraham, Isaac, and Jacob and his twelve sons.

Liturgical use: In the *Roman Missal,** Genesis is read on the 1st and 2nd Sunday of Lent* (A,B,C), Easter Vigil,* Pentecost,* Corpus Christi* (C), the 10th (B), 16th (C), 17th (C), and 27th (B) Sundays in Ordinary Time,* and the Immaculate Conception* as well as the Ritual Masses for Baptism* of Adults and Marriage* among others. It is also read on weekdays of the 5th and 6th Weeks and the 12th, 13th, and 14th Weeks in Ordinary Time (I), Common* and Votive Masses.* In the *Liturgy of the Hours,** it is read only on the feast of the Birth of Mary.*

Meaning: For Christians, the Mystery of Easter constitutes a new Creation, originating in the Cross* of Christ. Thereon is born "the new self created in God's way in righteousness and holiness of truth" (Eph 4:24). The people of Israel inherited the promises made to the patriarchs, but through the Mystery of Christ and the Church, all nations are invited to partake of the dignity of children of God and members of the chosen people and one day to inherit the benefits of the Promise.*

Genuflection (jen-yuh-FLEK-shuhn). The act whereby the right knee touches the ground near the left ankle in reverence or to show adoration* or homage. Today it occurs only at the Consecration,* before Communion,* when passing the Blessed Sacrament* reserved in the tabernacle,* when entering or leaving the church with the Blessed Sacrament present, and at specific ceremonies in honor of the Cross.* Genuflections may also be made to the Pope,* a cardinal,* and a bishop* in his diocese.

The double genuflection, that is kneeling on both knees and bowing the upper portion of the body slightly and then rising again, was the sign of adoration made before the Holy Eucharist* exposed. The current rubric* specifies only the simple genuflection before the Blessed Sacrament, reserved or exposed. *See also* KNEELING; POSTURES IN WORSHIP.

George, St. (johrj). ? - ca. 303. Veneration of this Saint* goes back to the 4th century at Lydda in Palestine, where a church was built in his honor. George was a soldier martyred for the Faith. He is always portrayed in military dress, as having donned the armor of God to combat the forces of evil. He is the Patron of England and usually represented as engaged in battle with a dragon. He is also the Patron of Boy

Scouts, Farmers, and Soldiers. *Liturgical celebration:* April 23 (Opt Mem.); *theme:* following Christ even in suffering and death.

Gertrude, St. (GUHR-trood). 1256-1301. Entrusted by her parents to the Cistercian nuns at Helfta at the age of five, Gertrude went on to become a nun and live there for the rest of her life. Until the age of twenty-four, she studied literature and philosophy, and then passed on to applied theology. She gave herself over to prayer* and contemplation and wrote numerous works on mystical theology. Her meditation centered on the Bible,* the Liturgy,* and the Fathers,* especially St. Augustine* and St. Bernard.* She had great devotion to the Sacred Humanity of Christ in His Passion* and in the Blessed Sacrament.* *Liturgical celebration:* November 16 (Opt. Mem.); *theme:* Life with God in Christ.

Gestures. *See* POSTURE IN WORSHIP.

Gifts of the Holy Spirit. *See* HOLY SPIRIT.

Gloria in Excelsis. *See* GLORY TO GOD.

Gloria Patri. *See* GLORY (BE) TO THE FATHER.

Gloria Tibi. *See* GLORY TO YOU, LORD.

Glory (GLOH-ree, GLAW-ree). In the Bible,* glory (Greek: *doxa;* Hebrew: *kabod)* means: honor, praise, reputation, splendor, majesty. The glory of God* the Father is at times associated with His presence and at other times intimately connected with His Divine essence or the Divine Being. Only the "Father of lights" (Jas 1:17) is the perfect source of this glory, and He pours it out in His Son, "the refulgence of [the Father's] glory, the very imprint of [the Father's] being" (Heb 1:3), the Word, Who renders glory to God in all truth. "The Spirit of glory" (1 Pt 4:14) is the mediator of the flow and reflow of glory in the Trinitarian life.

By the Incarnation* all of us have seen that glory, come from the Father, that aureoles the Son and shines on the face of Christ (2 Cor 4:6). Thanks to Him, "all of us, gazing with unveiled face on the glory of the Lord, are being transformed into the same image from glory to glory, as from the Lord who is the Spirit" (2 Cor 3:18). This exchange of glory that is at the heart of the

Trinity constitutes the structure of the Liturgy*: before rendering glory to God, we must receive glory. It comes to us from the Father through the Son and in the Spirit.

When Jesus says in His high priestly prayer, "Father, . . . give glory to your son, so that your son may glorify you" (Jn 17:1), He defines His whole being and His entire life as Son, as the sacrifice on Calvary will manifest in a supreme manner!

The Eucharist* places us at the core of this glory, as do all liturgical celebrations of which it is the center, while waiting to lead us to the heavenly Liturgy where we will be perfectly inserted into the praise of that glory (see Eph 1:6, 12, 14).

In the Eucharistic Prayer* we proclaim God's glory (Preface* of EP II* and Sanctus*), which God has revealed is also that of His Son and of the Holy Spirit (Trinity Sunday,* Preface). Christ is now living with the Father "in glory" (Opening Prayer,* 7th Sunday of Easter*), and He will come "in glory" (Opening Prayer, 2nd Sunday of Advent*). We hope "to enjoy for ever the vision of God's glory" (EP III*), and we ask the Father to enable us to "find the way to [His] glory" (Opening Prayer, 2nd Sunday of Lent*), for we want to "share" it (Opening Prayer, Christmas*—During Day), and it is in that glory that we will "find our joy" (Alternative Opening Prayer, 10th Ordinary* Sunday).

Glory (Be) to the Father (GLOH-; GLAW-; ree bee too thuh FAH-thuhr). A popular brief expression of praise to the Trinity* entitled the lesser Doxology.* The first half seemed to originate from the baptismal formula; the second part is an anti-Arian addition from the West that affirms the eternity of the Son. Its major use is to conclude each Psalm in the *Divine Office,** but it is also found in many devotions,* for instance, as a conclusion of each decade of the Rosary.*

Glory to God (GLOH-; GLAW-; ree too god). An ancient hymn of praise to the Trinity* during the Introductory Rites* of the Mass, following the Penitential Rite,* sung or recited in the vernacular on Solemnities,* Feasts,* most Sundays, and at solemn celebrations. Termed the major Doxology* because of its

length, it is also referred to as the Angelic Hymn because the introductory words come from the angels at Christ's birth in the Biblical narrative. Its corpus is a lyrical praise of the Incarnate Son, our Redeemer and our Intercessor with the Father. *See also* INTRODUCTORY RITES.

Glory to You, Lord (GLOH-; GLAW-; ree too yoo lohrd). The acclamation* by the people in response to the priest as he announces the reading from the Gospel,* in the Liturgy of the Word.* These words are a vivid reminder of Christ's presence in His Word. We acclaim Christ Himself Who comes among us to proclaim His Word to us today.

Gloves, Episcopal. (gluhvz, ee-PIS-kuh-puhl). At ordination,* bishops* receive gloves as a ceremonial vesture of their office. Made of silk, these gloves are worn during the celebration of the Pontifical Mass* up to the Preparation of the Gifts.* They are the color* of the day or season.

God (god). The Liturgy* is intimately connected with God—it is the public worship* of *God* by His people, the public prayer of His Church,* the religious dialogue between *God* and His children. And this relationship is directed toward the *Triune God,* the Mystery* of the Blessed Trinity that God has been pleased to reveal to human beings: "In His goodness and wisdom, God chose to reveal Himself and to make known to us the hidden purpose of His will by which through Christ the Word made flesh, we have access to the Father in the Holy Spirit and come to share in the Divine Nature" (DV,2).

There are three distinct Persons in one God—and they exist only in relation to one another. They are coequal, coeternal, and consubstantial. The Son proceeds from the Father by generation, and the Holy Spirit proceeds from the Father and the Son by spiration.

God the Father is the Creator, God the Son is the Redeemer, and God the Holy Spirit is the Sanctifier—but not in such a way that the Son and the Holy Spirit are excluded from creation, or the Father and the Holy Spirit from redemption, or the Father and the Son from sanctification.

God the Father

Traditionally, God the Father is known as the first Person of the

Blessed Trinity. He is truly Father as He begets a coeternal and coequal Son, to Whom He imparts the fullness of His nature and in Whom He contemplates His own perfect image.

By nature God is our Creator and Lord, and we are His creatures and subjects. As a result of sin, however, we have become His enemies and deserve His chastisements. Yet, through the grace* of Christ, the Father lovingly pardons us, adopts us as His children, and destines us to share in the life and beatitude of that same Christ, His only-begotten Son.

Thus, by Divine adoption God is our Father and we are His children. This adoption is effected through sanctifying grace, a Divine quality or supernatural habit infused into the soul by God, which blossoms into the vision of glory* in eternal life.* In the New Testament,* the word "God" as naming someone always means the heavenly Father.

Liturgical prayer is almost always addressed to the Father through the Son in the Holy Spirit. By such prayer we acknowledge the presence of the Spirit inspiring us to pray and we also acknowledge that our prayer would be valueless except for the love the Father has for His eternal Son.

God the Son

Jesus Christ is the center of the Father's work of salvation* because

He is the Son of God made Man so that as perfect man He might save all people and sum up all things in Himself. He summed up in Himself the Mysteries of our salvation by His Death and His Resurrection*; He had received all power in heaven and on earth; He founded His Church as a means for our salvation. Hence, in Christ our Redeemer we are joined to all human beings.

By becoming Man, Jesus consecrated human experience; God, now one of us, can be found in human loving, striving, and hoping. The risen Jesus is the firstfruits that includes the entire harvest of humankind, having died to a world where sin is at home and risen to the full humanity of the new Creation.

Jesus poured out on His people the Spirit of adoption by making us children of God. He made for Himself a new people, filled with the grace of God. United with Jesus, this new people of God constitutes "the whole Christ." He offers them to His Father and gives Him glory. This is the aim of His Father's plan for the salvation of all people.

Jesus does this most effectively through the Liturgy* which is "His work" and makes present for us the History of Salvation,* the saving love God has for us in His Son through the Holy Spirit. Jesus gave true worship to His Father throughout His earthly life and especially by His obedient Death. In so doing, He also effected our salvation. He was then raised up to the Father's right hand in eternal glory where He now offers perfect praise and continues to intercede for us (heavenly Liturgy).

The actions of the earthly Liturgy enable us to unite with Christ in His saving work. The actions of this Liturgy are not mere memorials in the sense of recalling the events of Salvation History. They are now portraying and making actual before our eyes as well as in our hearts the saving acts of Christ—His Passion, Death, and Resurrection. Christ's power is found in the Church, His Body, and is present and active in the Liturgy. (*See also* JESUS CHRIST.)

God the Holy Spirit

The Holy Spirit is the Third Person of the Blessed Trinity, really God just as the Father and the Son are really God. He is the Love of the Father and the Son. As Jesus is the center of the History of Salvation so the mystery of God is the center from which this history takes its origin and to which it is ordered as to its last end. The risen Jesus leads human beings to the Father by sending the Holy Spirit upon the People of God.

By His new and deeper coming into the world at Pentecost,* the Spirit was to accomplish the salvation of humanity. He came to sanctify the Church forever, giving life to all people because He is the Spirit of life. He is the very soul of the Church.

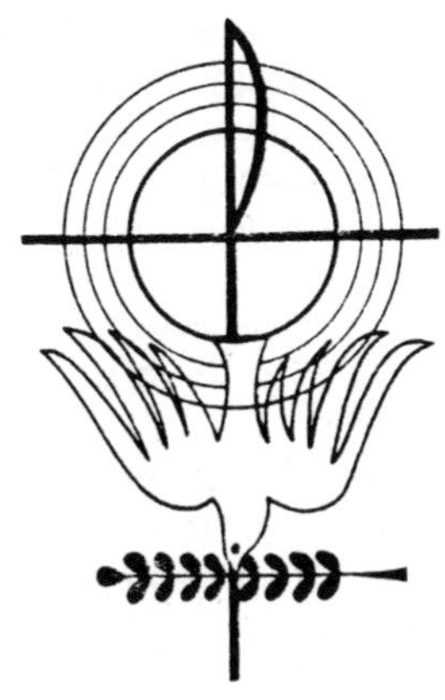

The Spirit prays and bears witness in the faithful* that they are adopted children of God. He guides the Church into the fullness of truth and gives her a unity of fellowship and service, furnishes and directs her with various gifts, and adorns her with the fruits of His grace. By the power of the Gospel* He makes the Church grow, renews her constantly, and leads her to perfect unity with her Spouse, Jesus Christ.

The Spirit has justly been called the *soul* of the Liturgy. It is He Who grants it the power to make present for us the History of Salvation, Who enables us to take full part in it, and Who effects our sanctification through the work of Christ. Every liturgical action takes place through the inspiration of the Holy Spirit.

It is the Spirit working through the Church Who supervises the fashioning of the Liturgical Year,* the development of the liturgical rites, and the implementation of the unending dialogue that the Church and each Christian carry on in the Liturgy—with the Father through Jesus. *See also* HOLY SPIRIT.

God, Come to My Assistance. *See* INTRODUCTORY VERSE.

Godparents (GOD-payr-uhnts). Some make this distinction between godparents and sponsors: the godparents are chosen by the elect, in consultation with the pastor, to escort them during the Initiation Rites*; sponsors are those chosen to accompany candidates who seek admission to the catechumenate* and remain with them to supervise their progress during this process until the Rite of Election, when they may also be chosen as godparents. Ordinarily the words are interchangeable and refer to those who at both Baptism* and Confirmation*

present the candidate with the intention of making sure that the person will be faithful to the meaning of the Sacrament.*

The function of the godparent is most obvious during the Baptism of Infants, where the sponsor requests the Sacrament for the infant, answers the Baptismal Promises* and affirms the Profession of Faith.* The godparents are expected to ensure Christian upbringing of the baptized, should the natural parents die or be lax in this regard. Consequently, the godparent is expected to be mature enough for the responsibility, a practicing Catholic who has received the Sacraments of Initiation, and be capable of fulfilling the office canonically. Only one godparent is prescribed, but two are allowed; however they must be of different sexes. A Christian from another communion may not be a sponsor but may be a witness to Baptism with a Catholic sponsor.

The revised Rite of Christian Initiation* brings a special dignity to this office emphasizing frequently the sponsor's obligation toward the education of the candidate. The godparent helps to instruct the catechumen,* and takes part in the judgment of the candidate's faith; as a delegate of the community the sponsor joins the candidate at the time of election to the catechumenate and counsels the person through the process of Illumination.* The godparent pledges willingness to aid the candidate to learn about and follow Christ during the Rite of Admission, when the sponsor testifies also to the neophyte's decision to follow Christ.

The godparent traces the cross on the senses of the candidate after the minister. At the Rite of Election, in close preparation for Baptism, the godparent testifies to the candidate's worthiness. During the scrutinies* and the actual Baptism the sponsor lays a hand on the recipient's shoulder during the prayers and the Baptism. The godparents hand the white garment and candle to the newly baptized, their names are mentioned during the Eucharistic Prayer,* and they receive Communion* under both species. During the mystagogia* they continue in their role.

In the Rite of Confirmation the godparent presents the candidate, places a hand on the candidate's shoulder at the anointing, and promises to aid the person in fulfilling the Baptismal Promises* validated by Confirmation. It is recommended that the sponsor at Confirmation be the same person who was godparent at Baptism. The sponsor may be different from the baptismal sponsor but may not be one of the parents of the candidate. Parents should not be called sponsors, even though they may bring or accompany the child to the bishop, whether the sponsor is present or not. The functions of the sponsor are different from those of the parents taking part in the Confirmation rite; in their role, the parents should be called presenters (Canons 893; 874). *See also* BAPTISM; CONFIRMATION; RITE OF CHRISTIAN INITIATION OF ADULTS.

Good Friday (gud FRAI-dee; -day). The Friday in Holy Week,* now called the Friday of the Passion and Death of Our Lord, is the only aliturgical* day in the Roman Rite.* It commemorates our redemption by Christ Who surrendered Himself totally to His Father's will by suffering death for us. This painful and grim phase of the Easter Mystery can only be understood in conjunction with the total celebration of the Sacred Triduum,* which includes the victory through Resurrection. Before 1955 a complex service was celebrated in the morning. Since then a more simple rite is celebrated in the afternoon or evening, usually between three and nine o'clock. In the United States because of the size or nature of a parish or community or for other pastoral reasons the bishop* may allow an additional service.

The Celebration

(1) *The Liturgy of the Word.* After an introductory prayer, there are three readings related to the Passion* of Christ, the final one being St. John's account of the Passion.

Thereafter the most solemn presentation of General Intercessions* during the Church Year* occurs. After an invitation to pray for a specific intention, the faithful* respond by an acclamation or the traditional period of kneeling at the invitation of the deacon,* but then the celebrant concludes each petition by singing or saying a prayer appropriate to the intention.

(2) *Veneration of the Cross.* The unveiling of the cross may take place in one of two methods. The cross may be taken to the front of the altar* with lighted candles. The priest uncovers the upper part and raises it up while singing the invitation "This is the wood of the cross, on which hung the Savior of the world," to which the people answer: "Come let us worship." All kneel to adore the cross for a short time in silence.

Then the right arm of the cross is unveiled and the rite is repeated. Finally the entire cross is uncovered and the acclamation is repeated. The cross and the lighted candles are placed at the entrance to the sanctuary* or some other suitable place while the veneration follows.

The second form, usually the more popular one, is a procession* from the church door where the celebrant repeats the previous actions, the first time at the entrance to the church, the second time in the middle of the church, and the third time at the entrance to the sanctuary.

During the adoration of the cross there is a procession of the people moving to the cross making a simple genuflection and usually kissing it. During this time appropriate songs are sung, including the Reproaches* or an alternate version. In larger churches, because of the crowd, several crosses may be used or the one cross may be held up after some have adored it individually for the rest to venerate; then finally it and the candles are placed on the altar.

(3) *The Communion Service.* The deacon or, lacking one, the priest brings the ciborium* from the place of reposition to the altar and says the Our Father* and the Introduction to Communion as done during Mass. All are encouraged to receive. A short prayer follows and finally the Dismissal,* which includes a Prayer over the People.*

Good News (gud nyooz). The Greek *euangelion* announces God's triumph in redeeming His people. It involves the total teaching of Christ that is accepted and put into practice by Christians. Glad tidings and Gospel* would be synonyms. This revelation from Jesus is considered *news* since it had been concealed from the time of Creation; it is considered *good* because all benefit from the saving grace bestowed on the fallen human race through Christ, the Incarnate Word. Today there is a move to replace the word Gospel with this term in popular parlance. *See also* GOSPEL.

Good Shepherd, The (gud SHEP-uhrd, thuh). One of the titles of Christ stemming from His words in Jn 10:7-18 and His Parable of the Good Shepherd in Lk 15:3-7 (Mt 18:12-14). The same theme is treated in Heb 13:20 and 1 Pt 2:25 and 5:4. Christ is represented as the Good Shepherd carrying a lamb upon His shoulders.

This theme is celebrated in the Liturgy* on Good Shepherd Sunday—the Fourth Sunday of Easter.* In the light of Easter, the Parable receives all its meaning. By portraying Himself as the Good Shepherd, Jesus identifies Himself with God, Who had so often been revealed by the Prophets* and the Psalms* as the Shepherd of Israel. But Jesus is the Shepherd Who gives His life for His sheep. The Liturgy combines these two aspects of the theme: in the Opening Prayer* it is the triumphant Christ Who appears as the Shepherd of His Church; in the Prayer after Communion* it is the omnipotent God Whom we invoke as our eternal Shepherd.

Good Works (gud wuhrks). The upright deeds or actions performed by human beings out of a living faith* in the observance of the commandments* and evangelical counsels.* The word is sometimes reserved for the observance of the counsels under the threefold category of prayer,* fasting,* and almsgiving.* The good works to which we should apply ourselves include (1) works of piety and penance, (2) works of love of neighbor, (3) conscientious work in our occupation, and (4) suffering borne for love of God. Especially important is frequent reception of Communion* because Christ in the Eucharist* is the food that nourishes the Divine life in our soul.

The Council of Trent decreed that acts of fear, hope,* initial love,* and sorrow are required in addition to faith for justification. In this sense, good works are necessary prerequisites for salvation.*

The Liturgy* is intimately connected with the active exercise of the theological virtues* (faith, hope, and love) and the moral virtues (prudence,* temperance,* justice,* and fortitude*) because of the twofold aspects of the sanctification that God works in His Church* and the worship* that the Church renders to God. The spirituality that is centered on the Liturgy and takes its tone from it is a spirituality in which the active expression of these virtues occupies a predominant place.

Thus, the theme of good works to be performed is always stressed in the Liturgy. The Prayers after Communion* continually petition God that the participation in the Liturgy may bear fruit for the faithful,* enabling them to lead lives of virtue and to meet all the needs of Christian existence, so that they may one day obtain the bliss of the beatific vision. The Opening Prayers* for the Masses of the Saints* continually ask that the faithful may imitate the virtues and labors for the cause of God practiced by the Saint of the day (for example, the Opening Prayer for the Mass at Midnight and Mass during the Day on Christmas,* for Friday of the Octave of Easter,* and for the Masses of St. Francis de Sales,* St. John Bosco,* and St. Francis Xavier*).

Indeed, participation in the Liturgy is itself an exercise of the virtue of religion (part of the virtue of justice). Religion is the response of human beings to the profound debt they owe God as the source, ultimate ruler, and end of all created beings. It thus surpasses all the other moral virtues and is closely allied with the theological virtues. In this sense the Liturgy may be said to be the chief good work that can be done by Christians. *See also* OPUS DEI.

Gospel (GOS-puhl). (1) *Biblical.* The word used to signify God's announcement of His plan to save humankind through Jesus Christ, His Son. The life, activity and Death of Jesus through His person, preaching, healing, and immolation assures us of salvation,* particularly through the Resurrection.*

The term usually refers to the four canonical Gospels of Matthew,* Mark,* Luke,* and John,* which depict the life and teachings of Christ. Beyond the four Gospels themselves the rest of the New Testament* relates much of the "Good News."*

(2) *Liturgical.* At Mass, a portion from the four Gospels concludes in a climactic way the Liturgy of the Word* as it is sung or proclaimed. Special marks of honor distinguish the reading of the Gospel, since only a minister no lower than a deacon,* who prepares himself by a blessing or prayer, may read it. Candles* may be brought to the pulpit* and the book may be incensed. During the proclamation of the Word, the congregation stands and by their acclamation at the conclusion the people indicate that Christ is present, speaking to them.

The choice of sections to be read is determined by the fact that some are more suitable to the particular occasion, but more usually the choice is made according to a continuous reading of the Gospels, which is spread over a three-year cycle on Sundays. Each year has one of the Synoptic Gospels assigned to it, whereas John's Gospel is placed annually in Lent* and the Easter Season.* The weekday Lectionary* chooses from all four Gospels each year; many choices are available for the Votive Masses,* the Common of the Saints,* and the Proper of the Saints.* *See also* CYCLES; GOOD NEWS; LECTIONARY.

Gospel Acclamation. *See* ACCLAMATIONS.

Gospel Book. *See* LECTIONARY.

Gospel Procession (GOS-puhl pruh-SESH-uhn). The second of five processions* that take place at Mass. During the singing of the Alleluia* or other chant before the Gospel,* the priest* (or deacon*) puts incense into the censer and says the prayer "Almighty God, cleanse my heart." He then takes the Book of Gospels* from the altar* and carries it solemnly to the lectern,* with the acolytes* holding the censer and candles* walking ahead of him. At the lectern, the priest opens the book, says the greeting, incenses the book, and proclaims the Gospel.

After the preparatory rites and after listening to the Word of God* through the writings of the Prophets* and the Apostles,* the people rise and outwardly demonstrate their love and admiration for Jesus Who comes to them in the Gospel. He comes to proclaim His Word to them and to enable them to apply it to their lives on the day in question. The acolytes represent the people in the procession, and the people show that although all the readings constitute the Word of God, it is the Gospel that holds the primary place in their lives. For it is the living Word of God's Son. *See also* GOSPEL; PROCESSIONS.

Gothic Rite *See* MOZARABIC RITE.

Grace (grays). An inward, supernatural help or gift that God bestows on human beings for the good of the soul. There are two principal types of grace: (1) helping and (2) sanctifying. Helping grace is also called actual or transient grace: actual because it is given to perform a supernatural act or acts, transient because it works on the soul in a passing manner. Sanctifying grace, on the other hand, remains in the soul and adorns and prepares the soul to be constantly pleasing in God's sight.

Helping grace inclines us to do good deeds and helps us to perform them. It enlightens our minds and moves and strengthens our will.

Sanctifying grace gives us a share in the Divine life,* makes us heirs of heaven, and gives value and merit to our good works.* It can be lost through mortal sin and regained through perfect contrition* and the resolve to go to confession* when opportunity offers (and through imperfect contrition combined with the Sacrament of Penance*). It can be preserved and increased by good works in our daily life.

The Liturgy* is a chief source of grace as well as worship.* "The Sacraments* [that is, the Liturgy] do indeed impart grace, but, in addition, the very act of celebrating them disposes the faithful* most effectively to receive this grace in a fruitful manner, to worship God duly, and to practice charity" (SC, 59).

"For well-disposed members of the faithful, the Liturgy of the Sacraments* and Sacramentals* sanctifies almost every event in their lives; they are given access to the stream of Divine grace that flows from the Paschal Mystery* of the Passion, Death, and Resurrection* of Christ" (SC, 61).

Thus, at every Eucharist* we pray to receive more grace and additional gifts of grace: e.g., a share in Christ's life (Prayer after Communion*: 11th Ordinary* Sunday); grace of forgiveness (Prayer over the Gifts*: 3rd Sunday of Lent*); and grace to follow Christ more closely (Opening Prayer*: 11th Ordinary* Sunday). *See also* GOOD WORKS.

Grace at Meals (grays at meelz). Prayers before and after meals are called *grace* from the Latin word for thanksgiving, *gratia,* because in them we thank God for the gifts He has given us. After the example of Christ, this Christian custom usually includes a request for His blessing on the food and the group present, together with gratitude to the Lord for His gifts and an expression of our total dependence upon Him even for food and drink. Sometimes there is a set formula; at other times any member of the family may be invited to improvise a prayer. In this fashion the mealtime, besides being a symbol of the charity that links the family and friends together, becomes an act of worship.*

Gradual. *See* RESPONSORIAL PSALM.

Gradual, Roman (GRAJ-oo-uhl, ROH-muhn). Authorized in 1972, this revised liturgical book contains the chants or choral sections of the Mass,* whether Ordinary* or Proper,* together with their notation. The translations from the Latin may need to have new musical settings in the various languages.

Graduale Simplex. *See* SIMPLE GRADUAL.

Gratias Agamus Domino Deo Nostro. *See* INTRODUCTORY DIALOGUE.

Gravissimum Educationis (grah-VEES-ee-moom e-du-kah-t[s]ee-OH-nees). Latin title (from the first two words "Grave [importance] of education") of the *Declaration on Christian Education* issued by the Second Vatican Council* on October 28, 1965. It states that the primary objective of a Christian education (which is the right of all Christians) is that the baptized, as they are led stage by stage to knowledge of the Mystery of Salvation,* may likewise grow in awareness of the gift of faith* they have received; that they learn to worship* the Father in spirit and in truth*—especially in the Liturgy*; that they be trained to live their own lives on the model of the new being created in righteousness and holiness of truth, thus developing into mature humanity, to the measure of the fullness of Christ, and contributing their part to the increase of the Mystical Body.* *See also* CATECHESIS AND LITURGY; VATICAN COUNCIL, SECOND.

Greater Litanies (GRAY-tuhr LIT-uh-neez). A day of prayer* and fasting* formerly observed on April 25 (though unconnected with the Feast of St. Mark*) to ask for God's blessing and protection upon the crops. It featured a procession* with the singing of the Litany of the Saints* followed by a Rogation Mass. (Originally, the procession was held in the fields.) With the passage of time, the procession itself became designated by the term "Litanies," known as "Greater" or "Major" since this celebration in Rome originated before the rise of the "Lesser Litanies" in Gaul. It began in the 4th century, taking the place of a similar pagan feast of the harvest. In the liturgical renewal of Vatican II,* such days of prayer* are no longer assigned in the Roman Calendar* but are entrusted to the National Episcopal Conferences.* *See also* DAYS OF PRAYER; LESSER LITANIES; ROGATION DAYS.

Greeting (GREET-ing). At the beginning of Mass,* and most of the other liturgical services, the celebrant* greets the assembly* by expressing the presence of the Lord to the community (GIRM, 28). Since the Lord is present in the community and in its members, the greeting and the people's response manifests the mystery* of the Church* that is gathered together.

The traditional formula is "The Lord be with you."* In Ruth* 2:4 these words appear as a greeting, but in Judges* 6:12 and elsewhere they constitute a simple statement of God's presence in the community. The response "And also with you" is found in Scripture in its more literal translation: "And with your spirit," for example, in Galatians* 6:18. Its meaning is generally accepted as one of reciprocity.

This greeting also appears at the end of Mass before the Dismissal* and throughout the service, usually as an introduction to a prayer of the celebrant.

There are two optional greetings for the beginning of Mass: "The grace of our Lord Jesus Christ and the love of God and the fellowship of the Holy Spirit be with you all" (2 Cor 13:13) and "The grace and peace of God our Father and the Lord Jesus Christ be with you" (Gal 1:3). *See also* LORD BE WITH YOU, THE.

Gregorian Calendar. *See* CALENDAR.

Gregorian Chant (gri-GAWR-ee-uhn; -GOHR; chant). Gregorian Chant is recognized as particularly suited to the Roman Liturgy,* and the *Constitution on the Sacred Liturgy** states that it should be given preference among musical forms, other things being equal. This official chant was revised and established by Pope Gregory the Great,* himself an outstanding musician. This expressive mode of singing probably has its origins in Hebraic art on the one hand and in Greco-Roman art on the other hand, as far as tonality and rhythm are concerned.

Chant is basically performed in unison, diatonic in nature and thus composed in the eight ecclesiastical tones. Other characteristics are that it is monophonic, that is, using a single melodic line, its range is not large, usually within an octave, the intervals are small, and the rhythm follows the natural accent of the words, like free verse. Accented syllables are sometimes stressed through high notes or several notes on them.

The most simple form is *syllabic,* in which each syllable has a single note, or perhaps a few small groups of notes. This type can be readily and easily sung by congregations. Another form is *neumatic,* where each syllable or the majority of them have a neum, that is, a group of notes to be sung on the same syllable. The most elaborate is *melismatic,* where one must sing many neumatic groups on one and the same syllable, and some of them quite prolonged. The Alleluias* and the Invitation to leave during the Concluding Rite* of Mass were fine examples of this form.

Earlier in the 20th century there was a reform of church music and the Pontifical Institute was to study Gregorian Chant. Critical texts were developed by the Solesmes Monks. The *Constitution on the Sacred Liturgy* asks for an edition of simpler melodies for use in smaller churches. Since chant is a natural and easy method of singing, it is a fine legitimate model for chanting a vernacular* text, and so musicians are begged to preserve this rich heritage for liturgical services. *See also* IUBILATE DEO; PLAINCHANT.

Gregorian Masses (gri-GAWR-ee-uhn; -GOHR; MAS-uhz). On thirty consecutive days, a Mass* is offered for one and the same deceased person with the intent to procure release from purgatory. The same priest* need not celebrate all the Masses nor must they be said at the same altar.* More than one series may be offered for a specific person, but not at the same time.

Gregorian Sacramentary (gri-GAWR-ee-uhn; -GOHR; sak-ruh-MEN-tuhr-ee). The name of a type of Sacramentary* that derives from the *Sacramentary* that St. Gregory the Great* (595) had composed for his own personal liturgical use as Roman Pontiff. Among its unique features are the uniting of the Temporal* and the Sanctoral* cycles, the indications of the Roman Stations,* and the absence of formularies on days when the Pope did not celebrate solemnly.

A version of this book known as the *Hadrian Sacramentary* was sent by Pope Adrian I in 785 to Charlemagne, and it became the official Mass Book in the Empire. It also served as an important source for the *Roman Missal** that began to appear in the 10th century. There are three types of *Gregorian Sacramentaries:* the *Hadrianum,* the *Paduenses,* and the *Supplemented Gregorian* (the last divided into two more types—the *Gregorian with Separated Supplement* and the *Gregorian with Attached Supplement). See also* GELASIAN SACRAMENTARY; LEONINE SACRAMENTARY; SACRAMENTARY.

Gregorian Water (gri-GAWR-ee-uhn; -GOHR; WAWT-uhr, WAHT-). Mixture of blessed water, wine,* ashes,* and salt* forming a lustrous liquid used in the *Roman Ritual** for the blessing of altars and churches. The name stems from an erroneous attribution of this "water" to St. Gregory the Great.*

Gregory Nazianzen, St. (GREG-uhr-ee naz-ee-ANZ-uhn). 330-390. Born in Nazianzen of Cappadocia, Gregory pursued knowledge as a youth and went on to become a hermit, a priest,* and a bishop*—of Sasima, Nazianzen, and Constantinople. The last nine years of his life were spent in Nazianzen in relative peace. He was called the Theologian because of his outstanding teaching and eloquence. Gregory is one of the greatest Doctors* of the Greek Church and is honored liturgically on the same day as his friend Basil the Great.* *Liturgical celebration:* January 2 (Memorial); *theme:* putting God's truth into action through faith and love.

Gregory the Great, St. (GREG-uhr-ee thuh grayt). 540-604. Born at Rome, Gregory held public office before entering the monastic life at the age of thirty-five and being ordained one of the seven deacons of Rome. In 590 he was elected Pope*

and began those labors that have earned for him the title "great." His zeal extended over the entire known world, he was in contact with all the Churches of Christendom, and, in spite of his bodily sufferings and innumerable labors, he found time to compose a vast number of works on moral and theological subjects. He is celebrated above all for his magnificent contributions to the Liturgy of the Mass* and the Office*—*Gregorian Sacramentary** and *Gregorian Chant** among others. He is one of the four great Doctors* of the Latin Church and the Patron of Musicians, Singers, and Teachers. *Liturgical celebration:* September 3 (Memorial); *theme:* the spirit of wisdom and growth in holiness.

Gregory VII, St. (GREG-uhr-ee thuh SEV-uhnth). 1028-1085. Born in Tuscany, Hildebrand was educated at Rome and became a Benedictine monk. He assisted the Popes* through many missions on behalf of Church reform, and in 1073 he succeeded to the Chair of St. Peter and took the name Gregory VII. He died at a refuge in Salerno besieged by King Henry IV. His last recorded words were: "I have loved justice and hated iniquity; therefore I am dying in exile." *Liturgical celebration:* May 25 (Opt. Mem.); *theme:* spirit of courage and love for justice.

Gremial(e) (GRAY-mee-uhl). The ceremonial apron, a silk lap-cloth, formerly placed on the lap of the bishop* at liturgical ceremonies is no longer used. However, a similar gremial may be retained when it serves a purpose functionally, as during the distribution of candles,* ashes,* and palm,* or when performing anointings.

Grille (gril). A grating used as a barrier between the cloistered part of a convent and the outside world, or as a screen in the confessional.* Since the 16th century such screens have separated priest* and penitent while not impeding dialogue between them. With the advent of the new Rite of Penance* in 1973 use of this grille is at the option of the penitent.

Guadalupe, Our Lady of. *See* OUR LADY OF GUADALUPE.

Guardian Angels (GAHR-dee-uhn AYN-juhlz). The Feast of September 29 presents the angels in their essential vocation: singing God's praises. The present Memorial brings out the second function of angels: to act as friends, protectors, and defenders of human beings. Faith teaches us that all individuals have a Guardian Angel who watches over each throughout this life. It is also a generally accepted doctrine that communities, the Church, dioceses, and nations have their tutelary angels.

The Guardian Angels defend those of whom they have charge against the assaults of the demons, endeavoring to preserve them from all the occasions of sin. They strive to keep us in the right path: if we fall, they help us to rise again, encourage us to become more and more virtuous, suggest good thoughts and holy desires, offer our prayers and good works* to God, and above all assist us at the hour of death. *Liturgical celebration:* October 2 (Memorial); *theme:* devotion to our Guardian Angels. *See also* ANGELS.

— H —

Habakkuk, The Book of (HAB-uh-kuk, huh-BAK-uk, thuh buk uhv). Forty-second Book of the Old Testament* and eighth of the Minor Prophets.* It was written toward the end of the 7th century B.C. (605-597), at a time when Israel was under heavy attack from the Chaldeans and in desperate straits. The prophet Habakkuk carries on a dialogue with the Lord and even dares to question His ways. After listening to the Lord's reply the prophet concludes that after bad times there will always be good times for those who are faithful to God. The third and last chapter is a magnificent religious lyric filled with reminiscences of Israel's past and expressions of authentic faith in the Lord.

Liturgical use: In the *Roman Missal,** this Book is read twice: on the 27th Sunday in Ordinary Time* (C) and on the Saturday of the 18th Week in Ordinary Time (II). In the *Liturgy of the Hours,** it is also read twice: on Tuesday and Wednesday of the 23rd Week in Ordinary Time. It also gives rise to a minor canticle* in the Psalter.* *Meaning:* Habakkuk calls for faith and complete confidence in God's power to rule earthly affairs and in His providence to protect His faithful. The just will live by their faithfulness, by their unwavering attachment to God. This was later reiterated and refined by St. Paul.*

Habemus ad Dominum. *See* INTRODUCTORY DIALOGUE.

Hadrian Sacramentary. *See* GREGORIAN SACRAMENTARY.

Haggai, The Book of (HAG-ee-ai, HAG-ai, thuh buk uhv). Forty-fourth Book of the Old Testament* and tenth of the Minor Prophets.* Postexilic prophecy begins with Haggai who received the word of the Lord in the second year of Darius (520 B.C.). The Jews who returned from the Exile in Babylonia had encountered formidable obstacles in their efforts to reestablish Jewish life in Judah. The Samaritans had succeeded in blocking the rebuilding of the Temple; but after Darius acceded to the throne permission was given to resume the work. At this critical moment, when defeatism and a certain lethargy had overtaken his repatriated compatriots, Haggai came forward with his exhortations to them to complete the great task.

Liturgical use: In the *Roman Missal,** this Book is read on Thursday and Friday of the 25th Week in Ordinary Time* (I). In the *Liturgy of the Hours,** it is read on Sunday and Monday of the 28th Week in Ordinary Time. *Meaning:* Haggai reminds us that we are to work unceasingly. Once it was to build God's Temple but today it is to build His Church,* a spiritual edifice, which is constructed by our acts of love. To build a Temple for God nowadays is above all to bring Him to all people. Thus, Haggai invokes the Messianic Hope, for in the conversion of the Gentiles that he announces is comprised the coming of the Messiah.*

Hagiographical Reading (haj-ee-uh-GRAF-i-kuhl;-hayj; REED-ing). From the Greek word meaning "holy," this term describes a reading used as a second lesson in the Office of Readings* on the feast of a Saint.* It may be a text from a Father* or from an ecclesiastical writer, which specifically refers to a Saint being honored or could be clearly applied to the Saint; it may also be an excerpt from the Saint's own writings, and rarely an account of the Saint's life. The intent is that true spiritual benefit should come to the one reciting the Office, by highlighting the spiritual qualities of the Saints and their importance in the life and spirituality of the Church. *See also* CYCLES; READINGS; TWO-YEAR CYCLE OF READINGS, ALTERNATE.

Hail Holy Queen. *See* SALVE REGINA.

Hail Mary (hayl MAY-ree). The well-known Marian prayer is comprised of three parts: the words of praise from the Archangel Gabriel* at the Annunciation*; the salutation of Elizabeth at the Visitation*; and the second half, beginning "Holy Mary," from the Carthusian Breviary of the Middle Ages. The first two greetings were used in the early centuries as an Offertory Prayer and during the Divine Office. The total Hail Mary was incorporated in the *Roman Breviary** by St. Pius V.* Today the prayer is used only in private devotions, such as the Rosary.* *See also* ROSARY.

Hail Queen of Heaven. *See* AVE REGINA CAELORUM.

Hallelujah. *See* ALLELUIA.

Hanc Igitur (hahnk IJ-i-tuhr, EEJ-ee-toohr). The fourth intercessory section of Eucharistic Prayer I* begging that the bread and wine may be accepted, beginning with the words: "Father, accept this offering." The intent of the prayer is to

show that the Eucharistic oblation includes the homage of the entire Church.* There are two proper Hanc Igiturs: (1) for Holy Thursday,* specifying the institution of the Eucharist by our Lord; (2) for the Octave of Easter,* mentioning the newly baptized.

While reciting the prayer, the priest holds his open hands palms down over the offerings, thus designating them in a respectful manner. Some give this gesture a mystical meaning or allegorical interpretation that Jesus, taking our faults upon Himself, immolated Himself for us. We therefore hope for forgiveness in Him alone. *See also* EPICLESIS; EUCHARISTIC PRAYER.

Hand Missal. *See* MISSAL.

Handicapped. *See* DISABLED.

Hands (handz). In the Liturgy,* as in other phases of human life, the gestures or positions of the hands have a specific meaning or implication. (1) Probably the oldest gesture, a very natural one, is with the hands open and elevated, as a sign of supplication.

(2) The joined hands, palms touching, much more recent and of possible feudal origin, expresses homage and is the more natural and expected position of the hands during liturgical services when the celebrant* has no other motion to make. It is also used as a sign of respect, signifying meditation, rather than a prayer of entreaty with outstretched hands and arms.

(3) In some areas it becomes a sign of accord in the marriage ceremony when, after the consent has been given, each spouse holds the other's right hand while the priest* blesses them.

(4) Hands are anointed in the ordination of a priest and bishop,*

and in the Sacrament of Anointing of the Sick.*

(5) The hand traces the Sign of the Cross* in blessings.* *See also* IMPOSITION OF HANDS; SIGN OF THE CROSS.

Hannah, Canticle of. *See* CANTICLE OF HANNAH.

Happiness (HAP-i-nuhs). Happiness is a recurring theme in the Liturgy.* Indeed, it is one of the purposes for which the Liturgy is carried out—to give glory to God and to *obtain human salvation,* that is, happiness.* The Liturgy is quick to point out that happiness belongs only to those who *hope in the Lord* (Responsorial Psalm,* 6th Sunday in Ordinary Time*—C) and those who practice the Beatitudes,* the eight Christian attitudes par excellence that Jesus delineated as "happy" in the Sermon on the Mount (November 1—All Saints*).

Such happiness is characterized by a *partial* joy here on earth and will be perfected in heaven (Prayer over the Gifts,* 3rd Sunday of Easter*). And at Mass, in the Eucharistic Prayer* the Church asks that we be freed from sin and be able to enter our heavenly Kingdom where "we shall sing [God's] glory with every creature through Christ our Lord" (EP IV*). Then at the Communion* the priest further specifies this spiritual happiness: "Happy are those who are called to [Christ's] supper." Hence, this happiness consists in union with Jesus through signs on earth and face to face in heaven: "Happy now are the dead who die in the Lord" (All Souls Day,* Reading II*—Rv 14:13).

This union is achieved by practicing good works* and cleansing oneself from sin: "Happy are they who wash their robes so as to have free access to the tree of life and enter the city through its gates" (7th Sunday of Easter, C—Reading II: Rv 22:12-14). Finally, this happiness is one of the themes of the new Solemn Blessings*: "May [God] free you from all anxiety and strengthen your hearts in His love. May He enrich you with His gifts of faith,* hope,* and love,* so that what you do in this life will bring you to the happiness of everlasting life"* (no. 13).

Headings (HED-ingz). In the *Lectionary,** individual sentences prefixed to each text. Every Heading is chosen carefully (usually from the words of the text itself) in order to point out the main theme of the Reading* and, when necessary, to make the connèction between the Readings of the same Mass clear. *See also* LECTIONARY.

Heart of Jesus. *See* SACRED HEART, FEAST OF.

Heart of Mary. *See* MARY, BLESSED VIRGIN—FEASTS.

Heaven (HEV-uhn). The Liturgy* is pervaded by the theme of heaven if not the word itself. Indeed, "in the earthly Liturgy, by way of foretaste, we share in that heavenly Liturgy which is celebrated in the holy city of Jerusalem* toward which we journey as pilgrims, and in which Christ is sitting at the right hand of God . . . ; we sing a hymn to the Lord's glory with all the warriors of the heavenly army; venerating the memory of the Saints, we hope for some part and fellowship with them" (SC, 8).

We carry on a dialogue with the God Who is "in heaven" (Our Father), although it cannot contain Him (Tuesday of 5th Week in Ordinary Time,* II, Reading I*—1 Kgs 8:27) and is inaccessible to human beings on earth (Tuesday of 2nd Week of Easter,* Gospel*—Jn 3:13). Heaven is a symbol of God's transcendence by its immensity and distance, its luminosity and transparence (6th Sunday of Easter, C, Reading II—Rv 21:10-14, 22-23). It is also a symbol of spiritual goods that surpass all earthly goods (6th Sunday in Ordinary Time, A, Reading II—1 Cor 2:9).

Heaven is the dwelling of the blessed after the universal resurrection and even now for those who have died (Wednesday of 33rd Week, II, Reading II—Rv 4:1ff). It is less a place, however, than a *state of intimacy* with God (32nd Sunday, A, Reading II—1 Thes 4:17) and of human freedom* now established in love by the vision of God and communion with the other blessed.

During His earthly life Jesus was a witness of this heaven, and He frequently alluded to it. He spoke of the Kingdom of Heaven, of the reward stored in heaven (4th Sunday in Ordinary Time, A, Gospel—Mt 5:12) for the righteous. Most of all, He spoke about His Father in heaven (Ash Wednesday,* Gospel—Mt 6:1ff). Jesus thus brought heaven to earth.

The Liturgy continues Christ's work of uniting heaven and earth. It tells us that our citizenship is in heaven, and it is from there that we expect the coming of our Savior, the Lord Jesus Christ. He will give a new form to this lowly body of ours and remake it according to the pattern of His glorified body, by His power to subject all things to Himself (2nd Sunday of Lent, C, Reading II—Phil 3:17—4:1).

Heaven is a new universe made up like ours of a "new heavens and a new earth" but nothing of death, tears, crying, or pain is there (5th Sunday of Easter, C, Reading II—Rv 21:1-5). We pray that the gifts of Christ may help us to rise with Him to the joys of heaven (Ascension,* Prayer over the Gifts*).

In the Ordinary,* the Creed* puts our faith plainly: "We look for . . . the life of the world to come" (that is, the life of heaven). We adore the God whose glory fills "heaven and earth" (Sanctus*), and we pray that His angel will bring the sacrifice to His altar "in heaven" (EP I*) and that He will grant us to enter into "our heavenly inheritance (EP IV*).

We ask our Father in heaven to sanctify His name, bring about His Kingdom, and effect His will on earth as in heaven. We ask Him for our daily bread and for forgiveness of our sins as we forgive others and to be spared temptation and delivered from evil (Lord's Prayer*). In the Solemn Blessing* for Ascension Day (no. 8), the Church asks that our lives may be blessed on this memorial of the day when Christ ascended into heaven "to prepare a place for [us]."

We also ask God to make us worthy to share "eternal life" (heaven) with the Saints and give glory to Him through Jesus (EP II*), and we express the hope that we may enjoy forever the vision of His glory (EP III*), finding "in [His] presence light, happiness, and peace" (EP I).

Hebdomadary. *See* CELEBRANT.

Hebrews, The Epistle to the (HEE-brooz, thee i-PIS-uhl too thuh). Sixty-fifth Book of the Bible* and nineteenth of the New Testament.* This Epistle, now commonly attributed to an anonymous disciple of Paul,* was written toward the end of the 1st century to a community of Christians afflicted with trials and in danger of lapsing into Judaizing practices. It eloquently expresses the eminent superiority of the new dispensation over the old. Inaugurated by the Son of God Himself, this new dispensation was God's final revelation to human beings. It completed the message of the Prophets* and brought to perfection all that was of permanent value in the Mosaic Covenant. The Incarnate Son of God was its High Priest, and His glorious sacrifice was truly efficacious before God in the forgiveness of sin.

Liturgical use: In the *Roman Missal,** this Epistle is read extensively: on the 27th through the 33rd Sundays in Ordinary Time* (B) and in the first three Weeks of Ordinary Time (I) as well as special Masses. In the *Liturgy of the Hours,** it is read on January 1, March 19, and throughout the last two weeks of Lent.* *Meaning:* As suffering and humiliation had an important place in the victory of Christ the High Priest, so we His followers are exhorted to forgo worldly advantage, to bear our trials patiently, and to persevere heroically in the Faith. For all of us are a "people of priests" and are to unite our priesthood* to Christ's whether that priesthood be ministerial or universal.*

Hedwig, St. (HED-wig). 1174-1243. Born in Bavaria, Hedwig was the daughter of the Duke of Croatia. In 1186, she was married to Henry I of Silesia and Poland and bore him seven children; after the birth of her last child, she and her husband vowed continence. She is best remembered for her great zeal for religion and her penitential mortifications, which led her to live like a hermit amidst her husband's court. She donated her entire fortune to the Church and the poor, and after her husband's death in 1234 entered the Cistercian convent of Trebnitz, which she had founded, among many others. *Liturgical celebration:* October 16 (Opt. Mem.); *theme:* practicing humility.

Henry, St. (HEN-ree). 973-1024. Born in Bavaria, Henry succeeded his father in ruling a duchy and later became Emperor of Germany and Head of the Holy Roman Empire. He was most remarkable for his work in Church reform and fostering missionary effort. Henry and his wife, St. Cunegundes, lived in perpetual celibacy to which they had vowed themselves. He established numerous pious foundations, gave liberally to religious institutions, and built the cathedral of Bamberg, where he is buried. *Liturgical celebration:* July 13 (Opt. Mem.); *theme:* simplicity of heart.

Heortology (hee-or-TOL-uh-jee). The name of the division of the science of Liturgy* (or Liturgiology) that studies the origin, history, and meaning of the feasts* and seasons* of the Liturgical Year.*

Heraldry (HER-uhl-dree). Ecclesiastical heraldry is the science of the coat of arms applied to the members of the clergy* both regular and secular. Everyone has the right to choose a coat of arms but must conform to the rules of heraldic art and to the traditions approved by the Holy See.*

At the time of his nomination, a bishop* has the duty to choose for himself a coat of arms if he does not already have one personally or in his family. He may not copy another's escutcheon but may add to his own. The coat of arms is the moral and ideal portrait of him who adopts it.

The motto is a brief sentence by which the owner of the coat of arms expresses a high thought that he intends to make his rule of conduct. It is placed under the escutcheon and is composed of very few Latin words.

Hermeneutics, Liturgical (huhr-muh-N[Y]OO-tics, luh-TUHR-ji-kuhl; li-). The study of the methodological principles of liturgical interpretation. Liturgiologists are aided in this effort by many of the same disciplines used in Biblical hermeneutics, e.g., philology, archeology, history, textual and literary criticism, ancient versions of classical texts, and oral and written traditions. This is a relatively new field of study and is of incalculable importance in reforming the Liturgy*—determining the meaning of previous rites and ceremonies and how they can be adapted or incorporated into today's Liturgy.

Hermit (HUHR-muht). A title retained by the reformed Liturgy* to designate a Saint* who out of religious motives retired to lead a solitary life in the desert. More often than not, hermits were monks who lived alone apart from the community although they remained obedient to an abbot. The eremetical life began around the 3rd century and attained its zenith during the centuries when the Roman Empire was coming apart. It then went downhill and finally lapsed completely in the West after the Protestant Reformation but remained viable in the East until our own day.

The hermits that do exist today still dedicate a consecrated life to God, particularly through a stricter separation from the world, the silence of solitude, and assiduous prayer* and penance.* They profess the three evangelical counsels,* either by vow or by sacred bond into the hands of the diocesan bishop,* and observe their plan of life under his direction. *See also* RELIGIOUS LIFE.

Heroic Virtue (hi-ROH-ik vuhr-choo). A technical name expressing the type of virtue* that a person must be shown to have had in order to be beatified or canonized and enjoy a liturgical cult in the Church. It means the practice of the Christian life and virtues to an eminent degree either throughout one's life or at least in death (by martyrdom)—a degree that is worthy of salvation* (holiness), acclamation, and emulation. Essentially, however, it refers to the faithful carrying out of the duties of one's state in life, based on the commandments* more than the evangelical counsels.* And as such, heroic virtue is open to all Christians.

Hierarchy (HAI-uh-rahr-kee; HAI-rahr-). The group of clergy* invested with ecclesiastical authority, organized in grades, orders, or ranks whose duty it is to administer sacred things. Their powers are priestly, pastoral, and teaching, corresponding to the triple office of Christ as priest, king, and prophet or teacher. These powers were transferred to the Apostles* and their successors and are received by an episcopal ordination.

There is a distinction made between the hierarchy of orders and the hierarchy of jurisdiction. (1) The hierarchy of orders, which deals with the total actions concerning worship,* is given to the men who receive Holy Orders,* namely, bishops,* priests,* and deacons.* (2) The hierarchy of jurisdiction refers to the pastoral aspects, the governing and teaching of Christians in a certain territory. Only the Pope,* bishops, and priests have ordinary jurisdiction. By Divine right the hierarchy of jurisdiction includes only the Pope and the episcopate. Jurisdiction held by priests and deacons is merely ecclesiastical, since they are delegated by the bishops.

Since the Church is essentially hierarchical, the Liturgy* which not only "makes" the Church but reflects it must also be hierarchical. The faithful* who come together for liturgical assembly* must possess a hierarchical structure of persons differing in rank and function. The distribution of liturgical roles is the strongest sign that the assembly is not a haphazard collection of people but a manifestation of the Church. It is the combined action of those present exercising different roles that comprises the Liturgy. *See also* LITURGY—PARTICIPATION.

High Mass (hai mas). A term to indicate a sung form of the pre-Vatican II* or Tridentine Mass (*Missa Cantata*) in opposition to the more usual Low Mass* (*Missa Lecta*) in which there was no singing and the Solemn High Mass* (*Missa Solemnis*) celebrated with singing and the aid of a deacon* and subdeacon.* With the appearance of the post-Vatican II fully participated Mass with music and song, this term is no longer meaningful and has disappeared from use. *See also* LOW MASS; MASS; SOLEMN HIGH MASS.

Hilary, St. (HIL-uh-ree). 320?-368? Born at Poitiers in Gaul, Hilary was married and had a daughter when he was converted to the Christian Faith through reading the Scriptures.* Chosen Bishop of Poitiers about 350, he zealously proclaimed the Divinity of Christ in opposition to the Arians and suffered four years of exile. During this time, he continued his ministry of teaching by writing solid works of wisdom and learning, among them the famous *Treatise on the Trinity.* He is a Doctor* of the Church and is invoked as a Patron against Snake Bites. *Liturgical celebration:* January 13 (Opt. Mem.); *theme:* witnessing to the Divinity of Christ.

Hippolytus, St. (hi-POL-i-tuhs). A priest and one of the most important theologians of the 3rd century, Hippolytus produced outstanding Scriptural writings, including the earliest known commentary on Sacred Scripture* (on Daniel*) and the *Apostolic Tradition** (a veritable *Roman Ritual**). After becoming involved in unfortunate controversies and even regarded as an antipope, he returned to the fold and con-

tinued to defend the Faith* against all her enemies. He was martyred together with Christ's Vicar on earth, St. Pontian,* and is honored with him by the Church. *Liturgical celebration:* August 13 (Opt. Mem.); *theme:* perseverance in faith during trials.

History of Salvation (HIS-t[uh-]ree uhv sal-VAY-shuhn). The History of Salvation is in the final analysis the eternal plan of the Father carried out in time* before being completed in glory.* It is basically the history of the Covenants* God made with the human race, as sketched by the Fourth Eucharistic Prayer.* This History starts with Creation,* which was quickly marred by original sin* and humankind's refusal of the first Covenant. Next comes the Covenant with Noah, which establishes, so to speak, the positive values of natural religions and their liturgies in spite of grave degradations.

The true beginning of friendly relations between God and the human race is found in the Covenant with Abraham.* It led to the Sinaitic Covenant at the time of Moses,* which gave birth to the People of God,* in the great liturgy of the desert. Israel's many infidelities (beginning with the Golden Calf and running throughout the history of the Exodus,* the Judges,* and the Kings*) prompted the Prophets* to proclaim a new Covenant—one of the heart.

The New Covenant was inaugurated by the Incarnation* of God, Jesus Christ, and was sealed with His Blood.* In the wake of Christ's Passion-Resurrection,* the History of Salvation progressively incorporates the children of adoption—who are engendered by the Church* through the Spirit* of the Lord—into the life of God until the heavenly Jerusalem* is complete: "When everything is subjected to him, . . . so that God may be all in all" (1 Cor 15:28).

Sinai, Calvary, and the heavenly Jerusalem are the essential stages of the History of Salvation. The Liturgy,* at the period when any participant is situated in the History, actualizes the preceding event while preparing for the one that is to come. It works a kind of telescopic effect on time.* Such is the meaning of Memorial* in Israel; and such is the meaning of the Eucharistic Memorial that Christ left us before His Death.

Each new stage in the History of Salvation "accomplishes" and assumes the preceding stages: that is why the Church still listens, in her Liturgy, to the Scriptures of the Old Testament,* while awaiting the consummation of the New Covenant in the Jerusalem on high, that vision of peace where there is no temple, for the Lord God of all is its temple as well as the Lamb (Rv 21:22).

In the state of glory, the History is not swallowed up but finds its full completion; the Liturgy has the perfect goal: to insert in the love of the Trinity the people who have been selected "to the praise of his glory" (Eph 1:14).

Therefore, the Liturgy is nothing more than a certain way in which Christ—in the present intermediate time that extends from Pentecost* to the Second Coming,* in this eschatological time already going on—communicates the fullness of His Divine Life to individual souls, reproduces His Mystery* in them, and draws them into His Mystery.

The liturgical action is itself an *event* of salvation because it puts the historic *today* in touch with the historic time of Christ, that is, with the reality already historically accomplished of salvation in Christ and through Christ. And it is a *Sacramental* event because its modalities of actuating that salvation differ from those of the historical fact itself.

Thus, in the Sacramental act of the Liturgy, the History of Salvation *reaches its ultimate moment of actuation.* All who, through the liturgical celebration, come into contact with the reality. of the Mystery of Christ and possess the proper interior sentiments (the chief among which is faith*) to freely cooperate with it, are rendered gradually conformed to this Mystery and enter into the History of Salvation in its Christological aspect. *See also* CHURCH AND LITURGY; CHURCH YEAR; LITURGY.

History of the Liturgy. *See* LITURGY—HISTORY.

Holiness (HOH-lee-nuhs). St. Thomas Aquinas* teaches that holiness in us has two elements: (1)

purity, which means the avoidance of all sin and imperfections, and detachment from all creatures; and (2) stability, in adhering to God. In God, holiness consists in His limitless perfections and the perfect love with which He loves the good that is Himself. Our holiness will be the higher the more we lovingly depend on God and conform our free will to our last end, which is the manifestation of His glory.*

The Liturgy* has as its purpose the praise of God's holiness and glory and the effecting of human holiness: "Christ always associates the Church with Himself in the great work [Liturgy] wherein God is perfectly glorified and all human beings are sanctified" (SC, 7). The Liturgy reminds us continually of God's great holiness: "Father, you are holy indeed, / and all creation rightly gives you praise. All life, all holiness comes from you / through your Son, Jesus Christ our Lord" (EP III*).

The Liturgy also reminds us of our call to holiness: "[Christ] gave himself up for [the Church] to make her holy" (21st Sunday in Ordinary Time,* B, Reading II*—Eph 5:25f); "God chose us in [Christ] before the world began, to be holy" (15th Sunday in Ordinary Time, B, Reading II—Eph 1:4). And it obtains that holiness for us: "Let us be filled with every grace and blessing" (that is, with the holiness of Christ) (EP I*). In fact, the Liturgy is the most powerful means of holiness at our disposal. It not only contains sanctifying grace* and dispenses it but also contains the Source of all grace, Jesus Christ, and enables us to encounter Him in a union of love* and holiness.

Holocaust (HOL-uh-kawst; HOH-; HAW-). In the ancient sacrifices of the Old Law, only the blood and certain parts of the victim were offered to God; the rest was divided among the priest and faithful who had offered it (Lv 7:11-21). A holocaust (from the Greek "wholly burned") was a sacrifice in which an entire animal except its hide was consumed in the fire on the altar, with the primary purpose of giving glory to God (Lv 1:1ff). In the New Law there is no holocaust and only one sacrifice—that of Jesus offering Himself on the Cross.* The Eucharist* is the perpetual unbloody sacrifice of the New Covenant* in which the Sacrifice of the Cross is made sacramentally present. *See also* SACRIFICE.

Holy Chrism. *See* CHRISM.

Holy Communion. *See* COMMUNION.

Holy Days of Obligation (HOH-lee DAYZ uhv ob-luh-GAY-shuhn). Besides Sundays, those solemn feasts of precept in the Church* on which Catholics are expected to participate at Mass* and to refrain from servile work. It is laudable to consecrate that day by works of piety, prayer,* and spiritual reading. Formerly there were many more Holy Days, but the industrial age led to a curtailment of the number, so that from century to century and from country to country the number has varied. In the United States there are currently six: the Solemnity of Mary* (January 1); Ascension* (forty days after Easter); Assumption* (August 15); All Saints Day* (November 1); Immaculate Conception* (December 8) and Christmas* (The Nativity) (December 25).

The Universal Church* celebrates ten Holy Days, but each Episcopal Conference* is free to reduce these in view of the circumstances of its particular country and people. The ten include the six days listed above plus: Epiphany* (January 6), Corpus Christi* (Thursday after Trinity* Sunday), Solemnity of St. Joseph* (March 19), and Solemnity of Sts. Peter and Paul* (June 29).

The Church in America celebrates two of the additional four Holy Days on Sundays (Epiphany and Corpus Christi). Thus, there are only two of the ten that are not Holy Days of Obligation in the United States (St. Joseph and Sts. Peter and Paul). However, the American Bishops recently gave some thought to a proposal to reduce the Holy Days for the reason, among others, that too many people must work and cannot observe them properly. Nevertheless, popular reaction was negative and the proposal was shelved. *See also* SERVILE WORK.

Holy Family, Feast of the (HOH-lee FAM-uh-lee; FAM-lee; feest uhv thuh). Devotion to the Holy Family, Jesus,* Mary,* and Joseph,* de-

veloped only in the 17th century. Built on the Gospel* accounts, this trio is looked upon as an excellent domestic unit representing the ideal family life. To promote family life and build up devotion to the Holy Family, a feast was established for the Universal Church* in 1921, and it is currently celebrated on the Sunday after Christmas or on December 30 when Christmas falls on Sunday.

Holy, Holy, Holy (HOH-lee, HOH-lee, HOH-lee). Concluding the Preface,* this chant of praise and adoration came into Christian Liturgies from the synagogue and couples the Preface* with the rest of the Eucharistic Prayer.* Since it shows how all are united in the Sacrifice of praise, being continuously offered to the Father, it should be sung by the entire congregation with the priest,* usually in a simple chant melody. In centuries past, the music of this text became so florid that specially trained choirs alone were capable of singing it, and the first part was sung before the Consecration* while the second came afterward. Now that separation is forbidden, since it disregarded the communal character of the acclamation.

This chant comes from Isaiah* 6:3 (with an allusion to Daniel* 7:10). It is the assembly's way of showing the unity of their Sacrifice of Praise with that of the angels* and Saints* in heaven. The second part: "Blessed is he who comes in the name of the Lord," is preceded and followed by the acclamation "Hosanna in the highest" (Ps 117:25f; Mt 21:9). Better than any other Mass text, this acclamation shows that our Eucharist* is above all a Sacrifice of Praise.

Holy Hour (HOH-lee owr). Adoration of the Blessed Sacrament,* ordinarily with exposition during a devotional nonliturgical service in reparation, with hymns, suitable prayers, a homily,* and Benediction.* This service was begun by St. Margaret Mary Alacoque* as a special devotion to the Sacred Heart* and was promoted by Popes. Usually a Thursday or a Friday evening is preferred; however any hour of any day is suitable.

Holy Innocents (HOH-lee IN-uh-suhnts). The children of Bethlehem who were "two years old and under" massacred by order of Herod the Great in his mad attempt to eliminate the Infant Jesus called the new King of the Jews by the Magi* (Mt 2:16-18). They have been commemorated as Martyrs* since the 1st century and since the 6th century have been honored during the days of the Lord's Birth. Their death is viewed as a prophecy of the Redemption and as a key to the nature of martyrdom, showing it to be a gratuitous gift of God. They are the Patrons of Choir Boys and Foundlings. *Liturgical celebration:* December 28 (Feast); *theme:* bearing witness to the Faith in deeds as well as words.

Holy Men. *See* SAINTS, LITURGICAL CATEGORIES OF.

Holy Name of Jesus, Feast of (HOH-lee naym uhv JEE-zuhs, feest uhv). The Holy Name of Jesus was invoked by the faithful* from the very beginning of the Church* (Phil 2:9ff). In the 14th century it began to be venerated with liturgical celebrations. St. Bernardine of Siena* and his disciples promoted this veneration, and in the 16th century the Holy Name was introduced as a liturgical feast in the Calendar* of the Franciscan Order. In 1721, it was inserted into the Universal Calendar* by Pope Innocent XIII—to be celebrated on the Sunday between January 2 and 5 or on January 2 when no Sunday occurred. In the liturgical reform of Vatican II,* this feast was taken out of the Universal Calendar in keeping with the elimination of duplications in the Liturgy,* since the memory of the Name of Jesus is already kept in the Gospel* of the Mass on January 1. However, the Votive Mass of the Holy Name was retained.

The emblem or monogram representing the Holy Name of Jesus consists of three letters—IHS—which are the first three letters of "Jesus" in Greek. This monogram is used very frequently in connection with the Liturgy—in churches, on vestments,* on hosts,* and on various other appurtenances.

Holy of Holies. *See* SANCTUARY.

Holy Oils (HOH-lee oilz). Used at the anointings during the celebrations of the Sacraments* and at the consecration of persons and things, these oils are blessed by the bishop* on Holy Thursday* morning in the Mass of the Chrism. Ordinarily olive oil is used, but recent legislation allows them to be made from any plant. Unctions with oil or other materials have been used throughout the centuries and are considered instruments for strengthening, beautifying, and healing. For Christians, their use symbolizes the gift of special grace of the Holy Spirit,* a source of spiritual energy and a procedure for consecration. The three kinds are: Oil of the Catechumens*; Holy Chrism*; and Oil of the Sick.*

The bishop is the ordinary minister in the consecration of the oils. However, some priests may have the faculty for blessing the Oil of Catechumens and the Oil of the Sick. Traditionally, the blessing of the Oil of the Sick occurs before the end of the Eucharistic Prayer,* while the blessing of the other two comes after Communion* of the Chrism Mass. For pastoral reasons all three may be blessed after the Liturgy of the Word.* Since the Mass of the Chrism is one of the main expressions of the fullness of the bishop's priesthood and reveals the close unity of the priests with him, many priests from various parts of the diocese concelebrate with him. The oils are to be kept in silver or pewter vessels, usually locked in the ambry* in the church; however, smaller oil stocks may be kept by priests in a more handy place. In fact, each priest may carry the oils with him, so as to be able to anoint the sick in case of necessity. *See also* ANOINTING; CHRISM; HOLY THURSDAY; OIL OF CATECHUMENS; OIL OF THE SICK.

Holy Orders (HOH-lee AWRD-uhrz). The Sacrament* which, by the imposition of the bishop's hands

and the designated formula, confers the spiritual faculty to sanctify others through the holy and proper administration of the Sacraments to the People of God* for their sanctification. Thus as president of the Christian community during liturgical functions, the priest* not only offers, confects, and administers the Sacrament of the Altar but also through his teaching of the Word and dispensing of the other Sacraments prepares the faithful,* the Mystical Body,* for the Eucharist.*

The plural form indicates that there are several degrees, grades, or ranks to this Sacrament, and at each level the grace* and power to act in accord with the various grades of ministry are given. Of Divine origin are the diaconate, priesthood, and episcopacy, three forms of the Sacrament but only one Sacrament administered separately with successively greater Sacramental effects. The subdiaconate and the former Minor Orders* were of ecclesiastical origin. With their abrogation in 1972, laymen and candidates for the diaconate and priesthood are now installed in the ministries of Acolyte* and Reader.* The former Tonsure* was replaced by an act of dedication to the Church* of God.

An indelible character* is believed to be imprinted on the recipient of Holy Orders. The Sacramental effect is an increase of grace,* whereby the one ordained acquires the helps and virtues* necessary to be an appropriate minister in the worthy exercise of his duties. *See also* ORDINATION.

Holy Saturday. *See* EASTER VIGIL.

Holy See. *See* APOSTOLIC SEE.

Holy Spirit (HOH-lee SPIR-it). The Third Person of the Blessed Trinity* is the result of the love that exists between Father* and Son.* On the first Pentecost* He was publicly revealed to all by glorifying Christ and establishing a new era in the Church,* that of the Spirit. The Liturgy* on that day celebrates the pouring out of the Holy Spirit upon the Apostles* and the Church. Of the three Divine Persons, He is the One Who gives life to the Church.

His name appears in all Trinitarian formulas. His role as Paraclete or Advocate is made obvious in the Epiclesis* in the Mass. In the Sacraments of Confirmation* and Holy Orders,* the Holy Spirit is solemnly invoked. (*See also* GOD.)

Gifts of the Spirit

Through the Liturgy, the Holy Spirit dispenses gifts to the faithful.* One type is given as powers or charisms to be used primarily for the sanctification of others—e.g., the gifts of miracles, prophecy, and tongues. The second type is primarily for the sanctification of the recipient—the so-called Seven Gifts of the Holy Spirit: wisdom, understanding, counsel, fortitude, knowledge, piety, and fear of the Lord. These are supernatural dispositions that make us more alert to discern and more ready to do the will of God.

Fruits of the Spirit

The effects of the Gifts of the Holy Spirit are the Twelve Fruits—supernatural works that are done with joy and with peace of soul: charity, joy, peace, patience, longanimity, goodness, long-suffering, mildness, faith, modesty, continence, and chastity.

Holy Thursday (HOH-lee THUHRZ-dee; -day). The anniversary of the Last Supper,* at which Christ instituted the Eucharist,* the Mass, and the priesthood, is celebrated on the Thursday before Easter* as part of the Sacred Triduum.* It is also entitled Maundy Thursday from the Latin for the new commandment of love Jesus gave His Apostles,* which He exemplified by the washing of the feet, a ceremonial action that takes place after the Liturgy of the Word* in the Mass of the Lord's Supper.

Mass of the Chrism

Only in the cathedral, the local Ordinary* concelebrates the Chrism Mass with many of his priests to exemplify the communion of the priests with their bishop; to show this unity of the presbyterate, priests from various parts of the diocese* should be present and receive Communion under both species.* This Mass emphasizes the institution of the priesthood.* At the end of the Liturgy of the Word,* there is a general renewal of commitment to priestly service by both the bishop and the priests. It is during this Mass that the blessing of oils and consecrating of chrism take place. (*See also* HOLY OILS.)

Mass of the Lord's Supper

Celebrated at a convenient hour in the evening, this Mass should have the complete participation* of the local community, including all priests and clergy who would exercise their ministry through concelebration.* Ordinarily only this one Mass is permitted; however, the bishop may permit another Mass in the evening, or out of genuine necessity even in the morning, for those who can in no way attend the evening ceremony.

Should the principal Mass of the day not be able to be celebrated even with simple ceremonies, for pastoral reasons permission may be granted for two Masses, which ought to be concelebrated at the stated time; these Masses end in the usual fashion.

During the singing of the *Glory to God,** church bells are rung and then remain silent until the Easter Vigil.* The Homily* is to dwell upon the principal Mysteries of this day, the Eucharist,* the priesthood, and the new commandment of brotherly love. Thereupon the Washing of the Feet* may follow, during which persons, usually chosen because of their service to the local church, have their feet washed by the celebrant. Meanwhile antiphons* or appropriate songs are sung.

Mass continues as usual, except that the ciborium* with Hosts for

the next day is left on the altar after Communion. Following the Prayer after Communion* these Hosts are then transferred to the altar of repose. Having incensed the Blessed Sacrament,* the celebrant takes the ciborium, covers it with the ends of the humeral veil,* and carries it accompanied by candles* and incense* to the chapel or place of reposition decorated for this occasion, while Eucharistic songs are sung. Arriving at the altar, the Blessed Sacrament is incensed again while the congregation sings the *Tantum Ergo.** After the tabernacle* is closed, the altar of sacrifice is stripped. The faithful* continue adoration during part of the night, usually not after midnight.

Holy Water (HOH-lee WAW-tuhr; WAHT-uhr). Blessed for religious purposes by a priest* who asks God's blessing on those who use it, this water is employed as a Sacramental.* Its use is beneficial against temptations from spiritual enemies and at times of physical danger. It is a symbol of spiritual cleansing, most obvious at the sprinkling* with water at the beginning of Sunday

Mass. Kept in the home, it not only is a symbol of Baptism* but reminds one of Divine blessings. Liturgically, it is used in all blessings* of persons and objects and during dedications* and exorcisms.* When it is blessed, a small amount of salt may be added. Other types of holy water are baptismal water* and Easter water.* *See also* SPRINKLING; WATER.

Holy Week (HOH-lee week). The last week in Lent,* immediately before Easter,* commencing with Passion (Palm) Sunday* and concluding with Holy Saturday.* As such it is the focus of the Church's* liturgical cycle, during which God's redeeming act of the Passion and Resurrection* of Christ is commemorated in a special way. Colored with sorrow, the ceremonies express gratitude to the Lord for His mercy in becoming man to suffer and die for us.

During this week many archaic liturgical rites are preserved, with a simplicity all their own. Through them we relive the occurrences at the end of Christ's life, in which we celebrate the Paschal Mystery* whereby Jesus reconciled the world to His Father.* In the recent liturgical revisions, the original simplicity of this week was restored while irrelevant characteristics of the rites were eradicated. Every effort was made to involve the faithful* more actively in the celebration of the Paschal Mysteries. *See also* EASTER VIGIL; GOOD FRIDAY; HOLY THURSDAY; PASSION SUNDAY.

Holy Women. *See* SAINTS, LITURGICAL CATEGORIES OF.

Holy Year. *See* JUBILEE.

Homiliary. *See* BREVIARY.

Homily (HOM-uh-lee). Vatican Council II* asserts that the Homily is an integral part of the Liturgy,* and it should develop its message primarily from the Scriptural and liturgical sources to show God's wonderful action in the History of Salvation,* particularly as it relates to the specific community being addressed. Thus a small informal type of instruction draws upon the Scriptures* to make practical applications to the spiritual life. Always an integral part of the Sunday Liturgy, it is recommended whenever a congregation is present, particularly during Advent,* Lent,* Christmas Season,* and Easter Season.*

The Homily is based on the usual practice in a synagogue, such as was followed by Jesus at Nazareth. The Apostles* also followed this custom when the faithful* gathered for the Eucharist.* The early Fathers* continued the practice and

several volumes of homilies are extant. The term relates primarily to preaching during Mass,* which is reserved to priests* and deacons.* The catechetical and thematic sermon, another method of fulfilling the teaching office of the priesthood, has its place apart from Mass at some special place or time. Lay persons may preach this type of sermon in certain circumstances or in particular cases as prescribed by the Conference of Bishops.* *See also* MINISTRIES; PREACHING.

Honorarium, Mass. *See* STIPEND.

Hope (hohp). This word expresses the firm expectation of a future possible good. Christian hope is the fulfillment of the Israelite Messianic hope, which was based not on human resource and initiative but on the all-powerful presence of God (Ps 18:7). This Israelite hope was unshakable in spite of all the vicissitudes of history (Mi 7:7-9; Ps 22:5-6; Jer 30:7), and formed the basis for the words of the Prophets* (Mi 4–5; Is 40ff; Jer 30–33; Ez 40ff).

Hence, Christian hope was confirmed and reinforced by the coming of the Messiah,* the Incarnation* and Redemption* of Christ.* It is characterized by the absolute witness of God's love and faithfulness to His promises. It brings the Gospel* to the far corners of the world and gives people a more complete assurance of salvation* (Rom 5:1-11; Heb 6:18-20) until the end of time (1 Pt 1:3-5)—eternal life and a likeness to God (1 Jn 2:25; 3:2).

Even now, the hope of Christ should be triumphant for the Invincible Word of God fights by our side (Rv 19:11-16; 20:1-6) and the decisive victory is near (Rv 1:1; 2:5; 3:11, 22:6, 12). Thus, we cry out: "Come, Lord Jesus!" (Rv 22:20), expressing the ardent desire of a love that hungers for the Lord's presence.

The Liturgy* itself is a liturgy of *hope*—it is permeated by this hope and continually alludes to it. In St. Thomas Aquinas'* classic description, the Eucharist is a "sacramental banquet in which Christ is our food, his passion* is recalled, our hearts are filled with grace,* and we receive a pledge of future glory*"—that is, our *hope* of glory is strengthened (Magnificat Antiphon for Corpus Christi*).

At every Mass we affirm that "we *hope* to enjoy forever the vision of [God's] glory" (EP III*) and "we wait in joyful *hope* for the coming of our Lord Jesus Christ" (Conclusion to the Our Father*). All along the line, the Liturgy is hope-directed, hope-filled and hope-inducing. In the words of the Preface* for Advent* (I), "we watch for the day *hoping* that the salvation promised us will be ours when Christ our Lord will come again in his glory."

Hope, Act of (hohp, akt uhv). A formula expressing the hope* for eternal happiness* based on God's goodness and His faithfulness to His promises. The Liturgy* is both permeated with acts of hope and fosters hope. The traditional Act of Hope is as follows:

> O my God, relying on Your almighty power and infinite mercy and promises, I hope to obtain pardon of my sins, the help of Your grace,* and life everlasting,* through the merits of Jesus Christ, my Lord and Redeemer.

Those who say an act of hope can gain a partial indulgence.*

Horologian (hawr-uh-LOHG-ee-uhn; hohr-). A liturgical book of the Byzantine Rite* that contains the Ordinary of the Divine Office* for every feast* and antiphons* for Mass.*

Hosanna (hoh-ZAHN-uh; -ZAN-uh). A Hebrew shout of triumph and joy, whose literal meaning is: "save, we pray," or "may God save." It was found in the Psalms* (118:25-26) and was used during the Feast of Tabernacles when the priest processed around the altar and the people waved palm branches. Since Ps 118 was regarded as announcing the coming of the Messiah,* who after suffering would appear as "the one who comes in the name of the Lord" (v 26), it was altogether natural for the people to shout this phrase in meeting Christ as He entered Jerusalem in a triumphal

manner on Passion Sunday.* The phrase was inserted into the Liturgy* at a very early date (see *Didache,** 10, 6) and is used today at every Mass as part of the Holy, Holy, Holy*; it is also sung during the solemn procession on Passion Sunday.

Hosea, The Book of (hoh-ZEE-uh; -ZAY-; thuh buk uhv). Thirty-fifth Book of the Old Testament* and first of the Minor Prophets.* Hosea's ministry to the Northern Kingdom followed closely upon that of Amos,* that is, after 746 B.C. While the latter had spoken as a southerner to the prosperous Israel enjoying an era of peace, Hosea spoke as a native to his own people who were suffering from war with Assyria and in virtual anarchy. The Prophet's personal life is an incarnation of God's redeeming love. He spoke out against the influence of pagan practices and is known as the cantor of God's redeeming love, which is opposed and frustrated by the people's infidelity. Hosea's revelation foreshadows that of Jesus, the revealer of the God of love.

Liturgical use: In the *Roman Missal,** this Book is read on the 8th Sunday (B) and the 10th Sunday (A) in Ordinary Time* as well as on Monday through Friday of the 14th Week in Ordinary Time (II), Friday and Saturday of the 3rd Week of Lent,* the Sacred Heart* (B), the Common of Virgins, and during the

Rites of Baptism* and Penance.* In the *Liturgy of the Hours,** it is read from Thursday of the 18th Week through Monday of the 19th Week in Ordinary Time. *Meaning:* The Christian God is a God of love. He loves us with a faithful and everlasting love and He desires our faithful love* in return—indeed, He desires love over sacrifice and knowledge of God over holocausts* (6:6). God's love knows no bounds and can forgive all our faults—provided we repent for our infidelity and return to Him.

Hosts. *See* BREAD.

Hours, Canonical. *See* CANONICAL HOURS.

Houses, Blessing of (HOW-ziz, BLES-ing uhv). This Sacramental* is one of many liturgical blessings whereby the pastor* or his dele-

gate, in sprinkling a house and the family living therein, begs God to sanctify the place and them. Where it is an annual event, it happens during Easter Season,* usually on Holy Saturday.* In some areas it occurs on Epiphany.*

Humeral Veil. *See* VEIL, HUMERAL.

Humiliate Capita Vestra Deo. *See* BOW YOUR HEADS....

Hymn of Praise. *See* GLORY TO GOD.

Hymnary. *See* BREVIARY.

Hymns (himz). Non-Biblical songs that praise God, usually in metric or strophic form. Most of the early Christian hymns are no longer extant. After the 4th century hymns appeared with two purposes, a doctrinal exposition or a devotional expression. Many of the Latin hymns by famous Saints* were entered into the Breviaries.

Vernacular hymns were introduced in the 13th century, and during the Reformation many German hymns were composed by no less than Martin Luther, a musician.

Catholic vernacular hymns in America were slow in developing, as they tried to represent the various cultures present. Hymnals of an unsatisfactory nature appeared in the 19th century, so that the reform by Pope St. Pius X* was happily received. Eventually better hymnals containing some of the best European hymns and some American compositions appeared.

The post-Vatican II* liturgical reform with its emphasis on singing by the congregation has put pressure upon musicians to be creative in developing songs of a religious nature that the people can readily sing. Success is not immediate and, unfortunately rather than building on a couple of centuries of music in their heritage, many have tried to begin anew with unsatisfactory results. Nevertheless, by this time, some good collections exist. Most try to blend the best from many traditions and styles of the past with contemporary composers. Groups and individuals try to satisfy the liturgical needs of our day. Some are ephemeral, others of an enduring nature. The great music of the past developed over centuries; we need a few more decades. *See also* CHOIRS (MUSIC); MUSIC.

Hypapante (hip-uh-PAHN-tee). The name given to the feast of the Presentation of the Lord* in the Eastern Liturgy. Stemming from the Greek word for "encounter" or "meeting," it refers to the meeting of Simeon and Anna with Mary*

and the Infant Jesus 40 days after His birth at the presentation in the Temple. In the West, a comparable title was used during the Middle Ages: *"Occursus Domini"*—"The Encounter with the Lord."

Hyperdulia (hai-puhr-doo-LAI-uh). The special form of homage given to Mary* in her role as Mother of God, Coredemptress with Christ, and Mediatrix of all graces. Different from the adoration* given to God, it stresses her unique sanctity, beyond that of all other creatures, angels,* and Saints.* *See also* DULIA; LATRIA.

— I —

ICEL. *See* INTERNATIONAL COMMISSION ON ENGLISH IN THE LITURGY.

Iconoclasm (ai-KON-uh-klaz-uhm). The heretical doctrine that opposed the veneration of icons, stylized paintings of Christ,* Mary,* and the Saints* generally done on wood and—except for the hands and face—covered with relief of pearls and silver or gold. The iconoclastic crisis affected principally the Eastern Church* and had two phases. The first began with Emperor Leo the Isaurian in 726 and ended in 787 when the Second Ecumenical Council of Nicaea condemned the heresy and allowed the veneration of sacred images. The second phase started in 814 under Leo V and ended in 842 when the Feast of Orthodoxy was established under Empress Theodora. St. John Damascene* and Theodore the Studite were the principal defenders of the veneration of these sacred images. *See also* IMAGES.

Iconostasis (ai-kuh-NOS-tuh-suhs). In the Eastern* churches this "picture-stand" separates the altar* from the nave.* Originally in stone, now more commonly in wood, with gates, it is usually covered with large pictures or icons.* It symbolizes a veil between heaven and earth, with the Saints* pictured on it acting as our mediators. The celebrant,* hidden by the screen, speaks from the altar* as if God were speaking to His people on earth.

Icons. *See* ICONOCLASM; IMAGES.

Ignatius of Antioch, St. (ig-NAY-shuhs uhv AN-tee-ok). ?-107. Bishop of Antioch after St. Peter,* Ignatius was sentenced to death by being thrown to the wild beasts. He was sent to Rome and suffered a glorious martyrdom under the Emperor Trajan. On his way to Rome, this saintly bishop wrote seven letters to the churches that are justly celebrated because of their wise and deep treatment of the theology of Christ, the constitution of the Church,* and the Christian life. *Liturgical celebration:* October 17 (Memorial); *theme:* courage in bearing witness to Christ.

Ignatius of Loyola, St. (ig-NAY-shuhs uhv loi-OH-luh; lai-). 1491-1556. Born in northern Spain, Ignatius lived a worldly early life at court and in the army before being converted to a life of holiness.* While studying theology at Paris, he gathered around him a group of

brilliant companions and after his ordination at Venice formed them into the Society of Jesus (Jesuits) at Rome. Ignatius carried on a most fruitful apostolate by his written work and by the formation of his disciples who won great praise for the renewal of the Church.* He left us his Society and his world-famous *Spiritual Exercises.* He is the Patron of Retreats and Soldiers. *Liturgical celebration:* July 31 (Memorial); *theme:* seeking ever the greater glory of God.

IHS. *See* HOLY NAME OF JESUS, FEAST OF.

Illumination. *See* ENLIGHTENMENT.

Images (IM-ij-uhz). An image is a representation in an art form, usually as a statue* through sculpture, or a painting through any of the various media. Such representations of Christ* and the Saints* may be venerated according to a decree of the Second Council of Nicaea. Icons* and images of any sort are expected to aid in devotion, to be instructive by complementing the written or spoken word, and to adorn the churches.

This veneration is allowed because the honor shown is not directed to the physical image but is referred to the person represented. Thus the reverence given is truly a worship* of Christ and a veneration of the Saints, who are displayed by the images. Ways of venerating would include incensation* of and kissing the images, placing lights* or candles* before them, and praying to the Lord through them as intercessors.

In its *Constitution on the Sacred Liturgy** (no. 125), the Second Vatican Council* upheld the practice of placing sacred images in churches so that they may be venerated by the faithful* but stipulated that their number should be moderate and their relative positions should reflect right order. As a result, there was a tendency to empty the churches of all sacred images. On June 30, 1965, Cardinal Lercaro wrote a letter to the presidents of episcopal conferences* in which he reiterated the Council's position. Without doubt the Mysteries* of the Redemption* and the Eucharistic Action must be at the center of worship; however, in perfect harmony and subordination there is room for the veneration of Mary* and the Saints through images. An enlightened zeal, in the spirit of the Church, is well aware that in the house of God everything has a meaning, everything speaks, and everything must preserve the stamp of the sacred and of mystery.

Images, Veiling of. *See* VEILING OF IMAGES.

Immaculate Conception (im-AK-yuh-luht kuhn-SEP-shuhn). The prerogative whereby the Blessed Virgin Mary* was sinless from the first moment of her existence. From the earliest times the Church formulated in her prayer the essentials of her faith concerning the Mother of Jesus (Council of Ephesus, 431). But it took a long time to uncover the wonders of grace* contained in those words.

St. Irenaeus,* in the 3rd century, foreshadowed Mary's Immaculate Conception by calling her the New Eve. By the 8th century, there was a feast in honor of this title in the Eastern Church. In the 11th century, it appeared in the Western Church and was celebrated in England. Two centuries later in Scotland, the Franciscan John Duns Scotus clarified the distinction whereby, though Mary deserved original sin like all other humans, she was preserved from it at the moment of conception by a pre-redemption.

This feast was included in the calendar of the Universal Church*

in the 14th century and made a feast of obligation in 1708, with an Opening Prayer* that declared: "God prepared a worthy dwelling place for [His] Son through the Immaculate Conception of the Virgin, preserving her from all sin in view of the foreseen Death of His [Son]." Finally, in 1854 Pius IX defined this prerogative as a dogma* of Faith and used practically the very words of the Liturgy* (found in the Opening Prayer).

The Immaculate Conception is more than just Mary's preservation from evil. It is her fullness of grace. Like her privilege of the Assumption,* it is based on Mary's Divine Motherhood. And in both Mary is the anticipated image of the Church without spot or wrinkle (Eph 5:27). This feast is a Holyday of Obligation* in the United States, and Mary is the Patroness of the country under her title of the Immaculate Conception. *Liturgical celebration:* December 8 (Solemnity); *theme:* purity of life before God.

Immaculate Heart of Mary. *See* MARY, BLESSED VIRGIN—FEASTS.

Immersion (i-MUHR-zhuhn; -shuhn). The oldest method of baptizing, through submerging the candidate as the form is pronounced. Although Baptism* by pouring of water is more common, the performance of the rite by immersion has been reintroduced recently. *See also* BAPTISM.

Impetration (im-puh-TRAY-shuhn). A synonym for petition,* meaning an act of requesting or entreating God for some good. It is one of the four ends of prayer* and the Sacrifice of the Mass.* *See also* ADORATION; MASS; PETITION; PRAYER; REPARATION; THANKSGIVING.

Imposition of Hands (im-puh-ZISH-uhn uhv handz). The ritualistic gesture of holding the hands on or over things or persons to transfer some power, duty, favor, or blessing is an ancient custom. Utilized by Jesus when curing and blessing people, the ritual entered into the Liturgy* readily and has been used with different meanings.

It is the essential part of the Sacrament of Holy Orders* when deacons,* priests,* or bishops* are ordained.* It accompanies most blessings* and exorcisms,* such as those before Baptism.* It is part of the blessing for healing and pardon when anointing the sick. In the Rite of Penance* it becomes a symbol of reconciliation.* During the epiclesis* the celebrant extends his hands over the gifts, as some say, to indicate the placing of the sins of the world on Christ Who becomes the expiatory Victim.

Imprecatory Psalms (IM-pri-kuh-tohr-ee; im-PREK-uh-tohr-ee; -tor). Certain Psalms* marked by strong language and denunciations of the foes of Israel and its God. Since the psalmists are often oppressed or persecuted by their enemies, they frequently cry out to God to give these enemies their just deserts: Ps 5:11; *6:11; 7:10; 10:15; 18:13-15;* 28:4; 31:19; 35:4-8; 40:15; 54:7; 58:7-11; 69:23-29; *70:3-4;* 79:6-7, 12; 83:10-19; 109; 110:5-6; *129:5-8;* 137:7-9; 139:19-22; 140:10-12; 141:10; 143:12).

These prayers are admittedly foreign to the teaching of Jesus, but we must remember that (1) the Old Testament* revelation was incomplete and a preparation for the New*; (2) the curse in the Near East was regarded as a legitimate means of defense; and (3) the language of Easterners is more impassioned than that of Westerners.

Nevertheless, these cursing Psalms pose a problem when intended to be used in the public prayer of the Church.* The texts in question can cause difficulty to the person praying. Hence, the *Liturgy of the Hours* has omitted Psalms 58, 83, and 109 altogether and dropped most of the other offending verses (the only ones that remain in liturgical use are those printed in *italics* above). On the other hand, some exegetes have objected that such excisions of the Biblical text cause harm to the meaning and the poetic balance and also water down the idea of struggle in the Christian life. *See also* PSALMS.

Imprimatur (im-pruh-MAH-too[uh]r; im-PRIM-uh-t[y]oo[uh]r). This Latin word means "Let it be printed"; by it approval of the bishop* is given to publish writings of any nature and to use material relating to religion and morality through the instruments of social communication. It merely states that there is nothing in this material contrary to Faith and morals. It indicates that appointed competent censors have passed favorable judgment on the material, so that the bishop may grant permission to publish or use. Among religious books affected by this law are not only the Scriptures* and translations of liturgical books* but also prayer books and devotional works. Authors may receive the imprimatur from the bishop of the place (1) where they reside or (2) where the book is published. The third option given in the 1917 Code—the bishop of the place of *printing*—has been eliminated (see Can. 824). Usually the censor's name and the bishop's name appear within the book with the date of approval.

IMPRIMI POTEST: **Robert J. Karris, O.F.M.**
Privincial Minister
NIHIL OBSTAT: **John J. Quinn, M.A.**
Censor Librorum
IMPRIMATUR: **Patrick J. Sheridan**
Vicar General, Archdiocese of New York

Imprimi Potest (IM-pruh-mee POH-test). This Latin phrase, "It may be printed," is obtained from a major Religious superior by one of his subjects, before a work is presented for an imprimatur.* It too, with the superior's name and date, is usually printed in the work.

Improperia. *See* REPROACHES.

In Saecula Saeculorum. *See* FOR EVER AND EVER.

Inaestimabile Donum (in-es-ti-MAH-bee-lay DOH-noohm). Latin title (from the first two words "Inestimable Gift") of the *Instruction on Certain Norms Concerning the Worship of the Eucharistic Mystery* issued by the Sacred Congregation for the Sacraments and Divine Worship* on April 3, 1980. The document notes the many positive results of the liturgical reform: more active participation* on the part of the faithful*; growth in the community sense of liturgical life; and successful efforts to close the gap between life* and worship,* between liturgical piety and personal piety, and between Liturgy* and popular piety.

The Instruction then goes on to list a series of abuses that had crept into liturgical services and indicates how to right them. It concludes with a call for priests* to acquire an ever deeper understanding of the Liturgy, especially the Mass,* as well as an adequate Biblical training so that they may present to the faithful the meaning of the Liturgy as an enactment, in signs, of the History of Salvation.*

Incarnation (in-kahr-NAY-shuhn). This word is used in two senses: (1) The action of taking human nature by the Second Person of the Blessed Trinity.* By the power of the Holy Spirit,* He was born of a human being with a human body and soul, i.e., a human nature. But He did not cease to be God. Hence, He is God-Man, true God and true Man, like us in all things except sin. His two natures, the human and the Divine, are inseparably united in the One Person of the Son of God. (2) The supernatural Mystery* covering the entire Life, Death, and Resurrection* of Christ and His Risen life in glory* interceding for us. In this sense, the word is equivalent to the Redemption.*

The Liturgy* is the public worship that the Incarnate Word, our Redeemer, as Head of the Church renders to the Father* as well as the worship that the Christian community renders to its Founder, the Incarnate Word, and through Him to the Father. Liturgy is the actualization, through sensible signs, of this Incarnation in its broad meaning as the Mystery of Salvation.*

Hence, the whole Liturgy is permeated by the Incarnation, speaks of the Incarnation, is powered by the Incarnation, and leads to the Incarnate Son of God, Jesus Christ. It is with Him that every part of the Liturgy is carried out, in Him that every prayer is recited, and through

Him that every action is performed—to the praise and glory of the Father in the unity of the Spirit.

Incensation (in-sen-SAY-shuhn). Within a thurible* burning charcoal covered with incense* creates smoke, which is wafted toward persons and things in a gesture that indicates liturgical honor.

Optional in any form of Mass,* incensations may take place during the Entrance Procession,* for the altar* is incensed at the beginning of Mass; in the procession and the proclamation of the Gospel*; at the Preparation of the Gifts,* when they, the altar,* the priest,* and the people are incensed; and during the elevation of the Host and chalice at the Consecration.*

After blessing in silence the incense placed on the charcoal in the thurible, the priest, swinging the censer, walks around a free-standing altar, but goes first to the right and then to the left if the altar is attached to a wall. A cross on the altar or near it is incensed prior to the altar; if it is behind the altar, it is incensed when the priest passes in front of it.

At Morning Prayer* and Evening Prayer,* during the Gospel Canticle,* the altar, then the priest and the people, may be incensed. During the Funeral Rites,* incensations of the altar and coffin occur. During Benediction* and processions of the Blessed Sacrament,* the Blessed

Sacrament is incensed. Incensations also take place at the blessing of many Sacramentals,* for instance, palms,* ashes,* candles,* and bells.*

Incense (IN-sens). Grains or powder from aromatic resinous gums, burned during church services, release a fragrant odor. Usually frankincense, native to Arabia, is used. Besides creating a worshipful atmosphere, incense provides a festive ambiance for processions* and similar ceremonies; it is an honor to the person and the objects being incensed, but primarily shows deep reverence and homage to the Lord God, particularly in incensations of the Blessed Sacrament,* where it is considered as a sacrifice to the Lord God. The ascending smoke serves as a symbolic representation of the prayer by the congregation rising to the throne of the Divine Majesty. Furthermore the grains of sand personify the individual Christians being poured out and consumed as they serve the Lord.

Thus, in the incensation of the altar,* the Gospel Book,* the crucifix,* icons,* and statues,* the clergy,* and the assembly,* it is really Jesus Himself Who is reverenced in the altar that stands for Him, in His living Word, in the images that represent Him to us, in the ordained ministers who act in His place, and in the people who through Baptism* are images of God because of the indwelling Trinity* and sharers of Christ's priesthood.* *See also* INCENSATION.

Incense Boat. *See* BOAT, INCENSE.

Incipit (IN-chi-pit). A Latin word (meaning "it begins") that refers to the initial formula of a prayer or the customary introductory phrase of a Scripture reading*: "At that time," "In those days," "Brothers and sisters," "Dearly beloved," or "Thus says the Lord." Such phrases may be changed or dropped by decree of the competent authorities (see LFMI, 124). *See also* INITIA.

Inclusive language (in-KLOO-siv LANG-gwij). Primarily in the English-speaking Church, where feminism is strong, and in Protestant churches where women are ordained to the ministry, there has been a controversy over the idea of inclusive language in both the Biblical translations and the Liturgy.* Present English usage is androcentric, that is, the male is understood to be the normative human person. "Man" denotes in English both the human being and the male. When generic pronouns are required, they are male; female pronouns are not used in this sense.

There are two reasons for this: (1) In the patriarchal social order, the male was head of the family legally, representing the whole family including the women. (2) In Latin, the common language when the Church was growing, the word *homo* stands for both male and female. The word *vir* stands for man as a male. Consequently, whenever the word *homo* appeared, it stood for all humankind, including men and women. When an author wanted to specify a male only, he used the term *vir.* Since today's speaking world is unfamiliar with Latin, we can understand its difficulty in accepting the fact that the word *homo,* man, stands for both men and women.

Inclusive language tries to avoid male generic language in different ways, for instance, by using neutral generics like "person" rather than "man"; by adding words to denote the female form, e.g., brothers and sisters; by adding "she" to "he" or writing the sentence in the plural, "they" for "he." Another method is to substitute the first or second person pronoun such as "we" and "you."

An *Inclusive Language Lectionary* is available (although it is not approved for use in the Catholic Liturgy) that embodies all these rules and adds words like "mother" to "father" in order to exemplify God's parental relation to us. To offset the male leadership titles of "Lord," "King," more neutral terms are used, such as "Ruler" or "Sovereign," and "Son of God" is changed to "Child of God."

The International Commission on English in the Liturgy* took note of this new sensitivity to sexist language when it was first becoming a part of the American consciousness. In an August 1975 meeting of the Advisory Committee, the following resolution was passed: "The Advisory Committee recognizes the necessity in all future translations and revisions to avoid words which ignore the place of women in the Christian community altogether or which seem to relegate women to a secondary role." Of course, the actual implementation of ths resolution will take much more work and even more time, but a beginning has been made.

Inclusive language arouses people's emotional feelings concerning their social and sexual identity. Implications are much more far-reaching and complex than many realize. Without inclusive language women feel deprived of a language they are familiar with as they pray or worship.

Independence Day Mass (in-duh-PEN-duhn(t)s day mas). In line with the civil holiday of independence in the United States, celebrated on July 4, the Mass* text for that occasion, with Presidential Prayers* and Preface,* was approved to be used for Independence Day and other civic observations—as part of the Proper* for the United States. A proper Mass was allowed in the bicentennial year, 1976.

Our secular holiday celebrates the inalienable right of all people to life,* liberty,* and the pursuit of happiness.* These three rights were upheld by Jesus Himself (Jn 10:10; Mt 8:32, 36; Mt 5:2-12). Thus, there is a natural affinity between our Independence Day and our spiritual independence, and between our celebration and the Jewish memorial of their freedom from Egyptian bondage. God guided that chosen band of people into the promised land, and He surely guided our forebears into making the United States "one nation under God with liberty and justice for all."

The Mass texts for this day take cognizance of the American Dream and exalt the thirst for social justice found therein. The Opening Prayer* asks God to open our hearts to greater love for His Son and to ensure that the boundaries of nations will not set limits to our love for others. Instead may they give us courage to build a land that serves Him in truth* and justice.*

In the Preface, we thank God and praise Him for His Son Who brought us a message of peace and taught us to live as brothers and sisters. His message took form in the vision of our forebears as they fashioned a nation whose people might live as one. This message lives on in our midst as a task for people today and a promise for tomorrow.

Indigenization. *See* ADAPTATION, LITURGICAL.

Indulgences (in-DUHL-juhn[t]s-ez). In the Rite of Penance* guilt for sins forgiven is taken away, but temporal punishment due for sins may be remitted through indulgences. The faithful* receive this remission through the ministry of the Church,* which dispenses in an authoritative manner the treasury of satisfaction earned by Christ and the Saints.* As for the rest the faithful must have the proper dispositions and fulfill certain conditions. The work that is indulgenced receives its effectiveness by the attitude and virtuous manner in which the task is completed and by how perfectly it is done. A *plenary* indulgence remits all temporal punishment, whereas a *partial* indulgence removes only a part of it. Indulgences may be gained for oneself or for the poor souls.

So as to encourage the faithful to inculcate the truly Christian spirit in many actions that they perform daily, three general grants of indulgences were given by Pope Paul VI in the *Apostolic Constitution on Indulgences.* These three partial indulgences are most fitting in our present milieu.

(1) The first is granted to those who in their regular duties and in enduring the trials of life say some pious invocation,* even mentally.

(2) The second goes to the faithful who out of charity and mercy give of themselves or their goods to help those in need.

(3) The third helps to bolster self-denial when people voluntarily deprive themselves, in a spirit of penance,* of things licit and pleasing to them.

Plenary indulgences can be acquired but once in a day, and three conditions are necessary besides the actual work itself, namely, Sacramental confession,* the reception of Communion,* and prayer for the intention of the Pope,* which can be satisfied by an Our Father* and Hail Mary*; one may choose another prayer out of piety or devotion. When Anointing of the Sick takes place in conjuction with Viaticum,* a plenary indulgence may be given by the priest after the Penitential Rite.*

Though some indulgences are attached to objects, gaining the indulgence is dependent upon the actions of the faithful. No longer is an amount of time attached to partial indulgences.

The whole doctrine on indulgences as well as the prayers and other good works to which indulgences are attached may be found in the *Enchiridion of Indulgences,** an authorized English edition of the *Enchiridion Indulgentiarum,* which was published in 1969. *See also* ENCHIRIDION OF INDULGENCES.

Indult (IN-duhlt; in-DUHLT). A special (and often temporary) dispensation granted to a physical or moral person by the Apostolic See (or the local Ordinary*), which confers faculties* contrary to or beyond the prescriptions of the law. An indult does not affect the law in any way but simply authorizes the person in question to act contrary to it because of special circumstances. For example, special liturgical feasts* or offices* not contained in the Calendar* of the Universal Church* are approved for certain places or societies by indult. *See also* LITURGICAL LAW, SOURCES OF.

Inerrancy. *See* INSPIRATION.

Infant Baptism. *See* BAPTISM.

Infulae (IN-fuhl-ay). Used mainly in this plural form (the singular is infula), the word refers to the two bands or tabs hanging from the back of a bishop's miter.* It may be used of a type of chasuble* found principally in France and England from the 11th to the 16th century.

Infusion (in-FYOO-zhuhn). That method of Baptism* whereby water is poured over the head of the candidate. Today it is the most common form employed during the Baptismal Ritual. *See also* BAPTISM.

Initia (in-ee-TSEE-ah). Latin plural meaning "beginnings," used by the *Lectionary* to refer to the beginnings of the readings,* especially when some words need to be deleted or supplied for intelligibility, inasmuch as the text has been separated from its context. It is important to make sure that these initia are taken care of any time a reading that does not appear in the *Lectionary* is to be used in the Liturgy.* *See also* INCIPIT.

Initiation Rites. *See* RITE OF CHRISTIAN INITIATION OF ADULTS.

Innovations, Liturgical (in-uh-VAY-shuhnz, luh-TUHR-ji-kuhl; li-). In the reform called for by the *Constitution on the Sacred Liturgy,** it was made clear that the Apostolic See* has the final authority with regard to all regulations, except insofar as it might be extended to local bishops' conferences.* Consequently not even a priest* may remove, add, or change anything on his own authority.

Any innovation adopted should be grounded in the fact that the good of the Church* certainly and genuinely requires it. Even then the changes are not to be made until thorough investigation has proceeded along theological, historical, and pastoral lines, preferably based on some experience from recent reforms. Since innovations are to develop organically from existing forms of worship,* certain factors are always to be considered: (a) the culture wherein the Liturgy* is celebrated; (b) the communal and hierarchical nature of the service; and (c) its pastoral and didactic purpose. *See also* ADAPTATION, LITURGICAL.

Inquirers (in-KWAI[uh]R-uhrz). In relation to the initiation rites,* those persons sincerely seeking to study the Faith of the Church.

INRI (ai-en-ahr-ai). An acronym from the title on Christ's Cross* as ordered by Pilate, from the Latin version of Jn 19:19—*Iesus Nazarenus Rex Iudaeorum* (Jesus of Nazareth, King of the Jews). After the 13th century it appears frequently in Western art, when representing the Crucifixion.

Inscription. *See* ENROLLMENT.

Insignia, Pontifical (in-SIG-nee-uh, pon-TIF-i-kuhl). The vestments and emblems worn by prelates, when they officiate at a liturgical ceremony. Pope Paul VI simplified their number and use and reduced privileges concerning them. Examples from the insignia of bishops and Popes are the miter,* gloves,* ring,* pectoral cross,* crozier,* and pallium.*

Inspiration (in-spuh-RAY-shuhn). The special influence of the Holy Spirit* on the hearts and minds of people prompting the exercise of one of His gifts* or an effect desired by the Trinity.*

Biblical Inspiration

Biblical inspiration is a Divine action or supernatural influence of the Holy Spirit on the sacred writers, moving and impelling them to write in such a manner that they first rightly understood, then willed faithfully to write down, and fully expressed in apt words with infallible truth all the things, and those only, that He ordered.

Thus, "the books of both the Old* and the New* Testaments in their entirety, with all their parts, are sacred and canonical because, written under the inspiration of the Holy Spirit, they have God as their Author" (DV, 11). This does not mean, however, that God used the sacred author as a secretary to whom He dictated. Nor did He simply reveal to the human author the contents of the Book and the way in which this should be expressed. Rather, the human author is a living instrument endowed with reason who under the Divine impulse brings his faculties and powers into play in such a way that all can easily gather from the Book produced by his work his distinctive genius and his individual characteristics and features. In other words, the sacred author, like every author, makes use of all his faculties—intellect, imagination, and will.

By virtue of the Divine condescension, things are presented to us in the Bible* in a manner that is in common use among human beings. For as the substantial Word of God* made Himself like human beings in all things except sin (Heb 4:15), so God's words, spoken by human tongues, have taken on all the qualities of human language except error.

The Israelites believed in the inspiration of Moses,* the Prophets,* and the authors of the Wisdom literature, the priests, in giving instruction. They ascribed the highest type of inspiration to the Pentateuch or Five Books attributed to Moses (also known as the Torah or Law*), a lower type to the Prophets, and an even lower one to the *Writings.*

The sacred writers of the New Testament cited the Old Testament about 350 times in such a way as to show that Christians shared the belief of the Israelites in the Divine origin of the sacred Books, but they made no distinction about the type of inspiration. In addition, the New Testament speaks of inspiration of the Old Testament Scriptures explicitly in 2 Timothy* (3:15-17) and 2 Peter* (1:19-21) and of the New Testament writings implicitly in 2 Peter (3:14-16).

The Fathers* of the Church accepted the Divine origin of the Bible. They see God as the Author of the Bible and the human author as His instrument. In the 2nd century, they begin to equate the New Testament with the Old as Scripture and Word of God.

The complete list of the inspired Canonical Books of both the New and the Old Testaments was given by the Church* at the Fourth Council of Rome (382) under Pope Damasus,* the Council of Hippo (393), the Third Council of Carthage (419), and the Gelasian Decree (Pope Gelasius, 494-496). The Ecumenical Council of Florence (1438-1445) also mentioned the complete Canon, and finally the Ecumenical Council of Trent formally defined the complete Canon of both Testaments on April 8, 1546.

This points out an important quality about inspiration. It does not follow from the religious enthusiasm produced in the reader, nor from the matter or form of the Books themselves, nor from the prophetic or apostolic origin of a Book, nor from the sacred writer's own witness to the inspiration of his Book. The criterion of inspiration follows solely from the Catholic Tradition* by which the formal witness of God to the inspiration of the Sacred Scriptures was revealed to the Apostles* and handed down to the whole Church.

Biblical inspiration leads directly to *inerrancy,* the quality whereby the Scriptures are—both in theory and in fact—free from all error in the message they convey. The words of the Bible are always true in the sense intended by their human authors.

The "truth" of an event or a subject is presented in a different fashion in each literary form—*but it is still the truth.* Thus, the whole Bible is true, absolutely true, every part of it, but it is true in the sense in which each kind of literary form bears witness to it. "Truth is proposed and expressed in a variety of ways, depending on whether a text is history of one kind or another or whether its form is that of prophecy, poetry, or another type of speech" (DV, 12).

Liturgical Inspiration

As far as the Liturgy* is concerned, the Biblical texts that are used during its celebrations possess that same inspiration. They are the

Word of God. They are rereadings of that inspired Word for the People of God today. They even take on a *deeper meaning* in their liturgical proclamation. We might almost term this a "liturgical inspiration." since it is the Church that rereads and redirects them to her members.

This quality may be viewed as a result of the general "inspiration" of the Holy Spirit in the Church (see 1 Cor 12:4-11). Such inspiration embraces the beginning and the development of revelation up to the time of its being set down in writing as well as the various ways in which the letter of Scripture is made actual by the living Church through the Liturgy and the Magisterium* and assimilated by believers. Hence, the apostolic Church in taking up the Old Testament in her life, Liturgy, and preaching acted as an author utilizing previous sources and can be equated to an author of the Old Testament. With the advent of Christ and the apostolic preaching the whole of the Old Testament received a new meaning. Thus, the *charism of inspiration* is part of the other charisms in the life of the Church.

Furthermore, every liturgical celebration, which is based primarily on the Word of God and sustained by it, becomes a new event and enriches the Word itself with new meaning and power (LFMI, 3). This deepening that the liturgical celebration gives to the Word of God is such that it brings the Liturgy into relation with Scripture as the reality of Christ is related to the "announcement" of Christ: Scripture contains the perennial *announcement* of the Divine plan of salvation while the liturgical celebration is the *ritual actuation* of this plan.

The revelation of salvation in Scripture is completed in the Liturgy—in the sense that the Word of God is brought to completion so that the Liturgy is always *revelation in act.* The happening that we read about in Scripture is the same happening that is actuated in the Liturgy. Scripture finds in the Liturgy its naturally correct interpretation and always on the level of the History of Salvation* not intellectual elaboration. Christ is the revelation announced in Scripture, and Christ becomes the revelation made present and communicated in the Liturgy.

The working or inspiration of the Holy Spirit in the liturgical assembly is needed so that the Word of God will make what we hear outwardly have its effect inwardly. Because of the Holy Spirit's *inspiration* and support, the Word of God becomes the foundation of the liturgical celebration and the rule and support of all our life. The working of the Holy Spirit *precedes, accompanies,* and *brings to completion* the whole celebration of the Liturgy. The Spirit also brings home to each person individually everything that in the proclamation of the Word of God is spoken for the good of the whole assembly of the faithful.* In strengthening the unity of all, the Holy Spirit at the same time fosters a variety of gifts and furthers their multiform operation (see LFMI, 9).

This "liturgical inspiration" gives forth "the specifically Christian reading of the Scriptures. It is the only reading which brings into play all the meaning which Scripture has in the eyes of its principal Author. It is the theological reading of the Bible. The philological, critical reading, which b, ɹefinition intends to confine itself to the sense of the contemporaries, is legitimate, useful, necessary, since every further reading must take its start from this; but such a reading is partial and incomplete" (C. Vagaggini, *Theological Dimensions of the Liturgy,* p. 486).

Installation (in-stuh-LAY-shuhn). The ceremony whereby a bishop*-elect takes possession of his diocese* by sitting on the episcopal chair in his cathedral,* while receiving the allegiance of his clergy.* Through this formal induction he may then exercise jurisdiction in the diocese. Usually an improvised ceremony takes place, including

that which is canonically required, namely, the bishop presenting his letters of appointment to the diocesan chapter.

In the United States the Bishops' Committee on the Liturgy* has developed four models for a Rite of Installation of a Bishop involving five basic elements: (1) reading the Decree of Appointment; (2) presentation of the crozier;* (3) the seating of the bishop in his cathedral chair; (4) welcome and acceptance by the local church; (5) the first address of the Ordinary* to his flock. These elements may be incorporated into the Eucharistic Liturgy.*

In recent times the coronation of the Pope* is replaced by a formal installation. Since the chair* is frequently called throne, this ceremony may be referred to as enthronization.

Institute for Pastoral Liturgy (IN-stuh-toot; -tyoot; fohr PAS-tuhr-uhl LIT-uhr-jee). Besides the Liturgical Commissions* set up by the local ecclesiastical authorities, an Institute for Pastoral Liturgy, made up of people competent in sacred music,* art,* liturgical science, and pastoral practice, should strive to make the pastoral-liturgical action within the Church* grow more vigorously. *See also* PASTORAL LITURGY.

Institutes, Secular. *See* SECULAR INSTITUTES.

Institution Narrative. *See* CONSECRATION.

Instruction (in-STRUHK-shuhn). A doctrinal explanation or set of directives, norms, rules, recommendations, and admonitions issued by the Roman Curia. Its purpose is to elaborate on prescriptions so that these will be more effectively implemented. It has the force of law only to the extent that it specifically declares such to be the case.

Since Vatican II* there have been a number of important instructions implementing the *Constitution on the Sacred Liturgy.** Some of them are: *Eucaristicum Mysterium*: On the Eucharistic Mystery* (May 25, 1967), *The Translation of Liturgical Texts* (January 25, 1969), *On Group Masses* (May 15, 1969), *The Manner of Administering Holy Communion* (May 29, 1969), and *The Priceless Gift of the Eucharist* (April 3, 1980). *See also* LITURGICAL LAW, SOURCES OF.

Instrumental Music. *See* MUSIC, INSTRUMENTAL.

Instrumentum Pacis (instroo-MEN-toom PA-cees) or **Instrument of Peace** (IN-struh-muhnt uhv pees). The name given to a small disc or tablet that has a sacred image* imprinted on it and is used to give the celebrant's kiss of peace* to the members of the assembly at Mass.* It is also known as the *pax* (peace) and the *deosculatorium* (from the Latin word for kiss, *osculum).* Begun in the Middle Ages, this usage has continued to our day among the Dominicans and Carthusians and is also found in some Pontifical Masses.*

Insufflation (in-suh-FLAY-shuhn). The exhalation or breathing upon a thing or person to signify the expulsion of an evil spirit and the conferring of the Holy Spirit.* Today this ritual action is used only in the consecration of the chrism* on Holy Thursday*; formerly it was used in the exorcisms* during the catechumenate* and in the blessing of the baptismal water* at the Easter Vigil.*

Intention (in-TEN-shuhn). This word is used in two main senses: (1) the purpose for which a person posits an action; (2) the purposeful action itself. The first kind of intention may be actual or virtual. An actual intention is one that a person actually wills at the moment when placing the action. A virtual intention (also called a habitual intention) is one that is not consciously willed but that *would be* if the person positing the action adverted to it.

Intention is very important in liturgical actions. The ministers* of a Sacrament* should have an actual intention of confecting and administering a Sacrament, "at least of doing what the Church does" (Council of Trent, Sess. 7, can. 1), although a virtual intention suffices for validity. The adult recipient of a Sacrament must have at least an implicit habitual intention to receive a Sacrament. In the case of Matrimony* and Penance,* how-

ever, this intention must be explicit since it constitutes the essence of the former and the matter of the latter.

Intentions, Mass (in-TEN-shuhnz, mas). Although the priest* must intend to effect the Consecration,* that is, determine to offer Mass,* this term ordinarily refers to the reason for which the priest offers the Mass or disposes of its fruits.* According to this former traditional theological rationale for Mass offerings, he formulates an intention whereby the ministerial fruits of the Mass are applied to a specific purpose. Most frequently it is offered for some living or deceased person(s) (Canon 901).

This intention may be (1) fixed by common law, e.g., one of the three Masses on All Souls Day* must be for the holy souls; (2) by specific precept, as the obligation of the pastor* to say Mass for the parish* on Sunday; (3) according to the intention of the one who gave the Mass stipend; or (4) in keeping with the priest's own devotion, for instance, when he has no obligations from any of the above. *See also* FRUITS OF THE MASS; STIPENDS.

Inter Mirifica (IN-turh mi-REEF-ee-kah). Latin title (from the first two words "Among the Wondrous") of the *Decree on the Media of Social Communication* issued by the Second Vatican Council* on December 4, 1963. Although this document dealt solely in general terms with

the media and did not touch upon their use in Liturgy,* it led to the formation of the Pontifical Commission for the Media of Social Communication, which in 1971 issued *Communio et Progressio,** a far-ranging *Pastoral Instruction on the Media of Social Communication* that gave principles on the media and the Liturgy. *See also* COMMUNIO ET PROGRESSIO.

Inter Oecumenici (IN-tuhr EK-oo-MEN-ee-chee). Latin title (from the first two words "Among the Ecumenical") of the *First Instruction on the Proper Implementation of the Constitution on the Sacred Liturgy* issued by the Congregation of Rites on September 26, 1964. This was the first of three such documents published by the Congregation to make the way of liturgical reform smooth until the new liturgical books* could be completed and published in accord with the stipulations of the Second Vatican Council.* It is a far-ranging document that sets out more sharply the functions of the Conferences of Bishops* in liturgical matters, explains more fully those principles stated in general terms in the *Constitution on the Second Liturgy,** and authorizes or mandates that those measures that are practicable before revision of the liturgical books go into effect immediately. *See also* LITURGIAE INSTAURATIONES; TRES ABHINC ANNOS.

Intercessions (int-uhr-SESH-uhnz). Supplications in behalf of others by mediation. By them, Christ, His Mother, Mediatrix of all graces, the angels,* the Saints,* the souls in purgatory, and the People of God* on earth intercede for each other by their prayers and merits. This is most obvious in that part of the Eucharistic Prayer* where it is clear that the Sacrifice is being offered not only for the Church* but for all her members, living and deceased. Prayers of this nature have been given their own proper prominent place in the Mass,* right before the Eucharistic Prayer, and in the Liturgy of the Hours* before the final oration at the end of each Morning Prayer* and Evening Prayer.* (*See also* GENERAL INTERCESSIONS).

In the Divine Office

Petitions restored to the Mass are entitled General Intercessions*; those in the Divine Office* are termed merely "Intercessions." They occur in Morning Prayer and Evening Prayer just before the Lord's Prayer.* As Morning Prayer commits the day to the Lord, these invocations during it dedicate the day to Him.

To satisfy the various ecclesial and human needs in different groups and peoples of divers climes at various times and in all ways of life, many formulas for the Intercessions are used; however they follow norms. Since the Liturgy of the Hours is a prayer by and for the whole Church, Intercessions should pray for general needs: the Church, the ministries of the Church, civil authorities, the sick, the poor, the sorrowing, for peace and other world needs. Beyond this, particular intentions are permitted, and in Evening Prayer the last intention would be for the dead.

Addressed directly to God, they are suitable both for community and for private recitation. The second part of each intention may be used as a variable response.* In that case after the priest says the first part, the congregation adds the second. Otherwise the minister may say both parts, and the community then adds a uniform response or merely pauses in silence.

Intercessory Prayers. *See* GENERAL INTERCESSIONS.

Intercommunion (int-uhr-kuh-MYOO-nyuhn). The relationship between Churches that allows members of one Church to receive Communion* in the other. In the Catholic Church it is presently authorized only in relation to the Eastern Churches, where the Sacrament of Orders* and apostolic succession have been preserved. Even then it is allowed only under specific circumstances and subject to the decision of the local Ordinary.*

In November 1986 the National Conference of Catholic Bishops* published guidelines for receiving Communion for Catholics and other Christians, which are also to be published in each Missalette.* The Conference clarifies the regulations for Catholics, with regard to proper

dispositions and, with regret, indicates that other Christians may not receive the Eucharist* but begs them to share our faith in Jesus by uniting themselves with us in prayer. *See also* ATTENDING NON-CATHOLIC SERVICES.

International Commission on English in the Liturgy (int-uhr-NASH-uhn-uhl kuh-MISH-uhn on IN-glish in thuh LIT-urh-jee). An international group responsible for making proposals on common English liturgical translations for all the English-speaking countries in the world. Representatives from the majority of the countries in which English is spoken work on this Commission. Their intent is to have translations of the highest literary quality, pastorally suited for use in the celebration of the Liturgy.*

The style of their translation tries to achieve accuracy and fidelity of meaning with suitability of the spoken or sung presentation to the liturgical assembly.* They strive after beauty and excellence in language expressed in clarity, simplicity, and dignity.

The Commission is customarily known by the acronym ICEL, and its people work closely with the Bishops' Committees on the Liturgy* of the English-speaking nations of the world. All translations made must be approved by each Bishops' Committee as well as by the Episcopal Conference* and then submitted to the Congregation for Divine Worship and the Discipline of the Sacraments* for final approval before they may be used in the Church's worship.

Intervenient Chants (int-uhr-VEEN-yuhnt chants). Traditional term for the chants of the Proper* that come between the readings* at Mass.* They were formerly the Tract,* Gradual,* Sequence,* and Alleluia.* In the *Roman Missal** of Paul VI they are the Responsorial Psalm* and Alleluia* or Verse before the Gospel.* They are sometimes called the Intermediate Chants.

Intinction (in-TING[K]-shuhn). One of the methods whereby Communion* is received under both kinds at the same time. Thicker, larger, consecrated Hosts* are dipped into the Precious Blood and administered to the recipients who hold the Communion plate* under their chins. Although this may be a convenient method, many object to it since it seems to be contrary to the method used by Christ at the Last Supper.* *See also* COMMUNION.

Introductions. *See* ADMONITIONS.

Introductory Dialogue (in-truh-DUHK-t[uh-]ree DAI-uh-log; -lahg). The dialogue between celebrant* and people* before the Preface* at the beginning of the Eucharistic Prayer.* This short dialogue is one of the most venerable elements of the Mass.* It is found in all the liturgies and may go back to the Apostles.* It provides the keynote of thanksgiving* that runs through every Eucharistic Prayer.

The dialogue is comprised of three versicles* and responses.* "The Lord be with you"* (*Dominus vobiscum*) with its response "And also with you" (*Et cum spiritu tuo*) has been a time-honored greeting among Christians. (*See also* GREETING.)

"Lift up your hearts" (*Sursum corda*) comes from a phrase found in Lamentations* 3:41 and indicates that our thoughts should be placed on a Divine plane. Its response "We lift them up to the Lord" (*Habemus ad Dominum*) shows our determination to pay attention to the things of God.

"Let us give thanks to the Lord, our God" (*Gratias agamus Domino Deo nostro*) was most likely taken from the Jewish invitation to the prayer of blessing over the cup. Its response "It is right to give him thanks and praise" (*Dignum et iustum est*) was originally a Greek acclamation of agreement. It has a juridic character with the idea of "duty" from the ancient Roman concept of religion. The meaning is that the thanksgiving* we are offering is a complete and perfect worship* and so we are thereby performing our duty toward God.

Therefore the whole thrust of the Introductory Dialogue is that the priestly people are "with" their Lord, whose presence is symbolized by the celebrant* who through ordination has received Christ's "spirit." Their attention is fixed on the "heights" where the risen Christ lives in glory,* and they are intent on entering with Him into His pas-

sage from the world to the Father (see Jn 13:1). *See also* DIALOGUE; GREETING; LORD BE WITH YOU, THE.

Introductory Rites (in-truh-DUHK-t[uh-]ree raits). The section of the Mass* preceding the Liturgy of the Word* that confers a quality of preparation and introduction on the

Eucharistic Sacrifice. The intent is that the assembled group unite as a community properly prepared to hear God's Word and celebrate the Eucharist.* The rite comprises the following parts: Entrance Antiphon* (or Entrance Song*), Greeting,* Penitential Rite* (or Rite of Blessing and Sprinkling Holy Water*), Lord Have Mercy,* Glory to God,* and Opening Prayer.* *See also* MASS.

Introductory Verse (in-truh-DUHK-t[uh-]ree vuhrs). The verse that opens the Hours of the Liturgy of the Hours. The first Hour begins with the verse "Lord, open my lips. And my mouth will proclaim your praise." It comes from Psalm 51:17 and was well known in its Latin form: *Domine, labia mea aperies. Et os meum annuntiabit laudem tuam.*

The other Hours begin with the verse "God, come to my assistance. Lord, make haste to help me." It comes from Psalm 70:2 and was even better known in its Latin form: *Deus, in adiutorium meum intende. Domine, ad adiuvandum me festina.* *See also* INVITATORY.

Introit. *See* ENTRANCE ANTIPHON; INTRODUCTORY RITES.

Investiture (in-VES-tuh-choor; -chuhr). The formal presentation of the Religious habit to the postulant at the beginning of the novitiate in any Religious Order or Congregation. The ceremony may vary from community to community but ordinarily takes place during Mass* after the Homily.*

Invitation to Pray. *See* PRAY, BRETHREN.

Invitatory (in-VAIT-uh-tawr-ee; -tohr-ee). To begin the day's Divine Office* an exhortation to praise God, starting with the verse: *Lord, open my lips. And my mouth will proclaim your praise,* is followed by Psalm 95 together with an antiphon* that varies. Psalms 100, 67, or 24 may be substituted for 95. The Psalm is more fittingly recited in responsorial fashion, with the antiphon said first and repeated after each strophe of the Psalm. Whether the day's prayer begins with Morning Prayer* or the Office of Readings,* the Invitatory always precedes the first Hour recited.

The term may also be applied to the invitations to prayer directed at the assembly by the celebrant* or commentator* at Mass. Some of these invitatories incorporate the announcement of the feast* and the intentions for which the particular Mass is being celebrated. Others call the people to exercise their universal priesthood* in the Prayer of the Faithful* and to unite themselves with the sentiments of the Eucharistic Prayer.* *See also* ADMONITIONS; COMMENTATOR; INTRODUCTORY VERSE.

Invocations (in-vuh-KAY-shuhnz; -voh-). Acts of entreaty either to God* or to the Saints* asking for help in spiritual and temporal need. The supposition is that the Saints, being near to God after having reached eternal life,* enjoy a special force in an intercessory way. Such entreaties may be long or short. When they are short, they are customarily termed aspirations—because they can be said in one breath or aspiration—or ejaculations.

The more familiar aspirations usually have indulgences* attached to them, and they are uttered in times of temptation or danger when it is difficult to say longer prayers. An example of a liturgical invocation or aspiration to God is the prayer by the priest* at the Gospel* during Mass*: "Almighty God, cleanse my heart and my lips that I may worthily proclaim your gospel." Examples of liturgical invocations made by the people at Mass are those uttered by many privately at the Consecration*: "My Lord and my God" at the elevation of the Host* and "My Jesus, mercy" at the elevation of the Chalice.*

Irenaeus, St. (ir-uh-NAY-uhs). 130-200. Born in Asia Minor, Irenaeus was educated at Smyrna and became the disciple of St. Polycarp,* who was bishop of that city and had known and followed St. John* the Apostle. In 177, Irenaeus was ordained a priest in Lyons, France, and shortly afterward became bishop there. He converted many to the Faith by his preaching, and his writings did much to combat the heresies that were rampant, especially Gnosticism and Valentinism. His principal works are: *Against Heresies* and *The Proof of the Apostolic Preaching,* which championed the idea of Apostolic Succession. Irenaeus was martyred for the Faith during the persecution of Decius. *Liturgical celebration:* June 28 (Memorial); *theme:* zeal for truth, Church unity, and peace.

Irregularity (ir-reg-yuh-LAR-uh-tee). An impediment to the reception of Holy Orders* or the exercise of an Order already received. Some irregularities are: apostasy, heresy, homicide, and attempted suicide. An irregularity makes the reception illicit (unlawful) but not invalid.

Isaac Jogues and Companions, Sts. (AI-zuhk joghz and kuhm-PAN-yuhnz). 1607-1647. In the 17th century both Franciscans and Jesuits came to New France to work as missionaries among the Hurons, a nickname given to the Wyandots. Both groups were expelled; after three years the Jesuits were allowed back in but the Franciscans had to wait several decades. Eight of these French missionaries (six Jesuits and two lay people) were killed for the Faith.

One group achieved martyrdom near Auriesville, New York, in the territory of the Iroquois: René Goupil, Patron of Anesthetists (b. 1606; d. September 29, 1642), and Isaac Jogues (b. 1607) and John de Lalande (b. ?; d. October 18, 1648). Another group were killed in Canada on the land of the Hurons: Anthony Daniel (b. 1601; d. July 4,

1648), John de Brébeuf (b. 1593) and Gabriel Lalemant (b. 1610; d. March 16, 1649), Noel Chabanel (b. 1613; d. December 1649), and Charles Garnier (b. 1605; d. December 7, 1649). They were all beatified in 1925 and canonized in 1930. Their feast is part of the Proper* for the United States.

Liturgical celebration: October 19 (Memorial); *theme:* growth of the Faith in North America.

Isaiah, The Book of (ai-ZAY-uh, thuh buk uhv). Twenty-ninth Book of the Old Testament* and first of the Major Prophets.* Isaiah is the greatest of the Prophets and one of the major witnesses of the Messianic hope in Israel. His ministry began in the second half of the 8th century B.C. which saw the collapse of the Northern Kingdom (722) and the constant peril of the Southern Kingdom at the hands of her foes. Isaiah was a man of great vision, ability, and political influence whose message is stamped by the majesty, holiness, and glory of the Lord and the pettiness and sinfulness of human beings.

His prophecies concerning Immanuel have earned him the title of the Fifth Evangelist and are important because of their Messianic character and their influence on Christian revelation. Isaiah also attacks social injustices as the most indicative sign of Judah's tenuous relationship with God. He exhorts his hearers to trust in their omnipotent God and to live accordingly. Justice and righteousness, teaching and word, and assurance of Divine blessing upon the faithful and punishment upon the faithless are recurrent themes in his message from the Holy One of Israel to a proud and stubborn people.

Chapters 40—55 (called *Second Isaiah)* are attributed to an anonymous poet who prophesied toward the end of the Babylonian Exile. From this section come the great Messianic oracles known as the Songs of the Servant,* whose mysterious destiny of suffering and glorification is fulfilled in the Passion and Glorification of Christ. Chapters 56-66 *(Third Isaiah)* contain oracles from a later period and were composed by disciples who inherited the spirit and continued the work of the great Prophet.

Liturgical use: This Book is used more extensively in the Liturgy* than any other Old Testament text except for the Psalms.* In the *Roman Missal,** it is read during Advent* and Christmas,* Lent* and Holy Week,* and also during the Season of Ordinary Time.* In the *Liturgy of the Hours,** it is also read during Advent-Christmas and during the 20th Week in Ordinary Time. Ten minor canticles* from it are used during the Four-Week Psalter* and five additional ones in Appendix I: for Vigils. *Meaning:* Isaiah reminds us that God is just and holy; He abhors sin and has put in motion a Divine plan to overcome it centering around the teachings and deeds of His Incarnate Son. All who adhere to faith in Him and live according to the Covenant* made in His Son Jesus will escape sin—for Jesus came in the flesh to be the sole bringer of salvation.*

Isidore, St. (IZ-uh-dohr). 560-636. Born in Seville, Spain, Isidore came from a family of Saints*—his brothers Leander and Fulgentius and his sister Florentina have also been canonized. He succeeded Leander as bishop of Seville about 600, governed the Church* wisely, and wrote many learned works, including the first encyclopedia. He called together and presided over several councils in Spain, led the Visigoths to Catholicism, and promoted the Mozarabic Rite.* He died at Seville and his learning made him one of the great Masters of the Middle Ages and a Doctor* of the Church. *Liturgical celebration:* April 4 (Opt. Mem.); *theme:* spreading God's truth.

Isidore the Farmer, St. (IZ-uh-dohr thuh FAHR-muhr). 1070-1130. A model of Christian perfection, this Patron Saint of Madrid and of farmers spent a good portion of his life laboring in poverty on a farm outside Madrid. He was considered a miracle worker during his time and the marvelous happenings did not cease upon his death. He wa

canonized in 1622. In 1947 he was proclaimed Patron of the National Rural Life Conference in the United States. Because of the importance of agriculture to this country, Isidore's feast is highly significant to farm communities. He is the Patron of Farmers and Laborers, and his feast is part of the Proper* for the United States. *Liturgical celebration:* May 15 (Opt. Mem.); *theme:* working for the corporal and spiritual welfare of others.

It Is Right to Give Him Thanks and Praise. *See* INTRODUCTORY DIALOGUE.

Ite Missa Est. *See* DISMISSAL.

Itinerarium or Itinerary (ai-tin-uh-RAHR-ee-uhm ohr ai-TIN-uh-rer-ee). A liturgical blessing* invoking God's help when embarking on a journey. Found among the blessings of the *Roman Ritual,** it consisted of the Canticle of Zechariah,* an antiphon,* a series of versicles* and responses,* and four prayers. Some missionary societies fashioned it into a departure ceremony.

The corresponding blessing found in the revised *Book of Blessings* (De Benedictionibus)* issued in Latin in 1984 is much different and fuller. Not only does it serve the same purpose as the old, but it offers another prayer upon the person's return.

Iubilate Deo (yoo-buh-LAH-tay DAY-oh). A Latin collection of the simpler Gregorian chants* that the faithful* should know, in keeping with the mind of the *Constitution on the Sacred Liturgy,** published by the Vatican Press in 1974. (A second typical edition* was issued in 1987.) The first section supplies all the chants for the Ordinary of the Mass* along with the responses* incorporated into the new *Roman Missal.** The second part contains chants for various celebrations (Eucharistic chants, hymns,* and canticles,* Marian antiphons,* the Te Deum,* etc.) *See also* GREGORIAN CHANT.

—J—

Jacobite Liturgy (JAY-kuh-bait LIT-uhr-jee). This is the Syriac Liturgy of St. James, an Antiochene* type practiced by the Syrian Churches who adhered to the Monophysite heresy after the Council of Chalcedon in 451. They united under Jacob Baradia in 543 and split later on. Many have now become reunited with Rome.

James, Liturgy of St. (jaymz, LIT-uhr-jee uhv). A form of the Antiochene Rite,* which is attributed to James, "brother of the Lord" and first bishop of Jerusalem,* and is used once a year in Greek by the Orthodox and in Syriac by the Jacobites and the Uniates. It is similar in many ways to the Liturgy of St. Cyril of Jerusalem* and contains an apparent reference to the finding of the true Cross at Jerusalem in 362.

James, The Epistle of (jaymz, thee i-PIS-uhl uhv). Sixty-sixth Book of the Bible* and twentieth of the New Testament.* Addressed to the Jewish-Christian Churches located in Palestine, Syria, and elsewhere, this Book has none of the characteristics of a true letter except the address. It is made up of aphorisms like those in the Wisdom Books of the Old Testament,* and at first glance it seems more Jewish than Christian since the name of Jesus occurs in it only twice. Yet it is wholly Christian, and certain passages seem to be reminiscences of the words of Jesus in the Sermon on the Mount.* It has no particular plan, but its unity stems from the prophetic spirit that permeates it. James has fittingly been termed the "Amos* of the New Testament."

The date of this Epistle is uncertain (possibly between the 60's and the 80's), and so is its author. It has been attributed to James the Less* and James "the brother of the Lord."

Liturgical use: In the *Roman Missal,** this Epistle is used on the 3rd Sunday of Advent* (A), the 22nd through 26th Sundays in Ordinary Time* (B), Weekdays of the 6th and 7th Ordinary Weeks (II), the Common* of Martyrs and of Men and Women, Masses for Various Needs and Occasions,* and the Ritual Masses for Reconciliation* and Anointing of the Sick.* In the *Liturgy of the Hours,** it occurs only in the alternate Two-Year Cycle* of Readings, during the 8th and 9th Weeks in Ordinary Time (I). *Meaning:* Christian perfection entails both faith* and good works.* Faith that is not confirmed by a concrete commitment is no faith at all. Faith is the root of salvation,* but good works are its fruit. The fervent Christian must attend to devotion and love but also to social justice, which is achieved only by a conversion* of heart.

James the Greater, St. (jaymz thuh GRAYT-uhr). ?-42. Son of Zebedee and brother of St. John the Apostle,* James was born at Bethsaida. He is called "the Greater" to distinguish him from the other Apostle James ("brother" of the Lord) who is known as "the Less"—because his vocation to follow Christ preceded that of James the

Less. So fiercely dedicated to Jesus were he and his brother John that our Lord styled them *Boanerges,* "sons of thunder." James was present at most of the miracles worked by Christ and was near Him in the Agony in the Garden.

After the dispersion of the Apostles, St. James preached the Gospel in Spain and then returned to Jerusalem, where by order of Herod Agrippa he was beheaded on Easter of 42. He is the Patron of Laborers, Pharmacists, Pilgrims, and Rheumatism Sufferers. *Liturgical celebration:* July 25 (Feast); *theme:* sharing Christ's sufferings.

James the Less, St. (jaymz thuh les). ?-62. James was the son of Alphaeus or Cleophas and the probable author of the first Catholic Epistle. His mother Mary was either a sister or a close relative of the Blessed Virgin,* and for that reason he was sometimes called the "brother of the Lord." The Apostle held a distinguished position in the early Christian community of Jerusalem. St. Paul calls him a "pillar" of the Church and tells us he was a witness of Christ's Resurrection.*

According to tradition, James was the first Bishop of Jerusalem, and was at the Council of Jerusalem about the year 50. He was martyred for the Faith in the spring of the year 62 by the Jews, although they greatly esteemed his person and had given him the surname of "James the Just." He is the Patron of Fullers and Hatters. *Liturgical celebration:* May 3 (Feast—in conjuction with St. Philip*); *theme:* witnessing to the Risen Christ.

Jane Frances de Chantal, St. (jayn FRAN-suhs duh SHAHN-tuhl; shahn-TAHL). 1572-1641. Born in Dijon, France, Jane was married to the Baron de Chantal, an army officer, and had six sons whom she reared in the Faith. At her husband's death after eight years of marriage, she provided for the welfare of her children and wholeheartedly embraced the Religious life under the guidance of St. Francis de Sales.* She performed works of charity especially for the poor and the sick and in 1610 established the Congregation of the Visitation. Jane suffered great inner trials while she labored to extend her Congregation and promote God's glory. She died at Moulins. *Liturgical celebration:* December 12; in the United States, August 18 (Opt. Mem.); *theme:* performing works of mercy, especially visiting the sick.

Januarius, St. (jan-yoo-AYR-ee-uhs). c. 275-305. Januarius (also known as Gennaro in English) was Bishop of Benevento, Italy. During the persecution of the Emperor Diocletian, he was arrested and with six other Christians was exposed in the Amphitheater. When they were left unharmed by the wild beasts, they were condemned to be beheaded; and the sentence was carried out near Puzzuoli. The relics of St. Januarius were later transferred to Naples and he became the Patron of that city. His blood is said to be contained in a vial preserved at the Naples Cathedral, and it liquefies numerous times a year when it is placed near the head of the holy Martyr (a phenomenon that has been attested since 1389 without scientific explanation). He is the Patron of Blood Banks. *Liturgical celebration:* September 19 (Opt. Mem.); *theme:* Christian patience in adversity.

Japanese Martyrs. *See* PAUL MIKI AND COMPANIONS, STS.

Jazz Mass (jaz mas). A Mass* during which jazz is performed. It arose during the sixties with the desire to make the Mass more relevant to people today. The best qualities of jazz (syncopated rhythms, polyphonic ensemble playing, structured improvisation, and modernity of sound) are brought to bear to increase the people's participation* in and appreciation of the Mass. The term is also used of a musical work of the Mass written in jazz. *See also* MUSIC; MUSIC, INSTRUMENTAL; NATIVE MUSIC.

Jeremiah, The Book of (je-ruh-MAI-uh, thuh buk uhv). Thirtieth Book of the Old Testament* and second of the Major Prophets.* The son of the Prophet Hilkiah, Jeremiah was born about 650 B.C. in Anathoth, three miles northeast of Jerusalem. He received his vocation when he was still very young, a vocation that included a renunciation of marriage and family, and he prophesied for about forty years (626-586 B.C.). This "Prophet of the Eleventh Hour" had the unpleasant task of foretelling the destruction of the Holy City and the Southern Kingdom—and of witnessing the fulfillment of his prediction. He also foretold the return from the Babylonian Exile and uttered the great oracle of the New Covenant (31:31-34), sometimes called "the Gospel before the Gospel." This passage

contains his most sublime teaching and is a landmark in Old Testament* theology.

The figure of Jeremiah is an image of the suffering just person and holds a very exceptional importance. The Prophet is a prefiguration of Jesus,* the "man of sorrows" acquainted with infirmity and grief (Is 33:3) because of the sins of His people. In Matthew 16:14 some people are seen to believe that Jesus was Jeremiah raised from the dead. Hence, Jeremiah predicts the coming of the Messiah* and His kingly mission by his life and works as well as by His words (23:5-6).

Liturgical use: In the *Roman Missal,** the Book of Jeremiah is used more than thirty times: in Ordinary Time* on the 12th and 22nd Sundays (A), the 16th and 30th Sundays (B), and the 4th, 6th, and 20th Sundays (C) as well as the 5th Sunday of Lent* (B) and the 1st Sunday of Advent* (C). It is also used on weekdays in the 16th, 17th, and 18th weeks of Ordinary Time (II) and a few weekdays in Lent as well as on June 24 (Vigil) and the Ritual Masses of Penance, Religious Profession,* Vocations, Marriage, and Baptism of Adults. In the *Liturgy of the Hours,** it is used from Tuesday of the 21st Week to Monday of the 23rd Week in Ordinary Time and on June 24. It also gives rise to two minor canticles* in the Four-Week Psalter* and two additional canticles in Appendix I: for Vigils. *Mean-*

ing: Jeremiah appears in the Liturgy as preacher, prophet, and theologian of Messianism and as the type of the suffering Messiah of the Songs of the Servant* of the Lord; he manifests his humanity so that we will seek holiness in conjunction with our own humanity. He calls us in times of trial to rely not on the Temple, the Law, circumcision, sacrifices, or any other human source but on God alone, for He saves His people. To rely on God, we must put on a new heart and manifest love and service toward Him.

Jerome, St. (juh-ROHM). c. 347-419/20. Destined to be a noted Scripture* scholar and Doctor* of the Church, Jerome studied grammar, rhetoric, and philosophy in Rome, theology in Trier, lived as a hermit in a Syrian desert while he studied Hebrew, and was eventually ordained in 379. He continued to study through listening to the lectures of St. Gregory Nazianzen* at Constantinople and attended the Council at Rome with St. Epiphanius to combat the Antiochene schism. He became friend and secretary to Pope Damasus* who suggested that he revise the Latin version of the Scripture. After the Pope's death, he left Rome and finally settled at Bethlehem, where he and some devout women founded a monastery for men and another for women.

Jerome's literary talents are evident from his monumental works, some historical, mainly biographies of the lives of prominent Christians; the letters written on a wide variety of subjects; and polemical writings in which most of the religious controversies of his times are argued, especially on Arius, Pelagius, and Origen. Because of his wide knowledge of Scripture and Tradition, his exegetical and homiletic writings are treasures. His translations were numerous, chiefly of ecclesiastical writers, but the most important is that for which he is best known, the translation of the entire Bible into Latin, commonly referred to as the Vulgate.* This was the official Latin text for Catholics since the Council of Trent, until a New Vulgate appeared in 1979. He is the Patron of Librarians. *Liturgical celebration:* September 30 (Memorial); *theme:* love of the Scriptures and the Christ Child. *See also* BIBLE, VERSIONS OF.

Jerome Emiliani, St. (juh-ROHM e-mee-li-AH-nee; e-mil-YAH-nee). 1481-1537. After several years as a wealthy commander in the Venetian army and an imprisonment, he changed his life and became a priest.* While helping plague and famine victims, he decided to lessen the plight of orphans, and he built several orphanages and a hospital. Later with two other priests he founded the Clerks Regular of Somascha, devoted to caring for abandoned children and educating them. He is the Patron of Orphans. *Liturgical celebration:* February 8: (Opt. Mem.); *theme:* living as children of God.

Jerusalem (juh-ROO-s[uh]luhm; -ROOZ-[uh]luhm). Capital of Israel, founded by David (also called City of David), and the scene of Christ's Passion* and Resurrection.* The

Liturgy* refers to the Church* as the image of the Heavenly Jerusalem (Rv 21:10-23—6th Sunday of Easter,* C), which is the city of the living God, the New Jerusalem (Heb 12:18-24—Thursday of the 4th Ordinary Week, I). Jerusalem is also the representation of the just soul,* especially in such hymns as *Jerusalem My Happy Home, Jerusalem the Golden,* and *Jerusalem Thou City Blest.*

Jerusalem, Liturgy of (juh-ROO-s[uh]luhm; -ROOZ-[uh]luhm, LIT-uhr-jee uhv). The Liturgy of St. James,* which was a form of the ancient Liturgy formulated at Antioch and is represented in the Liturgies of some Eastern Churches today. *See also* JAMES, LITURGY OF ST.

Jesse Window (JES-see WIN-doh). A stained glass window, found in some churches (for example, the Cathedral of Chartres), depicting the characters of our Lord's genealogical tree, starting with Jesse the father of King David.

Jesu, Dulcis Memoria (YAY-zoo, DOOL-chis me-MOH-ree-ah). A celebrated 11th-century poem attributed to St. Bernard,* sections of which were used in the Liturgy* at one time, for example, as a hymn on the feast of the Holy Name of Jesus* in the former Divine Office.* The complete hymn is 168 lines long and evinces deep mysticism combined with haunting beauty of language. It is known in its liturgical form in a variety of translations, one of which is as follows:

Jesus, the very thought of Thee
With sweetness fills the breast!
Yet sweeter far Thy face to see
And in Thy presence rest.

No voice can sing, no heart can frame,
Nor can the memory find,
A sweeter sound than Jesus' Name,
The Savior of humankind.

O hope of every contrite heart!
O joy of all the meek!
To those who fall, how kind Thou art!
How good to those who seek!

But what to those who find? Ah! this
No tongue nor pen can show—
The love of Jesus, what it is,
None but His loved ones know.

Jesus! our only hope be Thou,
As Thou our prize shalt be;
In Thee be all our glory now,
And through eternity.

Jesus Christ (JEE-zuhs; -zuhz; kraist). As already indicated in the entry on "God," Jesus is the Second Person of the Blessed Trinity* Who in accord with the Divine Will became Man, died, and rose again for the salvation* of all human beings. He established a Church* to bring that salvation to all people principally through the Liturgy.* This centrality of Christ in the History of Salvation* can be seen more vividly by utilizing four of His titles:

(1) *Mediator.* This title expresses in splendid fashion the saving work wrought by the Incarnate Word during His mission on earth from the Incarnation* to the Ascension,* above all through His Passion* and Resurrection.* Jesus now continues this mediation from His heavenly seat (Heb 7:25) and through the Eucharist* for the application of

salvation to individuals with the visible mediation of the Church.

(2) *Priest.* Jesus is a priest from the first moment of His Incarnation (see Heb 10:7ff). Indeed, He is the unique, true, supreme, perfect, and eternal priest. Jesus is also the victim for His priesthood, a victim offered for the redemption of the world, and His sacrifice reached its culmination on the altar of the Cross.*

(3) *Prophet.* Jesus is the Word of God manifested to the world through the Incarnation so that the Divine plan of salvation might be made known. Thus, He is the great Prophet of the Father. He fulfills Divine Revelation and proclaims to all humankind the truth that saves.

(4) *King.* Jesus is King because of the mysterious union that links His human nature with the Divine nature of the Second Person of the Trinity. He is King also by acquired right—because of the redemption of the human race that He accomplished. He is King too because of the glorification He received from the Father, in return for His total offering of self, in His Resurrection and Ascension. Jesus will exercise this Kingship for all eternity and in a special way at the Last Judgment.

Thus, Jesus is the Head of the Body, the Church (see Col 1:18), which He fills with His riches and which he continually infuses with the Divine Life,* through His humanity. From Christ, "the whole body, joined and held together . . . , brings about the body's growth and builds itself up in love" (Eph 4:16). This may be called the Mystery of Christ, conceived by God from all eternity, manifested in various ways in the Old Testament,* revealed fully in the New Testament,* and perpetuated in the Church until its definitive eschatological fulfillment.

The Liturgy—Christ in Mystery

The Liturgy* is a special realization of the Mystery of Christ. The person and redemptive act of Christ continue to flow in the Church, in humankind, in the cosmos, and especially in the Liturgy. The Liturgy "is considered as an exercise of the priestly office of Jesus Christ. In the Liturgy, by means of signs perceptible to the senses, human sanctification is signified and brought about in ways proper to each of these signs; in the Liturgy the whole public worship of the Church is performed by the Mystical Body* of Jesus Christ, that is, by the Head and His members" (SC, 7).

The Liturgy is also the "memorial,"* that is, the ritual recalling of a past event, that renders it present and makes way for its full realization in the future. The Liturgy is at the same time the aggregate Sacrament* of salvation, closely bound up with Christ and with the Church: Christ is the primordial Sacrament of salvation, and the Church is the universal Sacrament of salvation (see LG, 48).

As the Second Vatican Council* stated, the Liturgy makes Christ present in various ways: "Christ is always present in His Church, especially in her liturgical celebrations.

He is present in the Sacrifice of the Mass, not only in the person of His minister . . . but especially under the Eucharistic elements.* By His power He is present in the Sacraments,* so that when a man baptizes it is Christ Himself Who baptizes. He is present in His Word, since it is He Himself Who speaks when the Holy Scriptures are read in the Church. He is present, lastly, when the Church prays and sings, for He promised: 'When two or three are gathered together in My Name, there am I in the midst of them' (Mt 18:20)" (SC, 7).

This presence of Christ is unique but realized in various ways. It is *real,* even though the Eucharistic presence is the only one termed "real"—since, as Paul VI observed, this does not mean that the others are not real. Christ's presence is *Sacramental*—it takes place through signs of supernatural reality. It is *personal* and sets up a personal relationship between Christ and His faithful.*

This presence of Christ runs throughout the Liturgical Year.* Every week on the day that she has called the Lord's day, the Church keeps the memory of the Lord's Resurrection, which she also celebrates once in the year, together with His blessed Passion,* on the most solemn festival of Easter.* Within the cycle of a year, moreover, she also unfolds the whole Mystery of Christ, from the Incarnation and Birth until the Ascension, the day of Pentecost, and the expectation of blessed hope and of the coming of the Lord.

Encountering Christ

Recalling thus the Mysteries of the Redemption, the Church opens to the faithful the riches of her

Lord's powers and merits so that these are in some way made present for all time, and the faithful are enabled to lay hold of them and become filled with grace.

Jesus becomes present in every Sacrament. The Jesus Who pardons, heals, invests us with His priesthood or with His love is always the Jesus of the Paschal Mystery,* the Jesus eternally established in what is the culminating point of His life and His right to glory*—the event of His Death and Resurrection. Every Sacrament plunges us *spiritually but really* into the very act of Jesus dying and rising to new life.

We meet Jesus, we become transformed in Him, and we become conformed to Him in the manner proper to each Sacrament. However, this is true only if we participate* wholeheartedly in the Sacramental Action. In that case, every Christian can echo the words of St. Ambrose: "O Christ, . . . I come to know You in Your Sacraments." *See also* CHRIST; GOD; JESUS CHRIST, FEASTS OF.

Jesus Christ, Feasts of (JEE-zuhs; -zuhz; kraist, feests uhv). Days on which special commemoration and worship are rendered to Jesus* because of an event or Mystery* connected with Him. They are: Annunciation of the Lord,* Ascension,* Baptism of the Lord,* Body and Blood of Christ,* Christ the King,* Christmas,* Dedication of St. John

Lateran,* Easter,* Epiphany,* Holy Family,* Presentation of the Lord,* Sacred Heart,* Transfiguration, and Triumph of the Cross.* (*See the individual entries for more information.*)

Jewish Liturgy (JOO-ish LIT-uhr-jee). The Babylonian Exile gave rise to synagogues, which took the place of the Temple and kept alive Jewish liturgy. Yahweh's presence was now effected among His people through His Word. In front of the synagogue was a platform on which stood the holy Ark containing the Scriptures* and an eight-branch candlestick burning before it. Nearest the platform were the chief seats, where sat the leading men facing the congregation (Mt 23:6; Mk 12:39; Lk 11:43; 20:46). Among these were the ruler of the synagogue, the elders, and various functionaries whom they appointed.

The synagogue services were held chiefly on the Sabbath. They opened with the *Shema,** a profession of faith set within a framework of three blessings or prayers of thanksgiving. Next there followed the Eighteen Blessings* or *Tephillah,* accompanied by Psalms and prayers. Finally, there came a reading or readings from the Law* or the Prophets* (translated into Aramaic for the congregation). A sermon followed (Acts 13:15; 15:21). The ruler of the synagogue might grant permission to members of the congregation to speak, and sometimes he called upon one present to address the congregation. Jesus often spoke in synagogues. Then came the supplication known as the *Kaddish.** Finally, the blessing by a priest concluded the function.

JMJ (jay em jay). An emblem or monogram that represents the words "Jesus, Mary, and Joseph." It may be used as part of audiovisuals connected with the Liturgy.*

Joachim, St. (JOH-uh-kim). 1st century B.C. Husband of St. Ann* and traditionally the father of Mary.* His feast has been celebrated since the 16th century but is now joined with that of his spouse. *Liturgical celebration:* July 16 (Memorial); *theme:* the just person leads an irreproachable life.

Job, The Book of (johb, thuh buk uhv). Twenty-second Book of the Old Testament* and first of the Sapiential Books. Composed about the 5th century B.C., it is an artistic dialogue skillfully handling the problem of suffering though only from the standpoint of temporal life. Job, a just man, loses his wealth, his health, and his sons and daughters in lightning fashion and lies at death's door. Yet he refuses to curse God or to admit he has sinned in any way. In the end, although the author brings out many beautiful thoughts, the problem of the innocent person's suffering is left unresolved. It will be relieved only by the Gospel* account of the crucified and risen Redeemer,* although it is hinted at by God's response that He governs the world and the destinies of each person with wisdom and by His act of delivering His faithful servant Job from all his trials.

Liturgical use: In the *Roman Missal,** this Book is used on the 5th and 12th Sundays (B) and during the 26th Week in Ordinary Time* as well as the Masses for the Dead* and for the Anointing of the Sick.* In the *Liturgy of the Hours,** it is read during the 8th and 9th weeks in Ordinary Time. *Meaning:* The Book calls us to have patience in adversity and trust in God, for He governs the world with wisdom and justice. This is attained through an understanding of the majesty of God and the limited character of human knowledge. The best possible attitude for us is that manifested by Job's words: "Naked I came forth from my mother's womb, and naked I shall go back again. The Lord gave and the Lord has taken away. Blessed be the name of the Lord" (1:21). Thus, the problems of suffering we encounter can be solved by a broader and deeper awareness of God's power, presence, and wisdom.

Joel, The Book of (JOH-uhl, thuh buk uhv). Thirty-sixth Book of the Old Testament* and second of the Minor Prophets.* The Prophet Joel was from the Southern Kingdom and lived probably after the Babylonian Exile at the time of the Persian domination of Israel, possibly between 350 and 200 B.C. He is concerned with an invasion of locusts who threatened to eat the land dry. The Prophet calls the people to a great liturgical assembly of sincere repentance.* He refers to the eschatological "Day of the Lord" (or the last days) and to the effusion of the Spirit that took place on Pentecost* as well as the judgment of God on the universe.

Liturgical use: In the *Roman Missal,** this Book is used on Ash Wednesday,* Pentecost* (Vigil), Friday and Saturday of the 27th Week in Ordinary Time* (I), the Ritual Masses for Confirmation* and Penance,* and twice in Masses for Various Needs and Occasions* (After the Harvest and For Forgiveness of Sins). In the *Liturgy of the Hours,** it is read on the Sunday and Monday of the 33rd Week in Ordinary Time. *Meaning:* God stands ready to forgive our sins if only we repent. He is gracious and slow to anger, abounding in steadfast love.* He also orders all things, in His infinite wisdom, for the good of those who are devoted to Him, those who know how to maintain harmony with creatures and with God. Hence, we must be wise enough to read natural events and phenomena in the simple and honest language of truth.* We must see them as authentic signs of Yahweh's* liberating presence in the midst of His people.

John I, St. (jon thuh fuhrst). ?-526. Reigning as Pope from 523, John was seemingly forced by the King of Italy, Theodoric, to go to Constantinople to try to offset some of Emperor Justinian I's activities against the Arians. The Eastern clergy* there acknowledged his primacy, as the first Pope* ever to visit Constantinople. Theodoric felt his mission was a failure and imprisoned him at Ravenna, where he died of mistreatment. During his pontificate the system of reckoning years from Christ's birth was adopted, and the present Paschal

Cycle was originated. *Liturgical celebration:* May 18 (Opt. Mem.); *theme:* loyalty to the Faith.

John, Apostle, St. (jon, uh-POS-uhl). c.6-c.104. One of the first disciples of Christ, son of Zebedee and brother of James the Greater,* he became the beloved disciple, the only disciple at the Crucifixion, where He accepted the care of Mary.* After the Council of Jerusalem he went to Asia Minor, where he took care of Mary before she died. Later he traveled to Rome, escaped martyrdom from boiling oil, and lived in Patmos. Returning to Ephesus, he penned the Fourth Gospel* and three Epistles.* Because of his theological brilliance he is symbolized by an eagle in art. *Liturgical celebration:* December 27 (Feast); *theme:* love for one another is the basic law of being a Christian. *See also* JOHN, THE FIRST EPISTLE OF; JOHN, THE GOSPEL ACCORDING TO; JOHN, THE SECOND EPISTLE OF; JOHN, THE THIRD EPISTLE OF.

John Baptist de la Salle, St. (jon BAP-tist duh luh SAL). 1651-1719. This canon* of Rheims, of aristocratic background, became involved in educating poor boys and eventually dedicated his entire life to this work. After grouping some schoolmasters together, he realized that a Religious congregation would be the only answer, so he founded the Brothers of the Christian Schools, finally approved in 1725. Priests* were excluded from his Institute. He composed his own Rule adapting it to a brothers' apostolate. A pedagogical genius, he designed the educational program around religious instruction and made sure that his education would fit in the actual lives of poor youth. Class instructions took the place of individual instruction, and the vernacular was used instead of Latin and Greek. He also established teachers' colleges, and soon his schools spread throughout Europe and finally the whole world. He is the Patron of Teachers. *Liturgical celebration:* April 7 (Memorial); *theme:* all-consuming zeal for the souls of youth.

John Bosco, St. (jon BAH-sko). 1815-1888. A priest* of Turin, John became interested in providing education and housing for neglected boys and started a hospice that soon became the oratory of St. Francis de Sales.* Workshops were included in order to train the poor boys in manual skills. Of cheerful disposition his success occurred despite minimum restraint and discipline, for the love showed through his engaging personality. The boys developed because of all his personal encouragement and religious instruction. His need for assistants impelled him to found the Society of St. Francis de Sales (Salesians). Later he also founded the Daughters of Mary, Help of Christians, who took care of poor and neglected girls. He is the Patron of Editors and Laborers. *Liturgical celebration:* January 31 (Memorial); *theme:* wholehearted commitment to God's service and the salvation of humankind.

John Chrysostom, St. (jon KRIS-uhs-tuhm; kris-SOS-tuhm). c. 344-407. Born in Antioch of Christian parents he left the world to become a hermit under St. Basil.* Ill health brought him back to Antioch where as deacon* and priest* he earned his sobriquet Chrysostom (golden-mouthed). After being named patriarch of Constantinople, he started a reform, with fearless denunciations of whatever was morally wrong in Church or civil life. Such action brought about many exiles. Banished to a more distant exile, he died on the way. His many extant writings, including letters, treatises, and his exegetical homilies, earned this Father of the Church the title of Doctor.* He was responsible for the Eucharistic Rite of the Byzantine* tradition, which originated at Antioch but which he developed as Bishop of Constantinople. Today's general pattern of Christian worship,* a Liturgy of the Word,* followed by a Liturgy of the Eucharist,* is similar to it. Our more solemn liturgies are more like his with the singing and incense.* It differs most at the Anaphora* during which the people sing. He is the Patron of Preachers and Orators. *Liturgical celebration:* September 13 (Memorial); *theme:* suffering with patient endurance.

John Chrysostom, St., Liturgy of. *See* John Chrysostom, St.

John Damascene, St. (jon DAM-uh-seen). c. 650-750. John's Christian parents brought him forth in Damascus, and he lived under Mohammedan rule all his life. His talents lay primarily in preaching, hymnology, and scholarly works, whereby he compiled with the extraordinary gift of synthesis the teachings of the Fathers into a consistent theological system, thus earning for himself the title Doctor* of the Church. Championing the Catholic position concerning the veneration of images, he contributed significant original concepts. *Liturgical celebration:* December 4 (Opt. Mem.); *theme:* orthodox veneration of Christian images.

John de Brébeuf. *See* Isaac Jogues and Companions, Sts.

John Eudes, St. (jon yoodz). 1601-1670. This Frenchman became an Oratorian, preached parish missions successfully and founded with Madeleine Lamy the Visitation nuns, the Sisters of Our Lady of Charity of the Refuge, who care for wayward women. Leaving the Oratory, he founded the Congregation of Jesus and Mary with a common life for diocesan priests; its purpose is to upgrade the clergy.* The primary work of the members was staffing seminaries and preaching missions. With St. Margaret Mary Alacoque* he initiated devotion to the Sacred Heart* and built up devotion to the Heart of Mary,* composing Offices and Masses in their honor. *Liturgical celebration:* August 19 (Opt. Mem.); *theme:* devotion to the Hearts of Jesus and Mary.

John Fisher, St. (jon FISH-uhr). 1469-1535. This eminent scholar became Chancellor of the University at Cambridge where he improved the standard of scholarship. That same year, 1504, he became Bishop of Rochester and soon was internationally known for his writings: against Luther, on identifying Mary Magdalene on the Sacraments* and prayer,* and sermons. He vigorously defended the Eucharistic sacrifice, the real presence,* and the supremacy of the Pope,* when Henry VIII declared himself head of the Church of England. All this brought about his incarceration. While in prison he was named cardinal.* Less than a year later during a farce for a trial, he was convicted of treason and eventually beheaded. In the Liturgy,* his feast is coupled with that of St. Thomas More,* another great British martyr.* *Liturgical celebration:* June 22 (Opt. Mem.); *theme:* fidelity to the Church's teachings and to the Pope.

John Kanty, St. (jon KAN-tee). 1390-1473. Born at Kanty (Kanti), Poland, also known as John Cantius, he became a professor of Scripture.* Famous for his preaching, he was also renowned for his scholarship, learning, austerities, and concern for the poor. He is the Patron of Poland and Lithuania. *Liturgical celebration:* December 23 (Opt. Mem.); *theme:* understanding and kindness toward others.

John Leonardi, St. (jon lay-oh-NAHR-dee). 1541-1609. Born in Tuscany, John gave up pharmacy for the priesthood and eventually organized a group of laymen to work in hospitals and prisons; he also tried to implement the reforms of the Council of Trent. He started a community of priests,* living not according to the traditional monastic way of life, which eventually was recognized as the Clerks Regular of the Mother of God. He died of the plague in Rome while ministering to the stricken. He is regarded as one of the founders of the College for the Propagation of the Faith. *Liturgical celebration:* October 9 (Opt. Mem.); *theme:* true reform begins with self.

John Neumann, St. (jon NYOO-muhn; NOI). 1811-1860. Born in Bohemia, John completed his studies for ordination there, but since there were sufficient clergy in his diocese,* he decided to come to the United States and was accepted in the then Diocese of New York. Following four active years in the Buffalo area, he became the first Redemptorist to be professed in America. Besides serving in the parishes of New York, Baltimore, and Pittsburgh, he became head of the American Redemptorists in 1847. Consecrated Bishop of Philadelphia in 1852, he was much concerned about education and developed the diocesan system of parochial schools. He admitted the Christian Brothers and many communities of Sisters to his apostolate of education and founded the community of Franciscan Sisters of Philadelphia in Glen Riddle.

Besides Slavic dialects, French and German, John learned other languages including Gallic so as to communicate with immigrants. During a short episcopacy of eight years, eighty churches were built. He was the first bishop in the United States to inaugurate the Forty Hours' Devotion* on a diocesan basis. During the First Plenary Council of Baltimore, he was asked to revise his catechism which became an approved textbook. His

pastoral letters are well-written masterworks. Frequent illnesses did not foretell his sudden death at forty-eight on January 8, 1860. He was beatified in 1963 and canonized in 1977, and his feast is part of the Proper* for the United States. *Liturgical celebration:* January 5 (Memorial); *theme:* spreading the Faith through education.

John of Capistrano, St. (jon uhv kap-uh-STRAHN-oh). 1386-1456. The former Governor of Perugia entered the Order of Friars Minor and was ordained; immediately going into preaching, he brought about the conversion of many to a more spiritual way of living. Within the Franciscan Order he was active in trying to reunite the various groups, aided St. Colette in her reform of the Poor Clares, and was frequently an envoy for papal diplomatic missions. When the Moslems captured Constantinople, he preached a crusade against them and eventually exhorted the Hungarians to resist them and helped during the battle of Belgrade in 1456, which saved Europe from being taken over by the Turks. He is the Patron of Jurists and Military Chaplains. *Liturgical celebration:* October 23 (Opt. Mem.); *theme:* the Church militant* should be soldiers of Christ.

John of God, St. (jon uhv god). 1495-1550. Born in Portugal, John became a soldier and led a rather dissolute and varied life until he settled in Spain in 1536 and chanced to hear a sermon by St. John of Avila in 1538. His life took on a new purpose based on love for God and neighbor, which led him to help the sick and the poor; eventually he founded the Order of the Hospitallers of John of God. His dedication and holiness engendered donations from the wealthy to help his work among the destitute. He is the Patron of Booksellers, Heart Patients, Hospitals, Nurses, Printers, and the Sick. *Liturgical celebration:* March 8 (Opt. Mem.); *theme:* love and compassion for others.

John of the Cross, St. (jon uhv thuh kraws). 1542-1591. A Spanish Carmelite who collaborated with St. Theresa of Jesus* in reforming the Carmelite Order. All the usual difficulties of such a reform had to be met, because of the dissension between the Calced and Discalced Carmelites. His Thomistic studies were apparent in his spiritual teaching and writing. He is noted for his mystical poetry, some written during an imprisonment, and his ascetical-mystical theology and literature have earned him rightfully the title of Doctor of the Church.* *Liturgical celebration:* December 14 (Memorial); *theme:* love of the Cross* through the spirit of self-denial.

John the Baptist, St. (jon thuh BAP-tist). 1st century. The son of Zechariah and Elizabeth the kinswoman of Mary,* John was born at Ain Karim, and when Mary visited Elizabeth, he leapt with joy in his mother's womb, which signified his cleansing from original sin before birth (but not, as in Mary's case, from the first instant of conception). Because of this, he is the only Saint,* aside from Jesus and Mary,

whose birth is celebrated. In addition, his death—like that of every other Saint—is also commemorated. After many years of living as a hermit, he began his career on the banks of the Jordan by preaching repentance.* Following his baptism of Christ and his denunciation of Herod living in an incestuous marriage, John was imprisoned. Eventually, at the request of Salome, at the instigation of Herodias, her mother, he was beheaded.

This last of the Old Testament* Prophets* and the Precursor of the Messiah* identified Christ as the "Lamb of God."* Early veneration by the Church is obvious from the fact that his name is found in the Eucharistic Prayer,* the Litany of the Saints,* and the Confiteor* as well as from the witness of early Christian iconography. He is the Patron of Farriers. *Liturgical celebration:* June 24 ("Birth"—Solemnity) and August 29 ("Beheading"—Memorial); *theme:* God's call comes to us all and should be accepted with humility.

John, The First Epistle of (jon, thuh fuhrst i-PIS-uhl uhv). Sixty-ninth Book of the Bible* and twenty-third of the New Testament.* This Epistle is more like a doctrinal presentation than a letter. The style is that of a homily or catechesis. It was probably written at Ephesus toward the close of the 1st century by John the Apostle.* It seems to have been a kind of circular document to the faithful* of Asia Minor to remind them of what he had written and preached concerning the Divinity of Christ and to strengthen them against the heresies of the day. The basic thought of the Epistle is that God is made known to us in Jesus; hence, communion with the Father comes through the Son.

Liturgical use: In the *Roman Missal,** this Epistle is read during the Christmas Season* (weekdays) and the Sundays of the Easter Season* (B) as well as in the Common of the Saints* and Ritual Masses.* In the *Liturgy of the Hours,** it is read on December 27, in the Common of Holy Women, and during the 6th and 7th Weeks in the Easter Season. *Meaning:* At the center of salvation is communion with Jesus and of Christians with one another. This communion is realized in faith* in Christ and in love* for one another. God is light, justice, and love. Hence, if we wish to have communion with the Father through the Son we must walk in light, in justice and holiness, and in love.

John, The Gospel According to (jon, thuh GOS-puhl uh-kawrd-ing too). Fiftieth Book of the Bible* and fourth of the New Testament.* The last Gospel* written about 90 A.D. by John* the beloved disciple, it is the most sublime and theological of the Gospels and very different from the Synoptics in plan and content. It was written for Christians of Asia Minor, probably at Ephesus, and seeks to complement the Synoptics, which it presupposes are known to its readers. The tone is solemn, thought unfolds slowly, in cyclical fashion, and the same terms are repeated over and over creating a certain monotony, although there is also an almost liturgical rhythm in the sentences.

John shows the human characteristics of Jesus and the realism of His earthly existence, but more than the Synoptics he likes to reveal the spiritual, Divine, and glorious dimensions in the events of Jesus' life. He makes use of accounts of signs and long reflective discourses to reveal Christ's present mission as Word, Way, Truth, Life and Light. His purpose is to inspire belief in Jesus as the Messiah,* the Son of God (Jn 20:31).

Finally, the fourth Gospel is the Gospel of love.* No other Evangelist* has so clearly emphasized the love of the Father: "God so loved the world that he gave his only Son" (Jn 3:16); nor has any other so brought out the love of the Son for His own: "He loved them to the end" (Jn 13:1), that is, to the very limit. And no other Gospel has so insistently reduced the new law to the one precept of fraternal love: "As I have loved you, so you should love one another" (Jn 13:34; 15:12).

Liturgical use: In the *Roman Missal,** this Gospel is as well represented as those of Matthew,* Mark,* and Luke,* which are assigned to cycles A, B, and C respectively. In the Sunday Masses alone John occurs more than 40 times—at Christmas,* Easter,* Pentecost,* during the major seasons, and on the 17th through the 21st Sundays in Ordinary Time* (B). It is also used extensively in the continuous readings for weekdays, in the Proper of Saints,* in the Common of Saints,* and in Ritual Masses.* In the *Liturgy of the Hours,** it is used in Appendix I: "Canticles and Gospel Readings for Vigils."

Meaning: Jesus is the Son of God Who became Man and brought us eternal life,* which consists in the knowledge of the Father and the One He has sent, Jesus Christ, in the Holy Spirit. The way to obtain this life is to be born again through Baptism* and to practice the great commandment of love for God and neighbor. The power to do so is given by the Holy Spirit, Who renders us docile to the Word of God given us in Jesus, enables us to worship the Father in truth, and empowers us to follow in Christ's footsteps. We can encounter Jesus and remain united with Him through His Church,* the community of His followers founded on the Apostles,* who gives us the Eucharist* and the other Sacraments.*

John, The Second Epistle of (jon, thuh SEK-uhnd i-PIS-uhl uhv). Seventieth Book of the Bible* and twenty-fourth of the New Testament.* This is a very short Epistle written toward the close of the first century probably at Ephesus. Its author calls himself "the Preacher," and its vocabulary is like that found in John's Gospel* and First Epistle.* It is addressed to "the chosen Lady" and "to her children"—a literary image of a particular Christian community that reflects the specific destination and purpose of the Epistle. Unlike the First Epistle, this is not a theological treatise but a reply to problems within the Church. The Johannine themes of love* and truth* are used to support practical advice on Christian living.

Liturgical use: In the *Roman Missal,** this Epistle is read on Friday of the 32nd Week in Ordinary Time* (II). In the *Liturgy of the Hours,** it is read on Friday of the 7th Week of the Easter Season.* *Meaning:* Christians are to show their love by obedience to the Commandments,* especially love for others, for without love we do not know God; to keep the Faith,* especially concerning Christ's Divinity; and to avoid teachers who reject the truth.

John, The Third Epistle of (jon, thuh thuhrd i-PIS-uhl uhv). Seventy-first Book of the Bible* and twenty-fifth of the New Testament.* This is a very short Epistle written toward the close of the first century probably at Ephesus. Its author calls himself "the Preacher," and its vocabulary is like that found in John's Gospel* and First Epistle.* It is addressed to a Christian named Gaius, an official of a local Church, and vividly portrays certain features in the life of the early Church. Gaius is praised for his past good deeds, especially his hospitality* toward Christian missionaries, and for walking in the truth. Diotrephes, on the contrary, is censured for his ambition and lack of hospitality. A certain Demetrius is also commended for his virtue.

Liturgical use: In the *Roman Missal,** this Epistle is read on Saturday of the 32nd Week in Ordinary Time* (II). In the *Liturgy of the Hours,** it is read on Saturday of the 7th Week in the Easter Season.* *Meaning:* Christians are to walk in the truth and be faithful to their calling. They must imitate good not evil, for what is good is of God. Of particular importance is support and hospitality for those who bring the Faith* to others.

John Vianney, St. (jon vi-uhn-NAY; AN-ee). 1786-1859. His studies for the priesthood were slow and difficult, but finally through tutoring and a special examination, John was allowed to be ordained and served at first as a curate and eventually was sent to Ars, France, as pastor. He worked tirelessly to improve the religious attitude of his parishioners and eventually reformed the entire town. His reputation as a confessor* and spiritual director spread abroad and many came to him for advice so that he often spent sixteen hours a day in the confessional. Many claimed he could read hearts. Most trying were the thirty years of diabolical attacks with which he was plagued. He is the Patron of Parish Priests. *Liturgical celebration:* August 4 (Memorial); *theme:* zeal for souls, with the spirit of prayer* and penance.*

Jonah, The Book of (JOH-nuh, thuh buk uhv). Thirty-ninth Book of the Old Testament* and fifth of the Minor Prophets.* The Book of Jonah was written in the postexilic era, probably in the 5th century B.C., and is a didactic story with an important theological message. It is a parable of mercy, showing that God's threatened punishments are but the expression of a merciful will that moves all human beings to repent and seek forgiveness. The universality of the story contrasts sharply with the particularistic spirit of many in the postexilic community. The Book has also prepared the way for the Gospel* with its message of Redemption* for all, both Jew and Gentile.

Liturgical use: In the *Roman Missal,** this Book is read on the 3rd Sunday in Ordinary Time* (B), Wednesday of the 1st Week of Lent,* Monday, Tuesday, and Wednesday of the 27th Week in Ordinary Time (I), and Masses for Various Needs and Occasions* (For the Spread of the Gospel and Forgiveness of Sins). In the *Liturgy of the Hours,** it is only in the Two-Year Cycle*: Sunday and Monday of the 19th Week (II). *Meaning:* God is the God of all peoples, and He is loving and merciful. His love extends to Ninevites and pagans, and even to the beasts of the field and all that He has made. The vocation of the People of God* is to reveal to all nations the triune God Who loves them.

Josaphat, St. (JOH-zuh-fuht; -suh-fat). c. 1580-1623. This Polish youth entered the Ukrainian Order of St. Basil,* and as a priest* of the Byzantine Rite* preached well and became the leading advocate for uniting the Ukrainian Church with Rome. After being named bishop,* he instituted necessary reforms. Many, distrusting union with the Catholic Church, caused a ferment that eventually ended up in mob violence to him outside his Cathedral of Vitebsk, where he was murdered. The first Eastern Saint* to be formally canonized.* *Liturgical celebration:* November 12 (Memorial); *theme:* working for the honor and unity of the Church.*

Joseph Calasanz, St. (JOH-zuhf; -suhf; KA-lah-sanz). 1556-1648. Born in Aragon, Spain, Joseph received his law degree, was ordained, and served as vicar general of Trempe, but later went to Rome where he tried to improve the education of needy children. As the number of students grew, his teachers united in community. Eventually he founded the Religious Order called Clerks of Religious Schools. He is the Patron of Christian Schools. *Liturgical celebration:* August 25 (Opt. Mem.); *theme:* heroic patience* and fortitude.*

Joseph, Husband of Mary, St. (JOH-zuhf, -suhf, HUZ-buhnd uhv MAYR-ee). 1st century. The legal father of Jesus is of royal descent

from David. Reliable information can be found about him only in the Infancy Narratives. Apocryphal works added much to develop veneration of Joseph. His feast was not established until 1324. Pius IX proclaimed him Patron of the Universal Church in 1870. Leo XIII named him model for fathers of families in 1889. Pius XI called him the guardian of the spiritual battle against Communism and the Patron of Social Justice. To compete with the Communists' May Day celebration, Pius XII instituted the Memorial of St. Joseph the Worker. John XXIII designated him Protector of the Second Vatican Council* and inserted his name in Eucharistic Prayer I* in 1962. Devotion to him is quite widespread among Catholics. St. Joseph is also the Patron of Carpenters, the Dying, and Workingmen. *Liturgical celebration:* March 19 (Solemnity) and May 1 ("the Worker"—Opt. Mem.); *theme:* conjugal love and fatherly care.

Joshua, The Book of (JAHSH-[uh-] wuh, thuh buk uhv). Sixth Book of the Old Testament* named after the successor of Moses, who led the Israelites into Canaan, it contains a systematic account of the conquest of the Promised Land. Its purpose is to demonstrate God's fidelity in giving the Israelites the land He had promised them for an inheritance. It includes: (1) the conquest of Canaan; (2) division of the land; and

(3) return of the Transjordanian tribes and Joshua's farewell. Like the first five Books of the Bible,* Joshua was built up by a long and complex process of editing traditional materials. The whole history of the conquest of the Promised Land is a prophecy of the spiritual conquest of the world through the Church under the leadership of Jesus the Messiah.*

Liturgical use: In the *Roman Missal,** this Book is read on the 21st Sunday in Ordinary Time* (B), the 4th Sunday of Lent* (C), Thursday, Friday, and Saturday of the 19th Week in Ordinary Time (I), and the Rite of Baptism for Adults. In the *Liturgy of the Hours,** it is read from Monday to Saturday of the 10th Week in Ordinary Time. *Meaning:* Although the victories of Joshua are an action of God, they also call for the active collaboration and faith of His People. God's will is always done, for he controls the forces of nature and history. We must pray and ponder in order to make the right choices so as to be in tune with God's will.

Joy (joi). One of the fruits of the Holy Spirit,* Christian joy is the expectation or possession of more than simply any good. It is the expectation or possession of union with the Ultimate Good and source of joy, the triune God,* through the grace of Christ's Redemption.* The Liturgy* is totally concerned with this joy and helps the faithful* obtain it. The 3rd Sunday of Advent* (Gaudete Sunday*) and the 4th Sunday of Lent* (Laetare Sunday*) are completely given over to the inculcation of the joy of the *expected* Redemption. And the 2nd Sunday of Easter* alludes to the joy over the *accomplished* Redemption (Prayer over the Gifts*).

On earth this Christian joy can only be *partial,* but it will be perfected in heaven* (3rd Sunday of Easter—Prayer over the Gifts). This fullness of joy will be given us by Christ (Eucharistic Prayer for Masses of Reconciliation I*). We can also be aided in its attainment by the Eucharist* (Common of the Blessed Virgin Mary*—Mass 3, Prayer over the Gifts), and by the Saints* (All Saints*—Prayer after Communion*; Gospel*). Most important of all, this joy that Jesus gives is one that nobody can take away (Friday of the 6th Week in the Easter Season—Gospel). *See also* GAUDETE SUNDAY; HAPPINESS; LAETARE SUNDAY.

Jubilee (JOO-buh-lee). A holy year designated by the Holy See,* during which all who visit Rome and pray according to specified conditions may gain a plenary indulgence* under the usual conditions. The term is derived from the Hebrew word for ram-horn that was blown by the priest to announce their Jubilee year. The Jews celebrated such a Jubilee every fifty years considering it a year of thanksgiving, of liberty, of forgiveness and sanctification. Jubilation then expresses very well the feeling that should reign in this time of thanksgiving in the hearts of all Christians. Established in the year 1300, it was to be reiterated every hundred years. However, it was not long before, in imitation of the Jubilee of the Jews, the period was shortened to fifty years. Later it was shortened to twenty-five.

Extraordinary Jubilees occur between the ordinary Jubilees. For instance in the 20th century, there were extraordinary jubilees in 1904 on the occasion of the fiftieth anniversary of the promulgation of the dogma of the Immaculate Conception*; in 1913 on the occasion of the 16th centenary of the peace of the Church given by Constantine; in 1929 for the 50th anniversary of the priestly ordination of Pius XI; in 1933 for the 19th centenary of the Redemption*; and in 1974 when Paul VI asked for a year of prayer for reconciliation, peace, and social justice.

Each Jubilee usually is accompanied by a call for more fervent prayer and devotion on the part of the faithful,* especially through participation in the Eucharist* and the Sacraments.* The 1974 Jubilee was the occasion for the introduction of two new Eucharistic Prayers for Masses of Reconciliation,* which eventually became inserted into the *Roman Missal.** The opening and closing of each holy year is characterized by the opening and closing of the holy doors of St. Peter's in Rome. Since 1500 the Jubilee indulgence may be gained at home, without traveling to Rome, under special conditions once the period for visiting Rome is over.

Jubilee Sunday (JOO-buh-lee SUN-dee; -day). Another name for the 3rd Sunday of Easter,* whose Entrance Antiphon* begins with the Latin word *Iubilate* ("Cry out with joy"), formerly printed as *Jubilate.*

Jubilus (JOO-buh-luhs). A long melisma (group of notes) sung in plainchant on the final *a* of the second and third alleluias after the Gradual* in the Latin Mass.* It eventually gave rise to the *Sequence.** The name comes from the joyous character of the music.

Jude, St. (jood). 1st century. This Apostle,* the brother of James the Less,* is also called Thaddeus. Most

modern scholars believe that this Jude is distinct from Jude, a relative of the Lord, and author of the Epistle of Jude.* Legend has him working in Mesopotamia or Persia. He is the Patron of Hopeless Cases and Hospitals. *Liturgical celebration:* October 28 (Feast); *theme:* the Apostles as foundation stones of our faith.

Jude, The Epistle of (jood, thee i-PIS-uhl uhv). Seventy-second Book of the Bible* and twenty-sixth of the New Testament.* A very brief hortatory Epistle* written between 80 and 100 and attributed to Jude the

Apostle,* it is an attempt to warn various communities (possibly Gentile Christians) about some false teachers and their way of acting. It encourages the faithful* to be strong in prayer,* love,* and mercy* and concludes with one of the most beautiful doxologies* in the New Testament. A good part of the Epistle is quoted by 1 Peter.*

Liturgical use: In the *Roman Missal,** the Epistle is read on Saturday of the 8th Week in Ordinary Time* (II). In the *Liturgy of the Hours,** it is read on Saturday of the 34th Week in Ordinary Time—the last day of the Liturgical Year.* *Meaning:* The Christian way of life is one that pays no attention to false teachers of any kind. Following the Master, it concentrates on operative faith,* living prayer in the Spirit,* and unbounded love for God in the calm expectation of eternal life,* while showing mercy* to others.

Judges, The Book of (JUHJ-uhz, thuh buk uhv). Seventh Book of the Old Testament,* of unknown date and authorship. Its title stems from the twelve heroes of Israel whose deeds it records. They were not magistrates but military leaders sent by God to aid and to relieve His people in time of external danger. They exercised their activities in the interval of time between the death of Joshua* and the institution of the monarchy in Israel. The purpose of the Book is to show that the fortunes of Israel depended upon the

obedience of the people to God's Law. Whenever they rebelled against Him, they were oppressed by pagan nations; when they repented, He raised up Judges to deliver them.

Liturgical use: In the *Roman Missal,** this Book is read on Monday through Thursday of the 20th Week in Ordinary Time* (I) and on December 19. In the *Liturgy of the Hours,** it is read during the 11th Week in Ordinary Time. *Meaning:* God is faithful to His Covenant.* He never departs from us; it is we who depart from Him. If we remain faithful to Him, He will work with and through us to accomplish His Divine plan for us. God's Spirit* Who enabled the Judges to conquer the physical evils of their time will enable us to overcome the evil of every kind that confronts us today.

Judgment (JUHJ-muhnt). An act of the mind by which something is asserted or denied. Christians have to make a *moral judgment* about their lives and their actions—whether or not their lives and their actions are in conformity with the teachings of Jesus. The Liturgy* is concerned with moral judgment when it leads the worshipers to examine their consciences in the Introductory Rites* at Mass* and exhorts them to render true worship* to God and live authentic Christian lives. A confessor* is called upon to exercise judgment on his penitent in the Sacrament of Penance.* To be correct, judgment must proceed from an inclination to carry out justice,* be exercised by a superior authority, and follow the rules of prudence.*

It is God Who renders true judgment when the oppressed call upon Him (Friday of the 25th Ordinary

Week—Responsorial Psalm,* 43). He will fill with joy the ostracized and the forgotten but will be terrible toward the oppressors who ignore and crush them (2nd Sunday of Advent* (A)—Reading I*: Is 11:1-10). The judgment will be carried out by Jesus Who will take as criterion the person's attitude toward the least of His brothers and sisters (Christ the King,* A—Gospel*: Mt 25:31-46).

In reality, the people will judge themselves by the acts they do, for Jesus did not come to judge the world but to save it (Wednesday of the 4th Week of Easter*—Gospel: Jn 12:44-50). The judgment carried out by Jesus will take place at His Second Coming* and is called the *Last Judgment.* There will also be a *Particular Judgment* for each person at death,* which is equivalent to a Last Judgment for each.

Judica Sunday (JOO-di-kuh SUN-dee; -day). Another name for Passion Sunday (Palm Sunday),* whose Entrance Antiphon* begins with the Latin word *Iudica* ("Judge"), formerly printed as *Judica.*

Judith, The Book of (JOO-duhth, thuh buk uhv). Eighteenth Book of the Old Testament* and second of the Deuterocanonical Books that are accepted as canonical by the Catholic Church but not by the Protestant Churches, who

call them the Apocrypha.* Written between the 3rd and 1st centuries B.C., it is an edifying story recounting the preservation of the Israelites from conquest and ruin through the efforts of Judith. A deeply religious woman who observes all the commands of the Law,* she puts her trust in God, Who works with her to rescue her people from destruction. Judith is a figure of the Blessed Virgin Mary.*

Liturgical use: In the *Roman Missal,** this Book is read in the Common Mass for Holy Women (Widows*) and is used as the Responsorial Psalm* for Common Masses of the Blessed Virgin Mary. In the *Liturgy of the Hours,** it is used only as a minor canticle* in the Psalter* and an additional canticle in Appendix I for Vigils. *Meaning:* God is the Master of history Who makes use of both men and women to carry out His saving plan. Those who trust in Him and work with Him will attain salvation.

Julian Calendar. *See* CALENDAR.

Junipero Serra, Bl. (yoo-NEE-puh-roh SER-rah, Bles-uhd). 1713-1784. A Spanish Franciscan, Junipero came to Mexico at the age of 37. Working in California, he was responsible in large part for the foundation and spread of the Church* on the West Coast of the United States when it was still Spanish territory. He founded 21 missions and converted thousands of Indians. At the same time, the converts were taught agriculture, cattle raising, and arts and crafts. He was beatified by John Paul II on September 25, 1988, and his feast is part of the Proper* for the United States. *Liturgical celebration:* August 28 (Opt. Mem.); *theme:* zeal for souls is the supreme law.

Jurisdiction (juhr-uhs-DIK-shuhn). In Church law this power indicates official authority, namely the right to exercise public authority in some function. Hence a bishop* enjoys jurisdiction in his diocese,* a pastor* in his parish,* a Religious Superior over the members of his or her communities, a priest* in administering the Sacraments.* Liturgically, for instance, jurisdiction pertains to the validity of the absolution in the Sacrament of Penance* and the validity of Marriage* performed before a proper minister. Proper delegation must be given for other acts to be licit, such as a solemn Baptism,* Anointing of the Sick,* and certain solemn blessings.*

Jurisdiction also implies the right to wear certain pontifical insignia.* Signs of respect for jurisdiction include the use of chair* and the genuflection to the local Ordinary* in his diocese.

Jurist, The (JOO[uh]R-uhst, thuh). Semiannual publication of the Canon Law Society of America at Catholic University. It has appeared since 1940 and is regarded as one of the organs that can safely be followed in questions of liturgical practice. *See also* LITURGICAL LAW, SOURCES OF.

Justice (JUHS-tuhs). One of the four chief moral virtues* (together with fortitude,* prudence,* and temperance*), which dispose us to lead moral or good lives by aiding us to treat persons and things in the right way—that is, according to the will of God. They are also known as cardinal virtues because they are like hinges on which hang all other moral virtues and our whole moral life.

Justice inclines us to give whatever is due to God, to our neighbor, and to ourself. It includes many other virtues, for example, gratitude,* liberality, obedience, piety, religion,* and truthfulness.

Participating in the Liturgy* is an act of the moral virtue of religion (which is part of justice) that strengthens the other moral virtues, as indicated in the article on good works.* *See also* FORTITUDE; GOOD WORKS; PRUDENCE; TEMPERANCE; VIRTUES.

Justin, St. (JUHS-tuhn). c. 100-165. Born of pagan parents at Flavia Neapolis in Samaria, Justin was converted and, as a layman, became the first Christian apologist who wrote on Christianity at length, seeking to reconcile the claims of faith* and reason. He performed these duties in Asia Minor and in Rome, where he was eventually beheaded during the reign of Marcus Aurelius. Justin presents an important witness of faith and worship* in what he says about the Eucharist,* the observance of Sunday, and the Baptismal Liturgy. He is the Patron of Philosophers. *Liturgical celebration:* June 1 (Memorial); *theme:* the Mysteries* of the Faith must be vigorously defended.

— K—

Kaddish (KAY-dish). A Jewish doxology* exalting the holy Name of God recited in Aramaic at the daily ritual of the synagogue. Its name stems from the Aramaic term for "sanctified" or "hallowed" found in its opening words. The heart of the Kaddish comes from the words found in Ezekiel*: "I will prove my greatness and holiness and make myself known in the sight of many nations; thus they shall know that I am the Lord" (38:23). Similar sentiments are found in the Lord's Prayer.* *See also* JEWISH LITURGY.

Kairos (KAI-rohs). Word taken over from the Greek that means a "favorable or opportune time." It is used to indicate the intervention of the "time of God" in history through Jesus Christ. *See also* TIME, SANCTIFICATION OF.

Kateri Tekakwitha, Bl. (KAT-uhr-ee tek-uhk-WITH-uh, BLES-uhd). 1656-1680. Born in a Mohawk village, near the present Auriesville, New York, this Indian maiden was baptized by Fr. Jacques de Lamberville when she was twenty. Soon after, because of the hostility of her tribe over her conversion, Baptism,* and exemplary life, she fled to a Christian village in Canada and received her First Communion* there. Her life of austerity was steeped in virtue and charity, including a private vow of chastity. This "Lily of the Mohawks," filled with heroic dedication to the Christian Faith under difficult circumstances, was an inspiration, not only to the missionaries but to all who knew her. Beatified in 1980, she is the first Native American candidate for sainthood. Her feast is part of the Proper* for the United States and was originally placed on April 17, but since it was hardly ever celebrated because of Easter time, it was transferred to July 14. *Liturgical celebration:* (Memorial); *theme:* great holiness* and austerity.

Katharine Drexel, Bl. (KATH-uh-rin DREK-suhl, BLES-uhd). 1858-1955. Katharine inherited a large fortune and used it for the evangelization of black and Native American peoples. For this purpose she founded the Sisters of the Blessed Sacrament. From the age of 33 until her death over 60 years later, she dedicated her life and a fortune of 12 million dollars to this work. In 1915 she also founded Xavier University in New Orleans. Katharine was beatified by John Paul II on November 20, 1988, and her feast is part of the Proper* for the United States. *Liturgical celebration:* March 3 (Opt. Mem.); *theme:* dedicating one's life and possessions to the evangelization of peoples.

Kenosis (kee-NOH-sis). Greek word for "emptying" used in theology to refer to Christ's voluntary renunciation of His right to Divine privilege by appearing as a human being: "[Jesus] emptied himself, taking the form of a slave, coming in human likeness" (Phil 2:7). The Son of God so divested Himself of His glory* as to appear unrecognizable (see Is 53:2-3). Kenosis is the specifically Divine way of loving that pervades the Liturgy.*

Kerygma (kuh-RIG-muh). Proclamation or preaching as opposed to instruction or teaching. An authorized use of the message of salvation* from Christ to arouse a lively faith* in the listeners. The Liturgy* then is to convey the Christian message of God's part in our salvation rather than to place ethical requirements upon the faithful.*

In the Liturgy preaching occurs not only directly, as in the Homily,* but also indirectly, through the prayers,* rites, and symbols.* Liturgy is more than preaching. Although it can give instruction to people as during the Enlightenment,* still you can find devotional prayer texts in the Liturgy also. Liturgy, so as not to become a mere formality, assumes many kinds of preaching activities: catechesis,* private meditation* on Scripture,* personal prayer,* and pastoral care.

King. *See* JESUS CHRIST.

Kingdom of God (KING-duhm uhv god). The term "kingdom" signifies a state of things in which God is recognized as king to Whom everything must be submitted. Kingdom of God and Kingdom of heaven are equivalent. The Kingdom is preached by John the Baptist* (2nd Sunday of Advent,* A—Gospel*), inaugurated by Jesus* (Wednesday of 2nd Week of Lent*—Gospel), continued in the Church (Wednesday of 14th Week in Ordinary Time*—Gospel; 21st Sunday in Ordinary Time, A—Gospel), and will be definitively established in the glory of Christ's return at the Parousia* (1st Sunday of Advent, C—Gospel).

The members of the Kingdom are children of God and even in this life enjoy that eternal life* which will be completely expanded in the future world (4th Sunday of Lent, B—Gospel).

The Kingdom is explicitly treated in the Feast of Christ the King.* Christ rules an eternal and universal Kingdom, a Kingdom of truth* and life,* a Kingdom of holiness* and grace,* a Kingdom of Justice,* love,* and peace* (Preface*). It is a Kingdom that is imperfect on earth but perfect in heaven. If we live by His Gospel, we will be brought to the joy* of His Kingdom (Prayer after Communion*).

Kings, The First Book of (kingz, thuh fuhrst buk uhv). Eleventh Book of the Old Testament* that originally was combined with 2 Kings. This unit came out in two editions, one between 621 B.C. and 597 B.C. and the oher during the Exile, probably shortly after Jehoiachin was released from his Babylonian prison (561 B.C.).

The First Book of Kings carries the history of Israel from the last days and death of David to the accession in Samaria of Ahaziah, son of Ahab, near the end of the reign of Jehoshaphat, king of Judah, and includes the Cycle of Elijah. It shows the effects of the Deuteronomic influence *(see* GENESIS, THE BOOK OF) as it records the strivings of those who sought the worship of the one true God and the total regulation of life in accordance with loyalty to Him. The history given is pragmatic—being an historical account overlaid with an instructive message. The kings are judged not by their material accomplishments but by their moral purpose in the sight of Yahweh.*

Liturgical use: In the *Roman Missal,** this Book is read on the 17th and 19th Sundays in Ordinary Time* (A), the 19th and 32nd (B), and the 9th, 10th, and 13th (C) as well as on weekdays of the 4th, 5th, 10th, and 11th Weeks in Ordinary Time (II), and in Common and Ritual Masses* plus Masses for Various Needs and Occasions.* In the *Liturgy of the Hours,** it is read on

Friday of the 14th Week to Thursday of the 15th Week in Ordinary Time and in the Common for the Dedication of a Church. *Meaning:* God is the Lord of history despite its many vicissitudes, judging the moral conduct of His people in accord with the Covenant* made with them. God also shows much care for His people, for example, by sending Prophets* to bring them back to Him when they stray. Thus, if God is so involved in everyday life, it must have great value!

Kings, The Second Book of (kingz, thuh SEK-uhnd buk uhv). Twelfth Book of the Old Testament* that formed one unit with 1 Kings* *(see above entry).* It takes the story of Israel from the reign of Ahaziah to the destruction of Jerusalem in 587 B.C. and on to the release of Jehoiachin from prison in 561 B.C.

Liturgical use: In the *Roman Missal,** this Book is read on the 13th Sunday in Ordinary Time* (A), the 17th (B), and the 28th (C), Monday of the 3rd Week of Lent,* the Optional Readings for the 5th Week of Lent, Wednesday of the 11th Week in Ordinary Time to Friday of the 12th Week (II) as well as Mass of Christian Initiation* and Mass for the Sick. In the *Liturgy of the Hours,** it is read on Saturday of the 15th Week. *Meaning:* Same as First Book of Kings.

Kiss (kis). To touch with the lips to symbolize veneration of persons or things at the time of public worship* is long a liturgical tradition. All former kisses of the hand and objects that were presented or received have been abrogated; now only the altar* and the Gospel Book* are reverenced by a kiss. Where the kiss is out of harmony in certain cultures, some other sign may be substituted. *See also* ALTAR, VENERATION OF.

Kiss of Peace. *See* SIGN OF PEACE.

Kneeling (NEEL-ing). This posture of resting on both knees, comparable to a double genuflection,* is a gesture expressing an attitude of dependence, submission, or supplication. From early centuries it was a usual posture for private prayer. Penitential in style it conveys submission, humility, and reverence in accord with all types of prayer.* Present legislation in the United States requires that the congregation kneel after the Holy, Holy, Holy* until the final Amen of the Eucharistic Prayer.* *See also* GENUFLECTION; POSTURE IN WORSHIP.

Kyriale (keer-ee-AHL-ay). The liturgical book that contains the invariable Latin chants* (text and music) of the Mass*: *Kyrie,* Gloria,* Credo,* Sanctus,** and *Agnus Dei.**

In 1965, the Sacred Congregation of Rites published a *Kyriale Simplex* (Simple Kyriale) with simpler melodies than those found in the standard Kyriale. This was to facilitate the mandate of the Second Vatican Council* that "steps should be taken enabling the faithful* to . . . sing together in Latin those parts of the Ordinary* of the Mass belonging to them" (SC, 54). It contains the antiphons *Asperges Me* and *Vidi Aquam* followed by five simple settings for the Ordinary chants and the chant for the dismissal rite *(Ite, Missa Est** and *Benedicamus Domino*)* as well as an appendix with two tones for use by the congregation* in singing the Our Father* *(Pater Noster)* with the celebrant.*

Kyrie Eleison. *See* LORD HAVE MERCY.

—L—

Labor Day Mass (LAY-buhr day mas). Among the Days of Prayer* in the United States, this day is set aside to pray for workers. The Mass suggested is that of St. Joseph the Worker,* from May 1; however, the Mass for Various Public Needs #25, Blessing of Man's Labor, would seem apropos also.

The liturgical texts found in the Mass for the Blessing of Man's Labor provide a "concise theology of labor": (1) God is the ultimate source of all creativity (Entrance Antiphon*; Responsorial Psalm*). (2) We are God's coworkers although we can do nothing by ourselves (Opening Prayer*—A and B). (3) Work enhances human beings (Opening Prayer—A, alternate). (4) Human labor joins us to Christ's saving action (Prayer over the Gifts*—B). (5) Work builds up God's Kingdom* (Prayer after Communion*—A). (6) Labor in common leads to unity and brotherly love (Opening Prayer—B). (7) The earth has been given into human hands to cultivate (Reading I*—Gn 2:4-9, 15). (8) Work is a necessity for life (Reading II*—2 Thes 3:6-12, 16). (9) Work is never an end in itself but is always related to God's plan for us; it should be carried out with detachment and dependence on God (Gospel*—Mt 6:31-34). (10) Labor must not be allowed to consume us; there must be room for leisure activities and for meditation (Gospel—Mt 6:31-34). In this way, the Liturgy* helps us to keep our perspective about work,* about the world,* about salvation,* about leisure, and about our ultimate goal.

Laborem Exercens (lah-BOH-rem eks-AYR-chenz). Latin title (from the first two words "Exercising Labor") of the Encyclical *On Human Work* issued by Pope John Paul II on September 14, 1981. The Encyclical points out that human labor by the sweat and toil that go with it presents all who are called to follow Christ with the possibility of sharing lovingly in the *work* that Christ came to accomplish. This *work of salvation** came about through His Suffering and Death* on the Cross* and subsequent Resurrection* to glory.* In a sense, our work is an extension of sharing in the Eucharist,* which is a re-presentation of Christ's saving work. Indeed, the Eucharist takes our work and offers it to the Father for the salvation of the world.*

The Pope calls upon "Christians who listen to the Word of the living God, uniting work with prayer," to come to "know the place that their work has not only in earthly progress but also in the development of the Kingdom of God.* Thus, by combining work and worship Christians can "collaborate with the Son of God for the redemption of humankind"—not only through their Eucharist but also through their labor.

Lady Altar (LAY-dee AWL-tuhr). Side altar* of a church dedicated to the Blessed Virgin Mary* under one of her titles: Our Lady of Mount Carmel*; Our Lady of Sorrows*; etc.

Lady Chapel (LAY-dee CHAP-uhl). Chapel* dedicated to the Blessed Virgin Mary,* especially in the cathedrals* that stem from the Middle Ages.

Laetare Sunday (lay-TAH-ray SUHN-dee; -day). The 4th Sunday of Lent,* so designated by the first words of the Latin Entrance Antiphon*: *"Rejoice, Jerusalem!"* In mid-Lent the congregation pauses to revel in the ultimate victory to be won. Flowers may be used, the organ played, and rose vestments* are allowed. The custom of using rose vestments developed because that color* was proper to the blessing of the golden rose, which the Pope* performs that day in recognition of outstanding service to the Church. *See also* GAUDETE SUNDAY.

Laity (LAY-uht-ee). A word based on the Greek *laos,* "people," that refers to baptized Christian people who are not ordained or have not made Religious Profession* in an Order or Congregation approved by the Church.* They share in the universal priesthood* (1 Pt 2:5) and have rights and obligations to cooperate in the public worship* of the Church. Although certain Sacraments* cannot be celebrated without the priest, even the climax of the Liturgy,* the Eucharist,* brings Christ for one reason only, to become the sacrifice of the whole Church. Societal celebrations demand that the faithful* participate communally. The People of God* are to have an active part in listening, praying, sharing, and receiving in the Sacrifice.

It is the earnest desire of the Church that pastors promote the participation* of the People of God in the Liturgy, which is their right and duty by reason of Baptism,* by encouraging them to join in the acclamations,* responses,* psalmody,* antiphons,* and hymns,* and to show by actions, gestures,* and bodily attitudes, even at times by reverent silence,* their involvement. Furthermore many individuals can perform some special duties during Liturgies, such as those of acolytes,* commentators,* readers,* extraordinary ministers of Baptism,* of the Eucharist,* of exposition of the Blessed Sacrament,* delegates to assist at marriages,* ministers of Sacramentals,* singers in the choir,* and preachers (with the exception of homilies). Thus, the laity are to share in the Liturgy, which is the *laos-ergon,* "the work of the people."

Lay persons, moreover, may now exercise an increased number of nonordained ministries,* for instance, chancellor, notary, procurator-advocate, promoter of justice, defender of the bond, judge, diocesan business managers, members of diocesan or parish finance councils, recipients of the canonical mission to teach theology and other sacred sciences, missionaries, catechists, and they may represent the person of the Holy See* as members of pontifical missions, or as members of heads of delegations to international councils, conferences, or congresses.

Their ministry in and to the world carries a special responsibility to

proclaim and perform the rule of God for all in the world to see. The concept of laity should not have a negative connotation, but should be approached as a special form of Christian existence, having its own vocation with duties, privileges, dignity, and finally its guaranteed eternal recompense. *See also* APOSTOLICAM ACTUOSITATEM; CHRISTIFIDELES LAICI; LITURGY—PARTICIPATION; UNIVERSAL PRIESTHOOD.

Lamb of God (lam uhv god). (1) The title, given to Christ by John the Baptist,* which also appears several times in the New Testament.* It conjures up the double idea of the Servant of Yahweh,* compared to a lamb and the Paschal Lamb. Jesus, the Paschal Lamb immolated, remains forever the sacrificial Lamb of God.

(2) Employed as a symbol, an image either of the Blessed Sacrament* or of Jesus as victim. As a rule, the lamb is pictured with a cross or pennant and a halo.

(3) The series of invocations in the style of a litany* to be sung antiphonally by the chanter* or the choir* with the people during the Breaking of the Bread* at Mass.* The invocation: "Lamb of God, you take away the sins of the world, have mercy on us," is repeated until the consecrated Bread is broken in sufficient quantity to indicate a common sharing. Then in the final invocation the concluding phrase is changed to "grant us peace." The simultaneous breaking and singing intensifies the sign of unity, "for we all partake of the one loaf" (1 Cor 10:17).

The Lamb of God reminds us that Jesus is the Lamb of the New Covenant.* We "were ransomed . . . with the precious blood of Christ as of a

spotless, unblemished lamb" (1 Pt 1:18-19). Every Eucharist is a memorial* of the new Passover that brings forgiveness of sin and peace of mind and soul.

When it cannot be sung the Lamb of God is recited aloud, ordinarily led by the reader,* chanter, or commentator* while the people give the response; or the entire text is said in unison. Only when there is no one else to lead would the celebrant* begin it and then break the bread. *See also* BREAKING OF (THE) BREAD.

Lamentations, The Book of (lam-uhn-TAY-shuhnz, thuh buk uhv). Thirty-first Book of the Old Testament,* consisting of five poems written by an eyewitness (sometimes thought to be the Prophet Jeremiah*) of the national Jewish catastrophe that occurred with the fall of Jerusalem in 587 B.C. They combine confession of sin, grief over the suffering and humiliation of Zion, submission to merited chastisement, and strong faith in the constancy of Yahweh's* love and peace to bring about restoration.

Liturgical use: In the *Roman Missal,** this Book is read on Saturday of the 12th Week in Ordinary Time* (II) and in the Mass for Any Need and Mass for the Dead.* In the *Liturgy of the Hours,** it is read on Thursday, Friday, and Saturday of the 23rd Week in Ordinary Time. *Meaning:* Our God is the Lord of hope,* of love,* of faithfulness,* and of salvation*: "The favors of the Lord are not exhausted his mercies are never spent; they are renewed each morning, so great is his faithfulness" (3:22-23). He is willing to start over again whenever we are willing to acknowledge our errors and submit ourselves to Him.

Lamps. *See* CANDLES AND LIGHTS.

Language. *See* VERNACULAR.

Last Blessing (last BLES-ing). A blessing with a plenary indulgence* that is given to a dying person with Viaticum.* It is also known as the Apostolic Blessing. The new Rite of Anointing* found in *Pastoral Care of the Sick* terms it "Apostolic Pardon" and gives two formulas for it (no. 201). The plenary indulgence takes effect at the moment of death.

Last Gospel (last GOS-puhl). The passage from the Gospel* according to John* (1:1-14) formerly read at the end of Mass* in the Roman

Rite,* except during Lent,* on vigils,* on Sunday when a major feast* was celebrated, and on Christmas* at the Mass during the Day. The Last Gospel was suppressed in 1964 by the *Instruction on the Correct Implementation of the Constitution on the Sacred Liturgy, Inter Oecumenici.**

Last Sacraments. *See* ANOINTING OF THE SICK.

Last Supper (last SUHP-uhr). The farewell meal Jesus shared with His Apostles* the night before His Passion* and Death,* in which He instituted the priesthood* and the Eucharist.* It occurred during a festive Jewish meal having Passover characteristics, namely, beginning with a breaking of the bread and concluding with raising the cup of wine during a prayer of thanksgiving, while all present have done the same before drinking. Using these familiar actions Jesus prefigured the sacrifice He was to make the next day, thus instituting the Sacrament.* *See also* EUCHARIST.

Latin as Liturgical Language. *See* LITURGICAL LANGUAGE—LATIN.

Latin Rite. *See* ROMAN RITE.

Latria (la-TRAI-uh). The essential adoration* owed and offered to God alone because of His preeminent excellence and to show our total subservience to Him. This sign of interior reverence is usually shown outwardly by symbolic gestures of bowing and kneeling. Latria is uniquely distinct from veneration given to any creature. *See also* ADORATION; DULIA; HYPERDULIA; WORSHIP.

Lauda Sion (LOW-dah SEE-ohn). Latin title (from the first two words "Laud, O Zion") of the Sequence* for Corpus Christi* (which is optional in the new *Roman Missal**) written by St. Thomas Aquinas* (1225-1274). It is one of the five beautiful hymns the Angelic Doctor composed in honor of Jesus in the Blessed Sacrament* at the specific request of Pope Urban IV (1261-1264) for the new Feast of Corpus Christi in 1264.

The Sequence is a clear and concise summary of the Church's teaching about the Eucharist.* It is made up of 80 verses that may be divided as follows: (1) God is praised for having instituted the Eucharist, the Body and Blood of Jesus (1-18); (2) the Eucharist is shown to have replaced the Passover celebrated by the Israelites (19-30); (3) the doctrine of the Eucharist is reviewed (31-62); (4) this Bread is declared to have fulfilled the Old Testament* types* found in Isaac and the lamb and the manna (63-70); (5) a prayer is addressed to the Good Shepherd* that those who chant this hymn may enjoy the beatific vision (71-80). The following is one of the many translations that exist.

Zion, to Your Savior sing,
To Your Shepherd and Your King!
Let the air with praises ring!

All you can, proclaim with mirth,
For far higher is His worth
Than the glory words may wing.

Lo! before our eyes and living
Is the Sacred Bread life-giving,
Theme of canticle and hymn.

We profess this Bread from heaven
To the Twelve by Christ was given,
For our faith rests firm in Him.

Let us form a joyful chorus,
May our lauds ascend sonorous,
Bursting from each loving breast.

For we solemnly record
How the Table of the Lord
With the Lamb's own Gift was blest.

On this altar of the King
This new Paschal Offering
Brings an end to ancient rite.

Shadows flee that truth may stay,
Oldness to the new gives way,
And night's darkness to the light.

What at Supper Christ completed
He ordained to be repeated,
In His memory Divine.

Wherefore now, with adoration,*
We, the Host of our salvation,*
Consecrate from bread and wine.

Words a nature's course derange,
That in Flesh the bread may change
And the wine in Christ's own Blood.

Does it pass your comprehending?
Faith, the law of light transcending,
Leaps to things not understood.

Here beneath these signs are hidden
Priceless things, to sense forbidden;
Signs, not things, are all we see.

Flesh from bread, and Blood from wine,
Yet is Christ in either sign,
All entire confessed to be.

And whoe'er of Him partakes,
Severs not, nor rends, nor breaks:
All entire, their Lord receive.

Whether one or thousand eat,
All receive the selfsame meat,
Nor do less for others leave.

Both the wicked and the good
Eat of this celestial Food:
But with ends how opposite!

With this most substantial Bread,
Unto life or death they're fed,
In a difference infinite.

Nor a single doubt retain,
When they break the Host in twain,
But that in each part remain
What was in the whole before;

For the outward sign alone
May some change have undergone,
While the Signified stays one,
And the same forevermore.

Hail! Bread of Angels, broken,
For us pilgrims food, and token
Of the promise by Christ spoken,
Children's meat, to dogs denied!

Shown in Isaac's dedication,
In the Manna's preparation,
In the Paschal immolation,
In old types pre-signified.

Jesus, Shepherd mild and meek,
Shield the poor, support the weak;
Help all who Your pardon sue,
Placing all their trust in You:
Fill them with Your healing grace!

Source of all we have or know,
Feed and lead us here below.
Grant that with Your Saints* above,
Sitting at the feast of love
We may see You face to face.

Laudis Canticum (LOW-dees KAHN-tee-koom). Latin title (from the first two words "Hymn of Praise") of the *Apostolic Constitution* on the Divine Office** issued by Pope Paul VI on November 1, 1970, promulgating the *Liturgy of the Hours,** the Office revised in accord with the decrees of the Second Vatican Council.*

Lauds. *See* MORNING PRAYER.

Laus Tibi, Christe. *See* PRAISE TO YOU, LORD JESUS CHRIST.

Lavabo. *See* ABLUTIONS.

Law (law). (1) The first five Books of the Old Testament* (also called the Pentateuch): Genesis,* Exodus,* Leviticus,* Numbers,* and Deuteronomy,* which together with the Prophets and the Writings comprised the Jewish Scriptures. In liturgical writing, the First Reading* or Epistle* at Mass* was called the Law when it was taken from these Books. (2) The term also refers to the legislation contained in these Books, some of which Christ confirmed (e.g., the Ten Commandments*) and some of which he abrogated (e.g., legal uncleanness and profanation).

Law, Liturgical. *See* LITURGICAL LAW.

Lawrence, St. (LAWR-ents; LOR-). ?-258. Ordained by Pope St. Sixtus II* as deacon,* he served as one of the seven deacons of the Roman Church. The historicity of his death is in doubt. When called by the Prefect of Rome to deliver the treasury of the Church, he distributed it to the poor instead. Thereupon he was roasted to death on a red hot gridiron over a slow fire. He is the Patron of Cooks and of the Poor. *Liturgical celebration:* August 10 (Feast); *theme:* loving service to the poor.

Lawrence of Brindisi, St. (LAWR-ents; LOR-; uhv BRIN-dee-zi). 1559-1619. This Capuchin theologian, besides holding high offices in the order, was called upon by the Popes to act as diplomat in several difficult peace-making situations. He was also chaplain to the army that fought off the Turks in Hungary. His commentary on Genesis,* treatises against Luther, and volumes of sermons earned him the title of Doctor of the Church.* *Liturgical celebration:* July 21 (Opt. Mem.); *theme:* wisdom and fortitude in the service of the Church.

Lawrence Ruiz and Companions, Sts. (LAWR-ents; LOR-; roo-EEZ and kum-PAN-yuhnz). From 1633 to 1637 sixteen martyrs* (that is, Lawrence Ruiz and his companions) shed their blood out of love for Christ in the city of Nagasaki, Japan. This group was made up of members of the Order of Preachers and those associated with that Order; nine priests,* two religious,* two virgins,* and three lay people,* one of whom was Lawrence Ruiz the father of a family from the Philippine Islands. All had, at different times and under varying circumstances, preached the Christian Faith* in the Philippines, Formosa, and Japan. They manifested the universality of the Christian religion and by their example sowed the seed of future missionaries and converts. *Liturgical celebration:* September 28 (Opt. Mem.); *theme:* suffering patiently in the service of God and neighbor.

Lay Ministry. *See* LAITY.

Lay People. *See* LAITY,

Laying On of Hands. *See* IMPOSITION OF HANDS.

Leader of Song. *See* CHANTER.

Leap Year (leep yi[uh]r). In leap year a complementary day is added every four years to the conventional year, to compensate for the difference of five hours and forty-nine minutes needed to complete each solar year. It is also called bissextile year since the Church,* before the recent calendar* change, instead of considering February 29 as the intercalendar day, doubled the date of February 24, which is the sixth day before the kalends of March. Thus in leap year this sixth day occurred twice, on the 24th and the 25th. Formerly, when feasts* occurred on the dates from the 24th to the 28th, they were all advanced one date in leap year. The regular weekday Office* is said on the intercalendar day.

Lectern (LEK-tuhrn). A fixed elevated platform, usually between the sanctuary* and the nave,* used for reading and chanting the Scriptures,* the Exsultet,* the Homily,* and the General Intercessions.* Its placement indicates the relationship of the Word* to the Sacrament* and should allow the faithful* to see and hear the minister easily. To be worthy of its function as a suitable place to announce the message of the Lord, the lectern ought to be carefully proportioned, constructed of fine materials, and beautifully

designed. Its proper placement should insure visibility and audibility not only of the Word but also of the Homily. Also called *Chair for Preaching,* because of the connotation of authority in the word chair.*

Simple movable lecterns, which may be only a ledge supported on a post or column of wood or metal, and hence do not compete with the Gospel* lectern, may be used by commentators,* readers of announcements, chanters,* or the choirmaster.

Lectio Brevis (LEK-see-oh BRAY-vees). Latin name for the Scripture passage that follows the Psalmody* in the various Hours of the *Liturgy of the Hours** (formerly called the "Capitulum" or "Chapter"). The English edition calls it simply "[Short] Reading." *See also* READINGS.

Lectio Continua (LEK-see-oh kohn-TEE-noo-ah). Continuous reading of the Bible* in the Liturgy* consisting in starting each new reading* exactly where the reading in the previous celebration broke off. At times, this is really *semi-continuous* because of practical considerations, but the intent is to be continuous. In any case, this type of reading has enabled the Liturgy to implement the express desire of the Second Vatican Council*: "The treasures of the Bible are to be opened up more lavishly, so that richer fare may be provided for the faithful* at the table of God's Word.* In this way, a more representative portion of the Sacred Scriptures will be read to the people over a set cycle of years" (SC, 51). *See also* BIBLE AND LITURGY; LECTIONARY; READINGS.

Lectio Divina (LEK-see-oh dee-VEE-nah). The reading and meditation* of Sacred Scripture* oriented toward the deepening of the major themes of Biblical spirituality in strict relation with the liturgical life. This type of Bible reading started out in monastic settings and was regarded as exclusively religious,* but today it has become a vital part of the whole Christian community. It may be termed the *Christian reading of the Scriptures. See also* BIBLE AND LITURGY.

Lectionary (LEK-shuh-ner-ee). The liturgical book* that holds the Scriptural readings* used during the Liturgy of the Word* in the Mass.* An updated Latin edition of the 1969 *Lectionary* was published in 1981 and included an extended introduction with a more ample theology of the Word of God, more clear directives concerning the ministries in the Liturgy of the Word, and greater stress on the dignity of the Lectionary and the other elements of the Liturgy of the Word.

To the Israelites, the Word of God was that extremely personal communication by which He gave Himself to us in self-revelation. To them God's Word was dynamic, creative, prophetic, and salvific. When Christ came as the Word made flesh, He as the Divine Word assumed these same attributes. Therefore, Christ as the Word is always with us today, as the *Constitution on the Sacred Liturgy** states: "Christ is present in His Word because it is He Who speaks when Sacred Scripture is read in the Church" (no. 7).

Throughout the Liturgical Year* from Advent* on, the Mystery* of Christ is celebrated in word and action. As the great saving events are celebrated, we are sanctified. Between the Word proclaimed and the Word received is the dynamism of the Holy Spirit.* He is the transforming agent in the Liturgy of the Word. When the Word is proclaimed to the assembly,* the nature of the Church with her roles becomes apparent. All listen, some read, and others expound the Word of God, since they have the office of teaching.

Afterward when the members of the assembly break up, they become bearers of the Word as they go out into the world* and give witness by their way of life. Nourished spiritually at the table of God's Word and the table of the Eucharist,* all grow in wisdom and holiness; as the Word of God relates the History of Salvation,* the Eucharist embodies it through the Sacramental signs.* The two together offer one single act of Divine worship,* a sacrifice of praise to God, which makes the fullness of the Redemption* available to all creatures, primarily to those present and, through them, to those whom they seek out to bring into the Church.

History

Evidence exists that the Scriptures were read when Christians assembled on the Lord's Day as far back as the 2nd century. Once a Liturgical Year began to develop, a system of Scripture readings emerged. The first lectionaries then were a collection of Scripture references organized as readings for the Eucharist. They were called *Comes,* "companion." From them developed three types of books:

The *Epistulary* contained the texts proclaimed by the specially ordained readers,* preceding the proclamation of the Gospel.*

The *Evangeliary* contained the Gospel texts proclaimed by bishops,* priests,* or deacons,* following the other readings and prior to the Homily.*

The *Antiphonary* contained the antiphons* to be sung by the chanter,* namely, the Psalm* after the First Reading*; the responsorial texts sung during the Offertory*; the Psalms that were to be sung during the Entrance and Communion Processions.*

As time passed these texts of Scripture readings were added to the priest's distinct book of presidential prayers,* the *Sacramentary,** so that by the 13th century a so-called complete Missal* existed. It was made universal at the Council of Trent and lasted until Vatican II.* A lack of liturgical ministers and the increase of private Masses* brought this liturgically unacceptable development, wherein the Eucharist became the activity of the priest while the members of the community remained mere onlookers. The celebrant assumed all the roles of deacon, reader, chanter, and the like. In our current revised

Liturgy* the roles of several ministers bring about the return of various books: the *Sacramentary* for the celebrant, the *Lectionary* for the readers, the *Book of Gospels** for the deacons, the *Gradual** for the chanter. Although a separate *Book of Gospels* exists, the Gospels are ordinarily included within the *Lectionary* also.

Division

There are six major parts: (1) The *Temporal Cycle*:* for Sundays and weekdays of the entire year. (2) The *Sanctoral Cycle*:* readings for those days on which particular Saints* are celebrated and have their assigned Scripture readings. The arrangement is by calendar year. (3) The *Commons*:* whenever a feast day of the Blessed Virgin* or the Saints does not have its own proper assigned readings, one may choose from these. (4) *Ritual Masses*:* during the celebration of the many rites of the Church, such as the Sacraments* and Religious Profession,* a celebration of the Word of God occurs and choices are made from these readings; Masses for the Dead (funeral and anniversary Masses with readings appropriate to these occasions) are included in this section. (5) *Masses for Various Occasions*:* when the Church desires to celebrate the Eucharist for the needs of the Church (unity, spread of the Gospel, etc.), civil needs (for nations or those who serve them), various public needs (in time of famine, for the dying), and for particular needs (forgiveness of sins, a happy death), appropriate texts are available on such occasions. (6) *Votive Masses*:* occasionally the Church honors a Mystery or a Saint other than on the specific dates in the Liturgical Year, so these texts are available then.

Design and Structure

Some basic principles were involved in designing the revised *Lectionary.* To allow the faithful to become familiar with more of the Bible during the Mass, cycles were instituted so that the worshipers can hear more of the Scriptures and the celebrant has a greater variety on which to preach.

Sundays therefore have a three-year cycle—one for each of the synoptic Gospels, A: Matthew*; B: Mark*; C: Luke.* Year C is always divisible by three. John's* Gospel is used to supplement the year of Mark since the latter's Gospel is so brief. In Lent* and Easter* parts of John fit into all three cycles.

Weekdays have a two-year cycle of First Readings.* Thus on weekdays the Gospel selection is the same each year. Once this pattern of cycles was determined, two other principles became operative. In applying the principle of continuous reading* (*lectio continua**) or semicontinuous reading, that part of Scripture is read each day where the previous day ended, as one would read a book in an ordinary fashion. Sometimes certain sections are skipped, and thus we have a semicontinuous reading. During Sundays in Ordinary Time,* continuous and semicontinuous selections occur. During weekdays throughout the year, the assigned Gospel readings are almost totally continuous.

The other principle involved is that of harmonization, which means that there is a thematic connection between readings. To understand this principle it is necessary to remember the number of readings for the Liturgy of the Word. On Sundays and greater celebrations, three readings are chosen, one from the Old Testament,* the second from the Epistles* or Acts of the Apostles,* and the third from the Gospels. On other days when only two readings are used, the last is always from the Gospels and the first may be from either the Old or the New Testament* as described above.

In setting up the *Lectionary,* the Gospel for each day was settled first, then the other principles were applied, either the thematic harmony with the Gospel or the principle of continuous reading. Sundays usually incorporate both principles, because the First Reading harmonizes with the Gospel while the Second Reading* is usually continuous from Sunday to Sunday. On weekdays only continuous reading is applicable. Certain seasons of the year, e.g., Lent and Easter, influence the choice of Scripture texts. In a broader sense there is a harmony with the liturgical season.

The chants, namely, the Responsorial Psalm* and the Gospel Acclamation,* are part of the total scheme of the readings. As an integral part of the Liturgy, the Responsorial Psalm relates in a harmonious way to the First Reading; the Gospel Acclamation sets the tone or gives an insight to the content of the Gospel.

In the total arrangement of readings, some guiding principles were followed: (1) Certain books were reserved to specific liturgical seasons, ordinarily because of the intrinsic nature of the subject matter. (2) In considering the length of the texts, some narratives could hold the people's attention readily while others because of the depth of teaching would have to be shorter. Sometimes a shortened version is provided. (3) Truly difficult texts were shunned for pastoral reasons. (4) The omission of certain verses from the Scripture without distorting its meaning aided in deciding the length and allowed the inclusion of passages that contained high spiritual value.

In using the order of readings, options exist. On Sundays and greater feasts* an option seldom exists, and in the United States all three readings are prescribed. There may be a possibility to choose between the long and short forms, which should be done on pastoral grounds. In the weekday readings, texts are provided for each day, so unless a Solemnity or Feast occurs, there would be little option. When they do occur the readings for the entire week may be rearranged to allow the congregation a full view of the theme.

Some celebrations of the Saints have *proper* readings, others *accommodated* readings, and still others readings chosen from a Common.

For the other types of Masses, many texts are available so that the president may adapt the celebration to the situation and the concern of the groups attending the service.

Whenever the Responsorial Psalm and the Gospel Acclamation are not specifically assigned, the celebrant's choice will depend upon the pastoral benefit to the participating community.

Consultation on Common Texts

Established after Vatican II,* the North American Consultation on Common Texts prepared common liturgical texts for use among the Christian Churches of the United States and Canada. In 1978, the Consultation set up a committee entitled "The North American Commitee on the Calendar and Lectionary," which after four years has proposed a *Trial Lectionary.* Although the *Roman Lectionary* was adopted for Sunday celebrations by major Christian Churches, the Baptist and the Orthodox excepted, adaptations were made that resulted in four principal variants upon the Roman liturgical book.

Some characteristics of the CCT *Trial Lectionary* follow:

(1) Whereas the majority of readings have been retained, certain omitted verses and contextual verses have been furnished to make the beginnings of each reading

comprehensible. Thus, the use of a table of readings rather than a printed *Lectionary* also accommodated Churches that use a complete Bible* in their celebrations.

(2) Radical adaptation occurs only in the Old Testament readings of Ordinary Time, where the *Roman Lectionary's* choice was criticized as omitting some major readings, overemphasizing the thematic principle over the semicontinuous principle, and choosing selections that reflect excessive typology in relation to the Gospel readings. The *CCT Lectionary* respects the typological control, but in a broader way.

(3) Important pericopes* displaced by such adaptations appear elsewhere in the *CCT Lectionary.*

(4) Where Old Testament readings vary, the corresponding Responsorial Psalm has been changed.

(5) Various traditions of the liturgical calendar* have been respected with alternatives provided. The diverse numbering of Sundays in Ordinary Time includes a system for (a) Roman usage, (b) the numbering from Epiphany* to Pentecost,* and (c) Episcopalian usage.

The *CCT Lectionary* has been approved for trial use by a number of Churches in North America including the National Conference of Catholic Bishops.* When the Holy See confirms their decision, participation in the experimental use of this *Lectionary* would be on a voluntary basis. Norms for evaluation of the *CCT Lectionary* will be formulated, giving the general principles of the present *Roman Lectionary,* so that the examination may be rational rather than emotional.

Celebration of the Word

Because of the reinstitution of the ministerial roles during the Liturgy of the Word, several persons are involved: the readers* of the First Reading and the Second on Sundays and greater feasts; the chanter who leads the singing of the Responsorial Psalm and Gospel Acclamation; the deacon who proclaims the Gospel. The priest, who presides over the celebration, should have thorough understanding of the structure of the readings so as to develop an excellent response from the congregation in his presentations concerning it, particularly as he preaches the Homily. Making use of the various options available, he has the pastoral good of the community at heart. The members of the assembly* have a serious responsibility also; listening out of reverence to the Word allows them to grow spiritually. Their attentiveness and openness to the Word will permit the Spirit* to work well in achieving truly spiritual goals. The *Lectionary* and the *Book of Gospels* are signs and symbols of the sacred nature of our beliefs and ideals, so their binding and ornaments should be of high quality in order that the reverence and respect of the community may be given them.

Translations

In the United States the Conference of Bishops* has approved the following translations of the Bible for the *Lectionary:* (1) the *New American Bible,* a translation from the original languages; (2) the *Jerusalem Bible,* translated from Hebrew or Greek and compared to the French when variant interpretations arose; and (3) the *Revised*

Standard Version (Catholic Version), a revision of the 1901 American Standard Version, in turn a revision of the King James' version of 1611, which made use of Hebrew, Aramaic, and Greek texts; (4) for the Responsorial Psalms, the *Grail Psalter* is also allowed, since it was translated by Catholic laywomen to facilitate the *singing* of the Psalms. *See also* BIBLE; BIBLE AND LITURGY; BIBLE SERVICE; CELEBRANT; CHANTER; CYCLES; DEACON; LITURGY OF THE WORD; MISSAL; READINGS.

Lectors. *See* READING.

Lent (lent). A penitential season of prayer starting with Ash Wednesday* and continuing until Holy Saturday.* Besides preparing the people better for the feast of the Resurrection,* it predisposes them to receive more of the graces Christ has earned through His Passion* and Death.* It extends for a period of forty days, exclusive of Sundays, since fasting* never occurs on the Lord's Day. The period of forty days was established from our Lord's ex-

ample (Mt 4). Aptly the season begins with everyone receiving a sprinkling of blessed ashes* on Ash Wednesday.

Import

The twofold character of this season is (1) to perform penance* and (2) to recall or prepare for Baptism.*

(1) The penitential aspect includes various facets, primarily and originally as a period of fasting. The most recent prescription by Pope Paul VI explicitly names Ash Wednesday and Good Friday* as days of both fast and abstinence* and the other Fridays of Lent as days of abstinence. Besides these, penitential practices should be adapted in ways that are possible in our times for different regions, insofar as they fit the circumstances of the People of God.* Such would certainly include longer periods of prayer,* Bible services,* and periods of instruction and enlightenment, as may occur during the Lenten series of sermons, usually beyond those on Sundays. Prepared by eloquent preachers stressing the theme of the Passion,* they should also show consequences of sin and penance as a way to detest sin, since it offends God. More frequent attendance at Mass* and reception of the Sacraments* is expected. The penitential practices are not only internal and individual but social and external, such as almsgiving* and other practices of charity.*

(2) In the early Church one can readily see why the preparation for Baptism was predominant. A study of the Liturgy* of this season amply testifies to that fact; the baptismal features of former times are being restored as efforts toward reestablishing the Rite of Christian Initiation* increase.

The Lenten Liturgy calls us to deepen the sense of our condition as baptized people. We do this most of all by choosing to follow Christ more closely, by becoming in some sense "other Christs."

We are guided in this by our baptismal grace* that illumines us by faith,* renews us by newness of life, rules out all compromise with evil, leads us to community of life and responsibility with our brothers and sisters in the world, and orients us for the Lord's return in glory.*

Lent is thus a time of penance and renewal for the entire Church. It is not enough for us to make commitment to it individually. We must be one with the entire Mystical Body of Christ.*

Ultimately, then, Lent is a time of *doing*. After truly listening, we must *respond* and put into practice what we have learned. In this way, we will bring about the inner conversion to God that is the most fitting preparation for Easter.

Each day in Lent is a Station* day, signifying that the liturgical assembly* went to a specific church in procession to celebrate Mass in Rome. The Station affected the formulary of the Mass, so naturally the daily Lenten Stations are of liturgical interest.

Before the present liturgical calendar,* the two weeks before Easter were called *Passiontide,* for the Liturgy dwelt more heavily upon the Passion and Death of Christ. During this time the statues in churches were veiled, but that practice is now optional. In the United States it has been abrogated by the bishops. *See also* ASHES, BLESSED; BAPTISM; FASTING; RITE OF CHRISTIAN INITIATION OF ADULTS; STATION; VEILING OF IMAGES.

Leo, St. (LEE-oh). c. 400-461. This Pope,* also called "The Great," earned the title not only because of his contributions to the Church* in fighting off several heresies of his day, for which he was declared Doctor of the Church,* but also because of his wisdom in recognizing the need to forge an energetic central authority in the Church that stood for stability, authority, and action. His eloquence persuaded Attila not to sack Rome. He composed many liturgical prayers used in the *Leonine Sacramentary** and some of the Offices of Advent.* *Liturgical celebration:* November 10 (Memorial); *theme:* Papal primacy defends the Church against heresy.

Leonine Prayers (LEE-uh-nain prayrz). Prayers formerly recited in the vernacular* by priest* and people* at the end of Low Mass* by order of Pope Leo XIII (1884). The Hail Mary* was said three times followed by the Hail Holy Queen,* a versicle* and response,* and a prayer for the conversion of sinners and for the freedom and exaltation of the Church.* In 1886 Leo added a prayer to St. Michael* the Archangel, and in 1904 St. Pius X* appended an invocation to the Sacred Heart.* The original reason for the prayers was to right the wrong resulting from the loss of the Papal States. After 1928, when the Lateran Treaty achieved an equitable solution, Pope Pius XI directed that the prayers be continued to obtain the conversion of Russia.

Liturgists had always opposed the use of these prayers on the grounds that the whole Mass is a prayer that can be applied to any intention and there is no need for "extra" prayers. In the renewal brought about by the Second Vati-

can Council,* they were suppressed by the *First Instruction on the Proper Implementation of the Constitution on the Sacred Liturgy, Inter Oecumenici** (1964).

Leonine Sacramentary (LEE-uh-nain sak-ruh-MEN-tuh-ree). Also known as the *Veronese Sacramentary,* this is the oldest *Sacramentary** of the Latin Church. Only one manuscript is extant, dating from the 7th century. Found in the library of the Cathedral Chapter of Verona, it was published by Joseph Bianchini in 1735 and attributed to Pope St. Leo the Great.* The formulas are from the 4th to the 6th centuries, but only a few of them can be reasonably assigned to Pope Leo. There are a few texts of Pope Gelasius (492-496), a few of Pope Vigilius (537-555), and others that cannot be identified with certainty.

The formulas are distributed according to the months of the civil year (with the first three months missing) rather than the Liturgical Year.* There is no Canon* or Ordinary* but only a collection of prayers (Opening Prayer,* Prayer over the Gifts,* Preface,* Prayer after Communion,* and Prayer over the People*) of various Masses as well as ordination texts. Nevertheless, together with the *Gelasian Sacramentary** and the *Gregorian Sacramentary,** it lies at the basis of the *Roman Sacramentary.** *See also* GELASIAN SACRAMENTARY; GREGORIAN SACRAMENTARY; SACRAMENTARY.

Leper Window (LEP-uhr WIN-doh). Low window of a medieval church that provides a view of the altar* from the outside of the building. Lepers, anchorites, and others were thus able to participate in the Liturgy* without mingling with the general congregation.*

Lesser Litanies (LES-uhr LIT-uh-neez). Traditional days of prayer* and penance* that featured a procession* with the singing of the Litany of Saints* and a Rogation Mass* to ask for God's blessing and protection upon the crops of spring and were held on the Monday, Tuesday, and Wednesday before Ascension* Thursday. Known as the "Lesser Litanies" or "Rogation Days," they originated in Gaul at the request of St. Mamertus, Bishop of Vienne (470), but were not adopted by Rome until the 9th century. The liturgical renewal of Vatican II* dropped them from the Roman Calendar* and entrusted such days to the National Conferences of Bishops.* *See also* DAYS OF PRAYER; GREATER LITANIES; ROGATION DAYS.

Lessons. *See* READINGS.

Let Us Give Thanks to the Lord Our God. *See* INTRODUCTORY DIALOGUE.

Let Us Praise the Lord (let uhs prayz thuh lawrd). The translation of the Latin acclamation *Benedicamus Domino.* With its response "And give Him thanks" (*Deo gratias,* which is literally "Thanks be to God") it is the concluding formula for some Hours of the Divine Office.* However, it has been used widely in extraliturgical settings among Christians of all times.

Formerly, it replaced the usual Dismissal* at Mass* in non-festal celebrations. It was used whenever the Glory to God* was omitted. The substitution was made in order to invite the people to remain after Mass and join in with the services to follow. In times past, Masses celebrated during penitential seasons were followed by the singing of Evening Prayer,* so the people were invited to assist the clergy* in this Office. Likewise, after the Midnight Mass at Christmas* the faithful* were invited to stay and sing Morning Prayer* with the priests.

Let Us Pray (let uhs pray). An invitation by the priest* to the people* to prayer* that frequently occurs during Mass* and the Liturgy of the Hours* (in Latin: *Oremus).* Although it is made up of few words, it implies the whole Mystery* of the People of God,* of that People's priesthood* and the priesthood of its ministers. The priest invites the other faithful*—for the priest, being himself baptized, forms part of the faithful—to exercise their baptismal priesthood by prayer.

The priest's role as minister at the service of the community not only allows him to express this invitation but also gives him the right to gather together all the individual prayers and present them to the Father, as one offers several flowers in a bouquet. To this end, this phrase is followed by silence* during which the people may formulate their own petitions. As Father A.M. Roguet has said: "It is here that the faithful exercise 'active participation.' Let them bring to the Mass [and the other services wherein this phrase is used] their pains, their cares, the concerns of their family, and their lawful, professional, apostolic ambitions. Without that, the priest offers only a majestic but empty formula [in the prayer that follows]."

Levate. *See* FLECTAMUS GENUA.

Leviticus, The Book of (luh-VIT-i-kuhs, thuh buk uhv). Third Book of the Old Testament* that continues the ritual laws given by God to Moses on Mount Sinai. (*See* GENESIS, THE BOOK OF.) The name comes from the tribe of Levi, to which the hereditary priesthood belonged; thus it is also known as "the Priest's Handbook." Generally speaking the laws contained in this Book serve to teach the Israelites that they should always keep themselves in a state of legal purity, or external sanctity, as a sign of their intimate union with the Lord. Accordingly, the central idea is contained in the oft-repeated injunction: "You shall be holy, because I, the Lord, am holy."

Liturgical use: This Book is used sparingly in the Liturgy.* In the *Roman Missal,** it is read on the 7th Sunday of Ordinary Time* (A) and the 6th Sunday (B) as well as Monday of the 1st Week of Lent* and

Friday and Saturday of the 17th Week in Ordinary Time (I) and the Common of Saints.* In the *Liturgy of the Hours,** it is assigned to Sunday, Monday, and Tuesday of the 4th Week of Lent.* *Meaning:* God is holy and expects us to be holy, and the Liturgy is of primary help in this regard. All of life is God's and He is concerned with everything we do. His laws teach us how to live in a consecrated way before Him that includes love for neighbor and atonement for sin.

Lex Orandi—Lex Credendi (leks aw-RAHN-dee leks kray-DEN-dee). This is a short form of the celebrated axiom attributed to Pope St. Celestine I (422-432). It is given by Prosper of Aquitaine (d. 463) in its full form as follows: *"ut legem credendi statuat lex supplicandi"*—"that the rule of prayer may establish the rule of faith." The words pinpoint the vital relation that exists between faith* and Liturgy.* In *Mediator Dei** Pope Pius XII broadened the meaning of this axiom by citing a complementary one: "The rule of faith establishes the rule of prayer"—*"lex credendi legem statuat supplicandi"* (MD, 47).

In an address to a general audience on August 6, 1975, Pope Paul VI commented on the relationship in question: "We must all hold fast and joyously to the conviction that the *lex orandi* [rule of prayer] possesses in the *lex credendi* [rule of faith] its guiding light and measure; the rule of faith is the word received; the Liturgy is the word expressed."

The same Pontiff had spelled this out even further in an address to the liturgical experts who worked on the renewal of the Liturgy: "Intense effort must be brought to bear on the agreement of the *lex orandi* [rule of prayer] with the *lex credendi* [rule of faith], so that in its meaning prayer preserves the riches of dogma* and religious language is suited both to the dogmatic realities it bears and to the balanced expression of the scale of values among the realities celebrated" (October 13, 1966).

Libelli [Missarum] (lee-BEL-ee mee-SAH-room). A phrase that may be translated as "Little Mass Book." It contained one or more Mass texts for use of a particular church and came into prominence at the start of liturgical creativity in the Latin language. The best euchological compositions were then collected and gave rise to the *Sacramentary.** The *Leonine Sacramentary** is a prime example of a collection of libelli. *See also* GELASIAN SACRAMENTARY; GREGORIAN SACRAMENTARY; LEONINE SACRAMENTARY; SACRAMENTARY.

Liber Pontificalis (LEE-ber pon-tee-fee-KAH-lees). Latin ("Book of the Popes") book that contains notices about the lives and activities of the Popes from St. Peter* to Pius II (d. 1464). Although it is not an official Church book, it provides valuable information about liturgical practices.

Liber Usualis (LEE-ber oo-zoo-AH-lees). Latin liturgical book that contains the Gregorian Chant* for

℣. Dirigátur Dómine orátio méa.
℟. Sicut incénsum in conspéctu túo.
At Magn. Ant. Et qui praeíbant. *p.* 515.
Cant. Magníficat. 7. a. *p.* 211.

Tuesday.
Hymn. 1.
TEllú-ris álme Cóndi-tor, Múndi sólu

the Propers* of the Sunday Masses* and feasts* that supplant Sundays as well as the Hours of the Divine Office* except Matins* and Lauds.* It also includes the unsung parts. The liturgical renewal of Vatican II* has rendered it obsolete.

Libera Nos (LEE-be-rah nohs). The first two words in Latin ("Deliver Us") of the embolism* recited after the Lord's Prayer* at Mass.* *See also* EMBOLISM.

Liberation and Liturgy (lib-uh-RAY-shuhn and LIT-uhr-jee). Liberation may have various meanings because of the particular context in which it is used or the individual countries about which it is discussed. Basically it should express the all-embracing saving action of God in history, covering all dimensions of human life. The spiritual and cultural dimensions of liberation are based on theological reflection. In liturgical life it is necessary to restore the people's identity and sense of dignity by incorporating elements of their culture in creating a new spirituality* that they can fully recognize as their own. One might wonder if Western Christianity's elements of religious traditions must overshadow the symbolism* and rites* of other religions. Genuine spirituality must always be based on the centrality of the Eucharist,* which is the true celebration of us as humans in a community. Our struggles may be with ourselves or with others, against idolatries or against false spiritualities.

Spirituality thus developed is interrelated to commitment. It will occur differently in different places. For instance, in Latin America the basic Christian communities show how prayer and action mutually reinforce each other. The act of thanksgiving in the Mass* constantly challenges us to search for appropriate relationships in social, economic, and political life. Liberation in the Liturgy is not totally dependent on the text, but on the context of the situation, which then allows the worship* to be a liberating event. The spiritual force that results should lead all to help in the struggle against destitution and oppression. *See also* ADAPTATION, LITURGICAL.

Life (laif). The life of a Christian may be termed a Liturgy* in the sense that it is an offering made to God of one's whole existence in union with Christ (see Rom 1:9; 12:1; Phil 3:3). This liturgical orientation is possible only by active participation* in the life-giving Sacraments* of the Church. Christians are born to the Faith* in Baptism,* mature in that life through Confirmation,* are nourished in that life by the Eucharist,* and are restored to that life by Penance.* Holy Orders* provides the Church with qualified representatives of Christ to impart that life, Marriage* sanctifies all of family life, and the Anointing of the Sick* prepares Christians for the definitive encounter with the Lord that they have encountered in the Sacraments while on earth. Thus, the Christian life never ceases going from one Liturgy to another.

However, to live this liturgical life, Christians must also make good use of personal prayer* and contemplation* in preparation for liturgical celebrations* and in prolongation of them. In this way, the Liturgy will be sure to be the major part of their everyday lives. Pope John Paul II showed how this can be done with special emphasis on the Eucharist:

"It is from the Eucharist that all of us receive the grace* and strength for daily living—to live real Christian lives, in the joy of knowing that God loves us, that Christ died for us, and that the Holy Spirit* lives in us.

"Our full participation in the Eucharist is the real source of the Christian spirit that we wish to see in our personal lives and in all aspects of society. Whether we serve in politics, in the economic, cultural, social, or scientific field—no matter what our occupation is—the Eucharist is a challenge to our daily lives. . . .

"Our union with Christ in the Eucharist must be expressed in the truth of our lives today—in our actions, in our behavior, in our life style, and in our relationships with others. For each one of us the Eucharist is a call to ever greater effort, so that we may live as true followers of Jesus: truthful in our speech, generous in our deeds, concerned, respectful of the dignity and rights of all persons, whatever their rank or income, self-sacrificing, fair and just, kind, considerate, compassionate and self-controlled—looking to the well-being of our families, our young people, our country, Europe and the world.

"The truth of our union with Jesus Christ in the Eucharist is tested by whether or not we really

love our fellow men and women; it is tested by how we treat others, especially our families: husbands and wives, children and parents, brothers and sisters. It is tested by whether or not we try to be reconciled with our enemies, on whether or not we forgive those who hurt us or offend us. It is tested by whether we practice in life what our faith teaches us" (Homily at Phoenix Park, Dublin, September 29, 1979).

Lift Up Your Hearts. *See* INTRODUCTORY DIALOGUE.

Light (lait). As a natural phenomenon connected with the day, the sun, the moon, and the stars, light is one of the vital forces of nature that human beings master (though only partially) and utilize. The sun and light are the necessary conditions for all material life and growth. Used analogically, light means everything that is beautiful and good; that which is enlightenment, knowledge, and wisdom. "To come to the light" means to be born. "To see in the light" means to understand. "To be illumined" means to be open. "To receive the light" means to be transfigured.

In the Liturgy,* we learn that the Son is "Light from Light, true God from true God" (Nicene Creed* in the Ordinary*) for God is Light (Christmas Mass at Midnight—Reading I*; 3rd Sunday in Ordinary Time, A—Responsorial Psalm*). Light also are God's law (17th Sunday in Ordinary Time, A—Responsorial Psalm) and God's Word (1st Sunday of Advent, A—Reading I). Jesus is the Light of the world* (4th Sunday of Lent, A—Gospel*; Easter Vigil: Service of Light). Those who believe in and follow Him become themselves reflections of Christ's light to the world (5th Sunday in Ordinary Time, A—Gospel). *See also* CANDLES AND LIGHTS.

Lights. *See* CANDLES AND LIGHTS.

Lindisfarne Gospels (LIND-uhs-fahrn GOS-puhlz). Manuscript copy of the Gospels* from the Vulgate* written around 700 on the island of Lindisfarne off the coast of Northumbria, England. Noted for its illuminated initial letters, magnificent illustrations, and ornamental designs, it now rests in the British Museum in London.

The Gospels are each preceded by a table of contents and a list of feast days, which seem to have come from the Liturgy* of the Church of Naples around the beginning of the 7th century. Scholars believe the copied manuscript was brought to England by Hadrian abbot* of a monastery near Naples, when he came to visit in 688 with Archbishop Theodore of Tarsus. Others believe the bearer was Benedict Biscop.

The copier is thought to have been Bishop Eadfrid. Around 950 the priest* Aldred inserted an interlinear Anglo-Saxon translation (in the Northumbrian dialect) of the Latin, making it the earliest version of the Gospels in English.

Linens, Sacred (LIN-uhnz, SAY-kruhd). A collective term for the following furnishings used at Mass: altar cloth,* corporal,* pall,* purificator.*

Litanies (LIT-[uh-]neez). Popular responsorial prayers made up of petitions or invocations sung or said by a leader, to which the faithful* answer an affixed response. The Church* has utilized litanies (from the Greek word for "entreaties") from the beginning. The litany was a part of Jewish worship (note Psalm 136 with the repetition of the refrain: "for his mercy endures forever"), and it was recommended by St. Paul* to the Christians at Ephesus (1 Tm 2:1-4). It also figured prominently in the earliest extant accounts of the celebration of the Eucharist* (the *Apostolic Tradition** of Hippolytus and the *Anaphora* of Serapion*).

Prayers of the Faithful* were also included before the Offering of the Gifts. In the 4th century a similar prayer was recited at Antioch by the deacon* and people, and it was later incorporated into the Roman Liturgy. Pope Gelasius* (492-496) composed new texts of such litanies and assigned them to be used before the Readings.* Pope Gregory the Great* (590-604) restricted the use of the litanies to feast days and retained only the Kyrie* for every Mass. A vestige of the ancient use of litanies remains in the General Intercessions* of the Liturgy of the Word* on Good Friday.*

In time, litanies also came to refer to processions* during which they were said. This gave rise to the Lenten Stational Churches* (7th century) in which the Pope and people solemnly processed to a particular church (known as a *station* from the usual Latin word applied to Christians at worship) to celebrate Mass.* It also resulted in the Greater Litanies* on April 25 and the Lesser Litanies* on Rogation Days before the Ascension.*

In addition, more and more litanies came into vogue. In 1601 there were said to be some eighty in use. The Church stepped in to restrict their use in liturgical worship. Today, the Lord Have Mercy* and the Lamb of God* in the Mass are forms of litanies. The newly revised General Intercessions at the conclusion of the Liturgy of the Word is an ancient litany. In the *Pastoral Care of the Sick,** there is a very abbreviated form of a litany (of the Saints) with several optional formulas.

Most popular litanies have a precise structure, beginning with an invocation to each person of the Trinity,* followed by a series of petitions according to a specific theme; thereupon three invocations to the Lamb of God occur, and they conclude with a short oration that capsulizes the petitions enunciated above.

The litanies approved for use in public worship are found in the *Roman Ritual.** They are also named and given a partial indulgence in the *Enchiridion of Indulgences.** They now number seven: Holy Name,* Sacred Heart of Jesus,* Precious Blood,* Blessed Virgin Mary (two forms: Loreto* and Queenship, which is part of the *Order of Crowning an Image of the Blessed Virgin Mary*),* St. Joseph,* and All Saints* (two forms). Many other litanies have been approved for private use of the faithful. *See also* GREATER LITANIES; LESSER LITANIES; STATIONAL CHURCHES.

Litany of Loreto (LIT-[uh-]nee uhv luh-RET-oh). A litany sung in honor of Mary* at May services, Benediction,* and at the end of a common Hour of the Divine Office* by some congregations. Approved for use in public worship* in 1587 by Pope Sixtus V,* it takes its name from the famous Italian shrine where its use is attested for the year 1558 (but its existence far antedates this date). The last four invocations (concerning the Immaculate Conception,* Assumption,* Rosary,* and Peace) as well as the invocation "Mother of the Church"* are late additions made by the Holy See* itself, as occasion warranted. There seems little doubt that the Litany dates from between 1150 and 1200 and was probably of Parisian origins, or its environs. It is found in the *Roman Ritual** and *Enchiridion of Indulgences.**

The list of praises to Mary (49 titles) owes much to prayers of the Greek Church, in particular to the Akathist Hymn* (translated into Latin and first published at Venice, about the year 800). Originally, the Litany counted some 15 more invocations, among which were: Our Lady of Humility, Mother of Mercy, Temple of the Spirit, Gate of Redemption, and Queen of Disciples.

The first 20 invocations are Marian praises addressed to Mary as *Mother* and *Virgin;* the next 13 are remarkable descriptions of her *office, power,* or *virtues.* Four *common* titles follow, and then twelve address Mary as *Queen.* The Litany concludes with the Opening Prayer* from the Common* of the Blessed Virgin Mary. Although some people have criticized the titles as extravagant, they are based on the writings of the Fathers* of the first six centuries.

The alternation of admiring contemplation and confident supplication found in these titles makes the Litany a simple yet powerful prayer in honor of our Lady. *See also* LITANIES; LITANY OF THE BLESSED VIRGIN MARY.

Litany of St. Joseph (LIT-[uh-]nee uhv saynt JOH-zuhf; -suhf). Litany modeled after that of Loreto* and approved for use in public worship* by Pope St. Pius X* in 1909. It contains 21 specific invocations to St. Joseph detailing his virtues and his dignity as foster-father of the Word Incarnate. The charm and devotion that pervade these invocations make this Litany ideal for public or private prayer in honor of St. Joseph. It is found in the *Roman Ritual** and the *Enchiridion of Indulgences.** *See also* LITANIES.

Litany of the Blessed Virgin Mary (LIT-[uh-]nee uhv thuh BLES-uhd VUHR-juhn MAYR-ee). Newest approved Litany for use in public worship* that forms part of the new *Order of Crowning an Image of the Blessed Virgin Mary,** promulgated in Latin in 1981 and in English in 1987. It nicely blends traditional and modern elements in a Litany that is especially suited to be prayed privately and meditated upon.

It has been drawn up especially with the people in mind and includes well-known *traditional elements* that appeal to us at once: the opening threefold invocation, *Lord, have mercy;* the beloved response, *pray for us;* the first three invocations to Mary, *Holy Mary, Holy Mother of God, Most honored of virgins;* and the triple imploration of the *Lamb of God* at the end.

The heart of the Litany lies in its emphasis on Mary's Queenship. It defines the *specific area* of her Queenship: she is Queen of *charity,* because she excels in *love** (and love is essential for the follower of Christ). And she exercises her influence over the souls of the faithful* so that they may attain *love.* Finally, as Queen of love, Mary is also *Queen of mercy* and *Queen of peace,* for mercy and peace flow from love.

The Litany also sets down the *groups* (angelical, Old Testament,* and New Testament*) over whom Mary is Queen because of the depth of her service and the purity of her love. These are: *Angels, Patriarchs, Prophets, Apostles, Martyrs, Confessors, Virgins,* and *All Saints.*

Lastly, the *boundaries* of Mary's Kingdom are delineated and they are the same as those of her Son's Kingdom: she is *Queen of all the earth, of heaven,* and *of the universe.*

This modern and inspiring Litany is based on the *finest sources,* and they are clearly evident as we voice the invocations: (a) Sacred Scripture*: *Virgin Daughter of Zion; Handmaid of the Lord; Woman clothed with the stars.* (b) Formulas of Previous Litanies: the first three invocations are from the Litany of the Saints*; the group of invocations from *Queen of Angels* to *Queen conceived without original sin* are from the Litany of Loreto.* (c) Documents of Vatican II: *Finest fruit of the Redemption* (SC, 103); *Queen of the universe* and *Helper of the Redeemer* (LG, 59, 61). (d) Liturgical Texts: *Advocate of grace* (Preface for December 8), *Queen of heaven, Queen of all the earth,* and *Queen of mercy. See also* LITANY OF LORETO.

Litany of the Dying (LIT-[uh-]nee uhv thuh DAI-ing). Extremely short form of the Litany of the Saints* that forms part of the Anointing of the Sick* for those close to death. It calls down God's loving mercy on the person who will soon be judged by Him. *See also* LITANY OF THE SAINTS.

Litany of the Most Holy Name of Jesus (LIT-[uh-]nee uhv thuh mohst HOH-lee naym uhv JEE-zuhs; -zuhz). This Litany is patterned after the Litany of Loreto* and includes 51 invocations to the Name of Jesus. It was probably composed by St. Bernardine of Siena* and St. John Capistran* in the 15th century and approved for private use by Sixtus V in 1585. In 1862 the present form was approved by Pius IX for local usage, and in 1866 Leo XIII approved it for use in the public worship* of the Universal Church.* It is found in the *Roman Ritual** and the *Enchiridion of Indulgences.* * *See also* LITANIES.

Litany of the Precious Blood of Jesus (LIT-[uh-]nee uhv thuh PRESH-uhs bluhd uhv JEE-zuhs; zuhz). Litany promulgated by Pope John XXIII on February 24, 1960, to be inserted in the approved Litanies of the Church in the *Roman Ritual.** It was drawn up by the Sacred Congregation of Rites* to honor Jesus in His most Precious Blood,* a devotion popularized by St. Gaspar del Bufalo (1786-1837). It contains 24 invocations to the Precious Blood, to which the response is "Save us." The Blood refers to the physical Blood in some invocations, to the Humanity of Christ in others, and to both aspects in the remaining ones. The Litany is found in the *Enchiridion of Indulgences.* * *See also* LITANIES.

Litany of the Sacred Heart of Jesus (LIT-[uh-]nee uhv thuh SAY-kruhd hahrt uhv JEE-zuhs; -zuhz). This Litany was derived from one composed at Marseille in 1718 by Venerable Anne Madeleine Remuzat that had 27 invocations, 17 of which had come from a litany of Father Croiset (1691). The Sacred Congregation of Rites* added six more from a series composed by Sister Madeleine Joly at Dijon in 1686. This Litany was approved for public worship* by Pope Leo XIII in 1899. Its 33 invocations to the Heart* of Jesus each express some aspect of God's love for human be-

ings symbolized by the physical Heart of Jesus, the Son of God, Who became Man and died to save the world.* It is found in the *Roman Ritual** and the *Enchiridion of Indulgences.** *See also* LITANIES.

Litany of the Saints (LIT-[uh-]nee uhv thuh saynts). The oldest litany we possess, and the model for all the others. It was used as early as 590 by direct prescription of Pope St. Gregory the Great* for a public procession* of thanksgiving. Its name comes from the fact that in one part a number of Saints* are invoked, to each of which the congregation responds "Pray for us."

The recent revision of this Litany offers two versions, one short and the other long. The former is employed during Mass* at rites: for instance, the blessing of the baptismal font* during the Easter Vigil,* dedication of a church,* and ordinations.* Variations are allowed in the list of Saints and the petitions, to suit the occasion.

A very truncated form of this Litany is used in the Anointing of the Sick* when the person is at the point of death.

This most official type of Litany is divided into sections: (1) the introductory *Lord have mercy** with invocations to the Trinity*; (2) the series of Saints; (3) entreaties for deliverance; (4) supplications for deliverance because of events in Christ's redemptive life; (5) the intercessions, based on early Christian prayer forms; (6) the invocation Lamb of God*; (7) Psalm 70; and (8) a series of concluding prayers.

This Litany is found in the *Roman Ritual** and the *Enchiridion of Indulgences.** *See also* GREATER LITANIES; LESSER LITANIES; LITANIES; LITANY OF THE DYING.

Little Elevation. *See* ELEVATION, LITTLE.

Little Hours. *See* DAYTIME PRAYER.

Little Office of the Blessed Virgin (LIT-uhl OF-uhs uhv thuh BLES-uhd VUHR-juhn). An Office* recited in honor of our Lady, much shortened in form and differentiated from the Divine Office* obligatory upon priests* and nuns* and professed regular Religious.* It is comprised of seven Hours,* and its Psalms* do not vary from day to day. It developed as a private devotion in the 11th century, and at one time it was compulsory on Saturdays. Eventually the optional Office of the Blessed Virgin on Saturdays supplanted it; Pius V* relieved everyone of the obligation to say it on Saturday. After the Council of Trent, several modern congregations of Religious women adopted it as their sole choral Office in place of the Divine Office.

Recitation of any short Office after the pattern of the *Liturgy of the Hours,* by virtue of the Institute's Constitutions, is considered part of the public prayer of the Church according to the decision of Vatican II.* Because many of the newer versions allow for seasonal variations, the majority of such congregations have adopted the current one volume *Liturgy of the Hours* entitled *Christian Prayer.*

Nonetheless recent attempts have been made to revise the *Little Office.* One is an Italian edition with the approbation of the Sacred Congregation of Divine Worship.* Another is an English edition based loosely on it and drawing most of its material from the *Liturgy of the Hours.* Entitled the *Little Office of the Blessed Virgin Mary* (1988), it features the same elements as the *Liturgy of the Hours:* Biblical texts with more or less direct reference to the Mystery* of Mary, with variable Psalms with proper antiphons,* responsories,* intercessions,* and prayers*—all Marian in character.

Its originality lies precisely in this emphasis given to the person of Mary, who nonetheless never appears in isolated fashion. She is always portrayed as part of the History of Salvation,* as the admirable fruit of the Divine Power, as the Mother of the Lord, or as the image of the Church. Hence, the *Little Office* is a way of living—in praise and reflection—the principal moments of each day with Mary, who spent her life alongside her Son in ardent love, in joyous praise, and in deep faith. *See also* CHRISTIAN PRAYER; LITURGY OF THE HOURS.

Liturgicae Instaurationes (lee-toor-JEE-chay in-stow-rah-tsee-OH-nez). Latin title (from the first two words "Liturgical Renewal") of the *Third Instruction on the Proper Implementation of the Constitution on the Sacred Liturgy* issued by the Sacred Congregation for Divine Worship* on September 5, 1970. It gives a general review of the reasons for the liturgical renewal, speaks of the necessity of liturgical catechesis,* stresses that the rules must be obeyed by all, forbids the alteration, omission, or substitution of official texts (no secular texts may be used during the Liturgy of the Word*), and warns against the assembly* taking the parts of the celebrant* (for example, the Eucharistic Prayer*). It also lists the functions that may be performed by women: (1) reader*; (2) leader of song*; (3) commentator*; and (4) usher*—but not altar girl. *See also* INTER OECUMENICI; TRES ABHINC ANNOS.

Liturgical Actions (luh-TUHR-ji-kuhl, li-; AK-shuhnz). Sacred acts that by institution of Jesus or the Church,* and in the name of the whole Mystical Body* of Christ (both Head and members) in accord with what is written in liturgical books* approved by the Holy See,* are carried out by persons lawfully deputed by the authority of the Church. The New *Code of Canon Law* specifies them still further: "Liturgical acts are not private actions but celebrations of the Church itself, which is 'the sacrament of unity,' namely, a holy people assembled and ordered under the bishops; therefore liturgical actions pertain to the whole body of the Church and manifest and affect it, but they affect the individual members of the Church in different ways according to the diversity of orders, functions and actual participation" (Can. 837).

The power to perform liturgical acts stems from the Christians' share in Christ's priesthood*—either the ministerial priesthood* received through Holy Orders* or the universal priesthood* received through Baptism.* Such an action enables Christians to share in the redemptive power of Christ's acts that are being commemorated and renewed. *See also* LITURGY; LITURGY—PARTICIPATION; WORSHIP.

Liturgical Adaptation. *See* ADAPTATION, LITURGICAL.

Liturgical Apostolate. *See* LITURGICAL MOVEMENT.

Liturgical Archeology. *See* ARCHEOLOGY, LITURGICAL.

Liturgical Art. *See* ART AND LITURGY.

Liturgical Assembly. *See* ASSEMBLY, LITURGICAL.

Liturgical Books (luh-TUHR-ji-kuhl; li-; buks). Official collection (approved by competent authority) of texts to be chanted or recited, of rites to be practiced, and of rules to be followed in public worship.* Approbation to publish such official books is reserved to the Holy See* or to competent authority with the approval of the Holy See. Typical editions* are printed by the Vatican printing office under the control of the *Congregation for Divine Worship and the Discipline of the Sacraments.* * Reproduction of these editions, usually in the vernacular,* is entrusted to the Conference of Bishops* who have a censor verify their conformity to the typical edition. In this case the authorization given to the publisher to print includes a *Concordat Cum Originali,* "It agrees with the original."

Historically each liturgical book contained only the part of the Liturgy* that each player needed for his or her role in the religious drama. All were controlled by the master of ceremonies,* whose personal liturgical book, the *Ordo,* contained no text but the beginning of all the parts and the rubrics* or order to be followed.

In a decree* of August 10, 1946, the Congregation of Rites* listed the liturgical books of the Roman Rite* as: the *Roman Missal,* * *Roman Ritual,* * *Roman Pontifical,* * *Roman Martyrology,* * *Ceremonial* * *of Bishops, Memoriale Rituum,* * *Octavarium,* * and the collection of *Decreta Authentica* (Authentic Decrees) of the Congregation of Rites, not including books of chant, such as the *Roman Gradual** and the *Roman Antiphonary,* * and sections of these books, such as the *Roman Calendar.* *

The most important of these post-Tridentine liturgical books are: (1) the *Roman Missal* for the Eucharist (1570), (2) the *Roman Pontifical* (1596) and (3) the *Roman Ritual* (1614) for the other Sacraments* and Rites,* and (4) the *Roman Breviary* (1568) for the daily prayer of the Church.* These remained relatively unchanged till the 20th century. Then the reforms of St. Pius X,* Pius XII, and John XXIII-Paul VI (through the Second Vatican Council*) led up to their complete revision.

The Latin typical editions* began appearing in 1969. The *Roman Missal* was issued in three parts: (1) the *Order of Mass* (April 6, 1969), (2) the *Lectionary for Mass** (order of readings, May 25, 1969; second typical edition, January 21, 1981), and (3) *Missal* (presidential prayers or *Sacramentary,** March 26, 1970).

The *Roman Ritual* was issued in nine parts: (1) *Rite of Marriage** (March 19, 1969), (2) *Rite of Baptism* for Children* (May 15, 1969), (3) *Rite of Funerals** (August 15, 1969), (4) *Rite of Religious Profession** (February 2, 1970), (5) *Rite of Christian Initiation of Adults** (January 6, 1972), (6) *Rite of Anointing and Pastoral Care of the Sick** (December 7, 1972), (7) *Holy Communion and Worship of the Eucharist outside Mass** (June 21, 1973), (8) *Rite of Penance** (December 2, 1973), and (9) *Book of Blessings** (May 31, 1984).

The *Roman Pontifical* was issued in eight parts: (1) *Ordination* of Deacons, Priests, and Bishops* (August 15, 1968), (2) *Rite of Consecration* to a Life of Virginity* (May 31, 1970), (3) *Rite of Blessing* an Abbot or Abbess* (November 9, 1970), (4) *Rite of Blessing Oils,* Rite of Consecrating the Chrism** (December 3, 1970), (5) *Rite of Confirmation** (August 22, 1971), (6) *Rite of Institution of Readers* and Acolytes, etc.* (December 3, 1972), (7) *Dedication of a Church* and an Altar* (May 29, 1977), and (8) *Order of Crowning an Image of the Blessed Virgin Mary** (March 25, 1981). Its related volume, the *Ceremonial of Bishops,* was issued on September 14, 1984.

The *Roman Breviary* was issued under a new name, the *Liturgy of the Hours,** on April 11, 1971.

The *Simple Gradual* was published in 1967 and 1974 and the *Roman Antiphonary* in 1983.

On January 25, 1983, the new *Code of Canon Law** was promulgated as a means of enabling the Church to fulfill her mission in a manner more in keeping with the intent and teaching of the Second Vatican Council. As Canon 2 states, the existing liturgical books remain in force, but anything in them that is contrary to the new Code is to be emended. Thus, on September 12, 1983, the Congregation for the Sacraments and Divine Worship issued *Emendations in the Liturgical Books Following upon the New Code of Canon Law,* indicating the slight changes that were to be made upon new publication of the liturgical books.

All liturgical books should be attractively bound, a credit to the purpose for which they are made. Those that are carried in procession, such as the *Book of Gospels,** the *Sacramentary,* and the *Ritual,* which are commonly obvious to the congregation during liturgical services, may be ornamentally handsome. *See also* ANTIPHONARY; BREVIARY; CALENDAR; CEREMONIAL; FORMULAS, LITURGICAL; GRADUAL, ROMAN; MARTYROLOGY; MEMORIALE RITUUM; MISSAL; MISSALE PARVUM; OCTAVARIUM ROMANUM; ORDO; PONTIFICAL; PROPERS; RITUAL; SACRAMENTARY.

In the Eastern Church,* the offices are arranged in separate books, each containing only the parts of those who use them—the celebrant,* the deacon,* the choir,* and the like—which was formerly the case in the Latin Church.

The most important liturgical books of the Byzantine Church are: (1) the *Euchologion** (for priests and deacons), (2) the *Horologion** (containing the Ordinary of the canonical Hours* for readers* and singers), (3) the *Menaion** (the propers* of fixed feasts* throughout the year), (4) the *Typicon** (containing the ceremonies and rubrics like the Western *Ordo* in the past), (5) the *Archieratikon* (like the *Roman Pontifical**) and (6) the *Menelogion** (like the *Martyrology*).

There are also the books for the choir: (1) the *Oktoechos* or *Parakletike* (eight sets of Sunday propers), (2) the *Triodion* (propers for Lent*), and (3) the *Pentekostarion* (propers from Easter* to Pentecost*).

The liturgical books of the Maronite Rite* and the Malabar Rite* follow the Roman pattern.

Liturgical Calendar. *See* CALENDAR.

Liturgical Celebrations. *See* CELEBRATION; LITURGY—PARTICIPATION.

Liturgical Commissions (luh-TUHR-ji-kuhl; li-; kuh-MISH-uhnz). To promote and restore the Liturgy* is a distinguishing mark in the Church's life today. Liturgical commissions are set up to enable this pastoral-liturgical action to be more vigorous.

(1) The local bishops' conference in the United States is the National Conference of Catholic Bishops.* To aid them in this regard the bishops appointed the Bishops' Committee on the Liturgy*; later on the Federation of Diocesan Liturgical Commissions* was formed, from which they receive much input.

(2) At the diocesan level, a diocesan liturgical commission should exist, although sometimes several contiguous dioceses* may form one. Usually commissions for sacred music* and sacred art* may be part of this commission or at least work in close harmony with it. The duties of such commissions, under the direction of the bishop, are to remain informed about the pastoral-liturgical action in the diocese, to implement the programs, to promote practical undertakings in order to achieve this end, to suggest progressive steps in Pastoral Liturgy,* calling upon capable persons to help the ministers,* and to develop a harmonious spirit among other associations in order to expedite liturgical progress.

The bishop as high priest of his flock and moderator of the Liturgy should be anxious to receive help from this advisory body in his task as leader of worship* for the diocese. Owing to the size and diversity of this country, the NCCB has referred judgments or decisions to local bishops with regard to certain adaptations allowed them by the *Constitution on the Sacred Liturgy.**

In many of these cases the bishop will consult with the diocesan liturgical commission, or maybe even leave the administration of certain details in its hands, such as materials for sacred furnishings, the method of exchanging the Sign of Peace,* and the observance of days of prayer.* *See also* BISHOPS' COMMITTEE ON THE LITURGY; FEDERATION OF DIOCESAN LITURGICAL COMMISSIONS.

Liturgical Creativity. *See* CREATIVITY IN LITURGY.

Liturgical Dancing. *See* DANCING, LITURGICAL.

Liturgical Direction. *See* ORIENTATION.

Liturgical Drama (luh-TUHR-ji-kuhl; li-; DRAH-muh; DRAM-uh). During the Middle Ages plays on religious topics, usually in conjunction with the liturgical text* or Scripture reading,* were acted out during a service. At first they were at the introduction of the Mass,* but eventually they moved to the end of Matins,* which allowed greater liberty toward artistic development, so that they became rather elaborate stage productions with musical forms, costumes, and pageantry. They were intended to be instructive and entertaining. However, most participants and spectators eventually turned from them to secular drama. Recently a revival of interest has occurred, and there has been speculation as to whether liturgical reform will find some aspect of these dramatic presentations appropriate in the Liturgy of the Word* during Mass.

Liturgical Experimentation. *See* EXPERIMENTATION, LITURGICAL.

Liturgical Families (luh-TUHR-ji-kuhl; li-; FAM-uh-leez). Liturgies that possess similar characteristics. They derive from the differentiation and polarization in the liturgical nucleus based on complex historical, geographical, cultural, and linguistic factors. In the West, we can distinguish the Gallican, Celtic, Hispanic, Ambrosian,* and Roman* Families. In the East, there are the Antiochene* and the Alexandrian* Families.

Liturgical Formation (luh-TUHR-ji-kuhl; -li; fawr-MAY-shuhn). The procedure by which the total community, both laity* and clergy,* is instructed in the intent and objectives of the Liturgy* with its various rites.

For the Faithful

The purpose of such instruction is to promote not only the understanding of the Liturgy but also the active and full participation* of the faithful* together with an amalgamation of the true liturgical spirit* in their religious lives. In order that the pastors* may readily lead their flock by word and example as one of their chief duties, they are to take into consideration such matters as the age, the condition, the way of life, and the religious culture of the people. Naturally then, those already active in the pastoral ministry must update themselves with regard to the liturgical advancements, so that they truly understand their actions during sacred rites, living the liturgical life to the full as they share it with the faithful.

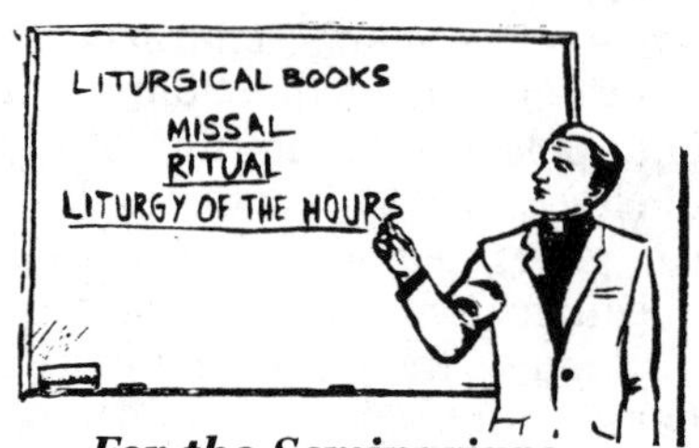

For the Seminarians

Liturgical instruction during seminary years has been raised from its ancillary position to one of prime importance. First of all, professors appointed to teach Liturgy are to be properly educated as specialists in this subject, since the Liturgy is now a compulsory and major course in theological studies. Furthermore, the other professors are to explain how their subjects relate to the Liturgy.

Over and beyond the formal education in Liturgy, the clerics are to experience a liturgical formation in their own spiritual lives. Not only must they understand the rites, but they must also take part in them enthusiastically and understand popular devotions in relation to the spirit of the Liturgy. Observance of liturgical law* ought to be able to influence seminary life in a truly religious manner. Liturgical formation, begun in seminary years, is to continue beyond the years of liturgical reform, and for the individual it becomes a continuing process. In-service liturgical education should always be in style. *See also* CATECHESIS AND LITURGY; LITURGY—PARTICIPATION; OPTATAM TOTIUS.

Liturgical Formulas. *See* FORMULAS, LITURGICAL.

Liturgical Functions. *See* LITURGY—PARTICIPATION.

Liturgical Innovations. *See* INNOVATIONS, LITURGICAL.

Liturgical Inspiration. *See* INSPIRATION.

Liturgical Instruction. *See* LITURGICAL FORMATION.

Liturgical Language. *See* VERNACULAR.

Liturgical Language—Latin (luh-TUHR-ji-kuhl; li-; LANG-wij—LAT-uhn). Although the celebrations of the Liturgy* used the vernacular* in the beginning, by the 4th century Latin became the liturgical language of the Western Church. To a certain extent it was the vernacular of the West, since it was the language of learning and culture there. With its stylistic beauty it overpowered the poorly developed argot of the barbarian nations. Later on other reasons were cited: tradition; the fact that Sacramental efficacy happens by virtue of the rite performed; a language common to all signifies Church unity.

By the time of Vatican II,* the realization that the proper performance of the Liturgy demands active participation* by the faithful* brought about an authorized extensive use of the vernacular in the Liturgy. Thus the congregation can easily understand the liturgical texts that are to declare clearly the holy things they signify.

According to a 1980 world survey of the use of Latin in the Liturgy, Latin is disappearing as the liturgical language of the Church. Its use is marginal, usually for practical reasons of celebrations occurring in multilingual regions or international meetings by priests* who do not know the language of the country they are visiting. Considering the total responses, less than 16 percent indicated a demand for Latin, these mostly by older people or those with an above-average level of intelligence. In those cases where the Mass in Latin was scheduled at the request of parishioners, low attendance eventually gave reason to cancel it.

In certain areas select groups show interest in the spiritual and musical value of Gregorian Chant,* but in most cases their repertory is limited to those chants easily performed.

The Tridentine Mass

The name "Tridentine Mass" refers to the Mass celebrated in Latin, according to the Apostolic Constitution *Quo Primum Tempore* of St. Pius V* published in 1570. This form of a Latin Mass was celebrated, with minor changes, up to the modifications that occurred as a result of Vatican II.

In the Church today, there are a very small, but active, minority insisting that they want only the Tridentine Mass, going so far as to repudiate the decisions of Vatican II. For the most part they are led by Archbishop Lefebvre. Some groups go their own way and are unwilling to try to resolve the issue, thus creating, as in the United States, autonomous "churches." The overwhelming consensus from the bishops* is that granting any concession with regard to the Tridentine Mass would not solve the problem. Instead it might develop an attitude of disdain for the decisions of the Council and wound the unity of the Church. Rather it would seem more wise to allow this group to die out.

Nevertheless, as of October 1984, Pope John Paul II has allowed the celebration of the Tridentine Mass under strictly controlled circumstances, and the bishops must report back to the Vatican on any requests. The decision is not meant to undermine the updated Mass rituals currently in vogue, nor as a concession to Archbishop Lefebvre. The 1962 Edition of the *Missale Romanum* for the United States is the one that includes all the changes of the *New Code of Rubrics of the Roman Breviary and Missal* of 1960 and must be followed according to this indult.*

Liturgical Law (luh-TUHR-ji-kuhl; li-; law). Ecclesiastical ordinances legislating worship.* Sections of the *Code of Canon Law* pertain. However, most laws are found in liturgical books,* in which rubrics* detail the ceremony. One book of this nature, a compendium of rubrics, is the *Ceremonial.** In the realm of

official cult, private initiatives might lead to fanciful novelties and could threaten the dignity and true meaning of the ceremonies. To legislate in liturgical matters is still reserved to the Holy See,* ordinarily exercised through the Congregation for Divine Worship and the Discipline of the Sacraments.* The collection of the *Decrees of the Sacred Congregation of Rites* (former name) contains the decisions, year after year, century after century, to form a record of the liturgical life of the Church.*

In keeping with the revision of liturgical books, ecclesiastical laws governing public worship are also revised. They occur in liturgical books, in Apostolic Constitutions* and other documents of the Popes, in decrees* and instructions* of the Roman Congregations, and as such have the force of law, unless they should be contrary to the legislation of the new *Code of Canon Law* (Can. 2). Actually the new Code contains a minimum of liturgical law. Certain aspects of liturgical law since the publication of the encyclical *Mediator Dei** in 1947 deserve consideration.

Changes

(1) *In style.* Rather than governing each detail, which would allow little freedom and flexibility, the legislation is directed to the rite as a whole and its effects. Details then fit into a pastoral context and should indicate the purpose the rite is to attain. Consequently, it implies a new type of obedience, for it almost insists that options* be used to reach the goal of the liturgical ceremony. In taking the whole rite into consideration, its symbolic function is to generate a truly spiritual effect in all those celebrating it.

(2) *In the theological context.* The flexibility allowed by the new legislation brings a different focus; rather than the Liturgy* being something the Church *does,* it now becomes a disclosure of what the Church *is.* Formerly concern was on things; now, beyond matter, form, prayers,* gestures,* it influences symbolic actions in the agents: namely, the persons involved, the minister,* the congregation,* Christ Himself. The Sacramental union of God and His people is brought about by the minister in his active role as the leader of prayer.

(3) *In the spirit.* In the past faithful observance to the rubrics sufficed; now pastors* must fulfill also the spirit of liturgical legislation. There are higher principles governing the choices of options and adaptations.* They are not expressly legislated but are seen more as intrinsic, implicit from the nature of the Church and the Liturgy and their interrelationship.

Principles

(1) *The Church as Mystery.* The Liturgy expresses the Mystery* of the Church, which needs continuous reexamination, since she is continually developing with the passage of time. After the Council of Trent, life moved on, but the Liturgy stagnated. Now new liturgical forms arise organically from existing ones, but in relation to cultural changes. With the same goals as the Church, the Liturgy directs itself first of all to the worship of God. Yet it may serve other needs too: ecumenical, missionary, catechetical. To be truly Catholic and universal, the Liturgy must express the Mystery of the Church in more than one prayer or rite. Adaptation and variety is expected to be offered to the different cultures by reason of the Church's catholicity.

Liturgy, as the prayer life of the Church, is closely related to its faith and morals; that is why the Church regulates the Liturgy. When the People of God experience liturgically the Paschal Mystery,* they find one of the principal sources of faith.* Thus, the Liturgy is a theological source and hence the

law not only governs the activity of the Church but also keeps authentic the essence of the Church

(2) *The hierarchic and communal nature of the Liturgy.* The entire Church prays in the Liturgy, in each member's particular role; consequently the community, which includes the active participation of the laity,* is to be an experience that expresses the total community's responsibility for the Liturgy. Because the Liturgy as a public prayer makes visible the Mystery, there is a sign value to every celebration. In its more central position in Christian life, the Liturgy should sustain the devotional life of the faithful. Although the Eucharist* and the Sacraments* communicate the nature of the Church in ways other prayers may not, other prayers can be enlivened by the liturgical spirit. Liturgy's centrality to spiritual life imposes a flexibility to suit the People of God, so that they will not turn away to nonliturgical devotions.*

The role of the bishop* as principal liturgist of the Local Church* reflects the hierarchic nature of the Church in every celebration. It is true that he is the guardian of the Liturgy, but in his role as leader of prayer for the diocese* there is reunited in one person the liturgical authority and the liturgical leadership. The priest* now has a new relationship with the bishop and the laity. The priest is to be seen as acting for the bishop who is absent. In large dioceses where the bishop is rarely seen by the laity, the pastoral perspective of the bishop must be such that he is aware of the needs of the local community; on the other hand, the priest must know the needs of the total diocese, even the whole Church.

(3) *The pastoral and instructive nature of the Liturgy.* A proper balance should preserve the double orientation of every true Liturgy, directed not only to God but to human beings. The prayers addressed to God are said in the name of the congregation, so that they can willingly add their "Amen." A homily* directed to the people instructs them, yet in a different way from school, since there is a dimension of worship and participation in the Paschal Mystery. Every liturgical celebration should be a human experience of beauty, variety, and sensitivity to the people participating. Liturgical celebrations governed by the communications arts become good, simple, comprehensible signs, humanly attractive.

Obedience to Liturgical Law

The knowledge of these general principles and the spirit of the legislation will allow priests to make proper decisions in these matters. Besides bringing the priests active in the ministry up-to-date on liturgical law, there is a different type of liturgical education in seminaries, allowing the Liturgy to take its place as a source of theology. Through dialogue and sharing of authority in priests' senates and lay councils, closer relationships may develop with the bishops. Liturgical commissions* aid much in this regard, since they do a great deal to provide materials of explanations of the rites and develop programs to educate both clergy and laity.

A new respect for the liturgical books can exist, since the new editions try to meet the contemporary needs as they fit into our traditions. They are written in such a way that they allow for necessary local adaptation. The law itself does not bring about the fullness of the Liturgy. Our understanding of the new style of legislation and the new type of obedience will make it possible to allow the Liturgy to meet our expectations: namely, to lead contemporary human beings into personal contact with the Father.* *See also* LITURGICAL LAW, SOURCES OF.

Liturgical Law, Sources of (luh-TUHR-ji-kuhl; li-; law, SAWR-suhz uhv). The new *Code of Canon Law,* promulgated January 25, 1983, does not go into details about the liturgical laws that govern the Liturgy.* It states: "For the most part the Code does not define the rites* which are to be observed in celebrating liturgical actions.* For this reason current liturgical norms retain their force unless a given liturgical norm is contrary to the canons" (Can. 2). The liturgical laws common to the universal Latin Church are found principally in the official liturgical books* (in the introductions and rubrics* that describe the rites and accompany the texts). They are also found in related juridic documents. Particular liturgical laws are found in the liturgical books proper to each nation or region and in the statutes of diocesan and particular Churches.

The "related juridic documents" may be Conciliar, Papal, or Curial.

Conciliar Documents

In descending order of importance Conciliar documents are:

constitutions, decrees, declarations, and messages.

Constitutions concern the Universal Church* and deal with doctrine, discipline, or pastoral.

Decrees deal with some aspect of the Church's life and mission. They are disciplinary in character but also include doctrine and policy.

Declarations deal with issues of the day. They are statements of the Church's stand.

Messages have no legislative function. They are exhortations addressed to specific groups at the beginning or end of the Council

The Second Vatican Council* issued four constitutions, nine decrees, three declarations, and a series of messages. Each of the documents in the first three categories is dealt with in an entry under its Latin name, and its relation to the Liturgy is given.

Papal Documents

The Pope* has many documents at his disposal through which to legislate on the Liturgy or to have an impact on liturgical law. His mind and will in the matter may be known principally from the character of the document, from his frequent repetition of the same doctrine, or from his manner of speaking. The following alphabetical listing gives an idea of the documents in question.

Addresses (Allocutions) are solemn forms of communication directed to the College of Cardinals on important matters or to any other group. They generally do not provide legislation although they may deal with the Liturgy.

Apostolic Constitutions may be termed the most solemn documents of the Pope addressed to the Universal Church on doctrine or discipline, and they are in very common use for liturgical legislation. Most of the new liturgical books after Vatican II were promulgated by Apostolic Constitutions.

Apostolic Epistles are less solemn documents addressed usually to particular persons or groups, not to the whole Church, with little legislative impact. An example of one that dealt with the Liturgy is Pope Paul VI's 1965 Apostolic Epistle *Investigabiles Divitias Christi* (The Unfathomable Riches of Christ) marking the second centenary of the institution of the Feast of the Sacred Heart.*

Apostolic Exhortations are directed to particular groups and are usually exhortative rather than legislative. One of those that dealt with Liturgy is *Marialis Cultus** (On Devotion to Mary) issued by Pope Paul VI in 1974.

Apostolic Letters Motu Proprio are documents issued by the Pope "on his own initiative" (*motu proprio*) concerning serious matters and addressed to the Universal Church. These are legislative. One such document is *Mysterii Paschalis* of February 14, 1969, approving the norms for the Liturgical Year* and the new General Roman Calendar.*

Briefs (*See* BRIEF, APOSTOLIC).

Bulls (*See* BULL, PAPAL).

Decretal Letters (also called Decretals) are very solemn documents setting forth dogmatic teaching or laying down authoritative decrees

on disciplinary matters or giving replies to queries about the latter. They are also used in beatifications* and canonizations.* For the most part, decretal letters do not legislate.

Encyclicals (*See* ENCYCLICALS).

Indults (*See* INDULT).

Motu Propio (Latin phrase meaning "on one's own initiative") is a term used to describe certain documents written by the Pope to meet a specific need in the Church. They are usually Apostolic Letters (see above) and many have been written after Vatican II to implement the changes in liturgical laws.

Curial Documents

The Roman Congregations, Secretariats, and Offices also issue many documents that have an impact on the Liturgy and liturgical law. The most important ones are the following (in alphabetical order).

Circular Letters are usually exhortatory in nature, but they can also set forth liturgical laws. For example, the November 20, 1972, Circular Letter *El 6 febrero* sent by Cardinal A. Tabera of the Congregation on Divine Worship to the Spanish-speaking conferences of Bishops in Latin America concerning the uniform translation of the parts of the Liturgy belonging to the people detailed the parts in question.

Declarations provide an interpretation for existing laws or facts or offer a response to a contested power of law. They may be *authentic* or *nonauthentic.* Authentic declarations are given by those empowered to give them in each instance. Thus, after the promulgation of the new Code the Pontifical Commission for the Authentic Interpretation of the Code of Canon Law considered several doubts concerning canonical legislation affecting liturgical practices and handed down authentic interpretations of them—e.g., Communion* more than once a day. Nonauthentic declarations are made by persons or organs that are concerned with Liturgy or law: *Ephemerides Liturgicae,* The Jurist,* La Maison-Dieu,* Notitiae,** and *Rivista Liturgica.**

Decrees constitute new laws promulgated with the special approval of the Pope. All the post-Vatican II liturgical books were promulgated by a decree. An example of a new law is the Decree *Cum de Nomine* of October 9, 1972, setting forth the laws governing mention of the bishop's name in the Eucharistic Prayer* (since this was not in the *Roman Missal**).

Directories provide guidelines for the application of principles that are accepted; thus they can have the force of law. One such in the field of Liturgy is the *Directory on Masses with Children* issued on November 1, 1973. It eventually became part of the *Roman Missal.*

Instructions (*See* INSTRUCTION).

Norms are laws that apply to specific instances. One example is found in the Norms *Pluries Decursu Temporis* on Crowning Images of the Blessed Virgin Mary issued on March 25, 1973.

Notifications resemble declarations and clarify existing law. One example is found in the Notification *Instructione de Constitutione* on the *Roman Missal,* the *Liturgy of the Hours,* and the *General Calendar,* issued on June 14, 1971.

Replies are answers to specific questions posed to the Congregations. One such was the Reply of the Pontifical Commission for the Authentic Interpretation of Canon Law on receiving Communion more than once a day (mentioned under "Declarations," above).

Liturgical Life. *See* LITURGICAL SPIRITUALITY.

Liturgical Movement (luh-TUHR-ji-kuhl; li; MOOV-muhnt). The name of a 20th-century movement working for liturgical renewal. A movement is an undertaking, a current of thought and action, an organism or a number of organisms inspired by identical principles, tending toward the same ideal. The ideal could be that of promoting autonomy, a reform, a restoration, or a renewal. This was the case with the Liturgical Movement, that is, the liturgical renewal of both the clergy* and the laity.* More specifically, the movement strove for making the Liturgy* known, loved, and

practiced in a better fashion, particularly by the full participation* of Christians in liturgical celebrations.

The term was coined in the 1894 edition of *Vesperale* by the German priest A. Schott and refers to a Movement that has "appeared as a sign of God's providential dispositions for the *present day,* as a Movement of the Holy Spirit* in His Church"* (Pope Pius XII, Address to the First International Congress on Pastoral Liturgy, September 22, 1956). The Second Vatican Council repeated these words, identifying the Movement with "zeal for the promotion and restoration of the Liturgy" (SC, 43).

Remote and Proximate Preparation

The *remote* preparation for this Movement was the whole history of alterations in the Liturgy from the beginning of the Church: the passage from the Aramaic of Jesus and His Apostles* to the Greek of Paul* and on to the Latin of Rome in the 4th century; (2) the changes from the classical Roman Liturgy of Gregory the Great* to the Roman-Frankish-Germanic Liturgy of the 11th century; (3) the further disposition of the Liturgy according to the use of the Roman Curia (13th century); and (4) the complete renewal of the Liturgy effected by the Council of Trent and St. Pius V.*

The *proximate* preparation may be found in the Catholic Enlightenment and in the Synod of Pistoia (18th century), the theological reawakening and monastic renewal (19th century), and the renewed idea of the Church (beginning of the 20th century). Catholics took the theme of the Enlightenment (rejection of *traditional* social, religious, and political ideas) and applied it to the Church. They sought to explain dogmas in all their purity and clarity in order to arrive at what is essential in doctrine and Catholic life.

The Synod of Pistoia, Italy (1786), among other things, applied this view to the Liturgy. Although this Synod was tinged with Jansenism and seven of its propositions were condemned by Pope Pius VI in 1794, many others of its propositions contained general liturgical and pastoral insights that have become part of the Vatican II liturgical renewal: (1) active participation of the people; (2) minimization of private Masses; (3) importance of liturgical prayer; (4) necessity of *Breviary** reform; (5) printing of vernacular* together with Latin in liturgical books, and many other similar points.

The theological reawakening of the 19th century can be termed the Catholic Restoration. In England, the Oxford Movement arose with Cardinal Newman, Keble, and

Pusey and became a concerted effort to restore to the Church of England certain principles of Catholic faith and works that had been lost. In Germany the post-Enlightenment writers such as Johan Sailor, Johan Moehler, and Matthias Scheeben stressed the doctrine of the Church as the Mystical Body* of Christ, a fundamental doctrine for the understanding of the Liturgy.

The monastic renewal at Solesmes (France) and Beuron (Germany) also played a large part. The moving figure behind it all was Dom Prosper Guéranger (1805-1875), the Father of the Liturgical Movement. Although he may be regarded by us today as too narrowly medieval, too limited in pastoral concern, and too immersed in archeologism,* Guéranger succeeded in recalling people to an interest in and concern for the Liturgy as something to be prayed and lived.

In 1882 another abbey (Maredsous) brought out a French Missal for the people and in 1884 Rev. A. Schott of the Abbey of Beuron published a German Missal for the people.

Beginnings

The Classical Period of the Liturgical Movement began when St. Pius X* on November 22, 1903 (scarcely three months after the beginning of his pontificate), formulated the revolutionary program for it in his Motu Proprio* *Tra le sollecitudini* ("Among the Concerns") on Church Music. He stressed that the right of "active participation in the sacred Mysteries* and in the public and solemn prayer of the Church" was the "first and indispensable source" of the true "Christian spirit." To achieve full participation by the people, the Pope two years later urged Christians to receive frequent and even daily Communion* (as the Council of Trent had done), and in 1910 he enabled even children to attain this full participation by receiving Communion as soon as they reached the age of reason.

Pius X also revised the *Breviary* so that the Psalter* would be read every week (1911) and reformed

the Calendar* so that Sundays took precedence over feasts of Saints.* He also published the first official edition of the *Roman Gradual** (1907) and an official edition of the *Antiphonary.**

The most important practical event in the history of the Liturgical Movement occurred in 1909 at a Catholic Conference in Malines, Belgium, when Dom Lambert Beauduin (1873-1960) proposed a program for liturgical renewal. He advocated the translation of the *Roman Missal** and its diffusion among the faithful as their principal prayer book, and he urged all Catholic piety to be based on the Mass and the *Breviary.* Finally, he called for the promotion of Gregorian Chant* and the spiritual and liturgical function of choirs. To this end, from his abbey of Mont César he published a Missal for the people (1920) and the periodical *La Vie liturgique* (The Liturgical Life, 1909ff), and the periodical *Questions Liturgiques et Paroissiales* (Liturgical and Parochial Questions, 1914ff) as well as the results of conferences (*Services Liturgiques).*

Another Belgian Abbey, Saint André in Bruges, published a Missal for the people by Dom Gaspar Lefebvre that became world-famous. In Austria, Pius Parsh (1884-1954) made the treasures of the Bible and Missal available to the people. In Germany, Ildefonse Herwegen (1874-1946) instituted the liturgical series *Ecclesia Orans* (The Church at Prayer), Romano Guardini (1885-1968) expounded the spirit of the Liturgy, and Odo Casel (1886-1948) developed his famous theory of the Mysteries. In Italy, another Benedictine abbey (at Savona) established the periodical *Rivista Liturgica* (Liturgical Review), which kept the people abreast of the Movement.

Growth

In 1936, one of the greatest workers in the Movement, Joseph A. Jungmann, S.J., published *The Good News Yesterday and Today,* which provided a basis of sound scholarship for the increasing demands for the renewal of the Liturgy (and Catechetics).

By the 1940s many countries were involved in the Movement. In 1943, the Center for Pastoral Liturgy was formed in France with the aid of Lambert Beauduin. Buttressed by theological, Biblical, and pastoral scholarship, it went on to become the exemplar for official liturgical organizations in other countries. It eventually started the periodical *La Maison-Dieu* (The House of God), which did yeoman work to further the Movement under A.M. Roguet and A.G. Martimort.

In the United States, the Movement was also growing. Dom Virgil Michel of St. John's Abbey, Collegeville, Minnesota, established the Liturgical Press and the periodical *Orate Fratres* (called *Worship* since 1951). Michael Ducey inspired the first Liturgical Week in 1940 sponsored by the Benedictine Liturgical Conference, which was replaced in 1944 by the National Liturgical Conference* in sponsoring other Liturgical Weeks until Vatican II. Collegeville and the Liturgical Conference gave rise to the two American liturgists who had great effect at the Council: Godfrey Diekmann and Frederick McManus.

Michael Mathis (1885-1960) was instrumental in making Notre Dame University a center for liturgical studies and in 1947 started the School of Liturgical Studies, the first Liturgical Institute in the world.

Church Endorsement

In the words of one of the foremost figures in the Movement, Archbishop Annibale Bugnini, "From 1920 to 1947 liturgical weeks and congresses, periodicals and publications, petitions, battles, fears and hopes followed upon each other in an ever-growing crescendo. Then in 1947 came the encyclical *Mediator Dei,** the truly great charter of the Liturgical

Movement that brought about its transformation. From individuals, from the growing legions of courageous pioneers, the Movement reached the bishops, the Apostolic See, and the Pope.* The Liturgy was no longer an elitist option or an isolated domain. It was an integral part of the activity of the Church. Vatican II was to call it the 'summit and source' of all ecclesial life" (*Notitiae* 92).

Thus, it was Pius XII by his encyclicals *Mystici Corporis** (1943) and *Mediator Dei* (1947—the first encyclical wholly dedicated to the Liturgy) who helped to clarify the theological foundations of the Liturgy and gave impetus to the Movement, making it a *pastoral apostolate.* He also instituted a commission within the Congregation of Rites* charged with preparing a general renewal of the Liturgy, mitigated the Eucharistic Fast,* returned the celebration of the Easter Vigil* to the holy night itself (1951), and issued restored rites for Holy Week* (1955).

Pius XII also wrote another encyclical, *De Sacra Musica* (Sacred Music, 1955), which set forth guidelines for increased participation of the faithful in liturgical rites. As a consequence of the Biblical Renewal, he authorized the reading of the Epistle* and Gospel* in the vernacular* at Mass after they were read in Latin. He also allowed publication of bilingual *Rituals* (1947), simplified the rubrics (1955), and had a simplification of rubrics prepared, which John XXIII promulgated in 1960. This latter Pope also published a simplification of the rite of the dedication of a church and altar in 1961 but decided to have the upcoming Council formulate the more important principles of a general reform of the Liturgy.

Fruits

The Second Vatican Council then issued the crowning achievement of the Liturgical Movement—the *Constitution on the Sacred Liturgy** (*Sacrosanctum Concilium,* 1963), and the reform that ensued is the practical fruit of that document. "From Mediator Dei to the Vatican II *Constitution on the Liturgy,* the transition was short. Between these two documents the continuity was unbroken. Both documents formed a natural evolution in the logical conclusions of the 'active participation' launched at the beginning of the century by St. Pius X. Thus, *Tra le sollecitudini, Mediator Dei,* and *Sacrosanctum Concilium* are three pillars of the same edifice that has Peter for its foundation" (*ibid.*).

Archbishop Bugnini then goes on to make an important point about the status of the Liturgical Movement today. "It is anachronistic to speak today of a 'Liturgical Movement' as if it were something that is parallel to the activity of the Church. The 'Liturgical Movement' belongs to history. *It has now become* the *pastoral action of the Church that aims at making the faithful participate in and live fully the Paschal Mystery* of Christ that the Liturgy celebrates.*

"To still ask oneself where the Liturgical Movement stands, or to anchor to its first glorious phases, is to move only in the realm of history. It is to seek to recuperate out of the past something that we would like to make present but which has no connection any longer with the present.

"Liturgical reform, liturgical adaptation,* liturgical life, and Pastoral Liturgy* are valid terms of the present . . . that have genuine and up-to-date significance" (*ibid.*).

However, the implementation of these new goals endorsed by the Church will take a "neo-Liturgical Movement," in the words of Archbishop Virgilio Noè, Secretary of the Congregation for Divine Worship,* speaking at Catholic University on June 7, 1984. This "neo-Liturgical Movement" calls for "scientific study and scholarly research." "Students should be encouraged to specialize in liturgical science. At the same time less specialized courses should be open to clergy* and laity* who have not the capacity or time for scientific work but who want a solid foundation in the subject."

We might sum up by saying that the Liturgical Movement was the result of the following five elements: (1) the rediscovery of the role of the People of God* and the communal nature of the Church; (2) renewed liturgical research; (3) the realization that worship must be the center of Christian life; (4) the

materialization of Biblical Theology; and (5) the Ecumenical Movement.

The goal of the Liturgical Movement was an intelligent and active participation of the people in the Liturgy that would lead them to final salvation.* The means was by accommodating the structures discovered by historical research to the cultural, social, religious, and psychological circumstances of today. And the fruition of much of the work of the Movement was found in the *Constitution on the Sacred Liturgy,* since its theology of the Liturgy explained the meaning and function of the life of the Church in a way that no other statement had done in the past. *See also* APOSTOLATE.

Liturgical Objects. *See* CHURCH FURNISHINGS.

Liturgical Participation. *See* LITURGY—PARTICIPATION.

Liturgical Renewal. *See* REFORM.

Liturgical Research Centers (luh-TUHR-ji-kuhl; li-; ri-SUHRCH; REE-suhrch; SENT-uhrz). In order that the Church* in America would have opportunities available to study liturgical celebrations* most suited to the average worshiping community, the Bishops' Committee on the Liturgy* designated certain centers with diversified interests to direct their studies to such broad needs. They are to help in adapting and creating liturgical rites and forms, decided upon through their own initiative, but these are to be judged by the National Conference of Catholic Bishops* before being put into practice.

(1) The Woodstock Center for Religion and Worship, Woodstock College, New York, existed from 1969 to 1975.

(2) St. John's University, Collegeville, Minnesota (1970). A long history of activity in the liturgical apostolate has well equipped this center for ongoing liturgical study and research, primarily intended for the formation of personnel in Pastoral Liturgy* at both diocesan* and parish* levels. Their twofold function is: "to coordinate, facilitate, and serve as a resource center for the various present and future abbey and university programs, as well as other forms of initiative and enterprise, in the area of Pastoral Liturgy; and to develop, and seek funding for, appropriate research projects" (*BCL Newsletter,* vol. 12, p. 71).

(3) The Murphy Center for Liturgical Research, University of Notre Dame, Indiana (1970). At first their research focused on ritual behavior, trying to determine the need of human beings for ritual structure in religious and civil life. The anthropological roots of worship* were studied in order to relate them to the significant changes in liturgical forms. Later the research took a more pastoral thrust, dialoguing with representatives from around the country to discover the tradition of Christian worship, particularly to understand how it is lived today.

(4) Composers' Forum for Catholic Worship, Sugar Creek, Missouri (1971). A wide range of talents is required to create music* for the Liturgy. To fulfill the pastoral need of quality vernacular* liturgical music, this group of Church musicians and liturgists help composers to develop new good music in a systematic way, which includes suggestions of a Biblical, theological, and liturgical nature. Their fourfold purpose is to: "(1) develop new music for worship by commissioning composers; (2) furnish a framework whereby liturgists, musicians, and experts from other disciplines may work together for the orderly development of music for worship; (3) test and evaluate the music thus composed; and (4) seek funds to support the Forum's projects" (*BCL Newsletter*, vol. 12, p. 71).

(5) Mexican American Cultural Center, San Antonio, Texas (1974). Since the pastoral needs in the United States must take into consideration the Spanish-speaking Catholics, which might be as much as one-third of our Catholic population, necessary adaptations should be considered. This center was founded to: "(1) do a serious study of the customs, heritage, and popular religious practices of the Mexican Catholics in the United States; (2) provide programs of formation for personnel working in Mexican American areas; (3) begin the preparation of materials which would incorporate the cultural expressions of the people in the liturgical celebrations; and (4) prepare catechetical materials which will take into account the natural wisdom of the people, their art, their tradition, and their popular piety" (*BCL Newsletter*, vol. 12, p. 73).

(6) The Center for Pastoral Liturgy, The Catholic University of America, Washington, DC (1976). Its nonacademic character proposes to help diocesan, parish, Religious, and other community liturgical commissions and committees in liturgical formation and celebration. Thus it meets liturgical needs in a practical, pastoral way. Nevertheless, it can develop academic programs leading to graduate degrees in related fields. To achieve its end, it will coordinate resources within The Catholic University and outside it to: "(1) conduct programs, first as pilot undertakings and then on broader scales, for the improvement of liturgical celebration; (2) offer special conferences or institutes for those engaged in the work of diocesan, parish, and community commissions; (3) gather, collate, and evaluate the materials employed for liturgical celebration and catechesis,* with a view toward raising the standards of celebration and integration of Liturgy with prayer life and with pastoral action; (4) stimulate or provide compositions and materials (artistic, audiovisual, musical, printed) for celebration and catechesis; and (5) focus attention, through major symposia and conferences, on the needs for liturgical development" (*BCL Newsletter*, vol. 12, p. 70).

(7) The Corpus Christi Center for Liturgy, 7575 N. 16th Street, Phoenix, Arizona, is a liturgical resource to parishes in the southwestern United States. It operates Turning Point Bookstore and offers two courses in Liturgy for parish liturgical leadership. Publications from the Center include *Liturgy Alive*, a bimonthly commentary on the Scripture readings, and *Liturgy Plus*, a computer software system for Liturgy planning.

(8) The Goergetown Center for Liturgy, Spirituality and the Arts, Washington, DC, is a teaching, research, and pastoral reflection institute working with parishes to enhance the quality of their worship. The Center conducts regional workshops in

Washington and Boston, a national conference on environment for worship, programs for parishes and dioceses, and the Certificate Program in Liturgical Studies at Georgetown University. Other activities include publications and the Georgetown Center Chorale, a performance chorus of singers from the Washington area. The center's work is supported, in large part, by its cosponsors, Georgetown University and Holy Trinity Parish, by the Society of Jesus, and by the contributions of friends concerned with parish worship.

(9) The Loyola Pastoral Institute, Seminary of the Immaculate Conception, Huntington, New York, provides an effective forum for pastoral reflection on the Liturgy for the Roman Catholic community in the greater New York area. The programs of the Institute are offered by the faculty of the Seminary of the Immaculate Conception, professional liturgists residing in the greater New York area, and highly renowned guest liturgists. The offerings of the Institute include opportunities for advanced research in conjunction with the Seminary's Doctor of Ministry and Masters programs, on site study weeks, and workshops throughout the New York area. The Institute's programs address a wide audience within the Roman Catholic community and provide service to those involved in the common prayer of the Christian community.

See also LITURGICAL COMMISSIONS.

Liturgical Rites. *See* RITES AND CEREMONIES.

Liturgical Spirituality (luh-TUHR-ji-kuhl; li-; spir-i-choo-AL-uh-tee). The attitude of Christians who base their lives on the authentic exercises of the Liturgy* so that it becomes the "source and summit" of all their actions (see SC, 10) and they become manifestations by their lives of the Paschal Mystery.* There are many types of spirituality (ways of living the Christian life) in the Church*—Benedictine, Carmelite, Ignatian, and the like—which aid Christians to live the life of grace according to the spirit rather than the flesh (see Gal 3:3-6; Rom 8:4-13). Liturgical spirituality may be termed the spirituality beyond compare, since it is an objective piety, a spirituality that consciously orients itself by the objective data of the liturgical celebrations, rites, and prayers of the Church (the Eucharist,* the Sacraments,* and the Liturgy of the Hours*) according to the rhythm of the Liturgical Year.*

However, the Sacramental acts must prolong themselves in personal prayer,* which will in turn ready us for the liturgical celebrations once again. The Liturgy must also become part of our everyday lives enabling us to fulfill our duties, to cultivate Christian virtues,* such as patience* and love,* and a continual disposition to help others. In short, it must help us fulfill the human, social, and political tasks entrusted to us in the world.*

Catholics imbued with a wholehearted and active liturgical life will find their spirituality characterized by a better realization of the corporate Church, the Communion of Saints,* and true contrition,* which leads to those virtues inculcated by liturgical celebrations with their Christocentric direction. *See also* APOSTOLATE; DEVOTION; DOMESTIC

CHURCH; EXERCISES, PIOUS; HOLINESS; LITURGY; LITURGY—PARTICIPATION; PARALITURGY; PRAYER; WORSHIP.

Liturgical Texts. *See* FORMULAS, LITURGICAL; LITURGICAL BOOKS.

Liturgical Use of the Alphabet. *See* ALPHABET, LITURGICAL USE OF THE.

Liturgical Year. *See* CHURCH YEAR.

Liturgiology (luh-tuhr-jee-OL-uh-jee). A rather arkward term for the scientific study of the rites,* symbols,* and actions* that comprise the worship* of the Church.* It is also known as Liturgics and Liturgy* (which then refers both to the science and to the practice of Christian worship). It deals with the theological, spiritual, historical, esthetic, and canonical aspects of the Liturgy and its parts: Mass,* Sacraments,* Sacramentals,* Liturgy of the Hours,* and Liturgical Year.* It makes use of history and the social sciences and is a distinct branch of theology.

The aim of Liturgiology is to impart a knowledge and appreciation of the worship of the Church, so as to create a liturgical spirit that will lead to full, conscious, and active participation* in the Liturgy resulting in the greater glory* of God and the salvation* of souls.

The method followed is to study both the present rites and their past so as to arrive at their true meaning. In this connection, the study of comparative rites is also important.

The divisions of Liturgiology are too numerous to list. The major divisions are general or fundamental Liturgy and special Liturgy. The former includes the notions and definitions of Liturgy, the relation between Liturgy and the Christian life (theology of the Liturgy), and everything that pertains to Liturgy as a whole. The latter focuses on one part of the whole (for example, the Liturgical Year, the rubrics,* or the texts).

Liturgy possesses a close relationship with the other divisions of theology. Dogmatic theology provides an indication of the Divine realities celebrated in the Liturgy. In turn, the Liturgy is a source of Church teaching for dogmatic theology; Pope Pius XI declared that in the Liturgy "the ordinary and privileged teaching of the Church is given." *(See also* LEX ORANDI—LEX CREDENDI; MAGISTERIUM.)

Moral theology provides the principles for spiritual growth that can be attained through worship. In turn, the Liturgy indicates the specific ways in which this growth can be attained.

Scripture* provides the content for the liturgical texts and rites as well as the principles for the interpretation of the Biblical texts used. In turn, the Liturgy makes the Bible intelligible to the people gathered for worship, bringing the Word of God* to people today.

Canon Law provides the principles for the interpretation of liturgical laws. In turn, the Liturgy details the liturgical laws that govern all its rites. *See also* ART AND LITURGY; BIBLE AND LITURGY; CATECHESIS AND LITURGY; GOOD WORKS; GRACE;

HOLINESS; LITURGICAL LAW; LITURGICAL LAW, SOURCES OF; LITURGY; THEOLOGY AND LITURGY.

Liturgy (LIT-uhr-jee). The public worship* carried out by the People of God,* the Mystical Body of Christ,* the Church.* Originally, the Greek word *leitourgia* denoted a voluntary work—political, technical, or religious—that was performed for the people as a whole. The Septuagint,* the Greek translation of the Jewish Scriptures completed in the 3rd century B.C., turned it into a reference to the priestly worship carried on in the Temple. The early Church and the Fathers* used this word to indicate a service of worship in which each member of the community offers to God on behalf of all in accord with his or her role. By the Middle Ages, it came to denote the official worship of the Church.

The Liturgical Movement* accentuated the fact that the Liturgy is the public worship of the People of God; it is prayer in action—the prayer of Christ and His Church.

Pius XII in his ground-breaking *Encyclical on the Sacred Liturgy* (*Mediator Dei**) provided the classic definition of the word:

> The Liturgy is the public worship that our Redeemer as Head of the Church renders to the Father as well as the worship that the community of the faithful* renders to its Founder, and through Him to the Father. It is, in short, the worship rendered by the Mystical Body of Christ in the entirety of its Head and members (no. 20).

The Second Vatican Council took a more descriptive approach and gave this practical definition:

> Rightly, then, the Liturgy is considered as an exercise of the priestly office of Jesus Christ. In the Liturgy, by means of signs perceptible to the senses, human sanctification is signified and brought about in ways proper to each of these signs; in the Liturgy, the whole public worship is performed by the Mystical Body of Jesus Christ, that is, by the Head and His members (SC, 7).

We can say, therefore, that the Liturgy is a number of things taken cumulatively:

(1) the worship of the Father, the Son, and the Holy Spirit;

(2) the exercise of the eternal priesthood* of Christ;

(3) the actualization of the Mystery of Salvation* through sacred signs*;

(4) a salvific "present" that makes us contemporaneous with Biblical History;

(5) a prophecy and foretaste of eschatology*;

(6) an action of the whole communitary and hierarchical ecclesial body in union with the angels* and the Saints*;

(7) a pedagogy of the Faith*;

(8) the moment of redemptive encounter with Christ in the Holy Spirit;

(9) the strengthening of the fraternal bonds among the members of the Church;

(10) a petition filled with hope*;

(11) a joyous feast and a profound contemplation*;

(12) a blessing* brimming with gifts;

(13) the extension of the Paschal Mystery* to all people and to the entire cosmos;

(14) a dialogue between God and human beings;

(15) the Christian community's celebration of God's saving deeds in Christ through the Holy Spirit.

The Liturgy makes use of (1) readings from the Bible* (the Word of God); (2) prayers based on the Bible; (3) spiritual songs*; (4) sacred actions and signs* or symbols* (ceremonies*); and (5) extemporaneous prayers of the individual community.

The Liturgy makes present for us the History of Salvation,* the saving love God has for us in His Son through the Holy Spirit. The actions of the earthly Liturgy are not mere memorials in the sense of recalling the events of that History. They are now portraying and making actual before our eyes as well as in our hearts the saving acts of Christ—His Passion,* Death,* and Resurrection.* Christ's power is found in the Church, His Body, and is present and active in the Liturgy.

Celebrants of the Liturgy

The principal celebrant* of the Liturgy is Christ Himself. The second celebrant is the general body of the faithful and the community here and now assembled in the Liturgy. The third celebrant is the bearer of the official priesthood who stands at the altar.*

In the Liturgy each person has an office to perform (as a result of the universal priesthood* received at Baptism*); the people take their part by means of acclamations,* responses,* psalmody,* antiphons,* and songs,* as well as by actions,* gestures,* bodily attitudes,* and a reverent silence* at the proper time. The participation of everyone involved in the Liturgy should be full, active, and conscious, internal as well as external, motivated by a deep religious sense of his or her office to be a sign of the Mystery of the Church.

Through the Liturgy, the faithful are enabled to encounter Christ in His Mysteries* and are filled with grace. "Recalling thus the Mysteries of Redemption, the Church opens to the faithful the riches of her Lord's powers and merits, so that these are in some way made present for all time, and the faithful are enabled to lay hold upon them and become filled with saving grace" (SC, 102). The greater is our love for Christ and the greater is the love we infuse into our participation, so much the greater will be our fruits.* Since Christ is acting in the Liturgy, the deeper our desire to be one with Him and His members, the more abundantly will He enrich our souls with graces.

Liturgy and Instruction

The Liturgy instructs us in the Faith, for the Church teaches as she sanctifies. In the Liturgy God speaks to His people and Christ is still proclaiming His Gospel* (SC, 33). In the words of Pius XI, "the ordinary and privileged teaching of the Church is given in the Liturgy" *(see* MAGISTERIUM). Together with Sacred History the Liturgy is one of the two sources of Catechesis.* The unfolding of the Liturgical Year* instructs and forms Christians by bringing them into contact with the person of the Savior through the actualization of successive events in the life of Christ.

The Liturgy comprises the sacred rites of the Eucharist* (both Mass and Sacrament*), Baptism, Confirmation,* Penance,* Holy Orders,* Marriage,* and Anointing of the Sick* as well as the Liturgy of the Hours* and the Sacramentals.* In performing these rites, the Liturgy makes use of signs and symbols in

order to convey invisible realities and reach the whole person who is made up not only of intellect and will but also of imagination, passions, appetites, and secular experiences. In this respect, the Liturgy may be termed the supreme art, which makes use of all the other arts. Architecture, sculpture, and painting prepare for it and adorn its surroundings; the vestment arts add to its beauty and majesty; eloquence and poetry sustained by music* provide its inspiration. Above all, faith and love for God inspire it and give it life.

Liturgy and Life

The Liturgy has a direct relation to our daily life. It is intended to celebrate and keep alive in the whole Christian community the meaning of our lives as Christians. We draw from the Liturgy the power and the strength to make Christ present and active in the world.* In our daily lives we show forth Christ's enduring love for all people and His constant concern for the betterment of humankind here on earth. By our faith in Christ's Second Coming* we keep alive in the world the blessed hope that human existence has ultimate and eternal significance.

Thus, the Liturgy surpasses all other actions of the Church since it is an action of Christ and His Church. "The Liturgy is the summit toward which the activity of the Church is directed; at the same time it is the fount from which all her power flows" (SC, 10).

Liturgy in the strict sense excludes private prayers and devotions of individuals and groups. However, in the broad sense one can say that for Christians there is no strictly individual prayer. Our most solitary, intimate, and private prayer is the prayer of a member of the Church, the Mystical Body of Christ. Liturgy is the life of Christians' souls, for it is the life of the Church to which all believers are associated, whether they are praying by themselves or in common, whether they are praying only mentally or using external signs with their body. It is like a stream of blood that circulates unceasingly through the whole body of the Church to manifest openly the religion of the human race toward God.

In some connotations Liturgy refers to the Eucharistic Celebration, particularly in the Eastern Church.* Usually, it has the broader sense of administering all the Sacraments to the faithful.

The word Liturgy is also used for the *science* of Liturgy, which makes use of history, theology, and human sciences to achieve a more profound and organic understanding of its subject. *See also* CATECHESIS AND LITURGY; CHURCH YEAR; CONSTITUTION ON THE SACRED LITURGY; HISTORY OF SALVATION; LITURGICAL MOVEMENT; LITURGY—HISTORY; LITURGY—PARTICIPATION.

Liturgy—History (LIT-uhr-jee—HIS-t[uh-]ree). The history of the Liturgy* is long and complex. What appears below is a general outline. For more detailed information, see Appendix 3: "Select Chronology of Major Events in the History of the Liturgy."

The history of the Liturgy can be divided into six periods: (1) Primitive Liturgy (1st to 3rd century); (2) Growth of Rites (4th to 6th century); (3) Fixation of the Roman Rite (7th to 9th century); (4) Clericalized Liturgy (10th to 15th century); (5) Age of Rubricism (16th to 19th century); (6) Liturgical Renewal (20th century).

(1) *Primitive Liturgy* (1st to 3rd century). Within this period the Liturgy first developed from the Last Supper* and teaching of Jesus, which contained elements from Jewish liturgy and table prayers. By the 2nd century a format of readings,* sermon,* prayer,* offering of gifts, thanksgiving, and Communion* was common to most congregations in the Western Church. The Eucharist* was celebrated on Sundays in the various houses of the Christians and later in houses of worship.*

At first, the celebrant* improvised the prayers, including the Eucharistic Prayer.* However, uniformity soon came into play, and by

the end of the 1st century there was a uniform Eucharistic Prayer after the image of the one found in the *Didache,** the *First Apology* of St. Justin,* and the *Apostolic Tradition** of St. Hippolytus.* A pattern of prayer in the morning and evening was also developing, along the lines of the Liturgy of the Hours.*

Entry into the Church was achieved through the Sacraments* of Christian Initiation: Baptism,* Confirmation,* and the Eucharist* with a catechumenate* of three years.

A liturgical calendar* gave rise to the keeping of the feasts of Easter* (2nd century), Pentecost and Epiphany (4th century), and Christmas (4th century) as well as the seasons of Lent* and Easter.*

(2) *Growth of Rites* (4th to 6th century). With the coming of the 4th century, the Church emerged into a new era of peace. By his Edict of 313 the Emperor Constantine made Christians legitimate in the Roman Empire. Churches were built. Bishops* attained the status of civic personalities. The Liturgy became more elaborate and structured. Greek was replaced by Latin, the language of the people, in the Liturgy, and liturgical emphasis was placed on the celebration of the events of salvation.*

The bishop celebrated surrounded by his college of priests* and assisted by his deacons.* Other ministers* were also present. The people were fully involved in the communal rite.

A number of liturgical families or rites arose, centered around the major cities of the Empire. Some of them were: (a) in *Alexandria:* the liturgy of St. Mark* as well as the Coptic liturgies of St. Cyril,* St. Basil,* and St. Gregory*; (b) in *Antioch:* the liturgy of St. James,* the liturgy of West Syria and the liturgy of East Syria; (c) in *Constantinople:* the Byzantine liturgy or the liturgy of St. John Chrysostom*; (d) in *Rome:* the Roman-North African liturgy stemming from Rome and Africa; and (e) Non-Roman Latin liturgies of the Gallican type: Spanish (Mozarabic) Gallican, Milanese, and Celtic.

In the 6th century, the season of Advent* was added to the calendar as a preparation for Christmas, and the calendar took greater shape. Collections of the prayers used during the Eucharistic celebration were made from the "libelli"* or booklets on which they had been written down. These collections, called "Sacramentaries,"* were later assigned by scholars to various Popes* who were thought to have had a hand in the composition of the texts. They became known as the *Leonine,** the *Gelasian,** and the *Gregorian** Sacramentaries.

(3) *Fixation of the Roman Rite* (7th to 9th century). Roman liturgical activity gradually came to a halt, and by the 7th century there was a fixed Liturgy. When Charlemagne became Emperor, he decided to unify the Empire in all things including the Liturgy. He imported Roman liturgical books* and put them into use in his kingdom. The Franco-German clergy adapted the Roman books to their own needs and culture. Alcuin,* a monk of the Carolingian court, laid down the bases of what was to become the *Roman Missal.** He added the texts of the Sundays after Pentecost,* inserted a liturgy for Palm Sunday,* included the rite of the New Fire on the Easter Vigil,* and effected other changes. Gradually, this *Roman Missal* became the dominant text read throughout the Empire.

The new mixed Liturgy was richer than the simple forms of the ancient Roman Liturgy. It contained the splendid Liturgy of the consecration of the Paschal Candle,* Votive Masses,* and a large number of more personal prayers, above all prayers in which the priest* made a private confession of his sins and asked forgiveness for them (the so-called apologies*), which little by little appeared at the beginning of almost all the parts of Mass.

Many other prayers also appeared directed to Christ rather than to the Father through Christ as in the classical form. A strong consciousness of sin was also apparent and an anguish in the face of the judgment.* The communal character was no longer dominant. The people took less part in the celebration. The priest began to celebrate with his back to the people and to assume the parts previously assigned to one or other minister.

As a result, there was need of only one book for the priest. This gave rise to the *"Missale Plenarium,"* the complete Missal, in which were included Antiphons,* Prayers,* Readings,* Prefaces,* Eucharistic Prayers,* and everything needed for Mass. In 950 at the monastery of St. Alban at Mainz, a book containing all these elements appeared entitled *Romano-German Pontifical,* for the use of the bishop for services apart from Mass.

(4) *Clericalized Liturgy* (10th to 15th century). The Franco-German Liturgy became the Liturgy of Rome. However, the desolation and chaos that followed the crumbling of civilization also affected the Liturgy. The clergy began to perfom their liturgical duties carelessly, and the people lost interest in the Liturgy. This period has been termed a time of dissolution, elaboration, reinterpretation, and misinterpretation.

The people no longer understood Latin and also lost some of the actions they once performed, such as the Offertory Procession.* They received Communion very infrequently and began to *watch* the Mass rather than take part in it. And in fact they could not even see very much since they were placed farther and farther from the sanctuary and the priest celebrated with his back to them. So they took comfort in looking at the elevation* of the Sacred Host from afar and then the elevation of the Chalice after the Consecration.* The Liturgy became the private domain of the clergy, and the people were more and more shut off from it.

The Liturgy of the classic Roman period and that of the Franco-German period used in monasteries and cathedrals were too rich to become a common patrimony. It was the genius of the clergy of the Roman curia that adapted and made it practicable in the smallest communities of the 12th and 13th centuries. It brought forth a *Missal, Breviary,* and *Pontifical,* which were adopted by the newly formed Franciscans who carried these books throughout Christendom.

(5) *Age of Rubricism* (16th to 19th century). The Council of Trent, reacting to the Protestant Reformation, carried out a liturgical reform that restored a recognizable Roman Liturgy to the Western Church. The Council deleted most of the medieval accretions, such as the multiplication of Masses of the Saints* and Votive Masses.* But it also kept some that did not conform to the Mass as a communal rite: Prayers at the Foot of the Altar* (Psalm 42) and the Last Gospel* at the end of Mass. Low Mass* was also given new emphasis Communion in the hand or from the Cup was not restored.

The Council did establish the restored rite in a rigid body of rubrics,* which everyone was obliged to keep under pain of sin. In so doing, the Council was able to preserve a Liturgy that could be improved later on.

The Council rejected the Breviary of Quinones because it did not correspond to the traditional chanting of community prayer and promulgated the Decree "On Things To Be Observed and Avoided in the Celebration of Mass." It undertook the liturgical reform—in order to overcome the chaotic state of the Liturgy—in continuity with Tradition.*

In the interests of greater uniformity, the Council made an Ordinary of the Mass* with set rubrics obligatory on all. The succeeding Popes quickly carried out the Council's wishes. The *Roman Breviary* (1568) and the *Roman Missal* (1570) appeared under Pius V*; the *Roman*

Pontifical (1596) and the *Ceremonial of Bishops* (1600) under Clement VIII; the *Roman Ritual* (1614) under Paul V; and the Sacred Congregation of Rites* was formed in 1598 under Sixtus V to guarantee the work of the reform.

It would be difficult to exaggerate the merits of such a reform. It freed the Church from the crises of the 16th century and provided valid bases for a genuine cult. Although the reform was made up of a mixed medieval form, at its core this Liturgy enshrined the essential patrimony of the ancient Roman Liturgy. It became a source of spiritual life for and a point of departure of the Liturgical Movement* in our day.

(6) *Liturgical Renewal* (20th century). In 1903 Pius X* began the last phase of the history of the Liturgy to our time with the statement that "the active participation [of the people] in the holy Mysteries* and in the public and solemn prayer of the Church" is "the foremost and indispensable fount" of the "true Christian spirit" *(Tra le Sollecitudini*)*. This gave rise to the Liturgical Movement* (which had its roots in many previous events, notably the work of Dom Prosper Guéranger in the 19th century).

After some forty years of grass roots liturgical ferment throughout the Catholic world, Pius XII issued his celebrated Encyclical *Mediator Dei** (On the Worship of the Church), which upheld the importance of the Liturgy and gave approval to the Liturgical Movement in progress. The same Pope went on to make reforms in the Easter Vigil* and in the celebration of the Eucharist. Pope John XXIII inserted the name of St. Joseph* in the Canon* (Eucharistic Prayer I*), laying the basis for further changes in a text that had been unchanged for some three hundred years.

International congresses of scholars and experts in Liturgy also paved the way for liturgical reform beginning in 1951, above all the International Congress on Pastoral Liturgy at Assisi in 1956 and the Eucharistic Congress at Monaco in 1960.

In 1962 the Second Vatican Council convened for its deliberations, and in 1963 it issued the first decree—the epoch-making *Constitution on the Sacred Liturgy,** which termed the Liturgy the fount and summit of the whole activity of the Church and called for a wholesale liturgical reform. Over the course of twenty-five years a thoroughgoing reform has been effected and is nearly complete. *See also* CONSTITUTION ON THE SACRED LITURGY; LITURGICAL BOOKS; LITURGICAL MOVEMENT; SACRAMENTALS; SACRAMENTS; VATICAN COUNCIL, SECOND; *and the listings of individual liturgical books, parts of Mass, Sacramentals, and Sacraments.*

Liturgy—Participation (LIT-uhr-jee puhr [pahr]-tis-uh-PAY-shuhn). Taking part in the Liturgy,* which is the celebration/memorial of the saving Mystery* of Christ. By such participation Christians lay internal and faith-filled hold of the redemptive action of the Risen Jesus present through the power of the Holy Spirit.* By this contact the faithful* are made holy and render to God true worship* in spirit and in truth (Jn 4:26). In the words of Pius X,* "the active participation of the people in the worship* of the Church* is the primary and indispensable source of the Christian spirit."

This act of taking part entails rapport, relationship, communication, imitation, union, and the like. In the case of the liturgical participation, it also involves an *inner spirituality* that is the soul of *external participation* and that must conform uniquely to the truth of the sanctification* of the faithful and the glory* of the Trinity. Hence, it entails a *personal response* of the faithful in the unique mystical presence of the Church to the call of the Father in, with, and through Christ by the power of the Holy Spirit.

Participation in the Liturgy is both the right and the duty of the faithful by reason of their Baptism* and Confirmation,* and (for some) Holy Orders,* which give each a share in

the priesthood of Christ—either the universal priesthood* (laity) or the ministerial priesthood* (priests).

> Mother Church earnestly desires that all the faithful should be led to that full, conscious, and active participation in liturgical celebrations that is demanded by the very nature of the Liturgy. Such participation by the Christian people as a "chosen race, a royal priesthood, a holy nation, a redeemed people" (1 Pt 2:9; see 2:4f), is their right and duty by reason of their Baptism (SC, 15).

This participation must be *full* as well as internal and external (as already mentioned). The faithful must respond with perfect attunement to the objective of the celebration,* thus giving full reign to the possibilities of the supernatural activities that form part of their supernatural existence as people deputed for the worship of God. The participation must engage the whole person with all the faculties required: mind, heart, and soul as well as body with tongue and lips, hands and feet, arms and legs, etc.

This participation must be *conscious.* The faithful must take part fully aware of what they are doing, actively engaged in the rite, and enriched by its effects (SC, 11). The prayer of the Church is not hermetically sealed, not divorced from the understanding of the people. Rather it goes out to meet the people's eagerness to know and understand; it fulfills the word of Christ: "They shall all be taught by God" (Jn 6:45).

This participation must be *active*—much more than simple assistance, no matter how attentive. The participants are not to be simple spectators, no matter how interested. They are to be doers in the action—responding, praying, worshiping!

In addition, participation must be *communitarian.* The intrinsic nature of the Liturgy as well as its psychological efficacy on the individual participant demands it. Liturgical services are not private functions but celebrations of the Church, which is the Sacrament of unity, namely the holy people united and arranged under their bishops* and priests.*

Finally, this participation must be *hierarchically structured.* Since the Liturgy is an epiphany (a manifestation) of the Church, it must possess a quality that is instrinsic to the nature of the Church—hierarchical structure. The Church is composed of members who differ in function, and so is the liturgical assembly. The Church as an organized body, a living society, prays in a collective cult, in which each member has a role to fulfill. All are to take part in the drama, but not in the same roles: priest, deacon,* reader,* chanter,* faithful—all perform in turn and listen to the others.

Active participation has the advantage not only of enabling everyone to understand the sense of the liturgical celebration and of Divine praise, that they may live the prayer of the Church, but also of empowering them to draw from the spiritual treasure earned by Christ for all of us.

Collaborating in the prayer of the community, the believers develop their Catholic sense rapidly and take from it a more efficient antidote against the multiple solicitations of the outside world.* They become conscious of the responsibility that all have toward the Church to which they belong. In the past several years, much has been accomplished along these lines because of the strenuous efforts made by those commissioned to follow up the wishes of the *Constitution on the Sacred Liturgy,** which called for the participation of all in liturgical worship. *See also* APOSTOLICAM ACTUOSITATEM; LAITY; UNIVERSAL PRIESTHOOD.

Liturgy and Art. *See* ART AND LITURGY.

Liturgy and Catechesis. *See* CATECHESIS AND LITURGY.

Liturgy and Contemplative Life (LIT-uhr-jee and kuhn-TEM-pluh-tiv laif). Contemplation* is an intellectual act in which an intuitive viewing of Divine things and God takes place, that is, the higher power of the mind is at work. Clearly then, contemplative life can be a part of everyone's life. However, it is expected of those who join a contemplative order, devoted almost exclusively to activities related to meditation and reflection. Lay* persons, Religious,* or members of contemplative orders should recognize the central dimension of the Liturgy* in their lives, particularly in the following cases.

(1) The solemn celebration of the Liturgy of the Hours,* the official prayer of the Church, should fill them with constant inspiration and nourishment as Religious and laity join together in a very intimate par-

ticipation of the Church's life. The spiritual riches of the Office of Readings* should be greatly appreciated as a source of devotion and a help to strengthen personal prayer, while the entire day is sanctified.

(2) Meditation on the Scriptures* should be a daily encounter, allowing for growth in the spiritual life, either in a personal or in a community commitment to mental prayer. Such activity allows one to contemplate the Word of God* in its objective richness as well as in our daily circumstances, particularly insofar as it reflects the teaching of the Church.

(3) The absolute center and life-giving force in any Religious community would necessarily have to be the celebration of the Eucharist.* Its daily solemnization should be paramount for any priest* or Religious; it is certainly expected that all Religious would actively participate in it each day, receiving the Lord from that same Sacrifice. Each day the communities are thus able to renew their self-offering to the Lord, as they are visibly assembled in their chapel* in the presence of the Blessed Sacrament,* fulfilling the main mission of their individual Religious family. Many cloistered Religious Communities who dedicate a good portion of their life to Eucharistic adoration are, by their silence* and recollection, allowing the Liturgy to work within them in a very effective manner.

(4) The Rite of Penance* has been frequently put forth by the bishops* and the Sacred Congregations as a significant aid for growth in the spiritual life.* Proper appreciation for this Sacrament can be established through the regular reception in a fraternal and ecclesial dimension, as the Sacrament is celebrated in a community rite, the actual confession being personal. *See also* CONTEMPLATION.

Liturgy and Creativity. *See* CREATIVITY IN LITURGY.

Liturgy and Education. *See* LITURGICAL FORMATION.

Liturgy and Eschatology (LIT-uhr-jee and es-kuh-TOL-uh-jee). Eschatology is the study of the "last things" of individuals, the Church,* and the cosmos. As far as Christian individuals are concerned, it deals with death,* the last judgment,* heaven,* and hell. At the center of eschatology is Christ Who by His glorious Resurrection* has inaugurated the *eschaton,* the new and definitive realities of history. Christ is the synthesis of all and He is the same "yesterday, today, and forever" (Heb 13:8), the "Alpha and the Omega," "the one who is and who was and who is to come" (Rv 1:8). In Him is contained as in germ the promises of the eschatology of the Church and the cosmos. His Resurrection is the guarantee of the promises about realities that must still be fulfilled: His coming in glory,* the final resurrection, and the final implementation of His Kingdom.*

The Liturgy has always set forth in an exemplary manner the eschatological vision centered on the Resurrection of Christ and the ex-

pectation of His coming, reducing all to the celebration of the Paschal Mystery,* synthesis of the History of Salvation.* Thus, the Liturgy is the essential locus of the confession of faith and the celebration of the experience of faith that illumines the meaning of life* and death, present and future.

In the liturgical experience it is eschatology that is lived: the presence of the Divine in the human, the invisible in the visible, the eternal in the temporal, that is, an anticipated eschatology, and the tension toward the future to attain the newness of the fullness of Christ (see Eph 4:13) in the future city toward which we are pilgrimaging (see Heb 13:14 and SC, 2). And although Jesus is present in the Liturgy, He is also still to come in His glory (SC, 8).

Thus, the Eucharist enables Christians to take part in an anticipated eschatology: it is the pledge of glory (SC, 47), presence of the Risen Christ and His Paschal Mystery, expectation of His coming, constitution of the eschatological community, seed of the resurrection, and anticipation of the renewal of creation in the transformation of the bread and wine.

The Sacraments* have this same eschatological dimension and so does the Liturgy of the Hours*: "When the Church offers praise to God in the Liturgy of the Hours she unites herself with that hymn of praise which is sung in the heavenly places throughout all ages. She also receives a foretaste of the song of praise in heaven . . . that is sung without ceasing before the throne of God and of the Lamb" (GILH, 16).

From one point of view, the Liturgy may be said to provide entry into the Kingdom, which for this world is still to come but of which the Church is the Sacrament, the beginning, and the anticipation. Hence, every celebration directs us toward the fulfillment, arousing Church hope in us. Anchored on Easter and Pentecost, the Liturgy tends toward the Second Coming as the decisive moment of its existence while at the same time it is already enjoying communion with the glory of the blessed.*

Hence, the Liturgy, since it combines time and eternity, can give a new meaning to the Christian commitment in the world with the practice of justice* and charity* in the service of others, contributing to the preparation of the Kingdom to come. *See also* CHURCH AND LITURGY; CHURCH YEAR; HISTORY OF SALVATION; KINGDOM OF GOD.

Liturgy and Liberation. *See* LIBERATION AND LITURGY.

Liturgy and the Bible. *See* BIBLE AND LITURGY.

Liturgy and Theology. *See* THEOLOGY AND LITURGY.

Liturgy Committee, Parish. *See* PARISH LITURGY COMMITTEE.

Liturgy of the Dead. *See* FUNERAL RITES AND CEREMONIES; MASS OF CHRISTIAN BURIAL.

Liturgy of the Eucharist (LIT-uhr-jee uhv thuh YOO-kuh-rist). The major part of Mass* that comes after the Liturgy of the Word* and ends before the Concluding Rite.* This part corresponds to the words and actions of Christ at the Last Supper.* Christ took bread and the cup, gave thanks, broke, and gave them to His disciples saying: "Take and eat; this is My Body. Take and drink; this is the cup of My Blood. Do this in memory of Me."

The Liturgy of the Eucharist includes: (1) Preparation of the Gifts* (Presentation); (2) Eucharistic Prayer* (Enactment and Offering of the Sacrifice); and (3) Communion Rite* (Partaking of the Sacrificial Meal).

(1) During the *Preparation of the Gifts,* the priest* prepares the altar* and the gifts, prays over the bread and wine, and helps the assembly* get ready for the tremendous Sacrifice* that will shortly take place in an unbloody manner. The following take place: (a) Offertory Song* and Procession*; (b) Preparation of the Altar*: (c) Preparation of the Bread*; (d) Preparation of the Wine*; (e) Washing of Hands*; (f) Invitation to Prayer*; and (g) Prayer over the Gifts.*

(2) The *Eucharistic Prayer* is the center and high point of the Mass that makes Christ present for us in His Passion,* Death,* and Resurrection.* During it, the entire assembly joins Christ in acknowledging the works of God and in offering the Sacrifice. The following take place: (a) Introductory Dialogue*; (b) Preface*; (c) Sanctus*; (d) Eucharistic Prayer*; (e) Consecration*; (f) Memorial Acclamation*; and (g) Great Amen.*

(3) The *Communion Rite* is the conclusion of the Mass. It is the part when God gives a gift to us after we have presented our gift to Him. In both cases the gift is the same—Jesus Christ, the Son of God and

Savior of the world. It includes: (a) Lord's Prayer*; (b) Sign of Peace*; (c) Breaking of the Bread*; (d) Lamb of God*; (e) Prayers before Communion*; (f) Reception of Communion*; (g) Communion Song* and Procession or Communion Antiphon*; (h) Silence after Communion*; and (i) Prayer after Communion.*

In summary, we might say that the members of the assembly, made ready by reflection on the Word of God, now through the Liturgy of the Eucharist enter into the Eucharistic Sacrifice itself, the Supper of the Lord. They celebrate the memorial that the Lord instituted at His Last Supper. They are God's new people, gathered by Him around His table. They are there to bless God and to receive the gift of Jesus' Body and Blood so that their faith* and life may be transformed. *See also* EUCHARIST; EUCHARISTIC PRAYER; EUCHARISTIC PRAYER I; EUCHARISTIC PRAYER II; EUCHARISTIC PRAYER III; EUCHARISTIC PRAYER IV; EUCHARISTIC PRAYERS FOR MASSES OF RECONCILIATION; EUCHARISTIC PRAYERS FOR MASSES WITH CHILDREN.

Liturgy of the Hours (LIT-uhr-jee uhv thee owrz). The official public prayer of the Church* comprised of hymns,* Psalms,* spiritual and Biblical readings,* and prayers.* Sung or recited by certain members of the Church particularly deputed to carry out this duty of thanksgiving,* reparation, and adoration* of God, this prayer at the same time also solicits graces that Christ's work on earth may continue. Because it is a prayer of the entire People of God, the Divine Office* is so arranged that not only those obliged to its recitation, the clergy* and Religious,* but also the laity* may participate in it.

Since this formal prayer is to sanctify the entire day, its recitation has been ordered to relate to the chronological hours of the day that we normally meet in contemporary life. Thus it becomes a complement to the Eucharistic Sacrifice* in order to bring about a fullness of Divine Worship, which overflows into all the hours of daily living.

History

Grounded on the daily liturgy of the Jews, everyday prayer became a routine for the early Christian communities. There was a firm tradition of scheduled times of prayer by assemblies, considered superior to private prayer. When religious freedom was granted to Christians, the rise of monasticism brought about a significant shift in spirituality and liturgical practice. With a more rigorous routine and formal community prayer of both day and night, a monastic office developed whereby they separated each day into sections by praying at the night office and seven times during the day. These hours were called: Matins,* Lauds,* Prime,* Terce,* Sext,* None,* Vespers,* and Compline.*

Simultaneously a cathedral office developed around the local bishop,* who limited the prayer routine because of his work and that of his priests. They, together with a relatively large number of faithful,* celebrated a Morning Prayer and an Evening Prayer. As time passed the Divine Office became more elaborate, more complicated, and the obligation for its recitation by the clerics and those in Religious Orders was stressed. Ultimately the Office from the Papal Curia, gathered into one book, the *Breviary,* was adopted because of its popularization by the Franciscans. Pope St. Pius V,* commissioned by the Council of Trent, revised the liturgical books* including the *Breviary.*

The Reform

After his revision, certain accretions occurred, but actual reforms did not take place until the 20th century. Before Vatican II,* the Sunday* was restored to its preeminence, the Psalms were redistributed, and much of the Office was simplified. Because of the Council, a more complete reform occurred, deleting Prime, allowing two of the Daytime Hours to be omitted, and placing more emphasis on the Scripture* and the Psalms, which were distributed over a four-week period.

To nourish personal prayer, much more variety was inserted and helps to meditation were included: titles,* Psalm-prayers,* antiphons,* and optional periods of silence.* Canticles* from both the Old* and the New Testament* were

added to Morning Prayer and Evening Prayer to increase their beauty and spiritual richness. The best readings from Christian authors were provided, and revisions in the hagiographical readings* helped to project the spiritual image of the Saints* together with their significance in the life of the Church. Intercessions* were added to Morning Prayer and Evening Prayer.

With the intent to make sure that the Office would relate to the time of the day and not be restricted to the clergy but offer opportunities for participation by many of the faithful* in its regular recitation, certain adaptations were made. Morning Prayer (Lauds) and Evening Prayer (Vespers) were designated as the hinges of each day's Office and necessarily of central importance. The Office of Readings* (Matins) was abbreviated and adapted to be said at any hour of the day. Night Prayer* (Compline) was called that since it was designed as a suitable prayer for the end of the day. Instead of the four Little Hours* (Prime, Terce, Sext, None) there was now Daytime Prayer* consisting of three sections: Midmorning,* Midday,* and Midafternoon.* However, unless one is obliged to celebrate the Office in choir, only one of these must be recited.

The structural elements of the Office are the following:

Opening Hymn. Aside from being a fitting introduction, the hymn serves to focus the time of day, the feast,* or the season* and stresses the importance of music* in the communal celebration of the Liturgy of the Hours.

Psalmody. The 150 Psalms display an array of human emotions. Helps to understand their various literary forms or types are given, such as titles, antiphons, and Psalm-prayers. They are distributed over a one-month period, that is, a four-week cycle.

Canticles. Canticles from the Old Testament are used in Morning Prayer and from the New Testament in Evening Prayer.

Readings. Although there is much Scripture in the Office of Readings, yet the Second Reading is non-Biblical, taken from patristic sources, significant ecclesiastical documents, or the writings of a Saint whose feast is being celebrated.

Intercessions. These are added to both Morning Prayer and Evening Prayer, which are the chief hours of formal public prayer; the needs of the Church should be met through this type of supplication on such an occasion.

The Lord's Prayer and *Concluding Prayer.* The Lord's Prayer is added to the important Hours of the Office, Morning Prayer and Evening Prayer, making them comparable to the Mass, which also includes this prayer. Usually the concluding prayer is identical to the Opening Prayer* at Mass.*

Dismissal. A formal dismissal occurs after the cardinal hours of Morning Prayer and Evening Prayer; a more brief formula concludes the other Hours.

Theology

Christ's prayer to His Father is obvious from the Scriptures, based on His intent to accomplish His Father's will to save us. In His Messianic ministry and throughout the Paschal Mystery,* prayer was a

vital force. Since He continues His priestly work through the Church, the official prayer of the Church becomes the eternal prayer of Christ. Thus all of us, sharing the priesthood* of Christ, join our voices with His. The Church as a community shows her communal nature by prayer,* a public act of worship.* Through the Liturgy of the Hours, praise, thanksgiving, and the remembrance of the Mysteries* of salvation are extended to the various hours of the day, so that the Divine Office becomes a prolongation of the Eucharistic celebration.

At the Eucharist and the Divine Office, the community recalls the saving works of God, and through the recitation of the Office, the Mass continues to be celebrated throughout the day as a great sacrifice of praise, which at the same time effects the sanctification of the Church in time. During its prayer, then, the Church not only remembers the past but looks toward the future as she stands in the present.

Just as the Holy Spirit* is called upon to change the bread and wine into the Body and Blood* of Christ during Mass, so during the Office does the Spirit transform the community into the Body of Christ,* giving it a character of unity. He helps us to pray properly, wording our entreaties better than we ever could.

Celebration

So that the Church can properly celebrate the Liturgy of the Hours, each parish* should choose certain times and occasions, preferably on a regular schedule, particularly for one or both of the hinge hours, Morning Prayer and Evening Prayer. Sundays, Solemnities,* and Feasts* offer opportunities for special local celebrations. Naturally, especially at the beginning, the celebration should be in some significant setting with proper planning preceding it. For instance, music* should be used, simple at first, and with sufficient practice to allow a rich and pleasing rendition. As to the proper setting, the selection of a place, vestments,* other accoutrements, and seating arrangement all must work together to bring about a suitable environment.

The ministers* should be carefully chosen, with sufficient ability to read, to sing, to lead, and to assist in the proper presentation of the particular Hour being celebrated. Since there is a ritual structure, the planned manner of procedure should be taken into consideration, and everything should flow smoothly and easily to allow for full participation* and a prayerful attitude on the part of all celebrating. The style should fit the occasion; for instance, Evening Prayer on a Solemnity in a Cathedral* Church is quite different from Night Prayer in a home.

The Future

The supposition of the reform is that the Liturgy of the Hours would become part of parish life. Although it may take a while to implement this, the hope is that the various types of celebration of the Liturgy of the Hours could become part and parcel of the Catholic devotional life as nonliturgical devotions were in the past. Once that is accomplished, Christian spirituality would be based upon a Biblical and sound theological foundation. For the Divine Office not only is the public and common prayer of the Church but also has an irreplaceable value of prayerful meeting with God at every moment and in every situation of daily life.

The Church wants all to understand that the Liturgy of the Hours is her prayer of worship and praise to the Father, through Christ and with Him, in the Holy Spirit, as she consecrates the time during which we live. In the regular recitation of the Office, this song of love is to become a meeting with God in unison by all those reciting, listening, and meditating on the various parts of the Office. Further, the Church hopes that the community will enjoy integrating the Liturgy of the Hours into its life, sanctifying its rhythms and cadences, and collaborating with God to bring about salvation.* *See also* BREVIARY; DAYTIME PRAYER; EVENING PRAYER; MORNING PRAYER; NIGHT PRAYER; OFFICE OF READINGS.

Liturgy of the Word (LIT-uhr-jee uhv thuh wuhrd). The major part of the Mass* between the Opening Prayer* and the Preparation of the Gifts,* during which the Word of God* is proclaimed (Readings*), responded to (Responsorial Psalm*), authoritatively explained (Homily*), accepted and held fast (Profession of Faith*), and appealed to (General Intercessions*). This liturgical proclamation is not simply a reading but an event, a happening—even more, it is a *salvific event.* It brings before the assembly* the Word that God wants to speak to us *today.* It enables us to encounter Christ Who "is present in His Word . . . when the Holy Scriptures* are read in the Church" (SC, 7).

> The many riches contained in the one word of God are admirably brought out in the different kinds of liturgical celebrations and liturgical assemblies. This occurs as the unfolding mystery* of Christ is recalled during the course of the liturgical year,* as the Church's sacraments* and sacramentals* are celebrated, or as the faithful* respond individually to the Holy Spirit* working within them. For then the liturgical celebration, based primarily on the word of God and sustained by it, *becomes a new event* and enriches that word itself *with new meaning and power.* Thus in the liturgy the Church faithfully adheres to the way Christ Himself read and explained the Scriptures, beginning with the "today" of His coming forward in the synagogue [at Capernaum] and urging all to search the Scriptures (LFMI, 3, *italics added*).

As a liturgical action, the Word is proclaimed in the midst of the gathering, which is a representation of the Church. This makes the act of hearing, receiving, and integrating that Word an *ecclesial action.* It constitutes the ever-new exchange and ratification of the Covenant* between God and His people.* It also manifests the nature of the Church with a distribution of proper roles. All are called to listen; some are delegated to proclaim; and others are empowered to "break the bread" of the Word (by expounding it through their office of teaching in virtue of their ordination or deputation to exercise that ministry).

However, the Word is not intended to remain within the liturgical assembly. "Baptism* and Confirmation* in the Spirit have made all the faithful messengers of God's word because of the grace of hearing they have received. They must therefore be the bearers of the same word in the Church and in the world,* at least by the witness of their way of life" (LFMI, 7).

Besides calling to mind the plan of salvation,* the Word expresses the Father's love for us, which becomes fully effective through the power of the Holy Spirit. All Scripture revolves around Christ, so that He becomes the center for the entire Liturgy. Indeed, the Risen Jesus becomes present to His Church in both parts of the Eucharistic Celebration: the Liturgy of the Word and the Liturgy of the Eucharist.* In both of these He is present under symbols.*

There are two tables of the Lord—the table of the Word and the table of the Eucharist. At the first, Jesus is present under the Veil of the words that impart the Word of God, and at the second He is present under the Species* of bread and wine that are His Body and Blood.

In both cases, Christ becomes present for us to help us become new human beings. We will in turn be able to transform others and eventually the whole world. Thus, the Word of God, listened to at the various liturgical celebrations by the faithful, enables them to participate more fully by a life of words and actions, which conforms to what they hear and celebrate in each Liturgy.

Those who have the office of teaching in the Church, through their exercise of this ministry, keep the teaching, life, and worship alive and adapt it to the needs of the Church at the present time. The Holy Spirit, working through them, enlightens the faithful to the applications proper to each.

Ideally, the proclamation of the Word of God together with its explanation leads automatically into the Liturgy of the Eucharist, which completes the Eucharistic Sacrifice.

Celebration

(1) *Readings.** These are taken from the Scriptures according to a definite pattern as explained under the entry "Lectionary."* Naturally the acme of the Liturgy of the Word is the presentation of the Gospel.*

(2) *Responsorial Psalm.** Following the First Reading* this Psalm

has pastoral significance and is an integral part of the Liturgy of the Word. If possible it should be sung; otherwise it is recited.

(3) *Acclamation.** This is an introductory verse to the Gospel and should be sung.

(4) *Homily.** Ordinarily the one who presides at the celebration of the Word is responsible for a carefully prepared explanation of the Scriptures proclaimed, which should be highly suited to the audience present.

(5) *Silence.** The Sacred Scriptures tend toward meditation, so intervals of silence can readily intersperse the Readings and certainly follow the Homily.

(6) *Profession of Faith.** The recitation of the symbol allows the faithful to give assent to the Word of God they have just heard and had explained to them.

(7) *General Intercessions.** This is an opportunity for the people to pray for the universal needs of the Church, the local community, and the special intentions that they may have.

Apart from Mass

The Liturgy of the Word is used apart from Mass where the Eucharistic Celebration is not possible because of lack of priests. It is also used in the nature of a Bible Service.*

The Sacraments and Blessings* of the *Ritual** are now also administered within the setting of the Liturgy of the Word in cases where Mass is not celebrated. *See also* ACCLAMATIONS; BIBLE; BIBLE AND LITURGY; BIBLE SERVICE; GENERAL INTERCESSIONS; GOSPEL; HOMILY; LECTIONARY; PROFESSION OF FAITH; READINGS; RESPONSORIAL PSALM; SILENCE; SUNDAY CELEBRATION IN THE ABSENCE OF A PRIEST.

Local Church (LOH-kuhl chuhrch). A local lawful congregation united with its pastor in which all the faithful* are gathered together by the preaching of Christ's Gospel* and the Mystery of the Lord's Supper is celebrated (see LG, 26). The whole of the liturgical assembly,* presided over by the priest* representing the bishop,* is the visible and efficacious sign* of the Church, and, like her, is one, holy, Catholic, and apostolic.

The Local Church is part of the Universal Church* and signifies the solidarity by which all Christians are united in the one Body of Christ* and all the assemblies in the one Church spread over all the earth. It is not autonomous within the unity of the Universal Church but is an integrated part, a living member, a flowering branch, endowed with its own vitality from the one source of faith* and grace.*

The Liturgy* stands out most strikingly as an ecclesial celebration when, through the bishop surrounded by his priests, and ministers, the Local Church celebrates it. For in the Local Church, the one, holy, Catholic, and apostolic Church is truly present and at work (see GILH, 20). The Church is, in a certain sense, Christ still living on in this world throughout the ages, ever engaged in saving and sanctifying people of every generation. And she is most clearly revealed when a full complement of God's holy people, united in prayer* and in a common liturgical service (especially the Eucharist*), exercise a thorough and active participation* at the very altar* where the bishop presides in the company of his priests and other ministers or at the altar where a pastor (or associate pastor) presides in the bishop's place surrounded by his ministers (see SC, 42).

Thus, each local assembly represents the visible Church constituted throughout the world, that is, the Universal Church. It is the Church in miniature, a manifestation of the whole Church. It is the Church made actual at a definite time and place; it can act for the Church by celebrating the Liturgy.

When the members of a Local Church celebrate the Eucharist, which is a covenant*-sacrifice,* each of them enters anew into a covenant making it their own. They are thus enabled to exercise whatever share in Christ's priesthood* has been conferred on them—either the *universal priesthood** through the Sacrament of Baptism* or the *ministerial priesthood** through the Sacrament of Holy Orders.* By repeating this action of the Church they build up the Church and keep her in being. *See also* CHURCH; CHURCH AND LITURGY; UNIVERSAL CHURCH.

Loculus (LOK-yuh-luhs). The diminutive form of the Latin word for "place" (*locus*) that has been retained in English in two senses. (1) It refers to a Christian grave in the catacombs,* which was formed in a horizontal rectangular niche, cut into the wall and closed at the front by a slab of stone that bore an epitaph. (2) It also refers to the hollowed-out space in the mensa of an altar* that contains the relics*—which goes by the additional name of "sepulcher."

Lord Be with You, The (lawrd bee with yoo, thuh). As a greeting,* invitation,* and blessing,* these words are employed frequently in various liturgies by the president of the congregation. The formula alerts the congregation to what is to follow, usually a prayer* or the Gospel,* and is normally joined with a gesture of extending the arms toward the congregation.

This formula is a translation of the Latin *"Dominus vobiscum,"* which is used frequently in Scripture.* In Ruth* 2:4 it appears as a greeting but in Judges* 6:12 and elsewhere constitutes a simple statement of God's presence in the community (notably in the salutation of the Angel Gabriel to Mary in Luke* 1:28). Thus, the phrase could have been translated as "The Lord *is* with you" with the understanding that the priest recognizes that he has before him a holy people assembled in the Name of Jesus and in which Jesus is present. However, in virtue of the fact that *"Dominus vobiscum"* is frequently repeated during the course of the service, it appears rather as a wish, hence as if it had a verb in the subjunctive!

The congregation's response conveys a return of the greeting, agreement with it, and a token of fellowship: *"Et cum spiritu tuo."* Formerly, the literal translation "And with your spirit" was used. The vernacular now uses the more free rendition: "And also with you."* *See also* GREETING.

Lord, Have Mercy (lawrd hav MUHR-see). The translation of the Greek invocation* *Kyrie eleison,* which is on the lips of those unfortunate people in the Gospel* who begged Jesus to cure them or their child. These included the blind (Mt 9:27 and 20:30-31; Mk 10:47), the lepers (Lk 17:13), the Canaanite woman whose daughter was possessed (Mt 15:22), and the father of the epileptic (Mt 17:14). It is also the prayer that Jesus places on the lips of the publican in the parable (Lk 18:14).

As in the Gospel, this supplication is directed to Christ. But the lepers or the blind, while they called Him "Son of David" or "Lord," saw in Him only the Messiah. For the first Christians, *Kyrios* ("Lord") was a Divine Name, the usual translation of *Yahweh,** and the proper title of the risen and glorious Christ, equal with the "Father."* St. Peter* says, at the end of his discourse on Pentecost: "Therefore let the whole house of Israel know for certain that God has made him both Lord and Messiah, this Jesus whom you crucified" (Acts 2:36; see also Phil 2:9-11).

In the 5th century an intercessory litany* using these words was inserted after the Introit* of the Mass,* and as such it shows the confidence of the congregation in the risen Lord together with an expression of joy.* Before the recent

liturgical reforms, this invocation was recited three times, its variant "Christ, have mercy" (*Christe, eleison*) was said three times, and that was followed by the triple "Lord, have mercy" for the second time, which was the congregation's way of petitioning for the entreaties in the celebrant's Opening Prayer* that followed immediately. Today, the same order is used, but the threefold form is changed to a responsorial twofold one and is incorporated in the Penitential Rite* of the Mass. (The liturgical formula leaves out the complement to the verb found in Scripture "have mercy on *me*" or "on *us*" since it is an imploration for all the miseries of humankind and not only for personal miseries.) *See also* PENITENTIAL RITE.

Lord, I Am Not Worthy . . . (lawrd ai am not WUHR-thee). Response of priest* and people to the invitation to receive Communion* voiced by the priest at Mass.* After the Breaking of the Bread,* the priest shows the Eucharistic Bread to the faithful.* He invites them to participate in the meal and leads them in an act of humility, reverence, confidence, and faith, using words from the Gospel*: "This is the Lamb of God* who takes away the sins of the world" (see Jn 1:36). "Happy are those who are called to his supper" (see Rv 19:9). The assembly accepts the invitation also in words from Scripture: "Lord, I am not worthy to receive you but only say the word and I shall be healed" (see Mt 8:9).

Lord, Open My Lips. *See* INTRODUCTORY VERSE.

Lord's Day. *See* SUNDAY.

Lord's Prayer (lawrdz prayr). The *Our Father* (Mt 6:9-13) was taught by Christ to the Apostles* at their request and has been a basic formula for Christian prayer* since then. Its seven petitions synthesize our Faith,* giving a balanced structure to our values, since the first three relate to the things of God and the last four to the needs of human beings. All in all, the Lord's Prayer has a unique status in the Liturgy* and is ordinarily not to be used in a repetitive fashion as was formerly the case when lay brothers and sisters in Religious Orders recited it in lieu of the Divine Office.*

Baptism

As a notable feature of the catechumenate, the Lord's Prayer is presented to the elect.* Since from antiquity the *Our Father* belongs to those who have received the spirit of adoption of children in Baptism,* the neophytes will join together with the rest of the baptized in reciting it during their first celebration of the Eucharist.* Usually this presentation takes place after the third scrutiny, but it may be celebrated during the catechumenate, particularly if the catechumens are mature. In some situations, it may be left to the time of the preparatory rites on Holy Saturday* itself.

Mass

At Mass the Communion Rite* begins with the Lord's Prayer, when the priest,* immediately after the Eucharistic Prayer,* invites the congregation to join with him in the *Our Father,* which preferably they should sing together. The priest adds the embolism* that expands the last petition; the people conclude with the doxology,* comprising the acclamation* that Protestants had added to the Lord's Prayer for many years: "For the kingdom, the power, and the glory are yours, now and for ever."

The *Our Father* is a natural preparatory prayer for Communion.* Summed up in its petitions we find all that we could request. In it we ask for our daily bread, the bread that gives access to eternity, the Bread of Life. For this purpose we beg forgiveness of our sins as we forgive others, so that "holy things may be given to the holy."

The *Our Father* formally entered the Mass in the late 4th century. Later, St. Gregory the Great,* influenced by St. Augustine,* transferred it from after the Breaking of the Bread* to before it. It used to be reserved to the celebrant with the people relegated to saying "Amen" at the end. In the Mass of Paul VI, the people now say the entire prayer with the celebrant, and the concluding "Amen" is no longer included.

Liturgy of the Hours

Historically, according to the *Didache,* the Lord's Prayer should be said three times a day. In keeping with this ancient custom, the Church in her present Liturgy* has specified the Lord's Prayer to be said, besides during the Communion Rite at Mass, as a conclusion to the Intercessions* during the hinge hours of the Divine Office, Morning Prayer* and Evening Prayer.* Thus all join together on these most important occasions to pray for the daily needs of the Church. *See also* MASS—COMMUNION RITE.

Lord's Supper, The (lawrdz SUHP-uhr, thuh). This term is used for the Sacrament of the Eucharist, particularly by Protestants, who rejected the Eucharistic teaching of the Roman Catholic Church. They consider it a true Sacrament* but usually exclude the sacrificial aspect of the Eucharist.*

It is also the name given to the final Paschal Supper that Jesus ate with His disciples* on the eve of His Death,* during which He consecrated the bread and wine for the first time and gave His Apostles* the power to continue this act. Now all priests,* when commemorating this action of Christ, renew it on the altar* at the Eucharistic table, which St. Paul calls the Lord's Supper (1 Cor 11:20). On Holy Thursday* the institution of the Eucharist is commemorated in a special way in the evening. The liturgical books* describe the action as "The Mass of the Lord's Supper." *See also* EUCHARIST; LAST SUPPER.

Louis, St. (LOO-uhs). 1214-1270. Louis became King of France when he was only twenty-two years old. He married and had eleven children whom he carefully instructed in the Christian life. He excelled in penance* and prayer* and in love for the poor. While ruling his kingdom he had regard not only for peace among peoples and the temporal good of his subjects but also for their spiritual welfare. He was sought by other rulers as an arbitrator because of his sanctity and fairness. This saintly ruler undertook two Crusades to recover the tomb of Christ and died near Carthage. He is the Patron of Barbers and of Franciscan Tertiaries. *Liturgical celebration:* August 25 (Opt. Mem.); *theme:* untiring effort toward peace.

Love (luhv). An affective tendency toward some good that leads to active communion with it. As a relational and unifying force, love may be either self-interested by being directed toward some object that enriches oneself or disinterested by manifesting gratuitous generosity through self-communication.

Put another way, love is the affinity of being with being. Love alone is capable of uniting living beings in such a way as to complete and fulfill them, for it alone takes them and joins them by what is deepest in themselves. Hence, love is the most universal, the most tremendous, and the most mysterious of the cosmic energies. Ultimately, it is the attraction exercised on each unit of consciousness by God in the creative process.

All being is a participation in the Divine Being, and it draws its reality from that participation. This means that the love or desire of participated being for fulfillment or more being is not something it has of itself but something it received from God. It means, too, that love, which is the fulfillment of this desire, is also a gift of God—but a specifically new and supernatural level of being. We call this Christian love.

In this sense, God is infinite Love. The Holy Spirit* is termed the mutual love of the Father and the Son, and it is He Who pours forth God's love on human beings and the whole created world.*

Christian love is a Divine virtue* infused into our souls by which we love God above all things for His own sake and our neighbor as ourselves for the love of God. This is the most excellent of all the virtues because it is eternal, it perfects all the other virtues, it makes everything we do pleasing to God, and it purifies us and establishes a true friendship between God and human beings.

It is called a theological virtue because like faith* and hope* it has God Himself for its immediate object, being a direct homage to all His Divine perfections, by which He is infinitely good in Himself and infinitely deserving of our love; and also because it is a virtue not acquired but infused by God into our souls.

With love all is possible. Love's victory is won through the strength not of coercion but of persuasion, attraction, or enticement, through the strength of unfailing love that never gives up.

The manifestations of love are revealed in Divine love, conjugal and friendship love, and societal love. When we love an individual in a center-to-center relationship, we in some measure love all humankind and the whole universe.

Liturgy: Love in Action

The Liturgy* may be termed Christian love in action together with faith and hope. "The worship* that the Church offers to God, all Good and Great, is a continuous profession of Catholic faith and a continuous exercise of hope and love, as Augustine* succinctly puts it: 'God is to be worshiped by faith, hope, and love' " (MD, 47). In the Liturgy, Christ draws to Himself by a most special title—in the worship that He renders to the Father*—the faithful and their acts of faith, hope, and love rendered in worshipful homage to the Father.

Furthermore, the whole of the Liturgy is directed always to the actuation of the love for God as the ultimate response of human beings to the prevenient and paternal love of God, which alone explains God's loving, gratuitous, and active interventions in history to draw human beings to Himself.

Thus, it is love that powers Christian participation* in the Liturgy.* Without love there is no true participation. At the same time, true liturgical participation increases love in Christians. The Liturgy also brings before us the many-faceted phases of this love.

God's Love for Human Beings

God's love for human beings is expressed in His many interventions in creation (Gn 1—Easter Vigil,* Reading I*) and in the history of Israel (Dt 4:37—Trinity Sunday,* B, Reading I; Jb 38—12th Ordinary Sunday, B, Reading I). It is a freely given elective love (Dt 7:7—Wednesday, 2nd Week in Ordinary Time* of *Liturgy of the Hours,** First Reading in Office of Readings*), working for the salvation of humankind and ever merciful in the face of human infidelity (Hos 14:2-10—Monday of 19th Week in Ordinary Time of *Liturgy of the Hours,* First Reading in Office of Readings).

This love led God to give His own Son up to death in order to save us

(Jn 3:16—4th Sunday of Lent,* B, Gospel*). Jesus' operative love was in perfect correspondence with the love of the Father and made the faithful the beloved of God (Jn 5:20-25—Wednesday, 4th Week of Lent, Gospel). In addition, this love in action is merciful as shown by the Cross* (Palm Sunday,* C, Passion; Jn 15:13—6th Sunday of Easter,* B, Gospel) and explained in the parables (Lk 15:11-32—4th Sunday of Lent, C, Gospel).

And the Liturgy requests this love for its participants, so that they may share in it and be counted among those God has chosen (Opening Prayer* for Mass of St. Matthias,* May 14).

Love for God

The Liturgy also indicates that we should have love for God above all things (Mt 22:37—30th Sunday in Ordinary Time, A, Gospel). We love God in this way when we value Him higher than anything in the world and are prepared to lose everything rather than offend Him by grave sin (*Rite of Penance,** Prayer of the Penitent). Our love for God is more perfect if we also strive to avoid venial sin: "I am convinced that neither death, nor life, nor angels, nor principalities, nor present things, nor future things, nor powers, nor height, nor depth, nor any other creature will be able to separate us from the love of God in Christ Jesus our Lord" (Rom 8:38-39—Common of Martyrs,* Reading II).

This love does not consist in tasting the sweetness of God. Since we cannot see God, our feelings for persons we can see, such as parents, may be stronger than our feelings for God. But love for God—or any true love, for that matter—is not primarily a matter of feelings. With regard to God, love means that in our mind we acknowledge Him as the highest good and in our will we are prepared to forsake everything else in order to adhere to Him. It is in this sense that Jesus said: "Whoever loves father or mother more than me is not worthy of me, and whoever loves son or daughter more than me is not worthy of me" (Mt 10:37—13th Sunday in Ordinary Time, A, Gospel).

Doubtless, there are moments when we also experience strong feelings for God, but we should not make them the touchstone of our love: "Whoever has my commandments and observes them is the one who loves me" (Jn 14:21—6th Sunday of Easter, A, Gospel).

The Liturgy asks for an increase in its participants' love for God (4th Sunday in Ordinary Time, Opening Prayer*) and for a truly operative love that will do God's will in all things (30th Sunday in Ordinary Time, Opening Prayer).

Love for Self

The Liturgy also points out that we should have a proper love for ourselves by indicating that our first concern must be the salvation* of our souls. With due regard for our spiritual welfare, we must also be concerned with the body and with things of this world: health, possessions, good name, job security. But we should always remember our Lord's words: "What profit would there be for one to gain the whole world and forfeit his [soul]?" (Mt 16:26—22nd Sunday in Ordinary Time, A, Gospel). For as Tobit said, "those habitually guilty of sin are their own worst enemies" (Tb 12:10—Saturday, 9th Week in Ordinary Time, Year I, Reading I).

However, we must be wary of self-love. Wrong self-love is egotism. It is the spirit of self-aggrandizement, when we use everyone and everything for our own advantage. If others must suffer in the process, so be it! Egotism makes people boastful, brazen, heartless, and offensive. This is not the way of Christian self-love.

All the texts in the Liturgy imply an ordered self-love, for they constantly ask that the participants attain union with God on earth and in heaven—in other words, the salvation of their souls! Almost every Prayer after Communion* has this idea as its theme. As an example, the Prayer after Communion of the 30th Sunday in Ordinary Time asks God to "bring to perfection within us the communion we share in this sacrament*" after the Opening Prayer has asked Him to "strengthen our faith, hope, and love. May we do with loving hearts what you ask of us and come to share the life you promise."

Love for Neighbor

The Liturgy also stresses that we are to have love for our neighbor, that is, for all people on earth: in the Parable of the Good Samaritan (Lk 10:25-37—Tuesday, 27th Week, Gospel) and in the Golden

Rule pronounced by Jesus: "Do to others whatever you would have them do to you" (Mt 7:13—Tuesday, 12th Week, Gospel). From this it follows that what we do *not* want done to us we should not do to others.

We should love all people because God has loved us with an unselfish love, because He commanded us to do so, and because all people are children of God, redeemed by the blood of Christ and called to eternal happiness in heaven: "This is my commandment: love one another as I have loved you" (Jn 15:12—6th Sunday of Easter, B, Gospel; see also Reading II: 1 Jn 4:7-10). He is "one God and Father of all and through all and in all" (Eph 4:6—17th Sunday, B, Reading II).

This love for others must be one "in deed and truth" and not only "in word or speech" (1 Jn 3:18—5th Sunday of Easter, B, Reading II). We must practice the corporal and spiritual works of mercy (*see* GOOD DEEDS).

Hence, the Liturgy prays that those who participate in it will grow in love for one another—a love that is operative—and come to perfection in the eternal life* prepared for them (25th Sunday, Opening Prayer).

This love for neighbor must include even enemies: "Love your enemies" (Mt 5:43ff—7th Sunday in Ordinary Time, A, Gospel). And the Liturgy prays that its participants may imitate St. Stephen* in this regard and love their enemies, thus attaining the same eternal glory* that is now his (Mass of December 26, Opening Prayer). *See also* COMMANDMENTS; FAITH; GOD; HOPE.

Love, Act of (luhv, akt uhv). (1) Any act that manifests a love for God stemming from supernatural motives. (2) An act by which we profess love for God because of His infinite Goodness and His love for us (in this case, the love is "perfect" and can blot out serious sin but does not remove the obligation to confess* the sin) or because of some self-regarding motive, such as gratitude for God's love for us or fear of hell (in this case, the love is "imperfect" and does not blot out grave sin but does remit venial sin and give glory to God).

The Liturgy* is both permeated with acts of love and fosters them. Indeed, conscious, full, and active participation* in the Liturgy is possible only through genuine acts of love. The traditional Act of Love is as follows:

> O my God, because You are infinite Goodness and worthy of infinite Love, I love You with my whole heart above all things, and for love of You I love my neighbor as myself.

Those who say any act of love can gain a partial indulgence.* *See also* CONVERSION; FAITH, ACT OF; HOPE, ACT OF.

Love Feast. *See* AGAPE.

Loving Mother of the Redeemer. *See* ALMA REDEMPTORIS MATER.

Low Mass (loh mas). A term to indicate a read form of the pre-Vatican II* or Tridentine Mass (*Missa Lecta*) in opposition to the less usual

High Mass* (*Missa Cantata*), in which there was singing, and the infrequent Solemn High Mass* (*Missa Solemnis*) celebrated with singing and the aid of a deacon* and subdeacon.* With the appearance of the post-Vatican II fully participated Mass with music* and song, this term is no longer meaningful and has disappeared from use. *See also* HIGH MASS; MASS; SOLEMN HIGH MASS.

Low Sunday. *See* DOMINICA IN ALBIS.

Lucernarium (loo-chuhr-NAH-ree-uhm). Direct from the Hebrew blessing of the evening lamp with thanksgiving to God for the day, this very old Christian blessing* of lights takes place at the start of evening services. A lamp (Latin: *lucerna*) is needed at the beginning of sunset. Usually it was part of the vigil celebrated by Christians in the first centuries every Saturday evening to commemorate the Resurrection* of our Lord and to await His Second Coming.* Today it is most obvious in the Light Service, that is, the blessing of the Paschal Candle,* at the beginning of the Easter Vigil.* However, there is currently a strong contingent of liturgists who are trying to revive this service during the

Evening Prayer,* where it is most fitting.

Lucy, St. (LOO-see). ?-304. This early martyr* of Sicily has been honored since the 6th century, with her name in the First Eucharistic Prayer.* She is invoked for protection against eye ailments. *Liturgical celebration:* December 13 (Memorial); *theme:* your light must shine before people.

Luke, St. (look). 1st century. A Greek from Antioch and a physician by profession, Luke met St. Paul* in Troas about 50 A.D. and accompanied him during the greater part of his missionary journeys through

Greece and Rome till his Roman captivity. Besides his Gospel,* Luke composed the Acts of the Apostles,* which describes the growth of the Church shortly after Christ's death to the year 63. He is venerated as a martyr,* but we have no details about his death.

Luke is typified as an ox, one of the creatures in Ezekiel's* vision (the sacrifice of an ox prefigured the death of Christ), since he starts his Gospel with Zechariah, a priest, and emphasizes the universal priesthood of Christ. There is a late tradition that he was a painter. He is the Patron of Artists, Brewers, Glassmakers, Notaries, Painters, Physicians, and Surgeons. *Liturgical celebration:* October 18 (Feast); *theme:* insight into the Gospel of love and mercy.

Luke, The Gospel According to (look, thuh GOS-puhl uh-KAWRD-ing too). The third Synoptic Gospel* and the forty-ninth Book of the Bible.* Many scholars discern in the Lucan Gospel and its sequel, the Acts of the Apostles,* an apologetic strain presumably directed against unfounded criticisms of Christian teaching. Written after the persecution of Nero that began in 64 A.D. and caused hostility toward Christians throughout the Empire, Luke-Acts reveal that Jesus Himself was accounted innocent by the Roman governor Pontius Pilate (Lk 23:4, 15, 22) and that St. Paul,* founder of many Christian communities in the Empire, was often acquitted by the Roman magistrates of charges against him (Acts 16:36; 18:12-17; 25:26; 26:32).

The Evangelist portrays Christianity, not as a political movement, nor as a sect organized for an initiated few, but as a religious faith open to all people, both Jews and Gentiles. His portrait of Jesus, drawn from the Gospel tradition, identifies Him as the expected Messiah,* Who is the Son of God and Son of Man, and manifests the Savior's concern for humankind and His identification with the poor, the outcast, and the criminal. Luke also gives prominence (especially via the 15 parables and six miracles exclusive to him) to Christ's teaching on prayer* and to the women who followed Him, as well as to women in general. Although the apologetic thought in Luke's writings must be acknowledged, it was nevertheless not his chief purpose to produce an apology for Christianity.

Luke wants to present the History of Salvation* from the beginnings of the world until the return of Christ

(Parousia*). For Luke, this History comprises three great periods, which he clearly distinguishes: (1) the time of expectation: "The law and the prophets lasted until John [the Baptist]" (16:16); (2) the time of Christ from His coming on earth until His Ascension*; and (3) the time of the Church,* whose foundations were laid in the preaching period, and which is unfolding fully from that time onward.

In this History it is the coming of Christ that marks the truly decisive turning point; it constitutes the "middle of the times." During the time of expectation people had their eyes fixed on the "middle of the times" that was to come. During the time of the Church, people look backward with their eyes on Jesus. The life of Jesus becomes for the Church a sort of prototype of her own life and a model for every member. It is a question of realizing, of fulfilling from day to day, what Jesus has lived and what He has taught (9:23), until His Second Coming.*

Liturgical use: In the *Roman Missal,** this Gospel is as well represented as those of Matthew,* Mark,* and John,* and it is assigned to Cycle C. It is also used extensively in the continuous readings for weekdays, in the Proper of Saints,* in the Common of Saints,* and in Ritual Masses.* In the *Liturgy of the Hours,** it gives rise to the three major canticles* (of Zechariah,* Mary,* and Simeon*) that form the climax of Morning Prayer,* Evening Prayer,* and Night Prayer.* It is also used in Appendix I: "Canticles and Gospel Readings for Vigils."

Meaning: God's Divine plan for human salvation* comes to us in a salvation history and was accomplished during the "time of Jesus," Who through the events of His life fulfilled the Old Testament* prophecies. This salvation is now extended to all humankind in the period of the Church through the power of the Holy Spirit.* If we wish to follow Christ, we must imitate His concern for the poor and lowly, the outcast, the sinner, and the afflicted—toward all who recognize their dependence on God. At the same time, we must share the Master's love for prayer and His spirit of detachment from material things, while responding with true faith* and repentance* as well as joy* to the word Jesus preaches. We will then attain salvation and peace.*

Lumen Christi (LOO-men KRIS-tee). Latin phrase meaning "the Light of Christ," which is used during the "Service of Light" on the Easter Vigil.* The official English translation is "Christ our Light" in keeping with the words of Jesus that He is the light of the world (Jn 8:12). *See also* EASTER VIGIL.

Lumen Gentium (LOO-men JEN-tsee-oom). Latin title (from the first two words "Light of the Nations") of the *Dogmatic Constitution on the Church* issued by the Second Vatican Council* on November 21, 1964. Among the many teachings it sets forth are the following connected with the Liturgy*: (1) Christians are the Body of Christ,* and His life is bestowed on them through the Sacraments.* (2) The baptized enjoy a universal priesthood* that does not infringe upon the ministerial priesthood* of the clergy.* (3) The Church* is truly present in all lawful local congregations of the faithful* that are gathered together by the preaching of Christ's Gospel* and in which the Mystery* of the Lord's Supper* is celebrated. (4) The bishop* is the regulator of the Liturgy in his particular church. (5) The laity* consecrate the world* to God through their participation* in the Eucharist.* (6) The Sacraments, especially the Eucharist, are the most important means available to the faithful for hearing the Word of God* and carrying it out in their works. (7) The Liturgy brings together the Church Militant* and the Church Triumphant.* (8) The liturgical cult of Mary* is to be fostered by all. *See also* VATICAN COUNCIL, SECOND.

Lunula (LOO-nuh-luh). A receptacle having the shape of a circle or semicircle which serves to hold the Host* in an upright position in the monstrance.* Its primitive shape resembles a crescent or growing moon (*luna*). Sometimes it is called luna or lunette. Usually made of gilt metal hinged together, it slides into a fitting that holds the Host firm and visible to all. As a sacred vessel,* it receives a blessing.*

LXX. *See* SEPTUAGINT.

— M —

Maccabees, Feast of the Holy (MAK-uh-beez, feest uhv thuh HOH-lee). Feast* formerly kept on August 1 to honor the seven Jewish brothers whose martyrdom is described in chapter 7 of the Second Book of Maccabees.* This event, alluded to in Hebrews* 11:35, became celebrated by many Fathers of the Church. The reputed relics* of the martyrs* were brought to Antioch and later to Rome (the church of St. Peter's in Chains). It became the only feast of an Old Testament* Saint* celebrated in the Latin Rite* with more than local observance. In the reform of 1960, the feast was deleted and assigned to local observance. *See also* MACCABEES, THE FIRST BOOK OF; MACCABEES, THE SECOND BOOK OF.

Maccabees, The First Book of [MAK-uh-beez, thuh fuhrst buk uhv). Twentieth Book of the Old Testament* and third of the Deuterocanonical Books that are accepted as canonical by the Catholic Church but not by the Protestant Churches, who call them the Apocrypha.* The two Books of Maccabees contain independent accounts in parts identical of the events that accompanied the attempted suppression of Judaism in Palestine in the 2nd century B.C. The vigorous reaction to this attempt established for a time the religious and political independence of the Jews.

The First Book was written about 100 B.C. and expresses the customary belief of Israel without the new elements that appear in 2 Maccabees* and in Daniel*: The people of Israel have been especially chosen by the one true God as His Covenant* partner, and they alone are privileged to know Him and wor-

ship Him. He is their eternal Benefactor and their unfailing source of help. The people, in turn, must be loyal to His exclusive worship* and must observe exactly the precepts of the Law* He has given them.

Liturgical use: In the *Roman Missal,** this Book is used on Monday, Thursday, Friday, and Saturday of the 33rd Week (I) as well as in the Dedication of a Church* and the Mass for Persecuted Christians. In the *Liturgy of the Hours,** it is used during the 31st Week. *Meaning:* Christians are the new People of God.* This calls for us to remain faithful to Him and His commandments, to have a zeal for His House and the Liturgy,* and a firm hope in times of trial.

Maccabees, The Second Book of (MAK-uh-beez, thuh SEK-uhnd buk uhv). Twenty-first Book of the Old Testament* and fourth of the Deuterocanonical Books that are accepted as canonical by the Catholic Church but not by the Protestant Churches, who call them the Apocrypha.* The Second Book of Maccabees has for its purpose to give a theological interpretation to the history of the period from 180 to 161 B.C. Of theological importance are the author's teaching on the resurrection of the just on the last day, the intercession of the Saints* in heaven for people living on earth, and the power of the living to offer prayers* and sacrifices* for the dead.

In the *Roman Missal,** this Book is used on Tuesday and Wednesday of the 33rd Week (I), Masses for the Dead,* and the Common of Martyrs.* In the *Liturgy of the Hours,** it is used on Friday of the 31st Week. *Meaning:* We must resist the domination of evil at all costs, even in the face of martyrdom, for God will never abandon us. At the same time, we must offer prayers and sacrifices for the dead and look forward to the resurrection on the last day.

Magi. *See* EPIPHANY.

Magic (MAJ-ik). The use of means (like charms or spells) that are believed to possess supernatural powers over natural forces. Nothing about the Liturgy* is magic. In fact, magic is the perversion of the Liturgy—it tries to *seize* God's grace* or privileges instead of *receiving* them from Him. Liturgical rites must constantly be verified in faith* to avoid all magical or simply mechanical contamination.

Magisterium (maj-uh-STIR-ee-uhm). The teaching authority of the Church,* which was originally bestowed on the Apostles* with St. Peter* at their head and now resides in the bishops* with the Pope* at their head. This Magisterium is twofold. (1) The *Solemn or Extraordinary Magisterium* is exercised in the formal declarations of the Pope or of the Ecumenical Councils of Bishops approved by the Pope. (2) The *Ordinary Magisterium* is exercised by the Pope or bishops in their normal means of instructing the faithful*—through word, writing, and action.

The *Extraordinary Magisterium* is always infallible when exercised. The *Ordinary Magisterium* may also be infallible when the Pope or bishops teach with moral unanimity. However, "no doctrine is understood as infallibly defined unless it is clearly established as such" (Canon 749). Infallible teachings are to be accorded the assent of faith by Catholics. Noninfallible teachings must be given a religious respect of intellect and will.

In a private audience, Pope Pius XI declared: "The Liturgy . . . is the most important organ of the Ordinary Magisterium of the Church. . . . The Liturgy is not the teaching of this or that individual, but the teaching of the Church" (cited by Cyprian Vagaggini, *Theological Dimensions of the Liturgy,* p. 512). (*See* CATECHESIS AND LITURGY *for a more extensive quote.)*

Magnificat. *See* CANTICLE OF OUR LADY.

Maison-Dieu, La (MAY-zohn d[y]uh, lah). A world-renowned liturgical periodical under the auspices of the National Center of Pastoral Liturgy of France. Begun in 1945, it has maintained such a high degree of scholarship in liturgical and pastoral studies that it is one of the organs whose opinions can safely be followed in matters of liturgical law. *See also* LITURGICAL LAW, SOURCES OF.

Malabar Rite (MAL-uh-bahr rait). Offshoot of the Chaldean Rite* with Latin modifications followed by the Eastern Christians of Malabar, India. Sometimes called the Syro-Malabar Rite, it constitutes the rite of the so-called St. Thomas Christians who until the 16th century were under Nestorian influence. They entered the Catholic Church with the arrival of the Portuguese missionaries in the 16th century. However, they were subjected to excessive Latinization, which led to the founding of the Malankarese Church in 1153 under the Jacobite Church of Syria. Since 1930 the Malankarese have been in the process of returning to the Catholic Church. *See also* ANTIOCHENE RITE; MALANKAR RITE.

Malabar Rites. *See* CHINESE RITES.

Malachi, The Book of (MAL-uh-kee; -kai; thuh buk uhv). Name of the forty-sixth and last Book of the Old Testament* (and the last of the twelve Minor Prophets*). It was probably written just before 455 B.C. by an anonymous Prophet who made a proper name out of the Hebrew expression "My Messenger" (Malachi), which occurs in 1:1 and 3:1. The author reminds the people of God's enduring love and then reprimands them for insincere worship* even though the Temple has been rebuilt. However, God's judgment is approaching, and on that day everything will be put into order once again. There will even be a perfect sacrifice* offered from morning till night (alluding to the Mass*). But first Elijah* will have to return to open the New Age. The New Testament* applies this description to John the Baptist,* the forerunner of Christ (see Mt 17:12 and Mk 9:13).

Liturgical use: In the *Roman Missal,** this Book is used on the 31st Sunday (A), and the 33rd Sunday (C), as well as on Thursday of the 27th Week (I), December 23, and February 2. In the *Liturgy of the Hours,** it is read on Friday and Saturday of the 28th Week.

Meaning: Worship of God must be sincere and according to His law. For God's promises are ever valid. True judgment will be rendered on the Day of the Lord when Jesus returns at the Second Coming.* The just will achieve full redemption and enter the definitive Kingdom of God.*

Malankar Rite (MAL-uhn-kahr rait). The rite practiced by the fraction of the Syrian Church of Malabar that joined the Jacobite Church* in 1653, adopting the West Syrian rite used by the latter. In 1930 the Malankarese Church began proceedings for union with Rome. *See also* ANTIOCHENE RITE; MALABAR RITE.

Mandatum. *See* WASHING OF THE FEET.

Maniple (MAN-uh-puhl). An ornamental vestment* of colored silk or damask once worn over the left forearm by the celebrant* at Mass.* Originally, it was a handkerchief carried in the left hand or thrown over the left arm. It came to be a symbol of good works*—the Latin word can mean a sheaf of grain—and the distinctive mark of the subdeacon,* with its color varying according to the liturgical color* of the day. The use of the maniple was suppressed by the 1967 Instruction *Tres Abhinc Annos.** *See also* VESTMENTS.

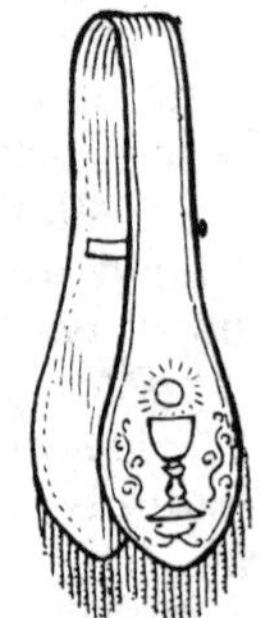

Manuterge (MAN-yoo-tuhrj) or **Manutergium** (man-yoo-TUHR-jee-uhm). A small linen towel used at the Washing of the Hands* at Mass.*

Maranatha (muh-RAN-uh-thah). An expression used by the first Christians (1 Cor 16:22 and reflected in Rv 22:20) probably as a liturgical refrain. A Greek transliteration from the Aramaic, it may be read as a prayer for the arrival of the Second Coming* of Christ: *Marana, tha,* "Lord, come"; or as an expression of hope* in the proximity of the Parousia,* *Maran atha,* "The Lord is coming."

Marcellinus, St. (mahr-sel-LEE-nuhs) ?-304. A priest who was arrested and imprisoned by Diocletian and eventually beheaded. He and his partner Peter are mentioned in Eucharistic Prayer I.* *Liturgical celebration:* June 2 (Opt. Mem.); *theme:* suffering for Christ brings eternal reward.

Margaret Mary Alacoque, St. (MAHR-guh-ruht MAYR-ee AL-uh-kohk). 1647-1690. A Visitation nun, who through revelations experienced in 1673-75 propagated the devotion to the Sacred Heart,* particularly the nine First Fridays* and the Holy Hour.* She, with St. John Eudes* and Blessed Claude de la Colombière, succeeded in bringing about the institution of the feast of the Sacred Heart, a devotion officially recognized in 1765. *Liturgical celebration:* October 16 (Opt. Mem.); *theme:* a devotion of love for the Sacred Heart.

Margaret of Scotland, St. (MAHR-guh-ruht uhv SKOT-luhnd). 1046-1093. Born in Hungary, this Queen of Scotland for thirty years, mother of eight, promoted reforms in the Church* and performed many acts of charity for the poor. She is the Patroness of Scotland. *Liturgical celebration:* November 16 (Opt. Mem.); *theme:* love for the poor.

Maria Goretti, St. (muh-REE-uh gaw-RET-ee). 1890-1902. A babysitter for farm workers in Italy, near Rome, she was stabbed to death by the son of her father's partner when she resisted his advances to seduce her. Her assailant reformed, worked for her beatification,* and was present at her canonization* in 1950. She is the Patroness of the Children of Mary. *Liturgical celebration:* July 6 (Opt. Mem.); *theme:* love of innocence and chastity.

Marialis Cultus (mah-ree-AH-lees KOOL-toos). Latin title (from the first two words "Marian Devotion") of the *Apostolic Exhortation on Devotion to the Blessed Virgin Mary* issued by Pope Paul VI on February 2, 1974. It is one of the most important documents of his pontificate and of the whole Marian Magisterium* of the Roman Pontiffs. The document sets forth the reasons and the means for devotion* to Mary* in a manner attuned to the needs of the mentality and custom of our age. To do so, it draws upon the liturgical reforms of Vatican II* and the great psychological and sociocultural changes that have overtaken the world.

Part One deals with devotion to Mary in the revised Liturgy* in the unfolding of the various seasons of the Liturgical Year* and in the special celebrations in honor of Mary

(Feasts* and Memorials*), both universal and particular. It treats references to Mary in the Eucharistic Prayer,* the theological and spiritual richness of the prayers,* readings,* hymns,* and the like in the *Sacramentary,* Lectionary,* Liturgy of the Hours,** and *Ritual.**

It speaks of the spiritual attitude with which the Church* celebrates and lives the Divine Mysteries,* taking as her Model Mary, who is the *attentive Virgin,* the *Virgin in prayer,* the *Virgin-Mother,* and the *Virgin presenting offerings* in perfect union with Christ. And with the Church as a whole, individual Christians are also called to imitate Mary in piety, spiritual life,* and worship.*

Part Two sets forth the reasons, norms, and means for the renewal of Marian devotion. It grounds them all on the Biblical, patristic, conciliar, and theological Magisterium of Christian Tradition.*

First it illustrates the Trinitarian, Christological, and ecclesial basis of Marian devotion and gives a valuable passage on Mary and the Holy Spirit.* It then adds four orientations for the devotion itself: it should be Biblical, liturgical, ecumenical, and anthropological in harmony with the best Tradition of the Church and with the most genuine needs of today's spirituality.

Part Three gives a few indications about the Angelus* and the Rosary,* explaining in detail the contents, forms, and methods of the latter.

A Conclusion nicely summarizes the theological and pastoral role of devotion to Mary. *See also* MARY, BLESSED VIRGIN; MARY, BLESSED VIRGIN—CULT; MARY, BLESSED VIRGIN—FEASTS; MARY, BLESSED VIRGIN—LECTIONARY; MARY, BLESSED VIRGIN—MASSES; MARY, BLESSED VIRGIN—MEMORIAL ON SATURDAY; MARY, BLESSED VIRGIN—ORDER OF CROWNING AN IMAGE; MARY, BLESSED VIRGIN—VOTIVE MASSES.

Marian Antiphons. *See* FINAL ANTIPHONS OF OUR LADY.

Marie Rose Durocher, Bl. (muh-REE rohz duh-ROH-shuhr; duh-ruh-SHAY). Born in Quebec, Canada, Eulalie Durocher established the first Canadian parish Sodality for young women. In 1843, she founded the Sisters of the Holy Names of Jesus and Mary, a new congregation of women dedicated to Christian education. Her community flourished in spite of great poverty and misunderstandings, and she exhibited unflagging concern for the poor. Marie was declared Blessed by Pope Paul II on May 23, 1982, and she forms part of the Proper for the United States.* *Liturgical celebration:* October 6 (Opt. Mem.); *theme:* teaching the Faith to others.

Mariolatry. *See* HYPERDULIA.

Mariology. *See* MARY, BLESSED VIRGIN.

Mark, St. (mahrk) ?-c. 75. A disciple of St. Paul,* Mark accompanied him and Barnabas* on missionary journeys. As author of the second Gospel,* he is said to be the interpreter of St. Peter.* Mark is represented by the lion, one of the symbolic living creatures of Ezekiel's* vision, that shakes the desert with his roars—because his account begins with the mission of John the Baptist* crying out in the desert. Tradition has him founding the Church at Alexandria in Egypt and martyred there. He is the Patron of Notaries. *Liturgical celebration:* April 25 (Feast); *theme:* may we be faithful to the preaching of the Gospel.

Mark, The Gospel According to (mahrk, thuh GOS-puhl uh-KAWRD-ing too). The second Synoptic Gospel* and the forty-eighth Book of the Bible.* Written about 70 A.D. by Mark, a companion of St. Paul* and later a coworker of St. Peter,* this Book is sometimes called the Gospel of Peter. It makes use of a familiar style that is occasionally awkward but always direct and that might be called photographic in its handling of details.

Mark is intent on showing that Jesus is the Son of God. He is the Messiah,* the anointed king of Davidic descent, who came to be called the "Christ" in Greek. At the same time, he presents Jesus as the Son of Man ordained to suffering and eventual vindication. On the one hand, this Son of Man is the superior personage conceived according to the vision of Daniel 7:13 who sits at the right hand of God (Dn 14:62) and comes on the clouds to dispense judgment (Dn 13:26). On the other hand, He is a human being, considered in human weakness with respect to the power of God (in the manner of Ez 2:1). Accordingly, Mark shows the authentic human emotions of Jesus: pity (1:44), anger (3:5), triumph (4:40), sympathy (5:36; 6:34), surprise (6:6), admiration (7:29; 10:21), sadness (14:33f), and indignation (14:48f).

Mark desires to establish a close bond between the Person of Jesus and His Lordship, showing that the Son of Man had to endure the Cross* before attaining His glory* and that His destiny is that of the Suffering Servant* prophesied by Isaiah* (ch. 53). Thus, all who follow Him must traverse this same path and endure the same suffering before attaining the same glory.

Finally, Mark shows forth the power of Jesus. He overcomes demonic possessions, disease, ignorance, enmities, and finally death. With the Father behind Him, Jesus accomplishes the task given Him.

Liturgical use: In the *Roman Missal,** this Gospel is as well represented as those of Matthew,* Luke,* and John* and it is assigned to Cycle B. It is also used extensively in the continuous readings for weekdays, in the Proper of the Saints,* in the Common of the Saints,* and in Ritual Masses.* In the *Liturgy of the Hours,** it is read in Appendix I: "Canticles and Gospel Readings for Vigils."

Meaning: Our craving for earthly happiness often distorts our vision and blinds us to what salvation* requires of us. Only faith* can restore to us a clear vision of the meaning

of our history. It constantly reminds us that the road to the glory of the Risen Lord passes through the humiliation of Calvary. Jesus is the Messiah—but not of the kind that was expected or of the type that we tend to seek. We must rethink our vision of Christ, the Son of God, and of the Father Himself—both of whom point us to glory through the Cross. *See also* MARK, ST.

Maronite Liturgy (MAR-uhn-ait LIT-uhr-jee). An Eastern Catholic worship* developed from the Syro-Antiochene Rite, with Arabic and Syriac as liturgical languages. Many of their anaphoras* were from the Apostles,* but during the Middle Ages they adopted many from the Holy Roman Church. Much of their Liturgy* became Latinized to the extent that Confirmation* was separated from Baptism,* unleavened bread was substituted for leavened, bishops* alone blessed the oil of the sick,* their chrism* simulated the Latin chrism, the form of the Sacraments* became like those of the Roman Church, and Communion* was given under one species. The greatest change constituted the insertion of the sanctoral* cycle, since in the beginning Saints* had not been incorporated into the Maronite calendar* though some Saints were found within the Eucharistic anaphoras.

In keeping with Vatican II's* desire for the Maronites to return to their original tradition, their new calendar reverts back as much as possible to a seasonal, liturgical celebration centered on Jesus and significant events of His life, such as Birth, Epiphany,* Passion,* Resurrection,* Sending of the Spirit,* and founding of the Church.* Thus they have discarded any sanctoral cycle to cling to their original idea of basic, healthy, vigorous and "Christly" vision and understanding of the Mystery of Salvation.*

Memorials* which are used to commemorate the Prophets,* Apostles,* angels,* Martyrs,* and the other Saints are to fit into the weekly cycle in such a way that they do not obscure or deviate from the central figure of the Liturgy, Jesus Christ. The various seasons, focusing on the saving events mentioned above, are based on cycles that flow from Sunday to the succeeding weekdays. Not happy with the term "Ordinary Time,"* they have opted for "the Season after Pentecost."* Meanwhile they are doing research on that period of time, composed of a changeable number of weeks without emphasis on any of the significant events of the Lord's life. Thus they are attempting to regain the originality, strength, and balance of the genuine Maronite spirituality.

Marriage (MAR-ij). A Sacrament* whereby a man and woman enter into a lasting contractual relationship, a matrimonial covenant,* which by giving them rights over each other for sexual relations not only fosters their mutual love but provides for the birth and upbringing of children in a family structure, the basis of society. To achieve these natural purposes of Marriage, two characteristics are essential: (1) *unity,* an exclusive relationship between one man and one woman, which is the result of the total commitment to the other human being in the Marriage, and (2) *indissolubility,* that is, the permanent union until death, namely a lifelong commitment. The resultant constancy, security, and dedicated love bring about the emotional well-being of children during their development.

Sacramentality

Because of its importance for Christian life, from the beginning Marriage was regarded as a Sacrament, imposing a sacred, indissoluble obligation, and became a religious symbol of the unity between the Church* and Christ. As a result of the conjugal bond, Sacramental grace* is conferred on the couple to allow them to live in accordance with their vocation and effectively enable them to fulfill the natural purposes of Marriage. *(See also* FAMILIARIS CONSORTIO).

Canon Law

Since the family is the foundation of society, Church law regulates the Marriage contract, stressing for the most part the purposes and the characteristics of Marriage mentioned above. The laws deal with the proper conditions for the celebration of Marriage. It should be celebrated in the parish* of either party, even after only one month's residence. With permission it may be performed elsewhere. The bishop,* priest,* or deacon* is the ordinary witness of the Church at a Marriage; where priests and deacons are lacking, the local bishop may choose lay persons to witness marriages, as long as the Conference of Bishops* has approved this practice and permission was obtained from the Holy See* for these specific lay* persons to minister at Marriages. Impediments flow either from Divine Law, such as a prior Marriage, or from ecclesiastical law, which affects only the baptized. Some impediments make the Marriage unlawful; others, the diriment impediments, result in nullity.

Nullity

An annulment can occur when the Church declares that a putative Marriage never existed. Requirements for validity must be present at the time of the Marriage. Such conditions are: (1) freedom from mental or emotional disorders: otherwise it would militate against the intimate marital union; (2) absence of diriment impediments, which preclude valid matrimonial consent; (3) consent on both sides to the Marriage as defined in the first paragraph with mutual, exclusive love and willingness to beget and educate children; and (4) consent exchanged in the presence of the authorized priest and two witnesses (canonical form).

Validation

An invalid Marriage may be rectified through canonical procedure. A simple convalidation renews the matrimonial consent that was not given or not correctly given. It could have been because of fear, force, moral pressure, error, or deception. Convalidation removes the nullifying impediment either by, for example, the passage of time, if one were too young, or by the death of a previous spouse in a prior valid Marriage. Convalidation may also occur by a dispensation that removes an impediment, allowing consent to be given. Failure to observe the canonical form is remedied by giving the consent again according to due form.

An extraordinary validation (healing at the root) is a juridical act by which the Church excuses from a diriment impediment, thus constituting the marriage a truly Sacramental one and making it retroactive. The supposition is that the partners were unaware of the invalidating impediment.

Mixed Marriage

Ecclesiastical law forbids a Marriage between a non-Catholic, baptized or not, and a Catholic. Thus mixed Marriages are discouraged, but in particular cases the Church relaxes the ecclesiastical discipline by dispensation. Such a Marriage may be celebrated in a church or any appropriate place with no need of permission. Pastoral care must be given to such couples, together with a prior information program to explain the restrictions and to seek the positive spiritual values that ought to be derived from Marriage.

More than the customary Marriage preparation, catechetical preparation should include a full explanation of the proprieties in Marriage and the promise given by the Catholic party to raise the children as Catholics. Under serious difficulties, a dispensation is some-

times granted from the canonical form of Marriage.

Marriage Rite

The preliminary preparations for Marriage occur through the preaching and catechesis* given by various means to the faithful* concerning the true meaning of Marriage and the duty of couples and parents. Shortly before Marriage, personal preparation takes place in the United States through pre-Cana instructions, which disposes the parties to the holiness and duties of their intended new state of life. With the cooperation of the couples, a fruitful liturgical celebration of Marriage is planned. Even after the Marriage, pastoral assistance should be given to help the couple maintain their faithfulness and protect the conjugal covenant, as they grow more holy day by day and lead a more full life with their families.

The Conference of Bishops may adapt the *Roman Ritual** to local customs and needs. Variations particularly as to the form of consent have been approved. Ordinarily, the Marriage is to take place during Mass, after the Liturgy of the Word* with a Homily.* It is expected that the spouses have chosen the prayers for the Mass from the three Mass formulas for weddings in the *Sacramentary** and the readings from the *Lectionary.** During the Introductory Rites* the priest greets the couple in a friendly manner, sharing the joy of the occasion. After the Homily, since the couple entering into this covenant are the primary ministers of the Sacrament, they state their willingness to accept the obligations of Marriage and their freedom to do so. Thereupon through an officially recognized local form of consent, the two accept each other as lifelong partners in the Sacrament, while the priest or deacon, the official witnesses, and the community gathered there affirm their entrance into the Church community in their new role as a married couple. The ring or rings are blessed. Thereupon the General Intercessions* occur, followed by the Liturgy of the Eucharist.* One of the three forms of the Nuptial Blessing* is given, and the Mass* concludes with a special blessing for the bride and bridegroom.

The wedding Mass with white vestments* is used, even on Sundays in Masses that are not parish Masses. On Solemnities* and during Sunday parish Masses, the Mass of the day is said with the Nuptial Blessing and special Final Blessing. Should a Marriage occur during Advent* or Lent,* the nature of those times should be taken into consideration.

If the couple opt for no Mass, the marriage ceremony is celebrated after the Liturgy of the Word,* which is then followed by the General Intercessions and the Nuptial Blessing. The rite may then be concluded with the Lord's Prayer* and the Final Blessing, even including the distribution of Communion. As a rule this is the form to be followed for mixed Marriages. However the Ordinary* may give permission for the ceremony to take place during Mass, without Communion for the non-Catholic. For Marriage between a Catholic and an unbaptized person, a more brief ceremony is prescribed, which is sensitive to and considerate of the feelings and beliefs of the unbaptized person.

Martha, St. (MAHR-thuh). 1st century. Sister of Mary* and Lazarus,* she was solicitous for the welfare of Jesus when He visited them in Bethany. Because of the incident in Luke* 10:38-42 she is the prototype for the activist Christian. She is the Patroness of Cooks, Hospital Dieticians, and Innkeepers. *Liturgical celebration*: July 29 (Memorial); *theme*: serving Christ in our brothers and sisters.

Martin I, St. (MAHRT-uhn thuh fuhrst). ?-c. 656. This Pope* presided over a Lateran Synod* in

which he courageously condemned a doctrinal decree, the *Type,* which the Emperor Constans II had issued; it contained the Monothelite heresy, that Christ had only one will. For that Martin was arrested in his cathedral,* taken to Constantinople, sentenced to death at a mock trial, sent to prison and eventually banished to Kherson in the Crimea where he died, the last of the Popes to be venerated as a martyr.* *Liturgical celebration:* April 13 (Opt. Mem.); *theme:* courage in defense of the truth and in enduring sufferings and death for the Lord.

Martin de Porres, St. (MAHRT-uhn duh POR-uhs; PAW-rez). 1579-1639. This mulatto, born in Peru, became a Dominican lay brother and quite active in caring for the sick throughout Lima. Besides establishing a foundling hospital and orphanage, he ministered to African slaves sent to Peru. He is the Patron of Interracial Justice and Hairdressers. *Litugical celebration:* November 3 (Opt. Mem.); *theme:* showing charity* toward the poor.

Martin of Tours, St. (MAHRT-uhn uhv toorz). c.316-397. A pagan Hungarian converted to Christianity, Martin left the army, lived as a hermit, eventually founded a monastic center, and was named

Bishop* of Tours in 371. As bishop he was an Apostle* of the rural area; noted as the glory of Gaul, he was the first person neither a martyr,* nor so-reputed, to be canonized. He is the Patron of France and of Soldiers. *Liturgical celebration:* November 11 (Memorial); *theme:* the power of love for God.

Martyrology (mahrt-uh-ROL-uh-jee). A term that signifies, strictly speaking, the list of names in chronological order of persons who have died for the Faith.* However, most martyrologies, like the *Roman Martyrology,* become the official calendar of feasts* celebrated in the Church;* each day's roll begins with the feast(s) celebrated that day and then lists those Saints* who have died on that particular date, called their birthday. Most martyrologies add an indication of the cemetery where the Martyr* lies together with a brief biography. Because the historical validity of much of this material is called into doubt, a general revision of the *Roman Martyrology* in its capacity as a liturgical book* is taking place now. Formerly the *Martyrology* was read during the Divine Office* at the Hour of Prime,* which has been abrogated with the advent of the new *Liturgy of the Hours.* *See also* LITURGICAL BOOKS.

Martyrology of St. Jerome (mahrt-uh-ROL-uh-jee uhv saynt juh-ROHM). Its title comes from the two spurious letters found at the head of the extant manuscripts—one to St. Jerome* and the other from him; it is also known as the *Hieronymian Martyrology* from the Latin word for Jerome. Composed in Italy in the middle of the 5th century, this martyrology gives the feasts celebrated in Rome, Africa, and the East. Intended for use in the Liturgy,* it also provided edifying reading for monasteries. In addition to the Saints* named for each day, it also gives the places where their tombs were or where they were venerated as well as other notes about their cult. Most important of all, it served as the basis for the *Roman Martyrology.**

Martyrs (MAHRT-uhrz). A Greek derivative, meaning witnesses, that indicates that those so named voluntarily suffered death for belief in Christ. High honor was given to these loyal imitators of Christ by people who preserved their relics,* frequently building altars* over the graves and eventually churches over the tombs. The cult of martyrs developed over the years. Until recent legislation relics* of martyrs were to be in every altar-stone, now prescribed only for stones of fixed altars. *See also* SAINTS, LITURGICAL CATEGORIES OF.

Mary, Blessed Virgin (MAYR-ee, BLES-uhd VUHR-juhn). The Mother of Jesus Christ* our Redeemer. The apostolic preaching (some of which is recorded in the early speeches in the Acts of the Apostles*—2:14-21; 3:12; 13:15ff) says not a word about Mary and practically nothing about Christ's earthly life. Some of the reasons for this reticence are: (1) Mary was known to all the faithful of Palestine, and there was little reason to refer to her; (2) her major role in Jesus' life had been carried out during his early years when there were no disciples to record it; and (3) the role of women in general was always downplayed in the East of that era.

St. Paul* provides the first allusion to Mary from among the apostolic preaching—in the Epistle to the Galatians* (4:4): "God sent his Son, *born of a woman" (italics added).* St. Mark* sketches a portrait of Mary as the Mother of Jesus (3:31ff; 6:3). St. Matthew* presents Mary as associated with Jesus in His birth in accord with Old Testament* prophecies (including her virginal conception)—a singular role that puts her in a personal relationship with the Spirit* (1:16-23; 2:11).

St. Luke* portrays Mary as the handmaid of the Lord, daughter of Zion, and closest follower of Christ—who hears God's Word and keeps it (1:38, 48; 2:19, 51; 11:28).

St. Luke (in Acts) makes mention of Mary gathered in prayer with the Apostles* in the Upper Room and so hints at her role in the formation of the Church* (1:14). St. John* portrays Mary as united with Jesus during His life (2:1-11) and at His Death* (19:25) and as His dying gift to His followers (19:26f). The Book of Revelation* puts the finishing touches to the primitive image of Mary, which focuses on her concrete fidelity, deep faith, ecclesial role, and singular grace. Mary is the servant par excellence, who did nothing other than accept, fashion, and offer Jesus (12:1-17).

In all the New Testament* recounts only seven words spoken by Mary (if we count the *Magnificat** as one word). Each of these words is filled with meaning and sums up some essential aspects of Mary's personality and religious functions: (1) "How can this be, since I have no relations with man?" (Lk 1:34—*virginal reserve);* (2) "I am the handmaid of the Lord" (Lk 1:38—*zealous service);* (3) "May it be done to me according to your word" (Lk 1:38—*faithful obedience);* (4) "My soul proclaims the greatness of the Lord . . ." (Lk 1:46-55—*joyful praise);* (5) "Son, why have you done this to us? Your father and I have been looking for you with great concern" (Lk 2:48—*authoritative gentleness);* (6) "They have no wine" (Jn 2:3—*tender charity);* and (7) "Do whatever he tells you" (Jn 2:5—*firm faith).*

The revered Mother of God is honored in the Church* today primarily by feasts* of a Christocentric nature. As the Mother of Christ she enjoys four great privileges: (1) Divine Maternity—as the Mother of Jesus, true God and true Man; (2) Immaculate Conception*—from the first moment of her existence preserved from the stain of original sin; (3) Perpetual Virginity—by virtue of being virgin before, during, and after the birth of Jesus; and (4) Assumption*—taken body and soul, after her earthly life, into the glory* of heaven.

Mary has a dual role. She is Coredemptrix, since she cooperated indirectly with her Son in the Redemption* and freely devoted her life to His service, even suffering with Him under the Cross.* She is also Mediatrix of All Graces, since she cooperated in subjective redemption and uses her maternal intercession in spreading the grace of redemption to all humankind.

Tradition* asserts that since Mary is the Mother of Christ she also became the Spiritual Mother of Christians. The dignity of Mother of God rates for her a devotion that is substantially less than the adoration* her Son receives yet singularly higher than veneration of other Saints*—it is called hyperdulia.*

Mary was venerated through the centuries with many Marian devotions,* not the least among them the Rosary,* the Litany,* the scapulars,* and since the 19th century the various shrines that mark apparitions of Mary. When the reformers rejected prayer to the Saints, devotion to Mary also became one of the differences between Catholics and Protestants. Recent pastoral, ecumenical, and Scriptural study indicates that Marian devotion still has a strong foundation but is in need of authentic contemporary expression.

Saturday has always been dedicated to Mary devotionally, especially First Saturdays with a Mass* in honor of the Immaculate Heart*; on each Saturday in Ordinary Time* not celebrated with an Obligatory Memorial* or higher feast, a Mass and an Office* of the Blessed Virgin are permitted. *See also* MARY, BLESSED VIRGIN—CULT; MARY, BLESSED VIRGIN—FEASTS; MARY, BLESSED VIRGIN—LECTIONARY; MARY, BLESSED VIRGIN—MASSES; MARY, BLESSED VIRGIN—MEMORIAL ON SATURDAY; MARY, BLESSED VIRGIN—ORDER OF CROWNING AN IMAGE; MARY, BLESSED VIRGIN—VOTIVE MASSES.

Mary, Blessed Virgin—Cult (MAYR-ee, BLES-uhd VUHR-juhn—kuhlt). Mary was involved in the Mysteries* of Christ. As the most holy Mother of God she was, after her Son, exalted by Divine grace* above all angels* and human beings. Hence, the Church* appropriately honors her with a special cult or devotion.

Indeed, from most ancient times the Blessed Virgin has been venerated under the title of "God-bearer." In all perils and needs, the faithful* have fled prayerfully to her protection. Especially after the Council of Ephesus (431) the cult of the People of God* toward Mary wonderfully increased in veneration and love, invocation and imitation.

This cult differs essentially from the cult of adoration* that is offered to the Incarnate Word* as well as to the Father* and to the Holy Spirit.* Yet devotion to Mary is most favorable to this supreme cult. While honoring Christ's Mother, her cult causes her Son to be rightfully known, loved, and glorified and all His commands to be observed.

Without a doubt the Mysteries of Redemption* and the Eucharistic celebration must be at the center of worship*; but according to the *Constitution on the Sacred Liturgy* (nos. 103, 104, 108, 111) there is a consonant and perfectly subordinate place for the veneration of the Virgin Mary. The Church's devotion to the Blessed Virgin is an intrinsic element of Christian worship. It is firmly rooted in the revealed Word and has solid dogmatic foundations.

This devotion is based on (1) the singular dignity of Mary, Mother of the Son of God, and therefore beloved Daughter of the Father and Temple of the Holy Spirit; (2) the part she played at decisive moments in the History of Salvation* that her Son accomplished; (3) her holiness,* already full at her Immaculate Conception* yet increasing all the time as she obeyed the Father's will and accepted the path of suffering; (4) her mission and the special position she holds within the People of God* as preeminent member, shining exemplar, and loving Mother; (5) her necessary and efficacious intervention for those who call upon her; and (6) her glory* that ennobles the whole of humankind.

St. Louis Grignion de Montfort* notes that this devotion to Mary is the ardor to serve her, the better to serve God. True Marian devotion must be (a) *interior,* more in the heart than in practices; (b) *steadfast,* based on faith* and not fluctuating with moods and feelings; (c) *disinterested,* more intent on God than the graces to be obtained (though the prayers of petition* and thanksgiving* are important elements in the general devotion that moves us to serve God); (d) *oriented toward Christ,* in whom we are brought to the Father; and (e) *confident and heartfelt,* since in us the spiritual itself is fleshly, i.e., communicates through the flesh.

Liturgical Cult

The Blessed Virgin Mary occupies a prominent place in the Liturgy* of the Church. The liturgies of both East and West bear witness to this fact by the ample space allotted to her memory in the Eucharistic Prayers,* in the Sacramental euchology, and in the diverse expressions of prayer.* Her presence is especially evident in the Marian feasts* that have grown over the years.

The Roman Rite,* with its traditional sobriety, has reserved to Mary a specific remembrance in the very heart of the Eucharistic Prayer—in the "Communicantes"* of the Roman Canon.* It has also slowly come to include a whole series of feasts that run throughout the Liturgical Year.*

As Pope John Paul II has put it, "Mary is present in the *memorial* because she was present in the *event!* . . . She is continuously united both with Christ the High Priest and with the Church, the worshiping community, in the saving event and in its liturgical memorial" (Not. 20 [1984], pp. 173f).

Consequently, she does not have a different cult but occupies a special place in the unique "Christian" cult, capable of making the Church community relive mysteriously in the present the historical past of the saving actions of Christ and (because of this) not dissociate the united action of Christ and His Mother even in its cultural-ritual-liturgical re-evocation. This enables the Church to celebrate the memorial of the Blessed Virgin not in her own special liturgical cycle but within the unique liturgical cycle of the Mysteries of Christ.

In addition to this aspect of the indissoluble union between Christ and Mary in the economy* of salvation and in its Sacramental realization, there is another aspect. Mary is united to the Mystery of the Church as her model in the celebration of the Mysteries. First of all, Mary is the *attentive Virgin* with respect to the Word of God; she thus appears as the model of the Church who meditates, is attentive to, accepts, lives, and proclaims the Word that became incarnate in Mary.

Secondly, Mary is the *Virgin in prayer,* because of her prayerful attitude as well as the sentiments that the Holy Spirit infused in her heart and that coincided with the grand divisions of ecclesial prayer, which has its roots in the Eucharistic Prayer: the *praise** and *thanksgiving** found in the *Magnificat,** the *intercession** at Cana, and the *petition** for the coming of the Spirit in the Upper Room.

Thirdly, Mary is the *Virgin presenting gifts* in the Temple of Jerusalem and on Calvary.* This experience both in its active aspect (*Mary offers*) and in its passive aspect (*Mary is offered)* becomes the exemplar for the Church in her sacrificial offering of the Eucharist and prayer.

Fourthly, Mary is the *Virgin-Mother.* As such she is the model of that active collaboration with which the Church also labors, through preaching and the Sacraments* (especially Baptism,* Confirmation,* and the Eucharist) to transmit the new life of the Spirit to human beings.

In this sense, every liturgical celebration must be *implicitly Marian,* insofar as it must be celebrated by the Church with the sentiments that were in Mary. The *Marian note* characterizes every celebration of the sacred Mysteries and makes liturgical spirituality* an authentically Marian spirituality in the best sense of the word.

Finally, Mary is not only an example for the whole Church on the exercise of Divine worship but also a teacher of the spiritual life for individual Christians. She is an example of the worship that consists in making one's life an offering to God. Her Yes is for all Christians a lesson and an example of obedience to the will of the Father, which is the way and means of one's sanctification.

Thus, at every liturgical celebration, Mary the Mother of God is with us—as our Model, our Intercessor, and our Mother. And she is even more each of these things in the Marian celebrations.

Each Marian celebration is also intended to give us a better understanding of Mary's part in our salvation, a true catechesis of Mary. As the Liturgy honors Mary over the course of a year, the Mysteries of Christ become present to us in their relationship with her.

Mary in the Eucharist

Mary is prominently mentioned every day in the Ordinary* of the Mass*: in the Introductory Rites* at the Confiteor,* in the Liturgy of the Word* at the Nicene Creed, and in the Eucharistic Prayer. Admittedly, the Roman Rite does not possess the admirable euchology of the Ethiopian Rite,* which enjoys two Marian anaphoras,* and the Byzantine Rite,* which reserves a special memorial for the Mother of God immediately after the epiclesis.* However, it does offer a valid synthesis of all the possible links between the celebration of the Eucharistic Mystery and the Blessed Virgin.

The Preface* of Eucharistic Prayer II* recalls the Incarnation* of the Word through the power of the Holy Spirit in the Virgin Mary: it is an ancient, universal, and essential mention because it unites the Eucharistic Mystery with the moment of the Incarnation, of which the Eucharist is also the recapitulation. The same remembrance is found in Eucharistic Prayer IV* after the *Sanctus.** Eucharistic Prayer I* solemnly expresses the union with Mary in the *Communicantes** in which her title of perpetual Virgin and her essential role as Mother of God are also recalled.

In a similar way, Eucharistic Prayer III* expresses with intense supplication the desire of those praying to share with the Mother the inheritance of the children: "May he make us an everlasting gift to you [the Father] and enable us to share in the inheritance of the saints with Mary, the Virgin Mother of God." Mary is also mentioned in each of the other five Eucharistic Prayers.

Mary in the Sacramental Rites

References to Mary in the Sacramental rites are restrained but important. In the *Rite of Ordination** there are prayers of supplication to Mary on behalf of the bishops,* priests,* and deacons* over whom the Litany of the Saints* is invoked. In the *Rite of Penance** Mary's help and intercession are invoked for

sinners in the Confiteor* and at the absolution,* and the *Magnificat** is suggested as a prayer of thanksgiving.*

In the *Rite of the Pastoral Care of the Sick** the sick person, before receiving Communion,* makes a profession of faith* in Jesus the Son of God, born of Mary; in the recommendation of the dying, Mary the Mother of God is invoked and a prayer asks God to grant the dying person an eternal dwelling with her in the new Jerusalem. In the *Rite of Marriage** one of the Gospel* readings is the passage from John 2:1-11 wherein Mary's intercession for the bridal couple comes to the fore. In the *Rite of Baptism** the Church invokes the Mother of grace before immersing candidates in the saving waters of Baptism. In the *Rite of Confirmation** the confirmands make a profession of faith in the Son of God, born of Mary, just before they are confirmed.

In the *Rite of Christian Burial** the Church asks that the grief of parents over a dead child may be assuaged by the maternal presence of Mary who stood by her dying Son on Calvary, and the Opening Prayer* for the Mass of Parents, Relatives, and Benefactors asks that those who have passed from this world may through Mary's intercession enjoy perfect happiness in heaven.

In the *Rite for the Dedication of a Church and an Altar** Mary's intercession is invoked in the Litany of the Saints and in the prayer that follows; the Preface speaks of the true temple in which there dwells the fullness of the Divinity, that is, the humanity of the Son born of the Virgin Mary. Finally, in the *Rite of Religious Profession** Mary's intercession is invoked in the Litany of the Saints and her example for those who consecrate themselves to God by a life of perfect chastity, obedience, and poverty, which was chosen by Christ the Lord and His Virgin Mother.

The *Order of Crowning an Image of the Blessed Virgin Mary** is completely Marian throughout. It provides a short summa on the theology of Mary after the Second Vatican Council and is filled with riches of Marian spirituality, including a new Litany.*

Mary in the Liturgy of the Hours

The *Liturgy of the Hours** also contains outstanding examples of the liturgical cult of Mary. These are found in the hymns*—which include several masterpieces of universal literature, such as Dante's sublime prayer to the Blessed Virgin—and in the antiphons* that complete the daily Office.

To these lyrical invocations there has been added the well-known prayer *Sub Tuum,** venerable for its antiquity and admirable for its content. Other examples occur at Morning Prayer* and Evening Prayer,* prayers that frequently express trusting recourse to the Mother of mercy. There are selections from the vast treasury of writings on our Lady composed by authors of the first Christian centuries, of the Middle Ages, and of Modern Times. Finally, the Church makes use of the *Magnificat* every day at Evening Prayer, using our Lady's words to give thanks for the wondrous gift of salvation.

Mary in the Liturgical Seasons

The *Season of Advent* has a typically Marian character, underlined especially in the Liturgy of the Hours where the hymns and antiphons frequently contain the name of Mary. There are many liturgical references to Mary besides the Solemnity of December 8, which is a joint celebration of the Immaculate Conception* of Mary, of the basic preparation (see Is 11:1, 10) for the coming of the Savior, and of the happy beginning of the Church without spot or wrinkle. In the Proper for the United States,* there is also the Feast of Our Lady of Guadalupe* showing Mary's love for her children.

Such liturgical references are found especially on the days from December 17 to 24, and more particularly on the Sunday before Christmas, which recalls the ancient prophecies concerning the Virgin Mother and the Messiah* and includes readings from the Gospel concerning the imminent birth of Christ and His Precursor.

The *Christmas Season* is a prolonged commemoration of the Divine, virginal, and salvific Motherhood of her whose inviolate virginity brought the Savior into the world. On the Solemnity of the Birth* of Christ the Church both adores the Savior and venerates His glorious Mother. On the Solemnity of the Mother of God* (January 1), the Church commemorates the part Mary played in the Mystery of Christ's Birth.

On the Feast of the Holy Family* the Church meditates upon the holy life led in the house at Nazareth by Jesus, the Son of God and Son of Man, Mary His Mother, and Joseph* the just man.

On the Epiphany* when she celebrates the universal call to salvation, the Church contemplates the Blessed Virgin, the true Seat of Wisdom and true Mother of the Redeemer, who presents to the Wise Men* for their adoration the Redeemer of all peoples.

On the Feast of the Presentation* (February 2) the Church highlights Mary's part in the suffering on Calvary, bringing the season to a close.

The *Season of Lent,** because of its preparatory character, has few references to Mary. It thus presents Mary as a model for us in living the preparation for Easter as disciples of Christ in such a way as to arrive with her at the Cross and the resurrection. It does contain the Feast of St. Joseph, Spouse of Mary (March 19), in which Mary has a great part, and the Feast of the Annunciation of the Lord* (March 25) in which Mary is also highly involved.

During the *Easter Triduum** Mary is also seen in various texts that serve to keep her before us. In the Office of Readings for Holy Thursday,* the Easter homily of Melito of Sardis is read, which refers to Mary and calls her "the fair ewe." She is also mentioned in the hymn sung at the reposition of the Blessed Sacrament* *Pange Lingua**: "From a noble womb to spring. / Of a pure and spotless Virgin / Born for us on earth below."

In the Veneration of the Cross* on Good Friday* the other hymn *Pange Lingua* recalls the Incarnation and the role of Mary in the History of Salvation*: "From a virgin's womb appearing, / clothed in our mortality. / All within a lowly manger, / lo, a tender babe he lies! / See his gentle Virgin Mother / lull to sleep his infant cries! / while the limbs of God incarnate / round with swathing bands she ties." The Passion* according to John also contains the passage on Mary at the Cross.

On Holy Saturday* Mary is invoked in the Litany of the Saints and mentioned in the profession of baptismal faith as well as the *Communicantes** of the Canon. At Morning Prayer there is a reference to the sorrowing Mother standing by Jesus at His Death and burial.

During the *Easter Season,* beginning with Holy Saturday the Liturgy of the Hours is concluded at Night Prayer* with the joyous *Regina Caeli,** the hymn that exults with Mary at the Resurrection of her Son. The Common of the Blessed Virgin (Mass no. 6) points to the Apostles who "were continually at prayer together with Mary" (Entrance Antiphon*) and thus reminds us that we should be too, for her Son "has arisen from his grave" (Communion Antiphon*). During this season there is also the great joy of the Month of Mary (May) and (when Easter comes late) the Feast of the Visitation (May 31) with its joy that anticipates the joy of the Resurrection. All this is topped off by the vigil of prayer in union with Mary that ends with the coming of the Holy Spirit at Pentecost.*

In *Ordinary Time,** Mary is always before us—in the Ordinary but also in the Proper feasts that occur throughout this time as well as the celebrations of Mary on Saturday. She is there as the Mother showing continual interest in her children (Our Lady of Lourdes,* February 11), as the praying Virgin teaching us to ponder God's Word in our hearts (Immaculate Heart of Mary,* 3rd Saturday after Pentecost), as the "garden-paradise" leading us to Christ (Memorial of Our Lady of Mount Carmel,* July 16), and as the temple of God and the new Jerusalem calling us home (Dedication of St. Mary Major,* August 5).

Mary is with us as the image and the commanding proof of the fulfillment of our final hope (Assumption,* August 15) and as the Queen and Intercessor sitting beside the King of Ages (Queenship of Mary,* August 22). She is with us as the hope of the world and the dawn of salvation (Birth of Mary,* September 8) and as the suffering Mother (Our Lady of Sorrows,* September 15).

Mary is with us in the victories of the History of Salvation (Our Lady of the Rosary,* October 7) and as the exemplar of dedication to God (Presentation of Mary,* November 21). *See also* LUMEN GENTIUM; MARIALIS CULTUS; MARY, BLESSED VIRGIN; MARY, BLESSED VIRGIN—FEASTS; MARY, BLESSED VIRGIN—LECTIONARY; MARY, BLESSED VIRGIN—MASSES; MARY, BLESSED VIRGIN—MEMORIAL ON SATURDAY; MARY, BLESSED VIRGIN—ORDER OF CROWNING AN IMAGE; MARY, BLESSED VIRGIN—VOTIVE MASSES.

Mary, Blessed Virgin—Feasts (MAYR-ee, BLES-uhd VUHR-juhn—feests). With the reduction of the Sanctoral Cycle* in the revision of the calendar* many feasts* in honor of the Blessed Virgin were eliminated. Thus, the Church* endeavored to strengthen the concept of Mary's Christocentric role as the Mother of our Redeemer, stressing her vocational role with Mother-Son feasts, such as the Annunciation* (March 25) and the Presentation of the Lord* (February 2), which now is not really considered the feast of her purification.

Solemnities

On the other hand, other feasts may be considered personal, such as the Immaculate Conception* (December 8). Her major feasts, or Solemnities, which are also Holy Days of Obligation* (as well as the two aforementioned feasts she shares with her Son) are treated under separate entries in this Dictionary: Assumption,* Immaculate Conception, and Solemnity of Mary Mother of God.*

Feasts

Two events in the life of Mary are celebrated by the Church with the rank of Feast: the Birth and the Visitation.

Visitation (viz-uh-TAY-shuhn). This feast commemorates Mary's visit—under the inspiration of the Holy Spirit*—to her cousin Elizabeth before the birth of St. John the Baptist* (Lk 1:39-56). It was instituted by Urban VI in 1389 after the Franciscans had celebrated it on July 2 from 1263 on. Sixtus IV (1471-1484) had a new Mass composed for it. The present calendar celebrates it on May 31, the last day of the month traditionally assigned to Mary and three weeks before the Solemnity of the Birth of John the Baptist* (June 24). *Liturgical celebration:* May 31 (Feast); *theme:* sharing feelings of joy by praising God.

Birth of Mary (buhrth uhv MAYR-ee). This feast derives from the dedication of the Church of Mary's Nativity (said to have been built on the house of St. Ann) at the end of the 5th century. In the 7th century it spread to Constantinople and Rome. From the 15th century on, the celebration assumed notable importance, becoming a Solemnity with a major Octave* and preceded by a Vigil* with fast. The Octave was reduced to a simple one during the reform of Pius XII in 1955. The date of celebration differed from place to place, but after the feast of the Immaculate Conception (which has a later origin than that of the Birth) was extended to the Universal Church,* the Birth came to be assigned to September 8, nine months after the conception. *Liturgical celebration:* September 8 (Feast); *theme:* joy at the birth of her who is the dawn of our salvation.

In the Proper of the United States* there is also another Feast, Our Lady of Guadalupe, which is treated under that name in this Dictionary.

Memorials

There are also eight Memorials of Mary in the calendar, some Obligatory and others Optional. They are inspired by episodes in the life of Mary or by theological ideas or by places venerated by the faithful.* In the order of their appearance in the Liturgical Year* they are as follows.

Our Lady of Lourdes (owr LAY-dee uhv loordz). Instituted by St. Pius X* in 1907, this feast celebrates the appearance of Mary to St. Bernadette* in 1858. The history of devotion and consolation that

Lourdes conjures up can lead to the contemplation of Mary as the Health of the Sick and the Comforter of the Afflicted. *Liturgical celebration:* February 11 (Opt. Mem.); *theme:* overcoming human weakness through the intercession of the Mother of God.

Immaculate Heart of Mary (im-AK-yuh-luht hahrt uhv MAYR-eè). This feast stems from the efforts of St. John Eudes* to inspire devotion to the Heart of Mary. In 1646 he

won approval for a Mass of the Immaculate Heart of Mary to be celebrated locally. In 1855 the Congregation of Rites* approved a Mass for the feast, and in 1880 Leo XIII extended it to the whole diocese of Rome. After the appearances of Mary to three children at Fatima in 1917, Pius XII consecrated the world to the Immaculate Heart of Mary in 1942 and in 1944 established the feast for the Universal Church on the octave day of the Assumption (August 22). *Liturgical celebration:* Saturday following the 2nd Sunday after Pentecost* (Opt. Mem.); *theme:* becoming worthy temples of God's glory* through devotion to the Immaculate Heart. *See also* APOSTLESHIP OF PRAYER.

Our Lady of Mount Carmel (owr LAY-dee uhv mownt KAHR-muhl). This feast was instituted about 1380 by the Carmelites in thanksgiving for the Order's successful establishment in the West after having been forced to leave their place of origin (Mount Carmel in the Holy Land). Benedict XIII extended it to the Universal Church in 1726. It is also connected with the scapular* and consecration to Mary. *Liturgical celebration:* July 16 (Opt. Mem.); *theme:* reaching Christ through the prayers of His Mother.

Dedication of St. Mary Major (ded-uh-KAY-shuhn uhv saynt MAYR-ee MAY-juhr). This feast recalls the 4th-century dedication in Rome of a replica of the basilica of Mary's Nativity in Bethlehem. In the 5th century Sixtus III offered the Church to the People of God,* and it became a monument to the dogmatic definition of Mary as the Mother of God handed down by the Council of Ephesus (431). St. Pius V* placed it in the Universal Calendar in 1568. *Liturgical celebration:* August 5 (Opt. Mem.); *theme:* Mary is the temple of God and the new Jerusalem who will obtain our salvation through her prayers.

Queenship of Mary (KWEEN-ship uhv MAYR-ee). This feast was inserted in the calendar for the Universal Church by Pius XII in 1954, the centenary of the proclamation of the Immaculate Conception as a dogma,* and assigned to May 31. It is now more felicitously assigned to August 22: "The Solemnity of the Assumption is prolonged in the celebration of the Queenship of . . . Mary, which occurs seven days later. On this occasion we contemplate her who, seated beside the King of Ages, shines forth as Queen and intercedes as Mother" (MC, 6). *Liturgical celebration:* August 22 (Memorial); *theme:* by honoring Mary our Queen, we honor Christ the King and obtain eternal life in the heavenly kingdom.

Our Lady of Sorrows (owr LAY-dee uhv SOR-ohz). A feast that recalls the sorrows of Mary at the foot of the Cross.* Originally granted to the Order of Servants of Mary in 1667, it was introduced into the Roman Calendar in 1814 and assigned to the third Sunday of September. In 1913 the date was changed to September 15. Until the recent reform, it was also anticipated on the Friday before Palm Sunday.* Occurring on the day after the Triumph of the Cross,* it is "a fitting occasion for reliving a decisive moment in the History of Salvation and for venerating, together with her Son lifted up on the Cross, His suffering Mother" (MC, 7). *Liturgical celebration:* September 15 (Memorial); *theme:* union with Christ in His sufferings.

Our Lady of the Rosary (owr LAY-dee uhv thuh ROHZ-[uh-]ree). This feast was instituted in 1573 as a special commemoration of the victory gained at Lepanto on Sunday, October 7, 1571, over the forces of Islam threatening to invade Europe. Prescribed by Gregory XIII for certain churches, it was inserted into the Roman Calendar by Clement XI in 1716 and assigned to the first Sunday of October. In 1913, it was assigned to October 7. *Liturgical celebration:* October 7 (Memorial); *theme:* following Christ by living His Joyful, Sorrowful, and Glorious Mysteries in union with Mary.

Presentation of Mary (pree-zen-TAY-shuhn; prez-uhn-; -preez-uhn-). This ancient feast was based on a pious tradition, recounted by the apocryphal Gospel known as the *Protevangelium of James,* that Mary was presented in the Temple of Jerusalem at the age of three

where she lived with other girls in the charge of holy women. This event was already commemorated in the 6th century in the East. Gregory XI in 1372 heard of the feast, kept in Greece on November 21, and instituted it at Avignon. In 1585, Sixtus V extended it to the Universal Church. *Liturgical celebration:* November 21 (Memorial); *theme:* total consecration to the Lord through Mary.

Other Feasts

In keeping with the principle to leave to particular calendars Marian feasts that do not possess universal interest, the new Liturgy suppressed the universal celebration of certain feasts. The *Seven Sorrows of Mary* on Friday before Passion Sunday* had been part of the Universal Calendar since 1727. However, since it duplicated the Memorial of Our Lady of Sorrows on September 15, it was dropped from the Calendar.

The *Holy Name of Mary* had been inserted on September 12 as a counterpart to the Feast of the Holy Name of Jesus (January 2). However, once the latter was eliminated and made a Votive Mass because it was part of the Solemnity of Mary, Mother of God on January 1, the *Holy Name of Mary* was also deleted and made a Votive Mass.

The feast of *Our Lady of Ransom* was celebrated on September 24 and was linked to a devotion spread by the Order of Mercedarians, which worked for the liberation of slaves. It was deemed to be of lesser interest for the Universal Church today and so returned to particular calendars.

Local Feasts

Many other feasts of Mary were celebrated in some dioceses and Religious Congregations from the 17th century to the reform of Vatican II.* Some of these were: Translation of the Holy House of Loreto (December 10); Our Lady of Guadalupe (December 12); Expectation of the Childbirth of Mary (December 18); Marriage of Mary and Joseph (January 25); Our Lady of Good Counsel (April 26); Mary, Help of Christians (May 24); Most Pure Heart of Mary (3rd Sunday after Pentecost); Our Lady of Perpetual Help (Sunday before June 24); Motherhood of Mary (2nd Sunday of October); Purity of Mary (3rd Sunday of October); Patronage of Mary (2nd Sunday of November); and Manifestation of the Miraculous Medal (November 27).

Common

The Common of the Blessed Virgin Mary in the *Roman Missal* comprises six Mass formularies and one Prayer formulary. These are used in the feasts mentioned above that do not have a complete formulary of their own. They are also utilized for the Mass of the Blessed Virgin on Saturday in Ordinary Time when there is no feast with a higher rank than Optional Memorial. They can also be used as Votive Masses.

The Common of the Blessed Virgin Mary in the *Liturgy of the Hours* contains complete formularies for all the Hours. These are used in the feasts mentioned above that lack a complete formulary. They can also be used as Votive Offices. *See also* ANNUNCIATION; ASSUMPTION; IMMACULATE CONCEPTION; MARY, BLESSED VIRGIN; MARY, BLESSED VIRGIN—CULT; MARY, BLESSED VIRGIN—LECTIONARY; MARY, BLESSED VIRGIN—MASSES; MARY, BLESSED VIRGIN—MEMORIAL ON SATURDAY; MARY, BLESSED VIRGIN—ORDER OF CROWNING AN IMAGE; MARY, BLESSED VIRGIN—VOTIVE MASSES; PRESENTATION OF THE LORD; SOLEMNITY OF MARY, MOTHER OF GOD.

Mary, Blessed Virgin—Lectionary (MAYR-ee, BLES-uhd VUHR-juhn—LEK-shuhn-er-ee). One of the major pluses of the new Liturgy is the "Marian Lectionary," comprising the readings* that are used in Marian celebrations. The previous *Lectionary** made only partial and disordered use of the Biblical material that has to do with Mary. A few readings (like Lk 1:26-38 and 11:27-28) were repeated too much while others (like Jn 2:1-11 and Acts 1:12-14) were never used in a Marian context. The non-Gospel readings made almost exclusive use of pericopes* from the Wisdom Books of the Old Testament* (Sir 24 and Prv 8) or the Book of Revelation* of the New Testament* (chs. 11 and 21).

Following the lead of Vatican II* (LG, 11), the new *Lectionary* includes texts that describe the preparation for salvation,* which, read in the Church* and interpreted in the light of complete revelation, aids our understanding of the Mystery* of the Mother of the Savior. New Testament texts then evoke the ecclesial traits of Mary. Thus, the *Lectionary* contains a larger number of Old and New Testament readings concerning the Blessed Virgin (around 55).

This numerical increase has not been based on random choice. Only those readings have been accepted which in different ways and degrees can be considered Marian, either from the evidence of their content or from the results of careful exegesis, supported by the teachings of the Magisterium* or by solid tradition (MC, 12).

Thus, the new *Lectionary* utilizes from the Old Testament the Protoevangelium (Gn 3:15), a few historical texts (Gn 12: the promises to Abraham, and 2 Samuel 7: the prophecy of Nathan—both of which are alluded to in the Annunciation*): 1 Chr 15 and 16 (the transferal of the Ark), and a certain number of prophetic oracles (Is 7: the virgin mother, and Is 9: Emmanuel—both of which are also alluded to by the angel* to Mary; Is 61: the spouse, as well as Mic 5: Emmanuel; Zep 3 and Zec 2: on the daughter of Zion).

The Gospel* texts are also better used. The accounts of the Infancy show Mary's person and function in relation to the events of the Savior's life. Luke* also brings out Mary's personality and her spiritual journey. He shows her faith,* obedience, complete openness, acceptance and interiorization of the Word of God, Who becomes flesh in her. She is the point of arrival for the faith and expectation of the just of the Old Testament, the place where God becomes man amid the poor. Then John* completes the portrait by the account of her standing by the Cross,* showing how she becomes the Model and Mother of the Messianic People of the New Covenant.*

Among the other New Testament pericopes the most important ones are those from the Book of Revelation (chs. 11 and 12: the Woman, and 21: Jerusalem); Acts 1 (Mary with the disciples) and four Pauline texts (Rom 5 and 8; Gal 4; Eph 1). These consistently bring out Mary's role in Salvation History, that is, her relation to Christ and to the Church. *See also* LECTIONARY; MARY, BLESSED VIRGIN; MARY, BLESSED VIRGIN—CULT; MARY, BLESSED VIRGIN—FEASTS; MARY, BLESSED VIRGIN—MASSES; MARY, BLESSED VIRGIN—MEMORIAL ON SATURDAY; MARY, BLESSED VIRGIN—ORDER OF CROWNING AN IMAGE; MARY, BLESSED VIRGIN—VOTIVE MASSES.

Mary, Blessed Virgin—Masses (MAYR-ee, BLES-uhd VUHR-juhn—MAS-uhz). On the Assumption* in 1986 the Congregation for Divine Worship* issued a decree* promulgating the *Collection of Masses of the Blessed Virgin Mary.* The Latin text appeared the following year, and the English text of some of the Masses was available in America in early 1988. The total collection in English is be published later.

Following the Church's teaching on the place of Mary within the Mystery* of Christ and His Church* by the Second Vatican Council,* churches and Religious Institutes composed new Mass Propers* from ancient liturgical sources and the writings of the Fathers of the

Church.* These Propers are outstanding because of their piety, teaching, and the significance of their texts. To promote properly the devotion to the Mother of God, the Roman Liturgy* integrates commemorations of her into the Liturgical Year,* to indicate her connection in the annual cycle of Christ's Mysteries.*

In celebrating the Sacred Mysteries, the Church is aware of the entire work of salvation.* Since Mary was intimately involved in the History of Salvation,* actively present during the Mysteries of Christ's life, the *Collection of Masses* has special meaning and purpose, commemorating her role as the Mother of the Lord in the work of redemption, as it celebrates the events of salvation in which the Blessed Virgin was involved in view of the Mystery of Christ. By honoring the Mother of God in this way, the Masses actually celebrate the action of God in our salvation, indicating Mary's intimate connection with her Son.

As Christ is present in our celebrations of the Liturgy, so also is Mary, now exalted in heaven at the side of her Son, where her intercession continues to obtain gifts for our salvation. She is ever present as the Mother of the Church and her advocate. Mary is considered the exemplar of the Christian life. She is considered a *figure,* because she exemplified how one should live as a virgin, spouse, and mother. She is referred to as an *image,* since she was perfectly fashioned after her Son, and thus as a flawless image, she is one to be emulated.

Nature of the Collection

Most of these texts are from local churches, Religious Institutes, or already in the *Sacramentary.** They would be intended primarily for the Marian shrines where Masses in her honor are celebrated frequently, but also for all Church communities, especially on Saturdays in Ordinary Time.* In other words there are no changes in the rubrics* governing such Masses as stated in the *General Instruction of the Roman Missal.*

Structure of the Collection

Forty-six of the Marian formularies are distributed over the seasons of the Liturgical Year: three in Advent,* six in Christmas,* five in Lent,* four in Easter,* and twenty-eight in Ordinary Time. The last mentioned are subdivided into three sections, the first (11 formularies) celebrates her under titles derived from Sacred Scripture,* or shows especially her bond with the Church; the second (9 formularies) honors her under titles that indicate her cooperation in fostering the spiritual life of the faithful*; the third (8 formularies) celebrates her under titles that indicate her compassionate interceding on behalf of the faithful. Published in two volumes, the first comparable to our *Sacramentary,* the second to our *Lectionary,** the collection, in volume 1, contains a liturgical, historical, and pastoral introduction to each formulary, so that one may prepare properly for the Eucharistic celebration.

Use of the Collection

The seasons of the Liturgical Year are to be respected, though there may be occasions to use certain Masses during another season for a just reason. Thus, Mary, Mother of Reconciliation, assigned to Lent, might be used during Ordinary Time to arouse a spirit of reconciliation. However, others, such as Mary and the Lord's Resurrection, would not ordinarily be allowed outside of the Easter Season.

The Marian shrines will benefit the most from this collection because of their privilege to have more frequent celebrations of Masses in her honor. Even though a shrine might be dedicated to a specific title of Mary, the liturgical season ought to be respected and the Biblical readings from those specific seasons should be proclaimed during such times. Even when there is a proper Mass of a shrine, during specific liturgical seasons, that same Mass should not be said every day and more than once the same day, in order to allow the faithful an overview of the entire History of Salvation. Even a pilgrimage, especially one that would spend several days at the shrine, should celebrate a variety of such Marian Masses.

Dedicating Saturday to the Blessed Mother is an ancient custom recognized by the recent liturgical reform, which bestowed new vigor on this type of celebration. These Masses allow a wide variety of ways for the ecclesial communities to honor Mary as a kind of introduction to the Lord's day. Genuine Marian devotion* is not merely a multiplication of such Masses but a celebration of a vital liturgical spirit accomplished with care and propriety.

Biblical Readings

In the *Lectionary* there are many readings relating to the life or mission of the Blessed Mother, or concerning prophecies about her. Some events, figures, or symbols foretell or suggest her life and mission; some readings may not refer specifically to Mary but extol virtues that flourished in Mary, who was the most perfect disciple of Christ. Although only two readings are provided, on some occasions three readings may be used, taken from the Common of the Blessed Virgin Mary or the appendix to the *Lectionary.* There may be occasions when the celebrants want to replace certain readings with more appropriate ones from these listings. *See also* MARY, BLESSED VIRGIN; MARY, BLESSED VIRGIN—CULT; MARY, BLESSED VIRGIN—FEASTS; MARY, BLESSED VIRGIN—LECTIONARY; MARY, BLESSED VIRGIN—MEMORIAL ON SATURDAY; MARY, BLESSED VIRGIN—ORDER OF CROWNING AN IMAGE; MARY, BLESSED VIRGIN—VOTIVE MASSES.

Mary, Blessed Virgin—Memorial on Saturday (MAYR-ee, BLES-uhd VUHR-juhn—muh-MAWR-ee-uhl on SAT-uhr-dee; day). The practice of dedicating Saturday to Mary is very old. The reason for the choice of Saturday is based on a legendary yet substantially accu-

rate account. On the Saturday after Christ's Death* and His disciples' abandonment of Him, Mary was the only one to preserve intact her faith* in the Divinity of her Son. As a result, she merited to receive an exceptional appearance of Jesus *on*

that day. Another explanation asserts that Divine Wisdom, becoming incarnate, *rested* (Saturday was the Sabbath = day of rest) in Mary as on a bed.

Hence, Saturday acquired its great Marian tone, and the existing fast on that day became associated with Mary. Today, the strongest trace of Mary's relationship with Saturday occurs in the Liturgy.* Saturday is dedicated to Mary by a Mass* or Office* of the Blessed Virgin Mary. Through these liturgical acts, Christians exalt the person of Mary in the action that renews the sacrifice* of Christ and in the action that prolongs His prayer.*

This liturgical attribution of Saturday to Mary was largely the work of the great Alcuin (735-804), the Benedictine monk who was "Minister of Education" at the court of Charlemagne and who contributed in a decisive manner to the Carolingian liturgical reform. Alcuin composed six formularies for Votive* (that is, devotional) Masses—one for each day of the week. And he assigned two formularies to Saturday in honor of our Lady. The practice was quickly and joyously embraced by both clergy* and laity.*

Gradually, the "Mass of the Blessed Virgin on Saturday" became simply the "Mass of the Blessed Virgin" and was celebrated even on other days, whenever liturgical legislation permitted. (Many aged priests* afflicted with diminishing sight were granted permission to celebrate daily this Marian Mass which they had committed to memory.)

The liturgical reform of Vatican II* did not abolish this traditional practice. It actually enriched the formularies with a greater variety of orations in accord with the spirit of the liturgical seasons and suggested the use of the weekday readings* in place of the invariable liturgical readings once used. The present *Roman Missal** gives three common formularies of the Mass plus one each for the seasons of Advent,* Christmas,* and Easter.*

In these texts Mary is seen as the image of the Church praying and as the model of the meditative hearing of God's Word.* There are also references to her lowly condition as an innocent, free, and grateful *woman;* as a faithful and praying *witness;* as a tender and attentive *mother.*

Hence, we can say that these new texts show respect for Marian devotion and insert it better into the annual liturgical cycle of Christ's Mysteries.* Christ's eternal light shines its rays on His Mother who, remaining intact in her virginal glory, has irradiated the whole world. The virginity and motherhood of Mary are stressed in many ways. At the same time, there is no lack of appeal to Mary's intercession to save her people from sin and lead them to eternal life.

We might ask in what the newness of the Mass of Our Lady consists—especially when we recall that it now contains only three orations, since the readings are of the day and do not speak of Mary. The newness consists in a development of the ancient and daily "commemoration," with the petition that Almighty God heed the constant intercession of Mary on our behalf.

Mary thus appears in the background, since the Eucharist* is a thanksgiving for the redeeming work wrought by Christ. But the liturgical texts still bring out the exceptional traits of this creature of God—her dignity as the virgin Mother of Christ and Mother of all Christians, and the one for whom God has done great things. She shows that even now in her condition of glory she does not cease to exercise a maternal function.

As we celebrate Christ's Passover, we commemorate the one who was intimately united with Him in His earthly life from conception to crucifixion and is also united with Him in heavenly bliss. We commemorate the perfect model of today's believers and the image of what we shall be in the new life of heaven. (These same themes are found in the Saturday Office of the Blessed Virgin Mary.) *See also* MARY, BLESSED VIRGIN; MARY, BLESSED VIRGIN—CULT; MARY, BLESSED VIRGIN—FEASTS; MARY, BLESSED VIRGIN—LECTIONARY; MARY, BLESSED VIRGIN—MASSES; MARY, BLESSED VIRGIN—ORDER OF CROWNING AN IMAGE; MARY, BLESSED VIRGIN—VOTIVE MASSES.

Mary, Blessed Virgin—Order of Crowning an Image (MAYR-ee, BLES-uhd VUHR-juhn—AWRD-uhr uhv KROWN-ing an IM-ij). One of the most recent Marian rites published by the Sacred Congregation for Divine Worship* in 1981 (English translation, 1987), which updates a traditional ceremony used in the Church* and sets forth the theological reasons for Mary's Queenship.* Both in the East and in the West the practice of depicting the Blessed Virgin Mary wearing a regal crown came into use in the era of the Council of Ephesus (431 A.D.). It is especially from the end of the 16th century that in the West the practice became widespread for the faithful, both Religious* and laity,* to crown images of Mary. The growth of this custom led to the composition of a special rite for the crowning, which was incorporated into the *Roman Pontifical** in the 19th century.

By means of this new rite the Church proclaims that Mary is rightly regarded and invoked as Queen for the following reasons. (1) She is the Mother of the Son of God, Who is the Messianic King. (2) She is the chosen companion of the Redeemer, Who made us a kingdom to our God (see Rv 5:10). (3) She is the perfect follower of Christ, who was taken up into heavenly glory and exalted by the Lord as Queen of all (see LG, 59). (4) She is the foremost member of the Church, who is rightly invoked as Queen of angels* and of Saints,* as our Lady and our Queen.

The rite of crowning is fittingly held on Solemnities* and Feasts* of Mary or on other festive days. But it is not to be held on the principal Solemnities of the Lord or on days having a penitential character. It may take place within Mass,* within the Liturgy of the Word* at Evening Prayer,* or within a celebration of the Word of God suited to the occasion.

The whole sense of the rite rests on the idea of the exaltation of the lowly chanted by Mary in the *Magnificat,** and it contains great theological and spiritual riches. Foremost among these is a new Litany* of the Blessed Virgin, which combines faithfulness to Biblical tradition and conformity with the spiritual sensibility of our times. *See also* LITANY OF THE BLESSED VIRGIN MARY; MARY, BLESSED VIRGIN; MARY, BLESSED VIRGIN—CULT.

Mary, Blessed Virgin—Votive Masses (MAYR-ee, BLES-uhd VUHR-juhn—VOHT-iv MAS-uhz). Masses of Mary that do not conform to the Office* or Mass* of the day, which are chosen by the celebrant* to fulfill a private devotion or to respond to the wish of the faithful.* These Masses are essentially those found in the Common* of the Blessed Virgin Mary plus the Mass of the Name of Mary (both of which have already been treated in the entry MARY, BLESSED VIRGIN—FEASTS) and the Mass of Mary, Mother of the Church, which was added in the 1975 edition of the *Missale Romanum* and the 1985 edition of the *Sacramentary.**

This latest Mass constitutes a notable enrichment of the doctrinal quality found in the Marian corpus of the Liturgy.* The Opening Prayer* recalls Mary at the foot of the Cross* at the moment when she becomes the Mother of Christ's disciples. The Preface* is taken from *Lumen Gentium** (the *Constitution on the Church). See also* MARY, BLESSED VIRGIN; MARY, BLESSED VIRGIN—CULT; MARY, BLESSED VIRGIN—FEASTS; MARY, BLESSED VIRGIN—LECTIONARY; MARY, BLESSED VIRGIN—MASSES; VOTIVE MASS.

Mary, Mother of God, Feast of. *See* SOLEMNITY OF MARY, MOTHER OF GOD.

Mary Magdalene, St. (MAYR-ee MAG-duh-len). 1st century. A native of Magdala, near Tiberius on the west shore of the Sea of Galilee, Mary was exorcised by Jesus, which

would not necessarily mean she had been a sinner. In gratitude, she became one of the ministering women, even accompanying Him on His last journey to Jerusalem, and was present on Calvary and at the entombment. After reporting the empty tomb, she was the first recorded person to see the risen Savior. *Liturgical celebration:* July 22 (Memorial); *theme:* the love of Christ impels us.

Mary Magdalene de Pazzi, St. (MAYR-ee MAG-duh-len duh PAHTS-see; PAHZ-ee). 1566-1607. An Italian Carmelite, who during a serious illness experienced many ecstasies, followed by years of depression and spiritual aridity. She was gifted with prophecy, healing powers, and the gift of reading minds. A critical edition of her mystical experiences and spiritual instructions exists. *Liturgical celebration*: May 25 (Opt. Mem.); *theme:* "To suffer and not to die."

Mass (mas). As the central act of worship* in the Catholic Church,* the Sacrifice of the Eucharist* is called the Mass, derived from the Latin word *missa*, meaning dismissal, enunciated at the end of the Liturgy of the Word* and the Liturgy of the Eucharist.* Under the appearances* of the bread and wine, the Body and Blood of Christ is sacrificed in a memorial fashion by His Church. Jesus, Who died once for all, by the ministry of and with His Church, offers a renewal of the sacrifice of the Cross* on the altar* as a perpetual application of merits He acquired by that immolation.

This liturgical reiteration does not increase the value of Christ's unique sacrifice, but since the members of the Church can thus co-sacrifice with their Head, it is more meaningful. The frequent celebration of the Mass stresses the objective sacrifice of the Church, which assumes significance through the participants offering themselves during each Mass. The Preparation of the Gifts* expresses this fact.

Always offered in the name of and for the entire Church, the Mass maintains a public and social character no matter where or under what circumstances it is performed. Consequently the dialogue form is always used in the plural. Present legislation stipulates celebrating Mass facing the people to accentuate this fact and to remind the people that the Mass is a celebration in which they are to participate* actively and fully, even to the extent of receiving Communion* during each Paschal meal, even if they attend Mass twice a day (Canon 917). Thus too, it gives sense to the duty of the community to join together for the Sunday Mass obligation.*

As a sacrifice, the Mass achieves four purposes: (1) to adore God, by acknowledging His infinite majesty and supreme dominion over creatures; (2) to be thankful for all God's benefits, hence the term Eucharist; (3) to atone for the sins of the human race, an act of expiation; (4) to beg new favors from His generosity in accordance with the many needs of the congregation. *See also* CONSECRATION; CONVENTUAL MASS; EUCHARIST; EUCHARISTIC PRAYER; FRUITS OF THE MASS; INTRODUCTORY RITES; LITURGY OF THE EUCHARIST; LITURGY OF THE WORD; MASS—COMMUNION RITE; MASS—CONCLUDING RITE; MULTILINGUAL MASSES; STIPENDS; TRANSUBSTANTIATION; *and the individual parts of Mass.*

Mass—Communion Rite (mas—kuh-MYOO-nyuhn rait). The Communion Rite begins after the Doxology* of the Eucharistic Prayer.* It expresses the unity within the Mystical Body* of Christ. All God's peo-

ple because of the intimacy of Communion* are united with God and Jesus. Such unity starts in the Lord's Prayer,* by which we call God "Our Father," because we are willing to relate to others as brother and sister; the Sign of Peace* should break down any division; symbolically, the Breaking of the Bread* means that we eat from one loaf; reception of Communion occurs at the same table.

The Lord's Prayer* prepares us for Communion by begging for bread and asking for forgiveness. It is followed by the embolism,* a sequel to the Our Father. Peace is experienced by the Christians, as the prayer ends with a brief doxology. The Sign of Peace gives the people an opportunity to express their love for one another and of God as they beg for peace in preparation for the reception of the Eucharist. Following it, the Breaking of the Bread should express the great unity and charity in a very concrete and explicit fashion. Further unity is symbolized by the Commingling* of the bread and wine, recalling that Christ is the living, risen Christ. Chanting the Lamb of God* during this rite stresses again the peace that is to come to all.

After some private prayers of the priest,* he invites the community to Communion and the people process to the altar* to symbolize their journey to the Kingdom of God.* Ordinarily a Communion Song* accompanies them. Their answer "Amen" to the presentation of the Host by the priest with the words "The Body of Christ" is a profession of faith.* Reception of the Eucharist is usually followed by a period of silence or a song of praise. Thereafter the Communion Rite concludes with the Prayer after Communion,* proper to that day.

Mass—Concluding Rite (mas—kuhn-KLOOD-ing rait). Immediately after the Communion Rite,* should there be any announcements,* these are made, but they should be kept brief. Then just as the people were greeted at the beginning of the Mass,* so now the president greets the people again and blesses them

in one of three forms, the simple one, or at his discretion a more Solemn Blessing,* particularly at various seasons or on specific feast days, or a Prayer over the People.* In the latter two cases the deacon* or the priest* asks the community to "Bow your heads and pray for God's blessing." After this they, having received the blessing, answer "Amen." They sign themselves with the Sign of the Cross,* concluding the ceremony in the same way that they began. Then the Dismissal* pleads with the congregation to do good works and leave praising and blessing the Lord.

Variants of the forms may be used by the celebrant. Should another liturgical function follow, naturally the faithful* would not be dismissed. In that case, the rite is usually omitted, although one might be permitted to say "Let us bless the Lord,*" which would be answered by "Thanks be to God.*"

Mass—Consecration. *See* CONSECRATION.

Mass—Eucharistic Prayer. *See* EUCHARISTIC PRAYER.

Mass—Introductory Rites. *See* INTRODUCTORY RITES.

Mass—Liturgy of the Eucharist. *See* LITURGY OF THE EUCHARIST.

Mass—Liturgy of the Word. *See* LITURGY OF THE WORD.

Mass—Penitential Rite. *See* PENITENTIAL RITE.

Mass—Preparation of the Gifts. *See* PREPARATION OF THE GIFTS.

Mass Card (mas kahrd). A card that indicates a Mass* will be offered for a particular person or intention and gives the name of the donor of the Mass. At times, it also

indicates the time and place of the service as well as the celebrant.* *See also* STIPENDS.

Mass, Conventual. *See* CONVENTUAL MASS.

Mass, Dialogue (mas DAI-uh-log). From 1922 to the Mass of Paul VI, this referred to a Low Mass* at which the Latin responses* customarily made by the server were spoken aloud by the congregation* in unison. The permission of the local Ordinary* was necessary in order to have such a Mass. Vatican II,* by its insistence on participation,* insured that every Mass would be a dialogue in the vernacular*—in keeping with the fact that the Mass is a dialogue between God and His people. *See also* DIALOGUE.

Mass, Ferial (mas FIR-ee-uhl; FER-). The seasonal Mass* proper to the day. The new Liturgy* has assigned a proper Mass to the weekdays of Advent,* Christmas Time,* Lent,* and Easter Time.* It is celebrated when there is no Mass of a Saint.* Thus, the Mass is ferial or optional. Ash Wednesday,* the ferias of Holy Week,* and the ferias of Advent from December 17 to December 24 are privileged ferias. During Ordinary Time,* the Mass of the preceding Sunday or any Sunday in Ordinary Time may be celebrated. *See also* WEEK; WEEKDAY.

Mass for Children and Special Groups (mas for CHIL-druhn and SPESH-uhl groops). With the advent of the vernacular,* the Church* was compelled to show special concern for children attending the liturgical services, particularly the Mass.* Words and signs used at the Mass should be sufficiently adapted to the capacity of the children. Since children are profoundly formed by the religious experience of infancy and early childhood, the Church introduced the *Directory for Masses with Children* in 1973. It concerns children who have not entered pre-adolescence, but does not pretend to suffice for children who are physically or mentally retarded. Further adaptations may need to be made for them.

Those working on the formation of children should develop the values of the Eucharistic gathering by including them in the activity of the community, exchange of greetings, experience of symbolic actions, expression of thanks, and the meal of friendship, which would allow them to enjoy a truly festive celebration. Naturally the family would have a great role in teaching these Christian and human values, helped as they can be by other educators. Special care should be taken in the catechesis* of children for first Penance* and first Communion,* so that they may actively participate in the Eucharist* with the People of God at the Lord's table. As they grow older, the Word of God* can readily have a more important place in their celebrations to allow them to enjoy a greater response to the Gospel* in their own daily lives.

In Masses with adults at which children also participate, great care should be taken that the children do not feel neglected. They can be spoken to directly in introductory comments and in the Homily.* When the physical circumstances allow, it might be advantageous to have the children relegated to a separate section during which they have an explanation, a reading from the Liturgy of the Word* and a special commentary or Homily for themselves. Good timing can allow them to participate in the Mass for adults with their joining the community at Preparation of the Gifts.*

In all this the intention is that the Eucharistic celebrations for children must lead toward the celebration of Mass with adults, particularly since most of the time this will occur on Sunday.*

Concerning the principles to be employed in such Masses, every effort should be made to make the experience more intense, which can occur as the children have special participatory action in the celebration,* such as preparing the altar,* being a chanter,* singing in the

choir,* playing the musical instruments, proclaiming the readings,* responding during a dialogue Homily, offering the General Intercessions, presenting the gifts, and similar activities. All of these external activities should serve to increase the internal participation* of the children, as the celebrant tries to be very festive, meditative, and as brotherly as Christ. Concerned with the dignity, clarity, and simplicity of his actions he strives to be readily understood by that age group.

Although normally the place for a celebration for children or special groups ought to be the church, there may be good reason to celebrate the Eucharist outside of the sacred place as long as the place for celebration is appropriate and worthy. Weekday Masses may be quite effective for children, wherein they may participate more fully and with greater effect and less problem with weariness. Usually a Children's Mass would not occur every day.

Singing and music should be used in a generous manner, since children take to that kind of participation readily, specifically in the acclamations.* Musical instruments, particularly when played by children themselves, can more readily express the festive joy and praise of the Lord.

Gestures and actions are extremely important in Masses for children, especially processions* in which they can join, and the use of many visual elements throughout the Liturgical Year* such as the Easter Candle,* liturgical ornaments and banners*; these have

special meaning for children. Related to this, silence* to be observed at the proper times gives the children a way of genuinely learning how to reflect on themselves and to praise God in their hearts.

Some parts of the Mass may be modified to suit the children in accordance with the *Directory*. For instance, certain elements of the Introductory Rites* may be stressed or omitted. In the Liturgy of the Word, the permission to choose readings more suited to the capacity of the children is given; the intent is to make the children more aware that the Biblical reading does apply to them and help them appreciate the value of God's Word more. The Homily then unfolds the Scriptures* and frequently may be more effective in dialogue form. For the Profession of Faith,* the Apostles' Creed* may be used, but the children should learn to recite the Nicene Creed* too.

Since the presidential prayers* might be too difficult for the children to understand in their usual form, the celebrant has the right to reword them in terms that can be better understood. Three versions of Eucharistic Prayers* for children are available as long as the Mass is one in which the majority of participants are children. These Eucharistic Prayers contain the elements of Eucharistic Prayer as prescribed, but in a simpler style of language more suitable to children. To keep the attention of children and for their more active participation, the number of acclamations have been increased without obscuring the nature of the Eucharistic Prayer as a presidential one.

Furthermore, Episcopal Conferences* are to make sure musical settings are prepared for the children in accord with the culture of the region. Catechetical instruction before and after the celebration should deepen the internal participation of the children. The rites before Communion* should have disposed those children who plan to receive the Eucharist* to do so with proper recollection, most probably accompanied by a procession during which there is singing. At the Dismissal* the connection between the Liturgy and life should be stressed, so that the children quickly and joyfully learn to encounter Christ at the Eucharistic celebration and make application to their daily living.

Mass for Special Gatherings. *See* MASS, PLACE OF.

Mass for the Dead. *See* MASS OF CHRISTIAN BURIAL.

Mass for the People (mas for thuh PEE-puhl). Pastors* are obligated to celebrate a Mass* for the intentions of their parishioners on Sundays and the other Holy Days of Obligation* celebrated in their particular country. During this gathering of the Christian community, they are to explain the Liturgy of the Word* for that day (Canon 534).

Mass for Various Needs and Occasions. *See* VARIOUS NEEDS AND OCCASIONS, MASSES FOR.

Mass in Homes. *See* MASS, PLACE OF.

Mass Intentions. *See* INTENTIONS, MASS.

Mass Media (mas MED-ee-uh). The artificial means for sharing aesthetic experience or communicating information to ear and eye. The principal ones are: the press, the cinema, radio and television, and the theater. These transform human communication into social communication. They offer new ways of confronting people with the message of the Gospel,* of allowing the faithful* to share in sacred rites and worship* even when they are far from the service.

The decree *Inter Mirifica** of Vatican II* defined the use of the media of social communication as a "duty" of the Church* (no. 3). The Pastoral Instruction of the Pontifical Commission for Social Communication *Communio et Progressio** (1971) indicated the structures needed for the fulfillment of such a duty (nos. 126-134) and alluded to the use of these media in the Liturgy* so that "they can bind the Christian community closer together and invite everyone to participate in the intimate life of the Church" (no. 128).

Audiovisuals such as videocassettes, audiocassettes, films, magnetic tapes, and photographic montages can be of great help in paraliturgical* services and Bible Services* as well as penitential celebrations,* pilgrimages,* and ecumenical gatherings. They can also be of use in the Liturgy, Sacramental preparation, evangelization, and the administration of the Sacraments.* In the past various means were used in the church to set the pastoral tone and spiritual climate of the day or season—stained glass windows, icons,* colored materials, tapestries, and the like. Perhaps a "photo-icon" art of the 20th century may one day be used in the same manner.

At the present time, the Church has indicated that audiovisuals can certainly be used in Masses of children as illustrations of a Homily, as visual expressions of the intentions of the General Intercessions,* or as inspirations to reflection *(Directory for Masses with Children* (nos. 35-36). *See also* MASS, TELEVISED.

Mass Obligation. *See* SUNDAY MASS OBLIGATION.

Mass of a Saint (mas uhv uh saynt). Mass* celebrated in honor of a Saint* in accord with the liturgical calendar.* The Mass is always addressed to God and offered to Him alone, however. The celebration is usually assigned to the Saint's birthday to heaven (date of death). The prayers, especially the Opening Prayer,* refer to the Saint and indicate the outstanding virtue that the faithful* should imitate so as to follow Christ more closely—since each Saint is a reflection in some way of the holiness of our Lord. *See also* MASS, FERIAL; PROPER OF THE SAINTS; SAINTS.

Mass of Christian Burial (mas uhv KRIS-chuhn BER-ee-uhl). Christian burial reflects two themes: joy* at the completion of the earthly pilgrimage of the dead persons, which begins their union with Christ; hope* that their rest will be hastened by the prayer and Eucharistic Sacrifice of the survivors. The Eucharistic Sacrifice is intended to offer prayers and petitions for the deceased and bring spiritual help and consoling hope to the survivors. The Mass of Christian Burial itself ranks as most important among those celebrated for the dead and is forbidden only on Holy Days of Obligation* and the Sundays of Advent,* Lent* and Easter* Seasons, on Ash Wednesday* and during Holy Week.* Even on Obligatory Memorials* Masses on the occasion of the news of a death, the final burial,

and the first anniversary are permitted. Daily Masses for the dead, as long as they are actually offered for them, are allowed on weekdays in Ordinary Time,* when anything less than an Obligatory Memorial is being celebrated. *See also* FUNERAL, RITES AND CEREMONIES.

Mass of the Catechumens (mas uhv thuh kat-uh-KYOO-muhnz). That part of the Mass which corresponds to what we today call the Liturgy of the Word.* It consists of the introductory prayers and the Scripture readings* together with a Homily.* This was the part of the Mass at which the catechumens,* who were preparing for Baptism,* were allowed to be present. *See also* CATECHUMENATE; MASS, ORDER OF.

Mass of the Faithful (mas uhv thuh FAYTH-fuhl). In the old terminology, that part of the Mass which followed the Mass of the Catechumens,* now referred to as the Liturgy of the Eucharist.* It received its name from the fact that those who were baptized, namely the faithful,* were the ones who were allowed to stay during the Eucharistic sacrifice for the Preparation of the Gifts,* the Consecration,* and the Communion.* *See also* MASS, ORDER OF.

Mass of the Presanctified (mas uhv thuh pree-SANGK-ti-faid). The term formerly used for the Communion* service of the Good Friday* Liturgy. *See also* GOOD FRIDAY.

Mass Offering. *See* STIPENDS.

Mass, Order of (mas, AWRD-uhr uhv). Historically the Liturgy of the Word* and the Liturgy of the Eucharist* were celebrated separately, but eventually they were united into one celebration called the Mass.* Expansion of rites during the centuries did not becloud the simplicity of structure by which the Mass was always characterized, centering as it did on the reading of the Scripture* and the celebration of the Sacrament.*

Complexities arose, particularly from a hybrid with Gallican rites; the Order of Mass was stabilized for the entire Church during the Council of Trent and through the introduction of Pius V's* *Roman Missal** in 1570. Even then the simplicity of the Roman Rite was superimposed with some Gallican elements, such as the Introductory Rites,* the Offertory,* and the Concluding Rites.*

Reforms enjoined by Vatican II* eventually resulted in the *Roman Missal* of Paul VI (1970) in which the intent was to restore the Roman Liturgy.

The focus on the Word and Sacrament is evident, but certain Gallican elements hallowed by time were preserved. With an emphasis on sacrifice, the role of others besides the priests was stressed. Terminology throughout has been changed to clarify the meaning and purpose of the structure of the Mass as well as the interrelationship of the two main parts. To help in its understanding, two tables are included, one a chronological table of Mass prayers, the other a comparative table between the Missals of Pius V and Paul VI. (*See* APPENDICES 1, 2.)

In the United States there was a nationwide study on the structural elements of the Order of the Mass. A book entitled *The Mystery of Faith* was circulated to various parishes* in the dioceses* willing to cooperate in the survey, and selected people of the parishes met regularly to answer the questions posed in the book. Thus there was a grass roots reaction to the Order of the Mass of 1970 about ten years after its implementation. The results reflect a high comfort level and satisfaction with the revision; furthermore, they indicate that an ever increasing number of people are closely involved in the Church's worship.*

After the study was completed, the North American Academy of Liturgy, during one of its workshops in January of 1983, reviewed the results of the study. Some of their observations follow. Some actions in the Mass* seem to have been retained for historical reasons rather than genuine symbolic content: washing of hands,* the commingling,* mixing water and wine.* More flexibility is desired, even though there are opportunities where the directions provide the option of using "these or similar words." The call for creativity is evident.

The Introductory Rites* seem too crowded; a greater variety of format is desired for the General Intercessions*; these are certainly areas that allow for greater flexibility, and models should be developed among the various types of Sunday Masses for a given parish. The positioning of the Sign of Peace* elsewhere and the ritual communication should be seriously considered. Verbal communication should reflect who is speaking to whom about what.

The difference between proclaiming presidential prayers* and uttering prayers of personal devotion already exists. Longer periods

of silence* should occur. Symbolic action should be more robust and lavish, such as real bread, the cup at all Masses, generous sprinkling with holy water,* willingness to use incense* as suggested. The desire for more effective homilies would call for a more thorough preparation at the seminary level in this area. The laity* is willing to accept the diversity of roles and ministries allowed, so that all members would be able to have the full active participation* the *Constitution on the Sacred Liturgy** desires.

Further suggestions included a hope that the catechesis on the Liturgy* and the Word of God* would continue, perhaps even making use of the workbook itself, *The Mystery of Faith*. Appropriate artistic and spatial setting in which the liturgical action can dynamically unfold means a constant concern for the principles explained in *Environment and Art in Catholic Worship*.

Most groups who enjoyed the study were extremely disappointed that they were not permitted to react to the *Eucharistic Prayer.** The Academy suggested more openness on the part of the Church to new and varying Eucharistic Prayers in keeping with liturgical tradition, including many sung acclamations* by the people. Further study needs to be accomplished in order to achieve a distinct Sunday Mass Eucharistic assembly of the Local Church.* Thus Sunday Mass could be looked upon in the context of a faith community, which tries to respond each day to the call of Christ, so that it could be, as His body, a sign and instrument of God's kingdom* at work in the world.* *See also* ABLUTIONS; ACCLAMATIONS; ADMONITIONS; ALLELUIA; AMEN; ANNOUNCEMENTS; COMMINGLING; COMMUNION; COMMUNION ANTIPHON; COMMUNION SONG; CONSECRATION; DISMISSAL; DOXOLOGY; ELEVATION; ELEVATION, LITTLE; EMBOLISM; ENTRANCE ANTIPHON; ENTRANCE SONG; EPICLESIS; EPISTLE; EUCHARIST; EUCHARISTIC PRAYER; GENERAL INTERCESSIONS; GLORY TO GOD; GLORY TO YOU, LORD; GOSPEL; GREETING; HANC IGITUR; HOLY, HOLY, HOLY; HOMILY; HOSANNA; INCENSATION; INTERCESSIONS; INTINCTION; INTRODUCTORY RITES; LAMB OF GOD; LET US PRAY; LITURGY OF THE EUCHARIST; LITURGY OF THE WORD; LORD BE WITH YOU, THE; LORD, HAVE MERCY; LORD'S PRAYER; MASS—COMMUNION RITE; MASS—CONCLUDING RITE; MASS OF THE CATECHUMENS; MASS OF THE FAITHFUL; MASS, ORDINARY OF THE; MASS, PROPER OF THE; OFFERING; OFFERTORY; OPENING PRAYER; PENITENTIAL RITE; PRAISE TO YOU, LORD JESUS CHRIST; PRAY, BRETHREN; PRAYER; PRAYER AFTER COMMUNION; PRAYER OVER THE GIFTS; PRAYER OVER THE PEOPLE; PREFACE; PREPARATION OF THE GIFTS; PROFESSION OF FAITH; READINGS; RESPONSORIAL PSALM; SAINTS IN EUCHARISTIC PRAYER I; SEQUENCE; SIGN OF PEACE; SILENCE; SPRINKLING; THANKS BE TO GOD; THROUGH CHRIST OUR LORD; VERSICLE.

Mass, Ordinary of the (mas, AWRD-[uh]n-er-ee uhv thuh). (1a) Those formulas which are common to every Mass* and have few variants, except for the Eucharistic Prayer* that currently allows nine forms. (1b) Those unvarying parts sung chorally, e.g., Glory to God,* Lamb of God.* *See also* MASS, PROPER OF THE.

(2) Formerly, it sometimes referred to the order of the Mass. *See also* MASS, ORDER OF.

Mass, Papal. *See* PAPAL MASS.

Mass, Parochial. *See* MASS FOR THE PEOPLE.

Mass, Place of (mas, plays uhv). Although the principal objective of pastoral activity is to insert the faithful* into the ecclesial community by liturgical celebrations, yet there are occasions when attention should be given to special gatherings, not with the intent of separating these from the total community, but to minister to their special needs and to deepen and intensify their Christian faith,* built upon some common spiritual or apostolic commitment. Permission can be given for the celebration of the Eucharist* for certain situations, such as retreats or pastoral studies; meetings of the lay apostolate or similar associations; meetings that occur for pastoral motives in sections of the parish*; young people or groups with certain similarities who gather periodically for formation or instruction, pointedly adapted to their mentality; special gatherings around the sick or the aged, which would include those friends who look after them; occasions such as wakes and other religious activities.

Since it is not always possible to celebrate these Eucharists in a sacred place, permission to celebrate them elsewhere in a fitting spot may be given, yet without preferring spacious or decorous places that might lead to a privileged class system. Ordinarily a good sized group should be invited to the celebration that may occur in much the same way that the Liturgy* in the sacred places occurs, including the use of musical compositions that relate to the congregation and would increase communal participation.* Deepening the spiritual informative

value of these celebrations will give the participants a greater awareness of the Christian Mystery,* and they will thus be able to insert themselves more fully into the total ecclesial community. Enriching programs of neighborhood Masses with newer modes and meaningful music can help this development along.

Mass, Pontifical. *See* PONTIFICAL MASS.

Mass, Proper of the (mas, PROP-uhr uhv thuh). The parts of the Mass* taken either from the Proper of the Season* or from the Proper of the Saints,* which then form the Proper of the Mass. They are: the Entrance Antiphon,* Opening Prayer,* Readings,* Intervenient Chants,* Preface,* Prayer over the Gifts,* Communion Antiphon,* and Prayer after Communion.* They make up the changeable parts of the Mass.

Mass Ritual (mas RICH-oo-uhl). Another term for the prescribed method celebrating the Mass,* which consists of four parts; the Introductory Rites,* the Liturgy of the Word,* the Liturgy of the Eucharist,* and the Concluding Rite.* *See also* MASS, ORDER OF.

Mass, Ritual. *See* RITUAL MASSES.

Mass Stipend. *See* STIPENDS.

At the Last Supper, Jesus said: "Do this as a remembrance of me."

THE HOLY SACRIFICE OF THE MASS

"AT the Last Supper, on the night when He was betrayed, our Savior instituted the Eucharistic sacrifice of His Body and Blood. He did this in order to perpetuate the sacrifice of the Cross throughout the centuries until He should come again.

Thus the Mass is:

1) the *true sacrifice* of the New Covenant, in which a holy and living Victim is offered, Jesus Christ, and we in union with Him, as a gift of love and obedience to the Father;

2) a *sacred meal* and *spiritual banquet* of the children of God;

3) a *Paschal meal,* which evokes the passage (passover) of Jesus from this world to the Father; it renders Him present and makes Him live again in souls, and it anticipates our definitive passage to the Kingdom of God;

4) a *communitarian meal,* that is, a gathering together of the Head and His members, of Jesus and His Church, His Mystical Body, in order to carry out a perfect divine worship.

Thus, the Mass is the greatest prayer we have. Through it we give thanks and praise to the Father for the wonderful future He has given us in His Son. We also ask forgiveness for our sins and beg the Father's blessing upon ourselves and our fellow human beings all over the world.

INTRODUCTORY RITES

THE Eucharist is made up essentially of (1) the Liturgy of the Word and (2) the Liturgy of the Eucharist. It also includes preliminary and concluding rites.

During the Introductory Rites acts of prayer and penitence prepare us to meet Christ as He comes in Word and Sacrament. We gather as a worshiping community to celebrate our unity with and in Him.

Beginning of Mass

AS a sign of adoration, the celebrant kisses the altar which represents Christ. Then He greets the people—thus connecting both parties of the Eucharistic dialogue: God and us. At the same time the Entrance Song or Antiphon provides us with the theme of the day.

KISSING THE ALTAR

OPENING PRAYER

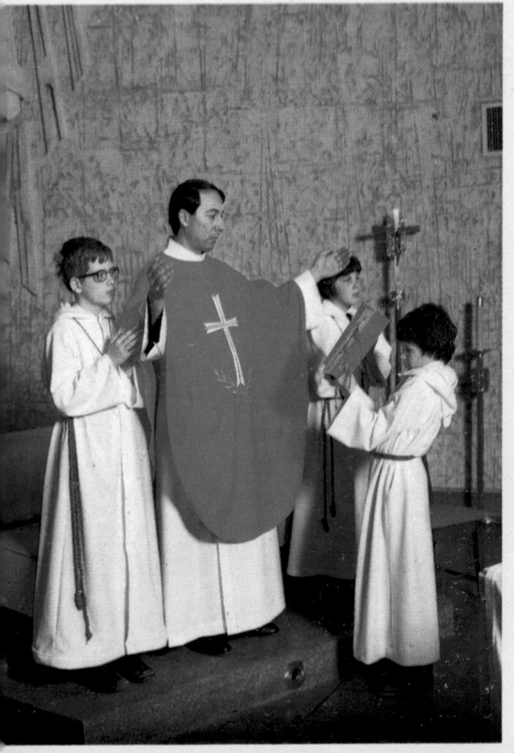

The Opening Prayer

WE then ask to be purified before hearing God's Word and celebrating His Eucharist. Next we turn our attention to praise and thanksgiving: the Kyrie and Gloria.

In the Opening Prayer, the priest invites us to pray for a moment and then in our name petitions God the Father through the mediation of Christ in the Holy Spirit. We bring to our prayer our pains, our cares, the concerns of our family, friends, and the whole world. We then ratify the prayer with our Amen.

Liturgy of the WORD

THE proclamation of God's Word is always centered on Christ. Jesus is the Word of God Himself and the Author of Revelation. It is He Himself Who speaks to us when the Sacred Scriptures are liturgically proclaimed.

First and Second Readings

CHRIST is present through His word as the Readings are proclaimed. The Old Testament writings prepare for Him, and the New Testament writings speak of Him directly.

In the Responsorial Psalm we reflect upon God's words and respond to them.

FIRST READING

The Gospel

WE then rise out of respect to show our love and admiration for Jesus Who will speak to us in the Gospel. He comes to proclaim His Word (through the priest or deacon) to us here and now and to enable us to apply it to our lives today.

God's Word is spoken again in the Homily. The Holy Spirit speaking through the lips of the preacher explains and applies the day's biblical readings to the needs of a particular congregation. He calls us to respond to Christ through the life we lead.

THE GOSPEL

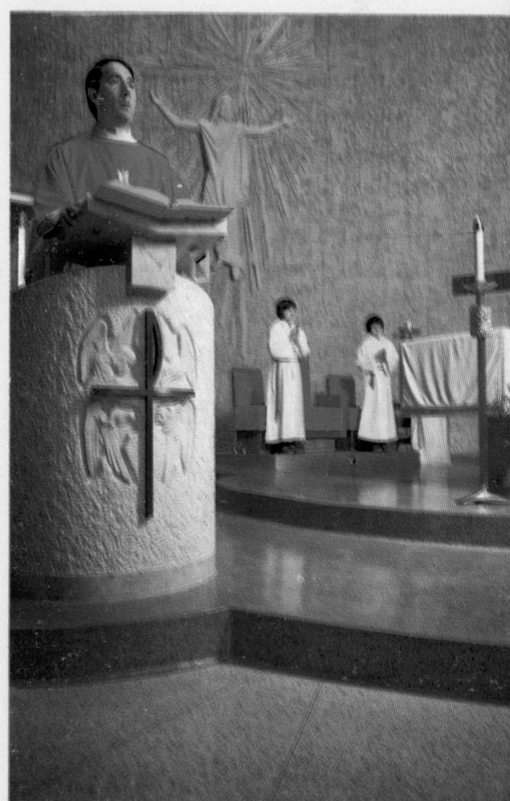

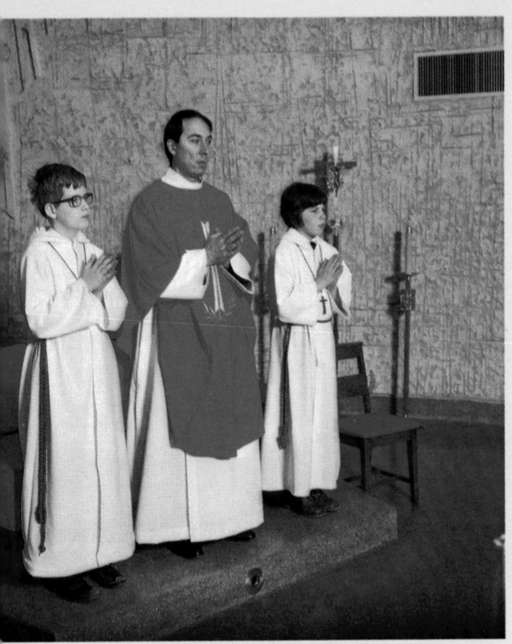

THE PROFESSION OF FAITH

The Profession of Faith (Creed)

AFTER listening to God's Word, reflecting on it, and responding in our hearts to it, we now make a corporate profession of faith. We publicly respond, assent, and adhere to that Word. This is a response not only to doctrinal propositions but also to the person of Christ present in the Word

The Creed used is the Nicene Creed (although the Apostles' Creed may also be used at times, especially in children's Masses). This is a summary of the faith expressed by the Councils of Nicaea (325) and of Constantinople (381) as ratified by the Council of Chalcedon (451).

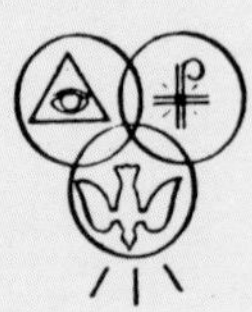

THE GENERAL INTERCESSIONS

The General Intercessions

INSTRUCTED, moved and renewed by the Word of God that brought Christ into our midst, we are now ready to exercise our priestly function by interceding for all mankind. We pray for the needs of the Church and the world as well as the current needs of our local parish community.

The celebrant sets the stage for the prayer and sums it up at the end, and the reader articulates its petitions, but it is the assembly that makes the prayer by its invocation.

Liturgy of the EUCHARIST

WE enter now into the Eucharistic sacrifice itself, the Supper of the Lord. We are God's new people, the redeemed brothers and sisters of Christ, gathered around his table.

Offering of the People's Gifts

THE people bring forward their gifts of bread and wine as well as their monetary offerings for the upkeep of the church building and the clergy, and the relief of the poor. These are but a symbol of their inner readiness to give God all of themselves with their hopes and disappointments, their work and leisure, and their whole everyday lives.

OFFERING OF THE PEOPLE'S GIFTS

PREPARATION OF THE GIFTS

Preparation of the Gifts

THESE are prayers of blessing of God's goodness. We bless God for the gifts of bread and wine (food and drink), for He is the creator of all things. We also bless Him for giving us the power to collaborate with Him in bringing forth His gifts by our dedicated labor and applied intelligence.

Afterward, we pray that our sacrifice will benefit all and then assent to the priest's prayer in our name that God will bless and accept our gifts.

CONSECRATION OF THE BREAD

CONSECRATION OF THE WINE

THE GREAT AMEN

The Eucharistic Prayer

THE Eucharistic service of praise and thanksgiving is the center of the celebration. We join Christ in His sacrifice, celebrating His memorial and acknowledging the wonderful works of God in our lives.

At the consecration of the bread and wine Christ's words spoken through the priest accomplish what they signify: His Eucharistic body and blood, His Real Presence with all the riches of the Kingdom.

The people now praise Christ in the Memorial Acclamation. We celebrate the fact that Christ has redeemed us, is with us now to apply that Redemption to each of us, and will return in glory to perfect that Redemption for all.

Continuing the Eucharistic Prayer, the Church offers the Victim to the Father in the Holy Spirit.

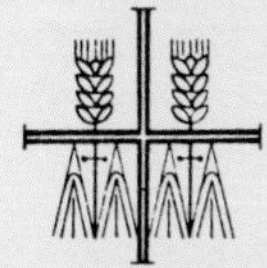

The Great Amen

AT the end of the Eucharistic Prayer the priest offers praise and honor to the Father through Christ Who is the High Priest, with Christ Who is present in the sacrificial memorial, and in Christ Who gives Himself to His members.

The people endorse these sentiments by their Great Amen. This Amen says that we have joined in praising the Father for all His wonderful works and have offered ourselves with Jesus to Him.

COMMUNION RITE

THE Communion Rite is the conclusion of the Mass. It is the part when God gives a gift to us after we have presented our gift to Him: Jesus Christ, the Son of God and Savior of the world.

The Our Father

THIS rite begins with the magnificent prayer left us by our Lord—the Our Father. In it we ask for our daily bread, the bread that gives access to eternity, the Bread of Life.

THE OUR FATHER

Communion of the Priest

AFTER prayers that stress brotherly love, the spirit of reconciliation, and the unity of Christians, the priest and people receive Communion. Communion is administered to the people via a procession accompanied by song. This expresses the real unity, spiritual joy, and brotherly love of those assembled to offer and communicate.

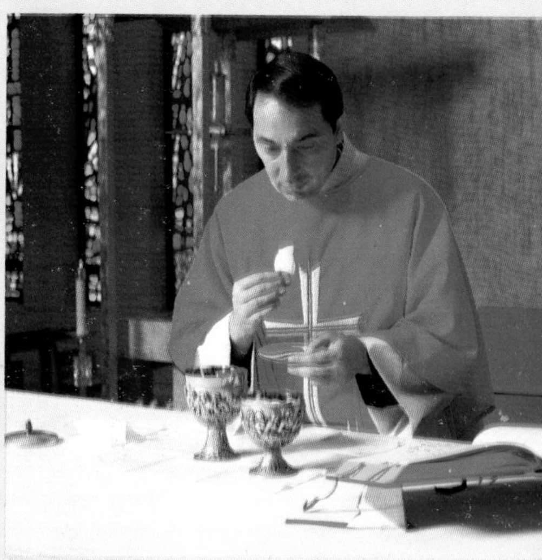

COMMUNION OF THE PRIEST

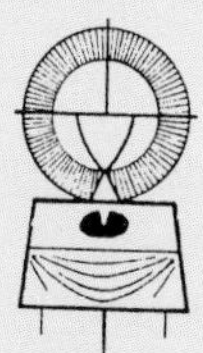

COMMUNION OF THE PEOPLE

Communion of the People

THE minister of communion says: "The Body of Christ" and the communicant says: "Amen." We should ever bear in mind St. Cyprian's words: "It is not idly that you say *Amen*. You are professing that you receive the Body of Christ. . . . Thus, keep in your heart what you profess with your lips!"

THE BLESSING

THE RECESSIONAL

CONCLUDING RITE

WE have heard God's Word and responded to it. We have received Christ's Body and Blood and achieved greater union with Him and others. Now it is time for us to leave to praise and bless the Lord in our daily lives.

The Blessing

TO bless God means to praise Him for His goodness and wonderful gifts. To bless people is an action asking God to continue to extend His generosity over them. The priest now asks that the greatest of all benefits be given to those who have shared in God's Word and Christ's Body.

The Recessional

THE Recessional usually takes place with a song that expresses praise or reflects the particular day or season. This song is our farewell to the ministers at the altar for being helpful in reenacting and representing the wondrous mystery of the Mass.

It is like the closing song of any gathering, the wish that all who came will arrive home safely, the end of a human ritual. Then we depart to try to apply the Eucharist to our lives.

Mass, Televised (mas, TEL-uh-vaizd). Not only will a televised Liturgy* offer a prayerful experience to shut-ins and interested viewers, but it may well foster evangelization through word and Sacrament.* Because of the medium, this prayer* experience must be both creative and artistic. The ministers* should be those who are capable of properly fulfilling their respective roles in the liturgical celebration in an almost ideal manner. The president* exhibits a pleasant and inviting celebration style, while his Homily,* derived from the Scriptural* texts and liturgical feasts* would appeal to the viewers. The acolytes* facilitate the flow of the liturgical action. The reader* proclaims the Scripture text and General Intercessions* clearly and distinctly; the commentator* becomes particularly valuable for explanation and ease of transition during the Mass.

Musicians, as ministers, will support the liturgical theme with music that never dominates the Liturgy. The varied audiences would determine the style of music, especially that which could encourage participation* by the worshipers in the studio and those at home. A music coordinator plans closely with the other ministers and the studio, so that the varied instruments may lead to a prayerful and reflective experience; the chanter* readily encourages congregational participation; a choir* supports and adds harmony to the congregational participation.

Art in its various forms and styles deepens one's religious experience; the medium of television can truly enhance the liturgical experience through use of aesthetic and artistic vestments,* banners,* lighting, slides, recordings, drama, gestures,* etc. Since the studio director oversees the presentation, all ministers and members participating should be responsive to the directives of the studio director. Prescribed reflective silence times, because of the special nature of a televised Mass, would be accompanied by background music, possibly with visuals, for instance, slides, film, and camera panning.

There are certain gains and losses for Christian worship* in television. Available to television is the best of architecture,* music,* Liturgy, preachers; yet there is more to worship than a splendid visual event. Silence which is increasingly important to modern worshipers must be filled in with some musical background or visuals. While television is tremendous to convey a spectacle or specific worldwide events, such as the Pope's visit to various countries, it finds it difficult to convey the incomprehensible behind the rite of worship.

Another important aspect of worship is the relationship with other worshipers. In television those who are unable or unwilling to go to church can watch in the seclusion of their own home, undermining the essential activity of community. Sacramental worship never occurs over television, since no one can be baptized or receive Holy Commu-

nion* in that way. The screen sets up a barrier that does not allow real participation and fellowship. Yet those who might not otherwise praise and honor God may be able to use this type of service in order to grow closer to Him. Hence, many believe it is better to continue than to refuse such service, particularly for the bedridden. *See also* MASS MEDIA.

Mass, Votive. *See* VOTIVE MASS.

Masses of the Blessed Virgin Mary. *See* MARY, BLESSED VIRGIN—MASSES.

Masses, Ritual. *See* RITUAL MASSES.

Master of Ceremonies (MAS-tuhr uhv ser-uh-MOH-neez). The person who directs and supervises religious ceremonies, in conformity with the rubrics* of the appropriate liturgical book,* so as to insure the exact observance of all ceremonial prescriptions during a liturgical function. Knowledgeable about the correct actions of the celebrants,* sacred ministers,* and others connected with the service, he guides the ceremonies so that they are executed with exactitude, dignity, and piety. In fulfilling his duties, he has complete authority over all those persons involved in carrying out the sacred rite.

Matins. *See* OFFICE OF READINGS.

Matrimony. *See* MARRIAGE.

Matter (MAT-uhr). The term used in Sacramental theology to denote one of the two essential elements of a Sacrament* (the other is the *form*). Matter is the sensible sign of the Sacrament whose meaning is indicated by the words (which constitute the form). The following is the matter for each Sacrament: (1) Baptism*: the pouring of the water on the forehead of the one being baptized or the immersing of the person in the baptismal water. (2) Confirmation*: the anointing of the forehead with chrism. (3) Eucharist*: bread and wine. (4) Penance*: the acts of the penitent* (contrition,* confession,* purpose of amendment,* and reparation). (5) Marriage*: the mutual consent of the spouses. (6) Holy Orders*: the imposition of hands on the ordinand. (7) Anointing of the Sick*: the anointing of the patient on the forehead and hands. *See also* SACRAMENTS.

Matthew, St. (MATH-yoo). 1st century. An Apostle,* called from his duties as tax collector to follow Christ,* who was considered an outcast of his society because of his position. Christ's healing love helped shape the way he composed the Gospel.* Probably written in the seventies, originally in Aramaic, it was penned by a Jewish-Christian for Jewish-Christians, proclaiming Christ's new law of love. After the Ascension* of our Lord, Matthew preached to pagan nations. He was martyred (possibly in Persia), and his body reposes in the Cathedral of Salerno, Italy. Matthew is represented in art by a young man, one of the symbolic living creatures in Ezekiel's* vision, because he begins his Gospel with Christ's earthly an-

cestry and stresses His human and kingly character. He is the Patron of Accountants, Bankers, Bookkeepers, and Tax Collectors. *Liturgical celebration:* September 21 (Feast); *theme*: faith is a shared experience; we can radiate spiritual energy to each other.

Matthew, The Gospel According to (MAT-thyoo, thuh GOS-puhl uh-KAWRD-ing too). The first Synoptic Gospel* and the forty-seventh Book of the Bible.* Written in its Aramaic form by Matthew,* one of the twelve Apostles,* about 80 or 85 A.D., it seems to have made use of the Gospel of Mark* with a few changes and additions. The Gospel gives a faithful and distinct image of Christ's teaching. Even today readers are struck by its clearness, its pedagogical direction, and the remarkable balance kept between the narrative sections and the five magnificent discourses in chapters 6–7, 10, 13, 18, and 24–25.

Beginning with a series of reflections relating Jesus and His parentage to the Messianism of the Old Testament* (1:1-25), the Gospel places His Birth* in the hostile political atmosphere of the time (2:1-23). Like the other Gospels, Matthew introduces the public ministry of Jesus with a summary of the mission of John the Baptist* (3:1-17). After the account of the temptation of Jesus (4:1-11), the Gospel reports His teaching and miracles, locating all these in Galilee and its vicinity, exclusive of Jerusalem* (4:12–20:34). It concludes with the final events and teaching of Jesus, locating them in Jerusalem and centering them around His Passion,* Death,* and Resurrection* (21:1–28:20).

While Mark probably addresses himself to the Romans and Luke* to the Greeks, Matthew writes for the Jews. It is the most Jewish of the Gospels, in its style, its methods of composition, and its way of arguing. Matthew wants to convince his people that Jesus is indeed the Messiah* who was expected by the Prophets,* and thus he tries to show that Jesus has fulfilled the Scriptures.*

This Gospel has been called the Gospel of the Church.* However, it is even more the Gospel of Jesus. Matthew constantly seeks to bring out the majesty of Jesus, His superhuman greatness, and His power. For Matthew, Jesus is the Lord. This title recurs some eighty times in his Gospel, while it appears only eighteen times in Mark. The term itself designates Jesus risen, working mightily, and always present in His Church.

For Matthew, Jesus is also the Christ, the Messiah, a title he gives Him as early as in the genealogy (1:16-18). But He is above all the Son of God (3:17; 8:29; 17:5; 26:63; 27:54, etc.). In a word, Matthew professes the Divinity of Jesus.

Liturgical use: In the *Roman Missal,** this Gospel is as well represented as those of Mark, Luke, and John.* It is assigned to Cycle A on Sundays. It is also used extensively in the continuous readings for weekdays, in the Proper of the

Saints,* in the Common of the Saints,* and in Ritual Masses.* In the *Liturgy of the Hours,** it is read in Appendix I: "Canticles and Gospel Readings for Vigils."

Meaning: Jesus is the Messiah Who fulfilled the promises transmitted by the Law* and the Prophets.* He is the Kingdom of Heaven* in person, and He inaugurates that Kingdom by founding His Church, which is its preparation and the fulfillment of God's Covenant* with His people. Jesus is the Emmanuel, God-with-us. We should acknowledge Him as the Master Who teaches us and the Lord Who gives us life. We must cling to the Church as the community that is inseparable from Him. She is the community of brothers and sisters living from the presence of her Lord, hidden in the hearts of the most lowly. She has a liturgical and Sacramental life and is guided by the descendants of the Apostles.* *See also* MATTHEW, ST.

Matthias, St. (muh-THAI-uhs). 1st century. Because numbers carry such a special significance in the mid-eastern culture, where the Bible* was written, the other Apostles* knew how important it was to replace Judas, to conserve the symbolic message of having twelve Apostles to match the number of the tribes of Israel, with twelve new patriarchs to be founders of the new Israel. The lot fell on Matthias, who had been with Christ from His Baptism* to His Resurrection.* He most probably preached in Cappadocia and was martyred at Colchis, a district of Asia Minor on the Black Sea. *Liturgical celebration:* May 14 (Feast); *theme*: we are to be witnesses of Christ's Resurrection* by our faith,* hope* and virtuous Christian life.

Maundy Thursday. *See* HOLY THURSDAY.

Maximilian Mary Kolbe, St. (mak-suh-MIL-yuhn MAYR-ee KOHL-bee). 1894-1941. A Conventual Franciscan, who was among the first to make use of the media* to promote the Christian Faith* and particularly devotion to the Immaculate Mary.* He founded presses to publish papers and magazines in Rome, India, Japan, and at his home in Warsaw. There he was arrested by the Gestapo and taken to Auschwitz, where he offered his life for a married man with a family. Thus, martyrdom is not limited to Roman times. He was canonized in 1982. *Liturgical celebration:* August 14 (Memorial); *theme*: precious in the eyes of the Lord are His faithful ones.

May, Month of Mary (may, muhnnth uhv MAYR-ee). The month of May is the "month that the piety of the faithful* has especially dedicated to our Blessed Lady," and it is the occasion for a "moving tribute of faith* and love* that Catholics in every part of the world [pay] to the Queen of Heaven. During this month Christians, both in church and in the privacy of the home, offer up to Mary* from their hearts an especially fervent and loving homage of prayer and veneration. In this month, too, the benefits of God's mercy come down to us from her throne in greater abundance"

(Paul VI: *Encyclical on the Month of May—Mense Maio**—no. 1).

This Christian custom of dedicating the month of May to the Blessed Virgin arose at the end of the 13th century. In this way, the Church* was able to Christianize the secular feasts that were wont to take place at that time. In the 16th century, books appeared and fostered this devotion.

The practice became especially popular among the members of the Jesuit Order—by 1700 it took hold among their students at the Roman College and a bit later it was publicly practiced in the *Gesù* Church in Rome. From there it spread to the whole Church.

The practice was granted a partial indulgence* by Pius VII in 1815 and a plenary indulgence* by Pius IX in 1859. With the complete revision of indulgences in 1966 and the decreased emphasis on specific indulgences, it no longer carries an indulgence; however, it certainly falls within the category of the First General Grant of Indulgences.

This pious practice has been especially recommended by the Popes. Pius XII made frequent reference to it and in his great *Encyclical on the Sacred Liturgy (Mediator Dei*)* characterized it as one of the "other exercises of piety that although not strictly belonging to the Sacred Liturgy* are nevertheless of special import and dignity and *may be considered in a certain way to be an addition to the liturgical cult:* they have been approved and praised over and over again by the Apostolic See* and by the Bishops" (no. 182, *italics added*).

In his encyclical, Paul VI, used the Month of Mary devotion as a means of obtaining prayers for peace. He urged the faithful to make use of this practice which is "gladdening and consoling" and by which the Blessed Virgin Mary is honored and the Christian people are enriched with spiritual gifts" (*Mense Maio,* no. 2).

There are no official prayers or rites for this practice. Many churches have a daily recitation of the Rosary* in public or some other prayers in honor of Mary, including the crowning of our Lady's statue. For private use, one can follow the format of a Liturgy of the Word*: entrance chant, opening prayer, Scripture* reading, and brief reflection or homily, with a concluding prayer of invocation. The only *necessary element* is that Mary be honored in a special way. *See also* Mary, Blessed Virgin; Mary, Blessed Virgin—Cult.

Medals, Devotional (MED-uhlz, di-VOH-shuhn-uhl). Coin-shaped objects, made of metal or plastic, bearing an inscription or an image of Christ,* Mary,* a Saint,* a religious symbol, some shrine, or a sacred event. Probably adapted from some secular custom, they were most likely used to identify Christians; in the Middle Ages they served as souvenirs for pilgrims to shrines or to commemorate an important event. Worn on neckchains or carried in purses or pockets, they are not considered lucky charms or

magical items. Their reasonable use was defended by the Council of Nicaea II and the Council of Trent.

Of themselves they have no intrinsic value, but the prayer of the Church* and the indulgences* connected with them intend to develop the faith,* hope,* and piety of the faithful.* Thus they have a value that only the self-righteous would disdain. From the 15th century papal medals honored the various Popes.* Besides these, some of the more popular ones are the Miraculous Medal, the scapular medal, the St. Benedict medal, the medal of the Child Jesus, and the medal of Our Lady of Guadalupe. *See also* INDULGENCES; SACRAMENTALS.

Media and Worship. *See* MASS MEDIA; MASS, TELEVISED.

Mediator (MEED-ee-ayt-uhr). An intermediary who intervenes between two other persons or groups to bring them together or reconcile them. Moses was thus a mediator between God and the people (Nm 14:13-20). Applied to Jesus, the term takes on even more profound meaning for Jesus is at the same time Divine and human. He belongs at once to both parties: "There is one God. There is also one mediator between God and the human race, Christ Jesus, himself human" (1 Tm 2:5).

Through Christ we have access to the Father, and through Christ the Father gives Himself to humankind (Heb 9:11-25; 12:24). Indeed, Christ's entire work is to enable us to know the Father and to unite us to Him by giving us God's life (Jn 17:2-3). He accomplished this reconciliation (2 Cor 5:18f) by His Death* (Rom 5:10) on the Cross* (Col 1:20). But this reconciliation is not applied to individuals without their consent and cooperation (2 Cor 5:20).

Christ's mediatorship is at the very heart of the Liturgy.* For Christ *is* the Covenant* (see Mt 26:26) and the messenger of the Covenant (Mal 3:1), and the Liturgy is the encounter of God with His people for the celebration of that Covenant. Christ's priesthood* is based on His mediatorship. His central action is the sacrifice of the Cross, which is unceasingly renewed in the Eucharist.* According to Vatican II,* "the Liturgy is an exercise of the priestly office of Jesus Christ" (SC, 7), which unites the Church and Jesus' life as Son.

The mediatorship of the Incarnate Word is linked to that of the Holy Spirit,* for their missions are coordinate. The Word gives the Holy Spirit to human beings. The mediating work of the Son and the Spirit in the History of Salvation* obtains for God's people the capacity to exercise the life of the Trinity as children of God. *See also* COVENANT; GOD; HISTORY OF SALVATION; JESUS CHRIST.

Mediator Dei (may-dee-AH-tawr DAY-ee). Latin title (from the first two words "Mediator of God") of the *Encyclical on the Sacred Liturgy* issued by Pius XII on November 20, 1947. Dealing with the Liturgy* and the Liturgical Movement,* it examined and showed the basis of liturgical worship* in the life of the Church,* while encouraging the renewal of the Liturgy that was taking place at that time. Beyond giving the historical development of the Liturgy up to that time, it laid the foundation for the reforms that occurred during the Second Vatican Council.* It defined Liturgy as the Church's official public worship but stressed the primacy of the interior dispositions from which the public act of worship flows.

Emphasizing the Mass as the acme of Christian religion, it urged the active participation* by the faithful,* suggesting many pastoral practices to make this possible. It reiterated the benefits from frequent Communion* and praised those who were devoted to the Real Presence,* particularly by devotion to the Blessed Sacrament.* Second only to the Eucharist is the Divine Office* in the Church's liturgical life; the Liturgical Year* should rotate around the Mysteries* of our Savior's Life, Passion,* and Resurrection.* Extraliturgical devotions* were sanctioned to intensify the piety of priests,* Religious,* and the laity.* *See also* CONSTITUTION ON THE SACRED LITURGY.

Meditation (med-uh-TAY-shuhn). A type of mental prayer, also known as discursive prayer. It consists of reflections on a particular spiritual theme with the practical aim of moving the will to make acts of faith,* hope,* love,* or any other virtue* and to form resolutions. There are various methods of mental prayer. One of them practices the ancient traditional ways of meditation in which the soul feeds on Scripture* and the teaching of the Liturgy.* Indeed, the Liturgy itself also contains a *discursive meditational* value. However, it is a *meditation-action* and cannot be used as a substitute for meditation. Instead, the exercise of meditation that forms part of the Liturgy must be prolonged outside the moments of our participation* in the Liturgy. *See also* CONTEMPLATION; LITURGY AND CONTEMPLATIVE LIFE; PRAYER.

Melchizedek (mel-KIZ-uh-dek). King of Salem and priest of God who offered bread and wine as an unbloody sacrifice in thanksgiving* for Abraham's* victory over the Four Eastern Kings (Gn 14:18-20). He is the type* of Christ: both are kings as well as priests; both offer bread and wine to God; and both have their priesthood directly from God. Thus, an antiphon* in the new rite of ordination of a priest* reads: "Christ the Lord, a priest for ever in the line of Melchizedek, offered bread and wine." Melchizedek's sacrifice is also a type of the Eucharist,* and in Eucharistic Prayer I* the Church prays that God will accept the offerings at Mass as He accepted the sacrificial gifts of Melchizedek. *See also* OFFERING.

Melisma (mi-LIZ-muh). In Gregorian Chant,* the more or less long succession of melodic notes on a single syllable or vowel. *See also* GREGORIAN CHANT.

Melkite Rite. *See* BYZANTINE RITE.

Melody, Gregorian. *See* GREGORIAN CHANT.

Memento (me-MENT-oh). A term derived from the first Latin word of two parts of Eucharistic Prayer I,* respectively at the beginning and after the Consecration,* in which the Church prays for the living and for the dead. By extension the word came to identify the part of Mass when the celebrant* recited these prayers. In the vernacular* Liturgy they are more customarily termed the Commemoration of the Living and Commemoration of the Dead or simply Intercessions.*

Memorial (muh-MAWR-ee-uhl). A term for the liturgical act that "recalls" to God's memory the assembly* celebrating the Covenant.* Since the memory of the participants joins the memory of God, the memorial serves to actualize the great foundational events of the Covenant. Every liturgical act makes the present the preceding Covenant and anticipates the more perfect Covenant to come.

The Sinaitic Covenant accomplished not only the Covenants with the Patriarchs but also the Covenant with Noah. At the same time, thanks to the action of the Prophets,* the liturgical Sinaitic Covenant manifested ever more its orientation toward a new and eternal Covenant. This last Covenant was effected by Jesus through the sacrifice of the New Covenant in His Blood, which inaugurated the end time (Acts 2:17).

The Eucharist re-presents for believers the central Hour of the History of Salvation* while anticipating the consummation of the last Covenant in the heavenly Jerusalem,* when God will "remember" His Messiah* and let Him return at the Parousia.* Thus declares the *Magnificat** Antiphon for Evening Prayer II* on the Solemnity of the Body and Blood of Christ*: "How holy is this feast in which Christ is our food; his passion* is recalled; grace* fills our hearts; and we receive a pledge of the glory* to come." This is the full meaning of the command given by Christ at the Last Supper*: "Do this in memory of me" (Lk 22:19).

If the liturgical memory concerned only our human memory, it would be simply a festive commemoration. But it involves the active "memory" of God for Whom the sacrifice of the Lamb has effect from the foundation of the world (Rv 13:8). Hence, the Liturgy renders present the Mystery* that comprises and surpasses our categories of past, present, and future. Every liturgical act, which joins our memory to God's memory, is for us a certain participation in God's eternity. *See also* ANAMNESIS; EUCHARIST; HISTORY OF SALVATION; LITURGY AND ESCHATOLOGY; MYSTERY.

Memorial Acclamation. *See* ACCLAMATIONS.

Memoriale Rituum (me-mawr-ee-AH-lay REE-too-oom). A liturgical book* that adapted ceremonies, particularly during Holy Week* and other unusual ceremonies of the year, for celebrations in small parish churches. In the recent liturgical reforms, it is superseded by provisions for pastoral adaptations necessary in such circumstances.

Memorials (muh-MAWR-ee-uhlz). Certain celebrations of the Saints are Memorials. When the word is found in the liturgical books* after the Saint's name, these memorials are *Obligatory*. When no indication occurs, the celebration is *Optional*. Less than 100 Optional Memorials occur during the year and while the Church* encourages their celebration, she does not strictly require their observance. The decision should not depend solely on the devotion of the person presiding but should take into consideration the common good and the devotion of the people attending. If more than one Optional Memorial in Ordinary Time* occurs on the same day, only one is celebrated, the others being omitted.

In celebrating the Liturgy of the Hours* for a Memorial, at Daytime Prayer* and at Night Prayer,* everything is from the weekday, nothing from the Saint. For the other hours, the Psalms* and antiphons* are from the weekday unless they are proper.* Everything else is taken from the Office of the Saint if it is proper; when not proper, it may be taken either from the Common* or from the weekday.

The priest* may choose the Mass of an Optional Memorial, bearing in mind the spiritual good of the faithful,* and at least one Mass* of such a Memorial should be celebrated in answer to popular piety. In choosing between a diocesan or a Religious calendar* having such Memorials, other things being equal, the Memorial in the particular calendar should have preference.

While no Memorials are celebrated in any way on Sundays, Solemnities* and Feasts,* Ash Wednesday,* during Holy Week* and the octave of Easter,* they have a partial celebration in other privileged seasons, namely weekdays between December 17 and 24, the octave of Christmas,* and the weekdays of Lent.* Memorials occurring during Lent are classed as Optional Memorials that year. To celebrate Memorials during these privileged seasons, the proper hagiographical reading* with its responsory* and the prayer* of the Saint is added at the end of the regular readings that were taken from the Proper of the Season. At Morning Prayer* and Evening Prayer,* the ending of the concluding prayer of the day may be omitted and the antiphon from the Proper or Common and the prayer of the Saint added. During the Mass of the day, the priest may substitute the prayer from the Memorial for the Opening Prayer.* *See also* FEASTS; SOLEMNITIES.

Memorization (mem-[uh-]ruh-ZAY-shuhn). Committing something to memory or learning it by heart. In every age and culture the Church* has recommended certain prayers, formulas, and practices to all her members. Memorization of these has had a special place in the handing-on of the Faith* throughout the ages. John Paul II dealt with the advantages and disadvantages of such memorization in *Catechesi Tradendae,** his *Apostolic Exhortation on Catechesis in Our Time* (no. 55), and concluded that it should still be used so that there would be a balance between reflection and spontaneity, between dialogue and silence, between written work and memory work. Indeed, he stressed we should attempt to put the faculty of human memory "back into use in an intelligent and even an original way in catechesis,* all the more since the celebration of the great events of the History of Salvation* requires a precise knowledge of them. A certain memorization of the words of Jesus, of important Bible* passages, of the Ten Commandments,* of the formulas of profession of the Faith,* of the *liturgical texts,* of the essential prayers,

of key doctrinal ideas, etc., far from being opposed to the dignity of young Christians . . . is a real need (*italics added*)."

The *National Catechetical Directory** issued by the National Conference of Bishops of the United States in 1979 recommended that memorization "be adapted to the level and ability of the child and introduced in a gradual manner, through a process which, begun early, continues gradually, flexibly, and never slavishly. In this way certain elements of Catholic faith, tradition,* and practice are learned for a lifetime and can contribute to the individual's continued growth in understanding and living the faith" (no. 176e).

The *Directory* spelled out the areas where memorization should be used:

(1) Prayers such as the Sign of the Cross,* Lord's Prayer,* Hail Mary,*

Apostles' Creed,* Act of Faith,* Act of Hope,* Act of Love,* and Act of Contrition.*

(2) Factual information contributing to an appreciation of the place of the Word of God* in the Church and the life of Christians through an awareness and understanding of (a) the key themes of the History of Salvation; (b) the major personalities of the Old* and New* Testaments, and (c) certain Biblical texts expressive of God's love and care.

(3) Formulas providing factual information regarding (a) worship,* (b) the Church Year,* and (c) major practices in the devotional life of Christians including the parts of the Mass,* the list of the Sacraments,* the Liturgical Seasons,* the Holy Days of Obligation,* the major feasts* of our Lord and our Lady, the various Eucharistic devotions,* the Mysteries* of the Rosary* of the Blessed Virgin, and the Stations of the Cross.*

(4) Formulas and practices dealing with the moral life of Christians including the commandments,* the beatitudes,* the gifts of the Holy Spirit,* the theological and moral virtues,* the precepts of the Church,* and the examination of conscience.*

In addition, the *General Instruction of the Roman Missal* (no. 19) states that since the faithful from different countries are together even more frequently in our day it is desirable that they know how to sing at least some parts of the Ordinary of the Mass* in Latin,* especially the Profession of Faith and the Lord's Prayer. Indeed, it might be well for the people to know the Latin responses* by heart, as *Musicam Sacram,** the 1967 Instruction by the Sacred Congregation of Rites* *On Music in the Liturgy,* declared: "Pastors should see to it that, in addition to the vernacular,* the faithful are also able to say or sing together in Latin those parts of the Ordinary of the Mass belonging to them" (no. 47). *See also* CATECHESIS AND LITURGY.

Menaion (me-NAI-uhn). Liturgical book* of the Byzantine Rite,* divided into months and containing the proper* parts of the Divine Office* for the immovable feasts* of

Christ,* Mary,* and the Saints* for the year beginning with September.

Menelogion (men-uh-LOHG-ee-uhn). In the Eastern Church* a liturgical book* containing the lives of the Saints* arranged according to months for the liturgical year* beginning with September.

Menology (men-OL-uh-jee). Term for several types of unofficial martyrologies that contain short lives of the Saints* arranged in calendar order for liturgical use.

Mensa. *See* ALTAR.

Mense Maio (MEN-say MAI-oh). Latin title (from the first two words "Month of May") of the *Encyclical on the Month of May* issued by Pope Paul VI on April 30, 1965. It describes May as "the month during which Christians, both in church and in the privacy of the home, offer up to Mary* from their hearts an especially fervent and loving homage of prayer and veneration. In this month, too, the gifts of God's mercy* come down to us from her throne in greater abundance" (no. 1). The *Encyclical* then goes on to ask for prayer to Mary for the peace of the world, for she is the Queen of Peace. *See also* MAY, MONTH OF MARY.

Mercy of God (MUHR-see uhv god). The willingness of God to draw near to human beings in a loving and saving encounter. In the past that mercy was shown in the Covenants* God made with human beings and in the New Covenant ratified by Jesus with His Death* and Resurrection.* As the re-presentation of Christ's Paschal Mystery* for the people of the third phase of Salvation History,* the Liturgy* is the way beyond compare in which God shows His mercy.

In his *Encyclical Rich in Mercy (Dives in Misericordia),* issued in 1980, John Paul II analyzed this mercy at length and concluded (no. 13) that the Church* professes and proclaims God's mercy in all its truth, as it has been handed down to us in Revelation.* In the daily life of the Church the truth about the mercy of God, expressed in the Bible,* resounds as a perennial echo through the many readings* of Sacred Scripture.*

Furthermore, the Church brings people close to the power of the Savior's mercy, of which she is the trustee and dispenser. Of great significance in this area is constant meditation* on the Word of God* and above all conscious and mature participation* in the Eucharist* and in the Sacrament of Penance.* Indeed, the Eucharist brings us ever nearer to that love which is more powerful than death. "For as often as we eat this bread and drink the cup," we proclaim not only the Death of the Redeemer but also the Resurrection, "until he comes in glory" (see 1 Cor 11:26; Memorial Acclamation*).

Christians share in this mercy of God through conversion.* Authentic

knowledge of the God of mercy is a constant and inexhaustible source of conversion, not only as a momentary interior act but also as a permanent attitude. Those who come to know God and experience Him in this way can live only in a state of being continually converted to Him. And they in turn will follow Christ's exhortation and show mercy to others: "Blessed are the merciful, for they will be shown mercy" (Mt 5:7). *See also* CONVERSION; COVENANT; GOD; HISTORY OF SALVATION; LOVE.

Merit (MER-uht). The right of human beings to be rewarded for a good work* done freely for God. It is a juridical term used in Catholic theology for the Biblical term "reward." Both in the Old Testament* and in the New* rewards are promised to the righteous for their good works (Ex 23:20-22; Dt 5:28-33; Mt 5:3-12; 6:4, 6; 6:19f; 7:21). By their good works Christians increase the justice* and grace* God has conferred on them. However, growth in the life of grace is not effected by the good works. It is only merited or striven for as a reward to be rendered by God. This "merit" comes from Christ's grace and merit, allowing His merit to bear fruit in His

members—for through His Redemption* He has gained grace for all human beings.

Participation* in the Liturgy* is the foremost way in which the faithful can gain merit—because of the surpassing sanctifying and purifying efficacy that the Mass* and the Sacraments* have in themselves. "Indeed, every other good work and every suffering patiently borne are by no means to be esteemed apart from the Mass and the Sacraments, the principal sources of sanctification and purification; for it is precisely their good works and sufferings that constitute the oblation that the faithful join to the oblation of Christ in the Eucharistic Sacrifice; it is also the Mass and the Sacraments that move the faithful* to perform the tasks laid upon them in such a way that they will hold fast in their lives to what they have received by faith" (EI, 3). *See also* GOOD WORKS; GRACE.

Messiah. *See* CHRIST.

Metanoia (me-tuh-NAW-yuh). Greek term for "change of heart." It appears in the *Apostolic Constitution On Fast and Abstinence (Paenitemini*—"Repent") issued by Paul VI on February 17, 1966. This document points out that "the Kingdom of God* announced by Christ can be entered only by a *metanoia,* that is to say, through the intimate and total change and renewal of the entire person—of the person's opinions, judgments, and decisions—which takes place in the light of the holiness* and love* of God, the holiness and love that were manifested to us in the Son and communicated fully." It is this *metanoia* that is the aim of the Liturgy* and the fruit of all full, active, and conscious participation.* *See also* CONVERSION.

Methodius, St. (me-THOHD-i-uhs). c.826-885. Methodius and his brother St. Cyril* were sent to the Volga region of Russia to convert the Khazars; because of their success, Photius sent them to convert the Moravians. They invented the Cyrillic alphabet and translated liturgical books* into Slavonic. Called to Rome to prove their orthodoxy, Methodius was made bishop* of Moravia and eventually became archbishop* of Velehrad, Czechoslovakia. As an apostle to the Slavs, he also fought for the unity of the Eastern and Western Churches. *Liturgical celebration:* February 14 (Memorial); *theme*: vernacular Liturgy draws people closer to God and to each other.

Metropolitan. *See* ARCHBISHOP.

Micah, The Book of (MAI-kuh, thuh buk uhv). The fortieth Book of the Bible* and the sixth of the Minor Prophets.* Micah carried out his ministry in the Southern Kingdom of Judah during the reigns of Jotham, Ahaz, and Hezekiah in the late 8th century B.C. He was thus a contemporary of Isaiah* and Amos.* He cried out against social injustice and foretold the fall of the Northern Kingdom because of the people's infidelity to God. He stressed God's judgment but also His loving mercy* and is known as the "Prophet of the Divine Compassion" (see 7:18-19).

Micah gives the fullest Old Testament* account of the coming of the Messiah* (5:2-15). The Messiah will come from Bethlehem and be a human being. He will have preexisted and will bring together a remnant of believers. He will inaugurate a Kingdom of peace and care for the needy. In Messianic times there will be universal peace. Swords will be beaten into plowshares and spears into pruning hooks. It will be an age of peace, prosperity, and plenty (4:1-5).

Liturgical use: In the *Roman Missal,** this Book is read on the 4th Sunday of Advent* (C), Saturday of the 15th Week (II), Monday of the 16th Week (II), Saturday of the 2nd Week of Lent,* and the Optional Mass for the 4th Week of Lent as well as September 8 (Birth of Mary*), Common* of the Blessed Virgin Mary, Common of Holy Men and Women,* Mass in Time of War and Civil Disturbance, and the Rite of Penance.* In addition, the complaints voiced by the Lord in chapter 6 (1-8) form the basis for the Reproaches* used on Good Friday.* In the *Liturgy of the Hours,** it is used on Tuesday through Saturday of the 19th Week. *Meaning:* The cause of war and individual unhappiness in the world is sin (both social and personal). God abhors idolatry, injustice, rebellion, and empty ritualism, but He delights in pardoning sinners who are determined to do justice,* love kindness, and walk humbly before Him (6:8). God has promised to take away sin and war at the coming of His Messiah. If we follow Jesus we will achieve peace and joy* in the Lord.

Michael, St. (MAI-kuhl). One of the three archangels, whose name means "who is like God!"* Appearing twice in the Old Testament* (Dn 10:13-21; 12:1), he is regarded as a

special protector of Israel by the Jews; appearing twice in the New Testament* (Jude 9; Rv 12:7), he is considered the protector of the Church,* usually depicted as battling Satan. He also functions as an intercessor for the Church, as an angel with censer* and incense* ascending before God,* and as our companion and guide at death. We pray that Michael may bring into the light of God's presence the souls of those who have died. He is the Patron of Grocers, Mariners, Policemen, Radiologists, and the Sick. *Liturgical celebration*: September 29 (Feast); *theme*: angelic help will defend us in battle, that we may not perish.

Micrologus (mai-KROHL-uh-guhs). Liturgical commentary of Bernold of Constance, a Benedictine monk of the 11th century, that had much success in the Middle Ages. It deals with the Mass,* the Ember Days,* and the Liturgical Year* from the standpoint of the Roman Liturgy.* It utilizes a moderate allegorical interpretation and provides useful information about the practices then in use. For example, the Gloria* was omitted during Advent* and Septuagesima,* and the prayer *Placeat tibi* ("May the tribute of my worship please You") was said after the Dismissal* though not yet in universal use. There was only one Opening Prayer,* the Creed* was not included, incense at the Offertory* was not recommended, and there was no Offertory prayer.

Milanese Rite. *See* AMBROSIAN RITE.

Ministers (MIN-uh-stuhrz). Those who fulfill or perform liturgical functions or spiritual offices in the Church.* Thus, the first minister

would be Christ, the One Who is the eternal high priest of the new law; then the Church or the Mystical Body* of Christ; for this Church the bishop,* priest,* and other ministers act in her name, deputed by her; finally, all of the faithful,* as they are members of the Church, the Mystical Body of Christ. In a restricted sense, those who assist the celebrant,* namely, the deacon,* acolytes,* lectors,* chanters,* and any others who serve the altar are also called ministers. Ministers may fulfill their spiritual functions at Sacramental rites or Eucharistic rites. In a broader sense, the term signifies those who aid in certain activities for the Church, such as catechetical ministers, youth ministers, pastoral ministers.

The term is also used to designate the heads of some Religious Orders, e.g., Franciscans; in the Jesuit Order, the second in charge of a community is the minister. Some Protestant denominations use this term to designate their ordained clergymen. *See also* EXTRAORDINARY MINISTERS OF HOLY COMMUNION; MINISTRIES; WOMEN AS MINISTERS.

Ministries (MIN-uh-streez). Forms of authorized service of God in active Christian service of others according to norms that Christ* revealed and that are further determined by the Church,* which designates or commissions certain persons to aid the community so that the Church may fulfill her mission of proclaiming the Good News* of salvation.* Thus defined, ministry was narrowed in some centuries, so that only the ordained ministers, bishops,* priests,* and deacons,* were exercising this function. Since Vatican II,* however, the original meaning has been reclaimed, for many laypersons now participate actively in Church ministries.

The forms of ministry include certain features: (a) they are used in the service of God; (b) they are authorized by the Church, through the Pope* or Ordinary* (this would include ordination* for the priestly ministry, consecration* for Religious life, or institution for readers,* acolytes,* and extraordinary ministers of Holy Communion*); (c) they are based on the teaching of Christ Who gave us an example of how to minister; and (d) they are guided by the directives and decrees of the Church.

Two formal ministries, formerly Minor Orders,* adapted to present-day needs, are preserved in the Latin Church, namely those of readers and acolytes. Since they are not reserved to candidates for the Sacrament of Holy Orders,* they may be given to lay Christians. Though these two ministries are not seen as steps to Holy Orders,* they are a requirement for ordination. All the laity* may be temporarily deputed to perform the duties of reader, commentator,* chanter,* and other ministries permitted by law in liturgical ceremonies.

When proper ministers are lacking and the necessity exists, even the laity who are not readers or acolytes may fulfill other offices, namely, proclaiming the Word of God,* presiding over liturgical prayer,* conferring Baptism,* and distributing Holy Communion,* in accordance with the prescripts of the law. If the Episcopal Conference* has formulated norms, and when necessity requires it or usefulness urges it, the laity may be permitted to preach in churches or oratories, as long as it is not a *Homily*,* which is reserved to the priest and deacon.

However, the approval of these two ministries does not preclude the possibility of the institution of others, particularly when the fulfillment of their duties would be necessary or very useful in certain regions. Looking to the future, we could very well consider possible ministries such as catechist,* or teacher of religion. Examples of a professional catechist would certainly include: (a) a properly prepared and qualified teacher of religion; (b) one who exercises the supervisory capacity in religious education; (c) a director or coordinator of religious education.

Another example could be the minister of church music. This liturgical ministry might include a number of functions, not always exercised by the same person: (a) the psalmist, the chanter who leads the Psalm between the first two readings*; (b) the chanter leading the assembly* in responsorial song and processional Psalms at other

times; (c) the leader of song for the congregation; (d) the choir leader or director of music; and (e) the organist. *See also* ACOLYTES; CHANTER; COMMENTATOR; HOMILY; MINISTERS; READERS; WOMEN AS MINISTERS.

Minor Orders (MAI-nuhr AWRD-uhrz). Formerly the inferior grades in the hierarchy of Orders: the doorkeeper (the modern sacristan), reader,* exorcist, and acolyte.* Never really considered part of the Sacrament of Holy Orders,* they were Sacramentals* leading up to the Major Orders. In 1973, all Minor Orders were abrogated; only two, acolyte and reader, were reduced to Church ministries, leaving other types of ministry in the Church open for consideration to be included in a similar category at a later date. *See also* ACOLYTES; MINISTRIES; READERS.

Miracle (MIR-i-kuhl). Traditionally defined as an extraordinary sensible effect produced by God outside the established order of things. A more contemporary definition identifies it as a religious sign whereby God testifies to His active presence through an extraordinary event. Thus, *physical miracles* signify God's special action in the sphere of things; *intellectual miracles* (such as prophecy) signify God's special action in the sphere of knowledge; and *moral miracles* signify God's special action in the sphere of human behavior.

The conversion of the whole substance of bread and wine into the Body and Blood of Christ at the Consecration* during Mass* is traditionally termed a miracle even though the transubstantiation* is not an observable event. In this sense, the Mass is sometimes called the *greatest miracle. See also* CONSECRATION; EUCHARIST; MASS; TRANSUBSTANTIATION.

Mirae Caritatis (MEER-ay kah-ree-TAH-tees). Latin title (from the first two words "Wondrous Love") of the *Encyclical On the Holy Eucharist* issued by Pope Leo XIII on May 28, 1902. It sets forth the teaching of the Church* on the Blessed Sacrament* and the wondrous spiritual and moral effects that flow from an authentic Eucharistic devotion.*

Miriam, Canticle of. *See* CANTICLE OF MIRIAM.

Miserere (miz-uh-RAY-ree; mee-say-RAY-ray). First word in Latin of Psalms 51, 56, and 57, meaning "Have mercy." It is generally used to refer to Psalm 51, which is the fourth and chief of the Penitential Psalms* and the most common prayer for mercy in the Liturgy.*

This Psalm is recited in the *Liturgy of the Hours** at Morning Prayer* for Friday in Weeks I, II, III, and IV as well as on Good Friday* and in the Office for the Dead.* It is also used as a Responsorial Psalm* in the *Roman Missal** some nineteen times, including Funeral Masses and Masses during Lent. *See also* PENITENTIAL PSALMS.

Misericord (muh-ZER-uh-kawrd). A small projection on the bottom of a hinged seat of a choir stall that gives support to the standing worshiper when the seat is turned up.

Missa Cantata. *See* HIGH MASS.

Missa Catechumenorum. *See* MASS OF THE CATECHUMENS.

Missa Fidelium. *See* MASS OF THE FAITHFUL.

Missa Lecta. *See* LOW MASS.

Missa Solemnis. *See* SOLEMN HIGH MASS.

Missal (MIS-uhl). The liturgical book* containing the texts, the readings* and the prayers,* recited in the celebration of the Mass.* In the first centuries of the Church,* the liturgical prayers were extemporized by the celebrating bishop.* The lessons or readings were taken directly from the Bible,* their choice also being made by the celebrant. Eventually, the prayers, following some of the better models, were brought together in a collection that was called a *Sacramentary.** The selection of Bible readings according to some fixed norm eventually appeared in a *Lectionary*;* if the readings were in individual books, they were called *Evangeliary** and *Epistulary.** Choirs used a *Gradual** or *Antiphonary.*

By the 10th century all these various prayers and readings were gathered together into one book, to enable the mendicant orders and members of the Roman Curia who traveled a great deal to be able to have this material in a single volume for convenient use at private Masses. Ultimately this *Roman Missal** came into popular use, and in 1570, Pius V published a revised edition. A revision of this 1570 Missal occurred in 1961, but liturgical reforms proposed by Vatican II* brought about a completely new text in 1970. At this time the readings and Scriptural responsories* were collected in the *Lectionary;* the presidential prayers* and other parts of the Mass in the *Sacramentary.*

The Hand Missal

About 100 years ago there appeared a "People's Missal" created by the pioneers of the liturgical movement. With it the faithful* could follow closely the actions and words of the priest* during the Latin Mass, and eventually the assembly, through it, was encouraged to participate even in the Latin Masses. It brought about a genuine spirituality of the Liturgical Year* and developed Eucharistic spirituality in the people. Once the vernacular* appeared, some people thought the Missal was obsolete, for the people presumably could understand what was going on. Yet we still hear the complaint that people are getting nothing out of the Mass. To know, love, and live the Mass, one must participate fully, consciously, and actively in the Liturgy.*

The new hand Missal, even though it requires three volumes, the first being the Sunday volume, has special features. Its purpose is to aid participation by allowing the people to meditate on liturgical texts prior to the Eucharist* and to

return to them afterward. Its value rests in the format or arrangement and particularly the explanatory introduction and comments that accompany the text of the Liturgy; thus the Missal presents a knowledge of the Mystery of Faith,* making it a textbook of the teaching of the Church, the living instrument of Christian knowledge. In spite of the liturgical reform, we know that explanations, commentaries, spiritual and catechetical preparations are still necessary. The popular Missal can reach this goal because the quantity and richness of the selections have increased greatly and its explanatory function helps every type of user.

Furthermore, the Missal is our own prayerbook, helping us to pray with the "mind of the Church." And by providing us with the Church's commentary on the Word of God,* it shows us the Bible in action through the Liturgy.

Finally, the Missal is a wonderful introduction to the Eucharist, showing its proper place in the Sacramental order. No other book can impart such liturgical culture. Naturally, it is a necessity for those who have a role in Liturgies, such as the Liturgy Committee,* readers,* extraordinary ministers,* and singers. It is the one single book that gives the essence of the Eucharist and thus is a sure guide to Eucharistic spirituality, the safe path to a real Christian life, for it embodies our catechism, our Bible, our prayerbook, and our book of worship. *See also* LECTIONARY; SACRAMENTARY.

Missale Francorum (mee-SAH-lay frahn-KOH-room). Literally, "Missal of the Franks," an incomplete *Sacramentary* written in France at the beginning of the 8th century that closely resembles the *Gelasian Sacramentary.** It contains ordination* rites, the blessing of virgins* and widows, and the consecration of altars* as well as eleven Masses and the Roman Canon* (up to the prayer *Nobis Quoque Peccatoribus*—"To Us Sinners"). It is kept in the Vatican Library.

Missale Gothicum (mee-SAH-lay GOHTH-ee-koom). Literally, "Missal of the Goths," because it was once thought to have originated in the province of Narbonne. In reality, it is a Gallican *Sacramentary* probably put together about 700 for the Church at Autun. Its arrangement follows the order of the Gallican Mass, although it does have some Roman formulas. It contains Masses of the season from Christmas Eve* to Pentecost,* which are interspersed with some Saints'* days and followed by Masses of the Common of Saints,* six Sunday Masses, and a fragment of a Mass for use on special ferias.* The manuscript is kept in the Vatican.

Missale Parvum (mee-SAH-lay PAHR-voom). Literally, "Small Missal," a selection of Latin Masses* to facilitate celebrations of Mass for priests who do not know the local language. Published on October 18, 1970, it includes the entire *Ordo Missae* (Ordinary* of the Mass) along with a selection of Prefaces* and Eucharistic Prayers I,* II,* III,* and IV* as well as several Mass formularies usable in accord with the different liturgical days and seasons. Vernacular* editions of the *Roman Missal** are to include some or all of this collection in an appendix.

Missalettes (MIS-uhl-ets). Booklets containing the liturgical texts for Mass* for a week, a month, or a season (e.g., Lent*) supplied by publishers to secure a better implementation of the vernacular.* They were readily accepted by the people who, in using both sight and hearing, proved the educational principle that the more senses used the greater is the understanding. Missalettes are also very helpful in the many churches that have poor acoustics. *See also* PUBLICATION OF LITURGICAL MATERIALS.

Missions. *See* AD GENTES; NATIVE CUSTOMS.

Miter or Mitre (MAI-tuhr). The liturgical headdress worn by cardinals,* bishops,* and abbots.* The front and back are stiff, shaped like inverted shields ending in a peak, which are pressed apart when the miter is on the head. These two pieces are sewn together at the lower part, but a cleft separates them on top and the two parts are held together by a folding cloth. Two wide lappets hang down from the back part over the shoulders. Its use originated in Rome during the 11th century.

Two forms exist, the precious miter richly adorned with jewels and made of silver or gold plate, and the plain miter of white linen or silk. During a liturgical service, the bishop uses only one, depending on the character of the celebration. It is always worn when he carries the pastoral staff and never during the Eucharistic Prayer* or whenever he prays.

Mixed Marriage. *See* MARRIAGE.

Mixing of Water and Wine (MIKS-ing uhv WAW-tuhr and wain). Ancient liturgical practice still used at the Preparation of the Gifts* at Mass.* Water was customarily used in the Palestine of Christ's day to dilute wine, which tended to be heavy. When used in the Liturgy* this utilitarian action came to be given a symbolic religious interpretation. In the West, the mixing represented our Lord's union with His faithful*—as wine receives water, so Christ takes us and our sins to Himself. In the East, the wine and water represented Christ's human and Divine natures. The accompanying prayer reminds us that through the Eucharist* we are to share in the Divine dignity of Christ Who became incarnate for us. *See also* PREPARATION OF THE GIFTS.

Monastic Breviary (muh-NAS-tik BREE-v[y]uh-ree; BREE-vee-uhr-ee). Variation of the *Roman Breviary** used by the Benedictines and other monks* and nuns. Based on the directives in the Rule of St. Benedict* and excluded from the reforms of St. Pius V* and Urban VIII, it differed from the Roman version in its distribution of the Psalms* and the number of readings among other things. After the publication of the Vatican II* *Liturgy of the Hours,** the Church let it be known through the Congregation on Divine Worship* that the monastic orders ought to safeguard their characteristic form of prayer—at a measured pace, in common, and somewhat prolonged. If monks were simply to adopt the prayer of the pastoral clergy,* the Church's spiritual life would be deprived of that distinctive note characterized by the monastic orders.

On February 10, 1977, the Congregation approved the *Thesaurus Liturgiae Horarum Monasticae* (Treasury of the Monastic Liturgy of the Hours) drawn up by the Benedictines, which contained a Directory for the Divine Office, Introduction, four plans for the Psalter,* Proper of Seasons,* Proper of Saints,* and Common of Saints.* The purpose of this *Thesaurus* is that there may be an aid and a model for each community of monks and nuns as the basis for its own renewal, suited to its region, and for its own more faithful celebration of the Divine Office. *See also* BREVIARY; LITURGY OF THE HOURS.

Monica, St. (MON-uh-kuh). c.331-387. As wife Monica handled her husband Patricius and her mother-in-law so well that they converted. She is probably best known for her continuous prayers for Augustine,* who was a Manichee, and led a dissolute life. Eventually, he was baptized by Ambrose* in 386; his conversion he attributed to her prayers. She is the Patroness of Married Women and Model for Christian Mothers. *Liturgical celebration*: August 27 (Memorial); *theme*: the efficacy of prayer.

Monk (muhnk). A person who lives in community with others dedicated to the quest for the one thing necessary. As stated by Vatican II,* "the main task of monks is to render to the Divine Majesty a service at once simple and noble, within the monastic confines. This they do either by devoting themselves entirely to Divine worship* in a life that is hidden or by lawfully taking up some apostolate or works of Christian charity" (PC, 9). Thus, the celebration of the Liturgy* holds top priority in the life of monks, and its meticulous implementation is a source of example for the whole Church.* *See also* MONASTIC BREVIARY.

Monstrance (MON-struhnts). A sacred vessel designed to expose the consecrated Host* to the faithful* either for adoration* in church or for carrying in procession,* particularly on the Solemnity of the Body and Blood of Christ.* In its early forms in the 13th century, it resembled a pyx* placed on a chalice base with openings or glass on the sides. Comparable devices displayed relics* of Saints* prior to this time. Eventually the monstrance grew larger and was extended at the sides, with small statues, with the apex being a crucifix,* and sometimes it had a gothic structure. During the baroque period, it took on a rayed form of a sun-monstrance with a circular window surrounded by a silver or gold frame with rays. The lunula* holding the Host fits into the window of the monstrance.

Months, Dedication of (muhnths, ded-uh-KAY-shuhn uhv). The unofficial and traditional practice of dedicating each month to a Mystery* of the Faith* or a special Saint.* Here is the most usual schema:

January: Holy Name* of Jesus
February: Passion* of Our Lord

March: St. Joseph*
Holy Family*

April: Resurrection* of Jesus
Holy Eucharist*

May: Blessed Virgin Mary*

June: Sacred Heart* of Jesus

July: Precious Blood* of Jesus

August: Assumption* of Mary

September: Holy Cross*
Mary, Queen of Martyrs

October: Holy Rosary*
Holy Angels*

November: Souls in Purgatory

December: Holy Infancy of Our Lord
Immaculate Conception*

Some of these dedications have been recognized and approved by the Church*: those for May, October, and November. Since Vatican II,* there is a concern that these dedications must be in full accord with the Liturgy.*

Month's Mind Mass (muhnths maind mas). A Requiem Mass* offered for a deceased person a month (30 days) after death. The *Missal of Pius V* provided Masses for the third, seventh, and thirtieth day after death. The new *Roman Missal** allows Masses for the Dead on the day news of death is received, on the day of burial, and on the anniversary. It does not mention the thirtieth day. *See also* MASS OF CHRISTIAN BURIAL.

Morning Offering (MAWRN-ing AWF-[uh-]ring). Prayer of offering of one's whole day to the Sacred Heart* of Jesus by members of the Apostleship of Prayer.* It makes the Mass* the center of the members' day, and it is intimately linked with the Liturgical Movement.* There are two versions of the prayer.

Traditional Morning Offering

O Jesus,
through the Immaculate Heart* of Mary,
I offer You my prayers, works, joys, and sufferings
of this day
in union with the Holy Sacrifice of the Mass
throughout the world.
I offer them
for all the intentions of your Sacred Heart:
the salvation* of souls,
reparation* for sins,
the reunion of all Christians.

I offer them for the intentions of our Bishops
and of all the Apostles of Prayer,
and in particular for those
recommended by our Holy Father for this month.

Contemporary Morning Offering

Eternal Father,
I offer You everything I do this day:
my work, my prayers, my apostolic efforts;
my time with family and friends;
my hours of relaxation;
my difficulties, problems, distress
which I shall try to bear with patience.

Join these my gifts to the unique offering
which Jesus Christ, Your Son, renews today
in the Eucharist.*

Grant, I pray, that,
vivified by the Holy Spirit*

and united to the Sacred Heart of Jesus,
my life this day may be of service
to You and to Your children
and help consecrate the world to You.

See also APOSTLESHIP OF PRAYER.

Morning Prayer (MAWRN-ing prayr). This first of the two hinge Hours in the Divine Office* was formerly called Lauds, because of the character of praise used in the Psalms* of that Hour. Designed to sanctify the beginning of the day, Morning Prayer as one of the chief Hours of the day, calls to mind new beginnings: day, light, work, and reminds us of the Mystery of the Resurrection* of Jesus.

Structure

Should this be the first Hour recited that day, the Office begins with the Invitatory.* Otherwise, following the Introductory Verse,* a Hymn* appropriate for that hour of the day is sung to provide a joyful beginning and lead readily into prayer. Morning Prayer's Psalmody* is made up of a morning Psalm, followed by an Old Testament* Canticle,* then another Psalm, the theme of which is in keeping with the tradition of the Church of morning praise, lauding God.

The Short Readings after each Psalm would emphasize some particular Christian message; if one opts for a longer Scripture reading, especially if people are present for this celebration, choose it from the Office of Readings* or the *Lectionary** for Mass. A short Homily* may interpret the Reading. A Response* follows, usually a responsorial hymn. The Canticle of Zechariah* is preceded and followed by an antiphon* that varies according to the liturgical season,* feast,* or day.

The Intercessions* during the Morning Prayer dedicates the day and its work to God. Because the Divine Office is a prayer for and by the whole Church, the Intercessions should pray for general needs of the Church, her ministries, for civil authorities, the sick, the sorrowing, the poor, peace and any other world needs. To these may be added particular intentions. In community celebrations there are variable methods of reciting these Intercessions.

The Lord's Prayer* has a place of honor at the end of the petitions and is followed immediately by the Concluding Prayer,* which is found in the Psalter* for weekdays in Ordinary Time,* otherwise in the Proper.* Then the deacon* or priest* dismisses the faithful* as at Mass* with a Greeting,* the Blessing* and the invitation to go in peace, with variations allowed. *See also* LITURGY OF THE HOURS.

Motet (moh-TET). A polyphonic musical composition, based on a Scriptural text, with two or more voices singing usually unaccompanied, although sometimes with organ accompaniment alone. It is considered extra-liturgical, having no proper place in the Mass* or Evening Prayer.* Nevertheless it is based on the Gregorian* tones used in Mass, and sometimes these songs would occur after the usual Offertory* text was sung in plainsong. Sometimes settings for the propers of the Mass were called Motets, but they should rather be given their proper liturgical title, e.g., Entrance Hymns.* *See also* MUSIC.

Mother of the Church (MUHTH-uhr uhv thuh chuhrch). This title given to Mary* was significant in patristic and medieval times. Recently it was formally recognized in the Second Vatican Council* and since then has gained prominence in Catholic theology.

Mary's role, rooted in the Bible,* is the prototype of redeemed humankind because of her willingness to be His Mother; her role is ecumenically promising since, as the Mother of the Christian community, she is not on the same level with her Son, but with us the community that witnesses to the gift of grace* given to the world by Christ.

Salvation,* as a social rather than an individual event, brings Mary into the Body of Christ* through the Spirit,* thus foreshadowing the incorporation of all human beings into Christ. Mary's activity is viewed as God's action in her through her Son and His Spirit.* In this way the Church* proves that Catholic Mariology is consistent with Biblical Christology, contrary to Protestant objections.

According to *Lumen Gentium** (chs. 60–65), this title belongs to Mary in a fivefold manner: (1) As "God bearer," she was the one who gave the human life to the Son of God that gives us the dignity of election. (2) The extension of her maternity was explicitly given to all of the faithful* through the disciple John* while Christ was on the Cross.* (3)

On Pentecost,* together with the Apostles,* she too received the Holy Spirit,* when the Church was born. (4) Generations of Christians, following the example of John, took Mary as their spiritual Mother. (5) Continuously she exercises her role as Mediatrix of all Grace because of her maternal care for the Church. *See also* REDEMPTORIS MATER; SOLEMNITY OF MARY, MOTHER OF GOD.

Motherhood of Mary. *See* MOTHER OF THE CHURCH.

Motto. *See* HERALDRY.

Movable Feasts. *See* FEASTS.

Movement, Biblical (Moov-muhnt, BIB-luh-kuhl). The 20th-century movement that has led to a renewed interest in and love for the Bible* among Catholics. It was inaugurated by the labors of outstanding Biblical scholars, such as Joseph-Mary Lagrange, O.P., and the pronouncements of the Church.* In 1890, Lagrange opened the Ecole Biblique at Jerusalem, which has been in the forefront of Catholic Bible studies ever since. He also established (in 1892) the *Revue Biblique* ("Biblical Review"), which has become one of the leading Biblical journals worldwide. In 1893, Pope Leo XIII issued the Encyclical *Providentissimus Deus* ("Most Provident God"), instituting a new era in

Catholic Biblical studies, and in 1902 he established the Pontifical Biblical Commission for the promotion of Bible studies among Catholics and the safeguarding of them from error.

In 1917, the Code of Canon Law authorized the study of any Bible that contained the Church's Imprimatur.* In 1943, Pius XII issued the Encyclical *Divino Afflante Spiritu* ("Inspired by the Divine Spirit"), which became the Magna Charta of the Biblical Movement. It urged Catholics to make use of the new discoveries in archeology, the greater knowledge of the original Biblical languages, and the better understanding of the customs and rites of the ancient peoples of the Near East of whom the Hebrews were a part.

Finally, Vatican II* by its Constitution *Dei Verbum** put a crowning touch to the Biblical Movement that was already in progress, spurring it on to even greater heights. It specifically urged all the faithful* to learn by frequent reading of the Divine Scriptures the excelling knowledge of Jesus Christ. They should gladly put themselves in touch with the sacred text, whether it be through the Liturgy,* rich in the Divine Word, or through devotional reading, or through instructions and other aids (see DV, 25).

The Biblical Movement thus succeeded in bringing out to all the faithful the paramount role of the Bible in the Liturgy, as the Council put it: "From the table of both the Word of God* and the Body of Christ,* the Church unceasingly receives and offers to the faithful the Bread of Life, especially in the sacred Liturgy" (DV, 21), *See also* BIBLE AND LITURGY; DEI VERBUM; LECTIONARY; LITURGY OF THE WORD.

Movement, Ecumenical (MOOV-muhnt, ek-yoo-MEN-i-kuhl; -yuh-). Those activities and enterprises that, according to various needs of the Church* and opportune occasions, are started and organized for the fostering of unity among Christians. According to Vatican II,* these are: (1) every effort to eliminate words, judgments, and actions that do not respond to the condition of "separated brethren" with truth and fairness and so make mutual relations between them more difficult and (2) dialogue between competent experts from different Churches and Communities. Through such dialogue, (a) everyone gains a truer knowledge and more just appreciation of the teaching and religious life of both Communions; (b) the Communions cooperate more closely in whatever projects a Christian conscience demands for the common good; (c) the Communions come together for common prayer, where this is permitted; and (d) all are led to examine their own faithfulness to Christ's will for the Church and, wherever necessary, to undertake with vigor the task of renewal and reform (UR, 4).

The beginning of the Ecumenical Movement is generally regarded as the Edinburgh Missionary Conference of 1910 wherein 159 missionary societies stipulated that competitive denominationalism was harmful to Christianity. When the World Council of Churches was formed in 1948 at Amsterdam, the Ecumenical Movement began to be funneled through that organization. The Catholic Church began to take part in the international aspect of the Movement in 1952 with the establishment of the Catholic Conference for Ecumenical Problems. In

1960 the Secretariat for Promoting Christian Unity was born, and in 1964 its Decree on Ecumenism was approved by Vatican II, which also called on all Catholics to participate in the work of ecumenism (see UR, 4).

The Ecumenical Movement has had a large effect on the Liturgy.* Prayer in common has been emphasized, and the rites of various Churches have been renewed. In English-speaking countries, there are a series of "Prayers We Have in Common" that are used as responses in the Eucharist* and the Liturgy of the Hours,* and the same cycle of readings is used in the Liturgy of the Word.* There is also a wide sharing of hymns* and even of translations of Scripture,* for example, the *Revised Standard Version.* However, Catholics still cannot participate in the full Eucharistic Communion at an Ecumenical worship of the Eucharist. *See also* ATTENDING NON-CATHOLIC SERVICES; UNITATIS REDINTEGRATIO.

Movement, Liturgical. *See* LITURGICAL MOVEMENT

Mozarabic Rite (moh-ZAR-uh-bik rait). A liturgical rite, established on the Iberian peninsula when it was under the Arabs, that flourished from the 6th through the 11th centuries. By the 11th century it was suppressed in favor of the Roman Rite* except for a few parishes.* Today it is still celebrated in a few churches in the Toledo diocese.* Oriental influences gave this Liturgy* a form quite different from the Roman and it in turn influenced the Gallican Liturgy. The anaphora* was not fixed; rather than to the Father, some of the priest's prayers were addressed to Jesus Christ.

Mozzetta (moh-ZET-uh). A small nonliturgical cape of silk or wool extending to the elbows and buttoned in front. A small hood is attached at the neck. The color* varies with the wearer's status and signifies jurisdiction.* Some Religious Orders have a similar cape as part of their monastic habit.

Mulieris Dignitatem (mool-YEE-e-ris deen-yee-TAH-tem). Latin title (from the first two words "Dignity of Women") of the *Apostolic Letter on the Dignity and Vocation of Women* issued by John Paul II on August 15, 1988. This document sketches the role of women in life and in the Church* by examining the Bible's* attitude toward them.

Most specifically, it shows that Jesus was a promoter of women's true dignity, without the slightest hint of the discrimination against women prevalent in his day. However, this did not include calling women to the ministerial priesthood.* Rather Jesus looks to them for the accomplishment of the "royal priesthood" (1 Pt 2:9)—that is, the universal priesthood*—which is the treasure He has given to every individual.

Multilingual Masses (muhl-ti-LIN-gwuhl MAS-uhz). Because many communities, at least in the United States, are faced with multilingual celebrations of the Eucharist,* the following guidelines offer an opportunity to use the rich diversity of cultural and linguistic expressions, when these assemblies come to one common act of worship.* Despite diversity of culture and language, unity should flow from liturgical celebrations. This type of Liturgy* could have particular value in celebrating weddings, funerals,* major feasts,* and certain special parish* or even diocesan* events. Not only language, but a choice of gestures,* vesture,* postures,* and even environmental design should be reflected throughout the celebration, with a commentator* giving the necessary instructions.

(1) The Introductory Rites* of Mass ought to be used properly to prepare the community for the Word of God* and the celebration of the Eucharist in a worthy manner. Thus the processional music,* introductory greetings, the penitential intercessions and the Glory to God* can be used effectively to allow all present to be aware of the cultural diversity of the gathering. Before the Opening Prayer* the typical invitation may be given in various languages; however the prayer itself would be in one language.

(2) The Liturgy of the Word* is a principal element of the Liturgy, so care must be taken that the assembly* will be able to understand the readings.* At least one reading preceding the Gospel* ought to be in the language of the majority present. If two readings are prescribed, one may be in another language. As to the Responsorial Psalm,* the antiphon* may be of a language not spoken by the majority, while the verses are sung by the chanter* or choir* in the language of the majority of the assembly. The Gospel would be in the language of the majority, although portions of it, to which the Homily* pertains, should be proclaimed also in the other languages. Yet, the entire Gospel should not be repeated in other languages, which would prolong the service. The Homily again, would be in the language of the majority; summaries may be given in other languages. The invitation to the

General Intercessions* can be given in various languages, but the conclusion to each intercession would be answered consistently in one language.

(3) For the Liturgy of the Eucharist,* at the Preparation of the Gifts,* only bread, wine, and gifts for the Church,* for the poor, are appropriate. In the Eucharistic Prayer,* only one language would be used for each of the chief elements, namely: Thanksgiving*; Acclamation*; Epiclesis*; Institution Narrative*; Anamnesis*; Offering*; Intercessions*; Final Doxology.* Both the Creed* and the Lord's Prayer,* being common to all Christians, may be recited simultaneously in the language of each person present.

(4) In the Concluding Rite,* when solemn forms of the Blessing* are used, each of the prayers may be given in languages appropriate to the assembly.

(5) As to music, it is hoped that such groups could sing short texts together even in a language foreign to them. Latin chants or antiphons can very effectively bring about musical unity. Basically, the languages of those assembled should be expressed in song, with music proper to each culture; alternating verses of those familiar hymns* that are known in several languages can be effective in antiphonal selections. The choir may sing the verses in various languages, while the

antiphon is sung by all present, in a common language. A blend of diverse languages, which nevertheless reflect an integral musical style, may be used for the Eucharistic Acclamations.

Munificentissimus Deus (moo-nee-fee-chen-TEES-ee-moos DAY-oos). Latin title from the first two words ("Most Bountiful God") of the Apostolic Constitution issued by Pius XII on November 1, 1950, defining the dogma of Mary's Assumption* with body and soul into heaven. He thus declared that the teaching of a liturgical feast* that had been celebrated for some fifteen centuries in the Church was a dogma* of the Faith.* *See also* ASSUMPTION OF MARY.

Music (MYOO-zik). Sacred music is needed in all aspects of liturgical and spiritual life, whether it makes prayer more pleasing, promotes unity of minds, or confers greater solemnity upon the sacred rites. When it is an integral part of worship* and combines both a spiritual superiority and an artistic dignity, music is sacred, therefore liturgical. Such music has the ability to cultivate, strengthen, and deepen the spiritual experience of the assembly* gathered for worship. Essential to the stability of authentic worship, liturgical music, in expressing Biblical and ritual texts, is usually a great, positive force of catechesis,* while it facilitates and nurtures prayers in the community.

Principles

(1) Sacraments* are celebrated within the Mass* or at a Liturgy of the Word.* Proper use of the musical instruments in the Liturgy of the Word allows the assembly's responses in song to become a normal pastoral practice.

(2) Each liturgical unit identifies the elements that could be enhanced by music. Sometimes rubrics* themselves indicate a place for song during the celebration of a rite, in some cases even suggesting an appropriate text to be rendered musically.

(3) Songs may have various functions: (a) they may accompany ritual actions, for instance, the procession* at Baptism,* or the anointing with chrism* at Confirmation,* or (b) the sung prayer may be a constituent element of the rite, so that no other ritual action is being performed during it; such might be the Song of Praise after Communion* and the Litany of the Saints* during Christian Initiation* or at a Religious Profession.

(4) Musical form should match the liturgical function. After the baptismal profession of faith,* a sung acclamation,* short, and as a strong, declarative statement, would be more suitable than verses of a hymn.

(5) A pastoral judgment in choosing music is important for Sacramental celebrations, though significant moments in the individual's life are equally important as a constitutive event in the community's life.

(6) Although music ought to be a normal and ordinary part of any liturgical celebration, the axiom of progressive solemnity should be considered. It takes into account the ability of the assembly, the relative importance of the rite and its parts, and the festivity of the day itself.

(7) Various languages and different musical idioms may occur during the same celebration. Some music may be classical, other music contemporary, or from plainsong. The music may be rendered variously, unaccompanied, or accompanied by organ or guitar. While employing musical plurality, musical integrity within the rite should be achieved.

Pastoral Planning

The planning committee ought to meet regularly to create and coordinate worship by using liturgical and musical options for the various liturgies. The unity derived from the liturgical feast* or season* can result in the skillful and sensitive

selection of options.* The planning group should have sufficient knowledge and artistic skills to achieve their purpose and should indicate, besides the choice of songs and options, the method of invitation to the assembly. Of concern should be the needs, the disposition, and the aptitude of the assembly, the group of worshipers.

Music should be within the competence of the congregation. Though there may be variations in the level of faith,* music may serve as a bridge to faith while even expressing it. Age level and cultural background may present a diversity of people. The planning team must be aware of and try to satisfy many types, both theologically and musically. If possible a variety of parish* Sunday celebrations should be offered.

The occasion might dictate a different way to celebrate, for one would expect well-polished musical song on great feasts while penitential seasons would be filled with more restraint. Furthermore, even Sunday should be celebrated with variety, but always in a prayerful and pastoral fashion.

The celebrant,* with his style, attitude, and bearing, can affect the Liturgy appreciably. Musical styles should increase his effectiveness, particularly when he himself is capable of singing his parts well.

Place of Music

Foremost in importance among signs and symbols* employed by the Church to celebrate her faith, sacred song plays an essential part in the Liturgy. Ministerial in function, it never dominates but serves. It brings joy and enthusiasm together with a sense of unity that sets the appropriate tone for each celebration. Because music displays a dimension of meaning and feeling that mere words cannot do, ideally each communal celebration ought to include music and singing.

The value of music in the liturgical celebration is to be judged on three levels:

(1) *The musical judgment.* It should be aesthetically, technically, and expressively good. Competent

musicians should create or search for quality music that fits the liturgical texts. One must judge value within each musical style, employing not only chant,* polyphony,* and choral hymns but also contemporary compositions, such as the folk idiom.

(2) *The liturgical judgment.* To help determine what type of music should be used, consider the nature of the Liturgy itself, which may indicate what parts should be sung and who should sing them. There should always be a balance, so that the relative importance of the various parts of the Mass is reflected in the music. The different texts dictate a type of musical presentation: proclamations, acclamations,* Psalms* and hymns, and prayers. Taken into account must be the roles of the chanter,* the choir,* the congregation, and the instrumentalists. Their capabilities should be understood so that they are comfortable in their renditions and all may feel that the celebration through their active participation enhances the Liturgy.

(3) *The pastoral judgment.* Pastoral concern makes decisions on whether or not, in a particular circumstance or concrete situation, music actually expresses the faith of the community in this place, at this age, in this culture. Sensitive to the social and cultural characteristics of the congregation, the pastoral decision, sometimes made by committee, will bring about a meaningful and genuinely human faith experience for the given worshiping community.

Music in the Eucharist

Clear understanding of the structure of the Liturgy is necessary to be aware of the relative importance of the various parts of the Mass and thus determine the overall rhythm in the liturgical action that would help in the decision as to what type of music should be used for the various sections. For instance, in the Introductory Rites,* the Entrance Song* and Opening Prayer* are important, just as in the Preparation of the Gifts,* the bringing of the gifts with the Prayer over the Gifts* is essential. In the climax during the Communion Rite,* the Lord's Prayer,* Communion Procession,* and Prayer after Communion* are primary.

During the Eucharistic Prayer,* the ratification and affirmation by the assembly through acclamations of faith prove that this Great Prayer of Praise is the center of the entire celebration. Varied musical patterns may be used within the liturgical structure of the Mass, so unlimited combinations of sung and recited parts can be chosen. Many parts of the Mass may be sung, and each should be rendered in accordance with its proper nature or function.

Five categories of singing occur: (a) Acclamations are meaningful assents to God's Word and action and are quite significant, e.g., the Alleluia* Verse, the Great Amen,* the doxology to the Lord's Prayer. (b) Processional songs are used at the entrance, during Communion,

and perhaps at the close of Mass. (c) The Responsorial Song, as a response to the First Reading,* should bring the Liturgy of the Word* more fully to life. (d) The Ordinary chants include the Lord Have Mercy,* Glory to God,* Lord's Prayer, Lamb of God,* and Profession of Faith.* (e) Supplementary songs are those chosen when no specific text needs to be used, for instance, during the Preparation of the Gifts, or the song after Communion, and even some litanies.

In all this one should not hesitate to use new patterns and combinations, as long as there is harmony. Flexibility has an important value, and the capable musician will be able to create an artistic rhythm in the liturgical action by combining the variety of options available into an effective whole.

Music and Sacrament as Celebrations

Since communal celebrations of the Sacraments* are encouraged by the *Constitution on the Sacred Liturgy,** a musical element should be involved. Even though some of the Sacraments may not occur within the Mass, the use of music is clearly indicated in the ritual.

In the *Rite of Christian Initiation of Adults,** opportunities exist for processional songs and acclamations. The same holds true for the *Rite of Baptism of Children.** During *Confirmation** the rite calls for song during the Profession of Faith and the anointings.

The Rites of *Anointing the Sick** and the *Sacrament of Penance** celebrated communally call for music. Their Introductory Rites and Liturgy of the Word follow the pattern of the Mass. Acclamations, songs, or even soft instrumental music may be fitting during the Sacrament.

Christian *Marriage** offers particular challenges that can be resolved by the couple working together with musician and pastor. The congregation should be involved at the important moments of the celebration, and the choice of music should follow and employ the musical, liturgical, and pastoral judgments mentioned above so that the Liturgy becomes prayer for all present, not a theatrical production.

At *funerals** music becomes particularly important to express the themes of hope* and resurrection.* An attempt should be made to involve the congregation with appropriate participation* aids. Retired parishioners and others home on weekdays may have a unique ministry of assisting musically at the funeral assembly to fit the Paschal theme, keeping in mind that a few things sung well might have priority at funerals in keeping with the principle of progressive solemnity.

The Liturgy of the Hours

Although Religious Communities have sung the Divine Office* for years, a large number of parishes may celebrate some of the Hours, either Morning Prayer* or Evening

Prayer,* possibly during one or other of the liturgical seasons. The Psalms and Canticles* as songs may be rendered in various ways: *responsorially,* perhaps the easiest for congregational use for the assembly responds with a brief antiphon; *antiphonally,* the assembly divided into two groups share the recitation of the Psalm; or *straight through*—a through-composed setting would rarely have any musical material repeated and is usually composed for soloists and choir, or choir alone. It is usually not designed for congregational use. The formula tones are either Psalm tones or especially composed for each Psalm or Canticle. Mixing the various musical idioms in the singing of the Psalms is certainly fitting, even to the extent that some parts may be performed unaccompanied and others accompanied by organ, guitar, or other instrument.

Other parts of the Liturgy of the Hours* are naturally to be sung, such as the Hymns, the Responsories,* the Introductory Greetings,* and the Versicles,* as well as the Lord's Prayer and the Intercessions.* Except on solemn occasions, the Readings are usually not chanted.

Music and Cultural Heritage

Certainly music from the past that can be adapted to current day needs should be relied upon. Many of the Gregorian Chants were quite simple and can readily be employed by the assembly participating in today's liturgies. In America there is a rich diversity of cultural heritage that should be recognized and fostered by celebrating events in song and music in accordance with the many peoples' cultural, ethnic, and racial roots. The musical gifts

of the various ethnic communities should enrich the whole Church. Folk music is one of collective or anonymous composition and shows unique characteristics, both ethnic and national. Recently much sacred music has passed into folk melodies, and these into hymn tunes. The academic discipline of ethnomusicology should help to bring fine folk tunes into the Liturgy for the various liturgical functions, carrying with it the spontaneity and cultural roots of the people.

Training for Sacred Music

Because sacred song is a necessary part of Liturgy, all seminarians are to be instructed and receive proper musical and voice training together with the study of their other disciplines. Adequate performance of Gregorian melodies and chants, especially the simple ones that are in traditional use, ought to be achieved. All seminarians should acquire basic principles for directing a choir. They should be part of the choir under a competent choirmaster, for this activity would also greatly increase their musical abilities. Opportunities for practice on organs and pianos and other instruments should be afforded them.

Singing

In public worship, singing is customary in every religion. Even in the New Testament* one can find evidence of congregational singing, which the *Constitution on the Sacred Liturgy* asks to be fostered during liturgical services. Throughout the centuries, chanting and Christian hymns were used by congregations regularly. There was always congregational singing during the Mass, particularly for those formulas common to all Masses, such as the Glory to God and the Holy, Holy, Holy.* During certain centuries the singing may have been usurped by specially trained musicians, but all reform tends to give back to the congregation its proper share in the chanting of the Ordinary* parts. Generally speaking, singing should be widely used during liturgical functions, taking into consideration the capability of the congregation, preference being given naturally to the more significant parts. *See also* ALLELUIA; ANTHEM; ANTIPHONAL CHANT; CANTICLE; CAROLS; CHANT; CHANTER; CHOIRS (MUSIC); COMMUNION SONG; CONGREGATIONAL SINGING; ENTRANCE SONG; GREGORIAN CHANT; HYMNS; MOTET; MUSIC, INSTRUMENTAL; MUSIC MINISTRY; NATIVE MUSIC; OFFERTORY SONG; PLAINCHANT; POLYPHONY; PSALM TONES; PSALMODY; RECESSIONAL SONG; SCHOLA CANTORUM.

Music Commissions (MYOO-zik kuh-MISH-uhnz). Diocesan commissions for sacred music were prescribed as early as 1967, when it was indicated that they should work closely with the liturgical commission* and quite possibly be combined into one. In some areas it might even be more fruitful for several dioceses* to set up one commission. The supposition is that experts should be appointed to these commissions, which would be involved in societies that deal in musical matters. The Popes* have met with many international societies and have praised their work and stressed the necessity of music in liturgical functions. *See also* LITURGICAL COMMISSIONS.

Music, Instrumental (MYOO-zik, in-struh-MENT-uhl). In the early years of Christianity the use of musical instruments was debated, because even though the Bible* exhorts us to praise God with all kinds of instruments (Ps 150), use of musical instruments in those years were connected with immoral practices and theatrical performances. The organ finally found its place in Christian worship,* together with some other instruments that help to embellish singing. By the 18th century orchestral instruments had a dominating influence, so that legislation tried to eliminate abuses. By the turn of this century the organ came back into esteem; by the time of the Second Vatican Council,* other instruments were permitted as long as they could be in accord with the dignity of the Liturgy.*

Many Conferences of Bishops* have allowed any musical instrument that can be played in a manner suitable to public worship. Thus the circumstances, the congregation, the culture, and the musical traditions of many races and peoples help determine the use of mu-

sical instruments in accord with the aforementioned criteria of musical, liturgical, and pastoral judgment.

Instrumental music grants the support when an assembly* is learning new music; it also assists when the congregation prepares for worship, meditates, and even gives full voice to praise during worship. At times it may bridge a gap between parts of ceremonies, and it may help to unify a liturgical action. Yet in every way instrumental music is ministerial, aiding the assembly to be of one mind, to rejoice, to be converted, and to pray. *See also* MUSIC; NATIVE MUSIC.

Music Ministry (MYOO-zik MIN-uh-stree). The whole congregation* exercises a ministry of music. However, certain members of the community have a special gift of leading musical praise for the worshiping assembly.* Any such pastoral musician is first of all a disciple and then a minister, a worshiper using musical talent, a believer who shares faith,* serves the community, and expresses love* of neighbor and of God through music. Although pastoral musicians may have developed fine musical skills, it may be necessary for them to study liturgical music so that they can be a valued part of the pastoral effort. The chanter* has perhaps the most crucial role among music ministers, that of developing congregational singing. Skills to introduce and teach new music, to encourage the assembly and yet not intrude on communal prayer, must be a special gift constantly employed.

The spirituality necessary for musicians, as is the case with any other artist, depends on their love of God, neighbor, and the world.* Ordinarily this is shown by the hospitality they emanate by creating an inviting environment for human beings to want to join in the music. They challenge us to stretch our human imagination about God and expect us to meditate on God with our whole being. Thus an artistic hospitality will occur in the Church* through the acoustic environment in which we can explore the Mystery* of God.

Musical Concerts in Church (MYOO-zi-kuhl KON-suhrts in chuhrch). Because church buildings are often ideal for concerts, music of a religious nature outside of liturgical services is often requested to be performed in them. Churches are set aside for Divine worship*—each is "a house of prayer" (Lk 19:46). According to Canon 1210 a church is used to promote "worship, piety, and religion," but the "Ordinary can . . . permit other uses . . . not contrary to the holiness of the place."

Sacred or religious musical performances, outside liturgical celebration, may be allowed when they:

(a) prepare for the major liturgical feasts,* or lend to these a more festive character beyond the moment of actual celebration;

(b) bring out the particular character of the different liturgical seasons*;

(c) create in churches a setting of beauty conducive to meditation,* so

as to arouse even in those who are distant from the Church* an openness to spiritual values;

(d) create a context that favors and makes accessible the proclamation of God's Word,* as for example, a sustained reading of the Gospel*;

(e) keep alive the treasures of Church music that must not be lost; musical pieces and songs composed for the Liturgy* but which cannot in any way be conveniently incorporated into liturgical celebrations in modern times; spiritual music, such as oratorios and religious cantatas, that can still serve as vehicles for spiritual communication;

(f) assist visitors and tourists to grasp more fully the sacred character of a church, by means of organ concerts at prearranged times.

Practical directives: Permission is to be requested for each concert, in writing with all details. The pastor* is to specify the requisite norms to be observed. No admission is to be charged and proper dress is to be worn. Musicians and singers must be outside the sanctuary.* The Blessed Sacrament* is to be transferred to a side chapel. The performance is to be presented to instill a deep understanding. The concert organizer must accept legal responsibility for all expenses, clean up, and damage.

Musicam Sacram (MOOZ-ee-kahm SAHK-rahm). Latin title from the first two words ("Sacred Music") of the *Instruction on Sacred Music* issued by the Sacred Congregation of Rites* on March 5, 1967. The document sets forth general norms and applies them to almost every aspect of liturgical music* as the following outline indicates: (1) general norms; (2) those with a role in liturgical celebrations*; (3) singing during Mass*; (4) singing the Divine Office*; (5) sacred music in the celebration of the Sacraments* and Sacramentals,* special services, celebrations of the Word of God,* and popular devotions*; (6) language for use in sung liturgies; preserving the treasury of sacred music; (7) composing musical settings for vernacular* texts; (8) sacred instrumental music; and (9) commissions in charge of promoting sacred music. *See also* Music.

Mustum (MUHS-tuhm). The freshly squeezed juice of grapes or juice in which the natural process of fermentation has been suspended by freezing or other methods that do not alter its nature. Alcoholic priests* may obtain permission to use mustum instead of wine at Mass* when intinction* is impossible as a method of communicating the Sacrament of the Eucharist.* The permission is to be sought by the Ordinary* from the Congregation for the Doctrine of the Faith by a petition for an individual priest that is accompanied by a medical certificate verifying that even the minimal amount of alcohol ingested by intinction would endanger the priest's health or recovery.

Myrrh (muhr). Extracted from the bark of certain species of trees, this gum resin solidifies into grains and because of its sweet smell is used as

a perfume. Mixed with incense* it may be used in the ceremony of blessing the bells.* From Christian tradition* it symbolizes suffering, and was one of the gifts from the Magi to the infant Jesus. *See also* EPIPHANY.

Mystagogia (mis-tuh-GOH-jee-ah; -jyah). The catechesis* received during the Easter Season* by the newly baptized, whereby the neophytes* and the Local Church* explore the meaning of the introductory Mysteries* and their own experience in the Church thus far. *See also* RITE OF CHRISTIAN INITIATION OF ADULTS.

Mysterium Fidei (mee-STAY-ree-oom FEE-day-ee). Latin title (from the first two words "The Mystery of Faith") of the *Encyclical on the Doctrine and Worship of the Eucharist* issued by Paul VI on September 3, 1965. To counter the perceived tendencies to depreciate private Masses,* adulterate the dogma* of Transubstantiation,* and devalue Eucharistic worship apart from Mass, Paul VI sets forth the importance of the Eucharistic Mystery* and recalls the traditional doctrine of Transubstantiation.

In the course of this Encyclical, the Pope* outlines the ways in which Christ is present to the Church* and then gives his celebrated definition of Christ's presence in the Eucharist: "This presence is called the *real presence* not to exclude the other kinds as though they were not real, but because it is real par excellence, since it is substantial, in the sense that Christ whole and entire, God and man, becomes present" (no. 39). *See also* ADORATION, EUCHARISTIC; EUCHARIST; EUCHARISTIC DEVOTIONS; TRANSUBSTANTIATION.

Mystery (MIS-t[uh-]ree). (1) A Divinely revealed truth, unable to be rationally conceived or fully understood by the finite mind. The Trinity* and Incarnation* are such Mysteries. Though incomprehensible, they are intelligible; in other words, a person can recognize that there is no contradiction in them, once revealed.

(2) Mystery, as understood in Greek patristic writings, is equivalent to the Latin *sacramentum*, and thus it expresses the meaning of Sacrament,* i.e., signs that declare that Christ followed the plan of salvation* for us; thus the Sacraments bring the Mystery of Christ's salvation into the present.

(3) Mystery in the liturgical sense is usually connected with two other words: "Mystery of Faith."* The term primarily refers to the Mass* in this context, and more especially to the words used after the Consecration,* which explicitly refer to the transubstantiation* that has just been enacted upon the altar.*

Mystery of Faith, The (MIS-t[uh-]ree uhv fayth, thuh). The Mystery of salvation,* principal object of Revelation* and of Christian belief (1 Tm 3:9). The Mystery of Faith is the Paschal Mystery,* the Mystery of Christ dying, rising, and present among His people. It is the whole plan of God realized in Christ's saving love, contained under the Sac-

ramental signs* of the Eucharist.* Formerly, this phrase was part of the words of Consecration.* Now it is proclaimed by the celebrant* when he invites the assembly* to proclaim the Memorial Acclamation,* which sums up the Paschal Mystery.

Mystical Body of Christ (MIS-ti-kuhl BOD-ee uhv kraist). The term used to identify the Catholic Church* founded by Christ as an expansion and continuance of the Incarnation.* Since the Church is visible, living, and a growing organism, enlivened by the Spirit* of God, she is a *body*. Her essential nature is a Mystery, while all her laws, teachings, and rites are Sacramental sources of grace,* and thus deserves the term "mystical." Christ as a Founder of the Church, remains the invisible Head, through Whom all blessings are communicated to the members, and so we have the full phrase "Mystical Body of Christ."

This term signifies the sacramentality of the Roman Catholic Church, for she is the great Sacrament of the New Law, instituted by Jesus in order to communicate grace to the whole world.* On the Cross,* Christ offered Himself alone to His Father; in the Eucharist,* He, as Priest and Victim, offers Himself in union with the Mystical Body. *See also* CHURCH.

Mystici Corporis (MEES-tee-chee KAWR-paw-rees). Latin title (from the first two words "Mystical Body") of the *Encyclical on the Mystical Body of Christ* issued by Pius XII on June 29, 1943. The Encyclical focused on a definition of the Church* that was not often used in its day. In doing so it prepared for many themes found in the teachings of Vatican II.* It stresses that

the Church is neither exclusively hierarchic nor exclusively charismatic. The Church is comprised of all the faithful,* each contributing to her life by a unique function, office, and gift.

The Encyclical indicates that just as God gave the human body its own means to provide for its life, health, and growth, so the Savior of humankind provided in a marvelous way for His Mystical Body by the Sacraments.* Through them, the members of the Church are given many consecutive, graduated graces* from the cradle to the grave. These unite them with their Head, Christ, in a union that reaches a climax in the Eucharist,* which the members offer through the hands of the priest* who represents their Head. *See also* MYSTICAL BODY OF CHRIST.

Mysticism (mis-tuh-SIZ-uhm). The experience of mystical union with God, which is attained only through a special Divine grace*; in a broader sense, it is an acute "awareness" of God and His activities and manifestations. In the first sense, the Liturgy* is no place for the practice of mysticism just as is true in the case of contemplation.* However, the Liturgy can prepare for it and lead up to it. In the second sense, the acute awareness of God has a very large place in the Liturgy, which also plays a large role in attaining this type of mysticism. *See also* CONTEMPLATION; LITURGY AND CONTEMPLATIVE LIFE.

— N —

Nahum, The Book of (NAY-huhm, thuh buk uhv). Forty-first Book of the Old Testament* and seventh of the Minor Prophets.* It was written by Nahum from Elkosh in Judah (about whom nothing else is known) between 664 and 612 B.C. The short contents (three chapters) is believed by scholars to be a "battle curse" (voiced shortly before an attack) that announces the coming punishment of the enemy Nineveh because of its unprecedented pride, idolatry, and oppression, especially against Israel. It thus becomes a word of comfort for the Prophet's people. Yet Nahum also indicates that God was willing to save the doomed city if its people repented. For He is always seeking the lost, is slow to anger (1:3), good (1:7), and a refuge for those who trust in Him (1:7). Indeed, God sends Good News* to those who will listen (1:15). All this is told with a matchless poetic style and great literary power.

Liturgical use: In the *Roman Missal,** this Book is read on Friday of the 18th Week in Ordinary Time,* Year II. In the *Liturgy of the Hours,** it occurs only in the alternate Two-Year Cycle of Readings* on Monday of the 29th Week, Year I. *Meaning:* God rules over all the earth, even over those who do not acknowledge Him as God. This one God holds us all accountable for our actions, whether we know it or not. Those who repent and rely on God will be saved, for He is their refuge in time of trial. He cares for all who trust in Him.

Name, Baptismal. *See* BAPTISMAL NAME.

Name Days. *See* PATRON SAINTS.

Nathaniel. *See* BARTHOLOMEW, ST.

Narthex (NAHR-theks). The vestibule or porch at the entrance of the church separated from the nave* by a wall, railing, or screen, acting as a buffer separating the secular life from contact with God. This area was used for two purposes at various times, for the catechumens* and penitents, or as the gathering place for those in the procession* to bring up the gifts in preparation for the Eucharist.*

National Catechetical Directory (NASH-uhn-uhl; NASH-nuhl; kat-uh-KET-i-kuhl duh-REK-t[uh-]ree). Directory* issued in 1979 that applies to the American Church the principles and guidelines of the *General Catechetical Directory* approved by Paul VI on March 18, 1971. The *General Directory* drew together and organized principles and guidelines for catechesis* for the Universal Church.* It emphasized the Church's concern that the faith* of Catholics be informed and living, and it urged Bishops' Conferences* to prepare national directories.

The American *Directory,* subtitled *Sharing the Light of Faith,* was one of the first national directories to appear. It deals with many aspects of catechesis, including the Liturgy.* It gives a fine summary of Liturgy and Catechesis in Chapter VI: Catechesis for a Worshiping Community. *See also* CATECHESIS AND LITURGY.

SHARING THE LIGHT OF FAITH
National Catechetical Directory for Catholics of the United States

National Conference of Catholic Bishops (NASH-uhn-uhl; NASH-nuhl; KON-f[uh-]ruhn[t]s uhv KATH-[uh-]lik BISH-uhps). Among the general principles in the *Constitution on the Sacred Liturgy** is the establishment of local Bishops' Conferences.* In the United States this group is called the National Conference of Catholic Bishops. Throughout the *Constitution* this same group is referred to frequently, indicating its duties and obligations, such as establishing liturgical and music commissions,* making artistic decisions, adaptations, vernacular translations, and carrying out many other activities related to the Liturgy.* In matters of Liturgy and liturgical books,* its decisions have the force of ecclesiastical law. Its membership includes the local Ordinaries* and their associate bishops,* who not only decide liturgical matters but also express statements of public policy on various matters of concern for Church* life. Closely related in some fashion to the Liturgy among these concerns are religious education and priestly formation.

Native Customs (NAY-tiv KUHS-tuhmz). Since the Universal Church* has a mission to spread the Gospel* message throughout the entire world, each member of the Church is called through Baptism* to help fulfill this overall mission of the Church. Dedicated individuals are sent as missionaries to those parts where the word has not yet become known. Priests* and laypeople* alike work in foreign cultures and countries, among the unchurched, evangelizing wherever possible. Others contribute medical supplies, goods, financial aid, and through prayer* and personal sacrifice sup-

port missionary activity. To ensure an easy transition for these people into the Church, special regulations are granted so that customs and traditions found in various regions of the world may be adapted to the various Christian rituals and rites as long as substantial unity with the Roman Rite* is preserved. Furthermore care must be taken that these native customs are not unalterably bound up with superstition and error. *See also* ADAPTATION, LITURGICAL; WORLD MISSION DAY.

Native Music (NAY-tiv MYOO-zik). Especially in mission territories, where people have their own musical traditions, these should be suitably adapted in accordance with their native genius to develop a proper attitude of worship* among the people and thus toward religion as a whole. Even in the United States, so rich in many cultural and ethnic heritages, new liturgical music in accordance with these cultures should be encouraged and used to enrich the Church's musical repertory. *See also* MUSIC.

Nativity of Christ. *See* CHRISTMAS.

Nave (nayv). The main body of the church reserved for worshipers is the central open space, distinct from the sanctuary* or choir* and extending to the rear of the church. It also includes the side aisles, should there be pillars, and the crossing transepts.* Less frequent use of pillars occurs today in modern construction, with emphasis on width rather than length for developing a greater sense of community among the congregation.* Derived from the Latin word for ship, nave symbolizes the Church battling toward its eternal goal. *See also* CHURCHES; TRANSEPT.

Nehemiah, The Book of (nee-[h]uh-MAI-uh, thuh buk uhv). The sixteenth Book of the Old Testament* and last of the Chronicler's four-volume work that includes 1 and 2 Chronicles* and Ezra.* It recounts the postexilic reconstruction of the walls of Jerusalem in 52 days

under Nehemiah, the cupbearer of the Persian King Artaxerxes I (464-423 B.C.). Nehemiah was appointed governor of Jerusalem in 444 B.C. and remained there for twelve years. After a short absence he returned for a second term. Nehemiah also established a reformation that brought the people, the aliens among them, and the priests back to the religious heritage of God's chosen. The Book makes clear that Nehemiah was the man of action who rebuilt the walls and introduced many administrative reforms while Ezra was the great religious reformer who succeeded in establishing the Law* as the condition of the returned community.

Liturgical use: In the *Roman Missal,** this Book is read on the 3rd Sunday in Ordinary Time* (C) as well as on Wednesday and Thursday of the 26th Week (I). It is also used in the *Rite of Penance** and in the Institution of Readers.* In the *Liturgy of the Hours,** it occurs only in the alternate Two-Year Cycle of Readings* from Friday of the 12th Week through Friday of the 13th Week. *Meaning:* Prayer* and work* go together. Recourse to God in prayer during times of trial is good. However, it must be accompanied by working to do God's will—even if that includes bearing sufferings and catastrophes. Christian leadership must be courageous, resourceful, and built on prayer. Laypeople like Nehemiah also must labor to carry out God's design for them.

Neo-Pentecostalism (nee-oh-pent-i-KAHS-tuh-liz-uhm; -KAWS-). Sometimes called the Catholic Charismatic Renewal, this movement emphasizes a spiritual experience of power from the Holy Spirit* that sanctifies and exhibits itself externally through charismatic gifts. This group assumes that the Holy Spirit is at work in the world sanctifying us and we should be expecting such reaction to His influence. It began in the late sixties at Duquesne University, Pittsburgh, and at the University of Notre Dame. Since then, it has spread widely throughout the states; national and international meetings have occurred, one at Rome in 1975, where it received approval from Pope Paul VI.

Manifestations of its members' spiritual renewal are taste for prayer,* praising God, contemplation,* much reading of Scripture,* and alertness to the grace* of the Holy Spirit. During their meetings, Charismatic prayer is essential; the gift of tongues, considered a gift of prayer and not communication, occurs during their prayer meetings, but in a truly self-possessed manner. The Spirit's presence and power are conveyed through the correlative gift of interpretation. Another identifying feature is the laying on of hands which brings peace,* joy,* or love* from the Holy Spirit. Such baptism in the Spirit brings about a moral transformation, a sense of rebirth, with a suffusion of the Spirit.

This type of Pentecostalism has deepened the spirituality of its members, with a more intense prayer life, a love for the Scriptures, a true sense of God's presence as Father, an emancipation from sin, attachment to the Eucharist* and devotion to Mary,* and strong fidelity to the Church.* Contrary to other Pentecostals, these Catholics reject rebaptism, in favor of Sacramental Baptism,* accept the Church and her teaching office, reject the certitude of one's salvation,* and do not profess Biblical fundamentalism. *See also* PENTECOSTAL MOVEMENT.

Neophyte (NEE-uh-fait). Although this term sometimes refers to a novice or postulant in the Religious community or even a newly ordained priest,* its primary use today is to designate the newly baptized person who is in the final period of Christian initiation, the postbaptismal catechesis or mystagogia.* Hence no longer are such persons catechumens. They used to wear their white garment during the octave of Easter* or Pentecost* while completing their catechesis.

Nereus, St. (NEER-ee-uhs). 1st century. A converted Roman soldier who left military service because of Christianity; an ancient cult* still honors his relics* in the Basilica* on Via Ardeatina. *Liturgical celebration:* May 12 (Opt. Mem.); *theme:* fortitude in professing the Faith.*

Neums (nyoomz; noomz). The signs, usually square in shape and sometimes rhomboidal, giving the notation of Gregorian Chant.* Positioned on a staff of four horizontal lines, they may be joined in groups of two or more; all the notes of a group are sung or played on one and the same syllable. *See also* GREGORIAN CHANT.

New Fire. *See* EASTER VIGIL.

New Testament. *See* TESTAMENT, NEW.

New Year's Day. *See* SOLEMNITY OF MARY, MOTHER OF GOD.

Nicene Creed. *See* PROFESSION OF FAITH.

Nicholas, St. (NIK-uh-luhs). 4th century. Bishop of Myra, Asia Minor, a run-down diocese,* Nicholas is distinguished for his zeal, holiness, charity, and liberality. Solicitous for the young, he is venerated as Patron of Bakers, Brewers, Brides, Children, Merchants, and Travelers as well as Patron of Greece. Apulia, Sicily, Lorraine and Russia. *Liturgical celebration*: De-

celebration: December 6 (Opt. Mem.); *theme*: genuine Christianity is joyous, loving, gift-giving.

Night Prayer (nait prayr). This last Hour of the Divine Office* is prayed before retiring for the day, at whatever hour of the night, even after midnight. In terminating the cycle of our daily prayers, it considers the themes of waking and sleep, death and life, sin and grace.* In preparing for rest, we beg the creator with filial confidence to watch over us like a faithful guardian. At first, Compline, as Night Prayer was called then, was a private prayer in monastic communities. Later it was said in common because Vespers,* the former name for Evening Prayer,* was said at an earlier time. It combined the evening spiritual reading, usually with a commentary and examination of conscience* with an hour of prayer based on the recitation of the Psalms.*

Structure

After the Introductory Verse,* an examination of conscience follows with or without one of the penitential rites as in the Mass.* Thereafter, an appropriate hymn* is sung. One or two Psalms that evoke confidence in God are recited. Thereupon there is a reading and the identical Response each day, *Into your hands*. The highpoint of the Hour is the Canticle of Simeon* with its antiphon*; the Concluding Prayer* and the Final Blessing* are standard for each day. In accord with ancient tradition, a hymn to Mary* concludes the Office.

Nihil Obstat (NEE-hil OHB-staht). An approval by a diocesan censor judging that a manuscript contains nothing detrimental to morals or Faith.* It must be given for liturgical books,* when it is usually written as *Concordat cum Originali*—which is the Latin for "Conforms to the Original" (usually a Latin volume). The date of approval together with the delegated censor is usually printed along with the Imprimatur,* which must be preceded by this approval. *See also* IMPRIMATUR.

Nine First Fridays. *See* FIRST FRIDAY DEVOTIONS.

Nocturnal Adoration. *See* ADORATION, EUCHARISTIC.

None. *See* DAYTIME PRAYER.

Norbert, St. (NOHR-buhrt). c.1080-1134. After reforming his life, Norbert became a monk and an itinerant preacher. Receiving land from a bishop* of France at Premontre he founded the Canon Regulars also known as Premonstratensians or Norbertines. As archbishop* of Magdeburg he effected reforms, continued preaching, and opposing heresy. He is the Patron of Bohemia. *Liturgical celebration:* June 6 (Opt. Mem.); *theme:* pastoral zeal in preaching leads a people to salvation.*

Norms. *See* LITURGICAL LAW, SOURCES OF.

North American Academy of Liturgy (nawrth uh-MER-uh-kuhn uh-KAD-uh-mee uhv LIT-uhr-jee). On the tenth anniversary of the publication of the *Constitution on* *the Sacred Liturgy,** seventy-five American liturgists met in December 1973 at the Franciscan Renewal Center in Scottsdale, Arizona, to discuss what progress liturgical reform had made since that time. The participants determined to form a professional society to serve as a continuing forum for similar exchanges, so in January of 1975 a definitive shape was given to this organization, which had opened its membership to Canadian participation.

The term academy is to signify its character as a learned society of professionals. They would be those who had developed expertise in any element of Liturgy,* such as music, ritual gesture,* architecture, administration, planning, and so forth. Attendees of the first two meetings were considered members; thereafter prospective members apply by having their names submitted and supported by a member. Although ecumenical in membership, it has received encouragement from the Bishops' Committee on the Liturgy.*

Because of its purpose, it does not consider itself duplicating any tasks or interfering in the work of other liturgical organizations within the Christian Churches of North America. Its threefold goal is: "(1) to provide channels for mutual professional assistance and for the sharing of methods and resources; (2) to provide technical information concerning recent developments in liturgical matters and research projects of its members; (3) to foster liturgical research, publication, and dialogue on a scholarly level, including exchanges with other religious traditions."

From these goals it is evident that the pastoral good of Churches is not its aim, yet the assumption is that the liturgical research by its members would contribute an important service to the pastoral ministry of the Churches. The group meets annually, usually the first week of the year.

North American Martyrs. *See* ISAAC JOGUES AND COMPANIONS, STS.

Nostra Aetate (NOHS-trah ay-TAH-tay). Latin title (from the first two words "In Our Age") of the *Declaration on the Relation of the Church to Non-Christian Religions* issued by the Second Vatican Council* on October 28, 1965. The document urges all Christians to promote fellowship with all non-Christians—such as tribal people, Hindus, Buddhists, Moslems, and Jews.

It states that the Church rejects nothing that is true and holy in "the teachings, rules of life, and *sacred ceremonies*" of other religions. Indeed, the Council mentions in an approving way the meditation* practiced in Hinduism. Therefore, it repudiates any type of discrimination and urges Catholics to enter into discussion and to collaborate with members of other religions. *See also* VATICAN COUNCIL, SECOND.

Notices. *See* ANNOUNCEMENTS.

Notifications. *See* LITURGICAL LAW, SOURCES OF.

Notitiae (noh-TEE-tsee-ay). A monthly journal, the official publication of the Sacred Congregation for Divine Worship and the Discipline of the Sacraments,* which includes reports on its activities. It prints significant documents dealing with the Liturgy,* appropriate studies and commentaries, and lists of official documents issued for various countries and of liturgical books* submitted to the Holy See.* It also gives replies to questions sent to the Congregation. Such replies are nonauthentic but worthy of being followed until official responses are given by the Congregation. *See also* LITURGICAL LAW, SOURCES OF.

Novenas (noh-VEE-nuhz). Nine successive days of public or private prayer* for a special intention, a special occasion, or in preparation for a feast.* Reminiscent of the nine days Mary and the disciples spent together in prayer between Ascension* and Pentecost,* this widespread and popular devotion* is not liturgical in character, but over the centuries it has been greatly indulgenced by the Church.* Currently only three public novenas are so recognized, namely the ones for Christmas,* Pentecost,* and the Immaculate Conception.* Private novenas continue to grow out of popular piety. *See also* PARALITURGY.

Novices (NOV-uhs-uhz). Persons admitted in a formal manner to a Religious Institute in preparation for the first temporary Religious Profession.* Clothed in the Religious habit for at least one full canonical year, they commonly undergo a period of formation and probation under the direction of a novice master or mistress, so that judgment as to their suitability as Religious can be made. *See also* INVESTITURE.

Nullity. *See* MARRIAGE.

Numbers, The Book of (NUHM-buhrz, thuh buk uhv). Fourth Book of the Old Testament* and of the Pentateuch (*see* DEUTERONOMY), which continues the story of the journey in the desert begun in Exodus.* It describes briefly the experiences of the Israelites for a period of thirty-eight years, from the end of their encampment at Sinai to their arrival at the border of the Promised Land. Numerous legal ordinances are interspersed in the account, making the Book a combination of law and history. The various events described clearly indicate the action of God, Who punishes the murmuring of the people by prolonging their stay in the desert, at the same time preparing them by this discipline to be His witnesses among the nations.

Liturgical use: In the *Roman Missal,** this Book is used on the 26th Sunday in Ordinary Time* (B), Monday through Thursday of the 18th Week (I), Monday of the 3rd Week of Advent,* Tuesday of the 5th Week of Lent,* Solemnity of Mary, Mother of God,* Triumph of the Cross,* and the Masses for Holy Orders* and the Beginning of the New Year. In the *Liturgy of the Hours,** it is said from Wednesday through Saturday of the 4th Week of Lent. *Meaning:* God is central to our lives. We should take comfort in relying on His power and might and be careful not to depart from Him. Our life is a pilgrimage, and the events of the Old Testament are an admonition to and an instruction for us.

Nunc Dimittis. *See* CANTICLE OF SIMEON.

Nuptial Blessing (NUHP-shuhl; -chuhl; BLES-ing). The formal blessing of spouses during their Marriage, given at Mass after the Lord's Prayer,* also during ceremonies outside of Mass and in mixed Marriages, even though one party may not be baptized. The priest* imposes the blessing with extended hands, using one of the forms chosen, praying for continued loyalty and fidelity between the couple and their continued growth in grace* and love*; furthermore it should impart to them the graces necessary to be good parents to the children God will send them. *See also* MARRIAGE.

Nuptial Mass. *See* MARRIAGE.

— O —

O Antiphons (oh AN-tuh-fuhnz). Seven antiphons,* each starting with the interjection "O," that consecutively lead off the Canticle of Our Lady* in Evening Prayer* during the Liturgy of the Hours* for the seven days preceding the vigil of Christmas,* December 17-23. Addressed to the Messiah* with an appeal that He come, each recognizes a Messianic attribute. Most of the texts can be derived from either prophetic or sapiential literature of the Old Testament.* The attributes used are: O Wisdom; O Sacred Lord; O Flower of Jesse's stem; O Key of David; O Radiant Dawn; O King of all the nations; O Emmanuel.

O Salutaris (oh sah-loo-TAH-rees). Latin title (from the first two words "O Saving") of a hymn* often sung during Benediction of the Blessed Sacrament.* It is composed

of the last two verses of *Verbum Supernum** ("The Heavenly Word"), one of the Eucharistic Hymns of St. Thomas.* It is also known by the first three words ("O Saving Victim") of the best-known English translation, which is given below:

O Saving Victim, opening wide
The gate of heaven to us below:
Our foes press on from every side;
Your aid supply; Your strength bestow.
To Your great Name be endless praise,
Immortal Godhead, One in Three!
O grant us endless length of days
With You in our true country.

See also EUCHARISTIC HYMNS OF ST. THOMAS; VERBUM SUPERNUM.

Obadiah, The Book of (oh-buh-DAI-uh, thuh buk uhv). Thirty-eighth and shortest Book of the Old Testament* (21 verses) and fourth of the Minor Prophets.* Nothing is known of the author, although his oracle against Edom, a long-standing enemy of Israel, indicates a date of composition around the 5th century B.C. His message is divided into two parts: (a) Edom has been judged by the Lord and will incur destruction for its social injustice (1-9) because it has taken part in the fall of Israel (10-14); (b) indeed, the Day of the Lord will come for all nations and Israel will be restored (15-21).

Liturgical use: In the *Roman Missal,** this Book finds no place. In the *Liturgy of the Hours,** it occurs only in the alternate Two-Year Cycle of Readings* on the 18th Sunday in Ordinary Time* (II). *Meaning:* Social injustice is just as abhorrent to God as personal sin. Yet God is always faithful to His promises, even when His people are unfaithful to Him and unworthy of them. Those who repent as Israel did will be blessed. Those who remain in indifference and rebellion as Edom did will incur the same fate—separation from God.

Objects, Liturgical. *See* CHURCH FURNISHINGS.

Oblations. *See* OFFERINGS.

Obligatory Memorial. *See* MEMORIALS.

Occurrence (uh-KUR-uhn[t]s). When two or more celebrations meet on the same day, occurrence takes place. It may be perpetual, when two feasts* always fall on the same date, as can occur with Optional Memorials.* In that case, one is chosen to be celebrated and the other omitted. Accidental occurrence may be frequent because of an intertwining of the two cycles, temporal* and sanctoral.* In such situations, the celebration that holds the higher rank according to the table of liturgical days is observed.

If Evening Prayer* is celebrated with the faithful,* when the Mass* would be of the Sunday, then the Evening Prayer would also be of the Sunday. Should a Solemnity* be impeded by a liturgical day that takes precedence over it, it is then transferred to the closest day not having a feast listed among the first eight in the table of liturgical days. Sundays can be displaced only by Solemnities or by Feasts of the Lord; Sundays in Advent,* Lent* and Easter* take precedence even over these, and in that case Solemnities are celebrated the preceding Saturday. Celebrations other than these described above are not observed in a year when there is a case of accidental occurrence. *See also* ORDER OF PRECEDENCE.

Octavarium Romanum (ohk-tah-VAH-ree-oom roh-MAH-noom). (1) Former liturgical book* that contained the Readings* for Matins* to be recited on days within the octaves* of Patrons and Titulars deprived of an octave in the *Roman Breviary.** Promulgated by Urban VIII in 1623, this book gradually went out of use and was for all practical purposes suppressed in 1955 by the simplification of rubrics for the Office. (2) A book that contained the complete Office for every day during one of the three octaves formerly found in the Liturgical Year*: Christmas,* Easter,* and Pentecost.* Since the publication of the *Liturgy of the Hours,** no octavarium has yet appeared.

Octave (OK-tiv; -tayv). The liturgical celebration of a feast* for eight days—on the day itself and the seven following days. This practice has its origins in the Old Testament* celebration of the Passover and the Feast of Tabernacles. Later in the Middle Ages many feasts had octaves, but they obscured the proper celebration of the Liturgical Year.* Eventually they were all suppressed except for the octaves of Easter* and Christmas.* Each has its own rules; the one for Easter does not allow any other celebration whereas that of Christmas allows the celebration of feasts and the Solemnity of Mary, Mother of God* on its octave day.

Offering (AW-fuhr-ing). The part of the Eucharistic Prayer* that follows the Anamnesis* and expresses the fact that the Church* here and now assembled offers the Victim to the Father* in the Holy Spirit.* The Church's intention is that the faithful* should not only offer the spotless Victim but also learn to offer themselves and daily to be drawn into ever more perfect union,

through Christ the Mediator, with the Father and with each other, so that at last God will be in all.

The idea of offering was included in the Offertory Prayers of the *Missal of Pius V,** which included sacrificial terminology and at times were even understood as anticipating the meaning of the Eucharistic Prayer. In the new *Roman Missal,** these have been dropped, and the prayers that make up the same section, now entitled the Preparation of the Gifts,* focus on praise rather than offering.

Right after the Anamnesis in Eucharistic Prayer I,* which petitions that God will accept the Bread of Life and the Cup from the many gifts He has given us, there is a request that the offerings may be accepted as were the sacrificial gifts of Abel,* Abraham,* and Melchizedek.* This is followed by a petition that the sacrifice may be taken to the altar* in heaven.* The same theme is also found in all the other Eucharistic Prayers. What is offered is the Church's Sacrifice of Praise, which is the Sacramental Action of the offering made once and for all by Christ. *See also* EUCHARISTIC PRAYER; OFFERINGS; OFFERTORY.

Offerings (AW-fuhr-ingz). Those gifts brought up by the people at the Preparation of the Gifts,* formerly called the Offertory.* Though in the past they may have included gifts for the poor, now commonly they are only the bread and wine consecrated by the priest* during the sacrifice, and on Sundays, the collection.*

Offertory (AW-fuhr-tohr [tawr]-ee). Formerly, this was the beginning of the Mass of the Faithful,* when the gifts were brought to the altar* and offered for the sacrifice. The word "offer" can mean simply to present, but in its stronger and more technical sense it means to immolate. The new Order of Mass takes cognizance of the fact that the point of immolation has not been reached at the Preparation of the Gifts* and thus avoids this terminology. The actual offering occurs during the Eucharistic Prayer.* *See also* OFFERING; OFFERINGS; PREPARATION OF THE GIFTS.

Offertory Antiphon (AW-fuhr-tohr [tawr]-ee AN-tuh-fuhn). A verse from the Bible* that the choir* sang at Mass* during the procession* at the Preparation of the Gifts.* With the disappearance of the procession only the Scriptural Verse or Antiphon* remained, and it was one of the Processional Chants* that were part of the Proper* and belonged to the people. The new Order of Mass specifies that this Antiphon is to be omitted if it is not sung. Hence, it is not included in the typical edition* of the *Roman Missal** or in vernacular editions such as the *Sacramentary** in English-speaking countries. The Latin Antiphon may be found in the *Roman Gradual.** The Offertory Antiphon has thus given way to the Offertory Song.* *See also* OFFERTORY SONG; PROCESSIONAL CHANTS.

Offertory Procession (AW-fuhr-tohr [tawr]-ee pruh-SESH-uhn). The third of five processions at Mass.* Historical evidence describes this procession with the gifts from the 4th century. It went through various phases, sometimes with gifts in kind and certainly after the 11th century with a money offering. The faithful* walked up to the sanctuary where the priest* received their gifts. Nothing expresses personal participation* in the sacrifice more readily than such a procession with gifts as a reminder that through this ritual the Mass becomes the sacrifice of all those present. The gifts brought to the altar also embrace all the joys and sorrows, labors and sufferings of the whole assembly.*

While Gallican influences embellished the rite, recent reforms have made it more subordinate. Now it is truly the symbolic procession of representatives of the assembly presenting the bread and wine with the money offering and is part of the Preparation of the Gifts.*

Offertory Song (AW-fuhr-tohr [tawr]-ee song). Musical accompaniment to the Offertory Procession.* Originally, Psalms* were sung antiphonally by two sections of a choir.* Later the singing became responsorial with a solo singer using an elaborate melody, being answered by the whole choir. Eventually after the Offertory Procession declined (10th century) the Offertory Song really became a rather ornate artistic polyphonic piece. Today a vernacular* song, which should express joyful giving, or praise or rejoicing, is chosen, preferably one that relates to the theme of the Mass*; it is more frequently called the Presentation Song.

The choice of texts for the Offertory Song is governed by the same rule as the Entrance Song.* If there is no Offertory Song, the Offertory Antiphon* found in the *Roman Gradual** (but not in the *Sacramentary**) is omitted.

The Offertory Song need not speak of bread and wine or of offering. The proper function of the Offertory Song is rather to accompany and celebrate the communal aspects of the procession. The text, therefore, may be an appropriate song of praise or of rejoicing in keeping with the liturgical season. Those texts are not acceptable which speak of the offering completely apart from the action of Christ.

In general, during the most important seasons of the Church Year,* Easter,* Lent,* Christmas,* and Advent,* it is preferable that most songs used during the Offertory be seasonal in character. During the remainder of the Church Year, however, topical songs may be used during the Offertory Procession, provided that these texts do not conflict with the Paschal character of every Sunday.*

Office, Cathedral. *See* CATHEDRAL OFFICE.

Office, Divine. *See* LITURGY OF THE HOURS.

Office for the Dead (AW-fuhs; OF-uhs; fawr thuh ded). A diversified rendition of the Liturgy of the Hours* celebrated on All Souls* Day. Originally it began in the 7th century with only the then Matins,* Lauds,* and Vespers.* Pius X* added the Little Hours, that is, the Daytime Prayer,* and eventually in 1971 it conformed completely with the *Liturgy of the Hours.** Centuries ago this votive Office would be prayed in addition to the Office of the day. This Office is recited, in whole or in part, at a funeral especially of a cleric* or a Religious.* Where the Office for the Dead is recited by law or custom, whether at the funeral rites or apart from them, it may still be celebrated out of devotion. Recently a wake service in the vernacular* patterned on the Office has been well received and is recommended in the current *Rite of Funerals.**

Many Religious Orders substitute this Office for the Dead for the usual Office of the day in Ordinary Time,* several times a year, for their deceased members and benefactors. A Mass* will also be offered that day for the same intention.

Office of Readings (AW-fuhs; OF-uhs; uhv REED-ingz). Originally called Matins, it derived from the offering of prayer* at midnight by the early Christians. They would meet in church and sing Psalms* until dawn when the public morning prayer of Lauds* was celebrated. Eventually the two Hours were amalgamated into one and said together either at night or very early in the morning. Priests* were allowed to anticipate Matins the previous afternoon. With the revision of the *Liturgy of the Hours,** this Office of Readings has the character of nocturnal praise but may be recited at any hour of the day, and it too may be anticipated the preceding evening after Evening Prayer.*

This Hour, although it contains the usual parts of the other Hours, such as Psalms, Hymn,* and Concluding Prayer,* consists primarily of Readings from Scripture* and Church writings. Thus by presenting the many riches of the Word of God,* and the application of it by the best of spiritual writers, this spiritual reading should benefit all the members of the Church.*

This reading is not so much a proclamation to move us to worship as it is a *lectio divina,** a reading and meditating of the Word of God. The Readings are primarily didactic. They are meant to be listened to in a spirit of openness and to shape our thinking as the Spirit wills.

We cannot approach this Word as mere spectators. We are not encountering a "piece of paper" or a "dead letter." We are attaining a personal encounter with the living God Who addresses us and wants us to respond to Him.

Structure

When the Office of Readings occurs before Morning Prayer,* it is preceded by the Invitatory*; otherwise the usual Introductory Verse* starts the hour. A Hymn appropriate to the time of the day should be chosen. The Psalmody* consists of either three Psalms* or three sections of longer Psalms. During the octaves* of Easter* and Christmas,* on Solemnities* and Feasts,* the Antiphons and Psalms are proper. Otherwise they are taken from the current week of the Psalter. A transitional verse is provided between the Psalms and the Readings. The First Reading is always from Scripture, whereas the Second may be patristic, or from an ecclesiastical writer, or is hagiographical.*

One principle in the reform was to extend the Biblical Readings in the Office of Readings, so they follow a pattern as explained in the *General Instruction of the Liturgy of the Hours* except for the Solemnities and Feasts that have Biblical Readings proper to them. The Second Reading and Responsory are in the *Liturgy of the Hours* or in the optional *Lectionary* (fifth volume—not yet issued) and are found in either the Proper of the Season* or the Proper of the Saints.* In the Proper of the Season, these are usually patristic writings or those of other ecclesiastical writers; in the Proper of the Saints, they are mostly hagiographical. On Solemnities, Feasts, during the octaves of Christmas and Easter, and on Sundays outside of Lent,* the Te Deum* is sung or said. The Prayer proper to the day concludes the Office of Readings, followed ordinarily by the acclamation: "Let us praise the Lord. And give Him thanks." *See also* READINGS; VIGIL.

Oil of Catechumens (oil uhv kat-uh-KYOO-muhnz). Oil, blessed by the Ordinary* during the Chrism Mass on Holy Thursday,* or by the priest* before anointing under certain conditions, is used to anoint the catechumens* during their initiation. Usually it is olive oil, but a vegetable oil is permitted. Besides its use in Baptism,* it is also employed during a coronation of Christian monarchs and to anoint the hands of priests at ordination.*

Oil of the Sick (oil uhv thuh sik). The olive oil blessed by the Ordinary* on Holy Thursday* to be used in the anointing of the sick. Recent legislation allows vegetable oil, and the blessing may be done by an authorized priest*—in an emergency, by any priest.

Oil Stocks (oil stoks). The phials or vessels in which the holy oils blessed on Holy Thursday* during the Chrism Mass* are kept. They are usually stored in a case with

three compartments labeled to fit the oil it contains. The oils are renewed each year and are preferably to be kept locked in the ambry.* However, the oil of the sick* may be kept personally by each priest* for cases of emergency according to the new Canon Law (1003:3).

Oils. *See* HOLY OILS.

Old Testament. *See* TESTAMENT, OLD.

Opening Prayer (OHP-uh-ning prayr). The oration by the celebrant* that concludes the Introductory Rites* of the Mass.* The mood, focus, and theme of each particular Mass are summarized in and through this prayer. With arms outstretched the president invites the

community to prayer, and after a sufficient period of silence for them to truly formulate petitions, he officially leads them in prayer. This solemn summary by the celebrant of the corporate prayer of the congregation* was formerly entitled the Collect, since it gathered together all the aspirations of the assembly.

The content and structure of the oration is unvarying. It begins with an address or invocation to the Father,* followed by praise of Him or reference to some Divine attribute or act as reason for the prayer; the petition, short, simple, and definite, usually supported by a motive, is of general nature since each individual has already formulated a particular petition during the previous silence.

The concluding doxology* offers the prayer to the Father through the priestly mediation of His Son and in unity with the Holy Spirit.* The congregation's assent is voiced with the "Amen"* to the prayer spoken by the celebrant in their name. The word is a Biblical affirmation, meaning "so may it be," and signifies ratification and acceptance.

The older Opening Prayers are truly notable for their preciseness of doctrine, aesthetic expression in a calm religious sense, together with genuinely human understanding. With all this, they are pithy of phrase and harmonious in diction. Such excellence causes considerable difficulty in translating the prayer into the vernacular.* The Prayer over the Gifts* and the Prayer after Communion* show a similar theological and literary pattern, yet with differences according to their function.

Optatam Totius (ohp-TAH-tahm toh-TSEE-oos). Latin title (from the first two words "Wished-for [Renewal] of the Whole [Church]") of the *Decree on Priestly Formation* issued by the Second Vatican Council* on October 28, 1965. The document points out that the whole training of seminarians must have as its objective to fashion genuine pastors of souls having as their model Jesus Christ—Teacher, Priest, and Shepherd. Their preparation should be aimed at the ministry of the Word—that they may grow in understanding of God's Word,* in possessing it by meditation,* and in expressing it in word and life.

It should also be aimed at the ministry of worship* and sanctification—that by prayer* and sharing in the celebration of the Liturgy* (especially the Eucharist* and the Liturgy of the Hours*) they may carry out the work of salvation* through the Eucharistic Sacrifice and the Sacraments.* Finally, it should be aimed at the pastoral ministry—that they may come to learn how to be the representative of Christ Who came not "to be served but to serve and to give His life as a ransom for many" (Mk 10:45). *See also* VATICAN COUNCIL, SECOND.

Optional Memorials. *See* MEMORIALS.

Options (OP-shuhnz). In the reform of the Liturgy,* explicit norms were set up for options. Without these it would not be possible to adapt the Liturgy to the various cultures throughout the world. The basic rule is from the *Constitution on the Sacred Liturgy* (no. 22): "No other person, not even a priest,* may add, remove, or change anything in the Liturgy on his own authority." However, freedom of choice is allowed in certain instances. Some examples follow.

(1) In the Liturgy of the Word,* no one is permitted to substitute readings from sacred or secular authors. However, aside from those assigned for Sundays, weekdays, and feasts,* many others are available for use when celebrating the Sacraments* or on other special occasions. One should choose texts most fitting to the particular celebration for Masses* with special groups, as long as these come from an authorized *Lectionary.**

(2) Many options are given for the sources for singing, especially the Entrance Antiphon* and Communion Antiphon,* and for other sections of the Mass. The types of music* should fit the culture of the people, so that congregational singing results. Music is to fit the spirit of the liturgical service, so that the members of the assembly* may be attentive to the service and that their sentiments will be truly prayerful. (*See also* MUSIC.)

(3) The choice of prayers (Opening Prayer*; Prayer over the Gifts*; Prayer after Communion*) is very broad. In Ordinary Time* on weekdays, the options allowed are from any of the 34 weeks in Ordinary Time, from the Masses for Various Occasions* or Votive Masses.* Even on Memorials,* the Opening Prayer may be from the Mass itself or the Common*; the Prayer over the Gifts and the Prayer after Communion, if not proper,* may be from the Common or even the weekday of the current season.*

(4) Admonitions* by the presider are certainly proper before the celebration begins to introduce the Mass, to comment on the Liturgy of the Word before the Readings, to introduce the Eucharistic Prayer* before the Preface,* and to conclude the entire service before the Dismissal.* These should be succinct and to the point.

(5) The General Intercessions* are a prayer of the people in their priestly function of interceding for all humanity. These should be included in all Masses. Although the sequence of intentions is regulated (for the needs of the Church, public authorities, those in need, for the local community), still the wording of these can be quite creative and varied from day to day. Naturally in particular celebrations such as Marriages* and Funerals,* the intercessions can refer more explicitly to the occasion.

(6) Several areas of the Eucharistic Celebration allow a wide variety of options. For instance, there are nine Eucharistic Prayers*; the Greetings* at the beginning of Mass

are quite varied; the Penitential Rite,* especially the third form, allows many opportunties for adapting it to suit the specific occasion; there is a variety of Alleluia Verses* for each season of the year and for many of the commons of the Saints*; the Final Blessing* has three options.

(7) In the Office of Readings* during Ordinary Time only on certain occasions for good reason one may choose readings different from those provided, e.g., during retreats, pastoral gatherings, prayers for Christian unity, etc. One may interchange the First and Second Readings* during the same season as long as they are taken from the *Liturgy of the Hours** or the alternate Two-Year Cycle of Readings* and *Optional Lectionary.* During weekdays, even outside of Ordinary Time, a semicontinuous reading from the Fathers* of the Church is allowed as long as it fits into the liturgical and Biblical context.

(8) Sunday's Psalms* from one week may be substituted for the Sunday Psalms of a different week, particularly when an Hour is celebrated with a congregation. For pastoral or spiritual reasons, Psalms for a specific day may be interchanged with others from the same Hour on a different day.

(9) Except on Sundays of the seasons of Advent,* Lent,* and Easter,* Ash Wednesday,* Holy Week,* the Octave of Easter, November 2, and Solemnities,* a votive Office may be celebrated in whole or in part. A good example would be a local feast,* the external solemnity of a Saint,* or a pilgrimage.

(10) When Optional Memorials are permitted, the office of any Saint listed that day in the *Martyrology,** or in an approved appendix, may be celebrated as a Memorial.

From December 17 to Christmas,* during its octave, and on weekdays of Lent, no Memorials are celebrated in the ordinary fashion. If desired, in the Office of Readings, after the Second Reading, the proper Reading for the Saint with its Responsory may follow, and one concludes with the prayer of the Saint. At both Morning Prayer* and Evening Prayer,* one may omit the ending of the Concluding Prayer and say the Saint's antiphon and prayer. This prayer of the Saint may be substituted for the Opening Prayer at Mass.

In Ordinary Time on Saturdays, when Optional Memorials are permitted, the Mass of the Blessed Virgin* may be celebrated with its own proper Reading.

Opus Dei (OH-poos DAY-ee). (1) A literal translation would be "the work of God." Liturgically it has always meant the Divine Office,* the obligation to recite it by those in Holy Orders* or in Religious* Orders.

(2) A worldwide association of laity* who live intensely spiritual lives in various situations; however they do not live in community or take vows. Founded in 1928, it received the Church's* approval in 1950. Priests* may also belong to this society. Besides charitable cen-

ters in underprivileged areas, it provides centers for conferences, nursing schools and clinics, and technical schools for workers and farmers.

Orate Fratres. *See* PRAY, BRETHREN.

Oratio super Populum. *See* PRAYER OVER THE PEOPLE.

Oration. *See* PRAYER.

Oratory (AWR-uh-tawr-ee; -tohr-ee; OR-). A place of prayer* set aside by the Ordinary* for the celebration of all liturgical functions and devotional exercises unless the liturgical laws forbid them or the Ordinary himself limits them. It is so designated for the use of a specific community or group of faithful* and any others that the competent superior will allow. A private chapel is a similar place of prayer, but for the use only of a private person or his/her household. Solemn public worship is not to be celebrated in it. *See also* BASILICA; CHAPEL; CHURCHES.

Order of Christian Funerals. *See* FUNERAL RITES AND CEREMONIES.

Order of Crowning an Image of the Blessed Virgin Mary. *See* MARY, BLESSED VIRGIN—ORDER OF CROWNING AN IMAGE.

Order of Mass. *See* MASS, ORDER OF.

Order of Precedence (AWRD-uhr uhv PRES-uhd-uhn[t]s; pri-SEED-uhn[t]s). Number fifty-nine of the *Roman Calendar** is the table of liturgical days in their order of precedence. The first section lists Solemnities,* the second Feasts,* the third Memorials.* After the major Solemnities pertaining to Christ's Life and Death,* including Sundays of Advent,* Lent,* Easter,* Holy Week,* and the octave of Easter,* come the Solemnities in the ordinary calendar and then proper Solemnities. Thereafter come the Feasts of Our Lord, other Sundays, Feasts of the Blessed Mother, the Saints,* and then the proper Feasts followed by the weekdays in privileged seasons. Lastly follow the Obligatory Memorials* and the Optional Memorials* and then the ferial* days. Number fifty-nine should be consulted for details concerning more exact precedence. *See also* CONCURRENCE; OCCURRENCE.

Orders, Holy. *See* HOLY ORDERS.

Orders, Minor. *See* MINOR ORDERS.

Ordinals (AWRD-nuhlz; -uhn-uhlz). Originally manuals giving the ritual* and rubrics* for liturgical ceremonies. They are important for the history of the Roman Rite* between the 6th and the 15th centuries. Today the name is given to the ritual book used in conferring Holy Orders.*

Ordinary (AWRD-[uh]n-er-ee). (1) The cleric* who has ordinary jurisdiction* in both the internal and the external forums. Local Ordinaries enjoy territorial jurisdiction. In exempt Religious Orders major superiors are personal or Religious Ordinaries with jurisdiction only over those individuals subordinate to them. (*See also* BISHOP.)

(2) The portion of the Liturgy, in contradistinction to the Proper,* that has comparatively few changes. (a) In the *Liturgy of the Hours,** the section that contains the unchanging parts of each Hour. (b) Ordinary of the Mass. *See* MASS, ORDINARY OF THE.

Ordinary Time (AWRD-[uh]n-er-ee taim). The name given to the part of the Liturgical Year* that does not fall within one of the major seasons (Advent,* Christmas,* Lent,* and Easter*) and does not observe any specific aspect of the Mystery* of Christ. It numbers thirty-three or thirty-four weeks (depending on the date of Easter) and is assigned to two periods of the year: (1) from the day after the Feast of the Baptism of the Lord* to the Tuesday before Ash Wednesday* inclusive and (2) from the Monday after Pentecost* to Evening Prayer I* of the First Sunday of Advent exclusive.

During this time the Church* continues to celebrate our Lord's Resurrection*—but in its application to our earthly lives. The time after the Baptism covers the beginning of Christ's preaching, His Baptism, and His first manifestation. The time after Pentecost covers Christ's Public Ministry of healing and preaching.

In contrast to the major seasons of the Church Year, which celebrate the various moments of the History of Salvation* and take on their coloration, Ordinary Time unfolds Sunday by Sunday bereft of any particular celebration, except for a few feasts of devotion or of Saints.* It is characterized by two themes: that of the Sunday and that of the Church.

Every *Sunday* is a little weekly Easter just as Easter is a great annual Sunday. Its name (in Latin) derives from *Dominus,* which means "Lord"—a title that the primitive Church bestowed on Jesus with respect to His Resurrection.

Sunday is thus the day on which we celebrate the victory of Jesus through His Cross.* But it is not a question merely of recalling a past event. With great joy* and faith* we celebrate the deed of the Resurrection, and at the same time Jesus gathers us around Him, present among His own, who have come together to listen to His Word* and celebrate His Eucharist.* And we become filled with the desire for Jesus' final coming in glory*; we

await the day on which He will come with His elect to celebrate the eternal Passover.

Each Sunday is thus a "feast" that is still incomplete. It is a joyous glimpse and timid anticipation of the life that will be ours when, united with God, we will be together in heaven.

This Season also introduces us in a special way into the *Mystery of the Church,* which was born on the day of Pentecost and is laboriously built up in our history.

We celebrate the barrier-ridden journey of the Church Militant* toward that final goal when we will all be members of the Church Triumphant* in heaven. Hence, the last Sunday of the Church Year is dominated by the thought of the end of the world and concludes with a vision of Christ's universal Kingship and the glory of all the Saints.*

Ordinary Time is thus a period of growth in the Faith* for all who follow the Liturgy.* It is a time for accentuating all the Christian virtues.* We are aided in this silent and gradual spiritual growth by the Holy Spirit.* It is He Who helps us live each Sunday, and each day, to the full. It is He Who makes of our seemingly ordinary lives *an eternal offering to the glory of God!*

Ordination (awrd-[uh]n-AY-shuhn). The liturgical act of conferring Holy Orders* upon a candidate, thus bestowing upon him an ecclesiastical office in order to minister to the Church.* The three orders are the diaconate, presbyterate, and episcopacy, which are granted to the individual by the laying on of hands* and the consecratory formula, for these two elements constitute the essential Sacramental Sign.*

An outline of the rite for ordination of deacons* and priests* is very similar: after the Liturgy of the Word,* there is a calling of the candidates, their presentation, and their election by the priests and the people. Following a Homily,* the examination of the candidates and their promise of obedience occur. Thereupon an invitation to prayer continues the service and the Litany of the Saints* is sung. The laying on of hands and the prayer of consecration follow. Then the deacon is invested with stole* and dalmatic,* is presented with the Book of Gospels,* and receives the kiss of peace.* The Mass proceeds with the Liturgy of the Eucharist.*

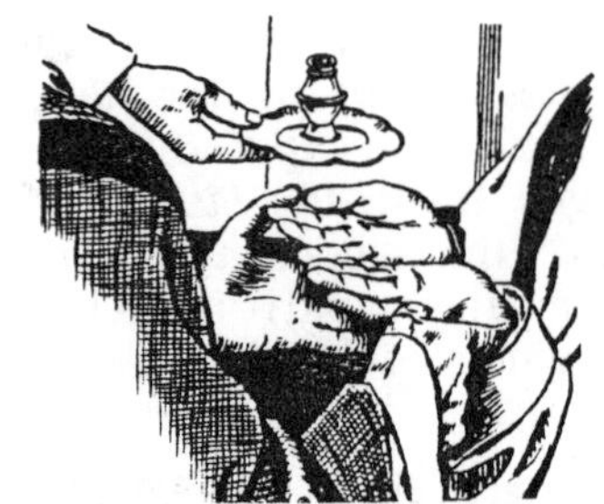

For the priest, there is investiture with the stole* and chasuble,* the anointing of the hands, the presentation of the gifts, and the Sign of Peace.* Again the Mass continues with the Liturgy of the Eucharist.

For episcopal ordination, after the Liturgy of the Word, the hymn to the Holy Spirit* is sung, and then there is a presentation of the bishop-elect, the apostolic letter is read, and consent is given by the people. Following the Homily, examination of the candidate, the invitation to prayer, the Litany of the Saints, the laying on of hands and the Book of Gospels, and then the prayer of consecration occur. Thereupon the bishop's head is anointed; he is presented with the Book of Gospels, invested with ring,* miter,* and pastoral staff.* Then he is seated in a chair to signify his authority; the Sign of Peace follows. The Mass continues with the Liturgy of the Eucharist, and at the end of Mass a special hymn of thanksgiving and a Solemn Blessing* conclude the ceremony. The Catholic Church has remained adamant in refusing to ordain women, although further study of this possibility continues. *See also* HOLY ORDERS; WOMEN AS MINISTERS.

Ordines Romani (AWR-dee-nez roh-MAH-nee). Literally, "Roman Orders," which during the Middle Ages referred to books containing directives for liturgical functions—in other words, a type of rituals. They originated in the needs of the clergy* of France to know how the ceremonies whose texts were in the Roman *Sacramentary* and *Lectionary* were carried out at Rome. Some 50 such *Ordines* have been distinguished divided into 10 sections and reducible to two families: (a) pure Roman and (b) Franco-Roman. The most important *Ordines* are: the first, which deals with the Papal Mass* in the 7th century; the eleventh, which describes the rites of the catechumenate*; and the fiftieth, also known as the *Ancient Roman Ordo,* which became the nucleus for the Roman-Germanic *Pontifical** of the 10th century. These *Ordines* are very important for the study of the Liturgy* in the medieval period.

Ordo (AWR-doh). (1) Ritual book describing the rites for the administration of a Sacrament* or another liturgical function, published by the Holy See.*

(2) The annual calendar that regulates the celebration of Mass* and the Liturgy of the Hours* for each day. Its purpose is to effect a uniform Liturgy* by giving proper directions for liturgical rites. Each diocese, or group of them, each Religious Order or Congregation, may have its own Ordo, though many may have only a supplement to the general Ordo.

Oremus. *See* LET US PRAY.

Organ (AWR-guhn). A keyboard musical instrument, the first to be approved and used regularly by the Church* in public worship.* The pipe organ was most popular, and only recently the pneumatic or electric organ gained some favor. Primarily all musical instruments,

the organ included, are to have only an ancillary role, namely to assist the singers and to provide interludes at the proper times. Music,* except to sustain the singing, is ordinarily forbidden during Advent* and Lent,* exceptions being the 3rd Sunday of Advent and the 4th Sunday of Lent, Holy Thursday* until the Gloria,* and Holy Saturday after the Gloria, Holy Days of Obligation* or some extraordinary Solemnity.* Although other musical instruments are allowed, the majestic tone of the organ is most suitable for Divine service. *See also* MUSIC; MUSIC, INSTRUMENTAL.

Orientalium Ecclesiarum (AW-ree-en-TAH-lee-oom ay-klay-zee-AH-room). Latin title (from the first two words "Of the Eastern Churches") of the *Decree on Eastern Catholic Churches* issued by the Second Vatican Council* on November 21, 1964. Intended as a complement to the *Decree on Ecumenism (Unitatis Redintegratio*)*, this document expresses the position and rights of the Eastern communities in the Catholic Church and reestablishes privileges and customs that have been abolished in the past. It also manifests the hope of the Council for a corporate reunion of the Eastern Churches presently separated from the Church of Rome.

The Council expresses its endorsement, praise, and hope for any needed reform of the discipline of the Sacraments* observed in the Eastern Churches and also of the practice connected with Sacramental celebration and administration. It lays down general rules for the control of Holy Days of Obligation,* a common date for Easter,* celebration of the Divine Praise, and the language to be used in liturgical services. Finally, it grants permission for intercommunion (along with the Sacraments of Penance* and Anointing*) between Catholics and those Eastern Churches that have valid orders but are separated from Rome. *See also* VATICAN COUNCIL, SECOND.

Orientation (awr-ee-en-TAY-shuhn; awr-ee-uhn-; ohr-). The practice or custom taken up by Christians of facing the East in prayer.* Since Christ lived in the East, and because the East was considered the cradle of human civilization, churches were erected with the apse* toward the East. When burying the dead, the lay person's feet were placed to the East. Eventually the East/West orientation of churches became impractical, and now Christians face the altar,* generally accepted as the symbol* of Christ.

Ornaments (AWR-nuh-muhnts). Those objects that encompass the material setting for Divine Worship.* Besides the clerical vestments,* it includes the appurtenances of the sanctuary* and altar.* *See also* ALTAR; ALTAR CLOTH; CANDLES AND LIGHTS; CANDLESTICKS; CHURCH FURNISHINGS; CROSS; VESTMENTS.

Orphrey (AWR-free). A strip of embroidery or painted symbols or images used in decorating ecclesiastical vestments,* probably originally employed to cover the seams or improve the appearance of borders. Though unessential they are still prominent parts of vestments.

Ostensorium. *See* MONSTRANCE.

Our Father. *See* LORD'S PRAYER.

Our Lady of Guadalupe (owr LAY-dee uhv GWAHD-uhl-oop). On December 9, 1531, Mary* the Virgin Mother of the true God appeared to an Aztec peasant, Juan Diego, on a hillside at Tepeyac, asking that a church be built there in her honor. When the bishop* demanded a sign, Mary told Juan to pick some roses, which should not be in bloom at that time, and bring them to the bishop. As he opened his cloak, the portrait of the Mother of God was miraculously painted on it and has remained brilliant, even now as the object of veneration at the shrine church in Guadalupe. The bishop built the first sanctuary* there, a suburb of Mexico City, and the devotion to Our Lady of Guadalupe spread to other parts of New Spain, especially southwestern United States and many Spanish colonies. Pius X* declared her the Patroness of all Latin America, and Pius XII called her "Queen of Mexico and Empress of the Americas."

Guadalupe is to Mexico and Americans what Lourdes and Fatima are to France and Portugal. She becomes the sign of God's presence and grace in the Americas and represents for all Americans the inculturation of the Gospel* in the New World. It was from Mexico that the missions of Texas, Arizona, New Mexico, and California developed. These Christian landmarks are honored as a rich legacy from Mexico, and consequently the Feast* of Our Lady of Guadalupe was chosen to be part of the Proper Calendar* for the United States in 1971 and raised from a Memorial* to the status of Feast in 1988. *Liturgical celebration:* December 12 (Feast); *theme:* the Mother of God is the Mother of the Americas and symbolizes the solidarity of the United States' Catholics with their compatriots of Mexico as well as Central and South America.

Our Lady of Lourdes. *See* MARY, BLESSED VIRGIN—FEASTS.

Our Lady of Mount Carmel. *See* MARY, BLESSED VIRGIN—FEASTS.

Our Lady of Sorrows. *See* MARY, BLESSED VIRGIN—FEASTS.

Our Lady of the Rosary. *See* MARY, BLESSED VIRGIN—FEASTS.

— P —

Paintings. *See* IMAGES.

Pall (pawl). (1) A square of linen, stiffened with starch, cardboard, or plastic, set on the chalice* to prevent dirt or insects from falling into it. With the advent of insecticides and air conditioning, its use has greatly diminished and is optional.

(2) An ample cloth covering, plain or ornamented, draped over the coffin at a funeral Mass.* Until recently it was purple or black, the color* of mourning, now ordinarily white, the color of resurrection* and hope*; usually it is decorated with baptismal symbols and/or a Cross,* for it is symbolic of the person having been clothed with Christ at Baptism,* and the promise of eternal life for each Christian. Consequently, even for veterans, the American flag should not be substituted for the pall at Mass. *See also* FLAGS.

Pallium (PAL-ee-uhm). A band of white cloth, woven from white wool of two lambs annually offered to the Holy Father on the feast* of St. Agnes,* worn over the chasuble* in the form of a collar, by the Pope,* patriarchs,* and archbishops.* This circular strip of white wool, about two and one-half inches wide, from which two short bands, made of the same material, hang down over the chest and the back, ending with black silk pendants, is decorated with six crosses of black taffeta, four placed in the circle and the two others in the hanging bands. Besides indicating a superior episcopal authority and dignity, it is also a symbol of communion with the Church.

Placed on the shoulders of the prelate,* the pallium symbolizes the profound humility of the Savior and the erring sheep that the Good Shepherd places on His shoulder to bring back to the flock. The four crosses in the circle symbolize the four cardinal virtues* of justice,* fortitude,* temperance,* and prudence*; the two hanging bands symbolize the active life of Martha* and the contemplative one of Mary.* In 1978 Paul VI restricted its use to metropolitan archbishops and the Latin patriarch in Jerusalem, who wear it at jurisdictional or Sacramental functions or ceremonies. Both Popes John Paul were invested with the pallium instead of the papal tiara.*

Palm Sunday. See PASSION SUNDAY.

Palms (pah[l]mz). Once blessed, palms become a Sacramental,* greatly revered by Christians and distributed to the People of God on Passion Sunday.* Branches from the date* bearing palm tree, greatly prized for its shelter, stately dignity, beauty, and shade, were carried as a symbol of victory and well-being in triumphal processions by Romans and Jews alike. The occasion of Christ's triumphant entry into Jerusalem, when such branches were strewn in His path, has brought them into decorative and liturgical use for Christian people. In the Psalms* (92:12-13) they symbolize the just person; in the Book

of Revelation* (7:9) they are related to martyrdom; in early Christian representations the Apostles* and Christ carried palms, a symbol of paradise. *See also* PASSION SUNDAY.

Pancras, St. (PAN-kruhs). ?-304? An orphan who suffered martyrdom at age fourteen in Rome and was buried in the cemetery* named after him. He is the Patron of Fidelity to Oaths. *Liturgical celebration:* May 12 (Opt. Mem.); *theme:* loyalty to baptismal vows.

Pange Lingua (PAHN-jay LEEN-gwah). Latin title ("Sing, My Tongue") of two hymns used in the Liturgy.* (1) The first is one of the famous Eucharistic Hymns of St. Thomas Aquinas* that is used in Evening Prayer I* on the Solemnity of the Body and Blood of Christ* and as a processional hymn on that day as well as Holy Thursday.* It is also used during the Forty Hours' Devotion,* and its last two stanzas (five and six) form the *"Tantum Ergo"* that is used at Benediction of the Blessed Sacrament.* The hymn combines literary artistry with theological accuracy in its six stanzas: (a) a lyrical summary of its teaching; (b) a brief outline of Christ's life; (c) institution of the Blessed Sacrament at the Last Supper*; (d) doctrine of Transubstantiation*; (e) praise and adoration of the present Christ; and (f) final doxology* for such a sublime gift. The following is one of many translation, that exist in English.

Sing, my tongue, the Savior's glory,
Of His Flesh the Mystery sing;
Of His Blood all price exceeding,
Shed by our immortal King,
Destined for the world's redemption,
From a noble womb to spring.

Of a pure and spotless Virgin,
Born for us on earth below,
He, as Man with man conversing,
Stayed the seeds of truth to sow;
Then He closed in solemn order
Wondrously His life of woe.

On the night of that Last Supper,*
Seated with His chosen band,
He, the Paschal victim eating,
First fulfills the Law's command;
Then as food to all His brethren
Gives Himself with His own hand.

Word made Flesh, the bread of nature,
By His word to Flesh He turns;
Wine into His Blood He changes:
What though sense no change discerns,
Only be the heart in earnest,
Faith* her lesson quickly learns.

Down in adoration falling,
Lo! the sacred Host we hail,
Lo! oe'r ancient forms departing
Newer rites of grace prevail;
Faith for all defects supplying,
Where the feeble senses fail.

To the everlasting Father,*
And the Son* Who reigns on high
With the Holy Spirit* proceeding
Forth from each eternally,
Be salvation,* honor, blessing,*
Might and endless majesty.

(2) The second hymn is the one composed by Venantius Fortunatus (530-609) that extols the triumph of our Savior's Cross* and is used on Good Friday* during the Adoration of the Cross and in the Liturgy of the Hours* on feasts* of the Cross. It is filled with sentiments of respect and love, penetrating tenderness and veneration, for the Cross and the Crucified One. *See also* EUCHARISTIC HYMNS OF ST. THOMAS.

Panis Angelicus (PAH-nees ahn-JEL-ee-koos). Latin title (from the first two words "Bread of Angels") of a Eucharistic hymn comprising the next-to-last stanza of *Sacris Sollemniis** composed by St. Thomas Aquinas* in honor of the Blessed Sacrament.* It exults at the fact that the Bread of angels has become the Bread of human beings, symbols have given way to the reality, and the poor and lowly can feed upon their Lord and Master. *See also* SACRIS SOLLEMNIIS.

Pantocrator (pahn-toh-KRAH-tawr). Name (taken from the Greek for "ruler of all") for a representation of Christ depicting Him ruling

from heaven, which is found in the dome of Byzantine churches. Sometimes, Christ is presented in full figure, seated on a throne and with His hand raised in blessing.* More often He is presented only in half figure, holding the Gospel* in His left hand and and raising His right hand in blessing. This title is the equal of Christ the King* in the Roman Rite.* *See also* CHRIST THE KING.

Papal Blessing. *See* BLESSING, APOSTOLIC.

Papal Bull. *See* Bull, PAPAL.

Papal Documents. *See* LITURGICAL LAW, SOURCES OF.

Papal Flag. *See* FLAGS.

Papal Mass (PAY-puhl mas). In the 4th century, after peace was restored to the Church* by Constantine the Great, solemn sacerdotal functions of the Pope* became possible. The Popes officiated in basilicas* of Rome until their exile to Avignon. Upon their return to the Vatican, they used the domestic chapels; eventually the Sistine Chapel was erected for this purpose. From the occupation of Rome in 1870 until the Concordat was signed in 1929 solemn liturgical functions were considered incompatible with the situation as it existed. Papal high Masses* before 1870 would take at least three hours. Today there is no official book for the papal Mass, for all papal rites are under review.

The recent public Masses of the Pope* are more in keeping with the current Liturgy* with a varied amount of singing, depending on the abilities of the congregation. Vestments* reserved for the Pope are the fanon,* an additional amice,* the falda, a voluminous white skirt, the subcinctorium, a girdle related to the maniple,* and instead of a crozier,* he carries a ferula,* a staff surmounted by a cross. Ceremonies peculiar to the papal Liturgy are the opening and closing of the holy door for a jubilee* year, the opening and closing of ecumenical councils, canonization,* the creation of cardinals, and the blessings of the following: wax medallions with the figure of the *Agnus Dei,** the golden rose, and the pallium* for archbishops.*

Papal Pronouncements, Liturgical. *See* LITURGICAL LAW, SOURCES OF.

Papal Tiara. *See* TIARA, PAPAL.

Paraliturgy (par-uh-LIT-uhr-jee). (1) A pedagogical method of liturgical instruction. It explains the rites* and liturgical ceremonies in the light of dogma,* history, spirituality,* and symbolism,* translating into living words the texts used in worship* and bringing the richness of the Liturgy* within the reach of all. Catechesis* is the term we use today in this sense. *(See also* CATECHESIS.)

(2) Celebrations or forms of worship in which liturgical elements are displayed, but which technically are not part of the official Liturgy* of the Church. As the *Constitution on the Sacred Liturgy** explicitly states, the spiritual life is not limited solely to participation* in the Liturgy; the Church does foster popular devotions,* as long as they are in accord with the norms of the Church. In fact, in some instances, bishops* approve books that have a collection of such devotions or pious exercises.* Such a manual of devotions, though usually intended for private use, is frequently utilized in devotions recited publicly in churches, but these prayers are never considered the official liturgical prayer of the Church. They are optional prayers and practices, bordering on the central themes of Christian worship, which many of the faithful* employ to arouse devotion within themselves. Some examples are: the Rosary,* the Stations of the Cross,* novenas,* and many monthly devotions.

Paraphrase. *See* ADAPTATION, LITURGICAL.

Pardon (PAHR-duhn). The excusing of an offense. Christians obtain God's pardon of their sins through the saving actions of Christ the Redeemer, which we encounter in the Liturgy.* Among other things, the Liturgy is concerned with granting pardon to those who have committed an offense against God or neighbor. This pardon is dispensed especially through Baptism* and Penance* in the case of grave sins and the Penitential Rite* of Mass for venial sins. The whole season of Lent* is a summons to repentance and a plea for pardon—an idea that runs all through the Mass for Ash Wednesday.* Indeed, every Mass is intended to effect a conversion* in the participants. *See also* BAPTISM; CONVERSION; LENT; METANOIA; PENANCE, RITE OF; PENITENTIAL RITE.

Parents (PAR-uhnts; PER-). Both the *Constitution on the Sacred Liturgy** and the *Declaration on Christian Education (Gravissimum Educationis*)* explicitly define the role of parents to provide physical, intellectual, and spiritual education of their children. Through a family atmosphere inspired by Sacred Scripture,* parents promote a so-

cial education for their children motivated by love and devotion to God and people alike. They are called to be a "domestic Church,"* to impart to their children the *liturgical dynamism* that summons Christians to chant the glory* of God and the *apostolic-missionary dynamism* that leads them to reveal and communicate Christ's salvation* to all human beings. *See also* DOMESTIC CHURCH; FAMILY PRAYER; GRAVISSIMUM EDUCATIONIS.

Parish (PAR-ish). (1) A geographical subdivision of a diocese* that has its own church building and a pastor,* appointed by and under the jurisdiction* of the bishop*; besides being the spiritual leader of the parish, the pastor is its administrator as well. To satisfy the needs of people of certain nationalities or races, national parishes exist with no relation to territory, though they are authorized by the Ordinary.*

(2) Any congregation or Local Church* with all its spiritual activities. Because of today's mobility, modern psychology, and current theology, which has defined the Church* as the assembled community of Christ, most people consider parish as that voluntarily gathered community in which Church is actively expressed and concretely present, for instance, when the congregation vivaciously participates* in a Eucharistic Celebration.

In either definition, because of the size of parishes and the lack of a sufficient number of priests, many parishes have associate pastors and depend heavily upon lay persons* and Religious* to share the work of the community. The latter do so by their appointments on parish councils and committees as well as by their service in many ministries, such as those connected with religious education, families, youth, and liturgical activities. *See also* LOCAL CHURCH.

Parish Liturgy Committee (PAR-ish LIT-uhr-jee kuh-MIT-ee). Responsible for liturgical and paraliturgical occasions in the parish,* this committee may attend to the following activities: plan and rehearse Sunday Mass* and other major liturgical occasions (more emphasis should be placed on Holy Week* and other major feasts* for the parish); evaluate the homilies of

priests* and deacons*; instruct lectors* and acolytes* on their duties; tend to proper decorations for seasonal liturgies; with the music director, help choose music suitable for various liturgical celebrations, bearing in mind the specific group of worshipers and the particular occasion; set up a program of continuing education, which would explain the liturgical rites together with the theology of community.

For the committee to be effective, it must have as members an artist, a musician, and people knowledgeable about Liturgy,* together with a pastor* or his representative among the clergy*; in addition, as many persons as possible are to accept the various roles in public worship* and be able to excel in their performance according to high standards set by the committee. In order to achieve a living, worshiping, universal Church, true pastoral concern should guide the liturgical celebrations, so that the People of God* may express their faith,* not only in these celebrations but in public nonliturgical devotions. Options* allowed by the Church are to be available to the community without becoming local law. *See also* CREATIVITY IN LITURGY; LITURGICAL COMMISSIONS; LITURGY—PARTICIPATION.

Parish Priests. *See* PASTORS.

Parishioners (puh-RISH-uhn-uhrz). Those faithful* who belong to a specific parish,* because of their enrollment therein, their habitual participation* in parish activities, primarily the Mass,* and their active support of the parish facilities insofar as their resources allow.

Parochial Mass. *See* MASS FOR THE PEOPLE.

Parousia (pahr-oo-SEE-uh; puh-ROO-zee-uh). A term (from the Greek for "arrival" or "presence") that refers to the Second Coming* of Christ in all His glory to judge the living and the dead, as stated in our Profession of Faith*: "He will come again in glory* to judge the living and the dead."

The New Testament* writers described the visible return of Jesus in ultimate triumph over His well established Kingdom*: "For as often as you eat this bread and drink the cup, you proclaim the death of the Lord until he comes" (1 Cor 11:26); "Then they will see the Son of Man coming in the clouds with great power and glory" (Mk 13:26); "The

Lord himself, with a word of command, with the voice of an archangel and the trumpet of God, will come down from heaven" (1 Thes 4:16). The angels at the Ascension* told the disciples: "This Jesus who has been taken up from you into heaven will return in the same way as you have seen him going into heaven" (Acts 1:11). Besides the above and other references, Christians believe in the Second Coming as Christ Himself described on the Mount of Olives to His disciples, indicating what signs of the times may occur (Mt 24:3-14).

Most liturgical acts have as at least a secondary intention the preparation of the faithful* for that Second Coming on the day of final judgment. *See also* JUDGMENT.

Partial Indulgences. *See* INDULGENCES.

Participation. *See* LITURGY—PARTICIPATION.

Particle (PAHRT-i-kuhl). The small, consecrated Hosts* for distribution to the people, particularly when the congregation is large. The ideal would be to break larger Hosts and give a particle to each, hence the name. Furthermore, it pertains also to the fragments that may be detached from the Eucharistic Species.* As long as each is recognizable as bread, the real presence* of Christ remains in it no matter how small. Such loose particles are to be consumed or flushed down the sacrarium.* *See also* BREAD.

Pasch. *See* EASTER.

Paschal Candle (PAS-kuhl KAN-duhl). The large wax candle,* usually decorated, blessed at the beginning of the Easter Vigil* ceremonies. It is placed on a special candlestick near the altar* or pulpit* and lighted during liturgical services. During the ceremony, five grains of incense,* representing the five wounds suffered by Jesus, are inserted in the form of a Cross.* An Alpha above the Cross and an Omega below indicate that Christ is really the beginning and end of all; on the four sides of the Cross are numbers of the current year, which are traced during the ceremony. The deacon,* or some assigned singer, proclaims the solemn hymn of praise, *Exsultet,** with its theme of the triumph of Christ over darkness; thus the Paschal Candle is the symbol of the risen Savior, the light of the world.*

During the Liturgy of Baptism* on Holy Saturday,* it leads the procession* of those to be baptized into the church, and during the Blessing of the Baptismal Water,* it may be lowered into it. After Pentecost,* the Paschal Candle is kept near the baptismal font* to be used during baptismal ceremonies and thus is also available for Funeral Rites,* being carried in the procession* and burning near the casket during the Mass. *See also* EASTER VIGIL.

Paschal Lamb. *See* LAMB OF GOD.

Paschal Mystery (PAS-kuhl MIS-t[uh-]ree). (1) A common term to express the redemptive act of Jesus including especially the time from the Last Supper* to the climax on Easter* Sunday.

(2) The English title of Pope Paul VI's 1969 document approving the restructuring of the Liturgical Year* and the calendar in the Roman Rite.* This new arrangement is expected to allow the People of God* to experience, in a more intense way, the whole of the Mystery of Christ,* as it unfolds throughout the cycle of the year.

Paschal Season. *See* EASTER SEASON.

Paschal Time (PAS-kuhl taim). The fifty-six days of the Easter Season,* during which the members of the Catholic Church, after having received First Holy Communion,* must communicate at least once a year (Easter duty). The Conference of Bishops* in the United States extended this period to its former length, from the First Sunday of Lent* to Trinity* Sunday. *See also* COMMUNION; EASTER SEASON.

Paschal Vigil. *See* EASTER VIGIL.

Passion (PASH-uhn). The episodes surrounding the suffering and Death* of Christ, which have been incorporated into the Liturgy* of Holy Week,* with those sections of the Gospels* read on Passion (Palm) Sunday* and Good Friday.* In the more solemn celebrations, these passages are chanted by priests,* deacons,* clerics,* or even lay people,* among whom the text is divided for dramatic purposes. One, preferably the celebrant,* takes Christ's part, another is a narrator, and the third takes the speaking parts of other characters and the crowd. Frequently the congregation* will join in with the responses from the crowd.

Devotion to the Passion

The Passion of Jesus is essential to redemption and as such should develop a Christian's devotional life and spirituality. Never should it distort the Paschal Mystery.* Together with the Death and Resurrection* of the Lord, the Passion is a part of the Paschal Mystery, which each Mass renews Sacramentally.

During the centuries, various Saints* indicated their willingness to carry the Cross,* to suffer along with Christ as a true disciple. A strong, personal devotion to His sufferings is obvious from the writings of many of the Fathers of the Church.* Cults to the wounds of the Savior, the Precious Blood,* the pierced Heart, together with the Stations of the Cross,* became popular.

Devotion to the Passion of Jesus is essential to the integral Paschal Mystery, should burgeon in a renewed Church, and be practiced by those pledged to walk the path Christ chose. Some such devotions are liturgical or at least paraliturgical.* Examples are: the Votive Mass* of the Passion; the blessing of crucifixes*; the Feast of the Triumph of the Holy Cross*; devotion to the relics* and instruments of the Passion. *See also* PASCHAL MYSTERY; PASSION SUNDAY.

Passion Sunday (PASH-uhn SUHN-dee; -day). Better known as Palm Sunday, the first day of Holy Week,* and not to be confused with the 5th Sunday of Lent,* formerly called Passion Sunday. Marked by contrast, the Liturgy* begins with triumphal joy during the blessing and procession* of the palms,* reenacting Christ's entry into Jerusalem, which emphasizes the dominant place of this triumphal procession to honor Christ the King* and allows a fuller participation* by all the faithful*; thereupon the antithetic sorrow portrayed during the Mass of the day leads into Holy Week.

The commemoration of the Lord's triumphal entry into Jerusalem is included in every Mass, with a procession before the principal Mass and a solemn or simple entrance before the others. If possible, the congregation assembles at another church or chapel or some suitable place apart from the church to which the procession will move. Carrying palm branches, the faithful greet the celebrant* with song, and he introduces the services with a special prayer blessing the palms, sprinkling them with holy water.* After an account of the Lord's entrance from one of the Gospels* and a brief Homily,* the priest* leads the procession to the church while proper hymns and antiphons are sung. After the altar is incensed, the Opening Prayer* of the Mass follows, and the Liturgy of the Word* continues as usual.

Should it be impossible to have a procession outside the church, a similar procession, called a solemn entrance, occurs from the front of the church or within the church. If a solemn entrance is not held, the simple entrance takes place with the usual introductory form of the Mass including the proper singing of the Entrance Antiphon* or other song of the same theme. In all Masses of this Sunday, the selection from the Gospel is the Passion* from one of the three evangelists* other than John, since his is read on Good Friday.*

Passiontide. *See* LENT.

Passover Seder (PAS-oh-vuhr SAY-duhr). Also known as the Pasch, the Passover is a seven-day Jewish feast, a sacred memorial, prescribed for all Jews by the Scriptures and tradition. As one of their major feasts, it is an integral part of Jewish family piety. Its main feature centers on a special meal, the seder supper, which the Synoptics* describe as the Last Supper* Jesus shared with the Apostles.* At it the first Eucharistic Celebration took place, on Holy Thursday,* together with the institution of the priesthood for the New Law.

Where it is customary for Christians to celebrate the Passover Seder during Holy Week,* they should respect the rites of this seder in its integrity, whether celebrated at home or as part of a parish activity. In any case, it demands a dignified manner and a sensitivity to the Jewish tradition in its celebration, which acknowledges our common roots in the History of Salvation.* Never should the Last Supper be restaged in this celebration, but the rite of the Haggadah for the seder should be followed explicitly. The rites of the Sacred Triduum* are the annual memorial of the Passion,* Death,* and Resurrection* of Christ. Only those editions of the Haggadah that are true to the tradition of Israel and contain the authentic meaning of the festival of Passover should be used.

Pastoral Care. (PAS-t[uh-]ruhl kay[uh]r). Pastoral care has greater implications than Liturgy.* Usually as a result of the Liturgy it functions by healing, reconciling, guiding, and sustaining. It should help in the personal transformation that occurs because of the liturgical services. It is the follow-up after the various Sacraments* are received, strengthening those who receive Baptism* and Confirmation,* aiding those who are sick, helping those with troubled marriages, being present at the time of sorrow at a funeral. All of these are usually linked with liturgical functions, but true pastoral care develops the fellowship that should exist within the community. It makes personal what the public nature of worship* has done for the community. Thus the liturgical functions are not centered totally on the Church,* but become relevant to human needs. One cannot attend liturgical functions and disregard the personal needs of those in the community. Worship generates pastoral implications and effects; pastoral situations may be the occasion for liturgical rites.*

Pastoral Care of the Sick (PAS-t[uh-]ruhl kay[uh]r uhv thuh sik). The Church in both the East and the West has an ancient liturgical tradition of anointing the sick. The whole person is helped and saved through the grace* of the Holy Spirit* in this Sacrament,* being strengthened against the temptation of the devil and anxiety over death. With this grace the person not only bears suffering bravely but also fights against it. The anointing is not intended to be miraculous; however, on occasions physical health may improve following the reception of this Sacrament. Furthermore the grace of the Sacrament takes away sin and any remnants of sin if some remain, provided this has not already been accomplished in the Sacrament of Penance.*

The Council of Trent indicated that the Sacrament should be given to the sick, especially those so seriously ill that they may be close to the end of their lives. Vatican Council II* definitely changed the name from "Extreme Unction" to the "Anointing of the Sick,"* with a clear indication that the Sacrament was not only for those at the point of death but also for anyone in danger of death from old age or sickness. The Sacrament consists in the laying on of hands,* the offering of the prayer of faith,* and the anointing of the sick with holy oil.*

Pastoral care, however, goes beyond this Sacrament, for it takes into consideration the Church's total need to care for the sick, including visits while they are ill, frequent Communion* during their sickness, the celebration of Viaticum* when necessary, together with the Commendation of the Dying,* and eventually the Prayers for the Dead.* Sickness is not to be considered a punishment for personal sin. The mystery of suffering should have meaning and value for the Christian's salvation.* Christ not only visited and healed the sick in His time but even today loves them in their illness. Not only He, but all Christians, doctors, friends, family, and priests,* should help the sick spiritually and physically, for in this way they fulfill the command of Christ to visit the sick, showing concern for the whole person, bringing physical relief and spiritual comfort.

Since the ministry to the sick is a common responsibility for all Christians, they should not only visit the sick, and pray for them, but also celebrate the Sacraments with them. The family especially should become accustomed to praying together with the sick person. Their words of encouragement and show of faith can help the sick unite themselves with the sufferings of Christ.

Recipients

As long as one's health is seriously impaired by old age or sickness, the Sacrament should be received, and it may be repeated if the sick person recovers after the anointing and falls ill again, or if the person's condition worsens during the same sickness. Before surgery brought about by serious illness, a sick person may be anointed. The elderly are to be anointed if they become noticeably weaker, even though a serious illness may not be obvious. Those sick children who have sufficient use of reason may be anointed. In danger of death or because of some other grave necessity, a non-Catholic Christian may receive the Sacraments of Penance,* Holy Eucharist,* and the Anointing of the Sick (Canon 844,4). When in doubt whether a person has the use of reason, is dangerously ill, or is dead, Anointing of the Sick is to be administered.

Minister

The bishop* and priest are the proper ministers of this Sacrament. Ordinarily pastors and their assistants perform this liturgical function regularly, or the hospital chaplain* does. When large groups receive the Sacrament together, several priests aid in the celebration. Several priests may also anoint a single sick person, one doing the anointing and the others taking the remaining parts of the service. The priest plays an important role in helping the sick person to prepare well for the reception of the Sacraments, and he should provide leadership to all who help in caring for the sick, whether they be deacons or ministers of the Eucharist. Furthermore, the pastor should make sure that the sick are mentioned in the General Intercessions* at Mass on the Lord's Day, and during Morning Prayer* and Evening Prayer* in the Intercessions.* Those who care for the sick could be remembered on these occasions as well.

Requirements

The proper matter for this Sacrament is olive oil, or if not available, some oil derived from plants. This oil is normally blessed by the bishop on Holy Thursday,* but in case of necessity any priest may bless it. The person who is ill is anointed on the forehead and hands, while the form is recited. A single anointing on the forehead suffices in the case of necessity, or in a particular case, on some other suitable part of the body, while the whole form is said.

Visits

Those who visit the sick, whether they be priests, deacons, or the laity dedicated to this work, should share the Word of God* with the ill, usually choosing some prayers to formulate a Liturgy of the Word,* which can be selected from the section on pastoral care in the *Roman Ritual.** Psalms,* litanies,* or other prayers may be suitable, and the minister should be willing to pray with the sick, encouraging them to offer their sufferings in union with Christ, joining in the prayer of the Church. Should a priest be present, he would probably perform the laying on of hands and give a blessing. Similar activities should occur in ministering to sick children, making sure that suitable elements from the Scripture and prayers familiar to the child be used.

Communion of the Sick

Opportunities for the persons who are ill to receive Communion frequently should be constant. Such celebrations could perhaps be better planned by allowing the sick person and friends and relatives to help in choosing the prayers and readings, frequently linking this visit with the community's Eucharistic Celebration, particularly should it occur on Sunday. Many times the Eucharistic ministers will take the Host to the sick immediately after Communion of the Sunday Mass as they receive a special blessing to do so from the celebrant. The Blessed Sacrament is carried in a pyx*; at the home a proper table

is covered with a linen cloth, and lighted candles and some holy water* should be available. Should sick persons be unable to receive Communion under the form of bread, they may receive it under the species of wine alone.

Occasionally provisions should be made to celebrate Mass in the homes of the sick with family and friends gathered around. In hospitals or institutions, when Mass would not be possible on each occasion, most probably it would be more suitable for the residents or patients to be gathered in groups in one or the other area, with additional ministers of Communion assisting. If such grouping were impossible, the more brief rite for Communion under these circumstances may be used, starting with the Eucharistic Antiphon in the church or chapel, the minister giving Communion to the sick in individual rooms, and the Concluding Prayer said in the church or chapel or the last room visited.

Anointing

When the proper conditions present themselves, namely that the Christians whose health is seriously impaired by sickness or old age are ready for the Sacrament, it may be given either outside of Mass, within Mass, or in a hospital or institution. In any case it should be made clear that by this anointing the Church supports the sick in their struggle against illness, while continuing Christ's Messianic work of healing. The priest should make sure about the physical and spiritual condition of the sick person, be acquainted with the family and friends, and choose the readings and the rest of the presentation in accordance with this knowledge. Should the sick person want to receive the Sacrament of Penance, it would probably be done during a previous visit. However, when it is necessary to celebrate the Sacrament of Penance during the Rite of Anointing, it supplants the Penitential Rite.*

Whenever a person is chronically ill or in a weakened condition, the anointing may be repeated at the pastoral judgment of the priest, when he believes the condition of the sick person warrants it.

The three distinct aspects of the celebration of this Sacrament are the prayer of faith, the laying on of hands, and the anointing with oil. All those present during the rites for the sick should join together as representatives of the entire Church in making the prayer of faith in response to God's Word. The sick persons should join in if they are capable of doing so. As Christ healed many of the sick by the laying on of hands, so with a similar gesture the priest indicates the power of the Church's prayer of faith by this sign. It further signifies that the Church is praying for the coming of the Holy Spirit* upon the sick persons. The actual anointing with oil follows, which signifies healing, strengthening, and the presence, power, and grace of the Holy Spirit. Generous use of oil is a most effective Sacramental symbol; it should not be wiped away.

Frequently, whether outside or within Mass, a large number of people may be anointed at the same celebration. Care must be taken that only those whose health is seriously impaired by sickness or old age are anointed. In these situations the full rite with all of the proper embellishments should take place, usually with several priests aiding the celebrant.

Whether for an individual or for a group, when the anointing takes place outside Mass, ordinarily the rite includes a Liturgy of the Word* and is followed if at all possible by reception of the Eucharist.*

When the condition of the sick person(s) permits, and particularly when Communion would be received, the Sacrament is celebrated within Mass, using the Ritual Mass, if at all possible according to the rubrics,* with its special Readings* culled from suitable sections of the Scriptures. The Sacrament is conferred between the Liturgy of the Word and the Liturgy of the Eucharist.* (*See also* ANOINTING OF THE SICK.)

Celebration of Viaticum

Whenever possible, a dying Christian should try to receive Viaticum* within Mass in order to receive under both species and to allow others to join in with the celebration more easily. This would probably happen in a small gathering at the home, hospital, or some institution, so effort should be made to involve the sick person, family, friends, and other members of the local community in the planning and celebration.

Distinctive to this celebration is the renewal of the baptismal Profession of Faith* by the dying person. At the reception of Viaticum, the special words are used: "May the Lord Jesus Christ protect you and lead you to eternal life." Naturally the special Mass for Viaticum should be used with its proper Readings, unless a Ritual Mass is not permitted that day. There is a special form of the Final Blessing* to be used to which the Apostolic Pardon* may be added at the discretion of the priest. Should the person linger on for several days after receiving Viaticum, opportunity should be given to receive the Eucharist later on, even daily. Should it be impossible to have a Mass, at least a brief Liturgy of the Word ought to accompany Viaticum outside Mass.

Commendation of the Dying

Although all Christians have the responsibility of joining with a dying person in prayer, the presence of a deacon or priest shows more clearly that a Christian dies in communion with the Church. Special prayers for the Commendation of the Dying* occur in the *Ritual,* and the selection of texts should relate to the condition and piety of the dying person and the family members present.

Prayers for the Dead

Also included here are prayers for use by a minister who is to attend to a person already dead, since

in that case he may not administer the Sacraments of Penance or Anointing of the Sick. It may be necessary to explain to the family that Sacraments are for the living and not for the dead, but prayers of the living help the deceased. Usually a symbolic gesture, such as a Sign of the Cross* on the forehead or sprinkling the body with holy water, may be a comfort to the family.

Rite for Exceptional Circumstances

Sudden illness or an accident may place one in proximate danger of death, and in this situation a continuous Rite of Penance, Anointing, and Viaticum is available. Ordinarily the Sacrament of Penance is celebrated first, though the confession may be generic. Thereupon Viaticum follows immediately, and if there is sufficient time, the Anointing of the Sick is celebrated. How much of each rite is used is dependent upon the priest's judgment in any particular circumstance. Should there be sufficient time, the ordinary order of the Sacraments would be the Rite of Penance, then the Anointing, and finally Viaticum. When there is doubt whether a person is dead or not, the priest should anoint the person, not conditionally as stated in number 15 of *Pastoral Care of the Sick*, but absolutely according to Canon 1005.

When Christian Initiation for the Dying is in order, normally it would be celebrated over a period of time. But when there is danger of death, the person should be baptized, and if the priest is present, he should confer Confirmation.* This should be followed by Communion. Should the person recover, the supposition is that the complete cycle of Initiation would take place.

Care of a Dying Child

In the case of a dying child, the Church's ministry is directed more to the parents and family than to the child. The Church tries to help the parents and family accept what God has allowed to happen, even beyond the time of the death of the child. Though the child may accept death more easily than adults, he or she can experience anguish because of the family's concern. The child's faith matures rapidly, so support for both child and family by visits, prayer, and any other form of assistance is important. Prayers and Readings by the ministers can help the family to see that the child, entering the Kingdom* of joy* ahead of them, becomes one of the family's great intercessors. Should it be necessary to celebrate the Sacraments of Initiation, the process should take place in its proper order. In this case as in any other, when death is imminent, one should remember that the Viaticum, rather than Anointing, is the Sacrament for the Dying. *See also* ANOINTING OF THE SICK; COMMENDATION OF THE DYING; VIATICUM.

Pastoral Liturgy (PAS-t[uh-]ruhl LIT-uhr-jee). The right linking of pastoral activity with the Liturgy* in such a way that the participants* in Divine worship* will be led to Christ and Christ to the participants through the means indicated by Christ Himself together with those determined by the Church.* Pastoral Liturgy takes seriously the fact that all the faithful,* by reason of their priestly dignity (LG, 10-11) and the "sense of faith" (LG, 12), must be taught how to interpret the Christian language of ritual signs* and how to perform symbolic actions that are meaningful to themselves. It also provides those who have ministerial tasks in the liturgical assembly with the "professionalism" required to carry out ritual actions that will clearly communicate the complex relations believers have with the God of Jesus in the Church pervaded by the Holy Spirit.*

The Church strongly recommends Pastoral Liturgy to the bishops* and priests* who are to implement it:

> The greatest care must be taken about rightly linking pastoral activity with the Liturgy not as if it were set apart and existing in isolation but as it is closely joined to other pastoral works.
>
> Especially necessary is a close, living union between Liturgy, catechesis,* religious formation, and preaching.
>
> Bishops and their assistants in the priesthood should, therefore, attach ever greater importance to their whole pastoral ministry as it is focused toward the Liturgy. Then the faithful* themselves will richly partake of the Divine Life through sharing in the sacred celebrations and . . . will proclaim that Divine Life and pass it on to others (IOE, 7-8).

This carrying out of Pastoral Liturgy is helped by the liturgical books,* which demand not only a ceremonial execution but also an interpretation with a view toward a pastoral implementation of what they contain. Their Introductions provide principles and norms that indicate the theological value, ecclesial function, and pastoral application of the rite. For example, the *General Instruction of the Roman Missal* states:

> The celebration of the Eucharist,* like the entire Liturgy, involves the use of outward signs that foster, strengthen, and express faith.* There must be the utmost care, therefore, to choose and to make wise use of those forms and elements provided by the Church which, in view of the circumstances of the people and the place, will best foster active and full participation and serve the spiritual well-being of the faithful (ch 1, no. 5).

In this respect, the liturgical signs must have a human truth about them. They must really make the people aware of the spiritual realities they signify. And the language of faith that is spoken must be intelligible on the experiential-cultural level of the participants.

The Church has set up organs to help carry out this Pastoral Liturgy: the *Congregation for Divine Worship and the Discipline of the Sacraments** on the international level; the National Liturgical Commissions on the national level; the Diocesan Liturgical Commissions* on the diocesan level; and the Parish Liturgical Commissions* on

the parish level. All of them labor long and hard to insure that the Liturgy in their regions will always be pastoral.

Pastoral Liturgy in the Parish

Within a parish* there are many private concerns that the pastor* must address. The pressures of the present moment upon the parishioners may distract them from truly well organized public worship.* Pastoral Liturgy is to relate the problem-centered crises found in pastoral ministry to the mutuality of worship. In caring for the personal needs of the parishioners, the pastor has to relate back to them in such a way that they recognize the need for Divine care also. The human needs of the parishioners must relate to the services in the church. No church service should be so centered on itself that it is unaware of the practical needs, difficulties, and trials besieging the community.

Occasionally situations within a parish will suggest liturgical rites. The celebration of the Eucharist* and the Sacraments* all have pastoral implications and should definitely reflect the particular needs of the Christian fellowship that develops from these actions. Major occasions in the parishioners' lives occur in some sort of natural transition, for instance, Baptisms,* Confirmations,* Marriages,* Funerals,* and so on. Even the Sacrament of Reconciliation* can be extremely important at various stages of people's lives, to say nothing of the moment for the Anointing of the Sick.* All these form special acts of Pastoral Liturgy that are most meaningful to the individuals who at the same time would normally find these Sacraments received in conjunction with other members of the community, so that they sense the whole Church praying for them. *See also* PASTORAL CARE OF THE SICK.

Pastoral Vicar (PAS-t[uh-]ruhl VIK-uhr). Canon law term for associate pastor.*

Pastors (PAS-tuhrz). Those individual priests* or moral persons, such as Religious Institutes, appointed by the Ordinary* with all the responsibilities and rights as described in Canon Law and the regulations of the diocese.* Besides conferring the Sacraments,* the pastor is responsible for related liturgical actions and administrative duties connected with them. Among these duties would be the spiritual care of all his parishioners, including the poor, visiting the sick, exercising charity toward his flock, promoting catechetical formation and Catholic education, performing funerals, proclaiming the Word of God,* keeping parish registers* up-to-date, and celebrating Mass* for his people on Sundays and Holy Days of Obligation.*

Because of the size of the parish, it is quite likely he may have associate pastors* and expect the service of many of the laity* with regard to the variety of ministries they can perform. They can be particularly helpful to him in his obligation of religious education of young and old, ministering to those in need,

and in encouraging any activity that could enhance the spiritual life* of the parish. *See also* CHRISTUS DOMINUS; MASS FOR THE PEOPLE; SAINTS, LITURGICAL CATEGORIES OF.

Paten (PAT-[uh]n). A round, thin, convex plate, of the same material as the chalice* and gold plated, large enough to extend over the lip of the chalice. The bread to be consecrated, at least for the priest,*

would be placed upon it. Recent liturgical instructions recommend a larger paten that could hold all the Communion bread necessary for the recipients at the Eucharistic Sacrifice. It receives a blessing comparable to that for the chalice, since it holds the bread not only before consecration but also afterward. *See also* CHALICE.

Pater Noster. *See* LORD'S PRAYER.

Patriarchs (PAY-tree-ahrks). (1) A word in the Bible* that identifies the father or ruler of a race, a tribe, or a family in Biblical history, ordinarily of the pre-Mosaic era, and usually refers to Abraham,* Isaac, and Jacob, though the founders of the twelve tribes of Israel are frequently considered patriarchs also.

(2) Those prelates* of the principal centers of the Roman Empire (Rome, Constantinople, Alexandria, Antioch, Jerusalem) who receive this title out of respect, whatever their hierarchical rank; thus they hold precedence over primates,* metropolitans,* and bishops.* There are minor patriarchs in both East and West.

Patrick, St. (PAT-rik). 389-c.461. Probably born in Scotland this Patron and Apostle of Ireland, after some years of slavery, was commissioned after ordination* to evangelize Ireland and eventually became its bishop* overcoming fierce opposition from the Druids. During his three decades in Ireland, he converted the country, raised the standards of scholarship, and developed closer relations with the Western Church. *Liturgical celebration:* March 17 (Opt. Mem.); *theme:* a life in loving service bears witness to the Faith.*

Patristic Readings (puh-TRIS-tik REED-ingz). The Second Readings of the Office of Readings* that frequently are from the writings of one of the Fathers of the Church,* that is, the great writers and preachers of the first six centuries of Church history. At times great Teachers* and Doctors* who lived in later periods are included in this category. *See also* READINGS.

Patron Saints (PAY-truhn saynts). The Blessed Virgin Mary,* a Saint* or Blessed,* who is considered the advocate before God and the protector of a specific place or territory, Religious Family, or moral person. Patron Saints are to be distinguished from the Titular Saint of any church, congregation, or community, although at times the Titular Saint may hold the title of Patron also.

Choice of a Patron

Patron Saints may be chosen by any place, as large as a nation or as small as a parish,* Religious

Families, moral persons, ecclesiastical or lay, such as institutes, sodalities, gatherings. The Blessed Virgin under any of her titles, the angels, the Saints, and Blesseds (by special indult) may be selected. Only one is allowed; where secondary Patrons existed before, they may continue in that role. Patrons of a place are chosen by the clerics* and faithful* who are placed under their protection. Patrons of Religious Families and moral persons are selected by those in charge or by the members of each such group, and the selection is done either by consultation or by election.

Approval and Confirmation

The chosen Patron should be approved by the competent local ecclesiastical authority; if the Patron is international in nature, the Holy See* approves. Confirmation is to be sought from the Congregation for Divine Worship and the Discipline of the Sacraments* through formal petition from a local authority, who includes a report of the proceedings, and the testimony of the competent ecclesiastical authority approving the election.

Liturgical Celebration

Only the Patron of a place, a city or town, a moral person, a sodality, institute, or gathering, is celebrated with the rank of Solemnity* taking precedence over all feasts* in the General Calendar and over Sundays of Christmas* and Ordinary Time.* Patrons of a diocese,* province, region, nation, or larger territory are ranked as Feasts and are to be celebrated even by Religious* who have a Proper calendar. Former secondary Patrons may be celebrated with the rank of Obligatory Memorial.* Other Patrons should no longer be honored. Religious Families are allowed the celebration of their Patron, Titular Saint, or founder ranked among Saints as a Solemnity. For special reasons they may request another Solemnity from among these. Patrons of a Religious Province are ranked as Feasts.

Patron Saints for Individuals

Names of Saints chosen by parents for their children at Baptism* are called Christian names in contradistinction to their surnames, and the Saint is expected to be a special intercessor with God for the child. The same holds good for additional names chosen during life as for Confirmation* or by a novice choosing a new name when entering Religious* Life. *See also* BAPTISMAL NAME.)

Patrons of Occupations

Specific Saints have been officially designated by the Church as Patrons of enterprises or professions, usually chosen because of some event or aspect of their lives. Examples would be St. Paschal Baylon for Eucharistic Congresses, St. Jerome* for librarians, St. Joseph of Cupertino for air travelers and pilots, and St. Emygdius for earthquakes.

Paul, Apostle, St. (pawl, uh-POS-uhl). ?-c.67. Apostle of the Gentiles and author of thirteen New

Testament* writings, this Jew, who was persecuting Christians, saw Christ in a vision, and it completely changed his life. The Church* realized she was to convert not only the Jews but also the pagans to Christianity. Paul fought for the latters' right to be Christian without following Jewish law. He built up a huge system of Christian communities through his missionary journeys. Eventually he was taken prisoner and martyred in Rome. He is the Patron of Hospital Public Relations. *Liturgical celebration:* June 29 (Solemnity); *theme:* the Church must be Catholic or universal. *See also* CONVERSION OF ST. PAUL; *and the individual Epistles:* COLOSSIANS; CORINTHIANS (1 and 2); EPHESIANS; GALATIANS; PHILEMON; PHILIPPIANS; ROMANS; THESSALONIANS (1 and 2); TIMOTHY (1 and 2); AND TITUS.

Paul Chong Hasang, St. *See* ANDREW KIM, ST.

Paul Miki and Companions, Sts. (pawl MI-ki and kuhm-PAN-yuhnz). 1562-1597. The son of a Japanese military leader, Jesuit and eloquent preacher, Paul with twenty-five other Catholics, including priests,* laity,* European missionaries, and Japanese Christians, was crucified near Nagasaki during a persecution by the ruler of Japan. Philip of Jesus, a Franciscan, was the first North American-born Saint* to be canonized. *Liturgical celebration:* February 6 (Memorial); *theme:* the blood of martyrs* is the seed of the Church.*

Paul of the Cross, St. (pawl uhv thuh kraws; kros). 1694-1775. Italian mystic and founder of the Passionists. Paul's austere life readily equipped him for the lifetime of preaching on the Mystery of the Cross.* He was elected superior

general, a post he held all his life, busy as it was with preaching and helping others. Eventually he founded a contemplative community of Passionist nuns. *Liturgical celebration:* October 19 (Opt. Mem.); *theme:* devotion to the Passion* and Death* of Christ.

Paulinus of Nola, St. (paw-LAI-nuhs uhv NOH-luh). c.354-431. Born in France, this successful, prominent lawyer married the Spanish Theresia, was baptized in Aquitaine, moved to Nola in Italy, where he was elected bishop* in 409, and became famous for his charities. His correspondence with leading churchmen is extant, together with his poetry, placing him among the foremost Christian Latin poets of that era. *Liturgical celebration:* June 22 (Opt. Mem.); *theme:* a love of poverty and a concern for others.

Pax. *See* SIGN OF PEACE.

Pax Brede (pahks breed). Another name for the *Instrumentum Pacis.**

Pax Domini. *See* SIGN OF PEACE.

Peace (pees). The tranquility of order. Sin has brought disorder into human beings both inwardly and outwardly. Through His Redemption* Christ has restored order into human life. This peace of Christ is the greatest fruit of the Paschal Mystery*: "Peace I leave with you;

my peace I give to you" (Jn 14:27); see also Jn 20:19, 20, 26 and Gal 5:22). It is communicated to the human heart and the world* by the Church,* especially through the Liturgy.* *See also* SIGN OF PEACE.

Peace, Kiss of. *See* SIGN OF PEACE.

Peace, Sign of. *See* SIGN OF PEACE.

Pectoral Cross. *See* CROSS, PECTORAL.

Penance (PEN-uhn[t]s). That virtue* or proclivity of spirit whereby one is sorry for one's sins and is converted to God. Externally many actions accompany such conversion* and indicate internal repentance. Conversion involves a concrete change to a different way of life, a turning around to go in a new direction. Repentance includes the feeling of remorse and regret, a change of mind that begins a trusting obedience to God. *See also* CONVERSION; FAMILIARIS CONSORTIO; PENANCE, RITE OF; PENANCES.

Penance, Public. *See* PENANCE, RITE OF; PENANCES.

Penance, Rite of (PEN-uhn[t]s, rait uhv). Penance is that Sacrament* instituted by Christ whereby sins committed after Baptism* are remitted if the sinner posits certain acts and receives absolution* from a qualified priest*; thus its purpose is to reconcile the faithful* to God. The new rite expresses the pastoral and reconciliatory meaning of Penance, with a new emphasis on the

ecclesial aspects of repentance and sin, for separation from God by sin lessens the inner unity of the Church community. To praise and worship* the Lord properly depends on our transformation by the healing and reconciling grace* of God, and with this experience of conversion, we as Christians change our way of life, repent, and believe.

A crucial issue in the modern world* is moral responsibility in our civic and personal lives, but we cannot have that without mutual forgiveness, peace,* healing, or in one word, reconciliation. The new rite helps us to recognize the Church as a reconciling community, performing its ministry of reconciliation as a sign of God's healing presence in the world.

Names

For most of us this Sacrament has been called Confession* for a long period of time, despite the fact that the official title was Penance, reinforced as early as the Council of Florence (1439-1443). To us it signifies that we admit our sins in confession. Early in the Christian era, however, penance had three meanings, not only the first just mentioned, but also praising God and affirming faith,* based primarily on the use of the word in the Psalms.* Before Christianity, the word meant that one acknowledged a fault or debt before a judge. So the Christians took this Latin juridical term and added to it the Biblical implications. Eventually then its usage came to mean almost totally confession of sins.

Penance is derived from the Latin word that translated a Greek term, *metanoia.** The Greek term denotes repentance, focusing on the deeply interior quality, a kind of interior renewal that accompanies forgiveness of sin.

The term that the Catholic Church prefers at the present time is reconciliation, which should signify the restoration of harmony between God and His people. Sin causes alienation; expiation achieves reconciliation. Christ by His Death* and Resurrection* brings about reconciliation, for it changes people's attitude; God's attitude is to hate sin, but not the sinner.

Reconciliation in this meaning occurs regularly throughout Paul's letters. Even in liturgical books* of the ancient Church, reconciliation designated the Sacramental act whereby Christians were reintroduced into the Christian community after the period of penance was completed. This Sacrament is seen as something of a second Baptism* for the remission and pardon of postbaptismal sin. Thus Penance reinserts us into the life and community of the Church, which we first entered through Baptism. Therefore the truly repentant sinner is reconciled not only with God but with the Church. The Christian is converted with reference to and within the reconciling community, the Church.

Relation to Other Sacraments

As we look to the total Sacramental context of the Church,* we find Baptism as the fundamental Sacrament of reconciliation and conversion. Through it, Christ's victory over death and sin is given to all who believe and repent. It changes our whole relationship with God. Through our conversion we become new creatures. Secondly the sacrifice of Christ, commemorated in the celebration of the Eucharist,* continues our reconciliation and brings about the forgiveness of sins, as long as we have an upright heart, true faith,* sorrow, and repentance.

For those who sin after Baptism, Penance becomes a second Baptism through repentance rather than water. Persons obtain God's merciful pardon* while simultaneously being reconciled with the Church, for they have wounded the Church by their sins, which not only disrupts their friendship with God but also harms their brothers and sisters. Furthermore, besides sin by individuals, there is also sin by social groups and nations. Consequently, there necessarily must be solidarity in grace through reconciliation, just as each one was hurt through the solidarity of sin. Hence communal celebration is basic to achieve this reconciliation with the total community.

Essential Parts

(1) *Contrition.* Of primary importance is this act, which is the result of a cold, hard look at oneself in relation to others and God, so that true sorrow for sin committed and aversion to it are accompanied with the firm resolve to sin no more.

(2) *Confession.* Having made the first step of contrition for sin, the sinner is expected to admit his or

her guilt with an outward accusation to the Church's minister. It implies openness on the part of the penitent and a fine tuned sensitivity and spiritual judgment by the priest.*

(3) *Act of Penance.* Despite the fact that God's forgiveness is unconditional and free, one is expected to amend one's life through expiation for sins committed and giving redress for injuries done. This satisfaction, another term for it, is not to appease God but to rectify things between oneself and others, including the Church. Consequently the form of expiation should be such that it assumes the aspect of a healing remedy for renewal and a new beginning, implying satisfaction for any fault. (*See also* PENANCES.)

(4) *Absolution.* The tangible expression of God's forgiveness is the visible sign of absolution, as the minister, placing his hand on the penitent, recites the formula and forgives sins with the Sign of the Cross.* Having reentered the sheepfold, the penitent is expected to partake of the banquet of the Eucharist as the culmination of the Father's love for all.

Frequency and Time

Whenever there is a rupture in the relationship between a person and God or two persons, reconciliation is necessary. Hence, each and every sin is to be confessed to a priest. However, repeated celebration of the Sacrament, more frequently than when needed by reason of serious sin, brings about correction of faults and lesser sins and indicates concern over one's state of sinfulness. The intent of frequent Confession is to perfect oneself, in striving to achieve likeness to Christ.

This Sacrament may be celebrated at any time in any day. Obviously hearing Confessions would be disruptive to any liturgical celebration, including the Mass, and should not take place then. Ordinarily stated times should be given to the community when the priest is available each week. The ideal penitential season is Lent,* but other periods are also suitable, such as Advent,* when we are preparing for the coming of the Lord. In each parish* situation, the more ideal time for the celebration of the Sacrament should be discussed and decided upon.

First Confession

The present discipline of the Church makes it amply clear that First Confession must take place before First Communion.* There was a period of time from 1970 to 1973 when experimentation was allowed in certain areas for First Communion to be given without Confession first. That period had to cease at the end of the 1972/73 school year, and all are obliged by the decree *Quam Singulari* of 1916, which states that children should receive Penance and Eucharist as soon as they reach the age of reason. The explanation in later documents indicates clearly that the Sacraments should be received in that order.

Minister

Juridical competence to hear Confession means that the priest has faculties from his own bishop to hear Confessions; this now gives him permission to hear Confessions anywhere in the world unless a bishop in another diocese explicitly revokes it for him. More than merely a judge, the priest-confessor, with discernment, wisdom, friendliness, and warmth, should not only understand disorders of souls but have the ability to recommend proper remedies for them. Awareness of the Sacramental seal of Confession builds trust and intimacy during the celebration of the Sacrament, so that the penitent may readily open up to a man imbued with Scripture and impregnated with personal and liturgical prayer.

Penitent

For the penitent the new rite expects an attitude signifying that this is a liturgical encounter between the Lord and the penitent. Therefore, sufficient preparation is necessary to avoid a routine Confession of personal sins and a disregard for the broad responsibilities to obey Gospel* injunctions to love and serve God and others.

Place

The new rite is such that it demands a different idea of space from that afforded Confession in the past in what was the conventional confessional box. To try to transform the former areas into a satisfactory space for today's celebration of Reconciliation is extremely difficult, particularly if there still remains available a screen or grille behind which those who would like to confess anonymously may remain. Larger rooms that give the penitent and the priest the opportunity to carry out the ritual in a comfortable way should be provided. Opportunities should be given for face-to-face exchange and proper spiritual counsel.

Furthermore since the rite asks for the extension of hands during absolution, a bigger area is more fitting for this situation. The time allotted for the reading of Scripture* and common prayer* requires a more open setting. Thought should be given also to the area surrounding the Reconciliation Room, so that there is ample space for waiting where one may do spiritual reading, be alone with thoughts and prayers, and offer an act of thanksgiving afterward. Access and safety should be taken into consideration; sufficient lighting, proper acoustics, and furnishings that will attract are to be supplied.

Various other areas might be adapted such as the baptistery,* particularly since Penance is seen as a second Baptism; chapels of the Blessed Sacrament,* because of the forgiveness and healing power of the Eucharist*; particularly during a communal Penance, the presidential seat* is likewise an option; a private outdoor court may prove desirable also. Creativity in adapting whatever space is available should be employed. (*See also* CONFESSIONAL; RECONCILIATION ROOM.)

Vestments

For communal celebrations, besides the alb* and stole,* a cope* may also be worn. These contribute to the visual impact and the overall beauty of the rite. In the first form, for individual penitents, the cassock* or clerical suit and stole is the common practice in the United States.

Three Forms of Celebration

(1) *Individual Penitents.* The warm greeting by the priest should welcome the penitents in a friendly manner that would allow them to experience the mercy* of God more readily. After the penitent's Sign of the Cross,* a short invocation by the priest reminds the penitent of God's mercy. Thereupon the penitent may indicate something from his state of life to make it easier for the priest to perform his duties. A brief reading from Scripture as an option follows and can be very effective in most cases. After this enlightenment, the penitents express their sins, with the priest aiding to make sure there is an integral Confession and a proper expression of sorrow. The counseling which follows is spiritual direction at its best.

A work of penance, called satisfaction, is given to the penitent, and should by its nature be not only a corrective for the sin committed but a true means to aid the process of continual conversion. Sometimes it is arrived at by consultation with the penitent. Never should the penitent be made to feel that performing the satisfaction earns or merits the forgiveness from God. That is totally gratuitous.

After the penitent's expression of contrition, the priest extends his hands, or at least his right hand, over the head of the penitent while saying the words of absolution. The Sign of the Cross accompanies the last part of the prayer, which is followed by a few words of praise to the Lord and a dismissal of the penitent. This enriched structure for the Rite of Penance can surely make individual celebration of Penance more fruitful and beneficial for the individual's growth in holiness.

(2) *Several Penitents, Individual Confession and Absolution.* This communal setting was anticipated in recent years by penitential liturgies that occurred. The second form allows individual Confessions within a context of community preparation and thanksgiving, thus making the ecclesial dimensions more evident. Usually this occurs at set times in the month or Liturgical Year.* The group gathers for introductory rites usually within the church and starts with a song expressing the proper mood. A short introduction makes clear to the participants the order of the service and the purpose of this celebration. Then an opening prayer concludes the introductory rites.

Thereupon the celebration of the Word occurs, and the choice of readings usually reflects God calling them back to conversion, the Mystery* of our reconciliation through the Passion* and Death* of Christ, the judgment of God on good

and evil in people's lives, all of which helps in the examination of conscience. A homily* puts the congregation into the proper frame of mind for their main duty to know and understand their sins. It should stress God's infinite mercy, the need for interior repentance, the social aspect of grace and sin, and the duty of making satisfaction for sin. Thereafter a period of silence occurs while all examine their consciences and build true contrition for sin.

The actual rite takes place first with a general confession of sinfulness, using some common formula such as the "I confess." Then all join in some litany* or suitable song expressing confession of sins, contrition, prayer for forgiveness, and trust in God's mercy, always to be concluded with the Lord's Prayer.* They are invited to go to priests at the places designated where they confess their sins, accept a fitting act of penance, and are absolved individually as in the first rite.

After the individual Confessions are completed the president invites all the reconciled to give thanks to the Lord for His mercy, either through the recitation of a Psalm or through the singing of a hymn.* One of the prayers of praise concludes this section immediately before the president blesses the faithful and dismisses the congregation.

(3) *Several Penitents, General Confession and Absolution.* Everything in this third rite occurs in the same manner as in the second rite with the exception of individual Confession and absolution. Following the homily, all are instructed in the proper dispositions necessary for absolution, their sorrow, their resolve to repair any harm, and particularly to confess every serious

sin at a later opportunity. An act of penance is suggested that everyone may perform. Then those who wish to be absolved show by some sign, e.g., kneeling, that they are ready for absolution. They make a general Confession, using a formula such as "I confess," followed by a penitential song or litany, which is concluded with the Lord's Prayer. The priest then gives the extended prayer of absolution provided for this occasion; he may also use the absolution for individual penitents in the plural.

Ordinarily speaking, the decision as to when this third rite may be used belongs to the Ordinary* of the diocese* unless there are exceptional conditions. For instance, in danger of death when there is not sufficient time for the Confessions of the individual penitents to be heard; or when the serious necessity exists as described below. The following three conditions must exist at the same time: a large number of penitents; a lack of sufficient confessors* to hear individual Confessions properly; the disadvantage to the faithful, through no fault of their own, of being forced to be without the grace of this Sacrament or Holy Communion* for a long time.

In every case, of course, those absolved must intend to go to individual Confession at an opportune time to mention their serious sins. The Rite of Penance indicates that one may not try to avoid individual Confession by use of this third rite, by stating that one may not receive general absolution again until individual Confession has occurred, unless there should be a just reason. These reasons may be individual, private, and personal, but they must be proportionate to the importance of the regulation. Naturally this rule binds only those who are conscious of serious sin. Others are free to share in communal reconciliation as frequently as they might like. *See also* GENERAL CONFESSION; RECONCILIATIO ET PAENITENTIA.

Penances (PEN-uhn[t]s-uhz). (1) A term applied to the parts of the Sacrament of Penance that have to do with satisfaction. They usually constitute some work or prayer assigned by the confessor* to the penitents who accept it to indicate their repentance and use it as a remedy for their weakness. In early Christian times there was an interval of rehabilitation, whereby conversion* took place in a liturgical context before reconciliation; sincerity in centering life on God rather than creatures was stressed. In the Middle Ages this part of the Sacrament of Penance was considered more expiation or reparation, something like a punitive debt. Contemporary theology envisions works of charity and something more in keeping with the type of sin committed to exhibit true conversion, particularly such that it will give the penitents a realization of the social and ecclesial effects of sin and Sacrament, especially with relation to everyday life. (*See also* PENANCE, RITE OF.)

(2) In the singular, a term applied to the internal consciousness of sin that induces a change of heart whereby sinners turn to God from their sin with regret. Normally there is some external manifestation of this, either through a confession of guilt or through the performance of difficult works that proclaim the depth of the conversion and show voluntary willingness for the acceptance of the punishment, since the penitents have violated God's law. (*See also* PENANCE.)

(3) A term applied to works of a similar nature performed for ascetical purposes rather than because of penalty for sins committed. Out of love that wants to share in the sufferings of Christ, the willingness to try to master disorderly inclinations might lead one to such practices as continence, abstinence,* fasting,* isolation, manual labor, privation of sleep, poverty, and the like. Obligatory penances have been downplayed in the contemporary Church, although the need for penance has been strongly reaffirmed by the Second Vatican Council and in the Apostolic Constitution *Paenitemini* of Paul VI. It allows the individual Catholic to choose the method of practicing penance.

Penitential Psalms (pen-uh-TEN-chuhl sah[l]mz). Seven Psalms* (6, 32, 38, 51, 102, 130, 143) that have traditionally been used to express sorrow for sin and desire for pardon* during penitential liturgies and seasons. The two that are penitential in their literal sense have been treated individually (Ps 51: the *Miserere,** and Ps 130: *De Profundis*)*. The others are less penitential in themselves, but they can be used as such in an accommodated sense. Psalm 6 is a prayer in time of distress; Psalm 32 hints at the blessedness of having one's sins forgiven; Psalm 38 is the prayer of an afflicted sinner; Psalm 102 is the prayer of a person who is very sick; and Psalm 143 is a plea for Divine assistance despite one's sinfulness.

Penitential Rite (pen-uh-TEN-chuhl rait). The part of the Introductory Rites* at Mass* wherein the congregation* joins with the priest* to ask God for mercy,* forgiveness* and healing. This rite prepares the community to listen to God's Word,* profess its faith,* join in the act of thanksgiving,* and share His graces and Communion.* The Penitential Rite begins with the presiding priest recalling the fact that we are sinners and invites us to ponder our faults so as to be sorry for them and seek pardon.* After a reasonable pause, there is a common confession, by which we proclaim that we are sinners before God and the Church.*

Our present version, more fraternal in character, is much less complex than the dialogue formerly used, the *Confiteor* (I confess), which consisted of two parts, a general confession and a supplication mentioning several Saints.* First said by the priest, it was then repeated by the acolytes.* It was followed by the *Misereatur*, which expressed the Church's intercessory prayer, and the *Indulgentiam*, a formula of absolution.

Aside from this ancient public confession of sins from the 11th century, much simplified in our current version, other formularies may be used, Biblical verses, or invocations that paraphrase the *Lord Have Mercy.** When these formulas are used, the *Lord Have Mercy* is not repeated later.

Before the Penitential Rite was established in a precise manner, the *Confiteor* with its absolution was used within many Sacramental rites. Present legislation limits its use to the Introductory Rites* of Mass and before the distribution of Communion Outside of Mass.*

Penitentials (pen-uh-TEN-chuhlz). Handbooks of directions for those hearing Confessions,* which were helpful because of the lists of sins with a proper penance* for each, questions the confessor should ask, and some prayers. Worked up by monks, they had no special authority, and depended mostly on the reputation of the compiler for holiness and wisdom. After they were brought into Frankish Europe from the Celtic Church, they were reworked more in keeping with Roman discipline. *See also* PENANCE, RITE OF; PENANCES.

Penitents (PEN-uh-tuhnts). (1) Persons who during the Rite of Penance* confess sin and seek absolution.* (*See also* PENANCE, RITE OF.)

(2) In the ancient penitential discipline, Christians who had fallen victim to serious fault and therefore were excluded for a certain length of time from the company of the faithful.* They were placed in a state of penance, a period of rigorous disciplinary law, and were given a separate place in the church. Their reconciliation was ordinarily performed on Holy Thursday.*

(3) Members of certain confraternities in parts of Europe during the Middle Ages who were obliged by statute to perform works of penance and mercy, similar to those in the previous definition. Thus, they contributed to society by visiting the sick, assisting prisoners, burying the dead, and doing similar acts of piety.

Pentecost (PENT-i-kawst; kahst). Derived from the Greek, the word means fiftieth day; in the Old Testament,* it was known as the Feast of Weeks, since it occurred after a week of weeks (7 times 7 = 49) after Passover. It was also known as the Feast of Harvest or the Day of Firstfruits. The Jews also commemorated the promulgation of the Law* on Mount Sinai on this day.

In the New Testament,* the Christians celebrated the completion of Christ's work through the coming of the Holy Spirit* on the Apostles* that gave birth to the Church.* The followers of Christ filled with the Holy Spirit and strengthened and encouraged by His grace* are fired up to spread the Gospel* to all nations as they themselves live and proclaim the Gospel. For them this feast also commemorates the promulgation of the New Law.

Sometimes Pentecost is referred to as Whitsunday. Before the recent Calendar,* Pentecost was celebrated with an octave.* The candidates for Baptism* who were not ready at Easter* were baptized on the vigil.* The second blessing of baptismal water on this day no longer occurs, though the vigil is still celebrated.

Pentecostal Movement (pent-i-KAHS-tuhl; -KAWS-tuhl; MOOV-muhnt). A form of Christianity, at first among Protestants, but since Vatican II* also among Roman Catholics, which holds that Baptism* with the Holy Spirit* allows speaking with tongues, healing of the sick, and similar charismatic gifts of the early Church,* and therefore a continuing outpouring of the Spirit should be among the ordinary happenings of Christian life. As the Holy Spirit brought special gifts then, a similar effusion of spiritual favors occurs today, usually manifested in three ways by the one who receives the Spirit (a) personal experience of the presence of the Spirit: (b) external signs of a preternatural character, comparable to the charismata of the Acts of the Apostles,* including speaking in tongues, the power of healing, the gift of prophecy; and (c) the need to extend these blessings to many others, by accepting the call of spreading the Spirit in the modern world.*

Their prayer meetings, which may last for several hours, are characterized by being free and spontaneous, with no set formula for praying, since they are being led by the Spirit. They dwell on Scriptural passages, possibly giving testimony of their own experiences, and many pray in whatever form or tongue they may choose. The results for these charismatic people is the increase of their confidence in the power of the Spirit, the assurance that they are in touch with the Divine, and the praise of the Father.* As a result an intensification of the community's unity in prayer occurs, the individual's prayer life deepens, and there is a more acute awareness of the Divine Presence. Should there be one in special need, the community laying on of hands takes place or praying for Baptism in the Spirit. Catholics prefer the term Charismatic Movement. *See also* NEO-PENTECOSTALISM.

Per Christum Dominum Nostrum. *See* THROUGH CHRIST OUR LORD.

Per Omnia Saecula Saeculorum. *See* FOR EVER AND EVER.

Peregrinatio Aetheriae (per-e-gree-NAH-tsi-oh ay-THER-ee-ay). Aetheria, from Gaul or Spain, traveled during the 5th century to Sinai, Mesopotamia, Asia Minor, Transjordan, and Jerusalem. Her diary contains the detailed description of the Liturgy* in Jerusalem and for historical studies is of major importance in Liturgy. Since the major feasts* were Epiphany* and Easter,* with octaves,* the rites she described seemed to be West Syrian, Byzantine, and Armenian. Pentecost* and Ascension* were linked; the special Liturgy of Lent* closed with the "greater week." Evidently she visited churches associated with sites and events in the Gospels.* This diary is the earliest witness to a developed daily Office* of liturgical prayer.*

Perfectae Caritatis (per- FEK-tay kah-ree-TAH-tees). Latin title (from the first two words "Perfect Charity") of the *Decree on the Appropriate Renewal of Religious Life* issued by the Second Vatican Council* on October 28, 1965. The document points out that Religious* should above all else seek and love God, for He has first loved us (see 1 Jn 4:10). In all circumstances they should be intent on developing a life hidden with Christ in God (see Col 3:3), the source and impetus of love of neighbor directed toward the salvation* of the world and the building up of the Church.*

They are also to cultivate the spirit and practice of prayer.* They should turn daily to Sacred Scripture,* there to learn by reading and meditation* the "supreme good of knowing Christ Jesus" (Phil 3:8). With heart and mind they should enter into the Liturgy,* especially the Mystery of the Eucharist,* and from this abundant source nurture their spiritual life. *See also* VATICAN COUNCIL, SECOND.

Pericopes (puh-RIK-uh-peez). Those passages selected from sacred books, primarily the Bible,* to be proclaimed during a liturgical service, expecially during Mass* and the Liturgy of the Hours.* Specific sections are appointed to be read on account of their aptness to the feast* or season*; during certain seasons, pericopes occur on successive days as a continuous* presentation of Scripture in their proper sequence. *See also* CYCLES; GOSPEL; LECTIONARY; READINGS.

Periods (PIR-ee-uhdz). During the initiation* process those times of maturation and investigation known as periods of: (1) evangelization* and precatechumenate*; (2) catechumenate*; (3) purification* and enlightenment*; (4) post-baptismal catechesis.* *See also* BAPTISM; RITE OF CHRISTIAN INITIATION OF ADULTS.

Permanent Deacons. *See* DEACON.

Perpetua and Felicity, Sts. (puhr-PECH-oo-ah and fi-LIS-uh-tee). ?-c.202. Of noble birth, Perpetua, a matron with one child, was taken prisoner in Carthage, with several others, including Felicity who was pregnant. She gave birth while they were imprisoned. Both were sentenced to death at the public games, but, when unharmed by the beasts, were killed by the sword. Perpetua wrote an account of their experiences, trial, and visions; an unknown eyewitness described their execution; these documents became an important record of the 3rd century Christian literature. Perpetua is mentioned in the Roman Canon (Eucharistic Prayer I*), but the Felicity mentioned with her is most likely the Roman martyr* of 162. St. Perpetua is the Patroness of Barren Women. *Liturgical celebration:* March 7 (Memorial); *theme:* dauntless in the face of martyrdom.

Perpetual Adoration. *See* ADORATION, EUCHARISTIC.

Peter, Apostle, St. (PEE-tuhr, uh-POS-uhl). ?-c.64. Simon, a fisherman, introduced to Jesus by Andrew* his brother, was called with him as one of the first Apostles* and surnamed Peter by the Lord. Most prominent of all of the Apostles, he is listed first among the Twelve and was their spokesman on many occasions. After the Ascension,* he assumed leadership, which, together with Tradition,* indicates his being head of the Church,* the first Pope.* The primacy had come to him in Scriptural passages; Tradition places him in Rome, where he died a martyr's death. *Liturgical celebration:* June 29 (Solemnity); *theme:* our weaknesses can be strengthened by trust in God. *See also* CHAIR OF ST. PETER; PETER, THE FIRST EPISTLE OF; PETER, THE SECOND EPISTLE OF.

Peter Canisius, St. (PEE-tuhr kuh-NEE-s[h]ee-uhs). 1521-1597. Born in the Netherlands, after his studies Peter joined the Jesuits and became noted for his preaching, teaching, writing, and being theological consultant during the Council of Trent. Ignatius Loyola* appointed him to the first Jesuit school at Messina. He became provincial of the southern German province and helped to establish colleges throughout Germany. Among his prolific writings are his catechisms, which have gone through innumerable editions. He was declared a Doctor of the Church* at his canonization in 1925. *Liturgical celebration:* December 21 (Opt. Mem.); *theme:* strive constantly to understand more perfectly the truths of your Faith.*

Peter Chanel, St. (PEE-tuhr sha-NEL). 1803-1841. After serving as a parish priest* near his home in France, he joined the Marists and was assigned as missionary to the Futuna Islands, Oceania, working among the savages, who eventually martyred him. The islands converted to Catholicism shortly thereafter. He is the first Marist martyr and the first martyr of Oceania. *Liturgical celebration:* April 28 (Opt. Mem.); *theme:* faithful witness to Christ even under adverse circumstances.

Peter Chrysologus, St. (PEE-tuhr kris-OL-uh-guhs). c.400- c.450. Born at Imola, Italy, Peter was a close friend of the Popes. He became bishop* of Ravenna, reformed his See, and used his rich friends to support his ambitious building program. His preaching dealt with the daily life of the people in a practical and moral manner; his many homilies earned for him the surname Chrysologus (golden-worded) and Doctor of the Church.* *Liturgical celebration:* July 30 (Opt. Mem.); *theme:* the Mystery* of our salvation* made clear out of love for others.

Peter Claver, St. (PEE-tuhr KLAY-vuhr). 1580-1654. This Spanish Jesuit, a missionary in Colombia, became the protector of Black slaves from Africa arriving in the Americas. Going into the infested holds of ships, Peter doctored

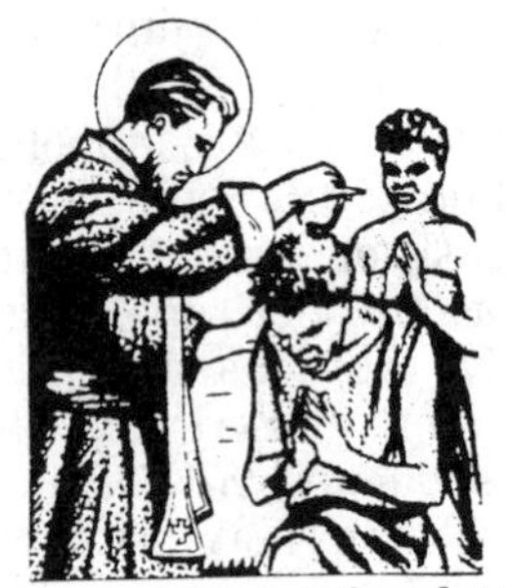

the slaves and later fought for their education and freedom. Through his miraculous works and his zeal in trying to ameliorate their condition, many slaves accepted Catholicism. At his canonization,* Leo XIII designated him the Patron of Catholic Missions for the Blacks. His feast is part of the Proper for the United States.* *Liturgical celebration:* September 9 (Memorial); *theme:* dedicated service to the downtrodden.

Peter Damian, St. (PEE-tuhr DAY-mi-uhn). c.1007-1072. An Italian Benedictine monk who later became Cardinal* of Austria. Besides strengthening community life in the monastery, he was active in diplomatic missions, synodal work, and ecclesiastical reform. His prolific writings covered many topics, and he is considered one of the greatest medieval Latin stylists. He is a Doctor of the Church.* *Liturgical celebration:* February 21 (Opt. Mem.); *theme:* service to Christ and His Church* should be our first love.

Peter, Martyr, St. (PEE-tuhr MAHR-tuhr). ?-304. Imprisoned during the persecution of Diocletian with Marcellinus,* a priest, Peter, an exorcist, converted many while in jail; they were eventually beheaded. Their names are mentioned in Eucharistic Prayer I.* *Liturgical celebration:* June 2 (Opt. Mem.); *theme:* concern for others even in stressful situations.

Peter, The First Epistle of (PEE-tuhr, thuh fuhrst i-PIS-uhl uhv). Sixty-seventh Book of the Bible* and twenty-first of the New Testament.* Written by St. Peter* the Apostle between 50 and 64 A.D., this little Book is like an encyclical* addressed to Christians enduring trials and overwhelmed by discouragement. It exhorts them to hope,* a holy life, irreproachable behavior, and submission to authorities in the fervent expectation of the proximate coming of the Lord. It is thus close to the great Epistles of Paul.* It also emphasizes Baptism* and alludes to various features of the baptismal Liturgy,* indicating that the author has incorporated into his exposition numerous homiletic, credal, hymnic, and Sacramental elements of the baptismal rite that had become traditional at an early date.

Liturgical use: In the *Roman Missal,** this Book is used especially during the Sundays of the Easter Season* (A), because of its baptismal emphasis; it is also read during the 1st Sunday of Lent* (B), the 8th Week of Ordinary Time* (II), in various Common* and Ritual* Masses as well as on the Chair of Peter,* the Feast of St. Mark,* and the Solemnity of Sts. Peter and Paul.* In the *Liturgy of the Hours,** it is used during the Octave* of Easter and in the Common* and gives rise to a minor canticle* in the Four Week Psalter.* *Meaning:* Christians have an inheritance reserved in heaven for us. It is unfading, unchanging, and protected by God. To attain it we must grow spiritually—by nourishing ourselves on prayer,* meditation,* reading God's Word,* and fellowship. Finally we must be ready to suffer as Jesus did. Indeed, we share the very priesthood of Christ—which has come to be

known as the Priesthood of the Faithful or universal priesthood* and is the basis for our participation* in the Liturgy.*

Peter, The Second Epistle of (PEE-tuhr, thuh SEK-uhnd i-PIS-uhl uhv). Sixty-eighth Book of the Bible* and twenty-second of the New Testament.* It was probably written by an unknown author about 100-125 A.D. and has a twofold purpose: to undergird faith in the Second Coming* of Christ and to warn against false teachers. In addition to foretelling the imminent doom of the false teachers, the author recalls the apostolic witness as the basis of the Church's* proclamation, points to the Messianic prophecis of the Old Testament,* which have been confirmed by Christ's coming, and attributes the delay of the Second Coming to God's patience and forbearance.

Liturgical use: In the *Roman Missal,** this Book is read on the 2nd Sunday of Advent* (B), the Transfiguration,* and Monday and Tuesday of the 9th Week in Ordinary Time* (II). In the *Liturgy of the Hours,** it is read during the 34th Week in Ordinary Time. *Meaning:* God's power has provided us with all that we need to live for Him. We must make use of this gift so that we can share in the Divine Nature through grace.* We should practice the virtues of faith,* knowledge, self-control, steadfastness, godliness, and love.* For the Lord desires that no one should perish but that all should come to repentance and life.

Petition (pe-TISH-uhn). This important and most used type of prayer* is also one of the four ends of the Eucharist.* Sometimes known as supplication, it is used also on behalf of others, and then termed intercession. Recall the General Intercessions* during the Eucharist.* People from all times and places use this type of prayer instinctively to ask God for special favors. It should not be belittled, for there are some liturgical acts that are devoted almost entirely to this type of petition, for example, the litany.* Most people find no difficulty in using this type of prayer, but some teachers of prayer may feel that it may be the only kind they know. In many instances it may seem quite selfish, but even Christ asked that the cup pass from Him in the Garden of Gethsemane.

Some wonder how God can answer our prayers, since presumably He knows all things and knows what is best for us. Others say that since He knows all things, it is quite possible that, realizing we would make this prayer of petition, He has already used His power to change the events. Since all prayers of petition should be constructed with the qualifying phrase "Thy will be done," one can expect the answer to be "no." Throughout the Bible,* people presume that a prayer of petition does not limit the freedom of God but strengthens the communication between God and the one who prays. *See also* ADORATION; IMPETRATION; MASS; PRAYER; REPARATION; THANKSGIVING.

Pews (pyooz). Fixed benches, usually with backs, to serve as seats for worshipers in church. Originat-

ing in early medieval times, they seem to have developed from stone seats attached to walls or nave piers to accommodate the infirm. Aligned to face the main altar,* many pews have elaborately carved ends or backs.

Pew rent was charged an individual or a family for reservation of a specific space at religious services. This source of revenue helped maintain the church and supported the clergy.* When the People of God began to enjoy a greater mobility in urban life, this practice gave way to a seat collection, which does not reserve space, but pays for a single use of the facility. *See also* CHURCH FURNISHINGS.

Philemon, The Epistle to (fuh-LEE-muhn; fai-; thee i-PIS-uhl too). Sixty-fourth Book of the Bible* and eighteenth of the New Testament.* During his first Roman imprisonment (61-63 A.D.), St. Paul* came to know a slave named Onesimus, who had deserted his master Philemon, a wealthy Christian of Colossae in Phrygia. After the Apostle* had won the fugitive over to Christianity, he looked for a favorable opportunity to send him back to his master. This opportunity offered itself when he was dispatching a letter to the Colossians* in the year 63. Onesimus accompanied St. Paul's messenger Tychicus. To Philemon, the Apostle addressed a touching appeal, entreating his friend to deal kindly with the runaway and in fact to set him free. For they are both servants of Christ and their union in Christ should overshadow their master-slave relationship.

Liturgical use: In the *Roman Missal,** this Book is read on the 23rd Sunday in Ordinary Time* (C) and Thursday of the 32nd Week (II). In the *Liturgy of the Hours,** it is used only in the alternate Two-Year Cycle* on Saturday of the 21st Week (I). *Meaning:* In Christ all Christians are brothers and sisters, for "there is neither Jew nor Greek, there is neither slave nor free person, there is not male and female; for you are all one in Christ Jesus" (Gal 3:28; see Col 3:11). Indeed, the Gospel* of Christ changes people's lives—as is shown by those named in the Epistle who went from not knowing Christ to following Him completely: Paul, Philemon, Onesimus, Apphia, Archippus, Timothy,* Epaphras, Mark, and Aristarchus.

Philip, Apostle, St. (FIL-ip, uh-POS-uhl). 1st century. From Bethsaida, Philip learned of Jesus through John the Baptist.* He was called individually by Jesus and brought Nathanael* to Him (Jn 1:43-47). Before Jesus multiplied the loaves, it was Philip who alluded to the great amount of food needed for such a crowd (Jn 6:7). After the Ascension,* Philip preached in Turkey and possibly France. He was martyred by being crucified and

stoned in Turkey about the year 80. *Liturgical celebration:* May 3 (Feast); *theme:* simplicity that allows faith* to grow.

Philip Neri, St. (FIL-ip NEER-ai). 1515-1595. Born in Florence, Philip started a social apostolate in Rome prior to his ordination.* Popular as a confessor,* he frequently also gave instructions to young men, imparting wisdom in a humorous way. This developed into an Oratory where spiritual reading, singing, and works of charity were practiced. Eventually he founded the Congregation of the Oratory and became its superior. He is called the Apostle* of Rome. *Liturgical celebration:* May 26 (Memorial); *theme:* cheerfulness and warm personal devotion to Christ.

Philippians, The Epistle to the (fuh-LIP-ee-uhnz, thee i-pis-uhl too thuh). Fifty-seventh Book of the Bible* and eleventh of the New Testament.* Philippians is a warm, friendly letter written by St. Paul* to the Christians of Philippi either from Ephesus (54-58) or from Rome during his captivity (61-63). Paul thanks the Philippians for their gift of money and commends Epaphroditus whom they had sent to care for him. At the same time, he takes the opportunity of exhorting them to put an end to their dissensions, and he warns them against Jewish converts who wished to make Old Testament* practices obligatory for Christians.

Paul recalls the example of Christ Who—in contrast with Adam who sought to assert himself and assure his life by his unaided efforts—wholly emptied Himself, renouncing all self-will and submitting entirely to the will of the Father* (2:6-11). This hymn, which in all probability antedates Paul and was a liturgical text, is one of the most extraordinary compositions of the ancient Church.* Christ's lot is exemplary. Those who live in and by Christ must, like Him, renounce their own interests, their will to power, and expect praise and glory from God alone.

Liturgical use: In the *Roman Missal,** this Book is read on the 2nd and 3rd Sundays of Advent* (C), 2nd and 5th Sundays of Lent* (C), Passion Sunday,* the 25th through the 28th Sundays in Ordinary Time (A), and Friday of the 30th Week to Saturday of the 31st Week (II). It is also read on the Triumph of the Cross* and October 17 as well as in Common,* Votive,* and Ritual Masses.* In the *Liturgy of the Hours,** it is read during the 26th Week in Ordinary Time and the Common of Holy Men and of Religious. It also gives rise to a minor canticle* in the Psalter.* *Meaning:* We are always to rejoice in the Lord for all that He has done for us. He obtained salvation* for us—all we need do is work it out "with fear and trembling" (2:12), pressing toward the goal of God's upward call in Christ (3:14). In doing so we must imitate the humility of Christ, which obtained His exaltation. We should have no anxiety but practice prayer, which will obtain true freedom for us (4:4-7).

Pictures. *See* IMAGES.

Pious Associations. *See* ASSOCIATIONS, PIOUS.

Pious Practices. *See* LITURGICAL SPIRITUALITY.

Piscina. *See* SACRARIUM.

Pius V, St. (PAI-uhs fifth). 1504-1572. Born Michele Ghisliere in northern Italy, this Dominican eventually became bishop,* and then a Cardinal Inquisitor General of the whole Church.* Upon his papal election, 1566, he put the decrees of the Council of Trent into effect, completed a new catechism,* revised the *Roman Breviary** and *Missal,** prescribed a new edition of Thomas Aquinas'* works, and proclaimed him a Doctor of the Church.* *Liturgical celebration:* April 30 (Opt. Mem.); *theme:* staunch defense of the Faith, together with fitting worship.*

Pius X, St. (PAI-uhs tenth). 1835-1914. Of humble parentage near Venice, Giuseppe Sarto was ordained, appointed bishop,* and then cardinal* of Venice, and finally elected Pope* in 1903. Warmly pastoral in his approach, he urged frequent and early Communion.* He

started codification of Canon Law, commissioned a revision of the Vulgate,* reorganized the Papal Court, and reformed the Psalter* and *Breviary.** His forthright, strong, and decisive intervention in modernism was providential. *Liturgical celebration:* August 21 (Memorial); *theme:* simplicity of life and humility of heart are indispensable for a perfect Christian life.

Place of Mass. *See* MASS, PLACE OF.

Plainchant (PLAYN-chant.) For those who do not want to consider this a synonym for Gregorian Chant,* the distinction is that it modifies Gregorian Chant. Composed on a scale of four lines, it has free rhythm and is sung in unison. Only natural intervals of the human voice are used, and melodies must be confined to the natural range of the voice. As a particular feature the "leading note" is ordinarily avoided. *See also* GREGORIAN CHANT.

Planeta. *See* CHASUBLE.

Plenary Indulgences. *See* INDULGENCES.

Polycarp, St. (POL-ee-kahrp). c.69-c.155. Personal disciple of John* the Apostle, who made him bishop* of Smyrna. Polycarp staunchly defended orthodoxy and opposed heresy, particularly Marcionism. During a persecution he refused to sacrifice to the gods, and when the flames did not consume him, he was stabbed to death. *Liturgical celebration:* February 23 (Memorial); *theme:* valor to suffer for the Lord at any age.

Polyphony (puh-LIF-uh-nee). The simultaneous singing of individual parts by two or more voices. In monophony, one part is sung by one or several voices. Although abuses in its use occurred in the past, polyphony is allowed today provided it is in accord with the spirit of the liturgical action being performed at that time. *See also* MUSIC.

Pontian, St. (PON-shi-uhn). ?-c.236. This Roman succeeded Pope Urban I and held a synod that confirmed the condemnation of Origen. Exiled to Sardinia, he met the anti-Pope Hippolytus* and most probably died of ill treatment. *Liturgical celebration:* August 13 (Opt. Mem.); *theme:* suffer out of love for the Lord.

Pontifical (pon-TIF-i-kuhl). A liturgical book* that includes the rites and prayers of liturgical functions reserved to the bishop,* except for the Mass.* It describes such sacred functions as Confirmation,* Ordination,* consecration of churches, altars,* and cemeteries,* various blessings,* and the like. Currently under revision, some sections are now available, for instance, Holy Orders.*

Pontifical Blessing (pon-TIF-i-kuhl BLES-ing). Whether during or outside of Mass* this blessing given only by a bishop* is characterized by the threefold Sign of the Cross* (a priest* makes only a single one)

and the specific formula that precedes it.

Pontifical Insignia. *See* INSIGNIA, PONTIFICAL.

Pontifical Mass (pon-TIF-i-kuhl mas). The solemn Mass celebrated by a bishop* (or an abbot*) either at the throne* with full ceremonial or at the faldstool* with less ceremonial. The prescribed ritual usually includes two deacons* and an assistant priest* besides the customary ministers.* Such a Mass, with the bishop surrounded by his clergy and congregation, is considered the sign of unity in the Church.*

Pontificals. *See* INSIGNIA, PONTIFICAL.

Poor Souls. *See* ALL SOULS.

Pope (pohp). The common English title for the visible head of the Catholic Church, derived from the Greek work, *pappas*, a colloquial child's word for father, since his authority is to be discharged in a paternal fashion. As Pope he is the supreme legislator for the Liturgy* but delegates most of this power to the Congregation for Divine Worship and the Discipline of the Sacraments.* In the Latin Rite* the Pope is prayed for during each Eucharistic Prayer*; a similar prayer for the Pope occurs in other Liturgies.

Popular Devotions. *See* PARALITURGY.

Postbaptismal (pohst-bap-TIZ-muhl). This adjectival term is usually connected with the noun catechesis,* indicating that special aspect of instruction for the catechumens* after they have been baptized. *See also* PERIODS.

Postcommunion. *See* PRAYER AFTER COMMUNION.

Postulancy (POS-chuh-luhn-see). That period, sometimes called the prenovitiate, during which a candidate for a Religious Order prepares to receive the Religious habit, that includes admission into the novitiate of a Religious community. The intent is to grow in the knowledge of Religious Life and of the institute one intends to join, and thereby to develop the proper attitudes and virtues* necessary for acceptance into the novitiate. The duration of the postulancy varies according to the Religious constitutions, usually no less than six months.

Posture in Worship (POS-chuhr in WUHR-shuhp). Natural movements of the body that express in some stylized form the love* of God during corporate worship* and give the important nonverbal manner of communicating during a liturgical celebration. The liturgical posture conveys personal relationships by means of directional movement. Ordinarily an up or down movement portrays the belief or feeling about relations between human beings and God. Horizontal movements communicate rather the relations between humans. These ritual actions may be of three types: (a) solely functional, for instance cleansing one's hands after the Preparation of the Gifts*; (b) an expression of a certain attitude, such as contrition,* by striking the breast; (c) merely symbolic, such as using oil* to display curative features of the Sacrament.*

Typical postures follow:

(1) *Standing.* Historically this was the normal attitude of prayer among pagans and Jews, adopted by the first Christians. It indicates a reverence* for God. For Christians it took on an added implication, referring to the Resurrection* of Christ, and frequently they faced the East toward the rising sun, regarded as a symbol of Christ Himself.

(2) *Kneeling.* This gesture indicates adoration,* or the expression of humility before the greatness of God, fervent entreaty in prayer,* a sign of penance* or sorrow, even mourning. Historically the congregation* gradually knelt more and more instead of maintaining its standing position. Recent rules limit kneeling at Mass.*

(3) *Prostration.* This occurs when one lies flat on the ground face downward. It is infrequently prescribed, primarily at the episcopal or sacerdotal ordinations* and at the beginning of the Good Friday* service.

(4) *Sitting.* This position is an exterior mark of dignity for the person seated during a liturgical function over which he presides; it is also the customary pose of a teacher. This same posture for a congregation allows it to be more relaxed during readings,* homilies,* and chants.* Clergy not engaged in some liturgical action may also sit. Custom has allowed most Religious Orders and canons* to sit during the singing or recitation of the Psalms* in the celebration of the Liturgy of the Hours.*

For a description of other liturgical postures see the following: BOWING; ELEVATION; GENUFLECTION; IMPOSITION OF HANDS; SIGN OF PEACE; SIGN OF THE CROSS.

Gestures of the Celebrant

It must be kept in mind that gestures of the celebrant during the Liturgy* are not peripheral but serve as signs that reveal Christ's presence in the assembly.* Such gestures, as any other art, must be learned. To stand properly, bow, genuflect, make the various signs, all these are to be done in a graceful but simple and unstudied manner. Liturgical gestures are to enhance with their beauty; hence they are done in an unhurried manner, without an affected slowness. Since the celebrant* himself is a sign of Christ, he therefore gives witness to Christ in the Church* insofar as his bearing, his gestures, and his words allow his own sanctity to show through his actions. They then are to be salvation* events through which the love of the Father,* as revealed in Christ, will be diffused through the Holy Spirit.*

Postures for the Faithful during Mass

Stand for the Entrance Song* or at the time the priest enters until the Opening Prayer* is concluded; sit during the Readings*; stand for the singing of the Alleluia Verse* or a Gospel Verse and during the proclamation of the Gospel*; sit during the Homily*; stand during the Profession of Faith* and the General Intercessions*; sit during the Preparation of the Gifts*; stand from the beginning of the Prayer over the Gifts* until the conclusion of the Holy, Holy, Holy* (*Sanctus*); kneel from the end of the Holy, Holy, Holy to the Amen* following the Eucharistic Prayer*; stand from the Lord's Prayer* until after the Lamb of God* and before the Prayer after Communion* until the end of Mass.* If there is a period of silent prayer after Communion, the congregation may sit.

Posture during the Liturgy of the Hours

Anyone who attends the Liturgy of the Hours* should stand during the Invitatory* and Introductory Verse* of each Hour, during the Hymn,* the Gospel Canticle,* the Intercessions,* the Lord's Prayer* and the Concluding Prayer. Be seated while listening to the Readings other than the Gospel. During the Psalms and non-Gospel Canticles and their Antiphons the community sits or stands according to custom. For the most part in the United States, the community sits. *See also* ATTITUDES.

Praise to You, Lord Jesus Christ (prayz too yoo, lawrd JEE-zuhs; -zuhz; kraist). The congregation's acclamation* at the end of the Gospel* in answer to the deacon's* or priest's* conclusion: "This is the Gospel of the Lord." *See also* MASS, ORDER OF.

Praises, Divine. *See* DIVINE PRAISES.

Pray, Brethren (pray, BRETH-[uh-]ruhn). This invitational appeal by the priest* to the faithful* near the end of the Preparation of the Gifts* together with their response reiterates what has gone before as they are asked to petition the Lord to accept the gifts; this they do by praising God and asking for His

blessing* on them, the community. Thus there is a reduplication of what the whole rite states, that the sacrifice of the priest is also the sacrifice of the people. To avoid sexist language, "Brethren" is omitted or a substitute found. *See also* PREPARATION OF THE GIFTS.

Prayer (prayr; pra[uh]r). (1) In its more specific meaning this word or its synonym, oration, frequently refers to the prayer immediately preceding the Liturgy of the Word* at Mass,* today called the Opening Prayer.* Ordinarily it is the same prayer that is said at the end of each of the Hours in the Liturgy of the Hours.* In a more extended meaning, and then usually in the plural, it refers not only to the Opening Prayer but to the Prayer over the Gifts* and the Prayer after Communion* at Mass.* (*See also* OPENING PRAYER; PRESIDENTIAL PRAYERS.)

(2) In a more general sense, prayer is any formal or informal prayer addressed to God; Catholics also apply the term to their supplications to the Blessed Virgin Mary* or the Saints.* It reflects the conscious relationship of human beings to God, whether that be done in a liturgical worship setting, meditation,* or individual prayer. Catechisms define it as the raising of the heart and mind to God, whether done mentally, vocally, individually, collectively, privately, or in public.

For the most part, prayer acknowledges the Divine goodness; nevertheless, it is a petition to seek from His Divine benevolence the benefits that are needed for life, both temporal and eternal. Though prayer is common to all cultures and times as a religious phenomenon, Christian prayer centers in the Incarnate Word and thus it becomes a personal communion with the Father* in the Son* through the Holy Spirit.*

Vocal prayer consists of a fixed formula in its approach to God; the free spontaneous expression is usually termed mental prayer and is divided into discursive prayer, meditation; affective prayer, which would have developed from meditation to a higher level; and finally contemplation,* a rather loving, intuitive type.

Traditionally, prayer is divided into four aspects or types. (a) Adoration* or praise* usually contemplates and worships God in Himself and stresses the totality of the Godhead with its self-sufficiency that demands our praise. Human beings offer this homage to God in many different ways; the most highly valued usually is through singing.

(b) In atonement for their sin based on their fallen nature, humans admit their guilt through general, personal, and Sacramental Confession.*

(c) Supplication, or interceding with the Lord to implore His favors and continuous generosity in fulfilling the needs of humankind, is the third form, and frequently the reason why the majority of people turn to prayer. Though many may consider it a low form of prayer, still it affects the daily living of the majority of people. To abandon the prayer of petition would seem to deny the basic definition of prayer from both the Latin and the Greek which denotes primarily the free approach to God to seek His benevolence for our daily living.

(d) Finally because of answers to our prayers of supplication, one strong feature should be and usually is thanksgiving, the gratitude shown to God for the personal experiences we have had of His goodness.

The Liturgy* is the highest form of prayer, since it is the prayer of Christ and of His members. It includes all types of prayer mentioned above, except for contemplation*—which is needed to prepare for authentic liturgical participation.* *See also* ADORATION; CONTEMPLATION; IMPETRATION; MASS; PARALITURGY; PENANCE; REPARATION; THANKSGIVING; WORSHIP.

Prayer after Communion (prayr; pray[uh]r; AF-tuhr kuh-MYOO-nyuhn). This prayer concludes the Liturgy of the Eucharist.* As in the other two presidential prayers,* the Opening Prayer* and the Prayer over the Gifts,* the celebrant* speaks in the name of the community by thanking the Father* for the gift received and petitions the Lord

that the fruits of the Sacrament* may be produced in us. We prepare to go forth and act, applying in our daily lives what we have learned, as we engage in our usual occupations. *See also* MASS—COMMUNION RITE; MASS, ORDER OF.

Prayer, Bidding. *See* GENERAL INTERCESSIONS.

Prayer Books (prayr; pray[uh]r; buks). In contradistinction to official liturgical books,* or service books, prayer books consist of a collection of prayers,* devotions,* and hymns* for private use. These are nonliturgical devotions, consisting of a variety of reflective readings, meditations, and authorized prayers. Recently some of these manuals contain paraphrases or substantial portions of liturgical texts. Many confraternities* and sodalities develop such prayer books, which in turn have strong influence on the spiritual growth of their members. Whether used by such groups or by individuals, these personal manuals of prayer enrich the religious piety of many, while they also serve as a tool for spiritual direction and religious instruction.

Prayer Endings (prayr; pray[uh]r; EN-dingz). The Opening Prayer,* which corresponds to the Concluding Prayer* in the *Liturgy of the Hours*,* enunciates the theme of the celebration. This petitionary prayer salutes God* the Father through Christ in the Holy Spirit.* In these two instances the longer conclusion is used:

—if the prayer is directed to the Father: *We ask this (Grant this) through our Lord Jesus Christ, your Son, who lives and reigns with you and the Holy Spirit, one God, for ever and ever;*

—if it is directed to the Father, but the Son is mentioned at the end: *Who lives and reigns with you and the Holy Spirit, one God, for ever and ever;*

—if it is directed to the Son: *You live and reign with the Father and the Holy Spirit, one God, for ever and ever.*

However, in the Mass* the shorter conclusion is used for the Prayer over the Gifts* and Prayer after Communion*:

—if the prayer is directed to the Father: *We ask this (Grant this) through Christ our Lord;*

—if it is directed to the Father, but the Son is mentioned at the end: *Who lives and reigns with you for ever and ever;*

—if it is directed to the Son: *You live and reign for ever and ever.*

Prayer, Lord's. *See* LORD'S PRAYER.

Prayer of the Faithful. *See* GENERAL INTERCESSIONS.

Prayer over the Gifts (prayr; pray[uh]r OH-vuhr thuh gifts). This presidential prayer* concludes the Preparation of the Gifts,* while it serves as a transition to the Eucharistic Prayer* during the Liturgy of the Eucharist.* With the material gifts properly prepared, this prayer is a symbolic expression

of the sacrificial intention of the congregation as these gifts are recommended to God through the functional nature of this Prayer over the Gifts. *See also* MASS, ORDER OF; OFFERING; OFFERTORY.

Prayer over the People (prayr; pray[uh]r; OH-vuhr thuh PEE-puhl). A dismissal blessing as a special invocation, used at the discretion of the priest,* at the end of the Mass* or in the Liturgy of the Hours* at the conclusion of the cardinal Hours, namely Morning Prayer* and Evening Prayer.* Preceding the Final Blessing,* it has a variety of formulas. Until recently it was used only in Lenten Masses. It begins with the invitation by the priest or deacon*: "Bow your heads* and pray for God's blessing."

Prayers. *See* INTERCESSIONS.

Prayers before Communion (prayrz; pray[uh]rz; bi-FAWR [FOHR] kuh-MYOO-nyuhn). After the Breaking of the Bread* and commingling, the priest* and people prepare privately for Communion.* The priest has a choice of two short prayers said quietly so others may not hear, begging that he may

worthily receive and that good may be effected thereby. The community is expected to join in silent prayer at this time. *See also* CELEBRANT, PRIVATE PRAYERS OF.

Prayers, Eucharistic. *See* EUCHARISTIC PRAYERS.

Preaching (PREECH-ing). The preaching ministry devolves upon bishops,* priests,* and deacons* as they exercise their office of proclaiming the Scriptures.* In the *Constitution on the Church* (LG, 28), this office is described as the first duty of priests, who are "consecrated to preach the Gospel."* Homilies* are prescribed for Sundays and Holy Days,* and strongly encouraged at weekday Masses, particularly during Advent* and Lent.* Although preaching has instructional, evangelizing, and exhortatory functions, recent decrees stress that liturgical preaching is to flow from the proclamation of the Scriptures in the assembly* and that, in the context of the occasion, the facet of the Mystery of Christ* expressed in the feast* or season* is to be proclaimed.

This richer theology of preaching acknowledges the union between Word and Sacrament, while the preaching brings to the present celebration essentially the Mystery of Salvation* as experienced here and now. It demands the extension of the call of God to Christian living, so that a concrete and direct response should be made. The result will be a commitment to greater faith* and love,* which shows itself in a greater Christian action in the world.* Lay persons may preach in certain circumstances or in particular cases as prescribed by the Conference of Bishops* except that they may not give a Homily. *See also* HOMILY.

Precatechumenate (pree-kat-uh-KYOO-muhn-uht). That period of time before the formal entrance into the catechumenate,* during which the person hears for the first time the preaching of the Gospel.* *See also* PERIODS.

Precedence (PRES-uhd-uhn[t]s; pri-SEED-uhn[t]s). The order of position or placement of physical persons based on a right of superior rank had been given by the former Canon Law; it has been deleted in the new Code. Its intent was to establish good order in assemblies* and processions.* Most likely for the same purpose, vestiges of the former law will probably be maintained in liturgical actions. For the most part, the ranking would be acceptable to most people, starting with the Pope,* cardinals,* bishops,* priests,* seculars,* Religious,* and finally lay people.*

Precedence of Feasts. *See* ORDER OF PRECEDENCE.

Precepts of the Church. *See* COMMANDMENTS.

Preces. *See* INTERCESSIONS.

Preconium. *See* EXSULTET.

Predella (pree-; pruh-; DEL-uh). The top of the platform on which an altar* is situated.

Preface (PREF-uhs; -is). Originally, any prayer solemnly pronounced by the celebrant* to the congregation during a liturgical action, but now restricted to the prologue of the Eucharistic Prayer.* Its main theme ascribes praise* and thanksgiving* to God. Obviously then it does not signify the usual sense of the word, preliminary, but a proclamation, similar to an overture in music, and as such ought to be sung. Introduced by an ancient invitational Introductory Dialogue,* it then proceeds to render general praise to God, continues with a special act of thanksgiving for the Mystery* being celebrated, usually always mentioning the Mediator Christ, and concludes with angelic praise, that introduces the singing of the Holy, Holy, Holy.*

Since the Preface contains reasons why the congregation has gathered to give thanks, various themes expressed commemorate events in God's plan of salvation,* or the life of Christ, or the lives of the Saints,* or even the People of God, as in marriage or death. Thus, the comparatively small number of Prefaces today (ninety-one) compared to the almost 300 of several centuries ago relate first of all to the liturgical seasons and feast days and then to the special liturgical celebrations. *See also* MASS, ORDER OF.

Prelate (PREL-uht; PREE-layt). An ecclesiastical official who enjoys ordinary jurisdiction over others, such as bishops,* abbots,* exempt Religious superiors, vicars general, and prelates nullius, who govern an area, usually a missionary territory, which is not part of an established diocese.* Some priests* receive this title as an indication of papal recognition for their service to the Church.*

Preparation of the Altar. *See* PREPARATION OF THE GIFTS.

Preparation of the Bread. *See* PREPARATION OF THE GIFTS.

Preparation of the Gifts (prep-uh-RAY-shuhn uhv thuh gifts). The part of Mass* that comes at the beginning of the Liturgy of the Eucharist,* after we have received the Word of God,* His Gift to us in the Liturgy of the Word.* In it we respond with a gift of our own in thanksgiving, namely that all-inclusive action without restriction or limit, the sacrifice of Christ under the appearance of bread and wine. Originally the preparation rite was very simple with the people gathering around the table and placing food upon it, but by the Middle Ages this communal dimension of the Mass, with its procession,* disappeared and the Rite of Preparation gave way to the Offertory Rite, based on the prayers of the priest.

Today our change in name to Preparation of the Gifts will surely correct the notion that the Offertory was something distinct from or anticipating the Eucharistic Prayer* itself, wherein the remembrance of the Lord's Passion* is the sacrificial offering.

The gifts are brought up in procession, usually accompanied by song, to the empty table of the Lord. The gifts as a rule are bread,* wine,* and water*; sometimes other gifts for the poor or items indicative of the sacrifice offered by the congregation are presented. Should money be collected during the Mass, it would be brought forward together with the elements of the Eucharist. Then the priest, elevating the paten* with the bread, pronounces the formula. Next, the wine is poured into the chalice* and a few drops of water are commingled with it, a rite rich in symbolism. For the Eastern Church, it symbolizes the Mystery of Christ,* the water Christ's humanity, the wine His Divinity. In the Western Church, it symbolizes the union of Christ (the wine) with His Church (the water). Then the chalice is elevated and a parallel formula pronounced.

This twofold formula is noteworthy in its origin, reflecting the fact that our Eucharistic sacrifice was grafted to the Jewish liturgy of repasts, as the one celebrated by Christ with His disciples on Holy Thursday.* The prayer is actually a blessing or benediction called *berakah.** Different from the blessing we think of when we ask the Lord to sanctify an object or an action of ours, this blessing ascends, thanking the Lord, congratulating Him for His greatness and His gifts.

If singing has not continued to this point in the Preparation, the formulas are recited in a loud voice and the faithful* participate in the blessing by the acclamation: "Blessed be God for ever."*

The quiet prayer of the priest that follows is taken from the Book of Daniel* as recited by Azariah, in which we are reminded that any material sacrifice is valueless if we do not have the desire of spiritual sacrifice to renounce evil and unite ourselves with God in loving obedience.

An optional rite of incensation* of the gifts and the altar may follow; this action, more than any other symbol, spiritualizes our sacrifice.* Thereafter follows the washing of the celebrant's hands because of handling the gifts and the censer.* An invitation to the faithful to pray that the gifts will be acceptable occurs next, and they respond affirmatively. As the Introductory Rites* are concluded with the Opening Prayer,* so the Preparation of the Gifts concludes with a similar oration, the Prayer over the Gifts.* Unlike the Opening Prayer,* which characterizes the Mystery of the day or the liturgical season, the Prayer over the Gifts is functional, having a purely Eucharistic purpose that is valid in any Mass and consequently may not necessarily be particularized by a feast. Thereupon the action moves to the Eucharistic Prayer.* *See also* OFFERTORY.

Preparation of the Wine. *See* PREPARATION OF THE GIFTS.

Presbyter. *See* PRIEST.

Presbyterorum Ordinis (prez-bee-te-ROH-room AWR-dee-nees). Latin title (from the first two words "Of the Order of Priests") of the *Decree on the Ministry and Life of Priests* issued by the Second Vatican Council* on December 7, 1965. It states that priests* possess the sacred power of orders to offer sacrifice in the community, to forgive sins, and in the name of Christ to exercise publicly the office of priests on behalf of the people. They are thus called to come to holiness* in the way proper to them by carrying out their offices sincerely and untiringly in the Spirit* of Christ. They are aided to do so by Scripture* and the Sacraments,* especially the Eucharist,* as well as by prayer* both public and private.

The Decree also states that the Eucharistic assembly* is central for the community of the faithful* over which the priest has charge. Thus, priests should instruct the faithful to offer the Divine Victim to the Father* in the sacrifice of the Mass* and with Christ to make an offering of their own life. Furthermore, priests should prolong the praise* and thanksgiving* offered in the Eucharist over the hours of the day by means of the Liturgy of the Hours.* At the same time they should devote themselves to the science and art of the Liturgy,* so that through their liturgical ministry the Christian communities in their care will offer an ever more perfect praise to God, Father, Son, and Holy Spirit. *See also* PRIEST.

Presbytery; Presbyterium (PREZ-buh-ter-ee; PRES-; prez-; pres-; buh-TER-ee-uhm). (1) That part of the church where bishops,* priests* and ministers* perform their ministry. Large enough to permit the sacred rites to be readily seen and carried out, it is usually in an elevated part of the church or set off by structure or decoration, so that the congregation* may readily attend with devotion. Same as CHOIRS (ARCHITECTURE).

(2) At one time the senate of priests who assisted a bishop in administering the diocese.*

(3) Popularly, a synonym for the rectory, clergy house, or residence of priests.

Presence, Real. *See* EUCHARIST.

Presentation of Mary. *See* MARY, BLESSED VIRGIN—FEASTS.

Presentation of the Lord (prez-uhn-TAY-shuhn; pree-zuhn-; uhv thuh Lawrd). This feast,* celebrated on February 2, commemorates the presentation of the infant Jesus in the Temple at Jerusalem by His parents. Since it coincides with the fortieth day after childbirth, it also designates the purification of Mary, as the feast was formerly called.

This purification rite was part of the Mosaic Law. Since 1969 the focus of the feast has emphasized the Presentation of the Lord, Jesus Christ, Who is considered the true light* of the world. Therefore this feast has popularly been called Candlemas Day, and at the beginning of Mass, candles* are blessed and a procession* occurs, honoring Jesus as our Savior Who sheds light upon us and offers salvation* to the whole world.*

The Ceremony

In some suitable place distinct from the church, the faithful* bring their unlighted candles. The priest, vested in white, comes with his ministers and the candles are lighted during the singing of a suitable song. After a greeting, a brief introduction follows, with the formal blessing of the candles, which are then sprinkled with holy water.* Immediately thereupon, the procession begins with an acclamation* by the priest: "Let us go forth in peace to meet the Lord." A processional antiphon* or canticle* is sung as the procession moves forward and enters the church. After the veneration of the altar, the Mass continues as usual with the *Glory to God.**

Should there not be a suitable place distinct from the church, the faithful holding their candles assemble either in front of the church or immediately inside the church and participate in the rite as described above, but with a much shorter procession to the altar.

Presentation, Rite of (prez-uhn-TAY-shuhn; pree-zuhn-; rait uhv). The presentations of the ancient documents of faith* and prayer,* the Profession of Faith* and the Lord's Prayer,* are usually given to the elect during Christian initiation after the scrutinies.* The rite takes place in the presence of the community after the Liturgy of the Word* at a weekday Mass with appropriate readings.* Sometimes these presentations are anticipated, for they could benefit the catechumens before the scrutinies. Thus the celebration would occur between the first and second stage. *See also* RITE OF CHRISTIAN INITIATION OF ADULTS.

Presentation Song. *See* OFFERTORY SONG.

President. *See* CELEBRANT.

Presidential Prayers (prez-uh-DEN-chuhl prayrz; pray[uh]rz). The prayers assigned to the celebrant* at Mass* as president of the assembly.* The most important part of the Mass reserved for the priest is the Eucharistic Prayer,* the apex of the whole celebration. As presider over the community in the person of Christ, the priest, in the name of the whole community, whether present or not, addresses the following prayers to God: the Opening Prayer,* the Prayer over the Gifts,* and the Prayer after Communion.* To keep children as attentive as possible, even during a somewhat lengthy Eucharistic Prayer,* the Eucharistic Prayers for Masses with Children* allow their participation* without obscuring the nature of it as a presidential prayer. All presidential prayers demand everyone's attention and so are proclaimed loudly and clearly, accompanied by no music, or any other prayer.

Presidential Seat (prez-uh-DEN-chuhl seet). The place for the one who presides at liturgical functions.

It is governed by the structure of the building, so that, to maintain the proper communication, the president, similar to a conductor of an orchestra, can see all the people and be seen and heard by them. It is here that the presider greets the people, performs the Penitential Rite,* says the first and last oration, listens to the Word of God* proclaimed by others, opens and closes the General Intercessions,* and dismisses the assembly* with blessings. *See also* CHURCH FURNISHINGS.

Priest (preest). The person who receives a second step in the Sacrament of Holy Orders,* the priesthood, whereby he becomes the mediator, authorized to offer the true sacrifice by which God's supreme dominion over human beings is acknowledged and atonement for their sins occurs.

The priest's essential power is to offer the Sacrifice of the Mass*; to distribute Divine graces* to the faithful* by the administration of the Sacraments, except for Holy Orders; and to preach the Word of God.* It is his duty to make sure that the Word is properly proclaimed, and with his familiarity with the structure of the *Lectionary,** he may be expected to plan Liturgies, making the proper choice of readings* for the pastoral good of the community. Through his homilies,* he is expected to lead the faithful to an effective knowledge of Sacred Scripture, opening their souls to the wonderful words of God, strengthening their faith* in the Word inspired by the Holy Spirit.*

The main function of the priest to offer the Body of Christ in sacrifice cannot be circumscribed. His secondary functions, serving the Mystical Body* of Christ through the administration of the Sacraments and preaching, can be exercised only with proper jurisdiction. *See also* BISHOP; CELEBRANT; DEACON; JESUS CHRIST; PRESBYTERORUM ORDINIS; PRIESTHOOD.

Priesthood (PREEST-hud). The major order between the diaconate and the episcopate.

The proper understanding of priesthood must include the relationship that should exist among the faithful,* the priests,* and Christ as the High Priest. In His role as the natural Mediator, by reason of the hypostatic union, Christ becomes the eternal High Priest between God and humankind, for He offered Himself once upon the Cross* as a Victim of infinite value. That sacrifice is constantly renewed on the altar* through the ministry of the Church,* the Mystical Body.*

The People of God are commissioned to continue Christ's saving work, sharing Christ's mediatorship in two ways, by offering spiritual sacrifices and by being co-offerers of the sacrifice of Calvary in the Mass.* The faithful by their "baptismal character" have participation in the priesthood and join with the ministerial priesthood exercised by the ordained priest, acting in the person of Christ, through whom the Church immolates again Christ by this re-presentation of His sacrifice.

In this way, an organic unity is developed concerning the priesthood of Christ, of the ordained priest, and of the faithful. Not only do the faithful have the right to receive other Sacraments,* but they participate in the Liturgy* uniting themselves with Christ, the eternal High Priest, as He offers Himself through the priest to the heavenly Father during the Eucharistic sacrifice.

Priesthood of the Faithful. *See* FAITHFUL; LAITY; LITURGY—PARTICIPATION; PRIESTHOOD; UNIVERSAL PRIESTHOOD.

Primates (PRAI-muhts; -mayts). Bishops* enjoying a certain preeminence over several other bishops, primarily a precedence of honor with no jurisdiction.* At times the title refers to the bishops of Sees* that are the oldest or most prominent in a country, such as Baltimore in the United States.

Prime. *See* DAYTIME PRAYER.

Pro-Cathedral (proh-ka-THEE-druhl). An edifice utilized by the bishop* while waiting for a more appropriate or permanent cathedral* to be built.

Processional Chants (pruh-SESH-nuhl; -uhn-uhl; chants). Traditional name for chants* of the Proper* that accompany processions at Mass.* It refers to the Entrance Antiphon* (or Song*), the Offertory Antiphon* (or Song*), and the Communion Antiphon* (or Song*). In the new *Roman Missal,** there are only two processional chants—the Offertory Antiphon is no longer given but has been relegated to the *Roman Gradual** since it is never used if it is not sung.

Processional Cross. *See* CROSS, PROCESSIONAL.

Processions (pruh-SESH-uhnz). Religious retinues going solemnly in ritual action from one place to another while singing. Secular parades are natural for many communities; the Christian Church adapted them, changed their significance, and used hymns* and prayers* while asking the community to walk with God on the pilgrimage of life. Processions occur in many liturgical contexts from Baptism* to funerals.*

Some occur regularly at specific times of the year and on anniversaries of certain events. Others grace certain specific occasions.

Some of the functional processions are at the Preparation of the Gifts,* the Entrance and Conclusion of the Mass, and the Gospel* and Communion.* Some of the ordinary processions would be those on Passion Sunday,* Candlemas Day,* and the Body and Blood of Christ.* The last mentioned has special importance for the pastoral life of a parish,* since, in keeping with local customs, the streets may be decorated and the Eucharistic blessing given at various stations. Thus people give public witness of faith* and devotion* toward the Blessed Sacrament.*

This rite, so universal, has its foundation in the religious instinct of human beings. Processions

translate marvelously the ordered, calm, trusting, and joyous life, the need of collective prayer, and the joy in the triumph of our Savior. Liturgy* employs all the arts for the glory of God and so could not leave out the art of movement, dignified and measured choreography, which appeals to all parts of the human body. *See also* COMMUNION PROCESSION; ENTRANCE PROCESSION; GOSPEL PROCESSION; OFFERTORY PROCESSION; RECESSIONAL PROCESSION.

Profession of Faith (pruh-FESH-uhn uhv fayth). In general, an externalized act of faith,* whether in word or in action, and sometimes prescribed for a Christian. Liturgically, it is a symbol of faith, summarizing the principal Christian beliefs. A former and still valid synonym is Creed; all creeds have a similar threefold construction, referring to the three persons in the Trinity,* and historically developed from baptismal rituals. During liturgical services the worshiping community recites them together to express their common faith. Several musical settings for the Latin *Credo* exist, and on more festive occasions, the Creed was treated in majestic style in polyphonic Masses.

Three Professions of Faith have been used by the Church.

(1) The Athanasian Creed, erroneously attributed to St. Athanasius,* more clearly stresses the belief in the Incarnation* and the Trinity; prior to the suppression of the Little Hour of Prime,* this Creed was said during it each Sunday.

(2) The Apostles' Creed,* the earliest simple statement of Christian belief, developed in connection with the Sacrament of Baptism,* and, at

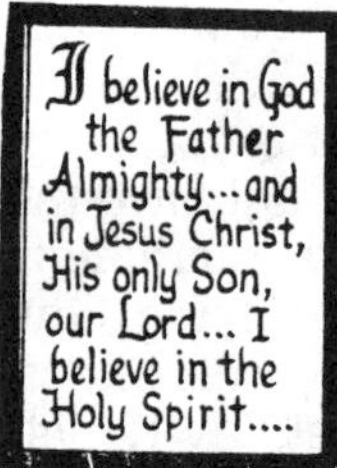

various times, it was used for that purpose. Today an interrogatory form is employed based on the tenets of the Apostles' Creed. At various times it was recited in the Divine Office* in certain Hours, and also at the ordination of a priest.* Today, it may replace the Nicene Creed at Mass.

(3) The Nicene Creed,* a fusion of the one drawn up at the Council of Nicaea in 325 and the symbol of Constantinople in 381, is found in the Eucharistic sacrifice as the Profession of Faith, ordinarily recited on Sundays and Solemnities.* It occurs near the end of the Liturgy of the Word*; as a summary of the whole of salvation* history, it constitutes a response to the Good News* as the congregation indicates its staunch attachment to Christ's message. Thus the gathered faithful* give assent to the Word of God heard in the Readings* and applied in the Homily,* before they start the Eucharist,* the Mystery of Faith. *See also* LITURGY OF THE WORD; MASS, ORDER OF.

Profession, Religious. *See* RELIGIOUS PROFESSION.

Promise (PROM-uhs). In the Bible* this word refers to God obligating Himself to help, both now and in the future, His chosen ones. In return, the people were expected to keep their promises to God, as exhorted by the Prophets.* The idea of promise in the Old Testament* is connected with Covenant,* e.g., God binding Himself to make a great people of Abraham* and his descendants (Gn 12:1-5, 15; 17:1-14). Through the Covenant at Sinai He promised the Hebrews a homeland, protection, a holy nation called Israel, a theocratic community (Ex 19; and Dt). They in turn were to be faithful in serving and loving God and their promises are in the Decalogue. God's promise to David of an eternal dynasty is an important Covenant.

The promises to Abraham are effected through his descendant Christ (Gal 3:16-19). David's son, the risen Christ, fulfills the Good News* promised in the Prophets (Rom 1:1-7). These promises to Abraham, Israel and David are fulfilled in the teachings concerning Jesus as the Messiah,* the one who brings salvation to the whole world. Pilgrim Christians undergo a priestly and sacrificial tension between their current activity and the assurance of future happiness* (Heb 4; 6:12-20; 9; 11:1–12:4).

Messianic salvation is guaranteed for all of us who persevere particularly through the use of the Liturgy,* the Sacraments,* and most of all the Eucharist.* The Son and the Father dwell in the Christian and will continue to do so in the life to come (1 Jn 2:24-28; 1:1-4). God has promised that they who love Him will receive the crown of life (Jas 1:12; 2:5). Furthermore we have God's promise of the coming of the Parousia* (2 Pt 3). *See also* COVENANT; HISTORY OF SALVATION.

Promises (PROM-uhs-uhz). Avowals declaring to God or some person that the avower will or will not undertake something. If made to God, a promise becomes a vow, binding according to the seriousness of the promise and the intention to bind oneself under pain of sin. If made to people, persons are obliged in justice and charity to keep the promises. (*See also* VOWS.)

Promises occur during the Rite of Baptism* when the candidates declare their faith* in the renunciation of sin immediately before Baptism.

In infant Baptism the sponsors* answer the interrogatory Creed.* The declaration of consent during a Marriage* ceremony might also be considered promises, but they result in a lifelong contract. In some areas it is possible to make a promise to marry in a formal Betrothal.* No formal action occurs to enforce such a promise, but the person would be bound in conscience to compensate the injured party for expenditures incurred because of an unkept promise. *See also* BETROTHAL.

Proper (PROP-uhr). (1) In the religious service of a Mass* or the Liturgy of the Hours,* those parts that vary according to the feast* or the liturgical season* and do not belong to the Ordinary* of the Mass or the Common of the Saints,* but rather to the particular day. The *Ordinary* of the Mass and of the Office supplies a uniform framework of celebration, filled out by the parts from the *Proper*.

(2) The chants, variable parts of the service, that are executed chorally, primarily composed of Psalmody.* In Mass this proper includes the Entrance and Communion Psalms, the Responsorial Psalm* and the Alleluia* Verse; in the Office, it embraces primarily those parts that would vary according to the day or the season. *See also* MASS, PROPER OF THE; PROPER OF THE SAINTS; PROPER OF THE SEASON.

Proper of the Mass. *See* MASS, PROPER OF THE.

Proper of the Saints (PROP-uhr uhv thuh saynts). That part of the *Roman Missal** and *Liturgy of the Hours** which contains the formularies for the cycle of the Saints,* who are celebrated in the Universal Church*; ordinarily they are listed in sequence from January to December. There is an interrelationship between this and the Common of the Saints,* for if certain prayers are not in the Proper, they are supplied from the Common of the Saints. *See also* ANNIVERSARY; COMMON OF THE SAINTS; PROPER; PROPERS.

Proper of the Season (PROP-uhr uhv thuh SEE-suhn). That section of the *Roman Missal** and *Liturgy of the Hours** which presents the formularies for the seasonal cycle, beginning with Advent,* moving to the Christmas Season,* Lent,* Holy Week,* Easter Season,* and Ordinary Time.* It would also include the Solemnities of the Lord throughout the year. *See also* ANNIVERSARY; CYCLES; PROPER.

Proper of the United States (PROP-uhr uhv thee yoo-NAIT-uhd stayts). Feasts* that are not part of the Universal Calendar* but are celebrated in all the dioceses* of the United States. They are:

January

4	Elizabeth Ann Seton, religious	Memorial
5	John Neumann, bishop	Memorial
6	*Bl. André Bessette, religious*	*Opt. Mem.*

March

3	*Bl. Katharine Drexel, virgin*	*Opt. Mem.*

May

15	*Isidore*	*Opt. Mem.*

July

4	*Independence Day*	*Opt. Mem.*
14	Bl. Kateri Tekakwitha, virgin	Memorial

August

18	*Jane Frances de Chantal, virgin*	*Opt. Mem.*
28	*Bl. Junipero Serra, priest*	*Opt. Mem.*

September

9	Peter Claver, priest	Memorial

October

6	*Bl. Marie-Rose Durocher, virgin*	*Opt. Mem.*
19	Isaac Jogues and John de Brébeuf, priests and martyrs, and companions, martyrs	Memorial

November

13	Frances Xavier Cabrini, virgin	Memorial
18	*Rose Philippine Duchesne, virgin*	*Opt. Mem.*
Fourth Thursday	*Thanksgiving Day*	*Opt. Mem.*

December

12	OUR LADY OF GUADALUPE	FEAST

Propers (PROP-uhrz). Appendices to the *Roman Missal** and the *Liturgy of the Hours** that comprise those feasts* not included in the general Calendar,* but observed only in a particular diocese,* country, region, Religious Order, or congregation. All of these formulas will have had prior approval from the

Congregation for Divine Worship and the Discipline of the Sacraments.* *See also* PROPER; PROPER OF THE SAINTS; PROPER OF THE UNITED STATES.

Prophet. *See* JESUS CHRIST.

Prophets (PROF-uhts). Spokespersons of God, intermediaries between Him and His people. The Prophetic Books of the Old Testament,* together with the oral preaching of the Prophets, were the result of the institution of prophetism, in which a succession of Israelites chosen by God and appointed by Him to be Prophets received communications from Him and transmitted them to the people in His name. These communications came through visions, dreams, and ecstasies and were transmitted to the people through sermons, writings, and symbolic actions.

The office of Prophet was due to a direct call from God. It was not a permanent gift but a transient one, subject entirely to the Divine will. The Prophets preserved and developed revealed religion, denounced idolatry, defended the moral law, gave counsel in political matters, and often in matters of private life. At times miracles confirmed their preaching, and their predictions of the future intensified the expectation of the Messiah* and of His Kingdom.

The literary form of prophecy uses warning and threat besides exhortation and promise to declare in God's name events of the near and distant future. Kindly and persuasive tones pervade the promises of reward and even the threats of punishment.

There were four major "writing Prophets" and twelve minor ones and Baruch,* who was a disciple of Jeremiah.* They are called Major and Minor Prophets because of the length of their writings and not because of any distinction among them. The Major Prophets are: Isaiah,* Jeremiah, Ezekiel,* and Daniel.* The Minor Prophets are:

Hosea,* Joel,* Amos,* Obadiah,* Jonah,* Micah,* Nahum,* Habakkuk,* Zephaniah,* Haggai,* Zechariah,* and Malachi.*

The Prophets in the Liturgy

On the evening of Easter,* Jesus said to His disciples: "Everything written about me in the law of Moses and in the prophets and psalms must be fulfilled" (Lk 24:44). He was referring to the order of the readings from the Bible* in the synagogue to signify that the whole Old Testament constituted a global prophecy of His coming (see Lk 24:26f). Hence, from the beginning, Christians read at their Sunday assemblies from "the memoires of the Apostles and the writings of the Prophets" (Justin,* *First Apology,* 67).

At the end of the 4th century, the Churches of Syria read successively the Law,* the Prophets, the Psalms,* the Writings of the Apostles, and the Gospels.* During the same period St. Ambrose* at Milan knew only one reading from the Old Testament before the Psalm, and he declared that at Mass "the Prophet, the Apostle, and the Gospel are read" *(Commentary on Psalm* 119, 17, 10). This arrangement has become the usage of the Roman Liturgy after Vatican II.*

On all Sundays outside the Easter Season,* the First Reading* is taken from the Old Testament. The Law and the Prophets thus lead to Christ. This is seen even more clearly during the time of Advent*-Christmas*-Epiphany* when the Messianic prophecies are read. Some might say that these prophecies have been fulfilled in Jesus and therefore can no longer interest us. This is not true. They have been fulfilled only in part by the First Advent or Coming, which we no longer wait for, but they have to be fulfilled completely by the Second Coming,* which we are still waiting for, so that the hope of the Prophets is still *our* hope.

This is why we say concerning the Holy Spirit* in the Creed,* "He spoke through the Prophets." The Prophets were waiting for a Messiah for Whom we no longer wait. They did not know *Who* that Messiah would be Whose name we know. But, in awaiting Him and in announcing Him, they teach us *what* that Messiah is, and they enable us to know Him better.

The Prophets are also used extensively in the Liturgy of the Hours both as readings* and as canticles.* These uses are listed under each Prophetic Book. *See also* LECTIONARY.

Prostration. *See* POSTURE IN WORSHIP.

Prot[h]onotary Apostolic (proh-T[H]ON-uh-ter-ee; proh-t[h]uh-NOH-tuh-ree; ap-uh-STOL-ik). Originally the title given to those responsible for listing the Acts of the Martyrs.* Today these men witness the signing of Papal bulls* and perform various ceremonial duties in Rome. Some canons* of basilicas* in Rome and other places receive this title. The vicars general of dioceses,* by reason of their office, have this title, to which ceremonial privileges are attached.

Proverbs, The Book of (PROV-uhrbs, thuh buk uhv). Twenty-fourth Book of the Old Testament* and third Sapiential Book whose purpose is to teach wisdom or moral conduct. The wisdom that the Book teaches covers a wide field of human and Divine activity ranging from matters purely secular to most lofty moral and religious truths, such as God's omniscience, power, providence, goodness, and the joy and strength resulting from abandonment to Him. The teaching of the Book is placed on a firm religious foundation by the principle that "the fear of the Lord is the beginning of knowledge" (1:7).

The Book was compiled between the 10th and 5th centuries B.C. beginning with Solomon and ending with an editor who composed the first nine chapters. It traces the path of the whole experience of a popular good sense. It also maintains a strong optimism in the face of the problem of evil.

Liturgical use: In the *Roman Missal,** this Book is read on the 20th

Sunday (B), 33rd Sunday (A), Trinity Sunday* (C), and Monday through Wednesday of the 25th Week (II) as well as July 11 (St. Benedict*), the Common of the Blessed Virgin Mary,* the Common of the Saints,* the Blessing of Abbots,* and the Votive Mass of the Holy Eucharist.* In the *Liturgy of the Hours,** it is read during the 6th Week in Ordinary Time* and the Common of Holy Women and gives rise to a canticle in Appendix I: for Vigils. *Meaning:* God is our Creator and Ruler. Life is filled with mysteries, but He understands them and invites us to turn to Him for guidance. Since God made all of life, all of it may be offered to Him. Serving God makes sense and leads to a full and satisfying life.

Prudence (PROOD-uhn[t]s). The first of the four chief moral virtues* (the other three are fortitude,* justice,* and temperance*), which dispose us to lead moral or good lives by aiding us to treat persons and things in the right way—that is, according to the will of God. They are also known as cardinal virtues because they are like hinges on which hang all other moral virtues and our whole moral life.

Prudence enables us to choose what has to be done and the best means to do it. It disposes us to choose in every circumstance the right means to attain our end by subordinating it to our last end. The rule of prudence is reason enlightened by faith.* This virtue comprises three aspects: (a) mature deliberation; (b) right judgment; and (c) positing of the action judged necessary or useful to the end envisaged.

Participating in the Liturgy* is an act of the moral virtue of religion* (which is part of justice) that strengthens the other moral virtues, as indicated in the article on good works.* *See also* FORTITUDE; GOOD WORKS; JUSTICE; TEMPERANCE; VIRTUES.

Psalm-prayers (sah[l]m-prayrz; pray[uh]rz). Prayers related to the Psalms* that have been introduced into the English Edition of the reformed *Liturgy of the Hours** (in the Latin Edition they are given in a supplement). They thus restore an ancient practice that provides help in understanding the Psalms in a Christian way. After the singing or recitation of a Psalm, a brief period of silence precedes the Psalm-prayer, which collects the aspirations and intercessions of those celebrating the Liturgy of the Hours. In the way they interpret the Psalms or in the doctrine they contain, the Psalm-prayers reflect the experience of celebrating the Liturgical Year.* However, in keeping with their genre, they exclude any reference to a particular feast* or liturgical season.*

Some of the subjects developed in these restored Psalm-prayers are directly theological as, for example, the Incarnation,* the Trinity,* grace,* and eternal happiness.* Others are theologico-moral in nature as, for example, faith,* bearing witness to the Faith,* hope,* patience, purity of heart, love,* the struggle against one's passions, repentance,* prayer,* and contemplation.* Still others are more closely related to the Liturgy* as, for example, the Christian assembly* as sign of the Universal Church,* the praise given God by the Church, the Liturgy of the Hours, the Eucharist,* Baptism,* and the ministry of preaching. *See also* LITURGY OF THE HOURS; PSALMS.

Psalm Tones (sah[l]m tohnz). Melodic formulas employed in singing the Psalms.* These eight tones relate to the eight Church modes of the Roman chant.* Each begins with an intonation that is used only at the start of the Psalm or canticle.* It is followed by the recitative note, the dominant of the tone that leads to the cadence, called the mediant at the conclusion of the half-verse. After a slight pause, the reciting note is resumed and concludes at the termination. Another tone, the mellifluous *tonus peregrinus* (wandering tone), consists of two recitative tones, the second for the later half being one-third lower than the first.

Psalmist. *See* CHANTER.

Psalmody (SAH[L]-muh-dee) (1) The art or practice of chanting Psalms* during worship.* The early Church* took over the custom from the synagogue; it has been a prominent part of Christian Liturgy* ever since. It became a major part in the monastic fulfillment of the Divine Office,* with certain sections or canticles* being sung in a more florid style, sometimes by the Schola Cantorum.* Today the usual pattern is that two choirs sing the verses alternately. (*See also* GREGORIAN CHANT; PSALMS; SCHOLA CANTORUM.)

(2) The term on occasion refers to a collection of Psalms, for instance, those chosen for one of the Hours in the Liturgy of the Hours.*

Psalms (sah[l]mz). Sacred hymns or songs of praise* chanted or sung during worship.* In a more strict sense it refers to the 150 poems and songs in the Old Testament Book of Psalms.* They are used profusely in the Mass,* the Divine Office,* and during the liturgical functions connected with all the Sacraments.* *See also* PSALMS, THE BOOK OF; PSALTER.

Psalms, The Book of (sah[l]mz, thuh buk uhv). The twenty-third, longest, and most beloved Book of the Old Testament* and second Sapiential Book. The 150 prayers,* poems, and hymns* it contains focus the worshipers on God's praise* and adoration.* Parts were used in the liturgical service of ancient Israel. A number of authors

took part in the composition of the Psalms, including King David, over the course of some five hundred years until its compilation by an editor after the Exile about 537 B.C.

The Psalms are the prayer of God's assembly, the public prayer par excellence of the People of God.* No prayer of Israel is comparable to the Psalter because of its universal character. The idea of the unity of the Chosen People's prayer guided its elaboration as well as its adoption by the Church.*

In giving us the Psalter that sums up the major aspects of the relationship of human beings to their Creator and Redeemer God puts into our mouths the word He wishes to hear and indicates to us the dimensions of prayer.

> The Psalms recall to mind the truths revealed by God to the Chosen People, which were at one time frightening and at another filled with wonderful tenderness; they keep repeating and fostering the hope of the promised Redeemer, which in ancient times was kept alive with song, either around the hearth or in the stately Temple; they show forth in splendid light the prophesied glory* of Jesus Christ: first, His supreme and eternal power, then His lowly coming to this earthly exile, His kingly dignity and priestly power, and finally His beneficent labors, and the shedding of His Blood for our redemption.
>
> In a similar way they express the joy and bitterness, the hope and fear, of our hearts and our desire of loving God and hoping in Him alone as well as our mystic ascent to Divine tabernacles (MD, 148).

The Psalms may be looked upon as the "Prayerbook of the Holy Spirit."* The Spirit of God inspired the Psalmists to compose magnificent prayers and hymns for every religious desire and need, mood and feeling. Thus, the Psalms have great power to raise minds to God, to inspire devotion,* to evoke gratitude in favorable times, and to bring consolation and strength in times of trial.

Liturgical use: The Psalms occupy a privileged position in the liturgical use of the Bible. Of all the Books of the Old and New Testaments, the Psalter is the most read liturgically. It customarily figures in every Liturgy of the Word*: Mass,* Sacraments,* Vigils,* and Liturgy of the Hours.* It is also used as a prayer-chant for various ritual actions.

The many reasons for this multiform use are all based on the poetic form of this Book. This allows these texts to express the religious experience of the People of the Covenant* in figures, images, and symbols that are valid for situations of all ages and all places. The Psalms thus constitute a kind of echo of the Law,* the Prophets,* the sacred history, and the wisdom of the Chosen People. At the same time, their poetic aspect also enables them to express prophetically all that has been accomplished in Christ: His Birth,* His Good News,* His Passion* and Death,* His Resurrection*

and Ascension,* and His Return in glory. It is also this poetic aspect that enables the psalmic imagery to show forth the wonderful works of God announced and celebrated in the Sacraments of the Church as well as the spiritual and mystical development of every Christian.

In the Liturgy of the Word, the Psalms form the link between the Old Testament and the New, between the whole Bible and the Sacraments of Christian worship, and between the Liturgy and the Christian life of believers.

In the *Roman Missal,** the Psalms are used as Responsorial Psalms and as antiphonal and processional chants.* In the *Liturgy of the Hours,** the Psalms are used in every Hour and form the basis of this Prayer of Praise by their arrangement in the Four-Week Psalter.

Meaning: The Psalms are filled with theological insights. Underlying the Psalmists' outlook is the power of God. Among other things, He is in full control at all times regardless of appearances. He acts at the right moment and in the proper way. We need only trust Him. God's providence is also at work continually—weaving His will with our free choices and bringing everything to an end in accord with His goodwill.

At the same time, God is ever compassionate toward those He has made. His love and understanding never fail to come to the aid of our weakness. In response, we are to lead lives of prayer,* praise,* humility, thanksgiving,* and faith.*

Psalter (SAWL-tuhr). (1) A stringed instrument used by the Jews to accompany the Psalms.*

(2) The Book of Psalms* itself.

(3) The collection of the Psalms* intended primarily for liturgical or devotional use, and later the section of the Breviary containing those Psalms. Today the *Liturgy of the Hours** incorporates the Psalms in the order in which they are distributed over a period of four weeks. Formerly all the Psalms were said once a week. *See also* PSALMS.

Public Confession. *See* PENANCE, RITE OF.

Publication of Liturgical Material (pub-li-KAY-shuhn uhv luh-TUHR-ji-kuhl; li-; muh-TIR-ee-uhl). Since the implementation of the *Constitution on the Sacred Liturgy,**

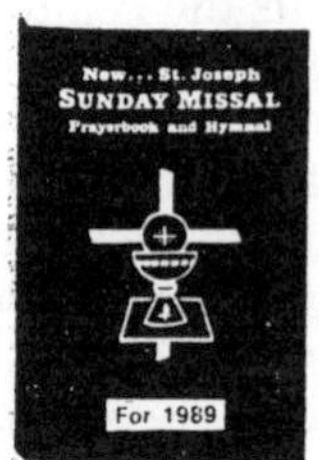

in the United States the Bishops' Committee on the Liturgy* regulates pastoral-liturgical action under the authority of the National Conference of Catholic Bishops.* Hence guidelines were issued not only for official liturgical books* but also for popular liturgical materials. The intent of the guidelines is the production of excellent liturgical materials in a style and format suitable for their purpose. General statements indicate who would be considered a publisher, that the committee does not issue the Imprimatur,* and that copyright permissions and contracts are obligations of the publisher.

Official Liturgical Books

Official liturgical books are books or parts thereof that will be used by the celebrant* or ministers* in the celebration of the Sacraments,* Mass,* or any other liturgical rite. Regulations stipulate how the publisher should apply for permission to publish, the submission of a manuscript and proofs, the dates for publication, the royalties to be paid, and the like.

Semiofficial Liturgical Publications

Semiofficial liturgical publications refer to materials that are neither official as stated above, nor participation* materials as stated below. Consequently they would be primarily study editions, such as hand Missals,* which would have the entire rite in the publication and be offered to the public in that guise. Again the definitive outline of the contents, the Ordinary* who is needed to grant the Imprimatur, the manuscript and proofs, the date of publications, and so forth are stipulated.

Participation Materials

To facilitate and promote participation of the people in the Liturgy,* participation materials with the necessary text and music are required so that they may fulfill their active role. When the texts become available, a suggested format, regulations with regard to options, the need for musical settings, the necessity for manuscripts and proofs, the need for copyrights, and the date for distribution are all regulated. Moreover special guidelines exist for Missalettes,* one of the more popular liturgical participation aids.

The intent of these guidelines is not to suppress initiative on the part of publishers but to regulate pastoral-liturgical action throughout the country, to enable the faithful* to achieve the full and active participation they should have in their respective role. The constraints put upon the publishers of this type of material were not well received by the public they were to serve. The People of God* do not like to be denied the option of having the texts readily available to them. They are not satisfied to sit and listen. They would rather use more than one of their senses to achieve the fullness of participation expected of them. *See also* IMPRIMATUR; LITURGICAL BOOKS; MISSAL; NIHIL OBSTAT; PARTICIPATION; TYPICAL EDITION.

Pulpit. *See* LECTERN.

Purification (pyur-uh-fuh-KAY-shuhn). During the second stage of initiation, that period which customarily coincides with Lent* and begins with the rite of election* when the catechumens,* chosen because of their proper dispositions, join a local community in spiritual recollection in preparation for the feast of Easter* and their reception of the Sacraments of Initiation. *See also* RITE OF CHRISTIAN INITIATION OF ADULTS.

Purification of Mary. *See* PRESENTATION OF THE LORD.

Purificator (pyur-uh-fuh-KAY-tuhr). A small piece of white absorbent linen, approximately eight by sixteen inches, folded in three lengthwise, and marked with a Cross* in the center, employed during the Mass.* It is used to wipe the lip of the chalice* after the reception of the Precious Blood* and to dry the chalice after it is washed at the end of or after Mass.

Purposes of the Mass. *See* MASS.

Pyx (piks). (1) Usually the small watch-shaped receptacle used to carry Communion* privately to the sick. Any vessel in which the Eucharist* is kept or carried, even of larger size, may also be called a pyx.

(2) The small, round, metal case in which the large consecrated Host* to be exposed in the monstrance* is kept inside the tabernacle.*

— Q —

Qahal (KAH-hahl). A Hebrew word for "assembly." It is with this term that Deuteronomy* designates the assembly of the people of Israel (5:22). The *qahal* is made up of brothers and sisters; its unity flows from the Divine election and is manifested by the obedience to God's commandments. After the exile, the *qahal* constitutes the ideal of the repatriates (Neh 5). In liturgical writings, the Church* is sometimes called the *qahal,* the assembly of God.

Qoheleth. *See* ECCLESIASTES, THE BOOK OF.

Quartodecimans (kwahr-toh-DAY-see-muhnz; -chee). Name given to the Eastern Christians who in the 2nd century were still celebrating Easter* on the 14th of Nisan (March), whereas in the West Easter was celebrated on the following Sunday. This difference led to the Easter Controversy during the pontificate of Victor I, which avoided becoming a schism largely through the efforts of Irenaeus* of Lyons.

Quas Primas (kwahs PREE-mahs). Latin title (from the first two words "Which First") of the *Encyclical on the Kingship of Christ* issued by Pius XI on December 11, 1925. The document makes use of Scripture* and the Fathers* to show that "Christ as Man deserves both the title and the power of King in strict reality" (no. 9). It links devotion to the Kingship with the veneration of the Eucharist* and the Sacred Heart.* Then it establishes the Feast of Christ the King* to foster recognition of Christ's kingly rights over the minds, hearts, and wills of human beings so that they will be able to overcome contemporary

secularism and atheism. It was also in this Encyclical that Pius XI made his famous statement that "the Liturgy . . . is the most important organ of the Ordinary Magisterium* of the Church." *See also* CATECHESIS AND LITURGY; MAGISTERIUM.

Quasimodo (kwa-si-MOH-doh). Name given to the Sunday after Easter,* Low Sunday, from the first Latin word ("Like) of the Entrance Antiphon.*

Queen of Heaven. *See* REGINA CAELI.

Queenship of Mary. *See* MARY, BLESSED VIRGIN—FEASTS.

Quia Tuum Est Regnum. *See* FOR THE KINGDOM, THE POWER, AND THE GLORY . . .

Quinquagesima (kwin-kwuh-JES-i-muh; -JAY-zuh-muh). Name formerly given to the last Sunday before Lent.* Because the Latin word for Lent is *Quadragesima,* meaning 40 days, the Sunday immediately before it was called Quinquagesima, namely 50 days before Easter.* Similarly the two previous Sundays are called Sexagesima* and Septuagesima.* These imprecise numbers signify the sixtieth and seventieth days before the Easter Triduum.* This pre-Lenten period of preparation began in the East and was not really accepted in the West until about the 6th century, when finally, under Gregory the Great,* Rome incorporated these three Sundays in the preparation for Lent.

A possible reason for its beginning is the practice in the East of not fasting* on Saturday and Sunday, so in order for Eastern Christians to fast 40 days before Easter, it was necessary for them to start ahead of time. Actually they started the Monday after Sexagesima. Fasting in the West however always began with Ash Wednesday.* This preparatory time for Lent was abolished by Vatican Council II* as not being necessary to embellish the penitential season. Lent alone can carry its essential role to prepare for the Paschal Mystery.*

—R—

Raphael, St. (RAYF-ee-uhl). One of the archangels, featured in the Book of Tobit,* in which he restores sight to the aged Tobit, and hence his name which means, "God has healed." Having guarded young Tobiah on his trip, he is on occasion depicted as the Patron of Travelers.

He is also the Patron of the Blind, Nurses, Physicians, and Travelers. *Liturgical celebration:* September 29 (Feast); *theme:* may Raphael heal our ills and guide and protect us on life's journey.

Raymond of Penyafort, St. (RAY-muhnd uhv PEN-yuh-fort). c.1175-1275. A Catalan, this Spaniard became a lawyer before joining the Dominicans. His first work for them was the first collection of cases of conscience, *Summa de Casibus*, used for the guidance of confessors.* Later in Rome after he had held several curial offices, Gregory IX had him compile the Decretals.* Elected Master General of the Dominicans, Raymond resigned at 65, but spent the rest of his life in Spain preaching and converting the Moors. *Liturgical celebration:* January 7 (Opt. Mem.); *theme:* a long life of dedicated service to the Lord.

RCIA. *See* BAPTISM; RITE OF INITIATION OF ADULTS.

Readers (REED-uhrz). Historically, the term reader or lector referred to one of the Minor Orders,* which were abrogated in 1972. The office of reading the Scriptures* was usurped years ago by the subdeacon* and deacon.* Today the office of reader is one of the ministries in the Church,* whereby men may be formerly instituted as readers, with the responsibilities to read the Sacred Scriptures in a liturgical assembly.*

The reader's liturgical function is to carry the *Lectionary** in the Entrance Procession* and read the lesson(s) before the Gospel,* even if ministers of a higher rank are present. If the chanter* is unavailable to lead the singing of the Responsorial Psalm,* the reader recites it. If the deacon or chanter does not make the intentions of the General Intercessions,* the reader also fulfills this function. If the reader is capable, for a reasonable cause, he may be permitted to preach in particular cases, as long as it is not a Homily.* The reader may also help in preparing other readers who are needed in the celebration of the Liturgy.*

Most parishes will have no instituted readers, so laypersons* are called upon to fulfill this function. They too should be carefully chosen, trained, and properly qualified to carry out the important task of proclaiming the Word of God,* so that the faithful* may develop a love for the Scriptures from listening to the sacred texts. Their spiritual preparation should include both Biblical and liturgical formation, so that they not only understand the readings in context but have a grasp of the meaning and structure of the Liturgy of the Word* and its significance in relation to the Liturgy of the Eucharist.* Their technical preparation should result in skillful, public reading.

Readers may also be called upon to proclaim any of the non-Gospel readings at Bible Services* or other devotions.* When sufficient readers are available, a different one should be assigned to the various readings, so that more members of the community may be engaged in the corporate act of worship.* Women may perform the duties of reader, but they may not be formally instituted. In many places, those who are not instituted are commissioned in recognition of their ministry.

Readings (REED-ingz). Selections proclaimed at liturgical services, always from Biblical passages during Mass.* However, during the Office of Readings,* in the Liturgy of the Hours,* certain sections are from the Bible* and others from patristic writings or papal documents. Formerly, the term lessons was used for these excerpts; patristic selections, historical narratives, or even lives of the Saints* were presented then. Currently, rather than a narrative biography, a hagiographical reading from some portion of the Saint's life or writings is employed. Thus today, the First Reading is always Biblical, while the Second is patristic, papal, or hagiographical.

In the Mass, Biblical Readings are used throughout the Liturgy of the Word,* with the Gospel* being the high point. On Sundays and Solemnities, the First Reading* from the Old Testament* is separated by a Responsorial Psalm* from the Second Reading* of the New Testament.* An acclamation,* in the form of an Alleluia Verse* (or the Verse before the Gospel* when the liturgical season requires it), precedes the proclamation of the Good News.* These Readings make up the essence of the Liturgy of the Word,* from which the Homily* is derived.

On days other than Sundays and the larger feasts,* before the Gospel there is only one Reading, either from the Old Testament or from the New Testament. How the selections were chosen and the options for the celebrant* in using them are explained in the entry entitled *Lectionary.**

In the Liturgy of the Hours, the Biblical Reading is not so much a proclamation to move us to worship as it is in the Mass and the Sacraments; it is a *lectio divina,** a reading and meditating of God's Word. It is primarily didactic. It is meant to be listened to in a spirit of openness and to shape our way of thinking as the Spirit wills. There is a kind of inspiration in this Reading (in accord with an important stream of patristic thought that looks upon it as an ever-present reality). God is still speaking to us today.

God's Word is now filled with the Spirit, whose influence is exercised no longer through the sacred writer but through the Word that is placed in our hands or sounded in our ears. However, this is true only if we read "in tune with the Church," which is the living organism that

transmits the Word to us and is alone able, as if by some instinct for the Divine, to grasp its full meaning.

This Reading is a dialogal, meditational, and prayerful one, going beyond mere scientific knowledge and wisdom. It also leads to action.

The use of hagiographical readings shows that the Saints are "sacred pages" through which God addresses the world. They are "Gospels" endowed with a new realism because they are filled inwardly with the Spirit of Christ! The Saints are living interpretations of Scripture, bits of authentically existential exegesis. *See also* CYCLES; FIRST READING; GOSPEL; LECTIONARY; LITURGY OF THE HOURS; LITURGY OF THE WORD; SECOND READING; TWO-YEAR CYCLE OF READINGS, ALTERNATE.

Real Presence. *See* EUCHARIST.

Reception of Baptized Christians (ri-SEP-shuhn uhv bap-TAIZD; BAP-taizd; KRIS-chuhnz). The new rite for admitting to communion within the Church* those who have already been validly baptized. It pertains to their admission, reception, and welcome into the fullness of Catholic communion. Two major changes replace the former regulations. No longer is the requirement of absolution from excommunication and the abjuration of heresy to be made. Furthermore, conditional Baptism,* should it be deemed necessary because of reasonable doubt, is celebrated privately.

The revised rite is a celebration of the Church,* climaxed by Eucharistic Communion,* during which any appearance of triumphalism should be avoided. Should it be impossible to celebrate the rite within Mass,* the one received into the Church should attend Mass as soon as possible in order to participate fully by Eucharistic Communion with the Catholic community.

The Rite

Usually the reception occurs at a Sunday Eucharistic celebration of the Local Church,* so that the entire Christian community can express its welcome and unity. Whether within the Mass, or outside Mass, the reception occurs in the context of the Liturgy of the Word.* On Sundays or Solemnities,* the Mass of the day is used, otherwise the Mass for the Unity of Christians is chosen. The Readings* are commonly from the Mass of the day, but if unsuitable, they could be taken from the *Lectionary* for the Mass for the Unity of Christians, or the Mass for Christian Initiation, or specific texts appearing in the *Roman Ritual** for this purpose. After the Homily,* which should treat of the significance of reception in the full communion, the entire community and the persons received into communion profess their faith.* Thereupon the declaration of reception occurs by the bishop* or the priest,* and unless the person has already been confirmed, the Sacrament of Confirmation* is conferred. General Intercessions* befitting the circumstances follow, and the Sign of Peace* is given at this point of the Mass rather than before Commu-

nion. Then the Mass continues with the Liturgy of the Eucharist* during which the candidates receive Communion for the first time with the Catholic community.

Recessional Procession (ri-SESH-nuhl; uhn-uhl; pruh-SESH-uhn). Last of the five processions* at Mass,* which is made up of the recession of priests* and ministers* from the altar* to the sacristy* at

the end of Mass. In the Middle Ages various texts were used to accompany the recession of the priest—for example, Daniel* 3:57-88 and Psalm* 150. These did not become part of the rite but came to be used as private prayers of the priest after Mass. In time, it became customary for the choir* and even the people to sing as the ministers left the sanctuary.* *See also* RECESSIONAL SONG.

Recessional Song (ri-SESH-nuhl; uhn-uhl; song). Song while the priests* and ministers* depart from the altar* to the sacristy.* It is the people's farewell to the ministers for their help in reenacting and re-presenting the wondrous Mystery of Faith.* It is like the closing song of any gathering, the wish that all who came will get home safely, the end of a human ritual. This Recessional Song is technically not a part of the rite. Hence, musicians are free to plan music that provides an appropriate closing to the Liturgy.* A song is one possible choice—to prolong the festive character of the celebration.* It expresses praise* or reflects the theme of the particular feast* or season.* Instrumental music may also serve to provide a joyous closing atmosphere. In times of penitential nature, silence* may also be appropriate. *See also* RECESSIONAL PROCESSION.

Reconciliatio et Paenitentia (ray-kohn-chee-lee-AHTS-ee-oh et pe-nee-TEN-tsee-ah). Latin title (from the first three words "Reconciliation and Penance") of the *Apostolic Exhortation on Reconciliation and Penance in the Mission of the Church* issued by John Paul II on December 2, 1984, as a summary document of the proceedings and recommendations of the 1983 Synod of Bishops. It is a far-ranging treatment of this topic. It defines penance as a conversion* that passes from the heart to deeds and then to the Christian's whole life. And it notes that penance is always related to reconciliation with God, with oneself, and with others.

The Church is the Sacrament,* that is, the sign and means, of reconciliation in different ways, which differ in value but all come together to obtain what the Divine initiative of mercy desires to grant to humankind. She is a Sacrament (1) by her very existence as a reconciled community, (2) through her service as the custodian and interpreter of Sacred Scripture,* which is the Good News* of reconciliation, (3) by reason of the seven Sacraments, (4) by her prayer,* (5) by her pastoral action, and (6) by her witness.

The document goes on to treat sin in its various forms and the three rites of the Sacrament: reconciliation of individual penitents (ordinary rite); reconciliation of a number of penitents with individual confession* and absolution*; and reconciliation of a number of penitents with general confession* and absolution (extraordinary rite). *See also* PENANCE, RITE OF.

Reconciliation. *See* PENANCE, RITE OF.

Reconciliation Room (rek-uhn-sil-ee-AY-shuhn room). A room where the Rite of Penance* can be carried out in accord with the Church's* current suggestion for a more personal administration of this Rite. She offers the option not only of receiving the Sacrament* in the traditional way in a confessional* but also of meeting the confessor* in a more informal manner face to face.

So that the symbols of peace and healing of the Rite of Penance can truly take effect, all those involved, including the total community, must be reeducated to the realization of the true symbolism. Only this type of space will allow the proper extending and laying on of hands* that is called for to convey the comforting experience of forgiveness during the Sacrament. Although it would be ideal to have a place of transition from the church to the reconciliation room wherein the penitent may read the Scripture* or other religious readings in thoughtful preparation, most churches or other places where confessions are heard will not be able to supply this function.

The reconciliation room itself ought to be such that the penitent may choose to receive the Sacrament anonymously or in the face-to-face relationship with the priest.* To try to adapt current confessional boxes to such a proper space is usu-

ally most difficult unless they can be enlarged somewhat. Consequently, many look for other methods of achieving this purpose, such as using an old baptistry,* shrine room, storage room, or classroom. A professional person should be consulted in all cases in order to convert properly existing space into a room that can richly symbolize the essentials of a good celebration of reconciliation. *See also* CONFESSIONAL; "Place," under PENANCE, RITE OF.

Records and Tapes, Use of. *See* MASS MEDIA; MASS, TELEVISED; MUSIC.

Rectors (REK-tuhrz). (1) Those priests* to whom the bishop* has confided the charge of a non-parochial church,* which is also neither a capitular church nor a church annexed to the house of a Religious Community for its religious functions. They may perform solemn liturgical celebrations* within the church, but they cannot carry out parochial functions, unless the pastor* consents. The local Ordinary* may allow the rector to celebrate certain church functions to benefit the people or at least certain groups of the faithful.* (*See also* PASTORS.)

(2) The term is also applied to the head of educational institutions of certain Religious Communities.

Red Mass (red mas). Ordinarily this relates to the color of the vestment* used on the occasion of the Votive Mass* in honor of the Holy Spirit,* celebrated at the opening of councils, deliberative groups, schools, and such similar occasions when guidance is invoked. Frequently, at the beginning of a judicial year, such a Mass is attended by judges and court officials for any civil court or legislative assembly with the intention that they might exercise equity and prudence while fulfilling their official capacities.

Redemption (ri-DEM[P]-shuhn). A word from the Latin *redimere,* signifying "to bring back or redeem," which describes the renewal of human beings through the Death* and Resurrection* of Jesus Christ. Redemption entails the liberation and reconciliation of the human race, the forgiveness of sins, and justification by grace.* The corresponding Hebrew term was used in the Bible* for the first time with reference to the exodus from Egypt (Ex 15:13); God has redeemed His people from the bondage of Egypt gratuitously, just as a master sets free his slave (Lv 19:20). In the New Testament,* it signifies that God, through Jesus, gratuitously redeems His people in order to establish His Kingdom* (Rom 3:24).

It is the Liturgy* that applies the Redemption to God's people throughout the ages, since Jesus redeemed all: "This is the cup of my blood, the blood of the new and everlasting covenant.* It will be shed for you and for all, so that sins may be forgiven. Do this in memory of me" (Institution Narrative in the Eucharistic Prayer*). It incorporates human beings into Christ's Paschal Mystery,* which unites all

mysteriously but really with the risen humanity of Christ.

Thus, the Redemption freed us from the evil in the world (Gal 1:4), the malediction of the Law* (Reading II* for January 1—Gal 4:5), the wrath of God (Reading II for Monday of the 21st Week, I—1 Thes 1:10), and the bondage of sin (Reading I for Wednesday of the 29th Week, I—Rom 6:16). This Redemption regards not only our soul but also our body (Reading II for Tuesday of the 30th Week, I—Rom 8:23). Our Redemption will be completed at Christ's Second Coming* (see Opening Prayer* for the Triumph of the Cross*). *See also* HISTORY OF SALVATION; REDEMPTOR HOMINIS.

Redemptionis Donum (ray-dem[p]-tsee-OH-nees DOH-noom). Latin title (from the first two words "The Gift of the Redemption") of the *Apostolic Exhortation on the Gift of the Redemption* issued by John Paul II on March 25, 1984, toward the close of the Holy Year in honor of the 1950th anniversary of the Crucifixion and Death* of Christ. It is addressed to men and women Religious* who are entirely consecrated to contemplation or vowed to the various works of the apostolate.* The document stresses that Religious Profession* is deeply rooted in baptismal consecration and is a fuller expression of it. Upon the Sacramental basis of Baptism* on which it is rooted, Religious Profession is a new burial in the Death of Christ.

The fundamental community nature of Religious life* must be nourished by the teaching of the Gospel* and by the Liturgy,* especially the Eucharist.* Then it will have a special way of accomplishing the interpersonal and social dimension of Religious life: by caring for one another and bearing one another's burdens, Religious will show by their unity that Christ is living in their midst. *See also* RELIGIOUS LIFE; RELIGIOUS PROFESSION.

Redemptor Hominis (ray-DEM[P]-tohr HOH-mee-nees). Latin title (from the first two words "The Redeemer of Humankind") of the *Encyclical on the Redeemer of Humankind* issued by John Paul II on March 4, 1979. It deals with the Mystery* of the Redemption* from various aspects: as a new creation, in its Divine and human dimensions, as the basis of the Church's* mission and of Christianity, and as reflecting the Church's mission and human freedom. It also sets forth the situation of redeemed human beings in the world—their fears, progress, and human rights.

The document goes on to show the Church's concern for the vocation in Christ of human beings and her responsibility for truth no matter what field it is found in. All members of the People of God* have their own part to play in Christ's prophetic mission and the service of Divine Truth, among other ways by an honest attitude toward truth in whatever field, while educating others in truth and teaching them to mature in love* and justice.*

In the Mystery of the Redemption, Christ's saving work, the Church not only shares in the Gospel* of her Master through fidelity to the Word* and the service of the truth but also shares—through a submission filled with hope* and love—in the power of His redeeming action expressed and enshrined by Him in a Sacramental form, especially in the Eucharist.* The essential commitment and, above all, the visible grace* and source of supernatural strength for the Church is to preserve and advance completely in Eucharistic life and Eucharistic piety and to develop spiritually in the climate of the Eucharist. And linked to this Eucharist is the Sacrament of Penance.*

Redemptoris Mater (ray-dem[p]-TOH-rees MAH-ter). Latin title (from the first two words "The Mother of the Redeemer") of the *Encyclical on the Mother of the Redeemer* issued by John Paul II on March 25, 1987. The document gives a comprehensive treatment of Mary's part in the Mystery of Salvation.* Mary is the Mother of the Church,* which is the Body of Christ* prolonged throughout the ages. Hence, the Church "looks to" Mary through Jesus, just as she "looks to" Jesus through Mary. As the Servant, Mother, and Disciple of the Lord, Mary is the model, guide, and strength of the pilgrim People of God,* especially during the most important stages of their journey through life.

The Encyclical does not go into the Liturgy* with reference to Mary, obviously because this had already been done in splendid fashion by Paul VI in his *Marialis Cultus.** However, it does call for a Holy Year in honor of Mary, setting in motion a whole series of liturgical celebrations that would bring out for all true participants Mary's special presence in the Mystery of Christ and the Mystery of the Church.

Reed. *See* TUBE.

Reform (ri-FAWRM). The intent of all reform is to effect change by improvement. Within the Catholic Church* reforms are constant and refer to various aspects of the life of the faithful.* For our sphere of interest, liturgical reform occurs through the rituals, and as indicated in the *Constitution on the Sacred Liturgy,** such a renewal should effect an increasing vigor in Christian life. The result of many of these changes is explained throughout this work, but more especially under the entry ADAPTATION, LITURGICAL.

Regina Caeli (ray-JEEN-ah CHAY-lee). Latin title (from the first two words "Queen of Heaven") of an antiphon* to the Blessed Virgin Mary* of unknown authorship that dates back to the 12th century. It replaces the *Angelus** during the Easter Season* and was prescribed to be recited in the *Liturgy of the Hours** after Night Prayer* from Holy Saturday* to the Saturday after Pentecost.* The text in the *Enchiridion of Indulgences** is as follows:

Queen of heaven, rejoice, alleluia:
For He whom you merited to bear, alleluia,
Has risen, as he said, alleluia.
Pray for us to God, alleluia.

℣. Rejoice and be glad, O Virgin Mary, alleluia.
℟. Because the Lord is truly risen, alleluia.

Let us pray.
O God,
Who by the Resurrection of Your Son,
our Lord Jesus Christ,
granted joy to the whole world:
grant, we beg You,
that through the intercession of the Virgin Mary, His Mother,
we may lay hold of the joys of eternal life.
Through the same Christ our Lord.
℟. Amen.

See also ANGELUS; FINAL ANTIPHONS OF OUR LADY.

Registers (REJ-uh-stuhrz). Record books in which are kept the names of those who receive certain Sacraments* and who died within the parish.* The register for the catechumens* includes their names, those of the minister and sponsor,* and date and place of admission; Baptism,* Confirmation,* and Marriage* records list comparable information. Other similar records are kept for deaths within the parish, those received into the Church* from a Christian religion, the distribution of Communion to

the Sick,* and the like, so that the spiritual condition of the parish may be easily ascertained.

Relics (REL-iks). Classified in three ways, relics can be the body or fragment of a Saint* or a beatified* person, and these are the ones placed in altar* stones; secondly, objects used by the Saint, such as clothing or instruments employed during martyrdom; and thirdly, other objects, such as a cloth that has touched a first class relic. Relics of the true Cross* and other instruments of Christ's Passion* also exist and are allowed to be venerated by permission of the Church.*

The veneration of all relics is legitimate as stated in current Canon Law under title 4. Only the cult of dulia* is accorded relics of the Saints, and that in a relative manner, addressing itself to the person and not to the object. Major relics may not be transferred without permission of the Holy See,* and relics may never be sold (Can. 1190). Local calendars usually include feasts* of the Saints whose relics are venerated in that locality. *See also* CROSS; RELIQUARIES.

Religion, Virtue of (ri-LIJ-uhn, VUHR-choo uhv). A moral virtue* by which human beings give Divine worship* and reverence to God as the Creator and Ruler of all things, acknowledging their dependence on Him by inner worship* (acts of devotion,* reverence,* thanksgiving,* and the like) and external worship (external reverence, liturgical actions, and the like). Religion is part of the moral virtue of justice,* which inclines us to give whatever is due to God, to our neighbor, and to our selves. It surpasses and strenthens all the other moral virtues and is closely allied with the theological virtues. Participation in the Liturgy* is an exercise of the virtue of religion. *See also* GOOD WORKS; JUSTICE; VIRTUES.

Religious. *See* SAINTS, LITURGICAL CATEGORIES OF

Religious, Consecration of. *See* CONSECRATION OF VIRGINS.

Religious Freedom. *See* DIGNITATIS HUMANAE; FREEDOM.

Religious Life (ri-LIJ-uhs laif). A fixed or institutionalized type of life by which people of the same sex live in common and observe the evangelical counsels,* usually by means of the vows of poverty, chastity, and obedience. Members of these groups are called brothers, Religious priests,* sisters, or nuns. Ordinarily each group has a specific charism from its founder through which its members give expression to Christ in the life that they lead in accordance with the counsels and along the lines of their specific way of serving the Lord. The majority of these groups are active in many liturgical functions, particularly the

priests, and liturgical functions are used to embrace this profession. *See also* CONSECRATION OF VIRGINS; PERFECTAE CARITATIS; REDEMPTIONIS DONUM; RELIGIOUS PROFESSION.

Religious Profession (ri-LIJ-uhs pruh-FESH-uhn). Dedication of individuals to a Religious community or secular institute by promise or vow in accord with the *Roman Ritual,** which is to be adapted by each Religious community in accordance with its own spirit and needs. Preferably the profession occurs during Mass* in the Rite of Initiation into Religious Life and comprises the candidates' declaration of intention, their vows whether temporary, perpetual, or in process of renewal, and the receiving of these vows by the official representative of the Church* or Religious community. Norms govern the profession of both men and women Religious, and also the more general Rite of Promise to serve the Word of God.* Usually it is given during Mass or joined to the celebration of the Divine Office.* An example of the formula of profession is given together with Masses for the first Religious profession, the perpetual profession, or the renewal of vows. *See also* CONSECRATION OF VIRGINS.

Reliquaries (REL-uh-kwer-eez). Vessels, cases, containers, or repositories in which a relic* is held and exposed. They vary in size and shape according to the relic itself,* and most have worked precious metal of exquisite design and value. Various metals, such as gold, silver, and copper, have been used and decorated with ivory, precious stones, or gilded wood. Pectoral crosses* and medallions worn around the neck also serve as reliquaries. If relics are placed alongside the tabernacle,* the small reliquaries used remind one of the base of the chalice* whose cup has been replaced by a small, transparent case, or medallion containing the venerated particle. *See also* RELICS.

Remission of Sin (ri-MISH-uhn uhv sin). A somewhat negative expression that refers actually to the pardon and forgiveness of sin and its guilt through the grace* of Christ, namely, justification through reconciliation.* Remitting sin is not so much a canceling of guilt as the conferring again of the gift of grace to end any turning away from God that serious sin caused. This infusion of grace is a positive restoration for the guilty sinner rather than a negative remittance of guilt. Ordinarily this would occur during the Sacrament of Penance,* yet sometimes the Sacrament simply ratifies the conversion and forgiveness already present. Since venial sin causes no complete break with God's love,* the forgiveness brings greater reaffirmation of love* for God and increases the intensity that the venial sin has lessened. *See also* PENANCE, RITE OF.

Remnant (REM-nuhnt). An expression often used by the Prophets* that designates the survivors of great catastrophes: the flood, the exile (Gn 7:1f; Is 6:13). God reserves this remnant for Himself to help in the restoration (Is 37:31). It is they who are and will remain the depositaries of the Messianic promise* (Mi 4:6-7). In the New Testament,* the Church* is represented as fulfilling the function of the faithful remnant, and the "Israel according to the flesh" is contrasted with the "Israel of God," which is the Church

(Rom 9:27; 1 Cor 10:18; Gal 6:16). It is this "remnant" that acts in the Liturgy* and is built up by the Liturgy. *See also* CHURCH.

Renewal of Vows (ri-N[Y]OO-uhl uhv vowz). The reaffirmation of temporary Religious vows at the end of the period of time for which they had been taken. This renewal may take place no more than a month before the time elapses, and the proper renewal rite occurs in the *Roman Ritual.**

However, renewal of vows for devotion may occur at any time by a Religious,* though most renewals of profession by devotion take place on certain days of the year as prescribed by the constitutions or statutes. These are optional, having no obligatory character.

Reparation (rep-uh-RAY-shuhn). Literally from the Latin to repair or restore. Theologically and liturgically it is more akin to reconciliation,* righting something that was wrong, to atone, to make it "at one," basically to expiate. In other words, we try through this act of reparation to appease God's wrath by our taking upon ourselves some penitential acts to help shoulder the Cross* that Christ bore for us. We know Christ accepted the burden of our sins (1 Pt 1:19; Jn 1:29; Acts 8:32-35). We on our part try to make up for our sins by various practices that not only are penitential but also have a positive value of love of God and others. It is primarily through our attendance at Mass,* the highest of all prayers, that this reparation can take place. Reparation is one of the four ends of the Eucharist* and all prayer. *See also* ADORATION; IMPETRATION; MASS; PENANCE; PETITION; PRAYER; THANKSGIVING.

Repentance. *See* PENANCE.

Replies. *See* LITURGICAL LAW, SOURCES OF.

Reposition. *See* BENEDICTION.

Repository (ri-poz-uh-tawr-ee; -tohr-ee). (1) The secondary chapel or side altar* where the Eucharist,* consecrated on Holy Thursday,* is reserved until it is to be distributed during the Good Friday* services. Ideally it should be outside the main body of the church, suitably but not elaborately decorated. Historically this reservation of the Blessed Sacrament* began to be celebrated with great solemnity and eventually gave rise to the Forty Hours' Devotion.* During the Middle Ages, it was considered a symbol of Christ's burial. Recent regulations deemphasize comparing the repository with the tomb or connecting it with the burial of Christ and allow solemn adoration only until midnight on Holy Thursday.

(2) The term also refers to the place where the Blessed Sacrament is reserved, other than in the tabernacle* on the altar. Ideally it should not be kept on the altar of sacrifice, but in some properly decorated and prominent place in the church.

(3) The term is sometimes also used for the place where holy oils are kept, the ambry.*

(4) Relics too are kept in a special, different repository, either in the

sacristry,* at a side chapel, or in the church itself.

Reproaches (Improperia) (ri-PROHCH-uhz) (im-proh-PER-ee-ah). Reproaches chanted during the veneration of the Cross* at the Good Friday Liturgy* that have been part of the Roman Rite* since the 11th

century. They are addressed by Christ to all people in the person of the Jews, reciting His mercies and their ingratitude. The twelve reproaches are interspersed with the Greek *Trisagion* (the "thrice-holy" hymn from the Byzantine Rite*: "Holy is God! Holy and strong! Holy immortal One, have mercy on us!") and the text of Micah* 6:3 ("My people, what have I done to you? How have I offended you? Answer me!"

Because we should have a genuine appreciation of the honor and dignity that belongs to the Jewish people, since they have a special place as God's first-chosen in the History of Salvation,* and because the Reproaches may be susceptible to poor interpretation and mishandling, other suitable songs may be sung at that time as the rubrics* prescribe, or the alternate version of the Reproaches, taken from Psalm 22, may be used.

Should one prefer to chant the reproaches, sufficient catechesis* should be given the people to explain that the Reproaches are a dialogue between God and the Church* today, and not a historical or theological indictment of Israel or Jews by God, and thus should not be considered anti-Semitic.

Requiem. *See* FUNERAL RITES AND CEREMONIES; MASS OF CHRISTIAN BURIAL.

Reredos. *See* ALTARPIECE.

Rescript (REE-skript). In answer to questions, petitions, or reports, a written reply from the Holy See* that grants a favor, dispensation, or gives an interpretation or information. Some rescripts pertain to judicial matters, others concede a favor. They may be directly communicated to the petitioner or sent through an executor, usually the bishop* or confessor.* Particular rescripts limited to particular cases or persons do not formulate any general ecclesiastical law. *See also* LITURGICAL LAW, SOURCES OF.

Research Centers, Liturgical. *See* LITURGICAL RESEARCH CENTERS.

Reservation of the Eucharist (rez-uhr-VAY-shuhn uhv thuh YOO-kuh-rist). The custom of keeping the Blessed Sacrament,* ordinarily under the species of Bread only, in a suitable place. Until recently this was considered to be the tabernacle,* ordinarily affixed to the altar* of sacrifice. Current regulation, however, prefers that some such repository* be a secure structure located in a prominent place within the church, with sufficient accommodations for people who wish to adore and pray to Christ present in the Eucharist.* The primary reason for reservation is to be able to administer Viaticum.* However, since Christians have the right to receive Communion* at any time, even outside of Mass,* it does allow for this function also. *See also* REPOSITORY.

Reserved Blessings. *See* BLESSING.

Responses (ri-SPON[T]S-uhz). The answers to the greetings of the priest* and his presidential prayers* made by the faithful* during the celebration of the Liturgy,* preferably sung, otherwise said. Such responses by the congregation express more clearly their participation* and develop the action of the entire community within the Liturgy. *See also* ACCLAMATIONS; INTRODUCTORY DIALOGUE.

Responsorial Psalm (ri-spon-SOH-ri-uhl sah[l]m). That Psalm,* or portion thereof, which serves as a responsorial between the lector* and the people and occurs after the First Reading* and before either the Second Reading* or the Gospel,* depending on the number of Readings during a Mass.* The Psalm with its recurring refrain echoes the dominant theme of the Reading and should be sung if at all possible, the chanter singing the Psalm-verse,* and the whole congregation joining in with the response. At times the entire Psalm can be sung straight through without the intervening refrain, and on occasion the entire community sings it together. If not sung, its recitation should be in a meditative mood. Formerly, it was called the Gradual, because it was sung on one of the steps of the altar* (*gradus* is Latin for step). *See also* INTERVENIENT CHANTS; LITURGY OF THE WORD.

Responsories (ri-SPON[T]S-[uh-]reez). Each Biblical Reading in the Divine Office* is followed by a Responsory. In the Office of Readings* it has a character of a sung meditation, shedding light on the passage just read, whether putting it in context with Salvation History* or indicating a relationship between the Old and the New Testaments*; it may aid in meditating or merely be a complementary poetic variation. The one following the Second Reading* is not so closely joined to the texts, so that there is a more free scope for thought. Each Responsory has a refrain that is not necessarily repeated if it is not sung. More simple Responsories follow the Readings of Morning and Evening Prayer,* Night Prayer,* and those in the Daytime Hours. They are more like an acclamation that allows God's Word* to penetrate more deeply into the hearts and minds of those reciting the Office. *See also* LITURGY OF THE HOURS.

Resurrection. *See* EASTER.

Retables. *See* ALTARPIECE.

Retreats (ri-TREETS). Those times when one withdraws from the regular setting of occupation and daily life to a place of solitude for more intense spiritual exercises, such as prayer,* meditation,* and self-examination, following the example of Jesus Who had special times of recollection. Clerics* and Religious* are required to make a

retreat once a year for usually a specified period of time. Retreats for the laity* are quite popular, usually for shorter periods, especially weekends. Retreats certainly foster the spirit of renewal propounded by Vatican II.*

Revelation (rev-uh-LAY-shuhn). God's self-manifestation to the human race. It is *natural* when it comes to us through the natural world of creation and our use of reason. It is *supernatural* when it comes to us through Scripture* (the Patriarchs and the Prophets* of the Old Testament* and Jesus and the Apostles* in the New Testament*) and Tradition.* Tradition is the Word of God given to the Apostles by Christ and the Holy Spirit* and handed down to their successors through the Church* by means of prayer* and creeds,* liturgical practices, and authoritative writings (Popes* and bishops* in union with the Holy Father). Thus, Scripture, Apostolic Tradition, and the Magisterium* guided by the Holy Spirit combine to bring us God's Revelation at any particular moment of time.

> As the community of believers grows in understanding, its faith* is expressed in creeds, dogmas,* and moral principles and teachings. The meaning of dogmatic formulas remains ever true and constant in the Church,* even when it is expressed with greater clarity or more developed. Because they are expressed in the language of a particular time and place, however, these formulations sometimes give way to new ones, proposed and approved by the Magisterium* of the Church, which express the same meaning more clearly or completely.
>
> What we believe is also expressed in the deeds of the Church community. The "deeds" in question are worship*—especially the celebration of the Eucharist,* in which the risen Christ speaks to His Church and continues His saving work—and acts performed to build up Christ's body through service to the community of faith or voluntary service in the universal mission of the Church (cf Eph 4:11f) (NCD, 59).

Hence, the Liturgy* may be termed a certain phase of Revelation, a way in which the meaning of Revelation is realized for people throughout the ages. It is a certain way in which Christ—in the present intermediate time that extends from Pentecost* to the Second Coming,* in this eschatological time already going on—communicates the fullness of His Divine Life to individual souls, reproduces His Mystery* in them, and draws them into His Mystery. The liturgical event is an *event* of salvation because it puts the historic *today* in touch with the historic time of Christ.

At the same time, Liturgy is itself an organ of Revelation, since it is in the words of Pius XI "the most important organ of the Ordinary Magisterium of the Church" *(Encyclical "Quas Primas"* on the Kingship of Christ).* In this sense, the rule of prayer establishes the rule of faith. *See also* CATECHESIS AND LITURGY; LEX ORANDI—LEX CREDENDI; MAGISTERIUM.

Revelation, The Book of (rev-uh-LAY-shuhn, thuh buk uhv). Last and most image-filled Book of the Bible.* Classified as a prophetic book, it is more properly an apocalyptic one. This was a type of writing that can best be described as "underground literature." It lasted from 200 B.C. to 200 A.D. and was very popular among both Jews and Christians while in vogue. Written about 95 A.D., and attributed to the Apostle John,* this mysterious Book cannot be adequately comprehended except against the historical background that occasioned its writing. Like the Book of Daniel* and other apocalypses, it was composed as resistance literature to meet a crisis. The Book itself suggests that the crisis was ruthless persecution of the early Church by the Roman authorities; the harlot Babylon symbolizes pagan Rome, the city on seven hills.

The Book is, then, an exhortation and admonition to Christians to stand fast in the Faith* and to avoid compromise with paganism, despite the threat of adversity and martyrdom; they are to await patiently the fulfillment of God's mighty promises.* The triumph of God in the world remains a mystery, to be accepted in faith and longed for in hope.* It is a triumph that unfolded in the history of Jesus of Nazareth and continues to unfold in the history of the individual Christian who follows the way of the Cross,* even, if necessary, to a martyr's death. The very forces of evil unwittingly carry out the Divine plan inasmuch as God is the sovereign Lord of history. And those who persevere will enjoy eternal life.*

Liturgical use: In the *Roman Missal,** this Book is read extensively: e.g., on Holy Thursday,* on the Sundays of the Easter Season* (C), the Assumption,* All Saints,* All Souls,* and Christ the King* as well as during the 33rd and 34th Weeks in Ordinary Time* (II) and in Common,* Votive,* and Ritual Masses.* In the *Liturgy of the Hours,** it is also widely used: from the 2nd through the 5th Week in Easter Time,* on Christ the King, August 15, September 29, and November 1, and the Common.* It also gives rise to four minor canticles* of the Four-Week Psalter.*

Meaning: Christ's overwhelming defeat of the kingdom of Satan has ushered in the everlasting Reign of God, and final victory is assured. Persecutions cannot take that triumph away, for God's servants will reign with Him forever. Thus, Christ gives meaning to all the realities of the world* and to all of human life. Our task is to discover that meaning by remaining faithful to Him in adversity as well as success while waiting for the definitive triumph to be ours.

Reverence (REV-[uh-]ruhn[t]s). A mark of respect with reference to persons or objects that are especially venerable. In the Liturgy,* the public cult includes various signs* that show our adoration* toward God, our veneration toward the Saints,* and our deference with regard to ecclesiastical authority. Liturgical books* prescribe a customary reverence, either the genuflection* or the bow* that is proper for the object venerated or the person reverenced.

Rings (ringz). Circular bands of metal ordinarily worn around the fourth finger as a sign of alliance or of power.

(1) The pastoral or episcopal ring is received by the bishop* at his episcopal ordination as a mark of his jurisdiction* and dignity. It clearly signifies the spiritual union and the alliance contracted by the bishop with his particular Church. In the earlier centuries, bishops, as well as cardinals* and the Pope* wore rings also for the practical need of using them as a seal on official documents. Prelates,* Religious* from some Orders, and those with pontifical doctoral degrees may wear rings.

(2) Most women Religious wear rings to remind them of their dedication to Christ; a pledge of the mystical union they contract with the Lord.

(3) The exchange of the nuptial ring(s) in the Marriage* ceremony signifies the mutual love of the wife and husband and the indissoluble bond that unites them during their entire life; thus it is a pledge of marital fidelity.

Rite of Admission to Candidacy for Diaconate and Presbyterate. *See* ADMISSION TO CANDIDACY FOR DIACONATE AND PRESBYTERATE, RITE OF.

Rite of Christian Initiation of Adults. (rait uhv KRIS-chun in-ish-ee-AY-shuhn uhv uh-DUHLTS). Currently each country is studying the *Rite of Christian Initiation of Adults,* so that it can be adapted properly to the cultural needs of the people of God.* The three Sacraments of initiation—Baptism,* Confirmation,* and the Holy Eucharist*—are solemnly celebrated on the Easter Vigil.*

Through Baptism the candidates become Christians, being formed into People of God,* adopted children of the Father,* with their sins forgiven. Through Confirmation they become more perfectly the image of the Lord, since they are signed with the gifts of the Spirit,* actually filled with the Spirit that thus allows them to give witness to their faith.* Then they share in Christ's sacrifice by receiving the Eucharist at the table of the Lord, expressing the unity of the People of God. Thus, through the three Sacraments, the recipients achieve Christian maturity, enabling them to fulfill their mission in the Church and the world.

The rite is looked upon as a spiritual journey for the adults. Three major stages occur:

(1) The persons learn of the Church,* indicate an interest and a desire to become Christians, and are eventually accepted as catechumens.*

(2) During the catechumenate* their faith grows while they are more fully instructed and receive various rites connected with catechesis.* The completion of this stage is the day of election.*

(3) Thereupon, the spiritual preparation being satisfactory, the persons receive the three Sacraments

ordinarily on the Easter Vigil. However, the follow-up period (during the Easter Season*) called mystagogia* allows the neophytes to understand the Paschal Mystery* better and to experience the reception of the Sacraments and life in a Christian community to bring about a more complete understanding of the Mysteries* they have acquired.

Precatechumenate

Technically the initiation starts with the catechumenate; yet the period preceding it is of great importance, since it is a time of evangelization.* The non-Christians are inspired by the Holy Spirit* to believe and really be converted to the Lord. During this evangelization come faith and the initial conversion,* so that the desire to seek Baptism matures.

These inquirers* or sympathizers are helped through the period by catechists,* deacons,* priests,* and the community. Locally some sort of reception for them can occur with-

out a specific rite, allowing the inquirers to feel the warmth of the community, since a sound intention to seek the Faith is evident.

Catechumenate

Before entering into this state the candidates should be grounded in the basic tenets of Christian teaching and experience a sense of repentance* with a desire to become a Christian. Sponsors* aid them through this period and help to judge their disposition.

At this juncture the candidates assemble publicly before the Church indicating their intention and are admitted to the catechumenate. Then their names are written into the register* with the name of their minister, sponsors, date, and place of admission.

The extended period of pastoral information that follows attempts to bring the catechumens to maturity. Their formation takes place through priests, deacons, catechists, and others, usually accommodated to the Liturgical Year* by celebrations of the Word.*

Thus their knowledge of dogmas,* precepts, and the Mystery of Salvation* increases. With the help of sponsors and the community, they learn to pray, to witness to the Faith, to practice virtue, to share in Christ's Death and Resurrection.*

Through liturgical rites the Church aids the catechumens, cleansing them little by little, strengthening them with blessings.* Furthermore, they learn how to work with others in spreading the Gospel* and building up the Church in a truly apostolic manner.

A Period of Purification and Enlightenment

A deeper spiritual preparation occurs during this time, commonly coinciding with Lent.* The entire community, together with the catechumens, ready themselves for the proper celebration of the Paschal Mystery. The assumption is that the catechumens have experienced a conversion of mind and morals, a deep sense of faith and charity, together with satisfactory knowledge of Christian teaching. The Church then decides on the admission of the catechumens because of their dispositions.

This stage is designated as the election* since they are chosen by God, and those admitted are called the elect.* These *competentes,* synonymous with elect, work toward the reception of the Sacraments, particularly Baptism, the Sacrament that is also called enlightenment* or illumination, for these neophytes will be illumined in the light of faith.

Spiritual recollection is stressed over catechesis, and the deeper knowledge of Christ is accomplished through various rites. The scrutinies,* solemnly celebrated on Sundays, reveal anything defective or sinful, with the intent of healing. The positive revealing of what is upright, strong, and holy is also strengthened. The presentations* proffer to the elect the documents of faith and prayer (the Creed* and the Lord's Prayer*).

In immediate preparation for the Sacraments, on the Easter Vigil these elect spend a day of recollection, during which some of the preparatory rites may be celebrated, e.g., profession of faith, Ephphetha* or opening of ears and mouth, choice of Christian name, and even anointing with the oil of catechumens.*

Sacraments of Initiation

Through the reception of these Sacraments the elect are admitted to the People of God with the promise of the eternal banquet. During the Easter Vigil, the high point of

adult Baptism, washing with water in the name of the Holy Trinity, occurs in its proper place.

With all its pastoral implications, following the complementary rites of Baptism, Confirmation is celebrated.

Then later in the Mass the first sharing of the Eucharist for the newly baptized occurs during Communion.

Mystagogia

This postbaptismal catechesis occurs during the Easter Season and is marked by a new experience of the Sacraments and the Christian community. Having been renewed in mind, sharing the spirit from the Word and the Food from the table, these Catholics now develop a new sense of faith, the Church, and the world.

During this time, the neophytes, helped by their sponsors, should grow into a closer relationship with all the faithful and receive a new impetus and renewed vision. The special Sunday Masses of the Easter Season should be able to develop these personal experiences more deeply.

Should it be impossible to use the customary times for the Rite of Initiation, adaptations may be made. Normally the Sacraments are to be celebrated on Sunday; the rite of the catechumenate depends on the local situation and the preparation and disposition of the candidates; the election should be celebrated six weeks or so before the Sacraments of initiation, and the scrutinies ought not to be celebrated on Solemnities, but on Sundays, and an attempt should be made to observe the usual intervals, using the readings* given in the *Ritual.*

Simple Rite

Under certain circumstances candidates may not be able to go through all the stages of initiation. Therefore the Rite may occur in one celebration, or one or another of the rites from the catechumenate may be carried out prior to the reception of the Sacraments. The simple rite authorizes the presentation and reception of the candidates, their public expression of the intention of receiving Christian initiation, plus the consent of the Church. After the Liturgy of the Word, the celebration of the Sacraments of initiation takes place, normally during the Mass,* preferably on Sunday, with the active participation* of the local community. *See also* BAPTISM.

Rite of Penance. *See* PENANCE, RITE OF.

Rites and Ceremonies (raits and ser-uh-MOH-neez). Gestures or external acts or movements that accompany prayers or liturgical exercises of Divine worship,* such as imposition of hands,* incensing the gifts, the sign of peace,* and any unction, ablution, or sprinkling.* Rite may also designate the form and manner of a total religious function, such as the rite of Confir-

mation,* or the rite of Consecration.* For supplying rites when a person has been baptized outside of the Church because of danger of death, see BAPTISM.

Rites are based on four concepts. (a) *Symbolism.* A natural action or object is emblematic of the Divine, for instance, the Eucharist* symbolizes Christ, the Bread of Life. (b) *Consecration.* A human situation shares in a principle that goes beyond it and is actually its basis. (c) *Repetition.* Representative actions bring Divine power into the present. Thus in the Eucharist, the Sacrifice of the Cross* is present through its effects. (d) *Remembrance.* Rites preserve and transmit the tradition of the community in a shared experience* and thus the community is perpetuated and renewed. *See also* CEREMONIAL; LITURGICAL LAW; PROCESSIONS; RITUAL.

Rites and Uses (raits and YOO-suhz). The term rites refers to the various groupings of Churches, identified by distinctive liturgical forms, traditions and customs, discipline and canonical organization, theological and spiritual heritage, while in communion with each other and the Pope.* The various rites originated in cultural, geographic, and political diversity that occurred during the development and spread of the Church.* The major distinctions lie between the Eastern and Western rites, and

each of these have several subdivisions or types. Certain Religious Orders also had specific rites.

When baptized, a person enters not only the Church but also a specific rite. Regulations then, with regard to the other Sacraments, would depend on Canon Law. *See also* ALEXANDRIAN RITE; AMBROSIAN RITE; ANTIOCHENE RITE; BYZANTINE RITE; CHALDEAN RITE; EASTERN RITE; GALLICAN RITE; MOZARABIC RITE; ROMAN RITE.

Rites of Presentation. *See* PRESENTATION, RITE OF.

Rites of Transition. *See* TRANSITION, RITES OF.

Rites, Sacred Congregation of. *See* CONGREGATION FOR DIVINE WORSHIP AND THE DISCIPLINE OF THE SACRAMENTS.

Ritual (RICH-oo-uhl; RICH-[uh-[wuhl). The liturgical book* that contains the rites for the Sacraments,* Sacramentals,* and any other liturgical actions the priest* may perform. Rites administered by a bishop* are found in the *Pontifical.** The *Ritual* is to be so constructed that it allows for variations and adaptations necessary in various regions and also with regard to the language employed. Particular *Rituals* for geographical areas or Religious Orders are nothing new, for the *Ritual* was never prescribed for the entire Latin Church.

The first *Roman Ritual** was promulgated in the early 17th century, and since then it has been frequently revised; the latest revision is that of Vatican II,* completed in 1984 with the publication of the *Book of Blessings.* Norms for the recent revision prescribe that a communal celebration should be preferred; active participation* of the faithful is to be fostered; no distinction should be made in favor of certain classes of people or private persons; simple rites that require little explanation are to be used; more reading of Sacred Scripture* should be introduced; opportunities for homilies* or brief explanations should be provided. *See also* CEREMONIAL; LITURGICAL BOOKS.

Ritual Masses (RICH-oo-uhl; RICH-[uh-]wuhl; MAS-uhz). Related to the celebration of certain Sacraments* or Sacramentals,* these Masses for the most part follow the rules of Masses for Various Needs and Occasions.* Seldom would the weekday Readings* and chants* be suitable for these special occasions, so it would be more fitting to choose Readings from those listed in the *Lectionary.** Ritual Masses are those connected with Christian initiation,* Holy Orders,* Marriage,* Viaticum,* consecration to a life of virginity, and Religious Profession.* Such Masses are prohibited on the days listed in the first four numbers of the table of precedence.* Norms in the ritual books or Masses also apply. Since these Masses are so specialized, unless the actual occasion for their use occurs, they are not permitted on those days in Ordinary Time* that would allow any Mass for Various Needs or Occasions.

Rivista Liturgica (ree-VEES-tah lee-TOOR-jee-kah). Italian liturgical periodical ("Liturgical Review") founded in 1914 at the Benedictine monastery of Finalpia in Savona. It is one of the organs whose opinions can safely be followed in matters of liturgical law. *See also* LITURGICAL LAW, SOURCES OF.

Robert Bellarmine, St. (ROB-uhrt BEL-uhr-min). 1542-1621. An Italian Jesuit who became a renowned theologian and Doctor of the Church.* After becoming a professor at Louvain, he was sent to Rome to teach, where he wrote his famous study refuting the Protestant work, *Centuries of Magdeburg*; his *Disputations on the Controversies* is a classic defense of the Catholic Faith*; created cardinal* and archbishop* of Capua he also wrote works of instruction and devotion.

He is the Patron of Catechists. *Liturgical celebration:* September 17 (Opt. Mem.); *theme:* wisdom and goodness used to defend the Faith.

Rochet (RAHCH-uht). A white linen vestment resembling a surplice* with close-fitting sleeves worn by bishops* and other prelates.*

Rogation Days (roh-GAY-shuhn dayz). Days of special prayer* and penance* formerly prescribed on the three days before Ascension.* The major Rogation however was April 25, but it had no connection with the feast* of St. Mark.* The primary purpose of the prayers was to ask for protection, appease Divine justice, and beg for a fruitful harvest. During a procession* the Litany of the Saints* was sung (hence the days were also named Greater Litanies and Lesser Litanies). The major Rogation day supplanted and Christianized a pagan festival in honor of the god, Robigus. The minor Rogation days began in France in the 5th century, primarily to beg for protection against earthquakes.

They were adopted by Rome in the 9th century. These specific days of prayer are no longer in the Roman Calendar* since its reform in 1969. However special days of prayer and thanksgiving, for productivity of crops, for human labor, for justice, and so forth, are to be established by the Episcopal Conferences* of the nation. Each diocese* in the United States chooses its own dates for these prayers. *See also* DAYS OF PRAYER; GREATER LITANIES; LESSER LITANIES.

Roles. *See* ASSEMBLY, LITURGICAL.

Roman Canon. *See* EUCHARISTIC PRAYER.

Roman Gradual. *See* GRADUAL, ROMAN.

Roman Rite (ROH-muhn rait). That manner of celebrating Mass and performing other liturgical functions, authorized for the Diocese* of Rome. By the 12th century, wherever Latin was used, the Roman Rite was in vogue. By the 16th century, it had firmly established itself under St. Pius V* and was adopted by the entire Church of the West with few exceptions. It had been influenced by both the Gallican and the Spanish rites.

The Latin Rite is characterized by sobriety and expression. Only about ten lines are required to comment on a Mystery* in a Preface,* while a page or more would be necessary in an Eastern Rite. The admirable conciseness should be noted in the ancient prayers of the Sundays in Ordinary Time,* wherein are expressed in a few words subjects that other Liturgies develop in long narratives. There is also a certain gravity proper to this Liturgy,* especially as compared with the pomp of Oriental ceremony. Compare the amplitude of gesture in certain Liturgies with the sobriety of gesture of the Roman celebrant.* It is truly Roman genius expressing itself with clarity, precision, order, practical sense, severity of line, absence of sentimentality, effusion, imagination, and mystery.

Liturgical presentation of the truth of our Faith is well-balanced and there is hardly any trace of the struggles that occurred against various heresies. Special features of the Roman Rite are the celibacy of priests,* unleavened bread for the Eucharist,* and, until recently, Communion under one kind, and the permission to receive Communion in the hand, where approved. (Most of the entries in this Dictionary have to do with the Roman Rite.) *See also* RITES AND USES.

Romans, Epistle to the (ROH-muhnz, i-PIS-uhl too thuh). Fifty-second Book of the Bible* and sixth of the New Testament.* It is unquestionably the most important Epistle Paul* wrote (around 57 A.D.). The Church of Rome was deeply divided and broken up into communities, one made up of converts from paganism and the other made up of converts from Judaism. Romans

contains a powerful exposition of the doctrine of the supremacy of Christ and of faith in Him as the source of salvation.* It is an implicit plea to the Christians of Rome to hold fast to that faith. They are to resist any pressure put on them to accept a doctrine of salvation through works of the Mosaic Law.* At the same time, they are not to exaggerate Christian freedom* through repudiation of law itself.

The implication of Paul's exposition by faith rather than by the Law is that the Divine plan of salvation works itself out on a broad theological plane to include the whole of humankind despite the differences of the given religious system to which a human culture is heir.

Liturgical use: In the *Roman Missal,** this Book is very extensively used, notably on the Easter Vigil,* Pentecost,* and the 9th through the 24th Sundays in Ordinary Time* (A) as well as Common,* Votive,* and Ritual* Masses. In the *Liturgy of the Hours,** it is sparsely used: on Easter Sunday,* Pentecost, Sacred Heart,* Immaculate Conception,* and the Common. *Meaning:* God never ceases to love us in Christ and in the Spirit.* (Indeed, Romans is a hymn to the glory* of Christ and His great love for sinful human beings.) Nothing in all of creation can separate us from the Ruler of creation.

God can work good out of evil for those who love Him, and He makes everything redound to their good.

Romuald, St. (ROM-yoo-uhld). c.950-1027. The son of an Italian nobleman, Romuald entered the monastery at twenty, searched for a more austere life among the hermits, and eventually founded the eremitical monasteries, based on the Benedictine rule, where the members live as hermits but in community. The most famous was at Camaldoli, and hence they are called the Camaldolese. *Liturgical celebration:* June 19 (Opt. Mem.); *theme:* self-denial through a life of solitude and prayer.*

Rosary (ROHZ-[uh-]ree). A liturgical devotion, consisting of the recitation of one Our Father,* ten Hail Marys,* and a Glory Be to the Father* for each of the fifteen decades, dedicated to fifteen Scriptural Mysteries* as the topic of mental prayer, which is the primary focus of this devotion. Separated into three sets of Five Mysteries, as they are called, actually meditations: joyful, sorrowful, and glorious, the Rosary focuses on the Incarnation,* the Sufferings, and the Glorification of Jesus. It is frequently called the Marian Psalter since the Hail Mary* is repeated 150 times instead of each of the 150 Psalms.

This devotion has been highly recommended by the Church,* with many of the Popes* praising it as a fine prayer* to develop a true Christological devotion, specifically because the Mysteries have their inspiration from Biblical and liturgical themes. Indulgences* have been attached to its recitation, and it certainly seems to fit the definition of the popular devotions spoken of in the *Constitution on the Sacred Liturgy** that are in some fashion derived from the Liturgy and lead people to it. We should appreciate the fact that the Rosary is a practice of piety that easily harmonizes with the Liturgy. Our Liturgy commemorates the same remembrances proper to the Rosary, although on different planes of reality, which have as their object the salvific events of Christ.

Thus the Rosary, as an exercise of piety that draws its motivating force from the Liturgy, familiarizes the hearts and minds of the faithful* with the Mysteries of Christ* and can therefore be a fine preparation for the celebration of the Mysteries in liturgical action. However, it is not to be recited during liturgical functions.

Rose of Lima, St. (rohz uhv LEE-muh). 1586-1617. From childhood Rose practiced remarkable austerity. Becoming a Dominican tertiary, she cared for destitute children and the elderly and, when not working, gave herself up to prayer* in a hermitage in the garden of her family home. Mystical experiences put her through further trials. First Saint of the New World, she is the Patroness of South America. *Liturgical celebration:* August 23 (Opt. Mem.); *theme:* a life of mortification and penance in contrast to the materialism of the world.

Rose Philippine Duchesne, St. (ROHZ FIL-uh-peen doo-SHAYN). 1769-1852. A member of the Society of the Sacred Heart in France, Rose was sent to the United States at the age of 49. She founded a boarding school for daughters of pioneers near St. Louis and opened the first free school west of the Missouri. At the age of 71, she began a school for Indians, who soon came to call her "the woman who is always praying." She was canonized by John Paul II on July 3, 1988, and her feast is part of the Proper* for the United States. *Liturgical celebration:* November 18 (Opt. Mem.); *theme:* love and zeal for the spread of God's Kingdom.*

Rubrics (ROO-briks). A term (taken from the Latin adjective *ruber,* "red") referring to the *directives* in liturgical books* that are printed in red so that they can be distinguished from the *text* (or prayers) printed in black. These regulations guide the bishops,* priests,* or deacons* in the performance of any Liturgy.* Some of them are of a more general nature and usually appear at the beginning of a book or a section, while others are special, inserted into the text itself. Some describe the essential rites of the liturgical service, while others merely regulate the actions.

Canon Law prescribes the observance of these rubrics in accord with the context, which should make clear whether they are preceptive, facultative, or nonpreceptive. Preceptive rubrics dictate the action, e.g., "anoint with chrism." Facultative rubrics give options, e.g., "in these or similar words." Nonpreceptive rubrics try to set the atmosphere, e.g., "The celebrant greets the candidate in a friendly manner. . . . He invites the candidates and their godparents* to come forward."

Rubricism is the practice of following the rubrics. Sometimes, it is used to indicate an attitude that accords more attention to the regulations for celebrations than to the meaning of the liturgical functions.

Ruth, The Book of (rooth, thuh buk uhv). Eighth Book of the Old Testament* named after the Moabite woman who was joined to the Israelite people by her marriage with the influential Boaz of Bethlehem.

Of unknown authorship and date, its aim is to demonstrate the Divine reward for true piety even when practiced by a foreigner. Ruth's piety, her spirit of self-sacrifice, and her moral integrity were favored by God with the gift of faith and an illustrious marriage whereby she became the ancestress of David and of Christ. In this the universality of salvation* is foreshadowed.

Liturgical use: In the *Roman Missal,** this Book is read on Friday and Saturday of the 20th Week in Ordinary Time* (I). In the *Liturgy of the Hours,** it is read only in the alternate Two-Year Cycle* of Readings from Wednesday of the 2nd Week of Advent* to the 3rd Sunday of Advent in Year I. *Meaning:* God's providence watches over the world.* Loyalty, love, kindness, esteem for persons, and understanding of others will lead to good even amid chaos. For God loves all whom He has made—even those who are inimical to us. We must be willing to risk all for God.

— S —

Sabbath. *See* SUNDAY.

Sacrament of the Sick. *See* ANOINTING OF THE SICK; PASTORAL CARE OF THE SICK.

Sacrament, Blessed. *See* EUCHARIST.

Sacramentals (sak-ruh-MENT-uhlz). Liturgical actions, sacred signs,* and objects introduced by the Church,* not instituted by Christ as the Sacraments* were, that resemble the Sacraments by signifying spiritual effects achieved through the intercession of the Church. The Sacraments, instituted by Christ, produce their effect by virtue of the ritual performed. Sacramentals, on the other hand, depend on prayerful petition,* the spiritual preparedness of the recipient, and the Church approving the Sacramentals by her intercession through the mediation of the minister's faith* and love.* The tangible symbols or signs bring effective sanctification because of the devotion, faith, and love of the user, whereas the Sacraments automatically channel grace* in an objective manner to the one receiving them.

Thus, the chief benefits obtained by the use of Sacramentals are: (1) actual graces; (2) forgiveness of venial sins; (3) remission of temporal punishment due to sin; (4) health of body and material blessings; and (5) protection from evil spirits.

Sacramentals range over the whole span of times and places, words and actions, objects and gestures, such as holy water,* candles,* blessings of the home, the sick, medals,* etc., blessings or actions connected with the Sacraments and the Mass,* prayers and exorcisms.* Exorcisms over the possessed can be performed only by a priest* who has obtained express permission from the Ordinary.* Ministers* of Sacramentals are clerics,* who have the necessary power, and deacons* who are allowed to impart only those blessings expressly permitted to them. Some Sacramentals may be administered by lay* people who have the appropriate qualities. Blessings for Catholics may also be imparted to catechumens,* and even non-Catholics, unless there is a Church prohibition.

Extensions and Radiations of the Sacraments

The Sacramentals are *extensions and radiations of the Sacraments* and have the same cause—the Passion,* Death,* and Resurrection* of Christ. They continue the work of the Sacraments or prepare for their reception.

Thus, *Baptism** can be followed by the Sacramentals of holy water,*

the sprinkling* of water at the beginning of the Sunday Eucharist, and the blessing of infants and children.

*Confirmation** is extended by the blessings of a school, library, archive, or typewriter.

The *Eucharist** may be prolonged by Benediction of the Blessed Sacrament.*

*Holy Orders** is followed by the consecration* or blessing of virgins.

*Marriage** is prolonged by the blessings of a bridal-chamber, an expectant mother, and a house and

the various blessings of material things used in a home.

*Penance** is extended in the Sacramental of the Confiteor,* absolutions,* the Papal Blessing* at the hour of death, and exorcisms.

The *Anointing of the Sick** flows into blessing of the sick, the blessing of oil,* medicine, and linens, and the blessing of a deceased at the grave.

Episcopal Conferences* may introduce new Sacramentals and perhaps change the rites of some that exist. They should make sure that the faithful can participate* intelligently, actively, and easily in the sanctifying action that Sacramentals bring to the well-disposed faithful because of the merits* and prayers* of the entire Mystical Body of Christ.* *See also* BLESSING; EX OPERE OPERANTIS; EX OPERE OPERATO; HOLY OILS.

Sacramentary (sak-ruh-MEN-tuhr-ee). The volume of presidential prayers* for the officiant of the Eucharist* and for any rites connected with the Mass.* Vatican Council II* restored the rule that all members of the worshiping community, whether ministers* or lay* persons, should perform only those parts which pertain to their office in accordance with the principles of the Liturgy.* Thus the *Sacramentary* has reemerged for the celebrant no longer absorbs the roles of the others, such as singers,* readers,* and the congregation.* The *Missal,** which it replaced, contained all the parts for the singers, readers, and even the congregation, namely what is now in the *Sacramentary, Lectionary** and *Gradual.** *See also* GELASIAN SACRAMENTARY; GREGORIAN SACRAMENTARY; LEONINE SACRAMENTARY, MISSAL; MISSALE FRANCORUM; MISSALE GOTHICUM.

Sacraments (SAK-ruh-muhnts). Outward signs* or sacred actions, instituted by Christ, through which grace* is channeled or communicated for inward sanctification of the soul. When the Sacraments are administered validly and the recipient is properly disposed, the Sacraments attain their ends infallibly, that is, grace is automatically communicated to the recipient. Thus, the Sacraments perpetuate Christ's Redemptive Action, making it present and effective throughout the ages.

Sanctifying grace is imparted in Baptism* and, when needed, is restored in both Penance* and the Anointing of the Sick.* If one is in the state of grace, sanctifying grace is always increased through the Sacraments. Each Sacrament gives actual grace, either at the time of reception or when the person needs help. Three Sacraments, Baptism, Confirmation,* and Holy Orders* imprint a Sacramental character.* Sacramental grace, corresponding to the specific purpose of each Sacrament, is transmitted to the soul to better its supernatural life.

The seven Sacraments were instituted by Christ—three of them (Baptism, Eucharist,* and Penance) directly and four of them (Confirmation, Holy Orders, Anointing of the Sick, and Marriage*) implicitly, through the Church.* They are intended to help us at every phase of our lives.

Sacraments of Initiation

Baptism is birth in the life of grace. It enables us to worship God *in spirit and in truth* as members of His Mystical Body,* the Church.

Confirmation gives us power to become adults in the life of grace. The Holy Spirit* enables us to *spread and defend the Faith** by word and by deed as true witnesses of Christ.

The *Eucharist* is the Body and Blood of Christ as the Food and Drink of our supernatural life. It is the *font and apex* of the whole Christian life. Taking part in the Eucharist, we offer the Divine Victim and ourselves along with Him. This Sacrament builds up the Mystical Body of Christ in unity.

Sacraments of Crisis

Penance is the *medicine of the soul* to heal sins. It grants pardon from the mercy* of God for offenses committed against Him. At the same time, it reconciles sinners to the Church, which they have also wounded by their sins.

The *Anointing of the Sick* is the spiritual remedy for sickness. It provides the grace of the Holy Spirit by which the whole person is brought to health, trust in God is encouraged, and strength is given to resist the temptations of the Evil One and anxiety about death. It enables us to join ourselves in sickness and death with the Pains and Death of Christ and thus to contribute to the welfare of the Church—the People of God.*

Sacraments of Vocation

Holy Orders provides *new priests to teach, rule, and sanctify* the Mystical Body. In that way it insures that the Church will continue for all time.

Marriage raises up new members for the Mystical Body by giving spouses a share in the *unity* and *fruitful* love *of Christ* and *His Church.* It enables the spouses to attain holiness* in the married state and to become as it were a Domestic Church.* In it parents should, by their word and example, be the first preachers of the Faith* to their children.

The Sacraments of Christ go with us throughout our lives and even throughout each day. If we know how to make use of the Sacramental graces at our disposal, we can convert everything into worship of God and into our good for eternity.

By words and objects the Sacraments strengthen, nourish, and express the faith* they presuppose; consequently, they are frequently called Sacraments of faith.

Recipients of the Sacraments

As a general rule Catholic ministers* are to administer the Sacraments to Catholics only. When it is physically or morally impossible to receive Penance, Eucharist, and Anointing of the Sick from a Catholic minister, the faithful* may receive them from non-Catholic ministers if their Churches have valid Sacraments. Christians not in full communion with the Catholic Church, who cannot approach a minister of their own, as long as they show Catholic faith in these Sacraments and are properly disposed, may, in danger of death or for some other grave necessity, receive them from Catholic ministers. The same Sacraments may be administered by Catholic ministers to the members of the Eastern Church not in full communion with the Catholic Church if they ask and are properly disposed.

Jesus and the Church as Sacraments

In a more general sense, any external sign of an internal blessing from God could be called a Sacrament. In that sense, Jesus would be the ultimate Sacrament, for He serves as the sign of the encounter between humans and God and becomes the principal minister for all the Sacraments. Also, the Church could be considered the universal Sacrament of salvation for all the faithful. *See also* CHARACTER (SACRAMENTS); EX OPERE OPERANTIS; EX OPERE OPERATO; *and the individual entries for each of the Sacraments.*

Sacraments and Divine Worship, Congregation for the. *See* CONGREGATION FOR DIVINE WORSHIP AND THE DISCIPLINE OF THE SACRAMENTS.

Sacrarium (suh-KRER-ee-uhm). A basin or sink, with a separate drainpipe directly to the earth for the disposal of water used for any sacred purpose, as when washing chalices* or altar linens.* The ashes of blessed, burnt objects, such as oils* used in the Sacraments,* are also washed down this drain. If the baptismal font* does not have its own sacrarium, the water is poured down the sacrarium which is usually located in the sacristry.*

Sacred Congregation of Rites. *See* CONGREGATION FOR DIVINE WORSHIP AND THE DISCIPLINE OF THE SACRAMENTS.

Sacred Heart, Cult of (SAY-krid hahrt, kuhlt uhv). The cult of the physical Heart of Jesus as a symbol of the love that Christ has for humankind. The real object of this devotion is the Divine Person, the Incarnate Word, as directed to His Heart that symbolizes His love, both human and Divine, for humankind. In the Biblical sense, the heart is the center of affection, and it also signifies the love of the Father* and the Holy Spirit* for the Church* and the world.*

Devotion to the Sacred Heart develops from the devotion to Christ's Sacred Humanity, since His human nature forms one person with the Divine Nature. Many Saints* have aided in the spread of this devotion, starting in the 11th century with strong emphasis by St.

John Eudes* and St. Margaret Mary Alacoque.* Claude de la Colombière, her spiritual director, led the Society of Jesus to promote the devotion, particularly by means of the Apostleship of Prayer.*

Three papal encyclicals are dedicated to the Sacred Heart: *Annum Sacrum* by Leo XIII in 1899 on consecration to the Sacred Heart; *Miserentissimus Redemptor* by Pius XI in 1928 on reparation to the Sacred Heart; and *Haurietis Aquas** by Pius XII in 1956 on devotion to the Sacred Heart, and an apostolic epistle: *Investigabiles Divitias Christi* by Paul VI in 1965 on the liturgical cult of the Sacred Heart. These deal, among other things, with the various forms of its cult, such as vigils of reparation, First Friday devotions,* and enthronement* of the Sacred Heart.

Act of Reparation

A partial* indulgence is attached to the recitation of the following Act of Reparation to the Sacred Heart and a plenary* indulgence to its public recitation on the Feast of the Sacred Heart (EI, 27).

> Most sweet Jesus, whose overflowing charity for human beings is requited by so much forgetfulness, negligence, and contempt, behold us prostrate before You, eager to repair by a special act of homage the cruel indifference and injuries to which Your loving Heart is everywhere subject.
>
> Mindful, alas! that we ourselves have had a share in such great indignities, which we now deplore from the depths of our hearts, we humbly ask Your pardon and declare our readiness to atone by voluntary expiation, not only for our own personal offenses, but also for the sins of those, who, straying far from the path of salvation,* refuse in their obstinate infidelity to follow You, their Shepherd and Leader, or, renouncing the promises of their Baptism,* have cast off the sweet yoke of Your law.
>
> We are now resolved to expiate each and every deplorable outrage committed against You; we are now determined to make amends for the manifold offenses against Christian modesty in unbecoming dress and behavior, for all the foul seductions laid to ensnare the feet of the innocent, for the frequent violations of Sundays and Holydays,* and the shocking blasphemies uttered against You and Your Saints.* We wish also to make amends for the insults to which Your Vicar on earth and Your priests* are subjected, for the profanation, by conscious neglect or terrible acts of sacrilege, of the very Sacrament* of your Divine love, and lastly for the public crimes of nations who resist the rights and teaching authority of the Church* which You have founded.
>
> Would that we were able to wash away such abominations with our blood. We now offer, in reparation for these violations of Your Divine honor, the satisfaction You once made to Your Eternal Father on the Cross* and which You continue to renew daily on our altars*; we offer it in union with the acts of atonement of Your Virgin Mother* and all the Saints and of the pious faithful* on earth; and we sincerely promise to

make recompense, as far as we can with the help of Your grace,* for all neglect of Your great love and for the sins we and others have committed in the past. Henceforth, we will live a life of unswerving faith,* of purity of conduct, of perfect observance of the precepts of the Gospel* and especially that of charity. We promise to the best of our power to prevent others from offending You and to bring as many as possible to follow You.

O loving Jesus, through the intercession of the Blessed Virgin Mother, our model in reparation,* deign to receive the voluntary offering we make of this act of expiation; and by the crowning gift of perseverance keep us faithful unto death in our duty and the allegiance we owe to You, so that we may all one day come to that happy home, where with the Father and the Holy Spirit You live and reign, God, forever and ever. Amen.

See also APOSTLESHIP OF PRAYER; ENTHRONEMENT; FIRST FRIDAY DEVOTIONS; SACRED HEART, FEAST OF.

Sacred Heart, Feast of (SAY-krid hahrt, feest uhv). Solemnity* honoring the Sacred Heart of Jesus that occurs on the Friday after the 2nd Sunday after Pentecost.* The institution of the feast was approved by Clement XIII in 1765, extended to the Universal Church* by Pius IX in 1856, and given new texts and the highest ranking by Pius XI in 1928. In the new liturgical books,* the texts of the Divine Office* and the Eucharist* have been revised in accord with the Scriptural and liturgical emphases set forth by Pius XII in his 1956 encyclical* on devotion to the Sacred Heart *(Haurietis Aquas).*

This feast, unlike most of the major liturgical Solemnities, does not celebrate a particular event in the History of Salvation.* It commemorates this salvation itself. It celebrates the truth that God is love and He desires all generations to discover Him through Christ and respond to His love. We can elicit such a response more readily by contemplating the sufferings of Christ for us. The pierced Heart on the Cross is a symbol of this suffering.

From it flowed "blood and water, the fountain of sacramental life in the Church" (Preface*).

There is also a Votive* Mass of the Sacred Heart, which is celebrated on the First Friday of each month when allowed by the rubrics.* *See also* ENTHRONEMENT; FIRST FRIDAY MASS; SACRED HEART, CULT OF.

Sacred Linens. *See* LINENS, SACRED.

Sacred Liturgy, Constitution on the. *See* CONSTITUTION ON THE SACRED LITURGY.

Sacred Scripture. *See* BIBLE.

Sacred Triduum (SAY-krid TRIJ-uh-wuhm; TRID-yuh-wuhm). Three day celebration of devotions,* prayer,* and preaching, preceding some special feast,* or in preparation for a major enterprise. Usually it is brought into conformity with the rites,* the calendar,* and the Biblical readings* of the Liturgy,* since basically each triduum imitates the Biblical three days that Christ spent in the tomb.

The Sacred Triduum (also called the Easter Triduum) refers to the celebration at the close of Holy Week.* It begins with the Evening Mass of the Lord's Supper on Holy Thursday,* reaches its high point in the Easter Vigil,* and closes with Evening Prayer* on Easter Sunday.* The Easter Triduum celebrates the Paschal Mystery* and so is the culmination of the entire Liturgical Year.*

Sacred Vessels (SAY-krid VES-uhlz). The containers or utensils employed during liturgical celebrations; those that touch the Sacred Species* are the paten,* chalice,* pyx,* ciborium,* lunula,* and monstrance.* Secondary vessels would be the oil stocks,* cruets,* thurible,* boat,* and sprinkler.* *See also* CHALICE; CIBORIUM; LUNULA; MONSTRANCE; PATEN; PYX.

Sacrifice (SAK-ruh-fais). That form of adoration* during which an authorized priest* offers a victim in the name of the people to recognize God's supreme dominion and our dependence on Him. The victim is at least withdrawn from human use, if not totally immolated.

Christ's Death on the Cross* has always been considered a sacrifice. Unlike the bloody sacrifices of animals in the Old Testament,* the sacrifice of the Mass in the New Law becomes the unbloody re-presentation of the sacrifice of Jesus on the Cross. *See also* MASS; OFFERINGS; WORSHIP.

Sacrifice of the Mass. *See* MASS.

Sacrilege (SAK-ruh-lij). The deliberate desecration of a place, a person, or an object set aside for the worship* of God. Violence perpetrated on Religious* or clerics,* using sacred vessels* for an unworthy purpose, a church* or shrine put to unseemly use, or desecration of the Sacred Species* are examples.

Sacring Bell. *See* BELL.

Sacris Sollemniis (SAHK-rees soh-LEM-nee-ees). Latin title (from the first two words "At This Our Solemn Feast") of a hymn composed by St. Thomas* Aquinas in honor of Jesus in the Blessed Sacrament* at the specific request of Urban IV (1261-1264) for the new Feast of Corpus Christi* in 1264. It is a reverent and lyrical depiction of the institution of the Eucharist* by our Lord at the Last Supper,* giving heavenly Bread to human beings as Food on their pilgrim way. It is used in the Latin edition of the *Liturgy of the Hours** at the Office of Readings* for Corpus Christi.

The following translation is one of the many that exist.

At this our solemn feast
Let holy joys abound,
And from the inmost breast
Let songs of praise resound;
Let ancient rites depart,
And all be new around,
In every act, and voice, and heart.

Remember we that eve,
When, the Last Supper spread,
Christ, as we all believe,
The Lamb, with leavenless bread,
Among His brethren shared,
And thus the Law* obeyed,
Of all unto their sires declared.

The typic Lamb consumed,
The legal Feast complete,
The Lord unto the Twelve
His Body gave to eat;
The whole to all, no less
The whole to each, did mete
With His own hands, as we confess.

He gave them, weak and frail,
His Flesh, their food to be;
On them, downcast and sad,
His Blood bestowed He:
And thus to them He spake,
"Receive this Cup from Me,
And all of you of this partake."

So He this Sacrifice
To institute did will,
And charged His priests alone
That office to fulfill:
In them He did confide:
To whom it pertains still
To take, and to the rest divide.

Thus Angels' Bread is made
The Living Bread for us today:
The Living Bread from heaven
With figures does away:
O wondrous gift indeed!
The poor and lowly may
Upon their Lord and Master feed.

You, therefore, we implore,
O Godhead, One in Three,
So may You visit us
Who worship You with glee;
And lead us on Your way,
That we at last may see
Where You dwell in Eternal Day.
Amen.

The last two stanzas have given rise to a famous hymn known as the *Panis Angelicus** and set to various music arrangements. *See also* PANIS ANGELICUS.

Sacristans (SAK-ruh-stuhnz). Usually lay* persons responsible for the care of the sacred vessels,* vestments,* altar utensils, or other items used in liturgical functions. The position developed at the time of the decline of the Minor Order* of doorkeeper.

Sacristy (SAK-ruh-stee). A room or annex of a church, commonly near the altar,* where furnishings for the altar are kept and where the ministers* vest and prepare themselves for Divine worship.* Besides the vesting table and storage space for the articles used in liturgical services, the sacristy also houses the sacrarium.* It should be possible to enter the sacristry without going through the church.

Sacrosanctum Concilium. *See* CONSTITUTION ON THE SACRED LITURGY.

Sainthood. *See* BEATIFICATION; CANONIZATION.

Saints (saynts). (1) In a general sense, a Saint is anyone who is in the state of grace.*

(2) In the strict sense, it refers to those who by their heroic virtue* during life are recognized by the Church* through canonization* or at least the Ordinary Magisterium* (universal Teaching Authority) of the Church. This official recognition indicates that such persons are in heaven and may be publicly invoked, since their virtues and death are an example and witness to Christians.

Humans, created in the image of God, through their saintly lives give glory to God. Their holiness* is the

ultimate flowering of baptismal grace, in the manner in which they unite with Christ in His Passover, in the very act of His Death* and Resurrection,* and thus the Paschal Mystery* is completed in these persons. Furthermore as Saints they become our models and protectors and are certainly among the living in the sense that their souls were not destroyed through death but fully possess Truth and Love in their eternal happiness.

(3) "By celebrating the passage of the Saints from earth to heaven the Church proclaims the Paschal Mystery achieved in those who have suffered and been glorified with Christ; she proposes them to the faithful* as examples drawing all to the Father through Christ, and through their merits she pleads for God's favors" (SC, 104).

Feasts of the Saints

Festive celebrations are held annually on the anniversary of a Saint's death. Such commemorations occurred early in the life of the Church, and eventually local celebrations spread to the entire Church in some instances. Because of their proliferation in recent centuries, the current calendar* reduced the list of Saints to more modest proportions, making sure through research of the authenticity of their existence. General rules are such that an encroachment by the cult of the Saints on the celebration of the Mysteries* of the Lord would be impossible. In conjunction with this reduction, the celebrations should occur on the anniversaries of their deaths.

Furthermore in the calendar, universality was stressed with regard to time and place: every century is represented and Saints from all geographic areas are included in the General Calendar. Dioceses* and Religious Orders are expected to choose Saints that relate to the locality or to their Order in accordance with special regulations for particular calendars. In this way, there can be true, joyous celebrations by the congregation as it has a living relationship to the Saint, either because its members live near the tomb, or because their life and work binds the Saint to them, or because they have chosen the Saint as their Patron.* *See also* LITANY OF THE SAINTS.

Saints, Commemoration of (saynts, kuh-mem-uh-RAY-shuhn uhv). The liturgical remembrance of a Mystery* or of a Saint* whose celebration is precluded by another Office of higher rank. This practice was developed after the 10th century, particularly by Frankish or Gallican influence, so much so that on one day there could be commemorations of many Mysteries or Saints, both in the Office and in the Mass.* In the revised calendar* the only celebrations reminiscent of this are Memorials* that occur on weekdays of Lent,* except Ash Wednesday* and Holy Week,* and from December 17 to December 31; they may be celebrated in the following way:

(1) *Office of Readings:* The Reading* and Responsory* in honor of the Saint follow the Second Read-

ing* of the day (with its Responsory); the Concluding Prayer* is only of the Saint.

(2) *Morning Prayer and Evening Prayer:* Omit the ending of the Concluding Prayer and add the Saint's Antiphon* and Prayer.

(3) *Mass:* The Opening Prayer* of the Saint is substituted for the Opening Prayer of the Day.

Saints, Common of the. *See* COMMON OF THE SAINTS.

Saints in Eucharistic Prayer I (saynts in yoo-kuh-RIS-tik prayr wuhn). Unique to Eucharistic Prayer I* is the listing of the Saints in two places. The intent is to add the names of those already in glory* to the remembrance we make of the present members of the Church.* Both lists were developed in the 5th century, but they may be abbreviated according to the current rubrics.*

The first group occurs in the prayer starting with *In union with the whole Church*, and includes Mary,* the twelve Apostles,* and twelve martyrs.* In 1962, John XXIII added the name of St. Joseph.* Besides Mary and Joseph and the Apostles, there are six bishops*: Linus, the successor of St. Peter*; Cletus, buried in the Vatican; Clement I,* who wrote a letter to the Corinthians and died in exile in the Crimea; Sixtus,* the second Pope of that name, who was captured celebrating Mass in the catacombs* and beheaded together with his four deacons in 258; Cornelius,* who upheld a milder view of the practice of penance against Novatian the anti-pope, and who died in exile and was buried in the catacomb of Callistus; and Cyprian,* the bishop of Carthage, renowned in Rome as one of the first Latin Doctors,* beheaded in 258.

The six nonbishops are: Lawrence,* the revered deacon, whose

feast is one of the oldest of Roman martyrs; Chrysogonus, founder of the church bearing his name in Trastevere; John and Paul, unknown Roman martyrs of the 3rd or 4th centuries; Cosmas* and Damian,* physicians martyred in Syria and highly honored in the East.

After the commemoration of the dead, in the section beginning *For ourselves too*, there are fourteen martyrs listed, seven men and seven women, in addition to John the Baptist,* sainted by Christ: Stephen,* the first martyr; Matthias* and Barnabas,* who represent the Apostles in this list; Ignatius,* second successor of Peter and author of seven famous letters, martyred in Rome; Alexander,* probably martyred with a group commemorated on June 10; Marcellinus* and Peter,* martyred under Diocletian; Felicity, a Roman lady whose tomb was marked by a basilica* but whose life is unknown (she is not to be equated with the slave-girl of the same name martyred together with her mistress Perpetua* who is next on the list; this Felicity is celebrated only in local calendars on November 23); Perpetua from North Africa, martyred with Felicity, representing their country; the Sicilian martyr virgins of the final persecution, Agatha* and Lucy*; Agnes,* Roman martyr, venerated from an early date, though her martyrdom is legendary; Cecilia,* martyred in the catacomb of Callistus, and venerated as a Patroness of Music because of an unauthenticated description of her sufferings; Anastasia, an Eastern martyr, included to represent the Byzantines. In the final analysis, the identity of these Saints is not as important as what they stand for—the anonymous multitudes of clergy* and laity* who have taught subsequent Christians by their martyrdoms to love Christ the Lord more than life itself.

Saints, Liturgical Categories of (saynts, luh-TUHR-ji-kuhl; li-; KAT-uh-gohr-eez; gawr; uhv). Categories into which the Saints* celebrated in the Liturgy* are placed according to time-honored custom.

These categories are based on the titles assigned to each Saint in the Liturgy. According to the Constitution *Lumen Gentium,** the following titles are assigned to the Saints:

(1) *Traditional titles:* Apostle,* Evangelist,* Martyr,* Virgin.*

(2) *Title of hierarchical rank:* Bishop* (Pope*), Presbyter (Priest*), Deacon.* (The word "Pope" indicates the full role of the office better than "Supreme Pontiff." The title "Doctor of the Church,"* while it does not specifically refer to members of the hierarchy, did in fact refer only to them until the conferral of that title upon St. Catherine of Siena* and St. Teresa* of Jesus.)

(3) *Titles of rank within an order:* Abbot* (Monk, Hermit), Religious.* (The title "Abbot" is given to those who governed a monastic community, even if they were presbyters, like St. Bernard*; "Religious" refers to those who were not presbyters and to women who were married before entering an Order; otherwise women Religious are known by the traditional title "Virgin."*)

These titles are found in the *Roman Missal** and *Liturgy of the Hours** and indicate the particular Common* to be followed for each Saint: Martyrs,* Pastors,* Doctors,* Virgins,* or Holy Men and Women.* Three titles formerly used in the Liturgy have been discontinued: "Confessor" and "Neither Virgin nor Martyr" because they present difficulties) and "Widow" (because it no longer carries the religious connotation it once had). Furthermore, in place of a title that would seem contemporary, for example, "Upright," "Lay Person," "Mother," or "Holy Woman," it seemed best not to insist on a title for each Saint in the new liturgical books.*

Thus, with the advent of the revised *Roman Missal* the Church has placed at the disposal of the faithful* a marvelous instrument for grasping the virtues* of the Saints and imitating them in their lives. She has provided a more complete series of Readings* for the different categories of Saints. It is the Word of God* that points to the road taken by each Saint. That Word enables us to see it more clearly and cling to it more tightly. At the same time, we are made to realize even more deeply how true it is that each Saint has something distinctive, some way of imitating Christ that is like no other!

Martyrs—Models of Christ the Martyr

The Common of Martyrs comprises ten Mass formularies and three Prayer formularies. Since the Martyrs were associated in a very special way with the Mystery* of Christ's Death* and Resurrection,*

their liturgies take on special significance when they are celebrated during the Easter Season.* Hence, the formularies are separated into those for Martyrs "outside the Easter Season" and those "in the Easter Season."

This Common shows that Christian Martyrs are not simply those who give their lives physically for the Faith.* They are also those who have entered fully into the Mystery* of love revealed to them by their Lord. They are not content simply to hope that after death their cause will triumph. They experience the living reality that life triumphs in their death, for they can share this love. They are caught up in the movement of love that comes from the Father, and they discover their identity with their Master, reliving the Paschal Mystery* in their bodies.

Pastors—In the Line of Christ the Good Shepherd

The Common of Pastors comprises twelve Mass formularies: two for a Pope or Bishop; two for a Bishop; one for a Pastor; two for several Pastors; one for a Founder of a Church; one for several Founders of Churches; and three for a Missionary Bishop.

Pastors are servants in imitation of Christ Himself. They are our fathers and brothers in the Faith. They are also members of the flock of Christ. St. Peter's* reaction to the cured sick man who prostrated himself at Peter's feet was: "I myself am also a human being" (Acts 10:26). Called out of the midst of God's people, Pastors prompt all of us to discover our own mission in the service of those around us.

Doctors—Imitators of Christ the Teacher

The Common of Doctors of the Church comprises only two Mass formularies. One of the reasons for this is the fact that the relatively few Saints who fit into this category also fit into another—for example, Pastors or Religious. Thus, a combination of the texts of these other categories offers ample opportunity for the desired variety.

Doctors of the Church teach us to utilize our talents to proclaim Christ to others, to pursue the world* for Christ, to find Him in every part of our lives—whether it be through formal knowledge or through the experience of everyday living. They inspire us to be "Doctors" of the everyday love of God in our lives.

Virgins—Imitators of Christ the Celibate

The Common of Virgins comprises four Mass formularies, three for one Virgin and the last for Several Virgins. The Saint who is a Virgin in many cases also fits into another category, e.g., Martyr, Doctor, Religious. One may use both categories in choosing the texts for each celebration.

Virgins as Saints bear witness to a love that surpasses all other loves. This love comes from God Himself and, although it is expressed in human relations, is much more fundamental. Virgins call the world back to the first love—God—in all other loves, telling us that the only reason for love is the God of love.

Men and Women Saints—Imitators of Christ's Humanity

The Common of Holy Men and Women comprises twelve Mass formularies. The first six refer to Saints in general; the other six refer to some specific state and field of endeavor: Religious; Those Who Worked for the Underprivileged; Teachers; and Those Who Were Especially Noteworthy for Holiness.

These Saints remind us that Christ lived life to the full. He was truly the complete human being, the Man for Others. Whoever "follows after Christ, the Perfect Man, becomes more of a human being" (GS, 41). They show us vividly how all the human can be transformed in Christ. While using the world *totally,* they used it for God, as a world that is "passing away" (1 Cor 7:31), one that looks forward to completion in the next life. *See also* COMMON OF THE SAINTS; PROPER OF THE SAINTS; SAINTS.

Saints, Proper of the. *See* PROPER OF THE SAINTS.

Salt (sawlt). Because of its qualities as a seasoning and a preservative, salt is a symbol used in religious rituals from early times. It is also a sign of integrity and wisdom. Until the new rite of Baptism* in 1969, a bit of salt was given to the person to be baptized. Today, blessed salt is used in ordinary holy water* and in the water used for consecration* of churches and altars.* In some areas, blessed salt itself was greatly esteemed as a Sacramental.*

Salutation. *See* GREETINGS.

Salvation (sal-VAY-shuhn). Preservation from destruction, particularly the deliverance of a soul or of the human race from the consequences of sin. The Incarnation* was the fitting means chosen by God. Christ fulfilled this mission as a Prophet Who taught human beings the truths they must believe (Jn 1:18; Col 2:3), as a King Who showed them the laws they must obey (Jn 18:37), and as a Priest Who offered a superabundant satisfaction to God by His Death on the Cross* (Rom 5:15-20).

Although Christ died to save all human beings, every individual must apply the fruits of the Redemption* to himself or herself. This is done principally through the Church* and her Liturgy.* The liturgical action is itself an event of salvation because it puts the historic *today* in touch with the historic time of Christ, that is, with the reality already historically accomplished of salvation in Christ and through Christ. In this saving event Christ communicates the fullness of His Divine Life to individual souls, reproduces His Mystery* in them, and draws them into that Mystery. The completion of this salvation will take place only at His Second Coming.*

Thus, the Liturgy is completely concerned with salvation. It speaks of the "bread of life" and the "cup of eternal salvation" (Eucharistic Prayer I*), of "the death your Son endured for our salvation" (Eucharistic Prayer III*), and of bringing "salvation to the world" (Eucharistic Prayer IV*). It also asks "life and salvation for us" (Opening Prayer* for Solemnity of Mary, Mother of God*) and prays that we may bring "salvation and joy to all the world" (Prayer after Communion* for 5th Sunday in Ordinary Time*). *See also* HISTORY OF SALVATION; LITURGY; REDEMPTION.

Salve Regina (SAHL-vay ray-JEEN-ah). A choral anthem that is a beautiful testimony to the flowering of Marian devotion in the 11th century. Since the 13th century it has been the last evening chant in many communities. After greeting our Queen and our Mother, who is full of mercy and tender love, we cry

out our misery. For she is our Advocate. We ask that when our time comes, she may show us Jesus born of her womb. This prayer of praise and supplication is a jewel that scarcely needs comment. One translation is as follows:

Hail, holy Queen, Mother of mercy;
hail, our life, our sweetness and our hope.
To you do we cry,
poor banished children of Eve.
To you do we send up our sighs,
mourning, and weeping in this valley of tears.
Turn then, most gracious Advocate,
your eyes of mercy toward us.
And after this our exile
show unto us the blessed fruit of your womb, Jesus.
O clement, O loving, O sweet Virgin Mary.

See also FINAL ANTIPHONS OF OUR LADY.

Salvifici Doloris (sahl-VEE-fee-chee doh-LOHR-ees). Latin title (from the first two words "Of Salvific Suffering") of the *Apostolic Constitution on the Christian Meaning of Suffering* issued by John Paul II on February 11, 1984. The document deals with the theme of suffering at the time of the Holy Year of the Redemption.* It states that Christian suffering is part of the redemptive suffering of Christ. Each person has a share in the Redemption, and each is called to share in that suffering through which the

Redemption was accomplished. It does not relate this theme to the Liturgy*—although the Liturgy is a re-presentation of Christ's suffering and allows us to share in it and its fruits.

Samuel, The First Book of (SAM-yoo-uhl, thuh fuhrst buk uhv). Ninth Book of the Old Testament* (and first Historical Book) that originally formed one with the Second Book of Samuel.* Both are named after the leading figure of the First Book, who was responsible for the enthronement of David. The author

is not known, but both Books may be assigned to the last part of the 7th century B.C. The First Book covers the lives of the last Judge,* Samuel, who was also a Prophet,* and introduces David as a warrior and possible successor to the throne. It speaks to us of the obedience of Samuel and Eli; Saul's disobedience; the beginning of prophetic ministry and the monarchy; David's battles with the Philistines; and the admirable friendship between David and Jonathan.

Liturgical use: In the *Roman Missal,** this Book is read on the 2nd Sunday in Ordinary Time* (B), the 7th Sunday in Ordinary Time (C), and the 4th Sunday of Lent* (A) as well as the 1st and 2nd Weeks in Ordinary Time (II); it is also used in the Common of Pastors,* Baptism of Adults,* Masses for Vocations and Religious Profession, and on December 22. In the *Liturgy of the Hours,** it is read during the 12th Week in Ordinary Time plus Sunday and Monday of the 13th Week and gives rise to a minor canticle* in the Four-Week Psalter.* *Meaning:* God is ever active in human history to work out His purposes, weaving His will through our free acts. He wants our action and our devotion to go together. Yet even when we fail to do His will, God deals with us through His mercy,* not according to our sins.

Samuel, The Second Book of (SAM-yoo-uhl, thuh SEK-uhnd buk uhv). Tenth Book of the Old Testament* (and second Historical Book) that originally formed one with the First Book of Samuel* and was named after the latter's leading figure. It picks up the narrative with David's anointing as king and focuses on him as the greatest of Israel's kings. He was a king after the heart of God, a king who knew how to maintain the domain of God on temporal structures. But he was also a fallible human being who knew how to repent and thus received God's great Messianic promise*: his House was to reign forever through the Messiah,* his descendant about whom the New Testament* says: "The Lord God will give him the throne of David his father" (Lk 1:32).

Liturgical use: In the *Roman Missal,** this Book is read on the 4th Sunday of Advent* (B), 11th Sunday in Ordinary Time* (C), Christ the King* (C), March 19, December 24, from Saturday of the 2nd Week to Wednesday of the 4th Week in Ordinary Time (II) as well as the Common of the Blessed Virgin Mary* and the Rite of Penance.* In the *Liturgy of the Hours,** it is read from Tuesday of the 13th Week through Thursday of the 14th Week in Ordinary Time. *Meaning:* David, God's anointed king, is a figure of God's Anointed One beyond compare: the Messiah, the living hope of Israel, Who will carry on the House of David. Just as David delivered Israel from its worldly enemies, so the Messiah will deliver His people from their spiritual enemies. We should follow David's example: we must be simple in faith* and deep trust while practicing true repentance* through liturgical worship* and prayer.*

Sanctification of Time. *See* TIME, SANCTIFICATION OF.

Sanctifying Grace. *See* GRACE.

Sanctoral Cycle. *See* CYCLES; PROPER OF THE SAINTS.

Sanctuary (SANG[K]-chuh-wer-ee). Literally, a holy place, which refers to the worship* area in the church, particularly around the altar.* As the center of liturgical ceremony, formerly it was distinct from the main body of the church, sometimes even separated by drapes or balustrades.* Today, following the prescriptions of renewal of the Liturgy,* the sanctuary is usually elevated but placed closer to the worshiping community.

Sanctuary Light (SANG[K]-chuh-wer-ee lait). A wax candle* or an oil lamp that burns constantly near the tabernacle,* wherever the Blessed Sacrament* is reserved in churches or chapels, as a sign of honor shown to the Lord. It depicts Christ's abiding love for us who in turn should respond with loving adoration.* It is true that oil and wax have a long history of tradition, for they truly represent this love of the Lord by their quality and appropriateness. These objects used in the Liturgy* in this fashion bear the weight of

mystery, reverence, awe, and wonder, truly serving the ritual action they should represent. Thus real candles and oil are preferable to, and should rule out, anything fake, pretentious, or lacking because of its artistic transparency, such as electric sanctuary lamps. *See also* CANDLES AND LIGHTS.

Sanctus. *See* HOLY, HOLY, HOLY.

Sanctus Candle (SANG[K]; SAHNG[K]-; tuhs KAN-duhl). Formerly, before the liturgical changes after Vatican II,* during a High Mass,* four to eight torchbearers would approach the altar* at the Sanctus* and remain until the Consecration.* At sung Masses and even at other Masses, the Low Mass,* for instance, at least one Sanctus candle was prescribed to burn from the Sanctus to the Consecration; later the regulation was that they were to burn until Communion* was finished. This occurred normally during the Solemn High Mass*; it fulfilled the obligation by the torchbearers.

Satanism (SAYT-uhn-iz-uhm). The cult of devil worship is primarily against Christianity; beginning in the 12th century, it built up to the Black Mass, a parody on the Eucharist.* There is a widespread devotion to Satan in modern times fashioned on rites comparable to those in the Church,* including the

Sacraments.* Based on a Manichaean idea of the universe, Satanists claim there are two creative principles, good and bad; they venerate the principle of evil.

Satisfaction. *See* PENANCE, RITE OF.

Scamnum. *See* SEDILIA.

Scapulars (SKAP-yuh-luhrz). Shoulder width outer garments worn front and back over the shoulders, as a portion of certain Religious habits. They first served as work aprons for monks; they are now classed as a distinctive part of a monastic habit. As such they symbolize the yoke of Christ.

When the laity* joined the Third Orders, they as tertiaries were invested with a scapular, much reduced in size, usually only two pieces of cloth two by three inches square joined by straps so that it could be worn over the shoulders under their clothes, indicating their affiliation with the Order. Usually the scapular is decorated with an image of the Blessed Virgin Mary,* some Saint,* or an emblem of devotion.* The esteemed practice of wearing a scapular symbolizes fellowship in being dedicated to a worthy cause. At least eighteen scapulars have been approved by the Church, but the best known are the following five: Our Lady of Mount Carmel,* brown; Seven Dolors, black; the Passion,* red; Immaculate Conception,* blue; the Holy Trinity,* white.

In 1910, Pius X* authorized the scapular medal as a substitute for the scapular. Bearing images of the Sacred Heart* on one side and of the Blessed Virgin on the other, it may replace any or all of the scapulars. However, the investiture must be done with a scapular and not the medal.

Schola Cantorum (SKOH-lah kahn-TOH-room). (1) A school for training or teaching ecclesiastical chant* or choral singing. In existence from the 4th century, even as late as the beginning of the 20th century such choir schools, wherever possible, were recommended by Pius X.*

(2) Select groups of singers during public worship* to render music in the church, particularly a more artistic presentation of the difficult chants and pieces. They are also expected to support congregational singing. *See also* CHOIRS (MUSIC).

Scholastica, St. (skuh-LAS-tuh-kuh). 480-c.543. A sister of St. Benedict,* Scholastica entered a life of contemplation at home at first and later established a second order of Benedictines near Monte Cassino following the rule of Benedict. She is the Patroness of Convulsive Children. *Liturgical celebration:* February 10 (Memorial); *theme:* prayerful meditation deepens love.

Scriptorium (skrip-TOHR [TAWR]-ee-uhm). That room in a monastery designated for copying and illuminating manuscripts. (Originally, it referred to the stylus with which one wrote on wax; later, it indicated the base on which the leaf was placed in the act of writing;

then, by extension, it became the room where the writing took place.) The monasteries were places of major book production, with a scriptorium handled by the librarian who watched over the scribes and made sure that supplies and equipment were available. Trained Religious did the copying, although visiting persons might be permitted to copy those books that were too valuable to loan. Once copied, the material was handed to a corrector. Most scribes were anonymous. Christian paleography isolates the characteristics of the known scriptoriums and is able to establish the origin, dating, and transcription of liturgical or other manuscripts.

Scripture Readings. *See* CYCLES; FIRST READING; LECTIONARY; LITURGY OF THE WORD; READINGS; SECOND READING; TWO-YEAR CYCLE OF READINGS, ALTERNATE.

Scroll of Ravenna (skrohl uhv Ruh-VEN-uh). Scroll (located in the city of northeast Italy) that is among the earliest sources for the *Sacramentary*.* It is about 12 feet long and one foot wide and contains on its back in uncial letters forty prayers relative to Christmas.* *See also* SACRAMENTARY.

Scrutinies (SKROOT-uhn-eez; SKROOT-neez). Rites celebrated on the 3rd, 4th, and 5th Sundays of Lent* by the priest* or deacon* with the elect* that are intended to purify the catechumens'* hearts and minds, strengthen them against temptation, purify their intentions, and firm up their decision, so that they may remain more closely united with Christ, and thus love God more deeply. These spiritual purposes are achieved through exorcisms* whereby the catechumens develop a spirit of repentance,* a more thorough understanding of sin, so as to become fully free as children of God.

Seal of Confession (seel uhv kuhn-FESH-uhn). The serious obligation that keeps sacred any information received during the Sacrament of Confession,* should such disclosure identify the penitent.* The obligation binds the priest* or anyone who may have heard this information, by natural law, Divine law, and Canon Law. The penitent may freely give permission to disclose the information. Ordinarily the seal of Confession ensures the penitents of peace of mind, since they are assured that the content of their confession is held in the strictest confidence.

Season, Proper of the. *See* PROPER OF THE SEASON.

Seasons of the Year. *See* CYCLES.

Seats. *See* PEWS.

Sebastian, St. (si-BAS-chuhn). 3rd century. This Roman Martyr,* somehow connected with Milan, according to legend was an officer in the guard of Diocletian. Discovered to be a Christian, he was presumably shot to death with arrows, recovered and was eventually cudgeled to death.* He is the Patron of Soldiers and Protector against the Plague. *Liturgical celebration:*

January 20 (Opt. Mem.); *theme:* courageous and faithful witness to God's law.

Second Coming. *See* PAROUSIA.

Second Reading (SEK-uhnd REED-ing). (1) *In the Liturgy of the Hours.** In the Office of Readings* the Second Reading is chosen from the Fathers* or Church writers. The Fathers and Doctors* enjoy distinctive authority in the Church. Since the purpose of the Second Reading is to provide meditation* on the Word* presented in the First Reading,* the Church looks to the tradition handed down by the ecclesiastical writers since they lead us to a more profound understanding of the Sacred Scriptures.* Through the readings, Christians can grasp the true sense of the liturgical seasons* and feasts.* These spiritual treasures provide a firm foundation for spiritual life and a bubbling source for increased devotion.*

Besides the Second Readings in the *Liturgy of the Hours* there is to be an optional *Lectionary* (in an Alternate Two-Year Cycle*) offering a much larger collection of similar readings to be used at the discretion of the person reciting the Office.* Furthermore, keeping in mind the culture and traditions of their own region, Conferences of Bishops* may include a supplement in this optional *Lectionary,* with texts taken from Catholic writers who are preeminent in their teaching.

When the Second Reading is in honor of the Saints,* the text may be from any ecclesiastical writer, as long as it refers specifically or is truly applicable to the Saint being commemorated. Sometimes even writings of the Saint are very fitting, and on some occasions they may be biographical. In these cases, historical accuracy must apply, with emphasis on some spiritual characteristic of the Saint in question, particularly as it relates to modern conditions. The readings should express how the Saint contributed to the spirituality and the life of the Church. (*See also* HAGIOGRAPHICAL READING.)

(2) *In the Mass.** On Sundays and major feasts (Solemnities and

Feasts of the Lord that fall on Sunday) each Mass will have three readings. The second one is from the Apostles,* that is, the New Testament,* e.g., an epistle or the Book of Revelation.* Two principles govern the choice of readings in the *Lectionary*:* thematic harmony and semicontinuous reading. In many cases, there is a relationship among the readings specified for a particular day. This is most obviously true between the Old Testament* choices and the Gospel* reading. This same thematic harmony occurs more regularly among all the readings during the major seasons of Advent,* Christmas,* Lent,* and Easter.* However, in Ordinary Time,* there is no particular theme, so the Second and Third Readings are actually arranged semicontinuously; yet even in these cases, the Old Testament readings will harmonize with the Gospel choices.

In honoring the Saints, for those celebrated as Solemnities* or Feasts,* and even some Memorials,* proper texts are presented. When these do not exist, there is a rich variety to choose from among the readings listed under the Common of the Saints.* The choices are abundant, and the celebrant should consider the pastoral needs of the group attending the service. For Memorials, there would be only the First Reading, either from the Old or from the New Testament, and a Gospel. On Solemnities and Feasts of the Lord that fall on Sunday, there may be three readings as on Sundays.

The choices that have been made from the *Lectionary,* besides broadening the scope of Sacred Scripture* that is read to the people during the Eucharistic Celebration, are intended to develop a hunger in the People of God* for listening to the Word and thus bringing about a more perfect unity in the Church. *See also* CYCLES; READINGS; TWO-YEAR CYCLE OF READINGS, ALTERNATE.

Secret. *See* PRAYER OVER THE GIFTS.

Secretarium (sek-ree-TAYR-ee-uhm). A room near the entrance to the cathedral* where the ministers,* concelebrants,* and bishop* vest, and from which the Entrance Procession* starts. Usually it is distinct from the sacristy,* and only if no secretarium exists may the sacristy or some other suitable place be used.

Secular Institutes (SEK-yuh-luhr IN-stuh-tyoots; -toots). Societies, with members, either lay* or cleric,* who profess the evangelical counsels* in striving for Christian perfection, but do so by living and working in the world,* without wearing a distinctive garb or living a community life. Their private vows* or promises are similar to the vows of other Religious communities or societies of common life. They are distinguished from the associations of the faithful* in ecclesiastical law (Canons 710-730). Their main purpose is to extend Christ's Kingdom* in the circumstances and marketplace of the secular world.

Secularization and Worship. *See* CULTURE AND WORSHIP.

Seder. *See* PASSOVER SEDER.

Sedilia (suh-DEE-lee-uh). A bench in the sanctuary* for the presiding ministers* at a liturgical rite. Formerly it was on the south

side of the sanctuary, but current regulations describe a president's chair situated so that the community can see him as he faces them while leading them in prayer.

See (see). This term indicates the jurisdiction vested in a bishop* who heads a territory. The word derives from the Latin word *sedes,* seat or chair, which symbolizes the bishop's authority, the episcopal throne. Sees have territorial boundaries, namely the local dioceses.* Only the Holy See* or the Apostolic See is worldwide, governed by the Pope.*

Sentences (SENT-uhn[t]s-uhz; -uhnz-uhz). In the *Liturgy of the Hours,** brief thoughts from the New Testament* or from the Fathers* added before each Psalm* (after the title*) to foster prayer in the light of Christ's revelation* and inviting one to pray the Psalms in their Christological meaning (see GILH, 111). For example, in the second Psalm (142) for Evening Prayer I* of Sunday of Week I there is the title: "You, Lord, are my refuge," and the sentence: "What is written in this Psalm was fulfilled in our Lord's Passion* (Saint Hilary)." *See also* TITLE.

Septuagesima (sep-tuh-wuh-JES-uh-muh; -JAY-zuh-). The 3rd Sunday* before Lent* was given this name, which translated means the seventieth day (before Easter*). It began a prelude to Lent that took on the aspects of a penitential season. With the revision of the Liturgy* after Vatican Council II,* this terminology is no longer used, and the period before Ash Wednesday,* starting with Septuagesima, has disappeared. *See also* QUINQUAGESIMA; SEXAGESIMA.

Septuagint (sep-T[Y]OO-uh-juhnt; SEP-tuh-wuh-jint). Translation into Greek of the Hebrew and Aramaic Old Testament* (including the Deuterocanonical Books*) made in Egypt by various authors during the period between 250 B.C and 100 B.C. Its name comes from the Latin word for seventy "septuaginta" and stems from the legend that ascribed the work to a group of seventy scholars. To be more precise, the group was said to be seventy-two men, six from each of the twelve tribes. Thus, it was termed *interpretatio septuaginta virorum,* "the translation of the seventy men."

The Septuagint is by far the most important Version of the Old Testament and until recently was our sole witness for the state of the original text of the Hebrew Old Testament before the Christian era. The Septuagint was the Version used by the Hebrews in Christ's time, by the Apostles* and New Testament writers, and by the Greek Fathers of the Church.* Many of the Fathers regarded it as inspired, and it is still the official liturgical text of the Greek Church. It is customarily designated by LXX, the Roman numeral for seventy. *See also* BIBLE, VERSIONS OF.

Sequence (SEE-kwuhn[t]s). A syllabic chant in the form of a liturgical poem, used as a hymn of joy to follow the final note of the Alleluia* of the Liturgy of the Word.* At one time five thousand existed, but most were abolished at the Council of Trent. Today only four are used; the two for Easter* *(Victimae Paschali Laudes*)* and Pentecost* *(Veni, Sancte Spiritus*)* are obligatory, the two for Corpus Christi* *(Lauda Sion*)* and Our Lady of Sorrows* *(Stabat Mater*)* are optional. Now they precede the Alleluia Verse instead of following it. *See also* MASS, ORDER OF.

Seraphic Blessing (suh-RAF-ik BLES-ing). St. Francis of Assisi* composed this blessing from a passage in Numbers 6:22-27 at the request of one of his brothers in 1224. Listed among the Solemn Blessings* in Ordinary Time,* it may be used at the end of Mass.*

Serapion, Euchologion of (suh-RAP-ee-uhn, yoo-kuh-LOH-jee-uhn uhv). A Byzantine liturgical book* compiled by Serapion, Bishop of Thmuis, in the 4th century. Besides the texts and rubrics* for the Divine liturgies of St. John Chrysostom,* St. Basil,* and the presanctified gifts, it contained also the ritual for the Sacraments,* the Office for the Dead,* the Ordinary* of the Divine Office,* Blessings,* Sacramentals,* prayers for the sick, and many other prayers. Thus it became a manual for bishops,* priests,* and deacons,* since it combined the *Pontifical,** the *Missal,** and the *Ritual.**

Sermons. *See* HOMILY.

Servant (SUHR-vuhnt). One who serves. The title "handmaid" or "servant" is the one applied by Mary* to herself at the time of the Annunciation*: "Behold, I am the handmaid [servant] of the Lord. . . . He has looked upon his handmaid's lowliness" (Lk 1:38, 48). *Servant* was a common Old Testament* designation for "slave" or "servant" of God. It was a title of honor for God's messengers in the Old Testament and for Paul* and the Apostles* in the New.*

Mary used it of herself to indicate her total openness to the work of salvation* held out to her. She pledged her positive cooperation in the redeeming Incarnation.* Hence, the title indicates certainty of God's transcendence and total obedience to His saving plan. In this sense Mary is in the line of God's servants: Israel, Abraham* (Gn 18:3), and the Poor of Yahweh (God's remnant*). Finally, Mary's "servant" is an echo of the Servant of Yahweh par excellence, Jesus Christ—the suffering Servant Who became obedient to death in order to bring God's salvation.

At the same time, this title highlights Mary's role as a model for all Christians. Each Christian is to be the servant of the Lord—by humility, poverty, service to Christ in life and worship,* and courage in following the suffering Christ.

Jesus spoke of His Apostles (and his other followers) as servants—people totally dedicated to Him and His mission. Indeed, He went so far as to call them "unprofitable" servants (Lk 17:10): they are doing only what it is their duty to do. In this way, Christians become freed people, possessing the liberty of children of God (Rom 6:15-23; Gal 4:1-10). They belong to their Redeemer, but the consent of their will makes service of God and neighbor the path of real freedom for them (Lk 12:35-38; Rom 6:22; 1 Pt 2:16).

Thus, service is the mark of the true disciple (Mt 20:26ff). Its greatest expression is to give up one's life for another (Mk 9:35). It is the response of a love* that is truly altruistic (1 Cor 16:15) in the service of God, which is expressed in justice,* peace,* joy* (Rom 14:17f), and love for one another (Gal 5:13). Central to this service is one's service to the Word of God* (Acts 6:4) and to the New Covenant* (2 Cor 3:6).

The Liturgy* makes use of the term servant to designate a person who has carried out this service to God and is pleasing to Him. It is found especially in the prayers of Masses for the Dead.*

Servant of God (SUHR-vuhnt uhv God). Title of a person who died "in the odor of sanctity" and into whose life and virtues* the Church has instituted an inquiry for the purpose of having the person declared Blessed*—which will bring with it the right to receive liturgical celebrations. *See also* BEATIFICATION; CANONIZATION; SAINTS.

Servant of Yahweh (SUHR-vuhnt uhv YAH-way). Protagonist of four passages in Isaiah* (42:1-4; 49:1-6; 50:4-9; 52:13—53:12) known as the "Songs of the Servant." They depict a Suffering Servant of God, thought to be the Messiah,* and foretell the ministry of Jesus; at another level, they are thought to refer to Israel, too, which was God's servant. They state that the Servant is to suffer for the world, establish justice, provide salvation* for the nations, act as a light to the Gentiles, instruct all in the truth, give sight to the blind, offer release to prisoners, be a Covenant* to the world, show compassion and care for the weak, pour forth the Spirit* of God, bear the sins of the world, intercede for sinners, bring knowledge of God to those who seek it, and obtain peace for all. These activities were all fulfilled in Christ.

In the *Roman Missal,** these four Songs are read respectively on the Baptism of the Lord,* Monday of Holy Week,* Wednesday of Holy Week, and Passion Sunday.* In the Fourth Song, the Passion* of Christ becomes almost more expressive than in the description of the Evangelists* themselves. It is possible in a certain sense to identify the stages of Christ's Passion in their various details: the arrest, the humiliation, the blows, the spitting, the contempt for the prisoner, the unjust sentence, and then the scourging, the crowning with thorns and the mocking, the carrying of the Cross,* the crucifixion, and the agony. The Song then adds that the Servant will be saved by Yahweh* Who will reward His obedience with exaltation. It is this factor that has earned for Isaiah the name of the "Fifth Evangelist." In the *Liturgy of the Hours,** the First and Second Songs are combined and used on the Baptism of the Lord.

The Liturgy* prays that the Servant not only may be for us the Light of the Nations and the gatherer of His people but also may aid us to accept suffering and death in union with Him so that we may share His Resurrection.* *See also* ISAIAH, THE BOOK OF.

Server. *See* ACOLYTE.

Service (SUHR-vuhs). Generally speaking this would define the obligation persons have as creatures toward God to show proper homage and pertains to those acts of the virtue of religion* by which they serve God personally and socially. Specifically, as a liturgical term, it is that ritual or form of worship* whereby one fulfills the obligation of serving God in a proper manner. *See also* SERVANT.

Service of the Light. *See* EASTER VIGIL.

Servile Work (SUR-vuhl; -vail; wuhrk). Originally derived from the

type of work done by servants, now indicative of the more strenuous labors performed during the week. Urbanization, plus the fact that many people do not have a day off on Sunday, makes the prohibition aspect (not to perform servile work) of the commandment to keep holy the Sabbath somewhat of an anomaly. The important aspect of this rule is that one should make sure that the Sunday is dedicated to the Lord by a good Liturgy,* a true solemn celebration of the Paschal Mystery.* It should thus also include avoiding activities such as needless work or business, or unnecessary housekeeping and shopping.

Seven Churches (SEV-uhn CHUHRCH-uhz). (1) From early times the seven basilicas* in Rome that were visited by pilgrims, particularly as a form of penance.* Today indulgences* can still be gained by visiting them for prayer. They are the basilicas of St. John Lateran,* St. Peter,* St. Mary Major,* Holy Cross* in Jerusalem (within Rome proper), and the three churches outside the walls of Rome—St. Lawrence,* St. Sebastian,* and St. Paul.*

(2) In the first chapter of the Book of Revelation,* John focuses on seven churches in Asia for praise or blame. They are at Ephesus, Smyrna, Pergamum, Thyatira, Sardis, Philadelphia, and Laodicea.

Sexagesima (sek-suh-JES-uh-muh; -JAY-zuh-). A word meaning sixtieth day (a round number) that refers to the 2nd Sunday before Lent*; it was a part of the pre-Lenten season that began with Septuagesima.* This preparation period for Lent is no longer in vogue since Vatican Council II.* *See also* QUINQUAGESIMA; SEPTUAGESIMA.

Sext. *See* DAYTIME PRAYER.

Sharing the Light of Faith. *See* NATIONAL CATECHETICAL DIRECTORY.

Shell (shel). A small vessel having the shape of a shell used to pour baptismal water on a catechumen's* head. The most common shape today is that of a seashell. Large, exotic shells have been and may still be used in some churches as holy water fonts.*

It has been used as an emblem for Baptism* since the 12th century; it is also the symbol for the pilgrim, hence for St. James* the Apostle, a famous place of pilgrimage; likewise one of the numerous symbols of Mary*; as an emblem for St. Augustine,* it refers to the vision in which Christ told him he could sooner empty the ocean with a shell than understand the Trinity.*

Shema (shuh-MAH). The Jewish name for the Hebrew profession of faith comprised of three passages from the Pentateuch*: Dt 6:4-9; 11:12-21; Nm 15:37-41. As we use the Creed* in Christian worship,* so do the Jewish people use the Shema in their synagogue service. The name comes from the first word of Dt 6:4: "Hear, O Israel, the Lord is our God, the Lord alone."

Short Office. *See* CHRISTIAN PRAYER.

Shrines (shrainz). Sacred places or churches to which pilgrimages of

the faithful* come for some pious reason. A shrine may be a place where a Saint* lived or died, the Saint's burial place, or a spot where an apparition took place. Certain privileges may be granted to shrines, particularly when the good of the faithful would suggest it. At such shrines, the Word of God* is to be carefully proclaimed, liturgical life fostered through the celebration of the Sacraments,* and approved forms of popular piety cultivated.

Sick Calls. *See* ANOINTING OF THE SICK; PASTORAL CARE OF THE SICK.

Side Altar (said AWL-tuhr). Also termed minor altar* or secondary altar, its erection in churches, other than the one main altar,* is the result of having a place to protect the body of Martyrs* from invaders. Later when Mass* was celebrated in private, many side altars emerged, usually far enough away from the main altar not to disturb the congregational Mass. Today some vestiges remain with usually a side altar in honor of the Blessed Mother and some other Saint,* which is then used to hold the tabernacle* in which the Blessed Sacrament* is preserved, to have an altar of reposition for Holy Thursday,* or to hold relics* of Saints. With the recent advent of concelebrated* Masses, the multiplicity of side altars dwindled.

Sign Language (sain LANG-gwij). A language based on signs rather than speech. As early as 1965 permission was granted for sign language to be used with and by deaf people throughout the Liturgy* whenever it was judged pastorally desirable. More and more celebrants* are capable of signing, but when they do not know the sign language, one who does signs for the deaf who also use sign language in answer. During the sung portions of the Mass,* simple and rhythmic melodies should accompany these portions in order to enhance the movement and grace of the signs.

Sign of Peace (sain uhv pees). A liturgical action that is a spontaneous greeting as a reciprocal token of neighborly love. Following the Lord's Prayer* at Mass,* the priest* extends a greeting of peace to the congregation adding that all should offer each other such a sign to show that they are at peace. As a symbol of union and love, they exchange a sign according to local custom. Not only does the Sign of Peace have a relationship to the Lord's Prayer, particularly the final petition of forgiveness, but it establishes an intimate link with the Communion* that follows.

All should consider this action a prayer,* a sincere pledge of reconciliation and peace on a personal level because of the Communion that follows and the forgiveness that took place. Thus it becomes a seal and pledge of the fellowship and unity of the Spirit,* found in the bond of peace. Each culture should seek the most meaningful expression of reconciliation and peace, and several methods might be used depending on the circumstances: the kiss, an embrace, bowing,* touching one another, a handshake.

The handclasp is most usual in the United States. With the gesture some greeting is usually formulated; "Peace be with you, N." "Grace and peace be yours, N." "The God of love and peace be with you, N." Normally connected with the Eucharistic Liturgy, it may occur during other rites, such as Baptism,* Confirmation,* and Penance.*

Early Jewish and Christian custom made use of this ritual of the Kiss of Peace as is evident from Luke* 7:45 and from Romans* 16:16. At first it followed the Liturgy of the Word*; still later it was associated with the Preparation of the Gifts,* as one must reconcile oneself with one's brother or sister before bringing a gift to the altar*; still later it was shifted to the close of the Eucharistic Prayer,* where as an extension of the Lord's Prayer it prepares one for Communion, and it has remained in this place in the revised Order* of the Mass.

The invitation given during the Sign of Peace calls for an exchange with others nearby, a genuine, reverent form of worship* and prayer, a true pledge and sign of reconciliation, peace, and unity. Neither people nor ministers are intended to greet personally each one in the congregation, but only those nearby. Since the celebrant* has addressed the community with the all-inclusive greeting, "The peace of the Lord be with you always," he need not offer the sign to the assembly* other than those near the altar. The amount of time spent in the exchange of this sign should be in proportion to the overall ritual flow and rhythm of the Mass. The celebrant should be wary of an imbalance caused by its length, musical accompaniment, a certain style, or any other elements that might exaggerate its importance.

Sign of the Cross (sain uhv thuh kraws; kros). This sign, which recalls the chief mysteries of religion, rightly has its place in the Liturgy.* Besides being a symbol of Christ's Passion,* His redemptive act, it signifies the whole Christian life that includes suffering in imitation of Christ. Making the Sign of the Cross* is a profession of faith* and a hope in the Redemption,* the result of His crucifixion.

In the small Sign of the Cross, persons sign their foreheads, mouths, and breasts with their thumbs at the beginning of the Gospel.* The large Sign of the Cross is made with the fingers of the hand together and raised to the forehead, then to the breast, and then to the left and right shoulders. The left hand is properly placed at the waist. This large Sign of the Cross is made at the beginning of most liturgical functions, such as the Mass,* the Sacraments,* at the beginning of the Hours* in the Divine Office, and upon entering a church. With the movement, belief in the Holy Trinity* is expressed by pronouncing the names of the three Divine Persons.

Blessings of persons or objects performed by a priest* or bishop*

are done by turning the little finger toward what is to be blessed and extending the hand, with fingers together and straight, to make the Sign of the Cross, whose dimension should be proportional to what is blessed. *See also* SIGNING.

Signing (SAIN-ing). The rite by which a bishop* or priest* marks a person or an object with the Sign of the Cross.* Ordinarily in these cases the small Sign of the Cross is used. It occurs in Baptism,* Confirmation,* Anointing of the Sick,* Holy Orders,* and in certain ceremonies such as the dedication of a church or an altar.* *See also* SIGN LANGUAGE; SIGN OF THE CROSS.

Signs and Symbols (sainz and SIM-buhlz). Material things that stand for spiritual things. Some authors make a distinction between these two words, indicating that the symbol is a sensible representation, a thing, or action that expresses an invisible reality, making it present. A sign, on the other hand, is arbitrary, taking its meaning from a factor extrinsic to the reality itself. The Liturgy* makes use of symbols to express the things of God. The God-Man would be the prototype of the symbol, for Divine Nature is joined with the sensibly perceptible humanity in one person.

Kinds of Symbols

(1) Reality-filled symbols are those by which something symbolized simultaneously comes to be, as in the Sacraments,* or through the Church's* intercession and by the spiritual preparedness of the one who puts the symbol into effect, as with the Sacramentals.*

(2) Natural symbols are those by which some process, such as washing, anointing,* or laying on of hands,* expresses an analogous happening of a supernatural nature, purification, strengthening, or conferring grace.

(3) Characterizing symbols are those in which a particular meaning is acquired by a certain action or thing by convention usually different from its original meaning and hence becomes a mark of distinction, such as the pallium.*

(4) Symbol in the remote sense would be the monograms or emblems, which in some way represent a Mystery of the Faith* or some sacred truth, such as a fish, a symbol of Christ because the five letters of the Greek word form the initials of the words: Jesus Christ, God's Son, Savior; the dove, which represents the soul or peace; certain letters like the *chi rho** in Greek (XP), the monogram for Christ,

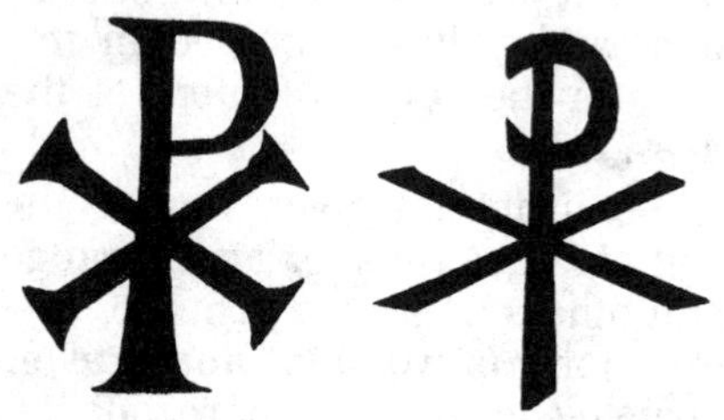

which stands for Christ, redeemer. *See also* SYMBOLISM.

Signum Magnum (SEEN-yoom MAHN-yoom). Latin title (from the first two words "The Great Sign") of the *Apostolic Constitution on the Great Sign* issued by Paul VI on May 13, 1967, on the occasion of the 50th anniversary of our Lady's appearances at Fatima. The document deals with two points of Marian doctrine and devotion: (1) the Biblical data concerning Mary,* Handmaid of the Lord, Mother of the Church, Teacher of redeemed humankind, and Exemplar of dedication to the service* of God and neighbor; (2) the true meaning of devotion to Mary in the teaching of the Church.*

Among other things, *Signum Magnum* points out that Mary is highly honored by the Church with a special veneration, particularly in the Liturgy,* not only as Mother of God who took part in the Mysteries of Christ but also as the Mother of the Church. It offers assurance that the liturgical reform (then in progress) will not be detrimental to the wholly singular veneration due to Mary and that the resultant greater veneration will in no way diminish the adoration* offered to the Incarnate Word* as well as to the Father* and to the Holy Spirit.*

Silence (SAI-luhn[t]s). The ascetical restriction from talking to achieve the quiet necessary for better thoughtfulness and prayerfulness. Silence has a special role to play in the Liturgy,* whose chief end is to bring us to union with God and procure for us the supernatural goods that flow therefrom. The physical stillness presumes the conscious effort to communicate with God. At designated times all should observe a reverent silence.

Typical instances are (1) during the Penitential Rite,* whether at Mass* or in the Liturgy of the Hours*; (2) after the celebrant's invitation to prayer, "Let us pray,*" during which all may reflect on the needs of the community and on personal and concrete petitions; (3) after Communion,* a time for praising God and expressing gratitude; (4) during the Liturgy of the Word,* after the First and Second Readings* and the Homily,* so that the

Holy Spirit* may dialogue with the people to take the Word of God to heart and to respond to it in prayer; (5) during the Eucharistic Prayer,* when the celebrant* pronounces the prayer as the interpreter of the voice of God and the voice of the people, who raise their hearts to God.

It is important to stress that this silence is in no way intended to reduce the faithful* to being present at the liturgical action like strangers and mute spectators. Rather its purpose is to insert the people more deeply into the Mystery* being celebrated. Liturgical silence attains its goal by means of the inner dispositions that flow from the Word of God that is listened to, from the chants and prayers that are voiced, and from the spiritual union with the celebrant who pronounces the parts that are his.

By this religious silence, which is now a real part of the sacred action, the faithful (1) reenter within themselves, (2) reflect briefly on what they have heard, or (3) praise God and pray to Him in the depths of their spirit. *See also* LITURGY—PARTICIPATION.

Silvester, St. *See* SYLVESTER, ST.

Simeon, Canticle of. *See* CANTICLE OF SIMEON.

Simon, St. (SAI-muhn). 1st century. One of the twelve Apostles,* also called the Canaanite and Zealot. Tradition has him preaching in the Near East, where he and St. Jude* suffered martyrdom. *Liturgical celebration:* October 28 (Feast); *theme:* changing the world* by converting our own hearts.

Simple Gradual (SIM-puhl GRAJ-oo-uhl). New liturgical book* for use in small churches (published in 1967 in its Latin edition and in 1969 in its English edition by ICEL*) that contains alternative antiphons* or refrains for use at Mass in place of the Intervenient Chants* and the Processional Chants* (Entrance, Offertory, and Communion). To bring about more effectively the active participation* of the assembly* with singing, a *Simple Gradual* was compiled to allow chants of a simpler form to be sung in place of the complex melodies of the *Roman Gradual.** Since members of the assembly of small churches may not be able to render correctly the ornate neums* of the chants in the *Roman Gradual,* simpler melodies that still maintain the devotional and admirable artistic qualities of Gregorian Chant* have been put together in this book to allow the small assemblies to enjoy sung celebrations with ease.

The use of the *Simple Gradual* does not preclude the use of melodies from the *Roman Gradual,* particularly the easier ones that are already familiar to certain congregations. Following the regulations given in the *Simple Gradual* is quite easy. A variety of choices exists, sometimes dependent on the season of the Liturgical Year.* Instead of each Sunday having a particular proper,* there are times when one or more formularies for the liturgical season are used throughout that season. Several options* are given in the Common of the Saints.*

Antiphons are intoned by a chanter,* who leads the Psalms* and invites the congregation to respond. Sometimes the congregation sings everything, other times the choir* might take over a section, or the two might sing together. The intent is always to include the congregation in the singing to the greatest extent. *See Also* GRADUAL, ROMAN; MUSIC.

Sin (sin). An offense against God by thought, word, deed, or omission. Every violation of the Commandments* of God or of the Church* is a sin: *mortal sin,* if three conditions are present—serious matter, sufficient reflection, and full consent of the will; *venial sin,* if the law violated concerns matter that is not grave or the offense is committed without sufficient reflection or full consent of the will. Venial sin does not deprive the soul of sanctifying grace.*

Mortal sin deprives us of sanctifying grace and brings eternal punishment to the soul, if we pass from this life before confessing this sin and obtaining forgiveness. However, an act of perfect contrition* (sorrow for offending a good and loving God) suffices if one is not able to go to Confession.*

Venial sin carries with it temporal punishment. It also weakens the will, thereby making it more difficult to resist temptation to mortal sin.

The Liturgy* is concerned with sin and forgiveness from it. In the Penitential Rite* at Mass* we ask God to forgive our sins, and before Communion* we pray for forgiveness to the Lamb of God* Who takes away the sins of the world. On Ash Wednesday,* we deplore our sins and ask for pardon, and throughout Lent* we do penance* for our sins. The Sacrament of Penance* is the usual manner in which Jesus forgives our sins, but He also does so in the Sacraments of Baptism* and Anointing of the Sick. *See also* ANOINTING OF THE SICK; BAPTISM; COMMANDMENTS; GRACE; HOLINESS; RITE OF PENANCE.

Singers. *See* CHOIRS (MUSIC); SCHOLA CANTORUM.

Singing. *See* MUSIC.

Sirach, The Book of (SIR-ak, thuh buk uhv). Twenty-eighth Book of the Old Testament and seventh Sapiential Book, written between 200 and 175 B.C. by a sage who lived in Jerusalem and was thoroughly imbued with love for the Law,* the Priesthood, the Temple, and Divine Worship. As a wise and experienced observer of life, he sets forth the true nature of wisdom and indicates the religious and social duties that must be performed in all the vicissitudes of life. Among other things, Sirach deals with the individual, the family, and the community in their relations with one another and with God as well as friendship, education, poverty, wealth, the Law, and religious worship. It culminates in the personification of Wisdom, which laid the basis for the revelation* of the Second Person of the Trinity, Who is the personalized Wisdom or Word of God.* The Book is also known as "Ecclesiasticus," part of its Latin title, which indicated that it was a "Church Book" extensively used in teaching catechumens* and the faithful.*

Liturgical use: In the *Roman Missal,** some 34 pericopes* are read from this Book, including those for the Holy Family,* 2nd Sunday after Christmas,* 6th and 24th Sundays in Ordinary Time* (A), 8th, 22nd, and 30th Sundays (C) as well as the 7th and 8th Weeks in Ordinary Time (I), Common,* Ritual,* and Votive* Masses. In the *Liturgy of the Hours,** it is read during the 1st Week in Ordinary Time, on the 10th Sunday, and on Saturday of the 14th Week as well as in the Common. It also gives rise to a minor canticle* in the Four-Week Psalter* and three additional ones in Appendix I: for Vigils. *Meaning:* The beginning of wisdom is the fear of the Lord, that is, reverence for the Lord. This means faith in and love* for the God of the Covenant* that is reflected in works, especially the practice of justice* and mercy* toward others. We should pray to God as a Father and forgive others if we would be forgiven, while doing good and fleeing from evil.

Sitting. *See* POSTURE IN WORSHIP.

Sixtus II, St. (SIK-stuhs SEK-uhnd). ?-258. Ordained Bishop* of Rome in 257, Sixtus upheld the rebaptism of heretics. He and his deacons* were taken prisoner during Mass* in the cemetery* of St. Callistus and beheaded. He is mentioned in the First Eucharistic Prayer.* *Liturgical celebration:* August 7 (Opt. Mem.); *theme:* tactful upholding of doctrine to avoid schism.

Skullcap. *See* ZUCCHETTO.

Slavorum Apostoli (slah-VOH-room ah-POHS-toh-lee). Latin title (from the first two words "Apostles of the Slavs") of the *Encyclical on the Apostles of the Slavs* issued by John Paul II on June 2, 1984. The Encyclical praises Sts. Cyril* and Methodius* for developing a Slavic alphabet and translating the Bible,* liturgical texts, and the writings of the Fathers* into it. The Pope calls their work a model of inculturation*—the incarnation of the Gospel* in native cultures and the introduction of these cultures into the life of the Church.*

The two brothers adapted to the Slavonic language the rich and refined texts of the Byzantine Liturgy.* In doing so, they conferred a capacity and cultural dignity upon the Old Slavonic liturgical language, which became for many hundreds of years not only the ecclesiastical but also the official and literary language, and even the common language of all the Slavs of the Eastern Rite.*

Social Character of the Mass. *See* MASS.

Societas Liturgica so-CHEE-uh-tahs li-TUHR-ji-kah). An international ecumenical liturgical society that meets every two years in different parts of the world. It encourages research in the field of worship* and allied subjects, and the pastoral implications thereof; facilitates the exchange of the results of research and liturgical knowledge; seeks to deepen the mutual understanding of the various liturgical traditions; and tries to show the relevance of Liturgy* in the contemporary world.

Sociology of Worship (soh-see-OL-uh-jee; -shee; uhv WUHR-shuhp). Sociologists consider worship* as a religious ritual, articulating the meaning of a social situation. It can be approached from different areas, such as its very structured annual cycle of the liturgical calendar*; its concern with the life cycle, from Baptism,* Confirmation,* and Marriage* to the funeral; its relationship to certain civic affairs, sometimes at the national level, such as Memorial Day ceremonies or Thanksgiving Day Mass*; and its effect on certain social issues, such as an anti-abortion rally or a peace movement.

Sociologists study social patterns of worship, for instance, attendance at various services, striving to determine why such high percentages of people will come to a Baptism or a Christian burial, over and against the small percentage of regular attendance at Sunday services. Attendance figures of cultural groups are also studied. Is there something in the Liturgy* that reinforces these social differences?

Sociologists also study social efficacy, how the official message is presented and accepted by those who participate.* Since these worshipers have their own beliefs and expectations, are they accepting of the official presentation? Another point deals with the reinforcement of their identity, for instance, with language, music, certain civil celebrations, and their closeness to the family during the life cycle events that occur in church. Social structure sometimes plays a part too, from the symbolic like the Sign of Peace* and the priest facing the community as over against the social position of those who have specific liturgical roles. This holds not only for the clergy* but also for the laity* who perform their specific function during the liturgical celebration.

One could consider nature and society as being explained in terms of the Divine and called the sacral universe. Human beings depend greatly upon God and His control over nature and His willingness to be our Protector and Savior. From such a public type of worship, well-being results and the dependence on Divine assistance and help is foremost in mind. In the secular universe, however, nature and society are explained in terms of human beings. There is less, if any, recourse to the Divine, and everyone looks to the material world and tries to control the laws of nature for his or her own benefit.

Religion, therefore, loses any function that it may have had in the sacral universe. In this case, religion tends to become private, and the public does not get together to honor the Deity. In this situation, any liturgical form created for a sacral universe does not have meaning in the modern world where the secular universe has taken over. The result is that the former types of worship, which were dependent upon neighborhood-based communities, now have to be left behind because of the variety of areas in which the family lives and works.

Therefore, we should leave the secular world behind and come together into another sacred world in which we find the presence of the All-Holy God and worship in that religious activity, usually in a church. Thereby we try to integrate our daily lives in the world in worshipful and prayerful celebrations of life together with others who have also come from such a variety of places.

Solemn High Mass (SOL-uhm hai mas). One of the three varieties allowed by the former Tridentine Mass along with Low Mass* and High Mass.* Known in Latin as *Missa Solemnis,* it was celebrated by a priest* with the help of a deacon* and subdeacon,* or priests taking these roles; hence, it was sometimes called a "Three-Priest-

Mass." Special ceremonies and music* were employed, together with incense.* It was built on the Pontifical Mass,* celebrated by the Pope* or bishop.* The term is no longer applicable since Vatican Council II's fully participated Mass with music* and song and is replaced by a concelebrated Mass. *See also* HIGH MASS; LOW MASS; MASS.

Solemnities (suh-LEM-nuh-teez). Liturgical celebrations that have the highest rank in the calendar.* Solemnities are days of greatest importance and begin with Evening Prayer I* of the preceding day. Some have a vigil* Mass, when Mass is celebrated on the preceding day in the evening. Easter* and Christmas* have an Octave* for their extended celebration.

In addition to the movable feasts like Easter and Pentecost,* the Calendar for the Universal Church* contains fourteen Solemnities: Mary, Mother of God,* Epiphany,* St. Joseph,* Annunciation,* Trinity Sunday,* Body and Blood of Christ,* Sacred Heart,* St. John the Baptist,* Sts. Peter and Paul,* Assumption,* All Saints,* Christ the King,* Immaculate Conception,* and Christmas.* *See also* FEASTS; LITURGY OF THE HOURS; MEMORIALS.

Solemnity (suh-LEM-nuh-tee). The exterior pomp with which a feast* may be enhanced, by decoration of the church and the altar,* richness of sacred vestments,* number of assistants, etc.

The term external solemnity is used for the transfer of a Solemnity* or Feast* to some other day when pastoral advantage or a serious need occurs. Examples would be the transfer of the Solemnity of Peter* and Paul* to the following Sunday, the transfer of the Feast of the principal patron,* the titular or the dedication of a church, the titular or Saint* who founded the Order, Congregation, or Religious Institute, to either the following Sunday or some day more fitting to the group for whom the celebration has special importance.

Solemnity of Mary, Mother of God (suh-LEM-nuh-tee uhv MAYR-ee, MUHTH-uhr uhv god). This feast* recognized Mary as the physical parent of Christ, the God-Man, defined at the Council of Ephesus in the 5th century. The third Mass of Christmas reflects the role of Mary in the Redemption,* so her role has always been connected with the Christmas Mystery.* Later from the 5th century to the 7th century, the feast was transferred to the Octave* Day of Christmas, January 1.

Prior to the time that this feast occurred on January 1, New Year's Day was observed as a day of prayer to offset pagan practices, since there were many riotous pagan celebrations. In the 5th century until the Middle Ages it honored Mary and her Divine Maternity. Then it was observed as the Octave of Christmas, which developed into the Feast of the Circumcision.* From 1961 to 1969 the title changed back to the Octave of the Nativity. Finally in 1969 the ancient Marian character was restored, so that we have its present title. It is a Holyday of Obligation.*

This Solemnity celebrates the part played by Mary in the Mystery* of Salvation,* exalts the singular dignity that this Mystery brings to the holy Mother, renews adoration* to the newborn Prince of Peace, and implores from God, through Mary's intercession, the supreme gift of peace.*

Sollicitudo Rei Socialis (sohl-lee-chee-TOO-doh RAY-ee soh-chee-AH-lees). Latin title (from the first three words "Social Concern") of the *Encyclical on Social Concern* issued by John Paul II on December 30, 1987. The Encyclical is a far-ranging treatment of the social teaching of the Church* in continuity with the teaching of the Popes from Leo XIII to Paul VI. It deals especially with relations between the developed and the underdeveloped countries. Development that is merely economic is incapable of setting people free; development that does not include the cultural, transcendent, and religious dimension of human beings is even less conducive to authentic liberation. The desire for profit and the thirst for power are the "structures of sin" that impede development while solidarity is the virtue* that aids development.

At the same time, the Encyclical points out that no temporal achievement is to be identified with the Kingdom of God*; such achievements simply reflect and anticipate the glory of that Kingdom. The Kingdom of God becomes present above all in the celebration of the Eucharist.* In it the fruits of the earth and the work of human hands—the bread and wine—are transformed into the Body* and Blood* of Jesus, through Whom the Kingdom of the Father has been made present in our midst. Thus, the Lord unites us with Himself and with one another in a bond stronger than any natural union. And He sends us thus united into the world to bear witness, by faith* and works,* to God's love,* preparing for the coming of the Kingdom and anticipating it. All who take part in the Eucharist are called to discover

the perfect meaning of our actions in the world in favor of development and peace; and to receive from it the strength to commit ourselves ever more generously.

Son of God. *See* GOD.

Song of Songs (song uhv songz). Twenty-sixth Book of the Old Testament* and fifth Sapiential Book. Attributed to Solomon, it was probably written by an unknown author in the 6th century B.C. It portrays the ideal human love of spouses for one another. It can also refer to God's love for His Chosen People and Christ's love for His Church* and the individual soul.

Liturgical use: The Liturgy* makes infrequent use of this Book because of its specialized subject matter. In the *Roman Missal,** it is read on December 21 and July 22, in the Common Masses of Virgins,* Ritual Masses* of the Consecration of Religious and Religious Profession, and the Mass for Marriage.* In the *Liturgy of the Hours,** it is read only on May 31 (Visitation*). *Meaning:* Love is stronger than death. God's love is always searching to bring us to Himself. At the same time, the structures of our humanity (psychological, physical, emotional, and the like) were created by God—for example, the love that unites man and woman is part of God's design and hence is something beautiful and worthy of honor. We should, then, always strive to use them in the way He intended and thank Him for making us in so wonderful a manner.

Soul (sohl). A spirit having understanding and free will and destined to live forever; the immortal essence, animating principle, and actuating cause of a person's life. It unites with the body to form a human being. Theologians usually identify three kinds of souls; (1) vegetative, the root of vital activity in plants; (2) sensitive, the root of vital activity in animals; and (3) intellectual, the root of vital activity in human beings. The third contains the first two and the second contains the first.

The human soul is created by God after His image and likeness and is the seat of grace* and glory.* Christ died to give eternal life* to human beings, and He stressed the importance of human salvation.* For a time after death the soul is separated from the body, but they will be reunited at the Second Coming.*

The Liturgy* is concerned with and carried out by both soul and body. Hence, the new texts do not speak of soul by itself but of the whole person. Even in the texts for All Souls Day,* the Church* does not speak of souls so much as deceased persons. In this way, she shows that although the state of the person is changed the person is identical to the person who lived on earth.

Special Groups, Mass for Children and. *See* MASS FOR CHILDREN AND SPECIAL GROUPS.

Species (SPEE-sheez; -seez). A Latin term, meaning external appearances, that identifies the accidents or form, that is, the weight, taste, color, size, odor, resistance, of the bread and wine which at the time of Consecration* remain when the substance is changed into the Body* and Blood* of Christ. The accidental properties, described above, remain after the conversion, which is called Transubstantiation*; the substance, namely the existing thing, changes. *See also* APPEARANCES; EUCHARIST; EUCHARISTIC ELEMENTS.

Spiritual Communion. *See* COMMUNION.

Spirituality, Liturgical. *See* LITURGICAL SPIRITUALITY.

Sponsors. *See* GODPARENTS.

Spoon (spoon). (1) A small spoon used in many Eastern Liturgies to distribute Holy Communion* under the species of bread imbibed with the Precious Blood.*

(2) In certain parts of the world a similar spoon is used to measure a few drops of water into the chalice* at the time of the Preparation of the Gifts.*

(3) A little spoon; of the same metal as the censer,* fits into the incense boat, and the minister uses it to put incense* on the charcoal in the censer.

Spouses (SPOW-suhz; -zuhz). Married persons. (1) Spouses are the ministers of the Sacrament of Marriage,* which they bestow upon each other by the exchange of vows before a duly ordained priest,* the delegated witness of the Universal Church,* and at least two other witnesses who represent the local community.

(2) It also refers to those women Religious* who vow their chastity to God to be more Christlike and to be intimately united with Him.

(3) The term, spouse of Christ, is used on occasion to identify the Church,* founded by Christ, which St. Paul* describes as espoused to Christ.

Sprinkler (SPRING-kluhr). A ritual object used to sprinkle holy water,* today usually made of metal with a hollow handle and a sponge at the ball-shaped top so that water can be sprinkled therefrom. Formerly it was frequently a branch of hyssop or some similar plant, like rosemary or boxwood. It is also called aspergill or aspersorium.

Sprinkling (SPRING-kling). The rite that consists of sprinkling holy water* on one or many persons, on a building, or on one or several objects in order to purify or bless them. At the principal Mass* on Sundays, this is the usual ceremony during which the people,* the ministers,* and the altar* are sprinkled during the Introductory Rites.* Formerly it was called *Asperges*, from the first Latin word of the antiphon* sung during the sprinkling. Whenever the sprinkling with holy water occurs on Sunday it takes the place of the Penitential Rite.*

This ceremony should remind the faithful* of their Baptism* and the inner spiritual purification with which they prepared themselves for the celebration of the Eucharist.* A similar rite is performed in the visitation of the sick, the consecration of churches, and the blessing* of houses and other mundane objects. Thus the ritual relives the faithful's conversion at Baptism and symbolizes a new birth or regeneration,

with concomitant cleansing and healing. This aspect, a reminder of Baptism with the renewal of grace,* is most obvious at the Easter Vigil* when the people are sprinkled after having renewed their baptismal promises.* *See also* INTRODUCTORY RITES.

Stabat Mater (STAH-baht MAH-ter). Latin title (from the first two words "The Mother Was Standing") of a hymn, *At the Cross Her Station Keeping,* consisting of twenty couplets in the Latin and describing with beauty and pathos the Sorrows of the Blessed Virgin Mary* at the Cross.* It is thought to have originated in the 13th or 14th century, in an atmosphere of ardent Franciscan devotion to the crucified Jesus. It has been variously attributed to Pope Innocent III (d. 1216), St. Bonaventure,* or most often Jacopone da Todi (d. 1306).

This hymn was introduced into the Liturgy* gradually until 1727 when it was prescribed as a Sequence* for the Mass of the Seven Sorrows of Mary* on September 15 and on the Friday before Holy Week,* as well as their corresponding Offices.* The *Stabat Mater* has been retained as an optional Sequence for September 15 in the reformed *Roman Missal** and as the hymn for the Office of Readings,* Morning Prayer,* and Evening Prayer* for that same date in the new *Liturgy of the Hours.**

The popularity of this world-famous writing is reflected by the more than sixty English translations that have been made and by its use in the popular devotion of the Stations of the Cross.*

The compassion of Mary—her presence and participation in the Sacrifice of the Cross—is part of the Mystery* of the Church* sharing in and offering the sacrifice of Jesus for the salvation* of the world.*

At the Cross her station keeping,
Stood the mournful Mother weeping,
Close to Jesus to the last.

Through her heart, His sorrow sharing,
All His bitter anguish bearing,
Lo, the piercing sword has passed!

O, how sad and sore distressed
Was that Mother highly blessed
Of the sole-begotten One.

Christ above in torment hangs,
She beneath beholds the pangs
Of her dying glorious Son.

Is there one who would not weep
'Whelmed in miseries so deep
Christ's dear Mother to behold?

Can the human heart refrain
From partaking in the pain,
In that Mother's pain untold?

Bruised, derided, cursed, defiled,
She beheld her tender Child,
All with bloody scourges rent.

For the sins of His own nation
Saw Him hang in desolation
Till His Spirit forth He sent.

O sweet Mother! fount of love,
Touch my spirit from above,
Make my heart with yours accord.

Make me feel as you have felt.
Make my soul to glow and melt
With the love of Christ, my Lord.

Holy Mother, pierce me through.
In my heart each wound renew
Of my Savior crucified.

Let me share with you His pain,
Who for all our sins was slain,
Who for me in torments died.

Let me mingle tears with you,
Mourning Him Who mourned for me,
All the days that I may live.

By the Cross with you to stay,
There with you to weep and pray,
Is all I ask of you to give.

Virgin of all virgins blest!
Listen to my fond request:
Let me share your grief Divine.

Let me, to my latest breath,
In my body bear the death
Of your dying Son Divine.

Wounded with His every wound,
Steep my soul till it has swooned
In His very Blood away.

Be to me, O Virgin, nigh,
Lest in flames I burn and die,
In His awe-full judgment day.

Christ, when You shall call me hence,
Be Your Mother my defense,
Be Your Cross my victory.

While my body here decays,
May my soul Your goodness praise,
Safe in heaven eternally.
Amen. Alleluia.

Staff, Pastoral. *See* CROZIER.

Stages (STAYJ-uhz). To achieve full initiation in the Church,* the catechumen* moves forward through various steps. Three stages occur in the process of adult initiation: (a) the candidate receives acceptance by the Church as a catechumen; (b) the catechumen having been found worthy is then elected or admitted into the Lenten* period of immediate preparation for the Sacraments of Initiation*; (c) the elected person after full preparation actually receives the Sacraments of Initiation. *See also* RITE OF CHRISTIAN INITIATION OF ADULTS.

Stalls. *See* CHOIR (ARCHITECTURE).

Standing. *See* POSTURE IN WORSHIP.

Stanislaus, St. (STAN-uhs-lows). c. 1030-1079. This Polish priest* was appointed Bishop* of Cracow. He excommunicated King Boleslaus who murdered him during a Mass.*

Liturgical celebration: April 11 (Memorial); *theme:* uniting one's own life with the sacrifice of the Mass.

Station (STAY-shuhn). A liturgical ceremony comprising a procession* followed by holy Mass* that the Pope* himself celebrates, ordinarily surrounded by his clergy* and the faithful,* in some outstanding church of the city of Rome. The term derives from the Latin *statio*, the word used for Christian assemblies of worship.*

The term station came to refer also to a specific church where on a fixed day the community gathered for the celebration of the Bishop's Liturgy.* Thus bishops celebrated in the churches under their jurisdiction on specific days. Pope St. Gregory the Great* organized the stational schedule, so that a special church was assigned to each station day. *See also* STATIONAL CHURCHES; STATIONAL MASS.

Stational Churches (STAY-shuhn-uhl CHURCH-uhz). Churches in which, on a specific day, the faithful* would gather to celebrate the Liturgy* with the bishop.* Early Christian literature indicated that this happened frequently. Though we hear of it more in Rome, it also occurred in Jerusalem and Constantinople. The people fasted on these days between twelve and three; there would be a procession* which would bring the Pope* (in Rome), the bishop, the clergy,* and the laity* together at that specific church at the appointed hour of the day.

St. Gregory the Great* organized the schedule, assigning a special church to each station day, so that there were stations for most of the Sundays and the Penitential Ferials of Advent* and Lent.* They were still listed in the *Roman Missal** before the Second Vatican Council,* and John XXIII reinstituted his visits to the stational churches in Rome. Symbolic of the type of Christian worship* in the beginning of the Church, this practice certainly does demonstrate the unity of a liturgical community, the shepherd in the midst of his flock. *See also* STATION; STATIONAL MASS.

Stational Mass (STAY-shuhn-uhl mas). The celebration of the Eucharist in a cathedral* by the diocesan bishop* in his role of high priest of the total diocese,* with the help of his presbyterate and ministers and with the active participation* of the entire People of God.*

The intent is to show both the unity in the Local Church* and the diversity of ministries around the Eucharist* and the bishop. *See also* STATION; STATIONAL CHURCHES.

Stations of the Cross (STAY-shuhnz uhv thuh kraws; kros). A pious exercise honoring the Passion* and Death* of Christ. Also known as the Way of the Cross, it originated through imitation of the practice in early times of visiting the scene of Christ's Passion and Death in Jerusalem. The term derived from the method of performing this devotion, namely standing or gathering at fourteen different places while meditating or praying on the Passion of Christ.

This practice was promoted energetically by the Franciscans during the 14th century, so that it became common by the 15th century even though the number and type of Stations varied. The Franciscan St. Leonard of Port Maurice frequently preached on this devotion in the 18th century, and finally Clement XII (1730-1740) gave the guidelines, fixing the number of Stations at fourteen, commemorating the events related in the Gospels* and from early tradition. The devotion may be public or private.

Usually the Stations are erected on the walls of the church, but they may be placed outdoors. For the plenary indulgence* to be gained, (a) different readings are to be made at each Station to which some vocal prayers are added; however, only a pious meditation on the Passion and Death of Christ is required at each Station; (b) movement from Station to Station is required; (c) the Stations must consist of fourteen wooden crosses, to which are frequently added pictures or images representing the Station; (d) if all the people cannot move readily from Station to Station, the one conducting the exercise does so while the others remain in their place; (e) those impeded from performing the exercise either through sickness or for some other reason may gain the indulgence by meditating for at least one-half hour on the Passion and Death of Christ.

The various scenes on the traditional Stations are: (1) Jesus is condemned to death; (2) Jesus accepts His Cross; (3) Jesus falls the first time; (4) Jesus meets His Mother;

(5) Simon of Cyrene helps Jesus carry His Cross; (6) Veronica wipes the face of Jesus; (7) Jesus falls the second time; (8) Jesus consoles the women of Jerusalem; (9) Jesus falls the third time; (10) Jesus is stripped of His garments; (11) Jesus is nailed to the Cross; (12) Jesus dies on the Cross; (13) Jesus is taken down from the Cross; (14) Jesus is laid in a tomb. In some areas there is an optional 15th Station consisting of the Resurrection.

During the Holy Year of 1975, Pope Paul VI approved a new series of Stations that are based on the Gospel. These Stations begin with the Last Supper* and conclude with the Resurrection.*

Statues. *See* IMAGES.

Stephen, Martyr, St. (STEE-vuhn, MAHR-tuhr). ?-c.35. A Greek-speaking Jew, converted to Christianity, and chosen to be one of the first deacons* ordained by the Apostles.* Because of his success in preaching and healing, he was charged with blasphemy; he defended himself against the Sanhedrin but was stoned to death, thus

becoming the First Martyr* of Christianity. He is the Patron of Bricklayers and Stonemasons. *Liturgical celebration:* December 26 (Feast); *theme:* proclaim and live the Faith fearlessly at whatever cost.

Stephen of Hungary, St. (STEE-vuhn uhv HUHNG-guh-ree). 975-1038. This son of Duke Geza, christened Stephen, became ruler of the Magyars at his father's death and eventually King of Hungary by vanquishing the rebels and consolidated the country. Besides establishing the Hungarian state, he helped build up the Hungarian Church by establishing Sees,* ordering financial support, making widespread reforms, ruling wisely, and being generous to the poor. *Liturgical celebration:* August 16 (Opt. Mem.); *theme:* fostering the growth of the Church* through the practice of virtue.*

Stipends (STAI-pendz; -puhndz). An offering, usually of money, received by the celebrant* or concelebrants* of Mass* with the understanding that the Mass will be celebrated for the donor's intention. Historically, these offerings were made at the time of the Procession* at the Preparation of the Gifts.* Thus this Offertory Gift is made for a public work, or in honor of God, or for assistance to the poor, totally in harmony with the nature of the Eucharistic Celebration. Never is it to be considered the price for the Eucharistic Sacrifice, but a voluntary donation to the priest* whose only source of sustenance is the service that he renders, and thus he would receive adequate income.

According to the new Code, the terminology has been changed from stipend (*stipendium*) to offering (*stips*). The former has a connotation of a mercantile transaction, imposing an obligation in justice.* The latter "offering" is interpreted as a donation to the poor, or for the honor of God, only gratuitous, and therefore with no contractual obligation in justice. Nevertheless it is the only offering a priest may accept for a single celebration of the Eucharist* at which he presides or concelebrates. Thus the offering for the support of the ministers* of the Church* or some worthy cause limits the celebrant insofar as he may take but one such offering for each celebration, but he has no strict contractual obligation to pray for the intention of the donor, worthy as the practice of praying for the intention is.

According to Canon 901 the celebrant is free to apply the Mass for anyone, living or dead. When he accepts an offering he is to apply the Mass according to that intention (Canon 945,1). Canon Law does not specify that the presider actually pray for that intention, because, as in the past, often the priest may not even know the precise intention for which he is celebrating the Mass. Some recent theologians postulate, based on the new Code of Canon Law and the apostolic letter of Paul VI *Firma in Traditione*, the following: Mass offerings are gratuitous donations given by the faithful* for the Church's ministry and not payments for services rendered.

The amount of the stipend or offering is normally determined by a diocesan standard. Usually it is given for a particular intention at one Mass; a foundation stipend may also be set up whereby the interest on money or property is used for annual Masses. Stipends or offerings accepted for a second or third Mass on the day must be given to the episcopal authority and are used ordinarily to support the seminaries. The current Code of Canon Law (canon 901, 945, and 946), however, clearly presumes the richness and value of the custom of applying the Mass for a definite intention, and the strict obligation in justice that binds the priest to offer Mass according to the intention of the one who offers the stipend.

Stockings (STAHK-ingz). Knit close-fitting covering for the feet and legs. Liturgical stockings are worn by the bishop* at solemn pontifical celebrations of the Mass.* They are made of silk conforming to the color* of the day and are worn with sandals (low-heeled shoes) of the same color. Both stockings and shoes are now optional.

Stole (stohl). The liturgical vestment, consisting of a long, narrow band of material several inches wide, worn around the neck by priests* and bishops,* from the left shoulder like a sash by deacons,* at liturgical services, e.g., the Mass,*

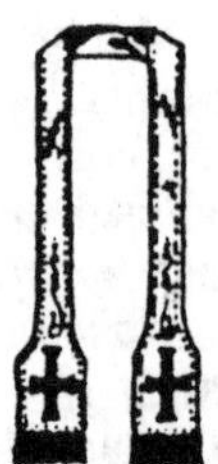

administration of the Sacraments* and Sacramentals,* and ceremonies with the Blessed Sacrament.* It is a mark of authority that the bishops, priests, and deacons wear in the exercise of these liturgical functions. It is worn over either the alb* or the surplice* and cowl, and in some cases directly over the habit* of mendicant Orders.

The sacerdotal stole, worn by the priest and bishop over the alb during liturgical services, hangs from the neck forward over the breast and is attached by the cincture.* Normally it is of the same material and color* as the chasuble.* Recently some priests have begun wearing a highly ornamental stole over the rather unadorned chasuble.

The pastoral stole resembles the sacerdotal stole in form, but its two hanging parts are joined, at the chest level, by a cord with tassels, so that the parts do not glide to one side more than the other. Normally it is worn over the surplice or rochet* and is not fixed by a cincture. Usually the pastoral stole is broader and more ornamented than the sacerdotal one. *See also* VESTMENTS.

Stole Fees (stohl feez). Offerings made by the faithful* on occasion of the administration of certain Sacraments* or Sacramentals.* They stem from the right of the clergy* to be supported by the laity* (1 Cor 9:7-13). Since the fees are related to the action of the ministerial priesthood,* they are termed "stole" fees, the stole being a sign of the office. However, the fees are not payment for the service but only offerings on the occasion of the service. Canon 848 clearly indicates this point: "The minister should ask nothing for the administration of the sacraments beyond the offerings by the competent authority, always being careful that the needy are not deprived of the help of the sacraments because of their poverty."

Stoup. *See* FONT.

Stowe Missal (stoh MIS-uhl). Parchment codex of 65 folios that constitutes the oldest known (between the 6th and 10th centuries) Mass Book of the Celtic Church. It contains extracts from the Gospel of St. John,* an Ordinary* and Canon* of the Mass, prayers for three proper Masses, an Ordo for Baptism,* the Visitation of the Sick, and an Irish treatise on the ceremonies of the Mass.

Striking the Breast (STRAI-king thuh brest). An ancient sign of sorrow and repentance (as in Lk 18:13: "The tax collector stood off at a distance and would not even raise his eyes to heaven but beat his breast and prayed, 'O God, be merciful to me a sinner,' " and 23:48) that still survives as a liturgical gesture. In the Liturgy,* striking the breast is symbolic, manifesting the feeling of repentance* and the idea of humility. It occurs during the "I Confess" at the Penitential Rite,* and in Eucharistic Prayer I* at the

words "Though we are sinners." At the words indicated, the striking is made with the right hand, fingers extended, not as a fist, with the left hand placed on the chest at a lower level.

Stripping of the Altar. *See* ALTAR, STRIPPING THE.

Subcinctorium. *See* PAPAL MASS.

Subdeacon (suhb-DEE-kuhn). Formerly one who received the Holy Order below that of deacon.* At one time it was considered a Major Order in the Western Church. In 1972 through the revision of the Orders by Paul VI, the Minor Orders* and that of the subdiaconate were abolished. In the Western Church when one became a subdeacon, he assumed the obligation of celibacy and the duty of the recitation of the Divine Office.* In the Eastern Church, the subdiaconate was listed among the Minor Orders. The ordinary duties of the subdeacon were to read the Epistle* at Mass* and prepare the elements and vessels at the time of the Preparation of the Gifts.* *See also* HOLY ORDERS.

Suffering (SUHF-[uh-]ring). The conscious and reflective experience of physical or mental pain. It is allied with the problem of evil, including sin* and death, in the world.* This can be answered only by a broader and deeper awareness of God's power, presence, and wisdom especially as seen in the Sufferings, Death,* and Resurrection* of Jesus. Christians must place themselves in the school of our Lord and learn to accept suffering in union with Him, uniting their suffering to His redemptive Sufferings for the world.

Christ affirmed the need of His Suffering (Lk 9:17). He took it upon Himself freely as an instrument of salvation* for all human beings and He invites us to do the same (1 Pt 2:21-25; Eph 5:1-9). All members of the Body of Christ* are accounted with Him in His Sufferings and must complete in their bodies what is lacking to the Sufferings of Christ; then the sufferings of this world will be changed into glory* in eternity (Rom 8:18-24; 2 Cor 5:1-5; Col 1:24).

The Liturgy* is a re-presentation of Christ's Sufferings and Death and allows its participants to share in it and in its fruits. The Liturgy constitutes the best means whereby the sufferings of Christians become endowed with a marvelous efficacy in expiating sin, in meriting actual and habitual grace,* and above all in producing a profoundly purifying effect in the soul. *See also* SALVIFICI DOLORIS.

Suffrages. *See* GENERAL INTERCESSIONS.

Sunday (SUHN-day; -dee). Name of the first day of the week, which was originally a day honoring the sun. For Christians, and specifically for liturgical purposes, the day has been renamed the Lord's Day (Rv 1:10). From the very beginning of the Christian era, Sunday supplanted the Jewish Sabbath as a day of worship,* primarily in commemoration of Christ's Resurrection* ("This is the day the Lord has made; let us be glad and rejoice in it" – Ps 118:24). Later it also was a memorial of the descent of the Holy Spirit* on Pentecost.* (Sunday may also be termed the eighth day of the week—in which case it evokes the hereafter, the eternity where the Risen Jesus awaits us.)

For Christians then, the first day of the week is dedicated to public worship, so that the community might satisfy its social obligation toward the Lord; only in the secondary manner is there an obligation to rest on that day, as the Jewish Sabbath dictated. Sunday has a unique preeminence over weekdays since it commemorates the Paschal Mystery* of Christ, the Lord, during which the assembly* is to listen to God's Word* and to partake of the Eucharist.*

Liturgically speaking, each Sunday must be regarded as a little Easter, relating to the rest of the week much as Easter does to the year as a whole. Therefore on Sundays, all the various groups in the community should attend the parish Mass, even if it means a reduction of the usual number of Masses to be held on the weekend. The bishop* should see that a sufficient number of services be provided on Sundays and Holy Days* for the convenience of those who must leave home early for places of recreation, amusement, or work. A suitable time should be allotted for the celebration of Mass in conjunction with transportation systems and businesses, such as shopping centers and urban centers, including the opportunity for the evening vigil* celebrations.

Furthermore, although the central point of the celebration of Sunday is through the offering of the Eucharistic Sacrifice, the day should offer sufficient opportunity to be kept holy by prayer,* works of charity,* and relaxation from work.* Certain Sacraments,* such as Baptism* and Confirmation,* might better be held on these days; opportunities for the faithful* joining with the pastors* in the recitation of the Divine Office* should be available. Religious education and discussion, Scripture* readings, family prayers, pilgrimages,* and the like are all good works* that should be able to find expression on Sunday. Furthermore, care must be taken to allow for sufficient healthy relaxation of both bodily and mental tension by experiencing art, literature, nature, and sensible, well-balanced activities. *See also* EASTER; ORDINARY TIME.

Sunday Celebration in the Absence of a Priest (SUN-day;-dee; sel-uh-BRAY-shuhn in thee AB-suhn[t]s uhv uh preest). In June 1988, a Directory* for *Sunday Celebrations in the Absence of a Priest* was published. It came in reply to requests from bishops* asking for guidelines to cover situations where the full celebration of the Sunday with the Eucharist* is impossible. Those elements essential to a Sunday celebration when Mass* cannot be celebrated are stipulated. Although recommending that the faithful* attend Mass at a neighboring church, it does give conditions if this cannot be done.

In that case the celebration of the Word* occurs, followed by a distribution of Holy Communion* if possible. However, such a service should not occur if there has been a celebration of the Mass on the previous evening. Also it may not occur if at least one Mass was celebrated on the given Sunday. The intent is that celebrations in the absence of the priest should bring about a greater desire for the Eucharist and should help the faithful prepare better for

the Eucharistic Celebration. The faithful are to pray with fervor for more vocations to the priesthood.

The diocesan bishop should stipulate the rules for Sunday celebrations in the absence of a priest, and all of them should occur under the supervision of a pastor.* All of these services are to be preceded by sufficient catechesis for the reasons behind such celebrations, be properly conducted, and be evaluated. Such Sunday celebrations may be led by deacons* or properly prepared lay persons.*

Morning Prayer* or Evening Prayer* from the *Liturgy of the Hours** may be used by inserting readings from the Mass in the Hours, with Communion* being distributed at the conclusion. The actual rites and texts are to be determined by the Conference of Bishops* according to the following structure: (1) Introductory Rites; (2) Liturgy of the Word; (3) Thanksgiving; (4) Rite of Communion; (5) Concluding Rites.

The *Lectionary** is used for the Liturgy of the Word. The thanksgiving could be the General Intercessions,* a Psalm,* a hymn,* or a litany.* Another alternative is placing the Eucharist* on the altar* before the Lord's Prayer* while all kneel and sing or recite a hymn, litany, or Psalm. The Prefaces and Eucharistic Prayers* are definitely not to be used; they are presidential prayers.* The Communion Rite follows the form in the *Roman Ritual** for Holy Communion Outside Mass. The Lord's Prayer is always sung or recited even if Communion is not distributed. Usually there would be announcements before the Dismissal.*

Sunday Mass Obligation (SUHN-day; -dee; mas ob-luh-GAY-shuhn). The Catholic's obligation to assist at Mass* on Sunday. Traditionally from apostolic times, the Church* gathered on Sunday* to share a common faith* and hope* in Jesus, the risen Savior, as the author of salvation.* Thus Sunday* is a day of feasting and joy in which to hear the Word of God* and participate* in the Eucharist,* while desisting from work. Therefore the observance of Sunday is not regarded so much as a law or obligation, but as a celebration of importance necessary for the faith of the entire Christian community; consequently, throughout history, despite difficulties and dangers, the Church assembles each Sunday. The Sunday gathering for the Eucharistic Celebration is distinguished from weekday Masses by its style, readings, and peculiar character. The faithful* of every category, age, and condition should feel invited and at ease during this service.

The passive attendance at Mass, as the old idiom "hearing Mass" suggests, has been disappearing since Vatican II,* because the emphasis has been on the active participation in the liturgical action by the faithful. Distinctive of the Roman Catholic Church, Sunday Mass observance became a mark of a practicing Catholic. Statistical surveys show the drop in fulfilling the Sunday Mass obligation from the time of the authority crisis in the '60s until the early '80s. Recently the trend has started upward, which would tend to signify that there has been a personal interiorization of the Faith. We could deduce that the congregation now attends Mass in active witness to and with formative participation in the Mystery of Faith,* the Mass.

One factor that may have helped the upward trend is the extension of allowing fulfillment of the Sunday Eucharist on Saturday evening. Some practical considerations for this action of the Church are the following. Vigils* have always been thought of as part of the following day. Many could celebrate Sunday more effectively were they permitted to take part in the obligatory Mass the evening before. This is particularly evident when we realize that Sunday should also be a day of mental, physical, and emotional rest, reflecting the image of the 7th day of creation. It allows people to entertain, to travel. Formerly the rhythm of the Church's life affected the rhythm of human life, but this is no longer so. The presence of unbelievers in the family, among friends, and in the community is a general experience; Church life is not the criterion for human relations anymore. In our society there are always some people who are obliged to work on Sun-

day; to attend Mass as well would be a serious inconvenience that day; consequently Saturday celebration is a gracious alternative.

These anticipated Masses are to be comparable to the Sunday Mass in every way. Some questions arise with regard to those occasions when Holy Days of Obligation* fall on either Saturday or Monday. In these cases, according to Canon 1248, #1, the Mass to be said will be the Mass of Obligation, independent of the liturgical rank of the concurring two celebrations. Unfortunately the Canon does not clarify what is to be done on Saturday and Sunday nights when Christmas,* Mary the Mother of God,* the Assumption,* and All Saints* fall either on Saturday or on Monday. However, an interpretation in *Notitiae* Vol. 20 (1984), pp. 603-605, grants to the Conference of Bishops,* or an individual bishop* of a diocese, the permission to make a decision in individual cases to suit the pastoral necessity and the local customs of the area.

The fulfillment of both the Holy Day and the Sunday Mass precept cannot be satisfied by attending only one Mass. When a Holy Day occurs on Saturday, a person may attend Mass in the morning for the Holy Day and in the evening for the Sunday, or attend one Mass on Saturday and one Mass on Sunday. When a Holy Day falls on Monday, a person may attend one Mass on Sunday and one Mass on Monday, or a Sunday Mass on Sunday and an anticipated Mass for the Holy Day on Sunday evening. *See also* SUNDAY.

Surplice (SUR-pluhs). A large-sleeved loose-fitting garment reaching almost to the knees, usu-

ally of linen or cotton, without cincture,* worn over the cassock* or habit.* It originated as a garment to be worn over the fur coats necessary in the northern countries. At times during the centuries, it was ornamented with lace or embroidery at the hem and sleeves. It is worn during processions,* while administering the Sacraments,* in choir,* and basically at any function when the alb* is not prescribed. At Mass* it is also used by the acolyte.*

Sursum Corda. *See* INTRODUCTORY DIALOGUE.

Sylvester, St. (Sil-VES-tuhr). ?-335. Pope after the Edict of Milan, whereby Constantine freed Christianity, he was overshadowed by the Emperor. He sent representatives to the Councils of Arles and of Nicaea, which condemned Donatism and Arianism. *Liturgical celebration:* December 31 (Opt. Mem.); *theme:* peace* will follow persecution.

Symbol of Faith. *See* PROFESSION OF FAITH.

Symbolism (SIM-buh-liz-uhm). The art or practice of investing external actions or things with inner meaning. As such, it is the universal language of any living religion. Early Christianity made use of such symbolisms because of the persecutions, hiding beliefs under emblems and figures. Most of the Church art, architecture, Liturgy,* and private devotions had definable religious meaning. Furthermore, since Catholic Christianity had Mysteries* of faith* so profound, such symbols allowed people to dwell upon these Mysteries in prayerful recollection for greater comprehension. This is particularly so in the sign value of the Sacraments,* wherein numer-

ous symbols can be found in Christian Liturgies. *See also* RITES AND CEREMONIES; SIGNS AND SYMBOLS.

Symbols. *See* SIGNS AND SYMBOLS.

Sympathizers. *See* INQUIRERS.

Synaxis (sin-AKS-is). Literally, a meeting or congregation. (1) For the Early Christian Church, it referred to a meeting or gathering of Christians for Divine worship* or any religious function. As such then it might also include, as it does certainly in the Eastern Church, any assembly for public worship, including the Mass.*

(2) In the Byzantine Rite* it refers to the celebration at a specific place to commemorate a particular feast,* corresponding to the Stations in the Latin Rite. (*See also* STATION.)

(3) In the Western Church it refers primarily to the gathering of an assembly* for only the first part of the Eucharist, the Liturgy of the Word,* based on the Jewish religious meeting in a synagogue. Therefore it consisted of Readings,* Psalms,* Prayer,* and a Sermon. Later on there were added the Introductory Rites,* the Lord Have Mercy,* the Glory to God,* and the Creed.* (*See also* CATHEDRAL OFFICE; MASS).

Synod (SIN-uhd). Literally, a meeting or assembly. (1) In general, a gathering of bishops.* The term is still used on occasions as an alternate for council.*

(2) Usually it is used specifically for a diocesan synod, that consultative body, consisting of selected clergy,* religious,* and laity,* convoked by a local bishop, to recommend legislation to improve the diocese.* Their conclusions receive force solely through the power of the bishop.

(3) The Synod of Bishops is the deliberative body of representatives from the whole world, convened by the Pope* to discuss serious Church* matters, and thus demonstrating the hierarchical communion of the bishops as they share in the responsibility of the Universal Church.* As a result of the deliberations during Vatican II,* Synods have been held every three years on topics of major interest, so that the bishops might work together in a collegial way in acting upon pressing issues that affect Church life.

— T —

Tabernacle (TAB-uhr-nak-uhl). (1) In the Christian sense, it refers to the shrine or receptacle either round or rectangular that serves as a place for the exclusive reservation of the Blessed Sacrament.* It should be of solid material, opaque, secure and inviolable, fitting the architecture of the church, in a preeminent place, yet not garish.

Reserving the Blessed Sacrament started in the 4th century, so that Communion* for the sick might be available. At times it was kept in the sacristy* or in a movable dove-shaped receptacle suspended by chains before the altar.* By the 16th century usually it was reserved in the tabernacle on the main altar.*

Since the reform brought about by Vatican II,* all agree that the proper place for the Blessed Sacrament would be a chapel* in the church suitable for private adoration* and prayer* of the faithful. Otherwise a side altar may be used or some noble and properly ornamented part of the church other than an altar, such as a pedestal or ledge. In this way the presence of the Eucharist* does not detract from the offering of the Sacrifice of the Mass* on the altar of sacrifice. The tabernacle is to be kept locked, with a sanctuary light* burning before it constantly. To indicate the presence of the Eucharist in the tabernacle, it should be covered by a veil,* unless another more suitable way is decided upon by a competent authority. (*See also* SANCTUARY LIGHT; VEIL TABERNACLE.)

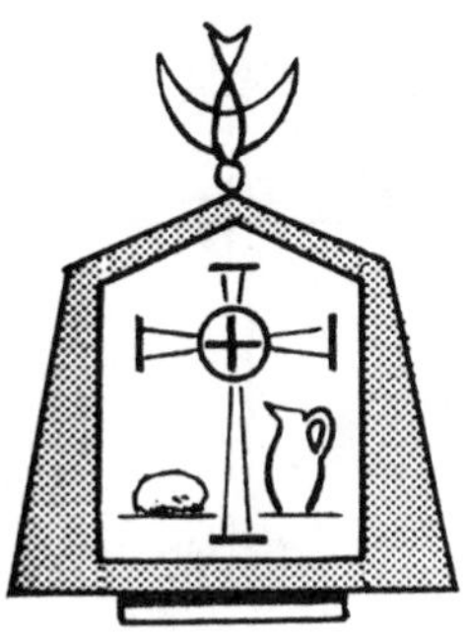

(2) The term sometimes is also used to describe the small, movable, metal vessels for reserving the Blessed Sacrament; sometimes these were used to carry the Eucharist to the sick; in this sense tabernacle is synonymous with pyx.*

(3) According to Jewish usage, the tabernacle was a shrine or sanctuary, shaped like a tent, built according to the detailed instructions given to Moses. During their wanderings in the wilderness and before the erection of the Temple of Jerusalem, this special tabernacle represented God's presence to His Chosen People. The tabernacle, set aside for religious observance, embraced a court with an inner shrine in which the Ark of the Covenant was kept.

Tabernacle Veil. *See* VEIL, TABERNACLE.

Table Blessing. *See* GRACE AT MEALS.

Tantum Ergo. *See* BENEDICTION; PANGE LINGUA.

Teachers. *See* SAINTS, LITURGICAL CATEGORIES OF.

Te Deum (tay DAY-uhm; tee DEE-uhm). Latin title (from the first two words "You, God") of a hymn* or canticle* of thanksgiving and praise, at first attributed to Sts. Ambrose,* Augustine,* or Hilary,* but now accredited to Nicetas, Bishop of Remesiana during the 4th century. Besides being used at extraordinary occasions as an expression of joy and thanks, at solemn ceremonies or liturgical functions, its liturgical use occurs at the conclusion of the Office of Readings* on Sundays outside of Lent,* during the Octaves* of Christmas* and Easter,* and on Solemnities* and Feasts.*

Originally the text could be seen as a poem in three strophes. The first verse states the theme: *You are God; we praise You.* Therefore it is a song of praise. The three strophes are sharply distinguished and are addressed successively to God, to the Trinity, and to Christ. The first strophe concludes with an act of Divine adoration,* the second with an act of faith* in the Trinity, and the third with a final supplication to Christ. A series of petitions taken from Psalm-verses* is another part of the hymn, though originally it did not belong to the hymn. This section may be added to the hymn, but it is not absolutely prescribed.

Te Igitur. *See* EUCHARISTIC PRAYER I.

Televised Mass. *See* MASS, TELEVISED.

Temperance (TEM-p[uh-]ruhn[t]s). Fourth and last of the chief moral virtues* (together with fortitude,* justice,* and prudence*), which dispose us to lead moral or good lives by aiding us to treat persons and things in the right way—that is, according to the will of God. They are also known as cardinal virtues because they are like hinges on which hang all other moral virtues and our whole moral life.

Temperance disposes us to control our desires and to use rightly the things that please our senses. It includes many other virtues, for example, continence, meekness, clemency, modesty, chastity, purity, studiousness, and playfulness.

Participating in the Liturgy* is an act of the moral virtue of religion* (which is part of justice) that strengthens the other moral virtues, as indicated in the article on good works. *See also* FORTITUDE; GOOD WORKS; JUSTICE; PRUDENCE; VIRTUES.

Temporal Cycle. *See* CHURCH YEAR.

Ten Commandments. *See* COMMANDMENTS.

Tenebrae (TEN-uh-bray). Before the Holy Week* reforms of 1955, the Office of Tenebrae was the celebration of Matins* and Lauds* for the last three days of Holy Week, Holy Thursday,* Good Friday,* and the Easter Vigil,* which were anticipated the preceding nights. The Latin term means shadows, and suggests symbolically the setting of the Sun of Justice, our Lord, and the spiritual darkness of the Jewish people. In addition to the kind of grief that characterized the entire Office, the accompanying rites were richly significant.

Fifteen candles were lit at the beginning of the service, and during the service candles were extinguished one by one at the end of each Psalm* of both Matins and

Lauds in order to denote the almost complete abandonment of Christ by the Apostles.* Nevertheless, the unrecognized light of Christ is not destroyed, as the 15th candle gives evidence. In the midst of the deepening darkness, the light of this candle still shone in order to die on Calvary, which was represented by the altar* on which the candle is placed for a moment. When it was hidden behind the altar at the end of Lauds,* we were reminded of Christ's burial. The confusion of sounds that followed then recalled the convulsions of nature that were associated with this period of great mourning: the earth trembled, rocks were rent, tombs opened. Suddenly the light reappeared, symbolizing clearly the Resurrection* and proclaiming the Savior's victory over death.

Recently, in the interests of holding services for the people on the mornings of Holy Thursday, Good Friday, and Holy Saturday, there has been a return to the use of Tenebrae—at least on the latter two days with the Office of Readings* used on Holy Thursday. In this respect, the New York Liturgical Commission has issued a booklet called *Parish Tenebrae Celebrations: Good Friday and Holy Saturday.*

Tephillah. *See* EIGHTEEN BLESSINGS.

Terce. *See* DAYTIME PRAYER.

Teresa of Jesus, St. (Te-REE-suh; -RES-uh; uhv JE-zuhs; -zuhz). 1515-1582. Also known as Teresa of Avila, where she was born and established the reformed convent of Carmelites. She spread her reform through many monasteries for nuns* and friars of Carmel, naturally encountering opposition. Meanwhile, she experienced many mystical ecstasies during contemplative prayer and as a result wrote extensively on prayer,* particularly discussing the many stages of prayer up to and including ecstatic union. Recently declared a Doctor of the Church,* she is also the Patroness of Headache Sufferers. *Liturgical celebration:* October 15 (Memorial); *theme:* charm, wit, and a sense of humor blend with contemplation.

Territorial Authority (ter-uh-TAWR-ee-uhl; -TOHR-ee-uhl; uh-THAWR-uh-tee; uh-THOR-). Regulating Sacred Liturgy* pertains to the purview of the Apostolic See,* but the laws also determine how far an individual bishop* may make revisions. Over and beyond that, in this same matter within certain defined limits legitimately established, local Bishops' Conferences* have territorial authority in this regard. They are entitled to regulate the Liturgy in their own regions as laid down by the law, making decisions concerning to what extent the vernacular* is to be used, the publishing of liturgical books,* and the adaptations called for by the *Constitution on the Sacred Liturgy.** In many instances their decisions need formal approval from the Apostolic See. *See also* NATIONAL CONFERENCE OF CATHOLIC BISHOPS.

Testament, New (TES-tuh-muhnt, nyoo; noo). (1) The alliance or Covenant* made between humanity and God through the mediation of Christ, our Lord. In this sense it is the fulfillment of the Old Covenant, that is, the fulfillment of the promise* made by God to the Jewish people. In this regard it means the New Law, now operative from the time of Christ and expected to remain in force until the last day.

(2) That part of the Christian Bible, including the Divinely inspired Books written after the coming of Christ, that informs us about the Life, Death,* and Resurrection* of Jesus Christ and the beginnings of His Church.* It consists of twenty-seven Books, including the Gospels,* that show the importance of the life and ministry of the Lord; the Epistles,* Acts,* and Revelation,* which demonstrate how the early Christians developed in their understanding of Christ as the Risen Savior and God's Son. One could also indicate a division of the Books into historical (the Acts and the Gospels), didactic (Epistles), and prophetic (Revelation). The Liturgy of the Word* at Mass* and many of the Readings* in the Liturgy of the Hours* are taken from the New Testament. *See also* BIBLE; BIBLE AND LITURGY; BIBLE SERVICE; TESTAMENT, OLD.

Testament, Old (TES-tuh-muhnt, ohld). (1) The Covenant* or alliance made between God and His chosen people through Abraham and the patriarchs to prepare them for the new and eternal pact, consummated in the New Testament* through Christ. It also refers to the primitive, prophetic, and patriarchal revelation from the origin of the human race until Christ.

(2) Most commonly it refers to the forty-six Books that the Catholic Church believes are Divinely inspired, and are not part of the New Testament. These Books, written over a period of 900 years, tell how God revealed Himself to us, His covenantal relationship with the Hebrews as His chosen people, and how the great plan for the salvation* of the whole human race was set in motion and eventually fulfilled in Jesus Christ.

The Jews divide the Books into the Law,* the Prophets,* and the Hagiographa (another term for the last is "Writings"). The Historical Books are the five in the Pentateuch*; the Prophets* contain twenty-one Books, and the Writings consist of a set of thirteen books. Catholics usually divide them into Historical, Prophetic, and Sapiential (or Didactic) Books. (*See* BIBLE.) Again, both in the Mass* and in the Liturgy of the Hours,* selections are made from the Old Testament, and a great portion of the Divine Office is derived from the Psalms.* *See also* BIBLE; BIBLE AND LITURGY; BIBLE SERVICE; TESTAMENT, NEW.

Texts, Liturgical. *See* FORMULAS, LITURGICAL; LITURGICAL BOOKS.

Thaddeus, St. *See* JUDE, ST.

Thanks Be to God (thangks bee too god). The response (in Latin: *Deo gratias*) given by the People of God to the Readings* and at the Dismissal* of the Mass.* This familiar theme of thanksgiving in Jewish prayer is continued by Christians as

they extend their praise and gratitude to the Lord liturgically, with the intent that it affect their daily lives. The same response frequently occurs in other ceremonies, and in some instances finds its way into everyday conversation. *See also* DISMISSAL; READINGS.

Thanksgiving (thangks-GIV-ing). One of the four ends of Mass,* this aspect of prayer,* whether public or private, is the result of the faithful* who offer thanks to the Lord for whatever personal experiences they have of His goodness. It is in a sense a direct result of praise, and flows readily from it, because the recipient of God's loving-kindness would like to indicate to the Lord the realization that the gifts have been thankfully received. In many ways the believers have experienced the Lord in their daily living in a very special way; they know God through this special blessing and wish to extend to Him the appropriate thanks. Most people believe that whatever good comes to us is the result of the direct influence of the Lord; consequently they develop this strong personal relationship with Him and are willing to indicate their full appreciation in this method of prayer. *See also* EUCHARIST; PRAYER; THANKSGIVING DAY MASS.

Thanksgiving Day Mass (thangks-GIV-ing day mas). A text prepared by the Bishops' Committee on the Liturgy* for the Prayers and Preface* of the Mass formulary for the annual Thanksgiving observance in America was approved in 1969. The formulary tries to interpret the American understanding of this celebration, and other parts of the Mass have Biblical allusions to the reasons for thanksgiving. Biblical readings* appropriate to the theme of thanksgiving are chosen from the *Lectionary.** It is celebrated as a Proper Mass on the fourth Thursday of the month of November.

Theandric Acts (thee-AN-drik akts). Literally from the Greek, "God human." It refers to those actions of the Lord that are both human and Divine, therefore very characteristic and distinctive of the God-Man alone. The operations of Christ are usually distinguished in a threefold manner:

(1) Acts performed in union with the Father* and the Holy Spirit,* such as the creation of the world.

(2) The purely human acts of speaking, breathing, walking, truly the acts done in the human nature alone. In one sense, very broadly, one might say these are theandric because they may have some redemptive merit.

(3) The strictly theandric operations, sometimes called mixed, which are those wherein the two natures, Divine and human, join to produce one common effect. The human power is the instrumental cause, whereas the Divine power is the principal cause. Examples are miracles, such as healing the sick by prayer alone, like the centurion's slave who was miles away (Lk 7), walking on water, and multiplying food by a mere blessing. The zenith of theandric action is the Suffering,*

Death* and Resurrection* of Christ, the truly redemptive act wherein Jesus, performing His priestly act in the Mystical Body,* has earned for us eternal glory.*

Theology and Liturgy (thee-OL-uh-jee and LIT-uhr-jee). The Church* has always acknowledged the mutual dependence between the Liturgy* and theology, recognizing that each is enriched by the other, especially in the broad sense when theology includes, beyond the Liturgy, spiritual life in the Scripture.* Limiting it to dogmatic theology, we find a strong relationship between that and the Liturgy also, particularly in that ancient dictum *lex orandi—lex credendi** (the norm of prayers [solidifies] the norm of faith). Thus the Liturgy transmits true doctrine; a believing community asserts its faith* through acts of worship.* Sacrificial death is demonstrated in the liturgical action of the Mass*; liturgical texts support the doctrine of the Immaculate Conception.* The Liturgy, a source of the Church's teaching, constantly delves into theology for a deeper understanding of the realities it celebrates. Worship is strongly related to theology.

Contemporary theologians emphasize that the Liturgy should control not only the structure and texture of theology but also the theme. C. Vagaggini places the prayers and rites within a framework of salvation history* and in the classical sections of Catholic theology. Recent liturgists have stressed the humanity of worship but have used rites and signs to come from and approach God. Whatever sociological tools they may employ, the Divine components in the communication occur through Christian Liturgy.

Theophany. *See* EPIPHANY.

Theresa of the Child Jesus, St. (te-REE-suh; -RES-uh; uhv thuh chaild JEE-zuhs; -zuhz). 1873-1897. Popularly known as the Little Flower, Theresa received permission to enter the Carmelite convent in Lisieux at age fifteen. Her autobiography explaining the Little Way of loving God in the ordinary things of life is a spiritual classic; her cult* became widespread in the twenties when she was canonized and made Co-Patron of the Missions and of

France. She is also the Patroness of Aviators and Florists. *Liturgical celebration:* October 1 (Memorial); *theme:* the Kingdom* is promised to those who become like little children.

Thessalonians, First Epistle to the (thes-uh-LOH-nyuhnz; -nee-uhnz; fuhrst i-PIS-uhl too thuh). Fifty-ninth Book of the Bible* and thirteenth of the New Testament.* Written in 51 or 52 A.D., this Epistle* is regarded as the earliest of Paul's* works. After reminding the Thessalonians of his work among them and of his affection for them, Paul urges them to preserve purity and charity, in expectation of the resurrection, which will happen when least expected. This points to the central theme of the Epistle, which is the Second Coming* of Christ (there is at least one verse about it in each chapter: 1:10; 2:19; 3:13; 4:13-18; 5:23). The Epistle is of great doctrinal value, revealing as it does the faith* of the community. It also manifests the care and labor that were expended in instructing the Christian communities in New Testament times.

Liturgical use: In the *Roman Missal,** this Epistle is read on the 1st Sunday of Advent* (C), 3rd Sunday of Advent (B), the 29th through 33rd Sundays in Ordinary Time* (A), and Monday of the 21st Week to Tuesday of the 22nd Week (I) as well as the Common* of Pastors and Ritual Masses.* In the *Liturgy of the Hours,** it is used during the 4th Week in Ordinary Time and in the Common of Pastors. *Meaning:* Confidence in Christ's return should enable us to be patient, create hope* and joy* in us, and spur us to lead pure and blameless lives. On the other hand, uncertainty as to the time of Christ's return should call forth alertness and watchfulness on our part.

Thessalonians, Second Epistle to the (thes-uh-LOH-nyuhnz; -nee-uhnz; SEK-uhnd i-PIS-uhl too thuh). Sixtieth Book of the Bible* and fourteenth of the New Testament.* This work was written soon after Paul's First Epistle* to quiet the doubts and fears of the Thessalonians. Paul hastened to supply them with fuller information on the subject of the Second Coming.* He informed them that it was not at hand and indeed could not take place until a great apostasy occurred and Antichrist appeared. Some of the Thessalonians who were convinced that the Second Coming was imminent thought it useless to work and consequently lived irregularly. Paul condemned this practice and ordered the offenders to be corrected. He urged all to adhere to his teachings, whether these were given orally or in writing.

Liturgical use: In the *Roman Missal,** this Epistle is read on the 31st, 32nd, and 33rd Sundays in Ordinary Time* (C), Monday, Tuesday, and Wednesday of the 21st Week (II), and the Mass for the Blessing of Man's Labor as well as the Mass for Labor Day* in the United States. In the *Liturgy of the Hours,** it is used on Thursday, Friday, and Saturday of the 4th Week in Ordinary Time. *Meaning:* The teaching of Christ's Second Coming is not intended to make us lazy, arrogant, and immoral. Rather, it demands that we be busy, humble, and pure, totally immersed in good works* so as to be ready to attain the reward for our labors at our Lord's Second Coming in glory.*

Thomas, Apostle, St. (TOM-uhs, uh-POS-uhl). 1st century. Probably a Galilean, with the nickname Twin, Thomas is best known

for doubting Christ's Resurrection,* but upon His second appearance explicitly acknowledging the Divinity of Christ. Tradition has him martyred in India, and he was declared Apostle of India in 1972. He is the Patron of Architects. *Liturgical celebration:* July 3 (Feast); *theme:* struggling with doubt can bring ardent faith.*

Thomas Aquinas, St. (TOM-uhs uh-KWAI-nuhs). c.1225-1274. This

Italian Dominican, disciple of St. Albert,* developed into a master theologian, known best for his *Summa Theologiae*. His voluminous writings are characterized by the sharp distinction between faith* and reason. He is a Doctor of the Church* and the Patron of Schools. *Liturgical celebration:* January 28 (Memorial); *theme:* learning and holiness authenticate each other.

Thomas Becket, St. (TOM-uhs BEK-it). 1118-1170. London-born Thomas was archdeacon of Canterbury and became chancellor to Henry II, who nominated him as Archbishop* of Canterbury. When elected, he changed his life, clashing with the king over ecclesiastical rights. Reconciliation did not succeed, and some knights murdered Thomas in the Cathedral. *Liturgical celebration:* December 29 (Opt. Mem.); *theme:* fearless struggle for the freedom of the Church.*

Thomas More, St. (TOM-uhs mawr; mohr). 1478-1535. Eminent lawyer and writer, Thomas moved up through various offices until he became lord chancellor of England under Henry VIII. Refusing to accept Henry's divorce of Catherine, he resigned the chancellorship, was arrested, imprisoned, and finally beheaded. He is the Patron of Lawyers. *Liturgical celebration:* June 22 (Opt. Mem.); *theme:* fidelity to Church* Law means more than life.

Those Who Worked for the Underprivileged. *See* SAINTS, LITURGICAL CATEGORIES OF.

Three Hours Service (three owrz SUR-vuhs). An extra-liturgical service begun in Peru in the 17th century to commemorate the three hours that Christ hung on the Cross* on Good Friday* from noon till three. (It is also called *Tre Ore* from the Italian title.) Normally the service consisted of a series of homilies on the Passion,* particularly the seven last words of Christ and the Stations of the Cross.* This allowed ample time for meditation; sometimes the Good Friday services became part of this celebration. Since the new regulations concerning Holy Week in 1956, the proper observance of this day was restored, so that today the Three Hours Service is usually not observed, and stress is put on the proper celebration of the current liturgical action for that day. It would seem that this is more in accord with changing social patterns; the need to adhere to these three hours appears quite uncertain. *See also* GOOD FRIDAY.

Throne (throhn). (1) A permanent seat of honor, placed on the right side of the altar, on a dais usually three steps high, and covered with a canopy, occupied by the bishop,* cardinal,* or abbot* in his own respective jurisdiction. (*See also* CHAIR; FALDSTOOL.)

(2) For exposition of the Blessed Sacrament* in a monstrance,* a throne may be used, as long as it is not too distant or lofty. It is a small stand with a canopy,* usually placed on the tabernacle* or in the center of the altar.* It is usually draped with red or white silk. *See also* BENEDICTION.

Through Christ Our Lord (throo kraist owr lawrd). The formal close of the presidential prayers* used in liturgical services. It stresses Christ's mediatorial function and the fact that we, the Church,* as the Body of Christ,* join in the prayer addressed to the Father in the unity of the Spirit.* In Latin, it is *Per Christum Dominum Nostrum.*

Thurible (THUR-uh-buhl). A vase or vessel wherein mixtures of various aromatics, incense,* are burned over lighted charcoal. (It is also called a censer.) Currently the spherical pan holding the charcoal is something of a deep dish placed in a cup-shaped metal body with a cover, somewhat bulged. The brazier is usually suspended by three chains, with a fourth one attached to the top of the cover so that the chain can pass freely into a handle to which the other three chains are attached. Thus by pulling that fourth chain, incense can readily be dropped on the hot charcoal. In some cases there is merely one chain, and the perforated cover, which allows the incense to exude, lifts up and out of the way at the time to put in incense.

The thurible is used during the more solemn celebrations of Mass,* but it may be used during all of them, during the canticles* at Morning Prayer* and Evening Prayer,* during processions,* and at other liturgical functions usually connected with the celebration of the Sacraments.* *See also* BENEDICTION; INCENSE; PROCESSIONS.

Thurifer (THUR-uh-fuhr). The minister* or acolyte* in charge of the thurible* whose duty is to make sure sufficient burning charcoal is available. He carries the thurible itself together with the incense boat,* so that incense can be added at the proper times.

Tiara, Papal (tee-AR-uh; -AYR-uh; -AHR-uh; PAY-puhl). A triple crown, or a tall canonical headdress, ornamented with precious stones, formerly placed on the Pope's head at his coronation. Symbolically it has meant different things to different people: (a) the three Churches, Militant,* Suffering,* and Triumphant*; (b) the Pope's universal episcopate, his primacy of jurisdiction, his temporal influence; (c) his power to rule, to teach, to sanctify. It was used only at nonliturgical ceremonies, and the miter* would be used at the liturgical services. Paul VI gave the tiara away for the poor, so it is no longer used. *See also* CORONATION OF A POPE.

Time, Sanctification of (taim, sanck-tuh-fi-KAY-shuhn uhv). For God to involve Himself in humanity, He, being eternal, would necessarily have to do so at a specific point in time. He did this by sending His Son to become incarnate in an historical period of time. The Liturgy* uses the Birth,* Life,* Death,* and Resurrection* of Jesus as a way of marking all temporal processes. It is as if the Incarnation* makes all time holy. The Liturgy, in reflecting upon Christ's Life, makes a Christian's life holy through the Church,* in so far as it sets aside specific times for

itself. Early on, it was the Sunday Eucharist,* the annual Pasch, and later developed into the total Christian calendar.*

Eventually there evolved also times of public and private prayer,* some not Eucharistic, all of which formed an elaborate pattern of frequent worship,* as shown in some monastic groups by sanctifying the whole day with prayer at specific hours. The devotional life of Christians, whether it is monastic meditation,* the Office of the clergy,* or any rule relating to corporate or community worship and private prayer, has moved toward this one end of making time holy so that all of life becomes holy. *See also* CALENDAR; CANONICAL HOURS; CHURCH YEAR; HISTORY OF SALVATION; LITURGY OF THE HOURS.

Timothy, First Epistle to (TIM-uh-thee, fuhrst i-PIS-uhl too). Sixty-first Book of the Bible* and fifteenth of the New Testament.* The First Epistle to Timothy (together with the Second* and with the Epistle to Titus*) is one of the "Pastoral Epistles." These three Epistles are addressed directly, not to any church as a group, but to its head or pastor* for his guidance in the rule of the church. This First Epistle was written between Paul's liberation from the first imprisonment (63 A.D.) and his death (67 A.D.) and has a twofold purpose: to provide guidance in the problems of Church administration and to oppose false teaching of a speculative and moralistic type. Among other things, it deals with liturgical celebrations and selections for the offices of bishop* and deacon.* It reminds Timothy, Paul's former co-voyager who is the Pastor of Ephesus, of the prophetic character of his office and expresses the principal motive that should guide his conduct—preservation of the purity of the Church's doctrine.

Liturgical use: In the *Roman Missal,** this Epistle is read on the 24th, 25th, and 26th Sundays in Ordinary Time* (C) and from Friday of the 23rd Week (I) to Saturday of the 24th Week as well as in Masses of the Common* of Holy Men and Women, Holy Orders,* Unity of Christians, Spread of the Gospel, After the Harvest, and Thanksgiving Day* in the United States. In the *Liturgy of the Hours,** it is used during the 27th Week in Ordinary Time and the Common of Pastors and gives rise to a minor canticle* for Epiphany* and the Transfiguration.* *Meaning:* As Christians, we should be aware that God made us with our basic human needs and we should not despise them. But they are not to dominate us, turning us into gluttons, drunkards, or adulterers. Rather, we must put everything in its proper place under the guidance of the Spirit* and with an attitude of humility.

Timothy, Second Epistle to (TIM-uh-thee, SEK-uhnd i-PIS-uhl too). Sixty-second Book of the Bible* and sixteenth of the New Testament.* Written in 66 or 67 A.D., while St. Paul was a prisoner for the last time, it is a moving pastoral like First Timothy* from a veteran missionary to a younger colleague urging endurance as the main quality of a preacher of the Gospel.* Paul presents the Resurrection* of Jesus and His Messianic role as the heart of the Gospel for which he is ready to lay down his life. He recommends that Christians rely on the power of the Scriptures,* on proclamation of the Word,* and on sound doctrine.

Liturgical use: In the *Roman Missal,** this Epistle is read on the 2nd Sunday of Lent* (A), the 27th through the 31st Sunday (C), and Wednesday through Saturday of the 9th Week (II) as well as the Proper of Saints* (January 26, June 28, June 29, September 30, and October 18), Common* of Saints, Holy Orders,* and Masses for the Dead.* In the *Liturgy of the Hours,** it is used only in the alternate Two-Year Cycle* of Readings from Wednesday through Saturday of the 22nd Week (II). *Meaning:* The Gospel is a spiritual inheritance that we have received from faithful witnesses and must in turn pass on to others. It brings about wholeness, a health, not only in beliefs but also in good works.* So vital is sound doctrine to the health of the Church* and individual Christians that it is something to be treasured and even suffered for.

Timothy, St. (TIM-uh-thee). 1st century. Son of a Christian Jewess and associate of Paul,* Timothy soon became his closest friend and confidant. He served as emissary of Paul, appearing in Thessalonica, Corinth, Macedonia, and Achaia. Tradition* sends him to Ephesus as first bishop,* where he was martyred. *Liturgical celebration:* January 26 (Memorial); *theme:* a model of authority as leader of the People of God.

Title. *See* TITULAR.

Titles (TAI-tuhlz). In the *Liturgy of the Hours,** titles added at the head of each Psalm* to explain its meaning and its human value for the life of faith. They are intended only as an aid to prayer.* *See also* LITURGY OF THE HOURS; PSALTER; SENTENCES.

Titles of Jesus (TAI-tuhls uhv JEE-zuhs; -zuhz). The titles of Jesus used in the Liturgy* are many, and they are taken mostly from the Bible.* The following are some of the main ones listed in alphabetical order (those that appear as separate entries are referred).

Alpha and Omega. See ALPHA AND OMEGA.

Christ. See CHRIST.

Everlasting Father. One of the four names of the Messiah* given by Isaiah* (9:6). It manifests that Christ is an enduring, corporate provider and protector for His people.

God. See GOD.

Good Shepherd. See GOOD SHEPHERD.

Emmanuel (Immanuel). A Hebrew word meaning "God is with us" used as a name by Isaiah* for the Child who was to be born of a Virgin (7:14). Matthew* identifies Jesus with Emmanuel (1:23). Christ fittingly bears this name because it means that God is with us personally by His Incarnation* and also through His assistance.

Jesus. This name, which was common in Israel in its root form, signifies "God saves." It was bestowed by God (Lk 1:31) on the Son of the Virgin Mary—Who was truly Man and later recognized as Lord (Phil 2:11) and Savior (2 Tm 1:10)—in consequence of His mission (Mt 1:21). *See also* CHRIST; JESUS CHRIST.

Judge. Actually, it is God Who judges. The Last Judgment will be shared in by all three Persons of the Trinity, each in a way consonant with His role in the Redemption.* Inasmuch as it is through the Incarnation* that the Trinity has saved humankind, it is Christ as Man Who is presented as supreme Judge of human beings. At the Second Coming,* He will judge the living and the dead. Jesus is also Judge in the Sac-

rament of Penance,* where the true characteristics of His judging shine forth: His judgment is not punitive or final but healing and redemptive.

King. See CHRIST THE KING; JESUS CHRIST.

Lamb of God. See LAMB OF GOD.

Lord. Originally, this title signified nothing more than "sir." From the 3rd century B.C. onward, the Jews replaced the ineffable name *Yahweh* with *Adonai* (Lord) in reading the Scriptures. Applied to Jesus by the first Christians, the name "Lord" was thus equivalent to an affirmation of His Divinity (Acts 2:36). It denotes the sovereignty of Christ and His headship over the individual believer, the Church, and all things.

Mediator. See JESUS CHRIST; MEDIATOR.

Messiah. See CHRIST; MESSIAH.

Mighty God. One of the four names of the Messiah given by Isaiah (9:6). It emphasizes Christ's Divine power as a warrior against sin and evil.

Priest. See JESUS CHRIST.

Prince of Peace. One of the four names of the Messiah given by Isaiah (9:6). It indicates that Christ's rule brings wholeness and well-being to individuals and to society.

Prophet. See JESUS CHRIST.

Savior. Christ's whole mission was to save, to be a Savior. His very name (Jesus) meant this. In Luke* 2:11 and John* 4:42 we see that aspect of Christ. He not only delivers from sins and all other woes that afflict humankind but also provides a state of wholeness and blessedness in which those saved recognize the purpose of God for them and are led to their highest destiny. This will be definitively manifested at the Last Judgment.

Servant. See SERVANT; SERVANT OF YAHWEH.

Son of David. This is a Messianic title, identifying Jesus as the One Who fulfilled the Davidic Covenant,* the One Who was expected to establish the Kingdom* and bring God's people to freedom,* peace,* and glory.*

Son of God. Jesus is God's Son in various ways. Among them we may list the following: (1) He has a Divine origin; (2) He has a filial relationship with the Father within the context of His human life, as any child of God has; (3) He is the Messiah, Who was appointed and sent by God in fulfillment of the Old Testament* prophecies; and (4) He is the only Son of the Father with a Divine relation to Him. *See also* GOD; JESUS CHRIST.

Teacher. The title by which Jesus is usually designated in the Gospels.* It indicates the impact of His instruction and the authority that lay behind it. Wisdom shines through His every word.

Wonder Counselor. One of the Messianic names given by Isaiah (9:6). It indicates Christ's royal program that will cause the whole world to marvel.

Word of God. Christ is the Second Person of the Blessed Trinity, the Speech of God, the Revealer of God. He opens to the understanding of the people the nature and purposes of God and discloses the Divine Wisdom to human beings.

Titular (TICH[-uh]-luhr). The titular of a church is the Divine Person, the Mystery,* or the Saint* whose name the church bears and in whose honor it has been consecrated or solemnly blessed. In the same manner, every fixed altar* would have a titular. Each year the clergy* of the church celebrate the Divine Office* and the Mass* as a Solemnity* on the feast day. The titular of the cathedral* church is celebrated in the same way by those attached to the cathedral. The rest of the diocese* celebrates that day only as a Feast,* diocesan and Religious Orders alike. A representation of the titular should be given the place of honor at the apse* of the church above the main altar.

A titular is not to be confused with a Patron Saint,* to whom a locality, a diocese, a city, or an area is dedicated. On occasions a titular and a patron may be identical. *See also* PATRON SAINTS.

Titular Bishop. *See* BISHOP.

Titus, St. (TAI-tuhs). 1st century. Convert, secretary, and companion to Paul,* this Gentile was sent to Corinth to settle divisions and strife there. Dispatched as bishop* to

Crete, he was to establish local hierarchy and most probably died there as an elderly man. *Liturgical celebration:* January 26 (Memorial); *theme:* assuming authority to allow the work of the Lord to prosper.

Titus, The Epistle to (TAI-tus, thee i-PIS-uhl too). Sixty-third Book of the Bible* and seventeenth of the New Testament.* Titus is one of the Pastoral Epistles mentioned in the entry on the First Epistle to Timothy,* and it gives instructions similar to those found in that Epistle. Paul* instructs Titus, Bishop* of Crete, about the character of the men he is to choose in view of the pastoral difficulties peculiar to Crete. He suggests the special individual and social virtues* that the various age groups and classes in the Christian community should be encouraged to acquire. The motives for improving one's personal character are to be found preeminently in the Mysteries* of the Incarnation* and the Second Coming* of Christ. The community is to be fashioned into a leaven for Christianizing the social world about it. Good works* are to be the evidence of their faith* in God; those who engage in religious controversy are, after suitable warning, to be ignored.

Liturgical use: In the *Roman Missal,** this Epistle is read on Christmas (Mass at Midnight* and Mass at Dawn*), on Monday, Tuesday, and Wednesday of the 32nd Week in Ordinary Time* (II), on January 26, and in Baptism of Adults.* In the *Liturgy of the Hours,** outside of the Common* of Pastors it is used only in the alternate Two-Year Cycle* on Sunday, Monday, and Tuesday of the 21st Week (II). *Meaning:* To be a Christian means that Christ has changed our lives. This change ought to be visible in our actions and our attitudes. Proper belief (in sound doctrine) gives rise to proper behavior. We must live as those saved by God's mercy who are to do good works, including being good citizens.

Tobit, The Book of (TOH-buht, thuh buk uhv). Seventeenth Book of the Old Testament* and first of the Deuterocanonical Books that are accepted as canonical by the Catholic Church but not by the Protestant Churches, who call them the Apocrypha.* Written in the 2nd century B.C., this charming Book uses the literary form of religious novel (as do Jonah* and Judith*) for the purpose of instruction and edification. It contains numerous maxims like those found in the Wisdom Books as well as the customary sapiential themes: fidelity to the Law,* the intercessory function of angels,* piety toward parents, the purity of marriage,* reverence for the dead, and the value of almsgiving,* prayer,* and fasting.*

Liturgical use: In the *Roman Missal,** this Book is read during the 9th Week in Ordinary Time* (I), the Common* of Holy Men and Women, and the Rite of Marriage.* In the *Liturgy of the Hours,** it is used as a minor canticle* in the Psalter* and an additional canticle in Appendix I for Vigils. (It is read during the 25th Week in Ordinary Time [II] in the alternate Two-Year Cycle.*) *Meaning:* Even when all seems lost, we must believe that God will not leave us. By His power He will come to our aid. We on our part must remain faithful to His commandments and cultivate a spirit of prayer, love for neighbor (especially love for children and parents), and patience in affliction as well as the sanctity of marriage.

Tono Recto. *See* MUSIC.

Tonsure (TON-shuhr). Formerly a ceremony performed by the bishop* of clipping the hair of a candidate at the time of admission into the clerical state. The resultant clerical crown was a narrow wreath-like circle of hair around the head, which served as a reminder that the ecclesiastics have

separated themselves from the world. It was a symbol of the renunciation of earthly vanities. Together with the Minor Orders* it was abolished by Pope Paul VI in 1972. *See also* ADMISSION TO CANDIDACY FOR THE DIACONATE AND PRESBYTERATE, RITE OF.

Torchbearers (TAWRCH-bayr-uhz). Ministers, either two, four, or six, who carry lighted candles at various liturgical functions, during processions,* during Benediction,* and at more solemn Masses.*

Torches (TAWRCH-uhz). The candles carried by the torchbearers in candlesticks during certain ritual functions. They are used primarily during processions,* at Benediction,* and during Mass.*

Towels (TOW-uhlz). Small cloths used by the celebrant* at various times in the Liturgy,* for instance, at the Preparation of the Gifts* in Mass,* or by the bishop* when administering the Sacraments of Confirmation* and Holy Orders.*

Tra Le Sollecitudini (trah le soh-le-chee-TOO-dee-nee). Italian title (from the first three words "Among the Concerns") of the *Motu Proprio on Church Music* issued by Pius X* on November 22, 1903. This document is regarded as inaugurating the Liturgical Movement* and formulating the revolutionary program for it. It stresses that the right of "active participation in the sacred Mysteries"* and in "the public and sacred prayer of the Church" is the "first and indispensable source" of the true "Christian spirit." It also speaks of sacred music to be used, the rules governing the form of sacred compositions, the singers, the use of instruments, and the length of the various chants. *See also* LITURGICAL MOVEMENT.

Tract (trakt). The Psalm* or verses* of a Psalm formerly sung or recited after the Gradual* in Masses* from Septuagesima* to Easter,* in Masses for the Dead,* and in other penitential Masses. The name derives from the fact that the Tract was drawn from a Psalm and executed by the chanter* "in one movement," without interruption or response. It is replaced in the new *Roman Missal** by the Alleluia Acclamation* or Verse before the Gospel.* *See also* INTERVENIENT CHANTS; RESPONSORIAL PSALM.

Tradition (truh-DISH-uhn). An inherited pattern of thought, action, or behavior. Catholic Tradition may be defined as the Word of God* given to the Apostles* by Christ and the Holy Spirit* and handed down to their successors through the Church* by means of prayer* and Creeds,* liturgical practices, and authoritative writings (Popes* and bishops* in union with the Holy Father).

Apostolic tradition can be defined as the way the Church understood and lived the teachings of Jesus up to the death of the last Apostle. Apostolic Tradition and Sacred Scripture* form the one deposit of the Word of God. Thus, Scripture, Apostolic Tradition, and the Magisterium* guided by the Holy Spirit combine to bring us God's revelation* at any particular moment of time. The following excerpt from the *National Catechetical Directory** gives a fine synopsis of the way Tradition works in the Church.

> Faith is expressed in words and deeds.
>
> What we are to believe is found in Tradition and Scripture, which together form one sacred deposit of the word of God which is committed to the Church. Scripture is the word of God inasmuch as it is consigned to writing under the inspiration of the divine Spirit. To the successors of the Apostles, Sacred Tradition hands on in its full purity God's word. Thus, led by the light of the Spirit of truth, these successors can in their preaching preserve this word of God faithfully, explain it, and make it more widely known.
>
> The Tradition which comes from the Apostles is unfolded in and by the Church with the help of the Holy Spirit. (Cf. 1 Cor 12:2f) Believers grow in insight through study and contemplation. Such growth comes about through the intimate understanding of spiritual things they experience, and through the preaching of those who have received through episcopal succession the sure gift of truth.*
>
> As the commuity of believers grows in understanding, its faith* is expressed in creeds, dogmas,* and moral principles and teachings. The meaning of dogmatic formulas remains ever true and constant in the Church, even when it is expressed with greater clarity or more developed. Because they are expressed in the language of a particular time and place, however, these formulations sometimes give way to new ones, proposed and approved by the Magisterium of the Church, which express the same meaning more clearly or completely.
>
> What we believe is also expressed in the deeds of the Church community. The "deeds" in question are worship*—especially the celebration of the Eucharist,* in which the risen Christ speaks to His Church and continues His saving work—and acts performed to build up Christ's body* through service to the community of faith or voluntary service in the universal mission of the Church. (Cf. Eph 4:11f) While it is true that our actions establish the sincerity of our words, it is equally true that our words must be able to explain our actions. In catechesis* Catholics are taught a facility in talking about their faith, lest they be silent when it comes to explaining what they are doing and why.
>
> Belief can also be expressed in the visual arts,* in poetry and literature, in music,* and architecture, in philosophy, and scientific or technological achievement. These, too, can be signs of God's presence, continuations of His creative activity, instruments by which believers glorify Him and give witness to the world concerning the faith that is in them (No. 59).

We see, therefore, that the Liturgy* is an organ of the Church's Tradition. In recent years theologians have been studying the Liturgy as a means of discovering the exact nature of the Church's teachings, for example, the precise nature of the Sacrament of Baptism.* *See also* ARCHEOLOGY, LITURGICAL; DEI VERBUM; DOGMA; MAGISTERIUM.

Transept (TRAN[T]S-ept). The transverse part of a cruciform church lying at right angles to the nave,* commonly between it and the chancel,* and including the high structural part, either a dome or a tower, in front of the apse.* It served two purposes: (1) to have space around the tomb of a Saint*; (2) to have an area for the tables that held gifts for the Offertory Procession* during the Mass.*

Transfiguration (tran[t]s-fig-[y]uh-RAY-shuhn). The Lord's Transfiguration celebrates that incident in Christ's life when His Divinity shone through His humanity.

Traditionally it occurred on Mt. Tabor and was intended to prepare the Apostles* for His Passion* and Death* on the Cross.* They found it difficult to accept His kind of Messiahship. In this feast we recognize His Kingship over creation, and especially the Divinity shining through His human nature. We anticipate our own future exaltation. *Liturgical celebration:* August 6 (Feast); *theme:*a renewed awareness of the invisible reality that will be ours in the future.

Transition, Rites of (tran[t]s-ISH-uhn, raits uhv). Various rites that may be used between the three major stages of the Rite of Christian Initiation of Adults.* Marked by liturgical rites, these more serious moments of initiation are: (a) the rite of becoming a catechumen*; (b) the rite of election or choice (even if anticipated); and (c) the celebration of the Sacraments.* *See also* RITE OF CHRISTIAN INITIATION OF ADULTS.

Transitional Deacons. *See* DEACON.

Translation of Feasts (tran[t]s-LAY-shuhn; tranz-; uhv feests). The practice of transferring the liturgical celebration of a feast* to a date other than that which is considered its normal date.

(1) *Fixed* translation occurs when the celebration is moved from the date of the death of the Saint,* considered the birthday of that Saint in heaven, to a different date because of the occurrence of a higher feast on that day of his death. It would then always be celebrated on the fixed date, chosen either because of some day associated with the Saint, such as ordination, discovery, or transfer of the body, or a day unimpeded by other celebrations and approved by the Apostolic See.*

(2) An *accidental* translation may occur in a specific year when more than one feast falls on the same date. In that circumstance the one that holds the highest rank according to the table of liturgical days is observed. If several Optional Memorials* occur on the same day, any one of them may be celebrated, but only one. Should a Solemnity,* however, be impeded by a liturgical day that takes precedence over it, then it would be transferred to the closest day, not listed in numbers one to eight in the table of liturgical days, except for the one rule that in Advent,* Lent,* and Easter* such Solemnities are to be observed on the preceding Saturday. *See also* CONCURRENCE; OCCURRENCE.

Translations. *See* LECTIONARY; VERNACULAR.

Transubstantiation (tran[t]s-uhb-stan-chee-AY-shuhn; -tsee-). That teaching of the Church* which signifies the conversion or complete change of the substance of bread and wine into the substance of Christ's Body* and Blood,* which occurs through the actions of a validly ordained priest* during the Eucharistic Prayer* at Mass,* with the result that only the accidents or appearances* of bread and wine remain. These accidents do not inhere in any substance whatever, but are sustained in a miraculous way. The terminology derives from Aristotelian philosophy. *See also* APPEARANCES; CONSECRATION; EUCHARIST.

Tre Ore. *See* THREE HOURS SERVICE.

Tres Abhinc Annos (trez AHB-heenk AN-ohs). Latin title (from the first three words "Three Years Ago") of the *Second Instruction on the Proper Implementation of the Constitution on the Sacred Liturgy* issued by the Congregation of Rites* on May 4, 1967. It was the second of three such documents published by the Congregation to make the way of liturgical reform smooth until the new liturgical books* could be completed and published in accord with the stipulations of the Second Vatican Council.*

The Instruction sets forth options,* establishes only one Opening Prayer* for each Mass, authorizes changes in the Ordinary,* gives variations in the Divine Office,* and suppresses the use of the maniple.* It also declares that the "competent territorial authority" may authorize the use of the vernacular* in the Liturgies celebrated with a congregation for (a) the Canon,* (b) all the rites of Holy Orders,* and (c) the Readings* of the Divine Office, even in choral recitation. *See also* INTER OECUMENICI; LITURGICAE INSTAURATIONES.

Tridentine Mass. *See* LITURGICAL LANGUAGE—LATIN.

Triduum, Sacred. *See* SACRED TRIDUUM.

Trination (trai-NAY-shuhn). The offering of Mass* by the same celebrant* three times in one day. Because of the shortage of priests,* this permission is granted only when the needs of the faithful* call for a celebration of the second and third Mass, or when a priest must concelebrate* on some special occasion.

Trinity, Blessed (TRIN-uh-tee, BLES-uhd). The dogma* of three Persons in one God.* Although in God there is one nature, there are three distinct Persons in that nature: the Father, the Son Who proceeds from the Father by generation, and the Holy Spirit* Who proceeds from the Father and the Son by spiration. The three Divine Persons are coequal, coeternal, and consubstantial; hence, they deserve coequal glory* and adoration.* All life* begins in the Trinity, comes from the Trinity, and is destined to end in the Trinity.

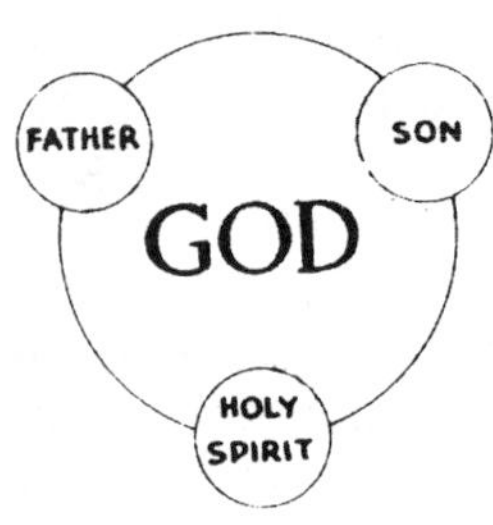

Every liturgical action begins "in the name of the Father, and of the Son, and of the Holy Spirit" and is accompanied by one or other trinitarian doxology,* such as "Glory be* to the Father, and to the Son, and to the Holy Spirit. . . ." It is because the faithful* are baptized "in the name of the Father, and of the Son, and of the Holy Spirit" that they can celebrate the Covenant* in virtue of their universal priesthood.* They can not only prepare themselves for the salvific action wrought by the Trinity but also enter into the very life of the Three Divine Persons (grace*). The Liturgy of the heavenly Jerusalem,* in which the earthly Liturgy really shares, is the perfect insertion of the Church,* the Spouse and Body* of Christ, into the life of the Son, begotten by the Father in the Holy Spirit and flowing back to the Father in the same Spirit. *See also* ASSEMBLY, LITURGICAL; COVENANT; GLORY; GOD; HOLY SPIRIT.

Trinity Sunday (TRIN-uh-tee SUHN-day; -dee). Solemnity* celebrated on the 1st Sunday after Pentecost* in honor of the Mystery* or dogma* of the Blessed Trinity or perhaps a solemn celebration of all the Paschal Mysteries put together. It evolved from a Votive Office* and Mass* around the 8th century. Eventually this Sunday was picked for its celebration in the 12th century because St. Thomas Becket* was consecrated Archbishop of Canterbury on the Sunday after Pentecost. Eventually in the 14th century, the feast was extended to the Universal Church.*

This feast is an opportune reminder of the source and goal of the whole Christian life. *See also* TRINITY, BLESSED.

Triumph of the Cross (TRAI-umf uhv thuh kraws; kros). This feast,* celebrated on September 14, also called the Exaltation of the Cross, indicates that the Cross was shown to people as a sign of salvation* and victory over evil. It commemorates the finding of the Holy Cross, the dedication of the Basilica of the Resurrection on the site of the Holy Sepulcher, and the recovery of the relics* of the Cross that had been carried off by the Persians in the early 7th century. For the faithful* the Cross has a profound meaning, for on the Cross Christ overcame the power of evil. Therefore no longer is the Cross the sign of shame or defeat, but of victory and salvation. *See also* CROSS.

Trope (trohp). A short series of words, by way of antiphons,* that were interpolated into liturgical chants of both the Mass* and the Divine Office.* They added some texts to something that existed, or created a new melody appending it to the chant, or changed the melody of an existing chant. Beginning in the 9th century, they became very popular in the Middle Ages and were much abused, so that at the Council of Trent, they were legislated out of existence. Currently the Second Vatican Council* allows their use during the "Lord, have mercy"* of the Mass.

True Cross. *See* CROSS.

Truth (trooth). Sincerity in action, character, and utterance; conformity of what one thinks or says with what one is. God is the Truth beyond compare, for in Him thought and word always represent reality. His word is truth, and this truth remains free (Jn 17:17; Rom 2:2). The Savior came full of grace* and truth (Jn 1:14). He is Truth in person (Jn 14:6), Who brings to the world the truth that makes people free (Jn 8:32) and sends the Spirit of Truth (Jn 16:13).

The Liturgy* enables us to worship God in spirit and in truth (EP I,* Prayer before Institution Narrative*). God sent us His Word to bring us His truth and His Spirit to make us holy (Trinity Sunday,* Opening Prayer*). We ask Him to keep us in the radiance of His truth (13th Sunday in Ordinary Time,* Opening Prayer), to drink of Christ's truth and expand our hearts with the joy of His promises* (33rd Sunday, Alternative Opening Prayer), for He came to testify to the truth (Christ the King,* Gospel,* B, and to present to the Father a "Kingdom of truth" (Christ the King, Preface*). By participating in the Liturgy, we too become filled with grace and truth.

Tube (tyoob; toob). A hollow, cylindrical silver tube used for Communion* under the species of wine. A sufficient number must be available for the celebrant* and each communicant. Necessarily there must be a container of water for purifying the tubes. The communicant goes to the minister of the chalice and, after the usual verbal exchange, receives a tube from the minister, puts it in the chalice, drinks a little, removes the tube, places it in a container of water held by the minister, sips a little water to purify the tube, then places it into another container. Though prevalent several centuries ago, this method of receiving the Precious Blood* is not very popular today. *See also* "Communion under Both Species" in the entry COMMUNION.

Tunic (T[Y]OO-nik). A vestment formerly worn by the subdeacon* as well as by cardinals,* bishops,* and abbots* under the dalmatic* at Pontifical Mass.* It is slightly smaller than a dalmatic but hangs like it from the shoulders and has wide, open sleeves that extend partway to the elbow. When used, it corre-

sponded in color to that of the chasuble.*

Turibius of Mogrovejo, St. (tuh-RI-bi-uhs uhv moh-groh-VAY-hoh). 1538-1606. This Spanish lawyer was named Archbishop* of Lima, Peru, in 1580 and was ordained and consecrated that year. As a tireless missionary he restored ecclesiastical discipline, founded churches, schools, hospitals, built the first seminary in the New World, learned to speak Indian dialects, published catechisms,* taught, preached, and confirmed many, including St. Rose of Lima* and St. Martin de Porres.* *Liturgical celebration:* March 23 (Opt. Mem.); *theme:* total dedication to apostolic work.

Two-Year Cycle of Readings, Alternate (too yeer SAI-kuhl uhv REED-ingz, AWL-tuhr-nuht). A set of optional Biblical and non-Biblical Readings for the Office of Readings* in the Liturgy of the Hours.*

(1) The Biblical Readings in the Office are complementary to the Readings at Mass* and so provide a conspectus of the whole History of Salvation.* This is true of the cycle of Readings incorporated in the four-volume *Liturgy of the Hours* (one-year) and the optional Two-Year Cycle that has been announced in the *General Instruction of the Liturgy of the Hours* (no. 145) and listed in *Notitiae** 119-123 (June-October 1976). A listing in English is found in *Christian Prayer,** and the full text is given in *Christian Readings,* an unofficial but approved six-volume work (Catholic Book Pub. Co., 1972-1973).

The Two-Year Cycle is like the cycle of Readings in Weekday Masses in Ordinary Time.* It is so arranged that each year nearly all the Books of the Bible* are read. The New Testament* as a whole is read each year, partly at Mass and partly in the Liturgy of the Hours; but a selection has been made of those parts of the Old Testament* that are of greater importance for the understanding of the History of Salvation and for deepening devotion.

(2) The Second Reading* from the Fathers and Ecclesiastical Writers also has a Two-Year Cycle. Besides the Reading assigned to each day in the four-volume *Liturgy of the Hours,* there is an alternate series with a larger selection of Readings so that the treasures of the Church's tradition may be made more widely available to those who pray the Office. The official series of non-Biblical Readings has not yet been published. There is a representative series of texts in *Christian Readings* to be used in conjunction with the Two-Year Cycle of Biblical Readings. *See also* CYCLE; FIRST READING; LECTIONARY; READINGS; SECOND READING.

Typical Edition (TIP-i-kuhl i-DISH-uhn). The form or version of a liturgical book* that is in the nature of a basic and exemplary edition, a type to be followed. Typical editions are printed usually in Latin by the Vatican Press under the control of the Congregation for Divine Worship and the Discipline of the Sacraments.*

The name typical edition belongs also to the edition of liturgical books containing the vernacular* translation that is published under the aegis of the Conference of Bishops* in each country. The decree declaring this to be the typical edition is issued by the president of the conference or of the national liturgical commission. The decree must make mention of the confirmation of the texts given by the Holy See.* *See also* IMPRIMATUR; LITURGICAL BOOKS; NIHIL OBSTAT; PUBLICATION OF LITURGICAL MATERIAL.

Typicon (TIP-i-kon). A liturgical book* of the Byzantine Rite* that contains the instructions for the recitation of the Divine Office* and the carrying out of various other liturgical services.

— U —

Umbrella. *See* BALDACHIN.

Unction. *See* ANOINTING.

Unitatis Redintegratio (oo-nee-TAH-tees re-deen-tay-GRAH-tsee-oh). Latin title (from the first two words "Restoration of Unity") of the *Decree on Ecumenism* issued by the Second Vatican Council* on November 21, 1964. This Decree sets forth Catholic principles on ecumenism, looking toward an eventual restoration of the unity of the Church.*

It endorses common prayer for unity but indicates that full *communicatio in sacris** cannot yet be practiced by Catholics. However, some form of it "is not only admissible but even admirable" with the Orthodox Churches "in the right circumstances and with the approval of Church authority." For the Orthodox "have true Sacraments* and especially, by virtue of apostolic succession, the Eucharist* and the priesthood" (no. 15). *See also* ATTENDING NON-CATHOLIC WORSHIP; MOVEMENT, ECUMENICAL.

United States Catholic Conference (yoo-NAIT-uhd stayts KATH-lik; -uh-lik; KON-f[uh-]ruhn[t]s). This is the secretariat and executive agency of the National Conference of Catholic Bishops.* As such, this corporation promotes and carries out the religious and civil work of the Church,* with major departments in education, communication, and social development and world peace. It has the structure and resources necessary for coordination, cooperation, and assistance in educational, public, and social concerns in the United States on national and interdiocesan levels. It serves as the publishing arm for the Bishops' Committee on the Liturgy,* which is under the NCCB. *See also* NATIONAL CONFERENCE OF CATHOLIC BISHOPS.

Universal Church (yoo-nuh-VUHR-suhl chuhrch). The one, holy, Catholic, and apostolic Church* established by Christ upon the Apostles* with Peter* as their chief without boundaries or limits except those that are found in the minds and hearts of sinful human beings. The Church was founded for all peoples and all times and as a matter of fact has spread over the whole world.* From her Roman base, this Church interacts with the Local Church,* particular churches that comprise this or that part of the human race, speaking this or that language.

The Church is universal by vocation and mission, but when she puts down her roots in a variety of cultural, social, and human terrains, she takes on different external expressions and appearances in each part of the world. An individual Church is attached to the Universal Church by solid bonds of communion, in charity and loyalty, in receptiveness to the Magisterium* of Peter, in the unity of the *lex orandi** which is also the *lex credendi,** and in the desire for unity with all the other Churches that make up the

whole. In this way, the individual Church will be capable of translating the treasure of faith* into the legitimate variety of expressions of the profession of faith, of prayer* and worship,* of Christian life and conduct, and of the spiritual influence on the people among which she dwells (*see Evangelii Nuntiandi,** 63-64).

The Local Church makes use of the liturgical calendar* of the Universal Church and enhances it with a particular calendar made up of local Saints* and Patrons*—always with the approval of the Congregation for Divine Worship and the Discipline of the Sacraments.* Furthermore in every liturgical celebration* it is the Universal Church that shines forth, for Christ is present there (LG, 26). Indeed, "the Liturgy is the summit toward which the activity of the [Universal] Church is directed . . . [and] the fount from which all her power flows" (SC, 10). Finally, "as [priests*] sanctify and govern under the bishop's* authority that part of the Lord's flock entrusted to them, they make the Universal Church visible in their own locality and lend powerful assistance to the upbringing of the whole Body of Christ" (LG, 28). *See also* CHURCH; CHURCH AND LITURGY; LOCAL CHURCH.

Universal Priesthood (yoo-nuh-VUHR-suhl PREEST-hud). The way the faithful* participate in the priesthood* of Christ for the salvation* of all. Through Baptism* the faithful are incorporated in the Church* and become the new People of God,* chosen to offer prayer* and sacrifice* through the ordained priest.* Not only this, but everything they do, all their work and activity,

can be made a spiritual sacrifice to God.

The Second Vatican Council* described the difference between the universal priesthood and the ministerial priesthood as follows:

> Though they differ from one another in essence and not only in degree, the common [or universal] priesthood of the faithful and the ministerial or hierarchical priesthood are nonetheless interrelated: each of them in its own special way is a participation in the one priesthood of Christ. The ministerial priest, by the sacred power he enjoys, teaches and rules the priestly people; acting in the person of Christ, he makes present the Eucharistic Sacrifice, and offers it to God in the name of all the people. But the faithful, in virtue of their royal priesthood, join in the offering of the Eucharist. They likewise exercise that priesthood in receiving the Sacraments,* in prayer and thanksgiving, in the witness of a holy life, and by self-denial and active charity (LG, 10).

In other words, the universal priesthood enables each person to make personally his or her own the sacrifice of Calvary, which Christ, by means of the hierarchical priesthood alone, actualizes Sacramentally in the Mass. This occurs when through active participation* we unite ourselves with the will of Christ in the sacrificial sacerdotal action and offer to God in union with Him our own lives in order to acknowledge God's sovereign dominion.

Scripture* and Tradition* call other liturgical and nonliturgical actions sacerdotal and sacrificial (such as mortifications, virginity, and the Religious life,* obligations of one's state in life, charity toward one's neighbor, private prayer, apostolate,* martyrdom,* and giving away one's possessions). These are such either because they are directed to the sacerdotal action of the Mass or because they are the effects and manifestations of it. *See also* CHRISTIFIDELES LAICI; LAITY; LITURGY—PARTICIPATION; LUMEN GENTIUM; PRIESTHOOD.

Unleavened Bread (uhn-LEV-uhnd bred). Bread from wheat, but without yeast, is used in the Western Church for the Eucharist.* Leavened bread, with yeast, is employed by the Eastern Church. Symbolically unleavened bread represents the faithfulness of the people to their new relationship with their God as St. Paul* states in 1 Corinthians* 5:7. The decision as to which type of bread Christ consecrated at the Last Supper* depends on whether or not that day occurred from the fifteenth day of Nisan to one of the following seven days, when the Jews did not eat fermented things. As yet the question has not been settled with a satisfactory answer.

Urbi et Orbi (OOR-bee et OHR-bee). The benediction at a public solemn occasion when the Pope blesses his visible audience in Rome (Urbi) and his invisible audience throughout the world (Orbi). Ordinarily given in jubilee* years and on important occasions, it carries a plenary indulgence.*

Ushers (UHSH-uhrz). The liturgical ministry of this group occurs outside the sanctuary,* as they greet the faith community at the highest moment of its self-realization, when it gathers to celebrate the Eucharist.* In taking over the abolished minor order of porter,* theirs is a ministry of hospitality, offering a joyous invitation to worship.* They show this not only in their warm friendliness and hospitality in greeting the members as they come to church but also by helping them be seated properly and making things comfortable for them with a welcome smile and a word of kindness, as well as ensuring that the physical surroundings are pleasant.

In their duties their reverent attitude should be contagious, as also their full participation* in the Divine service, by singing, listening, praying, reflecting, giving and receiving, all with the community. Some of their more explicit duties would be seating the congregation, taking up

the collection,* directing the Communion Procession,* so that the lines move smoothly, and finally voicing a pleasant good-bye as the community departs. Anyone from the laity* may perform this ministry.

—V—

Validation. *See* MARRIAGE.

Various Needs and Occasions, Masses for (VAYR-ee-uhs needz and uh-KAY-zhuhnz, mas-uhz fawr). The *General Instruction of the Roman Missal* indicates that there are three types of Masses for Various Needs and Occasions, namely Ritual Masses,* Votive Masses,* and Masses for Various Needs and Occasions. This entry will consider only the last class mentioned. Among these are the Masses that are used for the need or occasion when it arises or at some fixed time. They are divided into four sections: (a) for the Church; (b) for civil needs; (c) for various public needs; (d) for particular needs. Some are used only when the circumstance arises, for instance, in the first group, at the election of a Pope* or bishop*; others are used at fixed times, such as the Mass for the Spread of the Gospel on World Mission Day.* Types of Masses listed for civil needs are: for those who serve in public office; for peace and justice. Examples of public needs are: Masses for the blessings of man's labor on Labor Day*; for the sick; for rain; in thanksgiving. Samples of particular needs are: Masses for the family; for forgiveness of sins; for a happy death.

Ordinarily these Masses are allowed on weekdays* in Ordinary Time,* even if an Optional Memorial* occurs, but because of the specific occasion or need, the bishop may well allow some of these Masses to be celebrated when a higher ranking feast* occurs, in accordance with the rubrics* stated. *See also* RITUAL MASS; VOTIVE MASS.

Vatican (VAT-i-kuhn). Usually this term refers to the hundred and ten acres within the city of Rome, holding the cluster of buildings and churches that comprise the territorial see of the Pope* in the Catholic Church.* As a sovereign state, with a population of over 1000, it has diplomatic ties with many nations of the world. The Pope appoints a special pontifical commission to carry out the actual work of government within it.

The term on occasion is used as the central authority of the Church and its administration, or as a synonym for papacy.

Vatican Council, Second (VAT-i-kuhn KOWN-suhl, SEK-uhnd). The twenty-first Ecumenical Council. It was announced by John XXIII on January 25, 1959, convoked by him on December 21, 1961, and begun in the Basilica of St. Peter on October 11, 1962. After the death of Pope John on June 3, 1963, Paul VI ordered its continuance and brought it to a close on December 8, 1965. The Council held 168 general congregations in 10 public sessions and formulated 16 documents—two dogmatic and two pastoral Constitutions,* nine Decrees,* and three Declarations*—all reflecting its basic pastoral orientation toward Church* renewal. They are as follows (in the order of their promulgation):

*Constitution on the Sacred Liturgy**
(Sacrosanctum Concilium)
Third Session, December 4, 1963

Decree on the Media of Social Communication
(Inter Mirifica)*
Third Session, December 4, 1963

Constitution on the Church
(Lumen Gentium)*
Fifth Session, November 21, 1964

Decree on the Eastern Catholic Churches
(Orientalium Ecclesiarum)*
Fifth Session, November 21, 1964

Decree on Ecumenism
(Unitatis Redintegratio)*
Fifth Session, November 21, 1964

Decree on the Pastoral Office of Bishops in the Church
(Christus Dominus)*
Seventh Session, October 28, 1965

Decree on the Appropriate Renewal of Religious Life
(Perfectae Caritatis)*
Seventh Session, October 28, 1965

Decree on Priestly Formation
(Optatam Totius)*
Seventh Session, October 28, 1965

Declaration on Christian Education
(Gravissimum Educationis)*
Seventh Session, October 28, 1965

Declaration on the Relation of the Church to Non-Christian Religions
(Nostra Aetate)*
Seventh Session, October 28, 1965

Constitution on Divine Revelation
(Dei Verbum)*
Eighth Session, November 18, 1965

Decree on the Apostolate of the Laity
(Apostolicam Actuositatem)*
Eighth Session, November 18, 1965

Declaration on Religious Freedom
(Dignitatis Humanae)*
Ninth Session, December 7, 1965

Decree on the Missionary Activity of the Church
(Ad Gentes)*
Ninth Session, December 7, 1965

Decree on the Ministry and Life of Priests
(Presbyterorum Ordinis)*
Ninth Session, December 7, 1965

Constitution on the Church in the Modern World
(Gaudium et Spes)*
Ninth Session, December 7, 1965

The first document promulgated by the Council was the *Constitution on the Sacred Liturgy,* since its intent was to be a renewal in the life of the Church—whose summit and fount is the Liturgy. It went on to

formulate the essentials of the Liturgy in a striking and forceful manner, thus producing an enlightened revision of legislation unparalleled in Church history. The magnitude of the changes can be gauged by the words of Bishop John Dearden in the Foreword to *Thirty Years of Liturgical Renewal,* edited by Monsignor Frederick R. McManus (Washington, D.C.: USCC Publications, 1988):

> Looking back from the vantage point of today's liturgical celebrations enables us to appreciate how far we have come. The rigidly ordered liturgy of three decades ago—modified significantly by actions of Pope Pius XII—is a far cry from the joyous, reverent celebration of worship* now involving the entire Christian community. It is not only a matter of accidentals such as language; the spirit is different. The eucharis-

tic* liturgy is no longer the almost solitary action of the priest* witnessed by individuals in the congregation. It is, instead, an action of the total community presided over by the priest. And the entire event is an expression of the understanding of Church given us by the council.

See also CONSTITUTION ON THE SACRED LITURGY *and individual entries under Latin titles.*

Veil (vayl). A symbolic covering of sacred objects or persons as a sign of reverence. A bridal veil, usually white and long, is worn by the bride during the Sacrament of Marriage.* A Religious veil for the head and possibly the shoulders is considered part of the distinctive garb of Religious women, as is clear from the Church's *Order of Religious Profession.** The chalice* veil is to cover the chalice prepared for Mass* until the Preparation of the Gifts* as a sign of reverence.

Veil, Chalice. *See* CHALICE VEIL.

Veil, Humeral (vayl, HYOO-muhr-uhl). An oblong, rectangular cloth or vestment,* usually richly ornamented, placed over the shoulders and clasped in front of the chest, used in covering the hands when touching or carrying the monstrance* or other sacred vessels. The custom arose out of reverence of not touching a holy object directly. Its primary use is in giving Benediction* of the Blessed Sacrament, carrying sacred vessels* with their contents from one tabernacle* to another, or during processions* with the Sacred Host,* as on the Feast of the Body and Blood of Christ.* In some countries, viaticum* is carried to the sick in this fashion.

Veil, Tabernacle (vayl, TAB-uhr-nak-uhl). Unless competent authority determines otherwise, the presence of the Eucharist* in the tabernacle is shown by a veil.

Veiling of Images (VAYL-ing uhv IM-ij-uhz). The veiling of Crosses* and images during Passiontide,* that is, from the 5th Sunday of Lent until Good Friday,* is optional throughout the world. In the United States, the bishops suppressed this Passiontime observance.

Venerable (VEN-uhr[-uh]-buhl). Title of a Servant of God* whose cause of beatification* has been introduced and whose heroic virtue* or martyrdom has been officially established. However, Venerables cannot yet receive public liturgical veneration. *See also* BEATIFICATION; CANONIZATION.

Veneration of the Cross (ven-uh-RAY-shuhn uhv thuh kraws;-kros). Homage offered to an image of Christ crucified, with the realization that honoring the representation is honoring the person represented, not the material.

The formal liturgical occurrence of this action takes place on Good Friday,* when a veiled crucifix is brought to the altar* between two candles* and is unveiled in three stages, after each of which the words *This is the wood of the cross* are sung by the priest* and followed with a response of the faithful*: *Come, let us worship.* Then the

Crucified is kissed by the ministers and the congregation, while hymns* and chants are sung. This veneration of the Cross on Good Friday is an act of worship of Christ as Redeemer of the world,* with the crucifix as an aid to the devotion.

Veni, Creator Spiritus (VAY-nee, kray-AH-tohr SPEER-ee-toos). Latin title (from the first three words "Come, Creator Spirit") of one of the most widely used hymns* in the Church.* It is attributed to Rabanus Maurus (776-856) and is used at Evening Prayer* on Pentecost* and at the Dedication of a Church* as well as at Confirmation* and Holy Orders* and whenever the Holy Spirit* is solemnly invoked. The first stanza lauds the Spirit's part in creation; the second stresses His sanctification; the third alludes

to His seven gifts*; the fourth asks for His strength; the fifth calls upon His help; the sixth requests to know God better; and the seventh is a doxology* in honor of the Trinity.

A partial indulgence* is granted to the faithful* who recite this hymn in thanksgiving. A plenary indulgence is granted if the hymn is recited publicly on the last day of the year. The following translation is the one given in the *Enchiridion of Indulgences.**

Come, Holy Spirit, Creator blest,
And in our souls take up Your rest;
Come with Your grace and heavenly aid
To fill the hearts which You have made.

O Comforter, to You we cry,
O heavenly gift of God Most High,
O fount of life and fire of love,
And sweet anointing from above.

You in Your sevenfold gifts are known;
You, finger of God's hand we own;
You, promise of the Father, You
Who do the tongue with power imbue.

Kindle our senses from above,
And make our hearts o'erflow with love;
With patience firm and virtue high
The weakness of our flesh supply.

Far from us drive the foe we dread,
And grant us Your peace instead;
So shall we not, with You for guide,
Turn from the path of life aside.

Oh, may Your grace on us bestow
The Father and the Son to know;
And You, through endless times confessed,
Of both the eternal Spirit blest.

Now to the Father and the Son,
Who rose from death, be glory given,
With You, O holy Comforter,
Henceforth by all in earth and heaven. Amen.

Veni, Sancte Spiritus (VAY-nee, SAHNK-tay SPEER-ee-toos). Latin title (from the first three words "Come, Holy Spirit"*) of the Sequence* used in the Mass for Pentecost.* It is attributed to Stephen Langton (d. 1228), Archbishop of Canterbury. The first and second stanzas call upon the Holy Spirit to come; the third and fourth detail His strength to us; the fifth and sixth speak of Him as light and goodness; the seventh and eighth ask for His forgiveness; the ninth and tenth request grace* and eternal happiness.*

The following translation is one of the many that are extant.

Come, O Holy Spirit, come!
From Your bright and blissful Home
Rays of healing light impart.

Come, Father of the poor,
Source of gifts that will endure
Light of ev'ry human heart.

You of all consolers best,
Of the soul most kindly Guest,
Quick'ning courage do bestow.

In hard labor You are rest,
In the heat You refresh best,
And solace give in our woe.

O most blessed Light Divine,
Let Your radiance in us shine,
And our inmost being fill.

Nothing good by us is thought,
Nothing right by us is wrought,
When we spurn Your gracious Will.

Cleanse our souls from sinful stain,
Lave our dryness with Your rain,
Heal our wounds and mend our way.

Bend the stubborn heart and will,
Melt the frozen, warm the chill,
Guide the steps that go astray.

On the faithful who humbly
Trust in Your Divinity,
Deign Your sevenfold gift to send.

Give them virtue's rich increase,
Saving grace to die in peace,
Give them joys that never end. Amen. Alleluia.

Verbum Supernum (VER-boom soo-PER-noom). Latin title (from the first two words "Heavenly Word") of a hymn* used in Morning Prayer* on Corpus Christi* written by St. Thomas Aquinas* (1225-1274). It is one of the five beautiful hymns the Angelic Doctor composed in honor of Jesus in the Blessed Sacrament* at the specific request of Pope Urban IV (1261-1264) for the new Feast of Corpus Christi in 1264. The first four stanzas trace the eternal and temporal existence of the Son of God; then come an ardent and moving adjuration in the next stanza (*O Salutaris Hostia**: "O saving Victim") and a

doxology* that concludes an urgent prayer. It is a little poetic masterpiece. The last two stanzas were formerly used at Benediction of the Blessed Sacrament.*

The following is one of the many translations that exist.

The Word of God* proceeding forth,
Yet leaving not the Father's side,
Went forth upon His work on earth
And reached at length life's eventide.

By false disciple to be given
To foemen for His Blood athirst,
Himself, the living Bread from heaven,
He gave to His disciples first.

To them He gave, in twofold kind,
His very Flesh, His very Blood:
Of twofold substance are we made,
And He would freely be our Food.

By birth our fellowman was He,
Our Food while seated at the board;
He died, our ransomer to be;
He ever reigns, our great reward.

O saving Victim, opening wide
The gate of heaven to us below:
Our foes press on from every side;
Your aid supply, Your strength bestow.

To Your great Name be endless praise,
Immortal Godhead, One in Three!
O grant us endless length of days
With You in our true country.

See also EUCHARISTIC HYMNS OF ST. THOMAS.

Vernacular (vuh[r]-NAK-yuh-luhr). The language native to a region or country. Historically the liturgical language was the vernacular. After all, since Liturgy* is social worship,* involving communication between the members of the worshiping community and expressing their relationship to the Deity, the assumption should be that the form of speech used would be language intelligible to all present. However, even when the liturgical language is also the vernacular, there are usually some differences. Liturgical language will be more conservative in the method of expression, definitely avoiding

slang and even idiomatic phrases. Sometimes it may even employ older constructions in vocabulary, tending toward a more elaborate or ornate phraseology. The liturgical books* may have been written at a time of strong vitality, so a tendency is there to maintain the stability of that time, even though there have been changes in the vernacular with the passage of time.

In Christianity, the first Christians employed Aramaic. As the new communities developed, particularly in the Greek-speaking areas, they made use of their common Greek vernacular. There was great flexibility in the Church* in the early centuries, for the majority of the people eventually made use of the Greek, which was the language used throughout a great portion of the world. Eventually when Rome dominated the world, Latin became the common language, and most Greek liturgies were replaced by the Latin. At that stage, the historical contradiction seemed to arise that is common to practically all religions—the Church passed through a stage when she used almost totally language that the majority of the people did not understand.

The reasons for this strange phenomenon might be:

(1) When it comes to religion, most people are intrinsically conservative. Once the language settles into some definite form, since it deals with holy things, people think that thereby it partakes of the immutability of the Deity. Thus eventually the language certainly becomes archaic and frequently a dead language, as occurred with the use of Latin in the Catholic Church.

(2) Such a dead language is thought of as a sacred language, most probably because it is not a vernacular, but used exclusively in Liturgy with reverence proper to the Divinity.

(3) Since dead languages are practically unintelligible to the general populace, a mystique arises around the language, related to its sacredness that belongs alone to God.

(4) When foreign missionaries bring in their traditional Liturgy and impose it upon the converts, for the latter the language of the missionaries is totally foreign and unintelligible.

One of the factors involved in the use of Latin as the Church's liturgical language was the fact that in the West, as Rome conquered the various peoples, few of them had well developed languages. Therefore the

Roman empire imposed Latin as the language of the West. Eventually when Latin was no longer the vernacular and several other languages developed in Europe, much Christian Latin literature had already developed, so Latin was retained as the liturgical language. Furthermore all educated people were capable of speaking and writing Latin fluently until the 15th century. In commerce, government, theology, and in many of the more cultural activities, Latin was used heavily. But most of the common people at that time did not understand the Liturgy.

During the Council of Trent, bishops* recognized that replacing the Latin with the vernacular was desirable, and therefore did not condemn the vernacular as such. At that particular moment in history, they decided that it was not expedient to introduce the vernacular. Therefore Latin continued to be the official liturgical language in the Western Church until the Second Vatican Council* when, together with the radical liturgical reforms, adoption of the vernacular became commonplace.

The use of the mother tongue certainly aids the community in understanding and attending the liturgical worship in a more satisfactory manner and fulfilling for them the need that they have to relate to the Deity. Special regulations state that the vernacular translations, after having been accepted by the Bishops' Conferences,* would be approved by the Holy See (Canon 838). Rome was particularly careful with regard to the Sacramental* formulas, stating that they should be able to be understood according to the mind of the Church as the original Latin states them, making sure

that the texts express clearly the holy things that they signify. *See also* LITURGICAL LANGUAGE—LATIN.

Verse (vuhrs). (1) A hymn, without doxology,* that has a refrain between each strophe. Used primarily in processions,* some are still retained in the Liturgy,* such as the *Pange, Lingua** on Good Friday.*

(2) A short selection from the Scriptures* that is used as a sort of transition piece before the Gospel* during Mass. It is referred to as the Alleluia Acclamation,* or the Verse before the Gospel* (during Lent*). *See also* ACCLAMATIONS.

Versicle (VUHR-si-kuhl). (1) A phrase of a Psalm,* normally complete in itself, divided into two parts ordinarily equal in length and even symmetrical. The halves are divided by an asterisk in liturgical books,* to mark the pause that occurs during their recitation, or the inflection of the voice while singing.

(2) A short exclamatory sentence of prayer,* frequently taken from the Psalms, the first half of which is sung by the president or chanter,* the second half answered in response by the community. Such versicles occur most frequently in the Divine Office,* at the end of the Psalmody of the Office of Readings,* after the *Te Deum,** and after the Responsory* in Daytime Prayer,*

and several versicles are arranged in a series in the Intercessions* during Morning Prayer* and Evening Prayer.* Furthermore such versicles occur before the final prayer* in the formulas for blessings* in the *Ritual.**

Versions of the Bible. *See* BIBLE, VERSIONS OF THE.

Vesperal (VES-p[uh-]ruhl). The protective cloth spread over the table of altars* to keep them clean. So called because the front part, which hung over the table ledge, was folded back during the incensation at Evening Prayer,* which formerly was called Vespers.

Vespers. *See* EVENING PRAYER.

Vessels, Sacred. *See* SACRED VESSELS.

Vestibule. *See* NARTHEX.

Vestments (VEST-muhnts). The form of liturgical dress worn by the members of the clergy* during official priestly duties and religious ceremonies, such as the Mass,* processions,* the Sacraments,* and the blessing of objects or persons. The undergarments, worn over secular clothing or the Religious habit,* are usually of linen; they include the amice,* alb,* and cincture.* A surplice* on certain occasions may replace the alb; the amice, should it not be necessary to cover secular clothing, and the cincture, when the alb is form-fitting, are optional. For the outer garments, silk is the traditional fabric, but both natural and artificial fabrics, judged suitable for liturgical use by the Ordinary,* may be used. The outer garments consist of the stole,* proper to priests* and deacons,* the dalmatic* for the deacon, the chasuble* for the priest, and the cope* used in processions and other services.

A combination chasuble-alb is permitted, over which is worn the stole; its use is limited to concelebration,* Masses in particular groups, Masses outside of a church or oratory, and other local and personal circumstances which seem to be appropriate. It may not be used for the ordinary celebration of Mass in churches.

As ceremonial clothing, liturgical vestments express the nature of the occasion and to a certain extent clearly define the respective role or rank of each participant. They add a symbolism* and effectiveness in the communication pattern during worship,* reflecting concepts of majesty, mystery, revelation, incarnation, sacrifice, and communion. The modernization or modification of the historical style of vestments that has developed over the centuries is a good sign that allows the artists full opportunity to make use of their ability to bring about the significance that such a vesture offers to the various liturgical services. *See also* ALB; AMICE; CHASUBLE; CINCTURE; COLORS; COPE; DALMATIC; STOLE.

Vestry. *See* SACRISTRY.

Vexilla Regis (vek-SEEL-ah RAY-jees). Latin title (from the first two words "Royal Banners") of the hymn* sung at Evening Prayer* from Passion Sunday* to Holy

Thursday* and on the Feast of the Triumph of the Cross.* It was also sung formerly on Good Friday* when the Blessed Sacrament* was taken from the repository to the altar.* Attributed to Venantius Fortunatus (530-609), this hymn is essentially about the triumph of Christ through suffering.* The Cross becomes a throne for the Redeemer-King and the glory of the redeemed.

The following is one of the many translations that exist.

The royal banners forward go;
The Cross shines forth in mystic glow,
Where Life for sinners death endured,
And life by death for us procured.

Where deep for us the spear was dyed,
Life's torrent rushing from His side,
To wash us in that precious flood
Where mingled, Water flowed, and Blood.

Fulfilled is all that David told
In true prophetic song of old;
"Amid the nations, God," said he,
"Has reigned and triumphed from the Tree."

O Tree of beauty! Tree of light!
O Tree with royal purple dight!
Elect on whose triumphal breast
Those holy Limbs should find their rest.

On whose dear arms, so widely flung,
The weight of this world's ransom hung:
The price of humankind to pay
And spoil the spoiler of his prey.

O Cross, our one reliance, hail,
O glory of the saved, avail
To give fresh merit to the Saint,*
And pardon to the penitent.

To You, Eternal Three in One,
Let homage meet by all be done;
Whom by the Cross You do restore,
Preserve and govern evermore. Amen.

Viaticum (vai-AT-i-kuhm; vee-). The term given to Holy Communion* when someone near death receives it. It should not be deferred till such time that the sick person may lose consciousness. It may be received frequently so long as the danger of death exists; no laws of fasting* bind the recipient. All Christians in danger of death are bound by precept to receive Communion, so that they may be strengthened through the Body* of Christ, a pledge of the Resurrection,* in their passage from this life into the next. The last Sacraments*

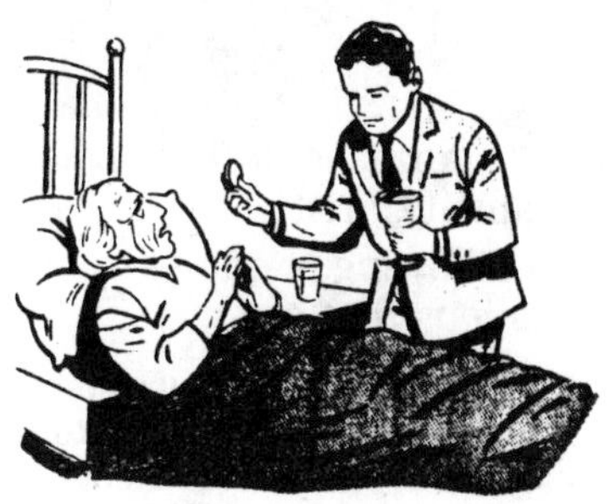

a person would receive are Penance, Anointing of the Sick,* and Viaticum. In extreme circumstances, after Sacramental Confession, even if generic, the person would receive Viaticum, and, if sufficient time exists, would then be anointed. *See also* ANOINTING OF THE SICK; PASTORAL CARE OF THE SICK.

Victimae Paschali (VEEK-tee-may pah-SKAH-lee). Latin title (from the first two words "Paschal Victim") of the Sequence* for Easter Sunday.* It is attributed to Wipo, chaplain of the German Emperor Conrad II in the 11th century, or Notker Balbulus (10th century), or Adam of St. Victor (13th century). Written specifically for the Mass,* this beautiful Sequence has a dialogue form in one of its stanzas that gives it dramatic quality. The first and second stanzas request praise for the Lamb Who has redeemed His sheep, the innocent Christ Who has reconciled sinners with God. The third stanza gives the dialogue between Mary Magdalene* and the Apostles* indicating Jesus' Resurrection.* The

fourth stanza is a hymn to the triumphant Christ.

The following is one of the many translations that exist.

Christ the Lord has risen today:
Christians, haste your vows to pay;
Offer now your praises meet
At the Paschal Victim's feet;
For the sheep the Lamb has bled,
Sinless in the sinner's stead.
Christ the Lord is risen on high;
Now He lives, no more to die.

Christ, the Victim undefiled,
Us to God has reconciled;
When in strange and awful strife
Met together Death and Life;
Christians, on this happy day
Haste with joy your vows to pay.
Christ the Lord is risen on high;
Now He lives, no more to die.

Say, O wond'ring Mary, say
What you did see on your way.
"I beheld where Christ had lain,
Empty tomb and angels twain;
I beheld the glory bright
Of the risen Lord of Light:
Christ my hope is risen again;
Now He lives, and lives to reign."

Christ, Who once for sinners bled,
Now the firstborn from the dead,
Throned in endless might and power,
Lives and reigns forevermore.
Hail, eternal hope on high!
Hail, O King of Victory!
Hail, O Prince of Life adored!
Help and save us, gracious Lord!

Vigil (VIJ-uhl). The eve or day before a specific feast* or holy day,* characterized by special offices and prayers, frequently even having a specific Mass* distinct from the one celebrated on the feast. Currently in the Roman Calendar,* the three major vigils of Easter,* Christmas,* and Pentecost* are the most important, and the custom of the specific services in preparation for these days should be maintained. The Easter Vigil* has the highest solemnity in the liturgical year,* particularly because of the formal celebration of Baptism* during it. Other feasts with vigils are those of the Birth of John the Baptist,* the Assumption of the Blessed Virgin Mary,* and the feast of Sts. Peter and Paul.* Formerly, in conjunction with the special offices and prayers, the eve was a day of fast.*

Today, the Office of Readings* is of moderate length, out of consideration for those engaged in apostolic work. It was the prayer used in the vigil services of earlier times. Should groups or individuals wish to have a longer vigil service on Sundays, Solemnities,* or Feasts,* the following directions are to be followed. After celebrating the Office of Readings up to the end of the Second Reading,* they may choose canticles* from Appendix I. Following that a Gospel* passage is read and a Homily* may reflect on that passage. This extended vigil ends with the sung *Te Deum** (You Are God) with the Concluding Prayer.* The Gospels chosen for these occasions on Solemnities and Feasts are from the *Lectionary,* otherwise from the series given in the Appendix. *See also* EASTER VIGIL; WAKE SERVICE.

Vigil of Easter. *See* EASTER VIGIL.

Vigil Lights. *See* CANDLES AND LIGHTS.

Vincent de Paul, St. (VIN-suhnt duh pawl). c.1580-1660. Son of French peasants, Vincent spent his early priesthood as chaplain* of wealthy families. Friendship with St. Francis de Sales* and others brought about conversion to a life of heroic charity.* Eventually he founded the Congregation of the Mission (Vincentians; Lazarists), helped found the Visitandines with St. Jane Frances de Chantal,* and founded the Daughters of Charity with Louise de Marillac. He established hospitals and orphanages, ransomed slaves, started a priest formation system with new

seminaries, and wrote much on spiritual topics. He is the Patron of Charitable Groups. *Liturgical celebration:* September 27 (Memorial); *theme:* showing charity to the poor.

Vincent, Deacon, St. (VIN-suhnt, DEE-kuhn). ?-c.304. One of the Church's* illustrious deacons,* and Spain's most renowned martyr,* Vincent was put to death during the persecution of Diocletian. *Liturgical celebration:* January 22 (Opt. Mem.); *theme:* courage in the face of torture and death for the Faith.*

Vincent Ferrer, St. (VIN-suhnt FER-uhr). c.1350-1419. This Spanish Dominican, teacher and ardent champion of the Avignon Popes,* eventually brought about the end of the Western Schism. Most of his life was spent preaching penance* through Western Europe in a rather charismatic atmosphere that brought a tremendous response from the people. He was also mediator in the Hundred Years' War. He is the Patron of Builders. *Liturgical celebration:* April 5 (Opt. Mem.); *theme:* preaching the Gospel* of repentance brings the Kingdom* of heaven.

Violated. *See* DESACRALIZATION.

Virgins. *See* SAINTS, LITURGICAL CATEGORIES OF.

Virgins, Consecration of. *See* CONSECRATION OF VIRGINS.

Virtues (VUHR-chooz). Beneficial habits, qualities, or powers. Christian virtues are supernatural powers given us by God through His grace* to make it possible for us to perform acts that help us attain salvation.* The most important virtues are the three *theological* virtues: faith,* hope,* and love,* which are so named because they have God for their proper object. There are also *moral* virtues, which dispose us to lead moral, or good, lives by aiding us to treat persons and things in the right way, that is, acording to the Divine Will. The chief moral virtues are: prudence,* fortitude,* justice,* and temperance* (also known as the cardinal virtues). Some of the other moral virtues are: patriotism, obedience, veracity, liberality, patience, humility, and purity.

The Liturgy* dispenses God's grace to us and hence increases and strengthens our virtues. At the same time, the moral virtue of religion* (which is part of justice*) enables us to give proper worship* to God. *See also* GOOD WORKS; RELIGION, VIRTUE OF.

Visitation. *See* MARY, BLESSED VIRGIN—FEASTS.

Visitation of the Sick. *See* ANOINTING OF THE SICK; PASTORAL CARE OF THE SICK.

Votive Candles. *See* CANDLES AND LIGHTS.

Votive Mass (VOHT-iv mas). Before the present *General Instruction of the Roman Missal*, this term included any Mass* that did not conform to the Office* of the Day and that the celebrant* chose to fulfill a personal devotion or to respond to the wish of certain faithful,* particularly those who may have offered a stipend* for the Mass. Thus it included not only what is defined today as a Votive Mass, namely, one that is of a Mystery* of Our Lord, in honor of the Blessed Virgin Mary,* or of a particular Saint* or all the Saints,* but also Masses for the Dead*; Ritual Masses* celebrated at the time that Sacraments* or Sacramentals* are administered; and the Masses for Various Needs and Occasions,* which depend on circumstances, with a specific fixed time for their celebration.

Votive Masses are allowed on weekdays* in Ordinary Time,* even if there is an Optional Memorial* that day. On other days, when there is a serious need or a pastoral advantage, such Masses may be allowed in accordance with the rubrics,* sometimes needing the permission of the Ordinary.* Examples of Votive Masses that are quite popular in many areas are those for the Sacred Heart,* the Immaculate Heart of Mary,* and Christ the Eternal High Priest.* *See also* FIRST FRIDAY DEVOTIONS; FIRST SATURDAY DEVOTIONS; FIRST THURSDAY DEVOTIONS; MASS OF CHRISTIAN BURIAL; RITUAL MASS; VARIOUS NEEDS AND OCCASIONS, MASS FOR.

Vows (vowz). Promises made to God, pertaining to a possible and better good, which is fulfilled under the virtue of religion.* Besides being implicit in the Sacraments* of Baptism* and Marriage,* vows are taken by those who enter Religious Life,* as they seek the state of greater perfection. These latter

vows are public as long as they are accepted in the name of the Church,* otherwise private. They are solemn when so acknowledged by the Church, otherwise simple. Actions performed under vows also become acts of religion, and therefore more meritorious. *See also* RENEWAL OF VOWS.

Vows, Renewal of. *See* RENEWAL OF VOWS.

Vulgate (VUHL-gayt; -guht). The official Latin translation of the Bible* that was prepared almost entirely by St. Jerome* from 382 to 405 A.D. Jerome borrowed heavily from Origen in translating the Psalter* and took Sirach,* Baruch,* and both Books of Maccabees* from Old Latin texts. He translated everything else from the existing Hebrew, Aramaic, or Greek manuscripts.

Jerome's translation eventually caught on with the people and became known as the *"vulgata"* (from the Latin word for "widespread"). From the 8th century onward this translation became the official Latin Version used in the Liturgy* by the Roman Rite.*

In 1546, the Council of Trent declared the Vulgate to be "authentic in public readings, disputations, preachings, and exposition" because it conforms to the original texts and contains no errors in faith* or morals. A revised version of the Vulgate was published by the Church* in 1979, and it is used in all Latin typical editions* of the liturgical books.* *See also* BIBLE, VERSIONS OF.

—W—

Wafer. *See* BREAD.

Wake Service (wayk SUHR-vuhs). This vigil* or watch takes place a day or so before the deceased is brought to the church for burial; during it, the mourners visit the body and offer condolences to the bereaved. In this country it occurs in funeral parlors, rather than the home; the wake service may take place in the home, the funeral parlor, or even in the church as long as it is separated from the funeral itself.

Though the Rosary* was the usual prayer at the wake in times past, the new *Rite of Funerals** schedules a vigil service in the form of the celebration of the Liturgy of the Word.* It begins with a greeting* including an explanation, a Psalm,* and a short prayer. Thereupon a suitable reading from Scripture* occurs, followed by a Homily.* General Intercessions,* particularly for the deceased person and the friends and relatives, conclude with either the Lord's Prayer* or some other appropriate prayer. Though the Homily is optional, it can be most effective in this situation for the friends and relatives. See also FUNERAL RITES AND CEREMONIES.

Washing of the Feet (WAHSH-ing uhv thuh feet). An optional portion of the Holy Thursday Liturgy.* After the Gospel* for that day,

which recounts Christ washing the feet of His disciples to teach them humility, the celebrant* performs a ceremonial washing of feet of members of the community chosen to represent the faithful.* For some centuries it was performed separately from the Eucharistic Celebration, but recent legislation has returned it to its proper position after the Homily.* This ceremony is also called the *Mandatum*, since it is the Latin word for the commandment given by Christ to His disciples to love one another. *See also* HOLY THURSDAY.

Washing of the Hands. *See* ABLUTIONS.

Water (WAWT-uhr; WOT-). Symbolizing both internal and external purification, water is frequently used in the Liturgy,* before Mass* on Sundays during the sprinkling* which then takes the place of the Penitential Rite,* during Mass as on the Easter Vigil,* at Funerals,* Marriages,* and similar functions. Furthermore, water is also mingled in limited quantity with the wine used at Mass. Our first exposure to water is in the administration of Baptism,* signifying the cleansing from original sin. *See also* HOLY WATER.

Water, Baptismal. *See* BAPTISMAL WATER.

Water, Holy. *See* HOLY WATER.

Way of the Cross. *See* STATIONS OF THE CROSS.

We Lift Them Up to the Lord. *See* INTRODUCTORY DIALOGUE.

Wedding. *See* MARRIAGE.

Week (week). The combination of seven successive days as a division of time, making it one of the units of time in a liturgical year*; the year is composed of fifty-two weeks. For the Church* the week begins with Sunday* and closes with Saturday or the Sabbath. Explanations for the choice of seven for the length of the week vary, some saying that the Pleiades total seven and that seven winds blow from seven directions; but Christians prefer to underline the fact that seven is a sacred and mystic number, more probably derived from the description in the Bible* of the work of creation taking six days with the seventh being a day of rest.

Jews and Christians alike designated the days of the week by numbers, rather than by names, so that even Sunday was called by them the first day; however the seventh day, was called the Sabbath. Astrologers assigned names of planets to the days, beginning with Sunday. Rome adopted this planetary week, using Latin names. Later Germanic tribes did the same but substituted Teutonic deities for the Roman ones. These are the names we know today. Only Sunday lends itself to Christian interpretation, for an early symbol of Christ in His Incarnation* and Resurrection* is the Rising Sun. *See also* SUNDAY.

Week of Prayer for Christian Unity (week uhv prayr for KRIS-chuhn YOO-nuht-ee). Formerly known as the Church Unity Octave, this is an annual period of eight days from January 18 to January 25, closing on the Feast of the Conversion of St. Paul,* during which all Christians are asked to pray that the unity Christ wants will be achieved when and how He wills.

The Chair of Unity Octave was founded by an American Episcopalian clergyman in 1908 with the special purpose of a union between the Anglican Church and the Catho-

lic Church, but including intentions for other Christians and non-Christians. At that time, January 18 was the Feast of St. Peter's Chair in Rome, hence the name. An early result was the reception of a group of Franciscans into the Catholic Church in 1909.

Later Benedict XV extended the Church Unity Octave to the whole Church, and Pius XII insisted on the name change to Week of Prayer for Christian Unity, a movement begun by Abbé Paul Couturier in the early 1930s who substituted a new formula of prayer for unity so that all persons, no matter what their faiths, could pray according to their own consciences. Yearly now the working groups of the World Council and the Catholic Secretariat for Promoting Christian Unity plan a common service during this week of prayer.

Weekday (WEEK-day). This term is the English equivalent of the Latinized term ferial day. The Latin meaning is a holiday or a day of rest and was originally used as a day on which no feast* or fast* was observed. The days of the week in the Christian terminology were called, first of all, the Day of the Lord for Sunday, then each of the following days, ferial two, three, and so forth, until the seventh day which was called Sabbath. Thus weekday is opposed to Sunday and ordinarily means day of the week on which no feast is assigned. Ferials in Advent,* Christmas Time,* Lent,* and Easter* are privileged, so that there is not as much freedom as to the choice of Masses allowed. The weekdays in Ordinary Time* allow almost any type of Mass to be celebrated, including that of any of the thirty-four Sundays in Ordinary Time to the Votive Masses,* Masses for the Dead,* and Masses for Various Needs and Occasions.* With the reduced number of Saints* in the recent Roman Calendar,* the significance of the weekday cycle is restored. *See also* WEEK.

Wenceslaus, St. (WEN-tsuhs-lows). c.903-929. Wenceslaus, a Bohemian raised a Christian, took over the kingdom after his father's death and ruled strictly, justly, suppressed oppression, and encouraged Christianity. Once his son was born, his jealous brother Boleslaus attacked him, and he died at the chapel door. He is the Patron of Bohemia. *Liturgical celebration:* September 28 (Opt. Mem.); *theme:* earthly kingdoms pale in light of the Kingdom of God.*

White Garment. *See* GARMENT, WHITE.

Wine (wain). The fermented juice of grapes, with no additives, used in the Christian Eucharist* as one of the elements to celebrate the Mass.* It is symbolic of our union with Christ, Who is the true vine (Jn 15) together with fellow Christians. Upon consecration* it is changed into the Blood* of Christ. A small quantity of water is mixed with the wine at Mass as was the custom in Palestine when Christ lived.

Alcoholic priests may use a weaker wine, even grape juice by indult. When they concelebrate,* they may receive only under the form of Bread.* At first all received Communion* under both forms; later Communion became more infrequent, and, for practical reasons, the reception from the cup by the laity* was prohibited. Recent regulations allow the laity to receive under both species* whenever practical. *See also* MUSTUM; PREPARATION OF THE GIFTS; WATER.

Wisdom, The Book of (WIZ-duhm, thuh buk uhv). Twenty-seventh Book of the Old Testament* and fifth of the Deuterocanonical Books that are accepted as canonical by the Catholic Church but not by the Protestant Churches, who call them the Apocrypha.* Written about 100 B.C. by an unknown member of the Jewish community at Alexandria, Egypt, this Book had for its primary purpose the edification of the author's coreligionists in a time when they were experiencing suffering and oppression, in part at least at the hands of apostate fellow Jews. To convey his message he made use of the most popular religious themes of his time, namely, the splendor and worth of Divine Wisdom, the glorious events

of the Exodus, God's mercy,* the folly of idolatry, and the manner in which God's justice is vindicated in rewarding or punishing the individual soul.

Liturgical use: In the *Roman Missal,** this Book is read on the 16th and 32nd Sundays in Ordinary Time* (A), the 13th, 25th, and 28th Sundays (B), and the 19th, 23rd, and 31st Sundays (C) as well as the 32nd Week in Ordinary Time (I), Friday of the 4th Week of Lent,* the Common of Martyrs* and Doctors,* Masses for the Dead,* and the Votive Mass* of the Holy Cross.* In the *Liturgy of the Hours,** it is used only in the Common of Martyrs,* Doctors,* and Holy Men.* It also gives rise to a minor canticle* in the Psalter* and three additional ones in Appendix I for Vigils. *Meaning:* We must not seek after worldly wisdom. True wisdom is of God. It comes from Him, is obtained by prayer,* and brings all good things to us. Israel's past is a manifestation of God's Wisdom and—in the light of New Testament revelation*—so is the life of Jesus, Who is the very Wisdom of God incarnate.

Witnesses (WIT-nuhs-uhz). Those persons who can present evidence, based on immediate and personal knowledge, of some event, experience, or fact. For this purpose, two witnesses are to be present at the exchange of vows during the Sacrament of Marriage,* who together with the celebrant* represent the Church* in this instance.

Women as Ministers (WIM-uhn az MIN-uh-stuhrz). A statement from the Bishops' Committee on the Liturgy,* based on the Third Instruction of 1970 (*Liturgicae Instaurationes**), allows the following. Except for service at the altar* itself, women may exercise liturgical ministries, for instance, reader,* chanter,* leader of song,* commentator,* director of liturgical participation. The president of the celebration* will judge this matter in view of the mentality and culture of the congregation.* As required for men, worthiness of character and life and any other qualifications are likewise expected of women. Women reading during the Liturgy of the Word* do so from the same lectern* where the other Readings* are proclaimed. Their position for the other ministries will depend on the circumstance or convenience.

Despite the fact that women may serve liturgically in these fashions, they have been denied the opportunity to be instituted into the ministry of Reader* and Acolyte.* Though these two ministries are no longer considered Minor Orders,* they are still reserved to men alone.

The possibility of ordination of women is highly controversial since Vatican Council II,* and certainly it is clear that research to develop a doctrine that could bring about the ordination of women is permissible. The Pontifical Biblical Commission and theologians put no obstacles in the way. Nevertheless, currently, statements from the last two Popes* indicate that the present stand of the Church* is based on an unbroken tradition, so that only men at this time may receive priestly ordination. (*See also* MULIERIS DIGNITATEM.)

There is a strong ecumenical feminist liturgical movement alive, particularly among Protestant and Catholic women. They try to promote the idea of having women in a priestly ministry, but with the strong opposition from the Vatican,* they are currently concentrating on renewal of ministry and Church, trying to open the eyes of the Church to their own social, personal, and spiritual needs. While the majority continue to be affiliated with their own Church traditions, they try to test experimentally, where allowed, various ideas to renew the ministry, so that eventually the current patriarchy may be definitely transformed from the existing religious tradition. *See also* EXTRAORDINARY MINISTERS OF HOLY COMMUNION; MINISTERS; MINISTRIES.

Word (of God) (wuhrd [uhv god]). A word may be defined as an utterance that communicates meaning. (1) St. John* (1:1) uses this term to designate the Son of God, for He is the complete "expression" of the Father. Christ, the Word of God, is the perfect Mediator of creation and the Divine Life* (Rv 19:11-16). As the Speech of God and Revealer of the Father, Christ opens to the understanding of the people the nature and purposes of God and discloses the Divine Wisdom to human beings.

(2) The term "Word of God" is also applied to the Bible* or to Scriptural Readings* in liturgical celebrations. *See also* BIBLE; BIBLE AND LITURGY; LITURGY OF THE WORD.

Work (wuhrk). Activity in which persons utilize strength or faculties to make or perform something. In the Old Testament,* the works of God are creation (Ps 104) and His revelation: His Covenant* and the active presence of the Creator in all sacred history. In the New Testament,* this expression designates the works and saving acts of Christ (Mt 11:2-19) that testified to His mission (Jn 5:36; 10:25; 14:11; 15:24; Rom 14:20).

The Greek word for work (*ergon*) together with the word for people (*laos*) lies behind our word Liturgy.* Hence, the Liturgy may fittingly be termed the "work of the people"—and specifically, God's People. It is the chief good work* Christians can accomplish and leads to all other good works.

The Liturgy of the Hours* has traditionally been called the "work of God" (*Opus Dei**). *See also* GOOD WORKS; LITURGY; OPUS DEI.

World (wuhrld). In the broad sense, the system of created things, all creation, the universe. As a result of sin, the unity and harmony of the world and the human community have suffered a disorder. In the Paschal Mystery* Christ has brought about reconciliation to

reestablish the cosmic order (Col 1:20). Through Christ, God Himself has accomplished this reconciliation (2 Cor 5:18ff), and the universe has been repacified. In the Liturgy* Christ becomes the "present" that renews the Mystery of cosmic reconciliation.

The Sacraments* and the Sacramentals* constitute the principal means by which this reconciliation of the world to God's creative plan takes place. The Sacraments, in particular, can be extended to practically every object with which human beings come in contact in their daily lives and can invest almost every situation in which they find themselves. As a result, Christians can be said to live in a "Christified" world, which they build up day after day by means of the Liturgy, prayer,* and good works.* *See also* GOOD WORKS; LITURGY; SACRAMENTS; SACRAMENTALS; SALVATION.

World Mission Day (wuhrld MISH-uhn day). The second last Sunday of October is chosen as World Mission Day, in which the special Votive Mass* (no. 14) is either allowed or prescribed. Proper prayers should be included in the General Intercessions,* and the significance of the day should be stressed in the Homily,* so that the People of God realize their commitment as a community to extend Christ's Church* throughout the world, particularly since evangelization is critical to the future of this world. A specific theme is chosen each year at the national level in the United States. *See also* NATIVE CUSTOMS.

World without End. *See* FOR EVER AND EVER.

Worship (WUHR-shuhp). The prayerful homage and recognition given to God by acts of the body or mind, or both, to acknowledge His dignity, superior position, worth, and primarily supreme dominion. These actions may be public and communal, or private. Worship is a genuine expression by which humanity exhibits its dependence upon the loving Creator. The term is certainly applied to the act of adoration* to God alone, also called latria.* However, when this term

occasionally is used in relation to the Saints,* because of their special relationship to God, it is a more properly termed veneration or dulia.*

The forms of worship are varied: praise,* petition,* repentance,* thanksgiving,* adoration, and sacrifice.* The highest form of worship would surely be considered the Sacrifice of the Mass,* since it commemorates the greatest act of worship by which Jesus gave Himself totally to God the Father. The reception of the other Sacraments* allows us not only to honor the supreme Deity but to receive through them the grace necessary to eventually achieve an abundant and everlasting life.

Fundamentally we can say that worship has three dimensions: (1) God's relation toward creation and particularly humans, through the coming of Christ His Son whose ministry, Death* and Resurrection* is totally an act of self-giving; (2) the Church* trying to live out within herself God's actions; (3) the life of the Church, symbolic of the world,* with God acting as Creator, Redeemer, and Sanctifier.

Whatever our culture may be, Christian worship, particularly the Eucharistic action as central to it, can be the transforming act that reshapes us despite any failures or brokenness. We try to be careful that in celebrating, we do not, through that activity, divorce ourselves from the concerns of the world and life itself. Furthermore, we become wary that the Church, in trying to transform the world, does not become so accommodated to it or conditioned by a cultural pattern that the transforming and ecstatic power coming from God might be lost.

Since there will always be at least a certain number of people trying to discover God as the basis, the center, of all our activity, the Church tries to respond to this situation. Thus the Church is open in her worship to any anxiety of the congregation; she realizes the constant tension between change and stability; she relates the personal with the broad scope of the Incarnation*; she willingly shapes and nurtures a faith* that is willing to explore and question so as to develop into true and full worship. *See also* ADORATION; CULTURE AND WORSHIP; DULIA; EUCHARISTICUM MYSTERIUM; HYPERDULIA; LATRIA; LITURGY.

—Y—

Yahweh (YAH-way). The proper personal name of the God of Israel, signifying, "I am who am" (Ex 3:14f). It is commonly explained in reference to God as the absolute and necessary Being. It may be understood of God as the Source of all created beings. Out of reverence for this name, the term *Adonai,* "my Lord," was later used as a substitute. The word LORD is substituted for "Yahweh" in Bible translations used in the Liturgy*: the *New American Bible,* the *Jerusalem Bible,* and the *Revised Standard Version* as well as the *Grail Psalter.*

Year, Liturgical. *See* CHURCH YEAR.

You Are God. *See* TE DEUM.

Youth Ministry (yooth MIN-uh-stree). Although the Church* must be aware of all groups within herself, she pays special heed to the youth, for the future of the Church depends upon the spiritual and personal growth of young persons. In

this ministry then the particular needs and challenges of modern youth must be met to draw them deeply into the ministry expected of the People of God* and to make them committed followers of Christ. Most dioceses* have a youth office called *Catholic Youth Organization.* Nationally there is a headquarters for them in Washington under the United States Catholic Conference. A document from that office, *A Vision of Youth Ministry,* presents the principles, goals, dimensions, philosophy, components, and hope for youth ministry. Basically youth ministry is *to* youth, *with* youth, *by* youth, and *for* youth.

—Z—

Zechariah, Canticle of. *See* CANTICLE OF ZECHARIAH.

Zechariah, The Book of (zek-uh-RAI-uh, thuh buk uhv). Forty-fifth Book of the Old Testament* and eleventh of the Minor Prophets.* Zechariah's initial prophecy is dated to 520 B.C., the same year in which Haggai* received the prophetic call. His prophecies promote the work of rebuilding the Temple and encourage the returned exiles, especially their leaders, Joshua and Zerubbabel. They also portray the Messiah* and the triumphant Messianic Age. He portrays the Messiah as a Good Shepherd* rejected by

the people (11:1-17), who would enter Jerusalem in great honor and riding on a donkey (9:9f), be sold for 30 pieces of silver (11:12f), have his side pierced (12:10), shed his blood for the sins of the world (13:17), and come to the world a second time (14:4).

Liturgical use: In the *Roman Missal,** this Book is read on the 14th Sunday in Ordinary Time* (A), the 12th Sunday (C), and Saturday of the 25th Week to Tuesday of the 26th Week (I) as well as the Common* of the Blessed Virgin,* the Votive Mass* of the Triumph of the Cross, the Masses for the Spread of the Gospel and In Time of War and Civil Disturbance, and the Rite of Penance.* In the *Liturgy of the Hours,** it is used on Tuesday, Wednesday, and Thursday of the 28th Week as well as Tuesday through Saturday of the 33rd Week. *Meaning:* God is in total control of life and history. Just as Jesus, the Messiah, did what God willed for Him (and had the Prophets prophesy about Him), so should we do whatever God wills for us. In this lies our earthly as well as our eternal happiness.*

Zephaniah, The Book of (zef-uh-NAI-uh, thuh buk uhv). Forty-third Book of the Old Testament* and ninth of the Minor Prophets.* Zephaniah's prophetic ministry took place during the first decade of Josiah's reign (640-609 B.C.). The Prophet details the judgment against Judah and Israel, the woes against other peoples, and the Messianic promise* for Israel (a remnant*) and eventually all nations. He is especially important for his delineation of the concept of the *Poor of Yahweh.* Instead of a social group within the Chosen People, he broadens the idea to include all the *oppressed* who see God as their only defense and all the *indigent* who know God as the only One Who can fill their needs.

Liturgical use: In the *Roman Missal,** this Book is read on the 3rd Sunday of Advent* (C), 4th Sunday in Ordinary Time* (A), Tuesday of the 3rd Week of Advent, December 21, and the Visitation* as well as the Common* of Holy Men and Women, Thanksgiving Day,* and the Masses for the Unity of Christians and In Thanksgiving. In the *Liturgy of the Hours,** it is used on Sunday and Monday of the 21st Week and also gives rise to an additional canticle* in Appendix I for Vigils. *Meaning:* Like the Poor of

Yahweh, we should be always cognizant of our insufficiency and put all our trust in God. We should repent for our sins, adore the Almighty Lord, and abandon ourselves to His will—for He seeks nothing else but our good.

Zucchetto (zoo-KET-oh). A small, semispherical headdress, skullcap, worn by the Pope,* cardinals,* bishops,* prelates,* and abbots.* It originated for hygienic reasons when clerics* had the tonsure.* It has a knot of braid in the center by which it can be grasped and is ordinarily made of cloth or silk. The color* is white for the Pope, red for cardinals, purple for bishops, and black for abbots.

APPENDICES

1. CHRONOLOGICAL TABLE OF MASS PRAYERS

1) The *first vertical column* gives the title or first few words of the prayer.
2) The *first horizontal column* lists centuries.
3) An *asterisk* identifies those prayers of Hebrew origin, which go back more than 1000 B.C.
4) The *crosses* indicate the century in which the existence of the prayer was known.
5) The *light shadings* refer to the period when the use of the prayer was optional.
6) The *heavy shadings* indicate when the prayer became obligatory in the Roman Rite.
N.B. This Table is, of course, only approximate.

Prayer	Century																			
	1	2	3	4	5	6	7	8	9	10	11	12	13	14	15	16	17	18	19	20
Prayers at Foot of Altar																				
Psalm 42 (Iudica me)*																				
Glory be					+															
Our help, etc. (Adiutorium)*																				
Confiteor																				
May almighty God (Misereatur)																				
May the Almighty (Indulgentiam)																				
O God, You (Deus tu)*																				
The Lord (Dominus)*																				
Let us pray (Oremus)																				
Take away (Aufer a nobis)					+															
We beseech You (Oramus te)																				
Incensation																				
Introductory Rites																				
Entrance Antiphon (Introit)*																				
Greeting																				
Penitential Rite																				
Confiteor																				
Other forms with Kyrie																				
Or sprinkling of holy water																				
Kyrie*																				
Gloria		+																		
Opening Prayer																				

Prayer	1	2	3	4	5	6	7	8	9	10	11	12	13	14	15	16	17	18	19	20
Liturgy of the Word																				
First Reading (OT)																				
Intervenient Chants																				
Gradual*																				
Alleluia*																				
Tract*																				
Cleanse my heart																				
Responsorial Psalm																				
Second Reading (NT)																				
Epistle																				
Alleluia Verse																				
Cleanse My Heart																				
Gospel	+																			
Homily																				
Creed/Profession of Faith				+																
General Intercessions																				
Liturgy of the Eucharist																				
Offertory Antiphon*																				
Offertory Prayers/Presentation of the Gifts'																				
Accept/Presentation of Bread									+											
O God/By the Mystery					+															
We Offer/Presentation of Chalice																				
In a humble/Lord God, we ask*											+									
Come, O Sanctifier (Veni, Sancte)											+									
Through (Per intercessionem)																				
May this incense (Incensum)																				
Let my prayer (Dirigatur)*																				
May the Lord (Accendat)																				

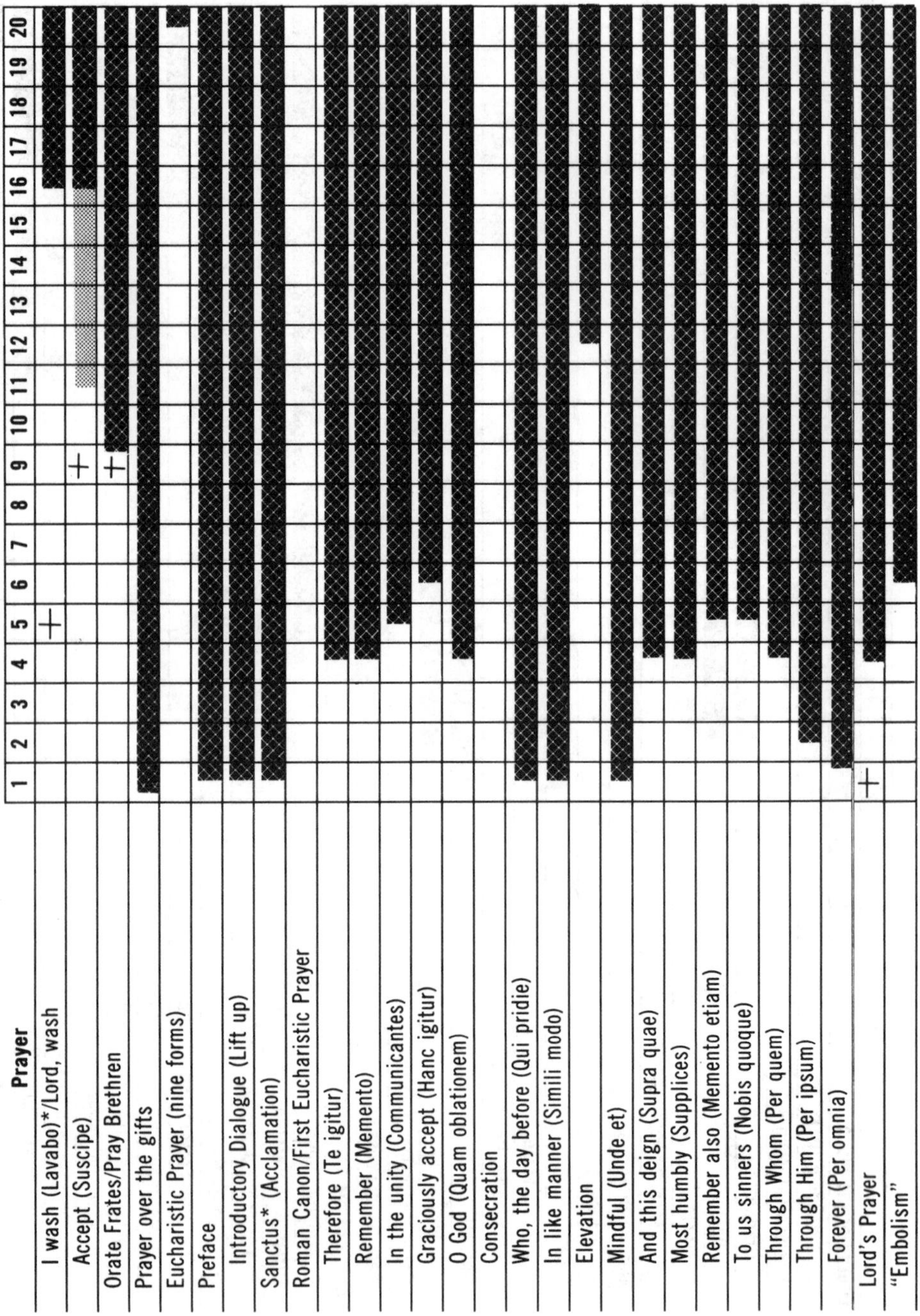

	Century																			
Prayer	1	2	3	4	5	6	7	8	9	10	11	12	13	14	15	16	17	18	19	20
I wash (Lavabo)*/Lord, wash					+															
Accept (Suscipe)									+											
Orate Frates/Pray Brethren									+											
Prayer over the gifts																				
Eucharistic Prayer (nine forms)																				
Preface																				
Introductory Dialogue (Lift up)																				
Sanctus* (Acclamation)																				
Roman Canon/First Eucharistic Prayer																				
Therefore (Te igitur)																				
Remember (Memento)																				
In the unity (Communicantes)																				
Graciously accept (Hanc igitur)																				
O God (Quam oblationem)																				
Consecration																				
Who, the day before (Qui pridie)																				
In like manner (Simili modo)																				
Elevation																				
Mindful (Unde et)																				
And this deign (Supra quae)																				
Most humbly (Supplices)																				
Remember also (Memento etiam)																				
To us sinners (Nobis quoque)																				
Through Whom (Per quem)																				
Through Him (Per ipsum)																				
Forever (Per omnia)																				
Lord's Prayer	+																			
"Embolism"																				

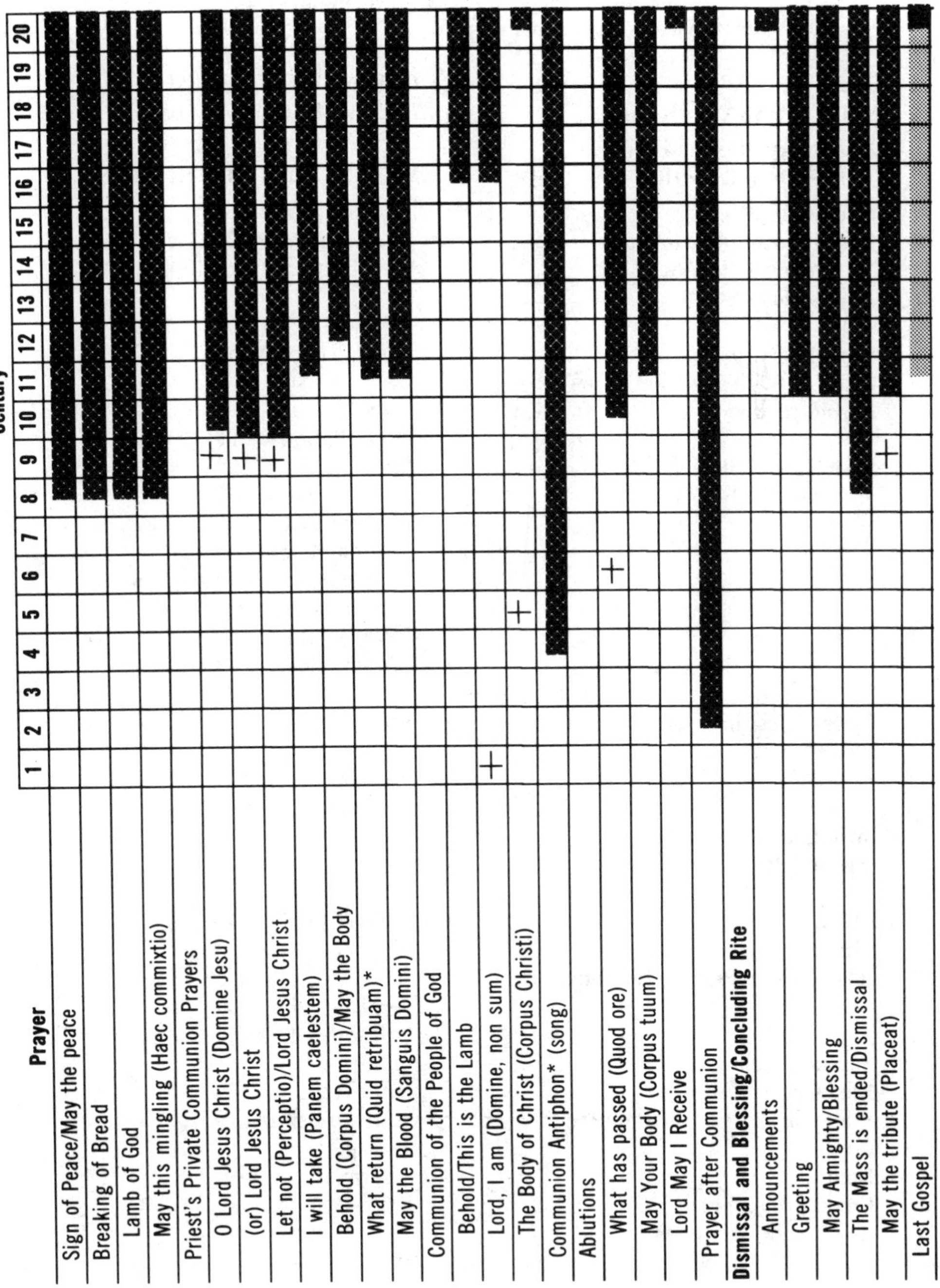

Prayer	Century 1	2	3	4	5	6	7	8	9	10	11	12	13	14	15	16	17	18	19	20
Sign of Peace/May the peace																				
Breaking of Bread																				
Lamb of God																				
May this mingling (Haec commixtio)																				
Priest's Private Communion Prayers																				
O Lord Jesus Christ (Domine Jesu)									+											
(or) Lord Jesus Christ									+											
Let not (Perceptio)/Lord Jesus Christ									+											
I will take (Panem caelestem)																				
Behold (Corpus Domini)/May the Body																				
What return (Quid retribuam)*																				
May the Blood (Sanguis Domini)																				
Communion of the People of God																				
Behold/This is the Lamb																				
Lord, I am (Domine, non sum)	+																			
The Body of Christ (Corpus Christi)					+															
Communion Antiphon* (song)																				
Ablutions																				
What has passed (Quod ore)						+														
May Your Body (Corpus tuum)																				
Lord May I Receive																				
Prayer after Communion																				
Dismissal and Blessing/Concluding Rite																				
Announcements																				
Greeting																				
May Almighty/Blessing																				
The Mass is ended/Dismissal																				
May the tribute (Placeat)									+											
Last Gospel																				

2. COMPARISON OF THE 1570 MASS WITH THE 1970 MASS

Explanation: Type, indention, size of type, typeface show relative importance
- - - - - - - - - - - corresponds to, but somewhat changed in form or position
boldface and *italics* indicates a changed position; also ________________
italics specifies an optional element

ORDER OF MASS: PAUL VI MISSAL (1970)	ORDINARY OF THE MASS: PIUS V MISSAL (1570)
Introductory Rites and LITURGY OF THE WORD	**MASS OF THE CATECHUMENS**
Introductory Rites	Entrance Rite
Entrance Antiphon (or song)	*Asperges (sprinkling rite)*
Veneration of the Altar & Kiss	Veneration of the Altar
Incensation of Altar	
	Prayers at the Foot of Altar
Sign of the Cross	Sign of the Cross
Greeting (with alternate forms)	
Introduction	
	Antiphon with Psalm 42
Sprinkling of Blessed Holy Water	
or Penitential Rite (3 forms)	
	Confiteor by Priest
	Confiteor by Servers
	Versicles and Responses
	Prayer going up to altar
	Prayer while kissing altar
	Incensation of Altar
	Introit
Kyrie (unless in penitential rite)	Kyrie
Gloria	Gloria
	Kissing of Altar
	Greeting
Invitation to Prayer with Silent Prayer	
Opening Prayer	Collect
LITURGY OF THE WORD	THE WORD OF GOD
First Reading: OT	
Responsorial Psalm with Antiphon	
	Epistle
	Gradual; Tract
Second Reading: NT	
Alleluia	Alleluia
Prayer before Gospel (quiet)	Prayer before Gospel
Gospel	Gospel
Homily	*Sermon*
Creed/Profession of Faith	Creed
General Intercessions	

LITURGY OF THE EUCHARIST and *Concluding Rites*		MASS OF THE FAITHFUL
LITURGY OF THE EUCHARIST		
PREPARATION OF ALTAR AND GIFTS		OFFERTORY
Procession		
Presentation of Bread (*aloud*)	----------------	Offering of Bread
Preparation of Wine (*silent*)	----------------	Preparation of Wine
Presentation of Wine (*aloud*)	----------------	Offering of Wine
Acceptance Prayer (*quiet*)	----------------	Acceptance Prayer
		Prayer to bless the sacrifice
Incensation of offerings, altar, priests and people (no prayers)	----------------	*Incensation of offerings, all priests and people (four prayers)*
Washing of Hands (*quiet*)	----------------	Washing of Hands and Psalm 25
		Our offering to the Trinity
Invitational Prayer with Response		Invitational Prayer with Response
Prayer over the Gifts		Secret Prayer
EUCHARISTIC PRAYER (nine forms) with people's acclamations	----------	PREFACE, SANCTUS, CANON
COMMUNION RITE		
The Lord's Prayer (congregation)		The Lord's Prayer (priest)
Embolism and Doxology	----------------	Embolism
Prayer for Peace with Sign of Peace		
Lamb of God; Breaking of the Bread		Breaking of Bread
		Lamb of God
Priest's Private Preparation (one prayer)	----------------	Priest's Private Preparation (three prayers)
Communion		
Invitation and Response		
Communion of the Priest	----------------	Communion of the Priest (three prayers)
Communion of the People (with singing)	----------------	Communion of the People (several prayers)
Cleaning of Vessels (one prayer; quiet) (may occur after Mass)	------------	Ablutions (two prayers)
Song of Praise or Period of Silence		
Prayer after Communion		Postcommunion Prayer
Concluding Rite		
Announcements		
Greeting		Greeting
		Dismissal
		Prayer of Priest
Blessing (several forms)	----------------	Blessing
Dismissal		
		Last Gospel

3. SELECT CHRONOLOGY OF MAJOR EVENTS IN THE HISTORY OF THE LITURGY

(Note: The origin of the individual parts of Mass is not detailed here since it is given in the Chronological Table of Mass Prayers, pp. 656-659.)

6 B.C.– 30 A.D. During His lifetime Jesus fulfills the requirements of the Mosaic Law: circumcision (Lk 2:21), purification (Lk 2:22), annual pilgrimage to the Temple for Passover (Lk 2:41). He is baptized by John the Baptist (Lk 3:21), teaches in the synagogue (Mk 1:21), and takes an active part in the synagogal worship (Lk 4:17-21). He spends whole nights in prayer (Lk 6:12) and teaches His disciples to pray (Lk 11:1-4). He celebrates the feasts of Israel and also makes use of the daily prayers of the pious Jews of His time: the Shema of Morning Prayer (Mk 12:29) and the *berakoth* (praises: Mk 6:41; 8:7; 14:22-23), transforming them into a prayer of His own (Messianic joy: Mt 11:25-27).

Jesus emphasizes purity of worship: by expelling the buyers and sellers from the Temple (Mk 11:15), by explaining the true observance of the Sabbath (Mk 2:18-28), by calling for a right inner attitude when offering sacrifice and above all when praying (Mt 5:23; 6:5ff; Lk 18:13). And He sets forth what the true worship of God comprises: "The hour is coming, and is now here, when true worshipers will worship the Father in Spirit and truth" (Jn 4:23).

30 Jesus institutes the Eucharist at the Last Supper. Within the context of a Jewish meal, most probably the Passover meal, Jesus sets down the core of the Christian Liturgy in a great prayer of blessing-thanksgiving in common use. This prayer was an invocation of God, using many of His Divine Names, and then a thanksgiving to Him for His gifts (bread and wine among them). Mention was explicitly made of God's saving deeds in the past—but in such a way that they were re-presented and their power was working in the present. Jesus undoubtedly inserts in this prayer references to His own saving actions, which He has been sent to accomplish by His Father (see Jn 17).

Jesus speaks of the new wine that He will drink in the Kingdom of His Father (Mt 26:29).

He then says: "Take and eat; this is My Body. Take and drink; this is the cup of My Blood. Do this in memory of Me."

On the evening of His Resurrection that manifested His victory over sin and death, Jesus breaks bread with two disciples whom He meets on the road to Emmaus (Lk 24:30), then He partakes of the remains of a meal with ten Apostles gathered in the city (Lk 24:41). Some time later, He approaches a group of His disciples on the shore of the Sea of Galilee and says: "Come, have breakfast" (Jn 21:12). Finally, it is after He has sat down with the Apostles at table that He takes leave of them to return to the Father (Acts 1:4).

30-100 The Apostles and other followers of Jesus are mindful of the *meal* that anticipated Christ's sacrifice of the Cross as well as of the *meal* they shared with the Risen Lord. They also keep in mind all the other *meals* that accompanied the announcement of the Good News: the Messianic meals of Cana (Jn 2:1-11) and the multiplication of the loaves in the desert (Mk 6:30-44; 8:1-10); meals shared with sinners (Mk 2:15-17); meals of friendship with Peter at Capernaum (Mk 1:31) and at the house of Martha and Mary in Bethany (Lk 10:38-42); meals taken in haste with the disciples worried about the crowds (Mk 6:32); and the meal that foreshadowed the Paschal victory held after the raising of Lazarus (Jn 12:1-8)—all are present in the minds of the Apostles when they come together at the home of one of the community in the expectation of the return of the Lord "at the wedding feast of the Lamb" Rv 19:9).

They thus keep alive the memory of the Lord's Death and Resurrection through a primitive Liturgy that will come to be called the Paschal Mystery.

It is first called the "Breaking of the Bread" (Acts 2:42) or the "Lord's Supper" (1 Cor 11:20). Toward the end of the 1st century it is termed the "Eucharist" (Letter of Ignatius of Antioch to the Smyrnians, 8). It is the Bread shared with the Lord of glory, the sacrificial meal of the New Covenant, the thanksgiving action of the community of believers, gathered joyfully around the table presided over by Christ in the person of His minister.

None of the Apostles is a Jewish priest, Levite, or leader of a synagogue. They are unversed in liturgical services. However, they are heads of families, very versed in presiding over the Passover meal and family meals (which were a ritual in themselves). Hence, while continuing to frequent the Temple services, they also hold a second service at home: "Every day they devoted themselves to meeting together in the temple area and to breaking bread in their homes" (Acts 2:46). Initially, this home service is combined with a meal called the agape but it eventually becomes a service by itself (see 1 Cor 11:18ff). The service follows the Jewish Temple and synagogue service, from which Christians are later barred (see Acts 21:27-32).

Christians continue the Jewish custom of reading from the Law, the Prophets, and the Psalms (representing the rest of the Old Testament) because they see these in reference to Christ (as He had taught them to do—Lk 24:44). At the same time they add accounts about the Lord's Passion, miracles, teachings, or discuss the Way that leads to God (Acts 9:22; 22:4), and they recite the Lord's Prayer. A sermon is given (see Acts 20:7) in imitation of the commentary in the synagogue. Then hymns are sung (see Eph 5:14; Phil 5:6-11; Rv 19:1-7).

The actions of Jesus at the Last Supper are repeated and the Christians receive the Body and Blood of the Lord in obedience to His words. This is also an outgrowth of the Jewish sacrifice-meal *Zebah Todah* in which the meal was shared with God—part burned up at the altar and part given back to the offerer. The Eucharist takes place especially on Sunday, the day of the Lord's Resurrection, which supersedes the Jewish Sabbath.

Baptism is associated with the Paschal Mystery (see Rom 6:4) and is celebrated at Easter (see 1 Pt *passim*).

Confirmation is given for the reception of the Holy Spirit (see Acts 19:2-6).

Confession is practiced in some degree (see Acts 19:18.

Holy Orders is administered by the Apostles to their successor (2 Tm 1:6).

Marriage is celebrated as a unique mystery, a symbol of the union of Christ and His Church (Mt 19:5; Eph 5:25, 31f; 1 Thes 4:4).

The Anointing of the Sick is celebrated for those who are ill and in danger of death (Jas 5:14f; Mk 6:12f).

The early disciples of the Apostles "pray without ceasing" (1 Thes 5:17), that is, continually, following the examples of the Old Testament and of other prayers in the Temple and synagogues at the time of Jesus: in the morning and in the evening and three times a day (Dn 6:11; Acts 3:1; 10:9). The formularies used are unstructured prayers (see Acts 4:24f) or the texts of the Psalms. They also follow the *berakoth* (praises) of the Old Testament: (1) laudatory mentions of the Name of God; (2) delineation of the reason for the praise: remembrance of God's wondrous deeds; and (3) final doxology (see Mt 11:25; Rom 16:25-27; Eph 1:3-14).

Jewish Christians conduct the Liturgy in Aramaic, and Hellenistic Christians carry it out in the Greek of the people, known as "Koiné."

70/100 The *Didache* (known as *The Teaching of the Disciples*) indicates that the traditional Jewish table blessings (*berakoth*) have been transformed into a *Eucharistia (thanksgiving)*. It presents a blessing of bread and wine and a final thanksgiving that scholars believe served as the framework of a Christian meal that in all likelihood included the Eucharist. It seems to be a prayerful preparation for "Mass in the home."

95-98 Pope Clement of Rome in his *Epistle to the Corinthians* defines a basic condition for the worthy celebration of the Eucharist: unity around the bishop and his priests.

107 St. Ignatius of Antioch, in his *Letter to the Smyrnaeans,* tells the people to participate in the Eucharist in unity with their bishop and his priests.

130-140 The *Epistula Apostolorum* (*Epistle of the Apostles*) speaks for the first time about the existence of Easter. It is celebrated annually like the Jewish Passover, and its liturgy consists in a nocturnal vigil, concluded at dawn with the celebration of the Eucharist.

150-300 The memorials of the martyrs on their "birthday" are kept by the celebration of the Eucharist in their tombs, followed by a common meal.

150 St. Justin Martyr presents the first description of the early Eucharist in his *First Apology.*

- A Liturgy of the Word (which concludes with the Prayer of the Faithful) precedes a Liturgy of the Eucharist.
- The Preparation of the Gifts flows right into the Eucharistic Prayer.
- The participation of the faithful is relegated to the acclamation Amen.
- There is a collection for the poor.

He also describes the rites of Baptism.

150 The *Shepherd of Hermas* allows only one public penance for Christians (a practice that will last until the 6th century).

175-200 Recognition by the ecclesiastical authorities of the cult of relics occurs as an aftermath of the cult of the martyrs.

190 Pope Victor I requires Christians of Asia to celebrate the feast of Easter on the Sunday following the Jewish Passover rather than on the day of the Passover itself.

200/300 A new form of the Mystery of Christ arises—the celebration of His Incarnation, His Epiphany, His luminous manifestation as Savior of the world, Light from Light, as mighty Lord, Who shows forth the Divine and redemptive glory in His Baptism and in His great miracles as the beginning of revelation that will reach its climax in the blessed Passion and glorious Resurrection.

Lent appears as a memorial of the 40 days spent by Jesus in the desert and as a preparation of the catechumens for the Sacraments of initiation: Baptism, Confirmation, and Eucharist.

The first manifestations of the devotion to Mary occur.

215 The *Apostolic Tradition* of Hippolytus informs us of the state of the Liturgy and Christian practices in the Church of Rome.

- It describes the ordinations of bishops, priests, and deacons.
- It indicates that Confirmation and First Communion are also given at the Baptism of adults by the bishop on Easter or Pentecost.
- It indicates the use of Sacramentals by recommending the blessing of oil, cheeses, olives, bread, honey, and the like.
- It details a type of "lucernarium" or evening worship, and advocates prayer in the morning, before heavy work, and at the third, sixth, and ninth hours of the day as well as before retiring for the night.

c. 230 The community of Rome begins using Latin in place of Greek for the celebration of the Divine Service. (However, Latin and Greek coexist until the reign of Pope Damasus I [366-384] when Latin wins out.)

c. 300 By the beginning of the fourth century a number of liturgical families arise, centering around the major cities of the Empire: (a) in *Alexandria:* the Liturgy of St. Mark as well as the Coptic Liturgies of St. Cyril, St. Basil, and St. Gregory; (b) in *Antioch:* the Liturgy of St. James, the Liturgy of West Syria and the Liturgy of East Syria; (c) in *Constantinople:* the Byzantine Liturgy or the Liturgy of St. John Chrysostom, (d) in *Rome:* the Roman-North African Liturgy stemming from Rome and Africa; and (e) *Non-Roman Latin Liturgies of the Gallican* type: Spanish (Mozarabic), Gallican, Milanese, and Celtic.

300/400 Easter, Pentecost, and Christmas become the poles of the Liturgical Year.

Beginning of the loss of participation in the Eucharist on the part of the people culminating in their complete separation from the rite during the Middle Ages.

The *De Sacramentis* (attributed to St. Ambrose) constitutes the earliest witness to the text of the Roman Canon.

Precious metals begin to be used side by side with glass for the ritual cups or chalices.

300 Public penitence is manifested with the solemn reconciliation of the penitents on Holy Thursday.

c. 306 The Council of Elvira in Spain forbids bishops, priests, deacons, and certain clerics from using the marital rights if they were married at the time of ordination.

313 By this date in the city of Rome alone, there are more than forty churches in which the Eucharist is celebrated.

The Edict of Milan brings peace for the Church in the West as well as the East and sets the stage for Latin to eventually replace Greek in the Liturgy.

321 A law of Constantine recognizes Sunday as a feast day absent of work.

325 The Council of Nicaea decrees that the celebration of the Paschal Mystery must take place on Sunday and not on the Jewish Sabbath.

330 Appearance of the feast of Christmas, fixed on December 25.

336 The inauguration of St. Peter's Basilica in Rome.

340-397 St. Ambrose, Bishop of Milan, contributes to the Liturgy by his hymns and marks the beginning of the Ambrosian Rite.

350 The *Euchologion of Serapion of Thmuis* appears, acting as a kind of *Pontifical, Missal,* and *Ritual* for the Byzantine Rite.

366-384 The changeover from Greek to Latin in the Liturgy is completed during the pontificate of Leo the Great. Christians begin to forge a Latin language proper to the teachings of the Church.

370 The earliest known Liturgy of Mary is composed in Syria.

385-406 St. Jerome completes a translation of the Bible into Latin, which becomes known as the Vulgate and is eventually the text used for the Scripture in the Latin Liturgy.

400/500 The Feast of the Commemoration of the Virgin is instituted in various places in Europe.

The Feast of the Annunciation is celebrated in Byzantium.

The Feast of the Hypapante (that is, Encounter between Christ and Simeon) is celebrated.

400/464 First mention of the Feast of the Ascension.

400 Before reception of Communion there is now an obligatory fast (which since the year 200 has been optional).

401-417 During the reign of Pope Innocent I, the Eucharistic Prayer becomes one fixed formula "by rule." It is called "the rule"—Canon.

417-418 Aetheria, a nun from Gaul, writes an account of her pilgrimage to the Holy Land that is of inestimable importance for our knowledge of the customs of the Church of Jerusalem, which had a manifold influence on the West.

428 Special "vestments" begin to be used at Mass. The regular clothes worn by the ministers previous to this time now come to be looked upon as liturgical ornaments, witnesses of a distant age.

431 The Council of Ephesus affirms the Divine Motherhood of Mary, and the first churches dedicated to the Blessed Virgin appear.

440-461 Pope Leo the Great has a profound influence on the Liturgy and lays the basis for what will become the *Leonine Sacramentary.*

Mary is introduced into the texts of the Mass. In the *Leonine Sacramentary* St. Leo adds to the Canon the reference to Mary: "In communion with and venerating in the first place the glorious ever-virgin Mary, Mother of God. . . ."

492-496 Pope Gelasius I gathers the prayers of the Eucharistic Liturgy into three books of a *Sacramentary:* a Proper of the Season, a Proper of the Saints, and a Book of Votive Masses.

The first traces appear of a Roman observance of Advent.

500/600 Emergence of a new kind of Penance—private confession of venial sins.

500 The Irish Monks (Columba and Gildas among them) initiate a scale of sins for confession: one accuses oneself of faults to the priest who then gives a proportionate penance.

523-526 St. Benedict in his *Rule* sketches the Divine Office, which conforms to the essentials of the Roman usage.

529 The Council of Vaison adds the words "As it was in the beginning" to the "Glory be to the Father and to the Son and to the Holy Spirit" in order to emphasize that the Divinity of the Son is from all eternity.

530-532 Earliest edition of the *Liber Pontificalis.*

547 The Divine Office has now become a monastic book (in addition to a book for the cathedrals), sharing the influence of the *Rule of St. Benedict.* It is made up of a Night and a Day Office, the latter consisting of Lauds, Prime, Terce, Sext, None, Vespers, and Compline.

550 The Feasts of the Birth of Mary, the Presentation of Jesus, and the Dormition are celebrated in Byzantium.

560 Appearance of the *Leonine Sacramentary,* which brings together texts attributed to Popes Leo, Gelasius, and Vigilius (537-555).

590-604 Pope Gregory the Great condenses the three books of Gelasius into a forerunner of our *Roman Missal* that develops into the *Gregorian Sacramentary* of the 7th century.

Pope Gregory also produces the *Book of the Antiphons of the Mass,* forerunner of the *Roman Gradual,* which contains the proper chants of the Mass.

590 Bishop Palladius of Saintes in Gaul sends a letter to Pope Gregory asking for relics of martyrs to be inserted into the 13 new altars he has introduced into his new church—an indication of the growing proliferation of private Masses.

Gregory the Great approves the use of the Liturgy of the Saints in public worship.

600/700 Ash Wednesday becomes the beginning of the Season of Lent.

First appearance of texts for the Common of the Mass (which will go on appearing until the fixation of the *Roman Missal* in 1600).

The *Brief Exposition of the Ancient Gallican Liturgy* is written, describing and explaining one Gallican Rite in detail, especially the Mass; it is erroneously attributed to St. Germanus of Paris (d. 576).

600/650 The Feast of the Purification (February 2) is celebrated at Rome (more as a Feast of Christ than as one of Mary).

600 The "Hail Mary" (first part) appears in the Offertory for the Sunday before Christmas.

601 St. Isidore becomes Archbishop of Seville. He writes a 20-volume encyclopedia of Christian and secular culture that includes two books on the Spanish Eucharistic Liturgy and the ecclesiastical ministers, among other things. It also brings to the West the allegorical and symbolic method of explaining the Liturgy (which will remain in vogue throughout the Middle Ages).

650/675 The Feast of the Annunciation (March 25) is celebrated at Rome (more as a feast of Christ than as one of Mary).

650 The Feast of the Assumption (August 15) is celebrated at Rome and goes on to become the principal Marian Feast.

675-700 The Feast of the Birth of Mary is celebrated at Rome (stemming from the dedication of the church of Mary's Nativity at Jerusalem, celebrated since the 5th century).

700/800 "Explanations of the Mass" begin to appear intended to encourage the people to relate to the Liturgy and to help the priest understand the Mass better.

726-843 The iconoclastic crisis riddles the Church.

747 The Council of Clovesho in England indicates that the complete cursus of all the Hours of the Divine Office should be celebrated every day in one and the same church.

754 The Emperor Pepin orders the compulsory introduction into the Frankish Empire of the current Gregorian form of the Roman Liturgy (but it does not come about until the time of his son Charlemagne).

787 The Second Council of Nicaea affirms the legitimacy of the cult of images and indicates the meaning that must be given to it.

795-804 At the behest of Charlemagne, Alcuin produces a new *Gregorian Sacramentary,* called the *Hadrianum* because its nucleus is a *Sacramentary* sent by Pope Hadrian from Rome. Alcuin works from copies of both the old and the new *Gelasian Sacramentary,* a Gregorian of the Paduan type, and other Gallican books.

Alcuin revises the *Roman Lectionary* and draws up an abridgment of the Divine Office for the laity—a few Psalms for each day with a prayer after each Psalm, on an ancient plan, and other prayers (without lessons or homilies).

800-1099 Romanization of the Gallican Liturgy, which becomes the Ambrosian Rite at Milan.

800/900 Appropriation of particular colors of vestments for individual feast days and classes of Saints begins with local variations.

800 Rise of auricular confession with the absolution preceding the penitence; avowal of faults passes on to the first rank as the penitential work beyond compare.

815/845 Existence of a full ritual for the Anointing of the Sick.

818 King Louis the Pious imposes the Roman Liturgy on French Brittany (but the Gallican Liturgy is not fully supplanted until 1172).

825-853 Amalarius of Metz writes a commentary on the whole Roman Liturgy (*On Ecclesiastical Offices*), which goes on to influence subsequent treatises. He popularizes the allegorical interpretation of the liturgical rites already in vogue in the East and makes it the standard of liturgical exegesis until the 16th century.

827-844 Gregory IV establishes the Feast of All Saints for the Universal Church.

843 The definitive triumph of the defenders of icons is celebrated on May 11 in Saint Sophia. It is commemorated in the Eastern Church by a liturgical feast ("Feast of Orthodoxy").

850 Leo IV prescribes the amice, alb, stole, maniple, and chasuble for Mass.

880 A Frankish monk witnesses to the fact that the Roman Office of St. Benedict has taken on Gallican features.

bef. 882 Hincmar of Reims declares that the Office is to be celebrated publicly if possible.

900/1000 The reshaped mixed Frankish-Roman Office is brought to Rome.

975-1025 The Feast of All Souls makes its appearance sponsored by Abbot Odilo of Cluny.

993 The canonization of Ulrich, Bishop of Augsburg, is held at Rome, becoming the first official canonization in the Church.

1000/1100 The *Lateran Roman Missal* shows that the Gallican additions have been incorporated into the Roman Liturgy.

The Feast of All Saints (celebrated here and there since the 7th century) becomes celebrated by the whole Church.

1072 St. Peter Damian bears witness to the general practice, in monastic circles, of the recitation of the Office in private.

1073/1085 Gregory VII replaces the Visigothic Rite with the Roman Rite.

1088-1099 During the pontificate of Urban II indulgences in the modern sense make their appearance: all penitents bound to perform certain works of piety in reparation for their sins are offered a reduction through another work that they are invited to accomplish.

1099 Date of the most ancient manuscript known as containing within one volume the whole of the Office, stemming from Monte Cassino.

1100/1300 Gregorian Chant at Mass becomes the business of the clergy and choir, with the people having no part in it.

1100/1200 Growth of a desire on the part of the people to see the consecrated Host at Mass, which becomes a kind of "visual Communion" substituting for the reception of Communion.

John Beleth enumerates the books needed for the performance of the Office—*Antiphonary,* Old and New Testaments, *Passionary* (Acts of the Martyrs), *Legendary* (Legends of the Saints), *Homiliary* (collection of homilies on the Gospels), *Sermologus* (collection of sermons), and the treatises of the Fathers (in addition to the Psalter, *Collectarum,* the prayers, and the *Martyrology*).

1172 The English Synod of Cashel calls upon all the churches of Ireland to adopt the Anglo-Roman Rite.

1198-1216 Innocent III succeeds in bringing forth a *Missal* that is a forerunner of the *Missal of Pius V.* (He also assigns liturgical colors for the various Masses.)

During his pontificate the use of the *Breviary* reaches Rome, not only in the basilicas but also in the Curia.

In addition to presiding over the Fourth Lateran Council, Innocent III also leaves a treatise on the Holy *Sacrament of the Altar,* hailed as the principal liturgical work of the Middle Ages.

1199 By this date the Benedictine Office is incorporated into the Roman Office.

1215 The Fourth Lateran Council makes the yearly confession ("to one's own priest") of grave sins obligatory.

1228-1238 The Dominican Rite is formulated and remains in existence till the reform of Vatican II.

1250/1500 The laity begin to make use of a prayerbook fashioned from the Liturgy that includes the *Little Office of the Blessed Virgin Mary,* the *Office for the Dead,* the 15 Gradual Psalms, and the Seven Penitential Psalms.

1260 The Franciscans adopt the Office of the Curia (the *Curial Breviary*) in one volume and popularize it throughout the places where they preach, authorized by Gregory IX.

1264 The Feast of the Body and Blood of Christ (Corpus Christi) is established by Urban IV (though it is not officially promulgated until 1312) with the Mass and Office composed by St. Thomas Aquinas.

1277 Pope Nicholas III prescribes a *Missal* to be observed in Rome.

1277-1280 The Church of Rome *adopts* the *Breviary* of the Franciscans not merely for the Curia but for the basilicas as well, and it becomes the *Breviary* of the Universal Church.

bef. 1280 St. Albert the Great writes his work *On the Mystery of the Mass* opposing the allegorical explanations of the Liturgy—but it falls on deaf ears.

1292-1295 William of Durand, Bishop of Mende, compiles for his own use a *Pontifical* that will become the official liturgical book for the whole Church.

1299 The practice of receiving Communion (under one or both species) begins to decline and is divorced from the Mass so that eventually many of the faithful will receive Communion only as Viaticum.

1300 Boniface VIII proclaims the first "Holy Year."

1334 The Feast of the Trinity is extended to the Universal Church by John XX.

1457 The first complete *Missal* is printed at Constance.

The Feast of the Transfiguration is extended to the Universal Church by Callistus III.

The *Little Office of the Blessed Virgin Mary* is printed.

1474 The *Missal for the Use of the Roman Curia* is published in Milan; it will become the *Missal of Pius V.* It repeats what Nicholas III prescribed for observance in Rome in 1277 based on the work of Innocent III (1198-1216).

1485 The *Pontifical* of William of Durand is adopted as an official text for Rome by Innocent VIII (and will be imposed on the whole Church by the Council of Trent).

1495-1517 Cardinal Ximenes, Archbishop of Toledo, publishes the classical edition of the Mozarabic books.

1535 The *Breviary* of Cardinal Francisco de Quiñones commanded by Clement VII (d. 1534) is published and becomes known as the *Breviary of the Cross.* It is intended for private recitation but is never adopted by the Church.

1551 The Council of Trent defends the Sacramental character of Penance.

1563 The Council of Trent stipulates that priests should celebrate Mass at least on Sundays and solemn feasts (session XXIII, ch. XIV).

The *Hail Mary* is introduced into the Divine Office.

1568 The *Roman Breviary* is published under Pius V.

1570 The *Roman Missal* is published under Pius V. It includes much that during the Franco-German period has been overlaid inartistically upon the austere form of the

Mass of Rome. Most important, it espouses absolute neglect of the assembly, the priest seeming to celebrate alone before the others.

1582 Gregory XIII reforms the Julian Calendar (which is ten days behind the position of the sun), and the Gregorian Calendar is adopted for everything, including liturgical feasts.

1584 The *Roman Martyrology* is published under Gregory XIII.

1588 Sixtus V establishes a special department of the Curia to rule over the Liturgy under the name of the "Congregation of Rites and Ceremonies."

1592 The *Maronite Missal* is published at Rome.

Clement VIII introduces the Forty Hours Devotion in Rome after it has been used from the 13th century on.

1592-1605 Completion under Clement VIII of the liturgical reform mandated by Trent.

1593 Publication of the *Clementine Vulgate.*

1596 The *Roman Pontifical* is published under Clement VIII.

1599 The Synod of Diamper revises the liturgical books of the Uniates.

1600/1700 The French school of the Oratory teaches that worship is the center of piety and private prayer is connected with public Liturgy.

1600 The *Ceremonial of Bishops* is published under Clement VIII.

1604 The use of the *Clementine Vulgate* is decreed for the Liturgy.

1614 The *Roman Ritual* is published under Paul V. With its rich repertory of Sacramentals it attests the frequency of their celebration by the Christian communities.

1615 Paul V authorizes the celebration of Mass and the Sacraments in Chinese (but in 1698 the Congregation for the Faith will prohibit it).

1623-1644 During the pontificate of Urban II, a proliferation of new feasts in the liturgical books frustrates the liturgical advances that had occurred under Pius V.

1630 The *Roman Martyrology* is revised under Urban VIII.

1644-1655 Under the pontificate of Innocent X more feasts are added and for all intents and purposes the Sunday Propers disappear except during Advent and Lent.

1650 The *Ceremonial of Bishops* is revised under Innocent X.

1656 A Decree of the Holy Office authorizes Chinese Catholics to continue the traditional practices.

1661 Alexander VI forbids translations of the *Roman Missal* into the vernacular (in resistance to the Reformers' attacks on the use of Latin and in the belief that the mystery of the Eucharist is to be safeguarded by a language unknown to the people).

1666 The *Maronite Office* begins to be published at Rome.

1675 The *Roman Martyrology* is revised under Clement X (but published only in 1681).

1716-1726 Pierre Le Brun of the Oratory publishes a four-volume work: *The Liturgical, Historical, and Dogmatic Explanation of the Prayers and Ceremonies of the Mass.* It explains the prayers of the Latin Mass, making frequent reference to medieval variants.

1725 The *Memoriale Rituum* (the Memorial of Rites or Little Ritual) is published under Benedict XIII for smaller churches of Rome.

1731 Clement XII issues an Instruction that regulates the

Forty Hours Devotion and becomes known as the Clementine Instruction.

1740-1758 Benedict XIV puts an end to the addition of Saints to the Liturgy, and the dream of a new reform begins.

1742 Benedict XIV takes a definitive position against the "permissions" granted to Chinese Catholics.

1748 The *Roman Martyrology* is revised under Benedict XIV.

bef. 1750 Luigi Muratori publishes *The Ancient Roman Liturgy,* a collection of Roman and Gallican Sacramentaries in wide use.

1752 The *Roman Ritual* is revised under Benedict XIV.

The *Roman Pontifical* is revised under Benedict XIV.

The *Ceremonial of Bishops* is revised under Benedict XIV.

1759 The Church issues a directive to missionaries in China that the prayers to be read in the vernacular by the people at Mass are not to be recited by the celebrant or deacon or altar boy or choir.

1774 The *Uniate Malabar Missal* is published at Rome.

1775 The *Uniate Order of Rites and Readings* is published at Rome.

1786 The Synod of Pistoia, Italy, sets forth liturgical and pastoral insights that foreshadow the Liturgical Movement, calling for: (1) active participation of the people; (2) minimization of private Masses; (3) importance of Liturgical prayer; (4) necessity of *Breviary* reform; and (5) printing the vernacular together with Latin in liturgical books.

1800/1900 The German *Singmesse* enables the people to sing parts of the Mass in the vernacular while the celebrant says them in Latin. (It will receive official Roman approval only in 1943.)

1821 Pius VII extends the use of the *Memorial of Rites* to all small churches of the Roman Rite.

1833 Dom Prosper Guéranger reopens the Abbey of Solesmes, which is then reconstituted by the Benedictines in 1837.

1839 A *Maronite Ritual* is published at Rome.

1841-1875 The Liturgy in France becomes uniform under the influence of Dom Guéranger, who has launched an attempt to reform the Liturgy by going back to the Middle Ages and to set the stage for a restoration of Gregorian Chant. (It is by the restoration of chant that Pius X will begin his reform of the Liturgy in 1903.) He also publishes *The Liturgical Year,* preparing the way for the Liturgical Movement.

1854 Pius IX proclaims the Immaculate Conception as a dogma of the Church.

1857 Pius IX renews the prohibition of translations of the prayers of the Mass for the people.

1865 Pius IX extends the Feast of the Sacred Heart to the Universal Church.

1866 The Litany of the Holy Name of Jesus is approved for public worship by Leo XIII.

1878-1885 The *Liturgical Institutions* of Guéranger is published posthumously.

1882 The *Ceremonial of Bishops* is revised under Leo XIII.

The Abbey of Maredsous publishes a *French Missal* for the people.

1884 Rev. A. Schott of the Abbey of Beuron publishes a German Missal for the people.

1887 The liturgical periodical *Ephemerides Liturgicae* is begun.

1888 The *Roman Pontifical* is revised under Leo XIII.

1890 The Maronite "Ferial Office" is published.

1898 Translations of the *Roman Missal* are no longer to be censured and put on the Index of Forbidden Books.

1899 The Litany of the Sacred Heart of Jesus is approved for use in public worship by Leo XIII.

1903 Pius X formulates the revolutionary program for the Liturgical Movement in his Motu Propio *Tra Le Sollecitudini,* stressing that the right of "active participation in the sacred Mysteries and in the public and solemn prayer of the Church" is the "first and indispensable source of the true Christian spirit."

1905 Pius X urges Christians to receive frequent and even daily Communion.

1907 Pius X publishes the first official edition of the *Roman Gradual* and an official edition of the *Antiphonary.*

1908 Pius X reorganizes the Congregation of Rites, dividing the work into three sections: (1) the rites of the Church; (2) the process of beatification and canonization; and (3) matters concerning relics.

1909 Dom Lambert Beauduin proposes a program for liturgical renewal.

The French periodical *Liturgical Life* is begun.

The Litany of St. Joseph is approved for use in public worship by Puis X.

1910 Pius X enables all children to receive Communion as soon as they reach the age of reason.

1911 Pius X revises the *Breviary* so that the Psalter will be read every week and reforms the calendar so that Sundays take precedence over feasts of Saints.

1914 The French periodical *Liturgical* and *Parochial Questions* is begun.

The liturgical periodical *Rivista Liturgica* is begun at Savona, Italy.

1920 Dom Lambert Beauduin publishes a French Missal for the people.

Dom Gaspar Lefebvre publishes a French Missal for the people that will become known worldwide.

1921 Benedict XV introduces the Feast of the Holy Family as a feast of the second class.

1922 The Dialogue Mass comes into use (and remains in vogue until the vernacular Mass of Vatican II).

1925 Pius XI writes an encyclical on the Sacred Heart of Jesus and establishes the Feast of Christ the King to be celebrated as a feast of the first class.

1928 Pius XI gives new texts and the highest ranking to the Feast of the Sacred Heart.

1936 Rev. Josef Jungmann publishes *The Good News Yesterday and Today,* which contains a powerful liturgical and pastoral vision that prepares for the renewal of Vatican II.

1940 The first Liturgical Week is held in the United States.

1942 Rev. Hugo Hoever of Notre Dame University publishes the Sunday Missal *I Pray the Mass* with the new Confraternity of Christian Doctrine translation for the Readings.

1943 The Center for Pastoral Liturgy is formed in France.

Rome officially approves the German *Singmesse* that has been used for over 100 years.

1947 Rev. Michael Mathis of Notre Dame University starts the School of Liturgical Studies, which becomes the first Liturgical Institute in the world.

Pius XII issues the epoch-making Encyclical *Mediator Dei,* which brings the Liturgy to center stage.

Pius XII allows the publication of *bilingual Rituals.*

1950 Pius XII declares the Assumption of Mary to be a dogma of the Church and issues a new Mass for the Feast.

1951 The *Restored Order of the Easter Vigil* is published under Pius XII.

1953 Pius XII mitigates the Eucharistic Fast so that the faithful will receive Communion more frequently.

1955 The *Restored Rites of Holy Week* are published under Pius XII.

The *Simplification of Rubrics* is published under Pius XII.

1956 The first International Congress of Pastoral Liturgy is held at Assisi.

1960 A further *Simplification of Rubrics* is published under John XXIII.

The Litany of the Precious Blood of Jesus is approved for use in public worship by John XXIII.

1962 John XXIII makes a change in the hitherto "unchangeable" Canon of the Mass, inserting the name of St. Joseph in the *Communicantes.*

1963 The Second Vatican Council promulgates the *Constitution on the Sacred Liturgy (Sacrosanctum Concilium)*, which lays the basis for the new Liturgy of Vatican II.

1964 The Congregation of Rites issues *Inter Oecumenici,* the First Instruction on the Proper Implementation of the Constitution on the Sacred Liturgy.

The Mass in English is introduced.

1965 The liturgical periodical *Notitiae,* a semiofficial organ of the Congregation for Divine Worship (new title for Congregation of Rites) is begun.

Paul VI issues his *Encyclical Mysterium Fidei* on the Eucharist.

The Holy See grants permission for sign language to be used in the Liturgy.

1967 The *Instruction on Music in the Liturgy* by the Congregation of Rites encourages congregational singing during liturgical celebrations and indicates that the distinctive lines traditionally drawn between the sung Liturgy and the spoken Liturgy are no longer in force. It also allows the use of instruments other than the organ in liturgical services, provided they are played in a manner suitable to worship.

The Congregation of Rites issues *Tres Abhinc Annos,* the Second Instruction for the Proper Implementation of the Constitution on the Sacred Liturgy.

The Congregation of Rites issues the Instruction *Eucharisticum Mysterium* on the Worship of the Eucharist, which among other things permits Communion under both kinds.

The *Simple Gradual* is published under Paul VI.

1968 The Congregation of Rites promulgates three new Eucharistic Prayers and eight new Prefaces.

The new *Enchiridion of Indulgences* is published under Paul VI.

The Vatican II Latin edition of the *Rites of Ordination of Bishops, Priest, and Deacons (Roman Pontifical)* is published under Paul VI.

1969 The Vatican II Latin edition of the *Roman Calendar* is published under Paul VI.

The Vatican II Latin edition of the *Rite of Marriage (Roman Ritual)* is published under Paul VI.

The Vatican II Latin edition of the *New Order of Mass* is promulgated under Paul VI.

Paul VI changes the Congregation of Rites to the Congregation for Divine Worship.

The Vatican II Latin edition of the *Rite of Baptism* (*Roman Ritual*) is published under Paul VI.

The Vatican II Latin edition of the *Lectionary for Mass* is published under Paul VI.

The Vatican II Latin edition of the *Rite of Funerals* (*Roman Ritual*) is published under Paul VI.

The Holy See begins to approve the practice of receiving Communion in the hand, for example, by giving the French Episcopal Conference permission to make use of it.

1970 The Congregation for the Clergy grants permission for the faithful to satisfy the precept of participating at Mass in the late afternoon or evening hours of Saturday and the days before Holy Days of Obligation.

The Vatican II Latin edition of the *Rite of Religious Profession* (*Roman Ritual*) is published under Paul VI.

The Vatican II Latin edition of the *Roman Missal* (actually, *Sacramentary*) is published under Paul VI.

The Congregation for Divine Worship publishes *Liturgicae Instaurationes*, the Third Instruction for the Implementation of the Constitution on the Sacred Liturgy.

The Vatican II Latin edition of the *Rite of Consecration to a Life of Virginity* (*Roman Pontifical*) is published under Paul VI.

The Vatican II Latin edition of the *Rite of Blessing an Abbot or Abbess* (*Roman Pontifical*) is published under Paul VI.

The Vatican II Latin edition of the *Rite of Blessing Oil, Rite of Consecrating the Chrism* (*Roman Pontifical*) is published under Paul VI.

1971 The Vatican II Latin edition of the *Rite of Confirmation* (*Roman Pontifical*) is published under Paul VI.

1971-1972 The Vatican II Latin edition of the *Liturgy of the Hours* (*Roman Breviary*) is published under Paul VI.

1972 The Vatican II Latin edition of the *Rite of Christian Initiation of Adults* (*Roman Ritual*) is published under Paul VI.

The Vatican II Latin edition of the *Rite of Institution of Readers and Acolytes, etc.* (*Roman Pontifical*) is published under Paul VI.

The Vatican II Latin edition of the *Rite of Anointing and Pastoral Care of the Sick* is published under Paul VI.

1973 Paul VI authorizes the designation of lay men and women to serve as extraordinary (or special) ministers of the Eucharist under certain conditions.

The Vatican II Latin edition of *Holy Communion and Worship of the Eucharist Outside Mass* (*Roman Ritual*) is published under Paul VI.

The Congregation for Divine Worship issues the *Directory of Masses with Children.*

The Vatican II Latin edition of the *Rite of Penance* (*Roman Ritual*) is published under Paul VI.

1974 Paul VI publishes the Apostolic Constitution *Marialis Cultus* on Marian devotion, which deals with our Lady in the Liturgy.

The *Congregation for Divine Worship* publishes *Iubilate Deo,* a collection of simple Latin chants.

The Congregation for Divine Worship publishes three new Eucharistic Prayers for Masses with Children and two for Masses of Reconciliation and grants permission for their temporary use.

1975 The second revised edition of the *Roman Missal* is published under Paul VI.

1977 The Vatican II Latin edition of the *Rite for the Dedication of a Church and an Altar* (*Roman Pontifical*) is published under Paul VI.

1979 The revised *Vulgate* is published under John Paul II and declared to be the Latin edition to be used in all typical editions.

1980 The Congregation for Divine Worship issues instructions concerning the use of the three new Eucharistic Prayers for Masses with Children and two new Eucharistic Prayers for Masses of Reconciliation.

1981 The second edition of the *Lectionary for Mass* is published under John Paul II.

The Vatican II Latin edition of the *Order of Crowning an Image of the Blessed Virgin Mary* (*Roman Pontifical*) is published under John Paul II, containing a new *Litany of the Blessed Virgin.*

1983 The new *Code of Canon Law* is published under John Paul II and gives general laws for the Liturgy.

The *Emendations in the Liturgical Books following upon the New Code of Canon Law* is published.

The Vatican II Latin edition of the *Roman Antiphonary* is published under John Paul II.

1984 The Vatican II Latin edition of the *Book of Blessings* (*Roman Ritual*) is published under John Paul II.

The Vatican II Latin edition of the *Ceremonial of Bishops* is published under John Paul II.

John Paul II grants an indult to all dioceses to celebrate the Tridentine Latin Mass according to the rite of the 1962 *Roman Missal.*

1985-1987 The revised edition of the *Liturgy of the Hours* is published.

1987 The Latin edition of the *Collection of Masses of the Blessed Virgin Mary* is published.

The revised edition of *Iubilate Deo* is published.

1988 The *Directory for Sunday Celebrations in the Absence of a Priest* is published.

4. GENERAL ROMAN CALENDAR

Includes proper feasts for the United States (U.S.A.)

JANUARY

1. Octave of Christmas
   SOLEMNITY OF MARY, MOTHER OF GOD — Solemnity
2. Basil the Great and Gregory Nazianzen, bishops and doctors — Memorial
3.
4. Elizabeth Ann Seton, religious (U.S.A.) — Memorial
5. John Neumann, bishop (U.S.A.) — Memorial
6. *Bl. André Bessette, religious (U.S.A.)*
7. *Raymond of Penyafort, priest**
8.
9.
10.
11.
12.
13. *Hilary, bishop and doctor*
14.
15.
16.
17. Anthony, abbot — Memorial
18.
19.
20. *Fabian, pope and martyr*
    Sebastian, martyr
21. Agnes, virgin and martyr — Memorial
22. *Vincent, deacon and martyr*
23.
24. Francis de Sales, bishop and doctor — Memorial
25. CONVERSION OF PAUL, APOSTLE — Feast
26. Timothy and Titus, bishops — Memorial
27. *Angela Merici, virgin*
28. Thomas Aquinas, priest and doctor — Memorial
29.
30.
31. John Bosco, priest — Memorial

Sunday between January 2 and 8: EPIPHANY — Solemnity

Sunday after January 6: BAPTISM OF THE LORD — Feast

*When no rank is given, it is an optional memorial.

FEBRUARY

1.
2. PRESENTATION OF THE LORD — Feast
3. *Blase, bishop and martyr*
   Ansgar, bishop
4.
5. Agatha, virgin and martyr — Memorial
6. Paul Miki and companions, martyrs — Memorial
7.
8. *Jerome Emiliani*
9.
10. Scholastica, virgin — Memorial
11. *Our Lady of Lourdes*
12.
13.
14. Cyril, monk, and Methodius, bishop — Memorial
15.
16.
17. *Seven Founders of the Order of Servites*
18.
19.
20.
21. *Peter Damian, bishop and doctor*
22. CHAIR OF PETER, APOSTLE — Feast
23. Polycarp, bishop and martyr — Memorial
24.
25.
26.
27.
28.

MARCH

1.
2.
3. *Bl. Katherine Drexel, virgin* (U.S.A.)
4. *Casimir*
5.
6.
7. Perpetua and Felicity, martyrs — Memorial
8. *John of God, religious*
9. *Frances of Rome, religious*
10.
11.
12.
13.
14.
15.
16.
17. *Patrick, bishop*
18. *Cyril of Jerusalem, bishop and doctor*
19. JOSEPH, HUSBAND OF MARY — Solemnity
20.
21.
22.
23. *Turibius de Mogrovejo, bishop*
24.
25. ANNUNCIATION OF THE LORD — Solemnity
26.
27.
28.
29.
30.
31.

APRIL

1.
2. *Francis of Paola, hermit*
3.
4. *Isidore, bishop and doctor*
5. *Vincent Ferrer, priest*
6.
7. John Baptist de la Salle, priest — Memorial
8.
9.

10.
11. Stanislaus, bishop and martyr — Memorial
12.
13. *Martin I, pope and martyr*
14.
15.
16.
17.
18.
19.
20.
21. *Anselm, bishop and doctor*
22.
23. *George, martyr*
24. *Fidelis of Sigmaringen, priest and martyr*
25. MARK, EVANGELIST — Feast
26.
27.
28. *Peter Chanel, priest and martyr*
29. Catherine of Siena, virgin and doctor — Memorial
30. *Pius V, pope*

MAY

1. *Joseph the Worker*
2. Athanasius, bishop and doctor — Memorial
3. PHILIP AND JAMES, APOSTLES — Feast
4.
5.
6.
7.
8.
9.
10.
11.
12. *Nereus and Achilleus, martyrs*
    Pancras, martyr
13.
14. MATTHIAS, APOSTLE — Feast
15. *Isidore* (U.S.A.)
16.
17.
18. *John I, pope and martyr*
19.
20. *Bernardine of Siena, priest*
21.
22.
23.
24.
25. *Venerable Bede, priest and doctor*
    Gregory VII, pope
    Mary Magadalene de Pazzi, virgin
26. Philip Neri, priest — Memorial
27. *Augustine of Canterbury, bishop*
28.
29.
30.
31. VISITATION — Feast

Thursday after Sixth Sunday of Easter: ASCENSION — Solemnity
First Sunday after Pentecost: HOLY TRINITY — Solemnity
Sunday after Holy Trinity: THE BODY AND BLOOD OF CHRIST — Solemnity
Friday following Second Sunday after Pentecost: SACRED HEART — Solemnity
Saturday following Second Sunday after Pentecost: *Immaculate Heart of Mary*

JUNE

1. Justin, martyr — Memorial
2. *Marcellinus and Peter, martyrs*
3. Charles Lwanga and companions, martyrs — Memorial
4.
5. Boniface, bishop and martyr — Memorial
6. *Norbert, bishop*
7.
8.
9. *Ephrem, deacon and doctor*
10.
11. Barnabas, apostle — Memorial
12.
13. Anthony of Padua, priest and doctor — Memorial
14.
15.
16.
17.
18.
19. *Romuald, abbot*
20.
21. Aloysius Gonzaga, religious — Memorial
22. *Paulinus of Nola, bishop*
    John Fisher, bishop and martyr, and Thomas More, martyr
23.
24. BIRTH OF JOHN THE BAPTIST — Solemnity
25.
26.
27. *Cyril of Alexandria, bishop and doctor*
28. Irenaeus, bishop and martyr — Memorial
29. PETER AND PAUL, APOSTLES — Solemnity
30. *First Martyrs of the Church of Rome*

JULY

1.
2.
3. THOMAS, APOSTLE — Feast
4. *Elizabeth of Portugal*
   Independence Day (U.S.A.)
5. *Anthony Zaccaria, priest*
6. *Maria Goretti, virgin and martyr*
7.
8.
9.

10.
11. Benedict, abbot — Memorial
12.
13. *Henry*
14. Bl. Kateri Tekakwitha, virgin (U.S.A.) — Memorial
    Camillus de Lellis, priest
15. Bonaventure, bishop and doctor — Memorial
16. *Our Lady of Mount Carmel*
17.
18.
19.
20.
21. *Lawrence of Brindisi, priest and doctor*
22. Mary Magdalene — Memorial
23. *Bridget, religious*
24.
25. JAMES, APOSTLE — Feast
26. Joachim and Ann, parents of Mary — Memorial
27.
28.
29. Martha — Memorial
30. *Peter Chrysologus, bishop and doctor*
31. Ignatius of Loyola, priest — Memorial

AUGUST

1. Alphonsus Liguori, bishop and doctor — Memorial
2. *Eusebius of Vercelli, bishop*
3.
4. John Vianney, priest — Memorial
5. *Dedication of St. Mary Major*
6. TRANSFIGURATION — Feast
7. *Sixtus II, pope and martyr, and companions, martyrs*
   Cajetan, priest
8. Dominic, priest — Memorial
9.
10. LAWRENCE, DEACON AND MARTYR — Feast
11. Clare, virgin — Memorial
12.
13. *Pontian, pope and martyr, and Hippolytus, priest and martyr*
14. Maximilian Mary Kolbe, priest and martyr — Memorial
15. ASSUMPTION — Solemnity
16. *Stephen of Hungary*
17.
18. *Jane Frances de Chantal (U.S.A.)*
19. *John Eudes, priest*
20. Bernard, abbot and doctor — Memorial
21. Pius X, pope — Memorial
22. Queenship of Mary — Memorial
23. *Rose of Lima, virgin*
24. BARTHOLOMEW, APOSTLE — Feast
25. *Louis*
    Joseph Calasanz, priest
26.
27. Monica — Memorial
28. Augustine, bishop and doctor — Memorial
    Bl. Junipero Serra, priest (U.S.A.)
29. Beheading of John the Baptist, martyr — Memorial
30.
31.

SEPTEMBER

1.
2.
3. Gregory the Great, pope and doctor — Memorial
4.
5.
6.
7.
8. BIRTH OF MARY — Feast
9. Peter Claver, priest (U.S.A) — Memorial
10.
11.
12.
13. John Chysostom, bishop and doctor — Memorial
14. TRIUMPH OF THE CROSS — Feast
15. Our Lady of Sorrows — Memorial
16. Cornelius, pope and martyr, and Cyprian, bishop and martyr — Memorial
17. *Robert Bellarmine, bishop and doctor*
18.
19. *Januarius, bishop and martyr*
20. Andrew Kim Taegon, priest and martyr, Paul Chong Hasang and companions, martyrs — Memorial
21. MATTHEW, APOSTLE AND EVANGELIST — Feast
22.
23.
24.
25.
26. *Cosmas and Damian, martyrs*
27. Vincent de Paul, priest — Memorial
28. *Wenceslaus, martyr*
    Lawrence Ruiz and companions, martyrs
29. MICHAEL, GABRIEL, AND RAPHAEL, ARCHANGELS — Feast
30. Jerome, priest and doctor — Memorial

First Monday *Labor Day*

OCTOBER

1. Theresa of the Child Jesus, virgin — Memorial
2. Guardian Angels — Memorial
3.
4. Francis of Assisi — Memorial
5.
6. *Bruno, priest*
   Bl. Marie-Rose Durocher, virgin (U.S.A.)
7. Our Lady of the Rosary — Memorial
8.
9. *Denis, bishop and martyr, and companions, martyrs*
   John Leonardi, priest

10.
11.
12.
13.
14. *Callistus I, pope and martyr*
15. Teresa of Jesus, virgin and doctor — Memorial
16. *Hedwig, religious*
Margaret Mary Alacoque, virgin
17. Ignatius of Antioch, bishop and martyr — Memorial
18. LUKE, EVANGELIST — Feast
19. Isaac Jogues and John de Brébeuf, priests and martyrs, and companions, martyrs (U.S.A) — Memorial
Paul of the Cross, priest
20.
21.
22.
23. *John of Capristrano, priest*
24. *Anthony Claret, bishop*
25.
26.
27.
28. SIMON AND JUDE, APOSTLES — Feast
29.
30.
31.

NOVEMBER

1. ALL SAINTS — Solemnity
2. ALL SOULS
3. *Martin de Porres, religious*
4. Charles Borromeo, bishop — Memorial
5.
6.
7.
8.
9. DEDICATION OF ST. JOHN LATERAN — Feast
10. Leo the Great, pope and doctor — Memorial
11. Martin of Tours, bishop — Memorial
12. Josaphat, bishop and martyr — Memorial
13. Frances Xavier Cabrini, virgin (U.S.A.) — Memorial
14.
15. *Albert the Great, bishop and doctor*
16. *Margaret of Scotland*
Gertrude, virgin
17. Elizabeth of Hungary, religious — Memorial
18. *Dedication of the churches of Peter and Paul, apostles*
Rose Philippine Duchesne, virgin (U.S.A.)
19.
20.
21. Presentation of Mary — Memorial
22. Cecilia, virgin and martyr — Memorial
23. *Clement I, pope and martyr*
Columban, abbot
24.
25.
26.
27.
28.
29.
30. ANDREW, APOSTLE — Feast

Last Sunday in Ordinary Time:
CHRIST THE KING — Solemnity
Fourth Thursday *Thanksgiving Day*

DECEMBER

1.
2.
3. Francis Xavier, priest — Memorial
4. *John Damascene, priest and doctor*
5.
6. *Nicholas, bishop*
7. Ambrose, bishop and doctor — Memorial
8. IMMACULATE CONCEPTION — Solemnity
9.
10.
11. *Damascus I, Pope*
12. OUR LADY OF GUADALUPE (U.S.A.) — Feast
13. Lucy, virgin and martyr — Memorial
14. John of the Cross, priest and doctor — Memorial
15.
16.
17.
18.
19.
20.
21. *Peter Canisius, priest and doctor*
22.
23. *John of Kanty, priest*
24.
25. CHRISTMAS — Solemnity
26. STEPHEN, FIRST MARTYR — Feast
27. JOHN, APOSTLE AND EVANGELIST — Feast
28. HOLY INNOCENTS, MARTYRS — Feast
29. *Thomas Becket, bishop and martyr*
30.
31. *Sylvester I, pope*

Sunday within the octave of Christmas or if there is no Sunday within the octave, December 30:
HOLY FAMILY — Feast

5. LATIN TEXTS FOR THE PEOPLE'S PARTS OF THE ORDINARY OF THE MASS

At the Greeting (3 forms)

℣. In nómine Patris et Fílii et Spíritus Sancti.
℟. **Amen.**

A

℣. Grátia Dómini nostri Iesu Christi, et cáritas Dei et communicátio Sancti Spíritus sit cum ómnibus vobis.
℟. **Et cum spíritu tuo.**

B OR

℣. Grátia vobis et pax a Deo Patre nostro et Dómine Iesu Christo.
℟. **Benedíctus Deus et Pater Dómini nostri Iesu Christi.**
or:
℟. **Et cum spíritu tuo.**

C OR

℣. Dóminus vobíscum.
℟. **Et cum spíritu tuo.**
Bishop: Pax vobis.
People: **Et cum spíritu tuo.**

At the Penitential Rite (3 forms)

After a brief silence one of the following is used.

A

Confiteor

Confíteor Deo omnipoténti et vobis, fratres,
quia peccávi nimis
cogitatióne, verbo, ópere et omissióne:
mea culpa, mea culpa, mea máxima culpa.
Ideo precor beátam Maríam semper Vírginem,
omnes Angelos et Sanctos,
et vos, fratres, oráre pro me
ad Dóminum Deum nostrum.

B OR

℣. Miserére nostri, Dómine.
℟. **Quia peccávimus tibi.**
℣. Ostende nobis, Dómine, misericórdiam tuam.
℟. **Et salutáre tuum da nobis.**

C OR

℣. Qui missus es sanáre contrítos corde: Kýrie, eléison.
℟. **Kýrie, eléison.**
℣. Qui peccatóres vocáre venísti: Christe, eléison.
℟. **Christe, eléison.**
℣. Qui ad déxteram Patris sedes, ad interpellándum pro nobis: Kýrie, eléison.

℣. Misereátur nostri omnípotens Deus
et, dimíssis peccátis nostris,
perdúcat nos ad vitam ætérnam.
℟. **Amen.**

Kýrie

℣. Kýrie, eléison.
℟. **Kýrie, eléison.**
℣. Christe, eléison.
℟. **Christe, eléison.**
℣. Kýrie, eléison.
℟. **Kýrie, eléison.**

Gloria

Glória in excélsis Deo
et in terra pax homínibus bonæ voluntátis.
Laudámus te,
benedícimus te,
adorámus te,
glorificámus te,
grátias ágimus tibi propter magnam glóriam tuam,
Dómine Deus, Rex cæléstis,
Deus Pater omnípotens.
Dómine Fili unigénite, Iesu Christe,
Dómine Deus, Agnus Dei, Fílius Patris,
qui tollis peccáta mundi, miserére nobis;
qui tollis peccáta mundi, súscipe deprecatiónem nostram.
Qui sedes ad déxteram Patris, miserére nobis.
Quóniam tu solus Sanctus, tu solus Dóminus,
tu solus Altíssimus,
Iesu Christe, cum Sancto Spíritu: in glória Dei Patris.
Amen.

After the Opening Prayer

℣. Per ómnia sǽcula sæculórum.
℟. **Amen.**

After the First and Second Readings

℣. Verbum Dómini.
℟. **Deo grátias.**

Before the Gospel

℣. Dóminus vobíscum.
℟. **Et cum spíritu tuo.**
℣. Léctio sancti Evangélii secúndum N.
℟. **Glória tibi, Dómine.**

At the end of the Gospel

℣. Verbum Dómini.
℟. **Laus tibi, Christe.**

Creed

Credo in unum Deum,
Patrem omnipoténtem, factórem cæli et terræ,
visibílium ómnium et invisibílium.
Et in unum Dóminum Iesum Christum,
Fílium Dei unigénitum,
et ex Patre natum ante ómnia sǽcula.
Deum de Deo, lumen de lúmine,
Deum verum de Deo vero,
génitum, non factum, consubstantiálem Patri:
per quem ómnia facta sunt.
Qui propter nos hómines et propter nostram salútem
descéndit de cælis.
Et incarnátus est de Spíritu Sancto
ex María Vírgine, et homo factus est.
Crucifíxus étiam pro nobis sub Póntio Piláto;
passus et sepúltus est,
et resurréxit tértia die, secúndum Scriptúras,
et ascéndit in cælum, sedet ad déxteram Patris.
Et íterum ventúrus est cum glória,

iudicáre vivos et mórtuos,
cuius regni non erit finis.
Et in Spíritum Sanctum, Dóminum et vivificántem:
qui ex Patre Filióque procédit.
Qui cum Patre et Fílio simul adorátur et conglorificátur:
qui locútus est per prophétas.
Et unam, sanctam, cathólicam et apostólicam Ecclésiam.
Confíteor unum baptísma in remissiónem peccatórum.
Et exspécto resurrectiónem mortuórum,
et vitam ventúri sǽculi. Amen.

Response at Preparation of the Gifts

℣. Benedíctus es . . . panis vitæ.
℟. **Benedíctus Deus in sǽcula.**
℣. Benedíctus es . . . potus spiritális.
℟. **Benedíctus Deus in sǽcula.**

Response to the Pray Brethren

℣. Orate, fratres . . . Patrem omnipoténtem.
℟. **Suscípiat Dóminus sacrifícium de mánibus tuis**
ad laudem et glóriam nóminis sui,
ad utilitátem quoque nostram
totiúsque Ecclésiæ suæ sanctæ.

After the Prayer over the Gifts

℣. Per Christum Dóminum nostrum.
or
In sǽcula sæculórum.
℟. **Amen.**

Introductory Dialogue before the Preface

℣. Dóminus vobíscum.
℟. **Et cum spíritu tuo.**
℣. Sursum corda.
℟. **Habémus ad Dóminum.**
℣. Grátias agámus Dómino Deo nostro.
℟. **Dignum et iustum est.**

Holy, Holy, Holy . . .

Sanctus, Sanctus, Sanctus Dóminus Deus Sábaoth.
Pleni sunt cæli et terra glória tua.
Hosánna in excélsis.
Benedíctus qui venit in nómine Dómini.
Hosánna in excélsis.

Memorial Acclamation

1. Mortem tuam annuntiámus, Dómine,
et tuam resurrectiónem confitémur, donec vénias.
2. Quotiescúmque manducámus panem hunc
et cálicem bíbimus,
mortem tuam annuntiámus, Dómine, donec vénias.
3. Salvátor mundi, salva nos,
qui per crucem et resurrectiónem tuam liberásti nos.

At the end of the Eucharistic Prayer

℣. Per ómnia sǽcula sæculórum,
℟. **Amen.**

Lord's Prayer

℣. Præcéptis salutáribus móniti,
et divína institutióne formáti,
audémus dícere:
All Pater noster, qui es in cælis:
sanctificétur nomen tuum;
advéniat regnum tuum;
fiat volúntas tua, sicut in cælo, et in terra.
Panem nostrum cotidiánum da nobis hódie;
et dimítte nobis débita nostra,
sicut et nos dimíttimus debitóribus nostris;
et ne nos indúcas in tentatiónem;
sed líbera nos a malo.

Acclamation after the Lord's Prayer

Quia tuum est regnum,
et potéstas, et glória
in sǽcula.

At the Sign of Peace

℣. Qui vivis et regnas in sǽcula sæculórum.
℟. **Amen.**
℣. Pax Dómini sit semper vobíscum.
℟. **Et cum spíritu tuo.**

Lamb of God

Agnus Dei, qui tollis peccáta mundi:
miserére nobis.
Agnus Dei, qui tollis peccáta mundi:
miserére nobis.
Agnus Dei, qui tollis peccáta mundi:
dona nobis pacem.

Lord, I Am Not Worthy

Dómine, non sum dignus ut intres sub tectum meum;
sed tantum dic verbo, et sanábitur anima mea.

At the Reception of Communion

℣. Corpus Christi *or* Sanguis Christi.
℟. **Amen.**

At the Prayer after Communion

℣. Dóminus vobíscum.
℟. **Et cum spíritu tuo.**
At the conclusion of the Prayer:
℣. Per Christum Dóminum nostrum.
or
In sǽcula sæculórum.
℟. **Amen.**

At the Concluding Rite

℣. Dóminus vobíscum.
℟. **Et cum spíritu tuo.**
℣. Benedícat vos omnípotens Deus,
Pater, et Fílius, ✠ et Spíritus Sanctus.
℟. **Amen.**
℣. Ite, missa est.
℟. **Deo grátias.**

SELECT BIBLIOGRAPHY

Adam, Adolf, and Berger, Rupert. *Pastoralliturgisches Handlexikon.* Freiburg, Germany: Herder, 1980.

Arent, Julian, OFM. *The Homily after Vatican II.* Wayne, IL: Assumption B.V.M. Province, 1982.

Bishops' Committee on Priestly Life and Ministry. *Fulfilled in Your Hearing.* The Homily in the Sunday Assembly. Washington, DC: USCC, 1982.

Bishops' Committee on the Liturgy. *Anointing and the Pastoral Care of the Sick.* Washington, DC: USCC, 1973.

Bishops' Committee on the Liturgy. *The Bishop and the Liturgy: Highlights of the New Ceremonial of Bishops.* Washington, DC: USCC, 1986.

Bishops' Committee on the Liturgy. *Catholic Household Blessings & Prayers.* Washington, DC: USCC, 1988.

Bishops' Committee on the Liturgy. *The Deacon, Minister of Word and Sacrament.* Washington, DC: USCC, 1979.

Bishops' Committee on the Liturgy. *Dedication of a Church and an Altar* (Provi sional Text). Washington, DC: USCC, 1978.

Bishops' Committee on the Liturgy. *Environment and Art in Catholic Worship.* Washington, DC: USCC, 1978.

Bishops' Committee on the Liturgy. *Eucharistic Worship and Devotion Outside Mass.* Study edition. Washington, DC: USCC, 1987.

Bishops' Committee on the Liturgy. *General Instruction of the Roman Missal.* Washington, DC: USCC, 1982.

Bishops' Committee on the Liturgy. *Holy Days in the United States: History, Theology, Celebration.* Washington, DC: USCC, 1984.

Bishops' Committee on the Liturgy. *Lectionary for Mass: Introduction.* Washington, DC: USCC, 1982.

Bishops' Committee on the Liturgy. *Liturgical Music Today.* Statement . . . 10th Anniversary of "Music in Catholic Worship." Washington, DC: USCC, 1982.

Bishops' Committee on the Liturgy. *The Liturgical Year: Celebrating the Mystery of Christ and His Saints.* Washington, DC: USCC, 1985.

Bishops' Committee on the Liturgy. *The Liturgy of the Hours.* Washington, DC: USCC, 1981.

Bishops' Committee on the Liturgy. *Ministries in the Church.* Washington, DC: USCC, 1974.

Bishops' Committee on the Liturgy. *Music in Catholic Worship.* Washington, DC: USCC, 1972.

Bishops' Committee on the Liturgy. *Newsletter 1965-1985; 1986- .* 3 vols. Washington, DC: USCC, 1976, 1981, 1986, 1987- .

Bishops' Committee on the Liturgy. *Pastoral Care of the Sick and Dying.* Study edition, revised. Washington, DC: USCC, 1984.

Bishops' Committee on the Liturgy. *Proclaim the Word: The Lectionary for Mass.* Washington, DC: USCC, 1982.

Bishops' Committee on the Liturgy. *Promoting Liturgical Renewal.* Guidelines for Diocesan Liturgical Commissions and Offices of Worship. Washington, DC: USCC, 1982.

Bishops' Committee on the Liturgy. *Rite of Confirmation.* Washington, DC: USCC, 1975.

Bishops' Committee on the Liturgy. *The Sign of Peace.* Washington, DC: USCC, 1977.

Bishops' Committee on the Liturgy, and Center for Pastoral Liturgy, eds. *The Environment for Worship.* A Reader. Washington, DC: USCC, 1980.

Bishops' Committee on the Permanent Diaconate. *Permanent Deacons in the United States.* Guidelines on their Formation and Ministry. Washington, DC: USCC, 1971.

Buono, Anthony M. *The Liturgy: Our School of Faith.* Staten Island, NY: Alba House, 1982.

Buono, Anthony M. *Spotlight on Liturgy.* New York: Catholic Book Publishing Co., 1981.

Cabaniss, Allen. *Liturgy and Literature.* University, AL: Univ. of Alabama Press, 1970.

Calabuig, Ignazio M. *The Dedication of a Church and an Altar.* A Theological Commentary. Washington, DC: USCC, 1980.

Casel, Odo. *The Mystery of Christian Worship.* Westminster, MD: The Newman Press, 1962.

Church at Prayer, The: A Holy Temple of the Lord. A Pastoral Statement Commemorating the Twentieth Anniversary of the Constitution on the Sacred Liturgy. Washington, DC: USCC, 1984.

Code of Canon Law. Washington, DC: Canon Law Society of America, 1983.

Codex Iuris Canonici. Auctoritate Ioannis Pauli PP. II promulgatus. Vatican City: Libreria Editrice Vaticana, 1983.

Comentarios a la Biblia Liturgica. 2 vols. Coedition: Libros de la Comunidad. Barcelona and Madrid, 1976.

Congregation for Divine Worship. *Circular Letter Concerning the Preparation and Celebration of the Easter Feasts* (January 16, 1988). Washington, DC: USCC, 1988.

Congregation for Divine Worship. *Directory for Sunday Celebrations in the absence of a Priest.* June 2, 1988. Washington, DC: USCC, 1988.

Congregation for Divine Worship. *Instruction on Masses for Special Gatherings.* Washington, DC: USCC, 1969.

Congregation for Divine Worship. *Instruction on the Manner of Administering Holy Communion.* Washington, DC: USCC, 1969.

Coulson, John, ed. *The Saints; a Concise Biographical Dictionary.* New York: Hawthorn, 1958.

Davies, J. G., ed. *The New Westminster Dictionary of Liturgy and Worship.* Philadelphia, Westminster Press, 1986.

Davies, J. G. *A Select Liturgical Lexicon.* Richmond: John Knox Press, 1965.

Delaney, John J. *Dictionary of Saints.* Garden City: Doubleday & Co. 1980.

DeMarco, Angelus A. *A Key to the New Liturgical Constitution.* An Alphabetical Analysis. New York: Desclée, 1964.

Deretz, J., and Nocent, A. *Dictionary of the Council.* Washington, DC: Corpus Books, 1968.

Dictionary of Mary. New York: Catholic Book Publishing Co., 1985

Dix, Gregory. *The Shape of the Liturgy.* Westminster: Dacre Press, 1945.

Documents of Vatican II, The. Walter M. Abbott, S.J., General Editor. New York, America Press, 1966.

Eisenhofer, Ludwig, and Lechner, Joseph. *The Liturgy of the Roman Rite.* New York: Herder and Herder, 1961.

Ekstrom, Reynolds R., and Ekstrom, Rosemary. *Concise Catholic Dictionary for Parents and Religion Teachers.* Mystic, CT: Twenty-Third Publications, 1982.

Enchiridion of Indulgences. Norms and Grants. English ed. New York: Catholic Book Publishing Co., 1969.

Enchiridion Vaticanum: Documenti Ufficiali della Santa Sede (1965 -). Bologna, Italy: Edizioni Dehoniane Bologna.

Evans, Francis. *Our Living Mass.* New York: Catholic Book Publishing Co., 1967.

Fiores, Stefano de, and Meo, Salvatore, eds. *Nuovo Dizionario di Mariologia.* Milan: Edizioni Paoline, 1986.

Fitzgerald, George. *Handbook of the Mass.* Ramsey: Paulist Press, 1982.

Funk, Virgil C., and Huck, Gabe. *Pastoral Music in Practice.* Washington, DC: National Association of Pastoral Musicians, 1981.

Gall, Robert Le. *Dictionnaire de Liturgie.* Paris: C.L.D., 1982

General Instruction of the Liturgy of the Hours, According to the Roman Rite. English Trans. ICEL. New York: Catholic Book Publishing Co., 1975.

General Instruction of the Roman Missal. Washington, DC: USCC, 1982.

Hardon, John A. *Modern Catholic Dictionary.* Garden City: Doubleday, 1980.

Holy Communion and Worship of the Eucharist Outside Mass. Roman Ritual Revised. New York: Catholic Book Publishing Co., 1976.

Huels, John M., O.S.M. *Liturgical Law: An Introduction.* Washington, DC: Pastoral Press, 1987.

International Commission on English in the Liturgy. *Documents on the Liturgy, 1963-1979, Conciliar, Papal, and Curial Texts.* Collegeville, MN: The Liturgical Press, 1983.

Jacobs, William. *A Young Person's Book of Catholic Words.* Garden City, NY: Doubleday, 1981.

John Paul II. *The Apostles of the Slavs*

(Slavorum Apostoli). Washington, DC: USCC, 1985.

John Paul II. *The Gift of the Redemption (Redemptionis Donum).* Washington, DC: USCC, 1984.

John Paul II. *Lord and Giver of Life (Dominum et Vivificantem).* Washington, DC: USCC, 1986.

John Paul II. *The Mother of the Redeemer (Redemptoris Mater).* Washington, DC: USCC, 1987.

John Paul II. *On Catechesis in Our Time (Catechesi Tradendae).* Washington, DC: USCC, 1979.

John Paul II. *On Human Work (Laborem Exercens).* Washington, DC: USCC, 1981.

John Paul II. *On Social Concern (Sollicitudo Rei Socialis).* Washington, DC: USCC, 1988.

John Paul II. *On the Christian Family (Familiaris Consortio).* Washington, DC: USCC, 1981.

John Paul II. *On the Christian Meaning of Human Suffering (Salvifici Doloris).* Washington, DC: USCC, 1984.

John Paul II. *On the Dignity and Vocation of Women (Mulieris Dignitatem).* Washington, DC: USSC, 1988.

John Paul II. *Pilgrimage of Peace: The Collected Speeches of John Paul II in Ireland and the United States.* New York: Farrar, Straus, Giroux, 1980.

John Paul II. *Reconciliation and Penance (Reconciliatio et Paenitentia).* Washington, DC: USCC, 1984.

John Paul II. *Redeemer of Man (Redemptor Hominis).* Washington, DC: USCC, 1979.

John Paul II. *Rich in Mercy (Dives in Misericordia).* Washington, DC: USCC, 1980.

Jounel, Pierre. *La Messe: Hier et Aujourd'hui.* Paris: O.E.I.L., 1986.

Jounel, Pierre. *Missel de la Semaine.* Paris: Desclée, 1973.

Jungmann, Josef A. *Pastoral Liturgy.* New York: Herder and Herder, 1962.

Jungmann, Josef A. *The Mass: An Historical, Theological, and Pastoral Survey.* Collegeville, MN.: The Liturgical Press, 1976.

Jungmann, Josef A. *The Mass of the Roman Rite: Its Origins and Development.* 2 vols. New York: Benziger Bros., 1951-1955.

Kapsner, Oliver K., ed. *Catholic Subject Headings.* A Modification of the 5th ed. Haverford, PA: Catholic Library Association, 1981.

Komonchak, Joseph A., Collins, Mary, and Lane, Dermot A. *The New Dictionary of Theology.* Wilmington, DE: Michael Glazier, 1987.

Krempa, S. Joseph. *Daily Homilies; Seasonal & Sanctoral Cycle.* New York: Alba House, 1985.

Lanz, Kerry J., and Post, W. E. *The Complete Server.* Wilton, CT: Morehouse-Barlow, 1978.

Lectionary for Mass. New York: Catholic Book Publishing Co., 1970.

Lee, Bernard J., General editor. *Alternative Futures for Worship.* 7 vols. Collegeville, MN: Liturgical Press, 1987.

Lercaro, Giacomo. *A Small Liturgical Dictionary.* Edited by J. B. O'Connell. Collegeville, MN: The Liturgical Press, 1959.

Liturgy Constitution, The. A Chapter by Chapter Analysis. Glen Rock: Paulist Press, 1964.

Liturgy of the Hours. 4 vols. New York: Catholic Book Publishing Co., 1975- 1976.

Lockyer, Herbert. *All the Apostles of the Bible.* Grand Rapids, MI.: Zondervan, 1975.

Lockyer, Herbert. *All the Divine Names and Titles in the Bible.* Grand Rapids, MI.: Zondervan, 1972.

McManus, Frederick R., ed. *Thirty Years of Liturgical Renewal.* Washington, DC: USCC, 1987.

Marsili, Salvatore, et al. *La Liturgia, Eucaristia: Teologia e Storia della Celebrazione.* Casale Monferrato, Italy: Casa Editrice Marietti, 1983.

Martimort, A.M., et al, eds. *The Church at Prayer.* 4 vols. Collegeville, MN: The Liturgical Press, 1986-87.

Meagher, P. K. et al, eds. *Encyclopedic Dictionary of Religion.* 3 volumes. Washington, DC: Corpus Publications, 1979.

Mistrorigo, Antonio. *Dizionario Liturgico-Pastorale.* Padova: Messaggero di S. Antonio, 1977.

Mistrorigo, Antonio. *La Liturgia.* Roma: Armando Armando, 1968.

Monloubou, Louis, and Du Buit, F.M. *Dictionnaire Biblique Universel.* Paris: Desclée, 1984.

Mystery of Faith, The: A Study of the Structural Elements of the Order of Mass. Washington, DC: Federation of Diocesan Liturgical Commissions, 1980.

New Catholic Encyclopedia. 15 vols. with 3 Supplements. Washington, DC: The Catholic University of America, 1967, 1974, 1979, 1989.

Newland, Mary Reed. *The Saint Book.* Minneapolis: Seabury, 1979.

Nocent, Adrien. *The Liturgical Year.* 4 vols. Collegeville, MN: The Liturgical Press, 1977.

Norms Governing Liturgical Calendars. Washington, DC: USCC, 1984.

Notitiae (1965 -). Rome, Italy: Congregation for Divine Worship, 1965- .

O'Carroll, Michael. *Corpus Christi: An Encyclopedia of the Eucharist.* Wilmington, DE: Michael Glazier, 1988.

O'Carroll, Michael. *Theotokos: A Theological Encyclopedia of the Blessed Virgin Mary.* Wilmington, DE: Michael Glazier, 1982.

O'Carroll, Michael. *Trinitas: A Theological Encyclopedia of the Holy Trinity.* Wilmington, DE: Michael Glazier, 1987.

Order of Crowning an Image of the Blessed Virgin Mary. Washington, DC: USCC, 1987.

Ordination of Deacons, Priests and Bishops. Study edition. Washington, DC: USCC, 1979.

Oury, Guy M. *The Mass: Spirituality, History, and Practice.* New York: Catholic Book Publishing Co., 1988.

Parsch, Pius. *The Church's Year of Grace.* 5 volumes. Collegeville: Liturgical Press, 1957.

Pastoral Care of the Sick. Rites of Anointing and Viaticum. New York: Catholic Book Publishing Co., 1983.

Paul VI. *Devotion to the Blessed Virgin Mary (Marialis Cultus).* Washington, DC: USCC, 1974.

Paul VI. *Encyclical on the Doctrine and Worship of the Eucharist (Mysterium Fidei).* Washington, DC: USCC, 1965.

Penance and Reconciliation in the Church. Washington, DC: USCC, 1986.

Podhradsky, Gerhard. *New Dictionary of the Liturgy.* Staten Island: Alba House, 1966.

Provost, James H., ed. *Code, Community, Ministry.* Selected Studies for the Parish Minister Introducing the Revised Code of Canon Law. Washington, DC: Canon Law Society of America, 1983.

Richstatter, Thomas. *Liturgical Law Today.* Chicago: Franciscan Herald Press, 1977.

Rite of Baptism for Children. Roman Ritual Revised. New York: Catholic Book Publishing Co., 1977.

Rite of Christian Initiation of Adults. Roman Ritual Revised. New York: Catholic Book Publishing Co., 1988.

Rite of Commissioning Special Ministers of Holy Communion. Provisional Text. Washington, DC: USCC, 1978.

Rite of Confirmation. Roman Ritual Revised. Washington, DC: USCC, 1973.

Rite of Funerals. Roman Ritual Revised. New York: Catholic Book Publishing Co., 1971.

Rite of Marriage. Roman Ritual Revised. New York: Catholic Book Publishing Co., 1970.

Rite of Penance. Roman Ritual Revised. New York: Catholic Book Publishing Co., 1975.

Rite of Reception of Baptized Christians into Full Communion with the Catholic Church. Roman Ritual Revised. Washington, DC: International Commission on English in the Liturgy, 1976.

Roguet, A. M. *The New Mass.* New York: Catholic Book Publishing Co., 1970.

Roman Calendar, The. Text and Commentary. Washington, DC: USCC, 1976.

Roman Pontifical, The. Roman Ritual Revised. Washington, DC: International Commission on English in the Liturgy, 1978.

Roulin, E. A. *Vestments and Vesture.* A Manual of Liturgical Art. Trans. Justin McCann. St. Louis: B. Herder, 1931.

Sacramentary. Roman Missal Revised. New York: Catholic Book Publishing Co., 1985.

Sacred Congregation for Divine Worship. *Letter to the Presidents of the National Conferences of Bishops concerning the Directory for Masses with Children.* Washington, DC: USCC, 1974.

Sacred Congregation for the Clergy. *General Catechetical Directory.* Washington, DC: USCC, 1971.

Sacred Congregation for the Sacraments and Divine Worship. *On Certain Norms concerning Worship of the Eucharistic Mystery (Inaestimabile Donum).* Washington, DC: USCC, 1980.

Sacred Congregation of Rites. *Instruction: On Music in the Liturgy.* Washington, DC: USCC, 1967.

Saint Joseph Edition of the New American Bible. New York: Catholic Book Publishing Co., 1987.

Saint Joseph Liturgical Bible. New York: Catholic Book Publishing Co., 1972.

Saint Joseph Sunday Missal. New York: Catholic Book Publishing Co., 1974-1986.

Saint Joseph Weekday Missal. 2 vols. New York: Catholic Book Publishing Co., 1974.

Salmon, Pierre. *The Breviary through the Centuries.* Collegeville, MN: The Liturgical Press, 1962.

Sartore, Domenico, and Triacca, Achille M., eds. *Nuovo Dizionario di Liturgia.* Rome: Edizioni Paoline, 1983.

Schraner, Anthony. *New St. Joseph Annotated Catechism.* New York: Catholic Book Publishing Co., 1981.

Seasoltz, R. Kevin. *New Liturgy, New Laws.* Collegeville, MN: The Liturgical Press, 1980.

Seasoltz, R. Kevin. *The New Liturgy: A Documentation, 1903-1965.* New York: Herder and Herder, 1966.

Selected Documentation from the New Sacramentary. Apostolic Constitution *Missale Romanum;* Forward to the Sacramentary; General Instruction of the Roman Missal; Appendix to the General Instruction for the Dioceses of the United States of America. Washington, DC: USCC, 1974.

Sharing the Light of Faith. National Catechetical Directory for Catholics of the United States. Washington, DC: USCC, 1979.

Simcoe, Mary Ann, ed. *The Liturgy Documents: A Parish Resource.* Rev. ed. Chicago, Liturgy Training Publications, 1985.

Smith, Gregory F. *The Ministry of Ushers.* Collegeville, MN: The Liturgical Press, 1980.

Smolarski, Dennis C. *Eucharistia.* A Study of the Eucharistic Prayer. Ramsey, NJ: Paulist Press, 1982.

Synod of Bishops, Rome, 1983. *Penance and Reconciliation in the Mission of the Church.* Washington, DC: USCC, 1984.

This Holy and Living Sacrifice: Directory for the Celebration and Reception of Communion under Both Kinds. Washington, DC: USCC, 1985.

Vagaggini, Cyprian. *Theological Dimensions of the Liturgy.* Collegeville, MN: The Liturgical Press, 1976.

Vosko, Richard S. *A Place for Reconciliation.* Albany: Liturgy Center, Diocese of Albany, 1976.

Webber, Robert E. *Worship, Old and New.* Grand Rapids, MI. Zondervan Publishing House, 1982.

Winkler, Jude. *Great People of the Bible.* New York: Catholic Book Pub. Co., 1985.